RAPID REVIEW
SELECTED CHAPTER TOPICS
Financial Accounting: Tools for Business Decision-Making, Seventh Canadian Edition

FINANCIAL STATEMENTS (Chapter 1)

Business Activities

1. Financing activities: Borrowing cash from lenders by issuing debt, or conversely, using cash to repay debt. Cash can also be raised from shareholders by issuing shares, or paid to shareholders by repurchasing shares or distributing dividends.
2. Investing activities: Purchasing and disposing of long-lived assets such as property, plant, and equipment and purchasing and selling long-term investments.
3. Operating activities: Result from day-to-day operations and include revenues and expenses and related accounts such as receivables, supplies, inventory, and payables.

Interrelationship of Financial Statements

Order of Preparation	Relationship	Date
1. Income statement		Period ended
2. Statement of changes in equity	Changes in common or preferred shares during current period added to (or deducted from) opening balance in common shares, and net income (loss) from income statement is added to (deducted from) opening retained earnings on statement of changes in equity	Period ended
3. Statement of financial position	Ending balance of each component of shareholders' equity from statement of changes in equity is reported in shareholders' equity section on statement of financial position	End of the period
4. Statement of cash flows	Cash balance reported on statement of financial position agrees with ending cash balance on statement of cash flows	Period ended

CONCEPTUAL FRAMEWORK (Chapter 2)

Objective of Financial Reporting
To provide financial information that is useful to existing and potential investors, lenders, and other creditors in making decisions about providing resources to the company and assessing management's stewardship of the company's assets.

Qualitative Characteristics of Useful Financial Information		
Fundamental Qualitative Characteristics	Enhancing Qualitative Characteristics	Constraint

1. Relevance
  • Predictive value
  • Confirmatory value
  • Materiality
2. Faithful representation
  • Complete
  • Neutral
  • Free from material error
	1. Comparability
	2. Verifiability
	3. Timeliness
	4. Understandability
		1. Cost

Underlying Assumption—Going Concern

Elements of Financial Statements	Measurement of the Elements
1. Assets 2. Liabilities 3. Equity 4. Income 5. Expenses	1. Historical cost 2. Current value

ACCOUNTING EQUATION WITH DEBIT/CREDIT RULES (Chapter 3)

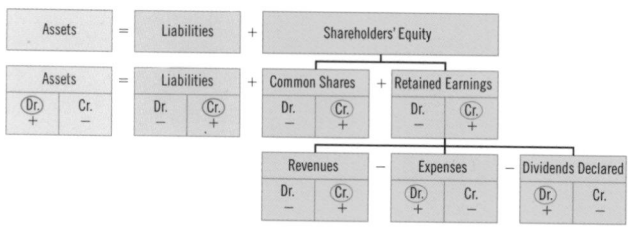

Note: Normal account balances are circled in red.

ADJUSTING ENTRIES (Chapter 4)

	Type	Original Entry	Adjusting Entry

Prepayments	1. Prepaid expenses	Dr. Prepaid Expense
		  Cr. Cash (or Accounts Payable)
			Dr. Expense
			  Cr. Prepaid Expense

	2. Unearned revenue	Dr. Cash
		  Cr. Unearned Revenue
			Dr. Unearned Revenue
			  Cr. Revenue

Accruals	1. Accrued expenses	No entry	Dr. Expense Cr. Payable
	2. Accrued revenues	No entry	Dr. Receivable Cr. Revenue

Note: 1. Each adjusting entry will affect at least one income statement account and at least one statement of financial position account.
    2. Adjusting entries never include the Cash account.

Selected Adjusting Entry Calculations

Straight-Line Depreciation = Cost ÷ Useful life (in years) × Time in terms of one year (Number of months ÷ 12)

Interest = Face value × Annual interest rate × Time in terms of one year (Number of months ÷ 12)

CLOSING ENTRIES (Chapter 4)

Temporary (These accounts are closed)	Permanent (These accounts are not closed)
All revenue accounts	All asset accounts
All expense accounts	All liability accounts
Dividends declared account	Shareholders' equity accounts (common or preferred shares and retained earnings)

Purpose

1. Update the Retained Earnings account by transferring net income (loss) and dividends declared to retained earnings.
2. Prepare the temporary accounts (revenue, expense, dividends declared) for the next period's postings by reducing their balances to zero.

Process

1. To close revenue accounts: Debit each individual revenue account for its balance and credit Income Summary for total revenues.
2. To close expense accounts: Debit Income Summary for total expenses and credit each individual expense account for its balance (assuming normal balances).
3. To close income summary: Debit Income Summary for the balance in the account (or credit if a loss) and credit (debit) Retained Earnings.
4. To close dividends: Debit Retained Earnings and credit Dividends Declared for the balance in the account.

STOP AND CHECK: (1) Is the balance in the Income Summary account, before transfer to the Retained Earnings account, equal to the net income (loss) reported in the income statement? (2) Does the balance in the Retained Earnings account equal the ending balance reported in the statement of changes in equity and statement of financial position? (3) Are all of the temporary account balances zero?

ACCOUNTING CYCLE (Chapters 3 and 4)

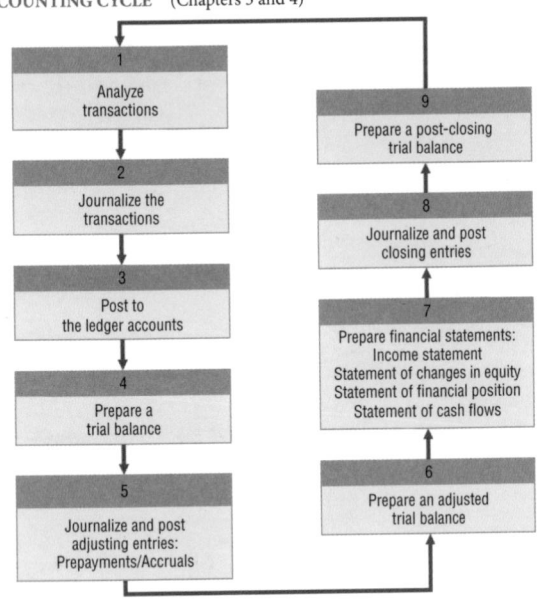

Formula for Cost of Goods Sold (Periodic Inventory System—Appendix 5A)

$$\boxed{\text{Beginning Inventory}} + \boxed{\text{Cost of Goods Purchased}} = \boxed{\text{Cost of Goods Available for Sale}} - \boxed{\text{Ending Inventory}} = \boxed{\text{Cost of Goods Sold}}$$

INVENTORY (Chapter 6)

Ownership of Inventory

	FOB Shipping Point	FOB Destination
Goods purchased in transit	Buyer's (once shipped)	Seller's (until they reach the buyer's destination)
Goods sold in transit	Buyer's (once shipped)	Seller's (until they reach the buyer's destination)

Inventory Cost Formulas

1. Specific identification: Used for goods that are not ordinarily interchangeable, or goods that have been produced and segregated for specific projects
2. Cost formulas: First-in, first-out (FIFO) or Average

Guidelines for Choice of Cost Formula

1. Choose method that best corresponds to physical flow of goods.
2. Report inventory cost on the statement of financial position close to inventory's recent cost.
3. Use same method for all inventories having similar nature and usage.

Financial Statement Effects of Cost Formulas (during period of rising prices)

	Specific Identification	FIFO	Average
Income Statement			
Cost of goods sold	Variable	Lower	Higher
Gross profit	Variable	Higher	Lower
Net income	Variable	Higher	Lower
Statement of Financial Position			
Cash (pre-tax)	Same	Same	Same
Ending inventory	Variable	Higher	Lower
Retained earnings	Variable	Higher	Lower

Inventory Errors (Perpetual Inventory System)

Errors Made in Determining the Cost of Inventory

If Inventory is:	Then Cost of Goods Sold is:	Then Gross Profit is:	Then Income Before Income Tax is:	Then Retained Earnings are:
Overstated	Understated	Overstated	Overstated	Overstated
Understated	Overstated	Understated	Understated	Understated

Errors Made in Recording Purchase of Inventory

If purchase of inventory on account is recorded:	Then Inventory is:	Then Cost of Goods Sold and Net Income are:	Then Accounts Payable is:	Then Retained Earnings are:
Too early	Overstated	Unaffected	Overstated	Unaffected
Too late	Understated	Unaffected	Understated	Unaffected

INTERNAL CONTROL AND CASH (Chapter 7)

Control Activities

Assignment of responsibility
Segregation of duties
Documentation
Physical controls
Review and reconciliation

Calculation of Deposits in Transit

$$\boxed{\begin{array}{c}\text{Deposits in transit at beginning of period}\end{array}} + \boxed{\begin{array}{c}\text{Deposits recorded in company's books this period}\end{array}} - \boxed{\begin{array}{c}\text{Deposits recorded on this period's bank statement}\end{array}} = \boxed{\begin{array}{c}\text{Deposits in transit at end of period}\end{array}}$$

Calculation of Outstanding Cheques

$$\boxed{\begin{array}{c}\text{Outstanding cheques at beginning of period}\end{array}} + \boxed{\begin{array}{c}\text{Cheques recorded in company's books this period}\end{array}} - \boxed{\begin{array}{c}\text{Cheques recorded on this period's bank statement}\end{array}} = \boxed{\begin{array}{c}\text{Outstanding cheques at end of period}\end{array}}$$

Calculation of Unadjusted Cash Balance per Books

Adjusted cash balance per books or per bank from prior period + Cash receipts – Cash payments = Unadjusted cash balance per books at beginning of period

INVENTORY (Chapter 5)

Perpetual vs. Periodic Journal Entries (buyer)

Transaction	Perpetual	Periodic (Appendix 5A)

Purchase of merchandise	Dr. Inventory
	  Cr. Cash or Accounts Payable
		Dr. Purchases
		  Cr. Cash or Accounts Payable

Freight on merchandise purchased (FOB shipping point)	Dr. Inventory
	  Cr. Cash or Accounts Payable
		Dr. Freight In
		  Cr. Cash or Accounts Payable

Return of purchased merchandise	Dr. Cash or Accounts Payable
	  Cr. Inventory
		Dr. Cash or Accounts Payable
		  Cr. Purchase Returns and Allowances

Paying creditors on account within discount period	Dr. Accounts Payable
	  Cr. Inventory
	  Cr. Cash
		Dr. Accounts Payable
		  Cr. Purchase Discounts
		  Cr. Cash

Adjustment of inventory in accounting records to lower physical count amount (entry is opposite for higher amount)	Dr. Cost of Goods Sold Cr. Inventory	No entry

Perpetual vs. Periodic Journal Entries (seller)

Transaction	Perpetual	Periodic (Appendix 5A)

Sale of merchandise	Dr. Cash or Accounts Receivable
	  Cr. Sales
	Dr. Cost of Goods Sold
	  Cr. Inventory
		Dr. Cash or Accounts Receivable
		  Cr. Sales
		No entry

Freight on merchandise sold (FOB destination)	Dr. Freight Out
	  Cr. Cash or Accounts Payable
		Dr. Freight Out
		  Cr. Cash or Accounts Payable

Return of sold merchandise (assuming resaleable)	Dr. Sales Returns and Allowances
	  Cr. Cash or Accounts Receivable
	Dr. Inventory
	  Cr. Cost of Goods Sold
		Dr. Sales Returns and Allowances
		  Cr. Cash or Accounts Receivable
		No entry

Collection of account from customer within discount period	Dr. Cash
	Dr. Sales Discounts
	  Cr. Accounts Receivable
		Dr. Cash
		Dr. Sales Discounts
		  Cr. Accounts Receivable

Period-end adjusting entry	No entry	Dr. Inventory (ending)
		Dr. Cost of Goods Sold
		Dr. Purchase Returns and Allowances
		Dr. Purchase Discounts
		  Cr. Inventory (beginning)
		  Cr. Purchases
		  Cr. Freight In

Bank Reconciliation

Bank	Books
Cash balance per bank statement (unadjusted) Add: Deposits in transit Deduct: Outstanding cheques Add (deduct): Bank errors = Reconciled cash balance	Cash balance per books (unadjusted) Add: EFT collections, interest and other deposits Deduct: EFT payments, service charges, and NSF cheques Add (deduct): Book errors = Reconciled cash balance

Note: 1. Errors should be recorded (added or deducted) on the side that made the error.
2. Adjusting journal entries should only be made on the books side.

STOP AND CHECK: (1) Do the reconciled cash balances per bank and per books agree? (2) Does the reconciled cash balance equal the balance in the general ledger Cash account after all journal entries have been made?

RECEIVABLES   (Chapter 8)

Bad Debts

Transaction	Journal Entry

Record credit sales	Dr. Accounts Receivable
	    Cr. Sales
	Dr. Cost of Goods Sold
	    Cr. Inventory

Estimate bad debts	Dr. Bad Debts Expense Cr. Allowance for Doubtful Accounts
Write off uncollectible account	Dr. Allowance for Doubtful Accounts Cr. Accounts Receivable

Subsequent recovery	Dr. Accounts Receivable
	    Cr. Allowance for Doubtful Accounts
	Dr. Cash
	    Cr. Accounts Receivable

Notes Receivable

Transaction	Journal Entry
Issue notes receivable	Dr. Notes Receivable Cr. Cash or Accounts Receivable
Record interest	Dr. Cash or Interest Receivable Cr. Interest Revenue

Record honouring (collection) of notes receivable)	Dr. Cash
	    Cr. Notes Receivable
	    Cr. Interest Revenue and/or Interest Receivable

Estimate bad debts	Dr. Bad Debts Expense Cr. Allowance for Doubtful Notes

Record dishonouring of notes receivable (eventual collection assumed)	Dr. Accounts Receivable
	    Cr. Notes Receivable
	    Cr. Interest Revenue and/or Interest Receivable

Record dishonouring of notes receivable (eventual collection not assumed)	Dr. Allowance for Doubtful Notes
	    Cr. Notes Receivable
	    Cr. Interest Receivable (if any)

LONG-LIVED ASSETS   (Chapter 9)

Recording Depreciation and Amortization

Property, plant, and equipment	Dr. Depreciation Expense Cr. Accumulated Depreciation
Limited life intangible assets	Dr. Amortization Expense Cr. Accumulated Amortization

Calculation of Annual Depreciation Expense

Straight-line	$\dfrac{\text{Cost} - \text{Residual value}}{\text{Useful life (in years)}}$
Diminishing-balance	Carrying amount (cost – accumulated depreciation) at beginning of year × Depreciation rate (straight-line rate × multiplier) Straight-line rate = 1 ÷ Useful life (in years)
Units-of-production	$\dfrac{\text{Cost} - \text{Residual value}}{\text{Estimated total units of activity}}$ × Actual units of activity during year

Note: 1. If depreciation is calculated for partial periods, the straight-line and diminishing-balance methods must be adjusted for the relevant proportion of the year. Multiply annual depreciation expense by the number of months expired in the year divided by 12 months.
2. The total depreciation for the diminishing-balance method is limited to depreciable cost (cost – residual value) and partial year adjustments are not needed as this effect is already in units produced.

Impairment Loss

Carrying amount (cost – accumulated depreciation) – Recoverable amount = Impairment loss

Dr. Impairment Loss
    Cr. Accumulated Depreciation (or Amortization, or asset if no contra account)

Derecognition of Property, Plant, and Equipment

1. Update depreciation for appropriate portion of current year	Dr. Depreciation Expense Cr. Accumulated Depreciation
2. Calculate carrying amount	Cost – Accumulated depreciation = Carrying amount
3. Calculate gain or loss	Proceeds – Carrying amount = Gain (loss)
4. Record disposal	Dr. Cash (or Receivable) Dr. Accumulated Depreciation Dr. Loss (or credit Gain) Cr. Property, Plant, and Equipment account

LIABILITIES   (Chapter 10)

Examples of Liabilities

Current Liabilities	Non-Current Liabilities
Bank indebtedness Corporate income tax payable Accounts payable Sales tax payable Property tax payable Salaries payable Payroll deductions (such as CPP payable, EI payable, employee income tax payable, union dues payable) Employee benefits (such as CPP payable, EI payable, health insurance benefits payable) Short-term notes payable Current maturities of non-current debt Provisions	Instalment notes payable Mortgage payable Bonds payable Finance lease liability Future income taxes Pension liabilities

Instalment Notes Payable—Payment Schedule

Payments	Interest Period	(A) Cash Payment	(B) Interest Expense	(C) Reduction of Principal	(D) Principal Balance
Fixed principal payments	Month	Variable B + C	D* × Annual Interest Rate × 1/12	Principal balance ÷ # of months	D* – C
Blended principal and interest	Month	Fixed B + C	D* × Annual Interest Rate × 1/12	A – B	D* – C

* From the prior period

Bonds Payable (Appendix 10A)

Premium	Market interest rate < Coupon interest rate
Face Value	Market interest rate = Coupon interest rate
Discount	Market interest rate > Coupon interest rate

Amortization of Bond Premium or Discount (Appendix 10A)

$$\underbrace{\text{Carrying Amount of Bonds at Beginning of Period} \times \text{Market (Effective) Interest Rate}}_{\text{(1) Bond Interest Expense}} - \underbrace{\text{Face Amount of Bonds} \times \text{Coupon Interest Rate}}_{\text{(2) Bond Interest Paid}} = \underbrace{\text{Amortization Amount}}_{\text{(3)}}$$

Continued on EP-4 at the end of the book

EP-3

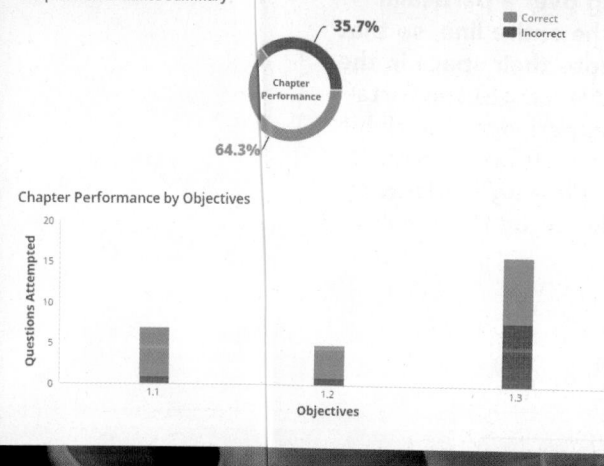
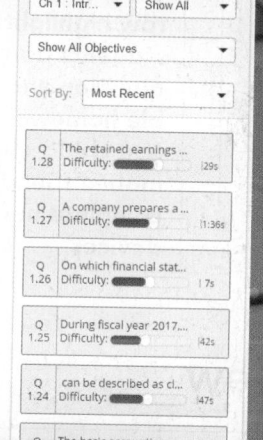

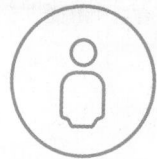
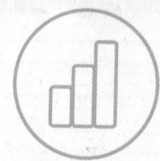

Applied Skills Videos

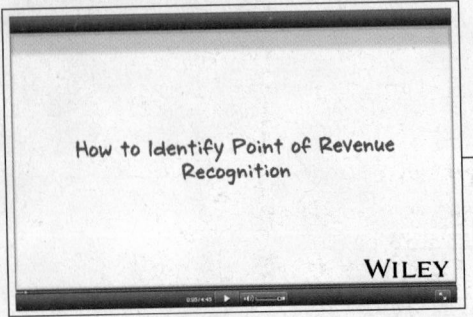

Applied skills videos cover general accounting concepts and provide an opportunity for students to get familiar with more challenging topics.

Improved Homework Aids

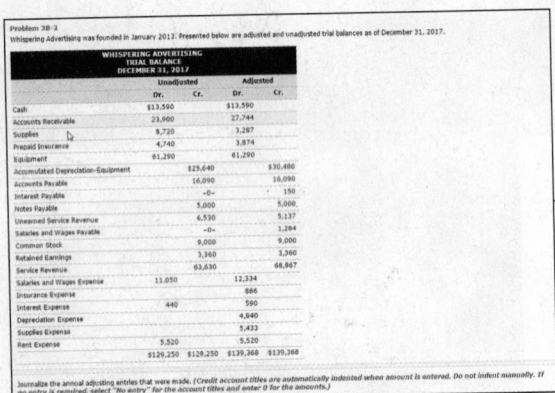

WileyPLUS has a new look for all end-of-chapter homework questions. The design features a clean sheet of paper effect with a larger field to input accounts so that nothing gets cut off. Hovering over a particular row highlights the entire line, so that students don't lose their space in the question and have a more comfortable homework experience. The debit and credit entry fields are also more mobile friendly, allowing students to complete homework on their mobile devices.

Accounting Cycle Review

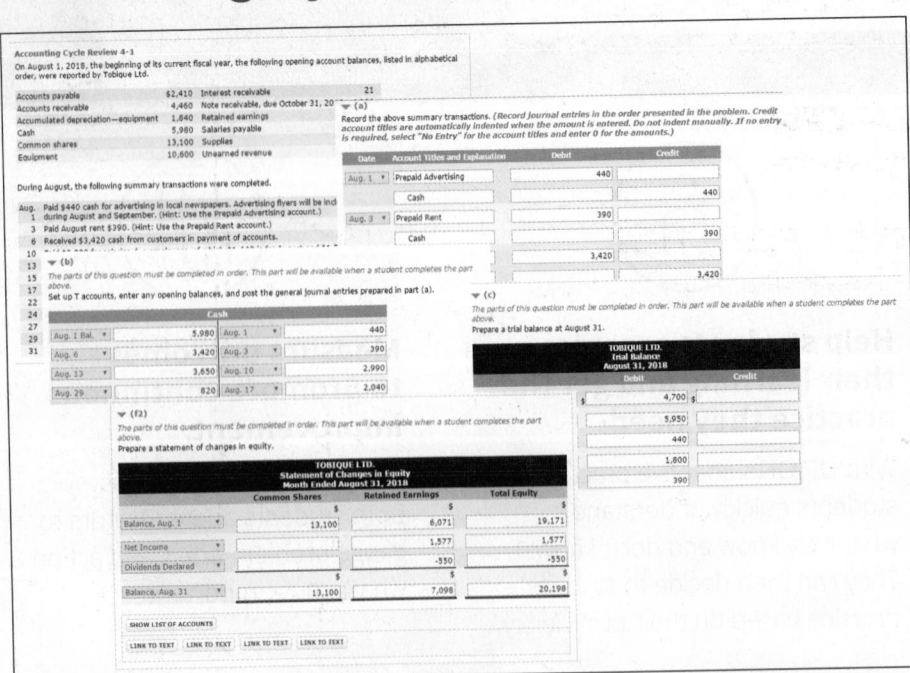

The Accouring Cycle Review hels students practise acounting fundamentls by integratingconcepts from multple chapters and stepsrom various parts of th accounting cycle.

FINANCIAL ACCOUNTING

Tools for Business Decision-Making

SEVENTH CANADIAN EDITION

Paul D. Kimmel Ph.D., CPA
University of Wisconsin—Milwaukee, Wisconsin

Jerry J. Weygandt Ph.D., CPA
University of Wisconsin—Madison, Wisconsin

Donald E. Kieso Ph.D., CPA
Northern Illinois University—DeKalb, Illinois

Barbara Trenholm FCPA, FCA, ICD.D
University of New Brunswick—Fredericton, New Brunswick

Wayne Irvine CPA, CA, CFA
University of Calgary—Calgary, Alberta

Christopher D. Burnley FCPA, FCA
Vancouver Island University—Nanaimo, British Columbia

Dedicated to our students—past, present, and future.

Library and Archives Canada Cataloguing in Publication

Kimmel, Paul D., author

Financial accounting : tools for business decision-making / Paul D. Kimmel, Ph.D., CPA, University of Wisconsin—Milwaukee, Wisconsin; Jerry J. Weygandt, Ph.D., CPA, University of Wisconsin—Madison, Wisconsin; Donald E. Kieso, Ph.D., CPA, Northern Illinois University—DeKalb, Illinois; Barbara Trenholm, FCPA, FCA, ICD.D, University of New Brunswick—Fredericton, New Brunswick; Wayne Irvine, CPA, CA, CFA; University of Calgary—Calgary, Alberta; Christopher D. Burnley, CPA, CA, Vancouver Island University—British Columbia.—Seventh Canadian edition.

Includes index.
Issued in print and electronic formats.
ISBN 978-1-119-21158-7.—ISBN 978-1-119-21157-0 (looseleaf).—ISBN 978-1-119-32062-3 (EPUB)

1. Accounting—Textbooks. I. Weygandt, Jerry J., author II. Kieso, Donald E., author III. Trenholm, Barbara, author IV. Irvine, Wayne, author V. Burnley, Christopher D., 1966- VI. Title.

HF5636.K55 2016   657'.044   C2016-906102-7
                                    C2016-906103-5

Production Credits
Director, Accounting and Finance, Global Education: Michael McDonald
Executive Editor: Zoë Craig
Senior Marketing Manager: Anita Osborne
Product Designer: Matt Origoni
Senior Manager, Learning Design and Content Development: Karen Staudinger
Developmental Editor: Daleara Jamasji Hirjikaka
Senior Content Manager: Dorothy Sinclair
Production Editor: Meaghan MacDonald
Media Editor: Elena Saccaro
Senior Photo Editor: Mary Ann Price
Typesetting: Aptara Corporation
Project Manager: Denise Showers (Aptara Corp.)
Interior Design: Joanna Vierra
Cover: Joanna Vierra/Wiley
Cover Photography: Front © Mimadeo/Getty; Back © Monkey Business Images/Shutterstock
Printing and Binding: LSC Communications, Inc.

WILEY

John Wiley & Sons Canada, Ltd.
90 Eglinton Avenue East, Suite 300
Toronto, ON, M4P 2Y3 Canada
Visit our website at: www.wiley.ca

Barbara Trenholm, FCPA, FCA, ICD.D, is a professor emerita at the University of New Brunswick, for which she continues to teach on a part-time basis. Her teaching and educational leadership has been widely recognized with numerous local, national, and international teaching awards. She also served a three-year term as a Teaching Scholar at the University of New Brunswick.

Barbara is a member of the boards of several public, Crown, and private corporations, including Plazacorp Retail REIT, NB Power, and the International Development Research Centre. She is a past board member of Atomic Energy of Canada Limited, the Canadian Institute of Chartered Accountants (now known as CPA Canada), and the Atlantic School of Chartered Accountancy (now known as CPA Atlantic School of Business), and past president of the New Brunswick Institute of Chartered Accountants (now known as CPA New Brunswick). She has extensive service as chair and a member of a wide range of committees at the provincial, national, and international levels of the accounting profession. In addition to her involvement with her profession, she has also served in leadership roles at the university and in the community.

She has presented at many conferences and published widely in the field of accounting education and standard setting in journals, including *Accounting Horizons, Journal of the Academy of Business Education, CAmagazine, CGA Magazine,* and *CMA Magazine.* She is also part of the Canadian author team of Weygandt, Kieso, Kimmel, Trenholm, Warren, and Novak, *Accounting Principles,* published by John Wiley & Sons Canada, Ltd.

Wayne Irvine, CPA, CA, CFA, teaches accounting at the Haskayne School of Business, University of Calgary. Prior to his full-time academic career, Wayne worked for 12 years at Price Waterhouse in the audit group and as manager of the Calgary office's continuing education program.

Wayne has over 25 years of teaching experience with several professional accounting programs, most recently as a session leader for CPA Western School of Business in its Professional Education Program.

Wayne has, in addition to other publishing projects, authored a number of case exams for CPA legacy programs and published a case in *Accounting Perspectives.*

Wayne is a four-time recipient of the University of Calgary's Students' Union Teaching Excellence Award and is the only member of his faculty to have been awarded a Hall of Fame Teaching award from that organization. He has also received over a dozen other teaching and service awards from other student organizations and from the CPA profession.

Chris Burnley, FCPA, FCA, is a professor in the Accounting Department at Vancouver Island University. Prior to his full-time academic career, Chris worked for 12 years in public practice and also audited government departments and United Nations agencies with the Office of the Auditor General of Canada. Chris also teaches in the CPA Professional Education Program for the CPA Western School of Business.

Chris has also taught in the Master of Professional Accounting Program at the Edwards School of Business, where he was recognized by the University of Saskatchewan with the Chartered Professional Accountants of Alberta teaching excellence award. He is active internationally, teaching and delivering guest lectures at Vancouver Island University's partner institutions in Europe, Asia, and the South Pacific. Chris has been awarded numerous internal and external grants in support of his academic work and has presented at national conferences.

Chris has been awarded a number of prizes by the Canadian Academic Accounting Association as a result of his academic work, including awards for case authoring and developing innovative ideas in accounting education.

Chris is active in the accounting profession, and chairs the board of the Chartered Professional Accountants of British Columbia's Education Foundation. He is a past recipient of the Ritchie W. McCloy Award for CA Volunteerism. Chris is also the author of the textbook *Understanding Financial Accounting,* published by John Wiley & Sons Canada, Ltd.

Paul D. Kimmel, Ph.D., CPA, received his bachelor's degree from the University of Minnesota and his doctorate in accounting from the University of Wisconsin. He is an Associate Professor at the University of Wisconsin—Milwaukee, and has public accounting experience with Deloitte & Touche (Minneapolis). He was the recipient of the UWM School of Business Advisory Council Teaching Award, the Reggie Taite Excellence in Teaching Award, and a three-time winner of the Outstanding Teaching Assistant Award at the University of Wisconsin. He is also a recipient of the Elijah Watts Sells Award for Honorary Distinction for his results on the CPA exam. He is a member of the American Accounting Association and the Institute of Management Accountants and has published articles in *Accounting Review, Accounting Horizons, Advances in Management Accounting, Managerial Finance, Issues in Accounting Education,* and *Journal of Accounting Education,* as well as other journals. His research interests include accounting for financial instruments and innovation in accounting education. He has published papers and given numerous talks on incorporating critical thinking into accounting education, and helped prepare a catalogue of critical thinking resources for the Federated Schools of Accountancy.

Jerry J. Weygandt, Ph.D., CPA, is the Arthur Andersen Alumni Emeritus Professor of Accounting at the University of Wisconsin—Madison. He holds a Ph.D. in accounting from the University of Illinois. Articles by Professor Weygandt have appeared in *Accounting Review, Journal of Accounting Research, Accounting Horizons, Journal of Accountancy,* and other academic and professional journals. Professor Weygandt is author of other accounting and financial reporting books and is a member of the American Accounting Association, the American Institute of Certified Public Accountants, and the Wisconsin Society of Certified Public Accountants. He has served on numerous committees of the American Accounting Association and as a member of the editorial board of *Accounting Review*; he has also served as President and Secretary-Treasurer of the American Accounting Association. In addition, he has been actively involved with the American Institute of Certified Public Accountants and has been a member of the Accounting Standards Executive Committee of that organization. He served on the FASB task force that examined the reporting issues related to accounting for income taxes and as a trustee of the Financial Accounting Foundation. Professor Weygandt has received the Chancellor's Award for Excellence in Teaching and the Beta Gamma Sigma Dean's Teaching Award. He is on the board of directors of M&I Bank of Southern Wisconsin. He is the recipient of the Wisconsin Institute of CPAs' Outstanding Educator's Award and the Lifetime Achievement Award. In 2001, he received the American Accounting Association's Outstanding Accounting Educator Award.

Donald E. Kieso, Ph.D., CPA, received his bachelor's degree from Aurora University and his doctorate in accounting from the University of Illinois. He has served as chairman of the Department of Accountancy and is currently the KPMG Emeritus Professor of Accounting at Northern Illinois University. He has public accounting experience with Price Waterhouse & Co. and Arthur Andersen & Co. and research experience with the Research Division of the American Institute of Certified Public Accountants. He is a recipient of NIU's Teaching Excellence Award and four Golden Apple Teaching Awards. Professor Kieso is a member of the American Accounting Association, the American Institute of Certified Public Accountants, and the Illinois CPA Society. He has served as a member of the Board of Directors of the Illinois CPA Society, the AACSB's Accounting Accreditation Committees, and the State of Illinois Comptroller's Commission; as Secretary-Treasurer of the Federation of Schools of Accountancy; and as Secretary-Treasurer of the American Accounting Association. Professor Kieso is currently serving on the Board of Trustees and Executive Committee of Aurora University, and is a member of various other boards. From 1989 to 1993, he served as a charter member of the national Accounting Education Change Commission. He is the recipient of the Outstanding Accounting Educator Award from the Illinois CPA Society, the FSA's Joseph A. Silvoso Award of Merit, the NIU Foundation's Humanitarian Award for Service to Higher Education, the Distinguished Service Award from the Illinois CPA Society, and in 2003 an honorary doctorate from Aurora University.

WHAT'S NEW?

Helping Students Learn Accounting Concepts

We have carefully scrutinized all chapter material to find new ways to engage students and help them learn accounting concepts. A new learning objective structure helps students learn concepts in more manageable "chunks," with 20% more Do It! exercises added to help students test their understanding before moving on to the next topic. Of these, more than 60% are new or updated. As well, we added and/or revised a significant number of explanations, examples, illustrations, and summaries throughout the text to better facilitate student learning.

Real-World Context

One of the goals of the financial accounting course is to orient students to the application of accounting principles and techniques in practice. Accordingly, we have expanded our practice of using current examples from real companies throughout the textbook by adding more high-interest companies that we hope will increase student engagement. This edition includes more than 300 references to real-world companies of interest to students. Nearly a quarter of the chapter-opening feature stories were replaced with new stories, while the remainder were updated. New feature companies for this edition are The North West Company and Sobeys, two well-known companies in the grocery industry. References to these companies have been included throughout the textbook in a variety of ways—in simplified financial statements in the chapter material, ratio analyses, Using the Decision Toolkit, end-of-chapter cases, and financial statements in Appendices A and B at the end of the textbook. In addition, our author team is active in delivering the CPA Professional Education Program and incorporated this real-world perspective as each chapter, including the end-of-chapter material, was written. International Financial Reporting Standards (IFRS) and Accounting Standards for Private Enterprises (ASPE) were also revised to reflect current and pending changes to standards.

Focus on the Accounting Cycle

For many students, success in an introductory accounting course hinges on developing a sound understanding of the accounting cycle and seeing how the material they are working with in a particular chapter fits in the accounting cycle. To help students improve their understanding, we have added new, recurring illustrations that show students the big picture of the accounting cycle and doubled the number of comprehensive cases that incorporate the accounting cycle. All of these changes provide students with more opportunities to learn and retain accounting fundamentals integrated across multiple chapters.

Review and Practice

A new review and practice section added to each chapter includes, in one place, an overview of the learning objectives, key terms, differences (if any) between IFRS and ASPE, and decision tools in addition to practice opportunities using the Decision Toolkit and a comprehensive Do It! The review and practice section also includes objective-format questions that allow students to self-assess their understanding of the topics in each chapter. These questions are comprehensive in their coverage, with detailed feedback provided at the end of the chapter to assist students in analyzing their results. Additional practice objective-format questions are available in the test bank for instructor use.

End-of-Chapter Material

The end-of-chapter material underwent a comprehensive updating to ensure that it continues to be relevant and fresh. Well over half of the questions, brief exercises, exercises, problems, and cases in the end-of-chapter material are either new or significantly updated. The cases in the Expand Your Critical Thinking section of each chapter have been reorganized into new categories, including financial reporting, financial analysis, ethics, student view, professional judgement, and serial cases. The serial case, which has been an important continuing feature in each chapter in past editions, has been completely revised in this edition to follow the evolution of a computer consulting company from a small private company to a large publicly traded company.

Key Features of Each Chapter

Chapter 1: The Purpose and Use of Financial Statements
- Feature story is about The North West Company and how accounting aids decision-making
- Identifies the users and uses of financial accounting information and forms of business organization—proprietorship, partnership, private corporation, and public corporation
- Describes the business activities—financing, investing, and operating activities—that affect companies
- Explains the content, purpose, and interrelationships of each of the financial statements—income statement, statement of changes in equity, statement of financial position, and statement of cash flows
- Uses financial statements of a hypothetical company (to keep it simple), followed by those for a real company, The North West Company (to make it relevant)
- *Key changes:* Clarified concept of internal users of financial information. Added discussion on why ASPE exists and why a private company may choose to use IFRS. Switched order of discussion of debt and equity financing and added context

to discussion of dividends. Revised discussion of investing activities related to investments in shares and debt securities and added information about asset disposals. Content added related to management discussion and analysis.

Chapter 2: A Further Look at Financial Statements
- Feature story is about CT Real Estate Investment Trust, its users, and use of accounting standards
- Presents the classified statement of financial position and the items typically found in each section
- Explains how ratio analysis is used to analyze a company's liquidity, solvency, and profitability
- Applies ratio analysis to CT REIT, Choice Properties REIT, and their industry (working capital, current debt to total assets, basic earnings per share, and price-earnings ratios)
- Describes the conceptual framework of accounting
- *Key changes*: Updated terminology relating to current value and income. Added explanation of future economic benefits. Added illustration of operating cycle. Expanded illustration of statement of financial position classifications. Expanded discussion of using price-earnings ratio to assess the price of a company's shares relative to the company's earnings. Added material on acceptance of IFRS-based financial statements by U.S. securities regulators. Included management stewardship of assets in objectives of financial reporting. Added discussion of users identified in conceptual framework and explanation of the difference between fundamental and enhancing qualitative characteristics. Revised conceptual framework illustration.

Chapter 3: The Accounting Information System
- Feature story is about BeaverTails' experiences with an accounting information system
- Covers transaction analysis, explaining how accounts, debits, and credits are used to record transactions
- Explains the first four steps in the accounting cycle, including analyzing, journalizing, and posting transactions and preparing the trial balance
- *Key changes*: Updated receivable transactions in the Sierra Corporation accounting cycle example. Expanded the discussion of when to record and not to record transactions in reference to the elements of financial statements. Clarified a number of concepts incorporated in this chapter, including the use of negatives in the accounting equation, the use of the chart of accounts, and the distinction between formal general ledger accounts and T accounts. Reformatted the accounting equation analysis to the same format used in Chapter 4 so that students can more easily compare information in different parts of the accounting cycle from one chapter to the next. Added a section on how opening balances affect accounting equation analyses. Repositioned the discussion of normal balances earlier in the chapter. Added a review of financial statement relationships to help students better understand the directional impact of shareholders' equity and how the statements fit together. Expanded the discussion about the preparation of a trial balance, including how to find errors.

Chapter 4: Accrual Accounting Concepts
- Feature story is about Western University's application of accrual accounting
- Explains revenue and expense recognition
- Emphasizes the difference between cash and accrual accounting
- Completes the accounting cycle, from adjusting entries to the closing process
- *Key changes*: Updated the revenue recognition section to incorporate new criteria consistent with anticipated changes to the revenue recognition standard and conceptual framework. Clarified and reordered discussion of accrued revenues and expenses. Added original transaction entries throughout adjusting entry section. Reorganized summary tables and added effects on net income and shareholders' equity. Expanded discussion and illustration of closing entries, using same format employed in Chapters 3 and 4.

Chapter 5: Merchandising Operations
- Feature story is about Loblaw Companies Limited's initiatives to improve its process of getting products from its suppliers to its shelves
- Identifies the key differences between service and merchandising companies
- Introduces inventory systems using perpetual inventory system (the periodic inventory system is presented in an appendix)
- Explains how to record purchases and sales of merchandise
- Presents single-step and multiple-step income statements
- Applies ratio analysis to Loblaw, Metro, and their industry (gross profit margin and profit margin)
- *Key changes*: Restructured multiple illustrations throughout the chapter, including income measurements, flow of costs, freight terms, cost of goods purchased, cost of goods available for sale, cost of goods sold, and net sales. Added table outlining the advantages of each type of inventory system. Included discussion on professional judgement required when classifying expenses by function.

Chapter 6: Reporting and Analyzing Inventory
- Feature story is about lululemon athletica inc.'s inventory management
- Explains how inventory quantities and ownership are determined
- Covers cost formulas and their financial statement effects using perpetual inventory system (the periodic inventory system is presented in an appendix)
- Discusses effects of inventory errors on financial statements
- Outlines how to value and record inventory at the lower of cost and net realizable value
- Applies ratio analysis to lululemon, Limited Brands, and their industry (inventory turnover and days in inventory)
- *Key changes*: Deleted section on detailed inventory count procedures. Revised discussion of errors to focus on two types of errors: errors made when determining the cost of inventory and errors made recording goods in transit. Expanded discussion of goods in transit and clarified

more specifically the nature of misstatements arising from errors in recording purchases of merchandise inventory as well as errors made when determining the cost of this inventory.

Chapter 7: Internal Control and Cash

- Feature story is about cash control at Nick's Steakhouse and Pizza
- Explains the components of an internal control system, including its control activities and limitations
- Identifies the key control activities over cash receipts and payments
- Discusses bank reconciliations in detail as a control feature
- Explains how cash is reported and managed
- *Key changes*: Revised control activities discussion to more closely align with Canadian Auditing Standard 315 and COSO (Committee of Sponsoring Organizations of the Treadway Commission). This resulted in changes to a number of control activities: authorization was changed to assignment of responsibility, independent checks were changed to review and reconciliation, and human resources controls was deleted. Added explanation of how assignment of responsibility and segregation of duties differ. Added discussion about internal controls being preventive or detective. Included a summary of the limitations of internal controls. Deleted discussion of Association of Certified Fraud Examiners fraud statistics, as well as the discussion of postage stamps and debit/credit card slips as cash. Expanded discussion of bank indebtedness and lines of credit.

Chapter 8: Reporting and Analyzing Receivables

- Feature story is about Canadian Tire's receivables
- Presents the basic types of receivables and how to record accounts receivable transactions, including the use of subsidiary ledgers
- Explains how to account for bad debt expense, write offs, and recovery of uncollectible accounts using the allowance method
- Outlines how to account for notes receivable, interest revenue, and derecognizing notes
- Explains statement presentation of receivables
- Identifies the principles of accounts receivable management
- Applies ratio analysis to Canadian Tire, Sears, and their industry (receivables turnover and average collection period)
- *Key changes*: Deleted discussion about nonbank credit card receivables. Enhanced discussion of the accounts receivable subsidiary ledger. Enhanced discussion on the percentage of receivables method. Revised summary of allowance method. Moved section comparing notes receivable and notes payable to Chapter 10. Enhanced discussion of bad debts related to notes receivable and the allowance for doubtful notes.

Chapter 9: Reporting and Analyzing Long-Lived Assets

- Feature story is about WestJet's property and equipment
- Covers the acquisition and derecognition of property, plant, and equipment
- Reviews buy or lease decisions

- Explains the calculation and implications of using different depreciation methods
- Discusses the accounting for intangible assets and goodwill
- Reviews the reporting of long-lived assets
- Applies ratio analysis to WestJet, Air Canada, and their industry (return on assets, asset turnover, and profit margin)
- *Key changes*: Incorporated concepts on value that are introduced in the IFRS conceptual framework, and covered new IFRS lease standards.

Chapter 10: Reporting and Analyzing Liabilities

- Feature story is about Canada Post's liabilities
- Covers current liabilities, including operating lines of credit, sales taxes, property taxes, payroll, short-term notes payable, current maturities of non-current debt, provisions, and contingencies
- Covers non-current liabilities, including instalment notes payable and bonds payable
- Applies effective-interest method of amortization to long-term instalment notes and bonds
- Reviews reporting and analysis of liabilities
- Applies ratio analysis to Canada Post, UPS, and their industry (debt to total assets and times interest earned)
- *Key changes*: Coverage of bonds, which is included in the appendix, has been split into two parts: the first dealing with the accounting for bond transactions without needing to determine bond prices and the second dealing with the calculation of bond prices. This gives instructors flexibility when covering bond topics.

Chapter 11: Reporting and Analyzing Shareholders' Equity

- Feature story is about Leon's Furniture Limited
- Discusses corporate form of organization and its advantages and disadvantages
- Covers issues related to common and preferred shares, including reasons why companies repurchase their own shares
- Explains cash dividends, stock dividends, stock splits, and implications for analysis
- Describes the presentation of equity items in the statement of financial position and statement of changes in equity (IFRS) or statement of retained earnings (ASPE)
- Applies ratio analysis to Leon's Furniture and BMTC, and their industry (payout ratio, dividend yield, earnings per share, and return on common shareholders' equity)
- *Key changes*: Increased emphasis on the comparison of debt versus equity financing. Included coverage of the entries recorded when reacquiring shares and expanded coverage of contributed surplus. Expanded coverage of preferred shares with dividend reset rates.

Chapter 12: Reporting and Analyzing Investments

- Feature story is about Scotiabank's management of investments
- Explains why companies purchase debt and equity securities as strategic or non-strategic investments
- Describes the various valuation models for non-strategic investments: fair value through profit or loss, fair value

through other comprehensive income, amortized cost, and cost
- Describes the accounting for strategic investments, including the use of the equity and cost valuation models
- Discusses other comprehensive income, including the statement of comprehensive income, and accumulated other comprehensive income
- Explains how investments are reported on the financial statements under each of the valuation models used for non-strategic and strategic investments, including the different reporting requirements under IFRS and ASPE
- Introduces consolidation accounting for financial reporting purposes at a conceptual level
- Discusses the accounting for investments in bonds and compares it with bonds payable in a chapter appendix
- *Key changes:* IFRS coverage updated to be consistent with IFRS 9.

Chapter 13: Statement of Cash Flows
- Feature story is about Teck Resources' cash flows
- Explains the purpose and content of the statement of cash flows
- Describes the preparation of the operating, investing, and financing activities of the statement of cash flows. Shows the use of the indirect method within the chapter and the direct method in the appendix to provide greater flexibility when determining which of these topics will be covered

- Applies ratio analysis to Teck and Freeport-McMoRan (free cash flow)
- *Key changes:* Moved coverage of the direct method to an appendix. Expanded coverage on how the life cycle of a business affects the statement of cash flows. Removed cash current debt coverage and cash total debt coverage ratios due to the adequacy of other ratios in the text for assessing debt coverage.

Chapter 14: Performance Measurement
- Feature story is about Hudson's Bay Company's business strategy, including its acquisitions and divestitures
- Demonstrates horizontal analysis, vertical analysis, and ratio analysis
- Applies ratio analysis to Hudson's Bay, Dollarama, and their industry (comprehensive analysis of all ratios)
- Discusses factors that can limit the usefulness of financial analysis, including the diversification of the company's operations, the use of alternative accounting policies, the use of estimates, and the impact of other comprehensive income items, discontinued operations, and non-recurring items
- Discusses the use of non-GAAP measures
- *Key changes:* Moved topics relating to sustainable income to the end of the chapter and reduced coverage of discontinued business losses. Increased coverage on the relationship between ratios.

ACTIVE TEACHING AND LEARNING SUPPLEMENTARY MATERIAL

WileyPLUS

www.wiley.com/go/kimmelcanada

Financial Accounting: Tools for Business Decision-Making, Seventh Canadian Edition, features a full line of teaching and learning resources. Driven by the same basic beliefs as the textbook, these supplements provide a consistent and well-integrated learning system. This hands-on, real-world package guides instructors through the process of active learning and gives them the tools to create an interactive learning environment.

WileyPLUS is an innovative, research-based online environment for effective teaching and learning. *WileyPLUS* builds students' confidence because it takes the guesswork out of studying by providing students with a clear roadmap: **what to do, how to do it, and if they did it right**. Students will take more initiative so you'll have a greater impact on their achievement in the classroom and beyond.

Among its many features, this online learning interface allows students to study and practise using the digital textbook, quizzes, and algorithmic exercises. The immediate feedback helps students understand where they need to focus their study efforts. We have standardized the chart of accounts to reduce complexity and to facilitate online practice.

Based on cognitive science, *WileyPLUS* **with ORION** is a personalized, adaptive learning experience that gives students the practice they need to build proficiency on topics while using their study time more effectively. The adaptive engine is powered by hundreds of unique questions per chapter, giving students endless opportunities for practice throughout the course. Orion is available with this text.

For Instructors

We offer several useful supplements and resources on the book's companion website (www.wiley.com/go/kimmelcanada) and in *WileyPLUS*. On these sites, instructors will find the Solutions Manual, PowerPoint presentations, Test Bank, Instructor's Manual, Computerized Test Bank, and other valuable teaching resources.

The supplements are prepared by subject matter experts and contributors who are often users of the text. Supplements are meticulously reviewed by the authors to ensure consistency with the textbook. Supplements like the test bank and the solutions manual are also rigorously checked to ensure accuracy.

For Students

Students will find selected support materials on the book's companion website (www.wiley.com/go/kimmelcanada) and an expanded list of resources in *WileyPLUS* that will help them develop their conceptual understanding of class material and increase their ability to solve problems. In addition to other resources, students will find:

- Multimedia tutorials
- Additional Demonstration Problems
- PowerPoint presentations
- Chart of accounts
- Checklist of key figures
- Financial Statement Analysis Primer
- Solution walk-through videos
- Applied skills videos
- Excel resources, including simulations and an Excel primer
- Practice questions in ORION

ACKNOWLEDGEMENTS

During the course of developing the seventh Canadian edition of *Financial Accounting: Tools for Business Decision-Making*, the authors benefited from the feedback from instructors and students of financial accounting across the country, including many users of the previous editions of this text.

The constructive advice and attention to accuracy by the following contributors to the seventh edition text and supplements provided valuable input to the development of this edition.

Jeremy Clegg, *Vancouver Island University*
Angela Davis, *Booth University College*
Rosalie Harms, *University of Winnipeg*
Rhonda Heninger, *Southern Alberta Institute of Technology*
Joanne Hinton, *University of New Brunswick*

Amy Hoggard, *Camosun College*
Sandy Kizan, *Athabasca University*
Cecile Laurin, *Algonquin College*
Debra Lee-Hue, *Centennial College*
Ross Meecher
Debbie Musil, *Kwantlen Polytechnic University*

Alison Parker, *Camosun College*
Joel Shapiro, *Ryerson University*
Marie Sinnott, *College of New Caledonia*
Amanda Wallace, *Ryerson University*

We appreciate the exemplary support and commitment given us by the talented team at Wiley Canada, including Zoë Craig, Executive Editor; Deanna Durnford, Supplements Coordinator; Daleara Hirjikaka, Developmental Editor; Anita Osborne, Senior Marketing Manager; Karen Staudinger, Senior Manager, Learning Design and Content Management; in addition to all of Wiley's dedicated sales managers and representatives, who continue to work diligently to serve your needs.

We also wish to specifically thank the many people who worked behind the scenes to improve the design and accuracy of this text, including Denise Showers, project manager at Aptara; Laurel Hyatt, copyeditor; Zofia Laubitz, proofreader; and Belle Wong, indexer.

It would not have been possible to write this text without the understanding of our employers, colleagues, students, family, and friends. Together, they provided a creative and supportive environment for our work.

We have tried our best to produce a text and supplement package that is error-free and that meets your specific needs. Suggestions and comments from users are encouraged and appreciated. Please don't hesitate to let us know of any improvements that we should consider for subsequent printings or editions. You can send us your thoughts and ideas by emailing KimmelAuthors@gmail.com.

Barbara Trenholm
Wayne Irvine
Christopher Burnley
November 2016

BRIEF CONTENTS

CONTENTS

1

The Purpose and Use of Financial Statements

CHAPTER PREVIEW   *The **Chapter Preview** describes the purpose of the chapter and highlights major topics.*

To be successful in business, countless decisions have to be made—and decisions require accounting information. The purpose of this chapter is to show you accounting's role in providing useful financial information for decision-making. The material in this chapter will help you answer a number of questions, including: Who uses accounting information and how do they use it? How are businesses formed? What are the main types of business activities and how are they reported in a business's financial statements? How can you begin to interpret the information in the financial statements and use it to make decisions?

*The **Chapter Outline** presents the chapter's learning objectives, topics, and practice opportunities to give you a framework for learning the specific concepts covered in the chapter.*

CHAPTER OUTLINE

LEARNING OBJECTIVES	READ	PRACTICE
1 Identify the uses and users of accounting information.	• Internal users • External users • Ethics and accounting information	**DO IT!** 1-1 Users of accounting information
2 Describe the primary forms of business organization.	• Proprietorships • Partnerships • Corporations • Generally accepted accounting principles for business organizations	**DO IT!** 1-2 Business organizations
3 Explain the three main types of business activity.	• Financing activities • Investing activities • Operating activities • Summary of business activities	**DO IT!** 1-3 Business activities
4 Describe the purpose and content of each of the financial statements.	• The financial statements • North West's financial statements • Elements of an annual report	**DO IT!** 1-4a Accounting equation 1-4b Financial statement relationships 1-4c Preparing financial statements

Simon Potter/Getty Images, Inc.

*The **Feature Story** helps you picture how the chapter relates to the real world of accounting and business. You will find references to the story throughout the chapter.*

The North West Company Inc. is one of the world's longest-running retail enterprises. It was established in Montreal in 1779 by European fur traders who helped map Canada's North. It was merged with the rival Hudson's Bay Company in 1821 and became the Northern Stores Division. A group of investors purchased the division in 1987 and, in 1992, the company began trading on the Winnipeg and Toronto Stock Exchanges as The North West Company, Inc.

The Winnipeg-based North West Company is still a fixture in Canada's North, serving communities ranging from 300 to 9,000 people—many of them former trading posts. Its stores carry food, clothing, housewares, appliances, and outdoor gear. Many of the stores also provide services such as fuel, a post office, pharmacy, and income tax return preparation. The challenges of operating in the far North are significant and about 40% of the company's stores cannot be accessed by all-weather roads.

In 1992, North West began operating internationally when it acquired stores in Alaska. This was followed by a 2007 acquisition of stores in the South Pacific and Caribbean. At January 31, 2016, North West operated 181 stores in Canada, 33 in Alaska, and 14 in the South Pacific and Caribbean. These stores are operated under a number of banners, including Northern, NorthMart, Quickstop, Giant Tiger, AC Value Centers, and Cost-U-Less. The

Trading on a Long Tradition

Giant Tiger stores are franchises, as is the one Tim Hortons restaurant that the company operates. Staying true to its roots, North West still has operations that purchase furs from trappers. For the fiscal year ending January 31, 2016, North West had sales of nearly $1.8 billion and profits of about $70 million. The company's international operations generated 39% of its total revenues.

How does a company like the North West Company decide whether to expand into a new market, change its product categories, or operate as a franchisee? How are decisions made regarding what types and quantities of inventory should be carried at each store? How are pricing decisions made given the significance of transportation costs and changing foreign currency values? How does the company track consumer demands in the disparate markets it serves? Management relies on accounting as its key decision-making tool. And it's not just the company that needs financial information for making decisions. External audiences, such as banks, potential shareholders, and suppliers, also need to see the company's financial information before deciding whether to lend to, invest in, or sell to the retailer. The way the North West Company and other businesses communicate their financial information is through financial statements.[1]

Go to the *REVIEW AND PRACTICE* section at the end of the chapter for a targeted summary and practice with solutions.

Visit **WileyPLUS** for more opportunities.

Identify the uses and users of accounting information.

Essential terms are printed in blue when they first appear. They are listed and defined again in the glossary at the end of the book. There are many new terms in the first few chapters of the book, as you learn the language of accounting. Developing an understanding of these terms is one of the keys to successfully learning the material.

Accounting is the information system that identifies and records the economic events of an organization, and then communicates them to a wide variety of interested users. Why does accounting matter to these users? The world's economic systems depend on highly transparent, reliable, and accurate financial reporting. Because of this, accounting has long been labelled "the language of business."

That's one of the reasons why many Canadians, even those who do not plan on becoming accountants, study accounting. For example, Mike Cassidy, president of Maritime Bus; Sabrina Geremia, managing director of Google Canada; Monique Leroux, president and CEO of Desjardins Group; Jennifer Maki, CEO of Vale Canada; Elizabeth Marshall, a senator; George Melville, chairman and owner of Boston Pizza International; and Joe Resnick, NHL hockey player agent, all have studied accounting in depth.

Whether you plan to become an accountant or not, a working knowledge of accounting will be relevant and useful in whatever role you assume as a user of accounting information—as an owner of your own business, working for someone else in their business, investing in a business, or simply understanding your own personal finances.

Users of accounting information can be divided broadly into two types: internal users and external users. We will discuss each of these in the sections that follow.

INTERNAL USERS

Internal users of accounting information manage companies, non-profits, and government organizations. They work for and manage these organizations. By virtue of their position in management, **internal users** have access to internal accounting information to help them make the decisions required to run the company. These include company officers (senior management), as well as managers and directors in finance, marketing, human resources, production, and other functional areas within a company. In other words, anyone who works for a company and has access to accounting information to assist them in managing and operating the company is considered to be an internal user.

In running a business, internal users must answer many important questions, as shown in Illustration 1-1.

▶Illustration 1-1
Questions asked by internal users

Finance
Is there enough cash to pay the bills?
Do we need to borrow more money?

Marketing
What price should we sell tablets
for to maximize profits?
Did our advertising campaign increase sales?

Human Resources
How many employees can we
afford to hire this year?
Can we afford to negotiate
salary increases?

Production
Which product line is the most profitable?
Should we contract out some of our production
or distribution operations?

To answer these and other questions, users need detailed accounting information on a timely basis; that is, it must be available when it is required. For internal users, accounting provides a variety of internal reports, such as financial comparisons of operating alternatives, projections of income from new sales campaigns, analyses of sales costs, and forecasts of cash needs. In addition, companies present summarized financial information in the form of financial statements for both internal and external use.

EXTERNAL USERS

External users are not involved in managing a company and do not have access to accounting information other than that which is available to the general public. There are several types of external users of accounting information. **Investors** use accounting information to make decisions to buy, hold, or sell their ownership interest. **Lenders**, such as bankers, use accounting information to evaluate the risks of lending money. Other **creditors**, such as suppliers, use accounting information to decide whether or not to grant credit (sell on account) to a customer. **Investors, lenders, and other creditors** are considered to be the primary users of accounting information.

Some questions that external users, such as investors, lenders, and other creditors, may ask about a company are shown in Illustration 1-2.

Alternative Terminology notes give synonyms that you may hear or see in the real world, as well as in this text.

> **Alternative Terminology**
> *Investors* are also known as *shareholders*. *Creditors* are also known as *lenders*.

▶ Illustration 1-2
Questions asked by external users

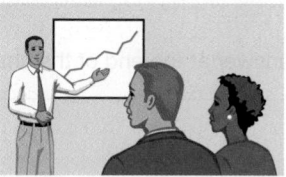

Investors
Should I purchase shares of this company?
What is the return from my investment?

Lenders and Other Creditors
Will the company be able to pay its debts as they come due?
How does the amount of funds invested by shareholders compare with the amount borrowed from creditors?

In addition to investors, lenders, and other creditors, there are many other external users with a variety of information needs and questions. For example, potential employees use annual reports to learn about the company and evaluate job prospects. Current employees who are not directly involved in managing the company, as well as any labour union that may represent them, use financial information to bargain for better salaries and benefits. And taxing authorities, such as the Canada Revenue Agency, use information from a company's financial statements in assessing a company's income tax return.

ETHICS AND ACCOUNTING INFORMATION

In order for financial information to have value to its users, whether internal or external, it must be prepared by individuals with high standards of ethical behaviour. Ethical decision-making is critical in the preparation of accounting information and to the decision makers who rely on this information.

Fortunately, most individuals in business are ethical. Their actions are both legal and responsible. They consider the organization's interests when they make decisions. Accountants and other professionals have extensive rules of professional conduct to guide their behaviour with each other and the public. In addition, most companies have codes of conduct that outline their commitment to ethical behaviour in their internal and external relationships.

To sensitize you to ethical situations and give you practice at solving ethical dilemmas, we highlight the importance of ethics in different ways in this text:

1. A number of the feature stories and other parts of the text discuss the central importance of ethical behaviour to financial reporting.
2. Many of the *Accounting Matters* boxes highlight ethics situations and issues in actual business settings.
3. Many chapters include an *Ethics Case* in the end-of-chapter material that simulates a business situation and asks you to put yourself in the position of a key decision maker.

DO IT! ▶ 1-1   Users of Accounting Information

Action Plan

✔ Understand the difference between internal and external users: Internal users work for the company at a management level and require access to internal accounting information to assist them in managing and operating the company. External users are not involved in running the company and do not have access to accounting information other than that which is available to the general public.

✔ Understand the types of information internal and external users require to make decisions.

Do It! exercises prompt you to stop and practise the key points you have just studied. The Action Plan offers you tips about how to approach the exercise. Related exercise material tells you which Brief Exercises (BE) and Exercises (E) at the end of the chapter have similar learning objectives.

The following is a list of questions that may be asked by different users of accounting information:

1. Will I be able to obtain enough cash to finance this month's cash shortfall?
2. Will the company be able to repay the money we lend them when the loan comes due?
3. What was the labour cost for the production of 1,000 board feet of lumber?
4. Will the company stay in business long enough to service the products I buy from it?
5. Will the company's share price go up or down in the near future?
6. In which geographical areas and age demographics are our sales increasing?

(a) Identify the type of user who would most likely ask each of the above questions from the following list of possible users: chief financial officer, customers, investors, lenders, production manager, or marketing manager.

(b) Indicate whether the user you chose is an internal or external user.

SOLUTION
Try this Do It! exercise on your own and then check your answer at the end of the chapter.

Related Exercise Material: BE1–1 and E1–1.

LEARNING OBJECTIVE ▶2   Describe the primary forms of business organization.

Businesses can be organized in different ways and the accounting standards they use can vary depending on the type of organization. There are three common forms of business organization: proprietorships, partnerships, and corporations.

PROPRIETORSHIPS

When you graduate, you might decide to start your own business. If you do, you may choose to set up a proprietorship. A **proprietorship** is a business owned by one person, known as a proprietor. It is often called a "sole" proprietorship because there is a single owner.

The proprietorship form of business organization is simple to set up and gives the owner control over the business. In most cases, only a relatively small amount of money (capital) is needed to start in business as a proprietorship. The owner receives any income, suffers any losses, and is personally liable (responsible) for all debts of the business. This is known as unlimited liability.

There is no legal distinction between the business as an economic unit and the owner. Accordingly, the life of the proprietorship is limited to the life of the owner. The business income is reported as self-employment income and taxed on the owner's personal income tax return. However, for accounting purposes, the business records of the proprietorship must be kept separate from those related to the owner's personal activities.

The separation of business and personal records is known in its simplest form as the reporting entity concept. The **reporting entity concept** requires that the economic activity that can be identified with a particular business be kept separate and distinct from the activities of the owner and of all other economic entities. This concept applies not only to proprietorships, but also to partnerships and corporations, which are discussed in the next sections.

Small service businesses such as hair salons, plumbers, and mechanics are often proprietorships, as are many small-scale farms and small retail stores.

PARTNERSHIPS

Another possibility after graduating would be for you to join forces with other individuals to form a partnership. A **partnership** is a business owned by more than one person. In most respects, a partnership is similar to a proprietorship except that there is more than one owner. Partnerships are often formed because one person does not have enough economic resources to start or expand the business, or because partners bring unique skills or other resources to the partnership.

Partnerships are normally formalized in a written partnership agreement that outlines the formation of the partnership, partners' contributions, how net income and losses are shared, provisions for withdrawals of assets and/or partners, dispute resolution, and partnership liquidation. The need to develop a partnership agreement makes establishing a partnership more complex than establishing a proprietorship. Although there are advantages to working with others, there are also disadvantages. Each partner generally has unlimited liability for all debts of the partnership, even if one of the other partners created the debt. However, there are certain situations where partnerships can be formed with limited liability for selected partners.

Similar to a proprietorship, the income of the partnership is reported as self-employment income and taxed on each partner's personal income tax return. In addition, the reporting entity concept requires that partnership records be kept separate from each partner's personal activities.

Partnerships are typically used to organize professional service businesses, such as the practices of lawyers, doctors, architects, engineers, and accountants.

CORPORATIONS

As a third alternative after graduating, you might choose to form a business as a corporation. A **corporation** is a business organized as a separate legal entity owned by shareholders and is the most complex form of business to establish. The North West Company in our opening feature story is a corporation. As an investor in a corporation such as The North West Company, you receive shares to indicate your ownership claim. It is often possible for individuals to become owners of shares (shareholders) by investing relatively small amounts of money.

> **Alternative Terminology**
> *Shares* are also known as *stock.*

Suppose that you are one of North West's shareholders. The amount of cash that you have in your personal bank account and the balance you owe on your personal car loan are not reported in North West's financial statements. Similar to proprietorships and partnerships, you and the company are separate reporting entities under the reporting entity concept.

Since a corporation is a separate legal entity, its life is indefinite. That means it continues on regardless of who owns its shares. It is not affected by the withdrawal, death, or incapacity of an owner, as is the case in a proprietorship or partnership. Consequently, buying shares in a corporation, especially a large corporation, is often more attractive than investing in a proprietorship or partnership because shares are easier to sell.

There are other factors that need to be considered when deciding which organizational form of business to choose. As we discussed earlier, if you choose to organize as a proprietorship or partnership, you are personally liable for all debts of the business. Shareholders are not responsible for corporate debts unless they have provided a personal guarantee to the lender for them. Most shareholders enjoy limited liability since their risk of loss is limited to the amount they have invested in the company's shares.

All of these advantages taken together—indefinite life, ease of transferring ownership when selling shares, and limited liability—can make it easier for corporations, especially large corporations, to raise capital (cash) compared with proprietorships and partnerships. Another potential advantage is that corporations may receive a more favourable income tax treatment than other forms of business organization such as proprietorships and partnerships. Because of the wide variety of income tax issues that apply to different companies in different jurisdictions, you would be wise to seek professional advice on taxation matters before choosing any form of business organization.

Although the combined number of proprietorships and partnerships in Canada is more than the number of corporations, the revenue produced by corporations is far greater. Most of the largest businesses in Canada—for example, Manulife Financial, Power, Weston, Loblaw, Alimentation Couche-Tard, Royal Bank, Suncor, and Empire—are corporations. Recently, the top 15 of Canada's largest corporations each reported annual revenues ranging from $24 billion to $53 billion.

Corporations such as these are publicly traded. That is, their shares are listed on Canadian, or other, stock exchanges such as the Toronto Stock Exchange (TSX). **Public corporations** are required to distribute their financial statements to investors, lenders, other creditors, other interested parties, and the general public on a quarterly (every three months) and annual basis. North West is a public corporation. Its financial statements are readily available on its own website, as well as that of the System for Electronic Document Analysis and Retrieval (SEDAR), which posts financial statements for all public corporations in Canada. We have also included North West's financial statements in Appendix A at the back of this textbook for your easy reference.

In addition to public corporations like North West, there are **private corporations**. Private corporations also issue shares, but they do not make them available to the general public nor are they traded on public stock exchanges. These shares are often said to be "closely held." Consequently, many private corporations, especially small ones, do not have the same advantages of raising capital as do large corporations. For example, a small, local incorporated business would likely have as much difficulty raising funds as a proprietorship or partnership would.

There are some very large private corporations, however, such as the Irving Group of Companies, the Jim Pattison Group, and McCain Foods. Some of these private corporations are equal in size to or larger than many public corporations. For example, the Pattison Group reported annual revenue of $8.4 billion, nearly equal to that of Canada's largest public corporations. Like proprietorships and partnerships, private companies seldom distribute their financial statements publicly. Unlike public corporations, private corporations are under no obligation to do so and most private corporations do not wish to disclose financial information to their competitors and the public. Sobeys is a private company and one of the few that does publish its financial information.

The form used to initially organize a business is not permanent and can be changed as the needs of the business and its owners change. Many businesses start as proprietorships or partnerships and eventually incorporate. Some major Canadian companies, including George Weston, Sobeys, Bombardier, and Dollarama, all started as proprietorships and eventually incorporated as the businesses grew.

Because most Canadian business is transacted by corporations, this book focuses on the corporate form of organization. We will discuss the accounting for both publicly traded and private corporations in this textbook.

GENERALLY ACCEPTED ACCOUNTING PRINCIPLES FOR BUSINESS ORGANIZATIONS

> **Alternative Terminology**
> *Accounting principles* are also commonly known as *accounting standards* or *accounting policies*.

How do businesses decide on the amount of financial information to disclose? In what format should financial information be presented? The answers to these questions can be found in accounting rules and practices that are recognized as a general guide for financial reporting purposes.

These rules and practices are referred to as **generally accepted accounting principles**, commonly abbreviated as GAAP. GAAP includes broad policies and practices as well as rules and procedures that have substantive authoritative support and agreement about how to record and report economic events.

Generally accepted accounting principles can differ depending on the form of business organization. Publicly traded corporations must use International Financial Reporting Standards

(IFRS), a set of global accounting standards developed by the International Accounting Standards Board. Private corporations, whose users can have different needs than those of publicly traded corporations, have a choice between using IFRS or Accounting Standards for Private Enterprises (ASPE), developed by the Canadian Accounting Standards Board. ASPE were developed to reduce the complexity and cost of financial reporting for private companies, recognizing that there are normally fewer users of private company financial statements. Generally, the users of private company financial statements also have access to financial information beyond that available to the users of public company financial statements.

Most private corporations choose to use ASPE, although there are exceptions. There are a number of reasons that a private company may adopt IFRS. These include: it is considering accessing public debt or equity markets in the future, it wants to be able to compare its financial results with competitors that use IFRS, or it has foreign subsidiaries that are required to use IFRS and it wants a common set of accounting standards across the company. Sobeys, which we will study in this text, is an example of a private corporation that uses IFRS rather than ASPE. We will learn more about IFRS and ASPE for corporations in Chapter 2.

Because proprietorships and partnerships are privately owned (even though they are not private *corporations*), these businesses generally follow ASPE for external financial reporting purposes. However, proprietorships and partnerships often prepare financial statements only for the internal use of the owner(s), in which case they don't have to follow any particular set of accounting standards.

*The **Accounting Matters** boxes give examples of how accounting is used in various business situations.*

ACCOUNTING MATTERS

What's in a Company Name?

How can you tell whether a company is a corporation or not? Corporations in Canada and the United States are identified by "Ltd." ("Ltée" in French), "Inc.," "Corp.," or in some cases, "Co." following their names. These abbreviations can also be spelled out. In Brazil and France, the letters used are "SA" (Sôciedade Anonima, Société Anonyme); in Japan, "KK" (Kabushiki Kaisha); in the Netherlands, "NV" (Naamloze Vennootschap); in Italy, "SpA" (Societá per Azioni); and in Sweden, "AB" (Aktiebolag).

In the United Kingdom, public corporations are identified by "plc" (public limited company), while private corporations are denoted by "Ltd." The same designations in Germany are "AG" (Aktiengesellschaft) for public corporations and "GmbH" (Gesellschaft mit beschränkter Haftung) for private corporations. There are no name distinctions between public and private corporations in Canada.

DO IT! ▶ 1-2　Business Organizations

In choosing the right organizational form for your business, you must consider the characteristics of each. Choose from the characteristics listed below for each of ownership, complexity, liability, life, capital, and income tax, and match the characteristic with the form of business organization—proprietorship, partnership, or corporation—they are normally associated with:

(a) Ownership: Choose among "one individual," "two or more individuals," or "many shareholders"
(b) Complexity: Choose among "simple," "moderate," or "complex"
(c) Liability: Choose between "limited" or "unlimited"
(d) Life: Choose between "limited" or "indefinite"
(e) Capital: Choose among "hard," "easier," or "easiest"
(f) Income tax: Choose between "paid by individual(s)" or "paid by entity"

Action Plan
✔ Understand the characteristics of each type of business organization.

SOLUTION
Try this Do It! exercise on your own and then check your answer at the end of the chapter.

Related Exercise Material: BE1–2 and E1–2.

3   Explain the three main types of business activity.

All businesses are involved in three types of activity: financing, investing, and operating. Each of these activities can result in inflows of cash (cash flowing into the company) or outflows of cash (cash flowing out of the company). For example, North West borrowed $13,081 thousand (an inflow) as part of its **financing** activities in 2016 as it continued to expand its operations. It also distributed $58,210 thousand in dividends to its shareholders, so it had a net outflow of cash related to financing activities. During the year, the company's **investing** activities included cash outflows of $63,179 thousand related to building new stores, undertaking major store renovations, and purchasing new fixtures and computer equipment. It also invested $12,804 thousand in new point-of-sale, merchandise management, and workforce management systems. As a result, it had an outflow from investing activities of $75,813 thousand. The company was able to use cash generated by its **operating** activities to finance the majority of these investments as the company generated a net inflow of $132,987 thousand in cash from its operations.

Let's now look at these three types of business activity in more detail.

FINANCING ACTIVITIES

Capital (money) is required to start any business. The two primary ways of raising outside funds for corporations are (1) issuing (selling) shares (equity financing) in exchange for cash (or other assets) and (2) borrowing money (debt financing).

The first transaction when establishing a corporation is the issue of shares to shareholders in exchange for cash or other assets. A corporation may obtain additional equity financing by selling additional shares to investors. The issue of shares for cash results in an inflow of cash. North West first issued common shares to the general public in 1992 when it became a publicly traded corporation and listed its shares for sale on the Winnipeg and Toronto Stock Exchanges. **Common shares** is the term used to describe the amount paid by investors for shares of ownership in a company. Common shares are just one class or type of shares (collectively known as **share capital**) that a company can issue. Owners of common shares are known as **shareholders**.

Shareholders seldom provide all of the financing required by a company. Additional financing, often a significant portion, is provided by lenders or creditors. It is important to understand that, if funds have been borrowed, shareholders have only a residual claim on the assets of the corporation. In other words, if a corporation was wound up (ceased operations), all debts have to be repaid before shareholders would have any legal right to a return of the capital they invested. Once shares are issued, the company has no obligation to buy them back, although it may choose to do so (unless it has committed to lenders not to). On the other hand, debt obligations must be repaid.

Many companies pay shareholders a return on their investment on a regular basis, as long as they are profitable and there is enough cash to cover required payments to lenders and other creditors. Payments that distribute a portion of income to shareholders are called **dividends** and are normally in the form of cash, although they can also take other forms. Dividends are declared by a company's board of directors. In 2016, North West declared and paid dividends of $58,210 thousand to its shareholders. The payment of dividends results in an outflow of cash.

Corporations can also repurchase shares that have been previously issued. Any share repurchases would result in an outflow of cash. North West did not repurchase any shares in 2016.

In addition to equity financing, corporations can access funds using debt financing, which involves borrowing money. Corporations can borrow money in a variety of ways. The persons or companies that a corporation owes money to are called lenders or creditors, one of the key user groups of accounting information. Amounts owed to lenders and other creditors—in the form of debt and other obligations—are called **liabilities**.

Specific names are given to different types of liabilities, depending on their source. For instance, a corporation may have received funds from an operating line of credit with its bank. An operating line of credit is a pre-arranged bank loan for a maximum amount that allows a company to draw more money than it has on deposit in its bank account. When a company uses its operating line of credit to cover cash shortfalls and overdraws its bank account, it results in a liability called **bank indebtedness**.

Corporations may borrow using a short-term **bank loan payable** (also known as a note payable) or using **long-term debt**. Long-term debt can include **mortgages payable**, **bonds payable**, **finance lease obligations**, and other types of debt securities borrowed for longer periods of time.

When funds are borrowed, the result is an inflow of cash from these financing activities. Conversely, the repayment of short-term or long-term debt results in an outflow of cash. In 2016, North West borrowed $13,081 thousand and did not repay any debt during the year. The claims of lenders and other creditors differ from those of shareholders. If a company borrows money from a lender or creditor, it must eventually be repaid with interest. The creditor and the company will agree to a repayment schedule at the time of borrowing. A lender or other creditor has a legal right to be paid at the agreed time. In the event of nonpayment, the lender or creditor may force the company to sell assets to pay its debts.

The payment of interest on borrowed funds may be treated as a financing activity or as an operating activity under IFRS. In either case, it will be an outflow of cash. North West paid interest of $5 million in 2016 and elected to report this as a financing activity.

INVESTING ACTIVITIES

After a company raises money through financing activities, it then uses that money for investing activities. Investing activities involve the purchase (or sale) of long-lived assets that a company needs in order to operate. **Assets** are resources that a company owns or controls. Every asset is capable of providing future economic benefits that can be short- or long-lived. Investing activities generally involve long-lived assets. For example, the purchase of long-lived assets such as furniture, equipment, computers, vehicles, buildings, and land are all examples of investing activities. Together, these assets are referred to as **property, plant, and equipment**, or "property and equipment," as North West calls this asset category.

> **Alternative Terminology**
> *Property, plant, and equipment* is also known as *capital assets* or *fixed assets*.

Other examples of long-lived assets include goodwill and intangible assets. **Goodwill** results when a company acquires another company, paying a price that is higher than the value of the purchased company's net identifiable assets. **Intangible assets** are assets that do not have any physical substance themselves but represent a privilege or a right granted to, or held by, a company. Examples of intangible assets include patents, copyrights, and trademarks.

For most companies, investing activities normally result in an outflow of cash as companies must continuously invest in long-term assets to grow or even to maintain their operations. Companies also dispose of long-term assets when they have finished using them. The sale of long-term assets results in an inflow of cash, though this is generally much less than the outflow of cash related to asset purchases. For example, North West had cash outflows of $75,983 thousand related to the purchase of long-term asset purchases, while inflows of only $170 thousand resulted from the sale of long-term assets.

Companies can also have investing activities related to the purchase (outflow) or sale (inflow) of shares or debt securities (such as bonds) of other companies. These **investments** may be related to generating returns (such as dividends or interest) in the short term or may be long-term strategic investments that enable the company to have a degree of influence or control over the other company. Many students misunderstand the term *investing activities*, thinking the term means "investments" only. For most companies, the vast majority of investing activities are normally related to the purchase and sale of long-term assets, rather than investments in the shares or debt securities of other companies.

OPERATING ACTIVITIES

Once a business has raised the necessary financing and invested in the long-term assets it needs to get started, it can begin its operations. For example, North West sells food, clothing, housewares, appliances, and outdoor products in its retail locations. The company also provides services to its customers, including income tax preparation, cheque cashing, money transfers, and postal services. We call the amounts earned from the sale of these goods and services **income**, also known as **revenue**. In accounting language, income results from increases in economic resources—normally an increase in an asset but sometimes a decrease in a liability—that result from the sale of a product or service in the normal course of business.

Income comes from different sources and can be identified by various names. As we will learn in later chapters, some of these sources of income are referred to as income and some as revenue—we use these terms interchangeably in this textbook. For instance, North West, which uses the term *revenue*, refers to the revenues it generates from the sale of goods and services as "sales." However, companies may also earn interest revenue on excess cash held as investments and rental revenue from unused space. Sources of income that are common to many businesses are **sales revenue, service revenue, interest revenue**, and **rent revenue**.

Some of North West's sales do not result in an immediate receipt of cash. Instead, credit is extended to its customers. This means they will pay their accounts in the future. This right to receive money in the future is called an **account receivable**. Accounts receivable are assets because they represent an economic resource—cash—which will be received when the amounts owed are eventually collected.

We first mentioned the term *assets* in the investing activities section above. A company's long-lived assets, such as property, plant, and equipment, are purchased through investing activities. Other assets—typically with shorter lives—result from operating activities, such as accounts receivable. Companies also have other types of receivables, such as interest receivable, rent receivable, and deferred tax assets that result from differences in how items are recorded for accounting and tax purposes.

Supplies are another example of a short-term asset used in day-to-day operations. These include items such as office and cleaning supplies, but do not include any items that are purchased to be resold to customers. Items that are held for future sale to customers are called **inventory** or merchandise inventory. When the goods (inventory) are sold, they are no longer an asset with future benefits but an expense. More specifically, the cost of the inventory sold is an expense called cost of goods sold. In accounting language, **expenses** are decreases in economic resources, normally the costs of assets that are consumed or services that are used in the process of generating revenues. As we will learn in Chapter 4, expenses are related to assets and liabilities. When an expense is incurred, an asset will decrease or a liability will increase.

There are many kinds of expenses and they are identified by various names, depending on the type of asset consumed or service used. For example, North West reports a number of types of expenses: **cost of goods sold** (which it calls "cost of sales"); **selling, operating, and administrative expenses**; **interest expense**; and **income tax expense**. North West's selling, operating, and administrative expenses item is a summary of individual expense accounts such as salaries, advertising, utilities, professional fees, rent, depreciation (the allocation of the cost of using property and equipment), amortization (the allocation of the cost of intangible assets), and other costs associated with running the business.

Short-term liabilities may result from some of these expenses. This occurs, for example, when a company purchases inventory or supplies on credit (on account) from suppliers. The obligations to pay for these goods are called **accounts payable**. A company may also have **interest payable** on the outstanding (unpaid) liability amounts owed to various lenders and other creditors, **dividends payable** to shareholders, **salaries payable** to employees, **property tax payable** to the municipal and/or provincial governments, and **sales tax payable** and **income tax payable** to the provincial and federal governments. Deferred tax liabilities are an example of another liability. They result from differences in how items are recorded for accounting and tax purposes.

The goal of every business is to sell a good or service for a price that is greater than the cost of producing or purchasing the good or providing the service, plus the cost of operating the business. This means that revenues should, normally, be greater than the expenses incurred to generate the revenues. When revenues exceed expenses, **net income** results, as shown in Illustration 1-3. Net income is also commonly known as *net earnings* or *profit*.

Alternative Terminology
Interest revenue is also known as *finance income*.

Alternative Terminology
Interest expense is commonly known as *finance costs*.

Revenues	−	Expenses	=	Net Income (Loss)

▶Illustration 1-3
Determination of net income (loss)

North West's revenues exceeded its expenses and it reported net income (which it calls "net earnings") of $69,779 thousand for the year ended January 31, 2016. When the opposite happens—that is, when expenses exceed revenues—a **loss** (also known as a *net loss*) results.

SUMMARY OF BUSINESS ACTIVITIES

To summarize our discussion in this section, there are three types of business activities that companies engage in: (1) financing, (2) investing, and (3) operating, as shown in Illustration 1-4.

▶Illustration 1-4
Business activities and examples

Financing Activities

Inflows: Issuing shares, taking out a loan

Outflows: Paying dividends, repurchasing shares, repaying loans

Investing Activities

Inflows: Buying long-lived assets, buying shares of other companies

Outflows: Proceeds from selling long-lived assets, proceeds from selling shares of other companies

Operating Activities

Inflows: Revenues, collection of receivables, sale of services or goods

Outflows: Expenses, payment of payables, purchase of inventory and supplies

1. **Financing activities** involve either equity or debt financing. Activities related to equity financing include issuing shares to shareholders, paying dividends to shareholders, or repurchasing shares. Activities related to debt financing include borrowing cash from lenders by issuing debt, or conversely, using cash to repay debt.
2. **Investing activities** include purchasing and disposing of long-lived assets such as property, plant, and equipment and long-term investments.
3. **Operating activities** result from day-to-day operations and include revenues and expenses and changes in related accounts, including receivables, supplies, inventory, and payables accounts.

DO IT! ▶ 1-3   Business Activities

For each of the following items (a) classify them as a financing, investing, or operating activity; (b) determine whether they resulted in an inflow or outflow of cash; and (c) classify them as an asset, liability, share capital, revenue, or expense.

1. An amount is paid to an employee for work performed
2. An amount is earned and received from providing a service
3. Common shares are issued
4. A vehicle is purchased
5. A bank loan is taken from the bank

Action Plan

✔ Classify each item based on its economic characteristics.

✔ Understand the differences among financing, investing, and operating activities.

✔ Consider whether cash flowed into or out of the company as a result of the transaction.

✔ Understand the distinctions among assets, liabilities, share capital, revenues, and expenses.

SOLUTION
Try this Do It! exercise on your own and then check your answer at the end of the chapter.

Related Exercise Material: BE1–3, BE1–4, E1–3, and E1–4.

LEARNING
OBJECTIVE ▶4

Describe the purpose and content of each of the financial statements.

You will recall that we learned about internal and external users of accounting information earlier in this chapter. Users, especially external users, are interested in a company's financial position (including assets, liabilities, and shareholders' equity, as well as its cash flow) in addition to the company's financial performance (such as revenues and expenses) and capital structure (components of shareholders' equity). For external reporting purposes, it is customary to arrange this information in four different financial statements that are the backbone of financial reporting.

1. **Income statement**: An income statement reports revenues and expenses, showing how a company's operations performed during a period of time.
2. **Statement of changes in equity**: A statement of changes in equity shows the changes in each component of shareholders' equity (including common shares and retained earnings), as well as total equity, during a period of time.
3. **Statement of financial position**: A statement of financial position presents a picture of what a company owns (its assets), what it owes (its liabilities), and the resulting difference (its shareholders' equity) at a specific point in time.
4. **Statement of cash flows**: A statement of cash flows shows where a company obtained cash during a period of time and how that cash was used.

Additional information is reported in **notes to the financial statements** that are cross-referenced to these four statements. These explanatory notes clarify information presented in the financial statements and provide additional detail. They are essential to understanding a company's financial performance and position.

While the above four financial statements are the statements most commonly provided by publicly traded companies, there are other financial statements. For example, a statement of comprehensive income must be prepared when a publicly traded company reports other comprehensive income earned from certain items. In addition, private corporations prepare a statement of retained earnings instead of a statement of changes in equity. We will wait until later chapters to illustrate these statements.

Financial statements must be produced annually, as well as quarterly, by public corporations. Financial statements are often produced monthly as well for internal use. An accounting time period that is one year in length is called a **fiscal year**.

> **Alternative Terminology**
> *Quarterly* financial statements are also called *interim* financial statements.

ACCOUNTING MATTERS

alexsl/iStockphoto

Fiscal Year Ends

While some companies choose to use December 31 for their fiscal year end, others do not. Many companies choose to end their accounting year when their inventory or operations are at a low. This is advantageous because gathering accounting information requires a lot of time and effort from managers. They would rather do it when business is slow (which is not the case for many retailers over the Christmas/New Year's holiday period, for example). Also, inventory can be more easily counted when it is low, reducing the cost of counting. Some companies whose year ends differ from December 31 are lululemon (Sunday closest to January 31), Jean Coutu (Saturday closest to February 29 or March 1), Canadian Tire (Saturday closest to December 31), Lions Gate Entertainment (March 31), and Shaw Communications (August 31). Most governments and government-related entities use March 31 for their fiscal year end.

THE FINANCIAL STATEMENTS

We will now look at the financial statements of a fictitious marketing agency, a service company called Sierra Corporation, to introduce you to the four primary financial statements: the income statement, statement of changes in equity, statement of financial position, and statement of cash flows.

Income Statement

The **income statement** reports the success or failure of the company's operations for a period of time—annually, quarterly, and/or monthly, as we mentioned in the previous section. In our example that follows, Sierra was incorporated (established) on October 1. It has been in operation for only one month, the month ended October 31, 2018, and reports its results monthly. To indicate that Sierra's income statement reports the results of operations for a period of one month, its statement is dated "Month Ended October 31, 2018."

The income statement lists the company's revenues first and then its expenses. We will learn about the order in which expenses can be listed in later chapters. For now, we have simply listed expenses in order of magnitude—that is, from the largest to the smallest. Expenses are deducted from revenues to determine income (or loss) before income tax. Income tax expense is shown separately, immediately following the income (or loss) before income tax line. Finally, net income (or net loss) is determined by deducting the income tax expense.

A sample income statement for Sierra Corporation is shown in Illustration 1-5.

▶Illustration 1-5
Income statement

SIERRA CORPORATION		
Income Statement		
Month Ended October 31, 2018		
Revenues		
Service revenue		$20,600
Expenses		
Salaries expense	$5,200	
Supplies expense	1,500	
Rent expense	900	
Depreciation expense	83	
Insurance expense	50	
Interest expense	25	7,758
Income before income tax		12,842
Income tax expense		1,800
Net income		$11,042

Note that cents are not included in the dollar figures recorded in financial statements. It is important to understand, however, that cents should be and are used in recording transactions in a company's internal accounting records. It is only for financial reporting purposes that financial statement amounts are normally rounded to the nearest dollar, thousand dollars, or million dollars, depending on the size of the company. For example, North West rounds amounts in its financial statements to the nearest thousand dollars. External reporting condenses and simplifies information so that it is easier for the reader to understand.

It also does not matter whether the data in the statements are listed in two columns, as they are for Sierra Corporation, or in one column. Companies use a variety of presentation formats, depending on their preference and what they think is easiest for the reader to understand.

Why are financial statement users interested in a company's net income? Investors are interested in a company's past income because these numbers provide information that may help predict future income. Income is required to generate cash to fund growth, repay debt, and pay dividends. Investors buy and sell shares based on their expectations about the future performance of a company. If you expect that Sierra will be even more successful in the future, and that this success will translate into a higher share price, you should buy Sierra's shares.

Like investors, lenders and other creditors also use the income statement to predict the future. When a bank lends money to a company, it does so because it believes it will be repaid in the future. If the bank thought it was not going to be repaid, it would not lend the money. Thus, before making the loan, the bank's loan officer must try to predict whether the company will stay in business long enough, and be profitable enough, to generate the cash required to repay the loan and interest charges. Thus, reporting recurring and increasing income amounts will make it easier for Sierra to raise additional cash either by borrowing or by issuing shares.

Statement of Changes in Equity

The **statement of changes in equity** shows the changes in total shareholders' equity for the period, as well as the changes in each component of shareholders' equity during the period. It starts with the account balances at the beginning of the period and ends with the account balances at the end of the period. The time period is the same as for the income statement—for the year, quarter, or month.

The ownership interest in a company is known as **shareholders' equity**. In its simplest form, total shareholders' equity includes (1) share capital and (2) retained earnings. It can also include other types of accounts, such as accumulated other comprehensive income that we will discuss later in this, and other, chapters.

Share capital represents amounts contributed by the shareholders in exchange for shares of ownership. All companies must have common shares. In Chapter 11, we will learn that many companies also have another class of shares, called preferred shares. Together, these two classes of shares—common and preferred—combine to form the company's share capital.

The statement of changes in equity starts with the beginning balance of share capital—common shares, in Sierra's case. This is zero for Sierra because it just began operations at the beginning of the month, October 1. The statement then goes on to add any changes in share capital due to new shares issued (or to deduct any changes in share capital due to shares repurchased) during the period to arrive at the ending balance of share capital, as shown in equation format below.

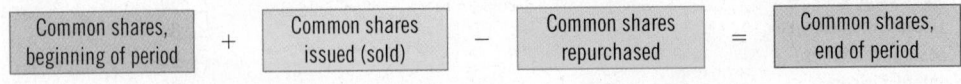

Retained earnings represent the cumulative amounts of net income that have been retained in the corporation. In other words, it is the income that has not been distributed as dividends to shareholders that has accumulated since the company's date of incorporation. If retained earnings is negative—that is, net losses have exceeded net income—it is known as a **deficit**.

In addition to showing the changes in share capital during the period, the statement of changes in equity also shows the amounts and nature of changes in retained earnings. The column for retained earnings starts with the beginning balance of retained earnings. Just as Sierra's beginning common shares balance was nil because it only began operations on October 1, so too is its beginning retained earnings balance. The net income for the period is added and dividends declared (if any) are deducted from the beginning balance to calculate the retained earnings at the end of the period, as shown in equation format below.

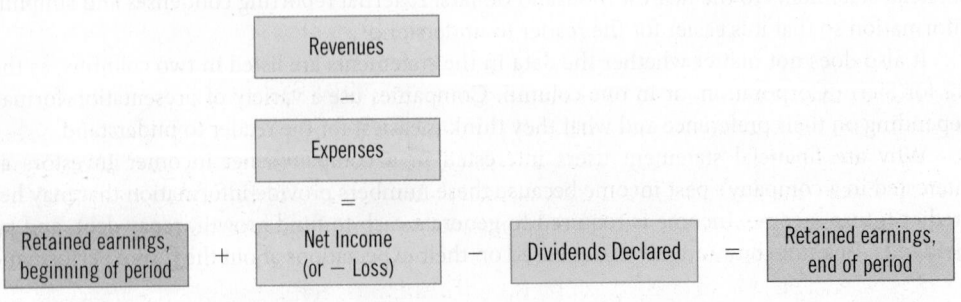

If a company reports a net loss, it is deducted (rather than added) to arrive at the ending balance of retained earnings. It is important to understand that dividends are not reported as an expense in the income statement. They are not an expense incurred to generate revenue. Instead, dividends are a distribution of retained earnings (or a distribution of accumulated net income) to shareholders and reported in the statement of changes in equity.

Illustration 1-6 presents Sierra's statement of changes in equity.

SIERRA CORPORATION Statement of Changes in Equity Month Ended October 31, 2018			
	Common Shares	Retained Earnings	Total Equity
Balance, October 1	$ 0	$ 0	$ 0
Issued common shares	10,000		10,000
Net income		11,042	11,042
Dividends declared		(500)	(500)
Balance, October 31	$10,000	$10,542	$20,542

► Illustration 1-6
Statement of changes in equity

Note that this statement adds both vertically (down; see "Total Equity" column) and horizontally (across; see "Balance, October 31" row). Also note that, as Sierra is a new company, all of its opening balances are zero.

By monitoring the statement of changes in equity for a publicly traded corporation, financial statement users can evaluate the use of equity for financing purposes. For example, using this statement, they can determine the amount of shares that were issued during the period. More importantly, the statement of changes in equity allows users to monitor a company's dividend practices. If Sierra is profitable, at the end of each period its board of directors must decide what portion of its retained earnings to pay to shareholders as dividends. In theory, it could pay all of its current period net income, but few companies choose to do this. Why? Because they want to retain part of the net income in the business so the company can expand when it chooses to or so it will have enough cash to repay debt.

Statement of Financial Position

The **statement of financial position** reports assets and claims to those assets at a specific point in time. This statement is also commonly known as the *balance sheet*, especially for those companies following ASPE, and we will use these two terms interchangeably in this textbook.

Claims to assets are subdivided into two categories: claims of lenders and other creditors and claims of shareholders. As noted earlier, claims of lenders and other creditors are called liabilities. Claims of shareholders, the owners of the company, are called shareholders' equity. This relationship is shown below in equation format and is known as the basic **accounting equation**.

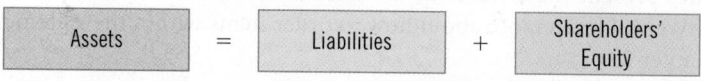

The relationship is where the name *balance sheet* comes from. Assets must be in balance with the claims to those assets by both creditors (liabilities) and shareholders (shareholders' equity). The right-hand side of the equation—the liabilities and equities—also shows how the assets have been financed. The financing could have occurred through debt by borrowing from lenders or other creditors or through equity by investments from shareholders (share capital) or net income retained in the company (retained earnings).

Sierra's statement of financial position is shown in Illustration 1-7.

►Illustration 1-7
Statement of financial position

SIERRA CORPORATION Statement of Financial Position October 31, 2018	
Assets	
Cash	$11,400
Accounts receivable	11,200
Supplies	1,000
Prepaid insurance	550
Equipment	4,917
Total assets	$29,067
Liabilities and Shareholders' Equity	
Liabilities	
Accounts payable	$ 1,500
Salaries payable	1,200
Interest payable	25
Unearned revenue	800
Bank loan payable	5,000
Total liabilities	8,525
Shareholders' equity	
Common shares	10,000
Retained earnings	10,542
Total shareholders' equity	20,542
Total liabilities and shareholders' equity	$29,067

▼ HELPFUL HINT
The statement of financial position is dated at a *specific point in time*. The income statement, statement of changes in equity, and statement of cash flows cover a *period of time*.

As you can see in the above illustration, Sierra's assets are listed first, followed by liabilities and shareholders' equity. Sierra's assets total $29,067 and include cash, accounts receivable, supplies, prepaid insurance (premiums paid in advance for insurance coverage in future periods), and equipment. Of these assets, only the purchase of equipment would be presented as an investing activity in the statement of cash flows, as we will see in the next section. The other items (except for cash) are examples of assets that result from operating activities.

Sierra's liabilities total $8,525 and consist of accounts payable, salaries payable, interest payable, unearned revenue (cash received in advance for which the service has not yet been provided and is therefore still owed), and a bank loan payable. Of these liabilities, only the bank loan payable is an example of a financing activity. The other items are examples of liabilities that arose from operating activities.

Sierra's shareholders' equity consists of common shares of $10,000 and retained earnings of $10,542, for total shareholders' equity of $20,542. Note that Sierra's total liabilities and total shareholders' equity equal its total assets of $29,067.

The items listed in the statement of financial position can be ordered in different ways. For example, Sierra presents its assets first, followed by liabilities and shareholders' equity. Some companies present these items in a different order, to better represent the nature of their business. We will learn more about how to order items within the statement of financial position in Chapter 2.

External users such as lenders and other creditors analyze a company's statement of financial position to determine the likelihood that they will be repaid. They carefully evaluate the nature of the company's assets and liabilities. For example, does the company have assets that could easily be sold, if required, to repay its debts? Do the company's assets exceed its liabilities in both the short and long term?

Internal users such as managers use the statement of financial position to determine whether inventory is adequate to support future sales and whether cash on hand is sufficient for immediate cash needs. Managers also look at the relationship between total liabilities and shareholders' equity to determine whether they have the best proportion of debt and equity financing.

Statement of Cash Flows

The main function of a **statement of cash flows** is to provide financial information about the cash receipts and cash payments of a business for a specific period of time. To help investors, lenders and other creditors, and others in their analysis of a company's cash position, the statement of cash flows reports the effects on cash of a company's (1) operating activities, (2) investing activities, and (3) financing activities during the period of time.

Recall from earlier in the chapter that operating activities result from transactions that create revenues and expenses. Investing activities involve the purchase or sale of long-lived resources such as property, plant, and equipment that a company needs to operate and the purchase or sale of investments in long-term securities. Financing activities involve borrowing (or repaying) long-term debt from (to) lenders and issuing (or repurchasing) shares or distributing dividends to shareholders.

Operating activities are normally presented first in the statement of cash flows, followed by investing and financing activities. In addition, the statement shows the net increase or decrease in cash during the period, and the cash amount at the end of the period.

The statement of cash flows for Sierra is shown in Illustration 1-8. Note that the positive numbers in the illustration indicate cash inflows. Numbers in parentheses indicate cash outflows.

SIERRA CORPORATION Statement of Cash Flows Month Ended October 31, 2018		
Operating activities		
Cash receipts from operating activities	$10,200	
Cash payments for operating activities	(8,300)	
Net cash provided by operating activities		$ 1,900
Investing activities		
Purchase of equipment	$ (5,000)	
Net cash used by investing activities		(5,000)
Financing activities		
Issue of common shares	$10,000	
Borrowing of bank loan	5,000	
Payment of dividends	(500)	
Net cash provided by financing activities		14,500
Net increase in cash		11,400
Cash, October 1		0
Cash, October 31		$11,400

▶Illustration 1-8
Statement of cash flows

In the above illustration, Sierra's statement of cash flows shows that overall cash increased by $11,400 during the month. Operating activities generated $1,900 in cash during the month, but this was not enough cash to fund the investing activities of $5,000 during the month. To help offset this shortfall, the company was able to generate $14,500 in cash from its financing activities. As a result, the company's cash inflows for the period exceeded its outflows, resulting in a net increase of $11,400.

For now, you should not worry too much about where the numbers came from. Our intention is to introduce this statement briefly at this point. We will learn more about the preparation of the statement of cash flows in Chapter 13.

KEEPING AN EYE ON CASH

Understanding where its cash comes from and where it goes is critical for a company. The statement of cash flows provides answers to these simple but important questions: (1) Where did cash come from during the period? (2) How was cash used during the period? (3) What was the change in the cash balance during the period?

The statement of cash flows answers these questions by summarizing cash flows as operating, investing, or financing activities. A user of this statement can then determine the amount of cash provided (or used) by operating activities, the amount of cash provided (or used) for investing purposes, and the amount of cash provided (or used) by financing activities.

Operating activities are activities the company performs to generate net income. It is desirable for operating activities to provide cash (positive balance) rather than use cash (negative balance). A positive source of cash from operating activities can help fund the investment in additional assets to grow the business and/or fund debt repayments or dividend payments.

Investing activities include the purchase or sale of long-lived assets used in operating the business, or the purchase or sale of long-term investment securities. For most growing companies, investing activities use cash (negative balance) rather than provide cash (positive balance), because growing companies purchase or replace more assets than they dispose of.

Financing activities include borrowing or repaying money, issuing or repurchasing shares, and paying dividends. For most growing companies, financing activities provide cash (positive balance) rather than use cash (negative balance). Most growing companies have to borrow money or issue shares rather than being able to repay financing. As companies mature, they are able to repay financing and this balance becomes negative (cash used) more often than positive.

*You will find a section called **Keeping an Eye on Cash** in selected chapters to help you understand the importance of cash.*

DO IT! ▶1-4a Accounting Equation

Action Plan

✔ Use the accounting equation to solve each question.

✔ Understand that total assets must always equal total liabilities plus total shareholders' equity.

✔ Remember that shareholders' equity is made up of share capital and retained earnings.

Answer each of the following using the accounting equation:

(a) The liabilities of Gillis Ltd. are $625,000, while its share capital is $250,000 and its retained earnings are $360,000. What is the amount of Gillis's total assets?

(b) Clegg Ltd.'s share capital is $315,000 and its retained earnings $525,000. If Clegg's total liabilities are $460,000, what is the amount of the company's total assets?

(c) The total assets of Mustafa Ltd. are $1.2 million, while its liabilities are $690,000 and its share capital is $150,000. What is the amount of Mustafa's retained earnings?

(d) Egeland Ltd.'s assets increased by $410,000 during the year, while its liabilities increased by $220,000. By what amount did Egeland's shareholders' equity change during the year?

(e) During the year, Haime Ltd.'s liabilities increased by $660,000, its share capital remained unchanged, and its retained earnings increased by $380,000. By what amount did Haime's assets change?

SOLUTION

Try this Do It! exercise on your own and then check your answer at the end of the chapter.

Related Exercise Material: BE1–5, BE1–6, E1–6, and E1–9.

Relationships between the Statements

Because the results on some statements are used as data for other statements, the statements are said to be interrelated (related to each other). These interrelationships are evident in Sierra's financial statements.

1. The statement of changes in equity depends, in part, on the results of the income statement. Sierra reported net income of $11,042 for the month, as shown in Illustration 1-5. This amount is added to the beginning amount of retained earnings as part of determining ending retained earnings—one of the components of total shareholders' equity shown in the statement of changes in equity in Illustration 1-6.
2. The statement of financial position and statement of changes in equity are interrelated. Note the ending balances of each component of shareholders' equity—common shares, $10,000, and retained earnings, $10,542—as well as total shareholders' equity of $20,542 at the end of the month reported on the statement of changes in equity in Illustration 1-6. These are reported in the shareholders' equity section of the statement of financial position in Illustration 1-7.
3. The statement of cash flows and the statement of financial position are also interrelated. The statement of cash flows presented in Illustration 1-8 shows how the cash account changed during the period by stating the amount of cash at the beginning of the period, the sources and uses of cash during the month, and the amount of cash at the end of the period, $11,400. The ending amount of cash shown on the statement of cash flows agrees with the amount of cash shown in the assets section of the statement of financial position in Illustration 1-7.

Study these interrelationships carefully. To prepare financial statements, you must understand the sequence in which these amounts are determined and how each statement affects the next. Because each financial statement depends on information contained in another statement, financial statements must be prepared in the following order: (1) income statement; (2) statement of changes in equity; (3) statement of financial position; and (4) statement of cash flows, as illustrated below:

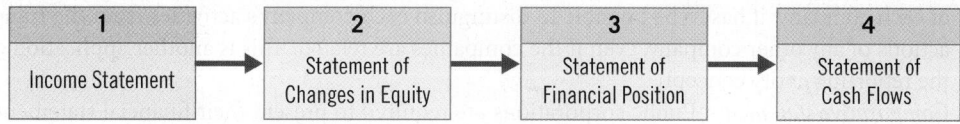

DO IT! ▶1-4b   Financial Statement Relationships

Using your understanding of the relationship within and between the financial statements, determine the seven missing amounts.

Income Statement	
Total revenues	$2,360,000
Total expenses	1,810,000
Net income	(a)
Statement of Changes in Equity	
Total shareholders' equity, beginning of year	980,000
Common shares, beginning of year	350,000
Issue of shares	(b)
Common shares, end of year	500,000
Retained earnings, beginning of year	630,000

Action Plan

✔ Remember the order in which the financial statements are prepared.

✔ Certain amounts, such as net income, appear on more than one financial statement.

✔ Remember that the accounting equation, which is the basis for the statement of financial position, must balance.

Net income	(c)
Dividends declared	(d)
Retained earnings, end of year	890,000
Total shareholders' equity, end of year	(e)
Statement of Financial Position	
Total assets	3,420,000
Total liabilities	(f)
Total shareholders' equity	(g)

NORTH WEST'S FINANCIAL STATEMENTS

The same relationships that you observed among the financial statements of Sierra Corporation can be seen in the 2016 simplified financial statements of The North West Company Inc., presented in Illustration 1-9.

North West's actual financial statements are presented in Appendix A at the end of the book. If you compare North West's actual financial statements with those presented in Illustration 1-9, you will notice some similarities and differences that we will clarify below.

1. *Statement titles:* North West uses different titles in some of its actual financial statements than we have used in this textbook and in Illustration 1-9. As explained earlier in this chapter, there are a number of statement titles that mean the same thing: "statement of earnings" is how North West refers to its income statement, "statement of changes in shareholders' equity" is how North West refers to its statement of changes in equity, and "balance sheet" is how North West refers to its statement of financial position.

2. *Consolidated financial statements:* North West presents consolidated financial statements. This means that the financial results include not only North West but also all the companies it owns or controls. Although the financial results of these companies are consolidated (combined) for reporting purposes, individual accounting records and financial statements are also produced for each specific company. In order to accurately assess the performance and financial position of each company, it has to be possible to distinguish each company's activities from the transactions of any other company, even if the companies are related. This is another application of the reporting entity concept.

3. *Comparative statements:* Public corporations are required to present their financial statements for at least two fiscal years. Financial statements that cover more than one period are called "comparative statements" and assist users in comparing the financial position and performance of one accounting period with that of the prior period(s).

4. *Unit of measure:* The numbers are reported in thousands of dollars on North West's financial statements; that is, the last three zeros (000) are omitted in both Illustration 1-9 and North West's actual financial statements.

5. *Condensed statements:* The statements included in Illustration 1-9 have been condensed and simplified to assist your learning—but they may look complicated to you anyway. Do not be alarmed by this. By the end of the book, you will have a lot of experience in reading and understanding financial statements such as these, and they will no longer look as complicated.

Income Statement

Take a look at the simplified version of North West's income statement presented in Illustration 1-9. While Sierra is a service company, providing services to earn its revenue, North West is a retail company. It sells products to earn its revenue, although it also provides some services from which it earns revenue as well.

THE NORTH WEST COMPANY INC.
Statement of Earnings
Year Ended January 31, 2016
($ in thousands)

Sales	$1,796,035
Cost of sales	1,273,421
Gross profit	522,614
Selling, operating and administrative expenses	415,293
Earnings from operations	107,321
Interest expense	6,210
Earnings before income taxes	101,111
Income taxes	31,332
Net earnings	$ 69,779

THE NORTH WEST COMPANY INC.
Statement of Changes in Shareholders' Equity
Year Ended January 31, 2016
($ in thousands)

	Share Capital	Retained Earnings	Accumulated Other Comprehensive Income	Other	Total Equity
Balance, February 1	$167,460	$140,527	$18,465	$2,831	$329,283
Net earnings		69,779			69,779
Other comprehensive income		4,583	11,953		16,536
Other changes to equity		(15)		124	109
Dividends declared		(58,210)			(58,210)
Issue of common shares	450			(335)	115
Balance, January 31	$167,910	$156,664	$30,418	$2,620	$357,612

THE NORTH WEST COMPANY INC.
Balance Sheet
January 31, 2016
($ in thousands)

Assets

Cash	$ 37,243
Accounts receivable	79,373
Inventory	211,736
Prepaid expenses	7,229
Property and equipment	345,881
Goodwill	37,260
Intangible assets	32,610
Other assets	42,463
Total assets	$793,795

Liabilities and Shareholders' Equity

Liabilities		
Accounts payable and accrued liabilities	$152,136	
Income taxes payable	3,365	
Long-term debt	225,489	
Other liabilities	55,193	
Total liabilities		$436,183
Shareholders' equity		
Share capital	$167,910	
Retained earnings	156,664	
Accumulated other comprehensive income	30,418	
Other equity items	2,620	
Total shareholders' equity		357,612
Total liabilities and shareholders' equity		$793,795

THE NORTH WEST COMPANY INC.
Statement of Cash Flows
Year Ended January 31, 2016
($ in thousands)

Operating activities		
Cash receipts from operating activities	$1,789,168	
Cash payments for operating activities	(1,656,181)	
Cash from operating activities		$132,987
Investing activities		
Purchase of property, plant and equipment	$(63,179)	
Purchase of intangible assets	(12,804)	
Proceeds from disposal of property, plant and equipment	170	
Cash used in investing activities		(75,813)
Financing activities		
Increase in long-term debt	$ 13,081	
Payment of dividends	(58,210)	
Payment of interest	(5,160)	
Issuance of common shares	115	
Cash used in financing activities		(50,174)
Net increase in cash		7,000
Effects of changes in foreign exchange rates on cash		1,114
Cash, beginning of year		29,129
Cash, end of year		$ 37,243

For 2016, North West reported sales of $1,796,035 thousand. As was mentioned earlier, North West reports its numbers in thousands of dollars. Thus, North West's total sales revenue is $1,796,035,000 and not $1,796,035. It then subtracts a variety of expenses related to operating the business. These expenses, totalling $1,694,924 thousand, include cost of sales; selling, operating, and administrative expenses; and interest expense. Recall that "cost of sales" is another term used for cost of goods sold.

Total expenses are deducted from revenue to determine income before income tax (which it calls "earnings before income tax") of $101,111 thousand. After subtracting the income tax expense of $31,332 thousand, the company reports net income (which it calls "net earnings") for the year ended January 31, 2016, of $69,779 thousand.

Statement of Changes in Equity

North West presents information next about its shareholders' equity in the simplified statement of changes in equity (which the company calls "statement of changes in shareholders' equity") in Illustration 1-9. This statement shows the changes in North West's share capital and retained earnings. During the year, North West issued shares for $450 thousand, which when added to its opening balance, resulted in a balance at the end of the year of $167,910 thousand. North West's opening retained earnings was increased by net income of $69,779 thousand and decreased by the declaration of dividends of $58,210 thousand. This, in addition to $4,568 thousand of other changes to retained earnings, resulted in a balance at the end of the year of $156,664 thousand. Note that the net income figure in the retained earnings column is the same as the net income reported on the income statement, as indicated with a ① in Illustration 1-9. No matter what order the financial statements are presented in, the income statement must be prepared first, because the net income (or loss) for the period is needed to prepare the statement of changes in equity.

North West's statement of changes in equity also includes a column for accumulated other comprehensive income (abbreviated by North West in its actual financial statements as "AOCI"). Companies such as North West reporting under IFRS may have complex items that are similar to revenues and expenses but, due to their nature, are not used to determine net income. Rather, they are included in **other comprehensive income**. If a company has other comprehensive income (or loss) during the period, it is added to (or deducted from in the case of a loss) a shareholders' equity account called **accumulated other comprehensive income**. Similar to the retained earnings account, which accumulates net income over time, the accumulated other comprehensive income account is also a shareholders' equity account that accumulates other comprehensive income over time.

We will learn more about other comprehensive income and accumulated other comprehensive income in Chapter 11. We will also learn in that chapter about differences in how changes that influence shareholders' equity, including other comprehensive income, affect public and private corporations.

Statement of Financial Position

North West's statement of financial position (which it calls "balance sheet") shown in Illustration 1-9 includes the types of assets mentioned in this chapter: cash, accounts receivable, inventory, prepaid expenses, property and equipment, goodwill, intangible assets, and other types of assets.

Similarly, its liabilities include accounts payable and accrued liabilities (we will learn about accrued liabilities in Chapter 2), income tax payable, and long-term debt, as well as other types of liabilities.

North West's statement of financial position shows that total assets equal $793,795 thousand and total liabilities equal $436,183 thousand at January 31, 2016. The ending balances of North West's share capital, retained earnings, accumulated other comprehensive income, and other items taken from the statement of changes in equity agree to (are equal to) the same items shown in the shareholders' equity section of the statement of financial position. Follow the arrow marked with a ② in Illustration 1-9 to confirm that the total shareholders' equity of $357,612 thousand reported in the statement of changes in equity as at January 31, 2016, agrees to the total shareholders' equity presented in the statement of financial position at the same date. Note also that total liabilities and total shareholders' equity equal total assets of $793,795 thousand.

You can see that North West relies more on debt financing than equity. It has 22% more liabilities than it has shareholders' equity. As you learn more about financial statements, we will discuss how to interpret the relationships and changes in financial statement items.

Statement of Cash Flows

North West's cash increased by $8,114 thousand in 2016. The reasons for the increase in cash can be determined by examining the statement of cash flows in Illustration 1-9.

As North West was opening new stores, renovating existing stores, and replacing equipment, it consequently spent considerable cash—$75,813 thousand—on investing activities. For example, it spent $63,179 thousand on new property and equipment and $12,804 thousand for new point-of-sale, merchandise management, and workforce management systems. Note that the cash provided by operating activities—$132,987 thousand—provided the vast majority of the funding for North West's investing and financing activities. The company also borrowed $13,081 thousand as part of its financing activities, which provided it with additional funding. North West also distributed $58,210 million in dividends and paid $5,160 million in interest, which both resulted in outflows from financing activities. The net result of the sources and uses of cash during the year was an increase in cash of $8,114 thousand.

This increase in cash is added to the opening balance of $29,129 thousand to result in an ending cash balance of $37,243 thousand. Trace the ending balance of cash reported in the statement of cash flows to the ending balance reported in the statement of financial position, as indicated by the arrow marked with a ③ in Illustration 1-9.

ELEMENTS OF AN ANNUAL REPORT

Public corporations must produce an **annual report** each year. The annual report is a document that includes financial information, as well as useful nonfinancial information about the company, for the previous fiscal year. Nonfinancial information may include the company's mission, goals and objectives, products, and people.

One of the most important pieces of financial information included in the annual report is the management discussion and analysis (often abbreviated as MD&A). The MD&A provides management's perspective on the financial results and can provide important context for interpreting them. In the MD&A, management also provides a forward-looking perspective (how the company's operations and results are expected to change in the future). Other important financial information in the annual report includes a statement of management responsibility for the financial statements, an auditors' report, the financial statements introduced in this chapter that are reported for at least two years, explanatory notes to the financial statements, and a historical summary of key financial ratios and indicators. No analysis of a company's financial situation and prospects is complete without a review of each of these items.

DO IT! ▶ 1-4c | **Preparing Financial Statements**

CSU Corporation began operations on January 1, 2018. The following account information is available for CSU Corporation on December 31, 2018: service revenue $22,200, accounts receivable $4,000, accounts payable $2,000, rent expense $9,000, bank loan payable $5,000, common shares $10,000, equipment $16,000, insurance expense $1,000, supplies $1,800, interest expense $200, cash $4,800, income tax expense $1,800, and dividends declared $600. Using this information, prepare an income statement, statement of changes in equity, statement of financial position, and statement of cash flows for the year.

For the operating activities section of the statement of cash flows, cash receipts from operating activities were $18,200 and cash payments for operating activities were $11,800. For the investing activities section, cash of $16,000 was paid for the purchase of the equipment. For the financing activities section, cash of $5,000 was received from the bank loan and $10,000 from the issue of common shares. Cash of $600 was paid for dividends.

SOLUTION
Try this Do It! exercise on your own and then check your answer at the end of the chapter.

Related Exercise Material:
BE1–7, BE1–8, BE1–9, E1–5, E1–10, E1–11, E1–12, E1–13, and E1–14.

Action Plan

✔ Classify each account into the following categories: revenues, expenses, dividends, assets, liabilities, and shareholders' equity.

✔ Report revenues and expenses for the period in the income statement and determine the amount of net income or loss.

✔ When preparing the statement of changes in equity, start with opening balances and show the amounts and causes of the changes in share capital and retained earnings for the period to determine ending balances. Ensure that net income or loss is included in retained earnings.

✔ List all assets and claims to those assets (liabilities and shareholders' equity) at a specific point in time

in the statement of financial position. Ensure that the share capital and retained earnings balances agree to the amounts reported on the statement of changes in equity.

✔ Show the changes in cash for the period, classified as operating, investing, or financing activities in the statement of cash flows. Ensure that the ending cash balance agrees with the amount of cash reported on the statement of financial position.

✔ Remember that the income statement, statement of changes in equity, and statement of cash flows cover a period of time, while the statement of financial position is reported at a specific point in time.

*The **Review and Practice** section provides opportunities for students to review key concepts and terms as well as complete a Using the Decision Toolkit case, a Comprehensive Do It! problem, and objective-format questions. Detailed solutions to these problems and questions are included at the end of the chapter.*

REVIEW AND PRACTICE

▶ LEARNING OBJECTIVE REVIEW

1. Identify the uses and users of accounting information. The purpose of accounting is to provide useful information for decision-making. There are two types of decision makers who use accounting information: internal users and external users. The primary internal users are managers, who work for the business and need internal accounting information to manage and run its operations. The primary external users are investors and lenders and other creditors. Investors (existing and potential shareholders) use accounting information to help decide whether to buy, hold, or sell shares. Lenders (such as bankers) and other creditors (such as suppliers) use accounting information to evaluate the risk of lending money or granting credit to a business. Other external users include non-management employees, customers, regulators, and taxing authorities.

2. Describe the primary forms of business organization. There are three types of business organizations: proprietorships, partnerships, and corporations. A proprietorship is a business owned by one person. A partnership is a business owned by two or more people. A corporation is a separate legal entity whose shares provide evidence of ownership. Corporations can be public, which means their shares trade on a stock exchange, or private, which means their shares are closely held and do not trade on a stock exchange.

Generally accepted accounting principles are a common set of guidelines that are used to record and report economic events. These can differ depending on the form of business organization. Public corporations follow International Financial Reporting Standards (IFRS) and private corporations have the choice of using Accounting Standards for Private Enterprises (ASPE) or IFRS. Proprietorships and partnerships generally use ASPE.

3. Explain the three main types of business activity. Financing activities involve obtaining the necessary funds (through the issue of equity or the assumption of debt) to support the business. Repayments of debt, the declaration and payment of dividends, and share repurchases are also financing activities. Investing activities primarily involve purchasing the long-term assets (such as property, plant, and equipment) that are needed to run the business, but also include the disposition of these items. Operating activities involve putting the resources of the business into action to generate net income. These involve the day-to-day activities of the business as it earns revenues and incurs expenses doing so.

4. Describe the purpose and content of each of the financial statements. The income statement presents the revenues and expenses of a company for a specific period of time. The statement of changes in equity summarizes the changes in shareholders' equity that have occurred for a specific period of time including those related to the issue of shares, generation of net income, and distribution of dividends. The statement of financial position reports the assets, liabilities, and shareholders' equity of a business at a specific date. The statement of cash flows summarizes information about the cash inflows (receipts) and outflows (payments) for a specific period of time. Notes to the financial statements add explanatory detail where required. The financial statements are included in an annual report, along with the management discussion and analysis (MD&A), and other nonfinancial and financial information.

▶ KEY TERM REVIEW

The following are key terms defined in this chapter with the corresponding page reference for your review. You will find a complete list of terms and definitions for all chapters in the glossary at the end of this textbook.

Accounting (p. 4)
Accounting equation (p. 17)
Assets (p. 11)
Corporation (p. 7)
Creditors (p. 5)
Deficit (p. 16)
Dividends (p. 10)
Expenses (p. 12)
External users (p. 5)
Financing activities (p. 13)
Fiscal year (p. 14)
Generally accepted accounting principles (GAAP) (p. 8)

Income (also known as revenue) (p. 12)
Income statement (also known as statement of earnings or statement of profit and loss) (p. 15)
Internal users (p. 4)
Investing activities (p. 13)
Investors (p. 5)
Lenders (p. 5)
Liabilities (p. 10)
Loss (also known as net loss) (p. 13)
Net income (also known as net earnings or profit) (p. 12)
Operating activities (p. 13)

Partnership (p. 7)
Private corporations (p. 8)
Proprietorship (p. 6)
Public corporation (p. 8)
Reporting entity concept (p. 6)
Retained earnings (p. 16)
Revenue (also known as income) (p. 12)
Share capital (p. 10)
Shareholders' equity (p. 16)
Statement of cash flows (p. 19)
Statement of changes in equity (p. 16)
Statement of financial position (also known as balance sheet) (p. 17)

▶ COMPARING IFRS AND ASPE REVIEW

Key Standard Differences	International Financial Reporting Standards (IFRS)	Accounting Standards for Private Enterprises (ASPE)
Accounting standards	Publicly traded corporations must use IFRS; private corporations normally use ASPE, but can choose to use IFRS.	Private corporations normally use ASPE, but can choose to use IFRS. Once the choice is made, it must be applied consistently. Proprietorships and partnerships generally follow ASPE.
Statement of changes in equity vs. statement of retained earnings	A statement of changes in equity must be presented that shows the changes in all components of shareholders' equity (for example, share capital and retained earnings).	A statement of retained earnings is presented that shows the change in only one component—retained earnings—of shareholders' equity.

*Every chapter presents useful information about how decision makers use financial statements. **Decision Toolkits** summarize discussions of key decision-making contexts and techniques.*

▶ DECISION TOOLKIT REVIEW

DECISION CHECKPOINTS	INFO NEEDED FOR DECISION	TOOLS TO USE FOR DECISION	HOW TO EVALUATE RESULTS
Are the company's operations profitable?	Income statement	The income statement indicates the success or failure of the company's operating activities by reporting its revenues and expenses.	If the company's revenues exceed its expenses, it will report net income; otherwise it will report a loss.
Is the company expanding or contracting its share capital?	Statement of changes in equity	Did the company issue or repurchase shares?	If share capital is increasing, the company may be gathering the funds for future expansion plans. If share capital is decreasing, the company has surplus cash and is returning it to shareholders by repurchasing some of their shares.
What is the company's policy on dividends and growth?	Statement of changes in equity	How much of the company's retained earnings was paid out in dividends to shareholders?	A company needing to finance growth or the repayment of debt will preserve the cash it generates from its operations and pay little or no dividends.

DECISION CHECKPOINTS	INFO NEEDED FOR DECISION	TOOLS TO USE FOR DECISION	HOW TO EVALUATE RESULTS
Does the company rely mainly on debt or on equity to finance its assets?	Statement of financial position	The statement of financial position reports the company's resources and claims to those resources. There are two types of claims: liabilities and shareholders' equity.	Compare the amount of liabilities as a percentage of total assets with the amount of shareholders' equity as a percentage of total assets to determine whether the company relies more on lenders and other creditors or on shareholders for its financing
Does the company generate enough cash from operating activities to fund its investing activities?	Statement of cash flows	The statement of cash flows shows the amount of cash provided or used by operating activities, investing activities, and financing activities.	Compare the amount of cash provided by operating activities with the amount of cash used by investing activities. Any deficiency i cash from operating activities must be made up with cash provided by financing activities

Using the Decision Toolkit cases ask you to apply business information and the decision tools presented in the chapter. Most of these cases are based on the company highlighted in the Feature Story or competitors of the feature company.

▶ PRACTICE USING THE DECISION TOOLKIT

Answers are at the end of the chapter.

Sobeys Inc. operates more than 1,500 stores across Canada. Just like North West, Sobeys has a long tradition—in this case, dating back to the early 1900s. While Sobeys' stores can be found in towns and cities across Canada, North West's stores are located in remote communities, including in Canada's far North and the Caribbean. While the two companies do not compete in the same markets, they are in a similar industry. Assume that you are reviewing the financial information of each company to determine if you should invest in North West or Sobeys.

INSTRUCTIONS

(a) Which financial statements should you review before you invest?

(b) What should each of these financial statements tell you? Which financial statement will you likely be most interested in?

(c) Sobeys' fiscal year end is the first Saturday in May. North West's fiscal year end is January 31. Do you believe it possible to compare these companies' financial statements since they have different fiscal year ends?

(d) Simplified financial statements for Sobeys follow. More detailed financial statements are included in Appendix B at the end of this textbook. What broad comparisons can you make between North West and Sobeys by reviewing their financial statements?

(e) How did the amount of cash generated by each company from operating activities compare with the amount of cash used for its investing activities? How did this relate to the cash flows each had from its financing activities?

SOBEYS INC.
Statement of (Loss) Income
53 and 52 Weeks Ended
(in millions)

	May 7 2016	May 2 2015
Revenues		
Sales	$24,618.8	$23,928.8
Other (loss) income, net	(14.2)	88.2
Total revenues	24,604.6	24,017.0
Expenses		
Cost of goods sold	18,661.2	17,966.3
Selling and administrative expenses	5,416.1	5,403.0
Finance expenses	134.6	150.7
Impairments of goodwill and long-lived assets	2,975.3	–
Total expenses	27,187.2	23,520.0
Income before income tax	(2,582.6)	497.0
Income tax (recovery) expense	(463.4)	130.3
Net (loss) income	$(2,119.2)	$ 366.7

SOBEYS INC.
Statement of Changes in Equity
Year ended May 7, 2016
(in millions)

	Share Capital	Retained Earnings (Deficit)	Accumulated Other Comprehensive Income	Other	Total Equity
Balance May 2, 2015	$2,752.9	$ 2,086.5	$ (7.1)	$146.1	$ 4,978.4
Net loss		(2,135.6)		16.4	(2,119.2)
Dividends declared		(130.3)			(130.3)
Other				(10.4)	(10.4)
Other comprehensive income		7.3	3.9		11.2
Balance May 7, 2016	$2,752.9	$ (172.1)	$ (3.2)	$152.1	$ 2,729.7

SOBEYS INC.
Statement of Financial Position
(in millions)

	May 7 2016	May 2 2015
Assets		
Cash and cash equivalents	$ 258.8	$ 295.6
Accounts receivable and loans receivable	614.9	625.5
Inventory	1,287.3	1,260.3
Assets held for sale	396.2	43.9
Investments	138.4	150.3
Property and equipment	3,096.8	3,448.4
Intangible assets	654.1	677.6
Goodwill	716.3	3,501.5
Other assets	797.8	257.9
Total assets	$ 7,960.6	$10,261.0
Liabilities and Shareholders' Equity		
Liabilities		
Accounts payable and accrued liabilities	$2,180.2	$ 2,245.4
Income taxes payable	57.8	74.3
Provisions	294.1	252.8
Long-term debt	2,371.9	2,368.9
Employee future benefits	326.9	341.2
Total liabilities	5,230.9	5,282.6
Shareholders' equity		
Share capital	2,752.9	2,752.9
Other	152.1	146.1
(Deficit) retained earnings	(172.1)	2,086.5
Other comprehensive income	(3.2)	(7.1)
Total shareholders' equity	2,729.7	4,978.4
Total liabilities and shareholders' equity	$7,960.6	$10,261.0

SOBEYS INC.
Statements of Cash Flows
53 and 52 Weeks Ended
(in millions)

	May 7 2016	May 2 2015
Operating activities		
Cash receipts from operating activities	$ 24,629.1	$ 23,928.8
Cash payments from operating activities	(23,791.4)	(22,862.4)
Net cash provided by operating activities	837.7	1,066.4
Investing activities		
Acquisition of property, equipment and investments	(616.2)	(497.2)
Proceeds on disposal of property, equipment	136.7	778.8
Additions to intangibles	(55.5)	(39.8)
Acquisition of business	(90.7)	(11.7)
Other assets and other long-term liabilities	(5.7)	(33.6)
Net cash (used) provided by operating activities	(631.4)	196.5
Financing activities		
Issue of long-term debt	581.3	373.5
Repayment of long-term debt	(594.4)	(1,511.8)
Payment of dividends	(130.3)	(119.2)
Payment of interest	(99.7)	(123.1)
Net cash used by financing activities	(243.1)	(1,380.6)
Net decrease in cash and cash equivalents	(36.8)	(117.7)
Cash and cash equivalents, beginning of year	295.6	413.3
Cash and cash equivalents, end of year	$ 258.8	$ 295.6

▶ PRACTICE COMPREHENSIVE DO IT!

*The **Comprehensive Do It!** is a final review before you begin your homework.*

Answers are at the end of the chapter.

Jeff Andringa, a former university hockey player, started Ice Camp Ltd., a hockey camp for children from ages 6 to 16. Eventually he would like to expand and open hockey camps across the country. Jeff has asked you to help him prepare financial statements at the end of his first year of operations. He tells you the following facts about his business activities.

In order to get the business off the ground, he decided to incorporate. On January 3, 2018, he incorporated Ice Camp Ltd., paying $5,000 in exchange for 500 common shares. The company subsequently borrowed $10,000 from a local bank. A used bus for transporting kids was purchased for $12,000 cash. Hockey nets and other miscellaneous equipment were purchased with $1,500 cash. The company earned camp tuition of $100,000 during the year but has collected only $90,000 of this amount far. Thus, at the end of the year the company was still owed $10,000 by some of its clients. The company rents time at a local rink. Total ice rental costs during the year were $14,000, insurance was $6,000, salaries were $20,000, and administrative expenses totalled $7,000—all of which were paid in cash. The company incurred $800 in interest expense on the bank loan, which it still owed at the end of the year. The company also owes $10,440 in income tax. The company paid Jeff dividends of $35,000 rather than salary during the year.

The balance in the corporate bank account at December 31, 2018, was $9,500 ($5,000 + $10,000 − $12,000 − $1,500 + $90,000 − $14,000 − $6,000 − $20,000 − $7,000 − $35,000).

INSTRUCTIONS

Prepare an income statement, statement of changes in equity, and statement of financial position for the year assuming Ice Camp uses IFRS. Note that, while it is unlikely that Ice Camp would follow IFRS, the resulting financial statements would not be very different from those that would be reported under ASPE.

*Practice **Objective-Format Questions** are multiple-choice questions that allow for more than one correct answer and better test your understanding of a concept.*

▶ PRACTICE OBJECTIVE-FORMAT QUESTIONS

Answers are at the end of the chapter.

1. For each of the following financial statement users, indicate whether they would be an "internal" or "external" user:

   (a) Bank (lender)
   (b) Shareholders
   (c) Employees (non-management)
   (d) Suppliers
   (e) Labour union
   (f) Canada Revenue Agency
   (g) Management

2. For each of the following questions that could be asked by a financial statement user, indicate which user (select from: management, shareholder, potential shareholder, supplier, labour union, and bank) would be most likely to ask it and whether they would be considered to be an "internal" or "external" user.

   (a) How do production costs compare across our two manufacturing plants?
   (b) If we lend the company money, will they be able to repay the loan, together with interest?
   (c) Should we allow the company to purchase materials on account?
   (d) Do the company's financial results justify the price I would have to pay to purchase shares in the company?
   (e) If we demand a 2% salary increase, would it make the company unprofitable?
   (f) Should we purchase or rent the new equipment we require?
   (g) If the company maintains its dividend policy (declares and pays the same dividends as it did in the previous year), what would be the dividend I would receive on the 100 shares I own?

3. Indicate which of the following statements are correct. (Select as many as are appropriate.)

   (a) A corporation is a separate legal entity and pays income tax on its net income.
   (b) In a partnership, there is a legal distinction between the business and the partners.
   (c) Shareholders are responsible for the debts of the corporation as they are the owners of the company.
   (d) The net income of a proprietorship is taxed on the owner's personal income tax return.

(e) Forming a corporation is the most complex way to structure a business.

(f) Each partner in a partnership generally has unlimited liability for all of the debts of the partnership.

(g) The reporting entity concept applies regardless of whether a business is organized as a proprietorship, partnership, or corporation.

4. Indicate which of the following statements are correct. (Select as many as are appropriate.)

(a) Public corporations are companies whose shares trade on a public stock exchange.

(b) Once the form of business is established (as a proprietorship, partnership, or corporation), it cannot be changed.

(c) Private companies can use either IFRS or ASPE to prepare their financial statements.

(d) It is normally easier for a proprietorship to raise capital than it is for a corporation.

(e) Private companies do not have to make their financial results public.

(f) The personal liability of shareholders in both private and public corporations is normally limited to the extent of their investment in shares of the corporation.

(g) Public companies can use either IFRS or ASPE to prepare their financial statements.

5. For each of the following, indicate what type of activity it is (financing, investing, or operating) and whether it would result in an inflow or outflow of cash.

(a) Paying dividends

(b) Collecting an account receivable from a customer

(c) Purchasing new equipment

(d) Issuing common shares

(e) Paying employee salaries

(f) Repaying a bank loan

(g) Selling equipment that the company has finished using

6. For each of the following, indicate what type of activity (financing, investing, or operating) it is related to.

(a) Property, plant, and equipment

(b) Dividends declared

(c) Intangible assets

(d) Accounts payable

(e) Loan payable

(f) Common shares

(g) Supplies

7. Indicate on which financial statement(s) (income statement, statement of changes in equity, statement of financial position, or statement of cash flows) each of the following would be reported. (Select as many as are appropriate.)

(a) Cash

(b) Unearned revenue

(c) Net income

(d) Cost of goods sold

(e) Dividends declared and paid

(f) Prepaid insurance

(g) Service revenue

8. Indicate which of the following statements are correct. (Select as many as are appropriate.)

(a) Total assets less total liabilities should be equal to shareholders' equity.

(b) The income statement is normally prepared before the statement of financial position.

(c) The declaration and payment of dividends would affect the income statement, statement of changes in equity, and statement of cash flows.

(d) A company's cash balance at the end of an accounting period is found on both the

statement of financial position and the statement of cash flows.

(e) If a company received a new bank loan, it would affect both the statement of financial position and the statement of cash flows.

(f) The statement of financial position is normally prepared before the statement of changes in equity.

(g) The issue of common shares would affect all four of the financial statements.

9. Indicate which financial statement(s) (income statement, statement of changes in equity, statement of financial position, or statement of cash flows) would have to be consulted to answer each of the following questions.

(a) Did the company declare dividends during the period?

(b) How did the company's salaries expense compare with its revenues?

(c) What was the company's income before income taxes?

(d) How much does the company owe its suppliers?

(e) Did the company issue shares during the period?

(f) Were the company's cash flows from operating activities sufficient to cover the cash required to purchase long-term assets?

(g) What amount was owed to the company by its customers?

10. For each lettered item below, indicate which of the following amounts it would be used to calculate: total assets, total liabilities, total shareholders' equity, net income, or retained earnings.

(a) Unearned revenue
(b) Common shares
(c) Cost of goods sold
(d) Bank indebtedness

(e) Dividends declared
(f) Goodwill
(g) Interest expense

WileyPLUS

Brief Exercises, Exercises, and many additional resources are available for practice in WileyPLUS.

The financial results of real companies are included in the end-of-chapter material. These company names are shown in **red**.

▶ QUESTIONS

(LO 1) 1. What is accounting?

(LO 1) 2. (a) Distinguish between internal and external users of accounting information. (b) Why are some people who work for a company considered to be internal users while others are considered to be external users?

(LO 1) 3. What kinds of questions might internal users of accounting information want answered? External users?

(LO 1) 4. Why are investors, lenders, and creditors considered to be the primary users of accounting information? Are these users considered to be internal or external users?

(LO 1) 5. Why is ethical decision-making important to the preparation of accounting information and to the decision makers who rely on this information?

(LO 2) 6. Identify the advantages and disadvantages of each of the following forms of business organization: (a) proprietorship, (b) partnership, (c) private corporation, and (d) public corporation.

(LO 2) 7. Identify the similarities and differences between a public corporation and a private corporation.

(LO 2) 8. (a) Identify the financial reporting standards a public and a private corporation may use. (b) Why do you think they differ?

(LO 2) 9. Why might a private corporation opt to prepare its financial statements using IFRS?

(LO 2) 10. Explain how the reporting entity concept applies to business organizations.

(LO 3) 11. Explain the following terms and give an example of each: (a) asset, (b) liability, (c) shareholders' equity, (d) revenues, and (e) expenses.

(LO 3) 12. Distinguish among operating, investing, and financing activities.

(LO 3) 13. Give two examples of each kind of business activity: (a) operating, (b) investing, and (c) financing. For each type of activity, identify at least one example that would result in a cash inflow and one that would result in a cash outflow.

(LO 3) 14. Name two local companies that provide services and generate service revenue. Name two local companies that sell products and generate sales revenue.

(LO 4) 15. What is a fiscal year end? Why does a company's fiscal year not always end on December 31?

(LO 4) 16. André is puzzled reading **Air Canada**'s financial statements. He notices that the numbers have all been rounded to the nearest million. He thought financial statements were supposed to be accurate and wonders what happened to the rest of the money. Respond to André's concern.

(LO 4) 17. The basic accounting equation is Assets = Liabilities + Shareholders' Equity. Replacing words with dollar amounts, what is **North West**'s accounting equation at January 31, 2016? North West's simplified financial statements can be found in Illustration 1-9 within this chapter.

(LO 4) 18. What are the primary components explained in a statement of changes in equity? What types of items generally increase each component? What types of items generally decrease each component?

(LO 4) 19. (a) What is the purpose of the statement of cash flows? (b) What are the three main categories of activities included in the statement?

(LO 4) 20. Explain whether cash flows from operating activities would normally be expected to be positive or negative in the early years of a company's life. What about cash flows from investing activities? Why is this the case?

(LO 4) 21. Why is a statement of financial position prepared as at a specific point in time, while the other financial statements cover a period of time?

(LO 4) 22. How are each of the following pairs of financial statements related?
(a) Income statement and statement of changes in equity
(b) Statement of changes in equity and statement of financial position
(c) Statement of financial position and statement of cash flows

(LO 4) 23. Identify the four financial statements used by corporations using (a) IFRS and (b) ASPE.

► BRIEF EXERCISES

BE1–1 The following list presents different types of evaluations made by various users of accounting information:
1. Determining if the company can pay for purchases made on account
2. Determining if the company has complied with income tax regulations
3. Determining if the company could afford a 1% salary increase
4. Determining if an advertising campaign was cost-effective
5. Determining if the company's net income will result in a share price increase
6. Determining if the company should use debt or equity financing

(a) Beside each user of accounting information listed in the left-hand column of the table that follows, write the number of the evaluation above (1 to 6) that the user would most likely make.
(b) Indicate if the user is internal or external. The first item has been done for you as an example.

Identify users of accounting information.
(LO 1)

	(a) Type of Evaluation	(b) Type of User
Investor	5	External
Marketing manager		
Creditor		
Chief financial officer		
Canada Revenue Agency		
Labour union		

BE1–2 Match each of the following forms of business organization—(1) proprietorship, (2) partnership, (3) public corporation, or (4) private corporation—with the set of characteristics that best describes it.
(a) _____ Simple to set up; founder retains control
(b) _____ Separate legal entity; shares closely held
(c) _____ Easier to transfer ownership and raise funds; no personal liability
(d) _____ Shared control; increased skills and resources
(e) _____ Issues shares; can choose to follow IFRS or ASPE accounting standards

Identify forms of business organization.
(LO 2)

BE1–3 Classify each item by type of business activity—operating (O), investing (I), or financing (F). Also indicate whether it results in an inflow or outflow of cash.
(a) _____/_____ Loan taken out from a bank
(b) _____/_____ Cash received from customers
(c) _____/_____ Sale of office equipment that company is done using
(d) _____/_____ Dividends paid to shareholders
(e) _____/_____ Common shares issued to investors
(f) _____/_____ Loan repayment
(g) _____/_____ Payment to supplier for inventory
(h) _____/_____ Purchase of an office building
(i) _____/_____ Salaries paid

Classify items by activity.
(LO 3)

BE1–4 For each of the following items, indicate (a) the type of business activity—operating (O), investing (I), or financing (F)—and (b) whether it increased (+), decreased (−), or had no effect (NE) on cash. The first one has been done for you as an example.

Identify business activity and effect on cash.
(LO 3)

	(a) Type of Activity	(b) Cash Effect
1. Sold goods on account.	O	NE
2. Borrowed money from a bank.		
3. Purchased inventory for cash.		
4. Provided a service for cash.		
5. Paid salaries in cash.		
6. Purchased a delivery truck for cash.		

BE1–5 Use the accounting equation to answer these independent questions:
(a) The shareholders' equity of Sansom Corporation is $120,000. Its total liabilities are $55,000. What is the amount of Sansom's total assets?
(b) The liabilities of Houle Corporation are $170,000. Houle's share capital is $100,000 and its retained earnings are $90,000. What is the amount of Houle's total assets?

Use accounting equation.
(LO 4)

(c) The total assets of Pitre Limited are $150,000. Its share capital is $50,000 and its retained earnings are $25,000. What is the amount of its total liabilities?

(d) The total assets of Budovitch Inc. are $500,000 and its liabilities are equal to half its total assets. What is the amount of Budovitch's shareholders' equity?

Use accounting equation.
(LO 4)

BE1–6 At the beginning of the year, Xul Ltd. had total assets of $720,000 and total liabilities of $420,000. Use this information to answer each of the following independent questions.

(a) If Xul's total assets increased by $250,000 during the year and total liabilities decreased by $80,000, what is the amount of shareholders' equity at the end of the year?

(b) During the year, Xul's total liabilities decreased by $100,000. The company reported net income of $90,000, sold additional shares for $125,000, and did not declare any dividends during the year. What is the amount of total assets at the end of the year?

(c) If Xul's total assets decreased by $90,000 during the year and shareholders' equity increased by $120,000, what is the amount of total liabilities at the end of the year?

Identify financial statement.
(LO 4)

BE1–7 Indicate which statement—income statement (IS), statement of financial position (SFP), statement of changes in equity (SCE), or statement of cash flows (SCF)—you would examine to find each of the following items:

(a) _____ Sales revenue

(b) _____ Supplies

(c) _____ Dividends declared

(d) _____ Cash provided by operating activities

(e) _____ Total liabilities

(f) _____ Cash used for financing activities

(g) _____ Salaries expense

(h) _____ Common shares issued during the year

Identify assets, liabilities, and shareholders' equity.
(LO 4)

BE1–8 Indicate whether each of these items is an asset (A), a liability (L), or shareholders' equity (SE):

(a) _____ Bank indebtedness

(b) _____ Accounts receivable

(c) _____ Salaries payable

(d) _____ Accounts payable

(e) _____ Inventory

(f) _____ Equipment

(g) _____ Goodwill

(h) _____ Common shares

(i) _____ Bank loan payable

(j) _____ Retained earnings

(k) _____ Cash

Determine effect of transactions on shareholders' equity.
(LO 4)

BE1–9 Determine whether each transaction would increase (+), decrease (−), or have no effect (NE) on each of the following components found in the statement of changes in equity: share capital, retained earnings, and total shareholders' equity. The first one has been done for you as an example.

	Share Capital	Retained Earnings	Total Shareholders' Equity
(a) Net income	NE	+	+
(b) Repayment of bank loan			
(c) Declared dividends			
(d) Issue of common shares			
(e) Cash			
(f) Repurchase of common shares			
(g) Net loss			
(h) Issue of long-term debt			

Calculate ending equity balances.
(LO 4)

BE1–10 Go-Ahead Limited began the year with common shares of $100,000 and retained earnings of $475,000. During the year, it issued an additional $50,000 of common shares, reported net income of $75,000, and declared dividends of $15,000. (a) Calculate the ending balances of (1) common shares, (2) retained earnings, and (3) total shareholders' equity. (b) Explain how your answer would change if the company had reported a loss of $75,000 rather than net income and not declared any dividends.

▶ EXERCISES

Identify users of accounting information.
(LO 1)

E1–1 Facebook, Inc. is a public corporation and has been one of the world's most active social networking sites. Its revenue is generated primarily from advertising.

Instructions

(a) Identify two internal users of Facebook's accounting information. Write a question that each user might try to answer by using accounting information.

(b) Identify two external users of Facebook's accounting information. Write a question that each user might try to answer by using accounting information.

E1–2 Consider the following statements.

Identify forms of business organization.

(LO 2)

	Proprietorship	Partnership	Public Corporation	Private Corporation
1. No personal liability	F	F	T	T
2. Owner(s) pay(s) personal income tax on company income				
3. Generally easiest form of organization to raise capital				
4. Ownership indicated by shares				
5. Required to issue quarterly financial statements				
6. Owned by one person				
7. Limited life				
8. Usually easiest form of organization to set up				
9. Required to use IFRS as its accounting standards				
10. Shares are closely held				

Instructions

Indicate if each of the statements listed in the left-hand column of the table above is normally true (T) or false (F) for each of the following types of business organization: proprietorship, partnership, public corporation, and private corporation. The first one has been done for you as an example.

E1–3 Consider the following business activities.

Classify business activities.

(LO 3)

1. Cash receipts from customers paying for daily ski passes — O
2. Payments made to purchase additional snow-making equipment
3. Payments made to repair the grooming machines
4. Receipt of funds from the bank to finance the purchase of the additional snow-making equipment
5. Issue of shares to raise funds for a planned expansion
6. Repayment of a portion of the loan from the bank (see #4)
7. Payment of interest on the bank loan
8. Payment of salaries to the employees who operate the ski lifts
9. Receipt of a grant from the government for training a group of disabled skiers
10. Payment of dividend to shareholders

Instructions

Classify each of the above items by type of business activity: operating (O), investing (I), or financing (F). The first one has been done for you as an example.

E1–4 Consider the following business activities.

Identify business activity and effect on cash.

(LO 3)

	(a) Type of Activity	(b) Cash Effect
1. Purchase of goods for resale	O	−
2. Issue of common shares		
3. Sale of equipment that the company has finished using		
4. Receipt of bank loan		
5. Purchase of long-term investment		
6. Purchase of equipment		
7. Sale of merchandise to customers		
8. Payment of salaries to employees		
9. Sale of long-term investment		
10. Repayment of loan owed to bank		
11. Payment of dividends		
12. Payment of interest on money borrowed from bank		

Instructions

(a) For each of the above items, indicate the type of business activity—operating (O), investing (I), or financing (F).

(b) Indicate whether each of the above items would increase (+) or decrease (−) cash. Assume all items are cash transactions. The first one has been done for you as an example.

Identify financial statement.

(LO 4)

E1-5 Consider the following typical accounts and statement items.

1. _____ Sales	9. _____ Merchandise inventory
2. _____ Cash	10. _____ Income tax expense
3. _____ Cash provided by operating activities	11. _____ Interest expense
4. _____ Service revenue	12. _____ Cash used by investing activities
5. _____ Common shares	13. _____ Equipment
6. _____ Dividends declared	14. _____ Retained earnings
7. _____ Net income	15. _____ Bank loan payable
8. _____ Accounts receivable	

Instructions

Indicate on which statement(s)—income statement (IS), statement of financial position (SFP), statement of changes in equity (SCE), and/or statement of cash flows (SCF)—you would find each of the above accounts or items. Note that there may be more than one correct statement for some of the above.

Calculate accounting equation.

(LO 4)

E1-6 K-Os Corporation reported the following selected information for the two years ended December 31:

	2018	2017
Total assets	$630,000	$550,000
Total liabilities	420,000	400,000

Instructions

(a) Calculate total shareholders' equity at December 31, 2017 and 2018.
(b) Calculate the change in total shareholders' equity for the year ended December 31, 2018.
(c) K-Os's shareholders' equity consists only of common shares and retained earnings. Using the change in total shareholders' equity calculated in part (b) above, calculate the net income or loss for the year ended December 31, 2018, assuming each of the following independent scenarios:
   1. K-Os issued no common shares during the year and did not declare any dividends.
   2. K-Os issued no common shares during the year and declared and paid dividends of $10,000.
   3. K-Os issued $30,000 of additional common shares during the year and did not declare any dividends.
   4. K-Os issued $20,000 of additional common shares during the year and declared and paid dividends of $10,000.

Determine missing amounts.

(LO 4)

E1-7 Summaries of selected data from the financial statements of two corporations follow. Both companies have just completed their first year of operations.

	Lumber Inc.	Trucking Inc.
Income statement		
Total revenues	$1,000,000	$ [7]
Total expenses	[1]	250,000
Net income	150,000	50,000
Statement of changes in equity		
Total shareholders' equity, beginning of year	0	0
Common shares, beginning of year	0	0
Issue of shares	100,000	[8]
Common shares, end of year	[2]	20,000
Retained earnings, beginning of year	0	0
Net income	[3]	[9]
Dividends declared	[4]	10,000
Retained earnings, end of year	100,000	40,000
Total shareholders' equity, end of year	[5]	[10]
Statement of financial position		
Total assets	1,050,000	[11]
Total liabilities	850,000	150,000
Total shareholders' equity	[6]	[12]

Instructions

Determine the missing amounts for [1] to [12]. Note that you may not be able to solve the items in numerical order.

Determine missing amounts.

(LO 4)

E1-8 Summaries of selected data from the financial statements of two corporations follow. Both companies have just completed their first year of operations.

	Heavy Lift Ltd.	Transport Ltd.
Income statement		
Total revenues	$ [1]	$3,200,000
Total expenses	1,700,000	[7]
Net income	1,100,000	1,500,000
Statement of changes in equity		
Total shareholders' equity, beginning of year	0	0
Common shares, beginning of year	0	0
Issue of shares	[2]	500,000
Common shares, end of year	200,000	[8]
Retained earnings, beginning of year	0	0
Net income	[3]	[9]
Dividends declared	300,000	[10]
Retained earnings, end of year	800,000	1,200,000
Total shareholders' equity, end of year	[4]	[11]
Statement of financial position		
Total assets	[5]	3,100,000
Total liabilities	1,600,000	[12]
Total shareholders' equity	[6]	1,700,000

Instructions

Determine the missing amounts for [1] to [12]. Note that you may not be able to solve the items in numerical order.

E1–9 The following amounts (in thousands) were taken from the December 31 statements of financial position of Maple Leaf Foods Inc.:

Calculate accounting equation.

(LO 4)

	2015	2014
Total assets	$2,630,865	$2,876,490
Total liabilities	577,731	631,994

Instructions

(a) How much is Maple Leaf Foods' shareholders' equity at December 31, 2015 and 2014?
(b) Write Maple Leaf Foods' accounting equation for each year.
(c) Calculate the change in total shareholders' equity for the year ended December 31, 2015.
(d) Assume that Maple Leaf Foods had the following changes to its shareholders' equity in 2015: dividends declared of $44,668 thousand, and other shareholders' equity items of $(188,274) thousand. How much net income did it report in 2015?

E1–10 The following list of accounts, in alphabetical order, is for Aventura Inc. at November 30, 2018:

Classify accounts and prepare statement of financial position.

(LO 4)

_____ Accounts payable	$ 26,200
_____ Accounts receivable	19,500
_____ Bank loan payable	34,000
_____ Buildings	100,000
_____ Cash	20,000
_____ Common shares	20,000
_____ Equipment	30,000
_____ Income tax payable	6,000
_____ Land	44,000
_____ Merchandise inventory	18,000
_____ Mortgage payable	97,500
_____ Retained earnings	48,500
_____ Supplies	700

Instructions

(a) For each of the above accounts, identify whether it is an asset (A), liability (L), or shareholders' equity (SE) item.
(b) Prepare a statement of financial position at November 30.

Classify accounts and prepare income statement.

(LO 4)

E1–11 The following selected accounts and amounts (in thousands) were taken from the January 30, 2016, financial statements of **Reitmans (Canada) Limited.**

_____	Administrative expenses	$ 46,950
_____	Cost of goods sold	410,035
_____	Dividends declared	12,917
_____	Finance expenses	16,443
_____	Finance income	7,998
_____	Income tax expense (recovery)	(1,426)
_____	Selling and distribution expenses	497,854
_____	Sales	937,155

Instructions
(a) For each of the above accounts, identify whether it is a revenue (R) or expense (E) account or an account that is not reported on the income statement (NR).
(b) Prepare an income statement for the year.

Prepare income statement and statement of changes in equity.
(LO 4)

E1–12 The following information is for Kon Inc. for the year ended December 31, 2018:

Common shares, Jan. 1	$20,000
Common shares issued during year	10,000
Retained earnings, Jan. 1	58,000
Office expense	1,600
Dividends declared	5,000
Rent expense	12,400
Service revenue	61,000
Utilities expense	2,400
Salaries expense	30,000
Income tax expense	3,000

Instructions
Prepare an income statement and statement of changes in equity for the year.

Calculate net income and prepare statements of changes in equity and financial position.
(LO 4)

E1–13 Sea Surf Campground, Inc. is a public camping ground near Ocean National Park. It has the following financial information as at December 31, 2018:

Camping revenue	$283,000	Dividends declared	$ 12,000
Cash	19,000	Operating expenses	245,000
Equipment	124,000	Supplies	2,500
Accounts payable	16,500	Common shares, Jan. 1	30,000
Bank loan payable	50,000	Common shares issued during year	15,000
Income tax expense	10,000	Retained earnings, Jan. 1	18,000

Instructions
(a) Determine net income for the year.
(b) Prepare a statement of changes in equity and a statement of financial position for the year.

Interpret financial information.
(LO 4)

E1–14 Consider each of the following independent situations:
1. The statement of changes in equity of Yu Corporation shows dividends declared of $70,000, while net income for the year was $75,000.
2. The statement of cash flows for Surya Corporation shows that cash provided by operating activities was $10,000; cash used by investing activities was $100,000; and cash provided by financing activities was $120,000.
3. Naguib Ltd.'s statement of financial position reports $200,000 of total liabilities and $250,000 of shareholders' equity.
4. Rijo Inc. has total assets of $100,000 and no liabilities.

Instructions
For each company, write a brief interpretation of these financial facts. For example, you might discuss the company's financial health or what seems to be its growth philosophy.

▶ PROBLEMS: SET A

Identify users of accounting information.
(LO 1, 4)

P1–1A Financial decisions made by users often depend on one financial statement more than the others. Consider each of the following independent, hypothetical situations:
1. The South Face Inc. is considering extending credit to a new customer. The credit terms would require the customer to pay within 30 days of receiving goods.

2. An investor is considering purchasing the common shares of Orbite Online, Inc. The investor plans on holding the investment for at least five years.
3. Caisse d'Économie Base Montréal is thinking about extending a loan to a small company. The company would be required to make interest payments at the end of each month for three years, and to repay the loan at the end of the third year.
4. The chief financial officer of Tech Toy Limited is trying to determine whether the company is generating enough cash to increase the amount of dividends paid to shareholders in this, and future, years. He needs to be sure that Tech Toy will still have enough cash to expand operations when needed.

Instructions

(a) Identify the key user(s) in each situation and determine whether they are internal or external users.
(b) State whether the user(s) you identified in part (a) would be most interested in the income statement, statement of financial position, or statement of cash flows to make their decision. Choose only one financial statement in each case, and briefly give reasons for your choice.

P1–2A Five independent situations follow:

Determine forms of business organization and accounting standards.

(LO 2)

1. Three computer science professors have formed a business selling technology that enables digital monitoring of cardiac patients outside of hospital settings. Each has contributed an equal amount of cash and knowledge to the venture. While their plans look promising, they are concerned about the legal liabilities that their business might confront.
2. Joseph LeBlanc, a student looking for summer work, has opened a bicycle rental shop in a small shed on the Trans Canada Trail system.
3. Robert Steven and Tom Cheng each owned businesses manufacturing customized snowboards and have now decided to combine their businesses. They expect that in the coming year they will need to raise funds to expand their operations.
4. Darcy Becker, Ellen Sweet, and Meg Dwyer recently completed their Chartered Professional Accountant training after articling with a public accounting firm. Friends since childhood, they have decided to start their own accounting practice.
5. Hervé Gaudet wants to install and then rent storage lockers in airports across the country. His idea is that customers will be able to leave their luggage at the airport if they have a long layover so they can explore the local surroundings without being burdened with luggage. This will require the rental of space in each airport as well as the hiring of employees and other operating costs.

Instructions

(a) In each of the above situations, explain what form of organization the business is likely to take: proprietorship, partnership, public corporation, or private corporation. Give reasons for your choice.
(b) Indicate which type of accounting standards—IFRS or ASPE—each of the business organizations you identified in part (a) is most likely to use for external reporting purposes.

P1–3A All companies are involved in three types of activities: operating, investing, and financing. The names and descriptions of organizations in several different industries follow:

Identify business activities.

(LO 3)

  Indigo Books & Music—book, gift, and specialty toy retailer
  High Liner Foods—processor and distributor of seafood products
  Mountain Equipment Co-op—outdoor equipment retailer
  Ganong Bros.—chocolate and candy manufacturer
  Royal Bank—banking and financial service provider

Instructions

(a) For each of the above organizations, provide a likely example of (1) one of its operating activities, (2) one of its investing activities, and (3) one of its financing activities.
(b) Which of the activities that you identified in part (a) are common to most organizations? Which activities are not?

P1–4A Slipstream Ltd. reports the following list of accounts, in alphabetical order:

Classify accounts.

(LO 4)

	(a)	(b)
Accounts payable	L	SFP
Accounts receivable		
Bank indebtedness		
Bank loan payable		
Cash		
Common shares		
Equipment		
Goodwill		
Income tax expense		
Income tax payable		
Interest expense		

Office expense	_____	_____
Prepaid insurance	_____	_____
Rent expense	_____	_____
Repair and maintenance expense	_____	_____
Salaries payable	_____	_____
Service revenue	_____	_____
Supplies	_____	_____
Vehicles	_____	_____

Instructions

(a) Classify each account as an asset (A), liability (L), share capital (SC), revenue (R), or expense (E) item. The first one has been done for you as an example.

(b) Identify on which financial statement(s)—income statement (IS), statement of changes in equity (SCE), and/or statement of financial position (SFP)—each account would be reported. Note that there may be more than one correct statement for some of the above. The first one has been done for you as an example.

Prepare accounting equation.

(LO 4)

P1–5A Craft Carpentry Limited reports the following statement of financial position accounts, in alphabetical order:

Accounts payable	$15,600	Interest payable	$ 300
Accounts receivable	13,100	Inventory	9,200
Bank loan payable	32,000	Prepaid insurance	1,000
Cash	9,350	Retained earnings	21,250
Common shares	20,000	Salaries payable	700
Equipment	30,500	Supplies	2,800
Income tax payable	1,800	Unearned revenue	1,800
Intangible assets	5,000	Vehicles	22,500

Instructions

(a) Classify each account as an asset (A), liability (L), or shareholders' equity (SE) item.

(b) Calculate total assets, total liabilities, and total shareholders' equity and prepare Craft Carpentry's accounting equation.

(c) Craft Carpentry's retained earnings were $18,000 at the beginning of the year. The company reported revenues of $296,750, expenses of $278,500, and dividends declared of $15,000 during the year. Prepare a calculation that proves how retained earnings of $21,250 at the end of the year were determined.

Determine missing amounts; answer questions.

(LO 4)

P1–6A Selected information (in millions) is available for **Sears Canada Inc.** and **Canadian Tire Corporation, Limited** for a recent fiscal year:

	Sears	Canadian Tire
Beginning of year		
Total assets	$ [1]	$14,553.2
Total liabilities	1,203.3	[4]
Total shareholders' equity	570.8	5,630.8
End of year		
Total assets	1,633.2	[5]
Total liabilities	[2]	9,198.1
Total shareholders' equity	554.2	[6]
Changes during year in shareholders' equity		
Repurchase of shares	–0–	434.6
Dividends declared	–0–	162.4
Total revenues	3,145.7	12,279.6
Total expenses	[3]	11,543.7
Other increases in shareholders' equity	51.3	20.0

Instructions

(a) Determine the missing amounts for [1] to [6].

(b) Which company has a higher proportion of debt financing at the end of its fiscal year? Of equity financing?

(c) Sears's year end is the last Saturday in January. Canadian Tire's year end is the last Saturday in December. How might these differing year-end dates affect your comparison in part (b)?

Prepare financial statements.

(LO 4)

P1–7A On June 1, 2018, One Planet Cosmetics Corp. was formed. Its assets, liabilities, share capital, revenues, expenses, and dividends as at June 30 follow:

Cash	$15,000	Supplies	$ 1,200
Accounts receivable	9,000	Equipment	52,000

Accounts payable	$ 7,300	Interest expense	$ 800
Bank loan payable	23,000	Office expense	1,500
Common shares	36,000	Utilities expense	1,500
Dividends declared	1,000	Income tax expense	700
Service revenue	24,200	Salaries expense	5,700
Supplies expense	2,100		

Instructions

(a) Prepare an income statement, statement of changes in equity, and statement of financial position for the month.

(b) Explain why it is necessary to prepare the financial statements in the order listed in part (a).

P1–8A Selected financial information follows for Maison Corporation for the year ended December 31, 2018:

Cash, Jan. 1	$ 12,000
Cash dividends paid	10,000
Cash paid to purchase equipment	35,000
Cash payments for operating activities	120,000
Cash receipts from operating activities	140,000
Cash received from issue of long-term debt	20,000
Cash received from issue of shares	20,000

Prepare statement of cash flows; comment on adequacy of cash.

(LO 4)

Instructions

(a) Classify each of the above items, except for cash at the beginning of the year, as an operating, investing, or financing activity.

(b) Prepare a statement of cash flows for Maison Corporation for the year.

(c) Comment on the adequacy of cash provided by operating activities to fund the company's investing activities.

P1–9A Incomplete financial statements for Baxter, Inc. follow.

Calculate missing amounts; explain statement interrelationships.

(LO 4)

BAXTER, INC.
Income Statement
Year Ended November 30, 2018

Service revenue	$225,000
Operating expenses	[1]
Income before income tax	45,000
Income tax expense	9,000
Net income	$ [2]

BAXTER, INC.
Statement of Changes in Equity
Year Ended November 30, 2018

	Common Shares	Retained Earnings	Total Equity
Balance, December 1, 2017	$ 0	$ 0	$ 0
Issued common shares	250,000		[5]
Net income		[3]	[6]
Dividends declared		(15,000)	(15,000)
Balance, November 30, 2018	$250,000	$ [4]	$ [7]

BAXTER, INC.
Statement of Financial Position
November 30, 2018

Assets		Liabilities and Shareholders' Equity	
Cash	$ 22,000	Liabilities	
Accounts receivable	34,000	Accounts payable	$ [10]
Land	[8]	Bank loan payable	600,000
Buildings	390,000	Total liabilities	693,000
Equipment	218,000	Shareholders' equity	
Total assets	$ [9]	Common shares	[11]
		Retained earnings	[12]
		Total shareholders' equity	[13]
		Total liabilities and shareholders' equity	$964,000

Instructions

(a) Calculate the missing amounts for [1] to [13]. Note that you may not be able to solve the items in numerical order.

(b) Explain (1) the sequence for preparing the financial statements, and (2) the interrelationships among the income statement, statement of changes in equity, and statement of financial position.

Prepare corrected statement of financial position; identify financial statements for ASPE.

(LO 4)

P1–10A GG Corporation, a private corporation, was formed on July 1, 2018. On July 31, Guy Gélinas, the company's president, prepared the following statement of financial position:

GG CORPORATION
Statement of Financial Position
July 31, 2018

Assets		Liabilities and Shareholders' Equity	
Cash	$ 20,000	Accounts payable	$ 34,000
Accounts receivable	50,000	Boat loan payable	40,000
Merchandise inventory	36,000	Common shares	50,000
Boat	24,000	Retained earnings	6,000
	$130,000		$130,000

Guy admits that his knowledge of accounting is somewhat limited and is concerned that his statement of financial position might not be correct. He gives you the following additional information:

1. The boat actually belongs to Guy Gélinas, not to GG Corporation. However, because Guy thinks he might take customers out on the boat occasionally, he decided to list it as an asset of the company. To be consistent, he also included as a liability of the company the personal bank loan that he took out to buy the boat.

2. Included in the accounts receivable balance is $10,000 that Guy personally loaned to his brother five years ago. Guy included this in the receivables of GG Corporation so that he wouldn't forget that his brother owes him money.

3. Guy's statements didn't balance originally. To make them balance, he adjusted the Common Shares account until assets equalled liabilities and shareholders' equity.

Instructions

(a) Identify any corrections that should be made to the statement of financial position and explain why.

(b) Prepare a corrected statement of financial position. (*Hint*: To get the balance sheet to balance, adjust Common Shares.)

(c) What other financial statements should GG Corporation prepare, assuming it follows Accounting Standards for Private Enterprises?

▶ PROBLEMS: SET B

Identify users of accounting information.

(LO 1, 4)

P1–1B Financial decisions made by users often depend on one financial statement more than the others. Consider each of the following independent, hypothetical situations:

1. An Ontario investor is considering purchasing the common shares of Fight Fat Ltd., which operates 13 fitness centres in the Toronto area. The investor plans on holding the investment for at least three years.

2. Comeau Ltée is considering extending credit to a new customer. The terms of the credit would require the customer to pay within 45 days of receipt of the goods.

3. The chief financial officer of Private Label Corporation is trying to determine whether the company is generating enough cash to increase the amount of dividends paid to shareholders in this, and future, years. She needs to ensure that there will still be enough cash to expand operations when needed.

4. Drummond Bank is considering extending a loan to a small company. The company would be required to make interest payments at the end of each month for five years, and to repay the loan at the end of the fifth year.

Instructions

(a) Identify the key user(s) in each situation and determine whether they are internal or external users.

(b) State whether the user(s) you identified in part (a) would be most interested in the income statement, statement of financial position, or statement of cash flows. Choose only one financial statement in each case, and briefly give reasons for your choice.

Determine forms of business organization and accounting standards.
(LO 2)

P1–2B Five independent situations follow:

1. Dawn Addington, a student looking for summer work, has opened a vegetable stand along a busy local highway. Each morning, she buys produce from local farmers, then sells it in the afternoon as people return home from work.
2. Joseph Counsell and Sabra Surkis each own a bike shop. They have decided to combine their businesses and try to expand their operations to include skis and snowboards. They expect that in the coming year they will need funds to expand their operations.
3. Three chemistry professors have formed a business that uses bacteria to clean up toxic waste sites. Each has contributed an equal amount of cash and knowledge to the venture. The use of bacteria in this situation is experimental, and legal obligations could result.
4. Abdul Rahim has run a successful but small co-operative health and organic food store for over five years. The increased sales at his store have made him believe that the time is right to open a chain of health and organic food stores across the country. Of course, this will require a substantial investment for inventory and property, plant, and equipment, as well as for employees and other resources. Abdul has no savings or personal assets.
5. Mary Emery, Richard Goedde, and Jigme Tshering recently graduated with law degrees. They have decided to start a law practice in their hometown.

Instructions

(a) In each of the above situations, explain what form of organization the business is likely to take: proprietorship, partnership, public corporation, or private corporation. Give reasons for your choice.
(b) Indicate which type of accounting standards—IFRS or ASPE—that each of the business organizations you identified in part (a) is most likely to use for external reporting purposes.

Identify business activities.
(LO 3)

P1–3B All companies are involved in three types of activities: operating, investing, and financing. The names and descriptions of organization in several different industries follow:

WestJet Airlines—airline
University of Calgary Students' Union—university student union
GlaxoSmithKline—pharmaceutical manufacturer
Maple Leaf Sports & Entertainment—professional sports company (including ownership of the Toronto Maple Leafs hockey team and Toronto Raptors basketball team)
Empire Company—food retailer and real estate investments (including ownership of Sobeys)

Instructions

(a) For each of the above organizations, provide a likely example of (1) one of its operating activities, (2) one of its investing activities, and (3) one of its financing activities.
(b) Which of the activities that you identified in part (a) are common to most organizations? Which activities are not?

Classify accounts.
(LO 4)

P1–4B Gulfstream Inc. reports the following list of accounts, in alphabetical order:

	(a)	(b)
Accounts payable	L	SFP
Accounts receivable		
Bank loan payable		
Buildings		
Cash		
Common shares		
Cost of goods sold		
Equipment		
Income tax expense		
Income tax payable		
Intangible assets		
Interest expense		
Land		
Merchandise inventory		
Mortgage payable		
Office expense		
Prepaid insurance		
Retained earnings		
Salaries payable		
Sales		
Unearned revenue		

Instructions

(a) Classify each account as an asset (A), liability (L), share capital (SC), revenue (R), or expense (E) item. The first one has been done for you as an example.

(b) Identify on which financial statement(s)—income statement (IS), statement of changes in equity (SCE), and/or statement of financial position (SFP)—each account would be reported. Note that there may be more than one correct statement for some of the above. The first one has been done for you as an example.

Prepare accounting equation.

(LO 4)

P1–5B D&K Delivery Limited reports the following statement of financial position accounts, in alphabetical order:

Accounts payable	$23,100	Interest payable	$ 500
Accounts receivable	6,950	Inventory	21,300
Bank loan payable	25,000	Prepaid insurance	950
Cash	17,750	Retained earnings	39,850
Common shares	20,000	Salaries payable	3,050
Equipment	66,200	Supplies	3,750
Income tax payable	1,900	Unearned revenue	3,500

Instructions

(a) Classify each account as an asset (A), liability (L), or shareholders' equity (SE) item.

(b) Calculate total assets, total liabilities, and total shareholders' equity and prepare D&K Delivery's accounting equation.

(c) D&K Delivery's retained earnings were $8,850 at the beginning of the year. The company reported revenues of $365,000, expenses of $333,000, and dividends declared of $1,000 during the year. Prepare a calculation that proves how retained earnings of $39,850 at the end of the year were determined.

Determine missing amounts; answer questions.

(LO 4)

P1–6B Selected information is available for **Restaurant Brands International**, which owns or franchises more than 19,000 Tim Hortons and Burger King restaurants around the world, and **Starbucks Corporation**, which owns and operates more than 12,000 stores around the world, for a recent fiscal year:

	Restaurant Brands International (in U.S. $ millions)	Starbucks (in U.S. $ millions)
Beginning of year		
Total assets	$21,343.0	$ [4]
Total liabilities	[1]	5,479.2
Total shareholders' equity	7,636.8	5,273.7
End of year		
Total assets	18,408.5	[5]
Total liabilities	12,198.4	6,626.3
Total shareholders' equity	[2]	[6]
Changes during year in shareholders' equity		
Issuance of shares	–0–	23.5
Repurchase of shares	293.7	–0–
Dividends declared	[3]	1,016.2
Total revenues	4,052.2	19,162.7
Total expenses	3,540.5	18,616.6
Other increases (decreases) in shareholders' equity	(1,167.8)	211.3

Instructions

(a) Determine the missing amounts for [1] to [6].

(b) Which company has the higher proportion of debt financing at the end of its fiscal year? Of equity financing?

(c) Restaurant Brands' year end is December 31. Starbucks' year end is the last Sunday in September. Is it appropriate to compare these two companies in part (b)?

Prepare financial statements.

(LO 4)

P1–7B On May 1, 2018, Aero Flying School Ltd. was formed. Its assets, liabilities, share capital, revenues, expenses, and dividends as at May 31 follow:

Cash	$ 26,900	Interest expense	$12,500
Accounts receivable	22,600	Rent expense	12,100
Supplies	15,000	Repair and maintenance expense	40,900
Equipment	372,500	Fuel expense	85,400
Accounts payable	6,400	Office expense	12,700
Bank loan payable	241,000	Salaries expense	36,600
Common shares	180,000	Income tax expense	2,800
Service revenue	215,300	Dividends declared	2,700

Instructions

(a) Prepare an income statement, statement of changes in equity, and statement of financial position for the month of May.

(b) Explain why it is necessary to prepare the financial statements in the order listed in part (a).

P1–8B Selected financial information follows for Furlotte Corporation for the year ended June 30, 2018:

Cash, July 1	$ 40,000
Cash payments for operating activities	109,000
Cash paid for equipment	40,000
Repayment of long-term debt	15,000
Cash dividends paid	13,000
Cash receipts from operating activities	158,000

Prepare statement of cash flows; comment on adequacy of cash.

(LO 4)

Instructions

(a) Classify each of the above items, except for cash at the beginning of the year, as an operating, investing, or financing activity.

(b) Prepare a statement of cash flows for Furlotte Corporation for the year.

(c) Comment on the adequacy of cash provided by operating activities to fund the company's investing activities.

P1–9B Incomplete financial statements for Wu, Inc. follow:

Calculate missing amounts; explain statement interrelationships.

(LO 4)

WU, INC.
Income Statement
Year Ended August 31, 2018

Service revenue	$325,000
Operating expenses	[1]
Income before income tax	116,000
Income tax expense	23,000
Net income	$ [2]

WU, INC.
Statement of Changes in Equity
Year Ended August 31, 2018

	Common Shares	Retained Earnings	Total Equity
Balance, September 1, 2017	$250,000	$440,000	$[5]
Issued common shares	60,000		[6]
Net income		[3]	[7]
Dividends declared		[4]	[8]
Balance, August 31, 2018	$310,000	$521,000	$[9]

WU, INC.
Statement of Financial Position
August 31, 2018

Assets		Liabilities and Shareholders' Equity	
Cash	$ [10]	Liabilities	
Accounts receivable	34,000	Accounts payable	$ 67,000
Equipment	364,000	Loan payable	453,000
Buildings	616,000	Shareholders' equity	
Land	310,000	Common shares	[12]
Total assets	$ [11]	Retained earnings	[13]
		Total liabilities and shareholders' equity	$1,351,000

Instructions

(a) Calculate the missing amounts [1] to [13]. Note that you may not be able to solve the items in numerical order.

(b) Explain (1) the sequence for preparing and presenting the financial statements, and (2) the interrelationships among the income statement, statement of changes in equity, and statement of financial position.

Prepare corrected statement of financial position; identify financial statements for ASPE.

(LO 4)

P1–10B The Independent Book Shop Ltd. was formed on April 1, 2017. It is a small private corporation, run by Joanna Kay. On March 31, 2018, Joanna prepared the following income statement:

INDEPENDENT BOOK SHOP LTD.
Income Statement
Year Ended March 31, 2018

Revenues		
Accounts receivable	$23,000	
Service revenue	41,000	
Total revenues		$64,000
Expenses		
Rent expense	$12,000	
Office expense	5,000	
Vacation expense	4,000	
Total expenses		21,000
Profit before income tax		85,000
Income tax expense		5,000
Net income		$90,000

Joanna admits that her knowledge of accounting is somewhat limited and is concerned that her income statement might not be correct. She gives you the following additional information:

1. Included in the Service Revenue account is $3,000 of revenue that the company expects to earn in April 2018. Joanna included it in this year's statement so she wouldn't forget about it.

2. Joanna operates her business in a converted carriage house attached to her parents' downtown home. They do not charge her anything for the use of this building, but she thinks that if she paid rent it would have cost her about $12,000 a year. She included this amount in the income statement as Rent Expense because of the "opportunity cost."

3. To reward herself after a year of hard work, Joanna took a vacation to Greece. She used personal funds to pay for the trip, but she reported it as an expense on the income statement since it was her job that made her need the vacation.

Instructions

(a) Identify any corrections that should be made to the income statement and explain why.

(b) Prepare a corrected income statement.

(c) What other financial statements should the Independent Book Shop prepare, assuming it follows Accounting Standards for Private Enterprises?

EXPAND YOUR | CRITICAL THINKING

CT1–1 Financial Reporting Case

Actual financial statements (rather than the simplified financial statements presented in the chapter) for **The North West Company Inc.** are presented in Appendix A at the end of this book.

Instructions

(a) What are the five financial statements that North West includes in its financial statement package? Which ones were discussed in this chapter?

(b) Look at North West's income statement (which it calls "statement of earnings"). Did its sales increase or decrease between 2015 and 2016? Did its net income (which it calls "net earnings") increase or decrease between the two years? Are its sales and net income moving in the same direction (that is, both increasing or both decreasing)? If not, explain why not.

(c) Look at North West's statement of financial position (which it calls "balance sheet"). Identify its total assets, total liabilities, and total shareholders' equity as at (1) January 31, 2016, and (2) January 31, 2015.

(d) Look at North West's statement of changes in equity (which it calls "statement of changes in shareholders' equity"). What were the balances in its share capital and retained earnings accounts at the end of 2016? At the end of 2015? Do these amounts agree to the same balances reported in the shareholders' equity section of the statement of financial position?

(e) How much cash did North West have at January 31, 2016? At January 31, 2015? Which financial statement(s) did you look at to answer this question?

CT1–2 Financial Analysis Case

The financial statements of **The North West Company Inc.** are presented in Appendix A followed by the financial statements for **Sobeys Inc.** in Appendix B.

Instructions
(a) Based on the information in these financial statements, determine the following for each company:
  1. Total assets, liabilities, and shareholders' equity at the end of the current and prior fiscal years
  2. Sales and net income (loss) for the current and prior fiscal years
(b) Calculate the percentage change between the current and prior fiscal years for each company for the assets, liabilities, shareholders' equity, sales, and net income amounts determined in part (a).
(c) What conclusions about the two companies can you draw from the data you determined in part (b)?
(d) Sobeys' fiscal year end is the first Saturday in May. North West's fiscal year end is January 31. Knowing that the year ends of Sobeys and North West are not the same, do you have any concerns about the comparisons you made in part (c)? If so, why?

CT1–3 Financial Analysis Case

The financial statements of **The North West Company Inc.** are presented in Appendix A followed by the financial statements for **Sobeys Inc.** in Appendix B.

Instructions
Based on the information in these financial statements, answer the following questions:
(a) Did both companies pay dividends during the year? If yes, how much did each company pay?
(b) Did each company generate positive cash flows from its operating activities? How much cash did each company generate from its operating activities? How did these amounts compare with the amount of cash each company required for its investing activities?
(c) How much, if any, long-term debt did each company repay during the year?
(d) Did either company issue common shares during the year? If yes, how much cash did this bring into each company?

CT1–4 Professional Judgement Case

In Canada, public corporations are required to adopt International Financial Reporting Standards (IFRS) as accounting standards. Private corporations are given a choice, and must decide between two sets of accounting standards: Accounting Standards for Private Enterprises (ASPE) or IFRS.

Instructions
(a) What is the key difference between public and private companies when it comes to their financial reporting?

(b) Who are the key users of public company financial statements? Who are the key users of private company financial statements?
(c) What is the difference between users of public company financial statements and users of private company financial statements?
(d) Why do you think public companies do not have a choice regarding which accounting standards they use?
(e) Why do you think private companies do have a choice regarding the accounting standards they use?

CT1–5 Financial Analysis Case

This case can be assigned as a group activity. Additional instructions and material for this activity can be found on the Instructor Resource site and in WileyPLUS.

Industrial Maids Service Ltd. (IMS) is a corporation based in Sarnia, Ontario, that focuses on cleaning commercial properties, which is a very competitive business. Although IMS tries to recruit highly trained employees, it is not able to pay a very high hourly wage. Cleaning services are charged to clients by the hour and the average rate is $17 per hour. Some of the cleaning done by this company is performed with larger equipment that is repaired by the company. The average employee will work an entire shift at one client's premises.

Prestige Cleaning Services Inc. (PCS) also operates a cleaning service in Sarnia but this company focuses on residential cleaning and targets large homes in high-income areas. The company is owned by a former NHL star who is very effective at securing cleaning contracts. Most of the cleaning work done by this company occurs during the day and the company is able to attract experienced cleaning staff and pay them a high wage. Cleaning services are charged to clients by the hour and the average rate is $30 per hour. The equipment used by this company is inexpensive. Most employees will clean two or three houses during a single shift. The company owns several vehicles.

Listed below are condensed income statements of the two corporations:

	IMS	PCS
Service revenue	$1,020,000	$900,000
Salaries expense	600,000	450,000
Rent expense	42,000	23,000
Other operating expenses	4,000	14,000
Interest expense	25,000	13,000
Income before income tax	349,000	400,000
Income tax expense	87,250	100,000
Net income	$ 261,750	$300,000

Instructions
(a) How many hours of cleaning service did each company provide to its clients?
(b) What is the average rate of pay per hour that each company pays its employees?
(c) Which company do you think uses larger facilities? Why do you think this is?

Optional collaborative learning activities in each chapter allow you to practice solving cases with classmates.

(d) Why does PCS likely have higher other operating expenses than IMS?

(e) One of the companies financed its start-up by taking out a higher amount of bank loan than the other company. Which company do you think this was? Both companies are charged the same rate of interest by their banks.

(f) What is the most significant factor that makes PCS more profitable than IMS?

CT1–6 Ethics Case

Chief executive officers (CEOs) and chief financial officers (CFOs) of publicly traded companies are required to personally certify that their companies' financial statements and other financial information contain no untrue statements and do not leave out any important facts. Khan Corporation just hired a new management team, and its members say they are too new to the company to know whether the most recent financial reports are accurate or not. They refuse to sign the certification.

Instructions

(a) Who are the stakeholders in this situation?

(b) Should the CEO and CFO sign the certification? Explain why or why not.

(c) What are the CEO's and CFO's alternatives?

CT1–7 Serial Case

*This **serial case** starts in this chapter and continues in each chapter of the book.*

As part of the requirements of her university entrepreneurship program, Emily Anthony had been operating Compu-Tech Consulting, a proprietorship, on a part-time basis. The purpose of Compu-Tech Consulting was to provide training and technical support to anyone who wished to learn how to use a computer, tablet, or smart phone, as well as to fix hardware or software issues. As Emily approaches her graduation from university, she is considering other opportunities in addition to continuing to operate Compu-Tech Consulting.

Emily's parents, Doug and Bev Anthony, have been operating Anthony Business Company Ltd. (ABC), a private corporation, for a number of years. ABC provides business services and sells related products and accessories. The company has been overwhelmed with the demand for its goods and services and has recently negotiated a number of new contracts.

In anticipation of Emily graduating, and in hope of spending a little more time away from the business, Doug and Bev have discussed with Emily the possibility of her moving back to her home province to become one of ABC's shareholders. In addition, Emily would assume the full-time responsibility of administrator. Emily could continue to provide computer training and technical support; however, that would be done through ABC in future rather than through Compu-Tech Consulting.

Instructions

(a) Discuss the advantages and disadvantages of each of these two forms of business organization: Compu-Tech Consulting, a proprietorship, and Anthony Business Company, a private corporation.

(b) What form of generally accepted accounting principles do you anticipate each of these business organizations is using? Explain.

(c) As ABC begins to meet the demands of its new contractual commitments, what accounting information will Emily need if she accepts the position with ABC as administrator, and why? How often will she need this information?

(d) What types of users do you anticipate will use ABC's accounting information? What information will these users require?

(e) Identify two examples each of operating activities, investing activities, and financing activities, that ABC would likely be engaged in. For each type of activity, identify at least one example that would result in a cash inflow and one that would result in a cash outflow.

► ANSWERS TO CHAPTER PRACTICE QUESTIONS

DO IT! 1-1
Preparing Financial Statements

(a) Type of User	(b) Internal or External User
1. Chief financial officer	Internal
2. Lenders	External
3. Production manager	Internal
4. Customers	External
5. Investors	External
6. Marketing manager	Internal

DO IT! 1-2
Business Organizations

	Proprietorship	Partnership	Corporation
(a) Ownership	One individual	Two or more individuals	Many shareholders
(b) Complexity	Simple	Moderate	Complex
(c) Liability	Unlimited	Unlimited	Limited
(d) Life	Limited	Limited	Indefinite
(e) Capital	Hard	Easier	Easiest
(f) Income tax	Paid by individual	Paid by individuals (partners)	Paid by entity (corporation)

(a)	(b)	(c)
1. Operating activity	Outflow	Expense (salary expense)
2. Operating activity	Inflow	Revenue (service revenue)
3. Financing activity	Inflow	Share capital (common shares)
4. Investing activity	Outflow	Asset (vehicles—property, plant, and equipment)
5. Financing activity	Inflow	Liability (bank loan payable)

DO IT! 1-3

Business Activities

(a) $1,235,000 ($1,235,000 = $625,000 + $250,000 + $360,000)
(b) $1,300,000 ($1,300,000 = $460,000 + $315,000 + $525,000)
(c) $360,000 ($1,200,000 = $690,000 + $150,000 + $360,000)
(d) Increased by $190,000 (Increased by $410,000 = Increased by $220,000 + Increased by $190,000)
(e) Increased by $1,040,000 (Increased by $1,040,000 = Increased by $660,000 + No change + Increased by $380,000)

DO IT! 1-4a

Accounting Equation

DO IT! 1-4b

Financial Statement Relationships

Income Statement	
Total revenues	$2,360,000
Total expenses	1,810,000
Net income	(a) 550,000
Statement of Changes in Equity	
Total shareholders' equity, beginning of year	980,000
Common shares, beginning of year	350,000
Issue of shares	(b) 150,000
Common shares, end of year	500,000
Retained earnings, beginning of year	630,000
Net income	(c) 550,000
Dividends declared	(d) 290,000
Retained earnings, end of year	890,000
Total shareholders' equity, end of year	(e) 1,390,000
Statement of Financial Position	
Total assets	3,420,000
Total liabilities	(f) 2,030,000
Total shareholders' equity	(g) 1,390,000

(a) $2,360,000 − $1,810,000
(b) $500,000 − $350,000
(c) See Item (a)
(d) $890,000 − $630,000 − $550,000
(e) $500,000 + $890,000
(f) $3,420,000 − Item (g)
(g) See Item (e)

DO IT! 1-4c
Preparing Financial
Statements

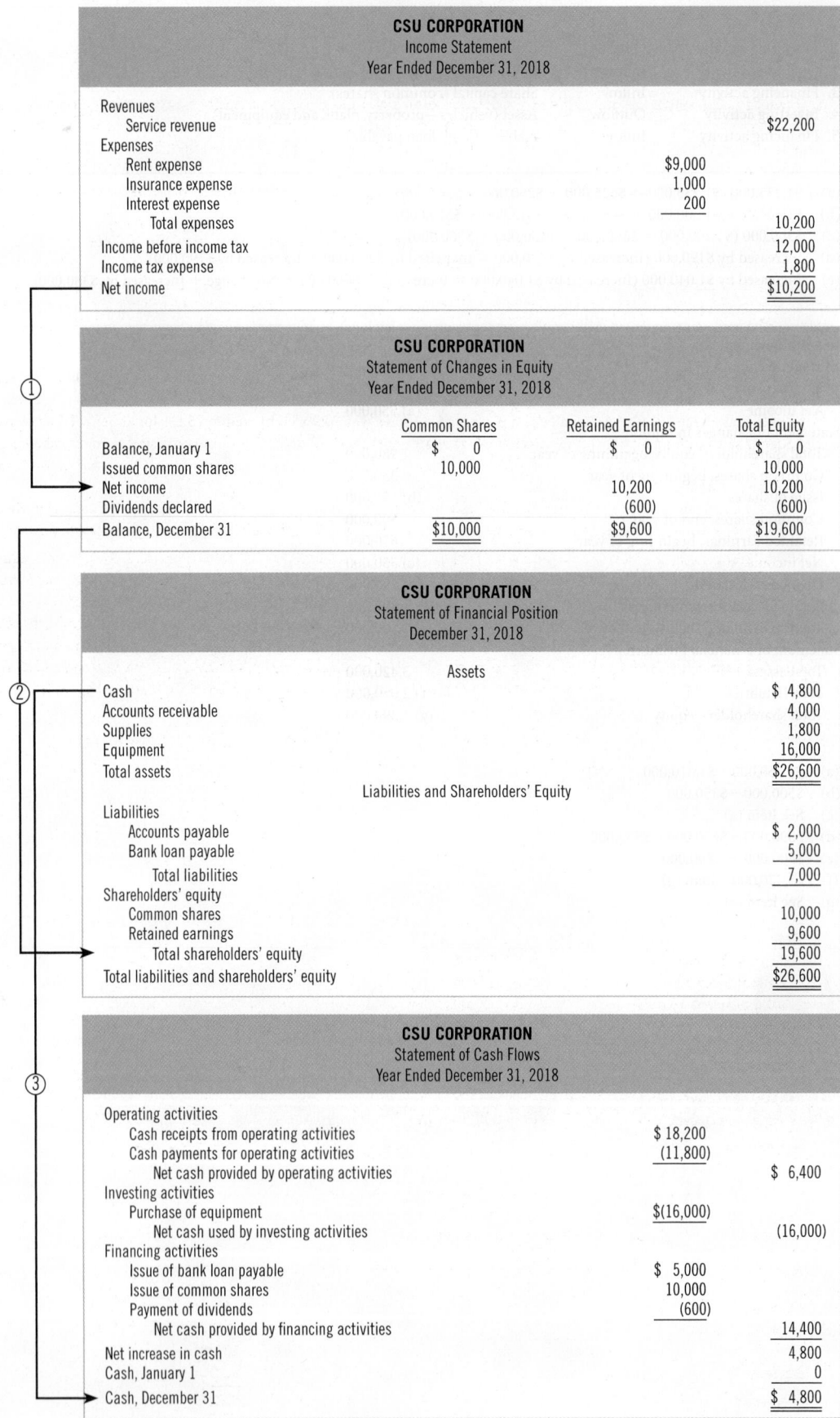

CSU CORPORATION
Income Statement
Year Ended December 31, 2018

Revenues		
Service revenue		$22,200
Expenses		
Rent expense	$9,000	
Insurance expense	1,000	
Interest expense	200	
Total expenses		10,200
Income before income tax		12,000
Income tax expense		1,800
Net income		$10,200

CSU CORPORATION
Statement of Changes in Equity
Year Ended December 31, 2018

	Common Shares	Retained Earnings	Total Equity
Balance, January 1	$ 0	$ 0	$ 0
Issued common shares	10,000		10,000
Net income		10,200	10,200
Dividends declared		(600)	(600)
Balance, December 31	$10,000	$9,600	$19,600

CSU CORPORATION
Statement of Financial Position
December 31, 2018

Assets

Cash	$ 4,800
Accounts receivable	4,000
Supplies	1,800
Equipment	16,000
Total assets	$26,600

Liabilities and Shareholders' Equity

Liabilities		
Accounts payable		$ 2,000
Bank loan payable		5,000
Total liabilities		7,000
Shareholders' equity		
Common shares		10,000
Retained earnings		9,600
Total shareholders' equity		19,600
Total liabilities and shareholders' equity		$26,600

CSU CORPORATION
Statement of Cash Flows
Year Ended December 31, 2018

Operating activities		
Cash receipts from operating activities	$ 18,200	
Cash payments for operating activities	(11,800)	
Net cash provided by operating activities		$ 6,400
Investing activities		
Purchase of equipment	$(16,000)	
Net cash used by investing activities		(16,000)
Financing activities		
Issue of bank loan payable	$ 5,000	
Issue of common shares	10,000	
Payment of dividends	(600)	
Net cash provided by financing activities		14,400
Net increase in cash		4,800
Cash, January 1		0
Cash, December 31		$ 4,800

▶ PRACTICE USING THE DECISION TOOLKIT

(a) Before you invest, you should investigate the income statement, statement of changes in equity, statement of financial position, and statement of cash flows for each company. In addition, you should carefully review the notes to the financial statements.

(b) The income statement shows a company's revenues and expenses and overall profitability for the current period. The statement of changes in equity shows any changes in share capital as well as the impact that the current period's net income and dividends declared have on the company's retained earnings. The statement of financial position reveals the company's financial position and the relationship among assets, liabilities, and shareholders' equity. Finally, the statement of cash flows reveals where the company is getting and spending its cash. This is especially important for a company that wants to grow.

Investors would probably be most interested in the income statement because it shows past performance and this can give an indication of future performance.

(c) Sobeys' fiscal year overlaps North West's for nine months (May 2015 through January 2016). If there have been no substantial changes to the economy that would affect their business during the three-month period in 2016 (February, March, and April) that Sobeys' financial results cover but North West's do not (or vice versa), it really does not matter when each company's fiscal year ends. It is more important that we compare what each company was able to achieve within an equivalent period of time—whether it be one year, six months, or one quarter. If, however, a major economic change does occur in the intervening period (the period where the statements do not overlap), such a change would likely reduce the usefulness of a comparison of the two companies' financial statements.

(d) Many interesting comparisons can be made between the two companies in spite of the unusual impairment loss recorded by Sobeys in 2016, which resulted in a substantial overall loss for the year. Sobeys is much larger than North West, with 10 times more assets and 13.7 times more revenues. It is interesting to note that North West's cost of sales as a percentage of sales was 70.9% compared to 75.8% for Sobeys. This means that North West makes more on each dollar of sales (it marks up its retail prices at a higher amount) than Sobeys. This is not surprising given the challenges of selling groceries and other goods in the far North. In addition, North West's selling, operating, and administrative expenses as a percentage of sales was 23.1%, a higher percentage than that of Sobeys at 22.0%.

While these comparisons are useful, these basic measures are not enough to determine whether one company will be a better investment than the other. In later chapters, you will acquire more tools to help you compare the relative profitability and financial health of these, and other, companies.

(e) North West generated $132,987 thousand cash from its operating activities, while Sobeys generated $837,700 thousand. Both companies generated significantly more cash from their operating activities than was required for their investing activities. It is important to note that Sobeys' cash provided by operating activities remained positive compared to its net earnings because the impairment loss it recorded did not use cash.

Sobeys used $631,400 thousand for investing activities and $243,100 thousand for financing activities during the current fiscal year. Together, Sobeys' use of cash by investing and financing activities was in excess of the cash it generated from operating activities, resulting in a net decrease of $36,800 thousand in overall cash and cash equivalents for the year. In comparison, North West used $75,813 thousand for investing activities and $50,174 thousand for financing activities during the current fiscal year. Its cash provided by operating activities was sufficient to offset the cash used by investing and financing activities, resulting in a net increase of $8,114 thousand cash for the year.

▶ PRACTICE COMPREHENSIVE DO IT!

ICE CAMP LTD.
Income Statement
Year Ended December 31, 2018

Revenues		
Camp tuition revenue		$100,000
Expenses		
Salaries expense	$20,000	
Ice rental expense	14,000	
Administrative expense	7,000	
Insurance expense	6,000	
Interest expense	800	
Total expenses		47,800
Income before income tax		52,200
Income tax expense		10,440
Net income		$ 41,760

ICE CAMP LTD.
Statement of Financial Position
December 31, 2018

Assets	
Cash	$ 9,500
Accounts receivable	10,000
Bus	12,000
Equipment	1,500
Total assets	$33,000

Liabilities and Shareholders' Equity

Liabilities	
Interest payable	$ 800
Income tax payable	10,440
Bank loan payable	10,000
Total liabilities	21,240
Shareholders' equity	
Common shares	5,000
Retained earnings	6,760
Total shareholders' equity	11,760
Total liabilities and shareholders' equity	$33,000

ICE CAMP LTD.
Statement of Changes in Equity
Year Ended December 31, 2018

	Common Shares	Retained Earnings	Total Equity
Balance, January 1	$ 0	$ 0	$ 0
Issued common shares	5,000		5,000
Net income		41,760	41,760
Dividends declared		(35,000)	(35,000)
Balance, December 31	$5,000	$ 6,760	$11,760

▶ PRACTICE OBJECTIVE-FORMAT QUESTIONS

1. (a) External   (e) External
    (b) External   (f) External
    (c) External   (g) Internal
    (d) External

2. (a) Management/Internal   (e) Labour union/External
    (b) Bank/External   (f) Management/Internal
    (c) Supplier/External   (g) Shareholder/External
    (d) Potential shareholder/External

3. (a), (d), (e), (f), and (g) are correct

Feedback
(b) Incorrect. A partnership does not establish a separate legal entity and there is no legal distinction between the business and the partners.
(c) Incorrect. Shareholders of a corporation are not responsible for the debts of the company unless they have personally guaranteed them with the lender.

4. (a), (c), (e), and (f) are correct

Feedback
(b) Incorrect. The form of business can be changed and many businesses initially established as proprietorships are eventually incorporated as the business grows.
(d) Incorrect. It is generally more difficult for a proprietorship to raise capital than it is for a corporation. Corporations can access the capital markets by issuing shares and/or debt, whereas proprietorships are limited to the capital of the owner and amounts that can be borrowed from lenders.
(g) Incorrect. Public companies must use IFRS to prepare their financial statements. The use of ASPE is not an option.

5. (a) Financing/Outflow   (e) Operating/Outflow
    (b) Operating/Inflow   (f) Financing/Outflow
    (c) Investing/Outflow   (g) Investing/Inflow
    (d) Financing/Inflow

6. (a) Investing   (e) Financing
    (b) Financing   (f) Financing
    (c) Investing   (g) Operating
    (d) Operating

7. (a) Statement of financial position (assets section)/Statement of cash flows
    (b) Statement of financial position (liabilities section)
    (c) Income statement/Statement of changes in equity
    (d) Income statement
    (e) Statement of changes in equity/Statement of cash flows
    (f) Statement of financial position (assets section)
    (g) Income statement

8. (a), (b), (d), and (e) are correct

Feedback
(c) Incorrect. The declaration and payment of dividends would have no impact on the statement of income, but would affect the statement of changes in equity (dividends declared) and the statement of cash flows (dividends paid).
(f) Incorrect. The statement of changes in equity is normally prepared before the statement of financial position because the ending equity balances are required in order to prepare the statement of financial position.
(g) Incorrect. The issue of common shares would have no impact on the statement of income, but would affect the other three financial statements.

9.   (a) Statement of changes in equity   (e) Statement of changes in equity/Statement of cash flows
     (b) Income statement   (f) Statement of cash flows
     (c) Income statement   (g) Statement of financial position
     (d) Statement of financial position

10.   (a) Total liabilities   (e) Retained earnings
     (b) Total shareholders' equity   (f) Total assets
     (c) Net income   (g) Net income
     (d) Total liabilities

▶ ENDNOTE

[1] Murray McNeill, "North West Company Shifts into Expansion Mode," *Winnipeg Free Press*, June 11, 2015; The North West Company website, www.northwest.ca; The North West Company 2015 annual report. The North West Company website, www.northwest.ca; The North West Company 2015 annual information form. The North West Company website, www.northwest.ca; Canadian operations, Fur marketing branch.

2

A Further Look at Financial Statements

CHAPTER PREVIEW

In this chapter, we take a closer look at the statement of financial position and introduce some useful ways for evaluating the information provided by the financial statements. We also examine the financial reporting concepts underlying the preparation and presentation of financial statements, including those used by publicly accountable enterprises such as CT Real Estate Investment Trust discussed in our feature story, as well as those used by private companies.

CHAPTER OUTLINE

LEARNING OBJECTIVES	READ	PRACTICE
1 Identify the sections of a classified statement of financial position.	• Assets • Liabilities • Shareholders' equity • Comprehensive illustration	**DO IT!** **2-1a** Statement of financial position classifications **2-1b** Statement amounts
2 Identify and calculate ratios for analyzing a company's liquidity, solvency, and profitability.	• Using the statement of financial position (balance sheet) • Using the income statement	**DO IT!** **2-2** Ratio analysis
3 Describe the framework for the preparation and presentation of financial statements.	• Objective of financial reporting • Qualitative characteristics of useful financial information • Cost constraint • Going concern assumption • Elements of financial statements • Measurement of the elements • Summary of conceptual framework	**DO IT!** **2-3** Conceptual framework

FEATURE STORY

Building Value for Investors

You no doubt are familiar with Canadian Tire, one of the country's most recognized brands and retailers. But you may not know that most of the company's retail locations are owned by CT Real Estate Investment Trust (CT REIT). CT REIT owns 290 income-producing commercial properties found mainly in Canada and the main tenants in those properties are Canadian Tire and other stores that are part of the Canadian Tire family, including Mark's and Sport Chek. While Canadian Tire Corporation, Ltd. does not own these retail locations, the company does own more than 80% of CT REIT, with the balance owned by other investors.

CT REIT's shares (which are called "units") trade on the Toronto Stock Exchange (TSX). Because it is listed on the TSX, CT REIT is considered a publicly accountable enterprise. It therefore must prepare financial statements that follow International Financial Reporting Standards (IFRS). It must also make these statements publicly available. In this way, external users of financial statements can understand the information being reported in a systematic way and compare financial information with that of competitors, who must use the same accounting standards. These factors are important for investors or potential investors, bankers that have lent or are interested in lending money, and current or potential tenants interested in leasing space.

As their name would imply, real estate is the most significant asset of all real estate investment trusts (REITs). External users of a REIT's financial statements want to know the amount of real estate assets (which are normally called "investment properties") reported on its statement of financial position.

This information is useful to current and potential investors to assess the value of the REIT's shares. It is also useful to current and potential lenders as they assess the REIT's level of debt relative to its assets. At December 31, 2015, CT REIT reported investment properties of $4.3 billion.

CT REIT and other REITs have a number of possible ways that they can use to determine the value at which they report their investment property. These include historical cost (what they paid for the real estate) and current value, which could either be its fair value (what the real estate could be sold for) or its value in use (based on the cash flows that are expected to be generated by these assets over their economic life). Accounting standard setters have considered this issue and included guidance on it in the conceptual framework for financial reporting. This framework identifies the characteristics of financial information that is useful to users, including relevance. In the case of investment properties, standard setters have determined that investment properties should be reported at current value, which is their value in use.

These types of decisions always involve trade-offs. For example, while the use of current value may result in information that is more relevant to users, it may also be less verifiable given the number of assumptions and the amount of judgement involved in determining the amount and timing of future cash flows.

In this chapter, we will introduce the conceptual framework for financial reporting, including a discussion of the trade-offs that must be made in applying it. One of the goals of this course is to equip you with the knowledge and tools to be able understand these trade-offs and apply your own judgement to the financial reporting issues we will cover.[1]

Go to the *REVIEW AND PRACTICE* section at the end of the chapter for a targeted summary and practice questions with solutions.

Visit **WileyPLUS** for more practice opportunities.

1 Identify the sections of a classified statement of financial position.

In Chapter 1, we introduced four financial statements: the statement of financial position, income statement, statement of changes in equity, and statement of cash flows. In this section, we will look at the statement of financial position in more detail and introduce standard statement classifications.

The statement of financial position, also commonly known as the balance sheet, presents a picture of a company's financial position—its assets, liabilities, and shareholders' equity—at a point in time. In Chapter 1, individual asset, liability, and equity items were listed in no particular order on the statement of financial position. To improve users' understanding of a company's financial position, companies group similar types of assets and similar types of liabilities together. A classified statement of financial position generally contains the standard classifications, ordered as shown in Illustration 2-1.

▶Illustration 2-1

Statement of financial
position classifications

Assets	Liabilities and Shareholders' Equity
Current assets	Current liabilities
Cash	Bank indebtedness
Held for trading investments	Accounts payable
Accounts receivable	Unearned revenue
Notes receivable	Notes payable
Inventory	Current maturities of long-term debt
Supplies	Non-current liabilities
Prepaid expenses	Bank loan payable
Non-current assets	Shareholders' equity
Long-term investments	Share capital
Property, plant, and equipment	Retained earnings
Intangible assets	
Goodwill	

These classifications or groupings help readers of the financial statements determine such things as (1) whether the company has enough assets to pay its debts as they come due and (2) the claims of short-term and long-term creditors and lenders on the company's total assets. The classifications are usually ordered as shown in Illustration 2-1. Some international companies, and a few Canadian companies, such as CT REIT and other REITs, use a reverse order. In the sections that follow, we explain each of these classifications and ordering possibilities.

ASSETS

Assets are the resources that a company owns or controls that will provide future economic benefits. These future economic benefits are related to the asset's ability to generate cash flows for the company. The asset may do this directly (itself) or indirectly (together with other assets). Assets include those resources whose benefits will be realized within one year (current assets) and those resources whose benefits will be realized over more than one year (non-current assets).

Current Assets

Current assets are assets that are expected to be converted into cash or to be sold or used up within one year of the company's financial statement date or its operating cycle, whichever is longer.

The **operating cycle** of a company is the average period of time it takes for a business to pay cash to obtain products or services and then receive cash from customers for these products or services. In a service business, this is the time it takes to pay employees, provide services on account, and then collect the cash from customers. For most businesses, the operating cycle is less than a year but for some businesses, such as vineyards, shipyards, or aircraft manufacturers, the operating cycle is longer than a year. For the purposes of this textbook, we will assume companies use a time frame of one year to determine whether an asset is current or non-current.

Illustration 2-2 depicts the operating cycle of a service company. We will learn more about operating cycles in Chapter 5, including how the operating cycle of a merchandising company differs from that of a service company.

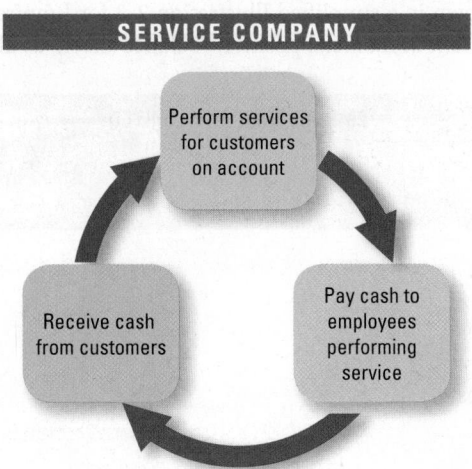

SERVICE COMPANY

▶Illustration 2-2
Operating cycle

Common types of current assets include:

1. Cash
2. Held for trading investments
3. Accounts receivable
4. Notes receivable, including loans receivable
5. Inventory
6. Supplies
7. Prepaid expenses

You are already familiar with cash, which includes both cash on hand and cash deposited in banks or other financial institutions. We will briefly discuss each of the other common types of current assets in the above list. **Held for trading investments** are investments in debt securities such as bonds of another company, or equity securities such as shares of another company, that are bought with the intention of reselling them after a short period of time in order to earn income from fluctuations in their price. We will learn more about held for trading investments in Chapter 12.

Accounts receivable are amounts owed to the company by customers who purchased products or services on credit (on account) and are normally supported with an invoice. Other types of receivables can arise from amounts owed to the company for interest, sales tax, rent, and like items. Normally they are not supported by an invoice and must sometimes be estimated. These types of receivables are often called **accrued revenues**, and arise when payments for revenues earned by the company have not yet been received in cash. We will learn more about accrued revenues in Chapter 4.

Notes receivable are amounts owed to the company by customers or others that are supported by a written promise to repay. Loans receivable are a type of note receivable. Notes receivable are normally interest-bearing, whereas accounts receivable are not.

Inventory is goods held for sale to customers. As we saw in the case of the North West Company in Chapter 1, its inventory consists of goods such as food, clothing, housewares, appliances, and outdoor products. **Supplies** include consumable items like office supplies (such as paper, toner, and pens) and cleaning supplies. They are a current asset because we expect that these will be used up by the business within the year.

Prepaid expenses represent the cost of expenses like rent and insurance paid in advance of use. They are current assets because they reflect unused benefits such as office space and insurance coverage available for future use during the year.

While total current assets must be disclosed, there is no prescribed order for current assets to be presented on the statement of financial position. North American companies normally list current assets in the order in which they are expected to be converted into cash; that is, in their order of liquidity. There is an exception to this. REITs in Canada and some international companies list current assets in a reverse order of liquidity. For the purpose of your assignments, you will be expected to list current assets in their order of liquidity unless specifically told otherwise.

Current assets are shown in a simplified Illustration 2-3 for Empire Company Limited. Note that Empire calls its statement of financial position "balance sheet," as do many companies.

▶Illustration 2-3
Current assets section

EMPIRE COMPANY LIMITED	
Balance Sheet (partial)	
May 7, 2016	
(in millions)	
Current assets	
Cash and cash equivalents	$ 264.7
Accounts receivable	489.4
Inventories	1,287.3
Prepaid expenses	117.3
Loans and other receivables	38.3
Assets held for sale	407.1
Total current assets	2,604.1

We have already learned about most of these accounts in Chapter 1, except for "cash equivalents," which is a new term. **Cash equivalents** are short-term, highly liquid investments with very little risk that can be easily sold. We will learn more about cash equivalents in Chapter 7.

Non-Current Assets

Non-current assets are not expected to be converted into cash, sold, or used up by the business within one year of the financial statement date or its operating cycle. In other words, non-current assets consist of all assets that are not classified as current assets.

Common types of non-current assets include:

1. Long-term investments
2. Property, plant, and equipment
3. Intangible assets
4. Goodwill
5. Other assets

Alternative Terminology
The terms *non-current* and *long-term* are used interchangeably in this text.

Long-term investments (also known as investments) include (1) multi-year investments in debt securities (for example, loans, notes, bonds, or mortgages) that management intends to hold to earn interest; and (2) equity securities (for example, shares) of other companies that management plans to hold for many years to generate investment revenue or for strategic reasons. These assets are classified as non-current because they are not readily marketable or because management is not intending to sell the investment and convert it into cash within one year. If the word "investments" is used without any modifier (held for trading or long-term), it is assumed to be non-current. We will learn more about long-term investments in Chapter 12.

As an example, BlackBerry Limited reports only long-term debt investments in the partial statement of financial position (which it calls balance sheet) shown in Illustration 2-4. BlackBerry describes these investments as consisting primarily of U.S. treasury bills, together with other types of investments.

▶Illustration 2-4
Long-term investments section

BLACKBERRY LIMITED	
Balance Sheet (partial)	
February 29, 2016	
(in U.S. $ millions)	
Long-term investments	$197

Property, plant, and equipment are tangible assets with relatively long useful lives that are being used in operating the business. This category includes items such as land, buildings, equipment, furniture, computers, and vehicles.

Although the order of property, plant, and equipment items can vary among companies, these items are often listed in the statement of financial position in their order of permanency. That is, land is usually listed first because it has an indefinite life, and is followed by the asset with the next longest useful life, normally buildings, followed by equipment, and so on. It is recommended that you use this order when preparing your homework assignments unless otherwise instructed.

Most companies record their property, plant, and equipment at cost. However, as was mentioned in the feature story, some companies may choose to record these assets at their current value (or fair value) instead. This is known as the **revaluation model**. This is often used in the real estate industry but seldom applied by other industries. For example, CT REIT, introduced in our feature story, uses the revaluation model. We will discuss the revaluation model in Chapter 9, but until then, we will assume that the cost model is used unless otherwise indicated.

Property, plant, and equipment, except land, have estimated useful lives over which they are expected to help generate revenues. Because these assets benefit future periods, their cost is allocated (expensed) over their estimated useful lives through a process called **depreciation**. Companies calculate depreciation by systematically assigning a portion of the asset's cost to depreciation expense each year (rather than expensing the full cost in the year the asset was purchased). We will learn how to calculate depreciation in Chapters 4 and 9.

Only assets with finite useful lives are depreciated. Land also contributes to the generation of revenue, but its estimated useful life is considered to be indefinite because the economic benefits represented by land are not used up or consumed. Consequently, the cost of land is never depreciated.

Assets that are depreciated should be reported on the statement of financial position at cost less their accumulated depreciation. Accumulated depreciation shows the cumulative amount of depreciation expense recorded to date over the *life of the asset*. It is a **contra asset account**; that is, its balance is subtracted from the balance of the asset that it relates to. The difference between cost and accumulated depreciation is referred to as the **carrying amount**, also commonly known as net book value or just simply book value.

Clothing retailer Reitmans details in a note to the financial statements its property, plant, and equipment—which it calls property and equipment because it does not own a plant—as shown in Illustration 2-5. Note that, except for land, all of Reitmans' property and equipment are depreciated. This company also has leasehold improvements, which are long-lived additions or renovations made to leased property that Reitmans rents in large shopping centres.

> **Alternative Terminology**
> *Property, plant, and equipment* are sometimes called *capital assets* or *fixed assets*.

> **Alternative Terminology**
> *Carrying amount* is sometimes called *net book value*.

REITMANS (CANADA) LIMITED Notes to the Financial Statements (partial) January 30, 2016 (in thousands)			
	Cost	Accumulated Depreciation	Carrying Amount
Property and equipment			
Land	$ 5,860	$ -	$ 5,860
Buildings	42,347	17,682	24,665
Fixtures and equipment	121,747	66,028	55,719
Leasehold improvements	121,427	73,308	48,119
	$291,381	$157,018	$134,363

▶Illustration 2-5
Property, plant, and equipment section

Many companies have assets that cannot be seen but that are of significant value. **Intangible assets** are non-current assets that do not have physical substance and that represent a privilege or a right granted to, or held by, a company. Examples of intangible assets include patents, copyrights, franchises, trademarks, trade names, and licences that give the company an exclusive right of use for a specified period of time. For companies in the technology, telecommunications, or entertainment industries, intangible assets can be their most significant asset.

Intangible assets are normally divided into two groups for accounting purposes: those with finite useful lives and those with indefinite useful lives. Similar to buildings and equipment, the cost of intangible assets with finite useful lives is allocated (expensed) over these future periods through the use of amortization. Amortization of intangible assets is the same as depreciation for property, plant, and equipment, even though a different term is used.

IFRS for publicly traded companies recommends the use of the term *depreciation* to refer to the allocation of cost over the useful lives of depreciable property, plant, and equipment and the term *amortization* to refer to the allocation of the cost of certain kinds of intangible assets. In contrast, Accounting Standards for Private Enterprises recommend the use of the term *amortization* to allocate the cost of both property, plant, and equipment and intangible assets. To complicate matters further, some publicly traded companies use the terms *depreciation* and *amortization* interchangeably. Regardless of what term is used, the cost of property, plant, and equipment and intangible assets with definite useful lives is allocated over these useful lives.

You will recall that land, which has an indefinite useful life, is not depreciated. Similarly, intangible assets with indefinite lives are not amortized. We will learn more about depreciating and amortizing both tangible and intangible long-lived assets in Chapter 9.

Goodwill is an asset that results from the acquisition of another company when the price paid to acquire the company is higher than the fair value of the purchased company's net identifiable assets. Net identifiable assets represents the value of the assets less the value of any liabilities assumed as part of the purchase. As such, goodwill is a residual amount—simply the difference between the price paid for the company and the fair value of the net assets acquired (fair value of assets acquired less fair value of any liabilities assumed). The difference, which is goodwill, represents a value not attributable to any recorded asset or liability and relates to something intangible like the reputation of the company and the quality of its employees.

Goodwill is similar to intangible assets in that it has no physical substance and will generate future value. It differs from intangible assets in that it cannot be separated from the company and sold—it is determined in relation to the acquired company as a whole. The only way it can be sold is to sell the acquired company. Goodwill is not amortized and is reported separately from other intangibles.

Illustration 2-6 shows, in a note to the financial statements, how Shaw Communications reports its goodwill and intangible assets, which consist of various rights and licences.

▶Illustration 2-6
Intangible assets and
goodwill section

SHAW COMMUNICATIONS INC. Notes to the Financial Statements (partial) August 31, 2015 (in millions)	
Intangibles	
Broadcast rights and licenses	$6,341
Program rights and advances	280
Other intangibles	838
Goodwill	1,506

Alternative Terminology
Deferred income tax is also called *future income tax*.

Some companies also report other types of assets that do not fit neatly into any of the above classifications. These can include non-current receivables, deferred income tax assets, and property held for sale, among many other items. Deferred income tax assets arise due to differences between accounting and tax treatment and represent the income tax that is expected to be recovered in a subsequent period due to deductions that a company will be able to take when preparing its corporate income returns in future periods.

Other assets are usually reported separately so that users can get a better idea of their nature and are accompanied by an explanatory note to the financial statements. Because these types of assets vary widely in practice, they are not illustrated here.

LIABILITIES

Liabilities are obligations that result from past transactions and will result in the transfer of an economic resource. Similar to assets, they are also classified as current (due within one year) and non-current (due after more than one year). Liabilities are typically settled through the sacrifice of an asset or the provision of a service.

Current Liabilities

Current liabilities are obligations that are to be paid or settled within one year of the company's statement date or its operating cycle, whichever is longer. As with current assets, companies use a period longer than one year if their operating cycle is longer than one year. For the purposes of this textbook, we will assume an operating cycle equal to, or shorter than, one year.

Common examples of current liabilities include:

1. Bank indebtedness
2. Accounts payable
3. Unearned revenue
4. Notes payable, including bank loans payable
5. Current maturities of long-term debt

You may recall from Chapter 1 that **bank indebtedness** is a short-term loan from a bank, typically occurring when a company uses an operating line of credit to cover cash shortfalls. **Accounts payable** represent amounts owed by the company to suppliers for purchases made on credit (account). They are usually supported by an invoice. Other types of payables can arise from amounts owed by the company for salaries, interest, sales tax, rent, income tax, and similar items. They are normally not supported by an invoice and may have to be estimated because of this. These types of payables are often called **accrued payables** and arise when expenses incurred by the company have not yet been paid in cash. We will learn more about accrued expenses and payables in Chapter 4.

Unearned revenue represents cash received from a customer in advance of any revenue being earned (before any goods or services have been provided). For example, airlines receive payments from passengers purchasing tickets in advance of any flights being provided. These payments are recorded as a current liability (unearned revenue) because the airline has an obligation to provide the flight in the future, normally within one year.

Notes payable are amounts owed, often to banks but also to suppliers or others, that are supported by a written promise to repay. Notes payable are normally interest-bearing, whereas accounts payable are not. Amounts owed to banks are usually known as bank loans payable. It is common to refer to notes and loans interchangeably, and we will do so in this text. Notes can be current or non-current. When a company has a non-current or long-term note or loan payable (such as a five-year bank loan), a portion of the loan is often repayable each year. The portion of the loan that is due within the next year is classified as **current maturities of long-term debt**. The remainder of the loan is classified as a non-current liability.

> **Alternative Terminology**
> *Current maturities of long-term debt* are also called *current portion of long-term debt.*

Similar to current assets, North American companies often list current liabilities in the order in which they are expected to be paid; that is, in their order of liquidity by due date. However, for many companies, the items in the current liabilities section are arranged according to an internal company custom rather than a prescribed rule. And some Canadian REITs and international companies list current liabilities in a reverse order of liquidity, similar to current assets. For the purpose of your assignments, we recommend that you list liabilities in the general order of liquidity unless instructed otherwise. We understand that you will not always know the due date of the liability, so you may have to make some assumptions.

The current liabilities section from the statement of financial position of Sears Canada is shown in Illustration 2-7.

►Illustration 2-7
Current liabilities section

SEARS CANADA INC. Statement of Financial Position (partial) January 30, 2016 (in millions)	
Current liabilities	
Accounts payable and accrued liabilities	$408.5
Unearned revenue	158.3
Income and other taxes payable	19.9
Current portion of long-term obligations	4.0
Total current liabilities	590.7

Users of financial statements look closely at the relationship between current assets and current liabilities. This relationship is important in evaluating a company's ability to pay its current liabilities. We will talk more about this later in the chapter when we learn how to use the information in the statement of financial position.

Non-Current Liabilities

Obligations that are expected to be paid or settled after one year are classified as **non-current liabilities**, or, as they are also commonly known, long-term liabilities.

Examples of non-current liabilities include:

1. Notes payable, including bank loans payable, mortgages payable, and bonds payable
2. Lease obligations
3. Pension and benefit obligations
4. Deferred income tax liabilities

We discussed notes payable in the current liabilities section above. **Mortgages payable** are similar to long-term notes but have property (such as land or a building) pledged as security for the loan. **Bonds payable** are used by large corporations and governments to borrow large sums of money. **Lease obligations** include amounts to be paid in the future on long-term rental contracts used for equipment or other property. **Pension and benefit obligations** are amounts companies owe past and current employees for retirement benefits. **Deferred income tax liabilities** arise due to differences between accounting and tax treatment and represent income tax related to the current year's net income that is expected to be paid in a subsequent period when a company prepares its corporate income returns for those periods.

Non-current liabilities reported on the statement of financial position are normally accompanied by extensive notes to the financial statements that describe the nature and terms of the obligation and other relevant details. For example, disclosure for a long-term mortgage payable would include the maturity date, interest rate, and any assets pledged as security to support the borrowing. Non-current liabilities will be discussed in detail in Chapter 10.

In Illustration 2-8, TELUS reported non-current liabilities of $14,458 million on a recent statement of financial position. There is no generally prescribed order for reporting non-current liabilities.

►Illustration 2-8
Non-current liabilities section

TELUS CORPORATION Statement of Financial Position (partial) December 31, 2015 (in millions)	
Non-current liabilities	
Provisions	$ 433
Long-term debt	11,182
Other long-term liabilities	688
Deferred income taxes	2,155
	14,458

Additional detail about its liabilities was reported by TELUS in the notes to its financial statements. There it indicated that its provisions related to legal claims, contract termination costs, and obligations it expects to incur when the company ceases using certain property, plant, and equipment. Its long-term debt consisted of notes, commercial paper, and debentures, and it gave details about the amounts, interest rates, and maturity dates. Its other long-term liabilities comprise liabilities for pensions and post-retirement benefits, as well as other items.

SHAREHOLDERS' EQUITY

Shareholders' equity is a residual amount and is the difference between a company's assets and its liabilities. Shareholders' equity is divided into two parts: share capital and retained earnings. As was mentioned in Chapter 1, some companies may include other items in the shareholders' equity section, such as accumulated other comprehensive income. We will learn more about accumulated other comprehensive income in Chapters 11 and 12.

Share Capital

As we learned in Chapter 1, shareholders purchase shares in a company by investing cash (or other assets). When the company receives these assets, it issues ownership certificates to these investors in the form of common or preferred shares. If preferred shares are issued in addition to common shares, the total of all classes of shares issued is classified as, or titled, **share capital**. Quite often, companies have only one class of shares and the title is simply "common shares." International companies often call these "ordinary shares."

> **Alternative Terminology**
> *Share capital* is also commonly known as *capital stock*.

Retained Earnings

The cumulative profits that have been retained for use in a company are known as **retained earnings**. Recall from Chapter 1 that the changes during the year (or period) to both share capital and retained earnings are detailed on the statement of changes in equity. The ending balances of share capital and retained earnings, determined on the statement of changes in equity, are combined and reported as shareholders' equity on the statement of financial position.

The shareholders' equity section of the Hudson's Bay Company's statement of financial position is shown in Illustration 2-9. In addition to share capital and retained earnings, Hudson's Bay also reports contributed surplus and accumulated other comprehensive income. Contributed surplus, also known as additional contributed capital, represents amounts contributed by shareholders (in addition to share capital) as a result of certain types of equity transactions. We will learn more about contributed surplus in Chapter 11. As we learned in Chapter 1, accumulated other comprehensive income is an account used to accumulate the company's other comprehensive income that arises under IFRS as a result of complex items that are similar to revenues and expenses.

HUDSON'S BAY COMPANY Statement of Financial Position (partial) January 30, 2016 (in millions)	
Shareholders' equity	
Share capital	$1,420
Retained earnings	1,029
Contributed surplus	86
Accumulated other comprehensive income	564
	3,099

▶Illustration 2-9
Shareholders' equity section

DO IT! ▶ **2-1a**   **Statement of Financial Position Classifications**

The following selected accounts were taken from a company's statement of financial position:

_____ Accounts payable
_____ Accounts receivable
_____ Accumulated depreciation—
        buildings

_____ Bank indebtedness
_____ Bank loan payable (due in 6 months)
_____ Buildings
_____ Cash

_____ Common shares	_____ Notes receivable (due in 3 months)
_____ Goodwill	_____ Prepaid insurance
_____ Held for trading investments	_____ Retained earnings
_____ Income tax payable	_____ Salaries payable
_____ Interest payable	_____ Sales taxes payable
_____ Inventory	_____ Supplies
_____ Land	_____ Unearned revenue
_____ Mortgage payable (due in 10 years)	_____ Vehicles

Classify each of the above accounts as current assets (CA), non-current assets (NCA), current liabilities (CL), non-current liabilities (NCL), or shareholders' equity (SE).

SOLUTION

Try this Do It! exercise on your own and then check your answer at the end of the chapter.

Related Exercise Material: BE2–1, BE2–2, and E2–1.

COMPREHENSIVE ILLUSTRATION

All of the standard classifications discussed above are illustrated in a comprehensive statement of financial position for a hypothetical company called Frenette Ltd. in Illustration 2-10.

▶Illustration 2-10

Classified statement of financial position in order of liquidity

FRENETTE LTD. Statement of Financial Position October 31, 2018			
Assets			
Current assets			
Cash		$6,600	
Held for trading investments		2,000	
Accounts receivable		7,000	
Inventory		4,000	
Supplies		2,100	
Prepaid insurance		400	
Total current assets			$ 22,100
Long-term investments			7,200
Property, plant, and equipment			
Land		$40,000	
Buildings	$75,000		
Less: Accumulated depreciation	15,000	60,000	
Equipment	$24,000		
Less: Accumulated depreciation	5,000	19,000	
Total property, plant, and equipment			119,000
Goodwill			3,100
Total assets			$151,400
Liabilities and Shareholders' Equity			
Liabilities			
Current liabilities			
Accounts payable		$ 2,100	
Salaries payable		1,600	
Interest payable		450	
Unearned revenue		900	
Bank loan payable		11,000	
Current portion of mortgage payable		1,000	
Total current liabilities			$ 17,050

Non-current liabilities		
Mortgage payable	$10,300	
Total non-current liabilities		10,300
Total liabilities		27,350
Shareholders' equity		
Common shares	$74,000	
Retained earnings	50,050	
Total shareholders' equity		124,050
Total liabilities and shareholders' equity		$151,400

Illustration 2-10 uses the common practice among North American companies of classifying the items in the statement classifications on the statement of financial position in order of liquidity (from the most to the least liquid). Accounting standards do not prescribe the order in which items are presented in the statement of financial position. As was mentioned earlier in the chapter, international companies often present items in this statement using a reverse order of liquidity. Some Canadian companies, especially real estate companies, use this reverse-liquidity-order format as well. CT REIT, our feature company in this chapter, presents items in its statement of financial position using a reverse order of liquidity. Its assets section starts with non-current assets, followed by current assets. Within the non-current assets section, the items are presented in reverse order of liquidity, from most permanent to least permanent. Within the current assets section, items are also presented in reverse order of liquidity; that is, cash is shown last. Liabilities are shown next, followed by shareholders' equity. The liabilities section presents non-current liabilities before current liabilities, and both non-current and current liabilities are listed in reverse order of liquidity.

Companies are allowed to choose how to order items so they can provide information that is most useful to their users. For your assignments, it is recommended that you use the standard order used by most North American companies—that is, in order of decreasing liquidity—unless specifically instructed to do otherwise.

DO IT! ▶ 2-1b   Statement Amounts

The following accounts and amounts were taken from Chawla Ltd.'s statement of financial position at November 30, 2018, the end of its fiscal year:

Accounts payable, $24,000
Accounts receivable, $15,000
Accumulated depreciation—buildings, $40,000
Accumulated depreciation—equipment, $58,000
Bank loan payable ($5,000 of which is due within the next year), $80,000
Buildings, $200,000
Cash, $10,000
Common shares, $60,000
Equipment, $147,000
Income tax payable, $5,000
Interest payable, $500
Inventory, $78,500
Land, $50,000
Mortgage payable ($7,500 of which is due within the next year), $150,000
Retained earnings, $74,000
Salaries payable, $8,000
Supplies, $1,000
Unearned revenue, $2,000

(a) Calculate the total amount of current assets, non-current assets, current liabilities, non-current liabilities, and shareholders' equity that would be reported on the statement of financial position at November 30.

(b) Using the amounts calculated in part (a), check that the accounting equation is in balance.

Action Plan

✔ First, classify each account as an asset, liability, or shareholders' equity item.

✔ Then, determine if asset and liability items are current or non-current by assessing whether the item is likely to be realized, paid, or settled within one year before totalling the amounts in each category.

✔ Recall that the accounting equation is assets = liabilities + shareholders' equity.

SOLUTION
Try this Do It! exercise on your own and then check your answer at the end of the chapter.

Related Exercise Material: BE2–3, BE2–4, E2–2, E2–3, E2–4, and E2–5.

2 Identify and calculate ratios for analyzing a company's liquidity, solvency, and profitability.

In Chapter 1, we briefly discussed how the financial statements give information about a company's financial position and performance. In this chapter, we continue this discussion by showing you specific tools, such as ratio analysis, that can be used to analyze two of the financial statements—the statement of financial position and income statement—in order to make a more meaningful evaluation of a company.

Ratio analysis expresses the relationships between selected items of financial statement data. Liquidity, solvency, and profitability ratios are the three general types of ratios that are used to analyze financial statements, as shown in Illustration 2-11. However, you may use additional types of ratios in other courses.

▶Illustration 2-11
Ratio classifications

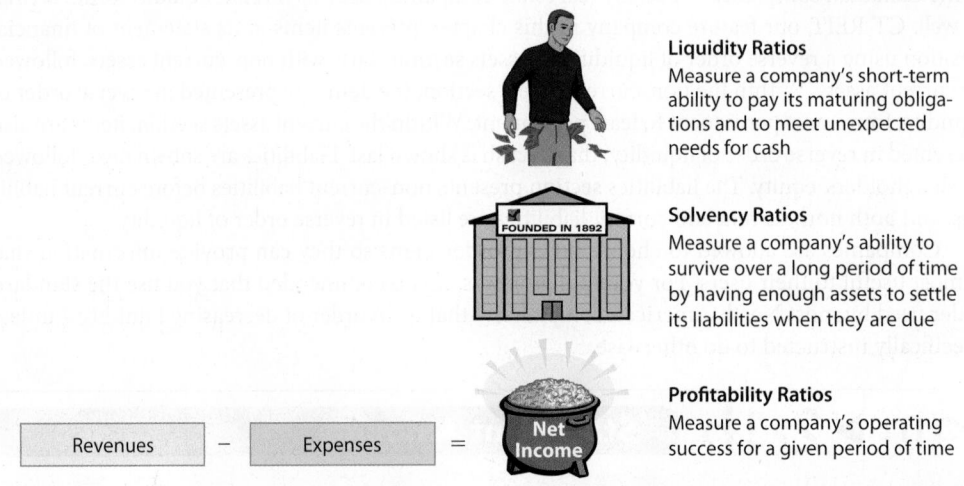

Liquidity Ratios
Measure a company's short-term ability to pay its maturing obligations and to meet unexpected needs for cash

Solvency Ratios
Measure a company's ability to survive over a long period of time by having enough assets to settle its liabilities when they are due

Profitability Ratios
Measure a company's operating success for a given period of time

Ratios can give clues about underlying conditions that may not be easy to see when the items of a particular ratio are examined separately. Since a single ratio by itself is not very meaningful, in this and later chapters we will use the following comparisons wherever possible:

1. **Intracompany comparisons** covering two or more periods for the same company
2. **Intercompany comparisons** based on comparisons with a competitor in the same industry
3. **Industry average comparisons** based on average ratios for particular industries with specific company ratios

In the following sections, we will introduce some examples of liquidity, solvency, and profitability ratios, using CT REIT's statement of financial position and income statement.

To broaden our analysis to include an intercompany comparison, we will then compare CT REIT's ratios for two years with those of one of its competitors, Choice Properties REIT. Choice Properties REIT owns the retail and commercial real estate in which Loblaw Companies Limited's stores (Loblaws, Superstore, No Frills, and others) are located. Finally, we will compare ratios for CT REIT and Choice Properties REIT with those from their industry.

USING THE STATEMENT OF FINANCIAL POSITION (BALANCE SHEET)

Purpose of the Statement of Financial Position

You can learn a great deal about a company's financial health by evaluating the relationships between its various assets and liabilities. A condensed statement of financial position for CT REIT with comparative data for two fiscal years is shown in Illustration 2-12.

CT REAL ESTATE INVESTMENT TRUST Balance Sheet December 31 (in thousands)		
Assets	2015	2014
Non-current assets	$4,321,602	$4,002,370
Current assets	29,301	15,050
Total assets	$4,350,903	$4,017,420
Liabilities and Shareholders' Equity		
Liabilities		
Non-current liabilities	$1,892,350	$1,705,058
Current liabilities	245,190	310,173
Total liabilities	2,137,540	2,015,231
Shareholders' equity	2,213,363	2,002,189
Total liabilities and shareholders' equity	$4,350,903	$4,017,420

► Illustration 2-12
CT REIT statement of financial position

Liquidity

Suppose you are a contractor entering into an arrangement to renovate some of the properties operated by CT REIT. You would be concerned about CT REIT's liquidity—its ability to pay obligations that are expected to become due within the next year. You would use liquidity ratios to look closely at the relationship of its current assets to its current liabilities. **Liquidity ratios** measure a company's short-term ability to pay its maturing obligations (usually its current liabilities) and to meet unexpected needs for cash. We will look at two examples of liquidity measures in this chapter—working capital and the current ratio—and others in later chapters.

WORKING CAPITAL One measure of liquidity is **working capital**, which is the difference between current assets and current liabilities. When working capital is positive, there is a greater likelihood that the company will be able to pay its liabilities. When working capital is negative, unless a company generates cash from its operations it may have to borrow money; otherwise, short-term creditors may not be paid. Positive working capital does not just reflect a company's ability to meets its liabilities, it also indicates that the company has liquid assets available to expand its operations.

Illustration 2-13 shows the calculation of working capital for CT REIT for 2015 and 2014, and compares it with that of Choice Properties REIT. Note that detailed calculations are not included for either Choice Properties—just the results for comparison purposes.

WORKING CAPITAL = CURRENT ASSETS − CURRENT LIABILITIES		
($ in thousands)	2015	2014
CT REIT	$29,301 − $245,190 = $(215,889)	$15,050 − $310,173 = $(295,123)
Choice Properties REIT	$(416,879)	$(142,356)
Industry average	n/a	n/a

► Illustration 2-13
Working capital

CT REIT reported negative working capital in both 2015 and 2014, which means that its current liabilities exceeded its current assets. Note, however, that the fact that its working capital is negative does not mean that this company is in difficulty. It obtains monthly cash flows from tenant rent payments that are sufficient to meet its current obligations. It is also important to understand that CT REIT's top tenant is Canadian Tire, from which it receives about 98% of its rent revenue. Canadian Tire is a national retailer that provides CT REIT with high occupancy rates and a reliable source of revenue. Despite showing a negative working capital, it is worth mentioning that CT

REIT reports a positive cash flow generated by operating activities (not illustrated here). Note that Choice Properties, which operates in the same industry, also had negative working capital.

When industry averages are not available for the ratios that we calculate in this text, such as working capital, this is indicated by "n/a" (not available).

CURRENT RATIO An important liquidity ratio is the **current ratio**, which is calculated by dividing current assets by current liabilities. The current ratio is a more dependable indicator of liquidity than working capital because it measures the relative relationship between current assets and current liabilities and therefore makes it possible to compare companies of different sizes. For example, we can compare CT REIT with Choice Properties REIT, which is larger (it has almost twice the assets). Furthermore, two companies with the same amount of working capital may have significantly different current ratios.

The 2015 and 2014 current ratios for our two companies and the industry average are shown in Illustration 2-14.

▶Illustration 2-14
Current ratio

($ in millions)	CURRENT RATIO $= \dfrac{\text{CURRENT ASSETS}}{\text{CURRENT LIABILITIES}}$	
	2015	2014
CT REIT	$\dfrac{\$29,301}{\$245,190} = 0.1{:}1$	$\dfrac{\$15,050}{\$310,173} = 0.0{:}1$
Choice Properties REIT	0.4:1	0.6:1
Industry average	0.3:1	0.4:1

What does the ratio actually mean? The 2015 current ratio of 0.1:1 means that for every dollar of current liabilities, CT REIT has 10 cents of current assets. Although there is a general belief that the current ratio should exceed a value of at least 1 to 1, we have to understand that this ratio will be different for companies in different industries. It is therefore more meaningful to compare the ratios of competitors within an industry than the ratios of companies operating in different industries. Unlike a company that produces and sells goods, real estate companies do not have a significant amount of inventory and since most tenants pay rent on time, their accounts receivable are usually low. Furthermore, since cash flows from rent are very predictable, large cash reserves are not needed. Therefore, compared with companies that sell inventory, a real estate company will have much lower current assets and this is the major reason for the lower current ratios we see above.

CT REIT's current ratio is lower than that of Choice Properties REIT and the industry, both of which declined slightly between 2014 and 2015 while CT REIT's current ratio increased marginally.

It is important to understand that the current ratio is only one measure of liquidity. It does not take into account the composition of the current assets. For example, a satisfactory current ratio may not reveal that a portion of the current assets is tied up in uncollectible accounts receivable or in slow-moving inventory. The composition of the assets matters because a dollar of cash is available to pay current liabilities, whereas a dollar of inventory would need to be sold before cash is available to pay current liabilities. For example, suppose a company's cash balance declined while its inventory increased by an even greater amount. To finance this increase in inventory, the company obtained long-term bank loans. Consequently, current assets will rise. If inventory increased because the company was having difficulty selling it, then the current ratio, which is rising, would not fully reflect the reduction in the company's liquidity. We will look at these effects in more detail in later chapters.

Solvency

Now suppose that, instead of being a short-term creditor, you are interested in either buying CT REIT's shares or making a long-term loan to the company. Investors and long-term lenders are interested in a company's long-run solvency—its ability to pay interest as it comes due and to repay the face value of debt at maturity. **Solvency ratios** measure a company's ability to survive over the long term by having enough assets to settle its liabilities as they fall due.

DEBT TO TOTAL ASSETS   The **debt to total assets** ratio is one source of information about long-term debt-paying ability. It measures the percentage of assets that are financed by lenders and other creditors rather than by shareholders. Financing provided by lenders and creditors (debt) is riskier than financing provided by shareholders (equity) because debt and the related interest must be repaid at specific points in time, whether the company is performing well or not. On the other hand, equity does not have to be repaid and there is no requirement for companies to pay dividends.

The debt to total assets ratio is calculated by dividing total debt (both current and non-current liabilities) by total assets. The higher the percentage of debt to total assets, the greater the risk that the company may be unable to pay its debts as they come due. The ratios of debt to total assets for CT REIT, Choice Properties REIT, and the industry average are shown in Illustration 2-15.

▼ **HELPFUL HINT**
Some users evaluate solvency using a ratio of debt divided by shareholders' equity. Similar to the debt to total assets ratio, the lower this "debt to equity" ratio, the better a company's solvency.

▶Illustration 2-15
Debt to total assets

($ in millions)	DEBT TO TOTAL ASSETS $= \dfrac{\text{TOTAL LIABILITIES}}{\text{TOTAL ASSETS}}$	
	2015	2014
CT REIT	$\dfrac{\$2,137,540}{\$4,350,903} = 49.1\%$	$\dfrac{\$2,015,231}{\$4,017,420} = 50.2\%$
Choice Properties REIT	90.5%	87.3%
Industry average	43.8%	45.9%

The 2015 ratio for CT REIT means that approximately 49 cents of every dollar that the company invested in assets was provided by its lenders and other creditors. CT REIT's ratio improved (fell) slightly in 2015. In 2015, approximately 90% of every dollar that Choice Properties REIT had invested in assets was provided by lenders and other creditors. This indicates that lenders and other creditors were much more exposed to risk with Choice Properties REIT than for CT REIT. The higher the ratio, the higher the amount of interest expense that a company will incur. If liabilities are too high, there is a lower equity "cushion" available to lenders and other creditors if the company becomes insolvent (unable to pay its debts). The equity cushion provides a margin of safety for lenders in the event that a company becomes insolvent and its assets are sold and the amounts received from their sale are less than the amounts they had been carried at on the statement of financial position. Thus, from the lenders' and other creditors' point of view, a high ratio of debt to total assets is undesirable and they would view the ratios of CT REIT favourably and the ratios of Choice Properties REIT unfavourably. Both companies' debt to total assets exceed (are worse than) the industry average.

USING THE INCOME STATEMENT

Purpose of the Income Statement

CT REIT generates profits for its shareholders by earning rent from tenants. The income statement reports how successful it is at generating income from its rental operations. Illustration 2-16 shows a condensed and simplified income statement for CT REIT, with comparative data. CT REIT provides additional details about its property revenue and property expenses in the notes to its financial statements.

▶Illustration 2-16
CT REIT's income statement

CT REAL ESTATE INVESTMENT TRUST Income Statement Year Ended December 31 (in thousands)		
	2015	2014
Property revenue	$378,180	$344,791
Property expense	(86,856)	(76,677)
General and administrative expense	(9,652)	(8,433)
Interest income	232	350
Interest and other financing charges	(87,334)	(82,991)
Other income (current value adjustment)	39,910	141,221
Net income	$234,480	$318,261

Profitability

Existing and potential investors, lenders, and other creditors are interested in a company's profitability. **Profitability ratios** measure a company's operating success for a specific period of time. We will look at two examples of profitability ratios in this chapter: basic earnings per share and the price-earnings ratio.

BASIC EARNINGS PER SHARE   **Basic earnings per share (EPS)** measures the income earned on each common share. It is calculated by dividing the income available to the common shareholders by the weighted average number of common shares.

Unless a company has preferred shares, the income available to common shareholders will be the same as the net income reported on a company's income statement. If a company has preferred shares, preferred share dividends (whether declared or not) must be deducted from net income. We will learn more about how to calculate income available to common shareholders and the weighted average number of shares in Chapter 11.

Shareholders usually think in terms of the number of shares they own—or plan to buy or sell—so reducing net income to a per-share amount gives a useful number for determining the investment return. In fact, earnings per share is such an important measure that it must be presented in the financial statements for publicly traded companies. It is the only ratio with this requirement. All publicly traded companies must report, at minimum, basic earnings per share. In certain circumstances, an additional type of earnings per share, diluted earnings per share, must also be reported. We will learn more about basic and diluted earnings per share in Chapter 11. Private corporations reporting under Accounting Standards for Private Enterprises are not required to report earnings per share.

Basic earnings per share for both CT REIT and Choice Properties REIT are shown in Illustration 2-17.

▶Illustration 2-17
Basic earnings per share

BASIC EARNINGS PER SHARE = $\dfrac{\text{INCOME AVAILABLE TO COMMON SHAREHOLDERS}}{\text{WEIGHTED AVERAGE NUMBER OF COMMON SHARES}}$		
	2015	2014
CT REIT	$1.25	$1.76
Choice Properties REIT	$(0.39)	$0.52
Industry average	n/a	n/a

While you can compare earnings per share between one year and another on an intracompany basis (within the same company), comparisons of earnings per share are not very meaningful on an intercompany basis (between different companies). This is because of the wide variation in the number of shares issued by each company and because some companies use financing structures with different levels of debt and equity, and it is why there is no industry average for the basic earnings per share in Illustration 2-17.

PRICE-EARNINGS RATIO   Although we cannot compare the earnings per share of two companies, we can use this amount to calculate a ratio that is comparable. This is the **price-earnings (P-E) ratio**. The price-earnings ratio is a frequently quoted statistic that measures the ratio of the stock market price of each common share to its earnings per share. It is calculated by dividing the market price per share by basic earnings per share.

The P-E ratio helps investors assess how a company's share price relates to the company's earnings. Share prices reflect investors' expectations about the company's future profits rather than just its current earnings. A higher price-earnings ratio indicates that investors consider that the company's earning potential will be higher in the future. Investors can also compare this measure to other companies to assess how expensive or inexpensive each company's shares are relative to their earnings.

The market price of CT REIT's shares at year end was $12.84 and $11.75, respectively, for 2015 and 2014. As was mentioned in the feature story, trust companies such as CT REIT and Choice Properties REIT call their shares "units." We will use the term "shares" for simplicity. If we take the share prices and divide them by the basic earnings per share amounts for each applicable year from Illustration 2-17, we can determine the price-earnings ratios as shown in Illustration 2-18.

▶Illustration 2-18
Price-earnings ratio

PRICE-EARNINGS RATIO = $\dfrac{\text{MARKET PRICE PER SHARE}}{\text{BASIC EARNINGS PER SHARE}}$		
	2015	2014
CT REIT	$\dfrac{\$12.84}{\$1.25} = 10.3$ times	$\dfrac{\$11.75}{\$1.76} = 6.7$ times
Choice Properties REIT	n/a* * The company had a loss in 2015	18.5 times
Industry average	28.0 times	22.4 times

The price-earnings ratio shows what investors expect of a company's future profitability. This ratio will be higher if investors think that current income levels will increase and it will be lower if investors think that profits will decline.

In 2015, CT REIT's other income decreased due to reduced current value adjustments on the company's investment properties compared with the previous year. This in turn reduced net income relative to the prior year, which was partially offset by increased income from new investment properties acquired during the year. In spite of the reduced net income, CT REIT's share price increased, resulting in a higher price-earnings ratio compared to 2014. Choice Properties REIT had a net loss in 2015. Given the absence of any earnings, no price-earnings ratio was determined. In spite of the loss in 2015, Choice Properties REIT's share price increased during the year, from $9.81 to $11.69.

Both companies' price-earnings ratios were less than those of the industry average in both years. It is difficult to compare these two companies with the industry average because not all companies in this industry use the revaluation model and adjust the value of their properties to current value each year.

ACCOUNTING MATTERS

© Ed Stock/istock.com

Using Ratios to Make Investment Decisions

Benjamin Graham was an economist who taught finance at Columbia University. In 1949 he authored one of the most famous books on investing, called *The Intelligent Investor*, in which he urged investors to buy stable, profitable companies

when their share prices were low. He also thought that the company's current ratio should be greater than 2:1, indicating that the company had good liquidity, which gave it a margin of safety. One of Graham's students was Warren Buffett (pictured), who bought shares in a company called Berkshire Hathaway in 1962 for just over U.S. $11 per share. He used that company to invest in other companies. By early 2016, one Berkshire Hathaway share was worth over U.S. $211,000, making Warren Buffett the second-richest U.S. citizen, behind Bill Gates, the co-founder of Microsoft.[2]

DO IT! ▶2-2   Ratio Analysis

Action Plan

✔ Use the formula for the current ratio: current assets ÷ current liabilities.

✔ Use the formula for debt to total assets: total liabilities ÷ total assets.

✔ Use the formula for basic earnings per share: income available to common shareholders ÷ weighted average number of common shares.

✔ Understand that higher is better for liquidity and profitability ratios and lower is better for certain solvency ratios, like debt to total assets.

SOLUTION

Try this Do It! exercise on your own and then check your answer at the end of the chapter.

Related Exercise Material: BE2–5, BE2–6, BE2–7, E2–6, E2–7, and E2–8.

Selected financial information is available for Drummond Inc.

	2018	2017
Current assets	$114,000	$75,600
Total assets	$1,100,000	$940,000
Current liabilities	$60,000	$42,000
Total liabilities	$528,000	$423,000
Net income	$240,000	$156,000
Weighted average number of common shares	80,000	60,000
Market price per common share	$24.00	$18.20

Drummond has no preferred shares, so net income is equal to the income available to common shareholders.

(a) Calculate the (1) current, (2) debt to total assets, (3) basic earnings per share, and (4) price-earnings ratios for each year.

(b) Based on the ratios calculated in part (a), state (1) whether there was an improvement or deterioration in liquidity, solvency, and profitability for Drummond in 2018, and (2) whether the shares of Drummond have become more expensive or more affordable for investors in 2018. Explain how you determined this.

LEARNING OBJECTIVE 3

Describe the framework for the preparation and presentation of financial statements.

How do CT REIT and Choice Properties REIT decide on the type of financial information to disclose? What format should they use? How should they measure assets, liabilities, revenues, and expenses? These and all other companies get guidance from a standardized framework for the preparation and presentation of financial statements called the conceptual framework for financial reporting. Standard-setting bodies, in consultation with the accounting profession and business community, determine this framework.

According to standard setters, the **conceptual framework** is "a coherent system of interrelated objectives and fundamentals that can lead to consistent standards and that prescribes the nature, function, and limits of financial accounting statements." In other words, the conceptual framework of accounting guides decisions about what to present in financial statements, alternative ways of reporting economic events, and appropriate ways of communicating this information.

Not every country uses the same conceptual framework or set of accounting standards. They can, and do, differ significantly from country to country. This lack of uniformity has arisen over time because of differences in legal systems, in processes for developing standards, in government requirements, and in economic environments. With more and more companies operating globally, differences in accounting systems create challenges and increase reporting costs.

The International Accounting Standards Board (IASB)—the standard-setting body responsible for developing IFRS—was formed to reduce these areas of difference and unify global standard setting. Its efforts have been very successful and there are currently more than 140 countries that either require or permit the use of IFRS. This includes Canada, which adopted IFRS in 2011. Two major economies, the United States and China, have yet to adopt IFRS. However, securities regulators in the United States accept financial statements prepared using IFRS from foreign companies registered on U.S. exchanges. More than 500 such companies report financial statements prepared using IFRS.

The IASB has been working on a project to update the conceptual framework. The chapter reflects the proposed changes to the conceptual framework as tentative decisions about these changes have been made by the IASB and at the time of writing, it is expected that the revised framework will be adopted in 2017.

Some of the key conceptual framework items we will cover in this chapter include:

- Objective of general purpose financial reporting
- Qualitative characteristics of useful financial information
- Underlying assumption
- Elements of financial statements
- Measurement of the elements of financial statements

There are other portions of the conceptual framework that will be discussed in future accounting courses. For the purpose of this textbook, we will concentrate on the sections outlined above.

The conceptual framework is fundamentally similar for publicly traded companies in Canada reporting under IFRS and private companies reporting under ASPE. While there are some differences, the Accounting Standards Board—the Canadian accounting standard setter—has committed to update the conceptual framework for private companies to remain consistent with the IASB conceptual framework. It does not believe that the differences between publicly accountable companies and private companies justify different conceptual frameworks.

OBJECTIVE OF FINANCIAL REPORTING

The **objective of financial reporting** is to provide financial information about a company that is useful to existing and potential investors, lenders, and other creditors in making decisions about providing resources to the company. Those decisions involve buying, selling, or holding equity and debt instruments and providing or settling loans and other forms of credit. They also include assessing management's stewardship of the company's assets. Although a wide variety of users rely on financial reporting, investors, lenders, and other creditors are identified as the main users of financial reporting. You will recall that we discussed these and other users and their needs in Chapter 1. The users identified in the conceptual framework are all external users and, as such, do not have access to the same financial information as internal users do, and it is important that the financial information they do receive be as useful as possible.

External users receive much of their financial information about a company through its general purpose financial statements, but the IASB acknowledges that it is not possible for these statements to provide all of the information these users require. General purpose financial statements provide information about the company's economic resources and the claims against these resources. They also provide information about the effects of transactions and other events that change a company's economic resources and claims. Both types of information provide useful input for decisions made by external users about providing resources to the company.

Financial statements are prepared using the **accrual basis of accounting**. Under the accrual basis of accounting, the effects of transactions on a company's economic resources and claims are recorded in the period when a transaction occurs and not when cash is received or paid. For example, a law firm would record revenue in the accounting period when the legal services are provided to the client and not necessarily in the accounting period when the client pays for the services. We will learn about the accrual basis of accounting in the next two chapters.

QUALITATIVE CHARACTERISTICS OF USEFUL FINANCIAL INFORMATION

The qualitative characteristics of useful financial information identify the types of information that are likely to be most useful to existing and potential investors, lenders, and other creditors in making their decisions. The qualitative characteristics are divided into those that are fundamental to useful information and those that enhance it. Fundamental qualitative characteristics are required for financial information to be useful, while enhancing qualitative characteristics enhance or increase the usefulness of financial information that is already considered useful for users.

Fundamental Qualitative Characteristics

The two fundamental qualitative characteristics of useful financial information are (1) relevance and (2) faithful representation. To be useful for decision-making, information must be relevant and faithfully represent the transactions represented by that information.

Accounting information has **relevance** if knowledge of it will influence a user's decision. Relevant information may have predictive value, confirmatory value, or both. Financial information has **predictive value** if it helps users make predictions about future events. Financial information has **confirmatory value** if it helps users confirm or correct their previous predictions or expectations. For example, information about a company's sales for the current year can be used as a basis to help predict sales in one or more future years. It can also be compared with sales predictions that were made in past years. The results of such comparisons can help a user to confirm or correct the processes that were used to make these previous predictions.

Materiality is an important component of relevance. Information is considered material if its omission or misstatement could influence the decisions of users. Materiality and relevance are both defined in terms of what influences or makes a difference to a decision maker. Materiality is determined in terms of both magnitude (normally dollar value) and/or nature (what the information is related to). A decision not to disclose certain information may be made because users have no need for that kind of information (it is not relevant) or because the amounts involved are too small to make a difference (they are not material). Magnitude by itself, without regard to the nature of the item and the circumstances in which the judgement has to be made, is not generally a sufficient basis for a materiality judgement. For example, if a company official receives a bribe, the amount involved may not be significant but, because of its nature, ethical and legal considerations are involved and knowledge of the bribe will affect the company as well as decisions that users will make.

For accounting information to be useful, it must not only be relevant but it must represent economic reality; that is, it must be a **faithful representation** of what really exists or happened. Often this requires accountants to report the economic substance rather than the legal form of an event. For example, if a company sells a product to a customer but agrees to buy it back at a later date, there really is no sale (the product was simply lent to the customer), and to faithfully represent this event, no sale would be recorded. To provide a faithful representation, information must have three characteristics. It must be **complete** (nothing important was omitted), **neutral** (not biased toward one position or another), and **free from error** (it provides an accurate description and no errors were made in the process used to determine it).

Complete, unbiased, and factual information that is faithfully represented is critical in financial reporting. Of course, perfection is seldom, if ever, achievable. Consequently, faithful representation does not necessarily mean accuracy in all respects. For example, as we will learn in later chapters, many estimates are required in accounting, and estimates are not exact. However, a representation of an estimate can be faithful if the amount is described as being an estimate, the nature and limitations of the estimating process are explained, and no errors have been made in the process used to develop the estimate.

ACCOUNTING MATTERS

Getting the Numbers Right

On November 4, 2011, Poseidon Concepts Ltd. shares began trading on the Toronto Stock Exchange. The Calgary-based corporation rented fluid holding tanks to companies engaged in horizontal drilling of oil and gas wells. The company's shares began trading at just over $11 and management planned to pay out more than $1 of dividends per share annually. This meant that, even if the share price did not change, an investor would receive a return on his or her investment of almost 10% per year. Since the dividend was attractive to investors and because the company was expected to grow rapidly, more shares were sold to the public at $13 each in February 2012. Following this, the share price rose to over $16 per share.

In its income statement for the nine months ending September 30, 2012, Poseidon reported revenues of over $148 million, which was more than triple the revenue reported in the same nine-month period in 2011. However, the company also reported accounts receivable of more than

$125 million. On December 27, 2012, the board of directors became aware that a significant amount of the company's revenue had likely been recorded in error. It appointed a special committee to investigate this issue and suspended all dividend payments. After an internal investigation, the company announced on February 13, 2013, that between $95 million and $106 million of the revenue reported should not have been recorded. On the following day, Poseidon shares ceased trading. At that time, the shares had a value of $0.27 each. By May 17, 2013, the shares were delisted from the Toronto Stock Exchange and the company's assets were up for sale. Some suppliers were left unpaid and shareholders lost the investment they had made in Poseidon's shares, which had a total value of $1.3 billion at the height of the company's valuation.

Accounting problems like the one at Poseidon have made it clear that those who prepare financial statements must get the numbers right in order to provide relevant and faithfully represented information that is useful to external users.[3]

Enhancing Qualitative Characteristics

In addition to the two fundamental qualities of relevance and faithful representation, the conceptual framework also describes four qualities that enhance the usefulness of information. These are (1) comparability, (2) verifiability, (3) timeliness, and (4) understandability.

In accounting, **comparability** results when users can identify and understand similarities in, and differences among, items. Comparability enhances the usefulness of financial information because it allows users to compare results from the same company from one period to the next or compare results across different companies as they make investing or lending decisions.

Information has **verifiability** if different knowledgeable and independent users can reach a consensus that the information is faithfully represented. Verifiability can be determined by verifying an amount directly; for example, by counting cash. It can also be determined by checking the inputs to a formula and recalculating the outputs. Public accountants perform audits of financial statements to verify that the information is fairly presented.

For accounting information to be useful, it must have **timeliness**. That is, it must be available to decision makers before it loses its ability to influence decisions. For example, regulators require that public companies listed on major stock exchanges provide their financial statements to investors within 45 days of their quarter end and within 90 days of their year end.

Information has the quality of **understandability** if it is classified, characterized, and presented clearly and concisely. Understandable information means that users with a reasonable knowledge of business can interpret the information and comprehend its meaning.

Applying the enhancing qualitative characteristics is an iterative process that does not have to follow a prescribed order. In addition, sometimes one enhancing qualitative characteristic may have to be given less emphasis in order to maximize another qualitative characteristic. For example, a new financial reporting standard may improve relevance or faithful representation in the longer term while comparability of results with prior periods is sacrificed in the shorter term.

COST CONSTRAINT

The **cost constraint** is a pervasive constraint that ensures that the value of the information provided in financial reporting is greater than the cost of providing it. That is, the benefits of financial reporting information should justify the costs of providing and using it.

For example, to achieve completeness, which we discussed along with the fundamental qualitative characteristic of faithful representation, accountants could record or disclose every financial event that occurs and every uncertainty that exists. However, providing additional information increases costs, and the benefits of providing this information, in some cases, may be less than the costs.

GOING CONCERN ASSUMPTION

A key assumption—the going concern assumption—creates a foundation for the accounting process. The **going concern assumption** assumes that a company will continue to operate for the foreseeable future. Of course, some businesses do fail. However, if a business has a history of profitable operations and access to financial resources, it is reasonable to assume that it will continue operating long enough to carry out its existing objectives and commitments.

The going concern assumption is essential to the way we record items in the financial statements. If a company is assumed to be a going concern, then reporting assets, such as equipment, as non-current makes sense because those assets are expected to be used for more than one year. If a company is assumed not to be a going concern, we would assume that the business is shutting down and is selling all of its assets as soon as possible. In that case, the equipment would be a current asset.

ELEMENTS OF FINANCIAL STATEMENTS

Financial statements portray the financial effects of transactions and other events by grouping them into broad categories or classes according to their economic characteristics. These broad classes are termed the **elements of financial statements**, which include **assets**, **liabilities**, **equity**, **income** (including gains), and **expenses** (including losses).

Because these elements are so important and are often interrelated, they must be precisely defined and universally measured and applied. You were briefly introduced to these definitions in Chapter 1. We will summarize them in Illustration 2-19 and will discuss these definitions in more detail in later chapters.

►Illustration 2-19
Elements of financial statements

Assets An asset is an economic resource controlled by the company as a result of past events. An economic resource is a right that has the potential to produce economic benefits.

Liabilities A liability is a present obligation of the company to transfer an economic resource as a result of past events.

Equity Equity is the residual interest in the assets of the company after deducting all its liabilities.

Income Income includes both revenue and gains. Revenue arises in the course of the ordinary activities of the company while gains may or may not arise from ordinary activities. Income is the increases in economic benefits during the accounting period in the form of inflows or increases in assets or decreases in liabilities that result in increases in equity, other than those relating to contributions from equity participants.

Expenses Expenses include losses as well as those expenses that arise from ordinary activities of the company. Losses may or may not arise from ordinary activities. Expenses are decreases in economic benefits during the accounting period in the form of outflows or decreases in assets or increases in liabilities that result in decreases in equity, other than those relating to distributions to equity participants.

MEASUREMENT OF THE ELEMENTS

Using the objective of financial reporting, the qualitative characteristics, and the underlying assumption described in the previous sections, standard setters have developed foundational principles that describe which, when, and how the elements of financial statements should be recognized, measured, and reported. These foundational principles are known as generally accepted accounting principles (GAAP), which were introduced to you in Chapter 1. In Canada, "generally accepted" means that these principles are widely recognized and have authoritative support through the Canadian and provincial business corporations acts and securities legislation.

Generally accepted accounting principles related to the *recognition* of the elements of financial statements will be introduced in Chapter 4. In this chapter, we introduce two bases of *measurement*—historical cost and current value. These are more commonly referred to as "measurement bases" rather than "principles," although both terms can be, and are, used interchangeably. It is worth noting that, although we discuss only two bases of measurement here, a number of different measurement models are used to different degrees and in varying combinations in financial statements.

> **Alternative Terminology**
> The words *principles, standards, policies, models,* and *bases* are used interchangeably in accounting.

Historical Cost

The **historical cost basis of accounting** states that assets and liabilities should be recorded at their cost at the time of acquisition. This is true not only at the time when the item is purchased, but also during the time that an asset or liability is held.

For example, if a company were to purchase land for $3 million, it would be recorded and reported on the statement of financial position at $3 million at the time of purchase. But what would the company do if by the end of the next year the land had increased in value to $4 million? The answer is that, under historical cost, the land would still be reported at $3 million. In this particular case, cost is the most **relevant** value because the land is intended for use in the business. It is not being held for resale. The land will continue to be reported at cost until either it is sold or the **going concern assumption** is no longer valid for the company.

Current Value

The **current value basis of accounting** states that certain assets and liabilities should be recorded and reported at **current value** (the price that would be paid to purchase the same asset or paid to settle the same liability). It is worth noting that at the acquisition date, cost and current value are generally the same. It is only as time passes that these two values diverge and current value may become a more useful measure than cost for certain types of assets and liabilities. For example, certain investment securities that are held for trading are reported at current value because market price information is readily available for these types of assets and they are intended to be sold, in which case the current value is more relevant for users' needs.

> **Alternative Terminology**
> The terms *current value, fair value,* and *current cost* are used interchangeably in accounting.

In choosing between cost and current value, two fundamental qualitative characteristics that make financial information useful for decision-making are applied: relevance and faithful representation. Recall that in our chapter-opening feature story CT REIT chose to use current value because it felt it was a more **relevant** measure for its income-producing properties.

In determining which basis of measurement to use, the factual nature of the cost figures must be weighed against the relevance of the current value figures. In general, standard setters require that most assets be recorded using historical cost because current value may not always be representationally faithful. That is, cost is the more faithful representation because it can be easily verified and is neutral. Only in situations where assets are actively traded, such as investment securities or investment properties in certain industries, such as the real estate industry, is the current value basis of accounting applied.

SUMMARY OF CONCEPTUAL FRAMEWORK

As we have seen, the conceptual framework for developing sound reporting practices starts with the objective of financial reporting—providing financial information that is useful for decision-making. Financial information is provided by general purpose financial statements that are prepared using the accrual basis of accounting. Qualitative characteristics help ensure that the information provided in these statements is useful. A key assumption—the going concern assumption—underlies the preparation of financial statements. The elements of the financial statements define the main terms used in the financial statements and measurement bases describe how the elements of financial statements should be measured and reported.

The conceptual framework is summarized in Illustration 2-20.

▶Illustration 2-20
Summary of conceptual framework

Objective of Financial Reporting
To provide financial information that is useful to existing and potential investors, lenders, and other creditors in making decisions about providing resources to the company and assessing management's stewardship of the company's assets.

Qualitative Characteristics of Useful Financial Information		
Fundamental Qualitative Characteristics	Enhancing Qualitative Characteristics	Constraint
1. Relevance • Predictive value • Confirmatory value • Materiality 2. Faithful representation • Complete • Neutral • Free from material error	1. Comparability 2. Verifiability 3. Timeliness 4. Understandability	1. Cost

Underlying Assumption—Going Concern

Elements of Financial Statements	Measurement of the Elements
1. Assets 2. Liabilities 3. Equity 4. Income 5. Expenses	1. Historical cost 2. Current value

DO IT! ▶ 2-3   Conceptual Framework

Action Plan

✔ Understand the fundamental and enhancing qualitative characteristics of accounting information:
 ✔ Fundamental: relevance and faithful representation.
 ✔ Enhancing: comparability, verifiability, timeliness, and understandability.
 ✔ Constraint: cost.

✔ Understand the underlying assumption of the accounting process: going concern.

✔ Understand the choice between how the elements of financial statements are measured: historical cost or current value.

The following is an alphabetized list of the qualitative characteristics, assumption, and measurement bases found in the conceptual framework for financial reporting.

1. Comparability
2. Cost constraint
3. Current value
4. Historical cost
5. Faithful representation
6. Going concern
7. Relevance
8. Timeliness
9. Understandability
10. Verifiability

Match each item above with a description below.

(a) _____ The qualitative characteristic that the use of the same accounting principles enables evaluation of one company's results relative to another company's.

(b) _____ The qualitative characteristic for describing information that indicates that the information makes a difference in a decision.

(c) _____ The basis of measurement that assets are reported at the cost incurred to acquire them.

(d) _____ The constraint that states that the value of information should exceed the cost of preparing it.

(e) _____ The qualitative characteristic that presents a true and transparent picture of what really exists or happened.

(f) _____ The qualitative characteristic that information can be recalculated and determined to be without errors or omissions.

(g) _____ The qualitative characteristic that information is available before it loses its ability to influence decisions.

(h) _____ The assumption that a company will continue to operate for the foreseeable future.

(i) _____ The qualitative characteristic that informed users are able to interpret information and comprehend its meaning.

(j) _____ The basis of measurement that assets are reported at the price that would have to be paid at present to acquire the asset.

SOLUTION

Try this Do It! exercise on your own and then check your answer at the end of the chapter.

Related Exercise Material: BE2–8, BE2–9, BE2–10, E2–9, and E2–10.

REVIEW AND PRACTICE

▶ LEARNING OBJECTIVE REVIEW

1. Identify the sections of a classified statement of financial position. In a classified statement of financial position, assets are classified as current or non-current assets. In the non-current asset category, they are further classified as long-term investments; property, plant, and equipment; intangible assets and goodwill; or other assets. Liabilities are classified as either current or non-current. There is also a shareholders' equity section, which shows share capital and retained earnings, and other equity items if any exist.

2. Identify and calculate ratios for analyzing a company's liquidity, solvency, and profitability. Liquidity ratios, such as working capital and the current ratio, measure a company's short-term ability to pay its maturing obligations and meet unexpected needs for cash. Solvency ratios, such as debt to total assets, measure a company's ability to survive over a long period by having enough assets to settle its liabilities as they fall due. Profitability ratios, such as basic earnings per share and the price-earnings ratio, measure a company's operating success for a specific period of time.

3. Describe the framework for the preparation and presentation of financial statements. The key components of the conceptual framework are (1) the objective of financial reporting; (2) qualitative characteristics of useful financial information, which include fundamental and enhancing characteristics and the cost constraint; (3) the going concern assumption underlying the accounting process; (4) elements of the financial statements; and (5) measurement of the elements of financial statements.

▶ KEY TERM REVIEW

The following are key terms defined in this chapter with the corresponding page reference for your review. You will find a complete list of terms and definitions for all chapters in the glossary at the end of this textbook.

Accounts payable (p. 61)
Accounts receivable (p. 57)
Bank indebtedness (p. 61)

Basic earnings per share (EPS) (p. 70)
Comparability (p. 75)
Conceptual framework (p. 73)

Contra asset account (p. 59)
Cost constraint (p. 76)
Current assets (p. 56)

Current liabilities (p. 61)
Current maturities of long-term debt (p. 61)
Current ratio (p. 67)
Current value (also known as fair value or current cost) (p. 77)
Current value basis of accounting (p. 77)
Debt to total assets (p. 69)
Elements of financial statements (p. 76)
Faithful representation (p. 74)
Going concern assumption (p. 76)
Held for trading investments (p. 57)
Historical cost basis of accounting (p. 77)
Intangible assets (p. 59)

Inventory (p. 57)
Liquidity ratios (p. 67)
Long-term investments (also known as investments) (p. 58)
Non-current assets (also known as long-term assets) (p. 58)
Non-current liabilities (also known as long-term liabilities) (p. 62)
Notes payable (also known as loans payable) (p. 61)
Notes receivable (p. 57)
Objective of financial reporting (p. 73)
Operating cycle (p. 56)

Prepaid expenses (p. 57)
Price-earnings (P-E) ratio (p. 71)
Profitability ratios (p. 70)
Property, plant, and equipment (p. 59)
Relevance (p. 74)
Solvency ratios (p. 69)
Supplies (p. 57)
Timeliness (p. 75)
Understandability (p. 75)
Unearned revenue (p. 61)
Verifiability (p. 75)
Working capital (p. 67)

▶ COMPARING IFRS AND ASPE REVIEW

Key Standard Differences	International Financial Reporting Standards (IFRS)	Accounting Standards for Private Enterprises (ASPE)
Basic earnings per share	Required to present in financial statements	Not required to present in financial statements
Conceptual framework for financial reporting	Still under development	Same general framework currently under development by international and U.S. standard setters anticipated to be applied to private enterprises when complete

▶ DECISION TOOLKIT REVIEW

DECISION CHECKPOINTS	INFO NEEDED FOR DECISION	TOOLS TO USE FOR DECISION	HOW TO EVALUATE RESULTS
Can the company meet its short-term obligations?	Current assets and current liabilities	Working capital = Current assets − Current liabilities $$\text{Current ratio} = \frac{\text{Current assets}}{\text{Current liabilities}}$$	A higher amount indicates better liquidity. A higher ratio suggests more favourable liquidity.
Can the company meet its long-term obligations?	Total debt and total assets	$$\text{Debt to total assets} = \frac{\text{Total liabilities}}{\text{Total assets}}$$	A lower percentage suggests favourable solvency.
How does the company's net income compare with previous years?	Income available to common shareholders and weighted average number of common shares	$$\text{Basic earnings per share} = \frac{\text{Income available to common shareholders}}{\text{Weighted average number of common shares}}$$	A higher measure suggests improved performance. Values should not be compared across companies.
How does the market see the company's prospects for future profitability?	Market price per share and basic earnings per share	$$\text{Price-earnings ratio} = \frac{\text{Market price per share}}{\text{Basic earnings per share}}$$	A high ratio suggests the market expects good performance, although it may also suggest that shares are overvalued.

▶ PRACTICE USING THE DECISION TOOLKIT

Answers are at the end of the chapter.

Condensed and simplified financial statements with comparative data for Canadian Tire Corporation, Limited for the years ended January 2, 2016, and January 3, 2015, are shown below.

CANADIAN TIRE CORPORATION, LIMITED
Balance Sheet
(in millions)

	January 2 2016	January 3 2015
Assets		
Current assets	$ 8,692.3	$ 8,510.2
Long-term receivables and other assets	731.2	684.2
Long-term investments	153.4	176.0
Goodwill and intangible assets	1,246.8	1,251.7
Investment property	137.8	148.6
Property and equipment	3,978.2	3,743.1
Other long-term assets	48.1	39.4
Total assets	$14,987.8	$14,553.2
Liabilities and Shareholders' Equity		
Liabilities		
Current liabilities	$ 3,883.8	$ 4,578.8
Long-term debt	2,971.4	2,131.6
Long-term deposits	1,372.2	1,286.2
Other long-term liabilities	970.7	925.8
Total liabilities	9,198.1	8,922.4
Shareholders' equity		
Share capital	671.2	695.5
Other equity items	946.5	860.2
Retained earnings	4,172.0	4,075.1
Total shareholders' equity	5,789.7	5,630.8
Total liabilities and shareholders' equity	$14,987.8	$14,553.2

CANADIAN TIRE CORPORATION, LIMITED
Income Statement
Years Ended
(in millions)

	January 2 2016	January 3 2015
Revenue	$12,279.6	$12,462.9
Total expenses	11,278.3	11,584.7
Income before income tax	1,001.3	878.2
Income tax expense	265.4	238.9
Net income	$ 735.9	$ 639.3

Additional information:

- Canadian Tire's net income is the same as its income available to common shareholders. The weighted average number of shares was 76.2 million in the year ended January 3, 2015 and 79.0 million in the year ended January 2, 2016. The share price was $199.36 at January 2, 2016, and $223.22 at January 3, 2015.
- Industry averages are as follows: current ratio, 2.1:1 in 2015 and 2.2:1 in 2014; debt to total assets, 39.0% in 2015 and 48.2% in 2014; and price-earnings ratio, 18.7 times in 2015 and 19.7 times in 2014. Industry averages are not comparable for basic earnings per share.

INSTRUCTIONS

(a) Calculate Canadian Tire's current ratio for both fiscal years. Discuss the company's liquidity generally, and compared with the industry.

(b) Calculate Canadian Tire's debt to total assets for both fiscal years. Discuss the company's solvency generally, and compared with the industry.

(c) Calculate Canadian Tire's basic earnings per share and price-earnings ratio for both fiscal years. Discuss the company's profitability generally, and compared with the industry.

▶ PRACTICE COMPREHENSIVE DO IT!

Answers are at the end of the chapter.

The following accounts and amounts are taken from the accounting records of the Paloma Corporation for the year ended January 31, 2018:

Accounts payable	$1,760,000	Income tax expense	$ 102,000
Accounts receivable	3,280,000	Interest expense	80,000
Accumulated depreciation—buildings	390,000	Land	526,000
Accumulated depreciation—equipment	122,000	Long-term investments	200,000
		Mortgage payable	1,068,000
Buildings	2,800,000	Operating expenses	17,708,000
Cash	118,000	Prepaid expenses	118,000
Common shares	3,500,000	Retained earnings, February 1, 2017	961,000
Dividends declared	100,000	Service revenue	18,300,000
Equipment	625,000	Supplies	373,000
Goodwill	206,000	Unearned revenue	135,000

Additional information:
$267,000 of the mortgage is due within the current year. There were no changes in common shares during the year.

INSTRUCTIONS

(a) Prepare an income statement, statement of changes in equity, and statement of financial position for Paloma Corporation.

(b) 1. Calculate Paloma's working capital at January 31, 2018, and determine the company's current ratio. Explain what you know about Paloma based on the current ratio you calculate.

  2. Calculate Paloma's debt to total assets ratio and comment on the percentage of the company's assets that have been financed using debt versus shareholders' equity.

▶ PRACTICE OBJECTIVE-FORMAT QUESTIONS

Answers are at the end of the chapter.

1. For each of the following items, identify whether it would be considered to be a current asset (CA), non-current asset (NCA), current liability (CL), non-current liability (NCL), or part of shareholders' equity (SE).

   (a) Unearned revenue
   (b) Intangible assets
   (c) Inventory
   (d) Bank indebtedness

   (e) Accounts receivable
   (f) Retained earnings
   (g) Accounts payable

2. Indicate which of the following statements are correct. (Select as many as are appropriate.)

   (a) Goodwill is similar to an intangible asset in that it has no physical substance, will generate future value, and is amortized over its useful life.

   (b) Loans payable can be treated as a current liability, a non-current liability, or part of both, depending upon when they have to be repaid.

(c) Items like office supplies and cleaning supplies are considered to be part of inventory because they will be used by the business within one year.

(d) Property, plant, and equipment are normally presented in order of permanency on the statement of financial position, with land being the last item listed because it has the longest life and is most permanent.

(e) Share capital is equal to the amount the company received when it issued common shares and any preferred shares.

(f) The difference between the cost of equipment and its accumulated depreciation is known as its carrying amount.

(g) Unearned revenue represents amounts owed to the company by its customers for goods and services provided to them but for which they have yet to pay.

3. Label the following items in the order that they would appear on a classified statement of financial position. The first item that would be presented should be labelled (1) and the last item to be presented should be labelled (7).

(a) Share capital
(b) Prepaid expenses
(c) Retained earnings
(d) Inventory
(e) Unearned revenue
(f) Goodwill
(g) Accounts receivable

4. The following accounts and amounts are taken from the accounting records of Martindale Ltd.

Cash	$ 16,200	Intangible assets	$25,000
Held for trading investments	3,000	Accounts payable	54,100
Accounts receivable	44,000	Salaries payable	3,200
Inventory	69,000	Unearned revenue	12,400
Prepaid rent	5,000	Long-term note payable	40,000
Supplies	2,500	Common shares	50,000
Equipment	213,000	Retained earnings	68,000
Accumulated depreciation	150,000		

Based on the above information, indicate which of the following statements are correct in relation to Martindale's classified statement of financial position. (Select as many as are appropriate.)

(a) Martindale's current liabilities would equal $69,700.
(b) Martindale's non-current assets would equal $238,000.
(c) Martindale's total shareholders' equity would be equal to $118,000.
(d) Martindale's total assets would equal $227,700.

(e) Martindale's total current assets would equal $136,700.
(f) Martindale's total liabilities would equal $109,700.
(g) Martindale's total liabilities and shareholders' equity would be $215,300.

5. Indicate which of the following statements are correct. (Select as many as are appropriate.)

(a) A higher debt to total assets ratio is considered superior to a lower one.
(b) The current ratio is an indicator of liquidity and measures the relationship between current assets and current liabilities.
(c) A higher price-earnings ratio indicates that investors are willing to pay more for shares of that company relative to its earnings than one with a lower price-earnings ratio.

(d) The price-earnings ratio must be presented in the financial statements of publicly traded companies.
(e) Intercompany ratio comparisons involve comparing two or more periods for the same company.
(f) Liquidity ratios measure a company's ability to meet its obligations over the next year.
(g) When working capital is negative, it means that total liabilities exceed total assets.

6. The following ratios are available for Campbell Ltd. and Kiedyk Corporation.

	Current ratio	Debt to total assets	Basic earnings per share	Market price per share
Campbell	1.4:1	59.8%	$1.76	$15.84
Kiedyk	0.9:1	49.2%	$0.87	$6.09

Based on the above ratios, indicate which of the following statements are correct. (Select as many as are appropriate.)

(a) Kiedyk has $0.90 in current liabilities for every $1 it has in current assets.

(b) Kiedyk would be considered to be more solvent than Campbell based on the debt to total assets ratios of the two companies.

(c) More of Campbell's total assets have been financed by shareholders than have been financed using debt.

(d) Campbell would be considered to be more liquid than Kiedyk based on the current ratios of the two companies.

(e) Shareholders of Campbell can expect to receive a dividend of $1.76 per share.

(f) Kiedyk's shares are more expensive than those of Campbell relative to each company's earnings.

(g) Based on the current ratios of the two companies, a user could conclude that Campbell has positive working capital, while Kiedyk has negative working capital.

7. For each of the following ratios, indicate which column's ratio would be considered superior.

		A	B
(a)	Debt to total assets	53.1%	61.2%
(b)	Working capital	$1.9 million	$1.3 million
(c)	Current ratio	0.8:1	1.6:1
(d)	Current ratio	0.7:1	0.6:1
(e)	Working capital	($16.1 million)	($8.9 million)
(f)	Debt to total assets	50.8%	42.6%
(g)	Current ratio	2.2:1	1.8:1

8. Indicate which of the following accounts would affect the calculation of a company's working capital. Indicate "Yes" if it would affect the calculation and "No" if it would not.

(a) Loan payable, due in two years

(b) Unearned revenue

(c) Equipment

(d) Cash

(e) Accounts payable

(f) Supplies

(g) Retained earnings

9. Indicate whether each of the following qualitative characteristics is fundamental (F), enhancing (E), or neither (N).

(a) Understandability

(b) Relevance

(c) Verifiability

(d) Neutrality

(e) Comparability

(f) Faithful representation

(g) Timeliness

10. Indicate which of the following statements are correct. (Select as many as are appropriate.)

(a) According to the cost constraint, if the cost of capturing and reporting financial information exceeds the benefits of doing so, then the information does not have to be reported.

(b) Enhancing qualitative characteristics cannot make useless financial information useful, they can only increase the usefulness of financial information that is already useful.

(c) Assessing whether an item is material or not is a matter of considering its magnitude or size (dollar value).

(d) The cost basis of accounting is supported by the going concern assumption.

(e) Financial information is considered to be a faithful representation if it is complete, neutral, and understandable.

(f) Materiality is a component of relevance.

(g) Financial information is considered to be relevant if it has predictive and/or confirmatory value.

WileyPLUS

Brief Exercises, Exercises, and many additional resources are available for practice in WileyPLUS.

▶QUESTIONS

(LO 1) 1. (a) What are current assets? (b) Give four examples of current assets a company might have and identify the order in which they would be listed on the statement of financial position.

(LO 1) 2. What is meant by the term *operating cycle*?

(LO 1) 3. (a) Distinguish between current assets and non-current assets. (b) Distinguish between current assets and current liabilities. Why does showing these items as current in nature matter?

(LO 1) 4. (a) What are current liabilities? (b) Give four examples of current liabilities a company might have and identify the order in which they would be listed on the statement of financial position.

(LO 1) 5. (a) Distinguish between current liabilities and non-current liabilities. (b) Explain how a bank loan can sometimes be classified as both a current liability and a non-current liability.

(LO 1) 6. (a) What does it mean if an account is a contra asset account? (b) Explain how a contra asset account is used to determine the carrying amount of property, plant, and equipment.

(LO 1) 7. Explain what it means to present current assets and current liabilities in order of liquidity and property, plant, and equipment in order of permanency on the statement of financial position.

(LO 1) 8. (a) Identify the two components of shareholders' equity normally found in a corporation and indicate the purpose of each. (b) Which financial statement(s) are these items presented on?

(LO 2) 9. Explain the difference between intracompany and intercompany ratio comparisons.

(LO 2) 10. Explain what each of the following classes of ratios measures and give an example of each: (a) liquidity ratios, (b) solvency ratios, and (c) profitability ratios.

(LO 2) 11. (a) How is working capital determined? (b) What does it mean if a company has positive working capital? (c) If a company has positive working capital, does it mean that it has lots of cash? Explain.

(LO 2) 12. Why is the current ratio a better measure of liquidity than working capital?

(LO 2) 13. "The current ratio should not be used as the only measure of liquidity, because it does not take into account the composition of the current assets." Explain what this statement means.

(LO 2) 14. Dong Corporation has a debt to total assets ratio of 45%, while its competitor, Du Ltd., has a debt to total assets ratio of 55%. Based on this information, which company is more solvent? Why?

(LO 2) 15. Jonathan Baird, the founder of Waterboots Inc., needs to raise $500,000 to expand his company's operations. He has been told that raising the money through debt by obtaining a bank loan will increase the riskiness of his company much more than by raising the money by issuing common shares. He doesn't understand why this is true. Explain it to him.

(LO 2) 16. Why can you compare the price-earnings ratio among different companies but not basic earnings per share?

(LO 2) 17. The **TD Bank** has a price-earnings ratio of 12.8 times, while **CIBC** has a price-earnings ratio of 11.3 times. Which company do investors appear to favour?

(LO 2) 18. Explain why increases in the basic earnings per share, price-earnings, and current ratios are considered to be signs of improvement in a company's financial health, but an increase in the debt to total assets ratio is considered to be a sign of deterioration.

(LO 3) 19. (a) Describe the conceptual framework and explain how it helps financial reporting. (b) Is the conceptual framework applicable to publicly traded companies reporting using IFRS, to private companies using ASPE, or to both?

(LO 3) 20. (a) What is the objective of financial reporting? (b) Who are the main users that rely on this objective?

(LO 3) 21. Explain how the going concern assumption supports the classification of assets and liabilities as current and non-current.

(LO 3) 22. Identify and explain the two fundamental qualitative characteristics of useful financial information.

(LO 3) 23. Explain the difference between a fundamental qualitative characteristic and an enhancing qualitative characteristic.

(LO 3) 24. How is materiality related to the fundamental qualitative characteristic of relevance?

(LO 3) 25. Identify and explain the four enhancing qualitative characteristics of useful financial information. Is there a prescribed order for applying these enhancing characteristics?

(LO 3) 26. Explain how the cost constraint relates to the quality of completeness.

(LO 3) 27. What are the elements of financial statements?

(LO 3) 28. Identify and explain the two bases used to measure the elements of financial statements.

(LO 3) 29. Explain how the qualitative characteristics of relevance and faithful representation relate to the historical cost and current value bases of accounting.

▶ BRIEF EXERCISES

Classify accounts.
(LO 1)

BE2–1 The following are the major statement of financial position classifications:

1. Current assets
2. Long-term investments
3. Property, plant, and equipment
4. Intangible assets

5. Current liabilities
6. Non-current liabilities
7. Share capital
8. Retained earnings

Classify each of the following selected accounts by writing in the number of its appropriate classification above:

(a) _____ Accounts payable
(b) _____ Accounts receivable
(c) _____ Accumulated depreciation
(d) _____ Buildings
(e) _____ Cash
(f) _____ Common shares
(g) _____ Current portion of mortgage payable
(h) _____ Patents
(i) _____ Dividends declared

(j) _____ Income tax payable
(k) _____ Long-term investments
(l) _____ Land
(m) _____ Inventory
(n) _____ Supplies
(o) _____ Mortgage payable, due in 20 years
(p) _____ Prepaid insurance
(q) _____ Unearned revenue

Classify accounts.
(LO 1)

BE2–2 The following are the major statement of financial position classifications:

1. Current assets
2. Property, plant, and equipment
3. Other non-current assets

4. Current liabilities
5. Non-current liabilities
6. Shareholders' equity

Classify each of the following selected accounts by writing in the number of its appropriate classification above:

(a) _____ Accounts receivable
(b) _____ Accumulated depreciation
(c) _____ Bank indebtedness
(d) _____ Bank loan payable, due in three years
(e) _____ Cash
(f) _____ Common shares
(g) _____ Equipment
(h) _____ Goodwill
(i) _____ Inventory

(j) _____ Notes receivable, due in six months
(k) _____ Prepaid rent
(l) _____ Retained earnings
(m) _____ Salaries payable
(n) _____ Supplies
(o) _____ Unearned revenue
(p) _____ Prepaid insurance
(q) _____ Accounts payable

Prepare assets section.
(LO 1)

BE2–3 A list of financial statement items for Shum Corporation includes the following: accounts receivable $14,500; cash $16,400; inventory $9,000; supplies $4,200; prepaid insurance $3,900; accumulated depreciation—buildings $33,000; accumulated depreciation—equipment $25,000; buildings $110,000; equipment $70,000; and land $65,000. Prepare the assets section of the statement of financial position.

Prepare current liabilities section.
(LO 1)

BE2–4 Hirjikaka Inc. reports the following current and non-current liabilities: accounts payable $22,500; salaries payable $3,900; interest payable $5,200; unearned revenue $900; income tax payable $6,400; mortgage payable (due within the year) $5,000; mortgage payable (due in more than one year) $50,000. Prepare the current liabilities section of the statement of financial position.

Calculate ratios and evaluate liquidity.
(LO 2)

BE2–5 **Indigo Books & Music Inc.** reported the following selected information for the years ended April 2, 2016, and March 2, 2015 (in thousands):

	2016	2015
Total current assets	$453,254	$421,955
Total current liabilities	235,400	223,239

(a) Calculate the working capital and current ratio for each year.
(b) Was Indigo's liquidity stronger or weaker in 2016 compared with 2015?

Calculate ratios and evaluate solvency.
(LO 2)

BE2–6 Convenience store operator **Alimentation Couche-Tard Inc.** reported the following selected information for the years ended April 24, 2016, and April 26, 2015 (in U.S. $ millions):

	2016	2015
Current assets	$2,934.8	$2,742.3
Non-current assets	9,369.1	8,286.1
Current liabilities	2,705.5	2,470.3
Non-current liabilities	4,554.8	4,655.1

(a) Calculate the debt to total assets ratio for each year.

(b) Was the company's solvency stronger or weaker in 2016 compared with 2015?

BE2-7 The following information is available for **Leon's Furniture Limited** for the years ended December 31 (in thousands, except for share price):

Calculate ratios and evaluate profitability.

(LO 2)

	2015	2014
Income available to common shareholders	$76,629	$75,524
Weighted average number of common shares	71,218	70,899
Share price	$13.99	$17.31

(a) Calculate the basic earnings per share and the price-earnings ratio for each year.

(b) Indicate whether profitability improved or deteriorated in 2015.

BE2-8 Presented below is a chart showing selected portions of the conceptual framework. Fill in the blanks from (a) to (f).

Identify components of conceptual framework.

(LO 3)

Qualitative Characteristics			Underlying Assumption	Measurement of the Elements
Fundamental Qualitative Characteristics	Enhancing Qualitative Characteristics	Constraint		
Relevance	Comparability	(d)	(e)	Historical Cost
(a)	(b)			(f)
	Timeliness			
	(c)			

BE2-9 The following selected items relate to the qualitative characteristics of useful financial information discussed in this chapter:

Identify qualitative characteristics.

(LO 3)

1. Comparability
2. Completeness
3. Confirmatory value
4. Cost constraint
5. Faithful representation
6. Freedom from error
7. Materiality
8. Neutrality
9. Predictive value
10. Relevance
11. Timeliness
12. Understandability
13. Verifiability

Match each characteristic to one of the statements below:

(a) _____ Information that has predictive value, confirmatory value, and is material is said to have this fundamental qualitative characteristic.

(b) _____ Information that is complete, neutral, and free of error is said to have this fundamental qualitative characteristic.

(c) _____ Public accountants perform audits to determine this enhancing qualitative characteristic.

(d) _____ This quality requires that information cannot be selected to favour one position over another.

(e) _____ This enhancing qualitative characteristic describes information that a reasonably informed user can interpret and comprehend.

(f) _____ When information provides a basis for forecasting income for future periods, it is said to have this quality.

(g) _____ This enhancing qualitative characteristic requires that similar companies should apply the same accounting principles to similar events for successive accounting periods.

(h) _____ This quality results in information that has nothing important omitted.

(i) _____ This restriction requires that the value of the information presented should be greater than the cost of providing it.

(j) _____ This quality describes information that confirms or corrects users' prior expectations.

(k) _____ This enhancing qualitative characteristic requires that information be available to decision makers before it loses its ability to influence their decisions.

(l) _____ Faithful representation means that information is complete, neutral, and this third quality.

(m) _____ This quality allows items of insignificance that would not likely influence a decision not to be disclosed.

BE2-10 For each of the situations discussed below, choose a basis of measurement to use and explain why.

Identify bases of measurement.

(LO 3)

(a) Sosa Ltd. is a real estate company that purchases and holds land for eventual sale to developers.

(b) Mohawk Inc. is a manufacturing company that purchased land on which it plans to construct a new plant next year. It expects the value of the land to rise rapidly over the next few years.

▶ EXERCISES

Classify accounts.

(LO 1)

E2–1 The following are the major statement of financial position classifications:

1. Current assets
2. Long-term investments
3. Property, plant, and equipment
4. Intangible assets

5. Current liabilities
6. Non-current liabilities
7. Shareholders' equity

Instructions

Classify each of the following selected accounts taken from **TELUS Corporation**'s statement of financial position by writing in the number of the appropriate classification above:

(a) _____ Accounts payable and accrued liabilities
(b) _____ Accounts receivable
(c) _____ Accumulated depreciation
(d) _____ Buildings and leasehold improvements
(e) _____ Common shares
(f) _____ Current maturities of long-term debt
(g) _____ Dividends payable

(h) _____ Patents
(i) _____ Income and other taxes payable
(j) _____ Income and other taxes receivable
(k) _____ Inventories
(l) _____ Land
(m) _____ Long-term debt
(n) _____ Prepaid expenses

Prepare assets section.

(LO 1)

E2–2 The assets (in thousands) that follow were taken from the December 31, 2015, balance sheet for **Big Rock Brewery Inc.**:

Accounts receivable	$ 2,221	Intangible assets	$ 456
Accumulated depreciation—buildings	1,817	Inventories	4,935
Accumulated depreciation—machinery and equipment	10,122	Land	8,377
Accumulated depreciation—mobile equipment	434	Machinery and equipment	24,860
Accumulated depreciation—office furniture and equipment	516	Mobile equipment	1,054
Buildings	17,692	Office furniture and equipment	1,286
Cash	540	Prepaid expenses and other	1,573

Instructions

Prepare the assets section of the statement of financial position.

Prepare liabilities and equity sections.

(LO 1)

E2–3 The liabilities and shareholders' equity items (in millions) that follow were taken from the March 31, 2016, balance sheet for **Saputo Inc.**:

Accounts payable and accrued liabilities	$ 896.6
Bank loans payable (current)	423.1
Common shares	821.0
Deferred income taxes payable (non-current)	475.6
Income taxes payable	37.1
Long-term debt	1,208.3
Other long-term liabilities	61.8
Retained earnings	3,180.8

Instructions

Prepare the liabilities and shareholders' equity sections of the statement of financial position.

Prepare statement of financial position.

(LO 1)

E2–4 These items are taken from the financial statements of Summit Ltd. at December 31, 2018:

Accounts payable	$ 21,050	Interest expense	$ 4,550
Accounts receivable	20,780	Interest payable	2,100
Accumulated depreciation—buildings	50,600	Land	194,000
Accumulated depreciation—equipment	21,470	Long-term investments	28,970
Service revenue	183,040	Mortgage payable	104,000
Buildings	133,800	Operating expenses	158,680
Cash	24,040	Prepaid insurance	1,420
Common shares	140,000	Retained earnings, January 1	116,520
Equipment	66,100	Supplies	1,240
Income tax expense	5,200		

Instructions

(a) Calculate net income and the ending balance of retained earnings at December 31, 2018. It is not necessary to prepare a formal income statement or statement of changes in equity.
(b) Prepare a statement of financial position. Assume that $30,500 of the mortgage payable will be paid in 2019.

E2–5 These financial statement items are for Batra Corporation at year end, July 31, 2018:

Prepare financial statements.

(LO 1)

Operating expenses	$ 32,500	Interest payable	$ 1,000
Salaries expense	44,700	Supplies expense	900
Unearned revenue	12,000	Dividends declared	12,000
Utilities expense	2,600	Depreciation expense	3,000
Equipment	62,900	Retained earnings, August 1, 2017	17,940
Accounts payable	4,220	Rent expense	10,800
Service revenue	113,600	Income tax expense	5,000
Rent revenue	18,500	Supplies	1,500
Common shares	25,000	Held for trading investments	20,000
Cash	5,060	Bank loan payable (due December 31, 2018)	21,800
Accounts receivable	17,100	Interest expense	2,000
Accumulated depreciation—equipment	6,000		

Additional information:

Batra started the year with $15,000 of common shares and issued additional shares for $10,000 during the year.

Instructions

Prepare an income statement, statement of changes in equity, and statement of financial position for the year.

E2–6 The chief financial officer (CFO) of Padilla Corporation requested that the accounting department prepare a preliminary statement of financial position on December 20, 2018. He knows that certain debt agreements with its lenders require the company to maintain a current ratio of at least 2:1 and wants to know how the company is doing. The preliminary statement of financial position follows:

Calculate ratios and evaluate liquidity.

(LO 2)

PADILLA CORPORATION
Statement of Financial Position
December 20, 2018

Assets			Liabilities		
Current assets			Current liabilities		
Cash	$ 25,000		Accounts payable	$20,000	
Accounts receivable	30,000		Salaries payable	20,000	$ 40,000
Prepaid insurance	5,000		Non-current liabilities		
Total current assets	60,000		Bank loan payable		80,000
Equipment	200,000		Total liabilities		120,000
Total assets	$260,000		Shareholders' equity		
			Common shares	$90,000	
			Retained earnings	50,000	140,000
			Total liabilities and shareholders' equity		$260,000

Instructions

(a) Calculate the current ratio based on the data in the preliminary statement of financial position.

(b) Based on the results in part (a), the CFO requested that $20,000 of the cash be used to pay off the balance of the accounts payable account on December 21. Calculate the current ratio after this payment is made, assuming there are no further changes to current assets and current liabilities.

(c) Is it ethical for the CFO to recommend this action?

E2–7 Crombie REIT is a competitor of **CT REIT** and **Choice Properties REIT**. Crombie owns retail properties in which many **Sobeys** stores are located and reported the following selected information (in thousands):

Calculate ratios and comment on liquidity and solvency.

(LO 2)

	2015	2014
Current assets	$ 167,816	$ 63,150
Non-current assets	3,304,377	3,350,264
Current liabilities	158,120	193,384
Non-current liabilities	2,166,843	2,036,716

Instructions

(a) Calculate the working capital, current ratio, and debt to total assets ratio for each year.

(b) Did Crombie REIT's liquidity and solvency improve or worsen during 2015?

(c) Using the data in the chapter, compare Crombie REIT's liquidity and solvency with that of CT REIT, Choice Properties REIT, and the industry for 2015 and 2014 (as shown in the chapter in Illustrations 2-13, 2-14, and 2-15).

Calculate ratios and evaluate profitability.

(LO 2)

E2–8 The following information is available for **Cameco Corporation** for the year ended December 31 (in thousands, except share price):

	2015	2014
Income available for common shareholders	$65,286	$185,234
Weighted average number of common shares	395,793	395,740
Share price	$17.07	$18.62

Instructions

(a) Calculate the basic earnings per share and price-earnings ratio for each year.

(b) Based on your calculations above, how did the company's profitability change from 2014 to 2015?

Identify qualitative characteristics.

(LO 3)

E2–9 Here are some fundamental and enhancing qualitative characteristics of useful financial information:

1. Comparability
2. Completeness
3. Confirmatory value
4. Faithful representation
5. Freedom from error
6. Materiality
7. Neutrality
8. Predictive value
9. Relevance
10. Timeliness
11. Understandability
12. Verifiability

Instructions

Match each characteristic to one of the following statements, using the numbers 1 to 12.

(a) _____ Accounting information cannot be selected, prepared, or presented to favour one set of interested users over another.

(b) _____ Accounting information must be available to decision makers before it loses its ability to influence their decisions.

(c) _____ Accounting information is prepared on the assumption that users have a reasonable understanding of accounting and general business and economic conditions.

(d) _____ Accounting information provides a basis to evaluate a previously made decision.

(e) _____ Accounting information includes everything it needs to and nothing important is omitted. This is an important component of faithful representation.

(f) _____ Accounting information helps users make predictions about the outcome of past, present, and future events.

(g) _____ Accounting information about one company can be evaluated against the accounting information from another company.

(h) _____ Accounting information is included if its omission or misstatement could influence the economic decisions of users. This is an important component of relevance.

(i) _____ All the accounting information that is necessary to faithfully represent economic reality is included.

(j) _____ Accounting information can be determined to be free of material error.

(k) _____ Accounting information is included if it will make a difference in users' decisions.

(l) _____ Accounting information about a company can be confirmed by two or more users to be a faithful representation.

Identify assumption or principle.

(LO 3)

E2–10 Marietta Corp. had the following reporting issues during the year:

1. Land with a cost of $208,000 that is intended to be used by the company as a building site was reported at its current value of $260,000.
2. A surplus parcel of land with a cost of $150,000 intended for resale in the near future is reported at its current value of $160,000.
3. The president of Marietta, Deanna Durnford, decided it wasn't necessary to classify assets and liabilities as current and non-current because she expects to operate the company for only another 10 years.

Instructions

For each of the above situations, identify (a) the assumption or principle involved, and (b) whether it is being followed correctly or has been violated.

▶ PROBLEMS: SET A

Classify accounts.

(LO 1)

P2–1A You are provided with the following selected balance sheet accounts for entertainment retailer **Live Nation Entertainment, Inc.**:

Accounts payable	Common shares
Accounts receivable	Computer equipment
Accumulated depreciation	Current portion of long-term debt
Cash	Furniture and equipment

Goodwill
Land, buildings and improvements
Long-term debt

Prepaid expenses
Unearned revenues

Instructions
Identify the balance sheet (statement of financial position) category for classifying each account. For example, accumulated depreciation should be classified as a contra asset in the property, plant, and equipment section of Live Nation's balance sheet.

P2–2A The following items are from the assets section of **WestJet Airlines Ltd.**'s December 31, 2015, statement of financial position (in thousands):

Prepare assets section.
(LO 1)

Accounts receivable	$ 82,136
Accumulated depreciation—aircraft	1,170,643
Accumulated depreciation—buildings	30,419
Accumulated depreciation—ground, property and equipment	196,829
Aircraft	3,912,617
Buildings	136,783
Cash	1,252,370
Ground and other property and equipment	821,753
Intangible assets	63,549
Inventory	36,018
Other assets	89,942
Prepaid expenses, deposits, and other	131,747

Instructions
(a) Identify the statement of financial position category in which each of the above items should be classified.
(b) Prepare the assets section of the statement of financial position.

P2–3A The following items are from the liability and shareholders' equity sections of WestJet Airlines Ltd.'s December 31, 2015, statement of financial position (in thousands):

Prepare liabilities and equity sections.
(LO 1)

Accounts payable and accrued liabilities	$ 545,438
Advance ticket sales	620,216
Current portion of long-term debt	227,391
Deferred income tax (long-term)	327,028
Long-term debt	1,276,475
Other current liabilities	158,880
Other long-term liabilities	13,603
Other shareholders' equity items	84,616
Retained earnings	1,292,581
Share capital	582,796

Instructions
(a) Identify the statement of financial position category in which each of the above items should be classified.
(b) Prepare the liabilities and equity sections of the statement of financial position.
(c) If you completed P2–2A, compare the total assets in P2–2A with the total liabilities and shareholders' equity in P2–3A. Do these two amounts agree?

P2–4A These items are taken from the financial statements of Mbong Corporation for the year ended December 31, 2018:

Prepare financial statements; discuss relationships.
(LO 1)

Retained earnings, January 1	$221,000
Cash	11,900
Salaries payable	3,000
Utilities expense	2,000
Equipment	66,000
Accounts payable	15,000
Buildings	72,000
Common shares	34,200
Dividends declared	5,000
Service revenue	213,900

Prepaid insurance	$ 2,000
Repair and maintenance expense	2,800
Land	156,000
Depreciation expense	6,200
Accounts receivable	14,200
Insurance expense	2,200
Salaries expense	129,800
Accumulated depreciation—equipment	17,600
Income tax expense	6,000
Supplies	200
Operating expense	39,400
Supplies expense	1,000
Bank loan payable, due 2021	15,000
Held for trading investments	20,000
Accumulated depreciation—buildings	18,000
Interest expense	1,500
Interest revenue	500

Additional information:
1. Mbong started the year with $30,000 of common shares and issued $4,200 more during the year.
2. $1,500 of the bank loan payable is due to be repaid within the next year.

Instructions
(a) Prepare an income statement, statement of changes in equity, and statement of financial position for the year.
(b) Explain how each financial statement is related to the others.

Calculate ratios and comment on liquidity, solvency, and profitability.

(LO 2)

P2–5A The financial statements of Johanssen Inc. are presented here:

JOHANSSEN INC.
Income Statement
Year Ended December 31, 2018

Service revenue		$2,218,500
Expenses		
Operating expenses	$1,918,500	
Interest expense	98,000	2,016,500
Income before income tax		202,000
Income tax expense		42,000
Net income		$ 160,000

JOHANSSEN INC.
Statement of Financial Position
December 31, 2018

Assets

Current assets		
Cash	$ 60,100	
Held for trading investments	54,000	
Accounts receivable	307,800	
Supplies	25,000	$ 446,900
Property, plant, and equipment		625,300
Total assets		$1,072,200

Liabilities and Shareholders' Equity

Current liabilities		
Accounts payable	$100,000	
Income tax payable	15,000	
Current portion of mortgage payable	27,500	$ 142,500
Mortgage payable		310,000
Total liabilities		452,500
Shareholders' equity		
Common shares	$307,630	
Retained earnings	312,070	619,700
Total liabilities and shareholders' equity		$1,072,200

Additional information:
1. Income available to common shareholders was $160,000.
2. The weighted average number of common shares was 40,000.
3. The share price at December 31 was $35.

Instructions
(a) Calculate the following values and ratios for 2018. We provide the results for 2017 for comparative purposes.
1. Working capital (2017: $260,500)
2. Current ratio (2017: 1.6:1)
3. Debt to total assets (2017: 31.5%)
4. Basic earnings per share (2017: $3.15)
5. Price-earnings ratio (2017: 7.5 times)
(b) Using the information in part (a), discuss the changes in liquidity, solvency, and profitability between 2018 and 2017.

P2–6A Selected financial statement data for a recent year for Chen Corporation and Caissie Corporation, two competitors, are as follows:

Calculate ratios and comment on liquidity, solvency, and profitability.
(LO 2)

	Chen	Caissie
Service revenue	$1,800,000	$620,000
Operating expenses	1,458,000	438,000
Interest expense	10,000	4,000
Income tax expense	85,000	35,400
Current assets	407,200	190,400
Non-current assets	532,000	139,700
Current liabilities	166,325	133,700
Non-current liabilities	108,500	40,700
Share price	$25	$15
Weighted average number of common shares	76,000	62,000

Instructions
(a) Calculate working capital and the current ratio for each company. Comment on their relative liquidity.
(b) Calculate the debt to total assets ratio for each company. Comment on their relative solvency.
(c) Calculate the net income, basic earnings per share, and price-earnings ratio for each company. Assume that the net income you calculate equals the income available to common shareholders. Comment on the two companies' relative profitability.

P2–7A Selected financial data for a recent year for two clothing competitors, **Le Château Inc.** and **Reitmans (Canada) Limited**, are presented here (in thousands, except share price):

Calculate ratios and comment on liquidity, solvency, and profitability.
(LO 2)

	Le Château	Reitmans
Current assets	$116,724	$319,362
Total assets	168,490	542,083
Current liabilities	36,038	121,172
Total liabilities	108,136	160,915
Loss to common shareholders	(35,745)	(24,703)
Share price	$0.27	$3.96
Weighted average number of common shares	29,964	64,079

Instructions
(a) For each company, calculate the following values and ratios. Where available, industry averages are included in parentheses.
1. Working capital (n/a)
2. Current ratio (1.8:1)
3. Debt to total assets (57%)
4. Basic earnings per share (n/a)
5. Price-earnings ratio (20.0 times)
(b) Compare the liquidity, solvency, and profitability of the two companies and their industry.

P2–8A Selected ratios for Pitka Corporation are as follows:

Comment on liquidity, solvency, and profitability.
(LO 2)

	2018	2017	2016
Working capital	$140,000	$155,000	$172,000
Current ratio	1.1:1	1.2:1	1.2:1
Debt to total assets	34.2%	42.3%	40.0%
Basic earnings per share	$3.50	$3.15	$3.40
Price-earnings ratio	6.7 times	6.2 times	6.5 times

Instructions

(a) Identify if the change in each value or ratio is an improvement or deterioration between (1) 2016 and 2017, and (2) 2017 and 2018.

(b) Briefly discuss the changes in Pitka's liquidity, solvency, and profitability over the three-year period.

Discuss financial reporting objective, qualitative characteristics, and elements.

(LO 3)

P2–9A Bobby Young is the accountant for the Blazers Ltd., which operates a new professional hockey team. He has just finished preparing the financial statements for the team's first year end, which falls on December 31, 2018. The chief financial officer (CFO) of the team is Bucky Ryan and he has just reviewed the financial statements and made the following requests of Bobby:

1. Because the team's bank has asked to have a final copy of the financial statements by January 15, 2019, Bobby recorded the utilities expense for December 2018 based on an estimate because he normally receives the utility bill three weeks after the month the bill pertains to. Bucky wants this removed from the financial statements because it is not a "solid" number based on an invoice.

2. The team has bought a small building near the arena. The area has recently been selected by the city for some significant development and consequently the value of the property has risen 15% in the past year. Bobby has not shown this increase in value on the financial statements but Bucky would like him to do so.

3. The team recently signed Wayne Crosby to play next year. Upon signing, the team paid Wayne a "no strings attached" signing bonus. Bobby recorded this as an expense but Bucky would like him to record it as an asset since it relates to a future period.

Instructions

(a) What is the objective of financial reporting? Do Bucky's suggestions for what should be reported on the financial statements meet the objective of financial reporting? Explain.

(b) For each of the items above, determine if the proposed changes enhance or diminish the qualitative characteristics of the team's financial statements. Also determine whether each item is dealing with the accounting issue in a manner that is consistent with the definitions for elements of financial statements.

Discuss bases of measurement.

(LO 3)

P2–10A In 2011, when publicly traded companies in Canada adopted IFRS, real estate companies were given the choice of using historical cost or current value to account for their real estate portfolios. This was not an easy decision for real estate companies to make because there were advantages and disadvantages to each choice. In the end, while many companies chose to revalue their real estate portfolios to current value, others chose historical cost.

Instructions

(a) Identify the advantages and disadvantages of each of the two bases of measurement: historical cost and current value.

(b) Speculate as to why a company might choose to adopt the current value basis of accounting for its real estate portfolio. What impact do you think this will have on the elements of its financial statements?

(c) Speculate as to why a company might choose to adopt the historical cost basis of accounting for its real estate portfolio. What impact do you think this will have on the elements of its financial statements?

(d) Do you believe you could effectively compare the financial statements of two competing companies using different bases of measurement?

▶ PROBLEMS: SET B

Classify accounts.

(LO 1)

P2–1B You are provided with the following selected balance sheet accounts for **L'Oréal Group SA**, the world's largest beauty products company:

Accumulated amortization—patents and trademarks	Inventories
Accumulated depreciation—industrial machinery and equipment	Land
Bank overdraft	Long-term investments
Cash	Non-current borrowings and debts
Common (ordinary) shares	Patents and trademarks
Current borrowings and debts	Prepaid expenses
Income tax payable (current)	Trade accounts payable
Industrial machinery and equipment	Trade accounts receivable

Instructions

Identify the balance sheet (statement of financial position) category for classifying each account. For example, accumulated amortization—patents and trademarks should be classified as a contra asset in the intangible assets section of L'Oreal's balance sheet.

P2–2B The following items are from the assets section of Devon Limited's December 31, 2018, statement of financial *Prepare assets section.*
position:

(LO 1)

Accounts receivable	$ 13,345
Accumulated depreciation—buildings	27,595
Accumulated depreciation—equipment	146,550
Buildings	58,275
Cash	100,460
Equipment	287,400
Goodwill	39,590
Held for trading investments	52,520
Inventory	105,320
Land	207,290
Patent	20,225
Prepaid expenses	13,950

Instructions
(a) Identify the statement of financial position category in which each of the above assets should be classified.
(b) Prepare the assets section of the statement of financial position.

P2–3B The following items are from the liability and shareholders' equity sections of Devon Limited's December 31, *Prepare liabilities and*
2018, statement of financial position: *equity sections.*

(LO 1)

Accounts payable	$ 13,100
Common shares	115,400
Current portion of mortgage payable (long-term portion)	29,000
Mortgage payable	231,255
Retained earnings	321,295
Unearned revenue	14,180

Instructions
(a) Identify the statement of financial position category in which each of the above items should be classified.
(b) Prepare the liabilities and equity sections of the statement of financial position.
(c) If you completed P2–2B, compare the total assets in P2–2B with the total liabilities and shareholders' equity in P2–3B.
     Do these two amounts agree?

P2–4B These items are taken from financial statements of Beaulieu Limited for the year ended December 31, 2018: *Prepare financial*
statements; discuss
relationships.

(LO 1)

Cash	$ 11,170
Buildings	105,000
Accumulated depreciation—equipment	19,200
Accounts payable	9,550
Salaries payable	6,170
Common shares	45,000
Accumulated depreciation—buildings	12,000
Accounts receivable	7,500
Prepaid insurance	250
Equipment	32,000
Income tax expense	5,000
Long-term investments	20,000
Retained earnings, January 1	34,000
Dividends declared	3,500
Service revenue	193,100
Depreciation expense	5,400
Insurance expense	2,400
Salaries expense	145,600
Utilities expense	3,700
Interest expense	8,000
Interest revenue	500
Land	145,800
Mortgage payable	175,800

Additional information:

1. Beaulieu started the year with $25,000 of common shares and issued $20,000 more during the year.
2. $35,100 of the mortgage payable is due to be repaid within the next year.

Instructions

(a) Prepare an income statement, statement of changes in equity, and statement of financial position for the year.
(b) Explain how each financial statement is related to the others.

Calculate ratios and comment on liquidity, solvency, and profitability.

(LO 2)

P2–5B The financial statements of Fast Corporation are presented here:

FAST CORPORATION
Income Statement
Year Ended December 31, 2018

Sales		$706,000
Expenses		
Operating expenses	$564,000	
Interest expense	10,000	574,000
Income before income taxes		132,000
Income tax expense		35,400
Net income		$ 96,600

FAST CORPORATION
Statement of Financial Position
December 31, 2018

Assets

Current assets		
Cash	$ 44,100	
Held for trading investments	64,930	
Accounts receivable	126,200	
Supplies	18,620	$253,850
Property, plant, and equipment		465,300
Total assets		$719,150

Liabilities and Shareholders' Equity

Current liabilities		
Accounts payable	$134,200	
Income tax payable	10,350	
Current portion of mortgage payable	12,000	$156,550
Mortgage payable		132,000
Total liabilities		288,550
Shareholders' equity		
Common shares	$100,000	
Retained earnings	330,600	430,600
Total liabilities and shareholders' equity		$719,150

Additional information:

1. Income available to common shareholders was $96,600.
2. The weighted average number of common shares was 40,000.
3. The share price at December 31 was $30.

Instructions

(a) Calculate the following values and ratios for 2018. The results for 2017 are provided for comparative purposes.
　1. Working capital (2017: $78,000)
　2. Current ratio (2017: 1.4:1)
　3. Debt to total assets (2017: 51.5%)
　4. Basic earnings per share (2017: $1.35)
　5. Price-earnings ratio (2017: 10.8 times)

Calculate ratios and comment on liquidity, solvency, and profitability.

(LO 2)

(b) Using the information in part (a), discuss the changes in liquidity, solvency, and profitability between 2017 and 2018.

P2–6B Selected financial statement data for a recent year for Belliveau Corporation and Shields Corporation, two competitors, are as follows:

	Belliveau	Shields
Service revenue	$450,000	$890,000
Operating expenses	390,000	679,000
Interest expense	6,000	10,000
Income tax expense	10,000	65,000
Current assets	180,000	700,000
Non-current assets	600,000	800,000
Current liabilities	75,000	300,000
Non-current liabilities	190,000	200,000
Share price	$2.50	$6.00
Weighted average number of common shares	200,000	200,000

Instructions

(a) Calculate working capital and the current ratio for each company. Comment on their relative liquidity.
(b) Calculate the debt to total assets ratio for each company. Comment on their relative solvency.
(c) Calculate the net income, basic earnings per share, and price-earnings ratio for each company. Assume that the income you calculate equals the income available to common shareholders. Comment on the two companies' relative profitability.

P2–7B Selected financial data for a recent year for two discount retail chains, **Walmart Stores, Inc.** and **Costco Wholesale Corporation**, are presented here (in U.S. $ millions, except for share price):

Calculate ratios and comment on liquidity, solvency, and profitability.

(LO 2)

	Walmart	Costco
Current assets	$ 60,239	$17,299
Total assets	$199,581	$33,440
Current liabilities	$64,619	$16,540
Total liabilities	$115,970	$22,597
Income available to common shareholders	$14,694	$2,377
Share price	$65.39	$133.58
Weighted average number of common shares	3,207	439

Instructions

(a) For each company, calculate the following values and ratios. Where available, industry averages have been included in parentheses.
   1. Working capital (n/a)
   2. Current ratio (1.2:1)
   3. Debt to total assets (74%)
   4. Basic earnings per share (n/a)
   5. Price-earnings ratio (26.4 times)
(b) Compare the liquidity, solvency, and profitability of the two companies and their industry.

P2–8B Selected ratios for Giasson Corporation are as follows:

Comment on liquidity, solvency, and profitability.

(LO 2)

	2018	2017	2016
Working capital	$159,000	$176,000	$168,000
Current ratio	1.5:1	1.7:1	2.0:1
Debt to total assets	40.5%	42.2%	36.1%
Basic earnings per share	$0.92	$1.33	$1.15
Price-earnings ratio	7.8 times	8.2 times	8.6 times

Instructions

(a) Identify if the change in each value or ratio is an improvement or deterioration between (1) 2016 and 2017, and (2) 2017 and 2018.
(b) Briefly discuss the changes in Giasson's liquidity, solvency, and profitability over the three-year period.

P2–9B Brenda Chan is the new accountant for a small private company called Ace Construction Limited. She has recently prepared the year-end financial statements for the company. Brenda's boss, Virginia Schwirtz, who is the chief executive officer (CEO), has asked her to make three changes to the financial statements as follows:

Discuss financial reporting objective, qualitative characteristics, and elements.

(LO 3)

1. Remove an expense and its related liability that Brenda recorded for damages expected to be paid from a lawsuit due to a poorly done construction job a few months ago. Virginia believes that, although it is highly likely that Ace will have to pay for these damages, because a final agreement about the exact amount of these damages will not be agreed to until next month, nothing relating to this issue should be recorded in the financial statements or disclosed in the notes to the financial statements.

2. Just prior to the end of the year, Ace signed a contract to build a new arena for the city for a fixed fee of $80 million. As long as the company can build the facility for less than this amount, the company will generate net income. Because the value of the contract is fixed and the city has always paid its bills on time, Virginia wants the revenue for this contract to be recorded in the current year because that was when the contract was signed.

3. The company has a chequing account that is allowed to go into an overdraft (negative) position. When the balance falls into an overdraft, the bank begins to charge interest on that amount as if it were a bank loan, which in essence it is. Since there is no due date on such a balance, Virginia would like the loan to be reported as a non-current liability.

Instructions

(a) What is the objective of financial reporting? Are Brenda's and Virginia's actions consistent with these objectives? Explain.

(b) For each of the items covered above, determine if the proposed changes enhance or diminish the qualitative characteristics of the company's financial statements and whether the company is dealing with these items in a manner that is consistent with the definitions for elements of financial statements.

Identify bases of measurement.

(LO 3)

P2–10B The following are hypothetical situations that require the choice of one of the two bases of measurement: historical cost or current value.

1. You purchase your textbooks at the university bookstore to use during the term, but plan on selling them at the end of the term.
2. You purchase a new iPad and plan on never parting with it, at least not until a new model comes out.
3. You purchase software for your computer under a special deal that allows you to upgrade it whenever a new version is released.
4. You purchase a used car.
5. You purchase land, which you eventually hope to build a home on.

Instructions

(a) Identify the advantages and disadvantages of each of the two bases of measurement: historical cost and current value.

(b) For each of the above situations, identify which basis of measurement would be the most appropriate to choose, and explain why.

EXPAND YOUR CRITICAL THINKING

CT2–1 Financial Reporting Case

The financial statements of **The North West Company Inc.** are presented in Appendix A at the end of this book.

Instructions

(a) What were the balances of North West's total current assets and total assets at the end of 2016 and 2015?

(b) In what order are North West's current assets listed? Non-current assets?

(c) What were the balances of North West's total current liabilities and total liabilities at the end of 2016 and 2015?

(d) In what order are its current liabilities listed? Non-current liabilities?

CT2–2 Financial Analysis Case

The financial statements of **The North West Company Inc.** are presented in Appendix A followed by the financial statements for **Sobeys Inc.** in Appendix B.

Instructions

(a) For each company, calculate or find the following ratios and values for the most recent fiscal year. Industry averages, where available, are shown in parentheses.
   1. Working capital (n/a)
   2. Current ratio (1.3:1)
   3. Debt to total assets (60.6%)

(b) Based on your findings for part (a), discuss the relative liquidity and solvency of the two companies and their industry.

CT2–3 Financial Reporting Case

McCain Foods Limited is a large multinational private company generating in excess of $7 billion in sales. It produces both frozen and non-frozen food products and makes one third of the frozen French fries produced worldwide. It has manufacturing operations on six continents, sales operations in over 160 countries, and employs more than 17,000 people.

Most private companies choose to use ASPE. However, some private companies like McCain have adopted IFRS. Because the company is so large, it treats itself for reporting purposes like a public company.

Instructions

(a) McCain has numerous subsidiaries located throughout the globe. How would this type of multinational structure motivate McCain to choose IFRS?

(b) Why would users of McCain's financial statements want them prepared using IFRS? Try to relate the users' needs to the four qualitative characteristics of accounting information: relevance, faithful representation, comparability, and understandability.

(c) It is often assumed that only large private companies would choose to adopt IFRS and small companies would avoid IFRS. Why do you think that is? Can you think of reasons why a small private company would want to adopt IFRS?

CT2–4 Financial Analysis Case

This case can be assigned as a group activity. Additional instructions and material for this activity can be found on the Instructor Resource site and in WileyPLUS.

Kenmare Architects Ltd. (KAL) was incorporated and began operations on January 1, 2017. Sheila Kenmare, the company's only employee, consults with various clients and uses expensive equipment to complete her work. When the company was formed, Sheila bought 10,000 common shares but at the beginning of 2018, another 1,000 common shares were sold to Sheila's mother.

In addition to selling shares, KAL received financing from Sheila's Uncle Harry in the form of a loan that was taken out on January 1, 2017. Her uncle required the company to pay only the interest on the loan and no principal in 2017, which KAL did. However, he wanted both interest and a portion of the principal to be paid during 2018. These payments were made evenly throughout 2018. Harry was surprised when Sheila paid down more of the loan balance in 2018 than he asked her to.

The following shows the financial statements of the company for the past two years:

KENMARE ARCHITECTS LTD.
Income Statement
Year Ended December 31

	2018	2017
Service revenue	$120,000	$100,000
Salaries expense	74,000	59,000
Rent and other office expenses	20,000	20,000
Depreciation expense	12,000	12,000
Interest expense	2,700	3,600
Income before income tax	11,300	5,400
Income tax	3,390	1,890
Net income	$ 7,910	$ 3,510

KENMARE ARCHITECTS LTD.
Statement of Financial Position
December 31

	2018	2017
Cash	$ 9,000	$ 22,000
Accounts receivable	37,000	9,000
	46,000	31,000
Equipment	84,000	84,000
Accumulated depreciation	(24,000)	(12,000)
	60,000	72,000
	$106,000	$103,000
Accounts payable	$ 29,580	$ 14,490
Current portion of loan payable	4,000	8,000
	33,580	22,490
Loan payable	26,000	52,000
	59,580	74,490
Common shares	35,000	25,000
Retained earnings	11,420	3,510
	46,420	28,510
	$106,000	$103,000

Instructions

(a) When the company was formed, how much did Sheila pay for her shares? How much did her mother pay for her shares?

(b) At the end of 2017, what portion of the loan did Uncle Harry want paid off in 2018? How much of the loan was actually paid off in 2018? What was the total amount of cash received by Harry in 2017 and 2018?

(c) Calculate the current ratio for each year. Has the company's liquidity improved or deteriorated?

(d) Calculate the debt to total assets ratio for each year. Did the company's solvency improve or deteriorate? What effect did the change in this ratio have on the income statement?

(e) Calculate the basic earnings per share of the company for each year. Why do you think that basic EPS changed in 2018?

(f) Assume that the price Sheila paid for her shares was the share price throughout 2017. Using that price, calculate the price-earnings ratio for that year. Assume that the price Sheila's mother paid for her shares was the share price throughout 2018. Using that price, calculate the price-earnings ratio for 2018. Why do you think the P-E ratio changed? Do you think that the share price change was justified?

(g) What was the major reason for the company to sell shares in 2018?

CT2–5 Ethics Case

Kathy Onishi, the controller at Redondo Corporation, a private corporation, discussed with Redondo's vice-president of finance the possibility of switching from ASPE to IFRS. She said it would result in a better comparison of the company's financial condition and net income with its competitors. Furthermore, some bankers preferred to see financial statements prepared under IFRS. When the vice-president determined that switching would decrease reported net income for the year, he strongly discouraged Kathy from implementing IFRS.

Instructions

(a) Who are the stakeholders in this situation?

(b) What, if any, are the ethical considerations in this situation?

(c) What could Kathy gain by adopting IFRS? Who might be affected by a decision not to adopt it?

CT2–6 Serial Case

(*Note*: This serial case was started in Chapter 1 and will continue in each chapter.)

After graduating from university in May 2017 and investigating the opportunities available to her, Emily becomes a shareholder of Anthony Business Company and assumes the position of administrator. She begins familiarizing herself with the business operation and all of the information that is available to help her run the business day to day.

While at a computer trade show, Emily is introduced to Michael Richards, operations manager of Software Solutions Inc., a publicly traded software development company. After much discussion, Michael asks if ABC would consider being one of Software Solutions' customer service support suppliers. He offers to provide Emily with Software Solutions' financial information to assist with her analysis of this offer. He anticipates that ABC will need to provide Software Solutions' customers with approximately 500 hours of support service each month. He suggests ABC provide a monthly invoice to Software Solutions, which will be paid approximately 30 days from the date the invoice is received in its Toronto head office.

Emily is excited about this offer. However, she is concerned that taking on this contractual commitment will be too much for ABC to handle given the other service contracts that have just recently been negotiated.

Instructions

Emily has come to you for advice and asks the following questions.

(a) Michael Richards has offered to provide me with Software Solutions' financial information. Can you please remind me about what financial statements I

should request and explain what type of information each one provides?

(b) How do I know that the information in the financial statements is verifiable and prepared on a timely basis?

(c) I would like to be sure that Software Solutions will be able to pay ABC's invoices. How can I determine if Software Solutions is able to satisfy its current liabilities? Are there any ratios and/or financial information I should look at to obtain that information?

(d) How can I assess if Software Solutions is profitable? Are there any ratios and/or financial information I should look at to get that information?

(e) How can I determine the extent of Software Solutions' total liabilities? I want to find out if Software Solutions is able to pay off both its liabilities and the related interest. Are there any ratios and/or financial information I should look at to get that information?

(f) If ABC were to sign a contract committing to provide 500 hours of service per month, what other factors should be considered before accepting the contract?

▶ANSWERS TO CHAPTER PRACTICE QUESTIONS

DO IT! 2-1a
Statement of Financial Position Classifications

CL	Accounts payable		CA	Inventory
CA	Accounts receivable		NCA	Land
NCA	Accumulated depreciation—buildings		NCL	Mortgage payable (due in 10 years)
CL	Bank indebtedness		CA	Notes receivable (due in 3 months)
CL	Bank loan payable (due in 6 months)		CA	Prepaid insurance
NCA	Buildings		SE	Retained earnings
CA	Cash		CL	Salaries payable
SE	Common shares		CL	Sales taxes payable
NCA	Goodwill		CA	Supplies
CA	Held for trading investments		CL	Unearned revenue
CL	Income tax payable		NCA	Vehicles
CL	Interest payable			

DO IT! 2-1b
Statement Amounts

(a) Current assets = $10,000 (cash) + $15,000 (accounts receivable) + $1,000 (supplies) + $78,500 (inventory) = $104,500

Non-current assets = $50,000 (land) + $200,000 (buildings) – $40,000 (accumulated depreciation) + $147,000 (equipment) – $58,000 (accumulated depreciation) = $299,000

Current liabilities = $24,000 (accounts payable) + $8,000 (salaries payable) + $5,000 (income tax payable) + $500 (interest payable) + $2,000 (unearned revenue) + $5,000 (current portion of bank loan payable) + $7,500 (current portion of mortgage payable) = $52,000

Non-current liabilities = $75,000 (bank loan payable $80,000 – $5,000) + $142,500 (mortgage payable $150,000 – $7,500) = $217,500

Shareholders' equity = $60,000 (common shares) + $74,000 (retained earnings) = $134,000

(b) $104,500 (current assets) + $299,000 (non-current assets) = $52,000 (current liabilities) + $217,500 (non-current liabilities) + $134,000 (shareholders' equity)

$403,500 = $403,500

DO IT! 2-2
Ratio Analysis

(a)

		2018	2017	Comparison
1.	Current ratio	$114,000 ÷ $60,000 = 1.9:1	$75,600 ÷ $42,000 = 1.8:1	Improved
2.	Debt to total assets ratio	$528,000 ÷ $1,100,000 = 48.0%	$423,000 ÷ $940,000 = 45.0%	Deteriorated
3.	Basic earnings per share	$240,000 ÷ 80,000 = $3.00	$156,000 ÷ 60,000 = $2.60	Improved
4.	Price-earnings ratio	$24.00 ÷ $3.00 = 8.0 times	$18.20 ÷ $2.60 = 7.0 times	Improved

(b) 1. **Liquidity:** The current ratio increased from 1.8:1 in 2017 to 1.9:1 in 2018. This would be viewed as an improvement, depending on how the composition of its current assets (such as receivables and inventories) changed.

Solvency: The debt to total assets ratio increased from 45% in 2017 to 48% in 2018. This would be viewed as a deterioration because the company has a higher debt, as a percentage of its assets, to repay in the future.

Profitability: Both the basic earnings per share and price-earnings ratios increased between 2017 and 2018. Both would be viewed as an improvement. Investors are viewing Drummond's potential to generate future income favourably, as indicated by the price-earnings ratio.

2. Drummond's shares have become more expensive for potential investors relative to the company's earnings. This is evidenced by the increase in the price-earnings ratio.

(a) 1 (b) 7 (c) 4 (d) 2 (e) 5 (f) 10 (g) 8 (h) 6 (i) 9 (j) 3

DO IT! 2-3
Conceptual
Framework

▶ SOLUTION TO PRACTICE USING THE DECISION TOOLKIT

(a) Liquidity
Current ratio (in millions)

	Canadian Tire	Industry
2015	$8,692.3 ÷ $3,883.8 = 2.2:1	2.1:1
2014	$8,510.2 ÷ $4,578.8 = 1.9:1	2.2:1

Based on the current ratio, Canadian Tire's liquidity appears strong because its current ratio has improved over the previous year and also exceeds that of the industry for the most recent year.

(b) Solvency
Debt to total assets (in millions)

	Canadian Tire	Industry
2015	$9,198.1 ÷ $14,987.8 = 61.4%	39.0%
2014	$8,922.4 ÷ $14,553.2 = 61.3%	48.2%

Canadian Tire's solvency remained almost unchanged in 2015. However, its reliance on debt financing is higher (worse) than that of the industry in both years. In contrast to what we observed with Canadian Tire's liquidity, which was above the industry average, its solvency is below average.

(c) Profitability
Basic earnings per share (in millions)

	Canadian Tire	Industry
2015	$735.9 ÷ 76.2 = $9.66	n/a
2014	$639.3 ÷ 79.0 = $8.09	n/a

Price-earnings ratio

	Canadian Tire	Industry
2015	$199.36 ÷ $9.66 = 20.6 times	18.7 times
2014	$223.22 ÷ $8.09 = 27.6 times	19.7 times

Canadian Tire's profitability improved in 2015 because its basic earnings per share rose. However, the share price fell and this is why the price-earnings ratio declined. One reason for the decline in this ratio is likely investor concerns about Canadian Tire's ability to continue to improve its profitability in the future. While both Canadian Tire's and the industry's price-earnings ratios declined in 2015, Canadian Tire's price-earnings ratio was still higher than the industry average.

▶ SOLUTION TO PRACTICE COMPREHENSIVE DO IT!

(a)

PALOMA CORPORATION Income Statement Year Ended January 31, 2018		
Service revenue		$18,300,000
Expenses		
Operating expenses	$17,708,000	
Interest expense	80,000	
Total expenses		17,788,000
Income before income tax		512,000
Income tax expense		102,000
Net income		$ 410,000

PALOMA CORPORATION
Statement of Changes in Equity
Year Ended January 31, 2018

	Common Shares	Retained Earnings	Total Equity
Balance, February 1, 2017	$3,500,000	$961,000	$4,461,000
Net income		410,000	410,000
Dividends declared		(100,000)	(100,000)
Balance, January 31, 2018	$3,500,000	$1,271,000	$4,771,000

PALOMA CORPORATION
Statement of Financial Position
January 31, 2018

Assets

Current assets			
Cash		$ 118,000	
Accounts receivable		3,280,000	
Supplies		373,000	
Prepaid expenses		118,000	
Total current assets			$3,889,000
Long-term investments			200,000
Property, plant, and equipment			
Land		$ 526,000	
Buildings	$2,800,000		
Less: Accumulated depreciation	(390,000)	2,410,000	
Equipment	$625,000		
Less: Accumulated depreciation	(122,000)	503,000	3,439,000
Goodwill			206,000
Total assets			$7,734,000

Liabilities and Shareholders' Equity

Liabilities			
Current liabilities			
Accounts payable		$1,760,000	
Unearned revenue		135,000	
Current portion of mortgage payable		267,000	
Total current liabilities			$2,162,000
Non-current liabilities			
Mortgage payable ($1,068,000 − $267,000)			801,000
Total liabilities			2,963,000
Shareholders' equity			
Common shares		$3,500,000	
Retained earnings		1,271,000	4,771,000
Total liabilities and shareholders' equity			$7,734,000

(b) 1. Paloma's working capital was $1,727,000 ($3,889,000 − $2,162,000) and its current ratio was 1.8:1 ($3,889,000 ÷ $2,162,000), meaning that it had $1.80 in current assets for every $1 in current liabilities.

2. Paloma's debt to total assets ratio was 38.3% ($2,963,000 ÷ $7,734,000), meaning that just under 40% of the company's assets were financed using debt, while just over 60% were financed using shareholders' equity.

▶ **PRACTICE OBJECTIVE-FORMAT QUESTIONS**

1. (a) CL   (d) CL   (f) SE
    (b) NCA   (e) CA   (g) CL
    (c) CA

2. (b), (e), and (f) are correct

Feedback
(a) Is incorrect because goodwill is not amortized.
(c) Is incorrect because only merchandise held for resale is classified as inventory. Office supplies and cleaning supplies will be used in the business, rather than being sold, so these items are presented as "supplies" rather than "inventory."
(d) Is incorrect because long-term assets, such as property, plant, and equipment, are usually presented in order of permanence, with the most permanent (land) being presented first.
(g) Is incorrect because the sentence describes accounts receivable, rather than unearned revenue. Unearned revenue represents cash received from customers in advance of their receiving goods or services.

3. (a) 6   (d) 2   (f) 4
    (b) 3   (e) 5   (g) 1
    (c) 7

4. (a), (c), (d), and (f) are correct

Feedback
(a) Correct. Current liabilities = Accounts payable + Salaries payable + Unearned revenue.
(b) Incorrect. Does not include accumulated depreciation. The correct amount is $88,000.
(c) Correct. Shareholders' equity = Common shares + Retained earnings.
(d) Correct. Total assets = Cash + Held for trading investments + Accounts receivable + Inventory + Prepaid rent + Supplies + Equipment – Accumulated depreciation + Intangible assets.
(e) Incorrect. Does not include held for trading investments. The correct amount is $139,700.
(f) Correct. Total liabilities = Accounts payable + Salaries payable + Unearned revenue + Long-term notes payable.
(g) Incorrect. Does not include unearned revenue. The correct amount is $227,700.

5. (b), (c), and (f) are correct

Feedback
(a) Incorrect. It is the opposite because a high debt to total assets ratio would mean the company has a high debt load relative to its total assets.
(d) Incorrect. It is the earnings per share ratio that must be presented in the financial statements of publicly traded companies.
(e) Incorrect. This would be an intracompany comparison.
(g) Incorrect. It would mean that current liabilities exceed current assets.

6. (b), (d), and (g) are correct

Feedback
(a) Incorrect. It is the opposite: the company has $0.90 in current assets for every $1 in current liabilities.
(b) Correct. It has a lower debt to total assets ratio.
(c) Incorrect. The debt to total assets ratio is 56.8%, which indicates that almost 60% of Campbell's assets have been financed using debt.
(d) Correct. A higher current ratio is considered superior.
(e) Incorrect. This is the basic earnings per share, but does not indicate that any dividends will be distributed. Companies seldom distribute all of their net income as dividends.
(f) Incorrect. Kiedyk's price-earnings ratio is 7.0 times ($6.09 ÷ $0.87), whereas Campbell's price-earnings ratio is 9.0 times ($15.84 ÷ $1.76), making Campbell's shares more expensive relative to net income.
(g) Correct. A current ratio greater than 1 indicates that current assets exceed current liabilities, while a current ratio less than 1 indicates the opposite.

7. (a) A   (d) A   (f) B
    (b) A   (e) B   (g) A
    (c) B

8. (a) No   (d) Yes   (f) Yes
    (b) Yes   (e) Yes   (g) No
    (c) No

9. (a) E   (d) N   (f) F
    (b) F   (e) E   (g) E
    (c) E

10. (a), (b), (d), (f), and (g) are correct

Feedback
(c) Is incorrect because the nature of the item must also be considered. It is possible for small dollar items to still be considered material.
(e) Is incorrect because understandability is an enhancing qualitative characteristic. The missing characteristic of faithful representation is free from error.

▶ ENDNOTES

[1] Doug Alexander, "Canadian Tire REIT Raises C$263.5 Million in Toronto IPO," Bloomberg, October 10, 2013; CT Real Estate Investment Trust 2015 annual report; CT Real Estate Investment Trust website, www.ctreit.com.

[2] Benjamin Graham, *The Intelligent Investor*, New York: Harper Business, 2003, p. 367; Alex Cuadros, Bloomberg News, "Warren Buffett Is Once Again the World's Third-Richest Person," *Financial Post*, March 22, 2013; Matthew J. Belvedere, "Buffett's Berkshire Stock: 'Bull' Gabelli vs. 'Bear' Kass," CNBC.com, May 3, 2013.

[3] "Poseidon Concepts Corp., Poseidon Concepts Ltd., Poseidon Concepts Limited Partnership and Poseidon Concepts Inc.: CCAA Filing," PricewaterhouseCoopers website, www.pwc.com/ca/en/car/poseidon/index.jhtml, updated July 4, 2013; Tim Kiladze, "Poseidon Concepts Dropped from TSX," *The Globe and Mail*, April 18, 2013; Barry Critchley, "Poseidon Concepts Dives to 27¢ from $16.03 in Less Than Five Months," *Financial Post*, February 14, 2013.

3

The Accounting Information System

CHAPTER PREVIEW

In Chapters 1 and 2, you were introduced to financial statements. The financial statements are the culmination of a process known as the accounting cycle. The accounting cycle is a systematized process to create accounting information and consists of a number of distinct steps. The preparation of financial statements is the final step in the accounting cycle, which begins with the analyzing, recording, and posting of transactions, followed by the preparation of a trial balance. These first four steps are illustrated in this chapter and the remaining steps, including the preparation of financial statements, will be discussed in Chapter 4.

CHAPTER OUTLINE

LEARNING OBJECTIVES	READ	PRACTICE
1 Analyze the effect of transactions on the accounting equation.	• Analyzing transactions • Analyzing transactions illustrated	**DO IT!** 3-1a Basic and equation analysis 3-1b Equation analysis
2 Explain how accounts, debits, and credits are used to record transactions.	• T accounts • Normal balances and debit and credit effects • Financial statement relationships	**DO IT!** 3-2 Accounts and debits and credits
3 Journalize transactions in the general journal.	• General journal	**DO IT!** 3-3 Debit–credit analysis and journal entries
4 Post transactions to the general ledger.	• Chart of accounts • Posting • The recording process illustrated	**DO IT!** 3-4a Posting 3-4b Posting
5 Prepare a trial balance.	• Preparing a trial balance • Limitations of a trial balance • Review of the accounting cycle—Steps 1–4	**DO IT!** 3-5 Trial balance

FEATURE STORY

For generations, grandmothers in Grant Hooker's family made a pastry of flattened whole-wheat dough stretched by hand to resemble the tail of a beaver as a special treat, called a BeaverTails pastry. In 1978, Mr. Hooker sold the family secret to the public for the first time at a music festival and agricultural fairs in the Ottawa Valley. The crowds loved it. Mr. Hooker trademarked the name "BeaverTails®" and built his own booth in Ottawa's Byward Market in 1980 to sell them full-time. However, sales weren't as swift as at the fairs.

Undaunted, Mr. Hooker secured permission to sell BeaverTails pastries on the Rideau Canal during Ottawa's Winterlude festival. Within three years, BeaverTails Canada Inc. had the contract to sell all the food on the Rideau Canal and employed 450 people. The business continued to grow; BeaverTails began franchising in 1990 and now includes an expanded menu served in more than 100 stores across Canada, with additional locations in the United States, Korea, Japan, and the UAE.

At first, keeping track of the money was straightforward for Mr. Hooker and didn't require a formal accounting system. It was merely a matter of staying on top of how much was owed to suppliers and staff, and in rent and utilities. Mr. Hooker, who has no formal business training, got along fine simply managing the chequebook.

But this changed with franchising. "We weren't just selling products to people for cash, putting the cash in the bank, and then writing cheques for what

Learning to Handle the Dough

we owed," says Mr. Hooker. "We were into receivables; people owed us money." The company also had liabilities—in the form of a bank loan.

Mr. Hooker hired a firm to set up an accounting information system for the business, an experience he describes as a "rude awakening" that cost him approximately $200,000. One of the accounting staff members was negligent, and the company's accounts weren't balanced properly.

"I realized how much improper accounting could cost me and how, if I didn't understand accounting, I'd have to trust somebody," Mr. Hooker says. He hired another accountant to rebuild the accounting system, working closely with him to learn how it worked.

The breakthrough point for him, he says, was in understanding that "cash is a debit." Assets (from the statement of financial position) and expenses (from the income statement) have normal debit balances. Liabilities and shareholders' equity (from the statement of financial position) and revenues (from the income statement) have normal credit balances. To increase the amount in an account, an entry has to be the same sign, he adds. In other words, only debits increase debit accounts and credits increase credit accounts.

Now that he understands the basics of the accounting system, Mr. Hooker monitors it very closely. He insists his accountant provide him with "TAMFS"—timely, accurate, monthly financial statements. "That is an absolute necessity any time a business grows to where the owner puts his trust in somebody else to handle the money," he says.[1]

Go to the *REVIEW AND PRACTICE* section at the end of the chapter for a targeted summary and practice questions with solutions.

Visit **WileyPLUS** for more practice opportunities.

Analyze the effect of transactions on the accounting equation.

| 1. Analyze transactions | 2. JOURNALIZE | 3. POST | 4. TRIAL BALANCE | 5. ADJUSTING ENTRIES | 6. ADJUSTED TRIAL BALANCE | 7. FINANCIAL STATEMENTS | 8. CLOSING ENTRIES | 9. POST-CLOSING TRIAL BALANCE |

*To help students see "The Big Picture" of the **accounting cycle**, we begin each learning objective in the accounting cycle chapters with a visual reminder of what stage of the accounting cycle they are about to enter.*

The system used to collect and process transaction data and communicate financial information to decision makers is known as the **accounting information system**. Accounting information systems can range from the basic to the complex. Factors that shape these systems include the type of business and its transactions, the size of the company, the amount of data, and the information that management and others need. For example, as indicated in the feature story, BeaverTails did not need a formal accounting system when it first began. However, as the business and the number and type of transactions grew, an organized accounting information system became essential.

Accounting information systems rely on a process referred to as the **accounting cycle**—a series of steps used to account for, and report, transactions. As you can see from the graphic above, the accounting cycle begins with the analysis of transactions and ends with the preparation of a post-closing trial balance. As mentioned in the Chapter Preview, we will explain the first four steps of the accounting cycle in this chapter and continue our discussion of the remaining steps in Chapter 4.

ANALYZING TRANSACTIONS

The first step in the accounting cycle is to analyze transactions. However, not all transactions that affect a company are recorded and reported. For example, suppose a new employee is hired. Should this transaction be recorded in the company's accounting records? The answer is "no" for accounting purposes. An *accounting* transaction will not occur in this particular situation until the new employee has started work and earned `his or her salary. In general, an **accounting transaction** occurs when an economic event results in a company's financial position (assets, liabilities, or shareholders' equity) changing in a measurable way. In the case of the new employee described above, no asset, liability, or equity item is affected simply by the act of hiring the employee, even if the employee signs an employment contract.

Illustration 3-1 provides examples of selected other transactions that should or should not be recorded.

▶Illustration 3-1
Transaction identification

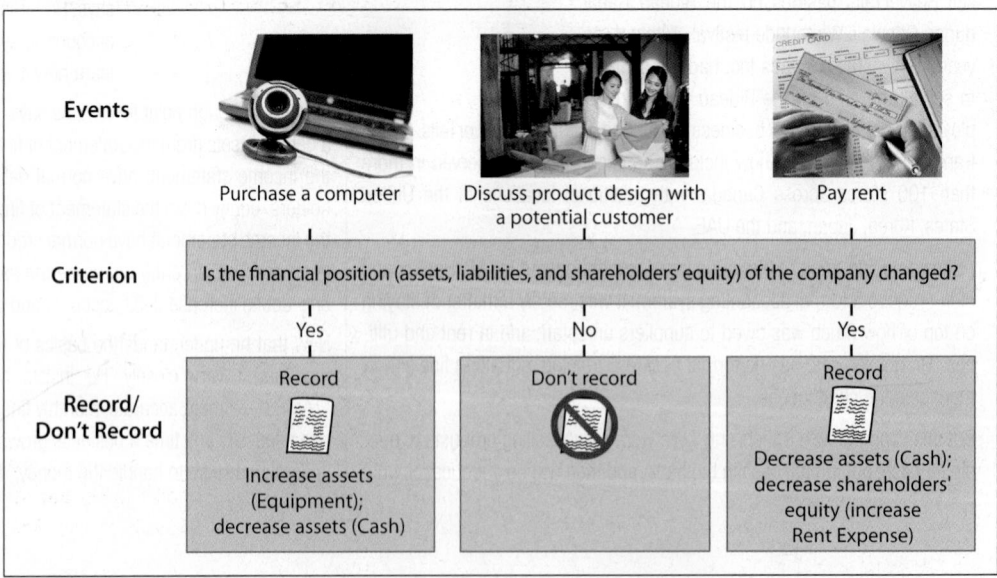

Photo credits for illustration 3-1 (from L-R): jcjgphotography/Shutterstock; Getty Images/Lane Oatey/Blue Jean Images; istockphoto.com/YinYang

Because transactions such as the purchase of a computer or the payment of rent are economic events that affect the company's financial position in measurable amounts, they must be recorded in the accounting records. While discussing a matter with a potential customer may affect a company's future financial performance if the customer becomes a real, and not just a potential, customer, it has no effect on the company's current financial situation. In addition, the act of discussing a matter with a customer (real or potential) by itself will not impact a company's financial position. Transactions such as these, although important to the company, are not recorded.

ACCOUNTING MATTERS

walik/iStockphoto

NHL Signing Bonuses

Does hiring a great hockey player add value to a National Hockey League (NHL) team? The owners, players, and fans would say so. However, the act of simply agreeing to sign a contract to play for a hockey team is not recorded as an accounting transaction because it does not change the team's assets, liabilities, or shareholders' equity. Despite the team's perceived value rising by the hiring of top talent, an accounting transaction does not occur until the player starts playing and earns his salary . . . and hopefully generates additional revenue for the team, as well.

On the other hand, signing bonuses to induce certain players to sign with the team can, in some cases, result in an accounting transaction. Part of the bonus may be paid up front or the bonus may be paid over a specified time period written into the player's contract, depending on certain limitations in a team's salary cap imposed by the NHL. If a player receives a portion of a signing bonus up front at the time of signing his contract, then the team's assets, liabilities, and equities would change and result in an accounting transaction.

In Chapter 1, you learned about the basic accounting equation:

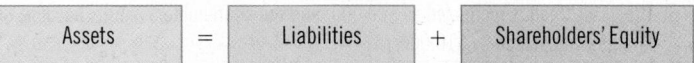

You will also recall that shareholders' equity is composed of common shares (which are one type of share capital) plus retained earnings. There are other possible items that can make up shareholders' equity, which we will discuss in later chapters. For now, we will focus only on these two items because they are common to all public companies: common shares and retained earnings. Further, retained earnings are equal to net income less any dividends declared. Net income, which is equal to revenues less expenses, increases retained earnings. (A net loss decreases retained earnings.) Dividends, when declared, are a distribution of retained earnings to shareholders and result in a decrease to retained earnings. We have expanded the basic accounting equation shown above to show the detailed components of shareholders' equity in Illustration 3-2.

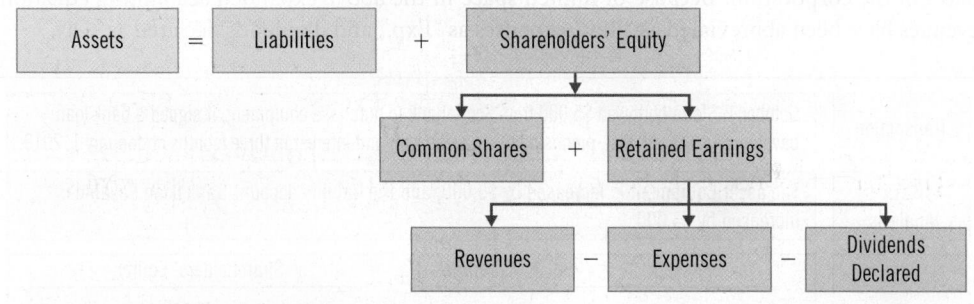

▶Illustration 3-2
Expanded accounting equation

By expanding the accounting equation, we have created a framework that can be used to record accounting transactions. You will recall that the components in the expanded accounting equation are known as the elements of financial statements, an important part of the conceptual framework introduced in Chapter 2.

Whether using the basic accounting equation or the expanded accounting equation, remember that the accounting equation must always balance. As a result, a recorded transaction will have, at minimum, a dual effect on the equation. For example, if an individual asset is increased, there must be either a corresponding:

- decrease in another asset, and/or
- increase in a specific liability, and/or
- increase in common shares or revenues, either of which would result in an increase in shareholders' equity.

Note that two or more items could be affected when analyzing the accounting equation. Assume that services of $200 have been provided, for which $50 has been received in cash and the remainder is owed on account. An asset (cash) would increase by $50, a different asset (accounts receivable) would increase by $150, and shareholders' equity (service revenue) would increase by $200. We call this type of thinking a **basic analysis** where the affected accounts and amounts are identified. This information is then inserted into the accounting equation in what we call an **equation analysis**.

ANALYZING TRANSACTIONS ILLUSTRATED

Chapter 1 presented the financial statements for Sierra Corporation, an advertising company, for its first month of operations, October 2018. We recommend you review these financial statements at this time. To illustrate the effects of economic events on the accounting equation, we will now examine some of the transactions that affected Sierra Corporation in its first month of operations and were ultimately reported on its financial statements in Chapter 1 in Illustrations 1-5, 1-6, 1-7, and 1-8. As shown below, we will use a basic analysis and equation analysis to analyze Sierra's transactions during the month of October.

▶ **Transaction (1)**
Investment of cash by shareholders

Transaction	October 1: Cash of $10,000 was invested in Sierra Corporation in exchange for 10,000 common shares.
Basic Analysis	The asset Cash is increased by $10,000, and the shareholders' equity account Common Shares is increased by $10,000.

	Assets	=	Liabilities	+	Shareholders' Equity			
							Retained Earnings	
Equation Analysis	Cash	=			Common Shares	+ Rev.	− Exp.	− Div.
(1)	+$10,000	=			+$10,000			

The above transaction results in an equivalent increase in assets and shareholders' equity, and the accounting equation remains in balance after this transaction.

Note that investments by shareholders are not recorded as revenue because they are not generated from the ordinary operating activities of the company. Rather, they are recorded as common shares of the corporation. Because of limited space in the above expanded accounting equation, revenues have been abbreviated as "Rev.", expenses as "Exp.", and dividends declared as "Div."

▶ **Transaction (2)**
Purchase of equipment and signing of bank loan

Transaction	October 1: Sierra borrowed $5,000 from Scotiabank to purchase equipment. It signed a bank loan payable, plus 6% interest, promising to repay the loan and interest in three months on January 1, 2019.
Basic Analysis	The asset Equipment is increased by $5,000, and the liability account Bank Loan Payable is increased by $5,000.

	Assets			=	Liabilities	+	Shareholders' Equity			
								Retained Earnings		
	Cash	+	Equipment	=	Bank Loan Payable	+	Common Shares	+ Rev.	− Exp.	− Div.
	$10,000						$10,000			
(2)			+$5,000	=	+$5,000					
	$10,000	+	$5,000	=	$5,000	+	$10,000			
		$15,000					$15,000			

Equation Analysis

This transaction results in an equal increase in assets and liabilities. Total assets are now $15,000 and the new liability of $5,000 plus shareholders' equity of $10,000 also total $15,000.

Interest is not recorded in the above example. That is because no interest is owed at October 1. Interest will accumulate over the next three months of the bank loan. We will learn when to record interest in situations such as this in Chapter 4.

▶Transaction (3)
Payment of rent

Transaction	October 2: Paid $900 for office rent for the month of October.
Basic Analysis	The expense Rent Expense is increased by $900 because the payment is only for the current month; the asset Cash is decreased by $900.

Equation Analysis

	Assets		=	Liabilities	+	Shareholders' Equity			
				Bank Loan		Common		Retained Earnings	
	Cash	+ Equipment	=	Payable	+	Shares	+ Rev.	− Exp.	− Div.
	$10,000	$5,000		$5,000		$10,000			
(3)	−900							−$900	
	$9,100	+ $5,000	=	$5,000	+	$10,000		− $900	

$14,100 $14,100

As there is not enough room to set up separate columns for each revenue and expense account in the expanded accounting equation shown above, individual revenues and expenses such as Rent Expense in this transaction are listed under the column headings Rev. and Exp. without specific account identification.

Note that, although the Rent Expense account increases, it is shown as a negative number in the equation because expenses decrease retained earnings, which in turn decrease shareholders' equity. Overall, assets (cash) decrease by $900 and shareholders' equity decreases by $900, keeping the equation in balance.

▶Transaction (4)
Purchase of insurance policy for cash

Transaction	October 5: Paid $600 for a one-year insurance policy effective October 1 that expires next year on September 30.
Basic Analysis	The asset Prepaid Insurance is increased by $600 because the payment extends to more than the current month; the asset Cash is decreased by $600.

Equation Analysis

	Assets			=	Liabilities	+	Shareholders' Equity			
					Bank Loan		Common		Retained Earnings	
	Cash	+ Pre. Ins.	+ Equipment	=	Payable	+	Shares	+ Rev.	− Exp.	− Div.
	$9,100		$5,000		$5,000		$10,000		$900	
(4)	−600	+$600								
	$8,500	+ $600	+ $5,000	=	$5,000	+	$10,000		− $900	

$14,100 $14,100

As shown in the expanded accounting equation above, the balance in total assets did not change; one asset account decreased by the same amount by which another increased.

Payments of expenses that will benefit more than one accounting period are initially recorded as assets known as prepaid expenses or prepayments. The asset account Prepaid Insurance (abbreviated as "Pre. Ins.") is increased by $600 because the payment is for more than the current month, which is the accounting period in our Sierra illustration. We will learn more about how to account for prepayments in the next chapter. In contrast, payments of expenses that benefit only the current accounting period, such as the rent expense paid in transaction 3, are recorded as expenses.

▶ Transaction (5)
Hiring of new employees

Transaction	October 8: Hired four employees to begin work on Monday, October 15. Each employee is to receive a weekly salary of $500 for a five-day workweek (Monday–Friday), payable every two weeks—first payment to be made on Friday, October 26.
Basic Analysis	An accounting transaction has not occurred. There is only an agreement that the employees will begin work on October 15.

▶ Transaction (6)
Purchase of supplies on account

An equation analysis is not required because the company's assets, liabilities, and shareholders' equity have not changed. (See transaction 10 for the first payment of salaries.)

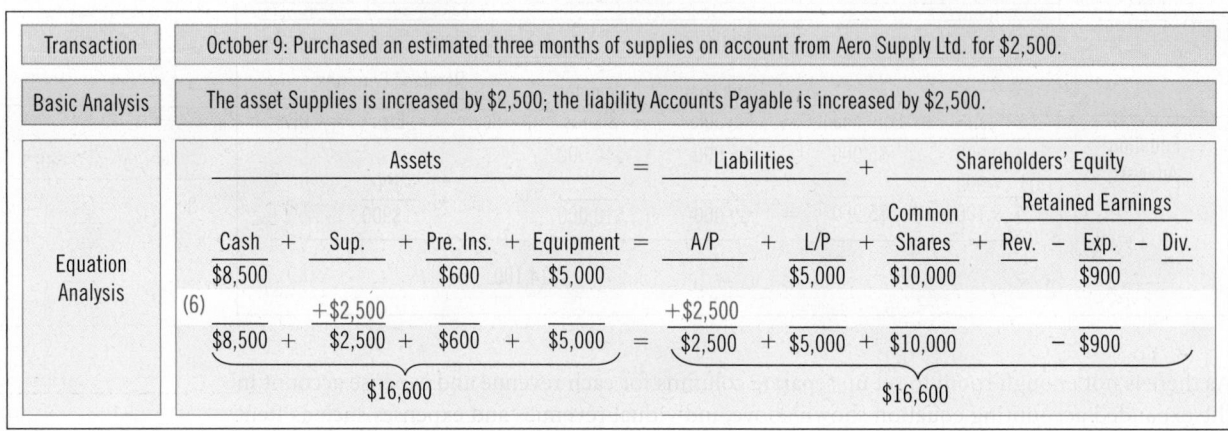

Transaction	October 9: Purchased an estimated three months of supplies on account from Aero Supply Ltd. for $2,500.
Basic Analysis	The asset Supplies is increased by $2,500; the liability Accounts Payable is increased by $2,500.

Equation Analysis

	Assets				=	Liabilities		+	Shareholders' Equity			
									Common	Retained Earnings		
	Cash +	Sup. +	Pre. Ins. +	Equipment =		A/P +	L/P +		Shares +	Rev. −	Exp. −	Div.
	$8,500		$600	$5,000			$5,000		$10,000		$900	
(6)		+$2,500				+$2,500						
	$8,500 +	$2,500 +	$600 +	$5,000	=	$2,500 +	$5,000 +		$10,000 +		− $900	
			$16,600						$16,600			

Purchasing goods or services "on account" or "on credit" means that the company receives goods or services that it will pay for at a later date. Assets are increased by this transaction because supplies (abbreviated as "Sup." in the equation above) represent a resource that will be used in the future in the process of providing services to customers. Instead of paying cash now, the company incurs a liability, an account payable, by promising to pay cash in the future. Note that Accounts Payable and Bank Loan Payable have been abbreviated as "A/P" and "L/P", respectively, in the equation above. **Unless you are told otherwise, you can assume in your assignments that goods or services purchased on account give rise to accounts payable (as opposed to another type of payable).**

▶ Transaction (7)
Provision of services on account

Transaction	October 15: A client, Copa Ltd., is billed $20,000 for advertising services.
Basic Analysis	The asset Accounts Receivable is increased by $20,000. The revenue account Service Revenue is increased by $20,000.

Equation Analysis

	Assets					=	Liabilities		+	Shareholders' Equity			
										Common	Retained Earnings		
	Cash +	A/R +	Sup. +	Pre. Ins. +	Equipment =		A/P +	L/P +		Shares +	Rev. −	Exp. −	Div.
	$8,500		$2,500	$600	$5,000		$2,500	$5,000		$10,000		$900	
(7)		+$20,000									+$20,000		
	$8,500 +	$20,000 +	$2,500 +	$600 +	$5,000	=	$2,500 +	$5,000 +		$10,000 +	$20,000 −	$900	
			$36,600							$36,600			

Companies often provide goods or services "on account" or "on credit" similar to purchasing goods or services "on account" or "on credit" as we saw in transaction 6. In this case, instead of receiving cash, the company receives a different type of asset, an account receivable (abbreviated as "A/R"). **Unless you are told otherwise, you can assume in your assignments that goods or services provided on account give rise to accounts receivable (as opposed to another type of receivable).**

You will recall that accounts receivable represent the right to receive payment at a future date. They are due from customers when a company provides the customer with the goods or services. Revenue is recorded when the services have been performed or goods delivered, even though cash has not been received. We will learn more about when to recognize revenue in Chapter 4. In the next transaction, transaction 8, we will see that revenue is not recorded when services have not been performed.

▶Transaction (8)
Receipt of cash in advance from client

Transaction	October 19: $1,200 was received in advance from Knox Ltd., a client, for advertising services that are not expected to be completed until November.
Basic Analysis	The asset Cash is increased by $1,200; the liability Unearned Revenue is increased by $1,200 because the services have not been provided yet.

Equation Analysis

	Assets					=	Liabilities			+	Shareholders' Equity				
												Retained Earnings			
	Cash +	A/R +	Sup. +	Pre. Ins. +	Equipment =		A/P +	L/P +	Unearned Revenue +		Common Shares +	Rev. −	Exp. −	Div.
	$8,500	$20,000	$2,500	$600	$5,000		$2,500	$5,000			$10,000	$20,000	$900	
(8)	+$1,200								+$1,200					
	$9,700 +	$20,000 +	$2,500 +	$600 +	$5,000 =		$2,500 +	$5,000 +	$1,200 +		$10,000 +	$20,000 −	$900	
			$37,800								$37,800			

In this transaction, even though Sierra received $1,200 cash, it should not record revenue until it has performed the work. Because cash was received before performing the services, Sierra has a liability or obligation to either perform the service or return the cash. We call this type of liability unearned revenue. Note that the placement of the word *unearned* in front of revenue indicates that this is a liability account rather than a revenue account. Although many liability accounts have the word *payable* in their title, not all do, and Unearned Revenue is a liability account even though the word *payable* is not used.

▶Transaction (9)
Partial payment of accounts payable

Transaction	October 22: Made a partial payment of $1,000 on the amount it owed for the supplies purchased from Aero Supply on October 9. (See transaction 6.)
Basic Analysis	The liability Accounts Payable is decreased by $1,000; the asset Cash is decreased by the same amount.

Equation Analysis

	Assets					=	Liabilities			+	Shareholders' Equity				
												Retained Earnings			
	Cash +	A/R +	Sup. +	Pre. Ins. +	Equipment =		A/P +	L/P +	Unearned Revenue +		Common Shares +	Rev. −	Exp. −	Div.
	$9,700	$20,000	$2,500	$600	$5,000		$2,500	$5,000	$1,200		$10,000	$20,000	$900	
(9)	−1,000						−1,000							
	$8,700 +	$20,000 +	$2,500 +	$600 +	$5,000 =		$1,500 +	$5,000 +	$1,200 +		$10,000 +	$20,000 −	$900	
			$36,800								$36,800			

Recall that the supplies and an account payable from this transaction were recorded earlier in transaction 6, when the supplies were purchased for $2,500 on October 9. Note the opening (beginning) balance in the Accounts Payable (A/P) account above of $2,500. Supplies should not be recorded again when the cash is paid. Rather, Accounts Payable is decreased by $1,000 and Cash is decreased by the same amount. Sierra still owes Aero Supply a remaining balance of $1,500 after this partial payment.

Transaction	October 26: Biweekly salaries are paid to four employees for the period October 15–26. (See transaction 5.)
Basic Analysis	The expense Salaries Expense is increased by $4,000; the asset Cash is decreased by $4,000.

Equation Analysis

	Assets				=	Liabilities			+	Shareholders' Equity			
								Unearned		Common	Retained Earnings		
	Cash +	A/R +	Sup. +	Pre. Ins. +	Equipment =	A/P +	L/P +	Revenue +		Shares +	Rev. −	Exp. −	Div.
	$8,700	$20,000	$2,500	$600	$5,000	$1,500	$5,000	$1,200		$10,000	$20,000	$ 900	
(10)	−4,000											−4,000	
	$4,700 +	$20,000 +	$2,500 +	$600 +	$5,000 =	$1,500 +	$5,000 +	$1,200 +		$10,000 +	$20,000 −	$4,900	
			$32,800								$32,800		

▶**Transaction (10)**
Payment of salaries

Recall that the employees hired in transaction 5 began work on Monday, October 15. Since then, the four employees have worked two weeks, earning $4,000 in salaries (4 employees × $500/week × 2 weeks). While the act of hiring the employees in transaction 5 did not result in an accounting transaction, the payment of the employees' salary is a transaction because assets and expenses are affected.

Transaction	October 29: Declared and paid $500 of dividends to shareholders.
Basic Analysis	Dividends Declared is increased by $500; the asset Cash is decreased by $500.

Equation Analysis

	Assets				=	Liabilities			+	Shareholders' Equity			
								Unearned		Common	Retained Earnings		
	Cash +	A/R +	Sup. +	Pre. Ins. +	Equipment =	A/P +	L/P +	Revenue +		Shares +	Rev. −	Exp. −	Div.
	$4,700	$20,000	$2,500	$600	$5,000	$1,500	$5,000	$1,200		$10,000	$20,000	$4,900	
(11)	−500												−$500
	$4,200 +	$20,000 +	$2,500 +	$600 +	$5,000 =	$1,500 +	$5,000 +	$1,200 +		$10,000 +	$20,000 −	$4,900 −	$500
			$32,300								$32,300		

▶**Transaction (11)**
Declaration and payment of dividends

▶**Transaction (12)**
Partial collection of accounts receivable

Recall that dividends, when declared, are a distribution of retained earnings to a company's shareholders. It is important to note that dividends are *not* an expense and are *not* included in the company's calculation of net income. In the above example, the Dividends Declared account is increased by $500. Similar to our use of minus signs in front of expense accounts, dividends are shown as a negative number, because this account reduces both retained earnings and shareholders' equity.

Transaction	October 30: Sierra collected $9,000 of the amount owing from Copa on its account. (See transaction 7.)
Basic Analysis	The asset Cash is increased by $9,000. The asset Accounts Receivable is decreased by $9,000.

Equation Analysis

	Assets				=	Liabilities			+	Shareholders' Equity			
								Unearned		Common	Retained Earnings		
	Cash +	A/R +	Sup. +	Pre. Ins. +	Equipment =	A/P +	L/P +	Revenue +		Shares +	Rev. −	Exp. −	Div.
	$4,200	$20,000	$2,500	$600	$5,000	$1,500	$5,000	$1,200		$10,000	$20,000	$4,900	$500
(12)	+9,000	−9,000											
	$13,200 +	$11,000 +	$2,500 +	$600 +	$5,000 =	$1,500 +	$5,000 +	$1,200 +		$10,000 +	$20,000 −	$4,900 −	$500
			$32,300								$32,300		

Recall that an account receivable and the revenue from this transaction were recorded earlier in transaction 7, when the service was provided and billed on October 15. Revenue should **not** be recorded again when the cash is collected. Rather, Cash is increased by $9,000 and Accounts Receivable is decreased by $9,000, bringing the balance in the Accounts Receivable account to $11,000—the amount still owing from Copa.

▶ Transaction (13)
Payment of income tax

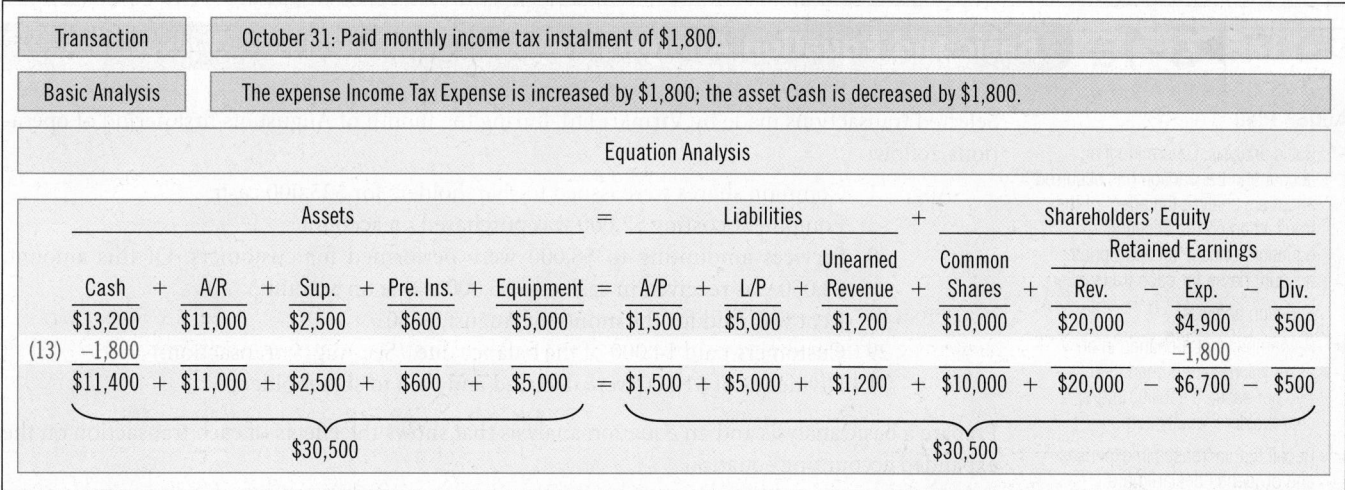

Transaction	October 31: Paid monthly income tax instalment of $1,800.
Basic Analysis	The expense Income Tax Expense is increased by $1,800; the asset Cash is decreased by $1,800.

Equation Analysis

	Assets					=	Liabilities			+	Shareholders' Equity				
									Unearned		Common		Retained Earnings		
	Cash	+ A/R	+ Sup.	+ Pre. Ins.	+ Equipment	= A/P	+ L/P	+ Revenue	+	Shares	+	Rev.	− Exp.	− Div.
	$13,200	$11,000	$2,500	$600	$5,000	$1,500	$5,000	$1,200		$10,000		$20,000	$4,900	$500
(13)	−1,800												−1,800	
	$11,400 +	$11,000 +	$2,500 +	$600 +	$5,000	= $1,500 +	$5,000 +	$1,200	+	$10,000	+	$20,000 −	$6,700 −	$500

$30,500 $30,500

Most companies pay monthly income tax instalments based on their prior year's income tax payable. They subsequently calculate the exact amount owed at year end when they prepare their income tax return, and submit any additional amount owing to the Canada Revenue Agency (CRA) at that time or receive a refund for any overpayment. Although this is the first year of operations for Sierra and it does not have a prior year income tax amount, we have assumed for illustration purposes that Sierra will pay an estimated amount of income tax monthly.

Summary of Transactions

The transactions of Sierra Corporation are summarized in Illustration 3-3 to show their cumulative effect on the accounting equation. The transaction numbers, the specific effects of each transaction, and the final balances are indicated. Remember that transaction 5—the hiring of employees—did not result in an accounting transaction, so nothing is recorded for that event.

▶ Illustration 3-3
Equation analysis

	Assets					=	Liabilities			+	Shareholders' Equity			
									Unearned		Common		Retained Earnings	
	Cash	+ A/R	+ Sup.	+ Pre. Ins.	+ Equipment	= A/P	+ L/P	+ Revenue	+	Shares	+	Rev.	− Exp.	− Div.
(1)	+$10,000									+$10,000				
(2)					+$5,000		+$5,000							
(3)	−900												−$900	
(4)	−600			+$600										
(6)			+$2,500			+$2,500								
(7)		+$20,000										+$20,000		
(8)	+1,200							+$1,200						
(9)	−1,000					−1,000								
(10)	−4,000												−4,000	
(11)	−500													−$500
(12)	+9,000	−9,000												
(13)	−1,800												−1,800	
	$11,400 +	$11,000 +	$2,500 +	$600 +	$5,000	= $1,500 +	$5,000 +	$1,200 +		$10,000 +		$20,000 −	$6,700 −	$500

$30,500 $30,500

The illustration demonstrates two important points:

1. Each transaction must be analyzed for its effect on the three primary components of the accounting equation (assets, liabilities, and shareholders' equity), as well as the specific effects within shareholders' equity items (revenues, expenses, and dividends).
2. The two sides of the equation must always be equal (assets = liabilities + shareholders' equity).

DO IT! ▶3-1a Basic and Equation Analysis

Action Plan

✔ Basic analysis: Determine if an accounting transaction has occurred and if so, analyze the effect of the transaction on the accounting equation. Choose an appropriate account name for each transaction.

Equation analysis:

✔ Remember that a change in an asset will require a change in another asset, a liability, and/or a shareholders' equity item.

✔ Recall that increases in expenses and dividends declared are shown as negative amounts in the accounting equation because they reduce retained earnings and shareholders' equity.

✔ Keep the accounting equation in balance.

Selected transactions made by Virmari Ltd. during the month of August, its first period of operations, follow:

Aug. 1 Common shares were issued to shareholders for $25,000 cash.
3 Equipment costing $7,000 was purchased on account.
9 Services amounting to $8,000 were performed for customers. Of this amount, $2,000 was received in cash and $6,000 is due on account.
10 Rent was paid for the month of August, $850.
29 Customers paid $4,000 of the balance due. (See Aug. 9 transaction.)
31 Dividends of $1,000 were declared and paid to shareholders.

Prepare a basic analysis and an equation analysis that shows the effects of each transaction on the expanded accounting equation.

SOLUTION
Try this Do It! exercise on your own and then check your answer at the end of the chapter.

Related Exercise Material: BE3–1 and BE3–2.

Balances at the Beginning of the Period

Note that Sierra did not have any opening balances in Illustration 3-3 because October was its first month of operations, and all opening balances were nil. Except for a company's first accounting period, it will have opening balances in some of its accounts. In such cases, when doing an equation analysis, a line would be added for opening balances and a column would be added for the balance in the Retained Earnings account. A separate column is used for the beginning balance (abbreviated as Beg. Bal.) of retained earnings in order to track the changes in revenues, expenses, and dividends declared during the period.

If we started to prepare an equation analysis for Sierra for the month of November, the month following that shown in Illustration 3-3, the first line would look like that shown in Illustration 3-4. We have assumed for illustration purposes that Sierra's accounting period is only a month, so opening retained earnings as at Sept. 30 (of which there were none) is combined with revenues, expenses, and dividends declared during October to form retained earnings as at October 31 (which is the same as the beginning balance on November 1) ($20,000 − $6,700 − $500 = $12,800). We will learn more about accounting periods and accumulating period information for revenues, expenses, and dividends in retained earnings in Chapter 4.

	Assets					=	Liabilities			+	Shareholders' Equity					
									Unearned		Common	Retained Earnings				
	Cash	+ A/R	+ Sup.	+ Pre. Ins.	+ Equipment	= A/P	+ L/P	+ Revenue	+	Shares	+ Bal.	− Rev.	− Exp.	− Div.
Oct. 31 bal.	+$11,400	+$11,000	+$2,500	+$600	+$5,000	+$1,500	+$5,000	+$1,200		+$10,000	+$12,800			

▶Illustration 3-4
Equation analysis with opening balances

The equation analyses shown in this section of the chapter and Illustrations 3-3 and 3-4 do not represent the actual method used to record transactions. However, understanding how to analyze transactions in this manner allows us to understand how accounting transactions change assets, liabilities, and shareholders' equity. This is fundamental to understanding the accounting cycle. Even if you are not formally asked to prepare a basic analysis in an assignment, thinking this through will help you better organize your answer. In the next section, we will apply this understanding and learn how to record these transactions.

DO IT! ▶3-1b   Equation Analysis

Green Lawn Care Ltd. had the following account balances at May 31: Cash $2,500; Accounts Receivable $1,000; Equipment $1,500; Common Shares $1,000; and Retained Earnings $4,000. Transactions for the month of June follow.

1. Received $1,000 cash from customers that had been billed in May.
2. Purchased $250 of supplies on account.
3. Billed customers $2,500 for services performed.
4. Declared and paid $100 of dividends to shareholders.
5. Purchased equipment for $3,500, paying $500 cash and signing a bank loan for the remainder.
6. Performed services for $1,200 cash.
7. Paid full amount owing for supplies purchased in transaction 2.
8. Paid $1,750 in salaries to employees.
9. Paid $600 for insurance coverage in advance.
10. Paid $400 for the monthly income tax instalment.

(a) Prepare an equation analysis that shows the effects of these transactions on the expanded accounting equation.

(b) Calculate the ending balances for total assets, total liabilities, and total shareholders' equity at June 30.

(c) Calculate net income for the month of June and retained earnings at June 30.

Action Plan

✔ Don't forget to enter opening balances in the accounting equation. Use a tabular summary format similar to that shown in Illustration 3-4.

✔ Remember that a change in an asset will require a change in another asset, a liability, and/or a shareholders' equity item.

✔ Recall that increases in expenses and dividends declared are shown as negative amounts in the accounting equation because they reduce retained earnings and shareholders' equity.

✔ Keep the accounting equation in balance.

✔ Remember the following formulas:
  ○ Net income = revenues − expenses
  ○ Ending retained earnings = Beginning retained earnings + net income − dividends declared

SOLUTION

Try this Do It! exercise on your own and then check your answer at the end of the chapter.

Related Exercise Material: E3-1 and E3-2.

LEARNING OBJECTIVE ▶2   **Explain how accounts, debits, and credits are used to record transactions.**

Instead of using an equation analysis like the one in Illustration 3-3 for Sierra Corporation, an accounting information system uses accounts. An **account** is an individual accounting record of increases and decreases in a specific asset, liability, or shareholders' equity item along with its opening and ending balances. For example, Sierra Corporation has separate accounts for cash, accounts receivable, accounts payable, service revenue, salaries expense, and so on.

T ACCOUNTS

In its simplest form, an account consists of three parts: (1) the title of the account, (2) a left or debit side, and (3) a right or credit side. The terms *debit* and *credit* don't have any meaning other than as a directional signal in the recording process. In other words, debits don't mean good and credits don't mean bad, nor do debits mean increases and credits decreases. **Debit** simply means left and **credit** simply means right. These terms are commonly abbreviated as Dr. for debit and Cr. for credit.[2]

Because the alignment of the three parts of an account resembles the letter T, it is referred to as a **T account**. A T account is also known as a **general ledger account**. The entire group of accounts maintained by a company (whether called a T account or a general ledger account) is referred to as the ledger. We will discuss the ledger in a later section of this chapter.

The T account form of an account is shown below.

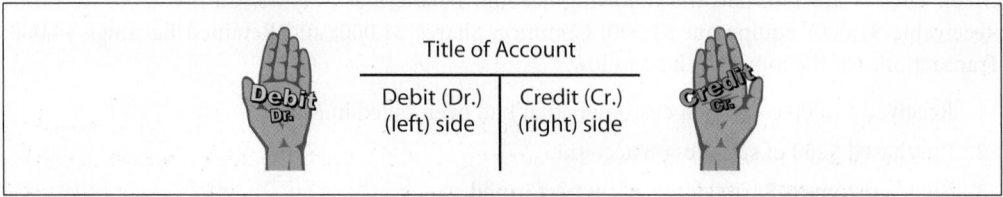

Quite often, a date will be included next to the debit or credit amount in order to identify the transaction.

The actual account form used in practice looks different from the above T account. As shown below, it usually has six columns that include information in addition to the two debit and credit columns included in T accounts.

TITLE OF ACCOUNT					
Date	Explanation	Ref.	Debit	Credit	Balance

The date and explanation columns make it possible to give more information about the transaction while the reference (abbreviated as "Ref.") column refers to the document that serves as evidence of the transaction. In addition, the balance in the account can be determined after each transaction. However, because of its simplicity, the T account is used for teaching and learning purposes and will be used throughout this textbook instead of the more formal six-column account form shown above.

NORMAL BALANCES AND DEBIT AND CREDIT EFFECTS

Accounts have normal debit or credit balances, depending on whether they are asset, liability, or shareholders' equity accounts. Recall the basic accounting equation:

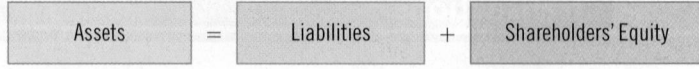

The **normal balance** of an account is always the side that is used to increase the account. If we overlay the accounting equation on a T account, we can better explain the concept of normal balances for each of assets, liabilities, and shareholders' equity.

T Account	
Debit (Dr.) Side	Credit (Cr.) Side
Assets	Liabilities + Shareholders' Equity

Assets

Assets are on the left side of the accounting equation and T account shown above. Consequently, if the normal balance of an account is always on its increase side, **asset accounts normally have debit (left-side) balances**. Increases in asset accounts are entered on the left or debit side of a T account while decreases in assets are entered on the right or credit side.

▼ HELPFUL HINT

Increases in asset accounts are recorded by debits and asset accounts normally have debit balances.

Assets	
Debit for increase	Credit for decrease
Normal balance	

When the totals of the two sides are added and netted against each other, an account will have a debit balance if the total of the debit entries recorded exceeds the total of the credit entries recorded. Conversely, an account will have a credit balance if the credit entries exceed the debit entries. Debits to a specific asset account usually exceed credits to that account, which results in a normal debit balance. It was a breakthrough for Mr. Hooker in the feature story when he learned that assets, such as cash, are normally debits.

Knowing an account's normal balance may help when you are trying to identify errors. For example, an asset account such as land would normally have a debit balance. If it had a credit balance, it would indicate a recording error. Occasionally, however, an account may not have its normal balance but still be correct. The Cash account, for example, will have a credit balance if the bank has authorized the company to have an overdraft, meaning the company can withdraw an amount in excess of its bank balance. If this occurs, then the Cash account will have a credit balance, which is called "bank indebtedness." You will recall that we learned in Chapter 2 that bank indebtedness is reported as a current liability rather than as a current asset. In addition to accounts like Bank Indebtedness, contra asset accounts, such as Accumulated Depreciation, have a normal credit balance.

We will illustrate using debits and credits for an asset account, Cash, using Sierra Corporation. The data shown in Illustration 3-5 are taken from the Cash column of the equation analysis shown earlier in Illustration 3-3. The data have also been inserted into a T account for comparison purposes.

Equation Analysis	T Account		
Cash	Cash		
+$10,000	(Dr.)	(Cr.)	
−900	10,000	900	
−600	1,200	600	
+1,200	9,000	1,000	
−1,000		4,000	
−4,000		500	
−500		1,800	
+9,000			
−1,800	Bal. 11,400		
$11,400			

▶ Illustration 3-5
Cash T account

Every positive item in the Cash column taken from the equation analysis represents a receipt of cash; every negative amount represents a payment of cash. In the T account, increases in cash are recorded as debits on the left-hand side of the account and decreases as credits on the right-hand side of the account. For example, in the first line of the T account, the $10,000 receipt of cash is debited to Cash and the $900 payment of cash is credited to Cash.

Having increases on one side and decreases on the other reduces recording errors and helps in determining the totals of each side of the account as well as the account balance. The balance is determined by netting the two sides (subtracting one amount from the other). The Cash account balance, a debit balance of $11,400, indicates that Sierra had $11,400 more increases (debits) than decreases (credits) in cash during the month.

Liabilities

Liabilities are on the right side of the accounting equation so **liability accounts normally have credit (right-side) balances**. Increases in liability accounts are entered on the right or credit side of a T account while decreases in liability accounts are entered on the left or debit side. Credits to a specific liability account should exceed debits to that account, which results in a normal credit balance.

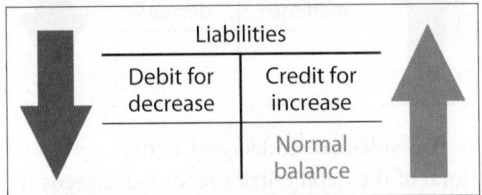

Compare the above T account with the one shown on the previous page for assets. Because liabilities are on the opposite side of the accounting equation from assets, it is not surprising that increases and decreases in liabilities are recorded opposite from assets.

Shareholders' Equity

All asset accounts are increased by debits and decreased by credits. All liability accounts are increased by credits and decreased by debits. However, shareholders' equity consists of different components, and they do not all move in the same direction. You will recall from Illustration 3-2 earlier in the chapter that shareholders' equity is usually composed of common shares (and possibly other types of share capital) and retained earnings. Retained earnings can be further subdivided into revenues and expenses (which together make up net income) and dividends declared. These components are then added to (in the case of revenues) or deducted from (in the case of expenses and dividends declared) retained earnings. You might find it helpful to review the expanded accounting equation shown in Illustration 3-2 to make sure you understand the directional impact of each component of shareholders' equity before we look at how debits and credits apply to each of these equity components.

INCREASES IN SHAREHOLDERS' EQUITY   Common shares and retained earnings both increase shareholders' equity. Retained earnings (and shareholders' equity in turn) are increased by revenues. Consequently, the common shares, retained earnings, and revenue accounts are increased by credits and decreased by debits. **The normal balance in these accounts is a credit balance.** This, and the effects that debits and credits have on these accounts is shown below:

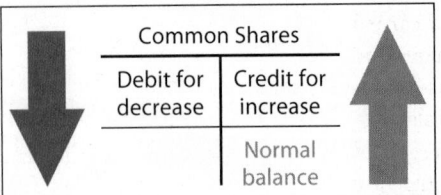

DECREASES IN SHAREHOLDERS' EQUITY   Expenses and dividends declared both decrease retained earnings (which in turn decrease shareholders' equity). Expenses combine with revenues to determine net income. Because expenses reduce net income and revenues increase net income, it is logical that the increase and decrease sides of expense accounts should be the opposite of revenue accounts. Thus, expense accounts are increased by debits and decreased by credits. If retained earnings are decreased by debits, it follows that increases in the Dividends Declared account are recorded with debits.

Because expense and dividends declared accounts are increased by debits, **the normal balance in these accounts is a debit balance.** This, and the effects that debits and credits have on these accounts is shown below:

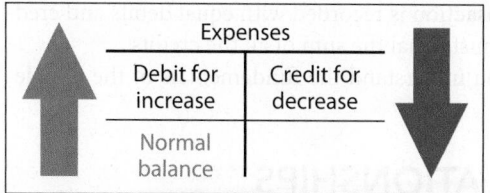

Summary of Normal Balances and Debit and Credit Effects

The normal balance of each of the T accounts shown in the preceding sections is on the account's increase side, as summarized in Illustration 3-6.

	Normal Balance	Increased By
Assets	Debit	Debits
Liabilities	Credit	Credits
Shareholders' equity		
Common shares	Credit	Credits
Retained earnings	Credit	Credits
Revenues	Credit	Credits
Expenses	Debit	Debits
Dividends declared	Debit	Debits

►Illustration 3-6
Summary of normal balances

Illustration 3-7 summarizes the debit and credit effects and shows the normal account balances (circled in red for your easy reference) in the expanded accounting equation. Recall Mr. Hooker's comment in our opening feature story that only debits increase debit accounts, only credits increase credit accounts, and that the normal balance of an account is always on its increase side.

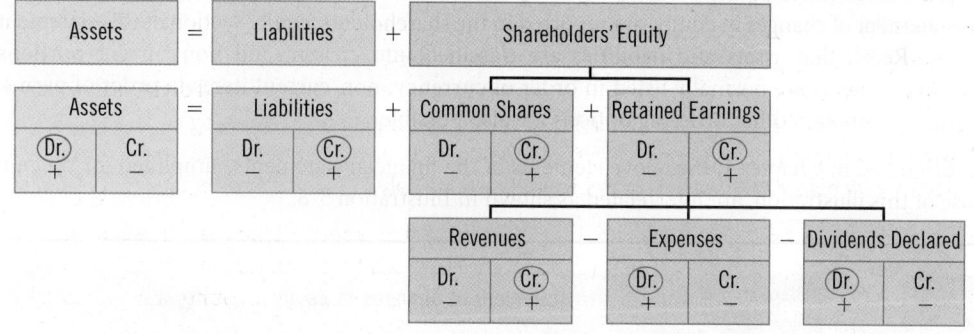

►Illustration 3-7
Summary of debit and credit rules for expanded accounting equation

Assets, on the left-hand side of the accounting equation, are increased by debits and consequently have a normal debit balance. Liabilities and shareholders' equity, on the right-hand side of the equation, are increased by credits and consequently have a normal credit balance. As we learned earlier, shareholders' equity is further divided into at least two components: common shares and retained earnings. Because shareholders' equity is increased by credits, both of these accounts—common shares and retained earnings—are also increased by credits and have a normal credit balance.

Retained earnings can be further subdivided into revenues and expenses (revenues and expenses combine to determine net income) and dividends declared, which increase (in the case of revenues) or decrease (in the case of expenses and dividends declared) any beginning balance in retained earnings. Because revenues increase retained earnings, which increase shareholders' equity, increases in revenue accounts are recorded by credits. Revenues have a normal credit balance. Expenses and dividends declared decrease retained earnings, and thus shareholders' equity. Decreases in shareholders' equity are recorded by debits. Because expenses and dividends declared decrease shareholders' equity, increases in each of these accounts are recorded by debits and they have a normal debit balance.

Like the basic accounting equation, the expanded equation must always be in balance (total debits must equal total credits). This equality of debits and credits is the basis for the **double-entry accounting system**, in which the dual (two-sided) effect of each transaction is recorded in appropriate accounts. This system provides a logical method for recording transactions and ensuring that amounts are recorded accurately. If every transaction is recorded with equal debits and credits, then the sum of all the debits to the accounts must equal the sum of all the credits.

Study Illustration 3-7 carefully. It will help you understand the fundamentals of the double-entry accounting system.

FINANCIAL STATEMENT RELATIONSHIPS

Assets, liabilities, and various components of shareholders' equity (common shares, retained earnings, revenues, expenses, and dividends declared) have been discussed in the above sections. It is timely to stop and review where companies report these items in the financial statements:

- Income statement: Revenues and expenses for the period are reported in this statement and combine to determine net income (loss). Although there are various conventions for listing revenues and expenses, we have generally chosen to list these items from largest to smallest. The exception is income tax expense, which is reported separately near the end of the statement. (Note that we will revisit the presentation of revenues and expenses in the income statement in Chapter 5.)

- Statement of changes in equity: The changes in all shareholders' equity items, including common shares and retained earnings, are reported in this statement. This statement starts with opening balances for the period (which are the same as the ending balances from the prior period) and shows any changes during the period to determine ending balances at the end of the current period. For example, additional common shares issued during the period will be shown in the common shares column. Net income (loss), determined from the income statement, and dividends declared for the period will be shown in the retained earnings column.

- Statement of financial position: The balances at the end of the period for assets, liabilities, and shareholders' equity are reported in this statement. Remember that assets must equal liabilities plus shareholders' equity. Note that common shares and retained earnings, determined from the statement of changes in equity, are reported in the shareholders' equity section of this statement. Recall that assets and liabilities are classified into current and non-current portions. Current items are normally listed in order of currency; non-current items in order of permanency, although other ordering options are also possible.

▶Illustration 3-8
Financial statement relationships

As discussed in Chapter 1, the above elements of the financial statements, simplified for the purpose of this illustration, are interrelated as shown in Illustration 3-8.

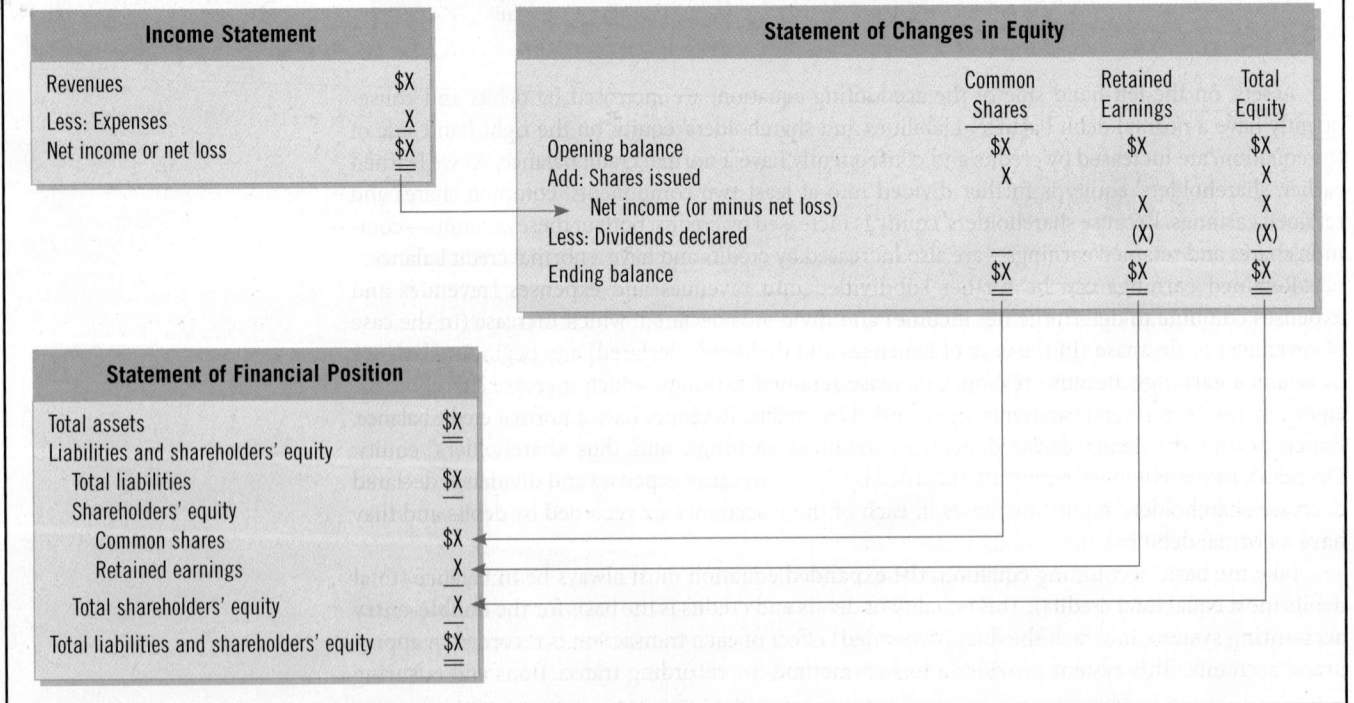

Revenues, expenses, and dividends declared are eventually transferred to retained earnings at the end of the period. We will learn how to do this in Chapter 4.

DO IT! ▶3-2 Accounts and Debits and Credits

Lin Ltd. has the following selected accounts:

1. Service Revenue
2. Income Tax Expense
3. Equipment
4. Accounts Receivable
5. Accumulated Depreciation
6. Unearned Revenue
7. Accounts Payable
8. Common Shares
9. Salaries Expense
10. Dividends Declared

(a) Indicate whether each of the above accounts is an asset, liability, or shareholders' equity account. If the account is an asset or liability, indicate its statement of financial position classification.

(b) Identify the normal balance.

(c) Indicate whether a debit would increase or decrease each account.

SOLUTION

Try this Do It! exercise on your own and then check your answer at the end of the chapter.

Related Exercise Material: BE3-3, BE3-4, BE3-5, E3-3, and E3-4.

✔ Classify each account into its place in the expanded accounting equation.

✔ Remember that the normal balance of an account is on its increase side. Note an exception for contra asset accounts. Even though they are assets, contra asset accounts move in the opposite direction from assets. That is, their normal balance is a credit as they are deducted from assets.

✔ Apply the debit and credit rules. Remember that assets are increased by debits, and liabilities and shareholders' equity are increased by credits. Don't forget that the individual components of shareholders' equity do not all move in the same direction.

LEARNING OBJECTIVE ▶ 3   **Journalize transactions in the general journal.**

| 1. ANALYZE | 2. Journalize the transactions | 3. POST | 4. TRIAL BALANCE | 5. ADJUSTING ENTRIES | 6. ADJUSTED TRIAL BALANCE | 7. FINANCIAL STATEMENTS | 8. CLOSING ENTRIES | 9. POST-CLOSING TRIAL BALANCE |

We have already discussed the first step of the accounting cycle. Recall that each transaction must be analyzed to determine if it has an effect on the accounts. Evidence of the transaction comes from a source document, such as a sales receipt, cheque, invoice, or cash register tape. As described in our feature story, Grant Hooker used cheques to begin the recording process for BeaverTails. Evidence supporting the transaction is analyzed to determine the effect on specific accounts. Deciding whether an accounting transaction has occurred, and if so, what to record, is the most critical point in the accounting process.

Most companies use computerized accounting systems. They may be as simple as a series of spreadsheets, such as Excel, or as sophisticated as an integrated accounting software package. These systems can be used to process all of the steps in the accounting cycle subsequent to the analysis of the transaction. The analysis of the transaction is one of the more difficult parts of the accounting cycle and must be done by a person in order to determine what accounts are affected, if any, and in what amount. Regardless of whether a manual or computerized accounting system is used, the underlying concepts are the same. In order to ensure that you understand the fundamentals of accounting systems, we will focus on manual accounting systems in this textbook.

GENERAL JOURNAL

After analyzing the transaction, the second step in the accounting cycle is to record accounting transactions. Although it is possible to enter transaction information directly into a T account, it is not practical to do so. Rather, the transaction information is recorded as a journal entry in the general journal (a book of original entry). Transactions are recorded in chronological order (by date) in a journal before continuing the recording process in step 3 of the accounting cycle.

For each transaction, the journal shows the debit and credit effects on specific accounts. Companies may use various kinds of journals, but every company has the most basic form of journal, a **general journal**. In a computerized accounting system, journals are kept as files and accounts are maintained in computer databases.

The general journal makes several contributions to the recording process:

1. It discloses the complete effect of a transaction in one place, including an explanation and, where applicable, identification of the source document.
2. It provides a chronological record of transactions.
3. It helps to prevent and locate errors, because the debit and credit amounts for each entry can be quickly compared.

Entering transaction data in the general journal is known as **journalizing**. To illustrate the technique of journalizing, we will look again at the first transaction of Sierra Corporation, where common shares were issued. To the basic and equation analysis illustrated in the previous sections, we will now add a third part to this analysis called a **debit–credit analysis**. This analysis will help us identify whether the accounts need to be debited or credited before we prepare the journal entry.

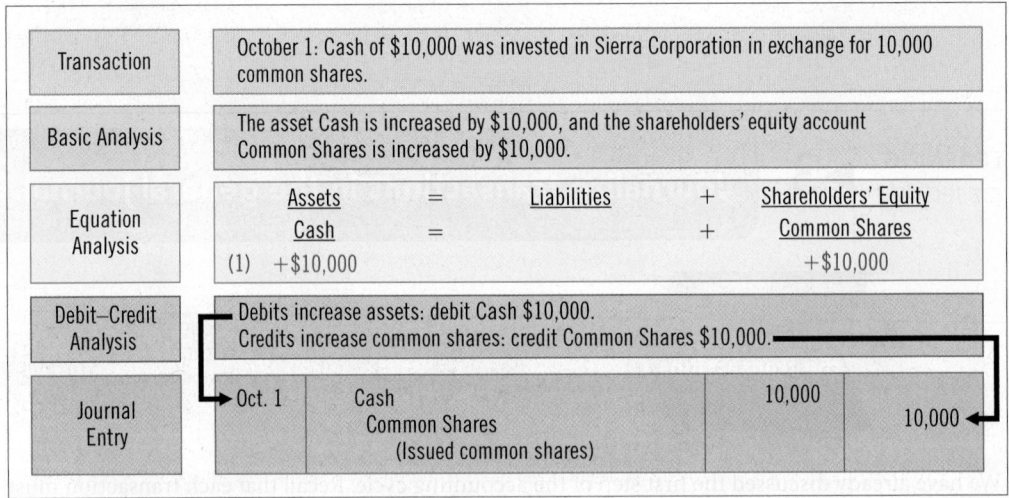

Note the following features of the journal entry:

1. The date of the transaction is entered in the Date column.
2. The account to be debited is entered first at the left. The account to be credited is then entered on the next line, indented under the line above. The indentation differentiates debits from credits and reduces the chance of switching the debit and credit amounts by mistake.
3. The amounts for the debits are recorded in the Debit (left) column, and the amounts for the credits are recorded in the Credit (right) column.
4. A brief explanation of the transaction is given.

If a journal entry affects only two accounts, one debit and one credit, it is considered to be a simple journal entry. When three or more accounts are required in one journal entry, the entry is called a compound entry. Regardless of the number of accounts used in the journal entry, **the total debit and credit amounts must be equal**.

In assignments, when specific account titles are given, they should be used in journalizing. When account titles are not given, you should create account titles that identify the nature and content of each account. Ambiguous or multiple account titles with similar names can lead to incorrect financial reporting. For example, a company could use any one of these account titles for recording the cost of delivery trucks: Automobiles, Delivery Trucks, Trucks, or Vehicles. However, if it uses more than one of these account titles, it will not be able to easily determine the total cost of its delivery trucks.

Once the company chooses the specific account title to use (say, Vehicles), all future transactions related to that account should be recorded in the Vehicles account. Note that an account title itself should not contain explanations or descriptions (such as Vehicles Purchased).

Although explanations are an important part of each journal entry, you may omit them unless otherwise instructed in your homework assignments. Including an explanation in an assignment is not a good use of your time because it simply involves copying the information from the problem to your assignment.

▼ **HELPFUL HINT**

It is important to use correct and specific account titles in journal entries.

DO IT! ▶3-3 Debit–Credit Analysis and Journal Entries

In Do It! 3-1a, you prepared a basic and equation analysis for Virmari Ltd. Prepare a debit–credit analysis and journal entry for each of the transactions analyzed in Do It! 3-1a.

Action Plan

✔ Refer back to the basic and equation analyses you prepared in Do It! 3-1a to review the effects of each transaction on the accounting equation.

✔ Apply the debit and credit rules to increases and decreases in the accounts.

✔ Prepare journal entries to record the transactions in the general journal. Recall that debits are normally recorded first, followed by credits, which are indented.

✔ As mentioned in the chapter, you may omit explanations for all journal entries unless you are explicitly requested to provide them.

SOLUTION

Try this Do It! exercise on your own and then check your answer at the end of the chapter.

Related Exercise Material: BE3-6, BE3-7, BE3-8, E3-5, and E3-6.

LEARNING
OBJECTIVE ▶ **4**   **Post transactions to the general ledger.**

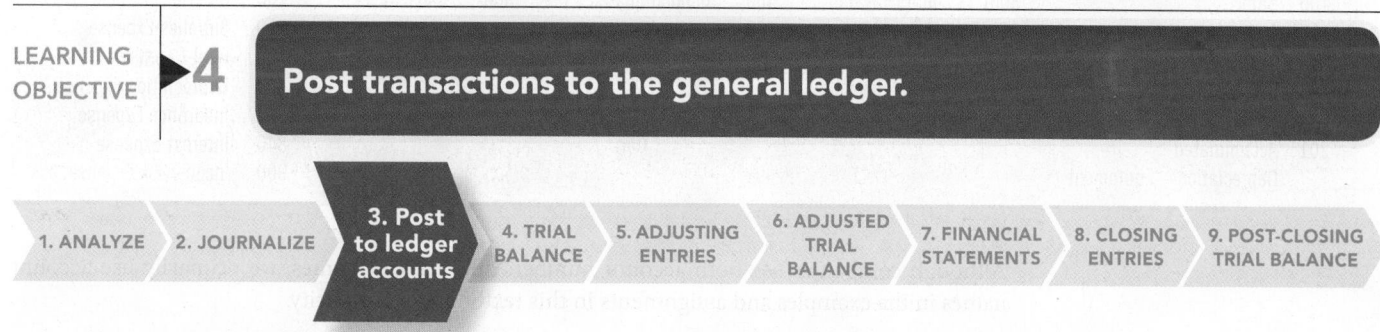

The third step in the accounting cycle is to transfer the journal entries recorded in the general journal to the appropriate accounts in the general ledger. The entire group of accounts (whether known as a T account or a general ledger account) maintained by a company is referred to as the ledger. The ledger keeps all the information about changes in specific account balances in one place.

Companies may use various kinds of ledgers, but every company has a general ledger. A **general ledger** contains all the asset, liability, shareholders' equity, dividends declared, revenue, and expense accounts. Each account has a number so that it is easier to identify. A company can use a loose-leaf binder or card file for the ledger, with each account kept on a separate sheet or card. A column in spreadsheet software can also be used as a general ledger account, but most companies today use a computerized accounting system where the entries from the journal are automatically recorded in the ledger by the software.

The ledger is normally arranged in the order in which accounts are presented in the financial statements, beginning with the statement of financial position accounts. The asset accounts come first, followed by liability accounts, and then shareholders' equity accounts, including common shares, retained earnings, and dividends declared accounts, followed by revenue and expense accounts. Of course, in a computerized accounting system, the accounts can easily be rearranged in whatever order is wanted.

CHART OF ACCOUNTS

Most companies list their general ledger accounts in a **chart of accounts**. The chart of accounts is the framework for the accounting information system. It lists the accounts and the account numbers that identify where the accounts are in the ledger.

The number and kind of accounts used can differ for each company, depending on the size, complexity, and type of business. For example, the number of accounts depends on the amount of detail desired by management. The management of one company may want one single account for all types of utility expenses. Another may keep separate expense accounts for each type of utility expenditure such as electricity, water, and telephone. A small corporation like Sierra will not have many accounts compared with a large company like Apple Inc. Sierra may be able to manage and report its activities using fewer than 50 accounts, whereas Apple requires thousands of accounts to keep track of its worldwide activities. As a result, the numbering system that is used to identify the accounts can be quite sophisticated or pretty simple.

Similar to the ledger, the chart of accounts usually starts with the statement of financial position accounts, followed by the income statement accounts. The chart of accounts for Sierra Corporation is shown in Illustration 3-9. Accounts shown in red are used in this chapter; accounts shown in black are explained in later chapters. Accounts 100 to 299 indicate asset accounts, 300 to 399 indicate liability accounts, 400 to 499 indicate shareholders' equity accounts, 500 to 699 indicate revenue accounts, and 700 to 999 indicate expense accounts. The three-digit numbering system allows room for new accounts to be created as needed during the life of the business.

▶Illustration 3-9
Chart of accounts

SIERRA CORPORATION—CHART OF ACCOUNTS									
Assets		**Liabilities**		**Shareholders' Equity**		**Revenues**		**Expenses**	
100	Cash	300	Accounts Payable	400	Common Shares	500	Service Revenue	700	Salaries Expense
110	Accounts Receivable	310	Salaries Payable	450	Retained Earnings			710	Supplies Expense
150	Supplies	320	Interest Payable	460	Dividends Declared			750	Rent Expense
155	Prepaid Insurance	330	Unearned Revenue					760	Depreciation Expense
200	Equipment	340	Bank Loan Payable					820	Insurance Expense
201	Accumulated Depreciation—Equipment							840	Interest Expense
								900	Income Tax Expense

Although companies use both account numbers and account names, we primarily use account names in the examples and assignments in this textbook for simplicity.

POSTING

The procedure of transferring journal entries from the general journal to the general ledger accounts is called **posting**. This phase of the recording process accumulates the effects of journalized transactions in the individual accounts. Posting involves transferring information from the general journal to the general ledger. For example, the date and amount shown on the first line of a general journal entry is entered in the debit column of the appropriate account in the general ledger. The same is done for the credit side of the entry—the date and amount are entered in the credit column of the general ledger account.

Posting should be done in chronological order. That is, all the debits and credits of one journal entry should be posted before going on to the next journal entry. Posting should also be done on a timely basis—at least monthly—to ensure that the general ledger is up to date. In a computerized accounting system, posting is usually performed simultaneously after each journal entry is prepared. Note that, as explained in the previous section, many general ledger accounts will have balances carried forward from the prior period and the posting will include only the transactions for the current period. We will learn more about which account balances carry over into subsequent periods in Chapter 4.

The first three steps in the accounting cycle—analyze, journalize, and post transactions—occur repeatedly in every company, whether a manual or a computerized accounting system is used. However, the first two steps—the analysis and entering of each transaction—must be done by a person even when a computerized system is used. The basic difference between a manual and computerized system is in Step 3 of the recording process—posting the information (and in some of the subsequent steps in the accounting cycle that we will learn about later).

ACCOUNTING MATTERS

Computerized Accounting Systems

Organizations of all shapes and sizes use computerized accounting systems. Lisa Hau, owner of the hair salon Lisa's Chop Shop in downtown Vancouver, uses the popular small-business accounting software Sage Accounting. "I'm confident that I can do the simple tasks like data entry, processing, payroll, and my accountant can focus on growing the business." The software also helps automate tax preparation and invoicing, leaving Ms. Hau more time to serve customers.

DO IT! ▶3-4a   Posting

Ahair Ltd. had opening balances at April 30 in selected accounts as follows: Cash $10,000; Accounts Receivable $5,000; Equipment $7,500; and Accounts Payable $6,000. The following journal entries were recorded in May:

May	1	Accounts Payable	5,000	
		Cash		5,000
		(Made partial payment on account)		
	4	Equipment	4,800	
		Bank Loan Payable		4,800
		(Purchased equipment in exchange for bank loan)		
	6	Supplies	600	
		Cash		600
		(Purchased supplies)		
	15	Cash	2,700	
		Accounts Receivable		2,700
		(Received partial payment of account)		

(a) Set up T accounts and enter the April 30 balances.

(b) Post the May journal entries to the general ledger and determine the ending balances in each account.

Action Plan

✔ Posting involves transferring the journalized debits and credits to specific T accounts in the general ledger.

✔ Don't forget to enter any opening balances.

✔ Remember to post debits on the left side of the T account and credits on the right side. Include the dates as well as the amounts when you post.

✔ Ledger accounts should be arranged in statement order.

✔ Determine the ending balances of each ledger account by netting (calculating the difference between) the total debits and credits.

SOLUTION

Try this Do It! exercise on your own and then check your answer at the end of the chapter.

THE RECORDING PROCESS ILLUSTRATED

The following transaction analyses illustrate the first three steps in the recording process—analyze, journalize, and post—using the October 2018 transactions for Sierra Corporation. Remember that, in Step 1 of the recording process, we first must determine if an accounting transaction has occurred. If so, the transaction is analyzed to identify (1) the types of accounts involved, (2) whether the accounts are increased or decreased, and (3) the impact on the accounting equation. Step 2 of the recording process is to prepare the journal entry and Step 3 is to post the journal entry to the general ledger (T) account. Note that, because Sierra started on October 1, 2018, there are no opening balances in its T accounts from prior transactions.

Study the following transaction analyses carefully. Doing so will help you understand the journal entries discussed in this chapter, as well as more complex journal entries described in later chapters.

▶Transaction (1)

Investment of cash by shareholders

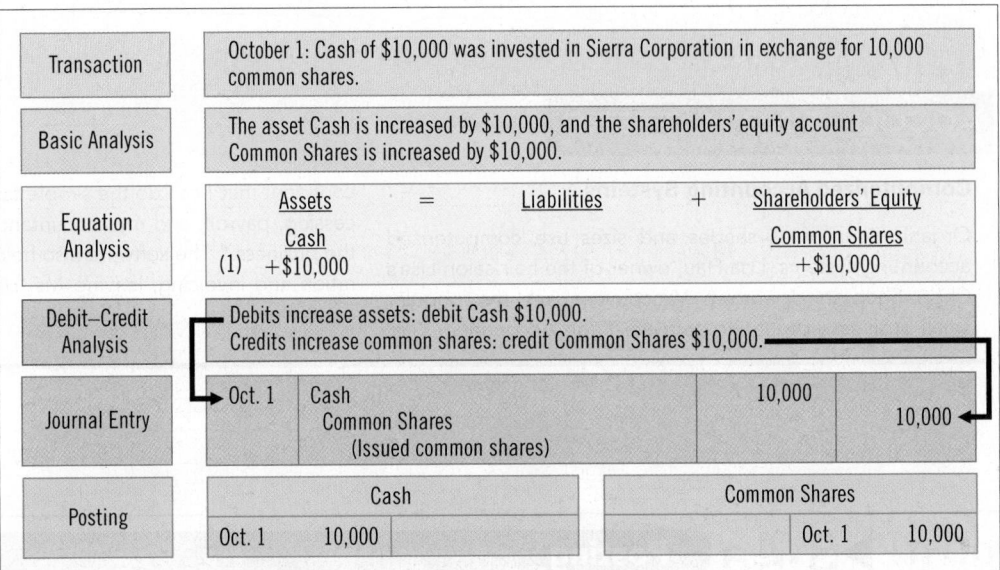

▶Transaction (2)

Purchase of equipment and signing of bank loan

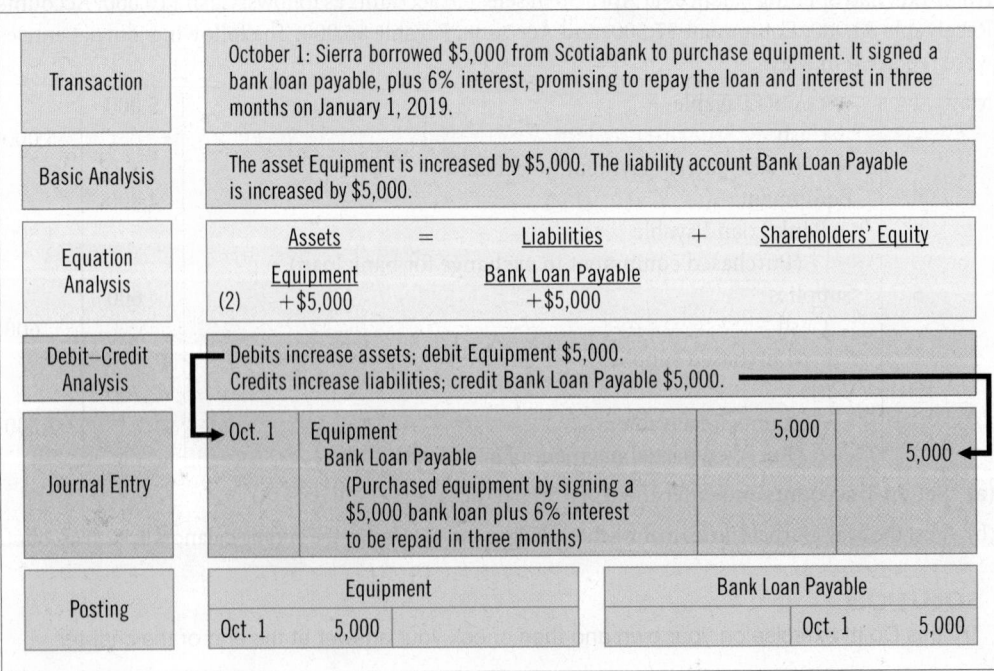

Transaction	October 2: Paid $900 for office rent for the month of October.
Basic Analysis	The expense Rent Expense is increased by $900 because the payment is only for the current month; the asset Cash is decreased by $900.

Equation Analysis

	Assets	=	Liabilities	+	Shareholders' Equity
					Retained Earnings
	Cash				Rent Expense
(3)	−$900				−$900

Debit–Credit Analysis	Debits increase expenses: debit Rent Expense $900. Credits decrease assets: credit Cash $900.

Journal Entry	Oct. 2	Rent Expense	900	
		Cash		900
		(Paid cash for October office rent)		

Posting

Cash				Rent Expense	
Oct. 1	10,000	Oct. 2	900	Oct. 2	900

▶ Transaction (3)
Payment of rent

Transaction	October 5: Paid $600 for a one-year insurance policy effective October 1 that expires next year on September 30.
Basic Analysis	The asset Prepaid Insurance is increased by $600 because the payment extends to more than the current month; the asset Cash is decreased by $600.

Equation Analysis

	Assets		=	Liabilities	+	Shareholders' Equity
	Cash	+ Prepaid Insurance				
(4)	−$600	+$600				

Debit–Credit Analysis	Debits increase assets: debit Prepaid Insurance $600. Credits decrease assets: credit Cash $600.

Journal Entry	Oct. 5	Prepaid Insurance	600	
		Cash		600
		(Paid one-year insurance policy; effective October 1)		

Posting

Cash				Prepaid Insurance	
Oct. 1	10,000	Oct. 2	900	Oct. 5	600
		5	600		

▶ Transaction (4)
Purchase of insurance policy for cash

Transaction	October 8: Hired four employees to begin work on Monday, October 15. Each employee is to receive a weekly salary of $500 for a five-day workweek (Monday–Friday), payable every two weeks—first payment to be made on Friday, October 26.
Basic Analysis	An accounting transaction has not occurred. There is only an agreement that the employees will begin work on October 15. Thus, an equation and further analysis is not needed because there is no accounting entry. (See transaction of October 26 for first entry.)

▶ Transaction (5)
Hiring of new employees

▶Transaction (6)
Purchase of supplies on account

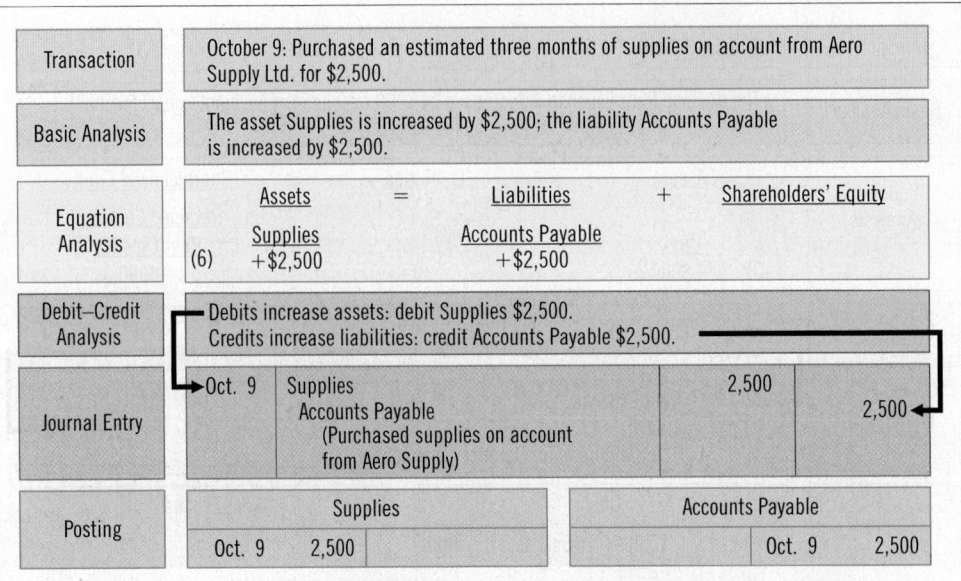

▶Transaction (7)
Provision of services on account

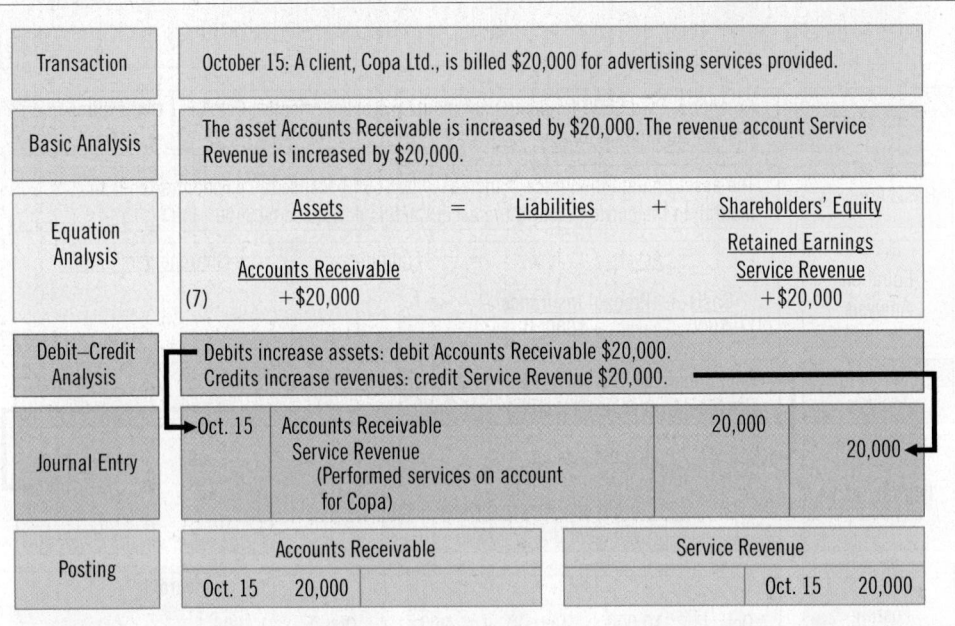

▶Transaction (8)
Receipt of cash in advance
from client

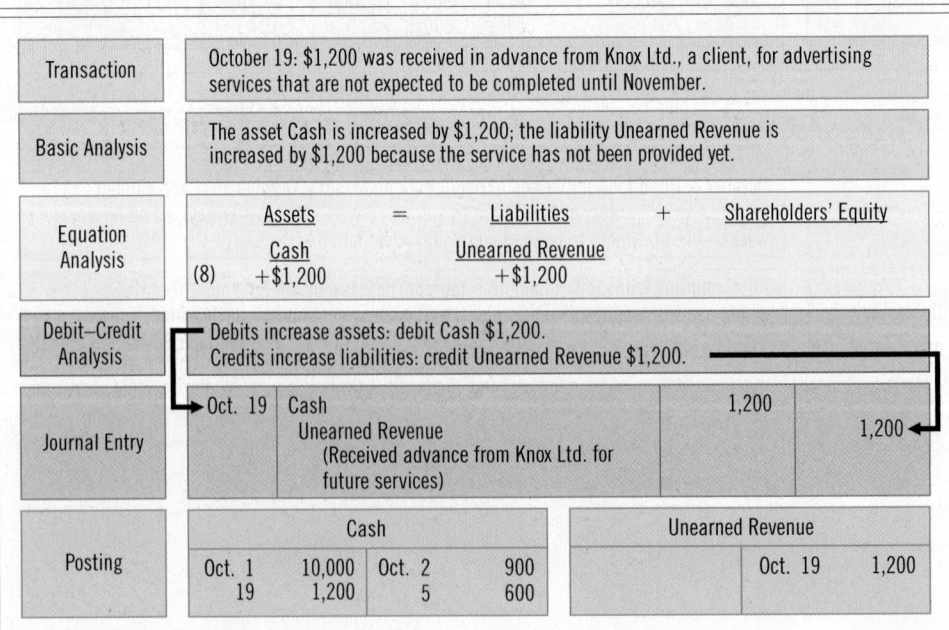

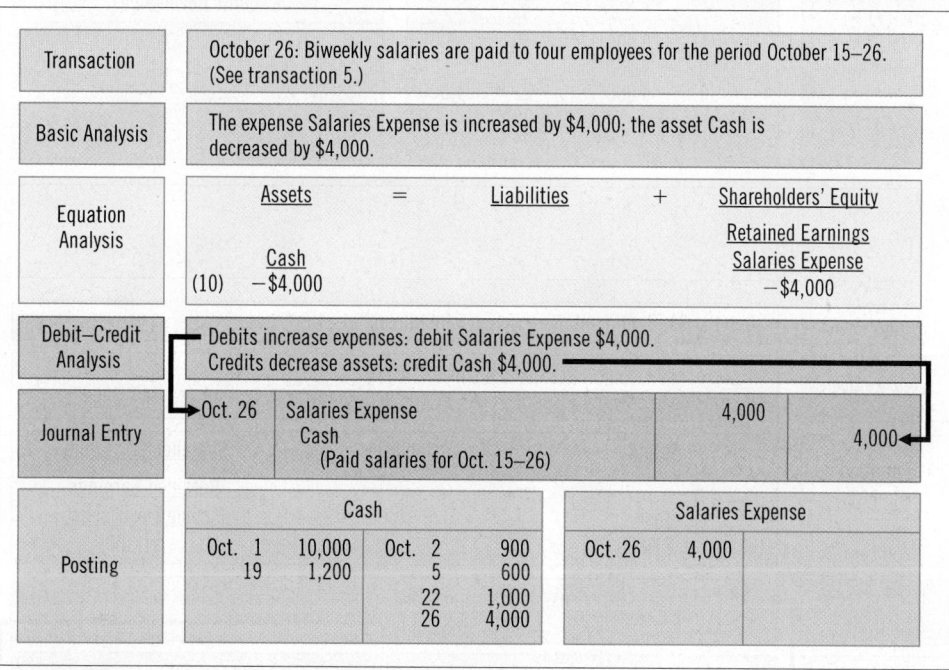

Transaction	October 22: Made a partial payment of $1,000 on the amount it owed for the supplies purchased from Aero Supply on October 9. (See transaction 6.)
Basic Analysis	The liability Accounts Payable is decreased by $1,000; the asset Cash is decreased by $1,000.

Equation Analysis

Assets	=	Liabilities	+	Shareholders' Equity
Cash		Accounts Payable		
(9) −$1,000		−$1,000		

Debit–Credit Analysis

Debits decrease liabilities; debit Accounts Payable $1,000.
Credits decrease assets; credit Cash $1,000.

Journal Entry

Oct. 22	Accounts Payable	1,000	
	Cash		1,000
	(Made partial payment on amount owing to Aero Supply)		

Posting

Cash					Accounts Payable			
Oct. 1	10,000	Oct. 2	900		Oct. 22	1,000	Oct. 9	2,500
19	1,200	5	600					
		22	1,000					

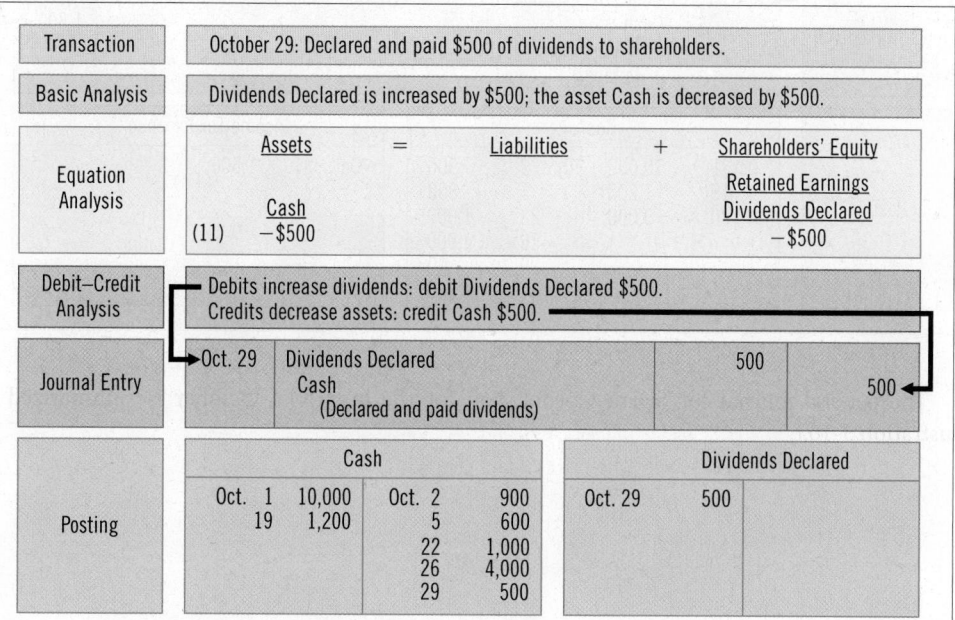

Transaction	October 26: Biweekly salaries are paid to four employees for the period October 15–26. (See transaction 5.)
Basic Analysis	The expense Salaries Expense is increased by $4,000; the asset Cash is decreased by $4,000.

Equation Analysis

Assets	=	Liabilities	+	Shareholders' Equity
				Retained Earnings
Cash				Salaries Expense
(10) −$4,000				−$4,000

Debit–Credit Analysis

Debits increase expenses: debit Salaries Expense $4,000.
Credits decrease assets: credit Cash $4,000.

Journal Entry

Oct. 26	Salaries Expense	4,000	
	Cash		4,000
	(Paid salaries for Oct. 15–26)		

Posting

Cash					Salaries Expense		
Oct. 1	10,000	Oct. 2	900		Oct. 26	4,000	
19	1,200	5	600				
		22	1,000				
		26	4,000				

Transaction	October 29: Declared and paid $500 of dividends to shareholders.
Basic Analysis	Dividends Declared is increased by $500; the asset Cash is decreased by $500.

Equation Analysis

Assets	=	Liabilities	+	Shareholders' Equity
				Retained Earnings
Cash				Dividends Declared
(11) −$500				−$500

Debit–Credit Analysis

Debits increase dividends: debit Dividends Declared $500.
Credits decrease assets: credit Cash $500.

Journal Entry

Oct. 29	Dividends Declared	500	
	Cash		500
	(Declared and paid dividends)		

Posting

Cash					Dividends Declared		
Oct. 1	10,000	Oct. 2	900		Oct. 29	500	
19	1,200	5	600				
		22	1,000				
		26	4,000				
		29	500				

▶ Transaction (12)

Partial collection of accounts receivable

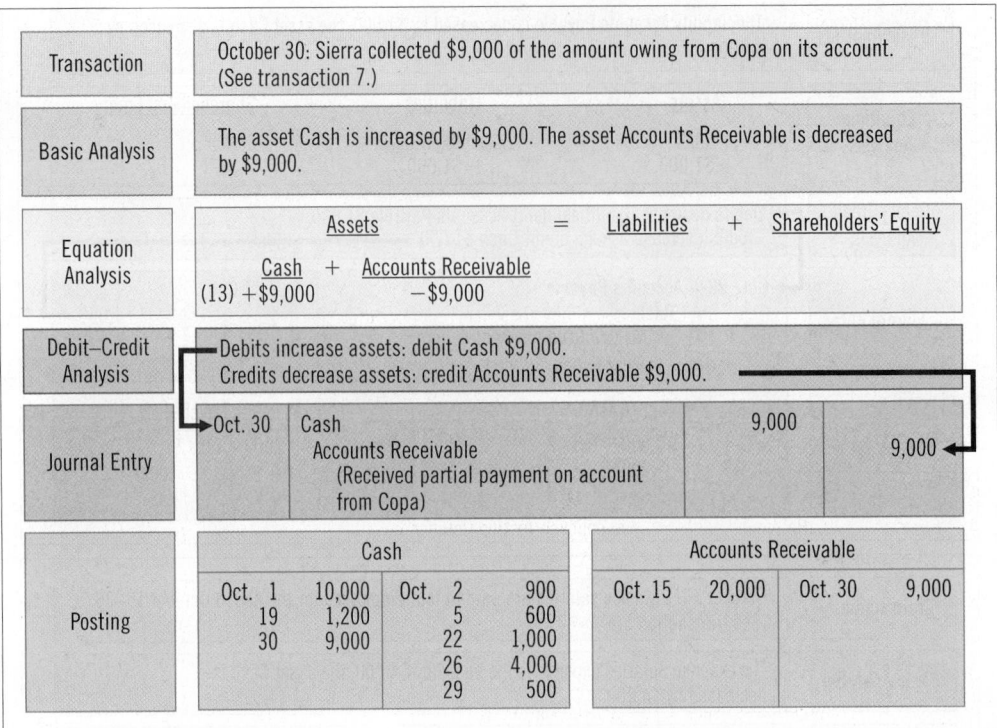

▶ Transaction (13)

Payment of income tax

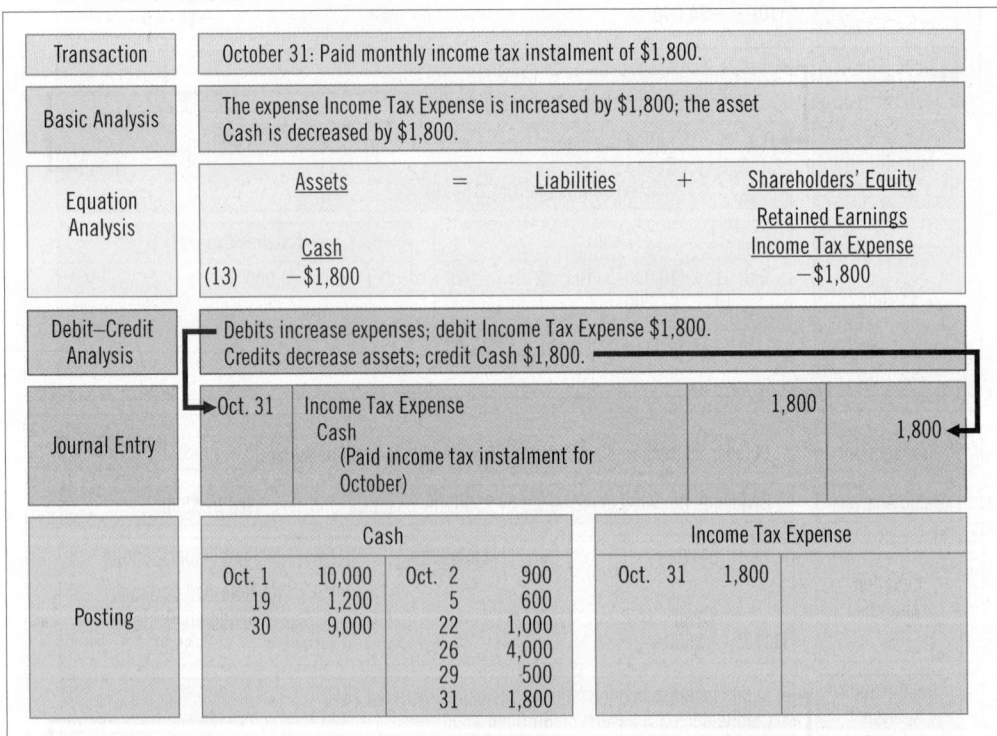

The general journal for Sierra Corporation for the month of October is summarized in Illustration 3-10.

	SIERRA CORPORATION General Journal			
Date	Account Titles and Explanation		Debit	Credit
2018				
Oct. 1	Cash		10,000	
	Common Shares			10,000
	(Issued common shares)			
1	Equipment		5,000	
	Bank Loan Payable			5,000
	(Purchased equipment by signing a $5,000 bank loan plus 6% interest to be repaid in three months)			
2	Rent Expense		900	
	Cash			900
	(Paid cash for October office rent)			
5	Prepaid Insurance		600	
	Cash			600
	(Paid one-year insurance policy; effective October 1)			
9	Supplies		2,500	
	Accounts Payable			2,500
	(Purchased supplies on account from Aero Supply)			
15	Accounts Receivable		20,000	
	Service Revenue			20,000
	(Performed services on account for Copa)			
19	Cash		1,200	
	Unearned Revenue			1,200
	(Received advance from Knox Ltd. for future services)			
22	Accounts Payable		1,000	
	Cash			1,000
	(Made partial payment on amount owing to Aero Supply)			
26	Salaries Expense		4,000	
	Cash			4,000
	(Paid salaries for Oct. 15–26)			
29	Dividends Declared		500	
	Cash			500
	(Declared and paid dividends)			
30	Cash		9,000	
	Accounts Receivable			9,000
	(Received partial payment on account from Copa)			
31	Income Tax Expense		1,800	
	Cash			1,800
	(Paid income tax instalment for October)			

▶Illustration 3-10

General journal for Sierra

The general ledger for Sierra Corporation is shown in Illustration 3-11.

SIERRA CORPORATION								
General Ledger								

▶Illustration 3-11

General ledger for Sierra

Cash						Unearned Revenue		
Oct.	1	10,000	Oct.	2	900		Oct. 19	1,200
	19	1,200		5	600			
	30	9,000		22	1,000	Bank Loan Payable		
				26	4,000		Oct. 1	5,000
				29	500			
				31	1,800	Common Shares		
Bal.		11,400					Oct. 1	10,000

(continued)

▶Illustration 3-11
General ledger for Sierra (continued)

Accounts Receivable						
Oct.	15	20,000	Oct.	30	9,000
Bal.		11,000			

Dividends Declared		
Oct.	29	500

Supplies		
Oct.	9	2,500

Service Revenue			
		Oct.	15	20,000

Prepaid Insurance		
Oct.	5	600

Salaries Expense		
Oct.	26	4,000

Equipment		
Oct.	1	5,000

Rent Expense		
Oct.	2	900

Accounts Payable					
Oct.	22	1,000	Oct.	9	2,500
			Bal.		1,500

Income Tax Expense		
Oct.	31	1,800

DO IT! ▶3-4b   Posting

SOLUTION
Try this Do It! exercise on your own and then check your answer at the end of the chapter.

Related Exercise Material: BE3-9, BE3-10, BE3-11, E3-7, E3-8, and E3-9.

In Do It! 3-1a and 3-3, a basic, equation, and debit–credit analysis and journal entries were prepared for Virmari Ltd. Set up T accounts, post the journal entries prepared in Do It! 3-3 to Virmari's general ledger, and determine the ending balances.

Action Plan

✔ Posting involves transferring the journalized debits and credits to specific T accounts in the general ledger.

✔ Remember to post debits on the left side of the T account and credits on the right side. Include the dates as well as the amounts when you post.

✔ Ledger accounts should be arranged in statement order.

✔ Determine the ending balance of each ledger account by netting (calculating the difference between) the total debits and credits.

LEARNING OBJECTIVE ▶5   **Prepare a trial balance.**

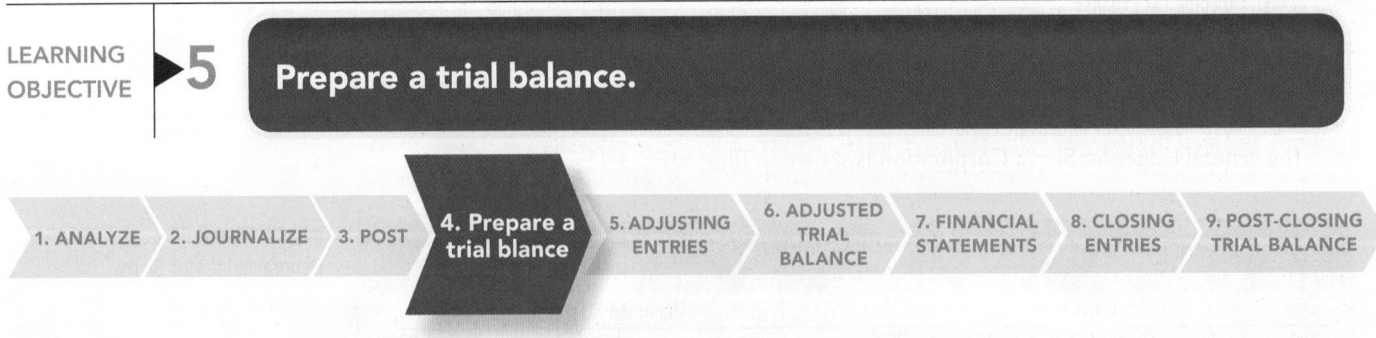

| 1. ANALYZE | 2. JOURNALIZE | 3. POST | **4. Prepare a trial blance** | 5. ADJUSTING ENTRIES | 6. ADJUSTED TRIAL BALANCE | 7. FINANCIAL STATEMENTS | 8. CLOSING ENTRIES | 9. POST-CLOSING TRIAL BALANCE |

▼ **HELPFUL HINT**
A trial balance proves that total debits equal total credits.

The fourth step in the accounting cycle is to prepare a trial balance. A **trial balance** is a list of general ledger accounts and their balances at a specific time. It is prepared at the end of an accounting period, which is usually monthly, but could also be quarterly or annually.

The main purpose of a trial balance is to prove (check) that the debits equal the credits after posting. That is, the sum of the debit account balances must equal the sum of the credit account balances. A trial balance is also useful in the preparation of financial statements, as we will explain in the next chapter.

PREPARING A TRIAL BALANCE

The procedure for preparing a trial balance is as follows:

1. List the account titles and their balances in the same order as in the general ledger and chart of accounts, which are usually in financial statement order. For assignment purposes, you will be expected to prepare trial balances in financial statement order unless otherwise advised.
2. Debit balances should be entered in the debit (left-hand) column and credit balances in the credit (right-hand) column.
3. Total the debit column and the credit column and ensure that the debit and credit column totals are equal (agree).

To illustrate a trial balance, we will continue with our Sierra Corporation example from previous sections of this chapter. We will use the information in Sierra's general ledger accounts shown in Illustration 3-11 to prepare the trial balance shown in Illustration 3-12. Note that the total debits, $37,700, equal the total credits, $37,700.

SIERRA CORPORATION Trial Balance October 31, 2018		
	Debit	Credit
Cash	$11,400	
Accounts receivable	11,000	
Supplies	2,500	
Prepaid insurance	600	
Equipment	5,000	
Accounts payable		$ 1,500
Unearned revenue		1,200
Bank loan payable		5,000
Common shares		10,000
Dividends declared	500	
Service revenue		20,000
Salaries expense	4,000	
Rent expense	900	
Income tax expense	1,800	
	$37,700	$37,700

► Illustration 3-12

Trial balance for Sierra

We wish to draw your attention to the fact that we have not used cents in the amounts recorded for Sierra for its journal entries, general ledger accounts, and trial balance. In practice, cents are used in the formal accounting records. We have chosen to omit them from this textbook for simplicity.

We will continue to use Sierra's trial balance in Chapter 4 to prepare adjusting journal entries in step 5 and an adjusted trial balance in step 6, and complete the remaining steps (7 through 9) of the accounting cycle. The trial balance shown in Illustration 3-12 above is often called an *unadjusted* trial balance to distinguish it from the adjusted trial balance we will learn about in the next chapter.

You might wonder why there is no Retained Earnings account included in the above trial balance. When a trial balance is first prepared, it is important to understand that the retained earnings account balance that is listed on the trial balance is not the retained earnings balance at the end of the period, even though the date on the trial balance is October 31. Rather, it is the retained earnings balance at the beginning of the period. In Sierra's case, its beginning retained earnings balance is zero because this is its first month of operations; accounts with zero balances are not normally included in a trial balance.

Why is the beginning balance used for the retained earnings account rather than the ending balance, as is the case in all the other accounts listed? Recall that retained earnings at the end of a period are equal to the beginning balance of retained earnings plus revenues less expenses and dividends declared for the period. When a trial balance lists revenues, expenses, and dividends declared account balances, the retained earnings balance has not yet been updated for these items and must therefore represent the balance in retained earnings at the beginning of the period. We will learn how to update retained earnings at the end of the accounting period in the next chapter.

LIMITATIONS OF A TRIAL BALANCE

We stated above that the totals of the debit and credit columns in a trial balance must agree—that is, the sum of the debit account balances must equal the sum of the credit account balances. If the debit and credit totals don't agree, the trial balance can help uncover errors in journalizing and posting. For example, the trial balance will not balance if debit and credit amounts are unequal in a journal entry, or if the amount is transferred incorrectly to the general ledger from a journal entry. If the trial balance does not balance, then the error must be located and corrected before proceeding.

If your trial balance does not balance, how can you locate the error? Sometimes the only way to find an error is to carefully retrace all of the steps in the accounting cycle. Other times, an error can be quickly located by applying the following tips after you determine the amount of the difference (the error) between total debits and total credits:

1. If the error is an amount such as $1, $100, or $1,000, re-add the trial balance columns.
2. If the error can be evenly divided by two, scan the trial balance to see if a balance equal to half the error has been entered in the wrong column.
3. If the error can be evenly divided by nine, retrace the account balances on the trial balance to see whether they have been incorrectly copied from the ledger. For example, if a balance was $12 but was listed as $21, a $9 error has been made. Reversing the order of numbers is called a transposition error.
4. If the error cannot be evenly divided by two or nine, scan the ledger to see whether an account balance in the amount of the error has been omitted from the trial balance. Scan the journal to see whether a posting in the amount of the error has been omitted.

Note that these suggestions will not always find the error, especially if there is more than one error.

In a computerized system, the trial balance is usually balanced because most computerized systems will not let you enter an unbalanced journal entry, and because the computer automatically posts journal entries and prepares the trial balance. In addition, the computer is usually programmed to flag violations of the normal balance and to print out error or exception reports.

Although a trial balance can reveal many types of errors in the recording process, it does not prove that all transactions have been recorded or that the general ledger is correct regardless of whether a computerized or manual system is in place. Errors may exist even though the trial balance column totals agree. For example, the trial balance may balance even when:

1. a transaction is not journalized,
2. a correct journal entry is not posted,
3. a journal entry is posted twice,
4. incorrect accounts are used in journalizing or posting, or
5. errors that cancel each other's effect are made in recording the amount of a transaction.

In other words, as long as equal debits and credits are posted, even to the wrong account or in the wrong amount, the total debits will equal the total credits. As a result, the trial balance will be in balance even though errors exist in account balances. Nevertheless, despite its limitations, the trial balance is a useful screen for finding many errors.

◀ ETHICS NOTE

When auditors become aware of misstatements in financial statements, they consider them to arise from either error or fraud. Unlike an error, fraud is an intentional misstatement that is viewed as being unethical and often illegal.

REVIEW OF THE ACCOUNTING CYCLE—STEPS 1–4

We learned about the first four steps of the accounting cycle in this chapter, and will learn the remaining steps (Steps 5–9) in the next chapter. Steps 1 through 4 of the accounting cycle begin with the analysis of business transactions and end with the preparation of the trial balance, as shown in Illustration 3-13.

THE ACCOUNTING CYCLE

▶Illustration 3-13
Steps 1–4 in the
accounting cycle

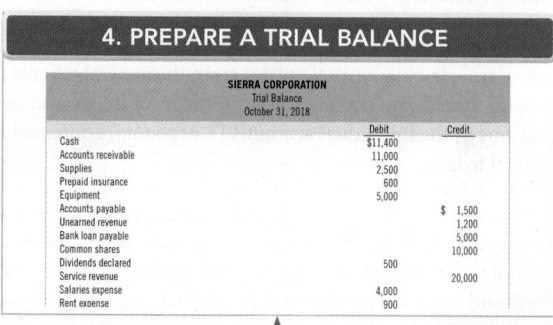

1. ANALYZE BUSINESS TRANSACTIONS

	Assets	=	Liabilities	+	Shareholders' Equity				
							Retained Earnings		
	Cash + Sup. + Pre. Ins. + Equipment = A/P + L/P +				Common Shares	+ Rev. – Exp. – Div.			
Equation Analysis	$8,500 $600 $5,000		$5,000		$10,000	$900			
(6)	+$2,500		+$2,500						
	$8,500 + $2,500 + $600 + $5,000 = $2,500 + $5,000 + $10,000 – $900								
	$16,600				$16,600				

4. PREPARE A TRIAL BALANCE

SIERRA CORPORATION
Trial Balance
October 31, 2018

	Debit	Credit
Cash	$11,400	
Accounts receivable	11,000	
Supplies	2,500	
Prepaid insurance	600	
Equipment	5,000	
Accounts payable		$ 1,500
Unearned revenue		1,200
Bank loan payable		5,000
Common shares		10,000
Dividends declared	500	
Service revenue		20,000
Salaries expense	4,000	
Rent expense	900	

2. JOURNALIZE THE TRANSACTIONS

SIERRA CORPORATION
General Journal

Date	Account Titles and Explanation	Debit	Credit
2018			
Oct. 1	Cash	10,000	
	Common Shares		10,000
	(Issued common shares)		
1	Equipment	5,000	
	Bank Loan Payable		5,000
	(Purchased equipment by signing a $5,000 bank loan plus 6% interest to be repaid in three months)		
2	Rent Expense	900	
	Cash		900
	(Paid cash for October office rent)		
5	Prepaid Insurance	600	

3. POST TO THE LEDGER ACCOUNTS

SIERRA CORPORATION
General Ledger

Cash						
Oct.	1	10,000	Oct.	2	900	
	19	1,200		5	600	
	30	9,000		22	1,000	
				26	4,000	
				29	500	
				31	1,800	
Bal.		1,400				

Unearned Revenue		
Oct. 19	1,200

Bank Loan Payable		
Oct. 1	5,000

Common Shares		
Oct. 1	10,000

Accounts Receivable				
Oct.	15	20,000	Oct. 30	9,000
Bal.		11,000		

Dividends Declared		
Oct. 29	500

The above steps must be done in sequence. Steps 1 and 2 may occur daily during the accounting period. Step 3 may also occur daily but most companies post monthly rather than daily to the general ledger unless a computerized accounting system exists. Step 4 is done on a periodic basis, such as monthly, quarterly, or annually.

DO IT! ▶3-5   Trial Balance

Koizumi Kollections Ltd. has the following alphabetical list of accounts and balances at July 31, 2018:

Accounts payable	$33,700	Equipment	$ 35,700
Accounts receivable	71,200	Income tax expense	12,000
Bank loan payable	49,500	Land	51,000
Buildings	86,500	Operating expenses	93,100
Cash	3,200	Service revenue	171,100
Common shares	99,400	Unearned revenue	3,000
Dividends declared	4,000		

Each of the above accounts has a normal balance. Prepare a trial balance.

Action Plan

✔ Reorder the accounts as they would normally appear in the general ledger and financial statements: statement of financial position accounts are listed first (assets, liabilities, and shareholders' equity), and then income statement accounts (revenues and expenses).

✔ Determine whether each account has a normal debit or credit balance.

✔ List the amounts in the appropriate debit or credit column.

✔ Total the trial balance columns. Total debits must equal total credits or a mistake has been made.

SOLUTION

Try this Do It! exercise on your own and then check your answer at the end of the chapter.

Related Exercise Material: BE3-12, BE3-13, E3-10, E3-11, E3-12, E3-13, E3-14, and E3-15.

REVIEW AND PRACTICE

▶ LEARNING OBJECTIVE REVIEW

1. Analyze the effect of transactions on the accounting equation. Each accounting transaction has a dual effect on the accounting equation: assets = liabilities + shareholders' equity. For example, if an individual asset is increased, there must be a corresponding decrease in another asset, an increase in a specific liability, or an increase in shareholders' equity.

2. Explain how accounts, debits, and credits are used to record transactions. An account is an individual accounting record of increases and decreases in specific asset, liability, and shareholders' equity (common shares, retained earnings, revenues, expenses, and dividends declared) accounts.

The terms *debit* and *credit* are synonymous with *left* and *right*. Assets, expenses, and dividends declared are increased by debits and decreased by credits. The normal balance of these accounts is a debit balance (the increase side). Liabilities, common shares, retained earnings, and revenues are increased by credits and decreased by debits. The normal balance of these accounts is a credit balance (the increase side).

3. Journalize transactions in the general journal. The initial record of an accounting transaction is entered in a general journal. The journal discloses in one place the complete effect of a transaction, provides a chronological record of transactions, and helps prevent or locate errors because the debit and credit amounts for each entry can be readily compared.

4. Post transactions to the general ledger. Posting is the process of transferring journal entries from the general journal to the general ledger. This accumulates the effects of the journalized transactions in the individual accounts (T accounts) contained in the general ledger.

5. Prepare a trial balance. A trial balance is a list of general ledger accounts and their balances at a specific time. The main purpose of the trial balance is to prove the mathematical equality of debits and credits after posting. A trial balance also can help uncover errors in journalizing and posting and is useful in preparing financial statements.

▶ KEY TERM REVIEW

The following are key terms defined in this chapter with the corresponding page reference for your review. You will find a complete list of terms and definitions for all chapters in the glossary at the end of this textbook.

Account (p. 115)
Accounting cycle (p. 106)
Accounting information system (p. 106)
Accounting transaction (p. 106)
Chart of accounts (p. 124)

Credit (p. 116)
Debit (p. 116)
Double-entry accounting
  system (p. 119)
General journal (p. 122)

General ledger (p. 123)
Normal balance (p. 116)
Posting (p. 124)
T account (p. 116)
Trial balance (p. 132)

▶ DECISION TOOLKIT REVIEW

DECISION CHECKPOINTS	INFO NEEDED FOR DECISION	TOOLS TO USE FOR DECISION	HOW TO EVALUATE RESULTS
Has an accounting transaction occurred?	Details of the transaction	Accounting equation	If the transaction affected assets, liabilities, or shareholders' equity, then record as an accounting transaction.
How do you determine an account's normal balance?	Type of account: asset, liability, shareholders' equity (common shares, retained earnings, revenue, expense, or dividends declared)	The normal balance of an account is always on its increase side. Accounts that normally have a debit balance: assets, expenses, and dividends declared. Accounts that normally have a credit balance: liabilities, retained earnings, common shares, and revenues.	Knowing an account's normal balance will help to determine debit and credit effects, in addition to helping to identify errors.
How do you determine that debits equal credits?	All general ledger account balances	Trial balance	List the account titles and their balances. Total the debit and credit columns and verify equality. If debits do not equal credits, then the error must be located and corrected before proceeding. Note that, even if debits equal credits, certain types of errors, such as not recording an entire transaction, may still exist.

▶ PRACTICE USING THE DECISION TOOLKIT

Answers are at the end of the chapter.

Nanaimo Ltd. hired a co-op student to prepare a trial balance for the company at year end from the following list of account balances, shown in alphabetical order.

NANAIMO LTD. List of Accounts December 31, 2018	
Accounts payable	$ 673,000
Accounts receivable	712,000
Bank loan payable	200,000
Buildings	1,291,000
Cash	32,000
Cost of goods sold	2,384,000
Equipment	83,000
Income tax expense	55,000
Income tax payable	5,000
Inventory	365,000
Land	110,000
Mortgage payable	685,000
Operating expenses	1,151,000
Retained earnings, beginning of year	892,000
Salaries payable	62,000
Sales revenue	3,741,000

The student couldn't get the trial balance to balance. He checked with various people responsible for entering accounting information and discovered the following:

1. The purchase of equipment, costing $7,000 and paid for with cash, was not recorded.
2. A data entry clerk accidentally deleted an account in the shareholders' equity section with a credit balance of $200,000. She couldn't remember the correct account name so the amount was added to the Mortgage Payable account in the trial balance.
3. December cash sales revenue of $75,000 was credited to the Sales Revenue account, but the debit side of the entry was not made.
4. Income tax expense of $5,000 was mistakenly charged to the Operating Expense account.
5. All accounts have normal balances.

INSTRUCTIONS

(a) Which mistake(s) have caused the trial balance to be out of balance?

(b) Should all of the mistakes identified in part (a) be corrected? Explain.

(c) What is the name of the account the data entry clerk deleted?

(d) Identify whether each of the accounts included in the list of accounts has a normal debit or credit balance.

(e) Make any necessary corrections and prepare a correct trial balance.

(f) On the trial balance, identify on which financial statement each account should be reported. Write "SFP" beside the accounts that should be shown on the statement of financial position, "IS" beside those that should be shown on the income statement, and "SCE" beside those that should be shown on the statement of changes in equity. (*Note:* Some accounts may be shown on more than one statement.)

▶ PRACTICE COMPREHENSIVE DO IT!

Answers are at the end of the chapter.

On August 31, 2018, Campus Laundry Ltd.'s general ledger showed the following accounts: Cash $20,000; Accounts Receivable $4,000; Equipment $15,000; Accounts Payable $2,000; Bank Loan Payable $10,000;

Common Shares $5,000; and Retained Earnings $22,000. During the month of September, the following transactions occurred:

Sept. 3   Paid $1,000 cash for rent for the month of September.
4   Purchased new washers and dryers for $25,000, paying $10,000 in cash and borrowing $15,000 from the bank for six months.
7   Paid $1,200 to renew a one-year insurance policy, effective September 1.
14   Paid biweekly employee salaries of $2,500.
15   Performed services on account for a nearby restaurant, $6,200.
21   Declared and paid $700 of dividends to shareholders.
26   Paid accounts payable owing to suppliers, $2,000.
28   Paid biweekly employee salaries of $2,500.
30   Total cash receipts for laundry services performed throughout the month were $5,000.
30   Received an invoice for utilities of $1,200 for the month of September.
30   Paid monthly income tax instalment of $600.

INSTRUCTIONS

(a) Journalize the September transactions.

(b) Prepare T accounts, enter the opening balances, post the September transactions, and determine the ending balances.

(c) Prepare a trial balance at September 30.

(d) Prepare an income statement, statement of changes in equity, and statement of financial position for September.

▶ PRACTICE OBJECTIVE-FORMAT QUESTIONS

Answers with feedback are at the end of the chapter.

1. Indicate which of the following transactions would *not* be recorded in the accounting records. (Select as many as are appropriate.)

(a) Purchased equipment on account.
(b) Obtained permission to purchase land from the board of directors.
(c) Issued common shares.
(d) Terminated an employee.
(e) Hired an employee.
(f) Performed services for customers on account.
(g) Entered into a contract to purchase inventory, with the supplier agreeing to deliver the goods in 15 days.

2. Indicate which of the following are correct. (Select as many as are appropriate).

(a) CKBW Ltd. started the year on January 1 with total assets of $70,000 and total liabilities of $40,000. During the year, the company recorded $100,000 in revenues, $65,000 in expenses, and dividends declared of $5,000, and issued $15,000 in additional common shares. The company's total shareholders' equity was $30,000 on January 1 and $75,000 on December 31.

(b) Carswell Ltd. started the year on January 1 with total assets of $105,000 and total liabilities of $50,000. During the year, the company recorded $150,000 in revenues, $75,000 in expenses, and dividends declared of $10,000, and issued $20,000 in additional common shares. The company's total shareholders' equity was $45,000 on January 1 and $135,000 on December 31.

(c) Willco Ltd. started the year on January 1 with total assets of $90,000 and total liabilities of $40,000. During the year, the company recorded $75,000 in revenues and $30,000 in expenses, did not declare any dividends, and issued $10,000 in additional common shares. The company's total shareholders' equity was $70,000 on January 1 and $125,000 on December 31.

(d) Farenholtz Ltd. started the year on January 1 with total assets of $115,000 and total liabilities of $67,000. During the year, the company recorded $95,000 in revenues, $75,000 in expenses, and dividends declared of $10,000, and did not issue any additional common shares. The company's total shareholders' equity was $48,000 on January 1 and $58,000 on December 31.

3. Indicate which of the following transactions would result in an increase in assets and an increase in shareholders' equity. (Select as many as are appropriate.)

(a) Received cash from a customer in advance of performing a service.
(b) Declared and paid dividends to shareholders.
(c) Performed services for a customer on account.
(d) Paid employee salaries.
(e) Purchased supplies on account.
(f) Prepaid an insurance policy for the year.
(g) Received cash from the issue of common shares.

4. Indicate which of the following accounts would normally have a debit balance and are asset accounts. (Select as many as are appropriate.)

(a) Accounts Receivable
(b) Accumulated Depreciation—Vehicles
(c) Common Shares
(d) Inventory
(e) Unearned Revenue
(f) Prepaid Insurance
(g) Vehicles
(h) Retained Earnings

5. Indicate which of the following accounts normally have a credit balance. (Select as many as are appropriate.)

(a) Unearned Revenue
(b) Dividends Declared
(c) Prepaid Insurance
(d) Retained Earnings
(e) Depreciation Expense
(f) Accounts Payable
(g) Accounts Receivable
(h) Common Shares

6. Indicate which of the following are correct. (Select as many as are appropriate.)

(a) Shareholders' equity includes common shares and retained earnings.
(b) Expenses decrease shareholders' equity and are recorded as credits.
(c) Liabilities normally have a credit balance and are increased by credits.
(d) Revenues increase shareholders' equity and are recorded as credits.
(e) Shareholders' equity is reduced by the declaration of dividends.
(f) Dividends declared and paid are an expense and are recorded as debits.
(g) Unearned revenue is a liability and increases net income.

7. A list of cash transactions is given in the left-hand column. Match the transaction with the account title given in the right-hand column that should be used to record the noncash side of each transaction. (Note that there are more account titles than required in the right-hand column.)

(a) Collected account due from a customer.
(b) Purchased inventory for future resale.
(c) Received an advance from a customer for future services.
(d) Received cash for services performed.
(e) Purchased supplies.
(f) Paid an account due to a supplier.
(g) Declared and paid dividends to shareholders.

1. Accounts Payable
2. Accounts Receivable
3. Dividends Declared
4. Dividends Expense
5. Equipment
6. Inventory
7. Service Revenue
8. Supplies
9. Unearned Revenue

8. Indicate which of the following statements are correct. (Select as many as are appropriate.)

(a) The general journal is also known as the book of original entry.
(b) Journal entries should be recorded in chronological order.
(c) A compound journal entry affects two accounts, one debit and one credit.
(d) It doesn't matter if debit and credit amounts equal in each journal entry as long as total debits equal total credits in the trial balance.
(e) The general ledger is often arranged in the order in which accounts are listed in the financial statements, starting with the statement of financial position accounts.
(f) Posting involves transferring information from the general ledger to the general journal.
(g) The first four steps in the accounting cycle can be completed in any order.

9. Indicate which of the following statements are correct regarding the retained earnings account shown on a trial balance prepared at the end of a company's first year of operations. (Select as many as are appropriate.)

(a) It represents the retained earnings at the end of the first year.
(b) It would be zero.
(c) It is equal to total assets less total liabilities.
(d) It is the same as total shareholders' equity at the end of the first year.
(e) It represents the income generated by the company during the first year (if no dividends were declared).

(f) It would be in the credit column of the trial balance.

(g) It would represent the amount received from the issue of common shares.

10. Indicate which of the following situations would result in the trial balance *not* being in balance. (Select as many as are appropriate.)

(a) A journal entry to record a cash sale is posted twice.

(b) The purchase of $400 of supplies on account is debited to Supplies and credited to Cash.

(c) The purchase of $275 of inventory on account was recorded as a debit to Inventory and a debit to Accounts Payable.

(d) A $100 cash dividend is debited to Dividends Declared for $1,000 and credited to Cash for $100.

(e) A $450 payment on account to a creditor is debited to Accounts Payable for $45 and credited to Cash for $45.

(f) A $125 collection on account was recorded and posted as a debit to Cash and a credit to Service Revenue.

(g) A $300 payment to a supplier to settle an outstanding account was posted as a debit to cash and a credit to accounts payable.

WileyPLUS

Brief Exercises, Exercises, and many additional resources are available for practice in WileyPLUS.

▶ QUESTIONS

(LO 1)   1. (a) Why are some events recorded as accounting transactions but others are not? (b) Give two examples of events that would not be recorded.

(LO 1)   2. Which of the following transactions should be recorded in the accounting records? Explain your answer in each case.
(a) The company wins an award as one of the top 50 companies in Canada to work for.
(b) Supplies are purchased on account.
(c) A shareholder dies.
(d) The company declares and pays dividends to its shareholders.
(e) A local lawyer agrees to provide legal services to the company for the next year.

(LO 1)   3. Can a company enter into a transaction that affects only the left (assets) side of the accounting equation? If so, give an example.

(LO 2)   4. Explain the relationship between the accounting equation and normal balances in assets, liabilities, and shareholders' equity.

(LO 2)   5. Given that both liabilities and shareholders' equity are on the same side of the accounting equation, why is it that all liability accounts are increased by credits but all shareholders' equity accounts are not?

(LO 2)   6. Emily Boudreau, an introductory accounting student, believes debit balances are favourable and credit balances are unfavourable. Is Emily correct? Discuss.

(LO 3)   7. (a) What is a general journal? (b) How does the journal facilitate the recording process?

(LO 3)   8. Meghan is recording the purchase of a truck in a journal entry and can't decide what account title to use for the truck. She is thinking about using "Truck Purchased," but

she also likes the account titles "Mack Truck" or "Big Rig," which better represent the type of truck the company purchased. Give Meghan advice about choosing an account title to use in a journal entry.

(LO 3, 4)   9. An efficiency expert who was reviewing the steps in the accounting cycle suggested dropping the general journal and recording and summarizing transactions directly into the general ledger instead. Comment on this suggestion.

(LO 3, 4) 10. Does it matter how frequently transactions are posted from the general journal to the general ledger? Explain.

(LO 4)   11. (a) What is a general ledger? (b) In what order are accounts usually arranged in a general ledger?

(LO 4)   12. (a) What is a chart of accounts and why is it important? (b) How does numbering the accounts help?

(LO 4)   13. Arrange the following accounts in their normal order in a chart of accounts: Accounts Payable, Accounts Receivable, Cash, Common Shares, Dividends Declared, Income Tax Expense, Prepaid Insurance, Salaries Expense, Service Revenue, Supplies, and Unearned Revenue.

(LO 5)   14. (a) What is a trial balance? (b) Does it matter in which order accounts are listed in the trial balance?

(LO 5)   15. On an unadjusted trial balance, why does the retained earnings balance shown relate to the beginning of the period rather than the end of the period?

(LO 5)   16. Claire Hart has just prepared a trial balance for a company and found that total debits were $100 higher than total credits. Assuming only one error was made, discuss the process Claire might use to find this error.

(LO 1, 3, 17. (a) Identify and describe the first four steps in the accounting cycle. (b) Does it matter in which order the steps are completed? Explain.
4, 5)

▶BRIEF EXERCISES

BE3–1 Presented below are a number of transactions. (a) Indicate whether each transaction increased (+), decreased (–), or had no effect (NE) on assets, liabilities, and shareholders' equity. (b) Which of the following are accounting transactions that should be recorded in the accounting records?

Determine effect of transactions on accounting equation.

(LO 1)

1. Purchased equipment for cash.
2. Completed the paperwork to hire a new employee; the employee will start work next week.
3. Fired the CEO.
4. Performed services on account.
5. A potential customer called to inquire about the availability of a product with limited availability and you are sure they will call back to place an order within the week.

BE3–2 Prepare an equation analysis of the effects of the following transactions on the expanded accounting equation, similar to that shown in Illustration 3-3.

Analyze effects of transactions.

(LO 1)

1. Purchased supplies on account, $250.
2. Provided a service on account, $500.
3. Paid salaries expense, $300.
4. Issued common shares in exchange for cash, $5,000.
5. Declared and paid $100 of dividends to shareholders.
6. Received cash from a customer who had previously been billed for services provided, $500 (see item 2).
7. Paid account owed to supplier on account, $250 (see item 1).
8. Paid for insurance in advance, $100.
9. Received cash in advance from a customer for services to be performed in the future, $300.
10. Performed the service that the customer previously paid for (see item 9).

BE3–3 For each of the following accounts, indicate (a) whether it is an asset, liability, or shareholders' equity account; (b) the normal balance of the account; (c) whether a debit will increase or decrease the account; and (d) whether a credit will increase or decrease the account.

Indicate normal balance and debit and credit effects.

(LO 2)

1. Accounts Payable
2. Accounts Receivable
3. Cash
4. Common Shares
5. Dividends Declared
6. Equipment
7. Income Tax Expense
8. Retained Earnings
9. Service Revenue
10. Unearned Revenue

BE3–4 Riko Ltd. has the following selected transactions:

Indicate debit and credit effects.

(LO 2)

1. Issued common shares to shareholders in exchange for $5,000.
2. Paid rent in advance for two months, $2,100.
3. Paid administrative assistant $500 salary.
4. Billed clients $1,200 for services provided.
5. Received $900 in partial payment from clients for services provided in item 4 above.
6. Purchased $500 of supplies on account.
7. Paid supplier amount owing on account, $500.
8. Borrowed $1,000 cash from the bank to purchase equipment.

For each transaction, indicate (a) the basic type of account debited or credited (asset, liability, shareholders' equity); (b) the specific account debited or credited; and (c) whether the specific account is increased or decreased when recording this transaction. Use the following format, in which the first one has been done for you as an example:

	Account Debited			Account Credited		
	(a)	(b)	(c)	(a)	(b)	(c)
Transaction	Basic Type	Specific Account	Effect	Basic Type	Specific Account	Effect
1.	Asset	Cash	Increase	Shareholders' equity	Common Shares	Increase

BE3–5 Transactions for Ing Ltd. for the month of June, its first month of operations, are presented below. For each transaction, prepare a (a) basic analysis, (b) equation analysis, and (c) debit–credit analysis.

Prepare basic, equation, and debit-credit analyses.

(LO 1, 2)

June	1	Issued common shares to shareholders in exchange for $2,500 cash.
	4	Purchased supplies on account for $250.
	7	Billed J. Kronsnoble $300 for welding work done.
	18	Received partial payment of $200 from J. Kronsnoble for work billed on June 7.

25	Hired a new employee to start work on July 3.
27	Received cash of $200 from Liu Controls Ltd. as a deposit for welding work to be done in July.
28	Paid for supplies purchased on June 4.
29	Paid $100 for monthly income tax instalment.

Record transactions

(LO 3)

BE3–6 Journalize the transactions given in BE3–2.

Record transactions.

(LO 3)

BE3–7 Journalize the transactions for Riko Ltd. given in BE3–4.

Record transactions.

(LO 3)

BE3–8 Journalize the transactions for Ing Ltd. given in BE3–5.

Determine missing amounts in ledger.

(LO 4)

BE3–9 Fill in the missing amounts from the following T accounts.

Accounts Receivable				Accounts Payable				Service Revenue			
Aug. 10	17,500					Aug. 5	(c)			Aug. 10	50,000
15	6,500					18	3,400	Aug. 12	500		
		Aug. 23	(a)	Aug. 29	5,800					15	45,000
Bal.	9,000					Bal.	3,600			Bal.	(e)
Sept. 5	(b)					Sept. 12	7,700			Sept. 5	(f)
		Sept. 15	8,000	Sept. 23	5,900					Sept. 25	450
Bal.	5,000					Bal.	(d)			Bal.	99,000

Post journal entries.

(LO 4)

BE3–10 Set up T accounts, post the journal entries recorded for Ing Ltd. in BE3–8 to the general ledger, and determine the ending balances in each account.

Post journal entries.

(LO 4)

BE3–11 Gushoe Ltd. had the following selected opening account balances at the end of April 30: Cash $1,500; Accounts Receivable $1,800; and Accounts Payable $900. Transactions during the month of May are presented in journal entry form below.

GENERAL JOURNAL

Date	Account Titles	Debit	Credit
May 4	Accounts Receivable	3,200	
	Service Revenue		3,200
7	Dividends Declared	500	
	Cash		500
11	Cash	1,900	
	Accounts Receivable		1,900
21	Cash	2,000	
	Service Revenue		2,000
25	Salaries Expense	2,500	
	Cash		2,500
28	Accounts Payable	200	
	Cash		200
30	Income Tax Expense	750	
	Cash		750

(a) Provide an explanation for each of the journal entries listed above. (b) Set up T accounts, enter the balances at April 30, post the May journal entries to the general ledger, and determine the ending balances.

Prepare trial balance.

(LO 5)

BE3–12 From the general ledger account balances given below, listed in alphabetical order, (a) identify the normal balance of each account, and (b) prepare a trial balance for Carland Inc. at June 30, 2018. All accounts have a normal balance.

Accounts payable	$ 3,000	Held for trading investments	6,000
Accounts receivable	4,000	Income tax expense	400
Accumulated depreciation—equipment	3,600	Rent expense	1,000
Cash	4,400	Retained earnings	12,650
Common shares	10,000	Salaries expense	4,000
Dividends declared	200	Service revenue	7,600
Equipment	17,000	Unearned revenue	150

Identify effects of errors on trial balance.

(LO 5)

BE3–13 Different types of posting errors are identified below:

1. A $1,200 debit to Supplies was posted as a $2,100 debit.
2. A $1,000 credit to Cash was posted twice as two credits to Cash.

3. A $5,000 debit to Dividends Declared was posted to the Common Shares account.
4. A journal entry debiting Cash and crediting Service Revenue for $2,500 was not posted.
5. The collection of $500 cash on account was posted as a debit of $500 to Cash and a credit of $500 to Accounts Payable.
6. The payment of $1,000 on an account payable owed to the insurance company was posted as a debit to the Insurance Expense account. No credit was posted.

For each of the above errors, indicate (a) whether the trial balance will balance (yes or no), (b) the amount of the difference if the trial balance will not balance, and (c) the trial balance column (debit or credit) that will have the larger total. Consider each error separately. Use the following format, in which the first error is given as an example:

Error	(a) In Balance	(b) Difference	(c) Larger Column Total
1.	No	$900	Debit

▶ EXERCISES

E3–1 An equation analysis of the transactions incurred by Wolfe Ltd. during August 2018 is shown below. Opening balances at July 31 are included as is a brief annotation beside each increase and decrease in shareholders' equity during August.

Analyze effects of transactions and calculate amounts.

(LO 1)

	Assets				=	Liabilities		+	Shareholders' Equity						
							Unearned		Common			Retained Earnings			
	Cash +	A/R +	Sup. +	Equipment =		A/P +	Revenue +		Shares +	Bal. +	Rev. −	Exp. −	Div.		
July 31 Bal.	+$6,500	+$5,000				+$2,000			+$5,000	+$4,500					
(1)	+1,000						+$1,000								
(2)	−1,000			+$5,000		+4,000									
(3)	−750		+$750												
(4)	+4,100	+5,400									+$9,500			Service revenue	
(5)	−2,000					−2,000									
(6)	−1,000												−$1,000	Dividends declared	
(7)	−4,800											−$4,800		Operating expenses	
(8)	+5,000	−5,000													
(9)	−300											−300		Interest expense	
(10)	−880											−880		Income tax expense	

Instructions
(a) Provide an explanation for each of the above transactions during the month of August.
(b) Calculate net income for the month of August and retained earnings at August 31.
(c) Calculate the ending balances for total assets, total liabilities, and total shareholders' equity at August 31.

E3–2 Wong Computer Corporation had the following opening account balances at the end of April: Cash $5,000; Accounts Receivable $6,000; Accounts Payable $2,000; Common Shares $5,000; and Retained Earnings $4,000. It entered into the following transactions during the month of May:

Analyze effects of transactions.

(LO 1)

1. Purchased equipment on account for $8,000.
2. Paid $1,600 for rent for the month of May.
3. Provided computer services for $3,800 on account.
4. Paid Ontario Hydro $300 cash for utilities used in May.
5. Borrowed $20,000 from the bank.
6. Paid supplier for equipment purchased in transaction 1.
7. Purchased a one-year accident insurance policy for $500 cash.
8. Received $3,000 cash in partial payment of the account owed in transaction 3.
9. Declared and paid $500 of dividends to shareholders.
10. Paid income tax of $250 for the month.

Instructions
Prepare an equation analysis of the effects of the opening balances and above transactions on the expanded accounting equation, similar to those shown in Illustrations 3-3 and 3-4.

E3–3 You are presented with the following alphabetical list of items, selected from the financial statements of **Saputo Inc.**:

Identify normal balance and statement classification.

(LO 2)

Bank loans payable
Buildings
Cash
Depreciation expense
Dividends declared
Finance income
Furniture, machinery, and equipment

Income tax expense
Income taxes payable
Interest expense
Inventories
Prepaid expenses
Receivables
Revenues

Instructions

For each of the above accounts, identify the following:

(a) the type of account (assets, liabilities, shareholders' equity [specify common shares, dividends, revenues, or expenses]);

(b) the normal balance of the account; and

(c) on which financial statement (income statement, statement of changes in equity, or statement of financial position) Saputo would report the account.

Prepare basic, equation, and debit–credit analyses.

(LO 1, 2)

E3–4 Selected transactions for Decorators Mill Ltd. during its first month of operations are presented below:

Mar.	2	Issued common shares for $11,000 cash.
	4	Purchased used car for $1,000 cash and $9,000 on account, for use in the business.
	10	Billed customers $2,300 for services performed.
	13	Paid $225 cash to advertise business opening.
	25	Received $1,000 cash from customers billed on March 10.
	27	Paid amount owing for used car purchased on March 4.
	30	Received $700 cash from a customer for services to be performed in April.
	31	Declared and paid $300 of dividends to shareholders.

Instructions

For each of the above transactions, prepare a (a) basic analysis, (b) equation analysis, and (c) debit–credit analysis.

Record transactions.

(LO 3)

E3–5 Data for Wong Computer Corporation were presented in E3–2.

Instructions

Journalize the transactions.

Record transactions.

(LO 3)

E3–6 Data for Decorators Mill Ltd. were presented in E3–4.

Instructions

Journalize the transactions.

Analyze, record, and post transactions.

(LO 1, 2, 3, 4)

E3–7 Selected transactions for the Basler Corporation during its first month of operations are presented below:

Sept.	1	Issued common shares for $20,000 cash.
	2	Performed $9,000 of services on account for a customer.
	4	Purchased equipment for $12,000, paying $5,000 in cash and borrowing the balance from the bank.
	10	Purchased $500 of supplies on account.
	25	Received $4,500 cash in advance for architectural services to be provided next month.
	30	Paid $300 on account in partial payment of amount owing for supplies. (See September 10 transaction.)
	30	Collected $5,000 on account owing from customer. (See September 2 transaction.)

Instructions

For each of the above transactions, do the following:

(a) Prepare a basic analysis.

(b) Prepare an equation analysis.

(c) Prepare a debit–credit analysis.

(d) Journalize the transactions.

(e) Set up T accounts, post the journal entries to the general ledger, and determine the ending balance in each account.

Post journal entries.

(LO 4)

E3–8 Data for Decorators Mill Ltd. were presented in E3–6.

Instructions

Set up T accounts, post the journal entries recorded in E3–6 to the general ledger, and determine the ending balances in each account.

Classify transactions as cash flow activities.

(LO 4)

E3–9 Review the transactions listed in E3–1 for Wolfe Ltd.

Instructions

Classify each August transaction as either an operating activity, investing activity, or financing activity.

Post journal entries and prepare trial balance.

(LO 4, 5)

E3–10 Kang Ltd. had the following opening account balances at July 31: Cash $4,000; Accounts Receivable $2,000; Equipment $2,500; Accounts Payable $1,500; Common Shares $2,000; and Retained Earnings $5,000. Kang's general journal for the month of August is presented here:

GENERAL JOURNAL			
Date	Account Titles	Debit	Credit
Aug. 7	Cash	1,800	
	Service Revenue		1,800
10	Equipment	4,000	
	Cash		1,500
	Bank Loan Payable		2,500

14	Accounts Receivable	1,450	
	Service Revenue		1,450
16	Cash	900	
	Unearned Revenue		900
28	Cash	700	
	Accounts Receivable		700
30	Salaries Expense	2,000	
	Cash		2,000
31	Dividends Declared	500	
	Cash		500

Instructions

(a) Prepare an explanation for each of the journal entries listed above.
(b) Set up T accounts, enter the opening balances at July 31, post the August journal entries to the general ledger, and determine the ending balances in each account.
(c) Prepare a trial balance at August 31.

E3–11 The following is the general ledger for Holly Corp. after its first month of operations:

Prepare trial balance.

(LO 5)

GENERAL LEDGER

Cash

Oct.	1	2,000	Oct.	5	400
	9	650		12	150
	17	500		16	300
				30	1,250
				31	500

Bank Loan Payable

| | | | Oct. 2 | 3,500 |

Common Shares

| | | | Oct. 1 | 2,000 |

Accounts Receivable

| Oct. | 3 | 800 | Oct. 17 | 500 |
| | 22 | 1,940 | | |

Dividends Declared

| Oct. 16 | 300 | |

Supplies

| Oct. | 5 | 400 | |

Service Revenue

| | | Oct. | 3 | 800 |
| | | | 22 | 1,940 |

Equipment

| Oct. | 2 | 3,500 | |

Salaries Expense

| Oct. 31 | 500 | |

Accounts Payable

| Oct. 12 | 150 | Oct. | 4 | 250 |

Advertising Expense

| Oct. 4 | 250 | |

Income Tax Payable

| | | Oct. 31 | 180 |

Rent Expense

| Oct. 30 | 1,250 | |

Unearned Revenue

| | | Oct. 9 | 650 |

Income Tax Expense

| Oct. 31 | 180 | |

Instructions

(a) Prepare an explanation for each ledger posting that was made above.
(b) Determine the ending balance in each of the T accounts.
(c) Prepare a trial balance at October 31.

E3–12 The following is a list of accounts, in alphabetical order, for Bourque Ltd. at December 31, 2018. All accounts have a normal balance.

Prepare trial balance.

(LO 5)

Accounts payable	$ 1,500		Office expense	$ 4,400
Accounts receivable	6,500		Rent expense	2,000
Accumulated depreciation—equipment	4,000		Retained earnings	16,000
Cash	10,000		Salaries expense	9,100
Common shares	5,000		Salaries payable	3,000
Depreciation expense	2,000		Service revenue	22,000
Dividends declared	4,500		Supplies	3,500
Equipment	10,000		Supplies expense	1,200
Income tax expense	500		Unearned revenue	2,200

Instructions
Prepare a trial balance.

*Prepare financial
statements.*
(LO 5)

E3–13 Refer to E3–12, where you prepared a trial balance for Bourque Ltd.

Instructions
Prepare an income statement, statement of changes in equity, and statement of financial position for the year ended December 31, 2018.

*Prepare trial balance and
financial statements.*
(LO 5)

E3–14 The following is a list of accounts, in alphabetical order, for Speedy Service Inc. at July 31, 2018:

Accounts payable	$ 9,500	Income tax expense	$ 3,000
Accounts receivable	14,000	Insurance expense	1,800
Accumulated depreciation—equipment	21,400	Interest expense	3,600
Bank loan payable, due 2020	39,000	Prepaid insurance	200
Cash	8,000	Rent expense	9,000
Common shares	38,000	Repairs and maintenance expense	10,450
Depreciation expense	9,700	Retained earnings	20,850
Dividends declared	800	Salaries expense	25,000
Equipment	99,000	Salaries payable	800
Held for trading investments	20,000	Service revenue	75,000

Additional information:
All accounts have a normal balance. During the year, the company issued common shares for $11,000.

Instructions
(a) Prepare a trial balance.
(b) Prepare an income statement, statement of changes in equity, and statement of financial position for the year.
(c) If you did not know the retained earnings amount at August 1, 2017, in the trial balance, could you have prepared the financial statements in part (b)? Explain.

*Identify effects of errors
on trial balance.*
(LO 5)

E3–15 The bookkeeper for Castle's Equipment Repair Corporation made these errors in journalizing and posting:
1. A credit posting of $400 to Accounts Receivable was omitted.
2. A debit posting of $750 for Prepaid Insurance was debited to Insurance Expense.
3. A collection on account of $100 was journalized and posted as a $100 debit to Cash and a $100 credit to Service Revenue.
4. A credit posting of $500 to Accounts Payable was made twice.
5. A cash purchase of supplies for $250 was journalized and posted as a $250 debit to Supplies and a $25 credit to Cash.
6. A debit of $465 to Advertising Expense was posted as $456.

Instructions
For each error, indicate:
(a) whether the trial balance will balance (yes or no),
(b) the amount of the difference if the trial balance will not balance, and
(c) the trial balance column (debit or credit) that will have the larger total.

Consider each error separately. Use the following format, in which the first error is given as an example:

	(a)	(b)	(c)
			Larger
Error	In Balance	Difference	Column Total
1.	No	$400	Debit

▶ PROBLEMS: SET A

*Analyze effects of trans-
actions and calculate
amounts.*
(LO 1)

P3–1A On April 1, Adventures Travel Agency Inc. began operations. The following transactions were completed during the month:
1. Issued common shares for $5,000 cash.
2. Obtained a bank loan for $20,000.
3. Paid $11,000 cash to buy equipment.
4. Paid $1,200 cash for April office rent.
5. Paid $1,450 for supplies.
6. Purchased $600 of newspaper advertising on account.
7. Earned $18,000 for services performed: cash of $2,000 was received from customers, and the balance was billed to customers on account.

8. Declared and paid $400 of dividends to shareholders.
9. Paid the utility bill for the month, $2,000.
10. Paid the amount due for newspaper advertising in transaction 6.
11. Paid $100 of interest on the bank loan obtained in transaction 2.
12. Paid employees' salaries, $6,400.
13. Received $12,000 cash from customers billed in transaction 7.
14. Paid income tax, $1,500.

Instructions

(a) Prepare an equation analysis of the effects of the above transactions on the expanded accounting equation, similar to that shown in Illustration 3-3.

(b) Calculate total assets, liabilities, and shareholders' equity at the end of the month and net income for the month.

P3–2A On July 31, 2018, the general ledger of Hills Legal Services Inc. showed these balances: Cash $4,000; Accounts Receivable $1,500; Supplies $500; Equipment $5,000; Accounts Payable $4,100; Common Shares $3,500; and Retained Earnings $3,400. During August, the following transactions occurred:

Analyze effects of transactions and prepare financial statements.

(LO 1)

Aug. 2   Collected $1,200 of accounts receivable due from customers.
      3   Received $1,300 for issuing common shares to new investors.
      6   Paid $2,700 on accounts payable owing.
      7   Earned fees of $6,500, of which $3,000 was collected in cash and the remainder was due on account.
      13 Purchased additional equipment for $1,200, paying $400 in cash and the balance on account.
      17 Paid salaries, $3,500, rent, $900, and advertising expenses, $275, for the month of August.
      17 Collected the balance of the fees earned on August 7.
      20 Declared and paid $500 of dividends to shareholders.
      22 Billed a client $1,000 for legal services provided.
      24 Received $2,000 from Laurentian Bank; the money was borrowed on a bank loan payable that is due in six months.
      27 Signed an engagement letter to provide legal services to a client in September for $4,500.
      28 Received the utility bill for the month of August in the amount of $275; it is due September 15.
      31 Paid income tax for the month, $500.

Instructions

(a) Beginning with the July 31 balances, prepare an equation analysis of the effects of the opening balances and above transactions on the expanded accounting equation, similar to those shown in Illustrations 3-3 and 3-4.

(b) Prepare an income statement, a statement of changes in equity, and a statement of financial position for August.

P3–3A Wood Maker Ltd. incurred the following selected transactions during the month of April:

Indicate debit and credit effects and normal balances.

(LO 2)

Apr. 2   Paid monthly rent, $800.
      3   Sold signs to a customer for $1,000 on account. (*Hint*: Use the Sales account for sales of all products.)
      5   Sold lawn furniture products for $1,250 cash.
      6   Purchased additional woodworking equipment for $3,000. The company paid cash of $500 and the balance was due on account in 20 days.
      12 Collected amount owed by customer for April 3 transaction.
      15 Declared and paid $150 of dividends to shareholders.
      16 Purchased lumber for $500 on account. (*Hint*: Use the Inventory account for lumber.)
      19 Paid $200 to repair equipment.
      20 Sold picnic tables to an RV park for $2,000 on account.
      25 Paid balance owing for purchase of woodworking equipment on April 6.
      27 Received $500 from a customer in advance to provide custom signs to be delivered next month.
      30 Paid salaries to employees of $1,800.

Instructions

(a) For each transaction, indicate (1) the basic type of account debited or credited (asset, liability, shareholders' equity); (2) the specific account debited or credited; and (3) whether the specific account is increased or decreased to record this transaction. Use the following format, in which the first one has been done for you as an example:

	Account Debited			Account Credited		
	(1) Basic	(2) Specific	(3)	(1) Basic	(2) Specific	(3)
Transaction	Type	Account	Effect	Type	Account	Effect
Apr. 2	Shareholders' equity	Rent Expense	Increase	Assets	Cash	Decrease

(b) Identify the normal balances for each of the accounts identified in part (a).

Identify normal balance and statement classification.

(LO 2)

P3–4A You are presented with the following alphabetical list of selected items from the financial statements of **Reitmans (Canada) Limited:**

Accumulated depreciation   Income tax expense
Administrative expenses   Income taxes recoverable
Buildings   Inventories
Common shares, beginning of year   Prepaid expenses
Cost of goods sold   Retained earnings, beginning of year
Dividends declared   Sales
Finance income   Trade and other payables
Goodwill   Trade and other receivables

Instructions

(a) For each of the above accounts, identify (1) whether the account is increased by a debit or a credit and (2) the normal balance of the account.

(b) For each of the above accounts, indicate on which financial statement (income statement, statement of changes in equity, or statement of financial position) the company would report the account.

(c) For the accounts identified in part (b) reported on the statement of financial position, indicate the appropriate classification (current assets, non-current assets, current liabilities, non-current liabilities, or shareholders' equity).

Prepare basic, equation, and debit–credit analyses and record transactions.

(LO 1, 2, 3)

P3–5A You are presented with the following transactions for Paddick Enterprises Ltd. for the month of February:

Feb.   2   Purchased supplies on account, $600.
        3   Purchased equipment for $10,000 by signing a bank loan due in three months.
        6   Earned service revenue of $50,000. Of this amount, $30,000 was received in cash. The balance was on account.
       13   Declared and paid $500 of dividends to shareholders.
       18   A customer paid $2,000 in advance for services to be performed next month.
       20   Paid the amount owing for the supplies purchased on February 2.
       23   Collected $20,000 of the amount owing from the February 6 transaction.
       24   Paid office expenses for the month, $22,000.
       27   Recorded salaries due to employees for work performed during the month, $14,000.
       28   Paid interest of $50 on the bank loan signed on February 3.

Instructions

(a) For each of the above transactions, prepare a (1) basic analysis, (2) equation analysis, and (3) debit–credit analysis.

(b) Journalize the transactions.

Record transactions.

(LO 3)

P3–6A Adventure Miniature Golf and Driving Range Inc. opened on May 1. The following selected events and transactions occurred during May:

May   1   Issued common shares for $120,000 cash.
      4   Purchased Henry's Golf Land for $270,000. The price consists of land $125,000; buildings $100,000; and equipment $45,000. Paid cash of $70,000 and signed a mortgage payable for the balance.
      4   Paid $1,500 for a one-year insurance policy; coverage begins next month.
      5   Advertised the opening of the driving range and miniature golf course, paying advertising expenses of $800.
      6   Purchased golf clubs and other equipment for $9,000 on account from Titleist Corporation.
     18   Received $8,800 from customers for golf fees earned.
     20   Declared and paid $500 of dividends to shareholders.
     22   Received $1,200 from a school board that paid for students' golf lessons that will be given in June.
     29   Paid Titleist in full for equipment purchased on May 6.
     30   Paid $800 of interest on the mortgage payable.
     30   Paid salaries of $3,400.

Instructions

Journalize the transactions.

Record and post transactions.

(LO 3, 4)

P3–7A During the first month of operations, the following transactions occurred for Virmani Architects Inc.:

Apr.   1   Invested cash of $10,000 and equipment of $6,000 in the company in exchange for common shares.
       1   Hired a secretary-receptionist at a monthly salary of $1,900.
       2   Paid office rent for the month, $950.
       3   Purchased architectural supplies on account from Halo Ltd., $1,900.
      10   Completed blueprints on a carport and billed client $1,200.
      13   Received $800 cash advance from a client for the design of a new home.
      20   Received $2,500 for services performed for a client.
      21   Received $600 from the client in partial payment for work completed and billed on April 10.

23   Received April's telephone bill for $135; due May 15. (*Hint:* Use the Utilities Expense account for telephone services.)

25   Declared and paid $160 of dividends to shareholders.

27   Paid 50% ($950) of the amount owed to Halo Ltd. on account. (See April 3 transaction.)

30   Paid secretary-receptionist for the month, $1,900.

30   Paid monthly income tax instalment, $100.

Instructions

(a) Journalize the transactions.

(b) Set up T accounts and post the journal entries to the general ledger.

(c) After the accountant finished journalizing and posting the above transactions, he complained that this process took too much time. He thought it would be more efficient to omit the journal entry step in the accounting cycle and record the transactions directly in the general ledger. Explain to the accountant whether you think this is a good idea or not, and why.

P3–8A On February 28, 2018, Star Theatre Inc.'s general ledger showed Cash $15,000; Land $85,000; Buildings $77,000; Equipment $20,000; Accounts Payable $12,000; Mortgage Payable $118,000; Common Shares $40,000; and Retained Earnings $27,000. During the month of March, the following transactions occurred:

Record and post transactions; prepare trial balance.

(LO 3, 4, 5)

Mar. 1   Received three movies to be shown during the first three weeks of March. The film rental was $27,000. Of that amount, $10,000 was paid in cash and the remainder was on account. (*Hint:* Star Theatre uses the account Rent Expense to record film rentals).

2   Hired M. Brewer to operate concession stand. Brewer agrees to pay Star Theatre 15% of gross receipts, payable on the last day of each month, for the right to operate the concession stand. (*Hint:* Star Theatre uses the account Concession Revenue to record concession receipts earned.)

5   Ordered three additional movies, to be shown the last 10 days of March. The film rental cost will be $300 per night.

12   Paid balance due on the movies rented on March 1.

13   Paid the accounts payable owing at the end of February.

15   Received $25,500 from customers for admissions for the first half of the month. (*Hint:* Star Theatre uses the account Fees Earned to record revenue from admissions.)

19   Paid advertising expenses, $950.

20   Received the movies ordered on March 5 and paid rental fee of $3,000 ($300 × 10 nights).

23   Paid salaries of $4,200.

26   Paid $1,250 of the balance due on the mortgage, as well as $750 of interest on the mortgage.

28   Paid $3,000 for the monthly income tax instalment.

30   Received statement from M. Brewer, showing gross concession receipts of $16,600, and the balance due to Star Theatre of $2,490 ($16,600 × 15%) for March. Brewer paid half of the balance due and will remit the remainder on April 5.

31   Received $25,800 from customers for admissions for the past two weeks.

Instructions

(a) Journalize the March transactions.

(b) Set up T accounts, enter the beginning balances in the ledger at February 28, and post the March journal entries to the general ledger.

(c) Prepare a trial balance at March 31.

P3–9A Pamper Me Salon Inc.'s general ledger at April 30, 2018, showed Cash $5,000; Supplies $500; Equipment $24,000; Accounts Payable $2,100; Unearned Revenue (from gift certificates) $1,000; Bank Loan Payable $10,000; Common Shares $5,000; and Retained Earnings $11,400. The following transactions occurred during May:

Record and post transactions; prepare trial balance.

(LO 3, 4, 5)

May 1   Paid rent for the month of May, $1,000.

4   Paid $1,100 of the accounts payable outstanding at April 30.

7   Issued gift certificates for future services for $1,500 cash.

15   Received $2,000 from customers for services performed to date.

15   Paid $1,200 in salaries to employees.

17   Customers receiving services worth $700 used gift certificates in payment.

18   Paid the remaining accounts payable from April 30.

22   Purchased supplies of $700 on account.

24   Received a bill for advertising for $500. This bill is due on June 22.

25   Received and paid a utilities bill for $400.

28   Received $2,100 from customers for services performed.

29   Customers receiving services worth $600 used gift certificates in payment.

30   Interest of $50 was paid on the bank loan.

31   Paid $1,200 in salaries to employees.

31   Paid income tax instalment for the month, $150.

Instructions

(a) Journalize the May transactions.

(b) Set up T accounts, enter the beginning balances in the general ledger at April 30, and post the May journal entries to the general ledger.

(c) Prepare a trial balance at May 31.

Prepare trial balance.
(LO 5)

P3–10A You are presented with the following alphabetical list of accounts and balances (in thousands) for Taggar Enterprises Inc. at June 30, 2018. All accounts have a normal balance.

Accounts payable	$ 3,500	Income tax payable	$ 100
Accounts receivable	3,000	Interest expense	100
Accumulated depreciation—buildings	4,000	Inventory	5,100
Accumulated depreciation—equipment	1,000	Land	7,400
Buildings	15,000	Long-term investments	3,550
Cash	1,800	Mortgage payable, due 2025	15,000
Common shares	5,000	Office expense	3,300
Cost of goods sold	13,700	Prepaid insurance	900
Dividends declared	2,000	Retained earnings	6,250
Equipment	3,000	Sales	25,000
Income tax expense	1,000		

Instructions

(a) Prepare a trial balance.

(b) If debits equal credits in Taggar's trial balance, do you have reasonable assurance that no errors exist? Explain.

Prepare financial
statements.
(LO 5)

P3–11A Refer to the trial balance for Taggar Enterprises Inc. prepared in P3–10A. In addition to this information, common shares in the amount of $2,000 were issued during the year and $1,250 of the mortgage is currently due.

Instructions

Prepare an income statement, statement of changes in equity, and statement of financial position for the year.

Identify effects of errors
and prepare correct trial
balance.
(LO 5)

P3–12A The following trial balance of Cantpost Ltd., at the end of its first year of operations, June 30, 2018, does not balance:

	Debit	Credit
Cash		$ 1,241
Accounts receivable	$ 2,630	
Supplies	860	
Equipment	3,000	
Accumulated depreciation— equipment		600
Accounts payable		2,665
Unearned revenue	1,200	
Common shares		1,000
Dividends declared	800	
Service revenue		8,440
Salaries expense	3,400	
Office expense	910	
Depreciation expense	600	
Income tax expense	365	
	$14,365	$13,346

Each of the listed accounts has a normal balance. However, each account may not have been listed in the appropriate debit or credit column. In addition, an examination of the general ledger and general journal reveals the following errors:

1. Cash received from a customer on account was debited for $570, and Accounts Receivable was credited for the same amount. The actual collection was for $750.

2. The purchase of equipment on account for $360 was recorded as a debit to Supplies for $360 and a credit to Accounts Payable for $360.

3. Services were performed on account for a client for $890. Accounts Receivable was debited for $890 and Service Revenue was credited for $89.

4. A transposition (reversal of digits) error was made when copying the balance in the Salaries Expense account. The correct balance should be $4,300.

5. A payment for rent in the amount of $1,000 was neither recorded nor posted.

Instructions

(a) Identify (1) any accounts listed in the wrong debit or credit column and (2) the effects of errors 1 to 5, if any, on the trial balance.

(b) Prepare a corrected trial balance.

▶ PROBLEMS: SET B

P3–1B On May 1, Marty's Repair Shop Ltd. began operations. The following transactions were completed during the month:

1. Issued common shares for $8,000 cash.
2. Paid $1,280 for May office rent.
3. Purchased equipment for $16,000, paying $4,000 cash and signing a bank loan payable for the balance.
4. Purchased supplies on account, $700.
5. Received $4,200 from customers for repair services provided.
6. Paid for supplies purchased in transaction 4.
7. Paid May telephone bill of $200.
8. Provided repair services on account to customers, $3,600.
9. Paid employee salaries, $2,000.
10. Received $700 in advance for repair services to be provided next month.
11. Collected $1,600 from customers for services billed in transaction 8.
12. Declared and paid $500 of dividends to shareholders.
13. Paid $80 of interest on the bank loan obtained in transaction 3.
14. Paid income tax of $600.

Analyze effects of transactions and calculate amounts.

(LO 1)

Instructions

(a) Prepare an equation analysis of the effects of the above transactions on the expanded accounting equation, similar to that shown in Illustration 3-3.

(b) Calculate total assets, liabilities, and shareholders' equity at the end of the month and net income for the month.

P3–2B The general ledger of Corso Care Corp., a veterinary company, showed these balances on August 31, 2018: Cash $4,500; Accounts Receivable $1,800; Supplies $350; Equipment $6,500; Accounts Payable $3,200; Common Shares $2,500; and Retained Earnings $7,450. During September, the following transactions occurred:

Analyze effects of transactions and prepare financial statements.

(LO 1)

Sept.	4	Paid the accounts payable owing at August 31.
	4	Paid $1,200 rent for September.
	5	Collected $1,450 of accounts receivable due from customers.
	6	Hired a part-time office assistant at $50 per day to start work the following week, on Monday, September 10.
	7	Received $2,300 cash for issuing common shares to new investors.
	10	Purchased additional equipment for $2,050, paying $700 in cash and the balance on account.
	12	Billed customers $500 for veterinary services provided.
	14	Paid $300 for advertising expenses.
	17	Received $2,500 from Canadian Western Bank; the money was borrowed on a bank loan payable due in nine months.
	18	Sent a statement reminding a customer that money was still owed from August.
	20	Earned veterinary service revenue of $4,500, of which $3,000 was received in cash. The balance is due in October.
	21	Paid part-time office assistant $750 for working two weeks in September.
	26	Received a bill for utility expenses in the amount of $175; it is not due until October 15.
	27	Declared and paid $500 of dividends to shareholders.
	28	Paid income tax for the month, $350.

Instructions

(a) Beginning with the August 31 balances, prepare an equation analysis of the effects of the opening balances and above transactions on the expanded accounting equation, similar to those shown in Illustrations 3-3 and 3-4.

(b) Prepare an income statement, a statement of changes in equity, and a statement of financial position for September.

P3–3B Pet Salon Ltd. incurred the following selected transactions during the month of March:

Mar.	1	Paid monthly rent, $1,000.
	3	Performed pet grooming services for $740 on account.

Indicate debit and credit effects and normal balances.

(LO 2)

5   Sold pet grooming products for $1,250 cash. (*Hint:* Use the Sales account for sales of pet products.)

8   Purchased additional grooming equipment for $700. The company paid cash of $70 and the balance was financed by a short-term bank loan.

12 Received $250 in payment from one of the customers for whom pet grooming services were performed on March 3.

15 Paid salaries to employees of $525.

16 Purchased $72 of supplies on account.

20 Paid $229 to repair grooming equipment.

22 Sold pet grooming products for $2,000 on account.

26 Paid balance owing for purchase of grooming equipment on March 8.

28 Received $500 from a customer in advance to provide pet grooming services at a dog show to be held next month.

31 Declared and paid $150 of dividends to shareholders.

Instructions

(a) For each transaction, indicate (1) the basic type of account debited or credited (asset, liability, shareholders' equity); (2) the specific account debited or credited; and (3) whether the specific account is increased or decreased to record this transaction. Use the following format, in which the first one has been done for you as an example:

	Account Debited			Account Credited		
Transaction	(1) Basic Type	(2) Specific Account	(3) Effect	(1) Basic Type	(2) Specific Account	(3) Effect
Mar. 1	Shareholders' equity	Rent Expense	Increase	Assets	Cash	Decrease

(b) Identify the normal balances for each of the accounts identified in part (a).

Identify normal balance and statement classification.

(LO 2)

P3–4B You are presented with the following alphabetical list of selected items from the financial statements of **High Liner Foods Incorporated:**

Accounts payable	Income taxes receivable
Accounts receivable	Interest expense
Bank loans payable (short-term)	Inventories
Cash	Prepaid expenses
Common shares, beginning of year	Retained earnings, beginning of year
Dividends declared	Sales
Furniture, fixtures, and production equipment	Selling, general, and administrative expenses
Income taxes expense	

Instructions

(a) For each of the above accounts, identify (1) whether the account is increased by a debit or a credit and (2) the normal balance of the account.

(b) For each of the above accounts, indicate on which financial statement (income statement, statement of changes in equity, or statement of financial position) the company would report the account.

(c) For the accounts identified in part (b) reported on the statement of financial position, indicate the appropriate classification (current assets, non-current assets, current liabilities, non-current liabilities, or shareholders' equity).

Prepare basic, equation, and debit–credit analyses and record transactions.

(LO 1, 2, 3)

P3–5B You are presented with the following transactions for Dankail Corporation for the month of January:

Jan. 2   Issued $5,000 of common shares for cash.

5   Provided services on account, $2,500.

6   Obtained a bank loan for $30,000.

7   Paid $40,000 to purchase a hybrid car to be used solely in the business.

9   Received a $5,000 deposit from a customer for services to be provided in the future.

12 Billed customers $20,000 for services performed during the month.

19 Paid $500 to purchase supplies.

20 Provided $1,500 of services for the customer who paid in advance on January 9.

23 Collected $5,000 owing from customers from the January 12 transaction.

26 Received a bill for utilities of $125, due February 26.

29 Paid rent for the month, $1,500.

31 Paid $4,000 of salaries to employees.

31 Paid interest of $300 on the bank loan from the January 6 transaction.

31 Paid income tax for the month, $3,600.

Instructions
(a) For each of the above transactions, prepare a (1) basic analysis, (2) equation analysis, and (3) debit–credit analysis.
(b) Journalize the transactions.

P3–6B Mountain Biking Corp. opened on April 1. The following selected events and transactions occurred during April:

Record transactions.
(LO 3)

Apr. 1 Issued common shares for $100,000 cash.
  3 Purchased an out-of-use ski hill costing $370,000, paying $60,000 cash and signing a bank loan payable for the balance. The $370,000 purchase price consisted of land $204,000; buildings $121,000; and equipment $45,000.
  8 Purchased advertising space for $1,800 on account.
  10 Paid salaries to employees, $2,800.
  13 Hired a park manager at a salary of $4,000 per month, effective May 1.
  14 Paid $5,500 for a one-year insurance policy.
  17 Declared and paid $600 of dividends to shareholders.
  20 Received $10,600 in cash from customers for admission fees.
  30 Paid $1,800 on account for the advertising purchased on April 8.
  30 Paid $2,000 of interest on the bank loan.
  30 Declared and paid an income tax instalment of $800.

Instructions
Journalize the transactions.

P3–7B During the first month of operations, the following transactions occurred for Astromech Accounting Services Inc.:

Record and post transactions.
(LO 3, 4)

May 1 Issued common shares for $20,000 cash.
  1 Paid office rent of $950 for the month.
  4 Hired a secretary-receptionist at a salary of $2,000 per month. She started work the same day.
  4 Purchased $750 of supplies on account from Read Supply Corp.
  11 Completed an income tax assignment and billed client $2,725 for services provided.
  12 Received $3,500 in advance on a management consulting engagement.
  15 Received $2,350 for services completed for Arnold Corp.
  20 Received $1,725 from client for work completed and billed on May 11.
  22 Paid one-third of balance due to Read Supply Corp. (See May 4 transaction.)
  25 Received a $275 telephone bill for May, to be paid next month. (*Hint:* Use the Utilities Expense account to record telephone services.)
  29 Paid secretary-receptionist $2,000 salary for the month.
  29 Paid monthly income tax instalment, $300.
  29 Declared and paid $250 dividend.

Instructions
(a) Journalize the transactions.
(b) Set up T accounts and post the journal entries to the general ledger.
(c) After the accountant finished journalizing and posting the above transactions, she complained that this process took too much time. She thought it would be more efficient to purchase and use accounting software instead of recording and posting transactions manually. Explain to the accountant whether you think this is a good idea or not, and why.

P3–8B On March 31, 2018, Lake Theatre Inc.'s general ledger showed Cash $6,000; Land $100,000; Buildings $80,000; Equipment $25,000; Accounts Payable $5,000; Mortgage Payable $125,000; Common Shares $50,000; and Retained Earnings $31,000. During the month of April, the following transactions occurred:

Record and post transactions; prepare trial balance.
(LO 3, 4, 5)

Apr. 2 Paid film rental fee of $800 on a movie ordered last month. (*Hint:* Lake Theatre uses the account Rent Expense to record film rentals.)
  3 Paid advertising expenses, $620.
  5 Hired Thoms Limited to operate concession stand. Thoms agrees to pay the Lake Theatre 20% of gross concession receipts, payable monthly, for the right to operate the concession stand. (*Hint:* Lake Theatre uses the account Concession Revenue to record concession receipts earned.)
  6 Ordered two additional films at $750 each.
  15 Received $1,950 from customers for admissions for the first half of the month. (*Hint:* Lake Theatre uses the account Fees Earned to record revenue from admissions.)
  16 Paid $2,000 of the balance due on the mortgage. Also paid $850 in interest on the mortgage.
  17 Paid $2,800 of the accounts payable.
  19 Received one of the films ordered on April 6 and was billed $750. The film will be shown in April.

20   Prepaid $700 rental fee on special film to be run in May. (*Hint:* Use the account Prepaid Rent to record rental fees paid in advance.)

26   Paid salaries, $2,900.

27   Paid $1,000 for the monthly income tax instalment.

30   Received statement from Thoms showing gross concession receipts of $5,600 and the balance due to Lake Theatre of $1,120 ($5,600 × 20%) for April. Thoms paid half of the balance due and will remit the remainder on May 4.

30   Received $7,300 from customers for admissions for the last half of the month.

Instructions

(a)   Journalize the April transactions.

(b)   Set up T accounts, enter the beginning balances in the ledger at March 31, and post the April journal entries to the ledger.

(c)   Prepare a trial balance at April 30.

Record and post transactions; prepare trial balance.

(LO 3, 4, 5)

P3–9B KG Skating School Inc.'s general ledger at March 31, 2018, showed Cash $23,000; Equipment $2,000; Accounts Payable $500; Unearned Revenue (for advance registration fees) $17,500; Common Shares $1,000; and Retained Earnings $6,000. The following transactions occurred during April:

Apr.   2   Paid for ice time for first two weeks of April, $5,000. (*Hint:* Use the account Rent Expense to record ice rentals.)

4   Booked ice with the city for the April session. It will cost $10,000.

6   Received and paid a bill for $500 for advertising of the April skating school.

9   Paid $300 of accounts payable outstanding at March 31.

13   Paid coaches and assistant coaches, $1,000.

16   Paid for ice time for remainder of April, $5,000.

18   Received a bill for Internet service for $100. This invoice is due on May 15. (*Hint:* Use the account Utilities Expense to record Internet costs.)

19   Paid $200 cash for supplies used immediately.

24   Received advance registrations for the next four-week skating session in May, $2,200.

25   Paid income tax instalment for the month, $880.

27   Purchased gifts for volunteers who helped out during April session, $300. (*Hint:* Use the account Advertising Expense to record gifts.)

30   Paid coaches and assistant coaches, $1,000.

30   Last day of April session. All of the advance registration fees have now been earned.

Instructions

(a)   Journalize the April transactions.

(b)   Set up T accounts, enter the beginning balances in the general ledger at March 31, and post the April journal entries to the general ledger.

(c)   Prepare a trial balance at April 30.

Prepare trial balance.

(LO 5)

P3–10B You are presented with the following alphabetical list of accounts and balances (in thousands) for Asian Importers Limited at January 31, 2018. All accounts have a normal balance.

Accounts payable	$ 46,300	Goodwill	$ 7,600
Accounts receivable	30,200	Income tax expense	10,000
Accumulated depreciation—buildings	13,000	Interest expense	2,150
Accumulated depreciation—equipment	3,600	Inventory	74,250
Bank loan payable (due 2021)	10,050	Land	42,500
Buildings	39,500	Mortgage payable	19,750
Cash	10,000	Office expense	67,750
Common shares	32,900	Other current liabilities	12,200
Cost of goods sold	244,200	Prepaid insurance	3,950
Dividends declared	1,850	Retained earnings	37,050
Equipment	10,900	Sales	370,000

Instructions

(a)   Prepare a trial balance.

(b)   If the trial balance doesn't balance, what steps should you take to find your error(s)?

Prepare financial statements.

(LO 5)

P3–11B Refer to the trial balance for Asian Importers prepared in P3–10B. In addition to this information, common shares in the amount of $12,900 were issued during the year and $6,300 of the mortgage is currently due.

Instructions

Prepare an income statement, statement of changes in equity, and statement of financial position for the year.

P3–12B The following trial balance of Messed Up Ltd., at the end of its first year of operations, May 31, 2018, does not balance:

Identify effects of errors and prepare correct trial balance.

(LO 5)

	Debit	Credit
Cash	$ 2,997	
Accounts receivable	2,630	
Equipment	9,200	
Accumulated depreciation—equipment	4,200	
Accounts payable	4,600	
Common shares	4,250	
Service revenue		$14,529
Salaries expense		8,150
Depreciation expense		2,100
Advertising expense		1,132
Insurance expense		600
Income tax expense		400
	$27,877	$26,911

Each of the listed accounts has a normal balance. However, each account may not have been listed in the appropriate debit or credit column. In addition, an examination of the general ledger and general journal reveals the following errors:

1. Prepaid Insurance, Accounts Payable, and Income Tax Expense were each understated by $100.
2. A transposition (reversal of digits) error was made in Service Revenue. Based on the posting made, the correct balance was $14,259.
3. A $750 dividend declared and paid to shareholders was debited to Salaries Expense and credited to Cash.
4. A $120 collection on account was recorded as a debit to Accounts Payable and a credit to Accounts Receivable.
5. A $2,000 bank loan was signed in exchange for the purchase of equipment. The transaction was neither journalized nor posted.

Instructions

(a) Identify (1) any accounts listed in the wrong debit or credit column and (2) the effects of errors 1 to 5, if any, on the trial balance.
(b) Prepare a corrected trial balance.

ACCOUNTING CYCLE | REVIEW

ACR3–1 Software Advisors Limited was organized on January 1, 2018. The company plans to use the following chart of accounts:

Record and post transactions; prepare trial balance and financial statements.

(LO 3, 4, 5)

*The **Accounting Cycle Review** is a comprehensive problem that helps students practice accounting fundamentals, and integrate concepts from multiple chapters.*

100	Cash		490	Dividends Declared
110	Accounts Receivable		500	Service Revenue
120	Supplies		700	Advertising Expense
130	Prepaid Insurance		710	Salaries Expense
200	Equipment		720	Interest Expense
300	Accounts Payable		730	Office Expense
310	Bank Loan Payable (non-current)		740	Rent Expense
400	Common Shares		900	Income Tax Expense
450	Retained Earnings			

The company had the following transactions in the month of January:

Jan. 2 Issued 1,000 common shares for $65 each.
4 Finalized a lease for office space and paid the first month's rent of $3,000.
5 Purchased $40,000 of equipment for $10,000 cash and financed the remainder with a long-term bank loan.
8 Paid for an advertisement in a local paper, $500.

Jan. 10   Purchased supplies on account, $1,000.
11   Paid for several advertising spots on the local radio station, $3,000.
12   Paid employees $7,500 for the first two weeks of work.
15   Summarized and recorded the billings to clients for the first two weeks of January. Billings totalled $15,000. These amounts are due by the 12th of the next month.
17   Paid $1,000 for office expenses.
19   Paid annual insurance policy with coverage up to December 31, 2018, for $6,000.
24   Received $10,000 from clients in partial settlement of accounts billed on the 15th.
25   Declared and paid $500 of dividends to shareholders.
26   Paid employees $7,500 for the previous two weeks of work.
29   Summarized and recorded the billings to clients for the prior two weeks. Billings totalled $18,000. These amounts are due by the 26th of the next month.
30   Made a payment to the bank of $200 for interest on the bank loan and $700 to pay on the amount owing for the bank loan.
31   Paid Canada Revenue Agency $1,500 for an income tax instalment.

Instructions
(a) Journalize the transactions.
(b) Set up T accounts and post the journal entries prepared in part (a).
(c) Prepare a trial balance.
(d) Prepare an income statement, statement of changes in equity, and statement of financial position for January.

Record and post transactions; prepare trial balance and financial statements; classify activities.

(LO 3, 4, 5)

ACR3–2 On July 31, 2018, the following alphabetically ordered list of accounts and amounts was available for B&B Repair Services Ltd.

Accounts payable	$ 2,300	Equipment	$10,000
Accounts receivable	3,200	Retained earnings	17,290
Accumulated depreciation—equipment	2,000	Salaries payable	1,420
Accumulated depreciation—vehicles	5,000	Supplies	1,030
Bank loan payable (non-current)	4,000	Unearned revenue	1,260
Cash	8,040	Vehicles	25,000
Common shares	14,000		

During August, the following summary transactions were completed:
Aug. 1   Paid $250 for advertising on Kijiji for the current month.
2   Provided $1,260 of services related to cash received in advance last month for services to be performed this month.
3   Paid August rent, $980.
6   Received $1,200 cash from customers in payment of accounts.
7   Signed a contract with Merrithew's Appliances Ltd. to provide future repair services for its customers as required.
10   Paid $3,120 for salaries due employees, of which $1,700 was for August and $1,420 for July salaries payable.
13   Received $2,800 cash for services performed to date in August.
15   Purchased new equipment for $2,000, which was financed with a bank loan.
20   Paid creditors $2,000 of accounts due.
22   Purchased supplies on account for $800.
24   Paid $2,900 for employees' salaries.
27   Billed customers $3,760 for services performed.
29   Received $780 from customers for services to be performed in the future.
30   Paid $500 on the bank loan, in addition to interest of $50.
31   Paid income tax of $380.
31   Declared and paid $400 of dividends to shareholders.

Instructions
(a) Journalize the August transactions.
(b) Set up T accounts, enter the opening balances in the general ledger at July 31, and post the journal entries to the general ledger.
(c) Prepare a trial balance at August 31.
(d) Prepare an income statement, statement of changes in equity, and statement of financial position for August.
(e) Review the Cash account in the general ledger. Classify each August transaction as either an operating activity, investing activity, or financing activity.

EXPAND YOUR | CRITICAL THINKING

CT3–1   Financial Reporting Case

The financial statements of **The North West Company Inc.** are presented in Appendix A, and those of **Sobeys Inc.** are presented in Appendix B.

Instructions

(a)   Using North West's financial statements, arrange the total amounts provided for assets, liabilities, and shareholders' equity into an accounting equation format (total assets = total liabilities + total shareholders' equity) at January 31, 2016. Further break down shareholders' equity into share capital, retained earnings, and other equity items.

(b)   Using Sobeys' financial statements, arrange the total amounts provided for assets, liabilities, and shareholders' equity into an accounting equation format at May 7, 2016. Further break down shareholders' equity into share capital (called capital stock by Sobeys), retained earnings (deficit), and other equity items.

(c)   Compare the two expanded accounting equations prepared in parts (a) and (b). Comment on any relevant comparisons between the two companies.

CT3–2   Financial Reporting Case

Uber Technologies Inc., a ride-sharing service, connects riders with drivers. It operates technology using a smart phone app or web browser, allowing users to request a ride and then uses GPS to guide the driver to the rider, and on to the rider's destination. Uber calculates the estimated fare ahead of time and transfers the money electronically, so no physical cash is exchanged and no one skips out on the fare. It keeps 20% of the fare for the use of its services.

The company was founded in 2009 and currently operates in 68 countries around the world, including Canada. In April 2016, the company's stock market value (market capitalization) had passed the U.S. $68-billion mark, surpassing Facebook as the most valuable venture-backed start-up in history.

Instructions

(a)   One of Uber's important economic resources is its network of riders and drivers. Do you expect this resource to be recorded in its accounting records?

(b)   Uber does not own any of the cars used to connect riders with drivers. What types of assets do you think Uber would report in its statement of financial position?

(c)   What information, if any, do you think Uber's statement of financial position would give to support its market value of U.S. $68 billion?

CT3–3   Financial Analysis Case

Melissa Young had always been encouraged by her accounting professor to apply her accounting skills as much as possible. When her uncle asked her to prepare his accounting records for a company he owns, called Bob's Repairs Ltd., she readily agreed.

The company has two employees who repair and service all computers used by four large companies in the area. Melissa spoke to her professor, who suggested that, due to the size of the business, she could record the company's transactions on a spreadsheet with the column headings representing the names of accounts that would appear in order on the income statement and statement of financial position. Each row of the spreadsheet could act like a journal entry. In addition, each column could act like a T account showing all debit and credit entries to an account. Melissa could add up the columns on the spreadsheet to determine the balance in each account at the end of the year. She could then build her financial statements on the spreadsheet by referencing the amounts for each item or category on the financial statements from the column totals.

Her uncle gave her the following information regarding its first year of operations, ending August 31, 2018:

1.   When the corporation was formed on September 1, 2017, common shares were sold to the sole shareholder, Uncle Bob, for $10,000 cash.

2.   Uncle Bob added up all of the invoices the company issued to its customers and the total came to $229,400. All of these were issued on credit.

3.   The company received $190,000 cash from customers when they paid their invoices.

4.   The company rents a small repair shop for $3,500 per month. The shop was rented for the full year and all rent was paid in cash. In addition, the landlord required the company to pay one month's rent in advance.

5.   Salaries to employees totalled $120,000 for the year and were paid in cash.

6.   Uncle Bob determined from a review of numerous invoices that the office expenses for the year were $36,400. Of these, all were paid except $4,000 that was still owing.

7.   In late August, a new customer approached the company and signed a contract for service to be done to its computers starting in October 2018. The customer paid the company $2,000 in advance to secure the service.

8.   Uncle Bob estimated that, given the net income earned by the company this year, income tax expense should be $6,200 but this would not have to be paid for another two months.

9.   The company declared and paid $1,000 of dividends to shareholders at the end of the year.

Instructions

(a)   Prepare an equation analysis of the effects of the above transactions on the expanded accounting equation. If you have access to spreadsheet software, prepare the analysis on a spreadsheet as suggested. If not, prepare the analysis manually as shown in Illustration 3-3.

(b)   Do you think that a spreadsheet could be used as described above and replace the requirement to journalize and post transactions? Explain.

(c)   Prepare an income statement, statement of changes in equity, and statement of financial position for the year.

(d)   There were seven transactions that affected cash. Which of these related to operating activities? What was their total effect? What would Uncle Bob think about the operating cash flow? Which cash flows would be considered financing activities? Did the company need these cash flows?

(e) The company could not borrow any money from a bank to help start operations. Why do you think this happened?

(f) If the income taxes were due next week, would the company be able to pay them?

(g) Why does the company have to pay income tax? Should Uncle Bob personally pay tax on any of the net income earned by the company?

CT3–4 Student View Case

You are a first-year university student and excited about moving away from home to go to university. You have saved $6,000 from your summer employment and your parents have agreed to match that $6,000. In addition, you have received a $9,000 student loan. All of this money is intended to last you for the academic year.

At September 1, you had $21,000 cash ($6,000 + $6,000 + $9,000), and a cellphone that cost $200. You have kept all of the receipts for all of your expenditures between September 1 and December 15. The following is a complete list of your cash receipts.

Residence and meal plan fees ($1,100 per month)	$4,400
Damage deposit on residence	400
Tuition for September to December	3,500
Textbooks	600
Personal costs (personal items, entertainment, eating out)	1,500
New clothes	1,500
Cellphone costs	250
Computer	1,000
Travel to go home at Christmas	450

On December 15, you checked the balance in your bank account and you only have $7,400 cash. You can't sleep, because you know residence for the second term will cost you $4,400 and your tuition will cost you $3,500 and you are $500 in the hole before purchasing textbooks or anything else for next term.

You need to figure out where you stand before you can talk to your parents about needing more money for the next term. You try to prepare a trial balance like you learned in your introductory accounting class, but it doesn't balance. You are getting more and more worried about what to do next.

PERSONAL TRIAL BALANCE
December 15, 2018

	Debit	Credit
Cash	$ 7,800	
Clothes	1,500	
Cellphone	200	
Computer	100	
Student loan		$ 9,000
Personal equity		12,200
Residence and meal expense	4,400	
Tuition for September to December	3,500	
Personal costs	1,500	
Textbooks for September to December	600	
Travel costs	540	
Cellphone costs	250	
	$20,390	$21,200

Instructions

(a) Calculate your personal equity (deficit) at September 1, 2018.

(b) Identify the errors in the above trial balance and prepare a corrected trial balance at December 15, 2018.

(c) Calculate your total expenses for the first term and your personal equity (deficit) at December 15, 2018. Assume the $200 cellphone you started with, the computer purchased, and damage deposit paid are assets, and that the remaining costs are expenses. Did your equity change? If so, by how much?

(d) Assuming you will have the same expenses in the second term, will you have enough cash to pay for them? If not, how much are you short?

(e) Are there any expenses you might be able to avoid in the second term to save cash? What are they? What did you overspend on in the first term?

(f) Will it be necessary for you to ask your parents for more money for the next term? If so, how much do you need to ask for? Explain.

CT3–5 Ethics Case

This case can be assigned as a group activity. Additional instructions and material for this activity can be found on the Instructor Resource site and in WileyPLUS.

Ron Hollister is a member of a group of students who have been given an accounting assignment by their professor. Ron is responsible for the portion of the assignment that requires the preparation of the trial balance and the financial statements. The assignment is due within an hour and Ron is working alone. All he has to do is complete his part of the assignment and hand the entire document in for grading. He has just prepared the trial balance and found out that it does not balance. The total credits are greater than the total debits by $810.

Without telling the other members of the group, Ron forces the trial balance to balance by adding $810 to the Salaries Expense account because it was the largest expense and he hoped no one would notice the difference. He wished that he had a few more hours to find out why the trial balance did not balance, but he knows he can't miss the deadline for handing in the assignment.

Instructions

(a) What advice would you give to Ron to help him find the error in the trial balance as quickly as possible?

(b) Who are the stakeholders in this situation?

(c) What ethical issues are involved?

(d) What are Ron's alternatives?

(e) Would your answer change if Ron was a professional accountant and was preparing financial statements for a public company?

CT3–6 Serial Case

(*Note:* This is a continuation of the serial case from Chapters 1 and 2.)

You will recall from Chapter 2 that Software Solutions Inc. had asked ABC to consider a proposal to provide it with approximately 500 hours a month of support services. After much discussion with her parents, Doug and Bev, Emily decides ABC should not accept Software Solutions' proposal.

At this point, Emily believes it too large a commitment for the current size of the business and that it is best to focus on providing quality service to the company's existing and other new clients. After becoming comfortable with these contractual commitments and determining the extent of service capacity available, ABC might later reconsider Software's offer.

Emily obtains a copy of ABC's partial trial balance at June 30, 2017, to start to become familiar with the organization's accounting position. The accounting records have not yet been fully updated for the month, so the trial balance is not yet complete.

ANTHONY BUSINESS COMPANY LTD.
Trial Balance (partial)
June 30, 2017

	Debit	Credit
Cash	$ 39,004	
Accounts receivable	5,900	
Inventory	16,250	
Supplies	1,875	
Prepaid insurance	12,000	
Land	100,000	
Buildings	165,000	
Accum. depreciation—buildings		$ 137,500
Equipment	42,000	
Accum. depreciation—equipment		14,000
Vehicles	52,500	
Accounts payable		3,540
Unearned revenue		100
Bank loan payable		22,500
Mortgage payable		53,200
Common shares		300
Retained earnings		146,788
Dividends declared	30,000	
Rent revenue		6,000
Sales revenue		633,768
Cost of goods sold	102,386	
Salaries expense	387,532	
Office expense	18,000	
Utilities expense	12,000	
Advertising expense	9,000	
Property tax expense	5,950	
Interest expense	5,299	
Income tax expense	13,000	
Total	$1,017,696	$1,017,696

While a number of transactions have already been recorded and posted for the month of June, there are other transactions listed below that have not yet been recorded in the accounting records:

June 5 Emily attends to the receipt of advertising supplies. 5,000 marketing brochures were purchased on account from Nakhooda Printing for $2,500. (Hint: Use the Supplies account.)

14 ABC purchases computer equipment for $2,520 cash to accommodate the growth of services. (Hint: Use the Equipment account.)

16 Emily's good friend is starting a tour boat business in July and wants ABC to set up the accounting system. A $1,000 cash deposit is received in advance.

19 Emily teaches a "Tips on using Facebook" class to a group of seniors that was booked a number of months ago. A $100 deposit had been received in advance and is included in the Unearned Revenue account. $300 is collected in cash at the end of the class, representing the remaining balance due. (Hint: ABC uses the Sales account for both the provision of services and the sale of goods.)

21 50 training manuals are delivered to a client in Calgary. An invoice of $2,040 for the preparation of these manuals is included.

27 A $200 invoice for use of Emily's cellphone is received. The cellphone is used exclusively for ABC's business. The invoice is for services provided in June and is due on July 21. (Hint: Use the Utilities Expense account.)

29 A new client has just had its computer data hacked. Emily has agreed to work with the client next month to help the company strengthen its firewall, tighten up its privacy controls, and document its procedures.

30 Emily receives her first paycheque from ABC, for $3,250.

30 The client for which 50 training manuals were delivered in the June 21 transaction requests another 50 manuals. These are delivered to its Calgary office and an invoice of $2,550 for the preparation of these manuals is included.

Instructions
(a) Journalize the above accounting transactions for June.
(b) Set up T accounts, enter the opening balances in the general ledger from the partially completed trial balance at June 30, and post the remaining June journal entries to the general ledger.
(c) Prepare an updated trial balance at June 30.

ANSWERS TO CHAPTER PRACTICE QUESTIONS

DO IT! 3-1a
Basic and Equation Analysis

Transaction	August 1: Common shares were issued to shareholders for $25,000 cash.
Basic Analysis	The asset Cash and the shareholders' equity account Common Shares both increased by $25,000.

Equation Analysis									
	Assets			= Liabilities +		Shareholders' Equity			
		Accounts			Accounts	Common		Retained Earnings	
	Cash +	Receivable +	Equipment =	Payable +		Shares +	Rev. −	Exp. −	Div.
Aug. 1	+$25,000					+$25,000			

Transaction August 3: Equipment costing $7,000 was purchased on account.

Basic Analysis The asset Equipment increased by $7,000; the liability Accounts Payable increased by the same amount.

Equation Analysis

	Assets			=	Liabilities	+		Shareholders' Equity			
					Accounts		Common		Retained Earnings		
	Cash	+ Receivable	+ Equipment	=	Payable	+	Shares	+ Rev.	− Exp.	− Div.
Aug. 3			+$7,000		+$7,000					

Transaction August 9: Services amounting to $8,000 were performed for customers. Of this amount, $2,000 was received in cash and $6,000 is due on account.

Basic Analysis The asset Cash increased by $2,000 and the asset Accounts Receivable increased by $6,000. The shareholders' equity account Service Revenue increased by $8,000.

Equation Analysis

	Assets			=	Liabilities	+		Shareholders' Equity			
					Accounts		Common		Retained Earnings		
	Cash	+ Receivable	+ Equipment	=	Payable	+	Shares	+ Rev.	− Exp.	− Div.
Aug. 9	+$2,000	+$6,000						+$8,000		

Transaction August 10: Rent was paid for the month of August, $850.

Basic Analysis The asset Cash decreased by $850. The shareholders' equity account Rent Expense increased by $850, which reduced retained earnings and shareholders' equity.

Equation Analysis

	Assets			=	Liabilities	+		Shareholders' Equity			
					Accounts		Common		Retained Earnings		
	Cash	+ Receivable	+ Equipment	=	Payable	+	Shares	+ Rev.	− Exp.	− Div.
Aug. 10	−$850								−$850	

Transaction August 29: Customers owing $6,000 on account paid $4,000 of the balance due. (See August 9 transaction.)

Basic Analysis The asset Cash increased by $4,000 and the asset Accounts Receivable decreased by the same amount.

Equation Analysis

	Assets			=	Liabilities	+		Shareholders' Equity			
					Accounts		Common		Retained Earnings		
	Cash	+ Receivable	+ Equipment	=	Payable	+	Shares	+ Rev.	− Exp.	− Div.
Aug. 29	+$4,000	−$4,000								

Transaction August 31: Dividends of $1,000 were declared and paid to shareholders.

Basic Analysis The asset Cash decreased by $1,000. The shareholders' equity account Dividends Declared increased by $1,000, which reduced retained earnings and shareholders' equity.

Equation Analysis

	Assets			=	Liabilities	+		Shareholders' Equity			
					Accounts		Common		Retained Earnings		
	Cash	+ Receivable	+ Equipment	=	Payable	+	Shares	+ Rev.	− Exp.	− Div.
Aug. 31	−$1,000									−$1,000

DO IT! 3-1b (a)

Equation Analysis

	Assets					=	Liabilities		+	Shareholders' Equity				
				Pre.						Common		Retained Earnings		
	Cash	+ A/R	+ Sup.	+ Ins.	+ Equip.	=	A/P	+ L/P	+	Shares	+ Bal.	+ Rev.	− Exp.	− Div.
May 31 Bal.	$2,500	$1,000			$1,500					$1,000	$4,000			
(1)	+1,000	−1,000												
(2)			+$250				+$250							
(3)		+2,500										+$2,500		
(4)	−100													−$100
(5)	−500				+3,500			+$3,000						
(6)	+1,200											+1,200		
(7)	−250						−250							
(8)	−1,750												−$1,750	
(9)	−600			+$600										
(10)	−400												−400	
	$1,100	$2,500	$250	$600	$5,000		$ 0	$3,000		$1,000	$4,000	$3,700	−$2,150	−$100

(b) Total assets = $1,100 + $2,500 + $250 + $600 + $5,000 = $9,450

Total liabilities = $0 + $3,000 = $3,000

Total shareholders' equity = $1,000 + $4,000 + $3,700 − $2,150 − $100 = $6,450

Check: Total assets = total liabilities + shareholders' equity

$9,450   = $3,000   + $6,450

(c)   Net income = $3,700 – $2,150 = $1,550
      Retained earnings = $4,000 + $1,550 – $100 = $5,450

	Account	(a) Classification	(b) Normal Balance	(c) Debit Effect
1.	Service revenue	Shareholders' equity	Credit	Decrease
2.	Income tax expense	Shareholders' equity	Debit	Increase
3.	Equipment	Assets	Debit	Increase
4.	Accounts receivable	Assets	Debit	Increase
5.	Accumulated depreciation	Assets (contra asset)	Credit	Decrease
6.	Unearned revenue	Liabilities	Credit	Decrease
7.	Accounts payable	Liabilities	Credit	Decrease
8.	Common shares	Shareholders' equity	Credit	Decrease
9.	Salaries expense	Shareholders' equity	Debit	Increase
10.	Dividends declared	Shareholders' equity	Debit	Increase

DO IT! 3-2
Accounts and Debits and Credits

Transaction — August 1: Common shares were issued to shareholders for $25,000 cash.

Basic Analysis — The asset Cash and the shareholders' equity account Common Shares both increased by $25,000.

Equation Analysis

	Assets		=	Liabilities +		Shareholders' Equity				
								Retained Earnings		
	Cash	+ Receivable + Equipment	=	Payable	+	Common Shares	+	Rev.	– Exp.	– Div.
Aug. 1	+$25,000					+$25,000				

Debit–Credit Analysis — Debits increase assets: debit Cash $25,000.
Credits increase common shares: credit Common Shares $25,000.

Journal Entry

Aug. 1	Cash	25,000	
	Common Shares		25,000

DO IT! 3-3
Debit–Credit Analysis and Journal Entries

Transaction — August 3: Equipment costing $7,000 was purchased on account.

Basic Analysis — The asset Equipment increased by $7,000; the liability Accounts Payable increased by the same amount.

Equation Analysis

	Assets		=	Liabilities +		Shareholders' Equity				
								Retained Earnings		
	Cash	+ Receivable + Equipment	=	Payable	+	Common Shares	+	Rev.	– Exp.	– Div.
Aug. 3		+$7,000		+$7,000						

Debit–Credit Analysis — Debits increase assets: debit Equipment $7,000.
Credits increase liabilities: credit Accounts Payable $7,000.

Journal Entry

Aug. 3	Equipment	7,000	
	Accounts Payable		7,000

Transaction — August 9: Services amounting to $8,000 were performed for customers. Of this amount, $2,000 was received in cash and $6,000 is due on account.

Basic Analysis — The asset Cash increased by $2,000 and the asset Accounts Receivable increased by $6,000. The shareholders' equity account Service Revenue increased by $8,000.

Equation Analysis

	Assets		=	Liabilities +		Shareholders' Equity				
								Retained Earnings		
	Cash	+ Receivable + Equipment	=	Payable	+	Common Shares	+	Rev.	– Exp.	– Div.
Aug. 9	+$2,000	+$6,000						+$8,000		

Debit–Credit Analysis — Debits increase assets: debit Cash $2,000 and debit Accounts Receivable $6,000.
Credits increase revenues: credit Service Revenue $8,000.

Journal Entry

Aug. 9	Cash	2,000	
	Accounts Receivable	6,000	
	Service Revenue		8,000

Transaction — August 10: Rent was paid for the month of August, $850.

Basic Analysis — The asset Cash decreased by $850. The shareholders' equity account Rent Expense increased by $850, which reduced retained earnings and shareholders' equity.

Equation Analysis

	Assets		=	Liabilities +		Shareholders' Equity				
								Retained Earnings		
	Cash	+ Receivable + Equipment	=	Payable	+	Common Shares	+	Rev.	– Exp.	– Div.
Aug. 10	–$850								–$850	

Debit–Credit Analysis — Debits increase expenses: debit Rent Expense $850.
Credits decrease assets: credit Cash $850.

Journal Entry

Aug. 10	Rent Expense	850	
	Cash		850

Transaction	August 29: Customers owing $6,000 on account paid $4,000 of the balance due. (See August 9 transaction.)
Basic Analysis	The asset Cash increased by $4,000 and the asset Accounts Receivable decreased by the same amount.

Equation Analysis

	Assets			=	Liabilities +		Shareholders' Equity			
									Retained Earnings	
	Cash	+ Receivable	+ Equipment	=	Accounts Payable	+ Common Shares	+ Rev.	− Exp.	− Div.	
Aug. 29	+$4,000	−$4,000								

Debit–Credit Analysis	Debits increase assets: debit Cash $4,000. Credits decrease assets: credit Accounts Receivable $4,000.

Journal Entry	Aug. 29	Cash	4,000	
		Accounts Receivable		4,000

Transaction	August 31: Dividends of $1,000 were declared and paid to shareholders.
Basic Analysis	The asset Cash decreased by $1,000. The shareholders' equity account Dividends Declared increased by $1,000, which reduced retained earnings and shareholders' equity.

Equation Analysis

	Assets			=	Liabilities +		Shareholders' Equity			
									Retained Earnings	
	Cash	+ Receivable	+ Equipment	=	Accounts Payable	+ Common Shares	+ Rev.	− Exp.	− Div.	
Aug. 31	−$1,000								−$1,000	

Debit–Credit Analysis	Debits increase dividends: debit Dividends Declared $1,000. Credits decrease assets: credit Cash $1,000.

Journal Entry	Aug. 31	Dividends Declared	1,000	
		Cash		1,000

DO IT! 3-4a
Posting

Cash

Apr. 30	10,000	May 1	5,000
May 15	2,700	6	600
Bal.	7,100		

Equipment

Apr. 30	7,500	
May 4	4,800	
Bal.	12,300	

Accounts Receivable

Apr. 30	5,000		
		May 15	2,700
Bal.	2,300		

Accounts Payable

		Apr. 30	6,000
May 1	5,000		
		Bal.	1,000

Supplies

May 6	600	

Bank Loan Payable

		May 4	4,800

DO IT! 3-4b
Posting

Cash

Aug. 1	25,000	Aug. 10	850
9	2,000	31	1,000
29	4,000		
Bal.	29,150		

Common Shares

		Aug. 1	25,000

Dividends Declared

Aug. 1	1,000	

Accounts Receivable

Aug. 9	6,000	Aug. 29	4,000
Bal.	2,000		

Service Revenue

		Aug. 9	8,000

Equipment

Aug. 3	7,000	

Rent Expense

Aug. 10	850	

Accounts Payable

		Aug. 3	7,000

KOIZUMI KOLLECTIONS LTD.
Trial Balance
July 31, 2018

	Debit	Credit
Cash	$ 3,200	
Accounts receivable	71,200	
Land	51,000	
Buildings	86,500	
Equipment	35,700	
Accounts payable		$ 33,700
Unearned revenue		3,000
Bank loan payable		49,500
Common shares		99,400
Dividends declared	4,000	
Service revenue		171,100
Operating expenses	93,100	
Income tax expense	12,000	
	$356,700	$356,700

▶ PRACTICE USING THE DECISION TOOLKIT

(a) Only mistake #3 has caused the trial balance to be out of balance.

(b) All of the mistakes should be corrected. The misclassification error (mistake #4) would not affect net income but it does affect the amounts reported in the two expense accounts, Income Tax Expense and Operating Expenses.

(c) There is no Common Shares account, so that must be the account deleted by the data entry clerk.

(d)

Account	Normal Balance
Accounts payable	Credit
Accounts receivable	Debit
Bank loan payable	Credit
Buildings	Debit
Cash	Debit
Cost of goods sold	Debit
Equipment	Debit
Income tax expense	Debit
Income tax payable	Credit
Inventory	Debit
Land	Debit
Mortgage payable	Credit
Operating expenses	Debit
Retained earnings, beginning of year	Credit
Salaries payable	Credit
Sales revenue	Credit

(e) and (f)

NANAIMO LTD.
Trial Balance
December 31, 2018

	Debit	Credit	Financial Statement
Cash ($32,000 − $7,000 + $75,000)	$ 100,000		SFP
Accounts receivable	712,000		SFP
Inventory	365,000		SFP
Land	110,000		SFP
Buildings	1,291,000		SFP
Equipment ($83,000 + $7,000)	90,000		SFP
Accounts payable		$ 673,000	SFP
Income tax payable		5,000	SFP
Salaries payable		62,000	SFP
Bank loan payable		200,000	SFP
Mortgage payable ($685,000 − $200,000)		485,000	SFP
Common shares (+$200,000)		200,000	SFP, SCE
Retained earnings, beginning of year		892,000	SCE
Sales revenue		3,741,000	IS
Cost of goods sold	2,384,000		IS
Operating expenses ($1,151,000 − $5,000)	1,146,000		IS
Income tax expense ($55,000 + $5,000)	60,000		IS
Totals	$6,258,000	$6,258,000	

▶ **PRACTICE COMPREHENSIVE DO IT!**

(a)

Date	Account Titles and Explanation	Debit	Credit
2018			
Sept. 3	Rent Expense	1,000	
	Cash		1,000
4	Equipment	25,000	
	Cash		10,000
	Bank Loan Payable		15,000
7	Prepaid Insurance	1,200	
	Cash		1,200
14	Salaries Expense	2,500	
	Cash		2,500
15	Accounts Receivable	6,200	
	Service Revenue		6,200
21	Dividends Declared	700	
	Cash		700
26	Accounts Payable	2,000	
	Cash		2,000
28	Salaries Expense	2,500	
	Cash		2,500
30	Cash	5,000	
	Service Revenue		5,000
30	Utilities Expense	1,200	
	Accounts Payable		1,200
30	Income Tax Expense	600	
	Cash		600

(b)

Cash

Aug. 31	20,000		
Sept. 30	5,000	Sept. 3	1,000
		4	10,000
		7	1,200
		14	2,500
		21	700
		26	2,000
		28	2,500
		30	600
Bal.	4,500		

Accounts Receivable

Aug. 31	4,000	
Sept. 15	6,200	
Bal.	10,200	

Prepaid Insurance

Sept. 7	1,200	

Equipment

Aug. 31	15,000	
Sept. 4	25,000	
Bal.	40,000	

Accounts Payable

		Aug. 31	2,000
Sept. 26	2,000	Sept. 30	1,200
		Bal.	1,200

Bank Loan Payable

		Aug. 31	10,000
		Sept. 4	15,000
		Bal.	25,000

Common Shares

		Aug. 31	5,000

Retained Earnings

		Aug. 31	22,000

Dividends Declared

Sept. 21	700	

Service Revenue

		Sept. 15	6,200
		30	5,000
		Bal.	11,200

Rent Expense

Sept. 3	1,000	

Salaries Expense

Sept. 14	2,500	
28	2,500	
Bal.	5,000	

Utilities Expense

Sept. 30	1,200	

Income Tax Expense

Sept. 30	600	

(c)

CAMPUS LAUNDRY LTD.
Trial Balance
September 30, 2018

	Debit	Credit
Cash	$ 4,500	
Accounts receivable	10,200	
Prepaid insurance	1,200	
Equipment	40,000	
Accounts payable		$ 1,200
Bank loan payable		25,000
Common shares		5,000
Retained earnings		22,000
Dividends declared	700	
Service revenue		11,200
Rent expense	1,000	
Salaries expense	5,000	
Utilities expense	1,200	
Income tax expense	600	
	$64,400	$64,400

(d)

CAMPUS LAUNDRY LTD.
Income Statement
Month Ended September 30, 2018

Revenues		
Service revenue		$11,200
Expenses		
Salaries expense	$5,000	
Utilities expense	1,200	
Rent expense	1,000	7,200
Income before income tax		4,000
Income tax expense		600
Net income		$ 3,400

CAMPUS LAUNDRY LTD.
Statement of Changes in Equity
Month Ended September 30, 2018

	Common Shares	Retained Earnings	Total Equity
Balance, September 1	$5,000	$22,000	$27,000
Net income		3,400	3,400
Dividends declared		(700)	(700)
Balance, September 30	$5,000	$24,700	$29,700

CAMPUS LAUNDRY LTD.
Statement of Financial Position
September 30, 2018

Assets		
Current assets		
Cash	$ 4,500	
Accounts receivable	10,200	
Prepaid insurance	1,200	$15,900
Property, plant, and equipment		
Equipment		40,000
Total assets		$55,900
Liabilities and Shareholders' Equity		
Current liabilities		
Accounts payable	$ 1,200	
Bank loan payable	25,000	$26,200
Shareholders' equity		
Common shares	$ 5,000	
Retained earnings	24,700	29,700
Total liabilities and shareholders' equity		$55,900

▶ PRACTICE OBJECTIVE-FORMAT QUESTIONS

1. (b), (d), (e), and (g) would not be recorded.

Feedback

(a) would be recorded because assets (equipment) and liabilities (accounts payable) are affected.

(b) would not be recorded because permission to purchase land does not result in a change in the accounting equation. Assets would have to decrease (for example, cash) or a liability increase (such as a mortgage payable) in order for the asset land to be recorded.

(c) would be recorded because assets (cash) and shareholders' equity (common shares) are affected.

(d) would not be recorded because the act of terminating an employee does not result in a change in the accounting equation. Once the employee is no longer with the company, no salary would be earned or paid.

(e) would not be recorded because the act of hiring an employee by itself does not result in a change in the accounting equation. Once an employee is hired and starts work and earns his or her salary, the transaction would be recorded.

(f) would be recorded because assets (accounts receivable) and shareholders' equity (service revenue) are affected.

(g) would not be recorded because the goods have not yet been received.

2. (a) and (d) are correct.

Feedback

(a) Assets = Liabilities + Shareholders' Equity (SE)

January 1: $70,000 assets = $40,000 liabilities + SE; SE = $30,000

December 31: $30,000 SE (Jan. 1 balance) + $100,000 revenues – $65,000 expenses – $5,000 dividends declared + $15,000 common shares = $75,000 SE (Dec. 31 balance)

(b) Assets = Liabilities + Shareholders' Equity (SE)

January 1: $105,000 assets = $50,000 liabilities + SE; SE = $55,000

December 31: $55,000 SE (Jan. 1 balance) + $150,000 revenues – $75,000 expenses – $10,000 dividends declared + $20,000 common shares = $140,000 SE (Dec. 31 balance)

(c)   Assets = Liabilities + Shareholders' Equity (SE)
       January 1: $90,000 (assets) = $40,000 liabilities + SE; SE = $50,000
       December 31: $50,000 SE (Jan. 1 balance) + $75,000 revenues – $30,000 expenses – $0 dividends declared + $10,000 common shares = $105,000 SE (Dec. 31 balance)
(d)   Assets = Liabilities + Shareholders' Equity (SE)
       January 1: $115,000 assets = $67,000 liabilities + SE; SE = $48,000
       December 31: $48,000 SE (Jan. 1 balance) + $95,000 revenues – $75,000 expenses – $10,000 dividends declared + $0 common shares = $58,000 SE (Dec. 31 balance)

3.   (c) and (g) would both result in an increase in assets and shareholders' equity.

Feedback
(a)   Assets (cash) increase and liabilities (unearned revenue) increase. Shareholders' equity is not affected.
(b)   Assets (cash) decrease and shareholders' equity decreases. (Dividends declared increases, so retained earnings decrease.)
(d)   Assets (cash) decrease and shareholders' equity decreases. (Salaries expense increases, so retained earnings decrease.)
(e)   Assets (supplies) increase and liabilities (accounts payable) increase. Shareholders' equity is not affected.
(f)   Assets (prepaid insurance) increase and assets (cash) decrease. Shareholders' equity is not affected.

4.   (a), (d), (f), and (g) are asset accounts and have normal debit balances.

Feedback
(b)   is a contra asset account and has a normal credit balance.
(c)   and (h) are shareholders' equity accounts and have a normal credit balance.
(e)   is a liability account and has a normal credit balance.

5.   (a), (d), (f), and (h) have normal credit balances.

Feedback
(b)   and (e) decrease shareholders' equity (retained earnings) and have normal debit balances.
(c)   and (g) are asset accounts and have normal debit balances.

6.   (a), (c), (d), and (e) are correct.

Feedback
(a)   Shareholders' equity consists of common shares (share capital) + retained earnings.
(b)   Expenses do decrease shareholders' equity (retained earnings) but are recorded as debits, not credits. The normal balance of shareholders' equity (retained earnings) is a credit and increases in shareholders' equity are recorded as credits.
(c)   Liabilities are increased by credits and have a normal credit balance.
(d)   Shareholders' equity is increased by credits and has a normal credit balance. Retained earnings are part of shareholders' equity (common shares + retained earnings) and also have a normal credit balance. Revenues increase retained earnings and are recorded as credits, and report a normal credit balance.
(e)   Retained earnings are part of shareholders' equity (common shares + retained earnings). Recall that retained earnings are increased by revenues and decreased by expenses and any dividends declared. When retained earnings are decreased by the declaration of dividends, shareholders' equity automatically decreases as well.
(f)   Dividends declared are recorded as debits but they are not an expense. They are a reduction of retained earnings and shareholders' equity.
(g)   Unearned revenue is a liability but it is a statement of financial position account and does not affect net income.

7.
(a)   2. Accounts Receivable
(b)   6. Inventory
(c)   9. Unearned Revenue
(d)   7. Service Revenue
(e)   8. Supplies
(f)   1. Accounts Payable
(g)   3. Dividends Declared

8.   (a), (b), and (e) are correct.

Feedback
(a)   The general journal is known as the book of original entry because it is the first place a transaction is recorded.
(b)   Journal entries should be recorded and posted in chronological (date) order.
(c)   A simple journal entry affects only two accounts; a compound journal entry affects three or more accounts.
(d)   Debits and credits must equal in each separate journal entry as well as in the trial balance.
(e)   Although other orders are possible, the most common order of a general ledger (T accounts) is in financial statement order.
(f)   Posting involves transferring information from the general journal to the general ledger, rather than the reverse.
(g)   The first four steps of the accounting cycle must be completed in this order: (1) analyze transactions, (2) journalize transactions, (3) post transactions from the general journal to the general ledger accounts, and (4) prepare a trial balance.

9.   (b) and (f) are correct.

Feedback
(a)   and (e) are not correct because the amount reported on the trial balance represents retained earnings at the beginning of the year, not the end of the year. Net income (revenues less expenses) and dividends declared are not yet included in retained earnings to determine the ending retained earnings balance.

(b)   is correct because opening retained earnings are zero the first year of a company's operations. After that, opening retained earnings of the current year equal ending retained earnings of the prior year.

(c)   and (d) are not the correct answers because shareholders' equity includes common shares in addition to retained earnings.

(f)   is correct because retained earnings are a component of shareholders' equity, both of which have normal credit balances.

(g)   is not correct because retained earnings do not include common shares.

10.   (c) and (d) would result in unequal debit and credit columns in the trial balance.

Feedback

All of the remaining choices, while incorrect, will not result in unequal debit and credit columns in the trial balance because the individual journal entries were balanced. (That is, debits equalled credits.)

▶ ENDNOTES

[1] "History," company website, www.beavertailsinc.com; Philip Fine, "A Sweet Story of Success," *The Montreal Gazette*, February 7, 2013, p. A28; Adam Kveton, "BeaverTails Opens Ottawa's Second Year-Round Store at Tanger Outlets," *Kanata Kourier-Standard*, May 8, 2015.

[2] It is generally assumed that the abbreviations Dr. and Cr. were coined by Luca Pacioli (known as the father of accounting) in 1494. These abbreviations are derived from the Latin words *debere* and *credere*, respectively. *Debere* means "to owe." *Credere* means "to entrust."

4

Accrual Accounting Concepts

CHAPTER PREVIEW

In Chapter 3, we examined the first four steps of the accounting cycle, which included the recording process up to and including the preparation of the trial balance. Although we prepared financial statements directly from the trial balance in that chapter, additional steps are normally necessary to properly update the accounts before the financial statements are prepared.

In this chapter, we introduce you to the accrual basis of accounting that guides the recognition of revenue and expenses in the appropriate time period. We will also describe the remaining steps in the accounting cycle.

CHAPTER OUTLINE

LEARNING OBJECTIVES	READ	PRACTICE
1 Explain the accrual basis of accounting and the reasons for adjusting entries.	• Revenue recognition • Expense recognition • Accrual versus cash basis of accounting • Adjusting entries	**DO IT!** 4-1a Accrual and cash basis accounting 4-1b Timing concepts
2 Prepare adjusting entries for prepayments.	• Prepaid expenses • Unearned revenues	**DO IT!** 4-2a Adjusting entries for prepaid expenses 4-2b Adjusting entries for prepayments
3 Prepare adjusting entries for accruals.	• Accrued expenses • Accrued revenues • Summary of basic relationships	**DO IT!** 4-3a Adjusting entries for accrued expenses 4-3b Adjusting entries for accrued revenues
4 Prepare an adjusted trial balance and financial statements.	• Adjusted trial balance • Financial statements	**DO IT!** 4-4 Adjusted trial balance
5 Prepare closing entries and a post-closing trial balance.	• Closing entries • Post-closing trial balance • Review of the accounting cycle	**DO IT!** 4-5 Closing entries

Jessie Parker/Getty Images, Inc.

School's Out, Time to Balance the Books

At Western University in London, Ontario, as at campuses across the country, classes for most students start in September and end in April. Likewise, the university's fiscal year end is April 30. So essentially, the university closes its books at the same time the students do. This cohesion helps the university to satisfy the criteria needed to recognize revenues and expenses at the appropriate time when services are performed and expenses incurred, respectively.

However, many students at Western take intersession courses. They pay their course fees before the year end of April 30, but the courses don't start until May or later. "We would get intersession fees and other fees in advance of our year end, so there is a deferral there," says Carter Scott, Western's controller. The university defers the recognition of that revenue until the following accounting period, the one in which it provides the teaching services.

Another example of the deferral of revenue is the advance fees students pay for residence admission to hold their spot for the coming year. The university defers recognition of this revenue until the start of the academic year in September, when the students move into the residences.

Research activities provide another example. "In a lot of cases, granting agencies' year ends are in March, so they send the funds in at the beginning of March," Mr. Scott points out. "For any faculty member who gets a grant,

it's deferred until they start expending it, because it's restricted for that purpose. Restricted revenues for which the related expenses have not been incurred are reported as unearned revenue on the university's balance sheet." The grant money is matched against expenses incurred over the course of the research project, which could go on for years.

Expenses, too, must be recorded in the year in which they were incurred. "Post-employment benefits [such as pensions and health care paid during retirement], at most universities, are a very large number that you accrue for," Mr. Scott explains. Other expenses that would have to be accrued at year end include utility bills, vacation pay, and outstanding salary for the approximately 3,900 full-time faculty and staff members.

"Accrual accounting is considered the most appropriate method of financial reporting because revenues and expenses are recognized in the period to which they relate, regardless of whether there has been a receipt or payment of cash," Mr. Scott explains. "A more meaningful picture of financial position and operations is provided under accrual accounting than on a cash flow basis."

Recording revenues and expenses in the correct period is a challenge, but one that must be met to best reflect the various activities of a large university like Western.[1]

Go to the *REVIEW AND PRACTICE* section at the end of the chapter for a targeted summary and practice questions with solutions.

Visit **WileyPLUS** for more practice opportunities.

LEARNING
OBJECTIVE   ▶1

Explain the accrual basis of accounting and the reasons for adjusting entries.

Users of accounting information require financial information on a regular basis. For example, management receives monthly reports on financial results, publicly traded corporations present quarterly and annual financial statements to shareholders, and the Canada Revenue Agency requires companies to file monthly sales tax reports and annual income tax returns.

As such, the economic life of a company is divided into periods of time. The longest accounting time period is normally one year, meaning that the company would generate financial statements for a one-year period. Shorter accounting time periods include monthly or quarterly (three-month) periods. You will recall from Chapter 1 that accounting time periods of one year are known as a **fiscal year**; monthly or quarterly periods are known as **interim periods**.

Many accounting transactions affect more than one of these time periods. For example, we saw in the feature story that research grants received by faculty at Western University can span multiple years. We also saw how Western collects intersession course fees in one fiscal year but delivers the courses in the next fiscal year. Determining the amount of revenue and expenses to report in a particular accounting period can be difficult. Two accounting standards are used as guidelines: revenue recognition and expense recognition.

REVENUE RECOGNITION

Recall from Chapter 2 that income is created by inflows of economic benefits (an increase in assets or decrease in liabilities) that result in increases in equity, with the exclusion of contributions from shareholders. As we learned in Chapter 2, the term *revenue* is often used interchangeably with the term *income*. *Revenue* is normally the term used for income that results from a company's **ordinary activities**, such as the provision of services in a service company or the sale of merchandise (goods) in a merchandising company. Income can also arise from activities that are not part of the company's ordinary activities, such as gains from the sale of land or investment income from sources such as interest, rent, or dividends. The term *gains* or *income* is normally used for this type of income.

It is important to understand that a type of income that is ordinary for one company may not be for another. For example, some companies (such as banks) might refer to interest received from loans as Interest Revenue while others (such as a company that is not in the business of lending money, but does grant occasional loans to employees) might refer to it as Interest Income. Many other companies use Interest Revenue regardless of whether it is part of its ordinary activities or not—we have chosen to use the account title Interest Revenue in this textbook for simplicity as it is often difficult to determine the source of the interest. As we learned in Chapter 3, it doesn't matter what your original choice of account title is as long as it is used consistently to record similar types of transactions.

Western University, in the chapter-opening feature story, earns income from a variety of activities. For example, it earns revenue from tuition and other student fees; government and research grants; the sale of goods and services from its bookstore, retail shops, and food and dining locations; the sale of parking passes; rental income from its student residences; donations; and investment returns; as well as from other sources, especially with respect to activities other than the provision of services or sale of goods.

Both ASPE and IFRS include **revenue recognition** standards which we will apply to the most common sources of revenue discussed in this textbook—service revenue and sales revenue (which will be discussed in more detail in the next chapter). Under ASPE, the performance of an obligation must be substantially complete in order for its revenue to be recognized. In addition, ASPE requires that revenue must be able to be reliably measured and collection is reasonably certain. Under IFRS, a new revenue standard will take effect January 1, 2018, or earlier if a company chooses. This pending standard, which has been incorporated into this textbook, describes a five-step process to use to measure and report revenue:

1. Identify the contract with the client or customer.
2. Identify the performance obligations in the contract.
3. Determine the transaction price.
4. Allocate the transaction price to the performance obligations in the contract.
5. Recognize revenue when (or as) the company satisfies the performance obligation.

Step 1 of the process is to identify the contract details. We learned in Chapter 3 that source documents are an important starting point to analyze the effects of a transaction, if any, on the accounting equation. A contract is another example of a source document. A contract—whether informal or formal—includes the terms of the transaction, the price of the transaction, and the promises that must be met by the seller and the buyer before the obligation is considered to be satisfied. This step also includes an evaluation of whether it is probable that the company will be able to collect the transaction price when due. The process to determine when, and how much (if any), revenue should be recognized may require a significant amount of professional judgement depending on the complexities of the contract and the nature of the service being performed or good being sold. It is often said that determining when to record revenue is one of the most difficult issues in accounting. We will leave the complexities and difficulties of this important standard to an intermediate accounting course and focus in this textbook on the more straightforward applications of this standard.

In general, in a service company, revenue is recognized (recorded) at the time the service is performed. In a merchandising company, revenue is recognized (recorded) when the merchandise is sold and delivered (normally at the point of sale). Regardless of whether cash is received at the point of delivery of service or sale or expected to be received at some point in future, an asset and revenue are recognized in the accounting period when or as the performance obligation is completed.

To illustrate, assume Wajax Ltd. signed a contract with a client to provide training on new equipment in September on an hourly basis at an agreed-upon rate schedule. The services were performed in September. In October, the company sent the client an invoice for $1,100, with payment due in 30 days. In November, the company received full payment from the client. In what month should Wajax record the revenue? Let's apply the five-step process described above to this situation to determine when to recognize revenue. The five steps of revenue recognition are outlined in Illustration 4-1.

▶ Illustration 4-1

Five steps of revenue recognition

Step 1: Identify the contract with the client or customer.	Wajax had a contract to provide training services to a client. This contract would include terms of service, pricing, and payment (for example, payment is due 30 days after receipt of the invoice). Collectibility is reasonably certain.
Step 2: Identify the performance obligations in the contract.	Wajax has only one performance obligation—to provide the training services in September.
Step 3: Determine the transaction price.	The transaction price is the amount that Wajax expects to receive from the customer for providing training services. In this case, the transaction price is $1,100.
Step 4: Allocate the transaction price to the performance obligations in the contract.	In this case, Wajax has only one performance obligation. If Wajax had also sold the equipment to the client in addition to providing training, it would have two separate performance obligations—one for the sale of the equipment and the other for the provision of the training.
Step 5: Recognize revenue when (or as) the company satisfies the performance obligation.	Wajax recognizes revenue of $1,100 when it satisfies the performance obligation—the completion of the provision of training services.

Wajax should recognize revenue in September because that was when the service was performed and obligation completed. An asset account, Accounts Receivable, would be increased, as would a revenue account, Service Revenue. At that time, the transaction price was determinable because, even though an invoice had not been prepared, the hours spent and rate per hour would have been known and agreed to by both parties.

Note that a signed contract is not necessarily required—a verbal agreement between two parties can also be considered to be a contract although a written contract may provide better protection for both parties in the case of a dispute. When you purchase merchandise at a retail store, you will see a posted price for the item and may also see a sign posted on the wall about merchandise returns and exchange policies. In effect, by purchasing the merchandise, you are agreeing to these terms of sale.

Recall also from Chapter 3 that the signing of a written contract by two parties does not, in itself, give rise to an accounting transaction. (In other words, it does not result in a journal entry.) Until performance occurs, no asset (or liability) is recognized as revenue.

EXPENSE RECOGNITION

Recall from Chapter 2 that expenses are the costs of assets that are consumed or services used in a company's **ordinary revenue-generating activities**. **Expense recognition** is linked to revenue recognition in that expenses are recognized, wherever possible, in the period in which a company makes efforts to generate revenues. This is sometimes known as **matching** because the effort (expenses) is matched with the results (revenues). And, similar to revenue recognition, expense recognition is not tied to the payment of cash. Expenses are recognized when incurred for the purpose of generating revenue regardless of whether cash is paid or not.

Expenses result in changes in assets and liabilities, similar to revenues. When an expense is incurred, an asset will decrease or a liability will increase. Consequently, just as revenues are related to increases in future economic benefits, expenses are related to decreases in future economic benefits, with the exclusion of distributions to shareholders. As such, the distribution of dividends to a shareholder is never an expense.

Consider again Wajax's provision of training services to learn how to use new equipment during the month of September discussed in the previous section. During the month of September, Wajax employees performed training services for a client. Because of this, the company owes these employees salaries. This obligation creates an increase in a liability, Salaries Payable (or a decrease in an asset, Cash), and a corresponding increase in an expense, Salaries Expense. In this case, the expenses are recognized in the same month as the revenues because the expenses were incurred at the same time and contributed to the earning of the revenue. This does not mean that revenues and expenses are always recognized at the same time.

Sometimes, it is not possible to directly associate expenses with revenue. For example, if a company rented office space, each month the rent would be due and this would increase a liability, Rent Payable (or decrease an asset, Cash) and increase an expense, Rent Expense, even if the company earned no revenue in a particular month. It is also difficult to match interest expense with the revenue that this finance cost might help earn. Other examples include losses and costs that help generate revenue over multiple periods of time, such as the depreciation of long-lived assets such as equipment. We will learn more about allocating expenses such as these later in this chapter.

ACCRUAL VERSUS CASH BASIS OF ACCOUNTING

The combined application of revenue and expense recognition results in accrual basis accounting. **Accrual basis accounting** means that transactions affecting a company's financial statements are recorded in the periods in which the events occur, rather than when the company actually receives or pays cash. This means recognizing revenues when they are earned rather than only when cash is received. Likewise, expenses are recognized in the period in which goods (such as office supplies) are consumed or services (such as employees' labour) are used, rather than only when cash is paid.

An alternative to the accrual basis is the cash basis. Under **cash basis accounting**, revenue is recorded only when cash is received, and an expense is recorded only when cash is paid. Cash basis accounting seems appealing because of its simplicity, but it can result in misleading information for decision-making because of timing differences between the occurrence of the actual event and its related cash flows. For example, revenues may be earned before cash is received (such as sales on account) or expenses may be incurred before cash is paid (such as the salaries owed to employees). Recording revenues and expenses simply on the basis of the receipt and payment of cash would be misleading in both of these circumstances.

Illustration 4-2 compares accrual-based results with cash-based results. Suppose that Colours Paint Ltd. paints a large building during year 1. In year 1, it incurs and pays total expenses (salaries, paint, and other costs) of $50,000. It also bills the customer $80,000 at the end of year 1, but does not receive payment until year 2.

Accounting Basis	Income Statement	Year 1	Year 2	Years 1 and 2 Combined
		Purchased paint, painted building complex, paid employees	Received payment for work done in year 1	
Accrual basis	Revenue Expense Net income	$ 80,000 50,000 $ 30,000	$ 0 0 $ 0	$ 80,000 50,000 $ 30,000
Cash basis	Revenue Expense Net (loss) income	$ 0 50,000 $(50,000)	$80,000 0 $80,000	$ 80,000 50,000 $ 30,000

► Illustration 4-2
Accrual versus cash basis accounting

On an accrual basis, revenue is considered to be earned, and therefore recorded, in the period when the service is performed (the performance obligation is satisfied). Expenses are recorded in the period in which they are incurred to earn revenue—the same period in which the employees provided their services and the paint and other costs were incurred. Net income for year 1 is $30,000, and no revenue or expense from this project would be reported in year 2.

If, instead, the cash basis of accounting was used, Colours Paint would record only expenses in year 1 (the period in which expenses were paid) and only revenues in year 2 (the period in which revenues were received). In year 1 there would be a net loss of $50,000, while net income for year 2 would be $80,000.

While total net income is the same over the two-year period ($30,000), cash basis measures are not very informative about the results of the company's efforts during year 1 or year 2. The total overall net income of $30,000 is the result of a net loss of $50,000 in year 1 and a big swing to a net income to $80,000 in year 2. As Carter Scott, the controller of Western University in our feature story, said, "Accrual accounting is considered the most appropriate method of financial reporting because revenues and expenses are recognized in the period to which they relate, regardless of whether there has been a receipt or payment of cash. A more meaningful picture of financial position and operations is provided under accrual accounting than on a cash flow basis."

The following schedule summarizes the differences between when revenues and expenses are recognized under the accrual and cash bases of accounting.

	Accrual Basis of Accounting	Cash Basis of Accounting
Revenue is recognized	When earned (generally when service performed or goods delivered and performance obligation satisfied)	When cash is received
Expense is recognized	When incurred to generate revenue (generally when service used or goods consumed)	When cash is paid

As we learned in Chapter 2, the accrual basis of accounting forms part of the conceptual framework and is required for the preparation of financial statements. Although different accounting standards are sometimes used in other countries, the accrual basis of accounting is central to all of these standards. The cash basis of accounting is not permitted for use in Canada.

ACCOUNTING MATTERS

© MichaelDeLeon/iStockphoto

Similar to most businesses, a university could not make timely decisions if its accounting records were prepared only on a cash basis. Imagine that you are sitting on the board of governors of a university and $1 million of tuition revenue (assume this is the only source of revenue) is received at the beginning of a four-month term. Each month, the university incurs $300,000 of expenses, which are paid almost immediately. This means that, over a four-month term, total expenses are $1.2 million. Knowing that the university is operating at a loss would be critical information for you and the other university governors. Even if monthly financial statements were prepared, this information would become known at different times depending upon whether the financial statements were prepared under accrual basis accounting or cash basis accounting.

Under accrual basis accounting, the loss would be known at the end of the first month, because reported revenues would be $250,000 (one quarter of the tuition will be recognized each month as it is earned) and expenses would be $300,000. At that time, you and your fellow board members could recommend that the university consider options such as borrowing money, seeking new revenue sources, and/or increasing tuition for the following term because it was anticipating a net loss in each of the next three months. However, if the cash basis of accounting was being used, revenues of $1 million would be reported in the first month, resulting in a net income of $700,000. It would not be until a month or two later that the board of governors might realize that the university is not profitable. It might be too late by then to meet expenses and continue to operate the university as originally planned.

DO IT! ▶4-1a   Accrual and Cash Basis Accounting

Action Plan

✔ For the cash basis of accounting, revenue is equal to the cash received.

✔ For the accrual basis of accounting, report revenue in the period in which it is earned, not when it is collected.

On December 31, 2017, customers owed Jomerans Ltd. $30,000 for services performed in 2017. During 2018, Jomerans collected $125,000 cash from customers, of which $30,000 was for services provided in 2017. At December 31, 2018, customers owed $19,500 for services provided in 2018. Calculate the revenue for 2018 using (a) the cash basis of accounting, and (b) the accrual basis of accounting.

SOLUTION

Try this Do It! exercise on your own and then check your answer at the end of the chapter.

Related Exercise Material: BE4–1, BE4–2, E4–1, E4–2, and E4–3.

ADJUSTING ENTRIES

For revenues to be recorded in the period in which they are earned and for expenses to be recorded in the period in which they are incurred, **adjusting entries** may be required to update accounts at the end of the accounting period. Adjusting entries ensure that revenue and expense recognition criteria are properly applied and make it possible to produce up-to-date and relevant financial information at the end of the accounting period.

Adjusting entries are necessary because the trial balance—the first pulling together of the transaction data—may not contain complete and up-to-date data. This is true for several reasons:

1. Some events are not recorded daily, because it would not be practical or efficient to do so. Instead, these events are recorded only at the end of the accounting period (that is, monthly, quarterly, or annually). Examples are the use of supplies and the earning of salaries by employees.

2. Some costs are not recorded during the accounting period because these costs expire with the passage of time rather than as a result of recurring daily transactions. Again, these costs are recorded at the end of the accounting period. Examples include rent, insurance, and depreciation.

3. Some items may be unrecorded during the accounting period because their amounts were unknown. Once they are known (or can be reasonably estimated), they can be recorded. An example is a utility service bill that is not received until after the end of an accounting period, but covers services delivered in that period.

Preparing adjusting entries requires an understanding of the company's operations and the interrelationship of accounts and can be a long and detailed process. For example, to accumulate the adjustment data for supplies, a company may need to count its remaining supplies. It may also need to prepare supporting schedules of insurance policies, rental agreements, and other contractual commitments.

In addition, as mentioned above, the information necessary to make adjustments is often not available until after the end of the accounting period. For example, telephone and other bills will not be received until after the month end or year end. In such cases, the information is gathered as soon as possible after the end of the period and adjusting entries are made. These entries would still be dated at the period end (in other words, the statement of financial position date).

Each account in the trial balance will need to be analyzed to see if it is complete and up to date. Because many of the amounts listed in the trial balance are incomplete until adjusting entries are prepared, this trial balance is commonly referred to as an **unadjusted trial balance**, which simply means it was prepared before adjusting entries have been made.

Adjusting entries are required every time financial statements are prepared. For public corporations, this means at least quarterly, because they are required to issue quarterly financial statements. For private corporations, this means at least annually, because they are required only to prepare annual financial statements. If public or private corporations wish to prepare monthly financial statements, then adjusting entries must be prepared monthly.

Adjusting entries can be classified as either prepayments or accruals. Each of these classes has two subcategories, as follows:

Prepayments	Accruals
Prepaid expenses	**Accrued expenses**
Expenses paid in cash and recorded as assets before they are used	Expenses incurred but not yet paid in cash or recorded through transaction journal entries
Unearned revenues	**Accrued revenues**
Cash received and recorded as liabilities before revenue is earned	Revenues earned but not yet received in cash or recorded through transaction journal entries

Subsequent sections give examples and explanations of each type of adjustment. Each example will be based on the October 31 trial balance of Sierra Corporation from Chapter 3, shown again below in Illustration 4-3. For our purposes, we have assumed that Sierra uses an accounting period of one month. Thus, monthly adjusting entries will be made, dated October 31.

▶Illustration 4-3
Unadjusted trial balance

SIERRA CORPORATION
Trial Balance
October 31, 2018

	Debit	Credit
Cash	$11,400	
Accounts receivable	11,000	
Supplies	2,500	
Prepaid insurance	600	
Equipment	5,000	
Accounts payable		$ 1,500
Unearned revenue		1,200
Bank loan payable		5,000
Common shares		10,000
Dividends declared	500	
Service revenue		20,000
Salaries expense	4,000	
Rent expense	900	
Income tax expense	1,800	
	$37,700	$37,700

Note that when a trial balance has no preceding adjective in its title, such as "unadjusted" trial balance (or "adjusted" trial balance or "post-closing" trial balance, which we will learn about in subsequent sections), it is assumed to be an unadjusted trial balance.

DO IT! ▶ 4-1b   Timing Concepts

Action Plan

✔ Review the terms given in this section.

✔ Review carefully the concepts of revenue recognition, expense recognition, accrual accounting versus cash basis accounting, and types of adjusting entries.

SOLUTION

Try this Do It! exercise on your own and then check your answer at the end of the chapter.

Match each of the concepts in the left-hand column with the most appropriate description found in the right-hand column. Each description is related to a single concept.

1. Accrual basis accounting
2. Adjusted trial balance
3. Adjusting entries
4. Cash basis accounting
5. Expense recognition
6. Fiscal year
7. Interim periods
8. Prepayments
9. Revenue recognition
10. Unadjusted trial balance

(a) Monthly and quarterly time periods

(b) Expenses are recorded in the period in which they are incurred by the company to generate revenues

(c) Revenues are recorded when cash is received and expenses when cash is paid

(d) An accounting time period of one year

(e) Revenues are recorded when earned (that is, when the performance obligation is satisfied)

(f) A trial balance prepared before adjusting entries are recorded and posted

(g) Prepaid expenses and unearned revenues

(h) A trial balance prepared after adjusting entries are recorded and posted

(i) Journal entries prepared at the end of the accounting period to update accounts

(j) Transactions recorded in period in which events occur

LEARNING OBJECTIVE ▶ **2**   Prepare adjusting entries for prepayments.

1. ANALYZE ▸ 2. JOURNALIZE ▸ 3. POST ▸ 4. TRIAL BALANCE ▸ **5. Journalize and post adjusting entries: prepayments/ accruals** ▸ 6. ADJUSTED TRIAL BALANCE ▸ 7. FINANCIAL STATEMENTS ▸ 8. CLOSING ENTRIES ▸ 9. POST-CLOSING TRIAL BALANCE

You will recall that we learned about the first four steps of the accounting cycle in Chapter 3. The fifth step in the accounting cycle is to journalize and post adjusting entries. We will discuss prepayments in this section and accruals in the next.

Sometimes a company will pay a cost in advance, such as paying for a 12-month insurance policy. This is called a **prepayment**. Prepayments increase current assets, such as prepaid expenses, and can also affect certain types of non-current assets, such as buildings and equipment. In such cases, the expense is recognized each month rather than when the cash is paid. With the insurance example, an asset (Prepaid Insurance) would be recognized at the time of payment, while an expense (Insurance Expense) would be recorded each month that the policy covers.

A company can also receive prepayments from its customers. Continuing the example above, cash is received in advance by the insurance company for the 12-month insurance policy. This type of prepayment increases current liabilities, such as unearned revenue. In such cases, revenue is recognized each month as the insurance coverage is provided, rather than when the cash is received.

Alternative Terminology
Prepayments are also known as *deferrals*.

For both of these types of prepayments—prepaid expenses (expenses paid in advance) and unearned revenues (revenues received in advance)—companies must make adjusting entries to record the expense incurred or revenue earned during the correct period. We will look at each of these in detail in the next sections.

PREPAID EXPENSES

We learned in earlier chapters that companies record payments of expenses that will benefit more than one accounting period as assets. These assets are known as **prepaid expenses**—expenses paid in cash before they are used or consumed. When expenses are prepaid, an asset (prepaid expenses) is increased (debited) to show the service or benefit that the company will receive in the future and cash is decreased (credited). Examples of common prepayments include insurance, supplies, advertising, and rent.

Prepaid expenses expire either with the passage of time (such as insurance) or through use (such as supplies). It is not practical to record the expiration of these costs on a daily basis. Instead, we record these expired costs whenever financial statements are prepared. At each statement date, adjusting entries are made for two purposes: (1) to record the expense applicable to the current accounting period, and (2) to record the offsetting reduction to the related asset (prepaid expenses) so that the account balance reflects only the benefits remaining from that asset.

The transaction journal entry to record a prepaid expense normally involves a debit to an asset (prepaid expenses) account and a credit to the Cash account. An adjusting entry for prepaid expenses is required to recognize the expense and reduction of the asset. Consequently, adjusting entries for prepaid expenses result in an increase (a debit) to an expense account and a decrease (a credit) to an asset (prepaid expenses) account, as shown below.

▼ HELPFUL HINT
A cost can be an asset or an expense. If the cost has future benefits (that is, the benefits have not yet expired), it is an asset. If the cost has no future benefits (that is, the benefits have expired), it is an expense.

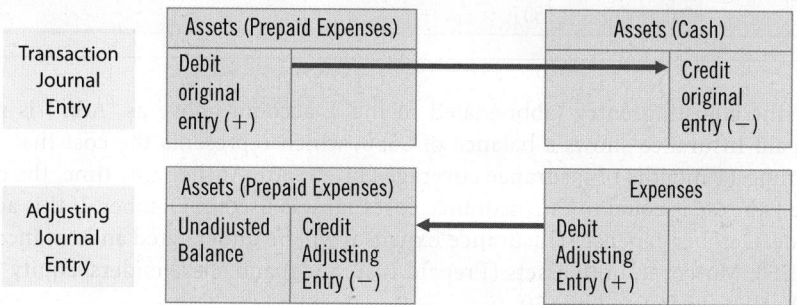

Until prepaid expenses are adjusted at the end of each accounting period, assets are overstated and expenses are understated. If expenses are understated, then net income, retained earnings, and shareholders' equity will be overstated.

In the following sections, we will look at three examples of prepaid expenses, beginning with insurance.

Insurance

Companies purchase insurance to protect themselves from losses caused by fire, theft, and unforeseen events. Insurance must be paid in advance, often for annual coverage. Insurance payments (premiums) made in advance are recorded in the asset account Prepaid Insurance. At the financial statement date, it is necessary to make an adjustment to increase (debit) Insurance Expense and decrease (credit) Prepaid Insurance for the cost of insurance that has been used (expired) during the period.

Recall from Chapter 3 that Sierra Corporation paid $600 for a one-year insurance policy on October 5. Coverage began on October 1 and expires next year on September 30. The original transaction was recorded as follows:

| Oct. 5 | Prepaid Insurance | 600 | |
| | Cash | | 600 |

A	=	L	+	SE
+600				
−600				
↓ Cash flows: −600				

The Prepaid Insurance account shows a balance of $600 in the October 31 trial balance. An analysis of the insurance policy reveals that $50 of insurance expires each month ($600 ÷ 12 months).

The following illustration outlines the basic analysis, similar to that shown in Chapter 3, used to determine the appropriate adjusting entry to record and post. Note that the debit–credit rules you learned in Chapter 3 also apply to adjusting and other types of journal entries.

▶ Adjustment (1)

Prepaid expenses—insurance

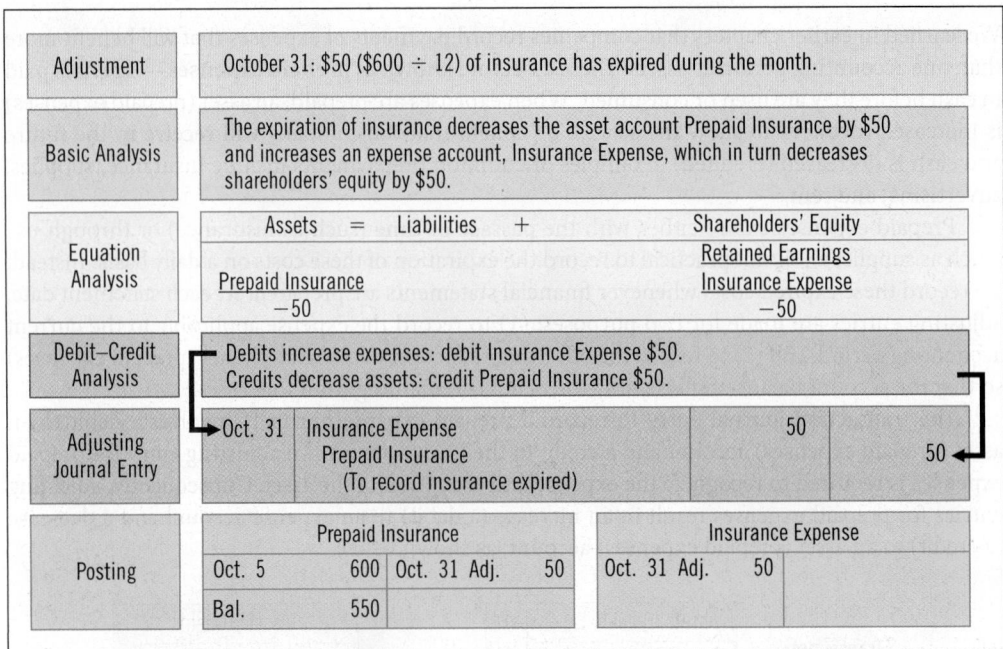

After the adjusting entry (abbreviated in the T account above as "Adj.") is made, the asset Prepaid Insurance shows a balance of $550, which represents the cost that applies to the remaining 11 months of insurance coverage (11 × $50). At the same time, the balance in Insurance Expense is equal to the insurance cost that was used in October. If this adjustment is not made, October expenses (Insurance Expense) will be understated and net income overstated by $50. Moreover, both assets (Prepaid Insurance) and shareholders' equity (Retained Earnings) will be overstated by $50.

Supplies

The purchase of supplies, such as paper and envelopes, results in an increase (a debit) to an asset (Supplies) account. During the accounting period, supplies are used. Rather than record supplies expense as the supplies are used, supplies expense is recognized at the *end* of the accounting period. At that time, the company must count the remaining supplies. The difference between the balance in the Supplies (asset) account and the actual cost of supplies on hand gives the supplies used (an expense) for that period.

Sierra Corporation purchased supplies costing $2,500 on October 9. This is an example of a prepayment made on account, rather than by cash, so Accounts Payable (a liability) is credited rather than the Cash account. The original transaction was recorded as follows:

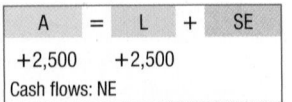

A	=	L	+	SE
+2,500		+2,500		
Cash flows: NE				

Oct. 9	Supplies	2,500	
	Accounts Payable		2,500

The Supplies account now shows a balance of $2,500 in the October 31 trial balance. A count at the close of business on October 31 reveals that $1,000 of supplies are still on hand. Thus, the cost of supplies used is $1,500 ($2,500 − $1,000). We need to update the Supplies Expense account by increasing it by $1,500 and reducing the Supplies account by the same amount.

►Adjustment (2)
Prepaid expenses—supplies

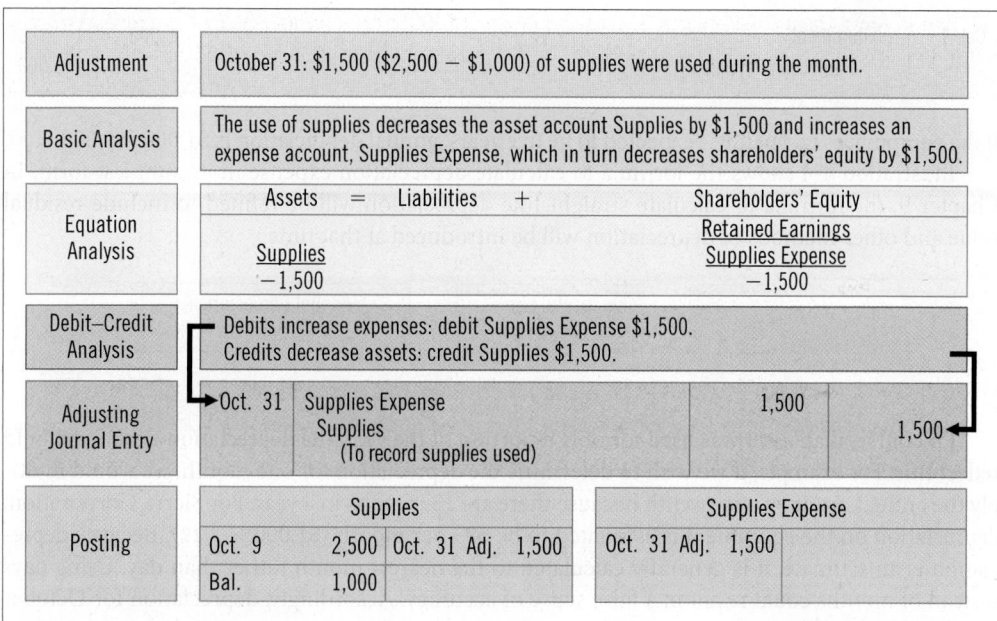

Adjustment	October 31: $1,500 ($2,500 − $1,000) of supplies were used during the month.		
Basic Analysis	The use of supplies decreases the asset account Supplies by $1,500 and increases an expense account, Supplies Expense, which in turn decreases shareholders' equity by $1,500.		

Equation Analysis

Assets	=	Liabilities	+	Shareholders' Equity
Supplies −1,500				Retained Earnings Supplies Expense −1,500

Debit–Credit Analysis	Debits increase expenses: debit Supplies Expense $1,500. Credits decrease assets: credit Supplies $1,500.		
Adjusting Journal Entry	Oct. 31	Supplies Expense	1,500	
		Supplies		1,500
		(To record supplies used)		

Posting

Supplies				Supplies Expense	
Oct. 9	2,500	Oct. 31 Adj.	1,500	Oct. 31 Adj. 1,500	
Bal.	1,000				

After adjustment, the asset account Supplies shows a balance of $1,000, which is equal to the cost of supplies on hand at the statement date. In addition, Supplies Expense shows a balance of $1,500, which equals the cost of supplies used in October. If the adjusting entry is not made, supplies will be overstated and October expenses (Supplies Expense) will be understated, and this will cause an overstatement of net income, retained earnings, and shareholders' equity.

Depreciation

A company typically owns a variety of assets that have long lives, such as buildings and equipment. Each one is recorded as an asset, rather than as an expense, in the year it is acquired because these long-lived assets provide a service for many years. The period of service is called the **useful life**.

From an accounting standpoint, the acquisition of certain types of long-lived assets is essentially a long-term prepayment for services. Similar to other prepaid expenses, the portion that has been used during the period must be expensed. In this case, the portion of the asset's cost that has been used to help generate revenues must be expensed during the period and the remaining (or unused) portion of the asset's cost is also adjusted at the end of the period. **Depreciation** is the process of allocating the cost of a long-lived or non-current asset, such as buildings and equipment, to expense over its useful life. Only assets with specified useful lives are depreciated. We call them *depreciable assets*. When an asset, such as land, has an unlimited useful life, it is not depreciated. As was mentioned in Chapter 2, some companies use the term *amortization* in place of *depreciation*, especially private companies reporting under ASPE.

One point about depreciation is very important to understand: depreciation is an allocation concept, not a valuation concept. That is, we depreciate an asset to allocate its cost to the periods over which we use it. We are not trying to record a change in the actual value of the asset.

CALCULATION OF DEPRECIATION   A common practice for calculating depreciation expense for a period of time is to divide the cost of the asset by its useful life. This is known as the **straight-line method of depreciation**. Of course, at the time an asset is acquired, its useful life is not known with complete certainty. It must therefore be estimated. Because of this, depreciation is an estimate rather than a factual measurement of the cost that has expired.

Sierra Corporation purchased equipment that cost $5,000 on October 1. The original transaction was recorded as follows:

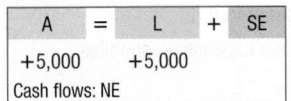

Oct. 1	Equipment	5,000	
	Bank Loan Payable		5,000

If the equipment's useful life is expected to be five years, annual depreciation is $1,000 ($5,000 ÷ 5).

Illustration 4-4 shows the formula to calculate depreciation expense in its simplest form. In Chapter 9, the formula to calculate straight-line depreciation will be refined to include residual value and other methods of depreciation will be introduced at that time.

►Illustration 4-4
Formula for straight-line depreciation

Cost	÷	Useful Life (in years)	=	Annual Depreciation Expense
$5,000	÷	5	=	$1,000

Of course, if an asset was used for only a portion of the year, the depreciation expense should reflect this. For example, if we wish to determine the depreciation for one month, we would multiply the annual result by one twelfth because there are 12 months in a year. For Sierra Corporation, depreciation on the equipment is estimated to be $83 per month ($1,000 × $1/12$). Because depreciation is an estimate, it is generally calculated to the nearest month rather than day. Using days instead of months could result in a false sense of accuracy. Accordingly, depreciation for October is recognized as follows:

►Adjustment (3)
Prepaid expenses—depreciation

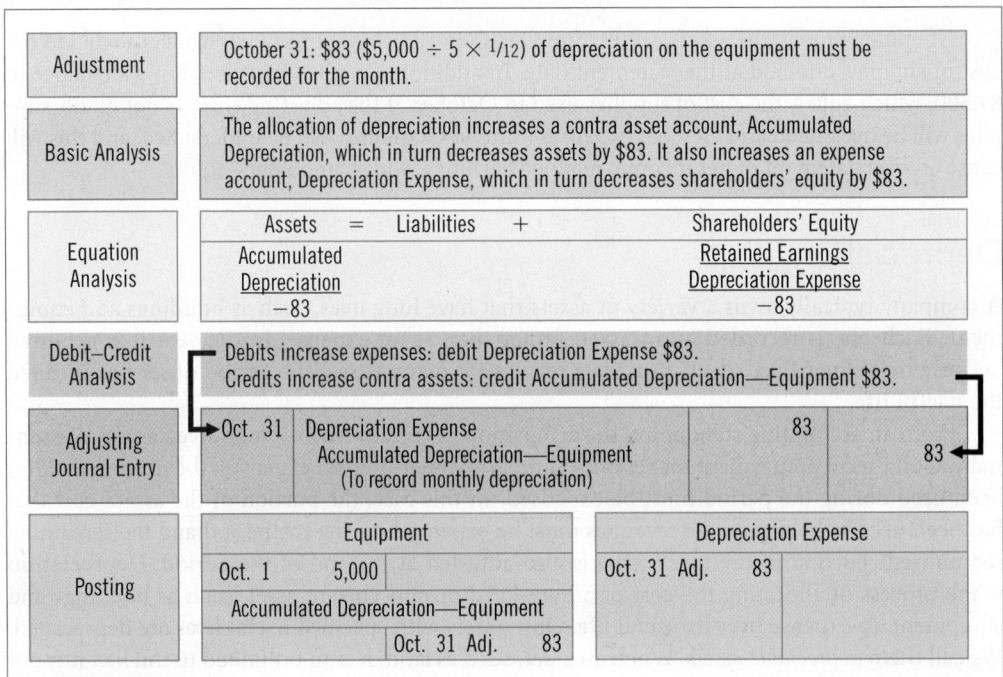

In the adjusting journal entry above, Depreciation Expense is debited (increased) and Accumulated Depreciation—Equipment is credited (increased) instead of crediting (decreasing) the Equipment account. Accumulated Depreciation—Equipment is a **contra asset account**. That means it is offset against an asset account, Equipment, on the statement of financial position. Its normal balance is a credit—the opposite of (contrary to) the normal debit balance of its related account, Equipment.

There is a simple reason for using a separate contra account instead of crediting Equipment directly for depreciation: using this account enables companies to disclose both the original cost of the equipment and the total estimated cost that has been expensed to date. This also helps separate actual amounts (cost) from estimated amounts (accumulated depreciation).

The balance in the Accumulated Depreciation account will increase by $83 each month ($1,000 each year) until the asset is fully depreciated in five years. Accumulated depreciation represents the cumulative total of the depreciation expense since the asset was purchased. The balance in the Equipment account will remain unchanged at $5,000 (unless existing equipment is later sold or new equipment purchased).

As in the case of other prepaid expenses, if this adjusting entry is not made, depreciation expense will be understated and net income overstated by $83. Total assets (because of the understatement in accumulated depreciation, a contra asset account) and shareholders' equity (because of the overstatement of net income) will also be overstated by $83.

STATEMENT PRESENTATION OF DEPRECIATION   In the statement of financial position, Accumulated Depreciation—Equipment is deducted from the related asset account as follows:

Equipment	$5,000
Less: Accumulated depreciation—equipment	83
Carrying amount	$4,917

The difference between the cost of a depreciable asset and its related accumulated depreciation is referred to as the **carrying amount** of that asset. The carrying amount is also commonly known as net book value, or simply book value. In the above illustration, the equipment's carrying amount at the statement of financial position date is $4,917. Be sure to understand that, except at acquisition, the asset's carrying amount and its current value (the price at which it could be sold) are two different amounts. As noted earlier, the purpose of depreciation is not to state an asset's value, but to allocate its cost over time.

The following summarizes the accounting for prepaid expenses. The accounting equation has been included in the "Accounts before Adjustment" column. "O" is an abbreviation for overstated, "U" for understated, and "NE" for no effect. Checking that the accounting equation is always in balance will help you ensure that you understand the directional impact on the accounts.

PREPAID EXPENSES				
Examples	**Original Transaction**	**Reasons for Adjustment**	**Accounts before Adjustment**	**Adjusting Entry**
Insurance, supplies, advertising, rent, depreciation	Expenses paid in cash and recorded as assets before they are used	Amounts recorded in asset accounts have been used	Expenses understated and net income overstated; assets and shareholders' equity overstated A = L + SE O = NE + O	Dr. Expense Cr. Asset (Prepaid Expenses) or contra asset account (Accumulated Depreciation)

DO IT! ▶4-2a   Adjusting Entries for Prepaid Expenses

Hammond, Inc.'s general ledger includes these selected accounts on March 31, 2018, before adjusting entries are prepared:

Prepaid rent	$ 3,600
Supplies	1,800
Equipment	24,000
Accumulated depreciation—equipment	5,750

An analysis of the accounts reveals the following:

1. Three months of rent ($1,200 per month) were paid in advance on March 1.

2. Supplies of $1,800 were purchased on March 2 for cash. A count determined that supplies on hand total $800 on March 31.

Action Plan

✔ Make sure you prepare adjustments for the appropriate time period.

✔ Adjusting entries for prepaid expenses require a debit to an expense account and a credit to an asset (or contra asset) account.

3. The equipment was purchased on April 1, 2016, for cash, and is estimated to have a useful life of eight years. Hammond uses straight-line depreciation.

For each of the above three items, do the following:

(a) Prepare the original transaction journal entry.

(b) Prepare the adjusting journal entries required at March 31, 2018, assuming entries are made monthly.

(c) Set up T accounts (you can omit the Cash account), enter any opening balances, post the transaction and adjusting journal entries prepared in (a) and (b), and check your work.

UNEARNED REVENUES

We know from earlier chapters that, when cash is received from customers before goods or services are provided to them, revenue is not recorded because it has not been earned. Instead, a liability, known as **unearned revenues**, is recorded because the related goods or services are still owed to the customer. To record this type of cash receipt, an asset account (Cash) is increased (debited) and a liability account (Unearned Revenue) is increased (credited) to recognize that the company has received cash in advance and has a performance obligation to provide a service in the future, or refund the cash. Examples of unearned revenues include magazine subscriptions, rent, and customer deposits. Airlines, such as Air Canada, treat cash received from the sale of tickets as unearned revenue until the flight service is provided. Similarly, tuition fees received by universities before the academic term begins are considered unearned revenue, as at Western University in our feature story.

Unearned revenues are the opposite of prepaid expenses. Indeed, unearned revenue on the books of one company is likely to be a prepaid expense on the books of the company that has made the advance payment. You will recall that we discussed this possibility with respect to an insurance policy earlier in this chapter. As another example, if identical accounting periods are assumed, a landlord will record unearned rent revenue, while the tenant would record prepaid rent.

It is not practical to make daily journal entries as the company performs services and revenue is earned. Instead, recognition of earned revenue and adjustment of the Unearned Revenue account is delayed until the adjustment process when financial statements are prepared. At that time, an adjusting entry is made to record the revenue that has been earned during the period and to show the liability related to unearned revenue that remains at the end of the accounting period.

As shown below, the journal entry to initially record unearned revenue results in an increase (debit) to the asset account (Cash) and an increase (credit) to the liability account (Unearned Revenue). The subsequent adjusting entry to record the revenue that has been earned results in a decrease (debit) to the liability (Unearned Revenue) account and an increase (credit) to a revenue account.

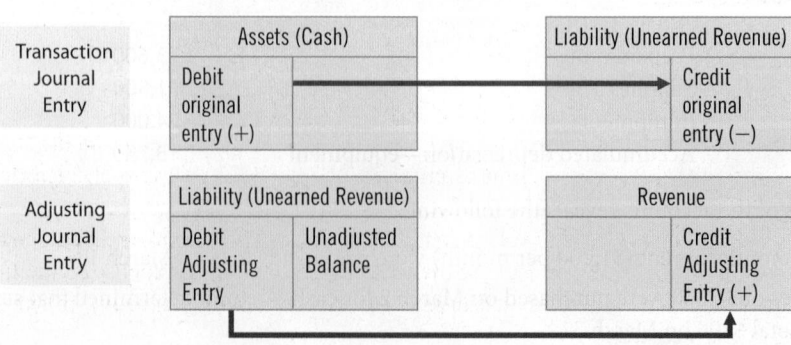

Typically, until the adjustment is made, liabilities are overstated and revenues and net income are understated. This in turn means that retained earnings and shareholders' equity are understated.

Returning to our Sierra example, we note that this company received $1,200 on October 19 from Knox Ltd. for advertising services not expected to be fully completed until November. The payment was credited to Unearned Revenue, and this liability account shows a balance of $1,200 in the October 31 trial balance. Sierra started work on this account in October and after a review of the work performed by Sierra for Knox to date, it is determined that $400 worth of service was performed, so this revenue should be recorded in October.

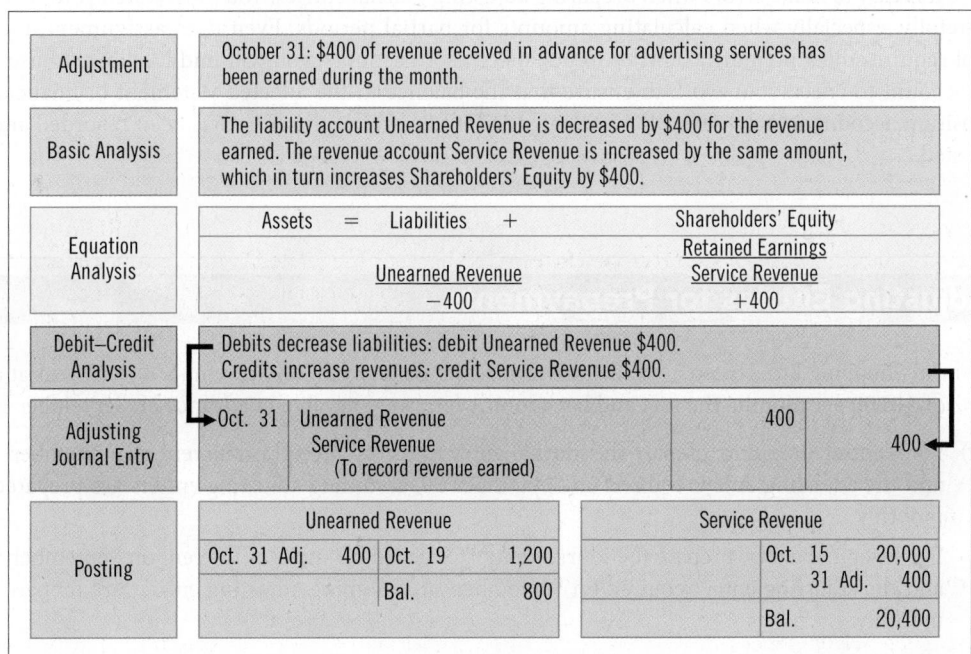

►Adjustment (4)
Unearned revenues—services

After adjustment, the liability Unearned Revenue shows a balance of $800, which represents the remaining advertising services that will be performed in the future. At the same time, Service Revenue shows total revenue earned in October of $20,400. If this adjustment is not made, revenues (Service Revenue) and net income will be understated by $400. Moreover, liabilities (Unearned Revenue) will be overstated by $400 and shareholders' equity (Retained Earnings) will also be understated by that amount.

The following summarizes the accounting for unearned revenues, including the impact on the accounting equation.

UNEARNED REVENUE				
Examples	Original Transaction	Reasons for Adjustment	Accounts before Adjustment	Adjusting Entry
Rent, magazine subscriptions, customer deposits for future service, all received in advance	Cash received and recorded as liabilities before revenue is earned	Unearned revenues recorded in liability accounts have been earned	Revenues and net income understated; liabilities overstated and shareholders' equity understated A = L + SE NE = O + U	Dr. Unearned Revenue Cr. Revenue

Note that we have assumed that prepayments, whether a prepaid expense discussed in the previous section or an unearned revenue discussed in this section, are originally recorded at some time during the period with an entry that affects cash and another account that is on the statement of financial position rather than an income statement account. For example, rent paid in advance is debited to Prepaid Rent, an asset account, rather than Rent Expense, an expense account. Similarly, rent received in advance is credited to Unearned Revenue, a liability account, rather than Rent Revenue, a revenue account.

An exception to this treatment may occur if only a short time will elapse between the initial cash flow and expiry of the prepaid expense or the earning of the revenue. If this is the case, some companies will simply record the initial payment or receipt as an expense or revenue and then adjust for any prepaid amount remaining at the end of the accounting period. Although either approach will work, as long as the appropriate adjusting journal entry is made so that the ending balances in each account are correct, it is considered to be better for control purposes to record the original transaction as a prepaid expense or unearned revenue and then adjust this at end of each accounting period. We follow this practice in this textbook.

It is easy to make errors when preparing adjusting journal entries. You must watch your dates carefully, especially when calculating amounts for partial periods. Even if an assignment does not require adjusting journal entries to be posted to T accounts, you will find it helpful to use a T account to check your work to ensure that the balance in the affected statement of financial position account actually says what you intended it to say after the entry has been recorded and posted.

DO IT! ▶ 4-2b   Adjusting Entries for Prepayments

Action Plan

✔ Identify which party is the tenant recording prepaid expenses and which party is the landlord recording unearned revenues.

✔ Recall that adjusting entries for prepaid expenses require a debit to an expense account and a credit to an asset account.

✔ Adjusting entries for unearned revenues require a debit to a liability account and a credit to a revenue account.

Central Shopping Ltd. rented a small store to Joseph's Bakery Ltd. on September 1 for a year at a rate of $1,200 per month. The first and last month's rent were payable in advance on September 1.

(a) For Central Shopping, prepare the journal entry to record receipt of the rent on September 1 and the adjusting entry required on September 30, assuming adjusting entries are prepared monthly.

(b) For Joseph's Bakery, prepare the journal entry to record payment of the rent on September 1 and the adjusting entry required on September 30, assuming adjusting entries are prepared monthly.

SOLUTION
Try this Do It! exercise on your own and then check your answer at the end of the chapter.

Related Exercise Material: **BE4–5** and **E4–4**.

LEARNING OBJECTIVE ▶ 3   Prepare adjusting entries for accruals.

| 1. ANALYZE | 2. JOURNALIZE | 3. POST | 4. TRIAL BALANCE | 5. Journalize and post adjusting entries: prepayments/ accruals | 6. ADJUSTED TRIAL BALANCE | 7. FINANCIAL STATEMENTS | 8. CLOSING ENTRIES | 9. POST-CLOSING TRIAL BALANCE |

▼ **HELPFUL HINT**
Unlike prepayments, for which a journal entry has been recorded during the accounting period and is later adjusted, accruals are recorded only by adjusting journal entries.

The second category of adjusting entries is **accruals**. Adjusting entries for accruals are required in order to record expenses incurred, or revenues earned, that have not yet been recorded during the accounting period. Unlike prepayments, accruals are not recognized through journal entries and thus are not yet reflected in the accounts prior to recording an adjusting entry. This is due to the fact that cash is paid or received during the accounting period for prepayments, while cash will be paid or received *after the end of the accounting period* for accruals.

Until an accrual adjustment is made, the expense account (and the related liability account which is usually a payable), or the revenue account (and the related asset account, which is usually a receivable), is understated. Thus, adjusting entries for accruals will increase both a statement of financial position account and an income statement account.

There are two types of adjusting entries for accruals: accrued expenses and accrued revenues. We now look at each type in more detail.

ACCRUED EXPENSES

Accrued expenses are expenses that have been incurred but not yet paid or recorded through transaction journal entries. Interest, salaries, property tax, and income tax are common examples of accrued expenses that are impractical to record on a daily basis. They are normally recorded when paid. However, if an accounting period ends before the accrued expense has been paid, then the expense and related liability must be recorded through an adjusting journal entry.

Because accrued expenses are not recorded by a transaction journal entry, an adjusting entry is required for two purposes: (1) to record the obligations that exist at the end of the period, and (2) to recognize the expenses that apply to the current accounting period. Until the adjustment is made, both liabilities and expenses are understated. Consequently, net income, retained earnings, and shareholders' equity are overstated.

An adjusting entry for accrued expenses results in an increase (debit) to an expense account and an increase (credit) to a liability (payable) account, as shown below.

> **Alternative Terminology**
> *Accrued expenses* are also referred as *accrued payables* because both are created in the same adjusting entry.

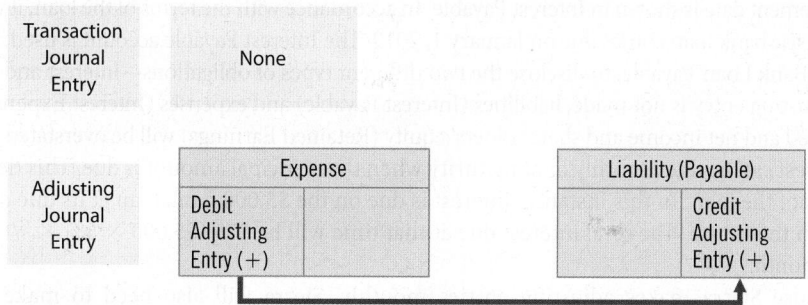

We now look in more detail at some specific types of accrued expenses, beginning with accrued interest.

Interest

Sierra Corporation signed a bank loan for $5,000 on October 1, with interest and principal repayable in three months. The bank loan incurs interest at 6%. Note that interest rates are always expressed in annual terms (also known as *per annum*). The amount of the interest incurred is determined by three factors: (1) the principal amount, or face value, of the loan ($5,000 for Sierra), which is the original amount received from the bank; (2) the interest rate (6% per annum for Sierra); and (3) the length of time that the loan is outstanding (unpaid) (three months for Sierra).

The formula for calculating interest, including how it applies to Sierra Corporation for the month of October, is shown in Illustration 4-5.

> **▼ HELPFUL HINT**
> To make interest easier to understand, this chapter uses a simplified method of interest calculation using months instead of days. In reality, interest is calculated by multiplying the principal amount by the interest rate by a ratio that uses the exact number of days in the interest period divided by the number of days in a year.

Principal Amount	$\times$	Annual Interest Rate	$\times$	Time in Terms of One Year	$=$	Interest
$5,000	$\times$	6%	$\times$	1/12	$=$	$25

▶ **Illustration 4-5**
Formula for calculating interest

The accrual of interest at October 31 is reflected as follows:

►Adjustment (5)
Accrued expenses—interest

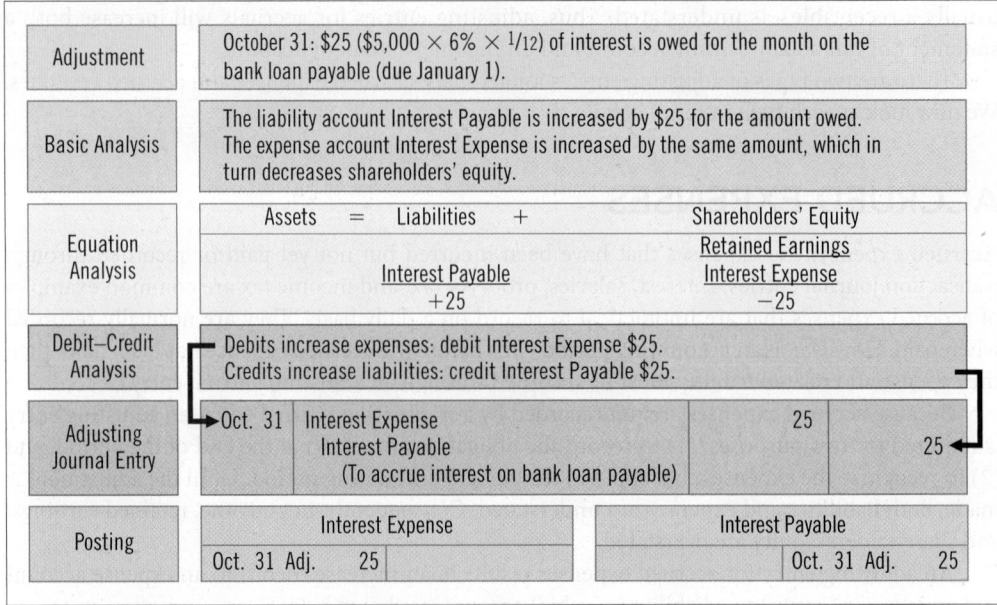

Adjustment	October 31: $25 ($5,000 × 6% × 1/12) of interest is owed for the month on the bank loan payable (due January 1).
Basic Analysis	The liability account Interest Payable is increased by $25 for the amount owed. The expense account Interest Expense is increased by the same amount, which in turn decreases shareholders' equity.

Equation Analysis	Assets	=	Liabilities	+	Shareholders' Equity
			Interest Payable +25		Retained Earnings Interest Expense −25

Debit–Credit Analysis	Debits increase expenses: debit Interest Expense $25. Credits increase liabilities: credit Interest Payable $25.		
Adjusting Journal Entry	Oct. 31 Interest Expense	25	
	Interest Payable		25
	(To accrue interest on bank loan payable)		

Posting	Interest Expense	Interest Payable
	Oct. 31 Adj. 25	Oct. 31 Adj. 25

Interest Expense shows the interest charges for the month of October. The amount of interest owed at the statement date is shown in Interest Payable. In accordance with the terms of the loan, it will not be paid until the bank loan comes due on January 1, 2019. The Interest Payable account is used, instead of crediting Bank Loan Payable, to disclose the two different types of obligations—interest and principal. If this adjusting entry is not made, liabilities (Interest Payable) and expenses (Interest Expense) will be understated and net income and shareholders' equity (Retained Earnings) will be overstated.

Interest can be due monthly or at maturity when the principal amount is due. This depends on the terms of the loan. In this instance, interest is due on the $5,000 bank loan at its due date, three months in the future. The total interest due at that time will be $75 ($5,000 × 6% × 3/12), or $25 for one month.

Because Sierra makes adjusting entries monthly, Sierra will also need to make identical adjustments similar to that shown in Adjustment (5) at the end of November and December to accrue for interest expense incurred in each of these months. After the three adjusting entries have been posted, the balance in Interest Payable will be $75 ($25 × 3). The following entry is made on January 1, 2019, when the loan and interest are paid:

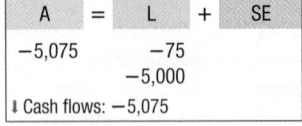

A	=	L	+	SE
−5,075		−75		
		−5,000		
↓ Cash flows: −5,075				

Jan. 1	Interest Payable	75	
	Bank Loan Payable	5,000	
	Cash		5,075
	(To record payment of bank loan and interest)		

This entry does two things: (1) it eliminates the liability for Interest Payable that was recorded in the October 31, November 30, and December 31 adjusting entries; and (2) it eliminates the bank loan payable as the loan principal has been repaid. Notice also that the account Interest Expense is not included in this entry, because the full amount of interest incurred was accrued in previous months.

Salaries

Some types of expenses, such as employee salaries, are paid for after the services have been performed and require an accrual adjustment if an accounting period ends prior to the payment of salaries incurred. For example, at its year end, Western University, described in our feature story, accrues salary and vacation pay for approximately 3,900 faculty and staff that will be paid out in the following period.

At Sierra Corporation, salaries are paid every two weeks. Sierra's four employees were last paid on October 26 for the period October 15–26. The next payment of salaries will not occur until November 9. As shown on the calendar below, there are three working days that remain unpaid for October (October 29–31).

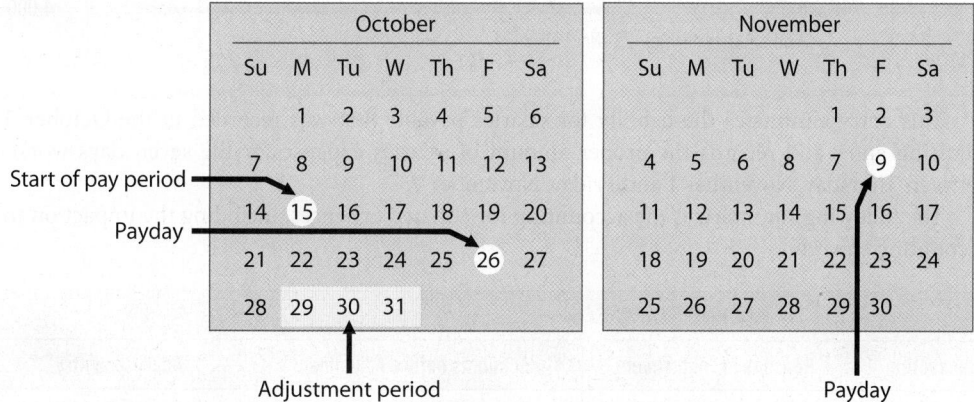

At October 31, the salaries for these three days (Monday, October 29, through Wednesday, October 31) represent an accrued expense and related liability for Sierra. Because the four employees each receive a salary of $500 a week for a five-day workweek from Monday to Friday, or $100 a day, accrued salaries at October 31 are $1,200 (3 days × $100/day × 4 employees).

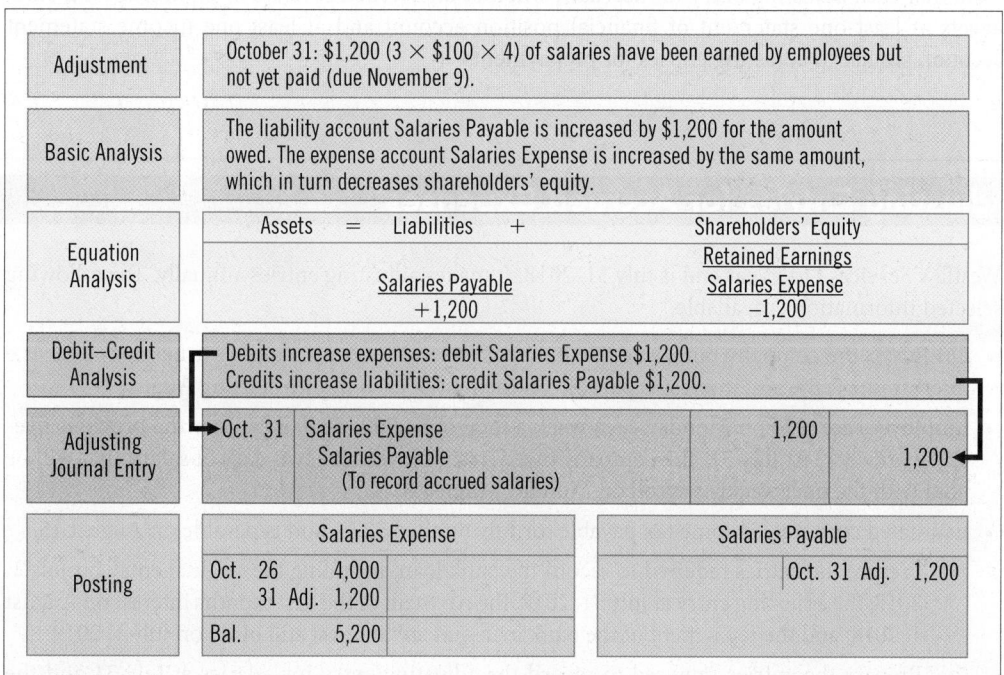

▶Adjustment (6)
Accrued expenses—salaries

After this adjustment, the balance in Salaries Expense of $5,200 (13 days × $100/day × 4 employees) is the actual salary expense for October for the period October 15–31. The balance in Salaries Payable of $1,200 is the amount of the liability for salaries owed as at October 31. If the $1,200 adjustment for salaries is not recorded, Sierra's expenses (Salaries Expense) and liabilities (Salaries Payable) will be understated by $1,200. Net income, retained earnings, and shareholders' equity will be overstated by $1,200.

At Sierra Corporation, salaries are payable every two weeks. Consequently, the next payday is November 9, when total salaries of $4,000 will again be paid. The payment consists of $1,200 of salaries payable at October 31 plus $2,800 of salaries expense for November 1–9 (7 days × $100/day × 4 employees). Therefore, the following entry is made on November 9:

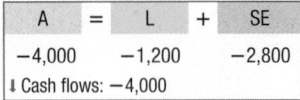

A	=	L	+	SE
−4,000		−1,200		−2,800
↓ Cash flows: −4,000				

Nov. 9	Salaries Payable (Oct. 29–31)	1,200	
	Salaries Expense (Nov. 1–9)	2,800	
	Cash		4,000
	(Paid salaries for Oct. 29–Nov. 9)		

This entry eliminates the liability for salaries payable that was recorded in the October 31 adjusting entry and records the proper amount of salaries expense for the seven days worked between Thursday, November 1 and Friday, November 9.

The following summarizes the accounting for accrued expenses, including the impact on the accounting equation.

ACCRUED EXPENSES				
Examples	Original Transaction	Reasons for Adjustment	Accounts before Adjustment	Adjusting Entry
Interest, salaries, property tax, income tax	None	Expenses have been incurred but not yet paid in cash or recorded	Expenses understated and net income overstated; liabilities understated and shareholders' equity overstated A = L + SE NE = U + O	Dr. Expense Cr. Payable

Note that each adjusting entry for accruals, whether an accrued revenue or an accrued expense, affects at least one statement of financial position account and at least one income statement account, similar to adjusting entries for prepayments.

DO IT! ▶ 4-3a ⬤ Adjusting Entries for Accrued Expenses

Action Plan

✔ Remember that accrued expenses are entries that initially record an expense whereas adjusting entries for prepayments adjust amounts that were previously recorded during the period.

✔ Adjusting entries for accrued expenses require a debit to an expense account and a credit to a liability account, causing both account balances to increase.

✔ Recall that interest rates are always stated as an annual rate.

Westlaw Services Ltd.'s year end is July 31, 2018. It makes adjusting entries annually. The following selected information is available:

- On July 1, the company borrowed $30,000 from a local bank on a one-year loan payable. The interest rate is 5% and interest is payable on the first of each month starting August 1.

- Employees are paid on Monday each week a total of $4,000 ($800 a day) for the previous five-day workweek. At July 31, the company owed its employees for two days of salary that will be paid with the next weekly payroll on Monday, August 6.

- Estimated corporate income tax payable for July totalled $275, and is payable on August 15.

(a) Prepare the entries required to record the bank loan, including the original entry on July 1, 2018, the adjusting entry at July 31, 2018, the payment of the first month's interest on August 1, 2018, and the repayment of the bank loan and any interest still owed on July 1, 2019.

(b) Prepare the entries required to record the adjusting entry for salaries at July 31 and the subsequent payment of salaries on August 6.

(c) Prepare the adjusting entry for corporate income tax at July 31 and the subsequent payment of tax on August 15.

SOLUTION

Try this Do It! exercise on your own and then check your answer at the end of the chapter.

Related Exercise Material: BE4–6, BE4–8, BE4–10, E4–8, and E4–9.

ACCRUED REVENUES

Accrued revenues are revenues that have been earned but not yet recorded through journal entries. For example, accrued revenues may be earned with the passing of time, as in the case of interest revenue. It is impractical to record interest daily, so it is normally recorded when collected. If an accounting period ends before the interest has been collected, then the receivable and related revenue must be recorded through an adjusting journal entry.

Accrued revenues may also result from services that have been performed but neither billed nor collected. For example, revenue from providing legal services may not have been recorded because only a portion of the service has been provided and the client will not be billed until the service has been completed. Or a service may have been provided but the invoices may not have been prepared before the end of the accounting period. Recall from prior chapters that journal entries are usually initiated by a source document such as an invoice or by the receipt of cash.

Because accrued revenues are not recorded by a transaction journal entry, an adjusting entry for accrued revenues is required for two purposes: (1) to show the receivable that exists at the end of the period, and (2) to record the revenue that has been earned during the period. Until the adjustment is made, both assets and revenues are understated. Consequently, net income and shareholders' equity will also be understated.

As shown below, an adjusting entry for accrued revenues results in an increase (a debit) to an asset (receivable) account and an increase (a credit) to a revenue account.

Alternative Terminology
Accrued revenues are also referred to as *accrued receivables* because both are created in the same adjusting entry.

Transaction Journal Entry	None	

Adjusting Journal Entry	**Asset (Receivable)**	**Revenue**
	Debit Adjusting Entry (+)	Credit Adjusting Entry (+)

In October, Sierra Corporation earned $200 for advertising services that were not billed to clients before October 31. Because these services have not been billed, they have not yet been recorded but they need to be because the revenue has been earned.

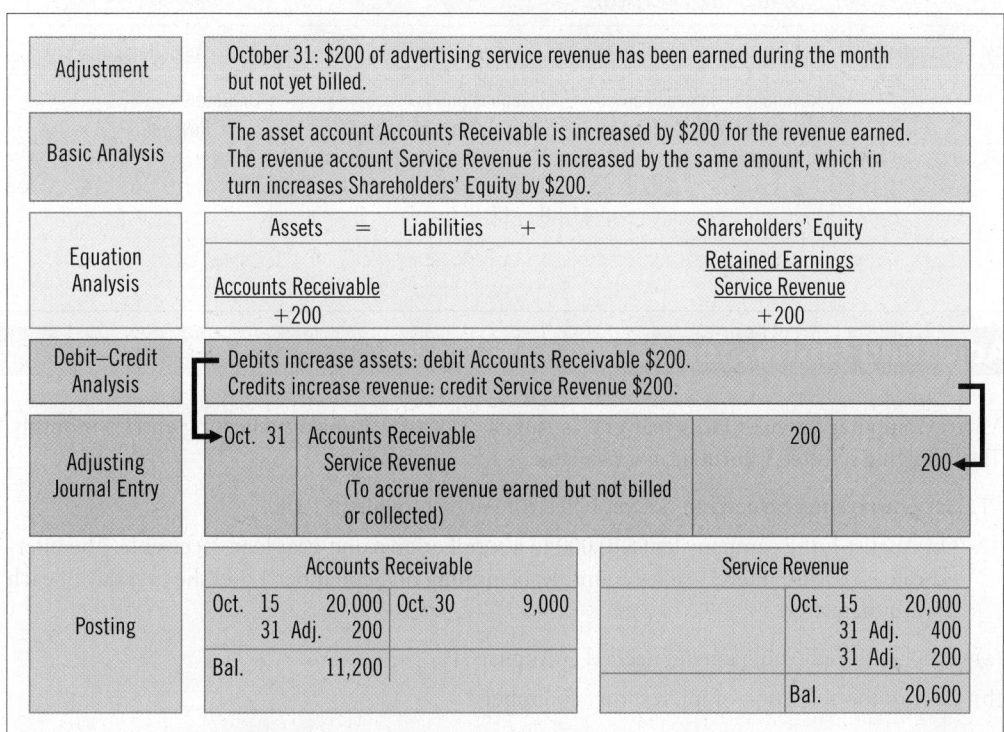

►Adjustment (7)
Accrued revenues—accounts receivable

Adjustment	October 31: $200 of advertising service revenue has been earned during the month but not yet billed.
Basic Analysis	The asset account Accounts Receivable is increased by $200 for the revenue earned. The revenue account Service Revenue is increased by the same amount, which in turn increases Shareholders' Equity by $200.

Equation Analysis

Assets	=	Liabilities	+	Shareholders' Equity
				Retained Earnings
Accounts Receivable				Service Revenue
+200				+200

Debit–Credit Analysis: Debits increase assets: debit Accounts Receivable $200. Credits increase revenue: credit Service Revenue $200.

Adjusting Journal Entry	Oct. 31	Accounts Receivable	200	
		Service Revenue		200
		(To accrue revenue earned but not billed or collected)		

Posting

Accounts Receivable				Service Revenue		
Oct. 15	20,000	Oct. 30	9,000		Oct. 15	20,000
31 Adj.	200				31 Adj.	400
					31 Adj.	200
Bal.	11,200				Bal.	20,600

The asset Accounts Receivable shows that $11,200 is owed by clients at October 31. The balance of $20,600 in Service Revenue represents the total revenue earned during the month. If the adjusting entry is not made, revenues (Service Revenue) and net income on the income statement will be understated, as will assets (Accounts Receivable) and shareholders' equity (Retained Earnings) on the statement of financial position.

An accrued revenue on the books of one company is an accrued expense to another company. For example, the $200 accrual of service revenue for Sierra Corporation discussed above is an accrued expense for the client that received the service.

In the next accounting period, cash will be collected from clients for services performed in October, as well as for services performed in November. When this occurs, the entry to record the collection should take into consideration the fact that $200 of the amount collected was previously recorded in the October 31 adjusting entry and this revenue should not be recorded a second time. For example, assume that on November 6, $2,500 cash is received. The $2,500 includes payment for the $200 owed for advertising provided in October and $2,300 for advertising provided in the first week of November. The collection of cash will be recorded as follows:

A	=	L	+	SE
+2,500				+2,300
−200				
⬆ Cash flows: +2,500				

Nov. 6	Cash	2,500	
	Accounts Receivable		200
	Service Revenue		2,300
	(To record collection of account and cash receipts from services performed)		

Some accountants prefer to reverse accrual entries at the beginning of a new accounting period rather than try to remember what entries had been made in the prior period. A reversing entry is made at the beginning of the next accounting period. It is the exact opposite of the adjusting entry made in the previous period. The accrual is reversed to ensure that revenue is not recorded a second time when the invoice is prepared. The preparation of reversing entries is an optional accounting procedure that is not a required step in the accounting cycle and will not be discussed here.

The following summarizes the accounting for accrued revenue, including the impact on the accounting equation.

ACCRUED REVENUE				
Examples	Original Transaction	Reasons for Adjustment	Accounts before Adjustment	Adjusting Entry
Interest and services performed but not yet billed	None	Revenues have been earned but not yet received in cash or recorded	Revenues and net income understated; assets and shareholders' equity understated A = L + SE U = NE + U	Dr. Receivable Cr. Revenue

DO IT! ▶ 4-3b   Adjusting Entries for Accrued Revenues

Micro Computer Services Ltd.'s year end is August 31, 2018. It makes adjusting entries monthly. The following selected information is available:

1. Service revenue earned but not yet billed for August totalled $1,100.

2. On August 1, the company lent $10,000 to a supplier on a one-year loan receivable. The interest rate is 6% and interest is due monthly, beginning on September 1 and the first day of each month thereafter.

(a) Prepare the adjusting entries needed at August 31.

(b) Record the collection of interest on September 1.

Action Plan (cont'd)

✔ Adjusting entries for accrued revenues require a debit to a receivable account and a credit to a revenue account.

✔ Recall that interest rates are always stated as an annual rate.

SOLUTION

Try this Do It! exercise on your own and then check your answer at the end of the chapter.

Related Exercise Material: BE4–7, BE4–9, E4-6, and E4-7.

SUMMARY OF BASIC RELATIONSHIPS

Illustration 4-6 summarizes the four basic types of adjusting entries. Take some time to study and analyze the adjusting entries and their impact on the accounting equation.

▶ Illustration 4-6
Summary of adjusting entries

Type of Adjustment	Transaction Journal Entry during Period	Accounts before Adjustment	Adjusting Entry
Prepayments			

Prepaid expenses	Dr. Prepaid Expense
	    Cr. Cash (or Accounts Payable)
		Expenses understated and net income overstated; assets and shareholders' equity overstated
		A = L + SE
		0 = NE + 0
			Dr. Expense
			    Cr. Prepaid Expense

Unearned revenue	Dr. Cash
	    Cr. Unearned Revenue
		Revenues and net income understated; liabilities overstated and shareholders' equity understated
		A = L + SE
		NE = 0 + U
			Dr. Unearned Revenue
			    Cr. Revenue

Accruals			
Accrued expenses	None	Expenses understated and net income overstated; liabilities understated and shareholders' equity overstated A = L + SE NE = U + 0	Dr. Expense Cr. Payable
Accrued revenues	None	Revenues and net income understated; assets and shareholders' equity understated A = L + SE U = NE + U	Dr. Receivable Cr. Revenue

Be sure to note that each adjusting entry above affects one statement of financial position account and one income statement account. **It is also important to understand that adjusting entries never involve the Cash account.** In the case of prepayments, cash has already been paid or received and recorded in the original transaction journal entry. The adjusting entry simply reallocates, or adjusts, amounts between a statement of financial position account (such as prepaid expenses or unearned revenues) and an income statement account (such as expenses or revenues). In the case of accruals, cash will be paid or received in the future and recorded then. The adjusting entry simply records the payable or receivable and the related expense or revenue.

Sierra Corporation Illustration

A summary of the adjusting entries described in this chapter for Sierra Corporation on October 31 is presented below in the general journal.

GENERAL JOURNAL			
Date	Account Titles and Explanation	Debit	Credit
2018 Oct. 31	Insurance Expense	50	
	Prepaid Insurance		50
	(To record insurance expired)		

(continued)

	GENERAL JOURNAL (cont'd)		
Date	Account Titles and Explanation	Debit	Credit
Oct. 31	Supplies Expense	1,500	
	Supplies		1,500
	(To record supplies used)		
31	Depreciation Expense	83	
	Accumulated Depreciation—Equipment		83
	(To record monthly depreciation)		
31	Unearned Revenue	400	
	Service Revenue		400
	(To record revenue earned)		
31	Interest Expense	25	
	Interest Payable		25
	(To accrue interest on bank loan payable)		
31	Salaries Expense	1,200	
	Salaries Payable		1,200
	(To record accrued salaries)		
31	Accounts Receivable	200	
	Service Revenue		200
	(To accrue revenue earned but not billed or collected)		

The above adjusting journal entries are then posted to the general ledger, as shown below. As you review the general ledger, notice that the adjustments are highlighted in colour. Note also that there is no account for retained earnings in the general ledger. Because this is Sierra's first month of operations, there is no balance in the Retained Earnings account (until we learn how to make closing entries later in this chapter).

GENERAL LEDGER

Cash			
Oct. 1	10,000	Oct. 2	900
19	1,200	5	600
30	9,000	22	1,000
		26	4,000
		29	500
		31	1,800
Bal.	11,400		

Accounts Receivable			
Oct. 15	20,000	Oct. 30	9,000
31 Adj.	200		
Bal.	11,200		

Supplies			
Oct. 9	2,500	Oct. 31 Adj.	1,500
Bal.	1,000		

Prepaid Insurance			
Oct. 5	600	Oct. 31 Adj.	50
Bal.	550		

Bank Loan Payable		
	Oct. 1	5,000

Common Shares		
	Oct. 1	10,000

Dividends Declared	
Oct. 29	500

Service Revenue			
		Oct. 15	20,000
		31 Adj.	400
		31 Adj.	200
		Bal.	20,600

Salaries Expense		
Oct. 26	4,000	
31 Adj.	1,200	
Bal.	5,200	

(continued)

GENERAL LEDGER (cont'd)

Equipment				Supplies Expense		
Oct. 1	5,000			Oct. 31 Adj.	1,500	

Accumulated Depreciation—Equipment				Rent Expense		
		Oct. 31 Adj.	83	Oct. 2	900	

Accounts Payable				Depreciation Expense		
Oct. 22	1,000	Oct. 9	2,500	Oct. 31 Adj.	83	
		Bal.	1,500			

Salaries Payable				Insurance Expense		
		Oct. 31 Adj.	1,200	Oct. 31 Adj.	50	

Interest Payable				Interest Expense		
		Oct. 31 Adj.	25	Oct. 31 Adj.	25	

Unearned Revenue				Income Tax Expense		
Oct. 31 Adj.	400	Oct. 19	1,200	Oct. 31	1,800	
		Bal.	800			

LEARNING
OBJECTIVE ▶4

Prepare an adjusted trial balance and financial statements.

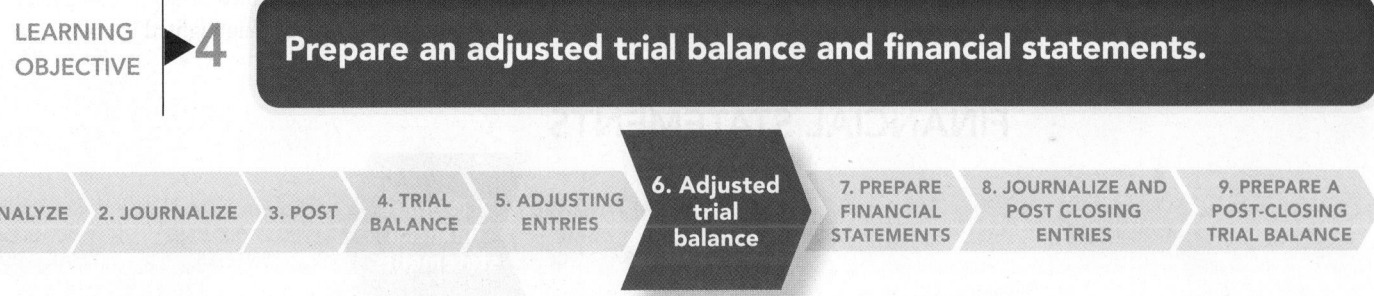

1. ANALYZE   2. JOURNALIZE   3. POST   4. TRIAL BALANCE   5. ADJUSTING ENTRIES   6. Adjusted trial balance   7. PREPARE FINANCIAL STATEMENTS   8. JOURNALIZE AND POST CLOSING ENTRIES   9. PREPARE A POST-CLOSING TRIAL BALANCE

After all adjusting entries have been journalized and posted to the general ledger, another trial balance is prepared in the sixth step of the accounting cycle. This trial balance is called an **adjusted trial balance**. It shows the balances of all accounts, including those that have been adjusted, at the end of the accounting period. Because the accounts contain all the data that are needed for financial statements, the adjusted trial balance is the main source for the preparation of financial statements.

ADJUSTED TRIAL BALANCE

The procedures for preparing an adjusted trial balance are the same as those described in Chapter 3 for preparing an unadjusted trial balance. An adjusted trial balance, similar to an unadjusted trial balance, lists the accounts in the general ledger and proves that the totals of the debit and credit balances in the ledger are equal after all adjustments have been recorded and posted.

The adjusted trial balance for Sierra Corporation is presented in Illustration 4-7 and has been prepared from the general ledger account balances shown in the previous section.

▶ Illustration 4-7
Adjusted trial balance

SIERRA CORPORATION Adjusted Trial Balance October 31, 2018		
	Debit	Credit
Cash	$11,400	
Accounts receivable	11,200	
Supplies	1,000	
Prepaid insurance	550	
Equipment	5,000	
Accumulated depreciation—equipment		$ 83
Accounts payable		1,500
Salaries payable		1,200
Interest payable		25
Unearned revenue		800
Bank loan payable		5,000
Common shares		10,000
Dividends declared	500	
Service revenue		20,600
Salaries expense	5,200	
Supplies expense	1,500	
Rent expense	900	
Depreciation expense	83	
Insurance expense	50	
Interest expense	25	
Income tax expense	1,800	
	$39,208	$39,208

Compare the adjusted trial balance with the unadjusted trial balance presented earlier in the chapter in Illustration 4-3. The amounts that are affected by the adjusting entries are highlighted in colour.

FINANCIAL STATEMENTS

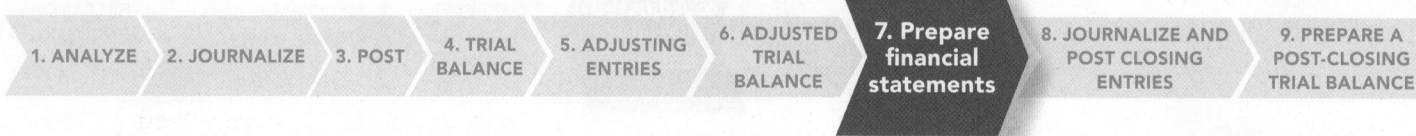

| 1. ANALYZE | 2. JOURNALIZE | 3. POST | 4. TRIAL BALANCE | 5. ADJUSTING ENTRIES | 6. ADJUSTED TRIAL BALANCE | 7. Prepare financial statements | 8. JOURNALIZE AND POST CLOSING ENTRIES | 9. PREPARE A POST-CLOSING TRIAL BALANCE |

In Chapter 3, we prepared financial statements from a trial balance, without adjusting entries. However, adjusting entries are necessary to prepare financial statements under the accrual basis of accounting. Therefore, you should always prepare financial statements from an adjusted trial balance rather than from an unadjusted trial balance, which is why "prepare financial statements" is now shown as step 7 in the accounting cycle graphic above.

We use the adjusted trial balance shown above in Illustration 4-7 to prepare Sierra's financial statements shown in Illustration 4-8. As we learned in prior chapters, the financial statements are prepared in the following order:

1. The income statement is prepared first using the revenue and expense accounts.
2. The statement of changes in equity is prepared next, using the common shares, retained earnings, and dividends declared accounts, and the net income (or loss) reported in the income statement. Note that none of these accounts had an opening balance because this is Sierra's first month of operations.
3. The statement of financial position is the third statement prepared, using the asset, liability, and shareholders' equity accounts. Note that shareholders' equity on the statement of financial position includes the *ending* common shares and the *ending* retained earnings account balances as reported in the statement of changes in equity.

SIERRA CORPORATION
Income Statement
Month Ended October 31, 2018

Revenues		
Service revenue		$20,600
Expenses		
Salaries expense	$5,200	
Supplies expense	1,500	
Rent expense	900	
Depreciation expense	83	
Insurance expense	50	
Interest expense	25	
Total expenses		7,758
Income before income tax		12,842
Income tax expense		1,800
Net income		$11,042

SIERRA CORPORATION
Statement of Changes in Equity
Month Ended October 31, 2018

	Common Shares	Retained Earnings	Total Equity
Balance, October 1	$ 0	$ 0	$ 0
Issued common shares	10,000		10,000
Net income		11,042	11,042
Dividends declared		(500)	(500)
Balance, October 31	$10,000	$10,542	$20,542

SIERRA CORPORATION
Statement of Financial Position
October 31, 2018

Assets		
Current assets		
Cash	$11,400	
Accounts receivable	11,200	
Supplies	1,000	
Prepaid insurance	550	
Total current assets		$24,150
Property, plant, and equipment		
Equipment	$ 5,000	
Less: Accumulated depreciation	83	
Total property, plant, and equipment		4,917
Total assets		$29,067
Liabilities and Shareholders' Equity		
Liabilities		
Current liabilities		
Accounts payable	$ 1,500	
Salaries payable	1,200	
Interest payable	25	
Unearned revenue	800	
Bank loan payable	5,000	
Total liabilities		$ 8,525
Shareholders' equity		
Common shares	$10,000	
Retained earnings	10,542	
Total shareholders' equity		20,542
Total liabilities and shareholders' equity		$29,067

▶Illustration 4-8
Sierra's financial statements

KEEPING AN EYE ON CASH

We learned earlier in this chapter the difference between accrual and cash basis accounting. If we were to compare Sierra's net income calculated on a cash basis with net income calculated on an accrual basis, we would have the following:

	Net Income	
	Cash Basis	Accrual Basis
1. Cash received in advance from customer	$ 1,200	$ 0
2. Unearned revenue received that was later earned (AJE)*	0	400
3. Cash received from customers for services performed	9,000	20,000
4. Services performed on account (AJE)	0	200
5. Payment of rent	(900)	(900)
6. Payment of insurance in advance	(600)	0
7. Use of insurance (AJE)	0	(50)
8. Payment for supplies purchased on account	(1,000)	
9. Use of supplies (AJE)	0	(1,500)
10. Payment of employee salaries	(4,000)	(4,000)
11. Salaries incurred, but not paid (AJE)	0	(1,200)
12. Payment of income tax	(1,800)	(1,800)
13. Depreciation (AJE)	0	(83)
14. Interest cost incurred, but not paid (AJE)	0	(25)
Net income	$ 1,900	$11,042

*AJE denotes an adjusting journal entry

(continued)

KEEPING AN EYE ON CASH (CONT'D)

Note that there is quite a difference between net income calculated on a cash basis and net income calculated on an accrual basis—much of which is created by adjusting journal entries. Sierra would have reported net income of $1,900 on a cash basis, compared with net income of $11,042 on an accrual basis. This is not surprising because a number of items in the accrual-basis income statement are recognized before or after the related cash flow.

Net income calculated on a cash basis is the equivalent of cash provided by operating activities, which is reported on the statement of cash flows. You will recall that operating activities were first introduced in Chapter 1 and will be discussed again in Chapter 13.

DO IT! ▶ 4-4   Adjusted Trial Balance

Action Plan

✔ The title of the adjusted trial balance includes the name of the company, the type of trial balance, and the date.

✔ Accounts are listed in the same order as in an unadjusted trial balance: assets, liabilities, shareholders' equity, revenues, and expenses.

✔ Apply the debit–credit rules to determine normal balances and list the amounts in the correct columns.

✔ Ensure that total debits equal total credits.

✔ Use the trial balance order of the accounts to help you identify which accounts should be reported on the income statement, statement of changes in equity, and/or statement of financial position and to calculate net income, total assets, and total liabilities.

✔ Make sure you understand the composition of total shareholders' equity (common shares + retained earnings; retained earnings = opening retained earnings + net income – dividends declared).

✔ The basic accounting equation is assets = liabilities + shareholders' equity.

Listed below, in alphabetical order, are the account balances (after adjustments) from the general ledger of KS Services Limited for the year ended December 31, 2018. All accounts have normal balances.

Accounts payable	$ 4,660
Accounts receivable	9,600
Accumulated depreciation—equipment	5,200
Bank loan payable	1,000
Cash	1,100
Common shares	5,000
Depreciation expense	2,600
Dividends declared	1,000
Equipment	20,800
Income tax expense	3,500
Interest expense	50
Other expenses	1,675
Rent expense	16,800
Retained earnings	3,700
Salaries expense	30,700
Salaries payable	710
Service revenue	67,200
Supplies	180
Supplies expense	475
Unearned revenue	1,010

(a) Prepare an adjusted trial balance.

(b) Beside each account listed in the adjusted trial balance, indicate whether it should be included on the income statement (IS), statement of changes in equity (SCE), and/or statement of financial position (SFP). (*Note*: Some accounts may be shown on more than one statement.)

(c) Calculate net income for the year.

(d) Calculate total assets, liabilities, and shareholders' equity at December 31.

(e) Present your answer in part (d) in the form of the basic accounting equation.

SOLUTION

Try this Do It! exercise on your own and then check your answer at the end of the chapter.

Related Exercise Material: BE4–11, BE4–12, E4–10, E4–11, and E4–12.

5 Prepare closing entries and a post-closing trial balance.

In previous chapters, you learned that revenue and expense accounts and the Dividends Declared account are components of retained earnings, which is reported in the shareholders' equity section of the statement of financial position. Because revenues, expenses, and dividends declared relate to activities over a particular accounting period, they are considered **temporary accounts**. In other words, these accounts are used *temporarily* to record activity for one accounting period and their balances are not carried forward into future accounting periods. Illustration 4-9 lists the types of temporary accounts and reminds you of their normal balances. Notice that all income statement accounts are temporary, along with the one temporary account that is not shown on the income statement, Dividends Declared.

Temporary Accounts	Normal Balances
Revenues	Credit
Expenses	Debit
Dividends Declared	Debit

►Illustration 4-9
Temporary accounts

In contrast, all statement of financial position accounts are considered **permanent accounts**. Asset, liability, and shareholders' equity (Common Shares and Retained Earnings) accounts are *not* closed at the end of the period because their balances are carried forward into future accounting periods. For example, if a company has cash at the end of the year, that cash balance will also exist at the beginning of the next year, so it is a permanent account. Illustration 4-10 lists the types of permanent accounts and reminds you of their normal balances.

Permanent Accounts	Normal Balances
Assets	Debit
Liabilities	Credit
Shareholders' equity accounts:	
Common Shares	Credit
Retained Earnings	Credit

►Illustration 4-10
Permanent accounts

CLOSING ENTRIES

| 1. ANALYZE | 2. JOURNALIZE | 3. POST | 4. TRIAL BALANCE | 5. ADJUSTING ENTRIES | 6. ADJUSTED TRIAL BALANCE | 7. PREPARE FINANCIAL STATEMENTS | 8. Journalize and post closing entries | 9. PREPARE A POST-CLOSING TRIAL BALANCE |

At the end of the accounting period, the temporary account balances are transferred to the permanent shareholders' equity account Retained Earnings through the preparation of closing entries in the eighth step of the accounting cycle. **Closing entries** are used to transfer the balances in the revenue, expense, and Dividends Declared accounts to the Retained Earnings account, thereby updating that account to its end-of-period balance. Before closing the books, the accounting equation is as follows, and includes the temporary accounts revenues, expenses, and Dividends Declared which have been circled for illustration purposes:

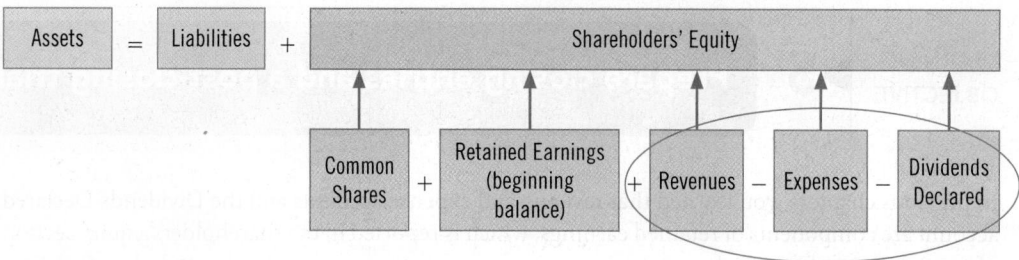

After closing entries are recorded and posted, the balance in Retained Earnings is the end-of-period balance. This ending balance in the general ledger account will then be the same as the ending balance reported on the statement of changes in equity in the retained earnings column and on the statement of financial position in the shareholders' equity section.

After closing entries are prepared, the accounting equation will be as follows:

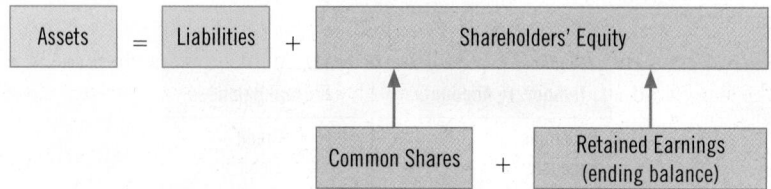

Closing entries produce a zero balance in each temporary account, in addition to updating Retained Earnings to its ending balance. For illustration purposes, the temporary revenue, expense, and Dividends Declared accounts have not been included in the above equation because they have zero balances. These accounts still exist in the general ledger though and are now ready to accumulate data about revenues, expenses, and dividends declared for the next accounting period. Permanent accounts are not closed because the future benefits relating to assets and the obligations relating to liabilities still exist.

When closing entries are prepared, each revenue and expense account could be closed directly to Retained Earnings. This is common in computerized accounting systems where the closing process occurs automatically when it is time to start a new accounting period. For our purposes, this practice can result in too much detail in the Retained Earnings account. Accordingly, the revenue and expense accounts are first closed to a new temporary account, **Income Summary**. Only the resulting total amount (net income or loss) is transferred from this account to the Retained Earnings account. Illustration 4-11 and the text that follows outlines the closing process.

▶Illustration 4-11
Closing process

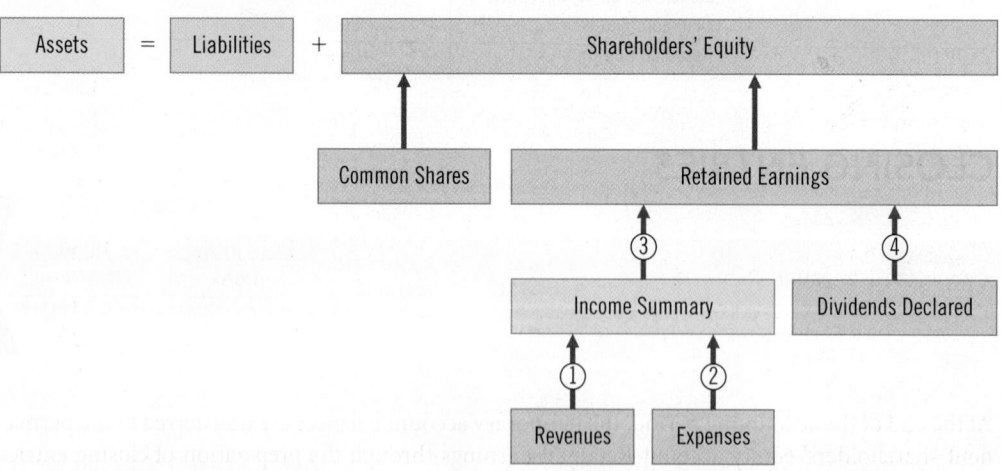

There are four closing entries necessary to close the temporary accounts:

1. Close all revenue accounts to Income Summary: Revenue accounts normally have a credit balance. As such, to close revenue accounts, each individual revenue account is debited by the balance in the account, with a credit to the Income Summary account for total revenues. After

this entry, all revenue accounts will have zero balances and the total of all revenue accounts will have been transferred into the Income Summary account.

2. Close all expense accounts to Income Summary: Expense accounts normally have debit balances. As such, the Income Summary account is debited for total expenses, and each individual expense account is credited by the balance in the account. After this entry, all expense accounts will have zero balances and the total of all expense accounts will have been transferred into the Income Summary account.

3. Close Income Summary to Retained Earnings: After recording the first two closing entries, the Income Summary account will normally have a credit balance because revenues normally exceed expenses. This balance is equal to net income. Income Summary will have a debit balance if there is a net loss (if expenses exceed revenues). The Income Summary account is debited for the balance in the account (or credited if there is a loss), while Retained Earnings is credited (debited if there is a loss). After this, the Income Summary account balance is zero because the net income or net loss has been transferred into the Retained Earnings account.

4. Close Dividends Declared to Retained Earnings: The Dividends Declared account has a normal debit balance, so it must be credited to be closed. In this final closing entry, Retained Earnings is debited for the balance in the Dividends Declared account, while Dividends Declared is credited by the same amount, bringing the account balance to zero. **Note: Do not close Dividends Declared to the Income Summary account along with expenses.** Dividends declared are not expenses and do not affect net income; they are a distribution of retained earnings.

Journalizing and posting closing entries are normally done after financial statements have been prepared, at the end of a company's *annual* accounting period. Closing entries can be prepared directly from the general ledger or the adjusted trial balance. If we were to prepare closing entries for Sierra Corporation, we would likely use the adjusted trial balance presented earlier in the chapter in Illustration 4-7 and reproduced below for your reference.

SIERRA CORPORATION Adjusted Trial Balance October 31, 2018		
	Debit	Credit
Cash	$11,400	
Accounts receivable	11,200	
Supplies	1,000	
Prepaid insurance	550	
Equipment	5,000	
Accumulated depreciation—equipment		$ 83
Accounts payable		1,500
Salaries payable		1,200
Interest payable		25
Unearned revenue		800
Bank loan payable		5,000
Common shares		10,000
Dividends declared	500	
Service revenue		20,600
Salaries expense	5,200	
Supplies expense	1,500	
Rent expense	900	
Depreciation expense	83	
Insurance expense	50	
Interest expense	25	
Income tax expense	1,800	
	$39,208	$39,208

In Sierra's case, all temporary accounts (Dividends Declared, Service Revenue, and its seven different expense accounts, which are highlighted in red in the illustration above for illustration purposes) must be closed. You will note that there is no Retained Earnings account in Sierra's adjusted trial balance. In this particular case, Retained Earnings has an adjusted balance of zero because this was Sierra's first month of operations and it started with a nil balance on October 1. Regardless of whether the company has just started, or has been in business for many years, the balance in Retained Earnings will be its balance at the beginning of the period in both the unadjusted and adjusted trial balances until closing entries are made.

Even though Retained Earnings is not a temporary account, we have seen that it is used in the closing process. This permanent account is not closed, but the net income (loss) and dividends declared for the period must be transferred into Retained Earnings through closing entries to update the account to its ending balance.

Let's now prepare closing entries for Sierra Corporation, using the information from its adjusted trial balance above.

►Closing entry (1)
Revenues to Income Summary

Basic Analysis	The Service Revenue account has a credit balance of $20,600. This account must be reduced by $20,600 to result in a zero balance and the Income Summary account increased by the same amount.
Debit–Credit Analysis	Debits decrease revenues: debit Service Revenue $20,600. Credits increase income summary: credit Income Summary $20,600.

Closing Journal Entry	Oct. 31	Service Revenue		20,600	
		Income Summary			20,600

Posting		Service Revenue			Income Summary	
			Oct. 15	20,000		Oct. 31 CE(1) 20,600
			31 Adj.	400		
			31 Adj.	200		
			Bal.	20,600		
	Oct. 31 CE(1) 20,600					
			Bal.	0		

The first closing entry transfers revenue to the Income Summary account. Sierra had only one revenue account. If there are more revenue accounts, they would be closed in one journal entry with a separate debit to each individual revenue account and one credit to the Income Summary account for the total amount. Note that in the T account above, we have used the notation "CE" to indicate that the entry is a closing entry (CE) and we have numbered the notations to match each closing entry.

►Closing entry (2)
Expenses to Income Summary

Basic Analysis	The expense accounts have debit balances totalling $9,558. Each individual expense account must be reduced by the appropriate amount to result in a zero account balance and the Income Summary account decreased by the total expense amount of $9,558.
Debit–Credit Analysis	Debits decrease income summary: debit Income Summary $9,558. Credits decrease expenses: credit each individual expense account for the balance in the account.

Closing Journal Entry	Oct. 31	Income Summary		9,558	
		Salaries Expense			5,200
		Supplies Expense			1,500
		Rent Expense			900
		Depreciation Expense			83
		Insurance Expense			50
		Interest Expense			25
		Income Tax Expense			1,800

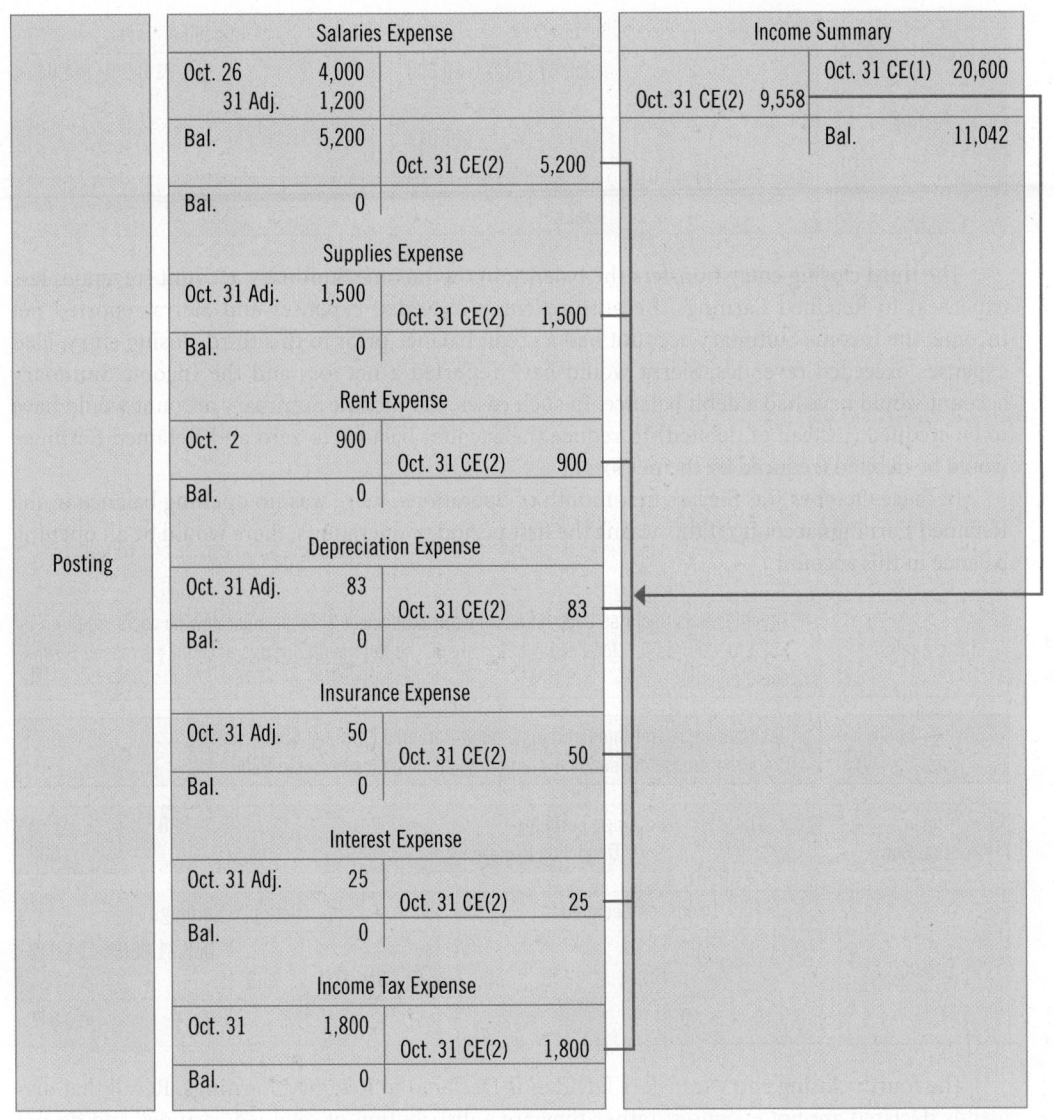

The second closing entry transfers expenses to the Income Summary account. Note that while the closing entry makes only one debit to the Income Summary account, it separately credits the balance in each individual expense account. You will recall from the last chapter that this is an example of a compound journal entry. The Income Summary account now reports a credit balance of $11,042, which is the difference between total revenues ($20,600) and total expenses ($9,558). It is important to understand that **the balance in the Income Summary account at this point should be equal to the net income** reported in Sierra's financial statements in Illustration 4-8. Check back and see if these two amounts agree. If not, then an error has been made.

▶ **Closing entry (3)**
Income Summary to Retained Earnings

Basic Analysis	The Income Summary account must now be reduced by the appropriate amount to result in a zero account balance and the Retained Earnings account increased by the same amount if net income exists (or decreased by the same amount if there is a net loss).
Debit–Credit Analysis	Debits decrease income summary: debit Income Summary $11,042. Credits increase retained earnings: credit Retained Earnings $11,042.
Closing Journal Entry	Oct. 31 Income Summary 11,042 　　Retained Earnings 11,042

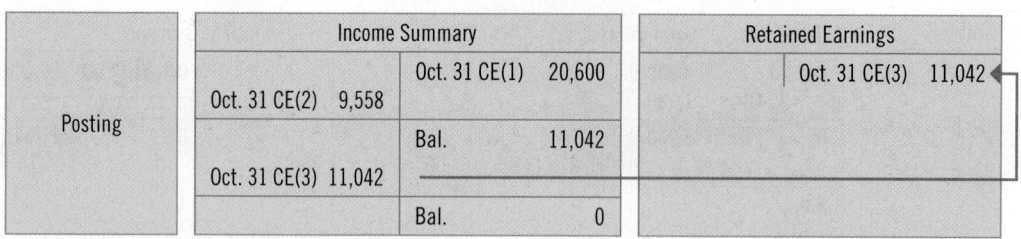

The third closing entry transfers the balance in the Income Summary account (revenues less expenses) to Retained Earnings. Because revenues exceeded expenses and Sierra reported net income, the Income Summary account had a credit balance prior to this third closing entry. Had expenses exceeded revenues, Sierra would have reported a net loss and the Income Summary account would have had a debit balance. In such cases, the Income Summary account would have to be credited (instead of debited) to reduce the account balance to zero and Retained Earnings would be debited (reduced by the net loss).

Because October was Sierra's first month of operations, there was no opening balance in the Retained Earnings account. If this wasn't the first period of operations, there would be an opening balance in this account.

► **Closing entry (4)**
Dividends Declared to Retained Earnings

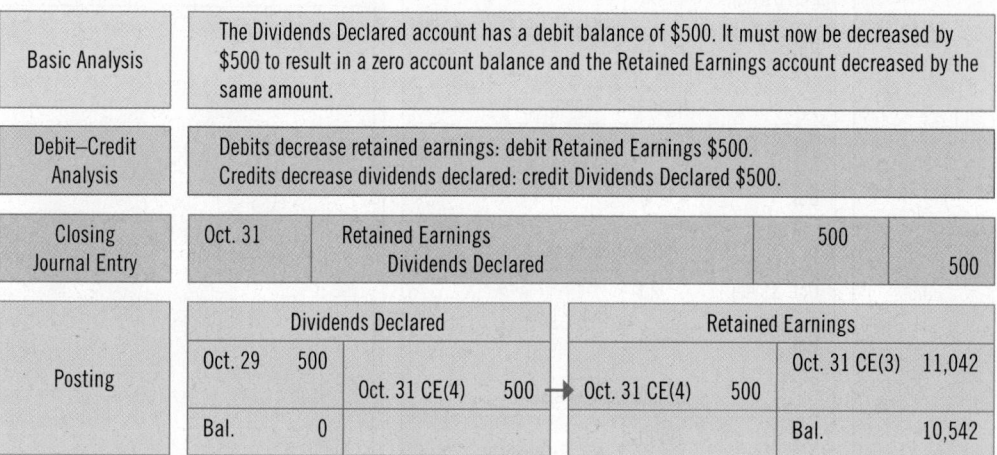

The fourth closing entry transfers Dividends Declared to Retained Earnings. Recall that dividends declared are not expenses; rather they are a distribution of retained earnings and do not affect net income (nor income summary). The ending balance of Retained Earnings now equals the balance reported in Sierra's financial statements in Illustration 4-8. This ending balance on Oct. 31 becomes the opening balance on November 1, because Retained Earnings is a permanent account whose balance carries over into the next period.

It is important to check your work during and after the closing process.

1. The balance in the Income Summary account, immediately before the final closing entry to transfer the balance to the Retained Earnings account (entry 3 above), should equal the net income (or loss) reported in the income statement.
2. All temporary accounts (revenues, expenses, Income Summary, and Dividends Declared) should have zero balances after closing.
3. The balance in the Retained Earnings account should equal the ending balance reported in the statement of changes in equity and statement of financial position after closing.

ACCOUNTING MATTERS

Closing the Books

Most companies work hard to prepare adjusting and closing entries as soon as possible so that their financial statements can be released promptly. World-class companies can close their books within five days. Why is it important to close the books quickly? A company's ability to do a quick close gives management enough time to analyze the results to make informed and timely decisions.

POST-CLOSING TRIAL BALANCE

1. ANALYZE	2. JOURNALIZE	3. POST	4. TRIAL BALANCE	5. ADJUSTING ENTRIES	6. ADJUSTED TRIAL BALANCE	7. PREPARE FINANCIAL STATEMENTS	8. JOURNALIZE AND POST CLOSING ENTRIES	**9. Prepare a post-closing trial balance**

After all closing entries are journalized and posted, another trial balance, called a post-closing trial balance, is prepared from the ledger in the ninth, and final, step of the accounting cycle. We have learned about the unadjusted and adjusted trial balances so far. The third and last trial balance, and final step in the accounting cycle, is the **post-closing trial balance**. It lists all permanent accounts and their balances after closing entries are journalized and posted. The purpose of this trial balance is to prove the equality of the permanent account balances that are carried forward into the next annual accounting period. Since all temporary accounts will have zero balances, the post-closing trial balance will contain only permanent—statement of financial position—accounts. Illustration 4-12 shows Sierra Corporation's post-closing trial balance.

▶Illustration 4-12
Post-closing trial balance

SIERRA CORPORATION
Post-Closing Trial Balance
October 31, 2018

	Debit	Credit
Cash	$11,400	
Accounts receivable	11,200	
Supplies	1,000	
Prepaid insurance	550	
Equipment	5,000	
Accumulated depreciation—equipment		$ 83
Accounts payable		1,500
Salaries payable		1,200
Interest payable		25
Unearned revenue		800
Bank loan payable		5,000
Common shares		10,000
Retained earnings		10,542
	$29,150	$29,150

DO IT! ▶ **4-5**   **Closing Entries**

The adjusted trial balance for Nguyen Corporation shows the following selected account balances at December 31: Dividends Declared $700; Common Shares $30,000; Retained Earnings $12,000; Service Revenue $18,000; Rent Expense $1,500; Supplies Expense $500; Salaries Expense $8,000; and Income Tax Expense $1,000. (a) Calculate net income and ending retained earnings. (b) Prepare the closing entries. (c) What would appear for each of the Income Summary and Retained Earnings accounts in the post-closing trial balance?

SOLUTION
Try this Do It! exercise on your own and then check your answer at the end of the chapter.

Related Exercise Material: BE4–13, BE4–14, BE4–15, E4–13, and E4–14.

Action Plan

✔ Close revenues and expenses to the Income Summary account.

✔ Stop and check your work: Is the balance in each individual revenue and expense account now zero? Does the balance in the Income Summary account equal the reported net income (loss)?

✔ Close the balance in the Income Summary account to the Retained Earnings account.

✔ Close the Dividends Declared account to the Retained Earnings account. Be sure **not** to close Dividends Declared to the Income Summary account.

✔ Stop and check your work: Does the balance in the Retained Earnings account equal the ending Retained Earnings balance reported in the statement of changes in equity and statement of financial position?

REVIEW OF THE ACCOUNTING CYCLE

The entire accounting cycle is shown in Illustration 4-13 for your information and review.

THE ACCOUNTING CYCLE

▶Illustration 4-13
Steps in the accounting cycle

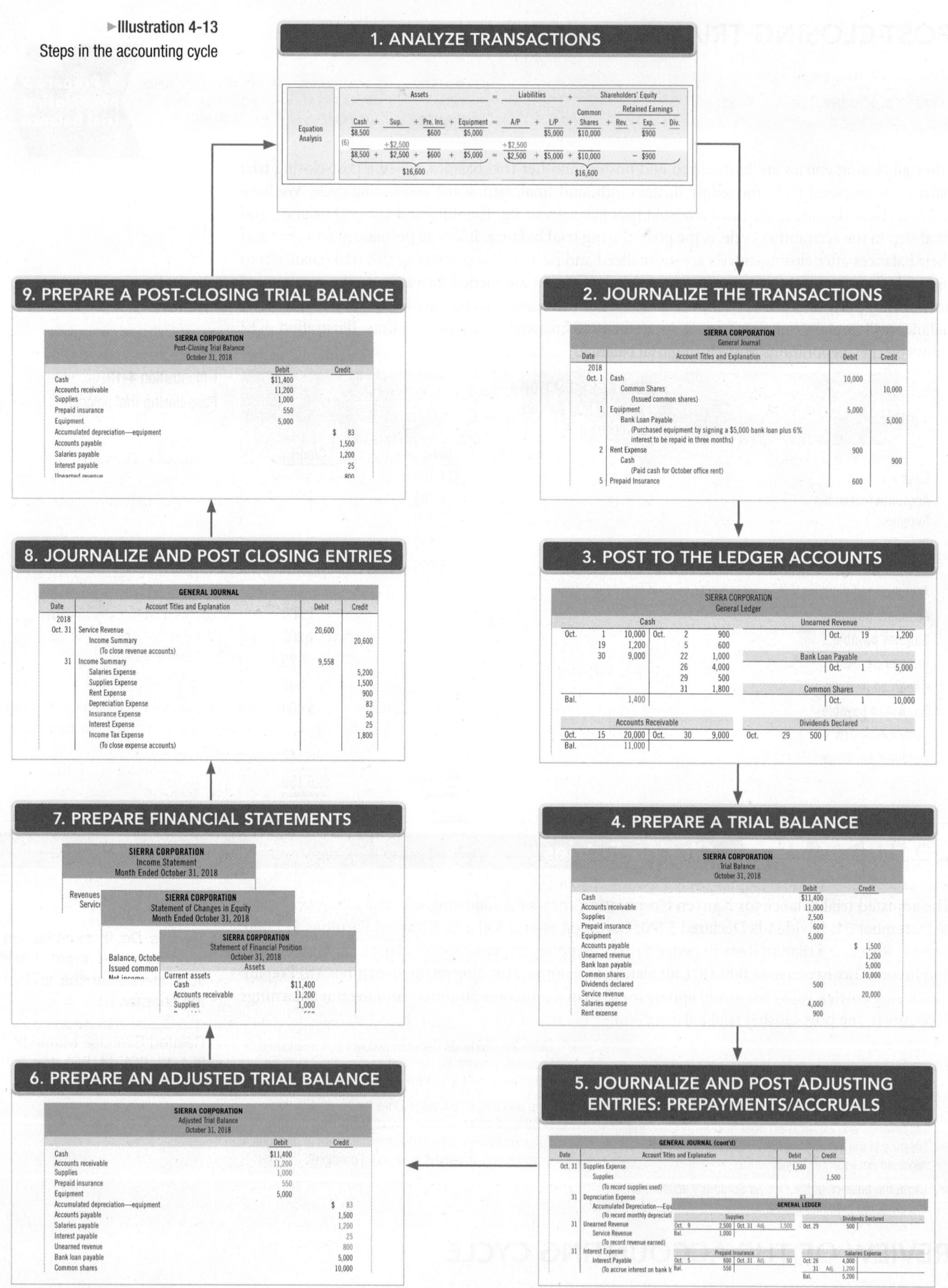

The accounting cycle begins with the analysis of business transactions and ends with the preparation of a post-closing trial balance. The steps are done in sequence and are repeated in each accounting period.

Steps 1 to 3 may occur daily during the accounting period, as we learned in Chapter 3, although some companies post monthly rather than daily to the general ledger. Steps 4 to 7 are done on a periodic basis, such as monthly, quarterly, or annually. Steps 8 and 9, closing entries and post-closing trial balance, are usually prepared only at the end of a company's annual accounting period.

REVIEW AND PRACTICE

▶ LEARNING OBJECTIVE REVIEW

1. Explain the accrual basis of accounting and the reasons for adjusting entries. Under the accrual basis of accounting, revenues are recognized (recorded) when they are earned, while expenses are recognized (recorded) when they are incurred. This means that revenues are recognized when or as performance obligations have been identified and satisfied, regardless of whether cash has been received. Expenses are recognized in the period when the company incurs them in an effort to generate revenue, regardless of whether cash has been paid.

This differs from the cash basis of accounting in which companies record events only in the periods in which the company receives (revenues) or pays cash (expenses).

Companies make adjusting entries at the end of each accounting period. There are two general types of adjusting entries: (1) prepayments, which allocate a portion of an asset's cost or unearned revenue to an expense or a revenue account on the income statement, and (2) accruals, which increase expenses or revenues in the income statement and the related payable or receivable in the statement of financial position.

2. Prepare adjusting entries for prepayments. Prepayments involve accounts that have previously been recorded as assets (such as when cash was paid in advance for prepaid expenses) or liabilities (such as when cash was received in advance for unearned revenues). The adjusting entry for prepaid expenses results in an increase (debit) to an expense account and a decrease (credit) to an asset account or an increase (credit) to a contra asset account. The adjusting entry for unearned revenues results in a decrease (debit) to a liability (Unearned Revenue) account and an increase (credit) to a revenue account.

3. Prepare adjusting entries for accruals. Adjusting entries for accruals are required in order to record the expenses and revenues that apply to the current accounting period and

that have not already been recognized through transaction journal entries. Accruals involve accounts for which there has been no cash received or paid as yet. The adjusting entry for accrued expenses results in an increase (debit) to an expense account and an increase (credit) to a liability (payable) account. The adjusting entry for accrued revenues results in an increase (debit) to an asset (receivable) account and an increase (credit) to a revenue account.

4. Prepare an adjusted trial balance and financial statements. An adjusted trial balance is a trial balance that shows the balances of all accounts at the end of an accounting period, including those that have been adjusted. It demonstrates that total debits equal total credits. An adjusted trial balance facilitates the preparation of the financial statements.

5. Prepare closing entries and a post-closing trial balance. One purpose of closing entries is to update the Retained Earnings account to its end-of-period balance. A second purpose is to reset the balance in all temporary accounts (revenue, expense, and Dividends Declared accounts) to zero for the beginning of the new accounting period. To accomplish this, entries are made to close each individual revenue and expense account to a specific purpose temporary account called Income Summary, which summarizes net income (or net loss). The Income Summary account is then closed to the Retained Earnings account. The Dividends Declared account is closed directly to Retained Earnings (and not via the Income Summary account, because dividends do not affect net income).

A post-closing trial balance lists only permanent accounts (statement of financial position accounts) because these account balances are carried forward to the next accounting period. The purpose of the post-closing trial balance, as with other trial balances, is to prove the equality of total debits and total credits.

▶ KEY TERM REVIEW

The following are key terms defined in this chapter with the corresponding page reference for your review. You will find a complete list of terms and definitions for all chapters in the glossary at the end of this textbook.

Accrual basis accounting (p. 172)	Cash basis accounting (p. 172)	Post-closing trial balance (p. 203)
Accrued expenses (p. 185)	Closing entries (p. 197)	Revenue recognition (p. 170)
Accrued revenues (p. 189)	Depreciation (p. 179)	Temporary accounts (p. 197)
Adjusted trial balance (p. 193)	Expense recognition (p. 172)	Unadjusted trial balance (p. 175)
Adjusting entries (p. 174)	Income Summary (p. 198)	Useful life (p. 179)
Carrying amount (p. 181)	Permanent accounts (p. 197)	

▶ COMPARING IFRS AND ASPE REVIEW

Key Standard Differences	International Financial Reporting Standards (IFRS)	Accounting Standards for Private Enterprises (ASPE)
Revenue recognition	The following process is used to measure and report revenue (pending standard effective Jan. 1, 2018): 1. Identify the contract with the client or customer. 2. Identify the performance obligations in the contract. 3. Determine the transaction price. 4. Allocate the transaction price to the performance obligations in the contract. 5. Recognize revenue when (or as) the company satisfies the performance obligation.	Revenue is recognized when performance is substantially complete, revenue amount is able to be reliably measured, and collection reasonably certain.

▶ DECISION TOOLKIT REVIEW

DECISION CHECKPOINTS	INFO NEEDED FOR DECISION	TOOLS TO USE FOR DECISION	HOW TO EVALUATE RESULTS
At what point should the company record revenue?	Need to understand the nature of the company's business, in particular when the performance obligation is considered to be complete.	Revenues are recognized when there is an increase in future economic benefits related to an increase in an asset or decrease in a liability in the course of ordinary activities, with the exclusion of those relating to shareholders. With respect to revenue from the provision of services or sales of goods, consider the contract terms of the transaction, the price of the transaction, and the promises that must be met by the seller and the buyer before the performance obligation is considered to be satisfied and revenue earned.	Recognizing revenue too early overstates current period revenue and net income; recognizing it too late understates current period revenue and net income.
At what point should the company record expenses?	Need to understand the nature of the company's business and whether the expense can be associated with revenue.	Expenses are recognized when there is a decrease in future economic benefits related to a decrease in an asset or increase in a liability in the course of ordinary activities, with the exclusion of those relating to shareholders. Often expenses can be associated with revenues; that is, recognized in the period in which a company makes efforts to generate revenues.	Recognizing expenses too early overstates current period expenses and understates net income; recognizing them too late understates current period expenses and overstates net income.

▶ PRACTICE USING THE DECISION TOOLKIT

Answers are at the end of the chapter.

Gift cards are among the hottest marketing tools in merchandising today. A gift card is a plastic card, similar to a credit card, with a magnetic strip on the back, which is loaded with a cash value when it is purchased. Customers purchase these cards and give them to someone as a gift for later use.

Although gift cards are popular with marketing executives, they raise accounting questions about when revenue should be recognized. Take, for example, Best Buy, whose gift cards range in value from $25 to $500. Suppose that Robert Jacobs purchases a $100 gift card at Best Buy on December 24, and gives it to his wife, Laurel Hyatt, as a present on December 25. On January 3, Laurel uses the card to purchase $100 worth of merchandise from Best Buy. Using the five steps for revenue recognition, when do you think Best Buy should recognize revenue and why?

▶ PRACTICE COMPREHENSIVE DO IT!

Answers are at the end of the chapter.

At March 31, 2018, the year-end unadjusted trial balance for the Blizzard Snow Removal Corporation shows the following balances for selected accounts:

Accounts receivable	$10,000	Unearned revenue	$ 3,150
Supplies	8,000	Retained earnings	37,000
Prepaid insurance	1,800	Service revenue	102,800
Equipment	25,000	Salaries expense	50,000
Accumulated depreciation—equipment	5,000	Interest expense	550
Bank loan payable	10,000	Income tax expense	9,600

Blizzard makes its adjusting entries annually. Analysis reveals the following additional data about these accounts:

1. Supplies were counted at year end and it was determined that $1,200 worth was on hand at March 31.
2. Prepaid insurance is the cost of a one-year insurance policy for $1,800, effective March 1, 2018.
3. The equipment was purchased on April 1, 2016, and is expected to have a useful life of five years. The company uses straight-line depreciation.
4. The bank loan was signed on April 1, 2017, and is repayable in two years. Interest on this 6% loan is due monthly, on the first day of each month. Interest was last paid on March 1.
5. Seven customers paid in advance to purchase the company's two-month (March and April), $300 spring special snow removal service package. These customers were serviced in March after several late storms.
6. Snow removal services provided to other customers but not billed at March 31 totalled $1,500.
7. Salaries are paid biweekly and were last paid up to and including Friday, March 23. Employees have worked one storm since March 23, and are owed $1,000 at March 31.
8. Income tax instalments of $800 have been made each month. Further calculations at year end determine that an additional $250 of income tax will be payable this year.

INSTRUCTIONS

(a) Prepare the adjusting entries at March 31.
(b) Set up T accounts, enter any opening balances, and post the adjusting entries prepared in part (a).
(c) Identify which of the accounts included in part (b) are permanent accounts and which are temporary accounts.
(d) Is the $37,000 balance shown in the Retained Earnings account above the ending account balance at March 31, 2018? Explain.

▶ PRACTICE OBJECTIVE-FORMAT QUESTIONS

Answers are at the end of the chapter.

1. Huahine Law LLP, a law firm, had the following activities:

   • Prepared a price quote for a proposed legal service to a client, Papeete Ltd., in February.
   • Performed the required service and sent an invoice to Papeete in March.
   • Received payment from Papeete in April.

Indicate which of the following statements is (are) correct related to this service. (Select as many as are appropriate.)

(a) Huahine would record revenue in February.
(b) Huahine would record revenue in March.
(c) Huahine would record revenue in April.
(d) Papeete would record expense in February.
(e) Papeete would record expense in March.
(f) Papeete would record expense in April.

2. Which of the following statements is (are) false? (Select as many as are appropriate.)

(a) Companies record events that change their financial statements in the period in which events occur according to revenue and expense recognition criteria, even if cash was not exchanged.

(b) Companies recognize revenue in the period in which the performance obligation is satisfied.

(c) Expenses are related to decreases in future economic benefits.

(d) Companies record revenue only when they receive cash, and record expenses only when they pay out cash.

(e) Companies have a choice of using accrual-based accounting or cash-based accounting, depending on the size of the company.

(f) Revenues arise in the course of a company's "ordinary" activities.

(g) Expense recognition is often linked to revenue recognition (that is, expenses are recognized in the same period as the related revenues are recognized), but not always.

3. Indicate which of the following statements is (are) true. (Select as many as are appropriate.)

(a) If adjusting entries are not recorded for prepaid expenses, then assets, shareholders' equity, and net income would be overstated and expenses understated.

(b) If adjusting entries are not recorded for unearned revenues, then liabilities would be understated and revenues, net income, and shareholders' equity overstated.

(c) If adjusting entries are not recorded for accrued revenues, then assets and shareholders' equity would be understated and expenses overstated.

(d) If adjusting entries are not recorded for accrued expenses, then liabilities and expenses would be understated and shareholders' equity and net income overstated.

4. (a) Indicate which of the following accounts would normally require an adjusting entry at year end. Insert "yes" if the account is normally adjusted; insert "no" if the account is not normally adjusted. (b) Indicate which of the following accounts are temporary (T) accounts and which are permanent (P) accounts by inserting a "T" or "P" in the space provided.

	(a)	(b)	
1.	_____	_____	Accumulated Depreciation
2.	_____	_____	Cash
3.	_____	_____	Dividends Declared
4.	_____	_____	Income Tax Payable
5.	_____	_____	Interest Receivable
6.	_____	_____	Prepaid Insurance
7.	_____	_____	Retained Earnings
8.	_____	_____	Salaries Expense
9.	_____	_____	Unearned Revenue

5. Indicate whether an adjusting entry to record an accrued revenue would result in an increase (I), decrease (D), or have no effect (NE) on the elements of the financial statements (assets, liabilities, shareholders' equity, revenues, expenses, net income) listed below.

_____ Assets   _____ Revenues

_____ Liabilities   _____ Expenses

_____ Shareholders' equity   _____ Net income

6. Indicate whether an adjusting entry to record an accrued expense would result in an increase (I), decrease (D), or have no effect (NE) on the elements of the financial statements (assets, liabilities, shareholders' equity, revenues, expenses, net income) listed below.

_____ Assets   _____ Revenues

_____ Liabilities   _____ Expenses

_____ Shareholders' equity   _____ Net income

7. Indicate which of the following statements about trial balances is (are) incorrect. (Select as many as are appropriate.)

(a) Companies can prepare at least four trial balances during the year: unadjusted trial balance, adjusted trial balance, closing trial balance, and post-closing trial balance.

(b) An unadjusted trial balance proves the equality of the total debit balances and total credit balances in the ledger.

(c) The post-closing trial balance is the main source for the preparation of financial statements.

(d) The post-closing trial balance is prepared after the closing entries have been journalized and posted.

(e) The adjusted trial balance is prepared after the adjusting entries have been journalized and posted.

(f) If total debits equal total credits in a trial balance, you are assured that there are no errors in the accounting process.

8. The Common Shares and Retained Earnings account balances in an unadjusted trial balance are $45,000 and $25,000, respectively. Revenues for the period are $33,000 and expenses $26,000. Dividends declared are $1,000. Indicate which of the following statements are correct. (Select as many as are appropriate.)

(a) Retained Earnings in the adjusted trial balance is $31,000.

(b) Retained Earnings in the post-closing trial balance is $31,000.

(c) Total shareholders' equity in the unadjusted trial balance is $70,000.

(d) Total shareholders' equity in the post-closing trial balance is $76,000.

(e) Dividends Declared in each of the unadjusted and adjusted trial balances is $1,000.

(f) Dividends Declared in the post-closing trial balance is $1,000.

9. Indicate which of the following accounts will have a zero balance after closing entries have been journalized and posted.

(a) Accumulated Depreciation
(b) Bank Loan Payable
(c) Cash
(d) Common Shares
(e) Dividends Declared
(f) Retained Earnings
(g) Service Revenue
(h) Supplies
(i) Salaries Expense
(j) Unearned Revenue

10. Number the steps in the accounting cycle in their proper sequence from 1 through 9.

_____ Prepare an adjusted trial balance.

_____ Journalize and post closing entries.

_____ Post transaction entries to general ledger accounts.

_____ Prepare an unadjusted trial balance.

_____ Prepare financial statements.

_____ Analyze business transactions.

_____ Journalize and post adjusting entries.

_____ Prepare a post-closing trial balance.

_____ Journalize the transactions.

WileyPLUS

Brief Exercises, Exercises, and many additional resources are available for practice in WileyPLUS.

▶ QUESTIONS

(LO 1) 1. Why are adjusting entries needed? Include in your explanation a description of the revenue and expense recognition criteria that relate to adjusting the accounts.

(LO 1) 2. (a) Describe the five-step process to measure and report revenue. (b) Apply these steps to the following situation: A law firm accepts a legal engagement for a firm price of $8,000 in March, does the work in April, bills the client in May, and is paid in June. When should the law firm recognize revenue from this engagement?

(LO 1) 3. In completing the engagement in question 2 (b), the law firm incurs expenses that are specifically related to this engagement as follows: none in March, $4,500 in April, and none in May and June. When should the law firm recognize these expenses? Explain.

(LO 1)   4. (a) What information do accrual-basis financial statements provide that cash-basis statements do not? (b) What information do cash-basis financial statements provide that accrual-basis statements do not? (c) Can companies choose between the cash and accrual bases of accounting for financial reporting purposes? Why or why not?

(LO 2)   5. The name "prepaid expense" implies that this type of account is an expense account and belongs on an income statement. However, these accounts actually appear on the statement of financial position as assets. Explain (a) why prepaid expense items are assets, and (b) why they require adjustment at the end of each period.

(LO 2)   6. The name "unearned revenue" implies that this type of account is a revenue account and belongs on an income statement. However, these accounts actually appear on the statement of financial position as liabilities. Explain (a) why unearned revenue items are liabilities, and (b) why they require adjustment at the end of each period.

(LO 2)   7. "Depreciation is a process of valuation that results in the reporting of the current value of the asset." Do you agree? Explain.

(LO 2)   8. Explain the difference between (a) depreciation expense and accumulated depreciation, and (b) cost and carrying amount.

(LO 2)   9. What is a contra asset account? Why do we use a contra asset account to record accumulated depreciation instead of directly reducing the depreciable asset account?

(LO 2, 3) 10. "An adjusting entry affects at least one statement of financial position and one income statement account." Do you agree? Why or why not?

(LO 2, 3) 11. "Adjusting entries for prepayments always include the Cash account, and adjusting entries for accruals never include the Cash account." Do you agree? Why or why not?

(LO 2, 3) 12. The original transaction journal entry must first be examined before an adjusting entry for a prepayment can be prepared. Why is this not also the case for an adjusting entry for an accrual?

(LO 3)   13. Picaroon's Ltd. owes $100 interest each month on a bank loan, payable the first of every month. The company's year-end is December 31, 2018, and adjusting entries are made annually. The company's bookkeeper decides not to record this interest on December 31 since it will be paid only a day later, on January 1. (a) Does it matter whether the interest is recorded on December 31 or January 1? Explain why or why not. (b) If a journal entry is not made on December 31, 2018, identify which accounts, if any, will be overstated or understated and by what amount for the 2018 fiscal year. If no accounts will be affected, say so.

(LO 4)   14. Why is it appropriate to prepare financial statements directly from an adjusted trial balance but not from an unadjusted trial balance?

(LO 2, 3, 5) 15. (a) How do original transaction entries differ from adjusting journal entries? (b) How do adjusting journal entries differ from closing journal entries?

(LO 4, 5) 16. Explain how an unadjusted trial balance, adjusted trial balance, and post-closing trial balance are similar, and how they differ. How often, and when, should each one be prepared?

(LO 4, 5) 17. Why is the retained earnings balance on the unadjusted trial balance the same amount that appears on the adjusted trial balance? Why is the retained earnings balance on an adjusted trial balance different from the amount that appears on the post-closing trial balance?

(LO 5)   18. What are two reasons for recording closing entries?

(LO 5)   19. Why is the account Dividends Declared not closed into Income Summary along with the expense accounts?

(LO 5)   20. Why is an Income Summary account used in the closing process rather than closing revenues and expenses directly to Retained Earnings?

(LO 5)   21. Identify whether the Income Summary account would be debited, credited, or not affected when making each of the four closing entries, assuming the company has (a) net income for the year, and (b) a net loss for the year.

(LO 5)   22. Which steps in the accounting cycle may be done daily, which steps are done on a periodic basis, and which steps are usually done only at the company's accounting period end?

▶ BRIEF EXERCISES

Indicate impact on cash and net income.

(LO 1)

BE4–1 Transactions that affect cash do not necessarily affect net income. Identify the impact, if any, of each of the following transactions on cash and net income. The first transaction has been completed for you as an example.

	Cash	Net income
	−$100	$0

(a) Purchased supplies for cash, $100.
(b) Made an adjusting entry to record use of $75 of the supplies in item (a).
(c) Performed services on account, $1,000.
(d) Received $800 from customers in payment of their account in item (c).
(e) Purchased equipment for cash, $5,000.
(f) Made an adjusting entry to record depreciation of the equipment in item (e), $1,000.
(g) Obtained a $1,000 bank loan.
(h) Made an adjusting entry to accrue interest on the loan in item (g), $50.
(i) Received $500 cash for services to be performed in the future.
(j) Made an adjusting entry relating to the amount received in item (i) to show that $200 of the services had now been performed.
(k) Made an adjusting entry to record utilities incurred but not yet paid, $250.

BE4–2 Blindleia Care Corporation had the following selected transactions in September:

1. Collected $200 cash from customers for services performed in August.
2. Collected $500 cash from customers for services performed in September.
3. Billed customers $600 for services performed in September.
4. Performed $100 of services to customers who paid in advance in August.
5. Received $100 from customers in advance for services to be performed in October.

(a) Calculate revenue for the month of September using the accrual basis of accounting.
(b) Calculate revenue for the month of September using the cash basis of accounting.

Calculate revenue on accrual and cash bases.

(LO 1)

BE4–3 Sain Advertising Ltd.'s opening trial balance on January 1 shows Supplies $1,500. On January 11, the company purchased additional supplies for $1,800 on account. On January 31, there are $1,100 of supplies on hand.

(a) Prepare the journal entry to record the purchase of supplies on January 11.
(b) Calculate the amount of supplies used during the month.
(c) Prepare the adjusting entry required at January 31, assuming adjusting entries are prepared monthly.
(d) Using T accounts, enter the opening balances in the affected accounts, post the journal entries in parts (a) and (c), and indicate the adjusted balance in each account.

Prepare and post transaction and adjusting entries for supplies.

(LO 2)

BE4–4 On January 2, 2018, Claymore Corporation purchased a vehicle for $50,000 cash. The company uses straight-line depreciation and estimates that the vehicle will have a five-year useful life. The company has a December 31 year end and adjusts its accounts annually.

(a) Prepare the journal entry to record the purchase of the vehicle on January 2.
(b) Prepare the adjusting entries required on December 31, 2018, and 2019.
(c) Indicate the statement of financial position presentation of the vehicle at December 31, 2018 and 2019.

Prepare transaction and adjusting entries for depreciation; show statement presentation.

(LO 2)

BE4–5 On June 1, 2018, Bere Ltd. pays $6,000 to Safety Insurance Corp. for a one-year insurance policy. Both companies have fiscal years ending December 31 and adjust their accounts annually.

(a) Record the June 1 transaction on the books of (1) Bere and (2) Safety.
(b) Calculate the amount of insurance that expired during 2018 and the unexpired cost at December 31.
(c) Prepare the adjusting entry required on December 31 by (1) Bere and (2) Safety.
(d) Post the above entries and indicate the adjusted balance in each account.

Prepare and post transaction and adjusting entries for insurance.

(LO 2, 3)

BE4–6 The total weekly payroll for Classic Auto Repairs Ltd. is $5,000 ($1,000 per day). The payroll is paid every Saturday for employee salaries earned during the same five-day workweek (Monday through Friday, inclusive). Salaries were last paid on Saturday, October 27. This year the company's year end, October 31, falls on a Wednesday. Salaries will be paid next on Saturday, November 3. Prepare the journal entries to record each of the following:

(a) Payment of the salaries on October 27
(b) The adjustment to accrue salaries at October 31
(c) Payment of the salaries on November 3

Prepare transaction and adjusting entries for salaries.

(LO 3)

BE4–7 Zieborg Maintenance Corp. has a $375 monthly contract with Crispy Treat Inc. for general maintenance services. Zieborg invoices Crispy on the first of the month for services that it performed in the previous month. Crispy must then pay for these services by the 10th of the following month. Zieborg has a November 30 year end and prepares adjusting entries monthly.

(a) Prepare any adjusting entry required on November 30 by Zieborg.
(b) Given your entry in part (a), will Zieborg also need to record a journal entry on December 1 when it invoices Crispy for services performed in November? Why or why not?
(c) Zieborg receives $375 from Crispy on January 10 for services performed in November. Prepare Zieborg's journal entry.

Prepare adjusting and subsequent entries for accrued revenue.

(LO 3)

BE4–8 On July 1, 2018, Nakhooda Limited received an 18-month loan for $40,000 from a bank at 6% and with these funds and another $10,000 cash, purchased a vehicle for $50,000. Prepare the journal entries to record each of the following on Nakhooda's books:

(a) The purchase of the vehicle on July 1, 2018
(b) The accrual of interest at Nakhooda's year end, December 31, 2018 and 2019, assuming adjusting entries are recorded annually and interest is due at maturity
(c) Repayment of the interest and the loan on January 1, 2020

Prepare adjusting and subsequent entries for interest expense.

(LO 3)

BE4–9 On July 1, 2018, the Canada Bank lent $40,000 to Nakhooda Limited. The 18-month loan bears interest at 6%. Prepare the journal entries to record each of the following on the Canada Bank's books:

(a) The issue of the bank loan on July 1, 2018
(b) The accrual of interest at the Canada Bank's year end, December 31, 2018 and 2019, assuming adjusting entries are recorded annually and interest is collected at maturity
(c) Collection of the interest and the loan on January 1, 2020
(d) If you completed BE4–8, compare your answers for Nahkooda and the Canada Bank.

Prepare adjusting and subsequent entries for interest revenue.

(LO 3)

Determine missing amounts for income tax.

(LO 3)

BE4–10 Fill in the missing amounts in the following income tax schedule for Ducharme Corporation. Assume that 2016 was the company's first year of operations.

	2018	2017	2016
Income tax expense	$ (c)	$3,600	$2,600
Income tax payable	700	500	(a)
Income tax paid	4,200	(b)	2,200

Prepare adjusted trial balance.

(LO 4)

BE4–11 Oromocto Corporation reports the following adjusted account balances, shown in alphabetical order, at the end of its fiscal year, February 28, 2018:

Accounts payable	$13,000	Income tax payable	$ 4,550
Accounts receivable	28,000	Insurance expense	3,500
Accumulated depreciation—equipment	5,400	Prepaid insurance	2,500
Cash	18,000	Rent expense	6,000
Common shares	10,000	Retained earnings	21,000
Depreciation expense	4,400	Salaries payable	3,000
Dividends declared	2,000	Salaries expense	46,400
Equipment	23,450	Supplies	1,000
Fees earned	89,500	Supplies expense	4,000
Income tax expense	4,800	Utilities expense	2,400

Prepare an adjusted trial balance at February 28.

Prepare financial statements.

(LO 4)

BE4–12 Refer to the data in BE4–11 for Oromocto Corporation. During the year ended February 28, 2018, common shares were issued for $5,000. Prepare (a) an income statement, (b) a statement of changes in equity, and (c) a statement of financial position.

Prepare closing entries.

(LO 5)

BE4–13 Refer to the data in BE4–11 for Oromocto Corporation. Prepare the closing journal entries.

Prepare and post closing entries.

(LO 5)

BE4–14 The income statement for Regina Cleaning Services Ltd. for the year ended November 30 shows Service Revenue $126,000; Salaries Expense $65,000; Repairs and Maintenance Expense $15,000; Supplies Expense $6,000; Utilities Expense $2,000; and Income Tax Expense $5,700. The statement of changes in equity shows an opening balance for Retained Earnings of $50,000 and Dividends Declared $5,000.
(a)   Calculate the net income or loss for the year.
(b)   Prepare the closing journal entries.
(c)   Using T accounts, post the closing entries, and determine the ending balances.

Identify post-closing trial balance accounts.

(LO 5)

BE4–15 The following selected accounts appear in the adjusted trial balance for **Maple Leaf Foods Inc.** Identify which accounts would be included in Maple Leaf Foods' post-closing trial balance.
(a)   Accounts payable and other accruals
(b)   Accounts receivable
(c)   Accumulated depreciation
(d)   Buildings
(e)   Common shares
(f)   Dividends declared
(g)   Income taxes payable
(h)   Interest expense
(i)   Interest income
(j)   Prepaid expenses
(k)   Retained earnings
(l)   Sales
(m)   Selling, general, and administrative expenses

▶ EXERCISES

Identify point of revenue recognition.

(LO 1)

E4–1 The following independent situations require professional judgement to determine when to recognize revenue from the transactions:
1.   **WestJet** sells you a non-refundable one-way airline ticket in September for your flight home at Christmas.
2.   You pay for a one-year subscription to **Maclean's Magazine** in March.
3.   The **Toronto Blue Jays** sell season tickets to games in the Rogers Centre. The season begins in April and ends in October. You purchase your tickets in February.
4.   The **RBC Financial Group** lends you money in August. The loan and the interest are repayable in full in November.
5.   In August, you order a sweater from **Sears** using its online catalogue. The sweater arrives in September and you charge it to your Sears credit card. You receive and pay the Sears bill in October.

Instructions
Identify when revenue should be recognized by the company in each situation.

E4-2 In its first year of operations, Athabasca Corp. earned $52,000 in service revenue. Of that amount, $8,000 was on account and the remainder, $44,000, was collected in cash from customers.

Calculate net income on accrual and cash bases.

(LO 1)

The company incurred various expenses totalling $31,000, of which $27,500 was paid in cash. At year end, $3,500 was still owing on account. In addition, Athabasca prepaid $2,000 for insurance coverage that covered the last half of the first year and the first half of the second year. Athabasca expects to owe $3,000 of income tax when it files its corporate income tax return after year end.

Instructions
(a) Calculate the first year's net income under the accrual basis of accounting.
(b) Calculate the first year's net income under the cash basis of accounting.
(c) Which basis of accounting (accrual or cash) gives the most useful information for decision makers? Explain.

E4-3 BizCon Inc., a consulting firm, has just completed its first year of operations. The company's sales growth was explosive. To encourage clients to hire its services, BizCon offered 90-day financing—meaning its largest customers do not pay for nearly three months. Because BizCon is a new company, its equipment suppliers insist on being paid cash on delivery. Also, it had to pay up front for two years of insurance. At the end of the year, BizCon owed employees for one full month of salaries, but due to a cash shortfall, it promised to pay them the first week of next year.

Identify differences between cash and accrual accounting.

(LO 1)

Instructions
(a) Explain how cash and accrual accounting would differ for each of the events listed above and describe the proper accrual accounting.
(b) Assume that at the end of the year, BizCon reported a favourable net income, yet the company's management is concerned because the company is short of cash. Explain how BizCon could have positive net income and yet run out of cash.

E4-4 Action Quest Games Inc. adjusts its accounts annually. The following information is available for the year ended December 31, 2018:

Prepare and post transaction and adjusting entries for prepayments.

(LO 2)

1. Purchased a one-year insurance policy on June 1, for $1,800 cash.
2. Paid $6,500 on August 31 for five months' rent in advance.
3. On September 4, received $3,600 cash in advance from a corporation to sponsor a game each month for a total of nine months for the most improved students at a local school.
4. Signed a contract for cleaning services starting December 1, for $1,000 per month. Paid for the first two months on November 30. (*Hint*: Use the account Prepaid Services to record this prepayment.)
5. On December 5, received $1,500 in advance from a gaming club. Determined that on December 31, $475 of these games had not yet been played.

Instructions
(a) For each of the above transactions, prepare the journal entry to record the initial transaction.
(b) For each of the above transactions, prepare the adjusting journal entry that is required on December 31. (*Hint*: Use the account Sponsorship Revenue for item 3 and Repairs and Maintenance Expense for item 4.)
(c) Post the journal entries in parts (a) and (b) to T accounts and determine the final balance in each account balance. (*Note*: Posting to the Cash account is not required.)

E4-5 Acadia Inc. owns the following long-lived assets:

Prepare adjusting entries for depreciation; calculate carrying amount.

(LO 2)

Asset	Date Purchased	Cost	Estimated Useful Life
Vehicles	Jan. 1, 2017	$33,000	3 years
Equipment	July 1, 2018	15,000	5 years

Instructions
(a) Prepare depreciation adjusting entries for each asset for the year ended December 31, 2018, assuming the company uses straight-line depreciation and adjusts its accounts annually.
(b) For each asset, calculate its accumulated depreciation and carrying amount at December 31, 2018.

E4-6 Greenock Limited has the following information available for accruals for the year ended December 31, 2018. The company adjusts its accounts annually.

Prepare adjusting and subsequent entries for accruals.

(LO 3)

1. The December utility bill for $425 was unrecorded on December 31. Greenock paid the bill on January 21.
2. Greenock is open seven days a week and employees are paid a total of $3,500 every Monday for a seven-day (Monday–Sunday) workweek. December 31 is a Monday, so employees will have worked one day (Monday, December 31) that they have not been paid for by year end. Employees will be paid next on Monday, January 7.
3. Greenock signed a $45,000, 5% bank loan on November 1, 2017, due in two years. Interest is payable on the first day of each following month and was last paid on December 1.
4. Greenock receives a fee from Pizza Shop next door for all pizzas sold to customers using Greenock's facility. The amount owing for December is $300, which Pizza Shop will pay on January 4. (*Hint*: Use the Fees Earned account.)
5. Greenock rented some of its unused warehouse space to a client for $6,000 a month, payable the first day of the following month. It received the rent for the month of December on January 2.

Instructions

(a) For each situation, prepare the adjusting entry required at December 31.

(b) For each situation, prepare the journal entry to record the subsequent cash transaction in 2019.

Prepare transaction and adjusting entries.

(LO 2, 3)

E4–7 The CCBC Corporation had the following opening trial balance at the beginning of its fiscal year, July 1, 2018:

	Debit	Credit
Cash	$ 4,400	
Accounts receivable	6,550	
Supplies	1,200	
Equipment	15,000	
Accumulated depreciation—equipment		$ 6,000
Unearned revenue		2,500
Common shares		5,000
Retained earnings		13,650
Totals	$27,150	$27,150

During the month of July, the following selected transactions took place:

July	2	Paid $1,500 for two months' rent in advance for July and August.
	7	Purchased $200 of supplies on account.
	14	Collected half of outstanding accounts receivable.
	15	Borrowed $1,000 from the bank for one year at an interest rate of 5%.
	21	Received $1,000 cash from a customer for services to be performed in August.
	28	Performed $1,500 of services to a customer on account.

Additional information:

1. At July 31, the company had performed $800 of services for a client that it had not billed or recorded.
2. Supplies on hand at July 31 were $500.
3. The equipment has a five-year useful life and uses straight-line depreciation.
4. Interest is due on the bank loan on the first day of each following month, beginning August 1.
5. As at July 31, the company owed $2,500 of salaries to its employees for the month just ended.
6. As at July 31, the company had earned $2,000 of revenue that had been paid in advance.

Instructions

(a) Record the July transactions.

(b) Prepare adjusting entries at July 31, assuming the company prepares adjusting entries monthly. Round all calculations to the nearest dollar.

Prepare adjusting entries.

(LO 2, 3)

E4–8 On March 31, 2018, Easy Rental Agency Inc.'s trial balance included the following selected unadjusted account balances. The company's year end is December 31 and it adjusts its accounts quarterly.

	Debit	Credit
Prepaid insurance	$14,400	
Supplies	2,800	
Equipment	21,600	
Accumulated depreciation—equipment		$ 5,400
Unearned revenue		9,600
Loan payable, due 2020		20,000
Rent revenue		30,000
Salaries expense	14,000	

An analysis of the accounts shows the following:

1. The equipment, which was purchased on January 1, 2017, is estimated to have a useful life of four years. The company uses straight-line depreciation.
2. One third of the unearned revenue related to rent is still unearned at the end of the quarter.
3. The loan payable has an interest rate of 6%. Interest is paid on the first day of each following month and was last paid March 1, 2018.
4. Supplies on hand total $850 at March 31.
5. The one-year insurance policy was purchased for $14,400 on January 1.
6. Income tax is estimated to be $3,200 for the quarter.

Instructions

Prepare the quarterly adjusting entries required at March 31.

E4-9 On December 31, 2018, Water Ltd. prepared an income statement and statement of financial position, but failed to take into account three adjusting journal entries. Prior to correcting this omission, the income statement reported net income of $90,000 and the statement of financial position reported total assets $170,000, total liabilities $70,000, and total shareholders' equity $100,000.

Correct for missing adjusting entries.
(LO 2, 3)

Information about the three missing adjusting entries is as follows:
1. Salaries owed amounting to $10,000 for the last two days worked in December were not accrued. The next payroll will be in January.
2. Rent of $8,000 was received for two months in advance on December 1. The entire amount was credited to Unearned Revenue when received.
3. Depreciation of $9,000 was not recorded.

Instructions
Complete the following table to correct the financial statement amounts shown. (Indicate deductions with parentheses.)

	Net Income	Total Assets	Total Liabilities	Total Shareholders' Equity
Incorrect balances	$90,000	$170,000	$70,000	$100,000
Adjustments:				
1. Salaries	___	___	___	___
2. Rent	___	___	___	___
3. Depreciation	___	___	___	___
Correct balances	___	___	___	___

E4-10 A partial adjusted trial balance follows for Nolet Ltd. at January 31, 2018. The company's fiscal year end is December 31 and it makes adjustments monthly. It has already recorded any required adjusting journal entries for the month of January and the amounts shown below are correct.

Analyze adjusted data.
(LO 2, 3, 4)

NOLET LTD.
Adjusted Trial Balance (partial)
January 31, 2018

	Debit	Credit
Supplies	$ 700	
Prepaid insurance	1,200	
Equipment	7,200	
Accumulated depreciation—equipment		$3,000
Income tax payable		150
Unearned revenue		750
Service revenue		2,000
Depreciation expense	120	
Insurance expense	400	
Supplies expense	950	
Income tax expense	100	

Instructions
(a) If $1,600 was received in December for services to be performed in January, and all of these services were performed as expected in January, what was the balance in Unearned Revenue at January 1? Assume there were no other transactions that affected Unearned Revenue during this period. (*Hint*: Prepare the December and January entries for this transaction, post to the Unearned Revenue T account, and work backwards to determine the opening balance.)
(b) If the amount in the Depreciation Expense account is the depreciation for the month of January, when was the equipment purchased? Assume that there have been no purchases or sales of equipment since this original purchase and that Nolet uses the straight-line method of depreciation. (*Hint*: Use the monthly depreciation and accumulated depreciation amounts to determine how many months the equipment has been depreciated.)
(c) If the amount in Insurance Expense is the amount of the January 31 adjusting entry, and the original insurance premium was for one year, what was the total premium (amount paid for the policy) and when was the policy purchased? (*Hint*: Use the prepaid insurance amount at January 31 and monthly insurance expense to determine how many months of insurance coverage remain. Once you know that, you can work backwards to determine the total amount paid for the policy and when.)
(d) If the amount in Supplies Expense is the amount of the January 31 adjusting entry, and $750 of supplies were purchased in January, what was the balance in Supplies on January 1? (*Hint*: Prepare the adjusting journal entry for this transaction, post to the Supplies and Supplies Expense T accounts, and work backwards to determine the opening balance.)
(e) If $100 of income tax was paid in January, what was the balance in Income Tax Payable at January 1? (*Hint*: Prepare the adjusting journal entry for this transaction, post to the Income Tax Expense and Income Tax Payable T accounts, and work backwards to determine the opening balance.)

Prepare adjusted trial balance.

(LO 4)

E4–11 Fraser Valley Services Ltd. reports the following adjusted account balances, shown in alphabetical order, at the end of its fiscal year, August 31, 2018:

Accounts payable	$ 2,800	Interest expense	$ 1,500
Accounts receivable	18,225	Interest payable	1,500
Accumulated depreciation—equipment	5,905	Prepaid insurance	3,450
Bank loan payable, due 2021	25,000	Rent expense	15,000
Cash	11,430	Rent payable	1,250
Common shares	5,000	Retained earnings	5,400
Depreciation expense	2,275	Salaries expense	19,200
Dividends declared	600	Salaries payable	2,200
Equipment	25,600	Service revenue	54,275
Income tax expense	2,000	Supplies	3,400
Income tax payable	1,500	Supplies expense	1,750
Insurance expense	1,100	Unearned revenue	700

Instructions

Prepare an adjusted trial balance.

Prepare financial statements.

(LO 4)

E4–12 The adjusted trial balance for Fraser Valley Services Ltd. was prepared in E4–11. Note that the company issued common shares for $1,000 during the year.

Instructions

Prepare (a) an income statement, (b) a statement of changes in equity, and (c) a statement of financial position.

Prepare and post closing entries.

(LO 5)

E4–13 Selected accounts from Betts Ltd.'s general ledger are presented below. Note that the account details for the year have not been included, only the account balance ("bal.") after adjustment but before closing is included.

Retained Earnings					Office Expense		
	Jan. 1 bal.	185,000		Dec. 31 bal.	21,500		

Dividends Declared				Depreciation Expense		
Dec. 31 bal.	10,500			Dec. 31 bal.	20,000	

Service Revenue				Utilities Expense		
	Dec. 31 bal.	396,000		Dec. 31 bal.	19,000	

Interest Revenue				Interest Expense		
	Dec. 31 bal.	9,000		Dec. 31 bal.	11,250	

Salaries Expense				Income Tax Expense		
Dec. 31 bal.	240,000			Dec. 31 bal.	18,650	

Instructions

(a) Prepare the closing entries at December 31.

(b) Post the closing entries to the T accounts, setting up new accounts as required.

Prepare closing entries and post-closing trial balance.

(LO 5)

E4–14 The adjusted trial balance for Fraser Valley Services Ltd. was prepared in E4–11.

Instructions

(a) Prepare the closing entries at August 31.

(b) Prepare a post-closing trial balance.

▶ PROBLEMS: SET A

Prepare transaction and adjusting entries for prepayments.

(LO 2)

P4–1A Ouellette Corporation began operations on January 2. Its year end is December 31, and it adjusts its accounts annually. Selected transactions for the current year follow:

1. On January 2, purchased supplies for $4,100 cash. A physical count at December 31 revealed that $700 of supplies were still on hand.

2. Purchased a vehicle for $45,000 on April 1, paying $5,000 cash and signing a $40,000 bank loan for the balance. The vehicle is estimated to have a useful life of five years and the company uses straight-line depreciation.

3. Purchased a $3,600, one-year insurance policy for cash on August 1. The policy came into effect on that date.

4. Received a $1,600 advance cash payment from a client on November 9 for services to be performed in the future. As at December 31, half of these services had been completed.

5. On December 1, the company rented additional office space for a six-month period starting on December 1 for $1,200 each month. It paid rent for the months of December and January in advance on this date.

Instructions

(a) For each of the above situations, prepare the journal entry for the original transaction.

(b) For each of the above situations, prepare any adjusting entry required at December 31.

P4–2A Zheng Corporation had the following selected transactions in the month of March. The company adjusts its accounts monthly.

Prepare adjusting and subsequent entries for accruals.

(LO 3)

1. The company has a 6%, $12,000 bank loan payable due in one year. Interest is payable on the first day of each following month and was last paid on March 1.

2. At the end of March, the company earned $250 interest on its investments. The bank deposited this amount in Zheng's cash account on April 1.

3. Zheng has five employees who each earn $200 a day. Salaries are normally paid on Mondays for work completed Monday through Friday of the previous week. Salaries were last paid on Monday, March 26. March 31 falls on a Saturday this year. Salaries will be paid next on Monday, April 2.

4. At the end of March, the company owed the utility company $550 and the telephone company $200 for services received during the month. These bills were paid on April 10. (*Hint:* Use the Utilities Expense account for the utility and telephone services.)

5. At the end of March, Zheng has earned service revenue of $3,000 that it has not yet billed. It bills its clients for this amount on April 4. On April 30, it collects $2,000 of this amount due.

Instructions

(a) For each of the above situations, prepare the adjusting journal entry required at March 31.

(b) For each of the above situations, prepare the journal entry to record the subsequent cash transaction in April.

P4–3A The following independent events for New Age Theatre Ltd. during the year ended November 30, 2018, require a transaction journal entry or an adjusting journal entry, or both. The company adjusts its accounts annually.

Prepare transaction and adjusting entries.

(LO 2, 3)

1. On June 1, 2017, the theatre purchased vehicles for $80,000 cash. The vehicles' estimated useful life is five years and the company uses straight-line depreciation.

2. The theatre has eight plays each season. This year's season starts in October 2018 and ends in May 2019 (one play per month). Season tickets sell for $320. On October 1, 400 season tickets were sold for the 2018–2019 season. The theatre credited Unearned Revenue for the full amount received on October 1 and uses a Ticket Revenue account to record revenue earned from season tickets.

3. Supplies on hand amounted to $1,000 at the beginning of the year. On February 16, additional supplies were purchased for cash at a cost of $2,100. At the end of the year, a physical count showed that supplies on hand amounted to $500.

4. On June 1, 2018, the theatre borrowed $100,000 from the Bank of Montreal at an interest rate of 6%. The principal is to be repaid in one year. The interest is payable on the first day of each following month, and was last paid on November 1.

5. The New Age Theatre rents a portion of its facilities for $400 a month to a local dance club that uses the space for rehearsals. On November 2, the dance club's treasurer made a mistake and accidentally sent a cheque for only $40 for the November rent. (*Hint:* Use the Unearned Revenue account to record the rent received in advance.) The dance club's treasurer promised to send a cheque in December for the balance when she returned from vacation. On December 4, the theatre received a $360 cheque for the balance owing from November.

6. The total weekly payroll is $7,000, paid every Monday for employee salaries earned during a seven-day workweek running from Sunday to Saturday. Salaries were last paid (and recorded) on Monday, November 26, and will be paid next on Monday, December 3. November 30 falls on a Friday this year.

7. Upon reviewing its income tax calculations on November 30, the theatre noted that an additional $1,250 of income tax was owed. This additional amount was paid on December 14.

Instructions

(a) Prepare the journal entries to record the original transactions for items 1, 2, 3, 4, and 5.

(b) Prepare the year-end adjusting entries required for items 1 through 7 on November 30.

(c) Record the subsequent cash transactions in December for (1) the interest paid on December 1 (item 4), (2) the cheque received on December 4 (item 5), (3) the payroll paid on December 3 (item 6), and (4) the income tax paid on December 14 (item 7).

P4–4A Roadside Travel Court Ltd. was organized on July 1, 2017, by Betty Johnson. Betty is a good manager but a poor accountant. From the trial balance prepared by a part-time bookkeeper, Betty prepared the following income statement for her fourth quarter, which ended June 30, 2018.

Prepare adjusting entries and a corrected income statement.

(LO 2, 3)

ROADSIDE TRAVEL COURT LTD.
Income Statement
Quarter Ended June 30, 2018

Rent revenue		$212,000
Expenses		
Salaries expense	$80,500	
Repair and maintenance expense	4,300	
Advertising expense	3,800	
Depreciation expense	2,700	
Utilities expense	900	92,200
Net income		$119,800

Betty suspected that something was wrong with the statement because net income had never exceeded $35,000 in any one quarter. Knowing that you are an experienced accountant, she asks you to review the income statement and other data.

You first look at the trial balance. In addition to the account balances reported above in the income statement, the trial balance contains the following additional selected balances at June 30, 2018.

Supplies	$ 8,200
Prepaid insurance	14,400
Mortgage payable	150,000

You then make inquiries and discover the following items:

1. Rental revenue includes advanced rental payments received for summer occupancy in July, in the amount of $57,000.
2. There were $800 of supplies on hand at June 30.
3. Prepaid insurance resulted from the purchase of a one-year policy for $14,400 on April 1, 2018.
4. The mail the first week of July brought the following bills: advertising for the week of June 24, $110; repairs made June 18, $4,450; and utilities for the month of June, $215.
5. Salaries are $300 per day. At June 30, four days' salaries have been incurred but not paid.
6. Interest on the mortgage payable is $1,875 for the quarter and due July 1.
7. Income tax of $8,000 for the quarter is due in July.

Instructions
(a) Prepare the adjusting journal entries required at June 30, assuming adjusting entries are made quarterly.
(b) Prepare a correct income statement for the quarter ended June 30, 2018.

Calculate and prepare adjusting entries.

(LO 2, 3)

P4–5A A review of the ledger of Chance Corporation at its year end, July 31, 2018, produces the following unadjusted data for the preparation of annual adjusting entries:

1. Prepaid Insurance, July 31, 2018, unadjusted balance, $9,600: The company purchased an insurance policy on December 1, 2016, with a two-year term, which expires November 30, 2018.
2. Buildings, July 31, 2018, unadjusted balance, $252,000: The company owns a building purchased on September 1, 2014, for $252,000, with an estimated 30-year useful life. The company uses straight-line depreciation.
3. Unearned Revenue, July 31, 2018, unadjusted balance, $42,500: The selling price of a digital magazine subscription is $60 for 24 monthly issues delivered over a two-year period. The company had sold 1,000 subscriptions on January 1, 2017, during a special promotion.
4. Salaries Payable, July 31, 2018, unadjusted balance, $0: There are nine salaried employees. Salaries are paid every Monday for the previous five-day workweek (Monday to Friday). Six employees receive a salary of $625 each per week, and three employees earn $750 each per week. July 31 is a Tuesday.

Instructions
(a) 1. How much insurance expires per month for the building?
    2. Prepare a calculation to show why the *unadjusted* balance in the Prepaid Insurance account is $9,600 at July 31, 2018.
    3. What was the original purchase price of the policy on December 1, 2016?
    4. How much should the adjusted balance in the Prepaid Insurance account be at July 31, 2018?
(b) 1. How much is annual depreciation expense for the building?
    2. Calculate the *unadjusted* balance in the Accumulated Depreciation—Buildings account as at July 31, 2018.
    3. How much should the adjusted balance in the Accumulated Depreciation—Buildings account be at July 31, 2018?
(c) 1. How much is earned by the company per month for the magazine subscriptions?
    2. Prepare a calculation to show why the *unadjusted* balance in the Unearned Revenue account is $42,500 at July 31, 2018.
    3. How much should the adjusted balance in the Unearned Revenue account be at July 31, 2018?
(d) 1. How much salary was paid on the last payday, Monday, July 30?
    2. How much, if any, salary is owed to the employees on July 31?
    3. How much salary will be paid on the next payday, Monday, August 6?
(e) Prepare the adjusting journal entries required for each of the above four items at July 31, 2018. (*Hint:* Use the account Subscription Revenue for item (c).)

P4–6A Near the end of its first year of operations, December 31, 2018, Creative Designs Ltd. approached the local bank for a $20,000 loan and was asked to submit financial statements prepared on an accrual basis. Although the company kept no formal accounting records, it did maintain a record of cash receipts and payments. The following information is available for the year ended December 31:

Convert cash to accrual basis; prepare financial statements.

(LO 1, 2, 3, 4)

	Cash Receipts	Cash Payments
Issue of common shares	$ 20,000	
Fees earned	157,600	
Equipment		$ 35,400
Supplies		8,600
Rent		20,000
Insurance		3,840
Income tax		6,000
Advertising		6,800
Salaries		59,800
Dividends declared		10,000
	$177,600	$150,440

Additional information:
1. Fees from design work earned but not yet collected amounted to $2,400.
2. The equipment was purchased at the beginning of January and has an estimated six-year useful life. The company uses straight-line depreciation.
3. Supplies on hand on December 31 were $1,260.
4. Rent payments included a $1,500 per month rental fee and a $2,000 deposit that is refundable at the end of the two-year lease. (*Hint:* Use the Prepaid Rent account for the refundable deposit.)
5. The insurance was purchased on February 1 for a one-year period expiring January 31, 2019.
6. Salaries earned for the last four days in December and to be paid in January 2019 amounted to $3,050.
7. At year end, it was determined that an additional $7,000 is owed for income tax.

Instructions
(a) Calculate the cash balance at December 31.
(b) Prepare an accrual-based (1) income statement, (2) statement of changes in equity, and (3) statement of financial position.

P4–7A In P4–6A, cash receipts and payments were given for Creative Designs Ltd. and converted to an accrual basis.

Compare cash and accrual-based income statements.

(LO 1)

Instructions
(a) Calculate total revenue, total expense, and net income that would be reported if Creative Designs used the cash basis of accounting.
(b) Compare the cash-based net income calculated in part (a) with the accrual-based net income calculated in P4–6A part (b) (1).
(c) Which method do you recommend Creative Designs use and why?

P4–8A The following is Wolastoq Tours Limited's unadjusted trial balance at its year end, November 30, 2018. The company adjusts its accounts annually.

Prepare and post adjusting entries; prepare adjusted trial balance.

(LO 2, 3, 4)

	Debit	Credit
Cash	$ 15,800	
Accounts receivable	7,640	
Supplies	965	
Prepaid rent	2,400	
Prepaid insurance	7,320	
Equipment	13,440	
Accumulated depreciation—equipment		$ 3,360
Vehicles	140,400	
Accumulated depreciation—vehicles		46,800
Accounts payable		1,925
Unearned revenue		14,000
Bank loan payable, due 2021		54,000
Common shares		10,000
Retained earnings		27,225
Fees earned		130,575
Salaries expense	69,560	
Repairs and maintenance expense	11,170	
Rent expense	13,200	
Interest expense	3,465	
Advertising expense	825	
Income tax expense	1,700	
	$287,885	$287,885

Additional information:
1. The insurance policy has a one-year term beginning April 1, 2018. At that time, a premium of $7,320 was paid.
2. The equipment was acquired on December 1, 2015, and has an estimated useful life of eight years. The vehicles were acquired on December 1, 2015, and have an estimated useful life of six years. The company uses straight-line depreciation.
3. A physical count shows $300 of supplies on hand at November 30.
4. The bank loan payable has a 7% interest rate. Interest is paid on the first day of each following month, and was last paid on November 1.
5. Deposits of $1,400 each were received for advance tour reservations from 10 school groups. At November 30, all of these deposits have been earned.
6. Employees are owed a total of $500 at November 30.
7. A senior citizens' organization that had not made an advance deposit took a river tour for $1,250. This group was not billed until December for the services performed.
8. Additional advertising costs of $260 have been incurred, but the bills have not been received by November 30.
9. On November 1, the company paid $2,400 rent in advance for November and December.
10. Income tax payable for the year is estimated to be an additional $300 beyond that recorded to date.

Instructions
(a) Prepare the adjusting journal entries required at November 30.
(b) Set up T accounts, enter the opening balances, and post the November adjusting entries to the general ledger.
(c) Prepare an adjusted trial balance at November 30.

Record and post transaction and adjusting entries; prepare unadjusted and adjusted trial balances and financial statements.

(LO 2, 3, 4)

P4–9A On October 31, 2018, Alou Equipment Repair Corp.'s opening trial balance was as follows. The company adjusts its accounts monthly.

	Debit	Credit
Cash	$15,580	
Accounts receivable	15,820	
Supplies	4,000	
Equipment	18,000	
Accumulated depreciation—equipment		$ 3,600
Accounts payable		4,600
Salaries payable		1,000
Unearned revenue		1,000
Common shares		10,000
Retained earnings		33,200
	$53,400	$53,400

During November, the following transactions were completed:

Nov. 9 Paid $2,200 to employees for salaries due, of which $1,000 is for October salaries payable and $1,200 for November.
13 Issued common shares for $5,000.
13 Received $12,400 cash from customers in payment of accounts.
19 Received $11,400 cash for services performed in November.
20 Purchased supplies on account, $600.

Nov. 21 Paid creditors $4,600 of accounts payable due.
23 Paid November rent, $600.
23 Paid salaries, $2,400.
27 Performed services on account, $3,800.
28 Declared and paid a cash dividend, $500.
30 Received $1,100 from customers for services to be performed in the future.

Adjustment data for the month:
1. Supplies on hand are $1,000.
2. Accrued salaries payable are $1,000.
3. The equipment has an estimated useful life of five years and Alou uses straight-line depreciation.
4. Unearned revenue of $800 was earned during the month.
5. Income tax payable is estimated to be $1,100.

Instructions
(a) Prepare journal entries to record the November transactions.
(b) Set up T accounts, enter any opening balances, and post the journal entries prepared in part (a).
(c) Prepare a trial balance at November 30.
(d) Prepare and post the adjusting journal entries for the month.
(e) Prepare an adjusted trial balance at November 30.
(f) Prepare (1) an income statement, (2) a statement of changes in equity, and (3) a statement of financial position.

P4–10A Refer to the data for Alou Equipment Repair Corp. in P4–9A. Assume that Alou closes its books monthly.

Prepare and post closing entries; prepare post-closing trial balance.

Instructions
(a) Prepare the closing journal entries.
(b) Post the closing entries to the T accounts prepared in P4–9A.
(c) Prepare a post-closing trial balance at November 30.

(LO 5)

P4–11A Accounts from the adjusted trial balance at September 30, 2018, are listed in alphabetical order below for Ozaki Corp.:

Prepare adjusted trial balance, closing entries, and post-closing trial balance.

(LO 4, 5)

Accounts payable	$ 4,460	Income tax payable	$ 200
Accounts receivable	8,435	Interest expense	105
Accumulated depreciation—equipment	750	Interest payable	105
Bank loan payable	7,800	Rent expense	1,500
Cash	3,250	Retained earnings	2,600
Common shares	7,000	Salaries expense	13,840
Depreciation expense	750	Salaries payable	840
Dividends declared	700	Supplies	1,265
Equipment	15,040	Supplies expense	485
Fees earned	22,485	Unearned revenue	550
Income tax expense	600	Utilities expense	820

Instructions
(a) Prepare an adjusted trial balance.
(b) Prepare the closing journal entries.
(c) Prepare a post-closing trial balance at September 30.

P4–12A The following is the unadjusted trial balance for Rainbow Lodge Ltd. at its year end, May 31, 2018. The company adjusts its accounts monthly.

Prepare and post adjusting entries; prepare adjusted trial balance and financial statements; assess financial performance.

(LO 2, 3, 4)

	Debit	Credit
Cash	$ 6,400	
Accounts receivable	11,800	
Supplies	4,880	
Prepaid insurance	4,550	
Land	106,370	
Buildings	168,000	
Accumulated depreciation—buildings		$ 24,500
Furniture	33,600	
Accumulated depreciation—furniture		19,600
Accounts payable		8,140
Unearned revenue		17,500
Mortgage payable, due 2021		126,000
Common shares		60,000
Retained earnings		41,580
Dividends declared	2,000	
Rent revenue		200,320
Salaries expense	98,700	
Utilities expense	23,870	
Depreciation expense	13,860	
Interest expense	9,240	
Insurance expense	6,370	
Advertising expense	1,000	
Income tax expense	7,000	
	$497,640	$497,640

Additional information:
1. An annual insurance policy was purchased for the first time on October 1, 2017, for $10,920 cash.
2. A count of supplies shows $1,340 of supplies on hand on May 31.
3. The buildings have an estimated useful life of 20 years and straight-line depreciation is applied.
4. The furniture has an estimated useful life of five years and straight-line depreciation is applied.
5. Customers must pay a $100 deposit if they want to book a room in advance during the peak period. An analysis of these bookings indicates that 175 deposits were received and credited to Unearned Revenue. By May 31, 25 of the deposits were earned.

6. On May 25, a local business contracted with Rainbow Lodge to rent one of its housekeeping units for four months, starting June 1, at a rate of $2,800 per month. An advance payment equal to one month's rent was paid on May 25 and credited to Rent Revenue.
7. On May 31, Rainbow Lodge has earned $1,780 of rent revenue from customers who are currently staying at the inn. The customers will pay the amount owing only when they check out in early June.
8. Salaries of $1,590 are unpaid at May 31.
9. Interest on the mortgage payable is $735 for the month of May and due June 1.
10. The May utility bill of $2,240 has not yet been recorded or paid.
11. Additional income tax is estimated to be $1,000.

Instructions
(a) Prepare adjusting journal entries for the month.
(b) Set up T accounts, enter any opening balances, and post the adjusting journal entries prepared in part (a).
(c) Prepare an adjusted trial balance at May 31.
(d) Prepare (1) an income statement, (2) a statement of changes in equity, and (3) a statement of financial position for the year. Note that $4,000 of common shares were issued during the month of May.
(e) A friend of yours is considering investing in the company and asks you to comment on the company's operations and financial position. Is the company performing well or not? Does the financial position look healthy or weak? Use specific information from the financial statements to support your answer.

Prepare and post closing entries; prepare post-closing trial balance.
(LO 5)

P4–13A Refer to the data for Rainbow Lodge Ltd. in P4–12A.

Instructions
(a) Prepare the closing journal entries.
(b) Post the closing entries to the T accounts prepared in P4–12A.
(c) Prepare a post-closing trial balance at May 31.

▶ PROBLEMS: SET B

Prepare transaction and adjusting entries for prepayments.
(LO 2)

P4–1B Bourque Corporation began operations on January 2. Its year end is December 31, and it adjusts its accounts annually. Selected transactions for the current year follow:
1. On January 2, purchased supplies for $2,100 cash. A physical count at December 31 revealed that $550 of supplies were still on hand.
2. Purchased equipment for $20,000 cash on March 1. The equipment is estimated to have a useful life of five years and the company uses straight-line depreciation.
3. Purchased a one-year, $4,200 insurance policy for cash on June 1. The policy came into effect on that date.
4. On November 15, received a $1,275 advance cash payment from three clients for services to be performed in the future. As at December 31, work had been completed for two of the clients ($425 each).
5. On December 15, the company paid $2,500 rent in advance for the next month (January).

Instructions
(a) For each of the above situations, prepare the journal entry for the original transaction.
(b) For each of the above situations, prepare any adjusting journal entry required at December 31.

Prepare adjusting and subsequent entries for accruals.
(LO 3)

P4–2B Hangzhou Corporation had the following selected transactions in the month of November. The company adjusts its accounts monthly.
1. Hangzhou has a biweekly payroll of $6,000. Salaries are normally paid every second Monday for work completed for the two preceding weeks. Employees work a five-day week, Monday through Friday. Salaries were last paid Monday, November 26, and will be paid next on Monday, December 10.
2. The company has a 7%, $20,000 bank loan payable due September 1 of the next year. Interest is payable on the first day of each following month, and was last paid on November 1.
3. At the end of November, Hangzhou has $1,000 of invoices for services provided to customers that have not yet been sent. It mails these invoices on December 1, and collects the amounts due on December 21.
4. At the end of November, the company earned $10 interest on the cash in its bank account. The bank deposited this amount in the company's cash account on December 1.
5. At the end of November, it was estimated that the company owed $1,000 of income tax. This amount was paid on December 18.

Instructions
(a) For each of the above situations, prepare the adjusting journal entry required at November 30.
(b) For each of the above situations, prepare the journal entry to record the subsequent cash transaction in December.

P4–3B The following independent events for Repertory Theatre Ltd. during the year ended December 31, 2018, require a transaction journal entry or an adjusting journal entry, or both. The company adjusts its accounts annually.

Prepare transaction and adjusting entries.

(LO 2, 3)

1. Supplies on hand amounted to $1,500 at the beginning of the year. On March 1, additional supplies were purchased for $4,250 cash. At the end of the year, a physical count showed that supplies on hand amounted to $1,000.

2. The theatre owns a vehicle that was purchased on January 2, 2018, for $120,000. The vehicle's estimated useful life is four years.

3. The theatre has nine plays each season, which starts in September 2018 and ends in May 2019 (one play per month). Season tickets sell for $360. On August 2, 600 season tickets were sold for the upcoming 2018–2019 season. The theatre credited Unearned Revenue for the full amount received on August 2 and uses a Ticket Revenue account to record revenue earned from season tickets.

4. On June 1, the theatre borrowed $30,000 from La Caisse Populaire Desjardins at an interest rate of 6%, to be repaid in one year. The interest is payable on the first day of each following month, and was last paid on December 1.

5. The total weekly payroll is $9,000, paid every Friday for employee salaries earned during the prior six-day workweek (Saturday to Thursday). This year, December 31 falls on a Monday. Salaries were last paid (and recorded) on Friday, December 28, and will be paid next on Friday, January 4.

6. Repertory Theatre rents a portion of its facilities for $600 a month to a local seniors' choir that uses the space for rehearsals. The choir's treasurer was ill during December, and on January 7, the theatre received a $1,200 cheque for both the amount owing for the month of December and the rent for the month of January.

7. Upon reviewing its books on December 31, the theatre noted that a telephone bill for the month of December had not yet been received. A call to Bell Aliant determined that the telephone bill was for $1,125. The bill was paid on January 11. (*Hint:* Use the Utilities Expense account for telephone services.)

Instructions

(a) Prepare the journal entries to record the original transactions for items 1, 2, 3, and 4.

(b) Prepare the year-end adjusting entries required for items 1 through 7 on December 31.

(c) Record the subsequent cash transactions in January for (1) the interest paid on January 1 (item 4), (2) payment of the payroll on January 4 (item 5), (3) receipt of the rent on January 7 (item 6), and (4) payment of the telephone bill on January 11 (item 7).

P4–4B Fly Right Travel Agency Ltd. was organized on January 1, 2016, by Joe Paul. Joe is a good manager but a poor accountant. From the trial balance prepared by a part-time bookkeeper, Joe prepared the following income statement for the fourth quarter, which ended March 31, 2018.

Prepare adjusting entries and a corrected income statement.

(LO 2, 3)

FLY RIGHT TRAVEL AGENCY LTD.
Income Statement
Quarter Ended March 31, 2018

Service revenue		$50,000
Expenses		
Salaries expense	$11,000	
Office expense	2,600	
Advertising expense	1,700	
Utilities expense	400	
Depreciation expense	400	16,100
Net income		$33,900

Joe knew that something was wrong with the statement because net income had never exceeded $8,000 in any one quarter. Knowing that you are an experienced accountant, he asks you to review the income statement and other data.

You first look at the trial balance. In addition to the account balances reported above in the income statement, the trial balance contains the following additional selected balances at March 31, 2018.

Supplies	$ 2,900
Prepaid insurance	3,360
Bank loan payable	12,000

You then make inquiries and discover the following items:

1. Service revenue includes advanced payments for cruises, in the amount of $20,000.

2. There were $800 of supplies on hand at March 31.

3. Prepaid insurance resulted from the purchase of a one-year policy for $3,360 on January 1, 2018.

4. The mail the first week of April brought in a bill for heat, light, and power for the month of March, $210.

5. There are two employees who receive salaries of $100 each per day. At March 31, four days' salaries have been incurred but not paid.

6. The bank loan was signed on January 1, 2018, for seven months, with 7% interest due at maturity, July 31.

7. Income tax of $1,990 for the quarter is due in April.

Instructions

(a) Prepare the adjusting journal entries required at March 31, assuming adjusting entries are made quarterly.

(b) Prepare a correct income statement for the quarter ended March 31, 2018.

Calculate and prepare adjusting entries.

(LO 2, 3)

P4–5B A review of the ledger of Greenberg Corporation at its year end, October 31, 2018, produces the following unadjusted data for the preparation of annual adjusting entries:

1. Prepaid Advertising, October 31, 2018, unadjusted balance, $8,400: On February 1, 2018, the company signed and prepaid $8,400 for a 12-month advertising contract for advertisements to run in a trade magazine that publishes monthly, with the first advertisement starting March 1.

2. Unearned Revenue, October 31, 2018, unadjusted balance, $135,000: The company began subleasing office space in its new building on September 1, 2018. At October 31, the company had five one-year contracts for rental space, signed September 1 at a monthly rent of $4,500. All five tenants paid six months' rent in advance on September 1 for the 12-month rental.

3. Bank Loan Payable, October 31 unadjusted balance, $90,000: This represents a one-year, 8% bank loan signed on April 1, 2018. Interest is payable at maturity.

4. Vehicles, October 31, 2018, unadjusted balance, $39,000: The company owns a vehicle, purchased for $39,000 on April 1, 2017. The vehicle has a five-year useful life and uses straight-line depreciation.

Instructions

(a) 1. How much advertising expires per month?
    2. Prepare a calculation to show why the *unadjusted* balance in the Prepaid Advertising account is $8,400 at October 31.
    3. How much should the adjusted balance in the Prepaid Advertising account be at October 31?

(b) 1. Prepare a calculation to show why the *unadjusted* balance in the Unearned Revenue account is $135,000 at October 31.
    2. How much should the adjusted balance in the Unearned Revenue account be at October 31?

(c) 1. How much is interest on the bank loan each month?
    2. How much interest is owed, if any, on October 31, 2018?
    3. How much interest will be paid on April 1, 2019, when the bank loan matures?

(d) 1. How much is annual depreciation expense?
    2. Calculate the *unadjusted* balance in the Accumulated Depreciation account as at October 31, 2018.
    3. How much should the adjusted balance in the Accumulated Depreciation account be at October 31, 2018?

(e) Prepare the adjusting journal entries required for each of the above four items at October 31, 2018.

Convert cash to accrual basis; prepare financial statements.

(LO 1, 2, 3, 4)

P4–6B The Sharp Edge Ltd., a ski tuning and repair shop, opened on November 1, 2017. Although the company did not keep any formal accounting records, it did maintain a record of cash receipts and payments. The following information is available at the end of the first ski season, April 30, 2018:

	Cash Receipts	Cash Payments
Issue of common shares	$20,000	
Ski and snowboard repair services	66,500	
Repair equipment		$47,040
Rent		9,100
Insurance		2,760
Advertising		920
Utility bills		1,900
Salaries		14,200
Income tax		5,000
	$86,500	$80,920

Additional information:

1. At the end of April, customers owe Sharp Edge $1,440 for services they have received and not yet paid for.

2. The repair equipment was purchased at the beginning of November and has an estimated useful life of eight years. Sharp Edge uses straight-line depreciation.

3. On November 1, the company began renting space at a cost of $1,300 per month on a one-year lease. As required by the lease contract, the company paid the first and last months' (November 2017 and October 2018) rent in advance, in addition to paying rent the first of each month for that particular month.

4. The insurance policy was purchased November 1 and is effective for one year.

5. At April 30, $4,240 is owed for unpaid salaries.

6. At April 30, it was determined that an additional $800 is owed for income tax.

Instructions

(a) Calculate the cash balance at April 30.

(b) Prepare an accrual-based (1) income statement, (2) statement of changes in equity, and (3) statement of financial position for the six months ended April 30.

P4–7B In P4–6B, cash receipts and payments were given for The Sharp Edge Ltd. and converted to an accrual basis.

Instructions

(a) Calculate total revenue, total expense, and net income that would be reported if Sharp Edge used the cash basis of accounting.

(b) Compare the cash-based net income calculated in part (a) with the accrual-based net income calculated in P4–6B part (b) (1).

(c) Which method do you recommend Sharp Edge use and why?

Compare cash and accrual-based income statements.

(LO 1)

P4–8B The following is Ortega Limo Service Ltd.'s unadjusted trial balance at its year end, December 31, 2018. The company adjusts its accounts annually.

Prepare and post adjusting entries; prepare adjusted trial balance.

(LO 2, 3, 4)

	Debit	Credit
Cash	$ 4,600	
Accounts receivable	8,220	
Supplies	2,500	
Prepaid insurance	3,600	
Prepaid rent	2,300	
Vehicles	58,000	
Accumulated depreciation—vehicles		$ 14,500
Furniture	16,000	
Accumulated depreciation—furniture		4,000
Unearned revenue		3,600
Bank loan payable, due September 1, 2021		27,475
Common shares		5,000
Retained earnings		7,600
Dividends declared	3,800	
Service revenue		125,600
Salaries expense	67,000	
Rent expense	12,650	
Repairs and maintenance expense	4,690	
Interest expense	2,415	
Income tax expense	2,000	
	$187,775	$187,775

Additional information:

1. The insurance policy has a one-year term beginning March 1, 2018. At that time, a premium of $3,600 was paid.
2. A physical count of supplies at December 31 shows $570 of supplies on hand.
3. The vehicles were purchased on January 2, 2017, and have an estimated useful life of four years. The company uses straight-line depreciation.
4. The furniture was purchased on July 2, 2015, and has an estimated useful life of 10 years.
5. Service revenue earned but not billed or recorded at December 31 is $1,750.
6. Interest on the 7% bank loan is paid on the first day of each following quarter (January 1, April 1, July 1, and October 1) and was last paid on October 1.
7. One of Ortega's customers paid $3,600 in advance for a six-month contract at the rate of $600 per month. The contract began on November 1 and Ortega credited Unearned Revenue at the time.
8. Drivers' salaries total $200 per day. At December 31, three days of salaries are unpaid.
9. On December 1, Ortega paid $2,300 ($1,150 per month) for the December 2018 and January 2019 rent in advance.
10. Income tax for the year is estimated to be $2,850. The company has paid $2,000 in income tax instalments to date.

Instructions

(a) Prepare the adjusting journal entries required at December 31.

(b) Set up T accounts, enter any opening balances, and post the December adjusting entries.

(c) Prepare an adjusted trial balance at December 31.

P4–9B On August 31, 2018, Rijo Equipment Repair Corp.'s opening trial balance was as follows. The company prepares adjusting entries monthly.

Record and post transaction and adjusting entries; prepare unadjusted and adjusted trial balances and financial statements.

(LO 2, 3, 4)

	Debit	Credit
Cash	$ 9,760	
Accounts receivable	7,440	
Supplies	1,600	

	Debit	Credit
Equipment	$30,000	
Accumulated depreciation—equipment		$ 3,000
Accounts payable		6,200
Salaries payable		1,400
Unearned revenue		800
Common shares		20,000
Retained earnings		17,400
	$48,800	$48,800

During September, the following transactions were completed:

Sept.	4	Paid employees $2,200 for salaries due, of which $1,400 was for August salaries payable and $800 for September.
	6	Received $5,400 cash from customers in payment of accounts.
	11	Received $8,800 cash for services performed in September.
	12	Issued common shares for $5,000 cash.
	17	Purchased supplies on account, $2,000.
	21	Paid creditors $7,000 of accounts payable due.
	24	Paid September and October rent, $2,000 ($1,000 per month).
	25	Paid salaries, $2,200.
	26	Performed services on account, $1,600.
	27	Received $1,300 from customers for services to be performed in the future.
	28	Declared and paid a cash dividend, $500.
	28	Paid income tax for the month, $600.

Adjustment data for the month:
1. Supplies on hand total $800.
2. Accrued salaries payable are $1,600.
3. Accrued service revenue for $600.
4. The equipment has a useful life of 10 years and the company uses straight-line depreciation.
5. Unearned revenue of $800 has been earned.

Instructions
(a) Prepare journal entries to record the September transactions.
(b) Set up T accounts, enter any opening balances, and post the journal entries prepared in part (a).
(c) Prepare a trial balance at September 30.
(d) Prepare and post the adjusting journal entries for the month.
(e) Prepare an adjusted trial balance at September 30.
(f) Prepare (1) an income statement, (2) a statement of changes in equity, and (3) a statement of financial position.

Prepare and post closing entries; prepare post-closing trial balance.

(LO 5)

P4–10B Refer to the data for Rijo Equipment Repair Corp. in P4–9B. Assume that Rijo closes its books monthly.

Instructions
(a) Prepare the closing journal entries.
(b) Post the closing entries to the T accounts prepared in P4–9B.
(c) Prepare a post-closing trial balance at September 30.

Prepare adjusted trial balance, closing entries, and post-closing trial balance.

(LO 4, 5)

P4–11B Accounts from the adjusted trial balance at December 31, 2018, are listed in alphabetical order below for Grant Advertising Agency Limited:

Accounts payable	$ 4,800	Income tax payable	$ 4,000
Accounts receivable	19,750	Insurance expense	1,600
Accumulated depreciation—equipment	39,600	Interest expense	700
Bank loan payable	10,000	Interest payable	700
Cash	11,000	Prepaid insurance	800
Common shares	20,000	Rent expense	7,200
Depreciation expense	13,200	Retained earnings	10,400
Dividends declared	2,000	Salaries expense	13,625
Equipment	66,000	Salaries payable	1,625
Fees earned	60,600	Supplies	1,265
Held for trading investments	10,850	Supplies expense	5,935
Income tax expense	4,000	Unearned revenue	6,200

Instructions
(a) Prepare an adjusted trial balance.
(b) Prepare the closing journal entries.
(c) Prepare a post-closing trial balance at December 31.

P4–12B The following is the unadjusted trial balance for Rocky Mountain Resort Inc. at its year end, August 31, 2018. The company adjusts its accounts annually.

Prepare and post adjusting entries; prepare adjusted trial balance and financial statements; assess financial performance.

(LO 2, 3, 4)

	Debit	Credit
Cash	$ 38,820	
Supplies	6,990	
Prepaid insurance	12,720	
Land	70,000	
Buildings	290,000	
Accumulated depreciation—buildings		$ 87,000
Furniture	57,200	
Accumulated depreciation—furniture		22,880
Accounts payable		13,000
Unearned revenue		71,000
Mortgage payable, due 2021		120,000
Common shares		40,000
Retained earnings		72,000
Dividends declared	10,000	
Rent revenue		497,000
Salaries expense	306,000	
Utilities expense	75,200	
Repairs and maintenance expense	28,250	
Interest expense	7,700	
Income tax expense	20,000	
	$922,880	$922,880

Additional information:
1. The one-year insurance policy was purchased on May 31 for $12,720.
2. A count of supplies on August 31 shows $1,380 of supplies on hand.
3. The buildings have an estimated useful life of 50 years and straight-line depreciation is applied.
4. The furniture has an estimated useful life of 10 years and straight-line depreciation is applied.
5. Customers must pay a $200 deposit if they want to book a cottage during the peak period. An analysis of these bookings indicates 355 deposits were received and credited to Unearned Revenue. Only 45 of these deposits have not been earned by August 31.
6. Salaries of $1,680 were unpaid at August 31.
7. The August utility bill of $3,120 has not yet been recorded or paid.
8. On August 25, a local business contracted with Rocky Mountain to rent one of the cottages for six months, starting October 1, at a rate of $3,000 per month. An advance payment equal to two months' (October and November) rent was received on August 31 and credited to Rent Revenue.
9. Interest on the mortgage payable is $700 for the month of August and due September 1.
10. Income tax payable is estimated to be $2,000.
11. During the month of May, $5,000 of common shares were issued. (*Note:* This has already been recorded.)

Instructions
(a) Prepare adjusting journal entries for the year.
(b) Set up T accounts, enter any opening balances, and post the adjusting journal entries prepared in part (a).
(c) Prepare an adjusted trial balance at August 31.
(d) Prepare (1) an income statement, (2) a statement of changes in equity, and (3) a statement of financial position. Note that there was no change in common shares during the year.
(e) A friend of yours is considering investing in the company and asks you to comment on the results of operations and financial position. Is the company performing well or not? Does the financial position look healthy or weak? Use specific information from the financial statements to support your answer.

P4–13B Refer to the data for Rocky Mountain Resort Inc. in P4–12B.

Instructions
(a) Prepare the closing journal entries.
(b) Post the closing entries to the T accounts prepared in P4–12B.
(c) Prepare a post-closing trial balance at August 31.

Prepare and post closing entries; prepare post-closing trial balance.

(LO 5)

ACCOUNTING CYCLE | REVIEW

*Record and post trans-
action, adjusting, and
closing journal entries;
prepare unadjusted,
adjusted, and post-closing
trial balances and finan-
cial statements.*

(LO 2, 3, 4, 5)

ACR4–1 On August 1, 2018, the beginning of its current fiscal year, the following opening account balances, listed in alphabetical order, were reported by Tobique Ltd.

Accounts payable	$ 2,300	Interest receivable	$ 20
Accounts receivable	4,310	Note receivable, due October 31, 2018	4,000
Accumulated depreciation—equipment	2,000	Retained earnings	6,400
Cash	6,020	Salaries payable	1,420
Common shares	12,000	Supplies	1,030
Equipment	10,000	Unearned revenue	1,260

During August, the following summary transactions were completed.

Aug. 1 Paid $400 cash for advertising in local newspapers. Advertising flyers will be included with newspapers delivered during August and September. (*Hint*: Use the Prepaid Advertising account.)
3 Paid August rent $380. (*Hint*: Use the Prepaid Rent account.)
6 Received $3,200 cash from customers in payment of accounts.
10 Paid $3,120 for salaries due employees, of which $1,700 is for August and $1,420 is for July salaries payable.
13 Received $3,800 cash for services performed in August.
15 Purchased additional equipment on account $2,000.
17 Paid creditors $2,000 of accounts payable due.
22 Purchased supplies on account $800.
24 Paid salaries $2,900.
27 Performed services worth $4,760 on account and billed customers.
29 Received $780 from customers for services to be provided in the future.
31 Declared and paid a $500 dividend.

Tobique records adjustments monthly. Adjustment data for the month of August are as follows:
1. One month's worth of advertising services have been received.
2. The August rent has expired.
3. Accrued salaries payable are $1,540.
4. Depreciation for the month is $200.
5. Supplies on hand at August 31 are $960.
6. Services were performed to satisfy $800 of unearned revenue.
7. One month of interest revenue related to the $4,000 note receivable has accrued. The note was issued on June 30 and is due October 31 and has a 6% annual interest rate. Interest is due at maturity.
8. Income tax of $300 is estimated to be owed for the month of August.

Instructions
(a) Record the above summary transactions.
(b) Set up T accounts, enter any opening balances, and post the general journal entries prepared in part (a).
(c) Prepare a trial balance at August 31.
(d) Prepare and post the August adjusting journal entries.
(e) Prepare an adjusted trial balance as at August 31.
(f) Prepare (1) an income statement, (2) a statement of changes in equity, and (3) a statement of financial position.
(g) Prepare and post the closing journal entries, assuming Tobique closes its books monthly.
(h) Prepare a post-closing trial balance.

*Record and post trans-
action, adjusting, and
closing journal entries;
prepare unadjusted and
adjusted trial balances
and financial statements;
calculate current ratio.*

(LO 2, 3, 4, 5)

ACR4–2 At June 30, 2018, the end of its most recent fiscal year, River Consultants Ltd.'s post-closing trial balance was as follows:

	Debit	Credit
Cash	$15,230	
Accounts receivable	1,200	
Supplies	690	
Accounts payable		$ 400
Income tax payable		500
Unearned revenue		1,120
Common shares		3,600
Retained earnings		11,500
	$17,120	$17,120

The company underwent a major expansion in July. New staff was hired and more financing was obtained. River conducted the following transactions during July 2018.

July   3   Issued $10,000 of common shares for cash.
       4   Purchased insurance coverage for a year, $3,600.
       5   Paid the first two (July and August 2018) months' rent for an annual lease of office space for $4,000 per month. (*Hint*: Use the Prepaid Rent account.)
       6   Purchased $3,800 of supplies for cash.
       6   Purchased equipment, paying $4,000 cash and signing a two-year bank loan for $20,000. The equipment has a four-year useful life. The bank loan has a 6% interest rate, which is payable on the first day of each following month.
      10   Visited client offices and agreed on the terms of a consulting project. River will invoice the client, Connor Productions Ltd., on the 19th of each month for work performed.
      12   Collected $1,200 on account from Milani Brothers Ltd. This client was invoiced in June when the service was provided.
      13   Completed services for Mactaquac Inc. This client paid $1,120 in advance last month. All services relating to this payment are now completed. (*Hint*: Use the Fees Earned account.)
      16   Paid salaries for the first half of the month, $11,000.
      17   Paid a utility bill of $400. This related to June utilities that were accrued at the end of June.
      18   Met with a new client, Bay Technologies. Received $12,000 cash in advance for future work to be performed.
      19   Invoiced Connor Productions for $28,000 of consulting fees provided on account. (*Hint*: Use the Fees Earned account.)
      20   Received an invoice for legal advice, $2,200. The amount is not due until August 20. (*Hint*: Use the Professional Fees Expense account.)
      23   Completed the first phase of the project for Bay Technologies Ltd. Recognized $10,000 of revenue from the cash advance previously received (see July 18 transaction).
      25   Paid $500 income tax payable owing at the end of June, in addition to $1,200 for the July income tax instalment.
      27   Received $15,000 cash from Connor Productions in partial payment of the invoice issued on July 19.
      30   Declared and paid a $5,000 dividend.

River Consultants records adjustments monthly. Adjustment data for the month of July are as follows:
1. Expiry of insurance coverage (see July 4 transaction)
2. Adjustment of prepaid rent (see July 5 transaction)
3. Supplies used, $1,250 (see July 6 transaction)
4. Equipment depreciation, using the straight-line method of depreciation (see July 6 transaction)
5. Accrual of interest on bank loan (see July 6 transaction)
6. Salaries for the second half of July, $11,000, to be paid on August 1
7. Estimated utilities expense for July, $800 (invoice to be received in August)

Instructions
(a) Record the above transactions.
(b) Set up T accounts, enter any opening balances, and post the general journal entries prepared in part (a).
(c) Prepare a trial balance at July 31.
(d) Record and post the July adjusting journal entries.
(e) Prepare an adjusted trial balance at July 31.
(f) Prepare (1) an income statement, (2) a statement of changes in equity, and (3) a statement of financial position.
(g) Prepare and post the closing journal entries, assuming River closes its books monthly.
(h) River needs to maintain a current ratio of 2:1 in order to maintain its financial standing with its bankers. Calculate the current ratio. Has it achieved the 2-to-1 benchmark?

EXPAND YOUR | CRITICAL THINKING

CT4–1 Financial Reporting Case

The financial statements of **The North West Company Inc.** are presented in Appendix A.

Instructions
(a) Identify two accounts presented on North West's balance sheet at January 31, 2016, or in the accompanying notes to this statement, that may have been used in an adjusting entry for prepayments. Identify the statement of earnings account most likely involved in each adjusting entry.

(b) Identify two accounts presented on North West's balance sheet at January 31, 2016, that may have been used in an adjusting entry for accruals. Identify the statement of earnings account most likely involved in each adjusting entry.

(c) Review Note 3 (c) Revenue Recognition in North West's financial statements. Comment on how North West likely applies the five-step process of revenue recognition with regard to the sale of groceries.

CT4–2 Financial Reporting Case

C Technologies Ltd. provides maintenance service for computers and office equipment. The sales manager is delighted because she closed a $300,000, three-year maintenance contract on December 29, 2017, two days before the company's year end. "Now we will hit this year's net income target for sure," she crowed. The customer is required to pay $100,000 on December 29 (the day the deal was closed). Two more payments of $100,000 each are also required on December 29, 2018, and 2019.

Instructions

Using revenue and expense recognition criteria, discuss the effect that this event will have on the company's financial statements for 2017, 2018, and 2019.

CT4–3 Professional Judgement Case

This case can be assigned as a group activity. Additional instructions and material for this activity can be found on the Instructor Resource site and in WileyPLUS.

Janice Tamagi is the accountant for Thin Dime Ltd., which retails low-priced household products through over 20 retail stores across Canada. The company's year end is December 31 and Janice is preparing the financial statements for the current year end. At this time, tension between management and staff is extremely high because a new collective agreement with the union representing most of the company's retail staff is being negotiated. Management is pleading with the union representatives to reduce their request for a salary increase, claiming that the company simply cannot afford it. Janice showed the draft financial statements with income before income tax of $2.8 million to her boss, Anna Chen, who is the corporate controller. The reported income had increased by 10% compared with the prior year. After reviewing the statements and discussing them with Janice, Anna asked her to do the following:

1. Most of the furniture owned by the company is depreciated over a 12-year life using straight-line depreciation. Depreciation expense this year was $600,000. Anna wants the useful life to be revised to 8 years, which would result in a revised depreciation expense of $900,000. Janice believes that it is possible for these assets to have a useful life of anywhere from 8 to 12 years.

2. One of the company's stores will probably be shut down next spring. The final decision to do so has not yet been made. If the store is to be shut down, severance pay for the employees who work there would be $400,000. Anna would like this amount accrued as salary expense in the current financial statements because it is highly likely to occur.

3. When Janice was preparing the financial statements, there were a few office expenses that related to December that she had not yet received the invoices

for. For example, none of the stores had received their utility bills yet for the month of December. Because the financial statements had to be finalized promptly due to the negotiations with the union, Janice estimated the amounts of these bills and recorded them in December. The total amount of this accrual was $150,000. Anna felt that it was more prudent to accrue $230,000 rather than $150,000 just to be safe.

Instructions

(a) Prepare the journal entries to adjust the financial statements as Anna has proposed.

(b) If Janice records these entries, what will the income before income tax for the current year now be?

(c) Why do you think Anna suggested that the useful life of the furniture be reduced?

(d) Do you think that it is appropriate to accrue an expense for the severance pay related to the possible store closure? Why or why not?

(e) Do you think that the increase in the office expense accrual is justified? Why was it done?

CT4–4 Ethics Case

Sundream Travel Agency Ltd. is a company that sells vacation packages and has a new chief executive officer (CEO) who is reviewing the draft December 31 year-end financial statements prepared by the company's controller. On these statements, the current assets total $400,000 while the current liabilities total $210,000, which results in a current ratio of 1.9:1. Several months ago, the company obtained some new bank financing that requires it to maintain a current ratio of at least 2:1. After reviewing the statements, the CEO suggests that the controller change the financial statements for two transactions.

The first transaction involves a vacation package that was sold to a ski club. The vacation starts in two months' time, in early March, and the club has paid $12,000 in advance for the trip. Because the cash has been received, the CEO suggests that the credit relating to this transaction be shown in revenue.

The second transaction relates to an accrual of $3,000 for December interest expense that is not due until early January. The CEO suggests that this accrual should not be made because the interest is not due until next year.

Instructions

(a) Who are the stakeholders in this situation?

(b) How will agreeing to the CEO's request have an impact on the financial statements?

(c) Is the CEO acting in an ethical manner? Why or why not?

(d) In what way does the existence of accounting standards enhance ethical behaviour?

CT4–5 Financial Reporting Case

First Capital Realty Inc. and the **Skyline Group of Companies** are both real estate investment trusts (REITs). However, First Capital Realty is a public company using IFRS and Skyline is a private company using ASPE. Because First Capital Realty is a publicly traded company, it is required to release quarterly financial statements to its shareholders. Skyline only releases its financial statements annually to its bankers and for the purposes of its annual tax filings.

Instructions

(a) Would you expect there to be any significant differences between the steps in the accounting cycle for each company? Explain.

(b) Based upon what you have read in the first four chapters of this text, identify any reporting differences you would expect to see in the two companies' financial statements.

CT4–6 Serial Case

(*Note*: This is a continuation of the serial case from Chapters 1 through 3.)

Emily reviews the updated trial balance prepared in Chapter 3. She recalls from her introductory accounting class that there are some adjustments that need to be prepared. She gathers up as much information as she can to enable the following adjusting journal entries to be prepared on June 30, 2017, ABC's year end. ABC prepares adjusting entries annually.

1. A count reveals that $600 worth of advertising brochures, recorded in the Supplies account, have been distributed during the month of June.

2. Depreciation, using the straight-line method, is to be recorded on the building for the year. The building was purchased 26 years ago for $165,000 and has an estimated useful life of 30 years. In addition, depreciation of $7,070 is to be recorded on the equipment with a cost of $44,520 for the year. Depreciation of $4,200 is also to be recorded on the company car, recorded in the Vehicles account, for the year. The company car was purchased on January 2 of the current year for $52,500 and no depreciation has been recorded to date.

3. Interest on the bank loan and mortgage payable was last paid on June 25. Interest accrued on the remaining days in the month of June is $50.

4. Six months' worth of the prepaid insurance has expired. This insurance policy was purchased on January 2 for an annual cost of $12,000.

5. At the end of June, electricity on the building, $1,025, was owed and due to be paid by July 14. (*Hint*: Use the Utilities Expense account.)

6. During the last week of June, an unexpected and urgent request for support services was received from Software Solutions. The services were provided and an invoice was prepared for $1,600. This invoice was not included in the accounting records at June 30.

7. Salaries for employees were paid on June 30. There were also two part-time employees who provided additional services to assist ABC in completing the Software Solutions job the last week of June; however, they did not submit their timesheets for that week until the first week of July. They each worked 20 hours and are to be paid $25/hour on the next payday.

8. An additional $5,000 of corporate income tax is estimated to be owed at June 30.

Instructions

(a) Prepare the adjusting journal entries required at June 30.

(b) Post the adjusting journal entries prepared in part (a) to the T accounts updated in CT3–6 in Chapter 3.

(c) Prepare an adjusted trial balance at June 30, 2017.

(d) Calculate the amount of net income ABC would report for the year ended June 30. How does this amount compare with the cash the company reports at June 30?

▶ ANSWERS TO CHAPTER PRACTICE QUESTIONS

(a)	Revenue using the cash basis of accounting	$125,000
(b)	Cash received from customers in 2018	$125,000
	Deduct: Collection of 2017 receivables (revenue recorded in 2017)	(30,000)
	Add: Amounts owing by customers at December 31, 2018	19,500
	Revenue using the accrual basis of accounting	$114,500

DO IT! 4-1a
Accrual and Cash Basis Accounting

1.	Accrual basis accounting	(j)	6.	Fiscal year	(d)
2.	Adjusted trial balance	(h)	7.	Interim periods	(a)
3.	Adjusting entries	(i)	8.	Prepayments	(g)
4.	Cash basis accounting	(c)	9.	Revenue recognition	(e)
5.	Expense recognition	(b)	10.	Unadjusted trial balance	(f)

DO IT! 4-1b
Timing Concepts

2018

1.	(a)	Mar. 1	Prepaid Rent	3,600	
			Cash		3,600
	(b)	31	Rent Expense ($3,600 ÷ 3)	1,200	
			Prepaid Rent		1,200

DO IT! 4-2a
Adjusting Entries for Prepaid Expenses

(c)

Prepaid Rent			
Mar. 1	3,600		
		Mar. 31 Adj.	1,200
Bal.	2,400		

Rent Expense			
Mar. 31 Adj.	1,200		

Check: Unexpired prepaid rent for the two months of April and May remains at March 31: $1,200 × 2 = $2,400

Check: Rent for one month was incurred at March 31: $1,200

		2018				
2.	(a)	Mar. 2	Supplies		1,800	
			Cash			1,800
	(b)	31	Supplies Expense ($1,800 − $800)		1,000	
			Supplies			1,000

(c)

Supplies					Supplies Expense		
Mar. 2	1,800				Mar. 31 Adj.	1,000	
		Mar. 31 Adj.	1,000				
Bal.	800						

Check: $800 of supplies are remaining at March 31 for future use

Check: $1,000 of supplies were used in the month of March

		2016				
3.	(a)	Apr. 1	Equipment		24,000	
			Cash			24,000
		2018				
	(b)	Mar. 31	Depreciation Expense		250	
			Accumulated Depreciation—			
			Equipment ($24,000 ÷ 8 × $^{1}/_{12}$)			250

(c)

Equipment					Depreciation Expense		
Apr. 1	24,000				Mar. 31 Adj.	250	

Accumulated Depreciation—Equipment			
		Bal.	5,750
		Mar. 31 Adj.	250
		Bal.	6,000

Check: At March 31, two years of accumulated depreciation should have been recorded (April 1, 2016 − March 31, 2018). $24,000 ÷ 8 years = $3,000 × 2 years = $6,000

Check: One month of depreciation of $250 was recorded in March.

DO IT! 4-2b
Adjusting Entries for Prepayments

(a)	Central Shopping Ltd. (landlord)				
	Sept. 1	Cash ($1,200 + $1,200)		2,400	
		Unearned Revenue			2,400
	30	Unearned Revenue		1,200	
		Rent Revenue			1,200
(b)	Joseph's Bakery Ltd. (tenant)				
	Sept. 1	Prepaid Rent ($1,200 + $1,200)		2,400	
		Cash			2,400
	30	Rent Expense		1,200	
		Prepaid Rent			1,200

DO IT! 4-3a
Adjusting Entries for Accrued Expenses

(a)	July 1, 2018	Cash		30,000	
		Bank Loan Payable			30,000
	July 31, 2018	Interest Expense ($30,000 × 5% × $^{1}/_{12}$)		125	
		Interest Payable			125
	Aug. 1, 2018	Interest Payable		125	
		Cash			125
	July 1, 2019	Interest Expense ($30,000 × 5% × $^{1}/_{12}$)		125	
		Bank Loan Payable		30,000	
		Cash			30,125

Note: Since adjusting entries are only recorded annually, interest would not have been accrued on June 30, 2019, as would have been the case if adjusting entries were recorded monthly. Note that only one month of interest is owed at July 1 because interest is paid monthly and would have been paid last on June 1, 2019.

(b)	July 31	Salaries Expense ($800 × 2 days)		1,600	
		Salaries Payable			1,600
	Aug. 6	Salaries Payable ($800 × 2 days)		1,600	
		Salaries Expense ($800 × 3 days)		2,400	
		Cash			4,000

(c)	July 31	Income Tax Expense	275	
		Income Tax Payable		275
	Aug. 15	Income Tax Payable	275	
		Cash		275

(a) 1.	Aug. 31	Accounts Receivable	1,100	
		Service Revenue		1,100
2.	Aug. 31	Interest Receivable ($10,000 × 6% × $\frac{1}{12}$)	50	
		Interest Revenue		50
(b)	Sept. 1	Cash	50	
		Interest Receivable		50

DO IT! 4-3b
Adjusting Entries for
Accrued Revenues

(a) and (b)

DO IT! 4-4
Adjusted Trial Balance

KS SERVICES LIMITED
Adjusted Trial Balance
December 31, 2018

	Debit	Credit	Statement
Cash	$ 1,100		SFP
Accounts receivable	9,600		SFP
Supplies	180		SFP
Equipment	20,800		SFP
Accumulated depreciation—equipment		$ 5,200	SFP
Accounts payable		4,660	SFP
Salaries payable		710	SFP
Unearned revenue		1,010	SFP
Bank loan payable		1,000	SFP
Common shares		5,000	SFP & SCE
Retained earnings		3,700	SCE
Dividends declared	1,000		SCE
Service revenue		67,200	IS
Salaries expense	30,700		IS
Rent expense	16,800		IS
Depreciation expense	2,600		IS
Other expenses	1,675		IS
Supplies expense	475		IS
Interest expense	50		IS
Income tax expense	3,500		IS
	$88,480	$88,480	

(c) Revenues − Expenses = Net income
$67,200 − ($30,700 + $16,800 + $2,600 + $1,675 + $475 + $50 + $3,500) = $11,400

(d) Total assets = $1,100 + $9,600 + $180 + $20,800 − $5,200 = $26,480
Total liabilities = $4,660 + $710 + $1,010 + $1,000 = $7,380
Total shareholders' equity = $5,000 + ($3,700 + $11,400 (from (c)) − $1,000) = $19,100

(e) Assets = Liabilities + Shareholders' Equity
$26,480 = $7,380 + $19,100

(a) Revenues − Expenses = Net income
$18,000 − ($1,500 + $500 + $8,000 + $1,000) = $7,000
Beginning retained earnings + Net income − Dividends declared = Ending retained earnings
$12,000 + $7,000 − $700 = $18,300

DO IT! 4-5
Closing Entries

(b)	Dec. 31	Service Revenue	18,000	
		Income Summary		18,000
		(To close revenue account)		
	31	Income Summary	11,000	
		Rent Expense		1,500
		Supplies Expense		500
		Salaries Expense		8,000
		Income Tax Expense		1,000
		(To close expense accounts)		
	31	Income Summary	7,000	
		Retained Earnings		7,000
		(To close income summary)		

(b)   (Continued)

Dec. 31	Retained Earnings	700	
	Dividends Declared		700
	(To close dividends)		

(c)   The Income Summary account would not appear in the post-closing trial balance because this account has a zero balance and accounts with zero balances are not normally included in trial balances. The Retained Earnings account would appear in the post-closing trial balance as a credit of $18,300.

Income Summary			
	11,000		18,000
CE	7,000	Bal.	7,000
		End. bal.	0

Retained Earnings			
		Beg. bal.	12,000
CE	700	CE	7,000
		End. bal.	18,300

▶ PRACTICE USING THE DECISION TOOLKIT

Let's apply the five steps of revenue recognition criteria to this situation:

Step 1: Identify the contract with the client or customer.	Best Buy sold a gift card to Robert Jacobs and promises that the card can be redeemed in exchange for up to $100 of merchandise purchased at Best Buy.
Step 2: Identify the performance obligations in the contract.	Best Buy has only one performance obligation—to provide merchandise up to a value of $100 when the card is presented.
Step 3: Determine the transaction price.	The transaction price is $100.
Step 4: Allocate the transaction price to the performance obligations in the contract.	In this case, Best Buy has only one performance obligation and the transaction price does not require allocation.
Step 5: Recognize revenue when (or as) the company satisfies the performance obligation.	Best Buy recognizes revenue of $100 when it satisfies the performance obligation—the provision of the merchandise on January 3.

In this particular case, revenue should be recorded when Best Buy provides the merchandise to its customer, Laurel. Although the transaction price was determined when the gift card was sold, the performance effort is not complete until the merchandise is sold. It is also at that time that the expense would be incurred to generate the revenue.

Thus, when Best Buy receives cash in exchange for the gift card on December 24, it should debit (increase) an asset, Cash, and credit (increase) a liability, Unearned Revenue, for $100. On January 3, when Laurel exchanges the card for merchandise, Best Buy should recognize revenue and eliminate the balance in the Unearned Revenue account by debiting Unearned Revenue and crediting Sales Revenue for $100.

Note that if Laurel had used the card on January 3 to purchase only $75 of merchandise, Best Buy would only record $75 of revenue on that date and the gift card would still be available for Laurel to purchase an additional $25 of merchandise at a future date.

Best Buy sells a significant number of gift cards and reported unearned revenue from the sale of gift cards of U.S. $409 million in a recent year.

▶ PRACTICE COMPREHENSIVE DO IT!

(a)   Adjusting Journal Entries

Mar. 31	Supplies Expense	6,800	
	Supplies		6,800
	(To record supplies used: $8,000 − $1,200)		
31	Insurance Expense	150	
	Prepaid Insurance		150
	(To record insurance expired: ($1,800 × $\frac{1}{12}$)		
31	Depreciation Expense	5,000	
	Accumulated Depreciation—Equipment		5,000
	(To record annual depreciation: $25,000 ÷ 5 = $5,000)		
31	Interest Expense	50	
	Interest Payable		50
	(To accrue interest on the bank loan: ($10,000 × 6% × $\frac{1}{12}$)		

(a)   (Continued)

Mar. 31	Unearned Revenue	1,050	
	Service Revenue		1,050
	(To record revenue earned: $300 ÷ 2 mos. × 7)		
31	Accounts Receivable	1,500	
	Service Revenue		1,500
	(To accrue revenue earned but not billed or collected)		
31	Salaries Expense	1,000	
	Salaries Payable		1,000
	(To record salaries owed)		
31	Income Tax Expense	250	
	Income Tax Payable		250
	(To accrue income tax payable)		

(b)   General Ledger (partial)

Accounts Receivable

Mar. 31	10,000	
31 Adj.	1,500	
Bal.	11,500	

Supplies

Mar. 31	8,000		
		Mar. 31 Adj.	6,800
Bal.	1,200		

Prepaid Insurance

Mar. 31	1,800		
		Mar. 31 Adj.	150
Bal.	1,650		

Equipment

| Mar. 31 | 25,000 | |

Accumulated Depreciation—Equipment

		Mar. 31	5,000
		31 Adj.	5,000
		Bal.	10,000

Bank Loan Payable

| | | Mar. 31 | 10,000 |

Salaries Payable

| | | Mar. 31 Adj. | 1,000 |

Unearned Revenue

		Mar. 31	3,150
Mar. 31 Adj.	1,050		
		Bal.	2,100

Interest Payable

| | | Mar. 31 Adj. | 50 |

Income Tax Payable

| | | Mar. 31 Adj. | 250 |

Retained Earnings

| | | Mar. 31 | 37,000 |

Service Revenue

		Mar. 31	102,800
		31 Adj.	1,050
		31 Adj.	1,500
		Bal.	105,350

Supplies Expense

| Mar. 31 Adj. | 6,800 | |

Insurance Expense

| Mar. 31 Adj. | 150 | |

Depreciation Expense

| Mar. 31 Adj. | 5,000 | |

Interest Expense

Mar. 31	550	
31 Adj.	50	
Bal.	600	

Salaries Expense

Mar. 31	50,000	
31 Adj.	1,000	
Bal.	51,000	

Income Tax Expense

Mar. 31	9,600	
31 Adj.	250	
Bal.	9,850	

(c)   Permanent accounts: Accounts Receivable, Supplies, Prepaid Insurance, Equipment, Accumulated Depreciation—Equipment, Bank Loan Payable, Salaries Payable, Unearned Revenue, Interest Payable, Income Tax Payable, and Retained Earnings. Temporary accounts: Service Revenue, Supplies Expense, Insurance Expense, Depreciation Expense, Interest Expense, Salaries Expense, and Income Tax Expense.

(d)   The $37,000 in the Retained Earnings account is the opening balance as at April 1, 2017. This balance will not change until closing journal entries for the revenue and expense accounts are prepared and posted.

▶ PRACTICE OBJECTIVE-FORMAT QUESTIONS

1.   (b) and (e) are correct.

Feedback

Huahine Law would debit Accounts Receivable and credit Service Revenue in the month of March, when the performance obligation had been satisfied. In April, it would debit Cash and credit Accounts Receivable when the cash was received from Papeete. No transaction has occurred in February so no entry would be made in that month.

Papeete would debit Legal Fees Expense and credit Accounts Payable in the month of March when the work had been completed and it received the invoice. In April, it would debit Accounts Payable and credit Cash when the invoice was paid. No transaction has occurred in February so no entry would be made in that month.

2.   (d) and (e) are false.

Feedback

(a), (b), (c), (f), and (g) are correct.

(d)   Recording revenue and expenses only when cash is received or paid describes the cash basis of accounting, which is not permitted in Canada.

(e)   Companies must use accrual-based accounting, regardless of their size.

(g)   This statement is correct even though expense recognition cannot always be linked to revenue recognition. Recall from the chapter that it is not always possible to directly associate expenses with revenue. Examples include interest expense and depreciation expense.

3.   (a) and (d) are correct.

Feedback

(a)   Adjusting entries for prepaid expenses increase an expense account and decrease an asset account. If such an entry was not recorded, then expenses would be understated (less than they should be), net income overstated (because expenses are less than they should be), assets overstated (more than they should be), and shareholders' equity overstated (because net income is overstated, which in turn overstates retained earnings).

(b)   Adjusting entries for unearned revenue decrease a liability (Unearned Revenue) account and increase a revenue account. If such an entry was not recorded, then liabilities would be overstated (more than they should be) and revenues understated (less than they should be). Net income would also be understated (because revenues are understated) as would shareholders' equity (because net income is understated, which in turn understates retained earnings).

(c)   Adjusting entries for accrued revenues increase an asset (receivable) account and a revenue account. If such an entry was not recorded, then assets and revenues would be understated (less than they should be). Net income would also be understated (because revenues are understated) as would shareholders' equity (because net income is understated, which in turn understates retained earnings). However, there would be **no** effect on expenses.

(d)   Adjusting entries for accrued expenses increase an expense account and a liability (payable) account. If such an entry was not recorded, then expenses and liabilities would both be understated (less than they should be). Net income would be overstated (because expenses are understated) and shareholders' equity overstated (because net income is overstated, which in turn overstates retained earnings).

4.

	(a)	(b)			(a)	(b)	
1.	Yes	P	Accumulated Depreciation	6.	Yes	P	Prepaid Insurance
2.	No	P	Cash	7.	No	P	Retained Earnings
3.	No	T	Dividends Declared	8.	Yes	T	Salaries Expense
4.	Yes	P	Income Tax Payable	9.	Yes	P	Unearned Revenue
5.	Yes	P	Interest Receivable				

Feedback

(a)   Adjusting entries for prepayments would affect the Accumulated Depreciation (Depreciation Expense), Prepaid Insurance (Insurance Expense), and Unearned Revenue (Revenue) accounts. Adjusting entries for accruals would affect the Income Tax Payable (Income Tax Expense), Interest Receivable (Interest Revenue), and Salaries Payable (Salaries Expense) accounts. The remaining accounts (Cash, Dividends Declared, and Retained Earnings) are not directly involved in the adjustment process.

(b)   Accumulated Depreciation, Cash, Income Tax Payable, Interest Receivable, Prepaid Insurance, Retained Earnings, and Unearned Revenue are all statement of financial position accounts and are considered to be permanent accounts. That is, their balances are not closed to zero at the end of the accounting period as is the case with temporary accounts. Dividends Declared and Salaries Expense are temporary accounts, whose balances are transferred into Retained Earnings at the end of the accounting period.

5.

I	Assets
NE	Liabilities
I	Shareholders' equity
I	Revenues
NE	Expenses
I	Net income

Feedback

An adjusting entry to record accrued revenue would debit (increase) an asset (receivable) account and credit (increase) a revenue account. Net income (revenues – expenses) would increase because revenues increase while expenses remain unchanged. Shareholders' equity would increase because net income increases, which in turn increases Retained Earnings, a shareholders' equity account.

6.

NE	Assets
I	Liabilities
D	Shareholders' equity
NE	Revenues
I	Expenses
D	Net income

Feedback

An adjusting entry to record an accrued expense would debit (increase) an expense account and credit (increase) a liability account. Net income (revenues – expenses) would decrease because expenses increase while revenues remain unchanged. Shareholders' equity would decrease because net income decreases, which in turn decreases Retained Earnings, a shareholders' equity account.

7.   (a), (c), and (f) are incorrect.

Feedback

(a)   Companies prepare three trial balances: an unadjusted trial balance (often known as just the "trial balance"), an adjusted trial balance, and a post-closing trial balance.

(c)   The post-closing trial balance cannot be used to prepare financial statements because it does not include any temporary accounts (revenues, expenses, dividends declared). Rather, the adjusted trial balance would be used to prepare financial statements.

(f)   Even if debits equal credits, errors can occur. An entire journal entry might be unrecorded or not posted, an equal debit and credit error might be made, or an entry with the correct amount might be recorded in the wrong account, in addition to other possibilities. As long as debits equal credits, you have some assurance that most errors have been caught, but not all.

8.   (b), (c), (d), and (e) are correct.

Feedback

(a)   is incorrect because retained earnings in the adjusted trial balance should equal beginning retained earnings (before revenues, expenses, and dividends declared have been closed into retained earnings). Retained earnings is $25,000 in the adjusted trial balance.

(b)   is correct because retained earnings in the post-closing trial balance would be $25,000 + $33,000 − $26,000 − $1,000 = $31,000.

(c)   is correct because shareholders' equity, beginning of period = $45,000 common shares + $25,000 retained earnings = $70,000.

(d)   is correct because shareholders' equity, end of period = $45,000 common shares + ($25,000 + $33,000 − $26,000 − $1,000) retained earnings = $76,000.

(e)   is correct because the Dividends Declared account is included in the unadjusted and adjusted trial balances. It is included in the trial balances until the account is closed and has a zero balance.

(f)   is incorrect because the balance in the Dividends Declared account should be zero in the post-closing trial balance because it is a temporary account whose balance is closed (transferred) into the Retained Earnings account.

9.   (e), (g), and (i) are temporary accounts and will have a zero balance after closing.

Feedback

(a), (b), (c), (d), (f), (h), and (j) are permanent accounts and not closed. Retained Earnings is involved in the closing process but only to be updated for revenues, expenses, and dividends declared for the period; it is not closed.

10.

6	Prepare an adjusted trial balance.
8	Journalize and post closing entries.
3	Post transaction entries to general ledger accounts.
4	Prepare an unadjusted trial balance.
7	Prepare financial statements.
1	Analyze business transactions.
5	Journalize and post adjusting entries.
9	Prepare a post-closing trial balance.
2	Journalize the transactions.

▶ ENDNOTE

[1] The University of Western Ontario Combined Financial Statements, April 30, 2015; "Facts & Figures 2013–14," university website, www.uwo.ca.

5

Merchandising Operations

CHAPTER PREVIEW

The first four chapters of this text focused primarily on service companies, like the fictional Sierra Corporation. In this and the next chapter, we turn our attention to merchandising companies. Merchandising is one of the largest and most influential industries in Canada. Merchandising companies such as Loblaw Companies Limited generate the majority of their profit from buying and selling merchandise rather than performing services. In this chapter, you will learn the basics of accounting for merchandising transactions. You will also learn how to prepare and analyze the income statement for a merchandising company.

CHAPTER OUTLINE

LEARNING OBJECTIVES	READ	PRACTICE
1 Identify the differences between service and merchandising companies.	• Income measurement process • Inventory systems	**DO IT!** 5-1 Inventory calculations
2 Prepare entries for purchases under a perpetual inventory system.	• Purchases • Summary of purchase transactions	**DO IT!** 5-2 Purchase transactions
3 Prepare entries for sales under a perpetual inventory system.	• Sales • Summary of sales transactions	**DO IT!** 5-3 Purchase and sales transactions—perpetual inventory system
4 Prepare a single-step and a multiple-step income statement.	• Single-step income statement • Multiple-step income statement	**DO IT!** 5-4 Multiple-step income statement amounts
5 Calculate the gross profit margin and profit margin.	• Gross profit margin • Profit margin	**DO IT!** 5-5 Calculating and evaluating profitability
6 Account for and report inventory in a periodic inventory system (Appendix 5A).	• Recording purchases of merchandise • Recording sales of merchandise • Calculating cost of goods sold • Adjusting entry at period end • Comparison of entries: perpetual vs. periodic • Income statement	**DO IT!** 5-6 Purchase and sales transactions—periodic inventory system

FEATURE STORY

Going with the Flow

Loblaw Companies Limited, Canada's largest retailer, has more than 2,300 corporate and franchised stores across the country. Its banners include the Loblaws grocery chain, Shoppers Drug Mart pharmacy chain, and Joe Fresh clothing line. With thousands of products, including those from its own labels such as President's Choice, "no name," and Life brand, managing inventory—much of which is perishable—is key to operations.

Historically, Loblaw's supply chain—the process of getting products from suppliers to store shelves—was based on a "stock and ship" model, which focused on product storage. Inventory was replenished based on warehouse shipment data. In other words, Loblaw used historical information to plan future shipments. This sometimes resulted in the company's warehouses overflowing while its store shelves were understocked. By the time a tub of yogourt appeared in a store dairy case, for example, it could already be two thirds of the way toward its best-before date. The company estimated that its outdated supply chain process resulted in tens of millions of dollars in lost sales because some competitors could get food to customers faster, fresher, and cheaper.

In 2007, Loblaw launched a five-year, multimillion-dollar plan to transform its supply chain from "stock and ship" to a "flow" model, where products would be ordered, stored, shipped, and shelved based on customer demand. The company also created a national supply chain with regional logistics centres, reduced the number of distribution centres, and created a single warehouse management system.

The company worked closely with suppliers, who can now package and ship items that are ready to be shelved without the need for warehouse staff to repackage and relabel them. This transformation isn't just for perishables, as Loblaw also improved how it manages inventory sold under its Joe Fresh clothing brand. It's important to stock the latest styles, which are constantly changing.

Loblaw continues to improve its supply chain, which grew even larger after it acquired Shoppers Drug Mart in 2013. For example, in 2015, Loblaw completed the rollout of one information technology system for all its food banners, which include the Real Canadian Superstore and No Frills. The company is using the system to try to reduce the amount of inventory it carries. The system will also help management see which products and categories are the biggest money-makers and money-losers. Loblaw says that some competitors' supply chains are so efficient, they lead to 20% higher profitability than Loblaw. In its 2015 annual report, the company said that its goal with supply chain improvement is to make its 27 distribution centres "part of the most responsive and customer-centric supply chain in North America."

The new IT system allowed Loblaw to move to a perpetual inventory system that can track the value of its inventory in real time. At the end of 2015, its inventory was valued at more than $4.3 billion, accounting for almost half of the company's current assets.

Loblaw has spent millions on investments in information technology and its supply chain. But the retailer has seen a strong return on investment. It estimates it saves up to $5 million a year thanks to improvements in such areas as labour efficiency, which increased by 5%. The company also reduced receiving time by approximately 25%, resulting in fresher products on its grocery stores' shelves. Having fresher items not only increases sales to customers wanting better-tasting food, but it also reduces shrinkage—the loss of inventory that plagues every retailer's bottom line—due to expired items that can no longer be sold.[1]

Go to the *REVIEW AND PRACTICE* section at the end of the chapter for a targeted summary and practice questions with solutions.

Visit **WileyPLUS** for more practice opportunities.

LEARNING OBJECTIVE ▶ 1

Identify the differences between service and merchandising companies.

Merchandising involves purchasing products (inventory) to resell to customers. Inventory for a merchandising company can consist of many different items. For example, in a Loblaws store, fresh fruit, canned goods, President's Choice frozen entrees, Joe Fresh clothes, cosmetics, and medications are just a few of the inventory items on hand. These items have two common characteristics: (1) the company owns them, and (2) they are in a form ready for sale to customers. Items with these characteristics are classified as **merchandise inventory** or just inventory.

Merchandising companies that purchase and sell directly to consumers are called **retailers**. Merchandising companies that sell to retailers are known as **wholesalers**. Companies that produce goods for sale to wholesalers (or others) are called **manufacturers**.

A manufacturing company also owns inventory, but differs from a merchandising company in that some of its inventory may not yet be ready for sale. This inventory is at some stage of the production process. As a result, manufacturing companies usually classify inventory into three categories: raw materials, work in process, and finished goods. **Raw materials** are the basic goods and materials that are on hand and will be used in production but have not yet been sent into production. **Work in process** is that portion of inventory on which production has started but is not yet complete. **Finished goods** inventory is manufactured items that are completed and ready for sale. Our focus in this chapter is primarily on merchandise inventory. Manufacturing inventory will be discussed in more detail in a managerial accounting course.

The steps in the **accounting cycle** for a merchandising company are the same as the steps for a service company. However, the **operating cycle**—the time it takes to go from cash to cash in producing revenues—is usually longer for a merchandising company than it is for a service company. You will recall that you were introduced to the operating cycle in Chapter 2. In a service company, the company performs services for cash or for an account receivable (which eventually results in cash when the account receivable is collected). In a merchandising company, the company first has to purchase merchandise for cash or on account (which it must pay) before it can sell it for cash or an account receivable. Often the merchandise must be held in stores or warehouses for a period of time before it is sold. Consequently, the operating cycle for a merchandising company covers the time between buying the inventory on account from suppliers and collecting the cash from its customers that buy the inventory.

KEEPING AN EYE ON CASH

A short operating cycle implies that a company needs to finance its inventory and accounts receivable for only a short period of time. Merchandising companies like The North West Company do a significant portion of cash sales. Thus they have greater liquidity and their operating cycles are shorter than those of companies that sell on account. A long operating cycle indicates lower liquidity; thus less cash is available at any point in time. The lower the liquidity, the longer the period of time over which a company must finance its inventory and accounts receivable.

Examples of operating cycles for three companies in different industries (a grocer, a book retailer, and an aerospace manufacturer) are presented below:

The North West Company Inc.	33.5 days
Indigo Books & Music Inc.	60.0 days
Bombardier Inc.	105.6 days

As a grocer, The North West Company has the shortest operating cycle because it is able to sell its inventory quickly and many of its sales are cash sales. While Indigo carries a significant level of inventory, which lengthens its operating cycle, the company has also been able to delay paying for these goods, so that its operating cycle is 60 days. As a manufacturer of aircraft and trains, Bombardier's operating cycle is even longer given the time required to manufacture these items, deliver them to customers, and receive payment.

INCOME MEASUREMENT PROCESS

Measuring net income for a merchandising company is basically the same as for a service company. That is, net income (or loss) is equal to revenues less expenses. In a merchandising company, the main source of revenue is from the sale of merchandise, which is often referred to simply as **sales revenue** or just sales. As we learned in Chapter 1, revenue is also called "income," especially by international companies that operate outside of Canada.

Expenses for a merchandising company are normally divided into two categories: (1) cost of goods sold and (2) operating expenses. This enables management and other financial statement users to easily monitor sales revenue relative to the cost of the goods that have been sold. Merchandising companies must ensure that they are making a sufficient income from the sale of goods to cover their other costs (such as salaries, rent, utilities, and the like) and provide a return to shareholders. Some merchandising companies may also have non-operating revenues and expenses, which we will learn about later in the chapter.

The **cost of goods sold** is the total cost of the merchandise that was sold during the period. This expense is directly related to the revenue that is recognized from the sale of goods. Sales revenue less the cost of goods sold is called **gross profit**. For example, Loblaw reported sales revenue of $45,394 million for the year ended December 29, 2015. It cost Loblaw $32,846 million to purchase this merchandise to sell (cost of goods sold), so the company earned a gross profit of $12,548 million ($45,394 million – $32,846 million) on these sales.

After gross profit is calculated, operating expenses are deducted to determine income before income tax. **Operating expenses** are expenses that are incurred in the process of earning sales revenue. The operating expenses of a merchandising company include many of the same expenses found in a service company, such as salaries, insurance, utilities, and depreciation.

Then, as is done for a service company, income tax expense is deducted from income before income tax to determine net income (loss). The income measurement process for a merchandising company, assuming it has no non-operating revenues or expenses, is shown in Illustration 5-1. The items in the two blue boxes are unique to a merchandising company; a service company does not use them. Also note that, in a service company, revenue is known as "service revenue" rather than "sales revenue."

Alternative Terminology
Gross profit is also called gross margin.

▶Illustration 5-1

Income measurement process for a merchandising company

Sales Revenue
− Cost of Goods Sold
= Gross Profit
− Operating Expenses
= Income (Loss) Before Income Tax
− Income Tax Expense
= Net Income (Loss)

INVENTORY SYSTEMS

A merchandising company manages its inventory so that management can determine what goods are available for sale (inventory) and what goods have been sold (cost of goods sold). This information may be available in dollars, number of units, or both. In terms of dollars, the flow of costs for a merchandising company is as follows:

The cost of the inventory on hand at the beginning of the period + cost of goods purchased during the period = the total cost of all of the goods that were available for sale during the period.

In accounting terms, *beginning inventory* plus the *cost of goods purchased* equals the *cost of goods available for sale*. As goods are sold, they are assigned to *cost of goods sold*. (We will learn how to assign these costs in Chapter 6.) Those goods that are not sold by the end of the accounting period represent what's left, or in accounting terms, *ending inventory*. Ending inventory (unsold goods) is reported as inventory, a current asset on the statement of financial position. The cost of goods sold (goods sold) is reported as an expense on the income statement (cost of goods sold). It is useful to remember that inventory can be in only one of two places: the company still has it (ending inventory) or it does not because it has been sold (cost of goods sold).

Illustration 5-2 describes these relationships.

One of two systems is used to account for inventory and the cost of goods sold: a **perpetual inventory system** or a **periodic inventory system**.

Perpetual Inventory System

In a **perpetual inventory system**, detailed records are maintained for the cost of each product that is purchased and sold. These records continuously—perpetually—show the quantity and cost of

►Illustration 5-2
Flow of costs for a
merchandising company

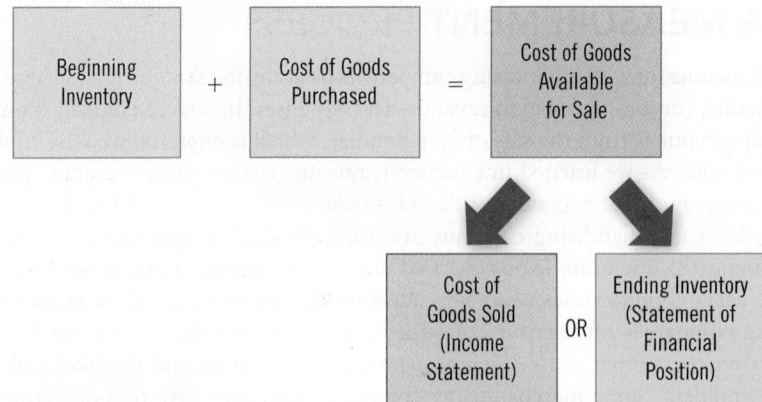

the inventory purchased, sold, and on hand. For example, an automotive dealership keeps separate inventory records for each car, truck, and van on its lot and showroom floor.

When inventory items are purchased under a perpetual inventory system, the purchase is recorded by debiting (increasing) Inventory. Whenever inventory is sold, the cost of those goods is obtained from the inventory system. This cost is transferred from the account Inventory (an asset) to the account Cost of Goods Sold (an expense). **Under a perpetual inventory system, the cost of goods sold and the reduction in inventory—both its quantity and cost—are recorded each time a sale occurs.** As a result, management knows the gross profit on each sale and for the period as a whole. In addition, the Inventory account is always up to date and reflects the cost and quantity of inventory on hand. This helps make it possible for management to monitor merchandise availability and maintain optimum inventory levels.

Inventory is usually the largest current asset for a merchandiser, as is the case with Loblaw Companies Limited in our feature story. The constant updating of inventory records that is a feature of perpetual inventory systems significantly enhances management's control over this important asset, which is one reason why Loblaw recently adopted a perpetual inventory system. Since the inventory records show the quantities that should be on hand, the merchandise can be counted at any time to see whether the amount actually on hand matches the inventory records. Any differences that are found can be investigated and adjusted, if required.

To adjust for any inventory shortages, the Cost of Goods Sold account would be debited and the Inventory account credited. Although the "missing" inventory has not been sold, the Cost of Goods Sold account is debited because inventory losses are considered part of the cost of selling the goods. The missing inventory must be removed from the Inventory account so that the account reflects the actual amount on hand.

For control purposes, a physical inventory count is always taken at least once a year and ideally more often, under the perpetual inventory system. We will learn more about counting inventory in the next chapter.

ACCOUNTING MATTERS

Managing Merchandise on Hand

The retail industry has always had to contend with unpredictable customer demand. The rise of social media has made inventory management even more challenging. In early 2016, for example, a Facebook post that went viral caused some Canadian grocers to run out of French's ketchup. A man in Orillia, Ontario, researched the ketchup and discovered that French's had picked up where Heinz had left off. Heinz stopped producing its ketchup in Canada, and the plant it left behind in Leamington, Ontario, was taken over by a private group that started making tomato paste used in French's ketchup. Brian Fernandez praised French's on Facebook for using Canadian ingredients, and his post was viewed thousands of times, with many people vowing to switch their ketchup loyalty to French's. The unexpected consumer frenzy caught several retailers unawares, including Walmart, which ran out of French's ketchup. Meanwhile, Loblaw Companies Limited had announced that it would stop selling French's ketchup due to low sales, but the social media support for the brand caused the retailer to reverse its decision.[2]

Periodic Inventory System

In a **periodic inventory system**, detailed inventory records of the merchandise on hand are not kept throughout the period. As a result, **the cost of goods sold is determined only at the end of the accounting period**—that is, periodically—when a physical inventory count is done to determine the cost of the goods on hand. The physical inventory count determines the quantities on hand, and then costs are assigned to these quantities. As was mentioned earlier, we will learn how to assign costs to quantities in Chapter 6.

In a periodic inventory system, the cost of the goods on hand (ending inventory) must be determined before we can calculate the cost of the goods sold. To determine the cost of goods sold under a periodic inventory system, the following steps are necessary:

1. Beginning inventory: Determine the cost of goods on hand at the beginning of the accounting period (beginning inventory). Note that this is equal to the previous accounting period's ending inventory.
2. Cost of goods available for sale: Add the cost of goods purchased (purchases) during the period to the beginning inventory. The total is the **cost of goods available for sale** during the period.
3. Ending inventory: Determine the cost of goods on hand at the end of the accounting period (ending inventory) from the physical inventory count. Subtract the ending inventory from the cost of goods available for sale. The result is the cost of goods sold.

Illustration 5-3 shows these relationships. Illustration 5-3 is similar to Illustration 5-2. The key difference is that, in a periodic inventory system, cost of goods sold is a residual number, determined by subtracting ending inventory from cost of goods available for sale. This means that any goods not included in ending inventory are assumed to have been sold. As discussed previously, this may not be the case, because goods may instead have been stolen. While theft can be easily quantified under a perpetual inventory system, it cannot be under a periodic inventory system.

How do companies decide whether to use a perpetual or periodic inventory system? They compare the cost of the detailed record keeping that is required for a perpetual inventory system with the benefits of having the additional information about, and control over, their inventory. The widespread availability of computerized perpetual inventory software and optical scanners has enabled the majority of companies to enjoy the benefits of perpetual inventory systems at a reasonable cost.

Some small businesses find it unnecessary or uneconomical to invest in a perpetual inventory system. Managers of these businesses can, in most cases, find other ways to control merchandise and manage day-to-day operations using a periodic inventory system.

▶Illustration 5-3
Determining cost of goods sold under a periodic inventory system

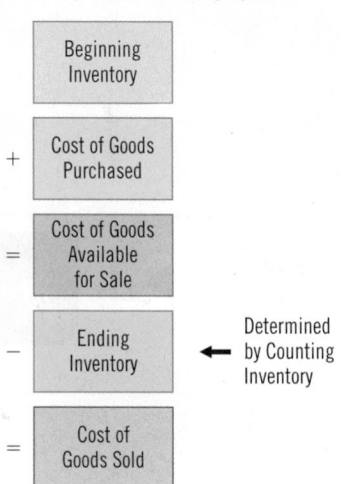

Advantages of Each Type of Inventory System	
Perpetual Inventory System	**Periodic Inventory System**
Provides up-to-date information on ending inventory and cost of goods sold.	Is less expensive in terms of cost of equipment and systems needed for inventory system.
Enables companies to establish automatic reordering based on predetermined minimum inventory levels.	Is simpler.
Enables companies to quantify the cost of goods lost to theft.	
Reduces the need for frequent inventory counts, saving salary costs and lost sales from closing the business to count inventory.	

Because the perpetual inventory system is widely used, we illustrate it in this chapter. The periodic inventory system is described in the appendix to this chapter.

DO IT! ▶5-1   Inventory Calculations

Maritime Audio Limited has 10 home audio systems on hand at January 1. Each unit cost $325. Maritime purchased 20 systems during the year for a total cost of $7,000. Twenty-five systems were sold during the year at a selling price of $579 each. According to the company's perpetual inventory system, the company had sold all of the systems that were on hand at the beginning of the year and 15 of the systems purchased during the year.

(a) Determine the following amounts in both units and dollars:
1. Beginning inventory on January 1
2. Cost of goods purchased during the year
3. Cost of goods sold
4. Ending inventory on December 31

(b) When company staff counted inventory at the close of business on December 31, there were five home audio systems on hand. Does this agree with your calculations in part (a)?

SOLUTION
Try this Do It! exercise on your own and then check your answer at the end of the chapter.

Related Exercise Material: BE5–1, BE5–2, and E5–1.

LEARNING OBJECTIVE ▶ 2   **Prepare entries for purchases under a perpetual inventory system.**

Purchases of merchandise for resale are recorded in the Inventory account in a perpetual inventory system. The purchase cost is increased by freight costs in certain circumstances and decreased by any purchase returns, allowances, and discounts. The net result of all of these costs is known as the **cost of goods purchased**. We will discuss each of these components of the cost of goods purchased in the next sections.

PURCHASES

Inventory purchases can be made for cash or credit (on account). The buyer normally records purchases when the goods are transferred from the seller to the buyer. Documentation, whether written or electronic, should support every purchase as evidence of the transaction. Invoices, purchase orders, receiving documents, and receipts are all examples of documentation that would be used to evidence inventory purchases. In many larger companies, purchase orders are used to document the types, quantities, and agreed prices for goods purchased. Receiving reports are completed when the goods that have been ordered are received, documenting the types and quantities of goods received. This is compared with the purchase order and invoice before the invoice is paid, to ensure that the goods that were ordered were received and were in appropriate condition and that the price being charged is as agreed. These documents also serve as the basis for updating purchase information in the inventory system.

Cash purchases are recorded by a debit (increase) to the Inventory account and a credit (decrease) to the Cash account. Credit purchases are recorded by a debit (increase) to the Inventory account and a credit (increase) to the Accounts Payable account.

To illustrate the recording of purchases on account, let's assume that PW Technologies, Inc. (the seller) prepares an invoice for the sale of equipment to Sauk Communications Ltd. (the buyer) on May 2 in the amount of $3,800.

Sauk Communications would make the following entry to record the purchase of merchandise:

May 2	Inventory	3,800	
	Accounts Payable		3,800
	(To record goods purchased on account from PW Technologies)		

A	=	L	+	SE
+3,800		+3,800		
Cash flows: no effect				

Only merchandise purchased for the purpose of selling to customers is recorded in the Inventory account. For example, Loblaw would record purchases of fresh produce, frozen food, household goods, clothes, pharmaceuticals, and anything else it purchased for resale to customers by debiting (increasing) the Inventory account. Purchases of assets that the company will use rather than resell, such as supplies and equipment, are recorded as increases to specific asset accounts rather than as increases to the Inventory account. For example, Loblaw would increase the Supplies account to record the purchase of cash register receipt paper or materials that it uses to make shelf signs.

Sales Taxes

Most merchandising and service companies pay sales taxes on the goods and services they purchase. Sales taxes in Canada include the Goods and Services Tax (GST), which is a federal sales tax, and the Provincial Sales Tax (PST). Several provinces, including Ontario and the Atlantic provinces, combine the GST and PST into a single Harmonized Sales Tax (HST). At the time of writing, GST was 5% and PST varied, depending on the province or territory, from 0% to 9.975%. For those provinces using an HST system, the rates can be as high as 15%.

When merchandising companies purchase goods for resale, they pay GST or HST on the cost of the goods. However, GST or HST does not form part of the cost of the merchandise because companies can get back any GST or HST they pay on purchases (by offsetting it against the GST or HST they collect from customers). Generally, retailers do not pay PST on purchases of goods for resale, because they are exempt for this purpose.

Sales taxes add much complexity to the accounting process because not all goods and services are taxable. The accounting transactions described in this chapter are therefore presented without the added complication of sales taxes. We will learn more about sales taxes in Chapter 10.

Freight Costs

Freight terms are agreed to by the buyer and seller. They indicate who is responsible for paying the freight charges (shipping costs) and who is responsible for the risk of loss or damage to the merchandise during transit. Understanding which party bears the risk of loss or damage is an important factor in determining when the goods cease being an asset of the seller and become an asset of the buyer. Freight terms can vary, but are often expressed as either FOB destination or FOB shipping point. The letters FOB mean "free on board" until the point where ownership is transferred.

FOB (free on board) destination means that the seller is responsible for delivering the goods to the destination. The seller pays the freight costs for transporting the goods to the buyer's destination and is responsible for any loss or damage that occurs along the way. As such, the goods would be included in the seller's inventory until they are delivered.

FOB (free on board) shipping point means that the buyer is responsible for the freight costs from the shipping point to the buyer's destination (normally the buyer's place of business). The buyer is also responsible for any loss or damage that occurs along the way. In other words, the goods become part of the buyer's inventory at the point of shipping even though the goods will not arrive at the buyer's destination for several days or even weeks.

Illustration 5-4 shows these shipping terms.

If the terms of the sale of the equipment from PW Technologies to Sauk Communications were FOB shipping point, it would mean that the buyer (Sauk Communications) paid the freight charges from the shipping point (likely PW Technologies' place of business) to the destination

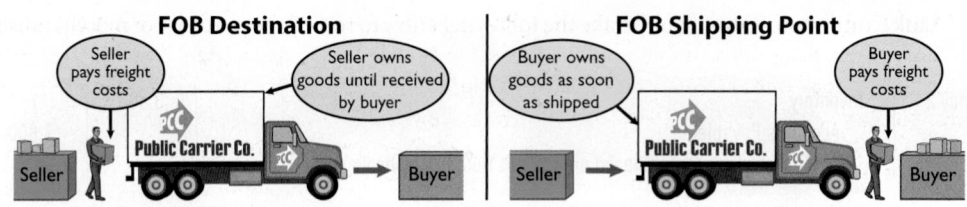

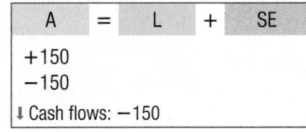

A	=	L	+	SE
+150				
−150				
↓ Cash flows: −150				

(Sauk Communications' place of business). Freight costs would be recorded by debiting (increasing) its Inventory account. Why? **The cost of inventory not only includes the purchase cost but also includes other costs incurred to transport the inventory and make it ready for sale.** As a result, any freight paid by the buyer is recorded as part of the cost of the merchandise purchased.

Assume that upon delivery of the goods on May 4, Sauk Communications (the buyer) pays CanTruck Ltd. $150 for freight charges. The entry on Sauk Communications' books is:

May 4	Inventory	150	
	Cash		150
	(To record payment of freight on goods purchased)		

In contrast, if the freight terms had been FOB destination rather than FOB shipping point, the seller (PW Technologies) would have paid the freight costs. Sauk Communications would not have recorded the purchase of these goods on May 2. Instead, this entry would not have been made until the goods were delivered on May 4. Sauk Communications would have no entry to record for freight and PW Technologies would record the freight costs it paid on outgoing merchandise as an operating expense. We will learn how to record freight costs incurred by the seller later in the chapter.

Purchase Returns and Allowances

A buyer may be dissatisfied with the merchandise received. The goods may be damaged or defective, of inferior quality, or might not fit the buyer's specifications. In such cases, the buyer may return the goods to the seller. The buyer may receive a cash refund if the purchase was made for cash. Credit is given if the purchase was made on account.

Alternatively, the buyer may choose to keep the merchandise if the seller is willing to give an allowance (reduce the purchase price). These types of transactions are known as **purchase returns and allowances**. In both cases, the result is a decrease in the cost of goods purchased.

Assume that Sauk Communications returned goods costing $300 to PW Technologies on May 8. Because these goods were originally sold on account, Sauk Communications received a credit (rather than cash) from PW Technologies for the return of this merchandise. The entry by Sauk Communications for the returned merchandise is:

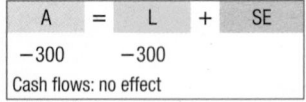

A	=	L	+	SE
−300		−300		
Cash flows: no effect				

May 8	Accounts Payable	300	
	Inventory		300
	(To record return of goods to PW Technologies)		

Because Sauk Communications increased the Inventory and Accounts Payable accounts when the goods were originally purchased, it will decrease these accounts when goods are returned, or when it is granted an allowance.

Discounts

The purchase terms for inventory items can include one or more discounts that are available to the buyer if certain activities occur. Companies may receive various discounts and allowances from sellers for volume (quantity) purchases or for paying for credit purchases before they are due.

Quantity discounts result in a reduced purchase price based on the volume or amount of goods purchased. **Quantity discounts are not recorded or accounted for separately**. For example, PW Technologies may offer a 10% price discount on orders of five or more pieces of equipment. So, if five pieces of equipment were ordered and the price of each piece was $300, the price per piece would be $270 ($300 × 90%) rather than $300. Sauk Communications would record the discounted price, $270, in its Inventory account.

Quantity discounts differ from purchase discounts. A **purchase discount** is offered to encourage customers to pay for goods purchased on account prior to the due date. A purchase discount offers advantages to both parties: the purchaser saves money, and the seller is able to shorten its operating cycle by converting accounts receivable into cash quicker.

The credit terms on the invoice or contract outline any purchase discounts that available to the purchaser. These terms specify the amount of the purchase discount and the time period during which it is offered. They also indicate the date by which the purchaser is expected to pay the full invoice price. Assume the invoice prepared by PW Technologies for the sale of equipment specified that the credit terms were 2/10, n/30, which is read "two-ten, net thirty." This means that a 2% cash discount may be taken on the invoice price, less ("net of") any returns or allowances, if payment is made within 10 days of the invoice date (the discount period). Otherwise, the invoice price, less any returns or allowances, is due 30 days from the invoice date.

Not every seller offers purchase discounts, although they are common in certain industries. When the seller chooses not to offer a discount for faster payment, credit terms will specify only the maximum time period for paying the balance due. For example, the period may be stated as n/30, meaning that the net amount must be paid in 30 days.

In contrast to quantity discounts, purchase discounts are recorded in the accounting records. When an invoice is paid within the discount period, the amount of the discount decreases the cost recorded in the Inventory account.

To illustrate, assume Sauk Communications pays the balance due of $3,500 (gross invoice price of $3,800 less purchase returns and allowances of $300) on May 12, the last day of the discount period. **Note that returns reduce the amount eligible for a discount. In addition, discounts are not taken on freight costs**, especially if the products were carried by an independent shipper. In this situation, the discount is $70 ($3,500 × 2%), and the amount of cash paid by Sauk Communications is $3,430 ($3,500 − $70). The entry to record the May 12 payment by Sauk Communications is:

May 12	Accounts Payable	3,500	
	Cash		3,430
	Inventory		70
	(To record payment to PW Technologies within discount period)		

A = L + SE
−3,430 −3,500
−70
↓ Cash flows: −3,430

Sauk Communications' payment of $3,430 would settle or extinguish the full $3,500 of accounts payable due to PW Technologies.

If Sauk Communications failed to take the discount and instead made full payment of $3,500 on June 1 (30 days after the date of sale), Sauk Communications would make the following entry rather than the one shown above:

June 1	Accounts Payable	3,500	
	Cash		3,500
	(To record payment to PW Technologies with no discount taken)		

A = L + SE
−3,500 −3,500
↓ Cash flows: −3,500

A merchandising company should take advantage of all available purchase discounts. Passing up the discount may be viewed as paying interest for use of the money. For example, if Sauk Communications passed up the discount, it would be paying 2% for the use of $3,500 for 20 days. This equals an annual interest rate of 36.5% (2% × 365 ÷ 20). It would be better for Sauk

Communications to borrow at bank interest rates, which are substantially lower than 36.5%, than to lose the discount.

Because of the importance of taking purchase discounts, some companies prepare journal entries to track the discounts not taken, or lost. Consequently, there are other ways to record discounts than shown in this section. These will be discussed in an intermediate accounting course.

SUMMARY OF PURCHASE TRANSACTIONS

A summary of the effect of the previous purchase transactions on Inventory is provided in the following T account (with transaction descriptions in parentheses). Sauk Communications originally purchased inventory with a cost of $3,800. It paid $150 in freight charges. It then returned goods costing $300. Finally, it received a $70 discount off the balance owed because it paid within the discount period. This results in a balance in the Inventory account of $3,580, as follows:

		Inventory			
(Purchase)	May 2	3,800	May 8	300	(Purchase return)
(Freight)	4	150	12	70	(Purchase discount)
	Bal.	3,580			

The $3,580 amount in the Inventory account represents the **cost of the goods purchased**. The cost of goods purchased includes the cost of the merchandise, increased by any freight costs incurred if the shipping terms are FOB shipping point, and decreased by any purchase returns and allowances and purchase discounts.

	Transactions	Recurring Journal Entries	Debit	Credit
Purchases	Purchasing merchandise for resale.	Inventory Cash or Accounts Payable	XX	XX
	Paying freight costs on merchandise purchased FOB shipping point.	Inventory Cash	XX	XX
	Receiving purchase returns or allowances from suppliers.	Cash or Accounts Payable Inventory	XX	XX

	Paying creditors on account within discount period.	Accounts Payable
		    Inventory
		    Cash
			XX	XX
				XX

	Paying creditors on account after discount period.	Accounts Payable Cash	XX	XX

DO IT! ▶5-2   Purchase Transactions

SOLUTION
Try this Do It! exercise on your own and then check your answer at the end of the chapter.

Related Exercise Material: BE5–3, BE5–5, E5–4, and E5–6.

On September 2, Brighthouse Corp. buys merchandise on account from Junot Inc. for $1,500, terms 2/10, n/30, FOB shipping point. Freight charges of $75 are paid on September 4. On September 8, Brighthouse returns $200 of the merchandise to Junot. On September 11, Brighthouse pays the total amount owing. Record the transactions on Brighthouse's books.

Action Plan

✔ Purchases of goods for resale are recorded in the asset account Inventory when a perpetual inventory system is used.

✔ Examine freight terms to determine which company pays the freight charges. Freight charges paid by the buyer increase the cost of the inventory.

✔ The Inventory account is reduced by the cost of merchandise returned.

✔ Calculate purchase discounts using the net amount owing for purchases (purchases less any purchase returns and allowances). Do not calculate purchase discounts on freight.

✔ Reduce the Inventory account by the amount of the purchase discount.

Prepare entries for sales under a perpetual inventory system.

You will recall from Chapter 4, when we discussed revenue recognition, that revenue is recorded (recognized) when there is an increase in assets (economic benefits) such as the receipt of cash or increase in accounts receivable as a result of the performance of a service or delivery of goods. A five-step process for measuring and reporting revenue was discussed. For a merchandising company, revenue will be recognized when the company satisfies its performance obligation(s), the fifth step in the recognition process. This occurs when the goods are transferred from the seller to the buyer.

We will discuss how to record sales revenue, including sales taxes, freight costs, sales returns and allowances, and sales discounts, in the next sections.

SALES

To record sales revenue, an asset account (typically Cash or Accounts Receivable) is debited (increased) and the Sales revenue account is credited (also increased). Alternatively, if a customer had previously paid in advance, a liability account (Unearned Revenue) is debited (decreased) and the Sales revenue account is credited (increased).

Similar to purchase transactions, every sales transaction—whether for cash or credit—should be supported by documentation—whether written or electronic—that provides evidence of the sale. Cash register tapes provide evidence of cash sales. A **sales invoice** provides support for a credit sale.

While only one journal entry is required to record the purchase of merchandise, **two journal entries are required to record each sale in a perpetual inventory system**. The first entry records the sales revenue: Cash (or Accounts Receivable, if it is a credit sale) is increased by a debit and Sales is increased by a credit for the selling (invoice) price of the goods. The second entry records the cost of the merchandise sold: Cost of Goods Sold is increased by a debit and Inventory is decreased by a credit for the cost of the goods. As a result, at all times, the Inventory account will show the amount of inventory that is (should be) on hand.

To illustrate a credit sales transaction, we will continue to use PW Technologies' sale of $3,800 of merchandise on May 2 to Sauk Communications that was illustrated earlier in the purchases section. Assume the merchandise cost PW Technologies $2,400 when it was originally purchased. The sale is recorded as follows:

▼ HELPFUL HINT
There are two journal entries when a sale is recorded by a company using a perpetual inventory system. The first entry records the cash and/or accounts receivable and the sales revenue. The second entry records the cost of goods sold and reduces the Inventory account.

May 2	Accounts Receivable	3,800	
	Sales		3,800
	(To record credit sale to Sauk Communications, terms 2/10, n/30, FOB shipping point)		
2	Cost of Goods Sold	2,400	
	Inventory		2,400
	(To record cost of merchandise sold to Sauk Communications)		

A	=	L	+	SE
+3,800				+3,800

Cash flows: no effect

A	=	L	+	SE
−2,400				−2,400

Cash flows: no effect

For internal decision-making purposes, merchandising companies may use more than one sales account. For example, PW Technologies may decide to keep separate sales accounts for its major product lines, rather than a single combined sales account. This enables management to monitor sales trends more closely and respond in a more strategic way to changes in sales patterns. For example, if sales of a certain type of equipment are increasing while sales of another type of equipment are decreasing, the company should re-evaluate both its advertising and pricing policies on each of these items to ensure that they are optimal.

On the income statement presented to external users, most merchandising companies provide only a single sales figure—the sum of all of their individual sales accounts. This is done for two reasons. First, providing detail on all of the individual sales accounts would make the income statement much longer. Second, companies generally do not want their competitors to know the details of their operating results.

Sales Taxes

Merchandising companies collect sales taxes on the goods they sell. You will recall from earlier in the chapter that sales taxes can include GST or HST.

When a company collects sales taxes from selling a product or service, these **sales taxes are not recorded as revenue**. The sales taxes are collected on behalf of the federal and provincial governments, and must be periodically remitted to these authorities. Sales taxes that are collected from selling a product or service are recorded as a liability until they are paid to the government. Further discussion of sales taxes is deferred until Chapter 10.

Freight Costs

As discussed earlier in the chapter, freight terms on the sales invoice—FOB destination and FOB shipping point—indicate who is responsible for shipping costs. If the terms are FOB destination, the seller assumes the responsibility for delivering the goods to their intended destination. Freight costs incurred by the seller on outgoing merchandise are an operating expense to the seller. These costs are debited to the expense account Freight Out. When the seller pays the freight charges, the seller will usually set a higher invoice price for the goods to cover the cost of shipping.

In PW Technologies' sale of electronic equipment to Sauk Communications, the freight terms (FOB shipping point) indicate that Sauk Communications (the buyer) must pay the cost of shipping the goods from the shipping point (likely PW Technologies' place of business) to their destination (Sauk Communications' place of business). PW Technologies makes no journal entry to record the cost of shipping, since the buyer, not the seller, incurred this cost.

If the freight terms had been FOB destination, PW Technologies would not have recorded the sale of these goods on May 2. Instead, this entry would have been made when the goods were delivered on May 4. PW Technologies would also have prepared a journal entry to record the freight costs as an operating expense, as shown below:

▼ HELPFUL HINT
The seller pays freight only when the shipping terms are FOB destination.

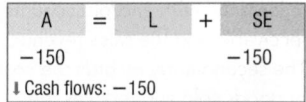

A	=	L	+	SE
−150				−150

↓ Cash flows: −150

May 4	Freight Out	150	
	Cash		150
	(To record payment of freight on goods sold)		

Sales Returns and Allowances

We now look at the "flip side" of purchase returns and allowances, because these are recorded as **sales returns and allowances** on the books of the seller. When customers (buyers) return goods, or are given price reductions, the seller will either return cash to the buyer, or reduce the buyer's accounts receivable if the goods were originally purchased on credit.

Just as a sale requires two entries in a perpetual inventory system, so too do returns unless the goods being returned cannot be resold. PW Technologies prepares the two separate journal entries shown below to record the $300 credit for goods returned by Sauk Communications. The first entry records a debit (increase) to the Sales Returns and Allowances account and a credit (decrease) to the Accounts Receivable account for the $300 selling price. Note that if the sales return had been for a cash sale, Cash would be credited instead of Accounts Receivable. The second journal entry required to record a sales return in a perpetual inventory system debits (increases) the Inventory account (assuming a $140 cost) and credits (decreases) the Cost of Goods Sold account. The goods are re-established in inventory until they are resold.

The Sales Returns and Allowances account is a **contra revenue account** to Sales. The normal balance of the Sales Returns and Allowances account is a debit. A contra account is used to disclose the amount of sales returns and allowances. A debit (decrease) recorded directly to Sales would make it more difficult for management to determine the percentage of total sales that ends up being lost through sales returns and allowances. It could also distort comparisons between total sales in different accounting periods.

This information is important to management. Excessive returns and allowances suggest the possibility of inferior merchandise, inefficiencies in filling orders, errors in billing customers, or mistakes in the delivery or shipment of goods.

Date	Account	Debit	Credit
May 8	Sales Returns and Allowances	300	
	Accounts Receivable		300
	(To record return of goods by Sauk Communications)		
8	Inventory	140	
	Cost of Goods Sold		140
	(To record cost of merchandise returned by Sauk Communications)		

A	=	L	+	SE
−300				−300

Cash flows: no effect

A	=	L	+	SE
+140				+140

Cash flows: no effect

The second entry shown above assumes that the merchandise is not damaged and can be resold. If the merchandise is not resaleable and is scrapped, a second entry is not made. Since the goods are defective and cannot be resold, the seller cannot increase its inventory and the original cost of goods sold recorded remains the correct amount.

A second entry is also not required when the seller gives the buyer an allowance. Giving a customer a sales allowance does not change the cost of the goods sold; it only changes the amount of revenue earned on the sale.

Discounts

When quantity discounts and sales discounts are given on invoice prices, they affect the seller, as well as the buyer. No separate entry is made to record a **quantity discount**. Sales are recorded at the invoice price—whether it is the full retail price, a sale price, or a volume discount price.

As discussed in an earlier section, the seller may offer the buyer a cash discount for paying for credit purchases prior to the due date. From the seller's point of view, this is called a **sales discount** and is offered on the invoice price less any sales returns and allowances.

Any sales discounts taken by customers are recorded in a new account, called Sales Discounts. Like the account for sales returns and allowances, Sales Discounts is a contra revenue account to Sales. Its normal balance is a debit. This account is used, instead of debiting Sales, so that management can monitor if customers are taking advantage of cash discounts and what the discounts are costing the company.

For PW Technologies, the sales discount is $70 ([$3,800 − $300] × 2%). The entry to record the cash receipt of $3,430 ($3,800 − $300 − $70) on May 12 from Sauk Communications within the discount period is:

Date	Account	Debit	Credit
May 12	Cash	3,430	
	Sales Discounts	70	
	Accounts Receivable		3,500
	(To record collection from Sauk Communications within discount period		

A	=	L	+	SE
+3,430				−70
−3,500				

↑ Cash flows: +3,430

If a customer does not take the discount, PW Technologies debits (increases) the Cash account for $3,500 and credits (decreases) the Accounts Receivable account for the same amount, as shown below:

Date	Account	Debit	Credit
June 1	Cash	3,500	
	Accounts Receivable		3,500
	(To record collection from Sauk Communications with no discount taken)		

A	=	L	+	SE
+3,500				
−3,500				

↑ Cash flows: +3,500

SUMMARY OF SALES TRANSACTIONS

PW Technologies sold merchandise for $3,800, and $300 of it was later returned. A sales discount of $70 was granted because the invoice was paid within the discount period. In contrast to the purchase transactions illustrated earlier in the chapter, which affected only one account, Inventory, sales transactions are recorded in different accounts. A summary of the effects of these transactions is provided in the following T accounts.

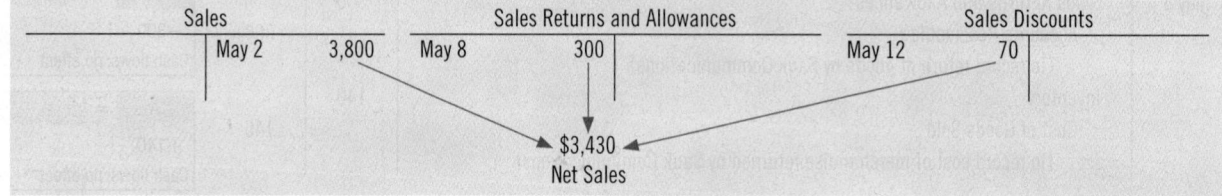

These three accounts combine to determine net sales. Illustration 5-5 shows the formula for the calculation of net sales.

▶Illustration 5-5

Formula for net sales

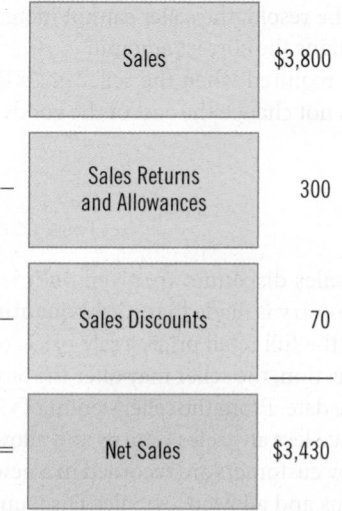

Total sales, before deducting any sales returns and allowances and sales discounts, are known as **gross sales**. Gross sales less returns and allowances and discounts are called **net sales**. The calculation of net sales is the same whether the company uses a perpetual or a periodic inventory system. Note that freight paid by the seller is recorded as an operating expense and does not affect net sales.

	Transactions	Recurring Journal Entries	Debit	Credit
Sales	Selling merchandise to customers.	Cash or Accounts Receivable	XX	
		Sales		XX
		Cost of Goods Sold	XX	
		Inventory		XX
	Sales returns by customers.	Inventory	XX	
		Cost of Goods Sold		XX
	Granting a sales allowance to customers.	Sales Returns and Allowances	XX	
		Cash or Accounts Receivable		XX
	Paying freight costs on sales, FOB destination.	Freight Out	XX	
		Cash		XX
	Receiving payment on account from customers within discount period.	Cash	XX	
		Sales Discounts	XX	
		Accounts Receivable		XX
	Receiving payment on account from customers after discount period.	Cash	XX	
		Accounts Receivable		XX

DO IT! ▶ **5-3** **Purchase and Sales Transactions—Perpetual Inventory System**

On September 4, Lalonde Ltée sells merchandise on account to Guerette Corp., terms 2/10, n/45. The selling price of the goods is $3,000, and the cost to Lalonde was $1,600. On September 8, goods with a selling price of $600 and a cost of $280 are returned for credit and restored to inventory. On September 13, Lalonde receives payment in full from Guerette. Record the transactions on the books of both companies, assuming a perpetual inventory system is used.

Action Plan

✔ Seller: Prepare two entries to record the sale of merchandise: one to record the selling price and one to record the cost of the sale. Prepare two entries to record the return of goods: one to record the selling price and one to record the cost of the return. Calculate sales discounts using the amount owing, net of any sales returns.

✔ Buyer: Record purchases of inventory, returned goods, and purchase discounts in one account—Inventory. Calculate purchase discounts using the amount owing, net of any purchase returns.

SOLUTION

Try this Do It! exercise on your own and then check your answer at the end of the chapter.

Related Exercise Material: **BE5-4, BE5-6, E5-2, E5-3,** and **E5-5.**

LEARNING OBJECTIVE ▶ **4** **Prepare a single-step and a multiple-step income statement.**

Two different forms of the income statement are widely used by merchandising companies. One is the **single-step income statement**. It has this name because only one step—subtracting total expenses (except for income tax expense) from total revenues—is required for determining income before income tax. A second form of the income statement is the **multiple-step income statement**. This statement gets its name because it shows multiple steps in determining income before income tax. We will look at each of these statement forms in the following sections.

SINGLE-STEP INCOME STATEMENT

In a **single-step income statement**, all data are classified into two categories: (1) revenues and (2) expenses. Revenues include both operating and non-operating revenues. Non-operating revenues are items not related to the company's main operations, such as interest revenue and gains. We will learn more about non-operating revenues (and expenses) in the next section of this chapter.

Expenses include cost of goods sold, operating expenses, and non-operating expenses (such as interest expense and losses). Income tax expense is usually disclosed separately from the other expenses in a single-step income statement. Illustration 5-6 shows a single-step income statement for PW Technologies, Inc., using assumed data.

►Illustration 5-6
Single-step income statement—
perpetual inventory system

PW TECHNOLOGIES, INC.
Income Statement
Year Ended December 31, 2018

Revenues		
Net sales	$460,000	
Interest revenue	3,400	$463,400
Expenses		
Cost of goods sold	$316,000	
Salaries expense	45,000	
Rent expense	19,000	
Utilities expense	17,000	
Advertising expense	16,000	
Depreciation expense	8,000	
Freight out	7,000	
Insurance expense	2,000	
Interest expense	1,600	
Loss on disposal	200	431,800
Income before income tax		31,600
Income tax expense		6,300
Net income		$ 25,300

Private companies following ASPE do not have to list their expenses in any particular order. Companies following IFRS must classify expenses by either their nature or function. Although expenses can be listed in any order within each classification, as we have done in past chapters, we have listed expenses in order of magnitude—from largest to smallest. Illustration 5-6 presents PW Technologies' expenses by nature.

Classifying expenses by **nature** means that expenses are reported according to their natural classification (such as salaries, transportation, depreciation, or advertising). Classifying expenses by **function** means that they are reported according to the activity (business function) for which they were incurred (for example, cost of goods sold, administrative expenses, and selling expenses).

Companies can choose between classifying expenses by nature or function, depending on whichever provides information that is more relevant. If a company chooses to present its expenses by function, it must also disclose additional information on the nature of certain expenses, such as depreciation and employee benefits expense. (We will learn about employee benefits expense in Chapter 10.)

The decision to classify expenses by function increases the extent of management judgement reflected in the statement of income. Management will need to determine what portion of each expense is allocated to the various functions. For example, while salaries expense would be a single line item when expenses are classified by nature, the expense would need to be allocated between classifications such as administrative expenses and selling expenses when expenses are classified by function. Using your university or college as an example, management would need to determine what portion, if any, of the salaries of the institution's deans or directors would be allocated to administrative expenses versus instructional expenses.

The single-step income statement is the form we have used in the text so far. There are two main reasons for using the single-step form:

1. A company does not realize any income until total revenues exceed total expenses, so it makes sense to divide the statement into these categories.
2. The single-step form is simple and easy to read.

Regardless of the simplicity of the single-step format, the majority of Canadian companies use the multiple-step form of income statement. We will learn why in the next section.

MULTIPLE-STEP INCOME STATEMENT

The **multiple-step income statement** is so named because several steps are presented in determining net income (or loss). It is considered more useful because it highlights the components of income separately.

The multiple-step income statement shows five main steps:

1. Net sales: Gross sales less sales returns and allowances and sales discounts.
2. Gross profit: Net sales less cost of goods sold.
3. Income from operations: Gross profit less operating expenses.
4. Income before income tax: Income from operations plus non-operating revenues and less non-operating expenses.
5. Net income: Income before income tax less income tax expense.

The first three steps involve the company's principal operating activities. The fourth step distinguishes between **operating and non-operating** activities and is necessary only if the company has non-operating activities. The last step is the same step shown in a single-step statement. We will now look more closely at the components of a multiple-step income statement using assumed data for PW Technologies.

Net Sales

The multiple-step income statement for a merchandising company begins by presenting sales revenues. The two contra revenue accounts, Sales Returns and Allowances and Sales Discounts, are deducted from gross sales in the income statement to arrive at **net sales**. The sales revenues section of the income statement is presented here.

Sales revenue		
Sales		$480,000
Less: Sales returns and allowances	$12,000	
Sales discounts	8,000	20,000
Net sales		460,000

This presentation shows the key aspects of the company's main revenue-producing activities. Most companies condense this information and publicly report only the net sales figure in their income statement.

Gross Profit

Earlier in the chapter, you learned that the cost of goods sold is deducted from net sales to determine **gross profit**. Based on the sales data presented above (net sales of $460,000) and the cost of goods sold amount of $316,000, the gross profit for PW Technologies is $144,000, calculated as follows:

Net sales	$460,000
Cost of goods sold	316,000
Gross profit	144,000

It is important to understand what gross profit is—and what it is not. Gross profit represents the **merchandising profit** of a company. Because operating expenses have not been deducted, it is not a measure of the overall profit of a company. Nevertheless, management and other users closely watch the amount and trend of gross profit. We will learn how to express gross profit as a rate in the next section and compare this rate on an intracompany, intercompany, and industry basis to determine the effectiveness of a company's purchasing and pricing policies.

Income from Operations

Income from operations, or the results of the company's normal operating activities, is calculated by subtracting operating expenses from gross profit.

At PW Technologies, operating expenses totalling $114,200 have been classified by nature rather than by function, as shown below. You will recall our discussion in the single-step income statement section about classifying operating expenses by either nature or function. This is required whether a company uses the single- or multiple-step format.

After subtracting operating expenses from gross profit, PW Technology's income from operations is determined to be $29,800, as shown below:

Gross profit		$144,000
Operating expenses		
Salaries expense	$45,000	
Rent expense	19,000	
Utilities expense	17,000	
Advertising expense	16,000	
Depreciation expense	8,000	
Freight out	7,000	
Insurance expense	2,000	
Loss on disposal	200	114,200
Income from operations		29,800

Reporting income from operations as a separate number from overall net income helps users in understanding the profitability of the company's continuing operations or typical business activities.

Non-Operating (Other) Revenues and Expenses

Non-operating items consist of other revenues (also known as other income), as well as other expenses, that are not related to the company's main operations.

Examples of other revenues include interest revenue, rent revenue (if the company's main activity is not rentals), and investment revenue. In addition, gains that are infrequent or unusual are normally reported in this section. An example of an other expense is finance (interest) costs. Losses that are infrequent and unusual are also reported in this section.

When a company has non-operating revenues and expenses, they are presented in the income statement right after "income from operations." The distinction between operating and non-operating activities is crucial to many external users of financial information. Income from operations is viewed as recurring and therefore long-term, and non-operating activities are viewed as nonrecurring and therefore short-term. When forecasting next year's income, analysts put the most weight on this year's income from operations because it has more **predictive value** and they put less weight on this year's non-operating activities.

PW Technologies' non-operating activities are presented below. Depending on whether the non-operating activities result in a net increase (other revenues exceed other expenses) or net decrease (other expenses exceed other revenues), they are added to or deducted from the income from operations. The result is income before income tax.

Income from operations		$29,800
Other revenues and expenses		
Interest revenue	$3,400	
Interest expense	1,600	1,800
Income before income tax		31,600

If there are no non-operating activities, income from operations will be the same as income before income tax.

Net Income

Net income is the final outcome of all the company's operating and non-operating activities. PW Technologies' net income is $25,300 after deducting its income tax expense of $6,300:

Income before income tax	$31,600
Income tax expense	6,300
Net income	$25,300

In Illustration 5-7, we bring together all the steps above in a comprehensive multiple-step income statement for PW Technologies. Note that the net income in Illustrations 5-7 (multiple-step) and 5-6 (single-step) is the same. The differences between the two income statements are the amount of detail displayed and the order of presentation.

▶Illustration 5-7

Multiple-step income statement— perpetual inventory system

PW TECHNOLOGIES, INC.
Income Statement
Year Ended December 31, 2018

Sales revenue		
Sales		$480,000
Less: Sales returns and allowances	$12,000	
Sales discounts	8,000	20,000
Net sales		460,000
Cost of goods sold		316,000
Gross profit		144,000
Operating expenses		
Salaries expense	$45,000	
Rent expense	19,000	
Utilities expense	17,000	
Advertising expense	16,000	
Depreciation expense	8,000	
Freight out	7,000	
Insurance expense	2,000	
Loss on disposal	200	114,200
Income from operations		29,800
Other revenues and expenses		
Interest revenue	$3,400	
Interest expense	1,600	1,800
Income before income tax		31,600
Income tax expense		6,300
Net income		$ 25,300

DO IT! ▶5-4   Multiple-Step Income Statement Amounts

Action Plan

✔ Recall the formula for net sales: Sales – sales returns and allowances – sales discounts.

✔ Recall the formula for gross profit: Net sales – cost of goods sold.

✔ Separate relevant accounts into operating (selling and administrative expenses) and non-operating (other revenues and expenses).

✔ Recall the formula for income from operations: Gross profit – operating expenses.

✔ Recall the formula for income before income tax: Income from operations + other revenue – other expenses.

✔ Recall the formula for net income: Income before income tax – income tax expense.

Tyrone Inc. reported the following selected information:

Administrative expenses	$ 200,000
Cost of goods sold	1,238,000
Income tax expense	23,000
Interest expense	4,000
Rent revenue	36,000
Sales	1,820,000
Sales discounts	30,000
Sales returns and allowances	170,000
Selling expenses	122,000

Calculate the following amounts for Tyrone Inc.: (a) net sales, (b) gross profit, (c) income from operations, (d) income before income tax, and (e) net income.

SOLUTION

Try this Do It! exercise on your own and then check your answer at the end of the chapter.

Related Exercise Material: **BE5–7, BE5–8, BE5–9, E5–8, and E5–9.**

LEARNING OBJECTIVE ▶5   Calculate the gross profit margin and profit margin.

In Chapter 2, we learned about two profitability ratios: earnings per share and the price-earnings ratio. We add two more examples of profitability ratios in this chapter: gross profit margin and profit margin.

GROSS PROFIT MARGIN

The **gross profit margin** expresses a company's gross profit as a percentage. It is calculated by dividing gross profit by net sales. For PW Technologies, the gross profit margin is 31.3% ($144,000 ÷ $460,000). This means that PW Technologies earns a gross profit of $0.31 for every $1 of net sales that is earned. The gross profit margin is generally considered more informative than the dollar amount of gross profit because the margin expresses a relationship between gross profit and net sales rather than a simple amount expressed in dollars. For example, a gross profit amount of $1 million may sound impressive, but if it is the result of sales of $100 million, the company's gross profit margin is only 1%. In other words, there was only $0.01 of gross profit available to cover operating expenses for every $1 of net sales. Because gross profit margin is expressed as a percentage, it also makes it easier for users to compare results period to period when the dollar amounts have changed.

In the following illustration, we will calculate the gross profit margin for Loblaw, and a major competitor, Metro Inc. The gross profit margins for Loblaw, Metro, and their industry for two recent fiscal years are presented in Illustration 5-8.

Loblaw's gross profit margin improved in 2015 compared with 2014 and the industry average. Loblaw (and the rest of the industry) tends to have a greater portion of its sales from non-grocery items than Metro. The gross profit on these items tends to be higher and this contributes to a higher gross profit than that experienced at Metro.

($ in millions)	GROSS PROFIT MARGIN = $\dfrac{\text{GROSS PROFIT}}{\text{NET SALES}}$	
	2015	2014
Loblaw	$\dfrac{(\$45{,}394 - \$32{,}846)}{\$45{,}394} = 27.6\%$	$\dfrac{(\$42{,}611 - \$32{,}063)}{\$42{,}611} = 24.7\%$
Metro	19.7%	19.1%
Industry average	24.4%	24.4%

▶Illustration 5-8
Gross profit margin

PROFIT MARGIN

Like gross profit, net income is often expressed as a percentage of sales. The **profit margin** measures the percentage of each dollar of sales that represents profit. It is calculated by dividing net income by net sales for the period.

What is the difference between gross profit margin and profit margin? Gross profit margin indicates how much higher the selling price is than the cost of goods sold. Profit margin indicates how well the selling price covers all expenses (including the cost of goods sold). A company can improve its profit margin by increasing its gross profit margin, by controlling its operating and other expenses, by earning other revenues, or by experiencing a decrease in the income tax rate.

Profit margins for Loblaw, Metro, and the industry average are presented in Illustration 5-9.

($ in millions)	PROFIT MARGIN = $\dfrac{\text{NET INCOME}}{\text{NET SALES}}$	
	2015	2014
Loblaw	$\dfrac{\$623}{\$45{,}394} = 1.4\%$	$\dfrac{\$53}{\$42{,}611} = 0.1\%$
Metro	4.2%	3.9%
Industry average	2.8%	2.8%

▶Illustration 5-9
Profit margin

Although Loblaw had a higher gross profit ratio, as shown in Illustration 5-8, it had a lower profit margin than Metro and the industry. This is primarily due to Metro's reputation for controlling its operating costs.

Both the gross profit margin and profit margin are **profitability measures** that vary according to the specific industry. Businesses with a high turnover of inventory, such as food stores, generally experience lower gross profit and profit margins. Low-turnover businesses, such as technology companies (Apple, for example), have higher gross profit and profit margins. In general, the higher the gross profit margin and profit margin, the better.

ACCOUNTING MATTERS

Danilin/Getty Images

Determining the Cost of an iPhone

It is important for companies to pay close attention to their costs, as cost is one of the biggest drivers of profitability. Research firm IHS estimates that the cost of manufacturing Apple's iPhone SE is about U.S. $156 for materials and another $4 for manufacturing. That's for the entry-level iPhone SE with 16 gigabytes of memory. When the iPhone SE went on sale in early 2016, the retail price of the 16 GB model was U.S. $399. Apple benefited from switching the SE model's screen to a Gorilla Glass one that cost $20, or about half the cost of the screen on a previous model, the iPhone 5. If IHS's estimates are correct, this means that Apple is most likely generating a gross profit of U.S. $239 for a 16 GB iPhone SE. This translates into a gross profit margin of 60% on that model.

That doesn't mean that Apple is making 60% profit, of course. There are development costs, marketing, and other operating expenses to take into account before arriving at its profit margin. Nonetheless, its profitability on this item would appear to be healthy, based on these estimates.[3]

DO IT! ▶5-5   Calculating and Evaluating Profitability

Action Plan

✔ Calculate gross profit and profit.

✔ Calculate the gross profit margin by dividing gross profit by net sales.

✔ Calculate the profit margin by dividing net income by net sales.

✔ A higher gross profit margin and profit margin indicate improved profitability.

Sports-R-Us Corporation reported the following information:

($ in thousands)	2018	2017
Net sales	$1,347	$1,331
Cost of goods sold	863	853
Operating expenses	439	407
Income tax expense	15	24

(a) Calculate the gross profit margin and profit margin for both years.

(b) Did Sports-R-Us's profitability improve or decline in 2018?

SOLUTION

Try this Do It! exercise on your own and then check your answer at the end of the chapter.

Related Exercise Material: BE5–10, BE5–11, E5–7, E5–10, E5–11, E5–12, and E5–13.

LEARNING
OBJECTIVE 6

Appendix 5A: Account for and report inventory in a periodic inventory system.

As noted in this chapter, there are two basic systems used to account for inventory: (1) the perpetual inventory system, and (2) the periodic inventory system. In the chapter, we focused on accounting for inventory in a perpetual system. In this appendix, the focus is on accounting for inventory in a periodic system, including a comparison of the journal entries used in each.

In both perpetual and periodic systems, revenues from the sale of merchandise are recorded when the performance obligation is complete—generally upon delivery of the merchandise. However, one key difference between the two systems is the point at which the cost of goods sold is calculated and recorded. In a periodic system, the cost of the merchandise sold is not recorded on the date of sale. Instead cost of goods sold is only determined at the end of each accounting period (month, quarter, or year) when an inventory count is taken. As such, an inventory count is required under a periodic inventory system anytime management is trying to determine cost of goods sold and/or ending inventory.

Another difference when using a periodic system is that purchases of merchandise are recorded in the temporary Purchases expense account rather than the permanent Inventory asset account. Also, in a periodic system, purchase returns and allowances, purchase discounts, and freight costs on purchases are recorded in separate temporary expense accounts. Consequently, if a periodic system is used, the Inventory account shown in an unadjusted trial balance represents the beginning inventory balance, which is the ending balance from the prior period.

To illustrate the recording of merchandise transactions under a periodic inventory system, we will use purchase and sale transactions between PW Technologies, Inc. (the seller) and Sauk Communications Ltd. (the buyer), as illustrated for the perpetual inventory system earlier in this chapter. You will recall that PW Technologies sold equipment to Sauk Communications on May 2 in the amount of $3,800. The terms of the sale are 2/10, n/30, FOB shipping point.

RECORDING PURCHASES OF MERCHANDISE

Sauk Communications records the $3,800 purchase of merchandise from PW Technologies on May 2 as follows:

May 2	Purchases	3,800	
	Accounts Payable		3,800
	(To record goods purchased on account from PW Technologies, terms 2/10, n/30, FOB shipping point)		

A	=	L	+	SE
		+3,800		−3,800
Cash flows: no effect				

The Purchases account is a temporary expense account reported on the income statement. Its normal balance is a debit.

Freight Costs

The freight terms for Sauk Communications' purchase of merchandise are FOB shipping point, which means that the buyer pays the freight costs. Upon delivery of the goods, Sauk Communications pays CanTruck Ltd. $150 for freight charges on its purchases from PW Technologies. The entry on Sauk Communications' books is as follows:

May 4	Freight In	150	
	Cash		150
	(To record payment of freight on goods purchased)		

A	=	L	+	SE
−150				−150
↓ Cash flows: −150				

Like Purchases, Freight In is a temporary expense account whose normal balance is a debit. Just as freight was part of the cost of the inventory in a perpetual inventory system, **freight is part of the cost of goods purchased** in a periodic inventory system. The cost of goods purchased includes any freight charges incurred in bringing the goods to the buyer. As a result, freight in is added to net purchases to determine the cost of goods purchased.

Purchase Returns and Allowances

When $300 of merchandise is returned to PW Technologies, Sauk Communications prepares the following entry to recognize the return:

May 8	Accounts Payable	300	
	Purchase Returns and Allowances		300
	(To record return of goods to PW Technologies)		

A	=	L	+	SE
		−300		+300
Cash flows: no effect				

Purchase Returns and Allowances is a temporary account whose normal balance is a credit. It is a **contra expense account** whose balance is subtracted from the Purchases account.

Purchase Discounts

Recall that the invoice terms were 2/10, n/30. On May 12, Sauk Communications pays the balance due on account to PW Technologies of $3,500 ($3,800 − $300), less the 2% cash discount allowed by PW Technologies for payment within 10 days. Note that freight costs are not subject to a purchase discount. Purchase discounts apply on the invoice cost of the merchandise purchased, less any returns. In this case, the purchase discount is $70, calculated as follows: ($3,800 − $300) × 2% = $70.

The payment and discount are recorded by Sauk Communications as follows:

May 12	Accounts Payable	3,500	
	Cash		3,430
	Purchase Discounts		70
	(To record payment to PW Technologies within discount period)		

A	=	L	+	SE
−3,430		−3,500		+70
↓ Cash flows: −3,430				

▶Illustration 5A-1
Formula for cost of goods purchased

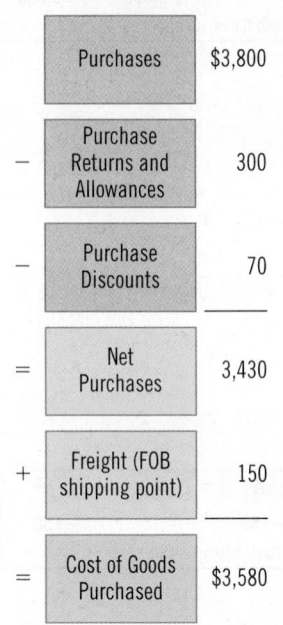

	Purchases	$3,800
−	Purchase Returns and Allowances	300
−	Purchase Discounts	70
=	Net Purchases	3,430
+	Freight (FOB shipping point)	150
=	Cost of Goods Purchased	$3,580

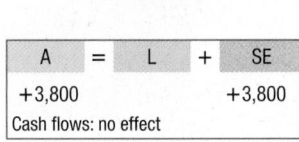

A	=	L	+	SE
+3,800				+3,800

Cash flows: no effect

Purchase Discounts is a temporary account whose normal balance is a credit. Like Purchase Returns and Allowances, it is a contra expense account subtracted from the Purchases account.

As was mentioned earlier, a temporary expense account is used in each of the above transactions to record purchases of merchandise instead of the Inventory account used in a perpetual inventory system. The Purchases and Freight In accounts are debited rather than Inventory in the first two entries, and Purchase Returns and Allowances and Purchase Discounts are credited in the last two entries rather than Inventory. These temporary accounts are needed for calculating the cost of goods purchased at the end of the period, as shown in Illustration 5A-1.

Purchases of merchandise, less returns and allowances and discounts, are commonly known as **net purchases**. Freight costs are then added to net purchases to determine the cost of goods purchased. Note that the cost of goods purchased, $3,580, is the same in a periodic inventory system as it is in a perpetual inventory system, as shown earlier in the chapter.

RECORDING SALES OF MERCHANDISE

The sale of $3,800 of merchandise to Sauk Communications on May 2 is recorded by the seller, PW Technologies, as follows:

May 2	Accounts Receivable	3,800	
	Sales		3,800
	(To record credit sale to Sauk Communications, terms 2/10, n/30, FOB shipping point)		

The sales entries illustrated in this section are exactly the same as those illustrated in the chapter for a perpetual inventory system, with one exception. In a perpetual inventory system, two journal entries are made for each sales transaction. The first entry records the accounts receivable and sales revenue, as illustrated above. The second journal entry records the cost of the sale by debiting Cost of Goods Sold and crediting Inventory in order to transfer the inventory to cost of goods sold.

In a periodic inventory system, there is only one journal entry made at the time of the sale (the entry to record the sales revenue). The cost of the sale is not recorded at the time of sale because this information is not available from a periodic inventory system at that time. Instead, the cost of goods sold is determined by calculation after an inventory count, normally at the end of the period (month, quarter, or year).

Freight Costs

Freight costs incurred by the seller on outgoing merchandise are an operating expense to the seller. There is no distinction in accounting for these costs between a perpetual and periodic inventory system. Under both systems, these costs are debited to the Freight Out account.

You will recall that Sauk Communications (the buyer) paid the shipping costs in our sales illustration, so PW Technologies (the seller) doesn't need to make a journal entry at this point. Note that the Freight Out account is not the same as the Freight In account. Freight Out is used by the seller to record freight costs. Freight In is used by the buyer to record freight costs.

Sales Returns and Allowances

When Sauk Communications returns merchandise on May 8, PW Technologies records the $300 sales return as follows:

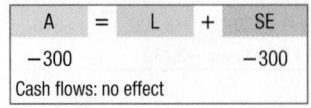

A	=	L	+	SE
−300				−300

Cash flows: no effect

May 8	Sales Returns and Allowances	300	
	Accounts Receivable		300
	(To record return of goods by Sauk Communications)		

Just as we observed that only one entry is needed when sales are recorded in a periodic inventory system, one entry is also all that is needed to record a return. In a perpetual inventory system, two entries are needed to record the sales return and the return of the goods to inventory.

Sales Discounts

On May 12, PW Technologies receives a payment of $3,430 ($3,800 − $300 − $70) on account from Sauk Communications. Because the payment was received within the discount period, the sales discount of $70 ([$3,800 − $300] × 2%) reduces the cash received. PW Technologies records the collection of the account as follows:

May 12	Cash	3,430	
	Sales Discounts	70	
	Accounts Receivable		3,500
	(To record collection from Sauk Communications within discount period)		

A	=	L	+	SE
+3,430				−70
−3,500				

↕ Cash flows: +3,430

All of the above accounts combine to determine net sales. The formula for net sales was shown in Illustration 5-5 in the chapter, and has been reproduced in Illustration 5A-2 for convenience.

CALCULATING COST OF GOODS SOLD

As was mentioned earlier, calculating the cost of goods sold is different in a periodic inventory system than in a perpetual inventory system. In a periodic inventory system, there is no running account (continuous updating) of changes in cost of goods sold and inventory as there is in a perpetual inventory system. Instead, the cost of goods sold for the period and the balance in ending inventory are calculated at the end of the period, after an inventory count has been completed.

To calculate the cost of goods sold in a periodic inventory, four steps are required:

1. Calculate the cost of goods purchased.
2. Determine the cost of goods available for sale by adding the cost of goods purchased to beginning inventory.
3. Determine ending inventory based on an inventory count.
4. Calculate the cost of goods sold by subtracting the ending inventory from cost of goods available for sale.

We will discuss each of these steps in the following sections.

▶Illustration 5A-2
Formula for net sales

	Sales	$3,800
−	Sales Returns and Allowances	300
−	Sales Discounts	70
=	Net Sales	$3,430

Cost of Goods Purchased

Earlier in this appendix, we used four accounts—Purchases, Freight In, Purchase Returns and Allowances, and Purchase Discounts—to record the purchase of inventory. These four accounts combine to determine the cost of goods purchased. You may find it helpful to review the formula to calculate cost of goods purchased shown earlier in Illustration 5A-1.

Using assumed data for PW Technologies, the calculation of net purchases and the cost of goods purchased is as follows:

Purchases		$325,000
Less: Purchase returns and allowances	$10,400	
Purchase discounts	6,800	17,200
Net purchases		307,800
Add: Freight in		12,200
Cost of goods purchased		$320,000

Cost of Goods Available for Sale

Cost of goods available for sale is determined by adding beginning inventory to the cost of goods purchased. If PW Technologies' ending inventory at December 31, 2017, was $36,000, then this will also be its beginning inventory at January 1, 2018. Using this information and the cost of goods purchased determined above, we can determine PW Technologies' cost of goods available for sale:

Inventory, January 1	$ 36,000
Cost of goods purchased	320,000
Cost of goods available for sale	$356,000

Cost of Goods Sold

Cost of goods sold is determined by subtracting the cost of ending inventory from the cost of goods available for sale. To determine the cost of the ending inventory on hand, PW Technologies must count inventory. Counting inventory involves these procedures:

1. Count the units on hand for each item of inventory.
2. Apply unit costs to the total units on hand for each item of inventory. (We will learn more about how to do this in the next chapter.)
3. Total the costs for each item of inventory to determine the total cost of goods on hand.

The cost of ending inventory is also known as the total cost of goods on hand. PW Technologies' physical inventory count on December 31, 2018, determines that the cost of its goods on hand, or ending inventory, is $40,000. Using this information and the cost of goods available for sale determined above, we can determine PW Technologies' cost of goods sold as follows:

Cost of goods available for sale	$356,000
Inventory, December 31	40,000
Cost of goods sold	$316,000

Illustration 5A-3 presents this as a formula and inserts the relevant data for PW Technologies.

▶ Illustration 5A-3
Formula for cost of goods sold

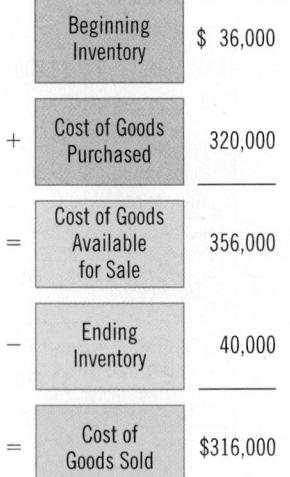

	Beginning Inventory	$ 36,000
+	Cost of Goods Purchased	320,000
=	Cost of Goods Available for Sale	356,000
−	Ending Inventory	40,000
=	Cost of Goods Sold	$316,000

ADJUSTING ENTRY AT PERIOD END

It is important to remember that, when using a periodic inventory system, no entries are posted to the Inventory account during the period. Because the Inventory account does not reflect an up-to-date balance and because the Cost of Goods Sold account does not have any balance as it was not used during the period, we need to record an adjusting entry at the end of each period to update the amounts in these accounts.

In the adjusting entry shown below for PW Technologies, the Inventory account is debited for the ending inventory amount of $40,000 that was determined when counting items at the end of the period and credited for the beginning inventory amount of $36,000. Cost of Goods Sold is also debited for $316,000, the amount we calculated above, and the balances of any purchase-related accounts are brought to zero as these amounts are now allocated to Cost of Goods Sold:

A	=	L	+	SE
+40,000				−316,000
−36,000				−10,400
				−6,800
				+325,000
				+12,200
Cash flows: no effect				

Dec. 31	Inventory (ending)	40,000	
	Cost of Goods Sold	316,000	
	Purchase Returns and Allowances	10,400	
	Purchase Discounts	6,800	
	Inventory (beginning)		36,000
	Purchases		325,000
	Freight In		12,200
	(To allocate purchase-related accounts and change in Inventory to Cost of Goods Sold)		

COMPARISON OF ENTRIES: PERPETUAL VS. PERIODIC

The periodic inventory system's entries for purchases and sales are shown in Illustration 5A-4 next to those that were illustrated in the chapter under the perpetual inventory system. Having these entries side by side should help you compare the differences. The entries that are different in the two inventory systems are highlighted in red.

ENTRIES ON SAUK COMMUNICATIONS' BOOKS (BUYER)

Transaction		Perpetual Inventory System			Periodic Inventory System		
May 2	Purchase of merchandise on credit	Inventory	3,800		Purchases	3,800	
		Accounts Payable		3,800	Accounts Payable		3,800
4	Freight costs on purchases	Inventory	150		Freight In	150	
		Cash		150	Cash		150
8	Purchase returns and allowances	Accounts Payable	300		Accounts Payable	300	
		Inventory		300	Purchase Returns and Allowances		300
12	Payment on account with a discount	Accounts Payable	3,500		Accounts Payable	3,500	
		Cash		3,430	Cash		3,430
		Inventory		70	Purchase Discounts		70

ENTRIES ON PW TECHNOLOGIES' BOOKS (SELLER)

Transaction		Perpetual Inventory System			Periodic Inventory System		
May 2	Sale of merchandise on credit	Accounts Receivable	3,800		Accounts Receivable	3,800	
		Sales		3,800	Sales		3,800
		Cost of Goods Sold	2,400		No entry required		
		Inventory		2,400			
8	Return of merchandise sold	Sales Returns and Allowances	300		Sales Returns and Allowances	300	
		Accounts Receivable		300	Accounts Receivable		300
		Inventory	140		No entry required		
		Cost of Goods Sold		140			
12	Cash received on account with a discount	Cash	3,430		Cash	3,430	
		Sales Discounts	70		Sales Discounts	70	
		Accounts Receivable		3,500	Accounts Receivable		3,500
Dec. 31	Period-end adjustment	No entry required			Inventory (ending)	40,000	
					Cost of Goods Sold	316,000	
					Purchase Returns and Allowances	10,400	
					Purchase Discounts	6,800	
					Inventory (beginning)		36,000
					Purchases		325,000
					Freight in		12,200

▶ Illustration 5A-4

Comparison of entries under perpetual and periodic inventory systems

INCOME STATEMENT

Once cost of goods sold is calculated in a periodic inventory system, gross profit, operating expenses, non-operating items, income before income tax, and net income are reported in a multiple-step or single-step income statement in the same way as they are in a perpetual inventory system. The only reporting difference in a multiple-step income statement is that the cost of goods sold section has more detail in a periodic inventory system than in a perpetual inventory system. (See red highlighted text in Illustration 5A-5.) Compare Illustration 5A-5 with the multiple-step income statement shown in Illustration 5-7 for a perpetual inventory system, where only one line is reported for the cost of goods sold.

▶Illustration 5A-5

Multiple-step income statement—
periodic inventory system

PW TECHNOLOGIES INC. Income Statement Year Ended December 31, 2018			
Sales revenue			
Sales			$480,000
Less: Sales returns and allowances		$12,000	
Sales discounts		8,000	20,000
Net sales			460,000
Cost of goods sold			
Inventory, January 1		$36,000	
Purchases	$325,000		
Less: Purchase returns and allowances	10,400		
Purchase discounts	6,800		
Net purchases	307,800		
Add: Freight in	12,200		
Cost of goods purchased		320,000	
Cost of goods available for sale		356,000	
Inventory, December 31		40,000	
Cost of goods sold			316,000
Gross profit			144,000
Operating expenses			
Salaries expense		$45,000	
Rent expense		19,000	
Utilities expense		17,000	
Advertising expense		16,000	
Depreciation expense		8,000	
Freight out		7,000	
Insurance expense		2,000	
Loss on disposal		200	114,200
Income from operations			29,800
Other revenues and expenses			
Interest revenue		$3,400	
Interest expense		1,600	1,800
Income before income tax			31,600
Income tax expense			6,300
Net income			$ 25,300

Using the periodic inventory system does not affect the content of the statement of financial position, statement of changes in equity, or statement of cash flow. As in the perpetual system, the ending balance of inventory is reported in the current assets section of the statement of financial position, and at the same amount.

DO IT! ▶5-6   Purchase and Sales Transactions—Periodic Inventory System

Action Plan

✔ Seller: Prepare only one entry to record the sale and do not record the cost of the sale. Prepare only one entry to record the return of goods and do not record the cost of the return. Calculate sales discounts using the amount owing, net of any sales returns.

✔ Buyer: Record purchases of inventory, returned goods, and purchase discounts in separate accounts. Calculate purchase discounts using the amount owing, net of any purchase returns.

On September 4, Lalonde Ltée sells merchandise on account to Guerette Corp., terms 2/10, n/45. The selling price of the goods is $3,000. On September 8, goods with a selling price of $600 are returned for credit and restored to inventory. On September 13, Lalonde receives payment in full from Guerette. Record the transactions on the books of both companies, assuming a periodic inventory system is used.

SOLUTION

Try this Do It! exercise on your own and then check your answer at the end of the chapter.

Related Exercise Material: *BE5–12, *BE5–13, *BE5–14, *BE5–15, *BE5–16, *E5–14, *E5–15, *E5–16, and *E5–17.

REVIEW AND PRACTICE

▶ LEARNING OBJECTIVE REVIEW

1. Identify the differences between service and merchandising companies. A service company performs services. It has service or fee revenue and operating expenses. A merchandising company sells goods. It has sales revenue, cost of goods sold, and gross profit in addition to operating expenses. Both types of company may also report non-operating items and each would report income tax expense.

There are two types of inventory systems: perpetual inventory systems and periodic inventory systems. In a perpetual inventory system, the cost of goods sold and ending inventory amounts are always known. This is not the case with a periodic inventory system in which these amounts can be determined only after an inventory count. In addition to providing more timely information, perpetual inventory systems have the added advantages of enabling management to determine the extent of any theft of inventory and establish automatic reordering points.

2. Prepare entries for purchases under a perpetual inventory system. The Inventory account is debited for all purchases of merchandise and for freight costs if those costs are paid by the buyer (freight terms FOB shipping point). The Inventory account is credited for purchase discounts, and purchase returns and allowances. Freight terms are used to determine when the ownership of inventory changes hands. If the terms are FOB destination, then the inventory remains an asset of the seller until it reaches the buyer's place of business. If the terms are FOB shipping point, then the inventory becomes an asset of the buyer as soon as it is shipped.

Purchase discounts are discounts provided by the seller to encourage the buyer to pay for credit purchases in advance of the due date. When they are taken, they must be accounted for because they reduce the cost of inventory purchases that have already been recorded. Quantity discounts are related to volume purchases of inventory and are offered at the time of purchase. They do not have to be separately accounted for because they simply reduce the purchase price, which is then used to record the inventory purchase.

3. Prepare entries for sales under a perpetual inventory system. When inventory is sold, two entries are required: (1) Cash or Accounts Receivable is debited and Sales is credited for the *selling price* of the merchandise, and (2) Cost of Goods Sold is debited and Inventory is credited for the *cost* of inventory items sold. Contra revenue accounts are used to record sales returns and allowances and sales discounts. Two journal entries are also required for sales returns so that both the selling price and the cost of the returned merchandise are recorded (if its condition would enable the company to resell it). Freight costs paid by the seller (shipping terms FOB destination) are recorded as an operating expense.

4. Prepare a single-step and a multiple-step income statement. In a single-step income statement, all data (except for income tax expense) are classified under two categories—revenues or expenses—and income before income tax is determined in one step. Income tax expense is separated from the other expenses and reported separately after income before income tax to determine net income (loss).

A multiple-step income statement shows several steps in determining net income. Step 1 deducts sales returns and allowances and sales discounts from gross sales to determine net sales. Step 2 deducts the cost of goods sold from net sales to determine gross profit. Step 3 deducts operating expenses (which can be classified by nature or by function) from gross profit to determine income from operations. Step 4 adds or deducts any non-operating items to determine income before income tax. Finally, step 5 deducts income tax expense to determine net income (loss).

5. Calculate the gross profit margin and profit margin. The gross profit margin, calculated by dividing gross profit by net sales, measures the gross profit earned for each dollar of sales. The profit margin, calculated by dividing net income by net sales, measures the income earned for each dollar of sales. Both are measures of profitability that are closely watched by management and other interested parties. Generally, management's aim is to maximize both gross profit margin and profit margin.

6. Account for and report inventory in a periodic inventory system (Appendix 5A). The periodic inventory system differs from the perpetual inventory system in that separate temporary accounts are used in the periodic system to record (1) purchases, (2) purchase returns and allowances, (3) purchase discounts, and (4) freight costs that are paid by the buyer (shipping terms FOB shipping point). The formula for cost of goods purchased is as follows: Purchases – purchase returns and allowances – purchase discounts = net purchases; and net purchases + freight in = cost of goods purchased.

Both perpetual and periodic systems use temporary accounts to record (1) sales, (2) sales returns and allowances, and (3) sales discounts. However, in a periodic inventory system, only one journal entry is made to record a sale of merchandise because the cost of goods sold is not recorded throughout the period. Instead, the cost of goods sold is determined at the end of the period, after an inventory count has been completed.

To determine the cost of goods sold, first calculate the cost of goods purchased, as indicated above. Then, calculate the cost of goods sold as follows: Beginning inventory + cost of goods purchased = cost of goods available for sale; and cost of goods available for sale – ending inventory = cost of goods sold.

At the end of the period, the Inventory account is adjusted to reflect its proper balance as determined from the inventory count results. The change in this account is allocated to the Cost of Goods Sold account as are the balances in the Freight In and Purchases accounts and any related contra accounts.

The statement of financial position, statement of changes in equity, and statement of cash flows are no different in a periodic inventory system than in a perpetual inventory system. However, a multiple-step income statement includes more detail in the cost of goods sold section in a periodic inventory system.

▶ KEY TERM REVIEW

The following are key terms defined in this chapter with the corresponding page reference for your review. You will find a complete list of terms and definitions for all chapters in the glossary at the end of this textbook.

Contra expense account (p. 261)
Contra revenue account (p. 250)
Cost of goods available for sale (p. 243)
Cost of goods purchased (p. 244)
Cost of goods sold (p. 241)
FOB (free on board) destination (p. 245)
FOB (free on board) shipping point (p. 245)
Function (p. 254)
Gross profit (p. 241)

Gross profit margin (p. 258)
Gross sales (p. 252)
Income from operations (p. 256)
Multiple-step income statement (p. 255)
Nature (p. 254)
Net purchases (p. 262)
Net sales (p. 252)
Operating expenses (p. 241)
Periodic inventory system (p. 243)

Perpetual inventory system (p. 241)
Profit margin (p. 259)
Purchase discount (p. 247)
Purchase returns and allowances (p. 246)
Quantity discount (p. 251)
Sales discount (p. 251)
Sales returns and allowances (p. 250)
Sales revenue (p. 241)
Single-step income statement (p. 253)

▶ COMPARING IFRS AND ASPE REVIEW

Key Standard Differences	International Financial Reporting Standards (IFRS)	Accounting Standards for Private Enterprises (ASPE)
Income statement	Expenses must be classified by nature or by function.	Expenses can be classified in any manner the company finds useful.

▶ DECISION TOOLKIT REVIEW

DECISION CHECKPOINTS	INFO NEEDED FOR DECISION	TOOLS TO USE FOR DECISION	HOW TO EVALUATE RESULTS
Are the selling prices of goods keeping pace with changes in the cost of inventory?	Gross profit and net sales	$\text{Gross profit margin} = \dfrac{\text{Gross profit}}{\text{Net sales}}$	If the ratio decreases over time, it suggests the company is not passing on increases in inventory costs to its customers by raising prices as fast as costs are rising. It can also mean that the company is reducing selling prices when costs have not fallen to the same extent. When compared across companies in the same industry, it can indicate which company does a better job of controlling product/production costs relative to sales revenue.
Is the company maintaining an adequate margin between sales and expenses?	Net income and net sales	$\text{Profit margin} = \dfrac{\text{Net income}}{\text{Net sales}}$	A higher ratio suggests a favourable return on each dollar of sales.

▶ PRACTICE USING THE DECISION TOOLKIT

Answers are at the end of the chapter.

The following selected information is available for **Costco Wholesale Corporation:**

(in U.S. $ millions)	2015	2014
Net sales	$113,666	$110,212
Cost of goods sold	101,065	98,458
Net income	2,377	2,058

INSTRUCTIONS

(a) Costco operates 686 stores in nine countries, while both Loblaw and Metro operate approximately 590 stores across Canada. Can a comparison of the financial results of these three companies be meaningful? Why or why not?

(b) Calculate the gross profit margin and profit margin for Costco for 2015 and 2014.

(c) Using the ratios calculated in part (b), compare the gross profit margin and profit margin with that of Loblaw, Metro, and their industry found in Illustrations 5-8 and 5-9 in the chapter.

▶ PRACTICE COMPREHENSIVE DO IT!

Answers are at the end of the chapter.

The adjusted trial balance at December 31, 2018, for Dykstra Inc. follows:

	Debit	Credit
DYKSTRA INC.		
Adjusted Trial Balance		
December 31, 2018		
Cash	$ 4,500	
Accounts receivable	11,100	
Inventory	29,000	
Prepaid insurance	2,500	
Land	150,000	
Buildings	500,000	
Accumulated depreciation—buildings		$ 40,000
Equipment	95,000	
Accumulated depreciation—equipment		18,000
Accounts payable		10,600
Property tax payable		4,000
Bank loan payable—short-term		25,000
Mortgage payable		551,000
Common shares		70,000
Retained earnings		61,000
Dividends declared	10,000	
Sales		536,800
Sales returns and allowances	6,700	
Sales discounts	5,000	
Cost of goods sold	363,400	
Administrative expenses	111,500	
Selling expenses	19,600	
Interest expense	4,600	
Interest revenue		2,500
Income tax expense	6,000	
	$1,318,900	$1,318,900

Additional information:
- $21,000 of the mortgage is due within the next year.
- Dykstra issued $5,000 of common shares during the year.

INSTRUCTIONS

Assuming Dykstra uses a perpetual inventory system, prepare a multiple-step income statement, statement of changes in equity, and statement of financial position for the year.

▶ PRACTICE OBJECTIVE-FORMAT QUESTIONS

Note: All questions marked with an asterisk (*) relate to material in Appendix 5A. Answers are at the end of the chapter.

1. Indicate which of the following statements are correct. (Select as many as are appropriate.)

   (a) Periodic inventory systems provide management with better information than perpetual inventory systems.

   (b) Selling goods to customers on account rather than for cash reduces a company's operating cycle.

(c) Both cost of goods sold and operating expenses are taken into account when calculating gross profit.

(d) Service companies do not use the Cost of Goods Sold account.

(e) Merchandising companies would normally have a longer operating cycle than service companies.

(f) Automated reordering of inventory is possible if a company is using a periodic inventory system.

(g) An inventory count is still required if a company is using a perpetual inventory system.

2. If inventory was purchased on account on October 10, with terms 2/10, n/30, FOB destination, indicate which of the following statements would be correct. (Select as many as are appropriate.)

(a) The buyer would be responsible for the freight costs.

(b) Payment in full would be due by October 20.

(c) If the goods were lost or damaged during shipping, the seller would be responsible and bear the cost.

(d) The goods would become part of the inventory of the buyer on October 10.

(e) Freight costs would be the responsibility of the seller and would be recorded as freight out.

(f) The goods would be included in the inventory of the seller on October 10 and would continue to be included until the goods were delivered at the buyer's place of business.

(g) If payment was made on or before October 20, the purchaser could take a 10% discount.

3. For each of the following journal entries, indicate whether they would be made by the buyer or seller of merchandise:

(a) Inventory
       Accounts Payable

(b) Cash
       Sales Discounts
       Accounts Receivable

(c) Cost of Goods Sold
       Inventory

(d) Inventory
       Cost of Goods Sold

(e) Accounts Payable
       Inventory
       Cash

(f) Freight Out
       Cash

(g) Inventory
       Cash

4. On January 2, Sawada Imports Ltd. sells merchandise on account to Hanneson Holdings Ltd., terms 1/10, n/30. The selling price of the goods is $8,500 and the cost to Sawada was $5,200. On January 7, Sawada received payment in full from Hanneson. If Sawada uses a perpetual inventory system, indicate which of the following journal entries are correct in relation to recording these transactions on Sawada's books. (Select as many as are appropriate.)

(a) Cash   8,500
       Sales   8,500

(b) Inventory   5,200
       Cost of Goods Sold   5,200

(c) Cash   8,415
       Sales Discounts   85
       Accounts Receivable   8,500

(d) Cost of Goods Sold   5,200
       Inventory   5,200

(e) Cash   8,500
       Accounts Receivable   8,500

(f) Cash   7,650
       Sales Discounts   850
       Accounts Receivable   8,500

(g) Accounts Receivable   8,500
       Sales   8,500

5. Indicate which of the following statements are correct in relation to the information from Al Mansour Imports Ltd. (AMI) presented below. Note: all accounts have their normal balance. (Select as many as are appropriate.)

Utilities expense	$ 7,000	Equipment	$206,000
Accounts payable	30,000	Loss on disposal	2,000
Cash	7,000	Sales	203,000
Sales discounts	9,000	Salaries expense	45,000
Retained earnings	28,000	Accounts receivable	32,000
Unearned revenue	3,000	Rent expense	12,000

Accumulated depreciation—equipment	$155,000	Dividends declared	$ 21,000
Salaries payable	13,000	Interest expense	1,000
Inventory	90,000	Sales returns and allowances	3,000
Depreciation expense	8,000	Cost of goods sold	88,000
Income tax expense	4,000	Common shares	103,000

(a) Net sales would equal $194,000.

(b) Interest expense would be included in administrative expenses if expenses were classified by function.

(c) Income from operations would equal $29,000.

(d) Income tax expense would be included in other revenues and expenses.

(e) Gross profit would equal $103,000.

(f) Dividends declared is included in other revenues and expenses.

(g) Net income would equal $25,000.

6. Indicate the effect (increase/decrease/no effect) that the following accounts would have on net income.

(a) Freight Out
(b) Accumulated Depreciation—Buildings
(c) Loss on Disposal
(d) Sales

(e) Depreciation Expense
(f) Sales Returns and Allowances
(g) Dividends Declared

7. Indicate which of the following accounts would be included in determining gross profit. (Select as many as are appropriate.)

(a) Freight Out
(b) Sales
(c) Depreciation Expense
(d) Sales Discounts

(e) Cost of Goods Sold
(f) Sales Returns and Allowances
(g) Salaries Expense

8. Indicate which of the following statements are correct in relation to the information from Skip Designs Ltd. presented below. (Select as many as are appropriate.)

	2018	2017	2016
Net sales	$978,000	$856,000	$765,000
Cost of goods sold	391,200	359,520	328,950
Net income	176,040	136,960	114,750

(a) The company's gross profit was $586,800 in 2018.

(b) Skip's operating and other expenses have increased as a percentage of net sales each year.

(c) Skip's gross profit margin has increased every year.

(d) Between 2017 and 2018, the company's selling prices have not kept pace with the changes in the cost of inventory.

(e) Skip has done a better job of controlling its operating and other expenses in 2018 than it did in prior years.

(f) Skip's profit margin has increased every year.

(g) The company's profit margin in 2018 decreased relative to the prior year.

9. Indicate which of the following statements are correct. (Select as many as are appropriate.)

(a) It is possible to quantify inventory theft if a company uses a perpetual inventory system.

(b) Cost of goods available for sale is equal to beginning inventory + cost of goods purchased – ending inventory.

(c) Raw materials are included in the inventory of a manufacturer.

(d) Inventory loss due to theft is included in cost of goods sold.

(e) Wholesalers produce goods for sale directly to consumers.

(f) Inventory counts are unnecessary if a company uses a perpetual inventory system.

(g) Gross profit is calculated without taking operating expenses into account.

*10. On August 8, Matchett Ltd. purchased merchandise on account from Beamen Ltd. for $20,000, terms 2/10, n/30, FOB shipping point. Matchett paid shipping charges of $525 on August 10. On August 17, Matchett paid the total amount owing to Beamen. Matchett uses a periodic inventory system. Indicate which of the following journal entries are correct in relation to Matchett's recording of these transactions. (Select as many as are appropriate.)

(a)	Purchases	20,000		(e)	Accounts Payable	20,000	
	Accounts Payable		20,000		Purchase Discounts		400
(b)	Accounts Payable	20,000			Cash		19,600
	Cash		20,000	(f)	Accounts Payable	20,000	
(c)	Freight In	525			Purchase Returns and		
	Cash		525		Allowances		20,000
(d)	Inventory	20,000		(g)	Inventory	525	
	Accounts Payable		20,000		Cash		525

WileyPLUS

Brief Exercises, Exercises, and many additional resources are available for practice in WileyPLUS.

Note: All questions, exercises, and problems below with an asterisk (*) relate to material in Appendix 5A.

▶ QUESTIONS

(LO 1) 1. (a) What is meant by the term *operating cycle*? (b) Why is the normal operating cycle for a merchandising company likely to be longer than that of a service company?

(LO 1) 2. (a) Explain the income measurement process in a merchandising company. (b) How does income measurement differ between a merchandising company and a service company?

(LO 1) 3. Suppose you are starting a company that sells used clothes. What factors would you consider in determining whether to use a perpetual or periodic inventory system?

(LO 1) 4. Song Yee wonders why a physical inventory count is necessary in a perpetual inventory system. After all, the accounting records show how much inventory is on hand. Explain why a physical inventory count is required in a perpetual inventory system.

(LO 1) 5. One of your classmates has come to you because he is struggling to understand the key differences between perpetual and periodic inventory systems. Prepare an explanation of the key differences for your classmate.

(LO 2) 6. Why are purchases of merchandise for resale not recorded in the same account as purchases of other items, such as supplies or equipment? Would it not be better to use one account to record all these purchases?

(LO 2) 7. Butler's Roofing Ltd. received an invoice for a purchase of merchandise for $48,000, terms 1/10, n/30. (a) Calculate the cost of missing this purchase discount to Butler's Roofing. (b) Should it take advantage of the cash discount offered or not? Explain.

(LO 2, 3) 8. Inventory was purchased on credit in April and paid for in May by Lebel Ltée. Lebel sold and delivered the merchandise, along with an invoice, to a customer in June. The customer paid Lebel for the merchandise in July. (a) In which month should Lebel record the sale as revenue and in which month should Lebel record the cost of goods sold as expense? (b) In which month should the customer record the purchase of inventory from Lebel?

(LO 2, 3) 9. (a) Distinguish between FOB shipping point and FOB destination. (b) What freight term will result in a debit to Inventory by the buyer? A debit to Freight Out by the seller?

(LO 2, 3) 10. Explain why purchase returns are credited directly to the Inventory account but sales returns are not debited directly to the Sales account.

(LO 2, 3) 11. (a) Distinguish between a quantity discount, a purchase discount, and a sales discount. (b) Explain how each kind of discount is recorded.

(LO 3) 12. Explain what contra revenue accounts are and why they are used. Be sure to identify one example of a contra revenue account in your response.

(LO 3) 13. If merchandise is returned and restored to inventory, the Cost of Goods Sold account is credited. However, if merchandise is returned but not restored to inventory (because it is not resaleable), Cost of Goods Sold is not credited. Why not?

(LO 3) 14. Explain why sales taxes collected by a merchandiser from customers when goods are sold are not recorded as sales revenue.

(LO 4) 15. Distinguish between a single-step and a multiple-step income statement for a merchandising company.

(LO 4) 16. Which type of income statement—single-step or multiple-step—does **The North West Company** use? You can find its financial statements in Appendix A at the back of this textbook.

(LO 4) 17. (a) What is the difference between classifying expenses in an income statement by nature or by function? (b) Does this classification apply only to a single-step income statement, to a multiple-step income statement, or to both?

(LO 4) 18. In British Columbia and Alberta, **Loblaws** has numerous competitors in the grocery marketplace. These include **The Jim Pattison Group**, Canada's second-largest private company, which owns the Overwaitea Food Group. The

Overwaitea Food Group operates grocery stores under a number of banners, including Save-On-Foods, Overwaitea Foods, and Urban Fare. Do you think that there might be a difference in how the expenses reported on Overwaitea's income statement, as a private company, might differ from those presented by a public company like Loblaws?

(LO 4) 19. Why is interest expense reported as a non-operating expense and not as an operating expense on a multiple-step income statement?

(LO 5) 20. Explain the difference, if any, between gross profit margin and profit margin.

(LO 5) 21. What factors affect a company's gross profit margin; that is, what can cause the gross profit margin to increase and what can cause it to decrease?

(LO 5) 22. Identify two types of companies that you would expect to have a high gross profit margin and two types of companies that you would expect to have a low gross profit margin.

(LO 6) *23. Identify the accounts that are added to or deducted from purchases in a periodic inventory system to determine the cost of goods purchased. For each account, indicate (a) whether its balance is added or deducted and (b) what its normal balance is.

(LO 6) *24. How is the cost of goods sold calculated and recorded in a periodic inventory system? In a perpetual inventory system?

(LO 6) *25. What differences would be found on an income statement prepared for a company using a periodic inventory system, compared with a company using a perpetual inventory system?

▶BRIEF EXERCISES

BE5–1 The operating cycles of three different companies are shown below.

Company	Operating Cycle (in days)
A	40
B	72
C	99

Compare operating cycles.
(LO 1)

(a) Which company has the most efficient operating cycle? (b) Identify which of the three companies is most likely a service company, a merchandising company, and a manufacturing company, and explain why.

BE5–2 Selected information from the income measurement process for a service company and a merchandising company is shown below.

Determine missing amounts for income measurement process.
(LO 1)

Company	Sales or Service Revenue	Cost of Goods Sold	Gross Profit	Operating Expenses	Income before Income Tax	Income Tax Expense	Profit
A	$100	$ 0	$ 0	$65	$ [1]	$ 9	$[2]
B	100	[3]	60	[4]	35	[5]	26

(a) Determine the missing amounts [1] through [5]. (b) Identify which of the two companies—A or B—is a service company and which is a merchandising company. Explain why you made the choices you did.

BE5–3 At the beginning of the year, Point Claire Shipping Ltd., a company that has a perpetual inventory system, had $55,000 of inventory. During the year, inventory costing $220,000 was purchased. Of this, $26,000 was returned to the supplier and a 5% discount was taken on the remainder. Freight costs incurred by the company for inventory purchases amounted to $2,700. The cost of goods sold during the year was $218,000. Determine the balance in the Inventory account at the end of the year.

Determine balance in Inventory account.
(LO 2)

BE5–4 On August 24, Pocras Corporation purchased inventory on account from Wydell Inc. The selling price of the goods is $32,000 and the cost of goods sold is $14,400. Both companies use perpetual inventory systems. Record the above transactions on the books of both companies.

Record purchase and sales transactions.
(LO 2, 3)

BE5–5 Prepare the journal entries to record the following purchase transactions in Xtra Inc.'s books. Xtra uses a perpetual inventory system.

Record purchase transactions.
(LO 2)

Jan. 2 Xtra purchased goods for $45,000 from Fundy Corp., terms 2/10, n/45, FOB destination.
  5 The appropriate company paid freight costs of $900.
  6 Xtra returned $6,000 of the goods purchased on January 2, because they were not needed.
  11 Xtra paid the balance owed to Fundy.

Record sales transactions.
(LO 3)

BE5–6 Prepare the journal entries to record the following sales transactions in Fundy Corp.'s books. Fundy uses a perpetual inventory system.

Jan. 2 Fundy sold $45,000 of goods to Xtra Inc., terms 2/10, n/45, FOB destination. The cost of the goods sold was $25,200.

5 The appropriate company paid freight costs of $900.

6 Xtra returned $6,000 of the merchandise purchased from Fundy on January 2, because it was not needed. The cost of the merchandise returned was $3,360, and it was restored to inventory.

11 Fundy received the balance due from Xtra.

Calculate amounts from income statement.
(LO 4)

BE5–7 Saguenay Limited reports the following information: sales $1,110,000; sales returns and allowances $22,000; sales discounts $18,000; cost of goods sold $658,000; administrative expenses $160,000; selling expenses $110,000; other revenues $26,000; other expenses $35,000; and income tax expense $27,000. Assuming Saguenay uses a multiple-step income statement, calculate the following: (a) net sales, (b) gross profit, (c) income from operations, (d) income before income tax, and (e) net income.

Identify placement of items on income statement.
(LO 4)

BE5–8 Explain where each of the following items would appear on (a) a single-step income statement and (b) a multiple-step income statement: depreciation expense, cost of goods sold, freight out, income tax expense, interest expense, interest revenue, rent revenue, salaries expense, sales, sales discounts, and sales returns and allowances.

Identify classification of expenses on income statement.
(LO 4)

BE5–9 A company presented its income statement using the following format:

Sales revenue	$x
Cost of goods sold	x
Gross profit	x
Administrative expenses	x
Selling expenses	x
Income from operations	x
Other revenues and expenses	x
Income before income tax	x
Income tax expense	x
Net income	$x

(a) Is this company using a single- or multiple-step form of income statement? (b) Is it classifying its expenses by nature or by function? Explain.

Calculate amounts from income statement, profitability ratios, and comment.
(LO 4, 5)

BE5–10 In 2018, Modder Corporation reported net sales of $250,000, cost of goods sold of $137,500, operating expenses of $50,000, and income tax expense of $20,000. In 2017, it reported net sales of $200,000, cost of goods sold of $114,000, operating expenses of $40,000, other revenues of $10,000, and income tax expense of $15,000. (a) Calculate the gross profit and net income for each year. (b) Calculate the gross profit margin and profit margin for each year. (c) Comment on Modder's changing profitability.

Calculate profitability ratios and comment.
(LO 5)

BE5–11 In 2015, **Canadian Tire** reported sales revenue of $12,279.6 million, cost of goods sold of $7,747.1 million, and net income of $735.9 million. In 2014, it reported sales revenue of $12,462.9 million, cost of goods sold of $8,033.2 million, and net income of $639.3 million. (a) Calculate the gross profit margin and profit margin for each year. (b) Comment on Canadian Tire's changing profitability.

Record purchase transactions.
(LO 6)

*BE5–12 From the information in BE5–5, prepare the journal entries to record the purchase transactions on Xtra Inc.'s books, assuming a periodic inventory system is used instead of a perpetual inventory system.

Record sales transactions.
(LO 6)

*BE5–13 From the information in BE5–6, prepare the journal entries to record the sales transactions on Fundy Corp.'s books, assuming a periodic inventory system is used instead of a perpetual inventory system.

Calculate amounts from income statement.
(LO 6)

*BE5–14 Bassing Corp. uses a periodic inventory system and reports the following information: sales $1,860,000; sales returns and allowances $124,000; sales discounts $28,000; purchases $880,000; purchase returns and allowances $13,000; purchase discounts $14,000; freight in $16,000; freight out $37,000; beginning inventory $96,000; and ending inventory $82,000. Assuming Bassing uses a multiple-step income statement, calculate (a) net sales, (b) net purchases, (c) cost of goods purchased, (d) cost of goods sold, and (e) gross profit.

*BE5–15 Halifax Limited reported the following selected data for the year ended December 31, 2018: purchases $195,000; purchase returns and allowances $6,600; purchase discounts $20,400; freight in $5,250; freight out $11,250; beginning inventory $105,000; and ending inventory $120,000. (a) Prepare the cost of goods sold section for Halifax in a multiple-step income statement. (b) Explain how the remainder of Halifax's income statement would differ, if at all, if it used a perpetual inventory system.

Prepare cost of goods sold section.

(LO 6)

*BE5–16 At the end of the year, Tunnel Mountain Resorts Ltd., a company that has a periodic inventory system, had the following account balances on its unadjusted trial balance: Inventory $75,000, Purchases $388,000, Purchase Discounts $6,000, Freight In $12,000. The inventory count at the end of the year determined that the inventory on hand at that time cost $68,000. Record the adjusting journal entry that would be made at the end of the year to update the Inventory and Cost of Goods Sold accounts.

Prepare period-end adjusting entry for periodic system.

(LO 6)

▶ EXERCISES

E5–1 Listed below are selected companies, accompanied by a brief description of their business.
1. **Toys "R" Us, Inc.** sells toys.
2. **Fasken Martineau LLP** is a law firm.
3. **Atlantic Grocery Distributors Ltd.** distributes food products to grocery stores.

Distinguish between service and merchandising companies.

(LO 1)

Instructions
(a) Identify whether the primary type of business for each of the above companies is as a service company, merchandiser (retailer) company, or merchandiser (wholesaler) company.
(b) Comment on how the operating cycles and income measurement processes of each of the above companies might differ, if at all.

E5–2 Listed below are selected examples of transactions related to the purchase and sale of inventory. Assume a perpetual inventory system is in use.
1. Purchase of $3,500 of inventory for cash.
2. Return of $750 of inventory to seller for credit on account.
3. Purchase of $4,000 of inventory on account, terms 2/10, n/45.
4. Payment of $400 cash for freight on purchase of inventory (FOB shipping point).
5. Payment of amount owed for purchase of $3,500 of inventory, terms 2/10, n/30, paid within discount period.
6. Sale of inventory on account, terms n/30. Selling price $10,000; cost $4,000.
7. Return of damaged inventory from buyer for cash. Selling price $750; cost $300. All of the goods were discarded because they are not resaleable.
8. Payment of $600 cash for freight on sale of inventory (FOB destination).
9. Return of unwanted inventory from buyer for credit on account. Selling price $1,000; cost $400. Goods restored to inventory for future resale.
10. Receipt of payment ($6,000) from customer on account, terms n/30.

Identify debit and credit effects of inventory transactions.

(LO 2, 3)

Instructions
For each of the above transactions, indicate: (a) the basic type (asset, liability, revenue, or expense) of each account to be debited and credited; (b) the specific name(s) of the account(s) to debit and credit (for example, Inventory); and (c) whether each account is increased (+) or decreased (−) and by what amount. The first one has been done for you as an example.

	Account Debited			Account Credited		
	(a)	(b)	(c)	(a)	(b)	(c)
	Basic Type of Account	Specific Account	Amount	Basic Type of Account	Specific Account	Amount
1.	Asset	Inventory	+$3,500	Asset	Cash	−$3,500

E5–3 On September 1, the beginning of its fiscal year, Campus Office Supply Ltd. had an inventory of 100 calculators at a cost of $20 each. The company uses a perpetual inventory system. During September, the following transactions occurred:

Record and post purchase and sales transactions.

(LO 2, 3)

Sept.   2   Purchased 750 calculators for $20 each from Digital Corp. on account, terms n/30.
     10   Returned 10 calculators to Digital for $200 credit because they did not meet specifications.
     11   Sold 260 calculators for $30 each to Campus Book Store, terms n/30.

Sept. 14   Granted credit of $300 to Campus Book Store for the return of 10 calculators that were not ordered. The calculators were restored to inventory.
    21   Sold 300 calculators for $30 each to Student Card Shop, terms 1/10, n/30.
    29   Paid Digital the amount owing.
    30   Received payment in full from the Student Card Shop.

Instructions

(a)   Record the September transactions.
(b)   Create T accounts for the Inventory and Cost of Goods Sold accounts. Enter the opening balances and post the September transactions.
(c)   Determine the ending balances of inventory and cost of goods sold in both dollars and quantities.

Record purchase transactions.

(LO 2)

E5–4   Olaf Corp. uses a perpetual inventory system. The company had the following inventory transactions in April:

Apr. 3   Purchased merchandise from DeVito Ltd. for $28,000, terms 1/10, n/30, FOB shipping point.
    6   The appropriate company paid freight costs of $700 on the merchandise purchased on April 3.
    7   Purchased supplies on account for $5,000.
    8   Returned damaged merchandise to DeVito and was given a purchase allowance of $3,500. The merchandise was repaired by DeVito and returned to inventory for future resale.
    30   Paid the amount due to DeVito in full.

Instructions

(a)   Record the above transactions in Olaf's books.
(b)   Assume that Olaf paid the balance due to DeVito on April 12 instead of April 30. Prepare the journal entry to record this payment on Olaf's books.

Record sales transactions.

(LO 3)

E5–5   Refer to the information in E5–4 for Olaf Corp. and the following additional information:

1.   The cost of the merchandise sold on April 3 was $19,000.
2.   The cost of the merchandise returned on April 8 was $2,300.
3.   DeVito uses a perpetual inventory system.

Instructions

(a)   Record the transactions in the books of DeVito.
(b)   Assume that DeVito received the balance due from Olaf on April 12 instead of April 30. Prepare the journal entry to record this collection on DeVito's books.

Calculate effect of purchase discount lost.

(LO 2)

E5–6   Broyle Ltd.'s main supplier offers it credit terms of 1/10, n/30 on its purchases. Because cash flow is tight for Broyle, the company's CFO is trying to determine what the annual interest rate would be if the company passes up this discount and pays at the end of the 30-day credit period instead. Also, if Broyle can access a short-term loan with interest of 8%, which would provide it with the funds to take advantage of the purchase discount, should it do so?

Record purchase and sales transactions; calculate gross profit.

(LO 2, 3, 5)

E5–7   The following merchandise transactions occurred in December. Both companies use a perpetual inventory system.

Dec. 3   Pictou Ltd. sold goods to Thames Corp. for $68,000, terms 2/10, n/30, FOB shipping point. The inventory had cost Pictou $36,000.
    7   Shipping costs of $900 were paid by the appropriate company.
    8   Thames returned unwanted merchandise to Pictou. The returned merchandise has a sales price of $2,100, and a cost of $1,150. It was restored to inventory.
    11   Pictou received the balance due from Thames.

Instructions

(a)   Record the above transactions in the books of Pictou.
(b)   Record the above transactions in the books of Thames.
(c)   Calculate the gross profit earned by Pictou on the above transactions.

E5–8 The following list of accounts is from the adjusted trial balance for Swirsky Corporation:

Classify accounts.
(LO 4)

Accounts payable	Equipment	Prepaid insurance
Accounts receivable	Income tax expense	Property tax payable
Accumulated depreciation	Interest expense	Salaries payable
Administrative expenses	Interest payable	Sales
Buildings	Inventory	Sales discounts
Cash	Land	Sales returns and allowances
Common shares	Mortgage payable	Unearned revenue

Instructions
For each account, identify whether it should be reported on the statement of financial position or income statement. Also specify where the account should be classified. For example, Accounts Payable would be classified under current liabilities on the statement of financial position.

E5–9 The following selected accounts from Blue Door Corporation's general ledger are presented below for the year ended December 31, 2018:

Prepare income statement.
(LO 4)

Accounts receivable	$ 265,000
Accumulated depreciation—equipment	783,500
Advertising expense	55,000
Common shares	250,000
Cost of goods sold	1,172,000
Depreciation expense	125,000
Dividends declared	150,000
Equipment	1,450,000
Freight out	25,000
Income tax expense	70,000
Insurance expense	23,000
Interest expense	62,000
Interest revenue	30,000
Inventory	97,000
Prepaid expenses	31,000
Rent revenue	24,000
Retained earnings	535,000
Salaries expense	705,000
Sales	2,650,000
Sales discounts	19,500
Sales returns and allowances	41,000
Unearned revenue	18,000

Instructions
(a) Prepare a single-step income statement.
(b) Prepare a multiple-step income statement.
(c) Are the expenses classified by nature or function in the list of accounts above? Explain.

E5–10 Income statement information is presented here for two companies:

Determine missing amounts and calculate profitability ratios.
(LO 4, 5)

	Young Ltd.	Rioux Ltée
Sales	$99,000	$ [6]
Sales returns and allowances	[1]	5,000
Net sales	89,000	100,000
Cost of goods sold	58,750	[7]
Gross profit	[2]	40,000
Operating expenses	19,500	[8]
Income from operations	[3]	18,000
Other revenues	750	0
Other expenses	0	2,000
Income before income tax	[4]	[9]
Income tax expense	2,300	[10]
Net income	[5]	12,800

Instructions
(a) Calculate the missing amounts for items [1] to [10].
(b) Calculate the gross profit margin and profit margin for each company.

Determine missing amounts and calculate profitability ratios.

(LO 4, 5)

E5–11 Income statement information is presented here for two companies:

	Marchant Ltd.	Dueck Ltd.
Sales	$1,460,000	$ [6]
Sales returns and allowances	28,000	48,000
Net sales	[1]	2,130,000
Cost of goods sold	657,000	1,172,000
Gross profit	[2]	[7]
Operating expenses	580,000	[8]
Income from operations	[3]	310,000
Other revenues	3,600	0
Other expenses	0	4,100
Income before income tax	[4]	[9]
Income tax expense	38,600	[10]
Net income	[5]	250,900

Instructions

(a) Calculate the missing amounts for items [1] to [10].

(b) Calculate the gross profit margin and profit margin for each company.

Prepare income statement; calculate profitability ratios.

(LO 4, 5)

E5–12 Montmorency Ltée reported the following condensed income statement data (in thousands) for the year ended August 31, 2018:

Administrative expenses	$ 670
Sales discounts	110
Cost of goods sold	4,030
Income tax expense	560
Sales revenue	7,200
Interest expense	270
Selling expenses	260

Instructions

(a) Prepare a multiple-step income statement.

(b) Are the expenses classified by nature or function in the list of accounts above?

(c) Calculate the gross profit margin and profit margin.

Calculate profitability ratios and comment.

(LO 5)

E5–13 **Best Buy** reported the following selected information for its three most recent fiscal years (in U.S. $ millions):

	2016	2015	2014
Net sales	$39,528	$40,339	$40,611
Cost of goods sold	30,334	31,292	31,212
Income from operations	1,375	1,450	1,144
Net income	807	1,246	695

Instructions

(a) Calculate the gross profit margin and profit margin for Best Buy for each of the three years.

(b) Comment on whether the ratios have improved or deteriorated over the past three years.

(c) Recalculate the profit margin for the three years using income from operations instead of net income. Does this result in a different trend than you saw in part (a)? If yes, what might be the reason for this change?

Record purchase and sales transactions.

(LO 6)

*E5–14 Data for Olaf Corp. and DeVito Ltd. are presented in E5–4 and E5–5.

Instructions

Repeat the requirements for E5–4 and E5–5, assuming a periodic inventory system is used instead of a perpetual inventory system.

Record purchase and sales transactions.

(LO 2, 3, 6)

*E5–15 Duvall Ltd. and Pele Ltd. incurred the following merchandise transactions in June.

June 10 Duvall sold $5,000 of merchandise to Pele, terms 1/10, n/30, FOB shipping point. The merchandise cost Duvall $3,000 when it was originally purchased.

　　11 Freight costs of $250 were paid by the appropriate company.

　　12 Duvall received damaged goods returned by Pele for credit. The goods were originally sold for $500; the cost of the returned merchandise was $300. The merchandise was not returned to inventory.

　　19 Duvall received full payment from Pele.

Instructions
(a) Prepare journal entries for each transaction in the books of Duvall Ltd., assuming (1) a perpetual inventory system is used, and (2) a periodic inventory system is used.
(b) Prepare journal entries for each transaction for Pele Ltd., assuming (1) a perpetual inventory system is used, and (2) a periodic inventory system is used.

*E5–16 Below are the cost of goods sold sections for the most recent two years for two companies using a periodic inventory system:

Determine missing amounts.
(LO 6)

	Company 1		Company 2	
	Year 1	Year 2	Year 1	Year 2
Beginning inventory	$ 200	$ [5]	$1,000	$ [14]
Purchases	1,500	[6]	[10]	8,550
Purchase returns and allowances	50	100	200	400
Purchase discounts	30	50	150	100
Net purchases	[1]	1,800	7,210	[15]
Freight in	130	[7]	[11]	550
Cost of goods purchased	[2]	[8]	7,800	[16]
Cost of goods available for sale	[3]	2,300	[12]	[17]
Ending inventory	[4]	350	1,250	1,500
Cost of goods sold	1,480	[9]	[13]	[18]

Instructions
Fill in the numbered blanks to complete the cost of goods sold sections.

*E5–17 The following selected information is presented for Lively Limited for the year ended February 28, 2018. Lively uses a periodic inventory system.

Prepare income statement.
(LO 6)

Accounts receivable	$ 32,500	Purchases	$273,000
Administrative expenses	120,900	Purchase discounts	39,000
Common shares	85,000	Purchase returns and allowances	20,800
Dividends declared	42,000	Sales	435,500
Freight in	8,450	Sales discounts	27,300
Income tax expense	9,300	Sales returns and allowances	15,600
Interest expense	7,800	Selling expenses	9,100
Inventory, Mar. 1, 2017	54,600	Unearned revenue	4,500
Inventory, Feb. 28, 2018	79,300		

Instructions
(a) Prepare a multiple-step income statement.
(b) Prepare the year-end adjusting entry that would be made to update the Inventory and Cost of Goods Sold accounts.

▶ PROBLEMS: SET A

P5–1A The Breeze Hair Salon Inc. began operations six months ago. The salon's main business is hair styling and other hair treatment services. The salon also purchases and sells all of the products it uses, plus hair accessories such as hair extensions and jewellery. The sale of the products, while secondary to the salon's main business, still constitutes a significant amount of revenue. Most sales are paid by the salon's customers with cash, or paid for by debit and bank credit cards, which are considered to be equivalent to cash.

Identify problems in operating cycle and use of perpetual inventory system.
(LO 1)

The salon purchases its products from a local wholesaler, on credit terms of n/30 days. Normally, the salon purchases a two-month supply of products at a time. Karen, the manager of the salon, is not comfortable with a high level of accounts payable so the salon pays the wholesaler much earlier than 30 days if it has cash on hand.

When the salon's accounting system was set up, a perpetual inventory system was established to track the products sold. Staff sometimes forget to scan the products that they use on customers.

Karen had a physical inventory count performed after the salon's first six months of operations. When the quantities of merchandise determined at the physical count were compared with the quantities per the perpetual system, there were a number of discrepancies.

Karen has noticed that the salon often runs out of the more popular products. She also noticed that, while some items sell fast, others seem to collect dust. To get rid of these slow-moving products, the salon has to mark down their selling prices, which is affecting the company's cash flow and gross profit.

Instructions
(a) Explain to Karen what an operating cycle is and why the salon is having problems with its cash flow and gross profit.
(b) Explain to Karen how she could be making better use of the company's perpetual inventory system to address the inventory concerns that have been identified.
(c) Explain to Karen the reasons for conducting an inventory count and advise her on the required frequency of counts.

Record purchase and sales transactions.

(LO 1, 2, 3)

P5–2A Phantom Book Warehouse Ltd. distributes hardcover books to retail stores. At the end of May, Phantom's inventory consists of 250 books purchased at $18 each. Phantom uses a perpetual inventory system.

During the month of June, the following merchandise transactions occurred:

June	1	Purchased 180 books on account for $16 each from Reader's World Publishers, terms n/45.
	3	Sold 220 books on account to The Book Nook for $25 each, with an average cost of $17, terms 2/10, n/45.
	5	Received a $160 credit for 10 books returned to Reader's World Publishers.
	8	Sold 80 books on account to Read-A-Lot Bookstore for $22 each, with an average cost of $17, terms 2/10, n/45.
	9	Issued a $264 credit memorandum to Read-A-Lot Bookstore for the return of 12 damaged books. The books were determined to be no longer saleable and were destroyed.
	11	Purchased 130 books on account for $15 each from Read More Publishers, terms n/45.
	12	Received payment in full from The Book Nook.
	17	Received payment in full from Read-A-Lot Bookstore.
	22	Sold 125 books on account to Reader's Bookstore for $25 each, with an average cost of $17, terms 2/10, n/45.
	25	Granted Reader's Bookstore a $375 credit for 15 returned books. These books were restored to inventory.
	29	Paid Reader's World Publishers in full.

Instructions
(a) Is the Phantom Book Warehouse a retailer or a wholesaler? Explain.
(b) Record the June transactions. (Record transactions to the nearest dollar.)
(c) Create a T account for the Inventory account. Enter the opening balance, post the June transactions related to Inventory prepared in part (b), and determine the ending balance in the account.
(d) Determine the number of books Phantom has on hand on June 30. What is the average cost of these books on June 30? (*Hint:* Divide the ending balance in the Inventory account calculated in part (c) and divide it by the number of books on hand at June 30. Round your answer to the nearest dollar.)

Record purchase and sales transactions.

(LO 2, 3)

P5–3A Presented here are selected transactions for Norlan Inc. during September of the current year. Norlan uses a perpetual inventory system.

Sept.	2	Purchased equipment on account for $65,000, terms n/30, FOB destination.
	3	Freight charges of $950 were paid by the appropriate party on the September 2 purchase of equipment.
	4	Purchased supplies for $4,000 cash.
	6	Purchased inventory on account from Hillary Corp. at a cost of $65,000, terms 1/15, n/30, FOB shipping point.
	7	Freight charges of $1,600 were paid by the appropriate party on the September 6 inventory purchase.
	8	Returned damaged goods costing $5,000 that were originally purchased from Hillary on September 4. Received a credit on account.
	9	Sold goods costing $15,000 to Fischer Limited for $20,000 on account, terms 2/10, n/30, FOB destination.
	10	Freight charges of $375 were paid by the appropriate party on the September 9 sale of inventory.
	17	Received the balance due from Fischer.
	20	Paid Hillary the balance due.
	21	Purchased inventory for $6,000 cash.
	22	Sold inventory costing $20,000 to Kun-Tai Inc. for $27,000 on account, terms n/30, FOB shipping point.
	23	Freight charges of $500 were paid by the appropriate party on the September 22 sale of inventory.
	28	Kun-Tai returned goods sold for $10,000 that cost $7,500. The merchandise was restored to inventory.

Instructions

(a) Record the September transactions on Norlan's books.

(b) Assume that Norlan did not take advantage of the 1% purchase discount offered by Hillary Corp. and paid Hillary on October 3 instead of September 20. Record the entry that Norlan would make on October 3 and determine the cost of missing this purchase discount to Norlan.

P5–4A At the beginning of the current golf season, on April 1, 2018, the general ledger of In the Pines Golf Shop showed Cash $4,200; Inventory $19,500; Common Shares $12,000; and Retained Earnings $11,700. In the Pines Golf Shop uses a perpetual inventory system.

The following transactions occurred in April:

Record and post purchase and sales transactions; prepare trial balance.

(LO 2, 3)

Apr.	3	Purchased golf bags, clubs, and balls on account from Balata Corp. for $3,200, terms 1/10, n/30, FOB shipping point.
	5	Freight of $286 was paid by the appropriate party on the April 3 purchase from Balata.
	7	Sold merchandise on account to members for $9,750, terms n/30. The cost of the merchandise sold was $5,850.
	9	Received a $320 purchase allowance from Balata for returned merchandise.
	11	Paid Balata in full.
	14	Received payments on account from members, $4,150.
	16	Purchased golf shoes, sweaters, and other accessories on account from Arrow Sportswear Limited for $1,300, terms 2/10, n/30.
	17	Received a $100 credit from Arrow Sportswear for returned merchandise.
	20	Sold merchandise on account to members for $11,100, terms n/30. The cost of the merchandise sold was $6,200.
	24	Paid Arrow Sportswear in full.
	25	Received payments on account from members, $4,375.
	27	Granted an $85 sales allowance to a member for a flaw in the clothing they had purchased. No merchandise was returned.

Instructions

(a) Record the April transactions.

(b) Set up T accounts, enter the opening balances, and post the transactions recorded in part (a).

(c) Prepare a trial balance as at April 30.

P5–5A Eagle Hardware Store Ltd. completed the following merchandising transactions in the month of May 2018. At the beginning of May, Eagle's ledger showed Cash $7,000; Accounts Receivable $1,500; Inventory $3,500; Common Shares $8,000; and Retained Earnings $4,000. Eagle Hardware uses a perpetual inventory system.

Record and post transactions and prepare partial financial statements.

(LO 2, 3, 4)

May	1	Purchased merchandise on account from Depot Wholesale Supply Ltd. for $5,800, terms 1/10, n/30, FOB shipping point.
	3	Freight charges of $145 were paid by the appropriate party on the merchandise purchased on May 1.
	4	Sold merchandise on account to Shep Ltd. for $3,500, terms 2/10, n/30, FOB destination. The cost of the merchandise was $2,100.
	7	Freight charges of $90 were paid by the appropriate party on the May 4 sale.
	8	Received a $200 credit from Depot Wholesale Supply when merchandise was returned.
	9	Paid Depot Wholesale Supply in full.
	11	Purchased supplies for $400 cash.
	14	Received payment in full from Shep Ltd. for merchandise sold on account on May 4.
	15	Collected $1,000 of the accounts receivable outstanding at the beginning of the month. All accounts were originally sold on terms of n/30, with no sales discounts.
	18	Purchased merchandise from Harlow Distributors Inc. for $2,000, terms n/30, FOB destination.
	21	Freight of $50 was paid by the appropriate party on the May 18 purchase of merchandise.
	22	Sold merchandise to various customers for $6,500 cash. The cost of the merchandise was $3,900.
	29	Paid a $100 cash refund to customers for returned merchandise. The cost of the returned merchandise was $60. It was restored to inventory.
	31	A physical inventory count was taken and determined that there was $5,100 of inventory on hand. Prepare any adjustment required.

Instructions

(a) Record the May transactions.

(b) Set up T accounts, enter the opening balances, and post the transactions recorded in part (a).

(c) Prepare a partial multiple-step income statement for the month ended May 31, through to gross profit.

(d) Prepare the current assets section of the statement of financial position as at May 31.

Prepare single- and multiple-step income statements.

(LO 4)

P5-6A The adjusted trial balance of Club Canada Wholesale Inc. contained the following accounts at December 31, the company's year end:

CLUB CANADA WHOLESALE INC.
Adjusted Trial Balance
December 31, 2018

	Debit	Credit
Cash	$ 12,275	
Accounts receivable	19,700	
Prepaid insurance	2,400	
Inventory	104,600	
Supplies	6,430	
Land	128,500	
Buildings	219,000	
Accumulated depreciation—buildings		$ 93,060
Equipment	95,500	
Accumulated depreciation—equipment		33,400
Accounts payable		60,900
Unearned revenue		9,650
Income tax payable		3,500
Bank loan payable		98,200
Common shares		50,000
Retained earnings		142,325
Sales		1,099,200
Sales returns and allowances	23,560	
Sales discounts	14,265	
Cost of goods sold	806,240	
Administrative expenses	88,515	
Selling expenses	42,100	
Interest expense	12,350	
Interest revenue		2,400
Income tax expense	17,200	
	$1,592,635	$1,592,635

Instructions

(a) Prepare a single-step income statement.

(b) Prepare a multiple-step income statement.

(c) Compare the two statements and comment on the usefulness of each one.

(d) Are the expenses in the statements classified by nature or by function? Explain.

Record and post adjusting entries; prepare adjusted trial balance and financial statements.

(LO 4)

P5-7A The unadjusted trial balance of Mesa Inc., at the company's year end of December 31, follows:

MESA INC.
Trial Balance
December 31, 2018

	Debit	Credit
Cash	$ 17,000	
Accounts receivable	31,700	
Inventory	28,750	
Supplies	2,940	
Prepaid insurance	3,000	
Land	30,000	
Buildings	150,000	
Accumulated depreciation—buildings		$ 24,000
Equipment	45,000	
Accumulated depreciation—equipment		18,000
Accounts payable		33,735

	Debit	Credit
Unearned revenue		4,000
Bank loan payable		147,100
Common shares		13,000
Retained earnings		31,425
Dividends declared	2,000	
Sales		265,770
Sales returns and allowances	2,500	
Sales discounts	3,275	
Cost of goods sold	171,225	
Salaries expense	30,950	
Utilities expense	5,100	
Interest expense	8,090	
Income tax expense	5,500	
	$537,030	$537,030

Additional information and adjustment data:

1. The 12-month insurance policy was purchased and was effective February 1, 2018.
2. There was $750 of supplies on hand on December 31.
3. Depreciation expense for the year is $6,000 for the buildings and $4,500 for the equipment.
4. Salaries of $750 are accrued and unpaid at December 31.
5. Accrued interest expense at December 31 is $735.
6. Unearned revenue of $975 is still unearned at December 31. On the sales revenue that was earned, the cost of goods sold was $2,000.
7. Of the bank loan payable, $9,800 is payable next year.
8. Income tax of $500 is due and unpaid.
9. A physical count of inventory indicates $23,800 on hand at December 31.
10. Common shares of $3,000 were issued during the year.

Instructions

(a) Record the required adjusting entries, assuming the company adjusts its accounts annually.
(b) Set up T accounts, enter the balances from the unadjusted trial balance, and post the adjusting entries prepared in part (a).
(c) Prepare an adjusted trial balance at December 31.
(d) Prepare a multiple-step income statement, statement of changes in equity, and statement of financial position for the year.

P5–8A Data for Club Canada Wholesale Inc. are presented in P5–6A.

Instructions

(a) Calculate the profit margin and gross profit margin.
(b) The vice-president of marketing and director of human resources have proposed that the company change its compensation of the sales force to a commission basis rather than paying a fixed salary. Given the extra incentive, they expect net sales to increase by 15%. They estimate that gross profit will increase by $27,000, operating expenses by $13,500, and income tax expense by $2,700. Non-operating expense is not expected to change. Calculate the expected new gross profit and net income amounts. (*Hint:* You do not need to prepare a formal income statement.)
(c) Calculate the revised gross profit margin and profit margin, using the information you calculated in part (b). Comment on the effect that this plan would have on profitability and evaluate the merit of this proposal.

Calculate profitability ratios and comment.

(LO 5)

P5–9A Psang Inc. purchases its inventory on credit and uses a perpetual inventory system. The company began operations on January 1, 2018, and during 2018 purchased merchandise costing $300,000. Of this amount, 80% was paid in 2018 with the balance paid in 2019. The company sold 90% of its inventory for $540,000 on credit. Of this amount, 70% was collected in 2018 with the rest collected in 2019. Operating expenses of $120,000 were incurred in 2018 and all were paid by the end of the year. The income tax rate is 30% and all income taxes relating to 2018 were paid in 2019. The following table indicates key amounts on the 2018 financial statements:

Calculate amounts and assess profitability.

(LO 4, 5)

	2018
Income statement data	
Sales	[1]
Cost of goods sold	[2]
Gross profit	[3]
Operating expenses	[4]
Income before income tax	[5]
Income tax expense	[6]
Net income	[7]

	2018
Statement of financial position data	
Accounts receivable	[8]
Inventory	[9]
Accounts payable	[10]
Income tax payable	[11]

Instructions

(a) Calculate the balances for Sales and Accounts Receivable (items 1 and 8 above).
(b) Calculate the balances for Cost of Goods Sold, Inventory, and Accounts Payable (items 2, 9, and 10 above).
(c) Calculate the gross profit, the balance in Operating Expenses, and the income before income tax (items 3, 4, and 5 above).
(d) Calculate the balances for Income Tax Expense, net income, and Income Tax Payable (items 6, 7, and 11 above).
(e) Calculate the gross profit margin and profit margin for the company. All companies in this industry sell their products at approximately the same price and incur income tax at the same rate. If the company's gross profit margin and profit margin are higher than the industry average, what are the most likely explanations for this?

Calculate ratios and comment.

(LO 5)

P5–10A The following selected information is available for **Canfor Corporation**, a British Columbia–based forest products company, for three fiscal years (in $ millions):

	2015	2014	2013
Current assets	$ 990.8	$ 902.6	$ 752.4
Current liabilities	635.1	425.9	440.5
Sales	3,925.3	3,347.6	3,194.9
Cost of goods sold	2,780.8	2,201.9	2,036.8
Net income	91.9	221.8	250.5

Instructions

(a) Calculate the current ratio, gross profit margin, and profit margin for each year.
(b) Comment on whether the ratios have improved or deteriorated over the three years.
(c) Compare the 2015 ratios calculated in part (a) with the following industry averages: current ratio 1.2:1; gross profit margin 20.8%, and profit margin 2.6%. Are Canfor's ratios better or worse than those of its industry?

Record purchase and sales transactions; discuss inventory systems.

(LO 1, 6)

*P5–11A Data for Phantom Book Warehouse Ltd. are presented in P5–2A.

Instructions

(a) Record the June transactions on Phantom Book Warehouse's books, assuming it uses a periodic inventory system instead of a perpetual inventory system. (Record transactions to the nearest dollar.)
(b) Identify the advantages and disadvantages of Phantom Book Warehouse using a periodic inventory system instead of a perpetual inventory system.

Record purchase and sales transactions.

(LO 6)

*P5–12A Data for Norlan Inc. are presented in P5–3A.

Instructions

(a) Record the September transactions on Norlan's books, assuming it uses a periodic inventory system instead of a perpetual inventory system.
(b) Assume that Norlan did not take advantage of the 1% purchase discount offered by Hillary Corp. and paid Hillary on October 3 instead of September 20. Record the entry that Norlan would make on October 3 and determine the cost of missing this purchase discount to Norlan.

Record and post purchase and sales transactions; prepare trial balance.

(LO 6)

*P5–13A Data for In the Pines Golf Shop are presented in P5–4A.

Instructions

(a) Record the April transactions for In the Pines Golf Shop, assuming it uses a periodic inventory system instead of a perpetual inventory system. Round all calculations to the nearest dollar.
(b) Set up T accounts, enter the opening balances, and post the transactions prepared in part (a).
(c) Prepare a trial balance as at April 30.
(d) The inventory count on April 30 determined that merchandise costing $11,763 was on hand. Prepare the adjusting journal entry needed at the end of the period to update the Inventory and Cost of Goods Sold accounts.

*P5–14A You have been provided with the following selected accounts for Feisty Ltd. for the year ended April 30, 2018:

Prepare partial income statement; calculate gross profit.
(LO 5, 6)

Inventory, May 1, 2017	$ 600,000	Interest expense	$ 30,000
Purchases	5,900,000	Interest income	20,000
Accounts receivable	780,000	Accounts payable	600,000
Sales	9,300,000	Administrative expenses	810,000
Purchase discounts	40,000	Selling expenses	150,000
Freight in	120,000	Cash	160,000
Land	900,000	Common shares	200,000
Sales returns and allowances	250,000		

Feisty conducted a physical inventory count on April 30, 2018. Inventory on hand at that date was determined to be $700,000.

Instructions

(a) Prepare a partial multiple-step income statement for the year ended April 30, 2018, through to gross profit.
(b) Prepare the period-end adjusting journal entry to update the Cost of Goods Sold and Inventory accounts.
(c) Calculate the gross profit margin. If the industry average gross profit margin is 30%, how does Feisty's gross profit margin compare?

*P5–15A Active Athletic Wear Inc.'s unadjusted trial balance amounts (prior to recording the adjusting entry to update Inventory and Cost of Goods Sold accounts) appear in alphabetical order as follows on December 31, 2018, the end of its fiscal year:

Prepare financial statements.
(LO 6)

Accounts payable	$129,450	Land	$112,500
Accounts receivable	66,300	Mortgage payable	187,500
Accumulated depreciation—buildings	77,700	Prepaid insurance	3,600
Accumulated depreciation—equipment	64,350	Property tax payable	7,200
Administrative expenses	271,350	Purchase discounts	33,750
Buildings	285,000	Purchase returns and allowances	9,600
Cash	25,500	Purchases	602,400
Common shares	112,500	Retained earnings	102,900
Dividends declared	12,000	Salaries payable	5,250
Equipment	165,000	Sales	955,500
Freight in	. 8,400	Sales discounts	22,500
Income tax expense	24,000	Sales returns and allowances	12,000
Interest expense	15,600	Selling expenses	11,250
Inventory, Jan. 1	60,750	Unearned revenue	12,450

Additional information:

1. Active Athletic Wear uses a periodic inventory system.
2. A physical inventory count determined that Inventory on December 31, 2018, was $108,900.
3. Of the mortgage payable, $18,750 is due in the next year.
4. Common shares of $37,500 were issued during the year.

Instructions
Prepare a multiple-step income statement, statement of changes in equity, and statement of financial position for the year.

▶ PROBLEMS: SET B

P5–1B The Fashion Palace Inc. sells a variety of home decorating merchandise, including pictures, small furniture items, dishes, candles, and area rugs. The company uses a periodic inventory system and counts inventory once a year. Most customers use the option to purchase on account and many take more than a month to pay. The company does not have any specific credit terms for its regular customers.

Identify problems in operating cycle and use of periodic inventory system.
(LO 1)

The general manager of The Fashion Palace, Rebecca Sherstabetoff, believes the company needs a bank loan because the accounts payable have to be paid long before the accounts receivable are collected. The bank manager is willing to give The Fashion Palace a loan but wants monthly financial statements.

Rebecca has also noticed that, while some of the company's merchandise sells very quickly, other items do not. Sometimes she wonders just how long some of those older items have been in stock. She has observed that the company seems to run out of some merchandise items on a regular basis. And she is wondering how she is going to find someone with the time to count the inventory every month so that monthly financial statements can be prepared for the bank. She has come to you for help.

Instructions

(a) Explain to Rebecca what an operating cycle is and why the company is having problems paying its bills.

(b) Make a recommendation about what inventory system the company should use and explain why.

(c) Explain to Rebecca the reasons for conducting an inventory count and advise her on the required frequency of counts.

Record purchase and sales transactions.

(LO 1, 2, 3)

P5–2B Travel Warehouse Ltd. distributes suitcases to retail stores. At the end of June, Travel Warehouse's inventory consisted of 60 suitcases purchased at $50 each. Travel Warehouse uses a perpetual inventory system. During the month of July, the following merchandising transactions occurred:

July	2	Purchased 75 suitcases on account for $60 each from Trunk Manufacturers Ltd., terms 2/10, n/30.
	3	Received a $240 credit from Trunk Manufacturers after returning four suitcases because they were damaged.
	6	Sold 55 suitcases on account to Satchel World Inc. for $90 each, with an average cost of $50, terms 2/15, n/45.
	7	Issued a $270 credit for three suitcases returned by Satchel World because they were the wrong model. The suitcases were returned to inventory.
	9	Sold three suitcases—this time the right model number—on account to Satchel World Inc. for $100 each, with an average cost of $60, terms 2/15, n/45.
	11	Paid Trunk Manufacturers the balance owing.
	13	Sold 25 suitcases on account to The Going Concern Limited for $100 each, with an average cost of $60, terms 2/15, n/45.
	16	Purchased 70 suitcases on account for $4,340 from Holiday Manufacturers, terms n/45.
	17	Issued a $500 credit for five suitcases returned by The Going Concern because they were damaged. These suitcases were not restored to inventory.
	20	Received payment in full from Satchel World for all transactions.
	27	Received payment in full from The Going Concern.

Instructions

(a) Is Travel Warehouse a retailer or a wholesaler? Explain.

(b) Record the July transactions. (Record transactions to the nearest dollar.)

(c) Set up a T account for the Inventory account. Enter the opening balance, post the transactions related to inventory prepared in part (b), and determine the ending balance in the account.

(d) Determine the number of suitcases Travel Warehouse has on hand on July 31. What is the average cost of these suitcases on July 31? (*Hint*: Divide the ending balance in the Inventory account calculated in part (c) and divide it by the number of suitcases on hand at July 31. Round your answer to the nearest dollar.)

Record purchase and sales transactions.

(LO 2, 3)

P5–3B Presented here are selected transactions for Shaoshi Inc. during October of the current year. Shaoshi uses a perpetual inventory system.

Oct.	1	Purchased merchandise on account from Micron Ltd. at a cost of $86,000, terms 1/15, n/30, FOB shipping point.
	1	Freight charges of $1,400 were paid by the appropriate party on the October 1 purchase of merchandise.
	2	Returned for credit $4,000 of damaged goods purchased from Micron on October 1.
	6	Purchased supplies for $2,800 cash.
	8	Sold the remaining merchandise purchased from Micron to Guidant Corp. for $140,000 on account, terms 2/10, n/30, FOB destination.
	9	Freight charges of $2,300 were paid by the appropriate party on the October 8 sale of merchandise.
	10	Purchased equipment on account for $62,000.
	12	Guidant returned damaged merchandise that was purchased on October 8 for a $3,500 credit on account. The merchandise originally cost $2,185 and was not restored to inventory.
	15	Purchased merchandise for $36,300 cash.
	17	Received the balance owing from Guidant.
	28	Sold merchandise for $30,000 on account to Deux Ltée, terms 2/10, n/30, FOB shipping point. The merchandise had a cost of $18,000.
	29	Freight charges of $750 were paid by the appropriate party on the October 28 sale of merchandise.
	30	Paid Micron the balance owing.
	31	Deux returned some of the merchandise that was purchased on October 28 for a $5,000 credit on account. The merchandise originally cost $3,000 and was restored to inventory.

Instructions

(a) Record the October transactions.

(b) Assume that Shaoshi took advantage of the 1% purchase discount offered by Micron Ltd. and paid Micron on October 14 rather than October 30. Record the entry that Shaoshi would make on October 14 and determine the cost of missing this purchase discount to Shaoshi.

P5–4B At the beginning of the current tennis season, on April 1, 2018, the general ledger of Grand Slam Tennis Shop showed Cash $16,400; Inventory $16,200; Common Shares $20,000; and Retained Earnings $12,600. Grand Slam Tennis Shop uses a perpetual inventory system.

Record and post purchase and sales transactions; prepare trial balance.

(LO 2, 3)

The following transactions occurred in April:

Apr.	2	Purchased racquets and balls from Roberts Inc. for $5,800, terms 2/10, n/30, FOB shipping point.
	3	The appropriate party paid $160 freight on the purchase from Roberts on April 2.
	5	Received credit of $100 from Roberts for a damaged racquet that was returned.
	9	Purchased supplies for $1,130 cash from Discount Supplies Limited.
	11	Paid Roberts in full.
	13	Purchased tennis shoes from Niki Sports Ltd. for $1,560 cash, FOB shipping point.
	16	The appropriate party paid $115 freight on the purchase from Niki on April 13.
	18	Received a $110 cash refund from Niki Sports for damaged merchandise that was returned.
	20	Sold merchandise to members for $11,100 on account, terms n/30. The cost of the merchandise was $6,660.
	21	Some of the merchandise purchased on April 20, with a sales price of $1,000 and a cost of $600, was returned by members. It was restored to inventory.
	23	Purchased equipment for use in the business from DomCo Ltd. for $11,700, terms n/45.
	25	Sold merchandise to members for $9,800, terms n/30. The cost of the merchandise was $5,880.
	27	Received cash payments on account from members, $9,800.
	28	Granted a $150 sales allowance on account to a member for slightly torn tennis clothing. No merchandise was returned.

Instructions

(a) Record the April transactions. Round all calculations to the nearest dollar.

(b) Set up T accounts, enter the opening balances, and post the transactions recorded in part (a).

(c) Prepare a trial balance as at April 30.

P5–5B Nisson Distributing Ltd. completed the following merchandising transactions in the month of April 2018. At the beginning of April, Nisson's general ledger showed Cash $4,000; Accounts Receivable $3,500; Inventory $2,500; Common Shares $5,000; and Retained Earnings $5,000. Nisson uses a perpetual inventory system.

Record and post transactions and prepare partial financial statements.

(LO 2, 3, 4)

Apr.	2	Purchased merchandise on account from Kai Supply Corp. for $8,900, terms 1/15, n/30, FOB shipping point.
	3	The appropriate party paid $225 freight on the April 2 purchase from Kai Supply.
	5	Sold $11,600 of merchandise on account to Kananaskis Supply Ltd., terms 2/10, n/30, FOB destination. The cost of the merchandise was $7,540.
	9	The appropriate party paid $290 freight on the April 5 sale of merchandise to Kananaskis Supply.
	10	Issued a $1,600 credit for merchandise returned by Kananaskis Supply. The merchandise originally cost $1,030 and was returned to inventory.
	11	Purchased merchandise on account from Pigeon Distributors Limited for $4,200, terms 1/10, n/30, FOB destination.
	12	The appropriate party paid $100 freight on the April 11 purchase from Pigeon Distributors.
	13	Received a $300 credit for merchandise returned to Pigeon Distributors.
	14	Received the balance owing from Kananaskis Supply.
	17	Paid Kai Supply in full.
	20	Paid Pigeon Distributors in full.
	23	Sold merchandise for $6,400 cash. The cost of the merchandise was $5,200.
	24	Made a $400 cash refund for damaged merchandise returned from the April 23 purchase. The cost of the merchandise returned was $260 and it was not restored to inventory.
	27	Purchased merchandise from Tipsea Inc. for $6,100 cash.
	30	Received a $500 refund for merchandise that was returned to Tipsea from the April 27 cash purchase.

Instructions

(a) Record the April transactions.

(b) Set up T accounts, enter the opening balances, and post the transactions recorded in part (a).

(c) Prepare a partial multiple-step income statement for the month ended April 30, through to gross profit.

(d) Prepare the current assets section of the statement of financial position as at April 30.

Prepare single- and multiple-step income statements.

(LO 4)

P5–6B The adjusted trial balance of Brigus Wholesale Ltd. contained the following accounts at November 30, the company's fiscal year end:

BRIGUS WHOLESALE LTD.
Adjusted Trial Balance
November 30, 2018

	Debit	Credit
Cash	$ 35,000	
Accounts receivable	96,300	
Notes receivable	28,200	
Inventory	115,600	
Supplies	4,900	
Land	580,000	
Buildings	452,000	
Accumulated depreciation—buildings		$ 45,200
Equipment	326,000	
Accumulated depreciation—equipment		81,500
Accounts payable		79,800
Income tax payable		18,200
Unearned revenue		32,100
Bank loan payable		205,000
Common shares		500,000
Retained earnings		546,700
Sales		2,234,800
Sales returns and allowances	12,800	
Sales discounts	11,400	
Cost of goods sold	1,387,200	
Administrative expenses	366,000	
Selling expenses	286,000	
Interest expense	12,300	
Interest revenue		2,800
Income tax expense	32,400	
	$3,746,100	$3,746,100

Instructions
(a) Prepare a single-step income statement.
(b) Prepare a multiple-step income statement.
(c) Compare the two statements and comment on the usefulness of each one.
(d) Are the expenses in the statements classified by nature or by function? Explain.

Record and post adjusting entries; prepare adjusted trial balance and financial statements.

(LO 4)

P5–7B The unadjusted trial balance of Fashion Centre Ltd. contained the following accounts at November 30, the company's fiscal year end:

FASHION CENTRE LTD.
Trial Balance
November 30, 2018

	Debit	Credit
Cash	$ 22,000	
Accounts receivable	30,600	
Inventory	27,500	
Supplies	1,650	
Prepaid insurance	1,800	
Long-term investments	37,000	
Equipment	26,800	
Accumulated depreciation—equipment		$ 10,720
Accounts payable		34,400
Unearned revenue		3,000
Bank loan payable		35,000
Common shares		16,400
Retained earnings		30,000
Dividends declared	10,000	

	Debit	Credit
Sales		248,500
Sales returns and allowances	4,600	
Sales discounts	4,520	
Cost of goods sold	157,000	
Salaries expense	32,600	
Rent expense	13,850	
Interest expense	4,000	
Advertising expense	2,100	
Income tax expense	2,000	
	$378,020	$378,020

Additional information and adjustment data:
1. The 12-month insurance policy was purchased on August 1.
2. There is $950 of supplies on hand at November 30.
3. Depreciation expense for the year is $5,360 on the equipment.
4. Salaries of $1,210 are unpaid at November 30.
5. Accrued interest expense at November 30 is $175.
6. Of the unearned revenue, $2,400 has been earned by November 30. The cost of goods sold incurred in earning this sales revenue is $1,560.
7. Of the bank loan payable, $5,000 is to be paid in the next year; the remainder is long-term.
8. Income tax of $1,100 is due and unpaid.
9. A physical count of inventory indicates $25,000 on hand at November 30.
10. Common shares of $5,000 were issued during the year.

Instructions
(a) Record the required adjusting entries, assuming the company adjusts its accounts annually.
(b) Set up T accounts, enter the balances from the unadjusted trial balance, and post the adjusting entries prepared in part (a).
(c) Prepare an adjusted trial balance at November 30.
(d) Prepare a multiple-step income statement, statement of changes in equity, and statement of financial position for the year.

P5–8B Data for Brigus Wholesale Ltd. are presented in P5–6B.

Instructions
(a) Calculate the profit margin and gross profit margin.
(b) The vice-president of marketing and director of human resources have proposed that the company change its compensation of the sales force to a commission basis rather than paying a fixed salary. Given the extra incentive, they expect net sales to increase by 10%. They estimate that gross profit will increase by $60,000, operating expenses by $32,000, and income tax expense by $4,000. Non-operating expense is not expected to change. Calculate the expected new gross profit and net income amounts. (*Hint*: You do not need to prepare a formal income statement.)
(c) Calculate the revised gross profit margin and profit margin, using the information you calculated in part (b). Comment on the effect that this plan would have on profitability and evaluate the merit of this proposal.

Calculate profitability ratios and comment.
(LO 5)

P5–9B Tsang Inc. purchases its inventory on credit and uses a perpetual inventory system. The company began operations on January 1, 2018, and during 2018 purchased merchandise costing $200,000. Of this amount, 75% was paid in 2018 with the balance paid in 2019. The company sold 80% of its inventory for $400,000 on credit. Of this amount, 80% was collected in 2018 with the rest collected in 2019. Operating expenses of $140,000 were incurred in 2018 and all were paid by the end of the year. The income tax rate is 30% and all income taxes relating to 2018 were paid in 2019. The following table indicates key amounts on the 2018 financial statements:

Calculate amounts and assess profitability.
(LO 4, 5)

	2018
Income statement data	
Sales	[1]
Cost of goods sold	[2]
Gross profit	[3]
Operating expenses	[4]
Income before income tax	[5]
Income tax expense	[6]
Net income	[7]
Statement of financial position data	
Accounts receivable	[8]
Inventory	[9]
Accounts payable	[10]
Income tax payable	[11]

Instructions

(a) Calculate the balances for Sales and Accounts Receivable (items 1 and 8 above).

(b) Calculate the balances for Cost of Goods Sold, Inventory, and Accounts Payable (items 2, 9, and 10 above).

(c) Calculate the gross profit, the balance in Operating Expenses, and the income before income tax (items 3, 4, and 5 above).

(d) Calculate the balances for Income Tax Expense, net income, and Income Tax Payable (items 6, 7, and 11 above).

(e) Calculate the gross profit margin and profit margin for the company. All companies in this industry sell their products at approximately the same price and incur income tax at the same rate. If the company's gross profit margin and profit margin are lower than the industry average, what are the most likely explanations for this?

Calculate ratios and comment.

(LO 5)

P5–10B The following selected information is available for **Volvo Group**, headquartered in Sweden, for three fiscal years (in SEK [Swedish krona] millions):

	2015	2014	2013
Current assets	170,687	177,302	163,612
Current liabilities	155,860	136,393	140,316
Net sales	312,515	282,948	272,622
Cost of goods sold	240,653	220,012	212,504
Net income	15,099	2,235	3,802

Instructions

(a) Calculate the current ratio, gross profit margin, and profit margin for each year.

(b) Comment on whether the ratios have improved or deteriorated over the three years.

(c) Compare the 2015 ratios calculated in part (a) with the following industry averages: current ratio 1.2:1; gross profit margin 16.3%; and profit margin 2.5%. Are Volvo's ratios better or worse than those of its industry?

Record purchase and sales transactions; discuss inventory systems.

(LO 1, 6)

*P5–11B Data for Travel Warehouse Ltd. are presented in P5–2B.

Instructions

(a) Record the July transactions on Travel Warehouse's books, assuming it uses a periodic inventory system instead of a perpetual inventory system. (Record transactions to the nearest dollar.)

(b) Identify the advantages and disadvantages of Travel Warehouse using a periodic inventory system instead of a perpetual inventory system.

Record purchase and sales transactions.

(LO 6)

*P5–12B Data for Shaoshi Inc. are presented in P5–3B.

Instructions

(a) Record the October transactions on Shaoshi's books, assuming it uses a periodic inventory system instead of a perpetual inventory system.

(b) Assume that Shaoshi took advantage of the 1% purchase discount offered by Micron Ltd. and paid Micron on October 14 rather than October 30. Record the entry that Shaoshi would make on October 14 and determine the cost of missing this purchase discount to Shaoshi.

Record and post purchase and sales transactions; prepare trial balance.

(LO 6)

*P5–13B Data for Grand Slam Tennis Shop are presented in P5–4B.

Instructions

(a) Record the April transactions for Grand Slam Tennis Shop, assuming it uses a periodic inventory system instead of a perpetual inventory system. Round all calculations to the nearest dollar.

(b) Set up T accounts, enter the opening balances, and post the transactions prepared in part (a).

(c) Prepare an unadjusted trial balance as at April 30.

(d) The inventory count on April 30 determined that merchandise costing $11,571 was on hand. Prepare the adjusting journal entry needed at the end of the period to update the Inventory and Cost of Goods Sold accounts.

Prepare partial income statement; calculate gross profit.

(LO 5, 6)

*P5–14B You have been provided with the following selected accounts for Severn Limited for the year ended June 30, 2018:

Inventory, July 1, 2017	$ 520,000
Purchases	6,280,000
Accounts receivable	660,000
Sales	7,800,000
Purchase returns and allowances	240,000
Freight in	80,000
Administrative expenses	740,000
Land	1,400,000
Sales discounts	100,000

Interest expense	$ 20,000
Interest revenue	40,000
Accounts payable	540,000
Selling expenses	120,000
Cash	500,000
Common shares	300,000

Severn conducted a physical inventory count on June 30, 2018. Inventory on hand at that date was determined to be $600,000.

Instructions

(a) Prepare a partial multiple-step income statement for the year ended June 30, 2018, through to gross profit.

(b) Prepare the period-end adjusting journal entry to update the Cost of Goods Sold and Inventory accounts.

(c) Calculate the gross profit margin. If the industry average gross profit margin is 26%, how does Severn's gross profit margin compare?

*P5–15B The Goody Shop Ltd.'s unadjusted trial balance amounts (prior to recording the adjusting journal entry to update Inventory and Cost of Goods Sold) appear in alphabetical order as follows on November 30, 2018, the end of its fiscal year:

Prepare financial statements.

(LO 6)

Accounts payable	$ 32,310	Land	$ 85,000
Accounts receivable	13,770	Mortgage payable	106,000
Accumulated depreciation—buildings	61,200	Prepaid insurance	4,500
Accumulated depreciation—equipment	19,880	Property tax payable	3,500
Administrative expenses	230,100	Purchase discounts	16,000
Buildings	175,000	Purchase returns and allowances	3,315
Cash	8,500	Purchases	684,700
Common shares	26,000	Retained earnings	82,800
Dividends declared	5,000	Salaries payable	8,500
Equipment	57,000	Sales	989,000
Freight in	5,060	Sales discounts	15,000
Income tax expense	10,000	Sales returns and allowances	10,000
Income tax payable	6,000	Selling expenses	8,200
Interest expense	11,315	Unearned revenue	3,000
Inventory, Dec. 1, 2017	34,360		

Additional information:

1. The Goody Shop uses a periodic inventory system.
2. A physical inventory count determined that inventory on November 30, 2018, was $37,350.
3. Of the mortgage payable, $5,300 is due in the next year.
4. Common shares of $25,000 were issued during the year.

Instructions

Prepare a multiple-step income statement, statement of changes in equity, and statement of financial position for the year.

ACCOUNTING CYCLE | REVIEW

ACR5–1 Heritage Furniture Limited reports the following information for 11 months of the year in its February 28, 2018, trial balance. The company's year end is March 31.

Record and post general, adjusting, and closing entries; prepare trial balances and financial statements.

(LO 2, 3, 4)

HERITAGE FURNITURE LIMITED
Trial Balance
February 28, 2018

	Debit	Credit
Cash	$ 65,000	
Accounts receivable	350,000	
Inventory	2,750,000	
Supplies	7,500	
Prepaid rent	5,000	
Equipment	145,000	
Accumulated depreciation—equipment		$ 29,000

	Debit	Credit
Accounts payable		$1,550,000
Unearned revenue		35,000
Bank loan payable		450,000
Common shares		200,000
Retained earnings		550,500
Dividends declared	$ 50,000	
Sales		5,479,400
Sales returns and allowances	107,000	
Sales discounts	65,000	
Cost of goods sold	3,843,900	
Advertising expense	75,000	
Freight out	180,000	
Office expense	26,000	
Rent expense	55,000	
Salaries expense	360,000	
Travel expense	12,500	
Utilities expense	20,000	
Interest expense	27,000	
Income tax expense	150,000	
	$8,293,900	$8,293,900

Heritage Furniture incurred the following transactions for the month of March. The company uses a perpetual inventory system.

Mar.	1	Received $125,000 on account from a major customer.
	2	Paid a supplier an amount owing of $200,000, taking the full discount, terms 2/10, n/30.
	5	Purchased merchandise from a supplier, $300,000, terms 2/10, n/30, FOB destination.
	6	Recorded cash sales, $285,000. The cost of goods sold for these sales was $200,000.
	7	Returned scratched merchandise to the supplier from the March 5 purchase, $25,000.
	8	The appropriate company paid freight for the March 5 purchase, $7,500.
	9	Sold $200,000 of merchandise on account, terms 2/10, n/30, FOB destination. The cost of goods sold was $140,000.
	9	The appropriate company paid freight for the March 9 sale, $5,000.
	12	Ordered custom merchandise for a local designer totalling $50,000. Received $12,500 as a deposit.
	13	Accepted returned merchandise from the sale on March 9, $20,000. The cost of the goods returned to inventory was $14,000.
	14	Paid for the merchandise purchased on March 5, net of merchandise returns on March 7.
	16	Paid salaries of $45,000.
	19	Received payment of merchandise sold on March 9, net of merchandise returns on March 13.
	20	Recorded cash sales, $255,000. The cost of goods sold for these sales was $179,000.
	27	Paid salaries, $50,000.
	30	Paid rent, $5,000.

Adjustment and additional data:
1. Accrued $10,000 for utilities, $10,000 for salaries, and $9,000 for interest on the bank loan.
2. Recorded depreciation on equipment, which has an expected useful life of 10 years.
3. Recorded an additional $50,000 of income tax payable.
4. Common shares of $1,000 were issued during the year.
5. $45,000 of the bank loan is due to be repaid in the next year.

Instructions
(a) Record the March transactions.
(b) Set up T accounts, enter the opening balances, and post the transactions recorded in part (a).
(c) Prepare a trial balance as at March 31.
(d) Record and post adjusting entries for the year ended March 31, assuming adjusting entries are made annually.
(e) Prepare an adjusted trial balance as at March 31.
(f) Prepare a multiple-step income statement, statement of changes in equity, and statement of financial position for the year.
(g) Prepare and post closing entries.
(h) Prepare a post-closing trial balance as at March 31.

EXPAND YOUR | CRITICAL THINKING

CT5–1 Financial Reporting Case

The financial statements of **The North West Company Inc.** are presented in Appendix A at the end of this book.

Instructions

(a) Is The North West Company a service company, merchandising company, or manufacturing company? Explain.

(b) Does The North West Company classify its operating expenses on its income statement by nature or by function? Explain.

(c) Are any non-operating revenues or expenses included in The North West Company's income statement? If so, identify the accounts included.

(d) Calculate The North West Company's gross profit margin for 2016 and 2015.

(e) Calculate The North West Company's profit margin for 2016 and 2015.

(f) Comment on the trend in The North West Company's gross profit margin and profit margin.

CT5–2 Financial Reporting Case

The financial statements of **The North West Company Inc.** are presented in Appendix A and the financial statements for **Sobeys Inc.** are presented in Appendix B.

Instructions

(a) Determine the following values for each company as follows:

   1. Percentage change in sales revenue for North West and for Sobeys for the most recent year shown.

   2. Gross profit margin.

(b) Which company had the bigger increase in sales? Was that company able to maintain its gross margin? What conclusions can be drawn from this?

(c) In spite of increasing sales, one of the companies experienced a decreased gross margin. Explain how this could occur.

CT5–3 Financial Reporting Case

Country Coffee Limited is a restaurant chain specializing in fresh, ready-to-serve coffee. Country Coffee is owned by its sole founder, who began the chain over 20 years ago. Today the business has expanded to 25 corporate locations and 30 franchise locations across Canada.

Country Coffee faces fierce competition from various other coffee chains. Happy Coffee Inc. is a major competitor that has successfully built a chain of over 500 restaurants. Happy Coffee enjoys strong brand recognition and customer loyalty in the Canadian market.

The founder of Country Coffee would like to compare his chain's results with those of Happy Coffee. Happy Coffee is publicly traded and prepares its financial statements in accordance with IFRS, whereas Country Coffee uses ASPE. The following are condensed versions of income statements for Happy Coffee and Country Coffee for the year ended December 31, 2018:

HAPPY COFFEE INC.
Income Statement
Year Ended December 31, 2018
(in millions)

Revenues		
Sales		$2,536
Operating expenses		
Cost of goods sold	$1,619	
Selling expenses	336	
Administrative expenses	81	2,036
Income from operations		500
Other revenues and expenses		
Interest expense		24
Income before income tax		476
Income tax expense		95
Net income		$ 381

COUNTRY COFFEE LIMITED
Income Statement
Year Ended December 31, 2018
(in millions)

Revenues		
Sales		$84
Operating expenses		
Cost of goods sold	$30	
Rent	15	
Salaries	10	
Depreciation	9	
Utilities	3	
Advertising	2	
Insurance	1	70
Income from operations		14
Other revenues and expenses		
Interest expense		1
Income before income tax		13
Income tax expense		3
Net income		$10

Instructions

(a) What is the main difference between the income statement presentation of Country Coffee and of Happy Coffee?

(b) Are these two formats acceptable under both ASPE and IFRS? Which of these methods requires a greater degree of judgement? Which of these two formats do you prefer and why?

(c) How will this difference affect the comparability of the two income statements?

(d) Will the use of different presentation formats affect the comparability of the gross profit margin and the profit margin of Country Coffee and Happy Coffee? Why or why not?

(e) What options does Country Coffee have if it wants to improve the comparability of its financial results with those of Happy Coffee?

CT5–4   Ethics Case

This case can be assigned as a group activity. Additional instructions and material for this activity can be found on the Instructor Resource site and in WileyPLUS.

Nazir Khan, the CEO of Peshawar Inc., signed an employment contract with the company that allowed him to earn a bonus if he increased Peshawar's gross profit margin by more than 3%. The draft income statement for 2018 has just been prepared and is shown below.

	2018	2017
Net sales	$113,000	$80,000
Cost of goods sold	62,000	48,000
Gross profit	51,000	32,000
Operating expenses	21,000	8,000
Income from operations	30,000	24,000
Income tax expense	9,000	7,200
Net income	$ 21,000	$16,800
Gross profit margin	45.1%	40.0%

The board of directors is about to meet and determine if Nazir is to be awarded his bonus. As one of the board members, you are surprised to receive an anonymous letter, supposedly from a member of the accounting department, that indicates that the CEO asked the staff member to do the following during 2018:
1. Record purchase returns of $7,000 as an increase of sales revenue.
2. Record freight of $5,000 paid on purchases of merchandise as an operating expense.
3. Record sales returns of $6,000 as an operating expense.

Instructions
(a) Assuming the staff member is right, correct the above adjustments and recalculate the gross profit margin. Is the CEO is eligible for his bonus?
(b) Did the adjustments requested by the CEO affect the profit margin?
(c) Based on the above, was any harm done to any users of the financial statements because of the adjustments made? Explain.

CT5–5   Ethics Case

Rita Pelzer was just hired as the assistant controller of Zaz Stores Ltd., a retail company. Among other things, the payment of all invoices is centralized in one of the departments Rita will manage. Her main responsibilities are to maintain the company's credit rating by paying all bills when they are due and to take advantage of all cash discounts.

Jamie Caterino, the former assistant controller, who has been promoted to controller, is training Rita in her new duties. He instructs Rita that she is to continue the practice of preparing all cheques for the amount due less

the discount and to date the cheques the last day of the discount period. "But," Jamie continues, "we always hold the cheques at least four days beyond the discount period before mailing them. That way we get another four days of interest on our money. Most of our creditors need our business and don't complain. And, if they scream about our missing the discount period, we blame it on Canada Post. We've only lost one discount out of every hundred we take that way. I think everybody does it. By the way, welcome to our team!"

Instructions
(a) What are the ethical considerations in this case?
(b) Which stakeholders are harmed or benefited?
(c) Should Rita continue the practice started by Jamie? Does she have any choice?

CT5–6   Serial Case

(*Note:* This is a continuation of the serial case from Chapters 1 through 4.)

Emily and her parents, Doug and Bev, are anxious to complete and analyze the updated June 30, 2017, financial statements. The following information represents additional adjustment data and information to enable the preparation of ABC's year-end financial statements.
1. The physical count of inventory indicates $18,000 on hand at June 30. ABC uses a perpetual inventory system.
2. Of the bank loan payable, $7,500 is to be paid in the next year; the remainder is non-current.
3. Of the mortgage payable, $5,000 is to be paid in the next year; the remainder is non-current.

Emily has obtained a copy of the financial statements of a major competitor, a public company, and has been able to determine several of their ratios: the current ratio is 2.5:1, the gross profit margin is 75%, and the profit margin is 8%.

Instructions
(a) Record and post any required adjusting entry for item 1 above to T accounts updated in CT4–6 in Chapter 4.
(b) Prepare a revised adjusted trial balance, if required, at June 30.
(c) Prepare a multiple-step income statement, statement of changes in equity, and statement of financial position for the year. (*Note:* Although ABC could prepare a statement of retained earnings, we have requested a statement of changes in equity. You will learn how to prepare a statement of retained earnings in detail in a later chapter.)
(d) Calculate the current ratio, gross profit margin, and profit margin for the year.
1. Are ABC's ratios better or worse than those of its major competitor?
2. Why do you expect there is a difference between ABC's ratios and those of its major competitor?

▶ ANSWERS TO CHAPTER PRACTICE QUESTIONS

DO IT! 5-1
Inventory Calculations

(a)

	Units		Dollars
1. Beginning inventory	10	(10 × $325)	$ 3,250
2. Cost of goods purchased	20	(20 × $350)	7,000
3. Cost of goods available for sale	30		10,250
4. Cost of goods sold	(10)	(10 × $325)	(3,250)
	(15)	(15 × $350)	(5,250)
5. Ending inventory	5	(5 × $350)	$ 1,750

(b) Yes, the physical inventory count of five units in ending inventory does agree with the calculations in part (a). If there was a shortage, an entry debiting Cost of Goods Sold and crediting Inventory would be made for an amount relating to the cost of the units that should be on hand.

Brighthouse (Buyer)

DO IT! 5-2
Purchase
Transactions

Sept. 2	Inventory		1,500	
	Accounts Payable			1,500
	(To record goods purchased on account from Junot, terms 2/10, n/30, FOB shipping point)			
4	Inventory		75	
	Cash			75
	(To record freight paid on goods purchased)			
8	Accounts Payable		200	
	Inventory			200
	(To record return of goods to Junot)			
11	Accounts Payable ($1,500 – $200)		1,300	
	Inventory ($1,300 × 2%)			26
	Cash ($1,300 – $26)			1,274
	(To record payment to Junot within discount period)			

Lalonde Ltée (Seller)

DO IT! 5-3
Purchase and Sales
Transactions—
Perpetual Inventory
System

Sept. 4	Accounts Receivable		3,000	
	Sales			3,000
	(To record credit sale to Guerette, terms 2/10, n/45)			
4	Cost of Goods Sold		1,600	
	Inventory			1,600
	(To record cost of goods sold to Guerette)			
8	Sales Returns and Allowances		600	
	Accounts Receivable			600
	(To record credit granted for receipt of returned goods from Guerette)			
8	Inventory		280	
	Cost of Goods Sold			280
	(To record cost of goods returned from Guerette)			
13	Cash ($2,400 – $48)		2,352	
	Sales Discounts ([$3,000 – $600] × 2%)		48	
	Accounts Receivable ($3,000 – $600)			2,400
	(To record collection from Guerette within discount period)			

Guerette Corp. (Buyer)

Sept. 4	Inventory		3,000	
	Accounts Payable			3,000
	(To record goods purchased on account from Lalonde, terms 2/10, n/45)			

8	Accounts Payable		600	
	Inventory			600
	(To record return of goods to Lalonde)			
13	Accounts Payable ($3,000 − $600)		2,400	
	Inventory ([$3,000 − $600] × 2%)			48
	Cash ($2,400 − $48)			2,352
	(To record payment to Lalonde within discount period)			

DO IT! 5-4
Multiple-Step Income Statement Accounts

(a) Net sales: $1,820,000 − $170,000 − $30,000 = $1,620,000
(b) Gross profit: $1,620,000 (from part (a)) − $1,238,000 = $382,000
(c) Income from operations: $382,000 (from part (b)) − ($200,000 + $122,000) = $60,000
(d) Income before income tax: $60,000 (from part (c)) + $36,000 − $4,000 = $92,000
(e) Net income: $92,000 (from part (d)) − $23,000 = $69,000

DO IT! 5-5
Calculating and Evaluating Profitability

($ in thousands)
(a) Gross profit
2018: $1,347 − $863 = $484
2017: $1,331 − $853 = $478
Net income
2018: $1,347 − $863 − $439 − $15 = $30
2017: $1,331 − $853 − $407 − $24 = $47

	2018	2017
Gross profit margin	$\dfrac{\$484}{\$1,347} = 35.9\%$	$\dfrac{\$478}{\$1,331} = 35.9\%$
Profit margin	$\dfrac{\$30}{\$1,347} = 2.2\%$	$\dfrac{\$47}{\$1,331} = 3.5\%$

(b) Sports-R-Us's gross profit margin remained unchanged in 2018. However, its profit margin declined. It appears that the company has good control of its cost of goods sold but needs to review its operating expenses, which appear to have increased faster than sales.

DO IT! 5-6
Purchase and Sales Transactions—Periodic Inventory System

Lalonde Ltée (Seller)

Sept. 4	Accounts Receivable		3,000	
	Sales			3,000
	(To record credit sale to Guerette, terms 2/10, n/45)			
8	Sales Returns and Allowances		600	
	Accounts Receivable			600
	(To record credit granted for receipt of returned goods from Guerette)			
13	Cash ($2,400 − $48)		2,352	
	Sales Discounts ([$3,000 − $600] × 2%)		48	
	Accounts Receivable ($3,000 − $600)			2,400
	(To record collection from Guerette within discount period)			

Guerette Corp. (Buyer)

Sept. 4	Purchases		3,000	
	Accounts Payable			3,000
	(To record goods purchased on account from Lalonde, terms 2/10, n/45)			
8	Accounts Payable		600	
	Purchase Returns and Allowances			600
	(To record return of goods to Lalonde)			
13	Accounts Payable ($3,000 − $600)		2,400	
	Purchase Discounts ([$3,000 − $600] × 2%)			48
	Cash ($2,400 − $48)			2,352
	(To record payment to Lalonde within discount period)			

▶ PRACTICE USING THE DECISION TOOLKIT

(a) It does not matter that Costco operates more stores than Loblaw and Metro or that it operates in more countries. Ratio analysis puts each company's financial information into the same perspective for a comparison. It is the relationship between the amounts that is meaningful.

(b) Gross profit margin:

(in U.S. $ millions)	2015	2014
Costco	$\dfrac{(\$113{,}666 - \$101{,}065)}{\$113{,}666} = 11.1\%$	$\dfrac{(\$110{,}212 - \$98{,}458)}{\$110{,}212} = 10.7\%$
Loblaw	27.6%	24.7%
Metro	19.7%	19.1%
Industry average	24.4%	24.4%

Profit margin:

(in U.S. $ millions)	2015	2014
Costco	$\dfrac{\$2{,}377}{\$113{,}666} = 2.1\%$	$\dfrac{\$2{,}058}{\$110{,}212} = 1.9\%$
Loblaw	1.4%	0.1%
Metro	4.2%	3.9%
Industry average	2.8%	2.8%

(c) Costco's gross profit margin showed a slight increase between 2014 and 2015. While this is an improvement, Costco's results are less than half the current industry average, but it should be noted that Costco's strategy is likely to sell a greater volume at lower prices. Both Loblaw and Metro's gross margins have increased as well, showing improvement. However, Loblaw's gross margin is even stronger than the industry average. This suggests that price increases were passed along to their customers.

From 2014 to 2015 all three companies saw an improvement in their profit margins. However, only Metro's profit margin was higher than the industry average. As Metro's gross profit margin was lower than the industry average and their profit margin was higher than the industry average, it suggests that Metro was better able to control its selling, general, and administrative expenses than its competitors.

▶ COMPREHENSIVE DO IT!

DYKSTRA INC.
Income Statement
Year Ended December 31, 2018

Sales		$536,800
Less: Sales returns and allowances	$ 6,700	
Sales discounts	5,000	11,700
Net sales		525,100
Cost of goods sold		363,400
Gross profit		161,700
Operating expenses		
Administrative expenses	$111,500	
Selling expenses	19,600	131,100
Income from operations		30,600
Other revenues and expenses		
Interest revenue	$ 2,500	
Interest expense	4,600	(2,100)
Income before income tax		28,500
Income tax expense		6,000
Net income		$ 22,500

DYKSTRA INC.
Statement of Changes in Equity
Year Ended December 31, 2018

	Common Shares	Retained Earnings	Total Equity
Balance, January 1	$65,000	$61,000	$126,000
Issue of common shares	5,000		5,000
Net income		22,500	22,500
Dividends declared		(10,000)	(10,000)
Balance, December 31	$70,000	$73,500	$143,500

DYKSTRA INC.
Statement of Financial Position
December 31, 2018

Assets

Current assets			
Cash		$ 4,500	
Accounts receivable		11,100	
Inventory		29,000	
Prepaid insurance		2,500	
Total current assets			$ 47,100
Property, plant, and equipment			
Land		$150,000	
Buildings	$500,000		
Less: Accumulated depreciation	40,000	460,000	
Equipment	$ 95,000		
Less: Accumulated depreciation	18,000	77,000	
Total property, plant, and equipment			687,000
Total assets			$734,100

Liabilities and Shareholders' Equity

Liabilities			
Current liabilities			
Accounts payable		$ 10,600	
Property tax payable		4,000	
Bank loan payable		25,000	
Mortgage payable—current portion		21,000	
Total current liabilities			$ 60,600
Non-current liabilities			
Mortgage payable			530,000
Total liabilities			590,600
Shareholders' equity			
Common shares		$ 70,000	
Retained earnings		73,500	143,500
Total liabilities and shareholders' equity			$734,100

▶ **PRACTICE OBJECTIVE-FORMAT QUESTIONS**

1.   (d), (e), and (g) are correct.

Feedback
(a)   is incorrect. It is the opposite: with periodic inventory systems, cost of goods sold and ending inventory are not known unless inventory is counted.
(b)   is incorrect. It is the opposite: it would make the operating cycle longer due to the need to wait to collect receivables.
(c)   is incorrect because only cost of goods sold is taken into account.
(f)   is incorrect because this is only possible if using a perpetual inventory system.

2.   (c), (e), and (f) are correct.

Feedback
(a)   is incorrect because these would be the responsibility of the seller under FOB destination freight terms.
(b)   is incorrect because payment of 98% of the receivable would be made on October 20, but the buyer could also choose to pay nothing until November 9.
(d)   is incorrect because the ownership of the goods would not change hands until they arrive at the buyer's place of business.
(g)   is incorrect because the purchaser would only be entitled to a 2% discount.

3.   *Feedback*
(a)   Buyer (buying on credit).
(b)   Seller (at time of sale).
(c)   Seller (at time of sale).
(d)   Seller (if goods are returned).
(e)   Buyer (paying for credit purchase within discount period).
(f)   Seller (if FOB destination). Note that, if the buyer were responsible and the shipping terms were FOB shipping point, the Inventory account would have been debited.
(g)   Buyer (cash purchase).

4.   (c), (d), and (g) are correct.

Feedback
(a)   is incorrect because the sale was on account, not cash.
(b)   is incorrect. The accounts should be switched.

(e)   is incorrect because Hanneson paid within the discount period.
(f)   is incorrect. This uses a 10% discount, rather than a 1% discount.

5. (c) and (e) are correct.

Feedback
(a) is incorrect because this number does not include sales returns and allowances. Net sales: $203,000 – $9,000 – $3,000 = $191,000.
(b) is incorrect because interest expense would be included in other revenues and expenses as a non-operating item.
(c) is correct. Income from operations: $191,000 net sales – $88,000 cost of goods sold = $103,000 gross profit – $7,000 – $2,000 – $45,000 – $12,000 – $8,000 = $29,000.
(d) is incorrect because income tax is shown separately after other revenues and expenses and income before income tax and immediately before net income.
(e) is correct. Gross profit = $103,000 [see (c)].
(f) is incorrect because dividends declared are not an expense, they are a distribution of retained earnings and are reported on the statement of changes in equity, not the income statement.
(g) is incorrect because this number does not include income tax expense. Net income: $29,000 [income from operations from (c)] – $1,000 interest expense – $4,000 income tax expense = $24,000.

6. *Feedback*
(a) Decrease.
(b) No effect.
(c) Decrease.
(d) Increase.
(e) Decrease.
(f) Decrease.
(g) No effect.

7. (b), (d), (e), and (f) are correct.

Feedback
(a) is incorrect because this is an operating expense.
(c) is incorrect because this is an operating expense.
(g) is incorrect because this is an operating expense.

8. (a), (c), (e), and (f) are correct.

Feedback
(a) is correct. $978,000 – $391,200 = $586,800.
(b) is incorrect. It is the opposite, because the profit margin has increased. Profit margin: 2016, $114,750 ÷ $765,000 = 15%; 2017, $136,960 ÷ $856,000 = 16%; 2018, $176,040 ÷ $978,000 = 18%.
(c) is correct. Gross profit margin: 2016 ($765,000 – $328,950) ÷ $765,000 = 57%; 2017 ($856,000 – $359,520) ÷ $856,000 = 58%; 2018 ($978,000 – $391,200) ÷ $978,000 = 60%.
(d) is incorrect. It is the opposite, because the gross profit margin has increased [see (c)].
(e) is correct because the profit margin was higher than in previous years [see (b)].
(f) is correct [see (b)].
(g) is incorrect because it was 18% in 2018 compared with 16% in 2017, so it increased rather than decreased.

9. (a), (c), (d), and (g) are correct.

Feedback
(b) is incorrect. Cost of goods available for sale = beginning inventory + cost of goods purchased.
(e) is incorrect because wholesalers sell to retailers, rather than consumers.
(f) is incorrect because inventory must still be counted at least once per year to quantify theft.

*10. (a), (c), and (e) are correct.

Feedback
(b) is incorrect because the 2% purchase discount should be recorded since payment was made within 10 days.
(d) is incorrect. The debit would have been to Inventory if a perpetual inventory system had been used; to Purchases in a periodic inventory system.
(f) is incorrect. The account was paid in full on August 17. The Purchase Returns and Allowances account is used if merchandise is returned, rather than retained.
(g) is incorrect. The debit would have been to Inventory if a perpetual inventory system had been used; to Freight In in a periodic inventory system.

▶ ENDNOTES

[1] Ron Margulis, "Loblaw Draws on the Latest Data Technology to Address Inventory Issues," *Canadian Grocer*, October 22, 2015; "Helping Loblaw Achieve High Performance Through Supply Chain Transformation," Accenture case study, 2013; Canadian Press, "Loblaws Claims Supply Chain Overhaul Successful," *Canadian Manufacturing*, March 1, 2012; Kathleen Lau, "Loblaw Hungry for Improved IT Supply Chain," *Computing Canada*, February 20, 2008; "Loblaw, Targeting Wal-Mart Like Efficiency, Still Battling Supply Chain Re-Design Woes," *Supply Chain Digest*, January 26, 2006; Loblaw Companies Limited 2015 annual report; Loblaw Companies Limited corporate website, www.loblaw.ca.

[2] Claire Brownell, "How a Misstep by Heinz Laid the Path for French's Quest to Become Canada's Ketchup King," *Calgary Herald*, March 21, 2016; Emma Prestwich, "French's Ketchup Is Selling Out in Canada After This Man's Viral Post," *The Huffington Post Canada*, March 1, 2016; Carolyn Thompson, "'Bye. Bye. Heinz': French's Ketchup Sells out after Online Post Praising It and Its Ontario-Grown Tomatoes," *National Post*, February 29, 2016.

[3] "iPhone SE Is Three iPhone Generations Rolled into One, IHS Teardown Reveals," IHS news release, April 4, 2016; Don Reisinger, "Here's What Apple Pays to Build the iPhone SE," *Fortune*, April 4, 2016.

6

Reporting and Analyzing Inventory

CHAPTER PREVIEW

In the previous chapter, we discussed the accounting for merchandise transactions. In this chapter, we first explain what companies need to consider when determining inventory quantities. We then discuss three cost formulas—specific identification; first-in, first-out (FIFO); and average cost—that can be used to assign amounts to the cost of goods sold and the cost of inventory on hand. We will also discuss the effects that these cost formulas and inventory errors can have on a company's financial statements. We will conclude with a discussion of the presentation of inventory on the statement of financial position and the introduction of a new liquidity measure called inventory turnover, which is used to analyze inventory.

CHAPTER OUTLINE

LEARNING OBJECTIVES	READ	PRACTICE
1 Describe the steps in determining inventory quantities.	• Determining ownership of goods • Taking a physical inventory	**DO IT!** 6-1 Rules of ownership
2 Apply the cost formulas using specific identification, FIFO, and average cost under a perpetual inventory system.	• Specific identification • First-in, first-out (FIFO) • Average cost	**DO IT!** 6-2a Specific identification—perpetual system 6-2b FIFO and average cost—perpetual system
3 Explain the effects on the financial statements of choosing each of the inventory cost formulas.	• Choice of cost formula • Financial statement effects	**DO IT!** 6-3 Cost formula effects on income statements
4 Identify the effects of inventory errors on the financial statements.	• Errors made when determining the cost of inventory • Errors made when recording goods in transit at period end	**DO IT!** 6-4 Inventory errors
5 Demonstrate the presentation and analysis of inventory.	• Valuing inventory at the lower of cost and net realizable value • Reporting inventory • Inventory turnover	**DO IT!** 6-5a Lower of cost and net realizable value 6-5b Inventory turnover
6 Apply the FIFO and average cost formulas under a periodic inventory system (Appendix 6A).	• First-in, first-out (FIFO) • Average cost	**DO IT!** 6-6 FIFO and average cost—periodic system

FEATURE STORY

lululemon athletica Stretches Inventory Levels

Most retailers try to have just the right amount of inventory on hand. Too much inventory can result in increased storage costs and excess merchandise that must be sold at a discount, resulting in inventory writedowns or write offs. Too little inventory can result in lost sales and disappointed customers.

Some retailers, however, deliberately carry too little inventory in order to create demand. This has long been a strategy of lululemon athletica inc., which designs and sells yoga, athletic, and lifestyle clothing and gear. Founded by surfer, skater, and snowboarder Chip Wilson, lululemon opened its first store in Vancouver in 2000. It developed a niche following among yoga enthusiasts who gravitated toward its stretchy, technical fabrics. It now has more than 360 stores in Canada, the United States, and countries such as Australia, United Kingdom, and Hong Kong. The stores are corporate-owned or franchised.

By carrying lower quantities than needed to supply customer demand, lululemon enticed customers to return to the store to check product availability, or to make impulse buys of in-stock items. With a more limited supply, the retailer notes that it also avoids excess inventory levels, which could result in discounted prices and "could impair the strength and exclusivity of our brand."

Despite the price of its merchandise (around $100 for yoga pants) and the absence of reduced-price sales, lululemon developed a loyal following of customers who appreciated its unique designs and materials, quality, and customer service. Revenues continued to increase even when the stores carried limited inventory in some products.

But in early 2013, lululemon experienced an inventory shortage that was not deliberate. The company identified quality issues with "luon," a proprietary fabric used in its clothing that resulted in a recall of women's yoga pants because they were too see-through. The recall amounted to 17% of its total supply of women's yoga pants. The company charged a $17.5-million inventory provision to cost of sales.

The company seems to have changed its inventory strategy, moving away from deliberate shortages. After its yoga pant recall, it launched a marketing and social media campaign to keep customers informed of the quality issues and inventory timeline. It also revamped its quality control process and ramped up production at its overseas factories to handle demand.

But inventory levels might have swung the other way, as the company finally gave in to a sales tactic used by other retailers to offload excess goods: starting in 2015, it opened seven outlet stores. That same year, it launched its first-ever warehouse sale, something rarely seen with premium brands. In the third quarter of 2015, lululemon's inventory levels rose 59% from the same period the year before, while sales growth was only expected to increase by 15% year over year. As at January 31, 2016 (its fiscal year end), the company had $284 million in inventory—up from $208 million the year before. The company said that its rise in inventory was due mainly to the opening of new stores and the timing of product deliveries. While the amount of its inventory is reported on lululemon's balance sheet as an asset, in the clothing business, where fashions can get stale fast, having too much inventory that can't be sold can significantly impact the value of that asset.[1]

Go to the *REVIEW AND PRACTICE* section at the end of the chapter for a targeted summary and practice questions with solutions.

Visit **WileyPLUS** for more practice opportunities.

Describe the steps in determining inventory quantities.

Whether they are using a perpetual or periodic inventory system, companies need to determine their inventory quantities at the end of each accounting period by physically counting their inventory.

You will recall from Chapter 5 that a perpetual inventory system continuously (perpetually) updates the inventory accounting records to show the quantity and cost of inventory that *should* be on hand. That does not mean that perpetual accounting records reflect what *is actually* on hand. Even if the accounting records are continuously updated, companies that use a perpetual inventory system must still physically count inventory at year end for two purposes: (1) to check the accuracy of their perpetual inventory records and (2) to determine the amount of inventory lost due to shrinkage or theft. If inventory shrinkage has occurred, the inventory account must be adjusted and an expense related to the shrinkage recorded. One common way this adjustment is recorded is to debit Cost of Goods Sold and credit Inventory.

In a periodic inventory system, inventory quantities are not updated on a continuous basis. Companies that use a periodic inventory system must therefore count inventory to determine the ending inventory (inventory on hand) at the end of each accounting period. Once the ending inventory amount is determined, the cost of goods sold for the period can be calculated.

Determining inventory quantities, whether in a perpetual or periodic inventory system, involves two steps: (1) determining the goods owned by the company (because those are the goods that need to be included in the physical inventory count) and (2) taking a physical inventory count.

DETERMINING OWNERSHIP OF GOODS

Prior to counting inventory, we need to consider the ownership of goods in order to ensure that all goods owned by the company are included in the inventory count and that goods on hand, but not owned by the company, are excluded from the count. To determine who owns the inventory, two questions must be answered: (1) Does the company own any goods that are not on hand, such as items in transit or on consignment? (2) Do all of the goods on hand belong to the company?

Goods in Transit

Goods in transit at the end of the period (on board a truck, train, ship, or plane) make determining ownership a bit more complicated. The company may have purchased goods that have not yet been received, or it may have sold goods that have not yet been delivered. To arrive at an accurate count, ownership of these goods must be determined.

The rule to follow is straightforward. **Goods in transit should be included in the inventory of the company that has legal title to the goods.** As we learned in Chapter 5, legal title, or ownership, is determined by the terms of the sale. If the shipping terms are FOB destination, the seller has legal title to the goods while they are in transit. If the shipping terms are FOB shipping point, the buyer has legal title to the goods while they are in transit. These terms are important in determining the exact date when a purchase or sale should be recorded and what items should be included in inventory, even if the items are not physically present at the time of the inventory count.

The following table illustrates the transfer of ownership (legal title) when inventory is shipped. Assume that the seller sells goods to the buyer and ships them on December 28. The goods do not reach the buyer until January. Both companies count their inventory on December 31. Depending on the shipping terms (FOB destination or FOB shipping point), the goods may or may not need to be included in the inventory count. Any goods owned, but in transit at the end of the accounting period, should be included in the final inventory balance by the party that owns them at that time.

Shipping Terms	Seller	Buyer
FOB destination	Inventory belongs to seller until it reaches the buyer's destination	Inventory belongs to buyer when it reaches the buyer's destination
FOB shipping point	Inventory belongs to the seller until shipped	Inventory belongs to the buyer once the shipment leaves the seller's place of business

Consigned Goods

In some lines of business, it is customary to hold goods belonging to other parties and sell them, for a fee, without ever taking ownership of the goods. These are called **consigned goods**. Under a consignment arrangement, the holder of the goods (called the **consignee**) does not own the goods. Ownership remains with the individual or company that wants to sell the goods (called the **consignor**) until the goods are actually sold to a customer. Because the consignee does not own consigned goods, the goods should not be included in the consignee's physical inventory count. Conversely, the consignor should include in its inventory any of its merchandise that is being held by the consignee.

For example, artists often display their paintings and other works of art in galleries on consignment. In such cases, the art gallery does not take ownership of the art—it still belongs to the artist. Therefore, if an inventory count is taken, any art on consignment should not be included in the art gallery's inventory. When the art sells, the gallery then takes a commission and pays the artist the remainder. Many craft stores, second-hand clothing stores, used vehicle dealerships, and antique dealers sell goods on consignment to avoid the risk of purchasing an item they will not be able to sell.

DO IT! ▶6-1 Rules of Ownership

The LaSalle Fashion House Corporation completed its inventory count at year end, August 31. It arrived at a total inventory amount of $400,000 after counting everything currently on hand in its warehouse. How will the following additional information affect the inventory count and cost?

1. Goods costing $30,000 and held on consignment for McQueen Dress Inc. were included in the inventory.
2. LaSalle's purchase of goods for $20,000 was in transit from Montreal as at August 31 (terms FOB shipping point) and was not included in the count.
3. LaSalle's purchase of $18,000 in goods from Deleau Ltd. was in transit from Winnipeg on August 31 (terms FOB destination) and was not included in the count.
4. LaSalle sold inventory for $36,000 that cost $24,000 when purchased. The items were in transit to a customer in Vancouver as at August 31 (terms FOB destination) and were not included in the count.

SOLUTION
Try this Do It! exercise on your own and then check your answer at the end of the chapter.

Related Exercise Material: BE6–1, BE6–2, E6–1, and E6–2.

Action Plan
- Apply the rules of ownership to goods held on consignment:
  - Goods held on consignment for another company are not included in inventory.
  - Goods held on consignment by another company are included in inventory.
- Apply the rules of ownership to goods in transit:
  - FOB destination: Goods sold or purchased and shipped FOB destination will belong to the seller until they reach their destination.
  - FOB shipping point: Goods sold or purchased and shipped FOB shipping point belong to the buyer after they have been shipped.

TAKING A PHYSICAL INVENTORY

Taking a physical inventory involves counting, weighing, or measuring each kind of inventory on hand. In many companies, taking a physical inventory is a formidable task. For example, clothing retailer lululemon, mentioned in our chapter-opening feature story, has hundreds of different

© Grzegorz Malec/istockphoto

Counting Inventory— Every Day

Dollarama is a family business that started in Montreal in 1910. It has grown since that time to become Canada's largest dollar store chain. Each of the approximately 1,000 store locations generates $2.5 million in sales from the 4,000 plus items in inventory. The maximum sales price of any item in the store at the time of writing was $3. Until 2012, the only way Dollarama could determine whether it needed to order more inventory was to count it. Store employees counted 10 to 15 product items every day and manually tracked the quantities on cards. Store managers used this information to decide whether or not they needed to order more of a particular item. If more items were required, they sent an email to head office and received them two weeks later. It took about 27 days to count all of the product items in inventory.

Counting inventory is a very labour-intensive process and there is no guarantee that the store will not run out of a popular item. For more than 15 years, Dollarama got by with a manual inventory system, but technology and competition caught up with it. In 2012, Dollarama completed a transformation of its inventory system from manual to electronic, and from periodic to perpetual. It put bar codes on every item and installed electronic scanners at the checkout counters. The scan data are now the primary source of information for stock replenishment.[2]

inventory items in each of its more than 360 stores located in six countries around the world. If goods are being sold or received during the physical inventory, the count becomes more complicated and the chance of errors increases. Consequently, companies often count inventory when the business is slow or when it is not open. And since most companies count their inventory at the end of the fiscal year, their year ends may coincide with slower periods. For example, lululemon's year end is the Sunday closest to January 31—following the holiday sales season when inventories are normally at their lowest level.

After the physical inventory is taken, the quantity of each kind of product is then multiplied by its cost to determine the total inventory cost. There are several ways to determine the cost of each product and these will be explained later in the chapter when we discuss the cost formulas used in inventory cost determination.

Inventory counts are part of a company's system of internal control. **Internal controls** are systems designed to help an organization achieve reliable financial reporting, effective and efficient operations, and compliance with relevant laws and regulations. Internal control systems include control activities, one of which is review and reconciliation. Counting inventory is a good example of this control activity. In a perpetual inventory system, the results of the physical inventory can be compared or reconciled with the information in the company's inventory system. As mentioned previously, this enables management to determine the extent of shrinkage or theft. If this is significant, management can put additional internal controls in place to safeguard inventory. These could include physical controls such as using garment sensors and security cameras. We will discuss internal controls in greater depth in Chapter 7.

LEARNING OBJECTIVE ▶ **2**

Apply the cost formulas using specific identification, FIFO, and average cost under a perpetual inventory system.

The physical inventory count we discussed in the last section determines the quantities on hand. If the perpetual inventory records reflect different quantities, these are adjusted to reflect the count results. Companies must then apply unit costs to the quantities to determine the total cost of the inventory.

Unfortunately, it is not all that easy to determine what cost to apply when we record the cost of merchandise sold in the accounting records throughout the period. The journal entries related to purchases and sales of merchandise were first illustrated in Chapter 5. At that time, however, you were either told the cost of the goods sold, or it was assumed, for simplicity, that all inventory items had the same unit cost. In practice, though, a company often purchases different items of inventory at different costs on different dates and from different suppliers. Costs differ for a variety of reasons, such as price changes, varying quantity discounts, and changes in exchange rates. The cost per unit of acquiring inventory can therefore be different every time there is a purchase.

Journal entries to record purchases of merchandise do not show the unit cost of each item of merchandise that was acquired. The account Inventory is simply debited for the total cost of all the units together, and Cash and/or Accounts Payable is credited. The entry to record the sales price is not directly affected by the unit cost. Cash and/or Accounts Receivable is debited and the Sales account is credited for the sales price of the merchandise sold, not its unit cost.

However, the unit cost is needed in order to prepare the entry to record the cost of goods sold and remove the cost of the items sold from inventory. Because units of the same inventory item are typically purchased at different prices, it is necessary to determine which unit costs to use in the calculation of the cost of the goods sold. There are three different cost formulas that can be used under IFRS and ASPE to determine inventory cost. These are specific identification; first-in, first-out (FIFO); and average cost. The first cost formula—specific identification—uses the actual physical flow of the goods to determine cost. We will look at this cost formula next.

SPECIFIC IDENTIFICATION

The **specific identification cost formula** tracks the actual physical flow of the goods in a perpetual inventory system. Each item of inventory is marked, tagged, or coded with its specific unit cost so that, at any point in time, the cost of the ending inventory and the cost of the goods sold can be determined. This cost formula is only used for inventories that are composed of unique, identifiable items. These items are typically also of high value.

Assume, for example, that a car dealership buys three different cars from a car manufacturer: a sedan at a cost of $45,200, a convertible at a cost of $70,500, and an SUV at a cost of $58,400. During the month, the dealership sells two of the vehicles, at the selling price of $50,800 for the sedan and $64,200 for the SUV. At December 31, the convertible is still on hand. The cost of goods sold is therefore $103,600 ($45,200 + $58,400) and the ending inventory is $70,500. This determination is possible because it was easy to track the actual physical flow of these three inventory items. Note that it is the *cost* of the car that is used to determine the cost of goods sold and not the selling price.

Specific identification is appropriate and required for goods that are not ordinarily interchangeable, and for goods that are produced and segregated for specific projects. It is used most often in situations involving a relatively small number of costly items that are easily distinguishable by their physical characteristics, serial numbers, or special markings. Examples include some types of jewellery, artwork, pianos, and automobiles. Specific identification is also suitable for many types of special orders.

While specific identification works well when a company sells high-unit-cost items that can be clearly identified from purchase through to sale, it cannot be used for goods that are interchangeable or that cannot be distinguished from one another.

The requirement that the specific identification cost formula be used only for goods that are not ordinarily interchangeable is an attempt to ensure that management does not use this cost formula to manage net income. If specific identification could be used for interchangeable goods, then management would be free to select the more expensive goods or the less expensive goods depending upon their motivation. If they were trying to minimize cost of goods sold, they would select the less expensive goods. If they were trying to maximize cost of goods sold, they would do the opposite.

▼ **HELPFUL HINT**
The specific identification cost formula must be used if the goods are not interchangable (that is, if they are unique and can be distinguished from one another). It cannot be used if the goods are interchangable.

It is important to note that companies can use more than one cost formula if they have different types of inventory. Consequently, car companies will use the specific identification cost formula to track the cost of their automobile inventory while using another cost formula to determine the cost of their parts inventory (because car parts are not unique or separately identifiable).

Finally, regardless of which type of inventory system—perpetual or periodic—is being used, specific identification will give the same results. The allocation of cost of goods available for sale between cost of goods sold and inventory will always be the same. This is because the exact (specific) costs of each unit, whether it is sold (part of cost of goods sold) or still on hand (part of inventory), are used.

DO IT! ▶6-2a   Specific Identification—Perpetual System

Action Plan

✔ Each time there is a purchase or sale of goods, cost of goods sold and ending inventory should be updated.

✔ Use the specific cost of the item being purchased or sold.

✔ Prove that the cost of goods sold and ending inventory equal the cost of goods available for sale.

✔ Remember to use the cost amounts and *not* the selling prices in your calculations.

Matchett Farm Equipment Ltd. began the month of February with five tractors in inventory that had the following costs:

	Cost
Tractor 1	$ 54,000
Tractor 2	78,000
Tractor 3	126,000
Tractor 4	95,000
Tractor 5	86,000
	$439,000

Matchett had the following transactions during the month:

Date	Explanation
Feb. 3	Sold Tractor 1 for $62,000
5	Sold Tractor 4 for $109,000
6	Purchased Tractor 6 at a cost of $140,000
10	Sold Tractor 3 for $145,000
13	Purchased Tractor 7 at a cost of $89,000
18	Sold Tractor 6 for $160,000
22	Purchased Tractor 8 at a cost of $132,000
27	Sold Tractor 8 for $152,000

Determine the cost of goods sold and ending inventory under a perpetual inventory system using the specific identification cost formula.

SOLUTION
Try this Do It! exercise on your own and then check your answer at the end of the chapter.

Related Exercise Material: BE6–3.

FIRST-IN, FIRST-OUT (FIFO)

If a company cannot use the specific identification cost formula, then it must use either the first-in, first-out (FIFO) or average cost formula. We will explain FIFO in this section, and then average cost in the next section. The **first-in, first-out (FIFO) cost formula** assumes that the earliest goods purchased (or oldest inventory) are the first ones to be sold. This does not necessarily mean that the oldest units are in fact sold first, only that the costs of the oldest units are recognized first in cost of goods sold. The cost formula chosen by a company should correspond as closely as possible to the actual physical flow of merchandise. FIFO generally does this because it is good business practice to sell the units that have been in inventory the longest (the oldest units) first.

To illustrate the application of FIFO in a perpetual inventory system, we will assume that The Tee-Shirt Corporation has the following information for one of its products, the University Soccer Shirt, as shown in Illustration 6-1.

THE TEE-SHIRT CORPORATION					
University Soccer Shirt					
Date	Explanation	Units	Unit Cost	Total Cost	Balance in Units
Jan. 1	Beginning inventory	100	$10	$ 1,000	100
Apr. 15	Purchases	200	11	2,200	300
May 1	Sales	(150)			150
Aug. 24	Purchases	300	12	3,600	450
Sept. 10	Sales	(400)			50
Nov. 27	Purchases	400	13	5,200	450
		450		$12,000	

▶Illustration 6-1

Inventory data for the University Soccer Shirt

Perpetual inventory schedules start with inventory on hand at the beginning of the year for each product. The schedule is updated for the quantity and cost of merchandise purchased and sold throughout the year. For example, we note in Illustration 6-1 that there were 100 units of merchandise costing $10 each on hand at the beginning of the year at a cost of $1,000 and 200 units of additional merchandise at $11 each that were purchased on April 15 at a cost of $2,200. This resulted, as of April 15, in 300 units available for sale at a total cost of $3,200 ($1,000 + $2,200), as shown in the partial inventory schedule below:

	Purchases			Cost of Goods Sold			Balance		
Date	Units	Cost	Total	Units	Cost	Total	Units	Cost	Total
Jan. 1							100	$10	$1,000
Apr. 15	200	$11	$2,200				100	10	} 3,200
							200	11	

On May 1, the date of the first sale, we will apply FIFO to determine whether the 150 units that were sold cost $10, $11, or a mix of both amounts. The cost must be determined on this date so that the Cost of Goods Sold account can be debited and the Inventory account credited for the cost of this sale. Note that the sale must also be recorded on this same date, which is done by debiting Cash or Accounts Receivable and crediting Sales. Although the sales price is required to record this entry, the above table does not include information about the sales price, because this is not needed to determine the *cost* of the goods sold or the *cost* of the ending inventory.

Under FIFO, the cost of the oldest goods on hand before each sale is allocated to the cost of goods sold under the assumption that they were sold first. Accordingly, the cost of goods sold on May 1 is assumed to consist of all 100 units of the January 1 beginning inventory and 50 units of the items purchased on April 15. This leaves 150 units of the April 15 purchase at a cost of $11 per unit remaining in ending inventory. In the table below, we have added this information (highlighted in red) to the inventory schedule that we started above.

	Purchases			Cost of Goods Sold			Balance		
Date	Units	Cost	Total	Units	Cost	Total	Units	Cost	Total
Jan. 1							100	$10	$1,000
Apr. 15	200	$11	$2,200				100	10	} 3,200
							200	11	
May 1				100	$10	} $1,550	150	11	1,650
				50	11				

After additional purchases are made on August 24, the cost of goods available for sale on this date now consists of 150 units at $11 each costing $1,650 and 300 units at $12 each costing $3,600, for a total of 450 units available for sale costing $5,250 ($1,650 + $3,600). This is shown below in the continuation of the perpetual inventory schedule:

Date	Purchases Units	Purchases Cost	Purchases Total	Cost of Goods Sold Units	Cost of Goods Sold Cost	Cost of Goods Sold Total	Balance Units	Balance Cost	Balance Total
Jan. 1							100	$10	$1,000
Apr. 15	200	$11	$2,200				100 / 200	10 / 11	} 3,200
May 1				100 / 50	$10 / 11	} $1,550	150	11	1,650
Aug. 24	300	12	3,600				150 / 300	11 / 12	} 5,250

On September 10, when 400 units are sold, the cost of goods sold is assumed to consist of the oldest units available for sale consisting of the 150 remaining units purchased on April 15 at $11 each costing $1,650, and 250 units purchased on August 24 at $12 each costing $3,000. The cost of goods sold for this sale is $4,650 ($1,650 + $3,000). This leaves 50 units in ending inventory at a cost of $12 per unit, or $600 in total, as shown below:

Date	Purchases Units	Purchases Cost	Purchases Total	Cost of Goods Sold Units	Cost of Goods Sold Cost	Cost of Goods Sold Total	Balance Units	Balance Cost	Balance Total
Jan. 1							100	$10	$1,000
Apr. 15	200	$11	$2,200				100 / 200	10 / 11	} 3,200
May 1				100 / 50	$10 / 11	} $1,550	150	11	1,650
Aug. 24	300	12	3,600				150 / 300	11 / 12	} 5,250
Sept. 10				150 / 250	11 / 12	} 4,650	50	12	600

After a purchase of 400 units on November 27, the ending inventory is 450 units consisting of 50 units at $12 costing $600 from the August 24 purchase and 400 units at $13 costing $5,200 from the November 27 purchase, for a total cost of $5,800 ($600 + $5,200). This transaction is included in Illustration 6-2, completing the inventory schedule shown above.

▶Illustration 6-2
Perpetual inventory schedule—FIFO

Date	Purchases Units	Purchases Cost	Purchases Total	Cost of Goods Sold Units	Cost of Goods Sold Cost	Cost of Goods Sold Total	Balance Units	Balance Cost	Balance Total
Jan. 1							100	$10	$1,000
Apr. 15	200	$11	$ 2,200				100 / 200	10 / 11	} 3,200
May 1				100 / 50	$10 / 11	} $1,550	150	11	1,650
Aug. 24	300	12	3,600				150 / 300	11 / 12	} 5,250
Sept. 10				150 / 250	11 / 12	} 4,650	50	12	600
Nov. 27	400	13	5,200				50 / 400	12 / 13	} 5,800
	900		$11,000	550		$6,200			

Check: Cost of Goods Sold + Ending Inventory = Cost of Goods Available for Sale (Beginning Inventory + Purchases)
Check: $6,200 + $5,800 = $12,000 ($1,000 + $11,000)

As at November 27, the total cost of goods sold is $6,200 and the ending inventory is $5,800. A useful check against calculation errors is to check whether the total of the cost of goods sold and ending inventory equals the total cost of goods available for sale of $12,000 (beginning inventory of $1,000 + purchases of $11,000).

In summary, FIFO assumes that the first goods purchased are the first ones sold. This cost formula always takes into consideration the order in which goods were purchased. As a result, FIFO also assumes that any ending inventory consists of the last goods purchased.

Whether a periodic or perpetual inventory system is used, FIFO will always result in the same cost of goods sold and ending inventory amounts. Recall from Chapter 5 that a key difference between these two inventory systems arises when the cost of goods available for sale (beginning inventory plus the cost of goods purchased) is allocated to the cost of goods sold and ending inventory. Under a perpetual inventory system, the cost of goods available for sale is allocated to the cost of goods sold as each item is sold. Under a periodic inventory system, the allocation is made only at the end of the period, with the cost of goods sold then calculated by deducting the ending inventory from the cost of goods available for sale. The same costs will always be first in, and therefore first out, whether the costs are allocated throughout the accounting period as in the perpetual inventory system or at the end of the accounting period as in the periodic inventory system. The periodic inventory system using FIFO is demonstrated in Appendix 6A.

AVERAGE COST

The **average cost formula** recognizes that it is not possible to measure a specific physical flow of inventory when the goods available for sale are homogeneous or interchangeable and cannot be distinguished from one another. Consider, for example, a fuel storage tank at a gas station. When the tank is refilled with gas that has a different cost than the gas that is currently in the tank, the gas mixes. As the gas is being sold, it is impossible to tell which batch of gas at which cost is being pumped and which batch of gas at which cost remains in the tank.

Under the average cost formula, the allocation of the cost of goods available for sale between cost of goods sold and ending inventory is made based on the **weighted average unit cost** of the merchandise available for sale. The calculation of this amount is shown in the formula in Illustration 6-3.

$$\boxed{\text{Cost of Goods Available for Sale}} \div \boxed{\text{Units Available for Sale}} = \boxed{\text{Weighted Average Unit Cost}}$$

Note that the weighted average unit cost is *not* calculated by taking a simple average of the costs of each purchase, but by weighting the quantities purchased at each unit cost. This is done by dividing the cost of goods available for sale by the units available for sale **at the date of each purchase**. Consequently, a new average is calculated, after each purchase (or purchase return). Because of this, when using the average cost formula for perpetual inventory systems, we often refer to this as a *moving* average cost formula as the average cost "moves" with each purchase.

We will use the same information provided in Illustration 6-2 for The Tee-Shirt Corporation to prepare a perpetual inventory schedule using the average cost formula so that you can compare the similarities and differences between the FIFO and average cost formulas. In the partial perpetual inventory schedule below, note that the beginning inventory of 100 units at $10 each costing $1,000 and the April 15 purchase of 200 units at $11 each costing $2,200 combine to total 300 units available for sale at a total cost of $3,200 ($1,000 + $2,200).

Using the formula shown in Illustration 6-3, the weighted average unit cost on April 15 is $10.67 ($3,200 ÷ 300) (highlighted in red in the table below). Accordingly, the unit cost of the 150 units sold on May 1 is shown at $10.67, and the total cost of goods sold is $1,600 (150 × $10.67). This unit cost is used in costing the units sold until another purchase (or a purchase return) is made, at which point a new unit cost must be calculated.

In practice, average unit costs may be rounded to the nearest cent, or even to the nearest dollar. This illustration uses the exact unit cost amounts in its calculations, as would a computerized

▼ HELPFUL HINT

Beginning inventory + Cost of goods purchased = Cost of goods available for sale

Cost of goods sold + Ending inventory = Cost of goods available for sale

Beginning inventory + Cost of goods purchased = Cost of goods sold + Ending inventory

►Illustration 6-3
Calculation of weighted average unit cost

▼ HELPFUL HINT

The weighted average unit cost is recalculated each time goods are purchased (or returned) under a perpetual inventory system.

schedule, even though the unit costs have been rounded to two decimal places for presentation purposes.

Date	Purchases			Cost of Goods Sold			Balance		
	Units	Cost	Total	Units	Cost	Total	Units	Cost	Total
Jan. 1							100	$10.00	$1,000.00
Apr. 15	200	$11.00	$2,200.00				300	10.67	3,200.00
May 1				150	$10.67	$1,600.00	150	10.67	1,600.00

On August 24, after 300 units costing $12 each are purchased for $3,600, a total of 450 units costing $5,200 ($1,600 + $3,600) are on hand. This results in a new average cost per unit of $11.56 ($5,200 ÷ 450). This new cost is used to calculate the cost of the September 10 sale and the units still on hand after the sale, as shown in the continuation of the inventory schedule below:

Date	Purchases			Cost of Goods Sold			Balance		
	Units	Cost	Total	Units	Cost	Total	Units	Cost	Total
Jan. 1							100	$10.00	$1,000.00
Apr. 15	200	$11.00	$2,200.00				300	10.67	3,200.00
May 1				150	$10.67	$1,600.00	150	10.67	1,600.00
Aug. 24	300	12.00	3,600.00				450	11.56	5,200.00
Sept. 10				400	11.56	4,622.22	50	11.56	577.78

A new unit cost will be calculated again after the November 27 purchase of 400 units for $5,200. After this purchase, there are 450 units on hand with a total cost of $5,777.78 ($577.78 + $5,200). This results in a new average cost of $12.84 ($5,777.78 ÷ 450), which will be used until another purchase is made (in the following year, in The Tee-Shirt Corporation's case).

These transactions, which complete the perpetual inventory schedule for the average cost formula, are shown in Illustration 6-4.

As at November 27, therefore, the total cost of goods sold is $6,222.22 and the total ending inventory is $5,777.78. The total of these amounts should agree with the cost of goods available for sale, $12,000 ($6,222.22 + $5,777.78). This is a useful check, or proof, of the accuracy of your calculations.

▶Illustration 6-4

Perpetual inventory schedule— average cost

Date	Purchases			Cost of Goods Sold			Balance		
	Units	Cost	Total	Units	Cost	Total	Units	Cost	Total
Jan. 1							100	$10.00	$1,000.00
Apr. 15	200	$11.00	$ 2,200.00				300	10.67	3,200.00
May 1				150	$10.67	$1,600.00	150	10.67	1,600.00
Aug. 24	300	12.00	3,600.00				450	11.56	5,200.00
Sept. 10				400	11.56	4,622.22	50	11.56	577.78
Nov. 27	400	13.00	5,200.00				450	12.84	5,777.78
	900		$11,000.00	550		$6,222.22			

Check: $6,222.22 + $5,777.78 = $12,000 ($1,000 + $11,000)

In summary, this cost formula uses the average cost of the goods that are available for sale to determine the cost of goods sold and ending inventory. When a perpetual inventory system is used, the average unit cost is determined after each purchase (or purchase return). When a periodic inventory system is used, the average unit cost is determined once, at the end of the accounting period. Because of the different times when the average unit cost is determined in perpetual and periodic inventory systems, different amounts will normally result for amounts allocated to cost of goods sold and ending inventory in each system when using the average cost formula. The use of the average cost formula in a periodic inventory system will be explained in Appendix 6A.

DO IT! ▶6-2b FIFO and Average Cost—Perpetual System

The inventory records of Ag Implement Inc. show the following data for the month of March:

Date		Explanation	Units	Unit Cost	Total Cost
Mar.	1	Beginning inventory	4,000	$3	$12,000
	10	Purchases	6,000	4	24,000
	19	Sales	(8,000)		
	22	Purchases	5,000	5	25,000
	28	Sales	(5,500)		
			1,500		$61,000

Determine the cost of goods sold and ending inventory under a perpetual inventory system using the (a) FIFO and (b) average cost formulas.

SOLUTION

Try this Do It! exercise on your own and then check your answer at the end of the chapter.

Related Exercise Material: BE6–4, BE6–5, and BE6–6.

Action Plan

✔ For FIFO, allocate the first costs to the cost of goods sold at the date of each sale. The latest costs will be allocated to the goods on hand (ending inventory).

✔ For average cost, determine the weighted average unit cost (cost of goods available for sale ÷ number of units available for sale) after each purchase. Multiply this cost by the number of units sold to determine the cost of goods sold, and by the number of units on hand to determine the cost of ending inventory.

✔ Prove that the cost of goods sold and ending inventory equal the cost of goods available for sale.

LEARNING OBJECTIVE ▶ 3 **Explain the effects on the financial statements of choosing each of the inventory cost formulas.**

Each of the cost formulas—specific identification, FIFO, and average cost—is acceptable for use by both publicly traded companies and private companies. However, there are guidelines that limit the choice of the formula that can be selected by management. We will discuss guidelines that influence the choice of the appropriate cost formula and the impact these choices can have on the financial statements in the sections that follow.

CHOICE OF COST FORMULA

If companies have goods that are not ordinarily interchangeable, or goods that have been produced and segregated for specific projects, they **must** use specific identification to determine the cost of their inventory. This formula is used when the goods are unique, high-value items. If the goods are interchangeable (cannot be specifically identified), then specific identification cannot be used and the company can choose to use either FIFO or average cost.

Some Canadian companies use specific identification, including Finning Equipment. Other Canadian companies use FIFO, including Jean Coutu, Magna International, Maple Leaf Foods, and Saputo. Still other Canadian companies use the average cost formula to determine the cost of their inventories, including Canadian Tire, Loblaw Companies Limited, and Sears Canada.

How should a company choose between FIFO and average cost? It should consider the following guidelines in making its choice:

1. Choose a cost formula that corresponds as closely as possible to the physical flow of goods.
2. Report an inventory cost on the statement of financial position that is close to the inventory's recent cost.
3. Use the same cost formula for all inventories of a similar nature and use.

After a company chooses a cost formula for determining the cost of its inventory, that cost formula should be used consistently from one period to the next. You will recall, from Chapter 2, that comparability of financial statements over successive time periods is an important enhancing characteristic of accounting information. Using FIFO in one year and average cost in the next year would make it difficult to compare the net income for the two years.

This is not to say that a company may never change from one cost formula to another. However, a change in cost formula may occur only if the nature and use of the inventory change and if a different cost formula would result in a more relevant or faithful representation in the financial statements. Such a change is unusual with respect to inventories. We will learn more about changing accounting policies in Chapter 11.

FINANCIAL STATEMENT EFFECTS

Inventory affects both the statement of financial position and the income statement because ending inventory is included as a current asset on the statement of financial position and cost of goods sold is included as an expense on the income statement. Cost of goods sold also affects gross profit and net income, which in turn will affect retained earnings in the statement of changes in equity as well as in the shareholders' equity section of the statement of financial position. We will look at the impact of inventory on both the income statement and the statement of financial position in the next two sections.

Income Statement Effects

To understand the impact of the FIFO and average cost formulas on the income statement, we will now examine their effects on The Tee-Shirt Corporation. The condensed income statements in Illustration 6-5 use the amounts we determined for cost of goods sold after applying the FIFO and average cost formulas earlier in the chapter. This illustration also assumes that The Tee-Shirt Corporation sold its 550 units for $11,500, had operating expenses of $2,000, and is subject to an income tax rate of 30%.

▶Illustration 6-5
Comparative effects of inventory cost formulas

THE TEE-SHIRT CORPORATION Condensed Income Statements		
	FIFO	Average Cost
Sales	$11,500	$11,500
Cost of goods sold	6,200	6,222
Gross profit	5,300	5,278
Operating expenses	2,000	2,000
Income before income tax	3,300	3,278
Income tax expense (30%)	990	983
Net income	$ 2,310	$ 2,295

The sales and operating expense figures are the same under both FIFO and average cost. But the cost of goods sold amounts (highlighted in red above) are different. This difference is because of the unit costs that are allocated under each cost formula. Each dollar of difference in cost of goods sold results in a corresponding dollar difference in income before income tax. For Tee-Shirt, there is a $22 difference between the FIFO and average cost amounts for cost of goods sold. A fixed percentage (30%) applied to determine income tax expense results in a difference in net income between the two cost formulas of $15.

In periods of changing prices, the choice of inventory cost formula can have a significant impact on net income. In a period of inflation (rising prices), as is the case for Tee-Shirt, FIFO produces higher net income because cost of goods sold is composed of the lowest-cost units and this in turn will maximize net income. As Illustration 6-5 shows, FIFO reports the highest net income ($2,310) and average cost the lowest ($2,295). This difference is not very large for Tee-Shirt, because prices are changing slowly and very few goods were involved. The more prices change and the greater the number of goods, the larger this difference will be.

If prices are falling, the results from the use of FIFO and average cost are reversed: FIFO will report the lowest net income and average cost the highest. If prices are stable, both cost formulas will report the same results.

Compared with FIFO, the average cost formula will result in more recent costs being reflected in the cost of goods sold. This will better identify or match current costs with current revenues and result in a better measurement of net income on the income statement. Of course, the specific identification cost formula provides the best match of costs and revenues, because it exactly matches each cost with the revenue it generates.

Statement of Financial Position Effects

One advantage of FIFO is that the costs allocated to ending inventory will approximate the inventory items' current (replacement) cost because the most recent purchases are assumed to be in ending inventory. For example, for Tee-Shirt, 400 of the 450 units in the ending inventory have a cost under FIFO at the most recent November 27 unit cost of $13. Since management needs to replace inventory when it is sold, a value that approximates the replacement cost is helpful for decision-making. That is why one of the guidelines in choosing an inventory cost formula is to "report an inventory cost on the statement of financial position that is close to the inventory's recent cost." FIFO provides a more relevant ending inventory value on the statement of financial position than does average cost.

By extension, one limitation of the average cost formula is that, in a period of inflation, the average cost results in older costs being included in ending inventory. For example, the average cost of Tee-Shirt's ending inventory, $12.84, includes the $10 unit cost of the beginning inventory as well as the cost of some of its earliest purchases in the period. The understatement becomes greater over extended periods of inflation if the inventory includes goods that were purchased in one or more earlier accounting periods.

Summary of Advantages and Financial Statement Effects of Each Cost Formula

The advantages of each of the three major cost formulas are summarized in Illustration 6-6.

Specific Identification	FIFO	Average Cost
• Exactly matches costs and revenues on the income statement.	• Ending inventory on the statement of financial position includes the most current costs (closest to replacement cost).	• Cost of goods sold on the income statement includes more current costs than FIFO.
• Tracks the actual physical flow.	• Approximates the physical flow of most retailers.	• Smooths the effects of price changes by assigning all units the same average cost.

▶ Illustration 6-6
Advantages of each cost formula

The key financial statement differences that will result from using the three cost formulas during a period of **rising prices** are summarized in Illustration 6-7. These effects will be the opposite if prices are falling and the same for all three cost formulas if prices are constant. In all cases, it does not matter whether a company uses the perpetual or periodic inventory system.

It is also worth remembering that all three cost formulas will give exactly the same result over the life cycle of the business or its product. **That is, the allocation between the cost of goods sold and ending inventory may vary annually, but it will produce the same cumulative results over**

▶Illustration 6-7
Summary of financial statement effects of cost formulas during a period of rising prices

	Specific Identification	FIFO	Average Cost
Income statement			
Cost of goods sold	Variable	Lower	Higher
Gross profit	Variable	Higher	Lower
Net income	Variable	Higher	Lower
Statement of financial position			
Cash	Same	Same	Same
Ending inventory	Variable	Higher	Lower
Retained earnings	Variable	Higher	Lower

time. Although much has been written about the impact of the choice of inventory cost formula on a variety of performance measures, in reality there is little real economic distinction among the cost formulas over time.

KEEPING AN EYE ON CASH

We have seen that both inventory on the statement of financial position and cost of goods sold on the income statement are affected by the choice of cost formula. It is very important to understand, however, that the choice of cost formula does *not* affect cash flow. All three cost formulas—specific identification, FIFO, and average cost—produce exactly the same cash flow before income tax.

Why is that? Sales and purchases are not affected by the inventory cost formula. The only thing that is affected is the allocation of the cost of goods available for sale between the cost of goods sold and ending inventory, which does not involve cash.

Let's consider this further. When a company records its sales, it uses the same selling price regardless of whether it uses specific identification, FIFO, or average cost. It doesn't change its selling price based on its cost formula. So cash receipts from cash sales, or collections of sales on account, are unchanged.

When a company records purchases of its merchandise for resale, it pays the same for the merchandise regardless of its cost formula. So cash payments for purchases, or payments on account, are unchanged.

In a perpetual inventory system, cost of goods sold is recorded by debiting the Cost of Goods Sold account and crediting the Inventory account. There is no cash involved in this entry. The only accounts affected by the choice of cost formula are inventory and retained earnings (and related amounts such as current assets, total assets, and total shareholders' equity) on the statement of financial position and cost of goods sold (and related amounts such as gross profit, income before income tax, income tax, and net income) on the income statement.

DO IT! ▶ 6-3 Cost Formula Effects on Income Statements

Action Plan

✔ Recall that FIFO allocates the earliest costs to the cost of goods sold at the date of each sale.

✔ Recall that average cost uses a weighted average unit cost to determine the cost of goods sold at the date of each sale. For this cost formula, use unrounded numbers in your calculations but round to the nearest cent for presentation purposes in an inventory schedule.

✔ In preparing comparative income statements, note that while the cost of goods sold will change between cost formulas, the sales figure does not.

On July 31, UFirst Inc. had the following merchandise transactions:

July	1	Beginning inventory, 2 units @ $75 each
	7	Purchases, 4 units @ $80 each
	19	Sales, 5 units @ $180 each
	25	Purchases, 6 units @ $100 each

(a) Calculate UFirst's cost of goods sold and ending inventory for the month of July assuming the use of (1) FIFO and (2) average cost in a perpetual inventory system.

(b) Prepare comparative income statements for each cost formula, assuming operating expenses of $300 and an income tax rate of 25%.

SOLUTION

Try this Do It! exercise on your own and then check your answer at the end of the chapter.

Related Exercise Material: BE6–7, E6–3, E6–4, E6–5, E6–6, and E6–7.

LEARNING
OBJECTIVE

4

Identify the effects of inventory errors on the financial statements.

Errors relating to inventory can arise in a number of ways. We will discuss two situations where inventory errors commonly occur. The first type of error arises when the quantity or costs assigned to inventory are incorrect. The second type of error we will discuss occurs when errors are made when recording goods in transit at the end of an accounting period. We will discuss both types of errors in more detail in the sections that follow.

ERRORS MADE WHEN DETERMINING THE COST OF INVENTORY

This first type of error occurs if a company uses incorrect quantity or cost information when determining ending inventory. Consider an example where a company has opening inventory of $20,000 and purchased inventory of $40,000 during 2018 for a total cost of goods available for sale of $60,000. If the correct cost of ending inventory is $15,000, this would mean that the cost of goods sold for the year would be $45,000 ($60,000 − $15,000). However, assume that an error in quantities or costs was made in determining the cost of inventory at the end of 2018 and the amount was calculated to be $12,000 rather than the correct amount of $15,000. In this case, cost of goods sold for 2018 would be $48,000 ($60,000 − $12,000), rather than the correct amount of $45,000.

An error made in determining the cost of inventory at the end of one period will also result in an error in the following period. As we have discussed, the ending inventory of one period automatically becomes the beginning inventory of the next period. Consequently, **an error in ending inventory of the current period will have a reverse effect on net income of the next accounting period** if it is not found and corrected.

Because of the $3,000 understatement in ending inventory at the end of 2018 ($12,000 instead of $15,000), it is also wrong at the beginning of 2019. If purchases made in 2019 were $68,000, the goods available for sale will be $80,000 ($12,000 + $68,000) when it really should be $83,000 ($15,000 + $68,000). Assuming that the cost of inventory on hand is determined correctly at the end of 2019 at $23,000, then the cost of goods sold would be determined as $57,000 ($80,000 − $23,000) when it really should be $60,000 ($83,000 − $23,000). Notice that the overstatement of cost of goods sold in 2018 is reversed by the understatement of cost of goods sold in 2019. Inventory errors relating to ending inventory will reverse in the following year as long as the inventory count is done correctly and the correct costs are assigned at the end of that subsequent year. Illustration 6-8 illustrates these effects.

▶Illustration 6-8

Effects of inventory errors on income statement for two years

SAMPLE COMPANY Extracts from Income Statements				
	2018		2019	
	Incorrect	Correct	Incorrect	Correct
Sales	$80,000	$80,000	$90,000	$90,000
Cost of goods sold	48,000	45,000	57,000	60,000
Gross profit	32,000	35,000	33,000	30,000
Operating expenses	10,000	10,000	20,000	20,000
Income before income tax	22,000	25,000	13,000	10,000

$(3,000)
Income understated

$3,000
Income overstated

The combined income before income tax for two years is correct because the errors cancel each other out.

The following table summarizes the effect of errors made when determining the cost of inventory:

If Inventory Is:	Then Cost of Goods Sold Is:	Then Gross Profit Is:	Then Income Before Income Tax Is:	Then Retained Earnings Are:
Overstated	Understated	Overstated	Overstated	Overstated
Understated	Overstated	Understated	Understated	Understated

Note that the effect on the statement of financial position is balanced. In other words, the overstatement or understatement error in the Inventory account equals the overstatement or understatement error in the Retained Earnings account. This, however, ignores the effect on income tax caused by the inventory error. In fact, if the error is not discovered and corrected beforehand and no further errors are made, the Inventory account will be correct at the end of the second year (because it is overstated and understated equally during each year). Similarly, the Retained Earnings account at the end of the second year will also be correct for the same reasons.

In all cases, it is helpful to use the accounting equation to help check that you have the direction of an error stated correctly. That is, if Inventory (assets) is overstated and Retained Earnings (shareholders' equity) is overstated (assuming no impact on liabilities), then the accounting equation is in balance. If Inventory (assets) is overstated, Retained Earnings (shareholders' equity) cannot be understated because the accounting equation (assets = liabilities + shareholders' equity) would not be in balance.

ERRORS MADE WHEN RECORDING GOODS IN TRANSIT AT PERIOD END

Another type of error that can affect the financial statements occurs when goods in transit at the end of the accounting period are recorded incorrectly. This could involve the company failing to record goods that it owned but that were in transit. Alternatively, it could involve the company incorrectly including goods in transit in its inventory when they were not owned by the company. These errors will cause the Inventory and Accounts Payable accounts to be misstated.

Consider an example where an accountant has not recorded an inventory purchase made on credit one day before year end for $5,000. The inventory was in transit with terms FOB shipping point at year-end so the purchase should have been recorded as the goods belonged to the purchaser once they were shipped. Because of this error, the Inventory account and the Accounts Payable account are both understated.

The following table summarizes the effect of purchase errors in a perpetual inventory system, ignoring any income tax effects.

If Purchase of Inventory Is Recorded:	Then Inventory Is:	Then Cost of Goods Sold and Net income Are:	Then Accounts Payable Are:	Then Retained Earnings Are:
Too early	Overstated	Unaffected	Overstated	Unaffected
Too late	Understated	Unaffected	Understated	Unaffected

DO IT! ▶6-4   Inventory Errors

On June 30, 2018, Wang Ltd.'s year end, it counted $800,000 of inventory. During the count, inventory costing $20,000 was counted twice. This count did not include $100,000 of goods in transit from Laughlin Inc. that were purchased on June 29 on account and shipped to Wang FOB shipping point. Wang recorded the purchase on July 2 when the goods were received.

(a) Determine the correct June 30 inventory amount.

(b) Identify any accounts that are in error at June 30, and state the amount and direction (understated or overstated) of the error. You can ignore income tax effects.

(c) Prepare the journal entry(ies) to correct any errors identified in part (b) for the year ended June 30, 2018.

(d) If the errors were not corrected immediately, explain how they would eventually be corrected during the year ended June 30, 2019.

SOLUTION

Try this Do It! exercise on your own and then check your answer at the end of the chapter.

Related Exercise Material: BE6–8, BE6–9, E6–8, and E6–9.

LEARNING OBJECTIVE ▶**5** **Demonstrate the presentation and analysis of inventory.**

Presenting inventory appropriately on the financial statements is important for merchandising companies because the Inventory account is usually the largest current asset on the statement of financial position while the largest expense on the income statement is cost of goods sold. For example, lululemon, introduced in our feature story, reported inventory of $284,009 thousand in 2016, which represented 31% of its total current assets. lululemon's cost of goods sold of $1,063,357 thousand is 59% of total expenses on its income statement.

In addition, these reported numbers are critical for analyzing a company's effectiveness in managing its inventory. In the next sections, we will discuss issues that are related to the presentation and analysis of inventory.

VALUING INVENTORY AT THE LOWER OF COST AND NET REALIZABLE VALUE

Before presenting inventory on the financial statements, we must first ensure that it is properly valued. While a company would hope to sell its merchandise for more than it cost, in some cases this is not possible when inventory is damaged or is becoming obsolete. Furthermore, the prices of some goods can drop dramatically with a change in season—few people want to buy a snow blower in the summer. And, in some industries, such as the commodities industry, prices are significantly affected by changes in supply and demand.

For example, Goldcorp, a Vancouver-based mining company, has inventories of ore in various stages of processing. Determining the value at which to report its inventory is complicated by the fact that the price of gold, like the price of any commodity, is constantly fluctuating. Goldcorp uses estimates of future metal selling prices as one of the ways to determine the value of its inventories. In 2015, the company recorded an expense of $274 million related to declines in the value of its inventory. This is one example of what happens when the current value of a company's inventory is less than its cost.

It does not matter if it is ore, smart phones, or yoga pants—if the carrying amount of a company's inventory exceeds the future economic benefits that are expected to flow from it, then its carrying amount must be adjusted. Assets should not be carried in excess of amounts expected to be realized from their sale or use. Consequently, when the net realizable value of inventory is lower than its cost, inventory is written down to its net realizable value. This is known as the **lower of cost and net realizable value (LCNRV)** rule. For a merchandising company, **net realizable value (NRV)** is the selling price, less any costs required to make the goods ready for sale.

The lower of cost and net realizable value rule is applied to the inventory at the end of the accounting period and results in an adjusting journal entry if NRV is lower than cost. To apply this rule, the following steps must be followed:

1. Determine the cost of the inventory, using specific identification, FIFO, or average cost.
2. Determine the net realizable value of the inventory.
3. Compare the two values—cost and net realizable value—determined in steps 1 and 2. Determine if net realizable value is lower than cost.
4. If net realizable value is lower than cost, adjust and report inventory on the financial statements at NRV rather than cost.

To illustrate the application of the LCNRV rule, assume that at March 31, 2018, New-2-You Autos Limited has the following inventory of used motor vehicles with costs and net realizable values as indicated:

	Cost	NRV	LCNRV
Vehicle A	$16,000	$15,500	$15,500
Vehicle B	14,500	15,300	14,500
Vehicle C	14,800	14,500	14,500
Vehicle D	13,200	14,800	13,200
Vehicle E	11,500	11,400	11,400
Total inventory	$70,000	$71,500	$69,100

In the above example, we compare the cost of each used motor vehicle with its net realizable value and choose the lower amount (which are circled). The lower of these two amounts, or LCNRV, is listed in the third column. For example, the NRV of $15,500 is the lower amount for Vehicle A, whereas the cost of $14,500 is the lower amount for Vehicle B. This comparison would continue for the remaining vehicles (C through E) in inventory until the total value using the lower of cost and NRV rule is determined. In this example, the lower of cost and net realizable value is $69,100.

The LCNRV rule should be applied to individual inventory items, rather than total inventory. In certain cases, it can be applied to groups of similar items. This may be the case with items of inventory relating to the same product line that have similar purposes or uses.

After the lower of cost and net realizable value has been determined—whether using individual inventory items or groups of inventory—the next step is to use the net realizable value, if it is lower than cost at the end of the accounting period, to adjust and report inventory. If New-2-You Autos uses a perpetual inventory system, an adjusting journal entry is required to write the inventory down by $900 ($70,000 − $69,100), as follows:

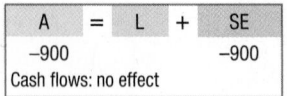

A	=	L	+	SE
−900				−900
Cash flows: no effect				

Mar. 31	Cost of Goods Sold	900	
	Inventory		900
	(To record decline in inventory value from original cost of $70,000 to net realizable value of $69,100)		

The Cost of Goods Sold account is directly debited for the loss in the above entry, even though no merchandise was sold. This is because a decline in the value of inventory is considered to be an overall cost of buying and selling merchandise, and is therefore reported as the cost of goods sold rather than as a non-operating "other revenues and expenses" item. The Inventory account is credited directly also to reflect the net realizable value of the inventory. There are other acceptable methods of recording a decline in inventory value, which will be discussed in an intermediate accounting course.

When the circumstances that previously caused inventories to be written down below cost no longer exist, or when there is clear evidence of an increase in net realizable value because of changed economic circumstances, the amount of the writedown is reversed. This occurs, for example, when an item of inventory that is carried at net realizable value, because its selling price had declined, is still on hand in a subsequent period and its selling price has increased. Reversals do not occur very often.

DO IT! ▶6-5a Lower of Cost and Net Realizable Value

E-Efficiency Inc. sells three different types of home heating stoves (wood, gas, and pellet). The cost and net realizable value of its inventory of stoves are as follows at March 31, the company's year end:

	Cost	NRV
Wood	$250,000	$280,000
Gas	84,000	79,000
Pellet	112,000	101,000
Total inventory	$446,000	$460,000

(a) What amount should E-Efficiency report for its inventory on its statement of financial position? (b) Prepare any journal entry required to record the inventory at its proper value.

Action Plan

✔ Compare the cost and NRV. Choose the lower value.

✔ Prepare a journal entry, if required, to adjust cost to net realizable value if it is lower.

SOLUTION

Try this Do It! exercise on your own and then check your answer at the end of the chapter.

Related Exercise Material: BE6–10, BE6–11, and E6–10.

ACCOUNTING MATTERS

© Vassiliy Mikhailin/Getty Images

Inventory Challenges

Food producers, such as Saputo Inc., can face widely varying inventory values based on changing commodity prices. For instance, in fiscal 2016, the Montreal-based manufacturer had an inventory writedown of $13 million as a result of a decrease in market selling prices. Commodities such as cheese and butter are traded on the Chicago Mercantile Exchange and affect the selling prices of those items. Cheese is traded based on a unit called average block market per pound of cheese, which is the average daily price paid for a 40-pound (18-kg) block of cheddar. The price can vary by 20 cents or more per pound over a quarter. For a manufacturer like Saputo, which has plants in Canada, the United States, and Argentina, these variations in price can cause large inventory writedowns.[3]

REPORTING INVENTORY

Ending inventory is reported in the current assets section of the statement of financial position at its lower of cost and net realizable value. Most companies do not separately disclose the cost and net realizable value of their inventory—they simply state that it is recorded at the lower of cost and net realizable value. For example, lululemon, our feature story company, discloses the following in the notes to its financial statements: "Inventories, consisting of finished goods, inventories in transit, and raw materials, are stated at the lower of cost and market value. Cost is determined using weighted-average costs."

Companies are required to disclose the following information related to inventory in the financial statements or the notes to the statements: (1) the total amount of inventory; (2) the cost of goods sold; (3) the cost formula(s) used (specific identification, FIFO, or average cost); (4) the amount of any writedown to net realizable value or reversals of previous writedowns, including the reason why the writedown was reversed; and (5) the amount of any inventory pledged as security.

In the significant accounting policy note for inventories, lululemon notes that it periodically reviews inventories and "makes provisions as necessary to appropriately value obsolete or damaged goods." In addition, it "provides for inventory shrinkage based on historical trends from actual physical inventory counts. Inventory shrinkage estimates are made to reduce the inventory value for lost or stolen items."

There are no significant differences at the introductory accounting level in the valuation or reporting of inventory between publicly traded companies reporting under IFRS and private companies reporting under ASPE. There are a few differences regarding specialized types of inventories that will be covered in an intermediate accounting course.

INVENTORY TURNOVER

A delicate balance must be kept between having too little inventory and too much inventory. Two ratios that can help a company manage its inventory levels are the inventory turnover and days in inventory ratios.

The **inventory turnover** ratio measures the number of times, on average, that inventory is sold ("turned over") during the period. It is calculated as the cost of goods sold divided by the average inventory. Whenever a ratio compares an account balance from the statement of financial position, such as inventory, with an account balance from the income statement, such as cost of goods sold, the account balance from the statement of financial position must be averaged. These averages are determined by adding the beginning and ending balances together and then dividing the result by two. Averages are used to ensure that the amount used for a statement of financial position account balance in a ratio is equal to the average balance throughout the period covered by the income statement account.

A complement to the inventory turnover ratio is the **days in inventory** ratio. It converts the inventory turnover into a measure of the average age of the inventory. It is calculated as 365 days divided by the inventory turnover ratio.

We will illustrate the calculation of the inventory turnover and days in inventory ratios for lululemon for two recent fiscal years using the following data (in thousands):

	2016	2015	2014
Cost of goods sold	$1,063,357	$883,033	$751,112
Inventory	$284,009	$208,116	$188,790

Using the amounts shown above, Illustration 6-9 presents the inventory turnover and days in inventory ratios for lululemon. We also include, for comparison purposes, the ratios for Limited Brands Inc., and its industry. Limited Brands owns La Senza and other apparel retailers that compete against lululemon.

▶Illustration 6-9

Inventory turnover and days in inventory

$$\text{INVENTORY TURNOVER} = \frac{\text{COST OF GOODS SOLD}}{\text{AVERAGE INVENTORY}}$$

$$\text{DAYS IN INVENTORY} = \frac{\text{365 DAYS}}{\text{INVENTORY TURNOVER}}$$

($ in thousands)		2016	2015
Lululemon	Inventory turnover	$\frac{\$1,063,357}{(\$208,116 + \$284,009) \div 2} = 4.3$ times	$\frac{\$883,033}{(\$188,790 + \$208,116) \div 2} = 4.5$ times
	Days in inventory	$\frac{365 \text{ days}}{4.3 \text{ times}} = 85$ days	$\frac{365 \text{ days}}{4.5 \text{ times}} = 81$ days
Limited Brands	Inventory turnover	6.4 times	6.0 times
	Days in inventory	57 days	61 days
Industry	Inventory turnover	4.2 times	4.2 times
	Days in inventory	87 days	87 days

In general, a company that is managing its inventory effectively will have a higher-than-average inventory turnover ratio and a lower-than-average days in inventory ratio because this indicates that the company can sell, or turn over, its inventory faster than average. The ratios in

Illustration 6-9 show that lululemon's inventory turnover decreased between 2015 and 2016 while Limited Brands' increased. In both years, Limited Brands' ratios indicate that it is turning its inventory over faster than lululemon. Overall, this analysis suggests that Limited Brands is more efficient in its inventory management than lululemon.

Both the inventory turnover and days in inventory ratios are liquidity ratios. Along with the current ratio, which was introduced in Chapter 2, these ratios are important in evaluating a company's liquidity, namely its ability to pay obligations that are expected to come due in the next year. Inventory is a significant component of the current ratio and a high level of inventory will result in a high current ratio. But if the inventory is not turning over very quickly, this will result in an "artificially" high current ratio.

Consequently, the current ratio should never be interpreted on its own. It should always be interpreted along with the inventory turnover ratio, because a high current ratio could mean good liquidity, or it could be artificially inflated by slow-moving inventory. Slow-moving inventory results in higher balances in the inventory account, which could also lead to excessive carrying costs (interest, storage, insurance, and taxes) or obsolete inventory.

Many companies have moved to streamline their supply chain operations, which include purchasing inventory and transporting it to the desired destination. One way of managing the amount of inventory on hand is to use a just-in-time approach. Rather than order large quantities of an inventory item, particularly one that is not in high demand, a company places a purchase order when the item is needed to fulfill a specific customer order. The company is then able to receive and sell the item at or about the same time. This has the effect of reducing inventory quantities on hand. It also positively affects the inventory liquidity ratios.

DO IT! ▶6-5b   Inventory Turnover

Webber Ltd. reported the following information for its three most recent fiscal years:

	2018	2017	2016
Cost of goods sold	$1,784,200	$1,719,500	$1,550,000
Inventory	405,500	439,000	466,000

(a) Calculate Webber's inventory turnover ratio and days in inventory for 2017 and 2018.

(b) Assess whether the company has improved its management of inventory in 2018.

Action Plan

✔ Determine the average inventory amounts for 2017 and 2018.

✔ Calculate the inventory turnover ratio by dividing cost of goods sold by average inventory.

✔ Calculate days in inventory by dividing 365 by the inventory turnover ratio.

✔ Remember that a higher inventory turnover ratio and a lower days in inventory indicate that a company has improved its management of inventory.

SOLUTION

Try this Do It! exercise on your own and then check your answer at the end of the chapter.

Related Exercise Material: BE6–12, E6–11, and E6–12.

LEARNING OBJECTIVE ▶6   **Appendix 6A: Apply the FIFO and average cost formulas under a periodic inventory system.**

Both of the inventory cost formulas—FIFO and average cost—described in the chapter for a perpetual inventory system may be used in a periodic inventory system. To show how to use each of these cost formulas in a periodic system, we will use the data below for The Tee-Shirt Corporation's University Soccer Shirt.

THE TEE-SHIRT CORPORATION				
University Soccer Shirt				
Date	Explanation	Units	Unit Cost	Total Cost
Jan. 1	Beginning inventory	100	$10	$ 1,000
Apr. 15	Purchases	200	11	2,200
Aug. 24	Purchases	300	12	3,600
Nov. 27	Purchases	400	13	5,200
	Total	1,000		$12,000

The details shown above are the same as those shown earlier in the chapter in Illustration 6-1, except that the number of units sold on specific dates has been omitted. In the periodic inventory system, we ignore the different dates of each of the sales because we are not recording cost of goods sold at those times. Instead we make the allocation **at the end of a period** and assume that the entire pool of costs is available for allocation at that time.

The Tee-Shirt Corporation had a total of 1,000 units available for sale during the period. The total cost of these units was $12,000. A physical inventory count at the end of the year determined that 450 units remained on hand. Using these amounts, Illustration 6A-1 shows the formula for calculating cost of goods sold that we first learned in Chapter 5.

▶Illustration 6A-1
Formula for cost
of goods sold

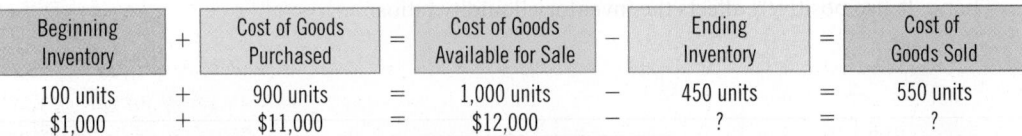

Beginning Inventory	+	Cost of Goods Purchased	=	Cost of Goods Available for Sale	−	Ending Inventory	=	Cost of Goods Sold
100 units	+	900 units	=	1,000 units	−	450 units	=	550 units
$1,000	+	$11,000	=	$12,000	−	?	=	?

If we apply this formula to the unit numbers, we can determine that 550 units must have been sold during the year. The total cost (or "pool of costs") of the 1,000 units available for sale was $12,000. However, we don't know yet how much of the cost of goods available for sale to allocate to ending inventory and to cost of goods sold. We will demonstrate the allocation of this pool of costs using FIFO and average cost in the next sections.

FIRST-IN, FIRST-OUT (FIFO)

The allocation of the cost of goods available for sale at The Tee-Shirt Corporation under FIFO is shown in Illustration 6A-2.

▶Illustration 6A-2
Periodic system—FIFO

COST OF GOODS AVAILABLE FOR SALE				
Date	Explanation	Units	Unit Cost	Total Cost
Jan. 1	Beginning inventory	100	$10	$ 1,000
Apr. 15	Purchases	200	11	2,200
Aug. 24	Purchases	300	12	3,600
Nov. 27	Purchases	400	13	5,200
	Total	1,000		$12,000

STEP 1: ENDING INVENTORY				STEP 2: COST OF GOODS SOLD	
Date	Units	Unit Cost	Unit Total		
Nov. 27	400	$13	$5,200	Cost of goods available for sale	$12,000
Aug. 24	50	12	600	Less: Ending inventory	5,800
Total	450		$5,800	Cost of goods sold	$ 6,200

Once we know the number of units in ending inventory, we assume it is composed of the last goods purchased. In this example, 450 units are on hand and because the last purchase was for

400 units at $13 on November 27, this "layer" of inventory is assumed to be in the ending inventory balance. The remaining 50 units are then assumed to come from the next most recent purchase, which is a layer of units purchased at $12, on August 24.

Once the cost of the ending inventory is determined, the cost of goods sold is calculated by subtracting the ending inventory (the cost of the units not sold) from the cost of all goods available for sale (the pool of costs).

The cost of goods sold can also be separately calculated as shown below by including in that amount the cost of the oldest 550 units. Do this by taking the cost of the oldest layer of inventory costs and adding the costs of subsequent layers purchased in order of purchase date until the total cost of the oldest 550 units is determined. Note that of the 300 units purchased on August 24, only 250 units are assumed to have been sold. This agrees with our calculation of the cost of the ending inventory, where 50 of these units were assumed unsold and thus included in ending inventory.

▼ HELPFUL HINT
Note the sequencing of the allocation: (1) Calculate ending inventory, and (2) determine cost of goods sold.

Date	Units	Unit Cost	Total Cost of Goods Sold
Jan. 1	100	$10	$1,000
Apr. 15	200	11	2,200
Aug. 24	250	12	3,000
Total	550		$6,200

Because of the potential for calculation errors, we recommend that the cost of goods sold amounts be separately calculated and proven in your assignments. The cost of goods sold and ending inventory totals can then be compared with the cost of goods available for sale to check the accuracy of the calculations. It would be as follows for The Tee-Shirt Corporation: $6,200 + $5,800 = $12,000. You will recall that we also did a similar check of our numbers under the perpetual inventory system.

Although the calculation format may differ, **the results under FIFO in a periodic inventory system are the same as in a perpetual inventory system**. (See Illustration 6-2 where, similarly, the ending inventory is $5,800 and the cost of goods sold is $6,200.) Under both inventory systems, the first costs in are the ones assigned to cost of goods sold and the last costs in are the ones assigned to ending inventory.

AVERAGE COST

When using a periodic system, the weighted average cost is calculated in the same manner that we used for a perpetual inventory system: by dividing the cost of goods available for sale by the units available for sale. However, with a periodic system, because we do not record cost of goods sold for each sale, we only calculate the average cost at the end of a period rather than after each purchase or purchase return, as shown in Illustration 6A-3.

Cost of Goods Available for Sale	÷	Units Available for Sale	=	Weighted Average Unit Cost
$12,000	÷	1,000	=	$12

►Illustration 6A-3
Calculation of weighted average unit cost

In this particular case, the weighted average unit cost does not require rounding. Similar to our discussion about rounding in the average cost perpetual system, it is important to use unrounded average unit costs in your calculations, even if the result presented is rounded to two decimal places (to the nearest cent).

The weighted average unit cost, $12 in this case, is then applied to the units on hand to determine the cost of the ending inventory. The allocation of the cost of goods available for sale at The Tee-Shirt Corporation using the average cost formula is shown in Illustration 6A-4.

COST OF GOODS AVAILABLE FOR SALE				
Date	Explanation	Units	Unit Cost	Total Cost
Jan. 1	Beginning inventory	100	$10	$ 1,000
Apr. 15	Purchases	200	11	2,200
Aug. 24	Purchases	300	12	3,600
Nov. 27	Purchases	400	13	5,200
	Total	1,000		$12,000

STEP 1: ENDING INVENTORY			STEP 2: COST OF GOODS SOLD	
$12,000 ÷ 1,000 = $12			Cost of goods available for sale	$12,000
Units	Unit Cost	Total Cost	Less: Ending inventory	5,400
450	$12	$5,400	Cost of goods sold	$ 6,600

We can verify the cost of goods sold under the average cost formula by multiplying the units sold by the weighted average unit cost (550 × $12 = $6,600). And, again, we can prove our calculations by ensuring that the total of the cost of goods sold and ending inventory equals the cost of goods available for sale ($6,600 + $5,400 = $12,000).

The results from applying the average cost formula under the periodic inventory system should be compared with Illustration 6-4 shown earlier in the chapter, which presents the results from applying the average cost formula under a perpetual inventory system. Notice that, under a periodic inventory system, the ending inventory of $5,400 and cost of goods sold of $6,600 are not the same as the values calculated under a perpetual inventory system. This is because in a perpetual system, a new (moving) average is calculated with each purchase or purchase return. In a periodic system, the same weighted average is used to calculate the cost of goods sold for all the units sold during the period.

DO IT! ► 6-6   FIFO and Average Cost—Periodic System

SOLUTION
Try this Do It! exercise on your own and then check your answer at the end of the chapter.

Related Exercise Material: *BE6–13, *BE6–14, *BE6–15, *E6–13, *E6–14, *E6–15, and *E6–16.

The accounting records of Hunton Ltd. show the following data:

Apr. 1	Beginning inventory	5,000 units at $3.00
12	Purchases	8,000 units at $4.00
15	Sales	11,000 units at $9.00
22	Purchases	7,000 units at $5.50
26	Sales	6,000 units at $9.00

Determine (a) the cost of goods available for sale, and (b) the cost of goods sold and ending inventory under a periodic inventory system using (1) FIFO, and (2) average cost.

Action Plan

✔ Ignore the selling price in allocating cost.

✔ Ignore the sales dates because cost of goods sold is only determined at the end of the accounting period.

✔ Calculate the number of units available for sale, cost of goods available for sale, and the ending inventory in units.

✔ Determine the cost of ending inventory first. Then calculate cost of goods sold by subtracting ending inventory

from the cost of goods available for sale for each cost formula.

✔ Understand the difference between FIFO and average cost.

✔ Round your answers to the nearest cent for presentation of your results in the average cost formula, but use unrounded numbers in any calculations.

✔ Check your work: Prove the cost of goods sold separately and then check that cost of goods sold plus ending inventory equals the cost of goods available for sale.

REVIEW AND PRACTICE

▶ LEARNING OBJECTIVE REVIEW

1. Describe the steps in determining inventory quantities. The steps are (1) determining the ownership of goods in transit, on consignment, and in similar situations; and (2) taking a physical inventory of goods on hand.

2. Apply the cost formulas using specific identification, FIFO, and average cost under a perpetual inventory system. Costs are allocated to the Cost of Goods Sold account each time that a sale occurs in a perpetual inventory system. The cost is determined by using the specific identification; first-in, first-out (FIFO); or average cost formula.

Specific identification must be used for goods that are not ordinarily interchangeable. This cost formula tracks the actual physical flow of goods, allocating the exact cost of each merchandise item to cost of goods sold and ending inventory.

If a company's goods are interchangeable (homogeneous), then either the FIFO or average cost formula may be used.

The FIFO cost formula assumes a first-in, first-out cost flow for sales. Cost of goods sold consists of the cost of the earliest goods purchased. Ending inventory consists of the cost of the most recent goods purchased.

Under the average cost formula, a new weighted (moving) average unit cost is calculated after each purchase or purchase return and applied to the number of units sold (and as a result, to the number of units remaining in ending inventory).

3. Explain the effects on the financial statements of choosing each of the inventory cost formulas. The specific identification cost formula must be used for goods that are not ordinarily interchangeable. (Typically the goods are unique, high-value items.) Either the FIFO or average cost formula can be used for goods that are interchangeable (that is, they are homogeneous or non-distinguishable from one another). Management should select the cost formula that most closely corresponds to the physical flow of goods and should report inventory on the statement of financial position at an amount that is closest to the cost of inventory recently purchased.

Specific identification results in an exact match of costs and revenues on the income statement. When prices are rising, the average cost formula results in a higher cost of goods sold and lower net income than FIFO. The average cost formula therefore results in a better allocation on the income statement of more current (recent) costs with current revenues than does FIFO. In terms of the statement of financial position, FIFO is considered to be superior because it results in an ending inventory that is closest to current (replacement) value. All three cost formulas result in the same cash flow before income tax.

4. Identify the effects of inventory errors on the financial statements. Ignoring the effects of income tax, an error made in determining the quantities and/or cost of inventory at the end of the year will also affect cost of goods sold. If ending inventory is overstated, cost of goods sold will be understated and this in turn will cause net income to be overstated. Therefore, an error

that overstates inventory will also overstate net income and after recording closing entries, the overstatement in net income will be reflected as an overstatement in retained earnings. In the following period, the overstatement in inventory will flow into cost of goods sold and overstate cost of goods sold and understate net income, thereby reversing the effect of the prior-period error. As long as the cost of inventory at the end of this subsequent period is determined properly, the reversal of the error will mean that both inventory and retained earnings are not misstated at the end of the following accounting period.

If an error is made by recording goods in transit as an inventory purchase in a period before title to the goods changes hands, both inventory and accounts payable will be overstated. If the purchase has actually occurred but is not recorded or counted, then both inventory and accounts payable will be understated.

5. Demonstrate the presentation and analysis of inventory. Inventory is valued at the lower of its cost and net realizable value, which results in the recording of an increase in cost of goods sold and a reduction in inventory when the net realizable value is less than cost.

Ending inventory is reported as a current asset on the statement of financial position at the lower of cost and net realizable value. Cost of goods sold is reported as an expense on the income statement.

The inventory turnover ratio is a measure of liquidity. It is calculated by dividing the cost of goods sold by average inventory. It can be converted to days in inventory by dividing 365 days by the inventory turnover ratio. In general, a higher inventory turnover and lower days in inventory ratio are desired.

6. Apply the FIFO and average cost formulas under a periodic inventory system (Appendix 6A). Under the FIFO cost formula, the cost of the most recent goods purchased is allocated to ending inventory. Cost of goods sold is calculated by deducting ending inventory from the cost of goods available for sale (or proven by applying the cost of the earliest goods on hand to determine the cost of goods sold). The cost of goods sold and ending inventory amounts under FIFO are the same regardless of whether a periodic or perpetual inventory system is used.

Under the average cost formula, the total cost of goods available for sale during the period is divided by the units available for sale during the same period to calculate a weighted average cost per unit. This unit cost is then applied to the number of units remaining in inventory to calculate the ending inventory. Cost of goods sold is calculated by deducting ending inventory from the cost of goods available for sale (or proven by applying the unit cost to the units sold to determine the cost of goods sold). The main difference between a periodic and a perpetual inventory system is that in a periodic system, average cost is only determined once (at the end of the accounting period), while average cost is determined at the date of each sale in a perpetual inventory system.

▶ KEY TERM REVIEW

The following are key terms defined in this chapter with the corresponding page reference for your review. You will find a complete list of terms and definitions for all chapters in the glossary at the end of this textbook.

Average cost formula (p. 309)
Consigned goods (p. 303)
Consignee (p. 303)
Consignor (p. 303)
Days in inventory (p. 320)

First-in, first-out (FIFO) cost formula (p. 306)
Internal controls (p. 304)
Inventory turnover (p. 320)
Lower of cost and net realizable value (LCNRV) (p. 317)

Net realizable value (NRV) (p. 317)
Specific identification cost formula (p. 305)
Weighted average unit cost (p. 309)

▶ DECISION TOOLKIT REVIEW

DECISION CHECKPOINTS	INFO NEEDED FOR DECISION	TOOLS TO USE FOR DECISION	HOW TO EVALUATE RESULTS
What is the impact of the choice of inventory cost formula?	Are prices increasing, or are they decreasing?	Income statement and statement of financial position effects	In periods of rising prices, net income and inventory are higher under FIFO than average cost. FIFO results in the best measure of ending inventory on the statement of financial position. Average cost provides opposite results—net income and inventory are lower compared with FIFO—but can smooth the impact of changing prices. Specific identification's impact on the financial statements will vary, depending on the actual cost. Specific identification results in the best allocation of costs to revenues on the income statement.
How long is an item in inventory?	Cost of goods sold; beginning and ending inventory	$\text{Inventory turnover} = \dfrac{\text{Cost of goods sold}}{\text{Average inventory}}$ $\text{Days in inventory} = \dfrac{365 \text{ days}}{\text{Inventory turnover}}$	A higher inventory turnover or lower days in inventory suggests efficiency, and that management is reducing the amount of inventory on hand relative to sales.

▶ PRACTICE USING THE DECISION TOOLKIT

Answers are at the end of the chapter.

Under Armour, Inc. specializes in the development, marketing, and distribution of athletic apparel, footwear, and accessories. Unlike lululemon, which sells primarily through its own stores, Under Armour generates most of its net revenue from product sales through national, regional, independent, and specialty retailers. It is one of lululemon athletica's key competitors in Canada, although it offers a broader range of athletic clothing than lululemon.

Selected financial information for Under Armour, Inc. (in U.S. $ thousands) for three recent fiscal years follows:

	2015	2014	2013
Cost of goods sold	$2,057,766	$1,572,164	$1,195,381
Inventory	783,031	536,714	469,006
Current assets	1,498,763	1,549,339	1,128,811
Current liabilities	478,810	421,627	426,630

Selected industry ratios:

	2015	2014
Inventory turnover	3.9 times	3.9 times
Days in inventory	94 days	94 days
Current ratio	3.2:1	3.7:1

INSTRUCTIONS

(a) Under Armour uses FIFO. Assume prices have risen over the last two years. If Under Armour used the average cost formula instead of FIFO, would its cost of goods sold and its inventory values be higher or lower than currently reported?

(b) Do each of the following:

1. Calculate the inventory turnover and days in inventory for 2015 and 2014.
2. Calculate the current ratio for each of 2015 and 2014.
3. Evaluate Under Armour, Inc.'s inventory management and overall liquidity over the most recent two years and in comparison with its industry.

▶ PRACTICE COMPREHENSIVE DO IT!

Answers are at the end of the chapter.

Englehart Ltd. uses a perpetual inventory system. The company has the following inventory data available for the month of March:

Date	Explanation	Units	Unit Cost/Price	Total Cost
Mar. 1	Beginning inventory	200	$4.30	$ 860
10	Purchases	500	4.50	2,250
15	Sales	(500)	9.00	
20	Purchases	400	4.75	1,900
25	Sales	(400)	9.00	
30	Purchase	300	5.00	1,500
		500		$6,510

INSTRUCTIONS

(a) Determine the cost of goods sold for March and the cost of the ending inventory at March 31 using (1) FIFO and (2) average cost. (For average cost, use unrounded numbers in your calculations but round to the nearest cent for presentation purposes in your answer.)

(b) Determine whether assets, liabilities, and shareholders' equity would be overstated, understated, or not affected if the March 30 purchase was recorded on March 30 in error and should not have been recorded until April 2. The goods were purchased on account with shipping terms of FOB destination, not FOB shipping point, and the goods were not received until April 2.

(c) Determine the amount of the error identified in part (b) on the ending inventory amounts calculated in part (a) using the FIFO and average cost formulas.

▶ PRACTICE OBJECTIVE-FORMAT QUESTIONS

Note: All questions marked with an asterisk (*) relate to material in Appendix 6A. Answers are at the end of the chapter.

1. As a result of a physical inventory count, Palermo Ltd. determined that it had inventory of $120,000 on hand at December 31. This count did not take into consideration the following:

1. Recoleta Ltd. was holding goods costing $24,000 on its sales floor that it was selling on consignment for Palermo.
2. Palermo purchased $10,000 of goods that were shipped on December 27, FOB shipping point, and that were expected to be delivered on January 3.
3. Palermo sold goods that had a cost of $26,000 on December 30 to Boyaca Ltd. with terms FOB destination. The goods are expected to be delivered on January 2.
4. Palermo purchased goods costing $18,000 with terms FOB destination. The goods are expected to be delivered on January 2.

Indicate which of the following statements are correct in relation to the above information. (Select as many as are appropriate.)

(a) Palermo's ending inventory should be $156,000.

(b) The goods on consignment with Recoleta [see (2) above] would not be included in Palermo's inventory at December 31.

(c) The goods sold on December 30 [see (3) above] should be included in Palermo's inventory at December 31.

(d) Palermo's ending inventory should be $180,000.

(e) Palermo's ending inventory should be $198,000.

(f) The goods sold to Boyaca [see (3) above] should be excluded from Palermo's ending inventory because they are no longer in Palermo's possession.

(g) The $18,000 of goods purchased with terms FOB destination [see (4) above] would not be included in Palermo's inventory at December 31 because they have not yet been received.

2. Madoc Inc. uses a perpetual inventory system and has the following beginning inventory, purchases, and sales in March:

		Units	Unit Cost	Total Cost
Mar. 1	Beginning inventory	10,000	$ 9	$ 90,000
9	Purchases	12,000	10	120,000
12	Sales	(20,000)		
18	Purchases	7,000	11	77,000

Indicate which of the following statements are correct in relation to the above information. (Select as many as are appropriate.)

(a) The weighted average cost per unit after the March 18 purchase would be $10.00 (rounded to the nearest cent).

(b) The weighted average cost per unit after the March 18 purchase would be $9.90 (rounded to the nearest cent).

(c) There were 9,000 units of inventory on hand at March 31.

(d) The cost of ending inventory at the end of March under the average cost formula would be $96,091.

(e) The weighted average cost per unit after the March 18 purchase would be $10.68 (rounded to the nearest cent).

(f) The cost of goods sold for the month of March under the average cost formula would be $198,000.

(g) The cost of goods available for sale for March was $287,000.

3. Skipper Ltd. uses a perpetual inventory system and had the following transactions during the month of October:

		Unit Cost	Total Cost
Oct. 1	Beginning inventory 6,000 units	$24/unit	$144,000
4	Purchased 12,000 units	$26/unit	$312,000
7	Purchased 14,000 units	$28/unit	$392,000
12	Sold 13,000 units at $40/unit		
17	Purchased 8,000 units	$30/unit	$240,000
22	Sold 18,000 units at $40/unit		

Indicate which of the following statements are correct in relation to the above information. (Select as many as are appropriate.) Round unit costs to the nearest cent.

(a) There were 3,000 units of inventory on hand at October 31.

(b) The weighted average cost per unit after the October 17 purchase would be $27.54.

(c) The cost of ending inventory at the end of October under the average cost formula would be $244,800.

(d) The cost of goods sold for the month of March under the average cost formula would be $1,088,000.

(e) The weighted average cost per unit after the October 17 purchase would be $27.20.

(f) The cost of ending inventory at the end of October under the average cost formula would be $247,860.

(g) The weighted average cost per unit after the October 17 purchase would be $27.00.

4. Indicate which cost formula (specific identification, FIFO, or average cost) is most closely linked to each of the following statements:

(a) Ending inventory includes the most current costs (closest to replacement costs).

(b) Cost of goods sold includes more current costs.

(c) Most closely matches costs and revenues on the income statement.

(d) Must be used if the goods being sold are unique, non-homogeneous items.

(e) Approximates the physical flow of most retailers.

(f) Smoothes the effects of price changes.

(g) Tracks the actual physical flow of goods.

5. In a period of rising prices, indicate which cost formula (FIFO or average cost) would have the highest:

(a) ending inventory.

(b) net income.

(c) cost of goods sold.

(d) current assets.

(e) retained earnings.

(f) gross profit.

(g) total assets.

6. Indicate whether each of the following would be "overstated," "understated," or "unaffected" if the purchase of inventory on account is recorded too early. (For example, goods purchased on account with terms FOB destination are recorded in inventory at year end, but prior to their delivery.)

(a) Accounts payable

(b) Retained earnings

(c) Inventory

(d) Current liabilities

(e) Net income

(f) Cost of goods sold

(g) Current assets

7. Indicate whether each of the following would be "overstated," "understated," or "unaffected" if inventory is understated because the company failed to include goods that were out on consignment in its year-end inventory count. Assume that an adjusting entry was made to record shrinkage equal to the cost of the goods on consignment, which adjusted both the Inventory and Cost of Goods Sold accounts.

(a) Sales revenue

(b) Net income

(c) Cost of goods sold

(d) Current assets

(e) Gross profit

(f) Current liabilities

(g) Retained earnings

8. Indicate which of the following statements are correct in relation to valuing inventory at the lower of cost and net realizable value. (Select as many as are appropriate.)

(a) This assessment is unaffected by the company's choice of cost formula.

(b) The requirement to carry inventory at the lower of cost and net realizable value is based on the concept that assets should not be carried at amounts in excess of the future economic benefits expected from them.

(c) For a merchandising company, net realizable value is selling price less any costs required to make the goods ready for sale.

(d) If net realizable value is less than cost, then Cost of Goods Sold should be adjusted by debiting it.

(e) The lower of cost and net realizable value rule can be applied to groups of similar inventory items rather than to individual inventory items.

(f) If net realizable value is less than cost, then Inventory should be adjusted by debiting it.

(g) If net realizable value is greater than cost, then no adjustment is required to Inventory.

9. The following data were gathered for two competitors: Nire Ltd. and Piks Ltd.:

Nire Ltd.	2018	2017	2016
Cost of goods sold	$768,750	$623,000	$580,000
Inventory	110,000	95,000	83,000

Piks Ltd.	2018	2017	2016
Cost of goods sold	$1,500,000	$1,000,000	$980,000
Inventory	250,000	210,000	190,000

Indicate which of the following statements is correct in relation to this information. (Select as many as are appropriate.)

(a) Nire's inventory turnover ratio was 7.0 in 2018, which was superior to Piks's ratio for the same period.

(b) Piks's inventory turnover was 6.5 in 2018 and the company shortened its days in inventory by 17 days from the previous year.

(c) Piks's inventory turnover ratio in 2018 was better than Nire's for the same period.

(d) Both companies improved their inventory turnover ratios in 2018 relative to the previous year.

(e) Piks's improvement in its days in inventory ratio in 2018 was superior to Nire's improvement for the same period.

(f) Piks's inventory turnover ratio was 4.8 in 2017 and its days in inventory ratio was 76 days.

(g) Nire's days in inventory was 52 in 2017, which worsened to 49 in 2018.

*10. Lin Ltd. uses a periodic inventory system and had the following transactions during the month of March:

			Unit Cost	Total Cost
Mar.	1	Beginning inventory 800 units	$2.50/unit	$2,000
	7	Purchased 2,000 units	$3.00/unit	$6,000
	12	Purchased 1,400 units	$3.40/unit	$4,760
	15	Sold 1,100 units at $7/unit		
	21	Purchased 800 units	$3.80/unit	$3,040
	26	Sold 1,200 units at $7/unit		

Indicate which of the following statements are correct in relation to the above information. (Select as many as are appropriate.)

(a) The cost of goods sold using the FIFO cost formula would have been $6,500 for March.

(b) The cost of goods available for sale for the month of March was $13,800.

(c) The 2,700 units in ending inventory would have a total cost of $10,157 under the average cost formula.

(d) The weighted average cost per unit after the March 21 purchase would be $3.16.

(e) The cost of goods available for sale for the month of March was $15,800.

(f) The cost of goods sold using the average cost formula would have been $7,302.50.

(g) The 2,700 units in ending inventory would have a total cost of $9,300 under the FIFO cost formula.

WileyPLUS   Brief Exercises, Exercises, and many additional resources are available for practice in WileyPLUS.

Note: All questions, exercises, and problems below with an asterisk (*) relate to material in Appendix 6A.

▶QUESTIONS

(LO 1) 1. Your friend Tom Wetzel has been hired to help take the physical inventory in Kikujiro's Hardware Store. Explain to Tom how to do this job, giving him specific instructions for determining the inventory quantities that Kikujiro's has legal title over.

(LO 1) 2. What is the difference between a consignee and a consignor? Would both parties include the goods in their inventory? If not, explain why and indicate which of the two should include the goods in their inventory.

(LO 1) 3. Janine Ltd. ships merchandise to Fastrak Corporation on December 30. The merchandise reaches Fastrak on January 5. Indicate the terms of sale (FOB shipping point or FOB destination) that will result in the goods being included in (a) Janine's December 31 inventory and (b) Fastrak's December 31 inventory.

(LO 1) 4. Explain whether each of the following should be included in the inventory of Kingsway Inc.: (a) consigned goods held by a craft shop for sale on Kingsway's behalf, (b) goods ordered from a supplier with terms FOB shipping point, but that have not yet been received by Kingsway, and (c) goods sold but held for alteration by Kingsway.

(LO 2) 5. (a) Explain why cost formulas are necessary. (b) When are cost formulas used in a perpetual inventory system? How does this differ from when they are used in a periodic inventory system?

(LO 2) 6. (a) Distinguish among the three cost formulas for determining cost for inventories: specific identification, FIFO, and average cost. (b) Give an example of a type of inventory for which each cost formula might be used.

(LO 2) 7. (a) Which of the three inventory cost formulas can be used if the goods available for sale are identical? (b) Which cost formula assumes that the first goods purchased are the first to be sold? (c) Which cost formula matches the actual physical flow of merchandise?

(LO 2) 8. Explain why a new weighted average unit cost must be calculated after each purchase when using the average cost formula in a perpetual inventory system, but not after each sale.

(LO 3) 9. What are the guidelines that a company should consider when choosing among the three cost formulas for determining cost for inventories: specific identification, FIFO, and average cost?

(LO 3) 10. Which inventory cost formula—FIFO or average cost—provides the better measure of cost of goods sold on the income statement? The better measure of ending inventory on the statement of financial position? Explain.

(LO 3) 11. Compare the financial effects (ignore income tax) of using the FIFO and average inventory cost formulas during a period of declining prices on (a) cash (pre-tax), (b) ending inventory, (c) cost of goods sold, (d) net income, and (e) retained earnings.

(LO 4) 12. If an error in counting ending inventory in one year will have the reverse effect in the following year, will this error need to be corrected when it is discovered? Explain.

(LO 4) 13. Mila Ltd.'s ending inventory at December 31, 2018, was understated by $43,000. Assuming that this error is not detected, what effect will it have on (a) 2018 income before income tax, (b) 2018 retained earnings, (c) 2018 total shareholders' equity, (d) 2019 income before income tax, (e) 2019 retained earnings, and (f) 2019 total shareholders' equity?

(LO 4) 14. Shediac Inc. purchased inventory from Bathurst Corp. four days prior to Shediac's year end. Bathurst shipped the goods to Shediac FOB destination two days before year end but Shediac did not receive the goods until three days after year end. The inventory clerk recorded the purchase of the inventory on credit prior to the year-end inventory count by debiting Inventory and crediting Accounts Payable. Shediac performs a physical inventory count each year end and makes any required adjustments. What overall effect will this error have on the components of the accounting equation—assets, liabilities, and shareholders' equity—at Shediac's year end (a) prior to any adjustment for the inventory count results, and (b) after any adjustment?

(LO 5) 15. (a) Explain the meaning of cost and net realizable value. (b) Explain when the lower of cost and net realizable value rule should be used to value inventory.

(LO 5) 16. (a) Describe the journal entry required to record a decline in inventory value under the lower of cost and net realizable value rule. (b) Why is an entry required even though no merchandise has been sold?

(LO 5) 17. Would an increase in the days in inventory ratio from one year to the next be viewed as an improvement or a deterioration in how efficiently a company manages its inventory?

(LO 5) 18. What are the consequences for a company when its inventory turnover ratio is (a) too high and (b) too low?

(LO 2, 6) *19. Your classmate does not understand the difference between the perpetual and periodic inventory systems. "The same cost formulas are used in both systems," he says, "and a physical inventory count is required in both systems. So what's the difference?" Explain to your confused classmate how the perpetual and periodic inventory systems differ.

(LO 6) *20. In a periodic inventory system, the ending inventory is counted and costed. This number is then used to calculate cost of goods sold. Emad asks, "Why can't you determine the cost of goods sold first instead of going through all of these steps?" Explain this to Emad.

(LO 2, 6) *21. Explain why, when a company uses FIFO with a periodic inventory system, the cost of goods sold and ending inventory costs are the same as they would be had FIFO been used with a perpetual system.

(LO 2, 6) *22. Explain why, when a company uses average cost formula with a periodic inventory system, the cost of goods sold and ending inventory costs are different from the amounts calculated when using the average cost formula with a perpetual inventory system.

▶ BRIEF EXERCISES

BE6–1 Helgeson Inc. identifies the following items as possibly belonging in its physical inventory count. For each item, indicate whether or not it should be included in the inventory.

Identify items in inventory.
(LO 1)

(a) Goods shipped on consignment by Helgeson to another company
(b) Goods held on consignment by Helgeson from another company
(c) Goods in transit to a customer, shipped FOB destination
(d) Goods in transit to Helgeson from a supplier shipped FOB shipping point
(e) Goods in transit to a customer, shipped FOB shipping point
(f) Goods in transit to Helgeson from a supplier, shipped FOB destination

BE6–2 The Village Hat Shop Limited counted the entire inventory in its store on August 31 and arrived at a total inventory cost of $95,000. The count included $7,500 of inventory held on consignment for a local designer; $500 of inventory that was being held for customers who were deciding if they actually wanted to purchase the merchandise; and $1,000

Calculate inventory cost.
(LO 1)

of inventory that had been sold to customers but was being held for alterations. There were two shipments of inventory received on September 1. The first shipment cost $4,000. It had been shipped on August 29, terms FOB destination. The second shipment cost $4,750, plus freight charges of $250. It had been shipped on August 28, terms FOB shipping point. Neither of these shipments was included in the August 31 count. Calculate the correct cost of the inventory on August 31.

Apply specific identification.

(LO 2)

BE6–3 On January 3, Piano Corp. purchased three portable electronic keyboards for $600 each. On January 20, it purchased two more of the same model keyboards for $475 each. During the month, it sold two keyboards; one was purchased on January 3 and the other was purchased on January 20. (a) Calculate the cost of goods sold and ending inventory for the month using specific identification. (b) Explain how management could manipulate net income, if it wished to, using this cost formula.

Apply perpetual FIFO.

(LO 2)

BE6–4 Akshay Limited uses the FIFO cost formula in a perpetual inventory system. Fill in the missing amounts for items [1] to [18] in the following perpetual inventory schedule:

Date		Purchases			Cost of Goods Sold			Balance		
		Units	Cost	Total	Units	Cost	Total	Units	Cost	Total
Apr.	1							15	$18	$270
	6	30	[1]	$450				[2]	[3]	
								[4]	[5]	[6]
	9				15	[7]				
					10	[8]	[9]	[10]	[11]	[12]
	14	[13]	12	144				[14]	[15]	
								[16]	[17]	[18]

Apply perpetual average cost.

(LO 2)

BE6–5 Akshay Limited uses the average cost formula in a perpetual inventory system. Fill in the missing amounts for items [1] to [13] in the following perpetual inventory schedule. (Use unrounded numbers in your calculations but round to the nearest cent for presentation purposes in your answer.)

Date		Purchases			Cost of Goods Sold			Balance		
		Units	Cost	Total	Units	Cost	Total	Units	Cost	Total
Apr.	1							15	$180	$2,700
	6	30	[1]	$6,000				[2]	[4]	[3]
	9				25	[5]	[6]	[7]	[9]	[8]
	14	[10]	205	2,460				[11]	[13]	[12]

Apply perpetual FIFO and average cost.

(LO 2)

BE6–6 Battery Limited uses a perpetual inventory system. The inventory records show the following data for its first month of operations:

Date	Explanation	Units	Unit Cost	Total Cost	Balance in Units
Aug. 2	Purchases	250	$ 70	$ 17,500	250
3	Purchases	500	100	50,000	750
10	Sales	(300)			450
15	Purchases	900	120	108,000	1,350
25	Sales	(325)			1,025

Calculate the cost of goods sold and ending inventory using (a) FIFO and (b) average cost. (For average cost, use unrounded numbers in your calculations but round to the nearest cent for presentation purposes in your answer.)

Discuss different cost formulas.

(LO 3)

BE6–7 Interactive.com just started business and is trying to decide which inventory cost formula—FIFO or average cost—to use. Assuming prices are falling, as they often do in the information technology sector, answer the following questions for Interactive.com:

(a) Which cost formula will result in the higher ending inventory? Will this cost formula also result in an ending inventory value that is closer to replacement cost? Explain.

(b) Which cost formula will result in the higher cost of goods sold? Will this cost formula also result in the most current cost of goods sold matched against revenue? Explain.

(c) What guidelines are important for Interactive.com to consider as it tries to select the most appropriate inventory cost formula?

Determine effect of inventory error.

(LO 4)

BE6–8 DuPlessis Corporation incorrectly recorded $25,000 of goods held on consignment for another company as a purchase on account during the year ended December 31, 2018. The physical inventory count, which included the consigned goods, agreed with the perpetual inventory accounting records at year end. What effect, if any, will this error have on total assets, liabilities, and shareholders' equity at December 31, 2018, assuming the error is not detected before year end?

BE6–9 In its year-end physical inventory count, Tire Track Corporation forgot to count tires it had stored outside its warehouse in a trailer. As a result, ending inventory was understated by $7,000. Assuming that this error was not subsequently discovered and corrected, what is the impact of this error on assets, liabilities, and shareholders' equity at the end of the current year? At the end of the next year?

Determine effect of inventory error for two years.
(LO 4)

BE6–10 The following information on cost and net realizable value of Tech-IT Ltd.'s various inventory categories was gathered at December 31:

Determine LCNRV valuation.
(LO 5)

Inventory Categories	Cost	NRV
Desktops	$347,000	$326,000
Tablets and readers	168,700	224,000
Laptops	221,020	285,000
Accessories and parts	97,400	94,300

(a) Calculate the lower of cost and net realizable value for each inventory category within Tech-IT's inventory.
(b) Prepare the entry needed to adjust Tech-IT's inventory value to the lower of cost or net realizable value at December 31.

BE6–11 The cost of Piper Music Inc.'s inventory at December 31, 2018, is $54,700. Its net realizable value on the same date is $52,500. (a) Prepare the adjusting journal entry required, if any, to record the decline in value of the inventory. (b) If Piper Music has the same inventory on hand at December 31, 2018, with a net realizable value of $55,000, what amount should it report its inventory at on that date?

Record LCNRV valuation.
(LO 5)

BE6–12 The following information is available for **Canadian Tire Corporation** (in $ millions):

Calculate inventory turnover and days in inventory.
(LO 5)

	2015	2014	2013
Inventory	$ 1,764.5	$ 1,623.8	$ 1,481.0
Net sales	12,279.6	12,462.9	11,785.6
Cost of goods sold	7,747.1	8,033.2	7,678.0

(a) Calculate the inventory turnover and days in inventory ratios for 2015 and 2014.
(b) Did Canadian Tire's inventory management improve or deteriorate in 2015?

*BE6–13 In its first month of operations, Queensland Inc. made three purchases of merchandise in the following sequence: (1) 370 units at $9 each, (2) 700 units at $12 each, and (3) 800 units at $11 each. A physical inventory count determined that there were 600 units on hand at the end of the month. Assuming Queensland uses a periodic inventory system, calculate the cost of the ending inventory and cost of goods sold using (a) FIFO and (b) average cost. (For average cost, use unrounded numbers in your calculations but round to the nearest cent for presentation purposes in your answer.)

Apply periodic FIFO and average cost.
(LO 6)

*BE6–14 G-Mac Corporation reports the following inventory data for the month of January:

Apply periodic FIFO.
(LO 2, 6)

Date	Explanation	Units	Unit Cost	Total Cost
Jan. 1	Beginning inventory	1,500	$45.00	$ 67,500
15	Purchases	1,800	50.00	90,000
27	Purchases	1,300	45.00	58,500
		4,600		$216,000

A physical inventory count determined that there were 1,500 units on hand at the end of January.
(a) Calculate the cost of the ending inventory and cost of goods sold under FIFO, assuming G-Mac uses a periodic inventory system. (Round your answers to the nearest cent.)
(b) Would your answers to part (a) differ if G-Mac used a perpetual inventory system? Explain.

*BE6–15 At the beginning of the year, Seller Ltd. had 900 units with a cost of $5 per unit in its beginning inventory. The following inventory transactions occurred during the month of January:

Record transactions under perpetual and periodic FIFO.
(LO 2, 6)

Jan. 3 Sold 700 units on account for $12 each.
9 Purchased 1,000 units on account for $6 per unit.
15 Sold 800 units for cash at $11 each.

Prepare journal entries assuming that Seller Ltd. uses FIFO (a) under a perpetual inventory system and (b) under a periodic inventory system.

► EXERCISES

Identify items in inventory.
(LO 1)

E6–1 Shippers Ltd. had the following inventory situations to consider at January 31, its year end:

1. Goods held on consignment for Boxes Unlimited since December 22
2. Goods that are still in transit and were shipped to a customer FOB destination on January 29
3. Goods shipped on consignment to Rinehart Holdings Ltd. on January 5
4. Freight costs due on goods in transit from item 2 above
5. Goods that are still in transit and were purchased FOB destination from a supplier on January 25
6. Goods that are still in transit and were purchased FOB shipping point from a supplier on January 25
7. Goods that are still in transit and were shipped to a customer FOB shipping point on January 29

Instructions

Identify which of the above items should be included in inventory. If an item should not be included in inventory, state where it should be recorded.

Determine correct inventory amount.
(LO 1)

E6–2 Gatineau Bank is considering giving Novotna Corporation a short-term bank loan. Before doing so, it decides that further discussions with Novotna's accountant may be desirable. One area of particular concern is the Inventory account, which according to a recent physical inventory count has a balance of $285,000 at December 31. This count agreed with the accounting records. Discussions with the accountant reveal the following:

1. Novotna sold goods costing $35,000 to India-based Moghul Company, FOB destination, on December 28. The goods are not expected to arrive in India until January 12. The goods were not included in the physical inventory count, because they were not in the warehouse.
2. The physical inventory count did not include goods costing $95,000 that were shipped to Novotna, FOB shipping point, on December 27 and were still in transit at year end.
3. Novotna received goods costing $28,000 on January 2. The goods were shipped FOB shipping point on December 26 by Cellar Corp. The goods were not included in the physical inventory count.
4. Novotna sold goods costing $49,000 to United Kingdom–based Sterling of Britain Ltd., FOB shipping point, on December 30. The goods were received by Sterling on January 8. They were not included in Novotna's physical inventory count.
5. On December 31, Schiller Corporation had $30,500 of goods held on consignment for Novotna. The goods were not included in the physical inventory count.
6. Included in the physical inventory count were $15,000 of parts for outdated products that the company had not been able to sell. It is unlikely that these obsolete parts will have any other use.

Instructions

(a) Determine the correct inventory amount on December 31.
(b) Explain why having an accurate inventory count is important to the bank in assessing whether to give Novotna a short-term bank loan or not.

Answer questions about specific identification.
(LO 2, 3)

E6–3 On February 28, Discount Electronics Ltd. has three ultra HD television systems left in stock. The purchase date, serial number, and cost of each of the three systems are as follows:

Date	Serial Number	Cost
Jan.　2	#1012	$2,400
Feb.　1	#1045	1,900
28	#1056	1,680

All three systems are priced to sell at $2,600. By March 31, two systems had been sold and one system remained in inventory.

Instructions

(a) Explain how Discount Electronics would use specific identification to determine the cost of goods sold and the cost of the ending inventory.
(b) Explain how Discount Electronics could manipulate its net income using specific identification by "selectively choosing" which home entertainment systems to sell to the two customers in the month of March. What would Discount Electronics' cost of goods sold and gross profit be if the company wished to minimize net income? To maximize net income? Ignore income tax.
(c) What guidelines should Discount Electronics consider when deciding whether to use specific identification or one of the other cost formulas to determine the cost of its inventory?

E6–4 Ohsweken Outdoor Stores Inc. uses a perpetual inventory system and has a beginning inventory, as at April 1, of 150 tents. This consists of 50 tents purchased in February at a cost of $210 each and 100 tents purchased in March at a cost of $225 each. During April, the company had the following purchases and sales of tents: *Apply perpetual FIFO.* *(LO 2, 3)*

Date		Purchases Units	Unit Cost	Sales Units	Unit Price
Apr.	3			75	$400
	10	200	$275		
	17			250	400
	24	300	290		
	30			200	400

Instructions
(a) Determine the cost of goods sold and the cost of the ending inventory using FIFO.
(b) Calculate Ohsweken Outdoors's gross profit and gross profit margin for the month of April.
(c) Is the gross profit determined in part (b) higher or lower than it would be if Ohsweken Outdoors had used the average cost formula? Explain.

E6–5 Basis Furniture Ltd. uses a perpetual inventory system and has a beginning inventory, as at June 1, of 500 bookcases at a cost of $125 each. During June, the company had the following purchases and sales of bookcases: *Apply perpetual average cost.* *(LO 2, 3)*

Date	Purchases Units	Unit Cost	Sales Units	Unit Price
June 6	1,200	$127		
10			1,000	$200
14	1,800	128		
16			1,600	205
26	1,000	129		

Instructions
(a) Determine the cost of goods sold and the cost of the ending inventory using the average cost formula. (Use unrounded numbers in your calculations but round to the nearest cent for presentation purposes in your answer.)
(b) Calculate Basis Furniture's gross profit and gross profit margin for the month of June.
(c) Is the gross profit determined in part (b) higher or lower than it would be if Basis Furniture had used FIFO? Explain.

E6–6 Lakshmi Ltd. uses the perpetual inventory system and reports the following inventory transactions for the month of June: *Apply perpetual FIFO and average cost; compare effects.* *(LO 2, 3)*

Date	Explanation	Units	Unit Cost	Total Cost
June 1	Beginning inventory	1,500	$5	$ 7,500
12	Purchases	2,300	6	13,800
15	Sale	(2,500)		
16	Purchases	4,500	7	31,500
23	Purchases	1,500	8	12,000
27	Sales	(5,700)		

Instructions
(a) Determine the cost of goods sold and the cost of the ending inventory using (1) FIFO and (2) average cost. Ignore the effect of income tax. (For average cost, use unrounded numbers in your calculations but round to the nearest cent for presentation purposes in your answer.)
(b) Which cost formula results in the higher cost of goods sold? Why?
(c) Which cost formula results in the higher net income? Why?
(d) Which cost formula results in the higher ending inventory? Why?
(e) Which cost formula results in the higher cash flow? Why?

*Apply perpetual FIFO
and average cost;
compare effects.*

(LO 2, 3)

E6-7 Glenmount Inc. is trying to determine whether to use the FIFO or average cost formula. The accounting records show the following selected inventory information:

	Purchases			Cost of Goods Sold			Balance		
Date	Units	Cost	Total	Units	Cost	Total	Units	Cost	Total
Oct. 2	9,000	$12	$108,000						
15	15,000	14	210,000						
29				22,000					

The company accountant has prepared the following partial income statement to help management understand the financial statement impact of each cost determination cost formula.

	FIFO	Average Cost
Sales	$525,000	$525,000
Cost of goods sold	_____	_____
Gross profit	_____	_____
Operating expenses	200,000	200,000
Income before income tax	_____	_____
Income tax expense (30%)	_____	_____
Net income	_____	_____

Instructions

(a) Complete the perpetual inventory schedule shown above, assuming the use of the FIFO cost formula.

(b) Complete the perpetual inventory schedule shown above, assuming the use of the average cost formula. (Use unrounded numbers in your calculations but round to the nearest cent for presentation purposes in your answer.)

(c) Fill in the missing information in the blanks shown in the partial income statement above.

(d) Explain whether the comparative net incomes of each cost formula determined in part (c) will be expected to increase, decrease, or not change if (1) costs fall, and (2) costs remain stable.

*Determine effects of
inventory errors for two
years.*

(LO 4)

E6-8 Seles Hardware Limited reported the following amounts for its cost of goods sold and inventory:

	2018	2017
Cost of goods sold	$168,000	$154,000
Ending inventory	37,000	30,000

Seles made two errors: (1) ending inventory for 2018 was overstated by $2,000 and (2) ending inventory for 2017 was understated by $4,000.

Instructions

(a) Calculate the correct ending inventory and cost of goods sold amounts for each year.

(b) Describe the impact of the error on (1) cost of goods sold, (2) income before income tax, (3) assets, (4) liabilities, and (5) total shareholders' equity for each of the two years.

(c) Explain why it is important that Seles Hardware correct these errors as soon as they are discovered.

*Correct partial income
statements and calculate
gross profit.*

(LO 4)

E6-9 Aruba Inc. reported the following partial income statement data for the years ended December 31, 2018 and 2017:

	2018	2017
Sales	$265,000	$250,000
Cost of goods sold	205,000	194,000
Gross profit	60,000	56,000

Inventory was reported in the current financial position at $44,000, $52,000, and $49,000 at the end of 2016, 2017, and 2018, respectively. The ending inventory amounts for 2016 and 2018 are correct. However, the ending inventory at December 31, 2017, is understated by $8,000.

Instructions

(a) Prepare correct income statements for 2017 and 2018 through to gross profit.

(b) What is the cumulative effect of the inventory error on total gross profit for these two years?

(c) Calculate the gross profit margin for each of these two years, before and after the correction.

E6–10 Calabogie Camera Shop Ltd. reports the following cost and net realizable value information for its inventory at December 31:

Record LCNRV valuation.
(LO 5)

	Units	Unit Cost	Unit NRV
Cameras:			
Sony	4	$175	$160
Canon	8	150	152
Light Meters:			
Gossen	12	135	139
Sekonic	10	115	110

Instructions
(a) Determine the lower of cost and net realizable value of the ending inventory.
(b) Prepare the adjusting journal entry required, if any, to record the lower of cost and net realizable value of the inventory assuming Calabogie Camera Shop uses a perpetual inventory system.
(c) A physical inventory count at December 31 found that two of the Canon cameras were badly damaged. It was determined that they had no resale value. Prepare the adjusting entry required, if any, to record the damaged cameras.

E6–11 The following information is available for **Gildan Activewear Inc.**, headquartered in Montreal, for three recent fiscal years (in U.S. $ thousands):

Calculate inventory turn-over, days in inventory, and gross profit margin.
(LO 5)

	2016	2015	2014
Inventory	$ 851,033	$ 779,407	$ 595,794
Net sales	2,959,238	2,359,994	2,284,303
Cost of goods sold	2,229,130	1,701,311	1,550,266

Instructions
(a) Calculate the inventory turnover, days in inventory, and gross profit margin for 2016 and 2015.
(b) Based on the ratios calculated in part (a), did Gildan's liquidity and profitability improve or deteriorate in 2016?

E6–12 The following comparative cost information is available for Kingswood Limited:

Determine effect of cost formulas on liquidity.
(LO 3, 5)

	Average Inventory	Cost of Goods Sold
FIFO	$222,500	$750,000
Average cost	227,500	735,000

Kingswood's current assets are $450,000, exclusive of inventory. Its current liabilities are $350,000.

Instructions
(a) Calculate Kingswood's inventory turnover ratio assuming (1) FIFO and (2) average cost is used to determine the cost of the ending inventory.
(b) Calculate Kingswood's current ratio assuming (1) FIFO and (2) average cost is used to determine the cost of the ending inventory.
(c) Does one cost formula result in a better measure of liquidity than the other for Kingswood? Explain.

*E6–13 Deala Ltd. ("DL") is a retailer of office equipment. The company uses a periodic inventory system and began October with 2,000 units with a total cost of $40,000. During the month of October, DL had the following inventory-related transactions:

Apply periodic FIFO and average cost.
(LO 3, 6)

Date	Explanation	Units	Unit Cost	Total Cost
Oct. 9	Purchase	5,000	$21.00	$105,000
12	Purchase	4,000	20.50	82,000
17	Sale (@ $40/unit)	(5,000)		
25	Purchase	4,000	20.80	83,200
28	Sale (@ $40/unit)	(6,000)		

(a) Determine the cost of goods available for sale for the month.
(b) Calculate ending inventory at October 31 and cost of goods sold for the month assuming that DL used (1) FIFO and (2) average cost.
(c) Determine which cost formula would result in the higher gross profit for DL.

Apply periodic FIFO and average cost.

(LO 6)

*E6–14 Lakshmi Ltd. reports the following inventory transactions in a periodic inventory system for the month of June. A physical inventory count determined that 1,600 units were on hand at the end of the month.

Date		Explanation	Units	Unit Cost	Total Cost
June	1	Beginning inventory	1,500	$5	$ 7,500
	12	Purchases	2,300	6	13,800
	16	Purchases	4,500	7	31,500
	23	Purchases	1,500	8	12,000

Instructions

(a) Determine the cost of the ending inventory and cost of goods sold using (1) FIFO and (2) average cost. (For average cost, use unrounded numbers in your calculations but round to the nearest cent for presentation purposes in your answer.)

(b) For item 2 of part (a), explain why the average unit cost is not $6.50 [($5 + $6 + $7 + $8) ÷ 4].

(c) By how much do the results for part (a) differ from E6–6, where the same information was used in a perpetual inventory system? Why?

Apply perpetual and periodic FIFO and average cost.

(LO 2, 6)

*E6–15 Powder, Inc. sells an Xpert snowboard that is popular with snowboard enthusiasts. The following information shows Powder's purchases and sales of Xpert snowboards during November:

Date		Explanation	Units	Unit Cost	Unit Sales Price
Nov.	1	Beginning inventory	30	$295	
	5	Purchases	25	300	
	12	Sales	(42)		$460
	19	Purchases	40	305	
	22	Sales	(50)		470
	25	Purchases	30	310	
			33		

Instructions

(a) Determine the cost of goods sold and ending inventory using (1) FIFO and (2) average cost, assuming Powder uses a perpetual inventory system. (For average cost, use unrounded numbers in your calculations but round to the nearest cent for presentation purposes in your answer.)

(b) Determine the cost of goods sold and ending inventory using (1) FIFO and (2) average cost, assuming Powder uses a periodic inventory system. (For average cost, use unrounded numbers in your calculations but round to the nearest cent for presentation purposes in your answer.)

Record transactions in perpetual and periodic inventory systems.

(LO 2, 6)

*E6–16 Refer to the data provided for Powder, Inc. in E6–15.

Instructions

(a) Prepare journal entries to record purchases and sales for Powder in a perpetual inventory system using (1) FIFO and (2) average cost.

(b) Prepare journal entries to record purchases and sales for Powder in a periodic inventory system using (1) FIFO and (2) average cost.

▶ PROBLEMS: SET A

P6–1A Kananaskis Limited is trying to determine the amount of its ending inventory as at February 28, the company's year end. The accountant counted everything in the warehouse in early March, which resulted in an ending inventory amount of $218,000. However, the accountant was not sure how to treat the following transactions, so he did not include them in the count. He has asked for your help in determining whether or not the following transactions should be included in inventory:

1. Feb. 1 Kananaskis shipped $1,800 of inventory on consignment to Banff Corporation. By February 28, Banff had sold half of this inventory for Kananaskis.

2. 19 Kananaskis was holding merchandise that had been sold to a customer on February 19 but needed adjustments before the customer would take possession. The merchandise cost $980 and alterations, which were completed on February 21, cost $120. The customer plans to pick up the merchandise on March 2 after the alterations are complete.

3. 22 Kananaskis shipped goods FOB shipping point to a customer. The merchandise cost $1,520. The appropriate party paid the freight costs of $90. The receiving report indicates that the goods were received by the customer on March 2.

4.   23   Kananaskis received $1,600 of inventory on consignment from Craft Producers Ltd. By February 28, Kananaskis had not sold any of this inventory.

5.   25   Kananaskis purchased goods FOB shipping point from a supplier. The merchandise cost $1,350. The appropriate party paid the freight costs of $95. The goods were shipped by the supplier on February 26 and received by Kananaskis on March 3.

6.   26   Kananaskis purchased goods FOB destination from a supplier. The merchandise cost $1,500. The appropriate party paid the freight costs of $150. The goods were shipped by the supplier on February 27 and received by Kananaskis on March 4.

7.   27   Kananaskis shipped goods FOB destination costing $1,900 to a customer. The appropriate party paid the freight costs of $200. The receiving report indicates that the customer received the goods on March 7.

8.   28   Kananaskis had $1,950 of inventory isolated in the warehouse. The inventory is designated for a customer who has requested that the goods not be shipped until March 5.

Instructions

(a)   For each of the above situations, specify whether the item should be included in ending inventory, and if so, at what amount. For each item that is not included in ending inventory, indicate who owns it and what account, if any, it should have been recorded in.

(b)   Calculate the revised ending inventory amount.

P6–2A Dean's Sales Ltd., a small Ford dealership, has provided you with the following information with respect to its vehicle inventory for the month of April. The company uses the specific identification cost formula.

Apply specific identification.

(LO 2)

Date	Explanation	Model	Vehicle Identification #	Unit Cost/Price
Apr. 1	Beginning inventory	Focus	C81362	$24,000
		F-150	F1883	25,000
		F-150	F1921	29,000
		Mustang	G62313	29,000
		Flex	X3892	31,000
8	Sales	Focus	C81362	26,000
		Mustang	G62313	32,000
12	Purchases	Mustang	G71811	30,000
		Flex	X4214	31,000
		Escape	E21202	29,000
		Mustang	G71891	28,000
		Flex	X4212	30,000
18	Sales	Mustang	G71891	33,000
		F-150	F1921	32,500
		Flex	X3892	34,000
		Escape	E21202	32,000
23	Purchases	Focus	C81528	27,000
		Escape	E28268	30,000

Instructions

(a)   Determine the cost of goods sold and ending inventory for the month of April.

(b)   Determine the gross profit for the month of April.

(c)   Discuss whether the specific identification cost formula is likely the most appropriate cost formula for Dean's Sales. Explain why this is, or is not, the case.

P6–3A Save-Mart Centre Inc. began operations on May 1 and uses a perpetual inventory system. During May, the company had the following purchases and sales for one of its products:

Apply perpetual FIFO and average cost; compare effects.

(LO 2, 3)

Date	Purchases Units	Unit Cost	Sales Units	Unit Price
May 1	120	$100		
3			80	$250
8	100	110		
13			80	275
15	60	115		
20			60	300
27			40	325

Instructions

(a) Determine the cost of goods sold and cost of ending inventory using (1) FIFO and (2) average cost. Ignore the effect of income tax. (For average cost, use unrounded numbers in your calculations but round to the nearest cent for presentation purposes in your answer.)

(b) What guidelines should Save-Mart consider in choosing between the FIFO and average cost formulas?

(c) Which cost formula produces the higher gross profit and net income?

(d) Which cost formula produces the higher ending inventory valuation?

(e) Which cost formula produces the higher cash flow?

Apply perpetual FIFO and answer questions about effects.

(LO 2, 3)

P6–4A Sandoval Skateshop Ltd. reports the following inventory transactions for its skateboards for the month of April. The company uses a perpetual inventory system.

Date	Explanation	Units	Unit Cost	Total Cost
Apr. 1	Beginning inventory	30	$50	$1,500
6	Purchases	15	45	675
9	Sales	(35)		
14	Purchases	20	40	800
20	Sales	(25)		
28	Purchases	20	35	700

Instructions

(a) Determine the cost of goods sold and cost of ending inventory using FIFO.

(b) Assume that Sandoval wants to change to the average cost formula. What guidelines must it consider before making this change?

(c) If the company does change to the average cost formula and prices continue to fall, would you expect the cost of goods sold and ending inventory amounts to be higher or lower than these amounts when using FIFO?

Apply perpetual average cost and discuss errors.

(LO 2, 4)

P6–5A Information for Sandoval Skateshop Ltd. is presented in P6–4A. Use the same inventory data and assume that the company uses the perpetual inventory system.

Instructions

(a) Determine the cost of goods sold and cost of ending inventory using average cost. (Use unrounded numbers in your calculations but round to the nearest cent for presentation purposes in your answer.)

(b) When the company counted its inventory at the end of April, it counted only 24 skateboards on hand. What journal entry, if any, should the company make to record this shortage?

(c) If the company had not discovered this shortage, identify what accounts would be overstated or understated and by what amount. Ignore the effect of income taxes.

Record transactions using perpetual average cost; apply LCNRV.

(LO 2, 5)

P6–6A You are provided with the following information for Amelia Inc., which purchases its inventory from a supplier for cash and has only cash sales. Amelia uses the average cost formula in a perpetual inventory system. Increased competition has recently reduced the price of the product.

Date	Explanation	Units	Unit Cost/Price
Apr. 1	Beginning inventory	50	$ 80
6	Purchases	110	90
8	Sales	(130)	120
15	Purchases	120	70
20	Sales	(120)	100
27	Purchases	20	60

Instructions

(a) Prepare all journal entries for the month of April for Amelia, the buyer. (Use unrounded numbers in your calculations but round to the nearest cent for presentation purposes in your answer.)

(b) Determine the ending inventory amount for Amelia.

(c) On April 30, Amelia learns that the product has a net realizable value of $50 per unit. What amount should ending inventory be valued at on the April statement of financial position?

Determine effects of inventory error for two years.

(LO 4, 5)

P6–7A In its physical inventory count at its February 28, 2017, year end, the Orange Sprocket Corporation included inventory that was being held for another company to sell on consignment. As a result, the company's inventory count showed the company having more inventory than its accounting records indicated it should have. The company adjusted its inventory and cost of goods sold accordingly. The merchandise was sold in the next year and inventory was correctly stated at February 28, 2018.

Instructions

Ignoring income tax, indicate the effect of this error (overstated, understated, or no effect) on each of the following at year end:

	2018	2017
(a) Cash		
(b) Cost of goods sold		
(c) Net income		
(d) Retained earnings		
(e) Ending inventory		
(f) Gross profit margin (40%)		
(g) Inventory turnover (10 times)		

P6–8A The records of Kmeta Inc. show the following data for the years ended July 31:

Determine effects of inventory errors for multiple years.

(LO 4, 5)

	2018	2017	2016
Income statement:			
Sales	$340,000	$320,000	$300,000
Cost of goods sold	233,000	220,000	209,000
Operating expenses	68,000	64,000	64,000
Statement of financial position:			
Inventory	40,000	40,000	24,000

After the company's July 31, 2018, year end, the accountant discovers two errors:

1. Ending inventory on July 31, 2016, was actually $33,000, not $24,000. Kmeta owned goods held on consignment at another company that were not included in the inventory count.
2. Kmeta purchased $15,000 of goods from a supplier on July 30, 2017, with shipping terms FOB shipping point. Kemta did not receive the goods until August 4, 2017 at which time the company recorded the purchase.

Instructions

(a) For each of the three years, prepare both incorrect and corrected income statements through to income before income tax.
(b) What is the combined (total) impact of these errors on retained earnings (ignoring any income tax effects) for the three years before correction? After correction?
(c) Calculate both the incorrect and corrected inventory turnover ratios for 2018 and 2017.

P6–9A Tascon Corporation sells coffee beans, which are sensitive to price fluctuations. The following inventory information is available for this product at December 31, 2018:

Determine and record LCNRV.

(LO 5)

Coffee Bean	Units	Unit Cost	Net Realizable Value
Coffea arabica	13,000 bags	$5.60	$5.55
Coffea robusta	5,000 bags	3.40	3.50

(a) Calculate Tascon's inventory at the lower of cost and net realizable value.
(b) Prepare any journal entry required to record the LCNRV, assuming that Tascon uses a perpetual inventory system.
(c) Explain whether Tascon should consider each type of coffee bean separately when determining the lower of cost and net realizable value. Identify an argument in support of both types of coffee beans being considered as part of one inventory grouping.

P6–10A You have been provided with the following information regarding Love Paper Ltd.'s inventory for June, July, and August.

Record and present LCNRV valuation for multiple periods.

(LO 5)

	Paper Inventory (in tonnes)	Cost/Tonne	NRV/Tonne
June 30	16,000	$790	$850
July 31	16,700	850	815
August 31	15,500	815	790

Instructions

(a) Calculate the cost and net realizable value of Love Paper's paper inventory at (1) June 30, (2) July 31, and (3) August 31.

(b) Prepare any journal entry necessary to record the LCNRV of the paper inventory at (1) June 30, (2) July 31, and (3) August 31. Assume that Love Paper uses a perpetual inventory system.

Calculate ratios and comment on liquidity.

(LO 5)

P6–11A The following information is available for **The Coca-Cola Company** (in U.S. $ millions):

	2015	2014	2013
Cost of goods sold	$17,482	$17,889	$18,421
Inventories	2,902	3,100	3,277
Current assets	33,395	32,986	31,304
Current liabilities	26,930	32,374	27,811

In the notes to its financial statements, Coca-Cola disclosed that it uses the FIFO and average cost formulas to determine the cost of its inventory.

The industry averages for the inventory turnover, days in inventory, and current ratios are as follows:

	2015	2014
Inventory turnover	8.7 times	9.1 times
Days in inventory	42 days	40 days
Current ratio	1.3:1	1.1:1

Instructions

(a) Calculate Coca-Cola's inventory turnover, days in inventory, and current ratios for 2015 and 2014. Comment on the company's liquidity over the two years, and in comparison with the industry.

(b) What might be the reason that Coca-Cola uses more than one cost formula to determine the cost of its inventory?

Compare ratios; comment on liquidity and profitability.

(LO 5)

P6–12A The following information is available for **The Wendy's Company** and **McDonald's Corporation**, and their industry, for a recent year:

	Wendy's	McDonald's	Industry Average
Inventory turnover	163.0 times	96.5 times	127.4 times
Current ratio	2.3:1	3.3:1	2.0:1
Gross profit margin	36.7%	38.5%	31.8%
Profit margin	8.6%	17.8%	11.9%

Instructions

(a) Comment on the liquidity of the two companies in comparison with each other, and with the industry.

(b) Comment on the profitability of the two companies in comparison with each other, and with the industry.

Apply periodic FIFO and average cost.

(LO 6)

*P6–13A Kane Ltd. had a beginning inventory on January 1 of 250 units of product SXL at a cost of $160 per unit. During the year, purchases were as follows:

	Units	Unit Cost	Total Cost
Mar. 15	700	$150	$105,000
July 20	500	145	72,500
Sept. 4	450	135	60,750
Dec. 2	100	125	12,500

Kane uses a periodic inventory system. At the end of the year, a physical inventory count determined that there were 200 units on hand.

Instructions

(a) Determine the cost of goods available for sale.

(b) Determine the cost of the ending inventory and the cost of the goods sold using (1) FIFO and (2) average cost. (Use unrounded numbers in your calculation of the average unit cost but round to the nearest cent for presentation purposes in your answer.)

*P6–14A Data for Kane Ltd. are presented in P6–13A. Assume that Kane sold product SXL for $200 per unit during the year.

Instructions

(a) Prepare a partial income statement through to gross profit for each of the two cost formulas: (1) FIFO and (2) average cost.

(b) Show how inventory would be reported in the current assets section of the statement of financial position for (1) FIFO and (2) average cost.

(c) Which cost formula results in the lower inventory amount for the statement of financial position? The lower gross profit amount for the income statement?

Prepare partial financial statements and assess effects.

(LO 5, 6)

*P6–15A You are provided with the following information about Lynk Inc.'s inventory for the month of August:

Apply perpetual and periodic FIFO.

(LO 2, 6)

Date		Description	Units	Unit Cost
Aug.	1	Beginning inventory	50	$90
	4	Purchase	180	92
	10	Sale	(160)	
	18	Purchase	70	94
	25	Sale	(100)	
	28	Purchase	40	95

Instructions

(a) Calculate the cost of ending inventory and cost of goods sold using FIFO in (1) a periodic inventory system, and (2) a perpetual inventory system.

(b) Compare your results for items 1 and 2 of part (a), commenting particularly on any differences or similarities between the two inventory systems.

*P6–16A Apple River Inc.'s inventory for the month of November was as follows:

Apply perpetual and periodic average cost.

(LO 2, 6)

Date		Explanation	Units	Unit Cost
Nov.	1	Beginning inventory	100	$40
	4	Purchase	500	42
	11	Sale	(450)	
	16	Purchase	750	44
	20	Sale	(800)	
	27	Purchase	600	46

Instructions

(a) Calculate the ending inventory and cost of goods sold using the average cost formula in (1) a perpetual inventory system, and (2) a periodic inventory system. (Use unrounded numbers in your calculations but round to the nearest cent for presentation purposes in your answer.)

(b) Compare your results for items 1 and 2 of part (a), commenting specifically on any differences or similarities between the two inventory systems.

▶ PROBLEMS: SET B

P6–1B Banff Limited is trying to determine the value of its ending inventory as at February 28, the company's year end. The accountant counted everything that was in the warehouse in early March, which resulted in an ending inventory amount of $161,000. However, the accountant was not sure how to treat the following transactions, so she did not include them in the count, with the exception of item 8. She has asked for your help in determining whether or not the following transactions should be included in inventory:

Identify items in inventory.

(LO 1)

1. Feb. 1 Banff received $2,000 of inventory on consignment from Kananaskis Limited. By February 28, Banff had sold one quarter of this inventory for Kananaskis.

2.   19 Banff purchased goods FOB shipping point from a supplier. The merchandise cost $2,500. The appropriate party paid the freight costs of $150. The goods were shipped by the supplier on February 21 and were received by Banff on March 1.

3.   22 Banff shipped goods FOB shipping point to a customer. The merchandise cost $2,600. The appropriate party paid the freight costs of $180. The receiving report indicates that the customer received the goods on March 1.

4.   23   Banff shipped $2,200 of inventory on consignment to a Jasper craft shop. By February 28, the craft shop had sold half of this inventory for Banff.

5.   24   Banff purchased goods FOB destination from a supplier. The merchandise cost $700. The appropriate party paid the freight costs of $35. The goods were shipped by the supplier on February 26 and received by Banff on March 2.

6.   26   Banff shipped goods FOB destination to a customer. The merchandise cost $1,800. The appropriate party paid the freight costs of $100. The receiving report indicates that the customer received the goods on March 3.

7.   27   Banff had $2,100 of inventory isolated in the warehouse. The inventory is designated for a customer who has requested that the goods not be shipped until March 2.

8.   28   Banff had damaged goods set aside in the warehouse because they were not saleable. These goods were included in the inventory count at their original cost of $800.

Instructions

(a)   For each of the above situations, specify whether the item should be included in ending inventory, and if so, at what amount. For each item that is not included in ending inventory, indicate who owns it and what account, if any, it should have been recorded in.

(b)   Calculate the revised ending inventory amount.

Apply specific identification.

(LO 2)

P6–2B   The Piano Studio Ltd. has provided you with the following information with respect to its piano inventory for the month of August. The company uses the specific identification cost formula.

Date	Explanation	Supplier	Serial #	Unit Cost/Price
Aug. 1	Beginning inventory	Yamaha	YH6318	$1,800
		Kawai	KG1268	1,800
		Kawai	KG1520	900
		Suzuki	SZ5716	1,400
		Suzuki	SZ5828	1,900
		Steinway	ST8411	2,900
		Steinway	ST0944	2,500
10	Sales	Suzuki	SZ5828	3,000
		Kawai	KG1268	2,100
15	Purchases	Yamaha	YH4418	1,600
		Yamaha	YH5632	1,900
18	Sales	Yamaha	YH4418	2,400
		Steinway	ST8411	4,000
22	Purchases	Suzuki	SZ6132	2,100
		Suzuki	SZ6148	1,900
26	Sales	Suzuki	SZ6132	3,200
		Yamaha	YH6318	2,800
		Yamaha	YH5632	2,900

Instructions

(a)   Determine the cost of goods sold and ending inventory for the month of August.

(b)   Determine the gross profit for the month of August.

(c)   Discuss whether the specific identification cost formula is likely the most appropriate cost determination cost formula for the Piano Studio. Explain why this is, or is not, the case.

Apply perpetual FIFO and average cost; compare effects.

(LO 2, 3)

P6–3B   Family Appliance Mart Ltd. began operations on May 1 and uses a perpetual inventory system. During May, the company had the following purchases and sales for one of its products:

	Purchases		Sales	
Date	Units	Unit Cost	Units	Unit Price
May 1	110	$190		
6	140	220		
11			200	$350
14	80	230		
21			100	400
27	50	250		

Instructions
(a) Determine the cost of goods sold and cost of ending inventory using (1) FIFO and (2) average cost. Ignore the effect of income tax. (For average cost, use unrounded numbers in your calculations but round to the nearest cent for presentation purposes in your answer.)
(b) What guidelines should Family Appliance Mart consider in choosing between the FIFO and average cost formulas?
(c) Which cost formula produces the higher gross profit and net income?
(d) Which cost formula produces the higher ending inventory valuation?
(e) Which cost formula produces the higher cash flow?

P6–4B BigFishTackle Co. Ltd. reports the following inventory transactions for its fishing rods for the month of April. The company uses a perpetual inventory system.

Apply perpetual FIFO and answer questions about effects.

(LO 2, 3)

Date	Explanation	Units	Unit Cost	Total Cost
Apr. 1	Beginning inventory	50	$230	$11,500
6	Purchases	35	240	8,400
9	Sales	(55)		
14	Purchases	40	245	9,800
20	Sales	(50)		
28	Purchases	30	250	7,500

Instructions
(a) Determine the cost of goods sold and cost of ending inventory using FIFO.
(b) Assume that BigFishTackle wants to change to the average cost formula. What guidelines must it consider before making this change?
(c) If the company does change to the average cost formula and prices continue to rise, would you expect the cost of goods sold and ending inventory amounts to be higher or lower than these amounts when using FIFO?

P6–5B Information for BigFishTackle Co. Ltd. is presented in P6–4B. Use the same inventory data and assume that the company uses the perpetual inventory system.

Apply perpetual average cost and discuss errors.

(LO 2, 4)

Instructions
(a) Determine the cost of goods sold and cost of ending inventory using average cost. (Use unrounded numbers in your calculations but round to the nearest cent for presentation purposes in your answer.)
(b) When the company counted its inventory at the end of April, it counted only 49 rods on hand. What journal entry, if any, should the company make to record this shortage?
(c) If the company had not discovered this shortage, identify what accounts would be overstated or understated and by what amount.

P6–6B You are provided with the following information for Geo Inc., which purchases its inventory from a supplier on account. All sales are also on account. Geo uses the FIFO cost formula in a perpetual inventory system. Increased competition has recently decreased the price of the product.

Record transactions using perpetual FIFO; apply LCNRV.

(LO 2, 5)

Date	Explanation	Units	Unit Cost Price
Oct. 1	Beginning inventory	60	$140
5	Purchases	100	130
8	Sales	(120)	200
15	Purchases	35	120
20	Sales	(60)	160
26	Purchases	15	110

Instructions
(a) Prepare all journal entries for the month of October for Geo, the buyer.
(b) Determine the ending inventory amount for Geo.
(c) On October 31, Geo learns that the product has a net realizable value of $108 per unit. What amount should ending inventory be valued at on the October 31 statement of financial position?

P6–7B In its physical inventory count at its March 31, 2017, year end, Backspring Corporation excluded inventory that was being held on consignment for Backspring by another company. As a result, the company's inventory count showed the company having less inventory than its accounting records indicated it should have. The company adjusted its inventory and cost of goods sold accordingly. The merchandise was sold in the next year and the inventory was correctly stated at March 31, 2018.

Determine effects of inventory error for two years.

(LO 4, 5)

Instructions

Ignoring income tax, indicate the effect of this error (overstated, understated, or no effect) on each of the following at year end:

	2018	2017
(a) Cash		
(b) Cost of goods sold		
(c) Net income		
(d) Retained earnings		
(e) Ending inventory		
(f) Gross profit margin (30%)		
(g) Inventory turnover (8 times)		

Determine effects of inventory errors for multiple years.

(LO 4, 5)

P6–8B The records of Pelletier Inc. show the following data for the years ended July 31:

	2018	2017	2016
Income statement:			
Sales	$320,000	$312,000	$300,000
Cost of goods sold	187,000	203,000	170,000
Operating expenses	52,000	52,000	50,000
Statement of financial position:			
Inventory	37,000	24,000	37,000

After the company's July 31, 2018, year end, the controller discovers two errors:

1. Ending inventory at the end of 2016 was actually $27,000, not $37,000. Pelletier included goods held on consignment for another company that were mistakenly included in the 2016 inventory account. As a result, the company's inventory count showed the company having more inventory than its accounting records indicated it should have. The company adjusted its inventory and cost of goods sold accordingly.
2. Pelletier purchased $5,000 of goods from a supplier on July 30, 2017, with shipping terms FOB shipping point. Pelletier did not receive the goods until August 4, 2017 at which time the company recorded the purchase.

Instructions

(a) For each of the three years, prepare both the incorrect and corrected income statements through to income before income tax.
(b) What is the combined (total) impact of the errors on retained earnings (ignoring any income tax effects) for the three years before correction? After correction?
(c) Calculate both the incorrect and corrected inventory turnover ratios for each of 2018 and 2017.

Determine and record LCNRV.

(LO 5)

P6–9B FlinFlon Limited sells three products whose prices are sensitive to price fluctuations. The following inventory information is available for these products at March 31, 2018:

Product	Units	Unit Cost	Net Realizable Value
A	25	$ 7	$ 7
B	30	6	8
C	60	11	10

Instructions

(a) Calculate FlinFlon's inventory at the lower of cost and net realizable value.
(b) Prepare any journal entry required to record the LCNRV, assuming that FlinFlon uses a perpetual inventory system.

Record and present LCNRV valuation for multiple periods.

(LO 5)

P6–10B You have been provided with the following information regarding R-Steel Inc.'s inventory for March, April, and May.

	Steel Inventory (in tonnes)	Cost/Tonne	NRV/Tonne
Mar. 31	30,000	$725	$740
Apr. 30	25,000	715	710
May 31	28,000	725	725

Instructions

(a) Calculate the cost and net realizable value of R-Steel's inventory at (1) March 31, (2) April 30, and (3) May 31.

(b) Prepare any journal entry required to record the LCNRV of the steel inventory at (1) March 31, (2) April 30, and (3) May 31. Assume that R-Steel uses a perpetual inventory system.

P6–11B The following information is available for **PepsiCo, Inc.** (in U.S. $ millions):

Calculate ratios and comment on liquidity.

(LO 5)

	2015	2014	2013
Cost of goods sold	$28,384	$30,884	$31,243
Inventories	2,720	3,143	3,409
Current assets	23,031	20,663	22,203
Current liabilities	17,578	18,092	17,839

In the notes to its financial statements, PepsiCo disclosed that it uses the FIFO and average cost formulas to determine the cost of the majority of its inventory.

The industry averages for the inventory turnover, days in inventory, and current ratios are as follows:

	2015	2014
Inventory turnover	8.7 times	9.1 times
Days in inventory	42 days	40 days
Current ratio	1.3:1	1.1:1

Instructions

(a) Calculate PepsiCo's inventory turnover, days in inventory, and current ratios for 2015 and 2014. Comment on the company's liquidity over the two years, and in comparison with the industry.

(b) What might be the reason that PepsiCo uses more than one cost formula to determine the cost of its inventory?

P6–12B **Magna International Inc.** is Canada's top manufacturer of auto parts and systems. Its top competitor is **Dana Holdings Inc.** The following information is available for these two competitors and their industry, for a recent year:

Compare ratios; comment on liquidity and profitability.

(LO 5)

	Magna	Dana	Industry Average
Inventory turnover	12.9 times	8.2 times	9.0 times
Current ratio	1.4:1	2.2:1	1.5:1
Gross profit margin	11.6%	13.5%	17.2%
Profit margin	3.6%	3.7%	4.6%

Instructions

(a) Comment on the liquidity of the two companies in comparison with each other, and the industry.

(b) Comment on the profitability of the two companies in comparison with each other, and the industry.

(c) It would appear from the above ratios that the inventory turnover ratio may have an impact on the current ratio. Please explain why.

***P6–13B** **Steward Inc.** had a beginning inventory on January 1 of 400 units of product MLN at a cost of $18 per unit. During the year, purchases were as follows:

Apply periodic FIFO and average cost.

(LO 6)

	Units	Unit Cost	Total Cost
Feb. 20	1,200	$19	$22,800
May 5	1,000	21	21,000
Aug. 12	1,200	20	24,000
Dec. 8	600	22	13,200

Steward uses a periodic inventory system. At the end of the year, a physical inventory count determined that there were 400 units on hand.

Instructions

(a) Determine the cost of goods available for sale.

(b) Determine the cost of the ending inventory and the cost of goods sold using (1) FIFO and (2) average cost. (Use unrounded numbers in your calculation of the average unit cost but round to the nearest cent for presentation purposes in your answer.)

Prepare partial financial statements and assess effects.

(LO 5, 6)

*P6–14B Data for Steward Inc. are presented in P6–13B. Assume that Steward sold product MLN for $40 per unit during the year.

Instructions

(a) Prepare a partial income statement through to gross profit for each of the two cost formulas: (1) FIFO and (2) average cost.

(b) Show how inventory would be reported in the current assets section of the statement of financial position for (1) FIFO and (2) average cost.

(c) Which cost formula results in the higher inventory amount for the statement of financial position? The higher gross profit amount on the income statement?

Apply perpetual and periodic FIFO.

(LO 2, 6)

*P6–15B You are provided with the following information about Bear River Inc.'s inventory for the month of May:

Date	Description	Units	Unit Cost
May 1	Beginning inventory	15,000	$2.30
6	Purchase	40,000	2.35
11	Sale	(30,000)	
14	Purchase	50,000	2.40
21	Sale	(65,000)	
27	Purchase	40,000	2.45

Instructions

(a) Calculate the ending inventory and cost of goods sold using FIFO in (1) a perpetual inventory system, and (2) a periodic inventory system.

(b) Compare your results for items 1 and 2 of part (a), commenting specifically on any differences or similarities between the two inventory systems.

Apply perpetual and periodic average cost.

(LO 2, 6)

*P6–16B You are provided with the following information about Lahti Inc.'s inventory for the month of October.

Date	Description	Units	Unit Cost
Oct. 1	Beginning inventory	50	$240
9	Purchase	125	260
15	Sale	(150)	
20	Purchase	70	270
29	Sale	(55)	

Instructions

(a) Calculate the cost of ending inventory and cost of goods sold using average cost in (1) a perpetual inventory system, and (2) a periodic inventory system. (Use unrounded numbers in your calculations but round to the nearest cent for presentation purposes in your answer.)

(b) Compare your results for items 1 and 2 of part (a), commenting specifically on any differences or similarities between the two inventory systems.

ACCOUNTING CYCLE | REVIEW

ACR6–1 Retro Productions Ltd. is a Vancouver-based furniture manufacturer. The company reported the following information on its trial balance for 11 months of the year ended November 30, 2018.

RETRO PRODUCTIONS LIMITED
Trial Balance
November 30, 2018

	Debit	Credit
Cash	$ 421,100	
Accounts receivable	1,390,000	
Inventory	2,780,000	
Supplies	39,000	
Prepaid rent	14,000	
Equipment	1,350,000	

	Debit	Credit
Accumulated depreciation—equipment		$ 35,625
Accounts payable		1,230,000
Unearned revenue		96,000
Bank loan payable—non-current		1,240,000
Common shares		600,000
Retained earnings		1,239,275
Dividends declared	120,000	
Sales		16,680,000
Sales returns and allowances	56,000	
Sales discounts	166,800	
Cost of goods sold	9,174,000	
Advertising expense	405,000	
Freight out	980,000	
Office expense	78,000	
Rent expense	154,000	
Salaries expense	3,436,000	
Travel expense	46,000	
Utilities expense	61,000	
Interest expense	70,000	
Income tax expense	380,000	
	$21,120,900	$21,120,900

Retro reported the following transactions for the month of December. The company uses a perpetual inventory system and began the month of December with 10,000 units in inventory.

Dec.	1	Received $315,000 on account from a major customer.
	1	Paid $14,000 in rent for the month of December.
	4	Paid $375,000 owing to a supplier from a purchase that had been made on account.
	6	Sold 4,200 units of merchandise to a Canadian furniture retailer for $2,121,000. Terms were n/30, FOB shipping point.
	15	Purchased 6,000 units of merchandise from a supplier at a cost of $290 per unit. Terms were n/30, FOB shipping point.
	18	Paid salaries of $125,000.
	21	Sold 8,000 units of merchandise for $4,092,000 on account, n/30, FOB shipping point.
	24	Paid $32,000 for advertising expenses incurred in the month.
	27	Purchased 5,000 units of inventory from a supplier at a cost of $300 per unit. Terms were n/30, FOB shipping point.

Adjustment and additional data:

1. Accrued $6,000 for utilities and $140,000 for salaries.
2. Accrued $6,200 of interest on the bank loan.
3. Recorded annual depreciation on equipment, which has an expected useful life of 8 years.
4. Carried out a physical inventory and determined that inventory with a cost of $2,594,000 was on hand in Retro Production's warehouse. The physical inventory correctly accounted for goods in transit and there were no goods on consignment.
5. Recorded an additional $112,000 of income tax payable.

Instructions
(a) Record the December transactions. The company uses the FIFO cost formula.
(b) Set up T accounts, enter any opening balances, and post the general journal entries prepared in part (a).
(c) Prepare an unadjusted trial balance at December 31.
(d) Record and post the December adjusting entries, assuming adjusting entries are made monthly except for depreciation.
(e) Prepare an adjusted trial balance at December 31.
(f) Prepare (1) a multiple-step income statement, (2) a statement of changes in equity, and (3) a statement of financial position for the year ended December 31.
(g) Record and post the closing journal entries.
(h) Prepare a post-closing trial balance as at December 31.

EXPAND YOUR CRITICAL THINKING

CT6–1 Financial Reporting Case

The financial statements of **The North West Company Inc.** the are presented in Appendix A at the end of this book.

Instructions

(a) What amounts did North West report for total inventories in its balance sheet at the end of 2016 and 2015?

(b) Calculate the change in the dollar amount of total inventories between 2016 and 2015 and the percentage change. Next, calculate inventory as a percentage of current assets for each of the two years. Comment on the results.

(c) North West uses the average cost formula to determine the cost of inventory in its warehouse and first-in, first-out for determining the cost of its food inventories. What do you think influenced North West's decision to select these cost formulas for each type of inventory?

(d) Refer to Note 6, Inventories in the financial statements. Did North West write down its inventories to net realizable value in either 2016 or 2015? If so, reproduce the journal entry for the most recent year that North West likely made.

CT6–2 Financial Analysis Case

The financial statements of **The North West Company Inc.** are presented in Appendix A, and those of **Sobeys Inc.** are presented in Appendix B.

Instructions

(a) Calculate the current ratio for each company for 2015.

(b) Calculate the inventory turnover and days in inventory ratios for each company for 2015.

(c) The 2015 industry average for the current ratio was 1.4:1, the inventory turnover was 7.7 times, and the days in inventory was 47 days. What conclusions about each company's liquidity in 2015 can you draw based on your results in parts (a) and (b) and the industry averages?

CT6–3 Financial Analysis Case

Gibson Lumber Limited is a small sawmill operation, servicing Atlantic Canada. It is a privately traded company, using ASPE. Gibson does not have a sophisticated costing system for its inventory. It estimates the cost of its inventory using the periodic average cost formula and performs a physical count at year end. The physical count is also performed using estimation techniques, such as measuring the piles of finished lumber and scaling the log piles.

Global Lumber Inc., an international lumber company, is a publicly traded company using IFRS that has just expanded into Atlantic Canada. It has a sophisticated inventory system including bar codes on each piece of lumber produced, along with detailed records of production costs. It uses the FIFO cost formula under a perpetual inventory system.

Lumber prices are controlled by a commodity market and have been increasing slightly over the past year.

Instructions

(a) Are there any specific differences related to the use of the two different accounting standards—ASPE and IFRS—that financial analysts should consider when evaluating the management of inventory by Gibson and Global?

(b) Would the use of the two different inventory systems—periodic and perpetual—affect the comparison of the financial statements of each company? If so, explain how.

(c) Would the use of the two different cost formulas—average cost and FIFO—affect the comparison of the financial statements of each company? If so, explain how.

CT6–4 Professional Judgement Case

On December 1, 2015, Athabasca Building Supplies Ltd. (ABS) purchased Dunbar Doors Inc. (DDI) from Kevin Osepchuk. This is the first time that ABS has operated in the door business and the company welcomed the opportunity to sell doors to existing customers. When DDI was acquired, ABS also agreed to take over a DDI loan with the Royal Dominion Bank. The loan has a limit equal to 80% of the inventory account balance at year end pertaining to doors. The loan has been held with that bank for a number of years and is currently at $200,000. The bank requires verification of the inventory balance at the end of every year. As part of the deal to acquire DDI, Kevin agreed to serve as the new manager of ABS's Door Division and to receive a bonus equal to 10% of the operating income of that division.

You are a student who is helping ABS prepare its year-end financial statements. At the inventory count on December 31, you noticed that the employees counting the inventory at that time found that there were 800 doors on hand. ABS uses the perpetual average cost formula.

In looking at the company's inventory records, you discover that 2,600 doors were purchased from DDI on December 1 at a cost of $310 each. Later in the month, 800 doors were purchased from a U.S. supplier at CAD$240 each and shortly after, 600 doors were purchased from China at CAD$190 each. Finally, on the last day of the year, 100 more doors were purchased at CAD$200 but these were in transit on December 31 with terms FOB destination. The only sale for the month occurred when 3,200 doors were sold at $400 each to a contractor developing the largest condominium project in the area. All sales occurred after the purchase of the doors from China. Kevin supervised the count and determined the cost of the ending inventory. He calculated the ending inventory to be 900 doors at $310 each. He added 100 doors to the amount counted because of the doors in transit. Kevin earned a bonus of $16,700 in December.

Instructions

(a) Determine the cost of goods available for sale in December.

(b) Determine the cost of ending inventory at December 31.

(c) Based on the above, should there be an adjustment to Kevin's bonus?

(d) Does this adjustment have any other implications?

(e) What do you think about Kevin's actions?

(f) Assume that the decrease in the cost of doors from China is indicative of future trends in the industry and that the cost savings will be passed along to customers through price reductions that will decrease the selling price of a door to $240. Will that have any impact on the December financial statements?

CT6–5 Ethics Case

You are provided with the following information for Swag Bags Ltd. Swag imports and wholesales one type of high-end Italian leather handbag—each bag is identical. Each shipment of bags purchased is carefully coded and marked with its purchase cost.

Mar.	1	Beginning inventory is 140 handbags at a cost of $500 per bag.
	3	Purchased 200 handbags at a cost of $540 each.
	5	Sold 170 handbags for $800 each.
	10	Purchased 340 handbags at a cost of $570 each.
	25	Sold 500 handbags for $850 each.

Instructions

(a) Assuming that Swag Bags uses the specific identification cost formula, do the following:

1. Show how Swag Bags could maximize its gross profit for the month by selecting which handbags to sell on March 5 and March 25.

2. Show how Swag Bags could minimize its gross profit for the month by selecting which handbags to sell on March 5 and March 25.

(b) Who are the stakeholders in this situation? Is there anything unethical in choosing which handbags to sell in a month?

(c) Assuming that Swag Bags uses a perpetual inventory system and the average cost formula, how much gross profit would Swag Bags report? (Round the average unit cost to the nearest cent—two decimal places.)

(d) Which cost formula—specific identification or average cost—should Swag Bags select? Explain.

CT6–6 Professional Judgement Case

This case can be assigned as a group activity. Additional instructions and material for this activity can be found on the Instructor Resource site and in WileyPLUS.

Suppose, after graduating, that you accept a job as a manager for a retail store that sells tablets and laptop computers, along with cases and bags for them. The inventory is purchased from other countries and is subject to currency fluctuation.

Instructions

(a) Identify some control measures that you think should be in place in your store to safeguard the inventory.

(b) Assume the store uses a perpetual inventory system. Do you think that taking a physical inventory count once a year is adequate? If not, how often do you think a physical inventory count should be taken? Identify any accounts that would be affected by an adjusting journal entry to update the inventory for any shortages or overages.

(c) Which cost formula would you recommend that the store use? Why? Would you recommend that the store use the same cost formula for all types of inventory the store carries? Why or why not?

CT6–7 Serial Case

(*Note:* This is a continuation of the serial case from Chapters 1 through 5. This case can be assigned as a group activity. Additional instructions and material for this activity can be found on the Instructor Resource site and in *WileyPLUS.*)

Zinski Supply Corp. has approached ABC to become a distributor of its time management software. The cost of the software is $550 and ABC would propose to sell the package for $995, including installation. ABC negotiates a discount of 2% after the first 20 software packages are purchased, and an additional 2% discount after the purchase of the next 20 software packages. Emily, Doug, and Bev believe that the time management software is top of the line and that many of their clients would be interested in purchasing this product.

Currently, all inventory at ABC is accounted for using the average cost formula in a perpetual inventory system. Emily remembers that there is another cost formula, FIFO, that can be used to determine the cost of inventory. Because this is a new type of inventory, she wonders if FIFO would make the accounting a little easier and better reflect ending inventory and cost of goods sold.

The following transactions occur between the months of July and October 2017:

July	4	Ten time management software packages are purchased on account and received from Zinski Supply for $5,500 ($550 each), FOB destination, terms n/30.
	14	Six packages are sold for $995, each paid in cash.
	25	Amount owing to Zinski Supply from the July 4 purchase is paid.
August	1	Ten more packages are purchased on account and received from Zinski Supply for $550 each, FOB destination, terms n/30.
	28	Nine packages are sold for a total of $8,955 ($995 each) cash.
	29	Amount owing to Zinski Supply from the August 1 purchase is paid.
September	4	Another 10 packages are purchased on account and received from Zinski Supply for $5,390 ($550 × 98% = $539 each), FOB destination, terms n/30.
	27	Eight packages are sold on account for a total of $7,960.
	29	Amount owing to Zinski Supply from the September 4 purchase is paid.

October   3   Another 20 packages are purchased on account and received from Zinski Supply for $10,672.20 (10 at $539 and 10 at $528.22 ($539 × 98%) each), FOB destination, terms n/30.

27   Seven more software packages are sold for $995, each paid in cash.

Instructions

(a) Prepare a perpetual inventory schedule, assuming use of the FIFO cost formula.

(b) Using the information you prepared in (a), prepare journal entries to record each transaction.

(c) Prepare a perpetual inventory schedule, assuming use of the average cost formula. Use unrounded numbers in your calculations but round to the nearest cent for presentation purposes in your answer.

(d) Using the information you prepared in (c), prepare journal entries to record each transaction.

(e) Calculate and compare the gross profit margin, assuming the use of the (1) FIFO, and (2) average cost formula.

(f) What guidelines should Emily consider when deciding which inventory cost formula to use?

▶ ANSWERS TO CHAPTER PRACTICE QUESTIONS

DO IT! 6-1
Rules of Ownership

Original count	$400,000
1. Consigned goods held at LaSalle for McQueen	(30,000)
2. Goods in transit (purchases FOB shipping point[a])	20,000
3. Goods in transit (purchases FOB destination[b])	–
4. Goods in transit (sales FOB destination[c])	24,000
Adjusted count	$414,000

[a]The title passed to LaSalle at the point of shipping for goods in transit purchased with the terms FOB shipping point. Therefore, these goods belong to LaSalle, even though they are still in transit.

[b]The title does not pass to LaSalle until the goods arrive at their destination for goods in transit purchased with the terms FOB destination. Therefore, these goods do not belong to LaSalle and should not be included in inventory.

[c]The title to these goods does not pass away from LaSalle until delivery for goods sold FOB destination. Therefore, these goods still belong to LaSalle.

DO IT! 6-2a
Specific Identification—
Perpetual System

Cost of Goods Sold:

			Cost
Feb.	3	Tractor 1	$ 54,000
	5	Tractor 4	95,000
	10	Tractor 3	126,000
	18	Tractor 6	140,000
	27	Tractor 8	132,000
			$547,000

Inventory:

	Cost
Tractor 2	$ 78,000
Tractor 5	86,000
Tractor 7	89,000
	$253,000

Check: Beginning inventory ($439,000) + Purchases ($140,000 + $89,000 + $132,000) = Cost of goods sold ($547,000) + Inventory ($253,000)

DO IT! 6-2b
FIFO and Average Cost—
Perpetual System

(a)   FIFO—Perpetual

Date	Purchases			Cost of Goods Sold			Balance		
	Units	Cost	Total	Units	Cost	Total	Units	Cost	Total
Mar. 1							4,000	$3	$12,000
10	6,000	$4	$24,000				4,000 6,000	3 4	} 36,000
19				4,000 4,000	$3 4	} $28,000	2,000	4	8,000
22	5,000	5	25,000				2,000 5,000	4 5	} 33,000
28				2,000 3,500	4 5	} 25,500	1,500	5	7,500
	11,000		$49,000	13,500		$53,500			

Check: $53,500 + $7,500 = $61,000 ($12,000 + $49,000)

(b) Average Cost—Perpetual

Date	Purchases Units	Cost	Total	Cost of Goods Sold Units	Cost	Total	Balance Units	Cost	Total
Mar. 1							4,000	$3.00	$12,000
10	6,000	$4	$24,000				10,000	3.60	36,000
19				8,000	$3.60	$28,800	2,000	3.60	7,200
22	5,000	5	25,000				7,000	4.60	32,200
28				5,500	4.60	25,300	1,500	4.60	6,900
	11,000		$49,000	13,500		$54,100			

Check: $54,100 + $6,900 = $61,000 ($12,000 + $49,000)

(a) (1) FIFO

DO IT! 6-3
Cost Formula Effects on
Income Statements

Date	Purchases Units	Cost	Total	Cost of Goods Sold Units	Cost	Total	Balance Units	Cost	Total
July 1							2	$75	$150
7	4	$80	$320				2	75	} 470
							4	80	
19				2	$75	} $390	1	80	80
				3	80				
25	6	100	600				1	80	} 680
							6	100	

Check: $390 + $680 = $1,070 ($150 + $320 + $600)

(a) (2) Average Cost

Date	Purchases Units	Cost	Total	Cost of Goods Sold Units	Cost	Total	Balance Units	Cost	Total
July 1							2	$75.00	$150.00
7	4	$ 80.00	$320.00				6	78.33	470.00
19				5	$78.33	$391.67	1	78.33	78.33
25	6	100.00	600.00				7	96.91	678.33

Check: $391.67 + $678.33 = $1,070 ($150 + $320 + $600)

(b)

UFIRST INC.
Condensed Income Statements

	FIFO	Average Cost
Sales (5 × $180)	$900	$900
Cost of goods sold	390	392
Gross profit	510	508
Operating expenses	300	300
Income before income tax	210	208
Income tax expense (25%)	52	52
Net income	$158	$156

DO IT! 6-4
Inventory Errors

(a) By counting inventory twice, an assumption will be made that inventory costing $40,000 (rather than $20,000) was on hand rather than sold. If not corrected, Inventory will be overstated and Cost of Goods Sold understated by $20,000. This, in turn, will result in Retained Earnings being overstated by $20,000 as well. The goods in transit should be included in Wang's inventory as they have already been shipped FOB shipping point. If not corrected, Inventory will be understated and liabilities (Accounts Payable) understated by $100,000. Because these goods in transit have not yet been sold, the failure to include them in the determination of ending inventory will have no impact on cost of goods sold or retained earnings.

The correct inventory balance at June 30, 2018 is $800,000 − $20,000 + $100,000 = $880,000.

(b) When inventory is counted twice, that error overstates the Inventory account balance and, as mentioned above, understates the Cost of Goods Sold account balance. By not recording the inventory in transit, the Inventory account is understated as is the Accounts Payable account balance.

The following table summarizes the effect of these errors on the statement of financial position using (U) for understated and (O) for overstated:

	Assets	=	Liabilities	+	Shareholders' equity
Count error	O $20,000	=	no effect	+	O $20,000
Purchase error	U $100,000	=	U $100,000	+	no effect

(c)

June 30	Cost of Goods Sold		20,000	
	Inventory			20,000
	(To correct for an overstatement in ending inventory arising from an error made when counting inventory)			
June 30	Inventory		100,000	
	Accounts Payable			100,000
	(To record merchandise purchased on June 29, FOB shipping point)			

(d) During the following year ended June 30, 2019, when an inventory count is performed, the count team will notice that the balance in the Inventory account is $20,000 higher than the amount on hand and will take steps to ensure that the error is corrected at that time. Also during the year ended June 30, 2019, when the invoice for the goods in transit is received from Laughlin Inc., the inventory purchase will be recorded and the Inventory and Accounts Payable accounts adjusted for the effect of this purchase. Therefore, the two journal entries recorded in part (c) above would eventually be recorded but in the wrong year, in essence reversing the effect of the error but in the subsequent year.

DO IT! 6-5a
Lower of Cost and Net Realizable Value

(a)

	Cost	NRV	LCNRV
Wood	$250,000	$280,000	$250,000
Gas	84,000	79,000	79,000
Pellet	112,000	101,000	101,000
Total inventory	$446,000	$460,000	$430,000

E-Efficiency should report its inventory at the lower of cost and net realizable value of $430,000.

(b)

Mar. 31	Cost of Goods Sold ($446,000 − $430,000)		16,000	
	Inventory			16,000
	(To record decline in inventory value from original cost of $446,000 to net realizable value of $430,000)			

DO IT! 6-5b
Inventory Turnover

(a)

	2018		2017	
Inventory turnover	$\dfrac{\$1,784,200}{(\$439,000 + \$405,500) \div 2} = 4.2$ times		$\dfrac{\$1,719,500}{(\$466,000 + \$439,000) \div 2} = 3.8$ times	
Days in inventory	$\dfrac{365 \text{ days}}{4.2 \text{ times}} = 87$ days		$\dfrac{365 \text{ days}}{3.8 \text{ times}} = 96$ days	

(b) Webber Ltd. has improved its inventory turnover in 2018 because it increased its turnover from 3.8 times to 4.2 times. This means that its days in inventory decreased from 96 days to 87 days, which is an improvement of 9 days. This indicates that, in 2018, the company's inventory was on hand for a little more than one week less than it was in 2017.

DO IT! 6-6
FIFO and Average Cost—Periodic System

(a) Total units available for sale = 5,000 + 8,000 + 7,000 = 20,000
Cost of goods available for sale = (5,000 × $3) + (8,000 × $4) + (7,000 × $5.50) = $85,500
Number of units sold = 11,000 + 6,000 = 17,000
Number of units in ending inventory = 5,000 + 8,000 − 11,000 + 7,000 − 6,000 = 3,000

(b) (1) FIFO

Ending inventory	Units	Unit Cost	Total Cost
Apr. 22	3,000	$5.50	$16,500

Cost of goods sold: $85,500 − $16,500 = $69,000

Proof of cost of goods sold:

	Units	Unit Cost	Total Cost
Apr. 1	5,000	$3.00	$15,000
12	8,000	4.00	32,000
22	4,000	5.50	22,000
	17,000		$69,000

Check: $69,000 + $16,500 = $85,500

(2) Average Cost

(Note that we have used unrounded numbers in the following calculations but rounded to the nearest cent for presentation purposes.)

Weighted average unit cost: $85,500 ÷ 20,000 = $4.28   Proof of cost of goods sold: 17,000 × $4.28 = $72,675
Ending inventory: 3,000 × $4.28 = $12,825   Check: $72,675 + $12,825 = $85,500
Cost of goods sold: $85,500 − $12,825 = $72,675

▶ PRACTICE USING THE DECISION TOOLKIT

(a) If Under Armour used the average cost formula rather than FIFO during a period of rising prices, its cost of goods sold would be higher and its inventory lower than currently reported.

(b) (in U.S. $ thousands)

1.

	2015	2014
Inventory turnover	$\dfrac{\$2,057,766}{(\$536,714 + \$783,031) \div 2} = 3.1$ times	$\dfrac{\$1,572,164}{(\$536,714 + \$469,006) \div 2} = 3.1$ times
Days in inventory	$\dfrac{365 \text{ days}}{3.1 \text{ times}} = 118$ days	$\dfrac{365 \text{ days}}{3.1 \text{ times}} = 118$ days

2.

	2015	2014
Current ratio	$1,498,763 ÷ $478,810 = 3.1:1	$1,549,339 ÷ $421,627 = 3.7:1

3. Under Armour's inventory turnover remained constant between 2015 and 2014. Consequently, the number of days in inventory was unchanged. The company's inventory turnover, however, is lower than the industry average and this is why its days in inventory is 24 days more than the average. This may be due to the fact that Under Armour sells most of its inventory to retailers rather than directly to consumers and has to have higher levels of inventory on hand as a result. Under Amour's current ratio was consistent with the industry average in 2014. It declined in 2015, meaning that the company was less liquid. This was consistent with a decline in the industry, with Under Armour's being slightly higher.

▶ PRACTICE COMPREHENSIVE DO IT!

(a) (1) FIFO

	Purchases			Cost of Goods Sold			Balance		
Date	Units	Cost	Total	Units	Cost	Total	Units	Cost	Total
Mar. 1							200	$4.30	$ 860
10	500	$4.50	$2,250				200	4.30	} 3,110
							500	4.50	
15				200	$4.30	} $2,210	200	4.50	900
				300	4.50				
20	400	4.75	1,900				200	4.50	} 2,800
							400	4.75	
25				200	4.50	} 1,850	200	4.75	950
				200	4.75				
30	300	5.00	1,500				200	4.75	} 2,450
							300	5.00	
	1,200		$5,650	900		$4,060			

Check: $4,060 + $2,450 = $6,510 ($860 + $5,650)

(2) Average Cost

	Purchases			Cost of Goods Sold			Balance		
Date	Units	Cost	Total	Units	Cost	Total	Units	Cost	Total
Mar. 1							200	$4.30	$ 860.00
10	500	$4.50	$2,250.00				700	4.44	3,110.00
15				500	$4.44	$2,221.43	200	4.44	888.57
20	400	4.75	1,900.00				600	4.65	2,788.57
25				400	4.65	1,859.05	200	4.65	929.52
30	300	5.00	1,500.00				500	4.86	2,429.52
	1,200		$5,650.00	900		$4,080.48			

Check: $4,080.48 + $2,429.52 = $6,510 ($860 + $5,650)

(b)   By incorrectly recording goods in transit as a purchase for which title has not yet transferred, the accounts Inventory and Accounts Payable are overstated. The following table illustrates the effect of the error on the statement of financial position:

Assets	=	Liabilities	+	Shareholders' Equity
Overstated	=	Overstated	+	No effect

(c)   Under FIFO, ending inventory should be $950 (200 × $4.75) rather than $2,450.

Under average cost, ending inventory should be $929.52 (200 × $4.65) rather than $2,429.52.

▶ PRACTICE OBJECTIVE-FORMAT QUESTIONS

1.   (c), (d), and (g) are correct.

Feedback
(a)   is incorrect because this calculation excludes the goods costing $24,000 that are on consignment but belong to Palermo.
(b)   is incorrect because the goods on consignment still belong to Palermo as consignor and should be included in the company's inventory count.
(c)   is correct because the goods were sold with terms FOB destination. Until they arrive at the customer's place of business, they belong to the seller. Because the goods had not been delivered at December 31, they should be included in Palermo's inventory at that date.
(d)   is correct; $180,000 = $120,000 + $24,000 + $10,000 + $26,000.
(e)   is incorrect because it includes goods costing $18,000 that were purchased with terms FOB destination, but that had not been received by December 31.
(f)   is incorrect because these goods were sold with terms FOB destination. They belong to Palermo and should be included in inventory until they are delivered.
(g)   is correct.

2.   (c), (d), (e), and (g) are correct.

Feedback
(a)   is incorrect because this number is based on a simple average [($9 + $10 + $11) ÷ 3 = $10], not a weighted average.
(b)   is incorrect because this is based on a periodic inventory system, rather than a perpetual system; ($90,000 + $120,000 + $77,000) ÷ (10,000 + 12,000 + 7,000) = $9.90.
(c)   is correct; 10,000 + 12,000 + 7,000 − 20,000 = 9,000.
(d)   is correct; [($90,000 + $120,000) ÷ 22,000] = $9.55 × 20,000 = cost of goods sold $190,909. $90,000 + $120,000 − $190,909 + $77,000 = ending inventory $96,091.
(e)   is correct; $96,091 [see (d)] ÷ 9,000 = $10.68.
(f)   is incorrect because this is based on a periodic inventory system, rather than a perpetual system; (20,000 × $9.90 [see (b)] = $198,000).
(g)   is correct; $90,000 + $120,000 + $77,000 = $287,000.

3.   (b) and (f) are correct.

Feedback
(a)   is incorrect because this does not include opening inventory.
(b)   is correct; ($144,000 + $312,000 + $392,000) ÷ (6,000 + 12,000 + 14,000) = $26.50 × 13,000 = $344,500. ($144,000 + $312,000 + $392,000 − $344,500 + $240,000) ÷ (6,000 + 12,000 + 14,000 − 13,000 + 8,000) = $27.54 ($27.537037037 unrounded).
(c)   is incorrect because this is based on a periodic inventory system rather than a perpetual system. The correct answer is: $27.537037037 [see (b) above] × 18,000 = $495,667. $144,000 + $312,000 + $392,000 − $344,500 + $240,000 − $495,667 = ending inventory $247,833.
(d)   is incorrect; $344,500 [see (b) above] + $495,720 ($27.54 [see (b) above] × 18,000) = cost of goods sold $840,220.
(e)   is incorrect because this is based on a periodic inventory system rather than a perpetual system. The correct answer is $27.54 [see (b) above].
(f)   is correct 9,000 × $27.54 [see (b) above] = $247,860.
(g)   is incorrect because this is based on a simple average rather than a weighted average.

4.

Feedback
(a)	FIFO	(e)	FIFO
(b)	average cost	(f)	average cost
(c)	specific identification	(g)	specific identification
(d)	specific identification		

5.

Feedback
(a)	FIFO	(e)	FIFO
(b)	FIFO	(f)	FIFO
(c)	average cost	(g)	FIFO
(d)	FIFO		

6.

Feedback
(a)	overstated	(e)	unaffected
(b)	unaffected	(f)	unaffected
(c)	overstated	(g)	overstated
(d)	overstated		

7.

Feedback
(a)	unaffected	(e)	understated
(b)	understated	(f)	unaffected
(c)	overstated	(g)	understated
(d)	understated		

8. (b), (c), (d), (e), and (g) are correct.

Feedback
(a) is incorrect because the choice of cost formula will affect the cost assigned to ending inventory.
(f) is incorrect because Inventory should be credited, not debited, because the account must be decreased.

9. (b), (d), and (e) are correct.

Feedback
(a) is incorrect. While Nire's inventory turnover ratio of 7.5 times was better than Piks's ratio of 6.5 times, its actual ratio was 7.5 and not 7.0 (which is the result if inventory is not averaged in the denominator).
(b) is correct. In 2017, the days in inventory was 73 versus 56 in 2018.
(c) is incorrect. Nire's ratio was better because its inventory turnover ratio was 7.5, which is higher than Piks's ratio of 6.5.
(d) is correct because both Nire improved (7.5 vs. 7.0) and Piks improved (6.5 vs. 5.0).
(e) is correct. Piks' improved from 73 days in 2017 to 56 days in 2018 (an improvement of 17 days). Nire's improved from 52 days in 2017 to 49 days in 2018 (an improvement of 3 days).
(f) is incorrect because this calculation did not use average inventory. Piks's inventory turnover was 5 in 2017 and its days in inventory ratio was 73 days.
(g) is incorrect. While the numbers are correct, this indicates an improvement rather than a worsening of inventory turnover.

*10. (a), (d), (e), and (g) are correct.

Feedback
(a) is correct; (800 units × $2.50) + (1,500 units × $3.00) = $6,500.
(b) is incorrect because it excludes beginning inventory. Cost of goods available for sale is $2,000 + $6,000 + $4,760 + $3,040 = $15,800.
(c) is incorrect. The weighted average price per unit is incorrectly calculated because it excludes the units in beginning inventory. Ending inventory $15,800 [see (b) above] ÷ (800 + 2,000 + 1,400 + 800) = $3.16 × 2,700 = $8,532.
(d) is correct; $15,800 ÷ 5,000 units = $3.16 [see (c) above].
(e) is correct [see (b) above].
(f) is incorrect because the calculation uses a simple average in determining cost rather than a weighted average. Cost of goods sold is (1,100 + 1,200) × $3.16 = $7,268.
(g) is correct; (500 units × $3.00) + (1,400 units × $3.40) + (800 units × $3.80) = $9,300.

▶ ENDNOTES

[1] Mallory Schlossberg, "Lululemon Is 'The Better House on a Bad Block' and That Has Investors Overlooking Its Problems," *Business Insider*, June 12, 2016; Hollie Shaw, "Does Lululemon Athletica Inc Have a Problem with Extra Inventory?", *Financial Post*, September 11, 2015; "Lululemon: Shares Tumble over Leadership Void and Inventory Problems," *Canadian Business*, June 11, 2013; Shelley DuBois, "Lululemon: The Downside of Selling Hot Pants," CNNMoney.com, March 22, 2013; The Canadian Press, "Lululemon Recalls Pants for Being See-Through," CBC.ca, March 19, 2013; Marina Strauss, "Lululemon's Problem? Customers Can't Get Enough," *The Globe and Mail*, March 17, 2011; lululemon athletica inc. 2015 Annual Report; lululemon corporate website, www.lululemon.com.

[2] John Daly, "A Man and His Merchandise," *Globe and Mail Report on Business*, April 2012, pp. 25–30; James Cowan, "Retail: The Genius of Dollarama," *Canadian Business*, April 7, 2011; Dollarama 2012 annual report.

[3] "Saputo Inc.: Financial Results for the Fiscal Year Ended March 31, 2016," Saputo news release, June 2, 2016; "Saputo Profit Falls on Inventory Writedown, Tough Markets," Reuters.com, July 31, 2012; Saputo corporate website, www.saputo.com.

7

Internal Control and Cash

CHAPTER PREVIEW

Cash is the lifeblood of any company and it must be managed carefully and safeguarded. Even companies that are successful in every other way can go bankrupt if they fail to manage their cash. In this chapter, we explain the essential features of an internal control system and describe how these controls apply to cash receipts and cash payments. We then explain how cash is reported in the financial statements, and describe ways to manage and monitor cash.

CHAPTER OUTLINE

LEARNING OBJECTIVES	READ	PRACTICE
1 Explain the components of an internal control system, including its control activities and limitations.	• Control activities • Limitations of internal control	**DO IT!** 7-1 Control activities
2 Apply the key control activities to cash receipts and payments.	• Control activities over cash receipts • Control activities over cash payments	**DO IT!** 7-2a Control activities over cash receipts 7-2b Control activities over cash payments
3 Prepare a bank reconciliation.	• Bank statements • Reconciling the bank account	**DO IT!** 7-3a Cash balance per company's books and errors 7-3b Bank reconciliation
4 Explain the reporting and management of cash.	• Reporting cash • Managing cash	**DO IT!** 7-4 Presentation of cash

Go to the ***REVIEW AND PRACTICE*** section at the end of the chapter for a targeted summary and practice questions with solutions.

Visit **WileyPLUS** for more opportunities.

FEATURE STORY

Controlling Cash at Nick's

Nick Petros, the founder of Nick's Steakhouse and Pizza in Calgary, came to Canada from Greece at age 17 with no money and speaking no English. For 25 years, he worked his way up in the restaurant industry, as a dishwasher, busboy, waiter, maître d', and then manager. In 1979, armed with a collection of his mother's homemade recipes, he opened his own restaurant. Nick's youngest child, Mark, and his wife, Michelle, took over the business in 2000, but Nick is still a welcome presence in the restaurant, greeting customers old and new.

Located across the street from McMahon Stadium, home to the CFL's Calgary Stampeders, Nick's has become a Calgary family tradition. The restaurant has more than 70 full- and part-time employees including servers, bartenders, and delivery drivers. On a busy Friday or Saturday evening, around a dozen servers and bartenders serve as many as 1,200 people in the 7,000-square-foot (650-square-metre) restaurant and bar, with more guests on the patios in the summer. Mark Petros says his point-of-sale (POS) system helps him keep track of the orders, inventory, and money.

After taking a table's order, servers enter the items into one of several computer terminals throughout the restaurant. The computer is preprogrammed with the price of each item and the server simply presses a labelled button, for example, "Caesar salad" or "lasagna," to enter an order. The POS system sends the order information to the bar, salad station, or line cooks and uses the information to track inventory. The servers collect payment from their tables. At the end of a shift, the POS system provides an employee report that itemizes the credit card, debit card, and cash sales that the server owes.

The bartenders and servers have a cash float of $400. The hosting staff also has a float to use for pickup orders and in case the servers need change for large bills. Mr. Petros explains, "When an employee with a float starts the shift, he or she makes sure that the cash on hand is equal to the float plus any orders taken so far that day. At the end of their shift, the same calculation is done to see if it balances out. If it does not balance, the employee is responsible for the missing money."

Similarly, before the bartenders start their shift, they have to count the beer in the fridges and note the levels in partially full bottles of alcohol. Everything must correspond to the POS system. For example, if three beers are missing from the fridge, three beers should have been entered in the system. If they weren't, the bartender is responsible.

"There's never a discrepancy," says Mr. Petros. If there ever is one, he adds, it's easy to find the problem, usually an error in pushing a button or entering information.

While cash is an obvious concern for internal control, Mr. Petros estimates that, at most, 10% of sales are paid for in cash, with the majority of customers paying by credit or debit card. Mr. Petros makes a cash deposit at the bank every day.

While there are fewer cash transactions than in the past, cash control remains crucial to a business like Nick's Steakhouse and Pizza. Fortunately, with an internal control system in place and the help of the latest technology, cash can be controlled reliably.[1]

Explain the components of an internal control system, including its control activities and limitations.

You were first introduced to the need for internal control in Chapter 6. As mentioned in that chapter, **internal control** consists of the systems within a company that help it achieve reliable financial reporting, operate effectively and efficiently, and comply with relevant laws and regulations. Internal controls can be preventive (which stop something the board of directors or management does not want to happen from occurring) or detective (which indicate when something that the board or management did not want to happen has occurred).

Good internal control systems have the following five primary components:

1. **Control environment:** It is the responsibility of the board of directors and management to make it clear that the organization values integrity, and that unethical activity will not be tolerated. (When the actions of a company's board and management demonstrate a commitment to integrity and ethical behaviour, it is often referred to as "setting the tone at the top.") An appropriate control environment is critical for internal controls to be effective.
2. **Risk assessment:** Management must identify and analyze the various factors that create risk for the business and determine how to best mitigate and manage these risks.
3. **Control activities:** To reduce the occurrence of unintentional and intentional errors, management must design policies and procedures to address the specific risks faced by the company.
4. **Information and communication:** The internal control system must capture and communicate all pertinent information to the appropriate internal and external users.
5. **Monitoring activities:** Internal control systems must be monitored periodically for their adequacy. To be effective, significant deficiencies must be communicated to management and the board of directors so they can be addressed.

CONTROL ACTIVITIES

Each of the five components of an internal control system is important. Here, we will focus on one component, the control activities. The reason? These activities form the backbone of a company's efforts to address the risks it faces. The specific control activities that are used by a company will vary depending on management's assessment of these risks. This assessment is also heavily influenced by the size and nature of the company.

We will review five control activities that apply to most companies, which are as follows:

1. Assignment of responsibility
2. Segregation of duties
3. Documentation
4. Physical controls
5. Review and reconciliation

Each of these control activities is explained in the following sections.

Assignment of Responsibility

An essential characteristic of internal control is the assignment of responsibility to specific employees. Responsibility may be assigned by employee level as well. For example, only managers may be authorized to perform certain tasks such as approving discounts or authorizing refunds. This control activity is most effective when only one employee (or level of employee) is authorized to perform a specific task and requires management to determine the activities that each employee (or manager) is responsible for. **This internal control enables responsibility to be assigned to specific employees, making them accountable for carrying it out appropriately.**

To illustrate, assume that a grocery store's system states that each cashier is assigned a separate cash drawer and they are the only employee authorized to access it. If the cash in the cash drawer at the end of the day is $100 less than the cash rung up on the cash register, it would be clear who is responsible for the error. If two or more individuals have used the same cash drawer, it may be impossible to determine who is responsible for the error.

In addition, it is important that an individual with the proper level of authority or an appropriate department develop the internal control system and related policies. For example, the vice-president of finance, not the vice-president of sales, should be responsible for establishing policies for credit sales because the vice-president of sales may be motivated to maximize sales—even to customers with poor credit ratings—in order to meet sales targets. A strong internal control system for credit sales should also require written credit approval for sales transactions above a certain value or to new customers. For example, sales on account for more than $5,000 would require written credit approval.

MISSING IN ACTION

Sundown Mattress Ltd. operates a medium-sized wholesaling business. The company has four employees who work in the company's purchasing department, each of whom is responsible for ordering goods from the company's suppliers. When goods are ordered, there is no indication which of the employees ordered them. When a shipment of mattresses arrived at Sundown's warehouse, it was discovered that the inventory was not needed and the employee who ordered the goods could not be identified. The company was forced to significantly discount the mattresses to sell them quickly because it had no room to store them in its warehouse. Management was unable to determine which employee had placed this order.

THE MISSING CONTROL
Assignment of Responsibility
The employees in the purchasing department should be required to note their name or employee number on each purchase order so that they can be held responsible for any concerns related to it in terms of order size, pricing, vendor selection, and terms.

Missing in Action boxes are introduced in this chapter to illustrate how a missing control activity can result in errors or misstatements.

Segregation of Duties

Segregation of duties is essential in a system of internal control. No one employee should be responsible for authorizing transactions, recording them, and having custody of the related assets. The responsibility for these activities should be segregated; that is, assigned to different individuals. **When the same individual is responsible for authorization, recording, and asset custody, the potential for unintentional and intentional errors increases.** Intentional errors to misappropriate (steal) assets or misstate financial information are commonly known as **fraud**.

As an example, consider what could happen if all purchasing activities—placing the orders, recording the transactions, and approving the payments—were carried out by one individual. That person could receive a bribe (a kickback) to buy merchandise at an inflated price from a dishonest supplier. The employee could record the transaction and approve payment without ever being discovered. The employee could also prepare fictitious invoices from a company they established, record them, approve them for payment, and when paid, receive the payment and deposit the money in bank accounts they control. If the employee had access to the merchandise, they could approve the purchase of merchandise and then steal it. When the responsibilities for approving orders and payments, receiving, and recording are assigned to different individuals, the risk of such abuses is much lower. Segregation of duties also reduces the risk of unintentional errors such as incorrectly recording the number of items received or the discount taken on the purchase of inventory because more than one person is involved in the process.

Just as purchase activities must be segregated, the same is true for sales-related activities such as approving credit for customers, shipping goods, and preparing and recording invoices. For example, a salesperson could make sales at unauthorized prices to increase sales commissions, a shipping clerk could ship goods to himself or herself, or a billing clerk could understate the amount billed for sales made to friends and relatives. These abuses are less likely to occur when the sales tasks are segregated: salespersons make the sale only after another employee checks the customer's credit, shipping department employees ship the goods based on the sales order, and billing department employees prepare the sales invoice after comparing the sales order with the report of goods shipped.

In small businesses, where the small number of employees makes it more challenging to segregate duties, it is important that the owner be actively involved in the business. They can then provide the oversight needed to ensure that the internal controls are working as intended. For example, Mark Petros of Nick's makes a daily bank deposit, which minimizes the opportunity for employees to misappropriate cash. He, or his delegate, should also review the bank reconciliation on a monthly basis and compare it with the daily sales reports. We will discuss the importance of bank reconciliations as a key control activity later in this chapter.

Understanding the difference between the assignment of responsibility and segregation of duties control activities can be a challenge. One way to make the distinction is to remember that assignment of responsibility means that specific employees can be held accountable for their actions. For example, if two or more employees are doing the same job, then the internal control system should include measures that enable the company to distinguish the actions of each employee. Assigning unique employee numbers that must be used when recording transactions would be an effective means of assigning responsibility. Segregation of duties involves the types of duties that should be spread across multiple employees. It involves the company ensuring that no single employee has the ability to authorize, record, and take custody of an asset. The two control activities work in combination. For example, multiple purchasing clerks could be assigned the responsibility to authorize purchases, each using their unique employee number (assignment of responsibility), while none of the clerks will have custody of the assets being purchased (segregation of duties).

MISSING IN ACTION

Tim Chan is the operations manager at a distribution centre for a sports equipment business. The company recently implemented a perpetual inventory system that provided management with the amount of inventory that should always be on hand. Tim was assigned to count the inventory once a month and compare the count with the perpetual inventory records to identify damaged and obsolete items. Tim found counting to be time-consuming so he asked one of the distribution clerks in the warehouse to do the count and send him a report. Tim reviewed the report and signed off the count adjustments based on the information provided by the clerk. The clerk appeared to be doing a good job so Tim never followed up or counted the inventory. However, when the external auditors performed the year-end count, they found that the perpetual inventory records for composite hockey sticks and professional sports team jerseys were higher than the physical inventory count, meaning that inventory was missing.

THE MISSING CONTROL
Segregation of Duties
The distribution clerk, who had access to the physical inventory, should not be responsible for the monthly counts because they can steal inventory and overstate the count results. Tim was asked to perform the inventory counts because he didn't work in the warehouse or the purchasing department.

Documentation

Documents provide evidence that transactions and events have occurred at specified times and at specified amounts. At Nick's, the point-of-sale system and employee reports provide documentation for the sale and the amount of cash received. Companies use shipping documents to indicate that goods have been shipped to customers and sales invoices to indicate that customers have been billed for the goods. If a signature (or initials) is added to a document, it also becomes possible to identify the individual responsible for the transaction or event, which links two control activities: documentation and assignment of responsibility.

Documentation (such as invoices and cheques) should be sequentially prenumbered. The prenumbering can be done either electronically (with electronically generated documents) or manually. Prenumbering helps prevent a transaction from being recorded more than once or, conversely, from not being recorded at all (because gaps in the sequential numbering can be determined and followed up).

Documentation can also be used as an internal control if companies require that any **original documents** (source documents) necessary for preparing accounting entries be promptly forwarded to the accounting department. This helps ensure timely and accurate recording of transactions. Photocopies should not be used to record transactions because this increases the risk of duplicate entries and payments.

MISSING IN ACTION

Sofas and More Ltd. operates a chain of furniture stores in Eastern Canada. All of the products sold by the company are ordered from overseas manufacturers and are received at the company's warehouse in Halifax, Nova Scotia, before being transferred to the company's various retail locations. Supplier invoices are used to record and update the company's inventory records. When these goods are received at the company's warehouse, the receiving employees do not complete any paperwork indicating the type, quantity, or condition of the goods received. The company has experienced product shortages when its inventory records indicate an item is in stock, but no such item can be found in its stores or warehouse. Management is uncertain whether goods are being stolen from its stores or warehouse or whether suppliers are billing the company for goods that were never received.

THE MISSING CONTROL
Documentation
The company should ensure that the employees receiving goods at the warehouse complete receiving reports, indicating the type, quantity, and condition of the goods. The receiving reports should be prenumbered. Completed reports should be sent to the accounting department, where they can be used to enter the goods received into the inventory system and can be compared with supplier invoices to ensure that the company does not pay for inventory it did not receive.

A good internal control system can require the use of two or more of the specific control activities in a particular situation. For example, documentation is the missing control activity in the above Missing in Action box. In addition, the employee completing the receiving report should sign it so they can be contacted about any issues related to it (which is the assignment of responsibility control activity). Changes to the company's inventory records are made by employees in the accounting department, not by warehouse staff, because this separates the recording and asset custody functions (which is the segregation of duties control activity). Comparing the receiving reports with the invoices received from suppliers prior to payment will ensure that the company is paying only for goods that it has received. This is an example of another control activity, review and reconciliation, which we will discuss later. The scenarios described in this, and other, Missing in Action boxes in this chapter focus on the main control activity that is missing.

Physical Controls

Physical controls can be used to safeguard assets and enhance the reliability of accounting records. Physical controls include the controls shown in Illustration 7-1.

► Illustration 7-1
Physical controls

Safes, vaults, and safety deposit boxes for cash and business papers

Locked warehouses and storage cabinets for inventories and records

Computer facilities that require a password, fingerprint, or eyeball scan

Alarms to prevent break-ins

Security cameras and garment sensors to deter theft

Time-tracking system for recording time worked

In addition to the physical controls shown above, a company should ensure that assets are adequately insured. Insuring assets is another form of safeguarding them—in this case, from risks related to theft or damage from fire or floods.

MISSING IN ACTION

Monique and Chantal are roommates who both work at a local bar. Sometimes they work the same shift. When employees begin their shift, they are supposed to swipe their employee cards at a time clock to register the time they arrived at work. Employees must do the same when they leave at the end of their shift. Quite often, Monique will arrive at the bar late. If Chantal knows that Monique will be late, she will swipe Monique's card along with her own card. Sometimes, Chantal leaves the bar early because she has another part-time job. Rather than swiping her card when she leaves early, Chantal asks Monique to swipe her card for her later in the evening. They have been swiping each other's cards for more than eight months.

THE MISSING CONTROL
Physical Controls
Time-tracking systems, such as the clock in this case, should be placed where they can be easily observed to prevent employees from committing payroll fraud by "punching in or out" with someone else's time card. Without this control, employers may end up paying wages for time that employees were not entitled to as they were not at work.

Review and Reconciliation

The four control activities that we just discussed—assignment of responsibility, segregation of duties, documentation, and physical controls—should be subject to review. This is most effective when the review is performed by someone who is not involved in the control activity being reviewed. This is an independent review and can be conducted by another employee (internal review) or by someone outside the company (external review). Reviews are necessary because employees can forget or intentionally fail to follow internal control activities, or they might become careless if there is no one to observe and evaluate their performance. Reconciliations are a key part of this control activity and involve comparisons between two or more documents, like comparing the receiving report with the sales invoices, as was discussed previously. Later in this chapter, we will learn about bank reconciliations, which are a key internal control related to cash.

INTERNAL REVIEWS   Internal reviews, which are conducted by employees or managers, are especially useful in comparing accounting records with existing assets to ensure that nothing has been stolen. The beer count at the beginning of each shift by the bartender in the feature story about Nick's Steakhouse and Pizza is an example.

For internal reviews to be beneficial, three measures are recommended:

1. The review should be performed regularly, with occasional reviews conducted on a surprise basis.
2. The employee performing the review should be independent of the personnel responsible for the information.
3. Discrepancies and exceptions should be reported to a management-level employee who can take appropriate corrective action.

Many large companies employ internal auditors. **Internal auditors** are company employees whose responsibilities include evaluating the effectiveness of the company's system of internal control. They periodically review the activities of departments and individuals to determine whether prescribed internal controls are being followed.

If a company is a public company (it lists its shares on a public stock exchange), a management report addressed to shareholders is included in the annual report that explains that management is responsible for the system of internal controls. The Chief Executive Officer (CEO) and Chief Financial Officer (CFO) must also provide certifications regarding the effectiveness of internal controls. Any identified control weaknesses of significance must be reported in the Management Discussion and Analysis (MD&A) section of the annual report.

EXTERNAL REVIEWS   It is useful to contrast *internal* reviews with *external* reviews. **External auditors** perform an important type of external review. They, in contrast to internal auditors, are independent of the company. They are professional accountants hired by a company to report on whether or not the company's financial statements fairly present its financial position and results of operations.

All public companies, including The North West Company, are required to have an external audit. A copy of North West's auditors' report is included in Appendix A. As you will see in the report, external auditors plan and perform an audit to obtain reasonable assurance that the financial statements do not have any material misstatements. In planning their audit, the external auditor will obtain an understanding of the company's internal control system related to financial reporting. Any deficiencies noted will be brought to the attention of management and the board.

In addition, as part of the company's governance processes, the independent audit committee of the board of directors is responsible for reviewing the company's internal control systems to ensure that they are adequate to result in fair, complete, and accurate financial reporting.

MISSING IN ACTION

Kevin Lin works in the IT department at Twillingate Inc. The company provides a laptop to all salespeople when they join the company. The laptop must be returned to the IT department when a salesperson leaves. Kevin is responsible for managing the laptops. He tracks them using an Excel spreadsheet that includes the date purchased, serial number, date assigned to a salesperson, date returned by a salesperson, and any repair information. The spreadsheet is sent to the asset clerk in the accounting department every month. After learning that no one in IT or accounting ever reviewed Kevin's spreadsheet, a new asset clerk, Angela Liu, decided to verify the information in the spreadsheet to laptops in the possession of salespeople. By doing this, Angela found that two salespeople had left the company without returning their laptops. In addition, a laptop was identified as being out for repairs for over a year and Kevin hadn't followed up with the repair company. Finally, a laptop listed as unassigned could not be located.

THE MISSING CONTROL
Review and Reconciliation
The asset clerk should reconcile the information from Kevin's spreadsheet to actual laptops on a regular basis to ensure all of Twillingate's computer assets are accounted for. Staff in the human resources department should verify that salespeople who resign or are terminated have returned their laptops.

LIMITATIONS OF INTERNAL CONTROL

No matter how well it is designed and operated, a company's system of internal control can only provide **reasonable assurance** (rather than a guarantee) that assets are properly safeguarded and that the accounting records are accurate and reliable. This is due to a number of limitations, which include:

1. Cost/benefit considerations
2. Human error
3. Collusion
4. Management override

Cost/Benefit Considerations

Cost/benefit considerations is the limitation that the costs of establishing control activities should not exceed the benefits that are expected to result from their use. In other words, if the benefits (such as reduced asset theft) that result from implementing an internal control are less than the costs of doing so, management would not implement the control.

To illustrate, consider shoplifting losses in retail stores. Such losses could be completely eliminated by having a security guard stop and search customers as they leave the store. Store managers have concluded, however, that the cost of doing so, along with the negative effects on customers' goodwill, outweighs the benefit achieved of reduced theft. Instead, stores have attempted to "control" shoplifting losses by using less costly procedures such as (1) posting signs saying, "We reserve the right to inspect all packages" and "All shoplifters will be prosecuted"; (2) using hidden cameras and store detectives to monitor customer activity; and (3) using sensor equipment at exits.

The size of the business affects the costs and benefits of implementing controls. In a small company, for example, it may be difficult to apply segregation of duties and independent internal verification because of the limited number of employees. In situations such as this, rather than incurring the cost of hiring more staff, it is often necessary for employees to assume the responsibility of performing or supervising incompatible functions. For example, at a small gas station, it is not unusual for a cashier to receive the cash and also prepare and make the night deposit at the bank. If the cash register tape is not locked, meaning that the cashier could tamper with the sales recorded in the cash register, it may be necessary for the owner to make the nightly bank deposits.

Human Error

The impact of human error is an important factor that limits the effectiveness of every system of internal control. A well-designed system can become ineffective as a result of lack of training, employee fatigue, carelessness, or indifference. For example, if a receiving clerk was not well trained or did not understand the importance of doing so, they may not bother to count goods received or just "fudge" the count, resulting in the wrong amount of inventory being added to the records.

Collusion

Occasionally, two or more individuals may work together to get around prescribed control activities, which is known as **collusion**. Such collusion can significantly lessen the effectiveness of internal control because it eliminates the protection expected from segregating the employees' duties. If a supervisor and a cashier collaborate to understate cash receipts and steal the shortfall, the system of internal control may be defeated (at least in the short run). The act of collusion is another example of fraud and one that no system of internal control can be designed to prevent.

Management Override

As management is responsible for a company's internal controls, it is also possible for management to override them. Managers may be able to ignore internal control policies and procedures without detection if they also provide the oversight function related to them. Management may override controls for personal gain or to improve the financial results of the company. These are both examples of fraud. The board of directors monitors this, normally through the audit committee. Management's actions and responsibilities are something that is assessed by the company's external auditors in planning the audit. As was noted in our discussions about the control environment, it is of utmost importance that a company's management demonstrate a commitment to internal control, setting the appropriate "tone at the top" for the organization.

DO IT! ▶7-1   Control Activities

Action Plan

✔ Understand each of the control activities: assignment of responsibility, segregation of duties, documentation, physical controls, and review and reconciliation.

In each of the following situations, identify the related control activity and state whether it has been supported or violated:

(a) The purchasing department orders, receives, and pays for merchandise.

(b) All cheques and receiving documents are prenumbered.

(c) The internal auditor performs surprise cash counts.

(d) Extra cash is kept locked in a safe that can be accessed only by the head cashier and supervisor.

(e) Multiple cashiers use a single cash drawer.

> ### SOLUTION
> Try this Do It! exercise on your own and then check your answer at the end of the chapter.
>
> ---
>
> Related Exercise Material: BE7–1, BE7–2, E7–1, and E7–2.

LEARNING
OBJECTIVE

▶2 Apply the key control activities to cash receipts and payments.

Cash is something that everyone desires, which makes it highly susceptible to theft. In addition, because companies can have large volumes of cash transactions, errors may easily occur in recording these transactions. To safeguard cash (protect it from theft) and to ensure the accuracy of the accounting records, effective control activities are essential.

Before we apply the control activities discussed in the previous section to cash, let's consider what cash is, and is not. **Cash** consists of coins, currency (paper money), cheques, and money orders. The general rule is that if the bank will accept it for deposit, it is cash. Cash can either be on hand in the company's cash registers, safe, or other secure place or on deposit in a bank or similar financial institution. Note that this definition of cash will likely change over time as various forms of digital or electronic cash, such as Bitcoin, continue to be developed and gain acceptance.

Cash does *not* include postdated cheques (cheques payable in the future), stale-dated cheques (cheques that will not be honoured because they are more than six months old), or returned cheques (cheques received from customers, but returned by the bank because the customer's account was lacking sufficient funds).

ACCOUNTING MATTERS

© Getty Images/Bloomberg

What Is Cash?

The way people have paid for transactions has changed over the centuries. Did you know that the first metal coins date back to 610–560 BC? A form of paper money first appeared in 1685. In the 1970s, debit and credit cards made their debut. In Canada, the $1 coin, the "loonie," replaced the $1 bill in 1987, followed by the "toonie" $2 coin in 1996. In 2012, the Royal Canadian Mint announced it would no longer make pennies and that the one-cent coin would be withdrawn from circulation. The federal government stopped issuing cheques as of April 1, 2016, switching entirely to direct deposits into individuals' and businesses' bank accounts.

New digital forms of money such as PayPal and Bitcoin—an open-source, peer-to-peer transaction processing system—have appeared. The Apple Pay service allows consumers to use their Apple devices, such as iPhones and the Apple Watch, to make payments in stores or online within apps via their credit card. Both Visa and MasterCard offer contactless cards or enabled devices that operate on radio frequencies so it isn't necessary to insert the card in a point-of-sale terminal. In mid-2015, roughly 25% of all store purchases made in Canada using a Visa or MasterCard were contactless. A Bank of Canada study found that cash accounted for just 44% of all transactions in the country in 2013, down from 54% in 2009. As digital forms of payment gain more acceptance, businesses will need to adapt their accounting and internal control processes to effectively control and manage their "cash" transactions.[2]

CONTROL ACTIVITIES OVER CASH RECEIPTS

Cash receipts come by way of a variety of methods:

1. Over-the-counter receipts
2. Electronic receipts
3. Cheque receipts (cheques received either at the time of sale or at a later date by mail)

The internal control procedures relating to cash receipts will vary from one company to another depending on the nature of their business. To illustrate some of these control activities, we will cover controls used in a typical service or merchandising business.

Over-the-Counter Receipts

As we saw with Nick's Steakhouse and Pizza in our feature story, most retail businesses receive payment with cash, credit cards, or debit cards. Staff members who operate cash registers (physical control) are each given a float (assignment of responsibility) to make change for customers who pay cash. All sales must be entered into the register through point-of-sale (POS) software, which records the sale at the proper price. In merchandising companies, the POS software also updates inventory records at the same time if the company is using a perpetual inventory system. Often the sale can be recorded simply by scanning the bar code on merchandise.

At the end of a shift, staff members must ensure that the cash in the register is equal to the float plus the cash sales that were recorded on the system. A supervisor will often double-check that this is the case (review and reconciliation). Access to the system should be restricted (physical control) so that cashiers cannot adjust the amount and type of sales recorded at that register to understate reported sales, which would hide the fact that they have taken cash. Employees must also ensure that the receipts are on hand for sales made by debit or credit cards and that these match sales that were recorded with this type of payment.

Let's assume that an employee steals the cash received from a customer and does not record the sale in the cash register. How will this theft be detected? After all, the cash collected from sales in the cash register will still equal the sales recorded. In this case, other internal control procedures, such as counting inventory, may detect the theft, particularly if this is done frequently (review and reconciliation). The count results will reveal a lower amount of inventory on hand than is shown in the POS system. The frequency of inventory counts depends on the type and cost of inventory. For example, the bar staff count the beer every shift at Nick's because of beer's cost and susceptibility to theft. A large box store, on the other hand, may count non-perishable items such as canned goods weekly or monthly. Thus it would take longer for the theft to be detected. Therefore some companies use security cameras (physical controls) to monitor staff to ensure that all sales are recorded in the system.

Not all businesses have converted to POS technology, for cost or other reasons. When a business doesn't use POS technology, the possibility of unintentional and intentional errors increases. For example, a staff member must manually enter the sales price into the register rather than having the prices preprogrammed in the system. This can lead to an unintentional error such as entering the price as $5.49 rather than the correct price of $9.45. It also allows the staff member to record the sale at a lower price for friends. Finally, because inventory is not automatically updated, intentional and unintentional errors may not be discovered until inventory is counted at a much later date.

Generally, internal control over cash receipts is more effective when **cash receipts are deposited intact into the bank account on a daily basis**. An authorized employee, such as the head cashier or general manager, should make bank deposits. **Increasing the amount of cash received by electronic funds transfer is also an effective control.**

Electronic Receipts

Electronic funds transfer (EFT) is a way of transferring money electronically from one bank account to another. Debit and bank credit card transactions are examples of electronic funds transfers. Another example is when customers use online banking to pay their accounts. When a customer pays his or her account, the cash is instantly transferred from the customer's bank account to the company's bank account.

Electronic funds transfers normally result in better internal control because company employees are not required to handle cash (or cheques, which will be discussed in the next section). This does not mean that recording errors or the opportunities for fraud are eliminated. For example, without proper assignment of responsibility and segregation of duties, an employee might be able to redirect electronic collections into a bank account that they control and conceal the theft with fraudulent accounting entries.

Cheque Receipts

Although the use of cheques has diminished, recent statistics from the Canadian Payments Association indicate that, although only 4% of all payments are made with cheques, they represent 46% of the value of all banking transactions. This makes sense because companies don't want to pay credit card fees on large-value transactions. We will discuss the fees charged by banks when credit cards are used later in this chapter.

When a cheque is received at the time of the sale, it will be included in the cash register and form part of an employee's reconciliation of daily sales to cash on hand. When a cheque is received in the mail, it is usually accompanied by a remittance advice, which is the detachable part of the sales invoice that customers are asked to send back with their cheque. Mailroom clerks will send the remittance advices to the accountants responsible for recording cash receipts while sending the cheques to another employee who will deposit them at the bank. The employee making the bank deposit should have no record-keeping duties so that they are prevented from stealing the cash and covering up the theft by understating the value of cash receipt journal entries. The person making the bank deposit will receive a bank-stamped deposit slip. Each day, an independent employee can then compare the amount of cash deposited per the deposit slip with the amount of cash receipts recorded that day to ensure that funds deposited were also recorded. If duties are segregated this way, no one employee would be able to steal cheques and also be able to record their receipt to cover up the theft. The review and reconciliation of the deposit slips further strengthens the controls over cheque receipts.

Illustration 7-2 shows examples of how the control activities explained earlier apply to cash receipts.

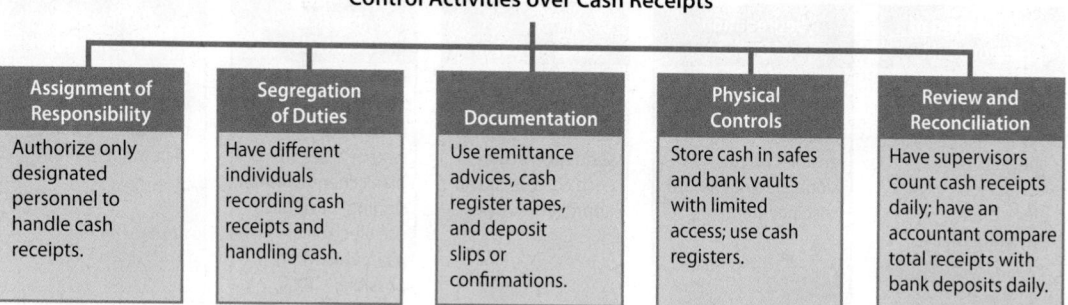

Control Activities over Cash Receipts

Assignment of Responsibility	Segregation of Duties	Documentation	Physical Controls	Review and Reconciliation
Authorize only designated personnel to handle cash receipts.	Have different individuals recording cash receipts and handling cash.	Use remittance advices, cash register tapes, and deposit slips or confirmations.	Store cash in safes and bank vaults with limited access; use cash registers.	Have supervisors count cash receipts daily; have an accountant compare total receipts with bank deposits daily.

►Illustration 7-2
Application of control activities to cash receipts

DO IT! ►7-2a   Control Activities over Cash Receipts

At Hamburger Heaven Restaurant, six employees working behind the counter share two cash registers. The owner says, "In an ideal situation, one person would be designated to ring in orders for each cash register, but when we get swamped, we all have to work together to keep things running smoothly." The prices of most items are preprogrammed into the cash register. At the end of the day, each register generates a sales report and one of the employees will count the cash in both registers, and after subtracting the float, will compare the total with the sales report. Then the employee puts the cash in an unlocked drawer in the office.

Identify any violations of control activities over cash receipts at this restaurant.

SOLUTION

Try this Do It! exercise on your own and then check your answer at the end of the chapter.

Related Exercise Material: BE7–3 and E7–3.

Action Plan

✔ Understand the application of each of the control activities to cash receipts: assignment of responsibility, segregation of duties, documentation, physical controls, and review and reconciliation.

CONTROL ACTIVITIES OVER CASH PAYMENTS

Cash is disbursed for a variety of reasons, such as to pay expenses, to settle liabilities, or to purchase assets. Generally, control activities over cash payments are more effective when **payments are made by cheque or by electronic funds transfer, rather than in cash**. Other control procedures (such as petty cash funds, which are not discussed here) are put in place for the few payments that cannot be made by cheque (for example, to reimburse customers for parking costs).

Good control for cheques includes having them signed by at least two authorized employees. The cheque signers should carefully review the supporting documentation for the payment before signing the cheque. There should be a clear segregation of duties between the cheque signing, which is an authorization function, and the accounts payable function, which is a recording function. This segregation helps ensure that accountants cannot record fraudulent invoices from companies they control and then sign cheques to pay these invoices. Cheques should be prenumbered (documentation) and all cheque numbers must be accounted for in the payment and recording process (review and reconciliation). Cheques should never be pre-signed (assignment of responsibility) and there should be restricted access to blank cheques and cheque-signing machines should be safeguarded (physical controls).

Payments can also be made electronically. For example, when a company pays its employees' salaries using a direct deposit option, the cash is instantly transferred from the company's bank account to each employee's bank account. As we discussed in the cash receipts section, as long as there is proper assignment of responsibility and segregation of duties, the use of EFT for cash payments will result in better internal control.

Examples of control activities applied to cash payments are shown in Illustration 7-3.

►Illustration 7-3
Application of control activities to cash payments

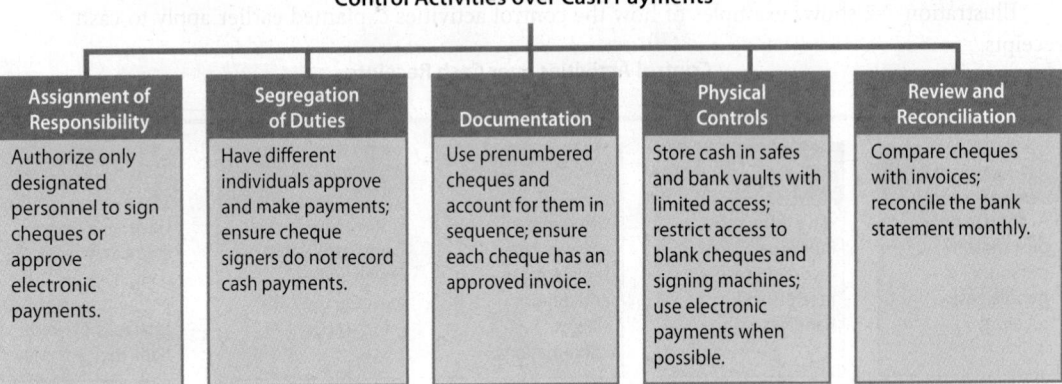

Control Activities over Cash Payments

Assignment of Responsibility	Segregation of Duties	Documentation	Physical Controls	Review and Reconciliation
Authorize only designated personnel to sign cheques or approve electronic payments.	Have different individuals approve and make payments; ensure cheque signers do not record cash payments.	Use prenumbered cheques and account for them in sequence; ensure each cheque has an approved invoice.	Store cash in safes and bank vaults with limited access; restrict access to blank cheques and signing machines; use electronic payments when possible.	Compare cheques with invoices; reconcile the bank statement monthly.

DO IT! ►7-2b   Control Activities over Cash Payments

Action Plan

✔ Understand the application of each of the control activities to cash payments: assignment of responsibility, segregation of duties, documentation, physical controls, and review and reconciliation.

During the short but very hectic ski season, High Peaks, the company that operates a local ski hill, struggles to pay its suppliers on a timely basis. This has resulted in upset suppliers, with some cutting off the company's access to credit purchases. To address this problem, the company's board of directors has agreed to let staff pay as many bills as possible with cash from the cash register if a supplier is on site. This had the added benefit of reducing the amount of cash on hand on the ski hill. All company cheques require the signatures of any two of the three authorized signing officers. However, because it was hard to find two signing officers who would be at the ski hill regularly, the signing officers agreed to have a series of pre-signed blank cheques that could be used to pay urgent bills. These are kept in an unlocked drawer in the manager's office.

Identify any violations of control activities over cash payments at High Peaks.

SOLUTION

Try this Do It! exercise on your own and then check your answer at the end of the chapter.

Related Exercise Material: **BE7–4** and **E7–4**.

LEARNING OBJECTIVE ►3   **Prepare a bank reconciliation.**

Several of the control activities discussed in the previous section involved the use of a bank— depositing cash on a regular basis, comparing cash receipts with bank deposit totals, and preparing monthly bank reconciliations. **In other words, the use of a bank contributes significantly to good internal control over cash.**

Aside from safeguarding cash, the use of a bank minimizes the amount of cash that must be kept on hand. In addition, control is strengthened because the bank's records (bank statement) provide a second record of the cash transactions that flowed into and out of the bank account. This enables the company to reconcile the transactions recorded in its Cash account with those recorded in the bank's records.

BANK STATEMENTS

Each month, the bank provides a bank statement showing the company's bank transactions and balance. With online banking, companies can access their bank statements whenever they are required. For example, in Illustration 7-4, the bank statement for Laird Ltd. shows the following: (1) dates; (2) a description of each transaction; (3) the amounts deducted (**debited**) from the bank account (for example, cheques and other payments); (4) the amounts added (**credited**) to the bank account (for example, deposits and other receipts); and (5) the account balance after each transaction.

▶**Illustration 7-4**
Bank statement

Your branch address:

505 King Street
Mississauga, ON L7A 2W9

Business Banking Statement

For the period ending April 30, 2018

Your Branch
Mississauga Main Office
Transit number: 0123

For questions about your statement call (905) 543-0820

Direct Banking
1-800-636-2999

Summary of account

Account	Opening balance ($)	Total amounts deducted ($)	+	Total amounts added ($)	Closing balance ($) on April 30, 2018
Interest Chequing Account # 0123 4567-890	13,256.90	11,719.70		13,069.53	14,606.73

Transaction details

Date	Description	Amounts deducted from account (debits)	Amounts added to account (credits)	Balance ($)
Owner:				
LAIRD LTD. 500 QUEEN STREET Mississauga, ON L6X 2Y3				
Apr 1	Opening balance			13,256.90
2	Deposit at BR. 0123		4,276.85	17,533.75
3	EFT, collection from M. Trask		2,137.50	19,671.25
6	Cheque, No. 436	1,185.79		18,485.46
7	Cheque, No. 439	3,260.00		15,225.46
13	Cheque, No. 441	2,420.00		12,805.46
14	Deposit at BR. 0123		425.60	13,231.06
16	Direct deposit, G. Jones		4,649.68	17,880.74
21	Returned cheque—NSF	425.60		17,455.14
21	NSF fee	40.00		17,415.14
23	Deposit at BR. 0098		1,579.90	18,995.04
26	EFT, payment of salaries	3,563.40		15,431.64
28	EFT, payment to Manulife Insurance	659.91		14,771.73
30	Bank service and debit/credit card fees	165.00		14,606.73

BANK OF ONTARIO

At first glance, it may appear that the debits and credits reported on the bank statement are backward. How can amounts deducted from a bank account, like a cheque, be a debit? And how can amounts added to a bank account, like a deposit, be a credit? The reason is that the bank statement reflects the *bank's* accounting, so the debits and credits are not really backward. While Cash is an asset account for the company, to the bank, the funds it holds for the company are a liability because the company can request them at any time. Liabilities are increased by credits and decreased by debits. When a company deposits money into its bank account, the bank's liability to the company increases. When a company writes a cheque or makes an electronic payment, the bank pays out this amount and decreases (debits) its liability to the company.

Amounts Deducted from a Bank Account (Debits)

Amounts deducted from a bank account include cheques and other payments. A cheque is a written order signed by an employee with signing authority that instructs the bank to pay a specific sum of money to a designated recipient (payee).

Many companies pay their employees' salaries using a direct deposit option. Laird pays its salaries this way. You can see the notation "EFT, payment of salaries" on April 26 in the bank statement in Illustration 7-4. When employee salaries are paid this way, the cash is automatically transferred from the company's bank account to each employee's bank account.

Other disbursements may appear on the bank statement. For example, pre-authorized payments relating to loans, rent, and insurance paid on a recurring basis are often made electronically. In Illustration 7-4, the notation "EFT, payment to Manulife Insurance" tells us that Laird authorized its insurance company to electronically withdraw the insurance premium on April 28.

Because the company initiated the transaction for salaries, and the transaction for the payment to Manulife, it can record them before receiving the bank statement. As we will learn later when we discuss deposits, sometimes a company will have to receive the bank statement before recording the transaction because another party initiated it. For example, a company won't know which customers have paid their accounts electronically until it receives the bank statement and supporting documentation.

There can also be deductions from a company's bank account related to customer cheques that were not honoured. These are cheques received from customers that have been deposited but subsequently returned by the bank as a result of the customers having insufficient funds to cover the cheques. When this happens, a customer's cheque is said to have "bounced." When this occurs, the customer's bank marks the cheque **NSF (not sufficient funds) cheque,** or returned cheque, and returns it to the depositor's bank. The bank then debits (decreases) the depositor's account, as shown by the notation, "Returned cheque—NSF" on the bank statement in Illustration 7-4 in the amount of $425.60 on April 21.

Note that the company previously deposited this cheque on April 14. The deposit was credited (added) to the account by the bank on April 14, but because the cheque was not honoured, this must be reversed and the account is debited (deducted) by the bank (see April 21 transaction). The bank returns the NSF cheque to the depositor as notification of the charge.

The company (depositor) will then advise the customer who wrote the NSF cheque that the payment was declined and that payment is still owed on the account. In addition, because the company's bank generally charges a service charge for processing a returned cheque, the company usually passes this on to the customer by adding the charged amount to the customer's account balance. You can see that the bank charged Laird a $40 NSF fee on April 21. In summary, the overall effect of an NSF cheque to the depositor is to create an account receivable and to reduce the cash in the depositor's bank account.

Another common deduction from a company's bank account is related to the fees charged by financial institutions related to transactions processed using debit and bank credit cards. Companies are willing to pay these fees for the almost instantaneous transfer of cash that occurs when a customer uses debit and bank credit cards. Some banks deduct debit and credit card fees from the company's bank account daily and others monthly, depending on the terms of the debit and credit card agreements. We have assumed a monthly service charge for debit and credit card fees for Laird. You can see the fees of $165 partly related to these transactions were removed from Laird's bank account on April 30.

Note that banks do not bill companies for their fees. Rather, the bank deducts this amount directly from the company's bank account. In addition to service charges such as the NSF fee and debit and credit card fees discussed above, banks also deduct a service charge for the account services they provide. For example, $165 was deducted directly by the bank from Laird's account on April 30 for this purpose as well as for the debit/credit card fees. Bank service charges vary widely depending on what kind of plan the company has with its bank.

Amounts Added to a Bank Account (Credits)

Deposits to a company's bank account can be made at the bank by authorized employees, which are documented by receipt of a deposit slip. Deposits can also be made by direct deposit, through an automated banking machine, or through an electronic funds transfer if the company allows customers to pay their accounts online. For example, in Illustration 7-4 Laird electronically collected $2,137.50 from a customer on April 3 in payment of an account. Another customer made a deposit directly to Laird's bank account on April 16 for $4,649.68.

In cases of electronic collections and direct deposits from customers, the company is often unaware of the collection until the bank statement is received. Why? When a customer pays their account using online banking or other electronic means, the cash is instantly transferred from the customer's bank account to the company's bank account. The primary evidence of these electronic cash receipts will be a line on the bank statement showing the amount, a reference number, and the name or account number of the person paying. Consequently, electronic receipts such as these may not be recorded until the company receives the bank statement.

Other additions to a company's bank account by the bank include any interest earned on the account balance, transfers from operating lines of credit, and funds received from any bank loans taken out in the period. No separate notification is usually given for these amounts either.

RECONCILING THE BANK ACCOUNT

Given that the bank and the company keep independent records of the company's chequing account, you might assume that the balances in both sets of records will always agree. In fact, the two balances are seldom the same because many transactions are not recorded at the same time on both records. It is therefore necessary to reconcile the company's Cash account balance and the balance reported on the bank statement and account for any differences as necessary.

There are two reasons that the bank and company records differ:

1. **Timing differences** that result in one of the parties recording the transaction in a different period (month) than the other and
2. **Errors** made by either party in recording transactions.

Except in electronic banking transactions, timing differences are common. For example, several days may pass between the time a company mails a supplier a cheque and the date the supplier presents the cheque to the bank for payment. Cheques written and mailed out (or otherwise distributed) by a company that have not yet cleared the bank (been deducted from the company's account) are called **outstanding cheques**.

Similarly, when a company uses the bank's night depository to make its deposits, there will be a difference of one day (or more, if holidays intervene) between the time the receipts are recorded by the company and the time they are recorded by the bank. Deposits recorded by the company that have not yet been recorded by the bank are called **deposits in transit**.

Errors can also occur. The frequency of errors depends on how effectively the company and bank have implemented internal controls. Bank errors are infrequent. However, either party could accidentally record a $450 cheque as $45 or $540. In addition, the bank might mistakenly charge a cheque to the wrong account if the code is missing or if the cheque cannot be scanned. Direct deposits and electronic funds transfers also depend on the correct account being keyed in to the system.

ACCOUNTING MATTERS

© istock.com/Sparky2000

Bank Errors

Bank errors may not occur as frequently as company errors, but they can still happen. Scotiabank's discount brokerage arm accidentally put $171 million of somebody else's money into a Toronto doctor's Scotiabank account. It took four months to find and correct the error. The red-faced bank admitted that many things went wrong—from posting the error to mistakes in reversals. And there are many more stories about banks making mistakes. However, they usually involve misplaced debits and rarely amounts as high as this.

Reconciliation Procedures

To get the most benefit from bank reconciliations, they should be prepared by an employee who has no other responsibilities related to cash (segregation of duties). Without segregation of duties, theft of cash by employees, which is also known as embezzlement, may go unnoticed. For example, a cashier who prepares the reconciliation can steal cash and hide the theft by misstating amounts on the reconciliation. In this way, the bank account would appear to reconcile with the company records and the theft would not be detected.

In reconciling the bank account, the balance per the bank statement is reconciled with the balance per the company's books. Reconciling items must be taken into account to arrive at the reconciled cash balance. The reconciliation is usually divided into two sections: one relating to the bank statement balance and one relating to the book balance. Because bank reconciliations are normally prepared at the end of every month, the starting point for preparing the reconciliation is to enter the ending cash balance per bank (found on the bank statement) and the cash balance per books (found in the Cash account in the general ledger) on the reconciliation.

Once the opening balances from the bank statement (for the bank) and the Cash account in the general ledger (for the company) are determined, the next step is to identify the reconciling items and determine how each reconciling item affects the bank's or the company's opening balances, respectively, to arrive at the reconciled cash balance. These procedures are shown in Illustration 7-5.

▶Illustration 7-5
Bank reconciliation procedures

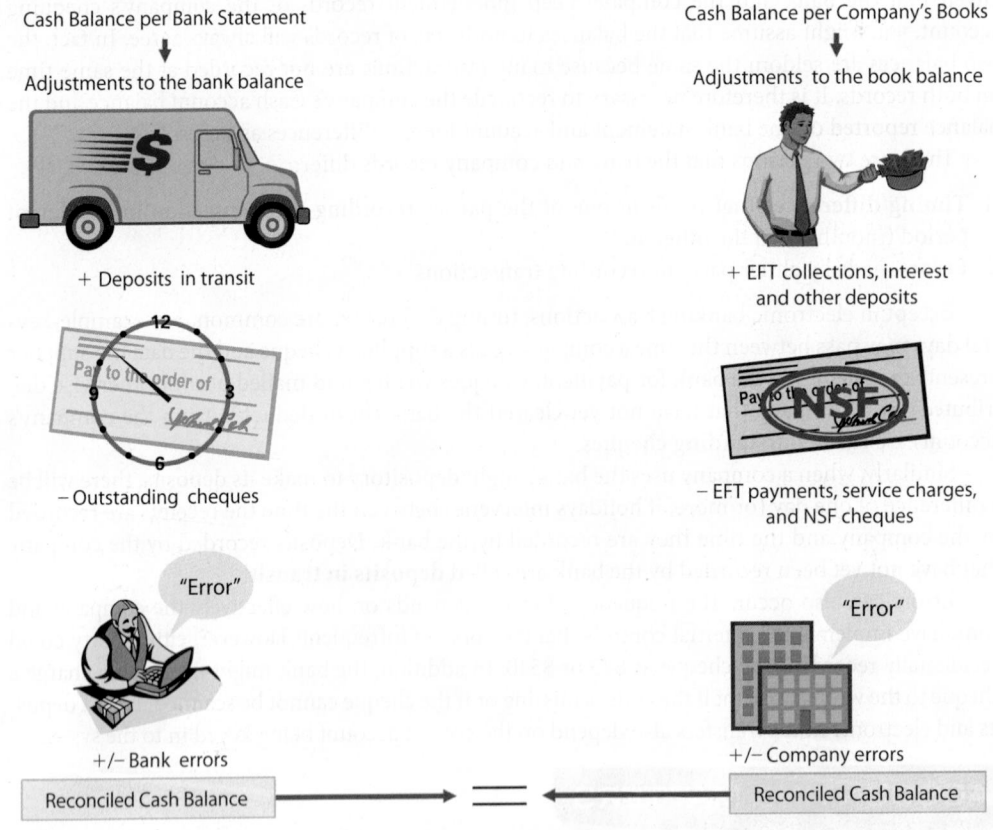

The following steps reveal the major reconciling items that cause the difference between the two balances.

Reconciling Items per Bank

The cash balance per the bank statement must be adjusted by the deposits in transit, outstanding cheques, and bank errors (if any). After these reconciling items are factored in, the reconciled cash balance reflects what the bank balance would have been if the bank had been aware of all of the reconciling items.

1. **Deposits in transit (+).** Compare the individual deposits on the bank statement with (1) the deposits in transit from the preceding bank reconciliation and (2) the deposits recorded in the books. Deposits in transit were recorded in the company's books when they were made but have not yet been recorded by the bank because it does not know about them yet. Once they are processed by the bank, the company's account balance will be increased. Therefore, they must be added to the balance per bank in the reconciliation process.

   Before determining the deposits in transit for the current period, you must check whether all deposits in transit that are outstanding from a prior period have cleared. For example, assume that Laird Ltd. used a night deposit slot (because the bank was closed for business) to deposit $2,201.40 on Monday, April 30. The bank will not receive or record this deposit until Tuesday, May 1. This amount would be treated as a deposit in transit at the end of April and would be added to the balance per bank in the reconciliation process. However, this outstanding deposit will clear the bank in May and will therefore no longer be a deposit in transit at the end of May. As at the end of May, this amount will have been recorded by both the company and the bank. The relationship between deposits in transit, deposits shown on the bank statement, and deposits recorded by the company is shown below:

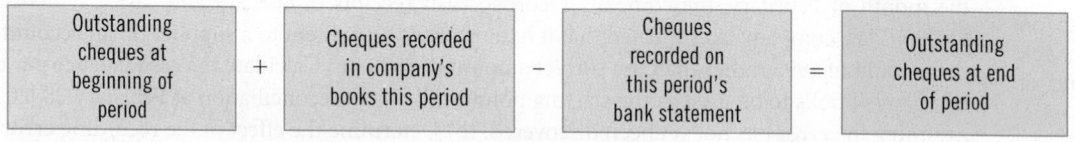

Deposits in transit at beginning of period	+	Deposits recorded in company's books this period	−	Deposits recorded on this period's bank statement	=	Deposits in transit at end of period

2. **Outstanding cheques (−).** Compare the paid cheques shown on the bank statement or returned with the bank statement with (a) cheques outstanding from the preceding bank reconciliation and (b) cheques issued by the company. Outstanding cheques were recorded on the company's books when they were prepared but have not yet cleared the bank account (because they have not been deposited by the recipient of the cheque, are still in the mail, or are still being processed by either the issuer's or recipient's bank). Once the issuer's bank becomes aware of these cheques, the company's account balance will be decreased. Therefore, these cheques must be deducted from the balance per bank in the reconciliation process.

   Note that an outstanding cheque from a prior period means that the cheque was deducted from the books in the prior period, but not paid by the bank in the same period. If the bank paid such a cheque in the current period, the cheque is no longer outstanding and will not be listed as a reconciling item on the reconciliation because both the company and the bank will have accounted for it. If the cheque has still not been presented to the bank for payment, it will continue to be outstanding. The relationship between outstanding cheques and cheques shown on the bank statement and recorded by the company is shown below:

Outstanding cheques at beginning of period	+	Cheques recorded in company's books this period	−	Cheques recorded on this period's bank statement	=	Outstanding cheques at end of period

3. **Bank errors (+/−).** Note any errors made by the bank that have been discovered in the previous steps. For example, if the bank processed a deposit of $1,693 as $1,639 in error, the difference of $54 ($1,693 − $1,639) is added to the balance per bank on the bank reconciliation because the bank will increase the account balance when it becomes aware of the error.

   Bank errors can be in either direction (increases or decreases). To determine whether the bank error should be added or subtracted in the reconciliation, consider what the bank balance would have been had the error not been made. If it would have been higher, then the error should be added in the reconciliation. If it would have been lower, then the error should be subtracted in the reconciliation.

Reconciling Items to Cash Balance per Company's Books

Reconciling items on the book side relate to amounts not yet recorded on the company's books. These adjustments are items that the company was unaware of until the bank statement was received and, therefore, had yet to record them.

1. **EFT collections, interest earned, and other deposits (+).** Compare the deposits on the bank statement with the company records. Any unrecorded amounts should be added to the balance per books. For example, if the bank statement shows electronic funds transfers from customers paying their accounts online, these amounts should be added to the balance per books on the bank reconciliation to update the company's records unless they had previously been recorded by the company. Any interest earned that is paid into the account would be noted on the bank statement and should be added to the balance per books to update the company's records.

2. **EFT payments, service charges, interest charges, and NSF cheques (−).** Similarly, any unrecorded payments should be deducted from the balance per books. For example, if the bank statement shows service charges (such as debit and credit card fees and other bank service charges) and these have not yet been recorded in the company's records, then these amounts are deducted from the balance per books on the bank reconciliation. If NSF cheques are returned with the bank statement, then they would also need to be recorded in the company's records, together with any fees charged by the bank in relation to them.

3. **Book errors (+/−).** Note any errors made by the company that have been discovered in the previous steps. For example, the company wrote cheque No. 439 to a supplier in the amount of $3,260 on April 7 but the accounting clerk recorded the cheque amount as $3,620. The error of $360 ($3,620 − $3,260) is added to the balance per books because the company reduced the cash account balance by $360 more than it should have when it recorded the cheque as $3,620 instead of $3,260. To determine whether the error made by the company should be added or subtracted in the reconciliation, consider what the book balance would have been had the error not been made. If it would have been higher, then the error should be added in the reconciliation. If it would have been lower, then the error should be subtracted in the reconciliation. Make sure that you include only errors made by the company, not the bank, as reconciling items in determining the reconciled cash balance.

DO IT! ▶7-3a   Cash Balance per Company's Books and Errors

SOLUTION

Try this Do It! exercise on your own and then check your answer at the end of the chapter.

Related Exercise Material: BE7–8, BE7–9, and E7–5.

Kariwak Limited's reconciled cash balance for the bank was $12,358 on January 31, 2018. During the month of February, the company recorded cash receipts of $68,319 and cash payments of $57,900. The company later learned that it had recorded a payment to a supplier on an account in the amount of $995 rather than the correct amount of $599. (a) Calculate the cash balance per the company's books to be used as the starting point in the bank reconciliation at February 28, 2018, assuming the error has not yet been discovered. (b) Determine the effect of the recording error in the bank reconciliation process.

Action Plan

✔ Recall that reconciled cash balances, whether for the bank or the company, are equal after the bank reconciliation process. So the company's cash balance in its general ledger account will equal the reconciled cash balance per bank reconciliation after adjusting entries have been made.

✔ Consider using a T account to help you.

✔ When determining which side of the bank reconciliation should be adjusted for the effect of the error, identify who knows about the error (the bank or the company). To determine the direction of the error, identify the impact of the amount made in error (for example, increased or reduced Cash account by which amount), identify the impact of the correct amount on the Cash account, and adjust for the difference.

Bank Reconciliation Illustrated

The bank statement for Laird Ltd. was shown in Illustration 7-4. It shows an unadjusted balance per bank of $14,606.73 on April 30, 2018. On this date, the cash balance per books is $4,387.55.

From the steps described above, the following reconciling items for the bank can be determined:

1. **Deposits in transit (+):** After comparing the deposits recorded in the books with the deposits listed in the bank statement, it was determined that the April 30 deposit of $2,201.40 was not recorded by the bank until May 1. $2,201.40
2. **Outstanding cheques (−):** After comparing the cheques recorded in the books with the cheques listed in the bank statement, it was determined that three cheques were outstanding: No. 437, $3,000.00; No. 438, $1,401.30; and No. 440, $1,502.70.   5,904.00
3. **Bank errors (+/−):** None

Reconciling items per books are as follows:

1. **EFT receipts (+):** Unrecorded electronic receipts from customers on account on April 3 and 16 determined from the bank statement: $2,137.50 + $4,649.68. $6,787.18
2. **Interest (+):** None
3. **EFT payments (−):** None. The electronic payments on April 26 and 28 were previously recorded by the company when they were initiated.
4. **NSF cheques (−):** Returned cheque plus NSF fee on April 21 ($425.60 + $40).   465.60
5. **Service fees (−):** Fees related to debit and credit cards, together with bank service charges on the company's accounts.   165.00
6. **Company errors (+/−):** Cheque No. 439 was correctly written by Laird for $3,260 and was correctly paid by the bank on April 7. However, it was recorded as $3,620 on Laird's books. The account is too low, so the error must be added back.   360.00

The bank reconciliation follows:

LAIRD LTD. Bank Reconciliation April 30, 2018		
Cash balance per bank statement		$14,606.73
Add: Deposits in transit		2,201.40
		16,808.13
Less: Outstanding cheques		
No. 437	$(3,000.00)	
No. 438	(1,401.30)	
No. 440	(1,502.70)	(5,904.00)
Reconciled cash balance per bank		$10,904.13
Cash balance per books		$ 4,387.55
Add: Electronic receipts from customers on account		
M. Trask	$2,137.50	
G. Jones	4,649.68	
Error in recording cheque No. 439 ($3,620 − $3,260)	360.00	7,147.18
		11,534.73
Less: Returned (NSF) cheque plus service charge ($425.60 + $40)	$(465.60)	
Bank service and debit/credit card fees	(165.00)	
		(630.60)
Reconciled cash balance per books		$10,904.13

Bank Reconciliation Journal Entries

The bank reconciliation shown above is only the first step in the reconciliation process. The reconciliation is not complete until the company's books are adjusted to agree with the adjusted (correct) cash balance. The company must record each reconciling item related to the cash balance per books. If these items are not journalized and posted, the Cash account will not show the correct balance.

No entries are necessary in relation to the cash balance per bank because these items will be accounted for by the bank when the outstanding deposits and outstanding cheques are processed. If any bank errors are discovered in preparing the reconciliation, the bank should be notified so it can make the necessary corrections on its records. **The bank cannot correct a company's errors on its books and a company cannot correct the bank's errors on its books.**

The journal entries for Laird Ltd.'s bank reconciliation at April 30 are as follows:

ELECTRONIC RECEIPTS ON ACCOUNT   A payment of an account by a customer is recorded in the same way, whether the cash is received through the mail or electronically. The entry is:

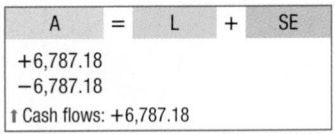

Apr. 30	Cash	6,787.18	
	Accounts Receivable		6,787.18
	(To record electronic collection of accounts for M. Trask, $2,137.50, and G. Jones, $4,649.68)		

In some cases, the company will have already recorded the EFT receipts. Some companies use online access to their bank accounts daily to monitor the activity. Other companies, such as Laird, wait until the bank statement is received to record transactions they were unaware of. When these transactions are recorded, Laird will post the receivable collection to each individual account in its subsidiary ledger as well as in total to the Accounts Receivable control account.

BOOK ERROR   An examination of the general journal shows that the incorrectly recorded cheque, No. 439, was a payment on account to a supplier. The correcting entry is:

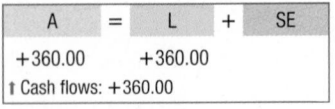

Apr. 30	Cash	360.00	
	Accounts Payable		360.00
	(To correct error in recording cheque No. 439)		

NSF CHEQUE   As indicated earlier, a cheque returned for not sufficient funds (NSF) along with the related service charge becomes an account receivable to the depositor. The entry is:

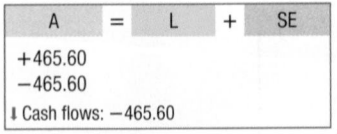

Apr. 30	Accounts Receivable ($425.60 + $40)	465.60	
	Cash		465.60
	(To re-establish accounts receivable for NSF cheque, and related service charge)		

BANK CHARGES EXPENSE   Fees for processing debit and credit card transactions are normally debited to the expense account Bank Charges, as are bank service charges.

Apr. 30	Bank Charges Expense	165.00	
	Cash		165.00
	(To record charges for debit and credit card fees and		
	bank service charges)		

A	=	L	+	SE
−165.00				−165.00

↓ Cash flows: −165.00

Our presentation assumes that all of the journal entries for reconciling items are made at the end of the month. In practice, a company may also make journal entries during the month as it receives information from the bank regarding its account, or as the company checks its bank account balances online. Once recorded, these items would no longer be reconciling items.

After the entries are posted, the Cash account will appear as in the T account that follows. The cash balance of $10,904.13 shown in the ledger should agree with the reconciled cash balance per books in the bank reconciliation shown earlier.

Cash

Apr. 30 Bal.	4,387.55	Apr. 30	465.60
30	6,787.18	30	165.00
30	360.00		
Apr. 30 Bal.	10,904.13		

DO IT! ▶7-3b   Bank Reconciliation

The Cash account of the Oakville Athletic Association showed a balance of $32,666 on December 31. The bank statement as at that date showed a balance of $36,168. After comparing the bank statement with the company records, the following information was determined.

1. Deposits in transit as at December 31 amounted to $7,286.

2. Cheques issued in December but still outstanding at the end of the month amounted to $6,000. Cheques still outstanding from the month of November totalled $560.

3. The bank made a mistake in recording a U.S. dollar payment received from a customer, overstating the Canadian funds deposited into the account received by $56.

4. Electronic receipts from customers in payment of their accounts totalled $4,699. These receipts have not yet been recorded by the company.

5. The company made an error in recording a customer's deposit in payment of its account. The company recorded the collection of the account as $209, when it should have been $290. The bank correctly recorded the deposit as $290.

6. The bank returned an NSF cheque in the amount of $478 that Oakville had deposited on December 20. The cheque was a payment on a customer's account.

7. The bank debited Oakville's account for service charges of $130. This included $45 for processing the NSF cheque (see item 6 above), and $85 for bank service charges and debit and credit card fees.

Prepare a bank reconciliation and any required journal entries for Oakville at December 31.

Action Plan

✔ Prepare the bank reconciliation in two sections: one for the bank and one for the company.

✔ Determine which reconciling items each side knows about and adjust the other side accordingly.

✔ Be careful when you determine the direction of an error correction.

✔ Prepare journal entries only for the book side, not the bank side.

✔ The reconciled cash balances must agree with each other when complete, and with the general ledger account after the journal entries are posted.

SOLUTION

Try this Do It! exercise on your own and then check your answer at the end of the chapter.

Related Exercise Material: BE7–5, BE7–6, BE7–7, BE7–10, BE7–11, E7–6, E7–7, E7–8, and E7–9.

4   Explain the reporting and management of cash

Business owners such as Mark Petros of Nick's and company managers must perform a difficult balancing act to manage cash. On one hand, it is critical to ensure that enough cash is available to pay bills as they come due, buy goods, and take advantage of opportunities as they present themselves. On the other hand, cash itself is an unproductive asset, in that it does not generate a return, unless it is invested in other assets (such as investments; inventory; or property, plant, and equipment). So it is critical that management know at all times exactly how much cash the company has and how much cash will be needed to fund future plans. In the next two sections, we will look at how cash is reported and will identify ways to manage and monitor cash.

REPORTING CASH

Cash is reported in two different financial statements: the statement of financial position and the statement of cash flows. The statement of financial position reports the amount of cash available at a specific point in time. The statement of cash flows shows the receipts and payments of cash during a period of time. These two statements are linked because the ending cash amount reported on the statement of cash flows agrees with the cash amount reported on the statement of financial position. The statement of cash flows was introduced in Chapter 1 and will be discussed in detail in Chapter 13.

Because it is the most liquid asset, cash is listed first in the current assets section of the statement of financial position, although the reverse order of liquidity can also be used under IFRS. Many companies combine cash with cash equivalents. **Cash equivalents** are short-term, highly liquid (easily sold) held-for-trading investments that are subject to an insignificant risk of changes in value. Examples of cash equivalents include debt investments such as government treasury bills (T-bills) that mature in 90 days or less, money market funds, and 90-day bank term deposits.

Some companies may be in a cash deficit or overdraft position at year end. Bank overdrafts occur when the bank has pre-approved the company to be able to write cheques for amounts greater than the cash balance in the company's bank account. These pre-approved amounts are referred to as **lines of credit** or **credit facilities**. They are, when used, a short-term loan from the bank. Most companies have overdraft protection or lines of credit up to a certain amount with their banks. When they have been accessed, the cash account (which is net of the line of credit) will show a credit balance in the general ledger that is reported as a current liability called **bank indebtedness**. This is because the bank has the right to request funds from the company to cover the overdraft (line of credit) at any time. We will discuss lines of credit in more depth in Chapter 10.

Bank overdrafts are deducted from cash and cash equivalents. In summary, cash equivalents include:

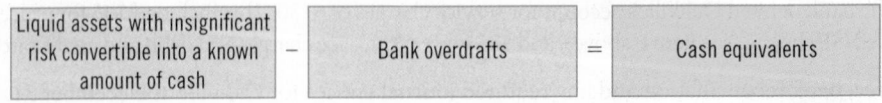

A company may have cash that is not available for general use because it is restricted for a special purpose. For example, landfill companies are often required to maintain a fund of restricted cash to ensure that they will have adequate resources to cover closing and cleanup costs at the end of a landfill site's useful life. Cash that has a restricted use should be reported separately on the statement of financial position as **restricted cash** so that users of the financial statements are aware that it is not available for use by the company. Restricted cash may be reported as a current or non-current asset, depending on when the cash will be required.

Banks can also require borrowers to maintain minimum cash balances when making loans to customers. These minimum balances, called a **compensating balance**, provide the bank with support for the loans in the event the borrower fails to make a payment. Compensating balances are a form of restricted cash and are reported as a current or non-current asset depending on the term (length) of the loan.

Illustration 7-6 shows how Sawada Technology presents its cash.

SAWADA TECHNOLOGY CORP. Statement of Financial Position (partial) December 31, 2018	
Current assets	
Cash and cash equivalents	$59,500,000
Restricted cash	6,850,000
Non-current assets	
Compensating cash balance	2,500,000

Sawada provides further information about the restricted cash in the notes to the financial statements. The company received customer deposits for high-tech equipment to be manufactured and shipped in the next 12 months. The contracts require Sawada to hold the deposits (totalling $6,850,000) in a separate bank account that cannot be used until the equipment is shipped. In addition, Sawada borrowed $50 million from the bank for expansion activities over the next five years. The bank requires Sawada to hold a compensating balance of 5% of the outstanding loan at all times.

MANAGING CASH

Many companies struggle, not because they cannot generate sales, but because they cannot manage their cash. We will use a hypothetical clothing manufacturing company to illustrate this point. Erin Martineau gave up a stable, high-paying marketing job to start her own company, Martineau Designs Ltd. Soon she had more clothing orders than she could fill. Yet she found herself on the brink of financial disaster: her company could generate sales, but it was not collecting cash fast enough to support its operations. To survive, a business must have cash.

To understand cash management, consider the operating cycle of a clothing manufacturing company. First, it purchases raw materials (fabric, buttons, thread, zippers, and the like). Let's assume that it purchases these on credit provided by the supplier, so the company owes its supplier money. Next, employees manufacture the clothing. Now the company also owes its employees their salary. Then, it sells the clothing to retailers, on credit. In spite of making the sale, the company will have no money to pay suppliers or employees until it collects money from its customers.

Ensuring that a company has sufficient cash to meet its needs is one of the greatest challenges management faces as it deals with the ebb and flow of cash. The following basic principles of cash management help ensure that companies will have a sufficient amount of cash.

1. **Increase the speed of collection on receivables.** Money owed to Erin Martineau by her customers is money that she needs as soon as possible. The sooner customers pay her, the faster she can use those funds. Thus, rather than having an average collection period (the time it takes to collect credit sales from customers) of 30 days, she may want an average collection period of 20 days. However, any attempt to force customers to pay earlier must be carefully weighed against the possibility that this may anger or alienate them. If her competitors are willing to provide a 30-day grace period, she may feel that her customers will expect the same terms. As noted in Chapter 5, a common way to encourage customers to pay quicker is to offer cash discounts for early payments under such terms as 2/10, n/30.

2. **Keep inventory levels low.** Maintaining a large inventory of raw material and finished goods is costly. Large amounts of cash are tied up if a company keeps large amounts of inventory on hand. There are also costs associated with storage, including operating and renting warehouse space. In addition, some types of inventory can become obsolete if held for a long period. In Erin Martineau's case, fashion trends may change, making the clothing more difficult to sell. Other types of goods may become obsolete due to changes in technology or as a result of spoilage. Many companies routinely use techniques to reduce their inventory on hand, thus conserving their cash. Of course, if companies have inadequate inventory, they will lose sales. The proper level of inventory is an important decision, as we learned in Chapter 6.

3. **Delay payment of liabilities.** By keeping track of when bills are due, Erin Martineau's company can avoid paying bills too early. Let's say her supplier allows 30 days for payment. If she pays in 10 days, she has lost the use of cash for 20 days. Therefore, she should use the full payment period, but she should not "stretch" payment past the point that could damage her credit rating (and future borrowing ability) or her ability to do business with suppliers.

4. **Plan the timing of major expenditures.** To maintain operations or to grow, all companies must make major expenditures that normally require some form of outside financing. In order to increase the likelihood of obtaining outside financing, Erin Martineau should carefully consider the timing of major expenditures in light of her company's operating cycle. If at all possible, expenditures should be made when the company normally has excess cash—usually during the off-season when inventory is low.

5. **Invest idle cash.** No return is earned on cash on hand. Excess cash should be invested, even if it is only overnight. Many businesses, such as Martineau Designs Ltd., are seasonal. During her slow season, if she has excess cash, she should invest it. To avoid an immediate cash crisis, however, it is very important that these investments be liquid and risk-free. A liquid investment is one that has an active market where someone is always willing to buy or sell the investment. A risk-free investment means there is no concern that the party will default on its promise to pay its principal and interest.

   For example, using excess cash to purchase shares in a company can be risky. If share values suddenly decreased, you might be forced to sell them at a loss in order to pay your bills as they come due. Common liquid, risk-free investments (albeit with lower rates of interest) are treasury bills or money market funds.

6. **Prepare a cash budget.** A cash budget is a critical tool, showing anticipated cash flows over a one- or two-year period. It can show when additional financing will be necessary well before the actual need arises. Conversely, it can indicate when excess cash will be available for the repayment of debts, for investments, or for other purposes.

   These principles of cash management are summarized in Illustration 7-7.

▶Illustration 7-7

Principles of cash management

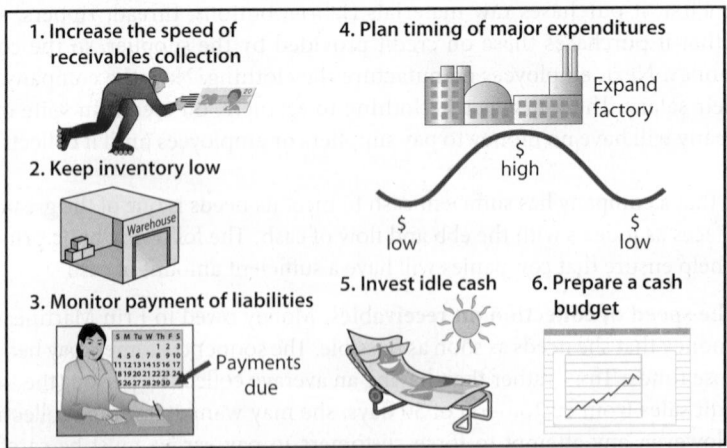

Because cash is so vital to a company, applying these principles of cash management to plan the company's cash needs is essential for any business. In a large company, one or more employees will be assigned responsibility for managing cash.

DO IT! ▶7-4   Presentation of Cash

Bay Resorts Limited reported the following selected items on May 31, 2018:

Accounts receivable	$29,000
Bank indebtedness	10,000
Cash	12,300
Cash (restricted for an upcoming plant expansion in the next few years)	50,000
Compensating balance (for a non-current loan)	5,000
Treasury bills, due in 30 days	1,500
Equity investment (in common shares)	4,000

(a) Calculate Bay Resorts' cash and cash equivalents.

(b) Identify where each of the above items not included in cash and cash equivalents should be reported on the statement of financial position.

Action Plan

✔ Understand the definition of cash equivalents: short-term, highly liquid held-for-trading investments – bank indebtedness.

✔ Understand the classifications on the statement of financial position.

SOLUTION
Try this Do It! exercise on your own and then check your answer at the end of the chapter.

Related Exercise Material: BE7–12, BE7–13, E7–10, and E7–11.

REVIEW AND PRACTICE

▶ LEARNING OBJECTIVE REVIEW

1. Explain the components of an internal control system, including its control activities and limitations. Internal control systems have the following components: the control environment, risk assessment, control activities, information and communication, and monitoring activities. Control activities include assignment of responsibility, segregation of duties, documentation, physical controls, and review and reconciliation.

2. Apply the key control activities to cash receipts and payments. Control activities over cash receipts include (a) designating only personnel such as cashiers to handle cash; (b) assigning the duties of receiving cash, recording cash, and custody of cash to different individuals; (c) obtaining remittance advices for mail receipts, cash register tapes for over-the-counter receipts, and deposit slips or confirmations for bank deposits; (d) using company safes and banks to store cash, with access limited to authorized personnel, and using cash registers in executing over-the-counter receipts; (e) depositing all cash intact daily in the bank account or using EFT; and (f) making independent daily counts of register receipts and daily comparisons of total receipts with total deposits.

Control activities over cash payments include (a) making all payments by cheque or by EFT; (b) having only specified individuals authorized to sign cheques; (c) assigning to different individuals the duties of approving items for payment, paying the items, and recording the payments; (d) using prenumbered cheques and accounting for all cheques; (e) storing blank cheques in a safe with access restricted to authorized personnel, and using electronic methods to print amounts on cheques; (f) comparing each cheque or EFT payment with the approved invoices before initiating payments; and (g) making monthly reconciliations of bank and book balances.

3. Prepare a bank reconciliation. In reconciling the bank account, the cash balance per the company's books is reconciled with the cash balance reported by the bank on the bank statement. There can be differences between the company's books and the bank due to timing differences and errors. Reconciling items for the bank include deposits in transit, outstanding cheques, and any errors made by the bank. Reconciling items for the company include EFT receipts, interest, EFT payments, service charges, NSF cheques, and any errors made by the company. Journal entries must be made for all items required to adjust the balance per books to the reconciled cash balance.

4. Explain the reporting and management of cash. Cash is usually the first current asset listed on the statement of financial position. Cash that is restricted for a special purpose is reported separately as a current asset or as a non-current asset, depending on when the cash is expected to be used. Compensating balances are a form of restriction on the use of cash and are reported as a current or non-current asset depending on the term of the restriction.

The six principles of cash management are to (a) collect receivables quicker, (b) keep inventory levels low, (c) delay the payment of liabilities, (d) plan the timing of major expenditures, (e) invest idle cash, and (f) prepare a cash budget.

► KEY TERM REVIEW

The following are key terms defined in this chapter with the corresponding page reference for your review. You will find a complete list of terms and definitions for all chapters in the glossary at the end of this textbook.

Cash (p. 367)
Cash equivalents (p. 380)
Collusion (p. 366)

Compensating balance (p. 381)
Deposits in transit (p. 373)
Fraud (p. 361)

NSF (not sufficient funds) cheque (p. 372)
Outstanding cheques (p. 373)
Restricted cash (p. 381)

► DECISION TOOLKIT REVIEW

DECISION CHECKPOINTS	INFO NEEDED FOR DECISION	TOOLS TO USE FOR DECISION	HOW TO EVALUATE RESULTS
Are the company's financial statements supported by adequate internal controls?	Auditor's report	Read the auditor's report and determine the opinion they reached with respect to the fairness of the information presented in the financial statements.	If the auditor's opinion states that the financial statements are fairly presented, then the auditor did not observe any control deficiencies that had a material impact on the financial statements.
Is all of the company's cash available for general use?	Statement of financial position and notes to financial statements	Does the company report any cash as being restricted or used as a compensating balance?	A restriction on the use of cash, or an amount that must be maintained as a compensating balance, limits management's ability to use those resources for general obligations. This should be considered when assessing liquidity.

► PRACTICE USING THE DECISION TOOLKIT

Answers are at the end of the chapter.

Sparks Basketball (SB) is a not-for-profit organization whose main purpose is to promote healthy living through sports activity. Its members are basketball associations throughout the province, for which SB provides a variety of services. These services include insurance coverage, the organization of provincial tournaments, and discounts from sponsor organizations. It is a volunteer organization with an independent board of directors, and one paid position—that of executive director. While the executive director was on parental leave, one of SB's board members, John Stevens, filled this position.

Unfortunately, some financial irregularities occurred while Mr. Stevens was acting as executive director. As the acting executive director, Mr. Stevens was responsible for paying invoices, making deposits, signing cheques, completing the bank reconciliation, and preparing financial statements for the annual general meeting.

It was also determined that Mr. Stevens handled all deposits and cash payments by himself for a national basketball tournament hosted by SB. He had promised to have an independent treasurer for the tournament but did not get one. He also coached a basketball team in a nearby city, and had full access to the team's bank account. During this time, to save on bank fees, Mr. Stevens had also stopped having the bank return SB's cancelled cheques.

An accountant was brought in to investigate further. She discovered many problems. The financial records were a mess, and there was almost no paper trail for many of the expenditures that were made. There were instances of "double dipping"—where one individual was reimbursed several times for the same expense claim. There were also several cheques made out to the team coached by Mr. Stevens. There was even a cheque where the payee's name had been scratched out and Mr. Stevens' name was inserted.

INSTRUCTIONS

(a) Identify the main weakness in control activities at Sparks Basketball.

(b) Discuss what steps should be taken to ensure that this situation does not happen again.

(c) Discuss the trade-off between implementing an extensive internal control system and the cost of having such a system for a volunteer organization that has limited funds.

▶ PRACTICE COMPREHENSIVE DO IT!

Answers are at the end of the chapter.

The Winnipeg Arts Society reports the following selected information with regard to cash at June 30:

From last month's bank reconciliation, at May 31:	
Reconciled cash balance	$34,080
From the general ledger Cash account:	
Cash receipts, June	34,000
Cash payments, June	39,520

From the bank:

WINNIPEG ARTS SOCIETY Bank Statement June 30			
	Amounts Deducted (Debits)	Amounts Added (Credits)	Balance
Opening balance, June 1			35,380
Deposits		30,496	65,876
Cheques cleared	36,200		29,676
EFT, payment of insurance	1,000		28,676
NSF cheque ($310 + $40 service charge)	350		28,326
Bank service charges and credit card fees	54		28,272
EFT, collection from Zukata		70	28,342

ADDITIONAL INFORMATION:

1. All cash receipts were deposited in the bank account. All cash payments were made by cheque.

2. There was a deposit in transit of $1,200 at May 31 that the bank recorded in June.

3. There were $1,500 of outstanding cheques at the end of May.

4. The pre-authorized EFT for insurance has already been recorded.

5. The NSF cheque was for $310, from Massif Corp., a customer, in payment of its account. The bank charged a $40 processing fee.

6. The EFT collection of $70 was incorrectly deposited by the bank to the society's account. It should have been deposited to the account of the Winnipeg Arts Council, a different organization with a similar name.

INSTRUCTIONS

(a) Calculate the cash balance per books at June 30, prior to reconciliation.

(b) Calculate the (1) deposits in transit and (2) outstanding cheques at June 30.

(c) Prepare a bank reconciliation at June 30.

(d) Prepare the journal entries required as a result of the reconciliation.

(e) Assume that the Winnipeg Arts Society has only one full-time employee. She is an experienced book-keeper and is responsible for handling all of the organization's receipts and payments. Directors on the society's board and other volunteers handle all of the other activities of the society.

Explain why it would be important to have the treasurer from the arts society's board review the bank reconciliation after it has been prepared each month. Identify the control activity (activities) that this step would relate to.

▶ PRACTICE OBJECTIVE-FORMAT QUESTIONS

Answers are at the end of the chapter.

1. Identify all of the controls from the list that follows that are related to the documentation control activity.

   (a) Using prenumbered cheques.
   (b) Maintaining a list of all of the signatures of employees who are authorized to sign cheques.
   (c) Having shipping clerks complete a shipping document each time goods are shipped, a copy of which is sent to the accounting department.
   (d) Preparing a monthly bank reconciliation.
   (e) Requiring employees to complete weekly time sheets.
   (f) Requiring departments to complete purchase requisitions forms when they wish to order goods.
   (g) Ensuring that only managers can override the price listed in the price guide provided to sales staff.

2. Indicate which of the following statements are correct. (Select as many as are appropriate.)

   (a) A bank reconciliation is an example of an external review.
   (b) Having a second cashier recount the cash drawer of another cashier would be an example of assignment of responsibility.
   (c) The control activity review and reconciliation can involve reviews that are conducted within the company and reviews conducted by persons outside or external to the company.
   (d) Physical controls include requiring employees to establish unique passwords to access the company's IT systems.
   (e) Having commission-based sales staff responsible for authorizing customer credit and shipment of goods would be an example of a control weakness related to assignment of responsibility.
   (f) Internal and external auditors are both considered to be independent of the company.
   (g) Tone at the top is a critical control activity.

3. Indicate which of the following controls would be considered to be examples of physical controls:

   (a) ID cards are issued to each employee.
   (b) Employees are required to change their computer passwords every two months.
   (c) Security cameras are used.
   (d) Only the Director of Human Resources is able to authorize the addition of a new employee in the company's payroll system.
   (e) Door access control systems are used, which restrict the areas unauthorized staff are able to access.
   (f) All cash received during the day is deposited at the bank on a daily basis by the manager.
   (g) Inventory in the warehouse is counted monthly by warehouse staff and the count results are provided to the company's bookkeeper.

4. Identify *all* of the controls that would be considered to be control activities over cash receipts:

   (a) Only specific employees are authorized to sign cheques.
   (b) An armoured car service picks up cash once per day on a varying schedule.
   (c) Cash floats are kept in a safe overnight.
   (d) The company uses prenumbered cheques.
   (e) Shift supervisors recount the amounts in each cashier's register drawer and agree them to the amounts reported by each cashier.
   (f) All cash registers keep an electronic record of all sales transactions, which is printed out daily and reconciled with the daily cash count.
   (g) Remittance advices are included with customer statements that customers fill in and send back with their payments.

5. Callum Prospecting Ltd.'s (CPL) bookkeeper is preparing a bank reconciliation for the month of September 2018. The company's account balance on its September 30, 2018, bank statement was $36,600. CPL's bookkeeper determined that eight cheques issued by the company to its suppliers for a total of $15,800 had not yet cleared the bank. Also, a deposit for $10,100 made by CPL on September 30 did not appear on the bank statement. Bank service charges of $80 appear on the bank statement, but have not yet been reflected in the general ledger. There was also an EFT receipt of $2,800 on the bank statement that had not been recorded by CPL's bookkeeper. While preparing the reconciliation, the bookkeeper also realizes that she had mistakenly recorded a cheque written for $2,100 as $1,200 in the general ledger. The balance in CPL's cash account in the general ledger was $29,080 prior to the reconciliation.

   Using the above information, identify *all* of the following statements that are correct regarding the bank reconciliation that would be prepared for CPL:

(a) The mistake made by the bookkeeper would be subtracted from the cash balance per books.
(b) The deposit in transit for $10,100 made by CPL on September 30 that did not appear on the bank statement would be added to the cash balance per books.
(c) The reconciled cash balance would be $30,900.
(d) The bank service charges of $80 would be subtracted from the cash balance per books.

(e) The eight outstanding cheques issued by CPL to its suppliers that have not yet been cleared through the bank would be a $15,800 deduction from the cash balance per bank statement.
(f) The EFT of $2,800 would be added to the cash balance per bank statement.
(g) The reconciled cash balance (after the reconciliation is completed and any required adjusting entries prepared) would be the balance that should be reflected in the company's records at September 30, 2018.

6. Indicate which of the following items would be reconciling items on a monthly bank reconciliation to the cash balance per bank statement ("Bank"), to the cash balance per company's books ("Books"), or would not be a reconciling item ("N/A"). For all reconciling items, indicate whether the item would be added ("+") or subtracted ("−").

(a) Service fees charged by the bank on the company's account
(b) NSF cheques returned with the bank statement
(c) EFT receipts from customers
(d) Funds deposited into the company's account in error by the bank

(e) Cheques written and mailed out by the company that have yet to be cashed
(f) A utility payment recorded by the company's bookkeeper as $463.91 rather than $436.91, which was the correct amount owing and paid
(g) A deposit made using the night deposit slot on the last day of the month

7. Indicate which of the following journal entries are correct in relation to the bank reconciliation below. (Select as many as are appropriate.)

Cash balance per bank statement		$10,916.39
Add: Deposit in transit		1,163.15
Deduct: Outstanding cheques		(528.67)
Reconciled balance		$11,550.87
Cash balance per books		$12,770.44
Add: EFT receipts from customers on account		312.98
Error in recording cheque No. 1187		180.00
Deduct: Bank charges		(25.75)
EFT payment for rent		(1,500.00)
NSF cheque		(186.80)
Reconciled balance		$11,550.87

Note: The error was related to the payment of an invoice for advertising. The bookkeeper mistakenly recorded the payment as $426.81 rather than $246.81, which was the amount actually owing and paid by cheque No. 1187.

(a) NSF Cheque Expense	186.80	
Cash		186.80
(b) Cash	312.98	
Accounts Receivable		312.98
(c) Cash	1,500.00	
Rent Expense		1,500.00
(d) Accounts Receivable	186.80	
Cash		186.80
(e) Cash	1,163.15	
Deposits in Transit		1,163.15
(f) Bank Charges Expense	25.75	
Cash		25.75
(g) Advertising Expense	180.00	
Cash		180.00

8. Identify which of the following would be reconciling items to the *cash balance per books in a company's bank reconciliation* and that would result in a journal entry that includes a *credit* to the company's Cash account:

(a) An EFT payment related to the monthly rent of its warehouse

(b) Cheques that had been mailed to suppliers but that they had yet to deposit

(c) A customer's cheque that was returned by the bank due to non-sufficient funds

(d) A payment for an invoice for supplies that was recorded by the bookkeeper as $471.15 rather than $417.15, which is the amount

of the cheque and the actual balance owing

(e) Service fees of $37 charged by the bank

(f) An EFT receipt of $1,700 related to a customer paying their account

(g) A deposit of $2,600 made on the last day of the month using the night deposit slot at the bank

9. Identify all of the following items that would be included in the amount of cash and cash equivalents reported on the statement of financial position.

(a) The amount the company is in overdraft in one of its bank accounts

(b) Money market funds held by the company

(c) Cash on deposit at a bank, but held in a savings account rather than in the company's chequing account

(d) A paycheque that has not been cashed by an employee who picked it up five days ago

(e) Government treasury bills maturing in 60 days

(f) Postdated cheques for future rent received from a tenant the company rents commercial space to

(g) Cash on hand in the company's safe

10. Indicate the effect (positive, negative, or no effect) that each of the following would have on the company's cash balance:

(a) The company changes the terms of credit sales from n/30 to n/45.

(b) The company makes arrangements with suppliers to deliver products directly to stores within 24 hours of ordering, reducing the need for the company to maintain inventory in its warehouse.

(c) The company's employees agree to accept 10% of their salaries in common shares of the company.

(d) A bank agrees to pay interest of 0.25% on balances in the company's chequing account in excess of $25,000, which occurs during

its peak sales period of October through December.

(e) One of the company's main suppliers stops offering purchase discounts and reduces its payment period.

(f) A primary overseas supplier introduces a requirement for a 20% deposit prior to shipping goods to the company.

(g) Sixty percent of the company's customers across the country agree to sign up for the company's direct payment option, meaning they would pay their accounts via electronic transfer rather than paying by cheque.

WileyPLUS

Brief Exercises, Exercises, and many additional resources are available for practice in WileyPLUS.

▶ QUESTIONS

(LO 1) 1. Identify and describe the five primary components of a good internal control system.

(LO 1) 2. Explain who is responsible for establishing a company's control environment.

(LO 1) 3. Explain why "tone at the top" is critical when considering a company's internal control environment.

(LO 1) 4. Identify the five control activities that apply to most companies.

(LO 1) 5. How do documentation procedures contribute to good internal control?

(LO 1) 6. One of the company's senior managers is questioning the need for the company to implement reviews of controls by the internal auditors if the company also segregates duties. What do you think about this?

(LO 1) 7. Explain why external auditors are required to be independent of the company, whereas internal auditors are not.

(LO 1) 8. Kim is trying to design control activities so that there is no possibility of errors or theft. Explain to Kim why this may be impractical, and even impossible.

(LO 1) 9. Explain collusion and the control activity that is most affected when it occurs.

(LO 2) 10. Explain how electronic funds transfers can result in better internal control.

(LO 2) 11. In the corner grocery store, all the clerks make change out of the same cash register drawer. Is this a violation of a control activity? Explain.

(LO 2) 12. Dent Department Stores Ltd. has just installed new electronic cash registers with scanners in its stores. How do these cash registers improve control activities over cash receipts?

(LO 2) 13. "To have maximum control over cash payments, all payments should be made by cheque." Is this true? Explain.

(LO 2) 14. At a dental office, the receptionist schedules appointments and can cancel them. She also collects payment from patients (about 10% of them pay cash) and maintains all of the accounting records for the practice. Comment on whether these arrangements can result in a violation of one or more control activities and give rise to fraud.

(LO 2, 3) 15. Who should be responsible for preparing a bank reconciliation? Why?

(LO 2, 3) 16. "The use of a bank contributes significantly to good internal control over cash." Is this true? Explain.

(LO 3) 17. Paul Pascal is confused about the lack of agreement between the cash balance per books and the balance per bank. Explain the possible causes for the lack of agreement to Paul, and give an example of each cause.

(LO 3) 18. Kari Mora asks for your help concerning an NSF cheque. Explain to Kari (a) what an NSF cheque is, (b) how it is treated in a bank reconciliation, and (c) whether it will require a journal entry and, if so, what accounts are typically debited and credited.

(LO 3) 19. The Diable Corporation wrote cheque #2375 for $1,325 on March 16. At March 31, the cheque had not cleared the company's bank account and was correctly listed as an outstanding cheque on the March 31 bank reconciliation. If the cheque has still not cleared the bank account on April 30, should it be included in the April bank reconciliation or not? Explain.

(LO 3) 20. Sam Wing is an accounting clerk who has stolen $1,700 in cash from the company he works for. He prepares the bank reconciliation each month. When he performs the reconciliation this month, he knows that the bank reconciliation will be out of balance by $1,700 because of his theft. He therefore decides to falsify the amount of outstanding cheques. Why would he do this and would he overstate or understate the amount of outstanding cheques?

(LO 4) 21. What account balances are included in cash and cash equivalents?

(LO 4) 22. What is restricted cash? What are compensating balances? How should these items be reported on the statement of financial position?

(LO 4) 23. At the end of its first quarter in the 2018 fiscal year, Brandon Corporation had an undrawn line of credit facility that allowed the company to borrow up to $16 million and pay it down whenever it wants to. How should this line of credit be reported on the statement of financial position?

(LO 4) 24. Describe the six principles of cash management.

(LO 4) 25. Glenn Green owns Green's Groceries Inc. He has been reading about companies having too much cash in the business press but doesn't understand how his company can have too much cash. Explain the concept of "too much cash" to Glenn and provide him with some suggestions for how the company could use the cash.

▶ BRIEF EXERCISES

BE7–1 Gina Milan is the new manager of Plenty Parking Ltd., a parking garage. She has heard about internal control but is not clear about its importance for the company. Explain to Gina the five control activities, and give her an example of an application of each control for Plenty Parking.

Identify control activities.
(LO 1)

BE7–2 Match each of the following control activities with its appropriate description.
1. Assignment of responsibility
2. Segregation of duties
3. Documentation
4. Physical controls
5. Review and reconciliation
   (a) _____ All transactions should include original, detailed receipts.
   (b) _____ Undeposited cash should be stored in the company safe.
   (c) _____ Surprise cash counts are performed by internal audit.
   (d) _____ Responsibility for related activities should be assigned to specific employees.
   (e) _____ Cheque signers are not allowed to record cash transactions.

Match control activities.
(LO 1)

BE7–3 Tene Ltd. has the following internal controls over cash receipts. Identify the control activity that is applicable to each procedure.
1. All over-the-counter receipts are recorded on cash registers.
2. Daily cash counts are performed by the accounting supervisor.
3. The duties of receiving cash, recording cash, and maintaining custody of cash are assigned to different individuals.
4. Only cashiers may operate cash registers.
5. All cash is deposited intact in the bank account every day.

Identify control activities for cash receipts.
(LO 1, 2)

Identify control activities for cash payments.
(LO 1, 2)

BE7–4 Rolling Hills Ltd. has the following internal controls over cash payments. Identify the control activity that is applicable to each procedure.
1. Company cheques are prenumbered.
2. The bank statement is reconciled monthly by the assistant controller.
3. Blank cheques are stored in a safe in the controller's office.
4. Both the controller and the assistant controller are required to sign cheques or authorize electronic payments.
5. Cheque signers are not allowed to record cash payments.
6. All payments are made by cheque or electronic transfer.

Identify location of items in bank reconciliation.
(LO 3)

BE7–5 For each of the items in the following list, identify where it is included on a bank reconciliation. Next to each item write "bank+" for an increase in the bank balance; "bank–" for a decrease in the bank balance; "books+" for an increase in the books balance; "books–" for a decrease in the books balance; or "NA" for not applicable, to indicate that the item is not included in the bank reconciliation.
_____ 1. Outstanding cheques from a prior month (May) that are still outstanding
_____ 2. Outstanding cheques from a prior month (May) that are no longer outstanding
_____ 3. A deposit in transit from the current month (June)
_____ 4. A company error in recording a cheque made out for $630 as $360
_____ 5. A bank error in recording a company cheque made out for $200 as $290
_____ 6. Bank service charges
_____ 7. A bank deposit for interest earned on an investment
_____ 8. Outstanding cheques from the current month (June)
_____ 9. A company error in recording a $1,280 deposit as $1,680
_____ 10. A bank service charge for an NSF cheque
_____ 11. A bank error in recording a $2,575 deposit as $2,755
_____ 12. An EFT collection on account

Analyze deposits in transit.
(LO 3)

BE7–6 For the months of January and February, Monde Ltd. recorded cash deposits in its books of $5,000 and $5,600, respectively. For the same two months, the bank reported deposits totalling $4,000 and $4,600, respectively. Assuming that there were no deposits in transit at the beginning of January, what was the amount of deposits in transit at the end of January and at the end of February?

Analyze outstanding cheques.
(LO 3)

BE7–7 In the month of November, its first month of operations, Singh Jaya Ltd. wrote cheques in the amount of $27,100. In December, cheques in the amount of $23,200 were written. In November, $25,900 of these cheques were presented to the bank for payment and $19,700 were presented in December. What is the amount of outstanding cheques at the end of November and at the end of December?

Analyze errors.
(LO 3)

BE7–8 Kashechewan Inc. mistakenly recorded a cheque as $569 that was written for $659 in payment of a payable owing to one of the company's suppliers. In addition, the company noticed that the bank had mistakenly deducted a cheque for $415 from its bank account that was written by another company. (a) Explain how each of these errors should be treated on the bank reconciliation. (b) Identify any entries required on Kashechewan's books to correct these errors.

Calculate the cash balance per Southco's books.
(LO 3)

BE7–9 The following information relates to Southco Limited's Cash account. The reconciled cash balance from June's bank reconciliation is $18,920. During the month of July, Southco recorded cash receipts of $21,700 and cash payments of $24,300 in the general ledger Cash account. Calculate Southco's cash balance per books at July 31, immediately prior to preparing the July bank reconciliation.

Prepare bank reconciliation.
(LO 3)

BE7–10 Using the data in BE7–9, determine or calculate the cash balance per Southco Limited's books. An examination of the company's July bank statement shows a balance of $19,260 on July 31; outstanding cheques $3,630; deposits in transit $1,450; EFT collections on account that were not yet recorded on the books $2,170; NSF cheque $1,270; NSF fee $50; and bank services charges $90. Prepare the bank reconciliation at July 31.

Prepare journal entries.
(LO 3)

BE7–11 Using the data in BE7–10, prepare the necessary journal entries required on July 31 for Southco.

Report cash.
(LO 4)

BE7–12 Ouellette Ltée reports the following items: cash in bank $17,500; payroll bank account $6,000; cash register floats $500; held-for-trading investments consisting of term deposits with maturity dates of less than 90 days $5,000; and cash restricted for plant expansion $25,000. Ouellette also maintains a $5,000 compensating bank balance in a separate bank account. Determine which accounts described above would be considered cash, cash equivalents, or other items to be reported on the statement of financial position. If "other" is chosen, indicate where on the statement of financial position the account would be classified.

BE7–13 Evergreen Inc. owns these assets at the statement of financial position date:

Calculate cash.
(LO 4)

Cash in bank (savings account)	$22,000 (1)
Cash on hand	1,700
Income tax refund due from the Canada Revenue Agency	2,000
Cash in bank (chequing account)	14,000
Postdated cheques received from customers	1,000

Notes: 1. As a condition of a loan, the bank requires Evergreen to maintain a minimum balance of $5,000 in the account.

(a) What amount should be reported as cash and cash equivalents in the statement of financial position? (b) For any item not included in part (a), identify where it should be reported.

▶ EXERCISES

E7–1 The following situations suggest either a strength or weakness in a control activity:

Identify control activities.
(LO 1)

1. At Tingley's, Iryna and Inder work alternate lunch hours. Normally, Iryna works the cash register at the checkout counter, but during her lunch hour Inder takes her place. They both use the same cash drawer and jointly count cash at the end of the day.
2. The Do It Corporation accepts both cash and credit cards for its sales. Due to privacy legislation that requires credit card information to be shredded within three months, it shreds all credit card slips after they are processed.
3. The mail clerk at Genesis Legal Services prepares a daily list of all cash receipts. The cash receipts are forwarded to a staff accountant, who deposits the cash in the company's bank account. The list is sent to the accounts receivable clerk for recording.
4. The Candy Store can afford only a part-time bookkeeper. The bookkeeper's responsibilities include making the bank deposit, recording transactions, and reconciling the bank statement.
5. The Decorator Shoppe counts inventory at the end of each month. Two staff members count the inventory together. It is then priced and totalled by the accounting department and reconciled to the perpetual inventory records. Any variances are investigated.

Instructions
(a) State whether each situation above is a control strength or weakness and explain why.
(b) For each weakness, suggest an improvement.

E7–2 Each of the following situations describes an instance of fraud:

Identify control activities to detect and prevent fraud.
(LO 1)

1. A bartender sells drinks to customers and, when they pay cash, he does not record the sale at the cash register and keeps the cash.
2. A bartender knows that there is a special on vodka tonight so he brings his own bottle of vodka to the bar. When a customer orders vodka and pays cash, the bartender pours the vodka from his own bottle, does not record the sale at the cash register, and keeps the cash.
3. The receptionist at a spa enters all appointments into a computerized schedule. After their appointment, the client pays the receptionist for the service received. For about half of the customers who pay with cash, the receptionist keeps the amount and deletes any record of the appointment from the schedule. The receptionist makes the bank deposits and records all sales in the accounting system.
4. The receptionist at a law firm has a key to a cabinet where company cheques are stored. She takes a cheque from the cabinet, makes it payable to herself, and forges the signature of the firm's managing partner on the cheque. She opens the mail every day and when the bank statement is received, she performs the bank reconciliation. She covers the theft by understating the amount of outstanding cheques on the bank reconciliation.

Instructions
(a) Is it possible to detect each of the above these types of fraud? Why or why not?
(b) Identify a control activity or activities that could help prevent each instance of fraud described above.

E7–3 The following control activities are used at Tolan Ltd. for over-the-counter cash receipts:

Identify control activities for cash receipts.
(LO 1, 2)

1. All over-the-counter receipts are received by one of three clerks. The clerks share a cash register with a single cash drawer.
2. To minimize the risk of robbery, cash in excess of $100 is stored in an unlocked strongbox in the stockroom until it is deposited in the bank.

3. At the end of each day, the total receipts are counted by the cashier on duty and reconciled to the cash register total.
4. The company accountant makes the bank deposit and then records the day's receipts.
5. If a customer has the exact change and does not want a receipt, the sale is not entered in the cash register. The money is kept in a loose change box.

Instructions

(a) For each of the above situations, explain the weakness and identify the control activity that is violated.
(b) For each weakness, suggest an improvement.

Identify control activities for cash payments.

(LO 1, 2)

E7–4 The following control activities are used in Sheera's Boutique Shoppe Ltd. for cash payments:
1. Blank cheques are stored in an unmarked envelope on a shelf behind the cash register.
2. The purchasing manager personally approves payments for purchases and signs the cheques issued to pay suppliers.
3. When the store manager goes away for an extended period of time, she pre-signs cheques to be used in her absence.
4. The company cheques are not prenumbered.
5. The company accountant prepares the bank reconciliation and reports any discrepancies to the store manager.

Instructions

(a) For each of the above situations, explain the weakness and identify the control activity that is violated.
(b) For each weakness, suggest an improvement.

Calculate reconciled cash balance.

(LO 3)

E7–5 The reconciled cash balance from Hudson Corporation's August 31 bank reconciliation was $34,780. Hudson recorded the following events in the general ledger Cash account during the month of September: (1) cheques totalling $176,978 were issued; (2) salaries of $39,170 were electronically deposited to employee accounts; (3) the monthly EFT payment of $2,600 was made for rent; and (4) deposits totalled $199,680.

Instructions

(a) Calculate Hudson's cash balance in the general ledger Cash account on September 30, prior to the bank reconciliation.
(b) Indicate the effects of items (1) through (4) in the bank reconciliation.

Indicate effects of items in bank reconciliation.

(LO 3)

E7–6 Ten items that may or may not be involved in the bank reconciliation process for April are listed in the table shown on the next page:

	Bank		Books			Journal
Item	Add (Credit)	Deduct (Debit)	Add (Debit)	Deduct (Credit)	Not Applicable	Entry Required
1. Deposits in transit at the end of April	✓					No
2. Deposits in transit at the beginning of April that cleared the bank in April						
3. Outstanding cheques at the beginning of April that cleared the bank in April						
4. Outstanding cheques at the end of April						
5. Bank service charges						
6. Deposit of $400 made in error by the bank to the company's account						
7. Cheque written for $250 recorded in error as $520 on the books						
8. NSF cheque received from customer						
9. EFT collection on account not previously recorded by company						
10. Interest earned on bank account						

Instructions

Complete the table shown above, identifying where each item should be included on a bank reconciliation prepared for the month of April. Insert a check mark (✓) in the appropriate column indicating whether the item should be added to, or deducted from, the bank or the books. If the item should not be included in the bank reconciliation, write "NA" for not applicable. Finally, indicate whether the item will require a journal entry on the company books by writing "yes" or "no" in the last column. The first item has been done for you as an example.

E7–7 The cash records of Lejeune Inc. show the following situations:

Deposits in transit:

1. The June 30 bank reconciliation indicated that deposits in transit total $2,000. During July, the general ledger account Cash shows deposits of $14,750, but the bank statement indicates that $15,820 in deposits were received during the month.
2. In August, deposits per bank statement totalled $22,500 and deposits per books were $22,900.

Outstanding cheques:

1. The June 30 bank reconciliation reported outstanding cheques of $570. During July, the Lejeune books showed that $18,200 of cheques were issued. The bank statement showed that $17,200 of cheques cleared the bank in July.
2. In August, cheques issued were $22,700 and cheques clearing the bank were $23,520.

Instructions
(a) What were the deposits in transit at July 31 and at August 31?
(b) What were the outstanding cheques at July 31 and at August 31?

Calculate deposits in transit and outstanding cheques.

(LO 3)

E7–8 The following information is for Neopolitan Ltd. in July:

1. Cash balance per bank, July 31, $10,670
2. Cash balance per books, July 31, $8,953
3. Bank service charge, $40
4. Deposits in transit, $1,968
5. Electronic receipts from customers in payment of their accounts, $1,276, not previously recorded by the company
6. Outstanding cheques, $2,359
7. Cheque #373 was correctly written in the amount of $890 but was incorrectly recorded by the company's bookkeeper as $980. The cheque was written for the purchase of office supplies.

Instructions
(a) Prepare the bank reconciliation at July 31.
(b) Prepare any journal entries required from the reconciliation.

Prepare bank reconciliation and journal entries.

(LO 3)

E7–9 The bookkeeper for Sharp Manufacturing Ltd. was trying to determine what items would be used in preparing the company's bank reconciliation that she is completing at May 31, 2018, which was the company's first month of operations. The company's bank statement showed the following:

Identify reconciling items and determine reconciled cash balance.

(LO 3)

SHARP MANUFACTURING LTD.
Bank Statement
May 31

Date		Description	Amounts Deducted from Account (Debits)	Amounts Added to Account (Credits)	Balance
May	1	Deposit		25,000	25,000
	3	Cheque, No. 001	1,620		23,380
	5	Cheque, No. 002	7,130		16,250
	15	Deposit		4,650	20,900
	19	Cheque, No. 004	8,289		12,611
	21	Cheque, No. 006	995		11,616
	25	Returned cheque—NSF, S. Gillis	1,350		10,266
	25	NSF fee	25		10,241
	27	Cheque, No. 009	2,125		8,116
	28	Cheque, No. 010	1,970		6,146
	31	Bank service charges	40		6,106

Sharp's cash receipts summary (which were all deposited) and cheque summary (which were all mailed out to suppliers) for the month of May showed the following:

Cash Receipts Summary			Cheque Summary		
Date		Amount	Date	Number	Amount
May	1	$25,000	May 2	001	$ 1,620
	15	4,650	3	002	7,130
	31	7,820	14	003	1,675
		$37,470	15	004	8,289
			18	005	360
			19	006	995
			22	007	2,130
			23	008	525
			25	009	2,125
			26	010	1,970
					$26,819

Instructions

(a) Review Sharp's cash receipts summary and determine the amount of any deposits not recorded by the bank. These will be deposits in transit. *Hint*: It can be useful to check off or cross out the deposits that appear on both the bank statement and the cash receipts summary because these will not be deposits in transit.

(b) Review Sharp's cheque summary and determine the amount of any cheques that have not yet cleared the company's bank account. These will be outstanding cheques. *Hint*: It can be useful to check off or cross out the cheques that appear on both the bank statement and the cheque summary because these will not be outstanding cheques.

(c) Review Sharp's bank statement and identify any items on it that are not included in either the company's cash receipts summary or cheque summary. These will be reconciling items to the "Cash balance per books."

(d) Determine the cash balance per books prior to the reconciliation. *Hint*: This would be equal to: Balance in the cash account at the beginning of the month + Deposits made during the month – Cheques issued during the month.

(e) Prepare Sharp's bank reconciliation at May 31 and determine the company's reconciled cash balance.

Calculate cash.
(LO 4)

E7–10 A new accountant at La Maison Ltée is trying to identify which of the following amounts should be reported as cash and cash equivalents in the April 30 year-end statement of financial position:

1. Currency and coin totalling $123 in a locked box used for incidental cash transactions
2. A balance of $4,325 in the Royal Bank chequing account
3. A balance of $5,000 in the Royal Bank savings account
4. A $25,000 government treasury bill, due the next month, May 31
5. April-dated cheques worth $750 that La Maison has received from customers but not yet deposited
6. A $185 cheque received from a customer in payment of its April account, but postdated to May 1
7. Over-the-counter receipts for April 30 consisting of $1,735 of currency and coin and $1,230 of cheques from customers, which were processed by the bank on May 1
8. A $50 IOU from the company receptionist
9. Cash register floats of $500

Instructions

(a) What amount should La Maison consider to be cash at April 30?

(b) What should it consider to be a cash equivalent?

(c) What combined amount would La Maison report as cash and cash equivalents on its year-end statement of financial position?

(d) In which financial statement(s) and in what account(s) should the items not included in part (a) be reported?

Discuss cash management.
(LO 4)

E7–11 Tory, Hachey, and Wedunn, three young lawyers who have joined together to open a law practice, are struggling to manage their cash flow. They have not yet built up enough clientele and revenues to support the cost of running their legal practice. Initial costs, such as advertising and renovations to the premises, all result in outgoing cash flow at a time when little is coming in! Tory, Hachey, and Wedunn have not had time to establish a billing system because most of their clients' cases have not yet reached the courts and the lawyers did not think it would be right to bill them until "results were achieved." Unfortunately, Tory, Hachey, and Wedunn's suppliers do not feel the same way. Their suppliers expect them to pay their accounts payable within a few weeks of receiving their bills. So far, there has not even been enough money to pay the three lawyers, and they are not sure how long they can keep practising law without getting some money into their pockets!

Instructions

Provide suggestions for Tory, Hachey, and Wedunn to improve its cash management practices, in particular with respect to accelerating the collection of its receivables and delaying the payment of its liabilities.

▶ PROBLEMS: SET A

P7–1A Red River Theatre has a cashier's booth located near the theatre entrance. There are two cashiers: one works from 1 p.m. to 5 p.m., the other from 5 p.m. to 9 p.m. The cashiers receive cash from customers and operate a machine that ejects serially numbered tickets. The rolls of tickets are inserted and locked into the machine by the theatre manager at the beginning of each cashier's shift.

Identify control activities over cash receipts.

(LO 1, 2)

After purchasing a ticket, which costs a different amount depending on the day of the week and the customer's age group, the customer takes the ticket to an usher stationed at the entrance to the theatre lobby, a few metres from the cashier's booth. The usher tears the ticket in half, admits the customer, and returns the ticket stub to the customer. The usher drops the other half of the ticket into a locked box.

At the end of each cashier's shift, the theatre manager removes the ticket rolls from the machine and makes a cash count. The cash count sheet is initialled by the cashier. At the end of the day, the manager deposits the total receipts in a bank night deposit slot. In addition, the manager sends copies of the deposit slip and the initialled cash count sheets to the head cashier for verification and to the accounting department for comparison with sales records. Receipts from the first shift are stored in a safe located in the manager's office.

Instructions
(a) Identify the control activities and their application to cash receipts at the theatre.
(b) If the usher and cashier decided to collude to steal cash, what actions might they take?

P7–2A High Tech Inc. began operations recently. Two friends from university, John Deol and Rehana Gerdman, jointly own the company's shares. John and Rehana have developed a new software application to track shipping. The two friends spend most of their time on developing new products and marketing the current product.

Identify control weaknesses over cash payments.

(LO 1, 2)

John and Rehana hired Fred Glass to be High Tech's controller. Fred has been given overall responsibility for the books and records of High Tech so that John and Rehana can spend their time on development and marketing.

Fred has one assistant, Asmaa. Both Fred and Asmaa have the authority to order goods for High Tech. Asmaa can approve invoices for payment up to $5,000. Fred can approve any invoice for payment. Fred, John, and Rehana are all signing officers on the company's bank account. Only one of the three signing officers needs to sign a cheque under $20,000. For cheques greater than $20,000, two signing officers must sign. Unsigned cheques are kept in the company safe. The safe is kept locked and access to the safe is limited to the signing officers. Fred is responsible for preparing the monthly bank reconciliations and making any necessary journal entries.

Instructions
(a) Identify the control weaknesses over the cash payments and the problems that could occur as a result of these weaknesses.
(b) List the improvements in control activities that High Tech should consider.

P7–3A Each of the following independent situations has one or more control activity weaknesses.
1. Board Riders Ltd. is a small snowboarding club that offers specialized coaching for snowboarders who want to improve their skills. Group lessons are offered every day. Members who want a lesson pay a $25 fee directly to the instructor at the start of the lesson that day. Most members pay cash. At the end of the lesson, the instructor reports the number of students and turns over the cash to the office manager.
2. Coloroso Agency Corp. offers parenting advice to young single mothers. Most of the agency's revenues are from government grants. The general manager is responsible for all of the accounting work, including approving invoices for payment, preparing and posting all entries into the accounting system, and preparing bank reconciliations.
3. At Nexus Corporation, each salesperson is responsible for deciding on the correct credit policies for his or her customers. For example, the salesperson decides if Nexus should sell to the customer on credit and how high the credit limit should be. Salespeople receive a commission based on their sales.
4. Algorithm Limited is a software company that employs many computer programmers. The company uses accounting software that was created by one of the employees. In order to be more flexible and share the workload, all of the programmers have access to the accounting software program in case changes are needed.
5. The warehouse manager at Orange Wing Distributors Ltd. is well known for running an efficient, cost-saving operation. He has eliminated the requirement for staff to create receiving reports and purchase orders because it was taking too long to prepare them.

Identify control weaknesses.

(LO 1, 2)

Instructions
(a) Identify the control weakness(es) in each of the above situations and the problems that could occur as a result of these weaknesses.
(b) Make recommendations for correcting each situation.

Identify control weaknesses over cash receipts and payments.

(LO 1, 2)

P7–4A Cedar Grove High School wants to raise money for a new sound system for its auditorium. The main fundraising event is a dance at which the famous disc jockey Obnoxious Al will play rap music. Roger DeMaster, the music teacher, has been given the responsibility for coordinating the fundraising efforts. This is Roger's first experience with fundraising. He decides to put the Student Representative Council (SRC) in charge of the event.

Roger had 500 unnumbered tickets printed for the dance. He left the tickets in a locked box on his desk and told the SRC students to take as many tickets as they thought they could sell for $20 each. To ensure that no extra tickets would be floating around, he told the students to destroy any unsold tickets in their possession. When the students received payment for the tickets, they were to bring the cash back to Roger, and he would put it in the locked box on his desk.

Some of the students were responsible for decorating the gymnasium for the dance. Roger gave each of them a key to the locked box and told them that if they took money out to purchase materials, they should put a note in the box saying how much they took and what it was used for. After two weeks, the locked box appeared to be getting full, so Roger asked one of the students, Praveen Patel, to count the money, prepare a deposit slip, and deposit the money in a bank account Roger had opened.

The day of the dance, Roger wrote a cheque from the account to pay Obnoxious Al. Al, however, said that he accepted only cash and did not give receipts. Having no alternative, Roger took $500 out of the locked box and gave it to Al. At the dance, Roger had a student, Sara Wu, working at the entrance to the gymnasium, collecting tickets from students and selling tickets to those who had not prepurchased them. Roger estimated that 400 students attended the dance.

The following day, Roger closed out the bank account, which had $750 in it, and gave that amount plus the $1,800 in the locked box to Principal Orlowski. Principal Orlowski seemed surprised that, after generating roughly $8,000 (400 tickets @ $20) in sales, the dance netted only $2,550 in cash. Roger did not know how to respond.

Instructions

(a) Identify the control weaknesses over cash receipts and payments and the problems that could occur because of these weaknesses.

(b) List the improvements in control activities that the school should consider.

Prepare bank reconciliation and journal entries.

(LO 3)

P7–5A On July 31, Beaupré Ltd. had a cash balance of $12,934 in its general ledger. The bank statement from the Caisse Populaire on that date showed a balance of $21,722. A comparison of the bank statement with the Cash account revealed the following:

1. The bank statement included service charges and credit card fees of $118.
2. The bank statement included electronic collections from customers on account totalling $5,230. Beaupré had not recorded the EFT.
3. A deposit of $3,100 made by another company was incorrectly added to Beaupré's account by the Caisse Populaire.
4. Salaries of $4,200 were paid electronically during the month. The company has already recorded these.
5. Cheques outstanding on June 30 totalled $2,738. Of these, $2,162 worth cleared the bank in July. All cheques written in July cleared the bank in July.

Instructions

(a) Prepare the bank reconciliation at July 31.

(b) Prepare any journal entries required from the reconciliation.

Prepare bank reconciliation and journal entries.

(LO 3)

P7–6A When Hirji Holdings Ltd. received its bank statement for the month of October, it showed that the company had a cash balance of $16,780 as at October 31. Hirji's general ledger showed a cash balance of $19,070 at that date. A comparison of the bank statement and the accounting records revealed the following information:

1. Bank service and credit card charges for the month were $65.
2. A cheque, in the amount of $575, from one of Hirji's customers that had been deposited during the last week of October was returned with the bank statement as "NSF."
3. Cheque #3421, which was a payment for utilities expenses, had been correctly written for $860 but had been incorrectly recorded in the general ledger as $680.
4. Hirji had written and mailed out cheques with a value of $2,650 that had not yet cleared the bank account.
5. During the month, the bank collected a $2,000 note receivable plus the outstanding interest of $180 on behalf of Hirji. The interest had already been accrued.
6. The cash receipts for October 31 amounted to $6,300 and had been deposited in the night drop slot at the bank on the evening of October 31. These were not reflected on the bank statement for October.

Instructions

(a) Prepare the bank reconciliation at October 31.

(b) Prepare any journal entries required from the reconciliation.

Prepare bank reconciliation and journal entries.

(LO 3)

P7–7A The bank portion of last month's bank reconciliation for Yap Ltd. at February 28 was as follows:

YAP LTD.
Bank Reconciliation
February 28

Cash balance per bank	$17,984
Add: Deposits in transit	3,140
	21,124
Less: Outstanding cheques	
#3451	1,960
#3470	2,135
Reconciled cash balance	$17,029

The reconciled cash balance per bank agreed with the reconciled cash balance per books after the bank reconciliation at February 28. The March bank statement showed the following:

YAP LTD.
Bank Statement
March 31

Date		Description	Amounts Deducted from Account (Debits)	Amounts Added to Account (Credits)	Balance
Feb.	28	Opening balance			17,984
Mar.	1	Cheque, No. 3451	1,960		16,024
	1	Deposit		3,140	19,164
	2	Cheque, No. 3470	2,135		17,029
	4	Deposit		1,971	19,000
	9	Cheque, No. 3471	1,682		17,318
	10	Returned cheque—NSF, J. Mustafa	870		16,448
	10	NSF fee	35		16,413
	15	EFT, loan payment	1,214		15,199
	19	Cheque, No. 3472	1,823		13,376
	26	Deposit		3,266	16,642
	31	EFT, collection on account from M. Boudreault		610	17,252
	31	Bank service charges and credit card fees	89		17,163

Yap's cash receipts and payments for the month of March showed the following:

Cash Receipts			Cash Payments		
Date	Amount		Date	Number	Amount
Mar. 4	$1,971		Mar. 7	3471	$1,682
26	3,266		15	3472	1,283
31	4,012		29	3473	4,947
	$9,249				$7,912

Additional information:

1. The EFT loan payment should have been recorded by the company on March 15, but this entry was missed. The payment included $84 of interest and a $1,130 payment on the loan principal.
2. The bank made an error processing cheque #3472.
3. The EFT collection was not previously recorded.
4. Bank service charges and credit card fees totalling $89 were not previously recorded.

Instructions

(a) Calculate the cash balance per books at March 31, prior to reconciliation.
(b) What is the amount of the deposits in transit at March 31?
(c) What is the amount of the outstanding cheques at March 31?
(d) Prepare the bank reconciliation at March 31.
(e) Prepare any journal entries required from the reconciliation.

*Prepare bank reconcilia-
tion and journal entries.*

(LO 3)

P7–8A The bank portion of last month's bank reconciliation for Hamptons Limited at October 31 is shown here:

HAMPTONS LIMITED		
Bank Reconciliation		
October 31		
Cash balance per bank		$24,890
Add: Deposits in transit		3,060
		27,950
Less: Outstanding cheques		
#2472	$1,440	
#2473	1,690	
#2474	1,008	4,138
Reconciled cash balance		$23,812

The reconciled cash balance per bank agreed with the reconciled cash balance per books after the bank reconciliation at October 31. The November bank statement showed the following:

HAMPTONS LIMITED				
Bank Statement				
November 30				
Date	Description	Amounts Deducted from Account (Debits)	Amounts Added to Account (Credits)	Balance
Oct. 31				24,890
Nov. 1	Cheque, No. 2472	1,440		23,450
1	Deposit		3,060	26,510
2	Cheque, No. 2473	1,690		24,820
3	Deposit		2,424	27,244
4	Cheque, No. 2475	3,282		23,962
7	Deposit		1,980	25,942
8	Cheque, No. 2476	5,660		20,282
10	Cheque, No. 2477	1,200		19,082
14	Deposit		5,150	24,232
15	Cheque, No. 2478	3,500		20,732
15	EFT, salaries	6,400		14,332
20	Deposit		5,890	20,222
25	Returned cheque—NSF, Giasson Developments	500		19,722
25	NSF fee	80		19,642
26	Cheque, No. 2479	1,390		18,252
27	Deposit		3,300	21,552
28	EFT, collection of note receivable and interest		5,008	26,560
30	Cheque, No. 2481	1,152		25,408
30	EFT, salaries	6,400		19,008
30	Bank service charges	50		18,958

The cash records per books for November showed the following:

Cash Receipts			Cash Payments		
Date	Amount		Date	Number	Amount
Nov. 3	$ 2,424		Nov. 1	2475	$ 3,282
7	1,980		2	2476	4,760
12	5,150		2	2477	1,200
20	5,908		8	2478	3,500
27	3,300		15	2479	1,390
30	2,676		15	EFT, salaries	6,400
	$21,438		18	2480	1,224
			20	2481	1,152
			29	2482	1,660
			30	EFT, salaries	6,400
					$30,968

Additional information:

1. The EFT collection was not previously recorded. The collection of the note on November 28 was for $4,400, plus $608 interest. Interest was not previously accrued.
2. EFT payments are recorded when they occur.
3. The bank did not make any errors.
4. Two errors were made by the company: one in recording a cheque and one in recording a cash receipt. The correction of any errors in the recording of cheques should be made to Accounts Payable. The correction of any errors in the recording of cash receipts should be made to Accounts Receivable.

Instructions

(a) Calculate the cash balance per books as at November 30, prior to reconciliation.
(b) Prepare the bank reconciliation at November 30.
(c) Prepare any journal entries required from the reconciliation.

P7–9A A first-year co-op student is trying to determine the amount of cash and cash equivalents that should be reported on a company's statement of financial position. The following information was provided to the student at year end:

Calculate cash.

(LO 4)

1. Cash on hand in the cash registers totals $2,920.
2. The balance in the commercial bank savings account is $57,800 and in the commercial bank chequing account, $25,000. The company also has a U.S. bank account, which contains the equivalent of $27,000 Canadian at year end.
3. A special bank account holds $200,000 in cash that is restricted for equipment replacement.
4. Amounts due from employees (travel advances) total $8,700.
5. Held-for-trading investments held by the company include $25,000 in a term deposit maturing in 120 days, a Government of Canada bond for $50,000 that falls due in 30 days, and $36,000 in shares of Loblaw Companies Limited.
6. The company has $1,230 of NSF cheques from customers that were returned by the bank. NSF fees charged by the bank for processing these cheques totalled $55.
7. The company keeps $12,000 as a compensating balance with respect to a long-term loan in a special account.

Instructions

(a) Determine which items listed above would be considered to be cash and which would be considered to be cash equivalents.
(b) What combined amount would the company report as cash and cash equivalents on the year-end statement of financial position?
(c) Identify where any items that were not reported as cash and cash equivalents in part (a) should be reported.

P7–10A Rupert Inc. reports the following selected information (in thousands) in its April 30, 2018, financial statements:

Discuss reporting of cash.

(LO 4)

	2018	2017
Cash and cash equivalents	$51,680	$42,290
Restricted cash	6,150	4,700

Additional information:

Restricted cash represents monies held for a potential lawsuit settlement.

Instructions

(a) Explain the difference between cash and cash equivalents. Why are they combined for reporting purposes?
(b) In which section of the statement of financial position would the restricted cash most likely be reported? Explain.
(c) Explain why it is necessary to report restricted cash separately when cash equivalents, such as highly liquid held-for-trading investments, are included in cash.

P7–11A Bev's Design Services Ltd. began operations approximately nine months ago. The company organizes the hall and table decorations for a variety of functions, including weddings, parties, and meetings. Bev's Design has completed 15 contracts so far and, with wedding season coming up, has 20 more signed contracts. However, the company has no cash in its bank account and its sole shareholder, Bev McDowell, has had to lend the company money from her personal funds.

Recommend cash management improvements.

(LO 4)

For each signed contract, the company requires a $50 non-refundable deposit. The balance of the account receivable is due three weeks following the function. For the weddings Bev has serviced, she has received the amount due on average five weeks after the function. All the decorations must be purchased about two months before the function or once the contract has been signed, whichever is earlier. The company pays for the decorations at the time of purchase. Recently, the company has learned that it can apply for an account, which will permit it to pay 30 days after purchase.

Instructions

Identify ways that Bev's Design Services Ltd. can improve its cash management practices, in particular with respect to accelerating the collection of its receivables and delaying the payment of its liabilities.

▶ PROBLEMS: SET B

Identify control activities over cash payments.

(LO 1, 2)

P7–1B Segal Office Supply Limited recently changed its control activities over cash payments. The new activities include the following features:

1. All cheques are prenumbered and written by an electronic cheque-writing system.
2. Before a cheque or electronic payment can be issued, each invoice must have the approval of Cindy van Bommel, the purchasing agent, and Ray Mills, the receiving department supervisor.
3. Cheques must be signed by either controller François Montpetit or assistant controller Mary Nishiyama. Before signing a cheque, the signer is expected to compare the amount of the cheque with the amount on the invoice.
4. After signing a cheque, the signer stamps the invoice "Paid" and writes in the date, cheque number, and amount of the cheque. The paid invoice is then sent to the accounting department for recording.
5. Blank cheques are stored in a safe in the controller's office. The combination to the safe is known only to the controller and assistant controller.
6. Each month, the bank statement is reconciled by a staff accountant who does not record payments.

Instructions

Identify the control activities and their application to cash payments at Segal Office Supply.

Identify control weaknesses over cash receipts.

(LO 1, 2)

P7–2B You are asked to join the board of elders of a local church to help with the control activities for the offerings collection made at weekly services. At a meeting of the board, you learn the following:

1. The board of elders has delegated responsibility for the financial management and audit of the financial records to the finance committee. This group prepares the annual budget and approves major payments but is not involved in collections or record keeping. No audit has been done in recent years, because the same trusted employee has kept church records and served as financial secretary for 15 years.
2. The collection at the weekly service is taken by a team of ushers who volunteer to serve for one month. The ushers take the collection plates to a basement office at the back of the church. They hand their plates to the head usher and return to the church service. After all plates have been turned in, the head usher counts the cash collected in them. The head usher then places the cash in the church safe along with a note that includes the amount counted. The safe is unlocked because no one can remember the combination, and after all, it is in a church.
3. The morning after the service, the financial secretary goes to the safe and recounts the collection. The secretary withholds $200 to pay for cash purchases for the week, and deposits the remainder of the collection in the bank. To facilitate the deposit, church members who contribute by cheque are asked to make their cheques payable to "Cash."
4. Each month, the financial secretary reconciles the bank statement and submits a copy of the reconciliation to the board of elders. The reconciliations have rarely revealed any bank errors and have never shown any errors per books.

Instructions

(a) Identify the control weaknesses in the handling of collections.
(b) List the improvements in control activities that should be recommended for (1) the head usher, (2) the ushers, (3) the financial secretary, and (4) the finance committee.

Identify control weaknesses.

(LO 1, 2)

P7–3B Each of the following independent situations has one or more control activity weaknesses:

1. Rowena's Cleaning Service Inc. provides home cleaning services for a large number of clients who all pay cash. Rowena collects the cash and keeps it in the glove compartment of her car until the end of the week when she has time to count it and prepare a bank deposit.
2. Hornet's Convenience Store Limited sells a variety of items, including cigarettes, non-alcoholic beverages, and snack foods. A long-term employee is responsible for ordering all merchandise, checking all deliveries, and approving invoices for payment.
3. At Ye Olde Ice Cream Shoppe Ltd., there are three sales clerks on duty during busy times. All three of them use the same cash drawer.
4. Most customers at Better Used Car dealership use the option to pay for their vehicles in 24 equal payments over two years. These customers send the company cheques or cash each month. The office manager opens the mail each day, makes a bank deposit with the cash and cheques received in the mail that day, and prepares and posts a journal entry in the accounting records.
5. Jimmy's Truck Parts Ltd. employs sales staff who visit current and prospective customers. The sales staff keep product samples in their vehicles so they can demonstrate the product to the customers. If a customer has a large order, the order is emailed to the warehouse. The warehouse then ships the product to the customer on account. If a customer wishes to purchase one or two sample items, the salesperson can sell these for cash or on account. To obtain more inventory, the salespeople go to the warehouse and restock the vehicle themselves.

Instructions

(a) Identify the control weakness(es) in each of the above situations and the problems that could occur as a result of these weaknesses.
(b) Make recommendations for correcting each situation.

P7–4B The president of a registered charity, the Helping Elderly Low-Income People Foundation (HELP), approaches you for help on a special project to set up the charity's accounting system. HELP is a relatively new organization that is regulated by both the federal and provincial governments. The organization is required to maintain current financial records for the public to scrutinize. In other words, the records must be available to anyone who is interested in reviewing them. It is now the end of the charity's first fiscal year, and HELP has come to you with a shoebox of receipts and bank statements. You notice that the bank statements are still in their envelopes—they have not been opened.

Identify control weaknesses over cash receipts and payments.

(LO 1, 2)

The charity's revenue is mostly from donations. A van driver takes volunteers around the city and they go door to door asking for donations. The volunteers give a donation receipt for amounts over $20. Since volunteering takes a lot of time, the charity has many short-term volunteers and anyone is welcome to be one.

Two car companies generously donated vans to the organization. The van drivers are paid $50 a day, which they take from the donations. Drivers keep a summary of the total donations collected by the volunteers, and at the end of the day the drivers take the money to a bank and deposit it. Drivers also pay for their gas out of the donated funds.

HELP also held a fundraising dance last month. The president said he was disappointed with the project, though, because it did not bring in much money. To keep costs down, the president made the dance tickets by photocopying tickets and cutting them up. He gave them out to volunteers to sell for $25 each. He estimates that he printed 500 tickets, but can only account for about $5,000 (200 tickets @ $25) of revenues turned in by his volunteers.

Instructions
(a) Identify the control weaknesses over cash receipts and payments.
(b) List the improvements in control activities that HELP should consider.

P7–5B On May 31, O'Hearne Limited had a cash balance per books of $13,126. The bank statement from Community Bank on that date showed a balance of $15,230. A comparison of the bank statement with the company's Cash account revealed the following:

Prepare bank reconciliation and journal entries.

(LO 3)

1. The bank statement included a bank service charge of $80.
2. The bank statement included electronic collections totalling $4,188. These were not previously recorded.
3. Outstanding cheques at April 30 totalled $2,900. Of these, $2,240 worth cleared the bank in May. There were $1,892 of cheques written in May that were still outstanding on May 31.
4. Included with the cancelled cheques was a cheque issued by O'Bearne Inc. for $1,200 that was incorrectly charged to O'Hearne by the bank.
5. On May 31, the bank statement showed a returned (NSF) cheque for $1,350 issued by a customer in payment of its account. In addition, the bank charged an $80 processing fee for this transaction.
6. The May 31 deposit of $1,926 was not included in the deposits on the May bank statement. The deposit had been placed in the bank's night deposit vault on May 31.

Instructions
(a) Prepare the bank reconciliation at May 31.
(b) Prepare any journal entries required from the reconciliation.

P7–6B You are a student intern at Island Milling Ltd. The bookkeeper has gathered all of the information necessary to complete Island Milling's bank reconciliation for October. She has asked you to complete it for her. Island Milling's general ledger showed a cash balance of $14,565 at October 31. The company's bank statement for the month of October showed that the company had a cash balance of $17,230 as at October 31. A comparison of the bank statement and the accounting records revealed the following information:

Prepare bank reconciliation and journal entries.

(LO 3)

1. Bank service and credit card charges for the month were $65.
2. The cash receipts for October 31 amounted to $3,600 and had been deposited in the night drop slot at the bank on the evening of October 31. These were not reflected on the bank statement for October.
3. During the last week of the month, one of Island Milling's customers made an electronic payment directly to Island Milling's bank in the amount of $2,650. Because the customer had not notified Island Milling of the payment, the company was unaware of it until it received the bank statement for October.
4. Island Milling had written and mailed out cheques with a value of $6,200 that had not yet cleared the bank account.
5. A cheque for $2,610 from one of Island Milling's customers that had been deposited during the last week of October was returned with the bank statement as "NSF."
6. Cheque #1926, which was a payment for legal fees, had been correctly written for $3,670 but had been incorrectly recorded in the general ledger as $3,760.

Instructions
(a) Prepare the bank reconciliation at October 31.
(b) Prepare any journal entries required from the reconciliation.

Prepare bank reconciliation and journal entries.

(LO 3)

P7-7B The bank portion of last month's bank reconciliation showed the following for River Adventures Ltd.:

RIVER ADVENTURES LTD.
Bank Reconciliation
April 30

Cash balance per bank		$12,612
Add: Deposits in transit		4,230
		16,842
Less: Outstanding cheques		
#533	$1,860	
#541	982	2,842
Reconciled cash balance		$14,000

The reconciled cash balance per bank agreed with the reconciled cash balance per books after the bank reconciliation at April 30. The May bank statement showed the following:

RIVER ADVENTURES LTD.
Bank Statement
May 31

Date	Description	Amounts Deducted from Account (Debits)	Amounts Added to Account (Credits)	Balance
Apr. 30	Opening balance			12,612
May 1	Deposit		4,230	16,842
3	Cheque, No. 541	982		15,860
4	Cheque, No. 533	1,860		14,000
6	Cheque, No. 542	1,620		12,380
6	Deposit		2,114	14,494
10	Cheque, No. 543	2,210		12,284
18	EFT, collection on account from A. Osborne		1,475	13,759
19	Cheque, No. 544	926		12,833
28	Deposit		1,819	14,652
28	Returned cheque—NSF, R. Lajeunesse	1,105		13,547
28	NSF fee	45		13,502
30	EFT, prepaid insurance payment	927		12,575
31	Bank service charges and credit card fees	95		12,480

River Adventures' cash receipts and payments for the month of May showed the following:

Cash Receipts			Cash Payments		
Date	Amount		Date	Number	Amount
May 6	$2,114		May 5	542	$1,620
28	1,819		7	543	2,120
31	1,524		15	544	926
	$5,457		31	545	1,535
					$6,201

Additional information:
1. The bank made an error when processing cheque #543.
2. The EFT collection was not previously recorded.
3. Because the EFT for prepaid insurance payment occurred near the end of the month, it has not been recorded yet.

Instructions
(a) Calculate the cash balance per books at May 31, prior to reconciliation.
(b) What is the amount of the deposits in transit at May 31?
(c) What is the amount of the outstanding cheques at May 31?
(d) Prepare the bank reconciliation at May 31.
(e) Prepare any journal entries required from the reconciliation.

P7–8B The bank portion of last month's bank reconciliation for Racine Limited at November 30 is shown here:

Prepare bank reconciliation and journal entries.

(LO 3)

RACINE LIMITED
Bank Reconciliation
November 30

Cash balance per bank		$14,368
Add: Deposits in transit		2,530
		16,898
Less: Outstanding cheques		
#3451	$2,260	
#3471	845	
#3474	1,050	4,155
Reconciled cash balance		$12,743

The reconciled cash balance per bank agreed with the reconciled cash balance per books after the bank reconciliation at November 30. The December bank statement showed the following:

RACINE LIMITED
Bank Statement
December 31

Date	Description	Amounts Deducted from Account (Debits)	Amounts Added to Account (Credits)	Balance
Nov. 30	Opening balance			14,368
Dec. 1	Deposit		2,530	16,898
1	Cheque, No. 3451	2,260		14,638
2	Cheque, No. 3471	845		13,793
3	Deposit		1,212	15,005
4	Cheque, No. 3475	1,641		13,364
7	EFT, salaries	1,427		11,937
8	Cheque, No. 3476	1,300		10,637
10	Cheque, No. 3477	2,130		8,507
15	Cheque, No. 3479	3,080		5,427
15	EFT, collection on account, R. Nishimura		3,145	8,572
17	Deposit		2,945	11,517
21	EFT, salaries	1,427		10,090
24	Returned cheque—NSF, Hilo Holdings	987		9,103
24	NSF fee	40		9,063
25	Deposit		2,567	11,630
27	Cheque, No. 3480	600		11,030
27	Cheque, No. 3482	1,140		9,890
30	Deposit		1,025	10,915
30	Cheque, No. 3481	475		10,440
31	Bank service charges	45		10,395

The cash records per books for December showed the following:

Cash Receipts			Cash Payments		
Date	Amount		Date	Number	Amount
Dec. 1	$1,212		Dec. 1	3475	$ 1,641
17	2,954		2	3476	1,300
27	2,567		2	3477	2,130
30	1,025		4	3478	538
31	1,197		7	EFT, salaries	1,427
	$8,955		8	3479	3,080
			10	3480	600
			20	3481	475
			21	EFT, salaries	1,427
			22	3482	1,140
			30	3483	1,390
					$15,148

Additional information:

1. The EFT collection was not previously recorded.
2. EFT payments are recorded when they occur.
3. The bank did not make any errors.
4. One error was made by the company. The correction of any errors in recording cheques should be made to Accounts Payable. The correction of any errors in recording cash receipts should be made to Accounts Receivable.

Instructions

(a) Calculate the cash balance per books as at December 31, prior to reconciliation.
(b) Prepare the bank reconciliation at December 31.
(c) Prepare any journal entries required from the reconciliation.

Calculate cash.

(LO 4)

P7–9B A new accounting student has been asked to determine the balance that should be reported as cash and cash equivalents as at December 31 for one of the firm's clients. The following information is available:

1. Cash on hand in the cash registers on December 31 totals $1,600. Of this amount, $500 is kept on hand as a cash float.
2. The balance in the bank chequing account at December 31 is $7,460.
3. Held-for-trading investments include $5,000 in a Government of Ontario bond that falls due in 80 days.
4. The company sold $250 of merchandise to a customer late in the day on December 31. The customer had forgotten her wallet and promised to pay the amount on January 2.
5. The company has a U.S. dollar bank account. At December 31, its U.S. funds were the equivalent of $2,241 Canadian.
6. In order to hook up utilities, the company is required to deposit $1,000 in trust with Hydro One. This amount must remain on deposit until a satisfactory credit history has been established. The company expects to have this deposit back within the year.

Instructions

(a) Determine which items listed above would be considered to be cash and which would be considered to be cash equivalents.
(b) What combined amount would the company report as cash and cash equivalents on the year-end statement of financial position?
(c) Identify where any items that were not reported as cash and cash equivalents in part (a) should be reported.

Discuss reporting of cash.

(LO 4)

P7–10B **Boardwalk REIT** reports the following selected information (in thousands) in its December 31, 2015, financial statements:

	2015	2014
Cash	$237,016	$139,564
Segregated tenants' security deposits	11,795	12,138

Additional information:

1. Cash consists of bank balances and term deposits.
2. Segregated tenants' security deposits are held on behalf of tenants and are returned at the end of a lease if the apartment rented to the tenant is undamaged. They are considered restricted cash because they are held in trust bank accounts.

Instructions

(a) Why do you think that the security deposits are not reported as part of cash?
(b) In which section of the statement of financial position would the segregated tenants' security deposits most likely be reported? Explain.

Recommend cash management improvements.

(LO 4)

P7–11B Jackie Ledbetter started a business, Jackie's Designs Inc., after finishing her interior design courses eight months ago. Jackie has been fortunate in that the company has already completed six contracts, has four more signed contracts, and has booked three meetings with prospective customers. The prospective customers are referrals from the six contracts she has already completed.

Jackie is having difficulty understanding why her business has no cash in the bank since it has been so successful. You asked her to explain the terms of the contracts and her system for purchases.

A contract is signed once the customer and Jackie agree on the work to be done. There is no deposit on signing the contract. The contract price is a flat fee for Jackie's work and cost plus a percentage for all items purchased by the company. The fee for Jackie's work is due once the contract is completed.

The amount for items purchased by the company is due three weeks after the items are delivered to the customer, in case the customer wants to return them. To date, an average contract takes four months to complete. The company does not have a formalized system for purchases. If a customer agrees that they would like to buy certain items, Jackie will purchase the items when she finds them. Generally, she uses cash to pay for the items at the time of purchase. The items are then delivered to the customer within a week.

Instructions

Identify ways that Jackie's Designs Inc. can improve its cash management practices, in particular with respect to accelerating the collection of its receivables and delaying the payment of its liabilities.

ACCOUNTING CYCLE | REVIEW

ACR7–1 Matchett Fabrications Ltd. sells greenhouse kits to retailers and garden centres. The company's post-closing trial balance at December 31, 2017, the end of its fiscal year, is presented below:

Record and post transaction, adjusting, and closing journal entries; prepare bank reconciliation; prepare unadjusted, adjusted, and post-closing trial balances, and financial statements.

(LO 3)

MATCHETT FABRICATIONS LTD.
Post-Closing Trial Balance
December 31, 2017

	Debit	Credit
Cash	$ 128,000	
Accounts receivable	920,000	
Supplies	3,000	
Inventory	457,000	
Equipment	2,280,000	
Accumulated depreciation—equipment		$ 380,000
Accounts payable		410,000
Interest payable		5,000
Salaries payable		34,000
Unearned revenue		120,000
Bank loan payable		2,000,000
Common shares		250,000
Retained earnings		589,000
	$3,788,000	$3,788,000

Matchett had the following transactions during January 2018:

Jan. 1 The bank loan bears interest at 3% and requires monthly payments on the first day of the month consisting of principal of $20,000 plus interest. The interest for December 2017 was properly accrued at the end of 2017.

8 Received payments of $178,000 from customers in payment of their accounts.

13 Made sales on account totalling $216,000 to garden centres. The greenhouse units sold had cost Matchett $122,000.

15 Purchased additional greenhouse kits from a supplier on account for $75,000.

17 Paid accounts payable that were due to creditors totalling $120,000.

18 Paid salaries of $70,000, which included the accrued salaries owing at the end of 2017 and $36,000 related to salaries earned to date in January.

21 Purchased supplies on account for $1,500.

24 Received a shipment of additional greenhouses from a supplier. The invoice for $98,000 is due in 30 days.

26 Made sales of $126,000, of which $58,000 was on account and the remainder was cash. The cost of the greenhouses sold was $68,000.

31 Delivered a custom greenhouse that a customer had ordered and put a $25,000 deposit down on. The total sales price was $50,000 and the greenhouse had cost Matchett $35,000. The customer paid the outstanding balance in cash.

Matchett reconciles its bank account at the end of every month and makes any necessary journal entries. The following information was gathered from reviewing the company's bank statement for the month of January:

1. There were outstanding cheques of $12,000.
2. The service charges on the account were $38 for the month.
3. A deposit for $25,000 was made using the night deposit slot on January 31. This deposit is not reflected on the company's bank statement for January.
4. A cheque from one of Matchett's customers for $9,800 that had been deposited during the month was returned by the bank due to the customer having insufficient funds in their account.
5. The company's account balance at January 31 was $161,162 according to the bank statement.

Matchett records adjustments monthly on the last day of the month. Adjusting entries were required for the following:

1. Record depreciation on the equipment assuming that Matchett uses the straight-line method to depreciate its equipment and the equipment is expected to have a useful life of six years.
2. Accrue interest for the month on the bank loan.
3. When supplies were counted, it was determined that supplies with a cost of $1,300 were still on hand.
4. Accrued salaries payable are $36,000.
5. The estimated income taxes owing for the month of January was $16,000.

Instructions

(a) Record the January transactions.

(b) Prepare the bank reconciliation at January 31, 2018, including any required journal entries.

(c) Set up T accounts, enter the December 31 opening balances, and post the journal entries prepared in parts (a) and (b).

(d) Prepare the necessary adjusting entries.

(e) Post the adjusting entries to the T accounts.

(f) Prepare an adjusted trial balance.

(g) Prepare the (1) income statement, (2) statement of changes in equity, and (3) statement of financial position.

EXPAND YOUR | CRITICAL THINKING

CT7–1 Financial Reporting Case

The financial statements of The North West Company Inc. are presented in Appendix A at the end of this book. Two reports are presented at the beginning of this appendix: a management report and a report from the independent auditors.

Instructions

(a) What comments, if any, about the company's system of internal control are included in management's report? In the independent auditors' report?

(b) Who is primarily responsible for the system of internal control—management or the auditors? Explain the responsibility of each with regard to internal control.

(c) Who is primarily responsible for the preparation and presentation of the financial statements? In which report(s) are these responsibilities identified?

CT7–2 Financial Reporting Case

The financial statements of The North West Company Inc. are presented in Appendix A and the financial statements for Sobeys Inc. are presented in Appendix B.

Instructions

(a) North West reports only "cash"; Sobeys reports "cash and cash equivalents." Refer to North West's statement of cash flows. What is the amount of its "cash" at the end of its most recent fiscal year?

(b) The notes to Sobey's financial statements specify that its cash equivalents consist of cash and guaranteed investments with a maturity less than 90 days at date of acquisition. Refer to Sobey's statement of financial position and identify the amounts of its "cash and cash equivalents" at the end of the most recent fiscal year.

(c) Compare the amount of the change in each company's cash and cash equivalents. Determine the percentage change over the previous year. Which company's cash position has improved the most?

CT7–3 Financial Reporting Case

Nick's Steakhouse and Pizza, described in the opening feature story of this chapter, is a privately held family-run restaurant located in Calgary. Imvescor Restaurant Group Inc. is a Canadian public company that operates more than 250 Pizza Delight, Mikes, Scores, and Bâton Rouge family restaurants across Canada.

Since Nick's and Imvescor are in the same industry, they have much in common. However, they are also very different. For instance, Nick's is an owner-operated single location, whereas Imvescor has multiple locations and multiple franchise owners. In addition, Nick's is a private company that follows ASPE while Imvescor is a public company that follows IFRS.

Instructions

(a) Do you think that, when a company chooses a particular set of accounting standards to use, this has any impact on its internal controls? If so, how?

(b) Because Imvescor is a public company, management is required to perform an annual in-depth evaluation of the company's internal controls over financial reporting. Imvescor must state in its annual report that the evaluation was performed and state the CEO's and CFO's conclusion on the effectiveness of internal controls. If there were any material weaknesses, they must be reported, along with how management plans to fix these weaknesses. Why do you think public companies are required to report on the effectiveness of their internal controls?

CT7–4 Professional Judgement Case

Patrick Chen is an entrepreneur who owns several businesses. His most recent acquisition several months ago was the Imperial Hotel, located in a resort community about 300 km from Patrick's residence. Because he is not usually at the hotel, Patrick hired a manager, Kevin Kildare, to run the hotel's operations. Patrick's daughter Vanessa is now studying accounting at university and asked her father if she could work at the hotel during the summer. He agreed and asked her to observe the operations at the hotel and report back to him at the end of her first week of work.

Vanessa Chen's first job was at the front desk working with Megan Kildare, who is Kevin's daughter. One evening, Kevin's friends dropped by the hotel to use one of the rooms for a poker party. Vanessa noticed the following day when reviewing room cleaning reports, that even though the room was cleaned by hotel staff, no record of a cash or credit card receipt for the use of the room that night appeared on the daily room sales report.

A couple of days later, Vanessa spent some time in the hotel lounge where Michael Kildare, Kevin's son, was the only bartender on duty during a very busy shift in the early evening. At that time, the lounge had a drink special with tequila on sale. Michael was very busy and sometimes was unable to ring drink sales into the cash register. Vanessa also noticed that he was using tequila bottles from a box under the bar instead of the ones that were on display over the bar. The following morning when the lounge manager, who works only during the day, performed the daily count of inventory, he concluded that tequila sales were not as high as he had hoped they would be given the fact that the tequila inventory had barely fallen over the past 24 hours.

Later that day, Vanessa reviewed a report showing that parking garage receipts had decreased during the past month. Kevin has resisted the installation of any automated payment systems for the parking garage because he is worried that they are not always reliable and prefers instead the more personable approach of having someone, like his nephew Tom, at the parking garage exit to collect the parking fees in cash. When a driver enters the parking garage, they get a ticket with the entry time and then they present this to Tom, who calculates the amount owed when exiting.

Instructions

(a) What control activity weaknesses will Vanessa report to her father?

(b) If Vanessa wanted to determine how much money has been stolen or lost from the hotel, how could she do this? Is it possible?

(c) What steps can the hotel take to avoid the possibility of fraud in the future?

CT7–5 Ethics Case

Banks charge fees of up to $45 for bounced cheques; that is, NSF cheques that exceed the balance in the payor's account. It has been estimated that processing bounced cheques costs a bank less than $5 per cheque. Thus, the profit margin on bounced cheques is high. Recognizing this, banks process cheques from largest to smallest within the same date range. By doing this, they maximize the number of cheques that bounce if a customer overdraws an account.

Instructions

(a) Who are the stakeholders in this case?

(b) A company had a balance of $1,500 in its chequing account on a day when the bank received the following five cheques for processing against that account:

Cheque Number	Amount
3150	$ 35
3158	1,510
3162	400
3165	890
3169	180

Assuming a $45 fee is charged by the bank for each NSF cheque, how much service charge revenue would the bank generate if it processed cheques (1) from largest to smallest and (2) from smallest to largest?

(c) Do you think that processing cheques from largest to smallest is an ethical business practice?

(d) Besides ethical issues, what else must a bank consider in deciding whether to process cheques from largest to smallest?

(e) If you were managing a bank, what policy would you adopt on bounced cheques?

CT7–6 Serial Case

(*Note:* This is a continuation of the serial case from Chapters 1 through 6. This case can be assigned as a group activity. Additional instructions and material for this activity can be found on the Instructor Resource site and in *WileyPLUS*.)

Emily is learning how ABC accumulates accounting information. The company has grown quickly and the controls for some transactions, especially cash, have not kept pace with the growth of the operation. Because Emily has taken a few accounting and auditing courses, she would like to take a more active role in ensuring that there are effective controls in place at the business.

Doug, Bev, and Emily discuss the accounting process that is currently in place and the following issues come up:

1. There are two employees who look after sales of computer products and accessories. There is only one cash register. Each employee has their own password. After a client chooses the computer software or supplies they wish to purchase, an employee will pull the inventory off the shelf and proceed to the cash register. After inputting a password, the employee will record what has been sold. The cash register calculates the amount owing, records how the client has paid, and prints a receipt. Sometimes, when the business is busy, the employee will not have a chance to log off a transaction before moving on to the next client. This can result in difficulty tracking which sale was made by which employee.

2. A summary of cash, credit card, and debit card receipts is printed daily. At the end of each day, Doug or Bev attempts to reconcile the summary of receipts to cash deposited. (The deposit is done nightly by Doug or Bev.) Lately, the reconciliation is being done once a week and done all at once. Because of the difficulty with passwords, if there is an error, it is difficult to determine who has made the error in processing a sale. Once they have finished the reconciliation, Doug or Bev enters the amounts into the accounting records.

3. Inventory is usually counted at the end of each month to determine what needs to be ordered and what is available for sale the next month. Purchases of inventory often occur during the month when someone alerts Doug or Bev that a particular product is running low. Sometimes this will result in overpurchasing if one of them has already recognized a shortage of a particular type of inventory but has not told the other that the purchase has already been made.

4. A work schedule is made at the start of each month and all overtime must be approved by either Doug or Bev. Lately, additional hours are being worked by all staff because of the demand for services. When the payroll is prepared, Bev attempts to reconcile the monthly schedule with the hours worked by each of

the staff members. Because Doug and Bev are not writing down which employee was authorized to work overtime, it is difficult to determine whether the overtime was in fact authorized.

5. Services are invoiced at the time the service has been performed. The invoices are manually prepared by the service manager. A photocopy is made to enable the invoices to be entered in the accounting records.

Instructions

(a) Identify the strengths in ABC's system of internal control. For each strength identified, describe the control activity that is being addressed.

(b) Identify the weaknesses in ABC's system of internal control, and for each weakness identified, suggest an improvement. As well, for each weakness identified, describe the control activity that is violated.

▶ ANSWERS TO CHAPTER PRACTICE QUESTIONS

DO IT! 7-1
Control Activities

(a) Segregation of duties; violated
(b) Documentation; supported
(c) Review and reconciliation; supported
(d) Physical controls; supported
(e) Assignment of responsibility; violated

DO IT! 7-2a
Control Activities over Cash Receipts

Assignment of responsibility: Because more than one person at Hamburger Heaven can use the same cash register, the assignment of responsibility control has been violated. If there is a cash shortage in the register at the end of the day, it will not be possible to determine who is responsible for it.

Segregation of duties: Segregation of duties has also been violated. Staff members who ring up the sale on the cash register and have access to cash should not be the ones to check the cash receipts against the sales report. They could choose to not ring up a sale and pocket the cash instead.

Review and reconciliation: Review and reconciliation has also been violated because the cash count should be verified by a second employee, or ideally the owner.

Physical controls: Physical controls are weak because cash should be deposited in a bank promptly, preferably as a night deposit. If this is not possible, it should be kept in a safe at the business or in a locked drawer at a minimum.

DO IT! 7-2b
Control Activities over Cash Payments

Assignment of responsibility: This has been violated in a couple of ways. First, allowing any High Peaks staff member to pay a supplier with cash means that it would not be possible to determine which staff member actually did so. Further, the use of pre-signed cheques also means that no one could be held accountable for payments made using a pre-signed cheque.

Segregation of duties: Allowing any staff member to make cash payments violates this control activity. Staff members currently have the ability to authorize cash payments, while also having custody of the cash. These two duties should be separated.

Documentation: Making cash payments also violates this control activity because it eliminates any record of the payment. Paying by cheque or even electronically creates a record to evidence payment.

Physical controls: Keeping the cheques in an unlocked drawer in the manager's office violates this control activity. Access to cheques should be restricted, with the cheques being kept in a locked drawer or safe.

DO IT! 7-3a
Cash Balance per Company's Books and Errors

(a)

Cash			
Reconciled balance at beginning of month (same as ending balance on January 31)	12,358		
Cash receipts in February	68,319	Cash disbursements in February	57,900
February 28 balance	22,777		

(b) The error was made by the company (not the bank), so the company's records will need to be adjusted. The error involved recording a payment to a supplier for $995, rather than the correct amount of $599. As such, the balance in the company's cash account is too low. It is $396 ($995 – $599) lower than it should be and a correcting entry should be made for this difference to increase the cash account.

After this correction, Kariwak Limited's cash balance at February 28, 2018, would be $23,173 ($22,777 + $396). This would be the balance before any items that would result from the bank reconciliation, such as interest, bank charges, or NSF cheques.

DO IT! 7-3b
Bank Reconciliation

OAKVILLE ATHLETIC ASSOCIATION
Bank Reconciliation
December 31

Cash balance per bank statement		$36,168
Add: Deposits in transit		7,286
		43,454
Less: Outstanding cheques ($6,000 + $560)	$(6,560)	
Error correction relating to conversion of U.S. dollar receipts to Canadian dollars	(56)	(6,616)
Reconciled cash balance		$36,838
Cash balance per books		$32,666
Add: Electronic receipts from customers on account	$4,699	
Deposit error correction ($290 – $209)	81	4,780
		37,446
Less: NSF cheque ($478 + $45)	$(523)	
Bank service charges and debit and credit card fees	(85)	(608)
Reconciled cash balance		$36,838

Dec. 31	Cash	4,699	
	Accounts Receivable		4,699
	(To record electronic receipts on account)		
31	Cash	81	
	Accounts Receivable		81
	(To correct deposit error)		
31	Accounts Receivable	523	
	Cash		523
	(To re-establish accounts receivable for NSF cheque and related service charge)		
31	Bank Charges Expense	85	
	Cash		85
	(To record bank service charges and debit and credit card fees)		

Check:

Cash

Dec. 31		32,666			
31		4,699	Dec. 31		523
31		81	31		85
Dec. 31	Reconciled bal.	36,838			

(a)
Cash in bank	$12,300
Add: Treasury bills	1,500
Less: Bank indebtedness	10,000
Cash and cash equivalents	$ 3,800

DO IT! 7-4
Presentation of cash

(b)
Accounts receivable	Accounts receivable (current asset)
Cash (restricted for an upcoming plant expansion)	Restricted cash (non-current asset)
Compensating balance (for a non-current loan)	Restricted cash (non-current asset)
Equity investment (in common shares)	Held-for-trading investments (likely a current asset)

▶ PRACTICE USING THE DECISION TOOLKIT

(a) The main control weakness at Sparks Basketball was the lack of segregation of duties. While the executive director was on parental leave, one person was responsible for all financial matters. There was also no review of Mr. Stevens' work, enabling him to make fraudulent transactions without anyone knowing about them.

(b) SB should require proper segregation of duties. Although it is often difficult to have proper segregation of duties in a not-for-profit organization such as this, at least two people should be involved in all financial transactions. SB could require that two people (the executive director and someone from the board) sign each cheque. The board member should be provided with supporting documentation that they can review prior to signing each cheque. SB should require monthly bank reconciliations that are prepared by someone other than the executive director. The cancelled cheques should be returned each month so that they can be reviewed as well. In addition, someone from the board of directors should review SB's transactions and financial statements regularly.

(c) Implementation of extensive control systems can be expensive. Not-for-profit organizations must carefully choose what control measures are most important for their specific needs. However, the value of some control activities, such as segregation of duties, often offsets the cost, as it would have for SB. In addition, the organization should use as many free controls as it can. Examples include proper screening of possible volunteers and employees, written policies for how transactions should be processed, and a requirement that employees and volunteers sign a formal statement of ethical guidelines.

▶ PRACTICE COMPREHENSIVE DO IT!

(a)

Cash

May 31		34,080		
June cash receipts		34,000	June cash payments	39,520
June 30	Reconciled bal.	28,560		

(b) 1. Deposits in transit: $1,200 + $34,000 − $30,496 = $4,704
2. Outstanding cheques: $1,500 + $39,520 − $36,200 = $4,820

(c)

WINNIPEG ARTS SOCIETY
Bank Reconciliation
June 30

Cash balance per bank statement		$28,342
Add: Deposits in transit		4,704
		33,046
Less: Outstanding cheques	$4,820	
Bank deposit error	70	4,890
Reconciled cash balance		$28,156
Cash balance per books		$28,560
Less: NSF cheque ($310 + $40)	$350	
Bank service charges	54	404
Reconciled cash balance		$28,156

(d)

June 30	Accounts Receivable	350	
	Cash		350
	(To re-establish accounts receivable for Massif Corp. for NSF cheque and related service charge)		
30	Bank Charges Expense	54	
	Cash		54
	(To record bank service and credit card fees)		

Check:

Cash

June 30		28,560	June 30		350
			30		54
June 30	Reconciled bal.	28,156			

(e) It would be important for a member of the Arts Society's board to review the bank reconciliation after it has been prepared each month because of the lack of any segregation of duties within the society's accounting area. Because the bookkeeper is responsible for authorization, recording, and asset custody, there is the potential for fraud to occur. Having the bank reconciliation reviewed is an example of the review and reconciliation control activity.

▶ PRACTICE OBJECTIVE-FORMAT QUESTIONS

1. (a), (c), (e), and (f) are correct and are all examples of the documentation control activity.

Feedback
(b) This is an example of assignment of responsibility.
(d) This is an example of review and reconciliation.
(g) This is an example of assignment of responsibility.

2. (c), (d), and (e) are correct.

Feedback
(a) A bank reconciliation is an example of review and reconciliation performed internally, not externally.
(b) Having a second cashier count the cash drawer of another cashier would be an example of review and reconciliation, not assignment of responsibility.
(f) While external auditors are considered to be independent of the company, internal auditors are not. This is because they are employees of the company.
(g) "Tone at the top" is an element of a company's control environment, rather than being a control activity.

3. (b), (c), (e), and (f) are correct. They are all examples of physical controls.

Feedback
(a) There is no indication of if or how the ID cards are being used. Therefore, they are not a physical control.
(d) This is an example of assignment of responsibility rather than physical control.
(g) This is an example of review and reconciliation rather than physical control.

4. (b), (c), (e), (f), and (g) are correct and would all be considered to be control activities over cash receipts.

Feedback
(a) This would be assignment of responsibility and is related to cash payments, not cash receipts.
(b) Cash receipts (physical control).
(c) Cash receipts (physical control).
(d) This would be documentation and is related to cash payments, not cash receipts.
(e) Cash receipts (review and reconciliation).
(f) Cash receipts (documentation, and review and reconciliation).
(g) Cash receipts (documentation).

5. (a), (c), (d), (e), and (g) are correct regarding CPL's bank reconciliation (prepared below).

Cash balance per bank statement	$36,600
Add: Deposit in transit	10,100
Deduct: Outstanding cheques	(15,800)
Reconciled balance	$30,900
Cash balance per books	$29,080
Add: EFT receipt	2,800
Deduct: Bank charges	(80)
Error in recording cheque	(900)
Reconciled balance	$30,900

Feedback
(b) The deposit for $10,100 would be added to the cash balance per bank, not the cash balance per books. The company would have recorded this on the date the night deposit was made, while the bank would not record it until the deposit was processed (the next day the bank was open for business).
(f) The EFT receipt would be added to the cash balance per books, not the cash balance per bank. The bank would be aware of the deposit and it would be reflected on the bank statement. The company would not be aware of it until it received the bank statement and would need to account for it at that time.

6. (a) Books   –   (e) Bank   –
    (b) Books   –   (f) Books   +
    (c) Books   +   (g) Bank   +
    (d) Bank   –

Feedback

(a) Bank has recorded; company has not. Therefore it is a reconciling item to the "Books balance." Service fees will reduce cash.
(b) Bank has recorded; company has not. Therefore it is a reconciling item to the "Books balance." The NSF cheque increased cash when it was initially deposited, so cash needs to be reduced to reflect the fact that no cash was actually received and there is still a receivable from the customer.
(c) Bank has recorded; company has not. Therefore it is a reconciling item to the "Books balance." EFT receipts from customers have been recorded by the bank, but not the company. Now that the company is aware of these payments, the cash balance can be increased.
(d) Bank has recorded in error and needs to correct its records. No accounting is required by the company.
(e) Bank has not recorded; company has. Once the outstanding cheques are deposited by the payees, the bank will reduce the company's account balance. Because the company has already accounted for these, there is no adjustment required to the company's accounts.
(f) Bank has recorded correctly; company has not. The cheque was written and cleared the bank account for the correct amount. It was accounted for incorrectly by the company's bookkeeper. Cash was reduced by $27 ($463.91 – $436.91) in the initial recording of the entry, so cash needs to be increased in the correcting entry.
(g) Bank has not recorded; company has. Once the bank becomes aware of the deposit (on the next day of operations), it will increase the company's account balance. Because the company has already recorded this, there is no adjustment required to the company's accounts.

7. (b), (d), and (f) are correct (they are all correctly prepared journal entries that would result from the bank reconciliation).

Feedback

(a) NSF Cheque Expense is not a valid account. Instead, the debit should be to Accounts Receivable.
(c) The debit and credit are reversed in this entry. Rent Expense should be debited and Cash credited.
(e) There would not be any journal entry related to deposits in transit because this would be a reconciling item to the cash balance per bank.
(g) The debit and credit are reversed in this entry. Cash should be debited and Advertising Expense credited. This is necessary because the payment was recorded for more than the actual payment amount.

8. (a), (c), and (e) are correct. They are all reconciling items to the cash balance per books and would result in a journal entry with a credit to the Cash account.

Feedback

(b) These are outstanding cheques, which would be deducted from the cash balance per bank.
(d) While this would be a reconciling item to the cash balance per books, it would result in a debit to the Cash account (not a credit) because the bookkeeper recorded the payment for more than the actual amount of the cheque.
(f) While this would be a reconciling item to the cash balance per books, it would result in a debit to the Cash account (not a credit) because it was related to the receipt of cash.
(g) This is an outstanding deposit, which would be added to the cash balance per bank.

9. (a), (b), (c), (e), and (g) are correct and would be included in cash and cash equivalents.

Feedback

(d) A paycheque that has not been cashed is an outstanding cheque and would not be included in cash and cash equivalents.
(f) Postdated cheques, which are cheques dated in the future, are not considered to be cash or a cash equivalent because they cannot be deposited until the date on the cheque.

10. (a) –   Customers would have longer to pay their accounts, meaning slower collection of accounts receivable and less cash available.

     (b) +   Having to carry less inventory in the warehouse will increase the cash the company has available for other activities.

     (c) +   This will reduce the amount of cash being paid as salaries.

     (d) +   The additional interest that will be received on the company's account will increase cash.

     (e) –   This will mean that the company will not receive purchase discounts and will need to settle its payables more quickly, reducing cash.

     (f) –   Having to pay the 20% deposit prior to shipment will reduce cash.

     (g) +   This would mean the company would receive these customer payments more quickly, increasing cash.

▶ ENDNOTES

[1] Sources: "Interview with Nick's Steakhouse & Pizza," eh Canada travel and adventure website and blog, February 17, 2016, www.ehcanadatravel.com/blog/2016/02/27/interview-with-nicks-steakhouse-pizza/; Julie Van Rosendaal, "Five Restos That Have Stood the Test of Time," *Calgary Herald*, February 26, 2014; Nick's Steakhouse and Pizza website, http://nickssteakandpizza.com/.

[2] Sources: Jamie Sturgeon, "'Tap and Go' Credit Card Purchases Are Surging in Canada," Global News online, October 29, 2015; Rebecca Burn-Callander, "The History of Money: From Barter to Bitcoin," *The Telegraph*, October 20, 2014; Apple Canada website, www.apple.com/ca/apple-pay/; Bitcoin website, https://bitcoin.org/; MasterCard website, www.mastercard.ca/contactless.html; Royal Canadian Mint website, http://www.mint.ca/store/mint/learn/background-6800008#.VzDjWmNvCfc.

8

Reporting and Analyzing Receivables

CHAPTER PREVIEW

The management of receivables is important for any company that sells on credit. In this chapter, we will learn how companies record various receivables, collect receivables when due, estimate the receivables that may not be collected, and then, in some cases, collect their receivables that were thought to be uncollectible. We will also discuss how receivables are reported on the financial statements and how they are managed.

CHAPTER OUTLINE

LEARNING OBJECTIVES	READ	PRACTICE
1 Identify the types of receivables and record accounts receivable transactions.	• Recording accounts receivable • Subsidiary ledgers • Interest revenue	**DO IT!** 8-1 Receivables transactions
2 Account for bad debts.	• Measuring and recording estimated uncollectible accounts • Writing off uncollectible accounts • Collecting uncollectible accounts • Summary of allowance method	**DO IT!** 8-2a Bad debts 8-2b Write offs and recoveries
3 Account for notes receivable.	• Recording notes receivable • Derecognizing notes receivable	**DO IT!** 8-3 Notes receivable
4 Explain the statement presentation of receivables.	• Statement of financial position • Income statement	**DO IT!** 8-4 Statement presentation
5 Apply the principles of sound accounts receivable management.	• Extending credit • Establishing a payment period • Monitoring collections • Evaluating liquidity of receivables	**DO IT!** 8-5 Managing receivables

FEATURE STORY

Receivables are generally a company's third-largest asset, after its property, plant, and equipment and inventory. For large retail operations like Canadian Tire, it is essential to manage, and monitor the collection of, receivables on an ongoing basis.

The nearly century-old Canadian Tire Corporation has almost 1,700 locations across the country, including the iconic Canadian Tire stores and gas bars, as well as clothing retailer Mark's, and sporting goods chains Sport Chek and Sports Experts—part of the former FGL Sports Ltd., which the corporation acquired in 2012.

Canadian Tire's major receivables fall into three broad categories. First, there are the corporation's own credit cards, such as the Canadian Tire Options MasterCard, which it issues to some 4 million customers. Second are the receivable accounts created by the 480 Canadian Tire associate dealers and hundreds of franchisees of the other chains across the country that buy merchandise from the company and operate their stores under the company banners. The third category is vendor receivables, which would be money due from vendors in support of various programs such as product launches or new store openings.

The largest receivable amount is Canadian Tire's credit card programs, which represented about $4.8 billion in receivables in 2015. Canadian Tire is one of the few retailers in Canada that has its own financial services

Varying Degrees of Credit

division, which manages and finances its credit card receivables. The criteria for issuing a card are similar to any credit card program. The company assesses applications, does a credit score, and decides whether to issue a card and at what credit limit.

Canadian Tire has a large call centre that deals with customer service collections, although certain collections are outsourced to collection agencies. Despite efforts to collect its credit card accounts, Canadian Tire writes off about $350 million per year in bad debts.

Fortunately, the company's dealer and vendor receivables carry virtually no bad debts. Canadian Tire essentially acts as a wholesaler, where dealers and franchisees acquire from Canadian Tire all the merchandise they sell. At any point in time, dealers owe the corporation hundreds of millions of dollars for products that it has shipped to them. Canadian Tire has a dedicated system that tracks shipments to each store, immediately recording the receivable and billing the dealer for the amount owed. It's very unusual for a dealer not to be able to repay the money it owes the corporation, and it's also unusual for a vendor not to pay, since the corporation usually owes them money as well.

So, for a large retail operation like Canadian Tire, it pays to have its receivables in more than one category.[1]

Go to the *REVIEW AND PRACTICE* section at the end of the chapter for a targeted summary and practice questions with solutions.

Visit **WileyPLUS** for more practice opportunities.

Identify the types of receivables and record accounts receivable transactions.

The term *receivables* refers to amounts that are owed to a company by its customers, employees, the government, and others. Receivables are claims that are expected to be collected in cash, and they are frequently classified as (1) accounts receivable, (2) notes receivable, and (3) other receivables. Receivables, along with certain types of investments, are considered **financial assets**. These assets represent a contractual right to receive cash or another financial asset. We will learn more about investments and financial assets in Chapter 12.

Accounts receivable are amounts owed by customers on account. They result from the sale of goods and services. Receivables are normally evidenced by a sales invoice issued to a customer rather than any separate formal document. They are generally expected to be collected within 30 days or so, and are classified as current assets. You will recall that we learned in Chapter 5 that **credit terms** set out the time period in which a receivable is due (such as 30 days), in addition to any possible discounts for early repayment.

Notes receivable are claims where formal instruments of credit—a written promise to repay—are issued as evidence of the debt. The credit instrument normally requires the debtor to pay interest and is for time periods of 30 days or longer. Notes receivable may be either current assets or non-current assets, depending on their due dates. Accounts and notes receivable that result from sales transactions are often called **trade receivables**.

Other receivables include **nontrade receivables** that do not result from the operations of the business. These can include interest receivable, loans to company officers, advances to employees, sales tax recoverable, and income tax receivable.

We will focus our discussion in this section and the next on accounts receivable before turning our attention to notes receivable.

RECORDING ACCOUNTS RECEIVABLE

As we discussed in Chapter 4, accounts receivable are recognized or recorded when revenue has been earned, but payment has yet to be received from the customer. For a service company, a receivable is recorded when a service is provided on account. For a merchandising company, a receivable is recorded at the point of sale of merchandise on account.

You will recall from Chapter 5 that the seller may offer terms, such as providing a discount, to encourage early payment. If the buyer chooses to pay within the discount period, the seller's account receivable is reduced in full by the amount of cash received plus the amount of the sales discount. Also, the buyer might find some of the goods unacceptable and choose to return them or ask for a price reduction which also results in a reduction of the account receivable.

To review, assume that Jordache Corp., which uses a perpetual inventory system, sells merchandise on account to Polo Limited for $1,000 on January 2, terms 2/10, n/30. The goods had cost Jordache $580. On January 5, Polo returns merchandise worth $100 to Jordache. This merchandise had a cost of $55 and is still in saleable condition, so it was put back on the shelf. On January 11, Jordache receives payment from Polo for the balance due. The journal entries to record these transactions on the books of Jordache are as follows:

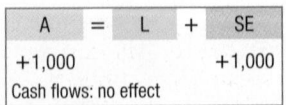

A	=	L	+	SE
+1,000				+1,000

Cash flows: no effect

Jan. 2	Accounts Receivable	1,000	
	Sales		1,000
	(To record sale of merchandise on account to Polo Limited, terms 2/10, n/30)		

Jan. 2	Cost of Goods Sold	580	
	Inventory		580
	(To record cost of merchandise sold to Polo)		
5	Sales Returns and Allowances	100	
	Accounts Receivable		100
	(To record merchandise returned by Polo)		
5	Inventory	55	
	Cost of Goods Sold		55
	(To record cost of merchandise returned by Polo)		
11	Cash [($1,000 − $100) × 98%]	882	
	Sales Discounts [($1,000 − $100) × 2%]	18	
	Accounts Receivable ($1,000 − $100)		900
	(To record collection of accounts receivable from Polo)		

A	=	L	+	SE
−580				−580

Cash flows: no effect

A	=	L	+	SE
−100				−100

Cash flows: no effect

A	=	L	+	SE
+55				+55

Cash flows: no effect

A	=	L	+	SE
+882				−18
−900				

↕ Cash flows: +882

SUBSIDIARY LEDGERS

In Chapter 3, we learned about the general ledger. In many cases, the accounts in the general ledger provide a sufficient level of detail for management. However, there are accounts, like Accounts Receivable, for which management requires the information to be captured differently. Imagine what would happen if a company like Canadian Tire recorded the accounts receivable for each of its customers in only one general ledger account. If it did, the details for thousands and thousands of customers would be mixed together and it would be very difficult to determine the balance owed by any one customer at a specific point in time. As such, using the Accounts Receivable account in the general ledger only works for companies with a very limited number of customer accounts.

Companies like Canadian Tire use a subsidiary ledger, known as the accounts receivable subsidiary ledger, in addition to the general ledger. A **subsidiary ledger** is a ledger that is used to manage detailed information that would be difficult to track in a general ledger account. For example, the accounts receivable subsidiary ledger contains the individual account detail for each of a company's customers. Each subsidiary ledger is controlled by a single general ledger account, which is known as the **control account**. This means that the balance in the control account must always equal the total of the subsidiary ledger. Because Accounts Receivable is the control account for the accounts receivable subsidiary ledger, the account balance must be equal to all of the individual customer receivables balances recorded in the subsidiary ledger. When receivables transactions are recorded in the subsidiary ledgers on a customer-by-customer basis, summaries of these transactions are also recorded in the general ledger. In this way, the subsidiary ledger provides supporting detail to the general ledger, freeing it from excessive detail. This also means that an entry cannot be made to a control account without making an entry in the subsidiary ledger, nor can an entry be made in the subsidiary ledger without making a corresponding entry in the control account. You should also note that the entry made in the control account is often a summary entry. This summary entry is the total of all of the detailed entries made to the customer accounts in the subsidiary ledger.

In addition to Accounts Receivable, other accounts that are supported by subsidiary ledgers include Inventory (to track inventory quantities and balances), Accounts Payable (to track individual creditor balances), and payroll (to track individual employee pay records).

To illustrate the accounts receivable subsidiary ledger, consider the following simplified example for Jordache Corp.

> **Alternative Terminology**
> *A subsidiary ledger* is also known as a *subledger.*

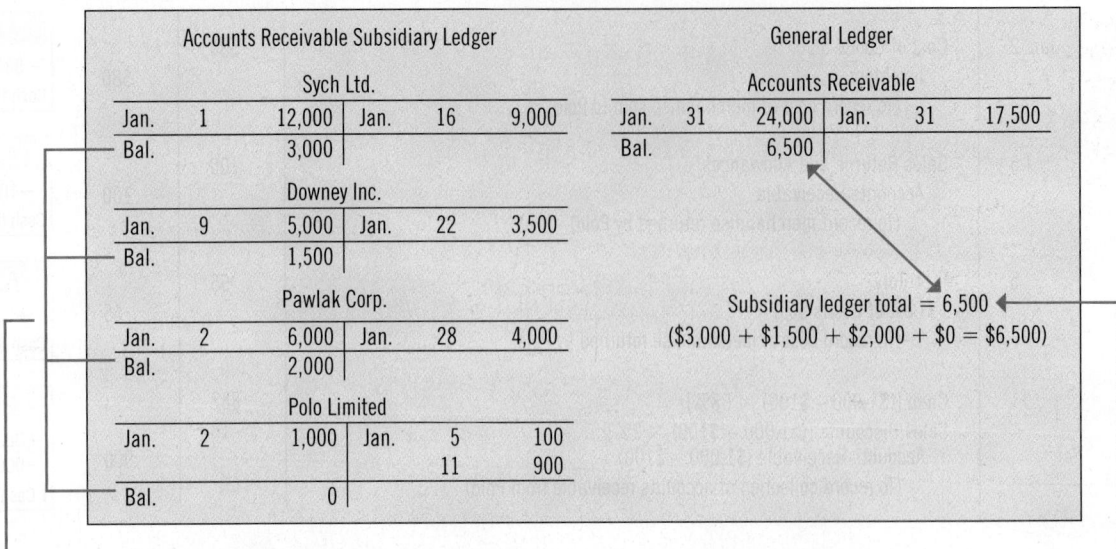

Jordache posts individual transactions to its subsidiary ledger daily and posts summary transactions to its general ledger monthly. Notice that the debit of $24,000 to the general ledger Accounts Receivable account represents the total of all debits made to customer accounts in the subsidiary ledger in January ($12,000 + $5,000 + $6,000 + $1,000 = $24,000). Likewise, the credit entry of $17,500 represents the total of all credits made to customer accounts in the subsidiary ledger in January ($9,000 + $3,500 + $4,000 + $100 + $900 = $17,500). Because of this, the sum of all customer account balances in the subsidiary ledger is equal to the balance in the Accounts Receivable general ledger account at the end of January.

INTEREST REVENUE

At the end of each month, a company can use the subsidiary ledger to easily determine the transactions in each customer's account and then send the customer a statement of transactions that occurred that month, along with the balance outstanding.

If the customer does not pay in full within the **credit term** period (usually 30 days), an interest (financing) charge may be added to the balance due. When financing charges are added, the seller recognizes interest revenue and increases the account receivable amount owed by the customer. This can be a substantial amount for some companies.

For example, assume that Jordache Corp. charges 28% interest on the balance due if not paid by the end of the month. If Sych Ltd., in the previous section, does not pay its outstanding balance of $3,000, Jordache would record interest revenue for the month of February of $70 ($3,000 $\times$ 28% $\times$ $^{1}/_{12}$) as follows:

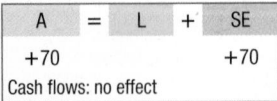

Feb. 28	Accounts Receivable	70	
	Interest Revenue		70
	(To record interest on amount due from Sych Ltd.)		

The above debit to Accounts Receivable would be posted individually to Sych Ltd.'s account in the subsidiary ledger. It would also be posted as part of a summary entry to the Accounts Receivable general ledger control account at the end of the month for the interest revenue recorded on all accounts. Note that the Accounts Receivable account is debited for the interest due, rather than a separate Interest Receivable account. Interest will be charged on interest the following month (that is, $3,070) if the account continues to be unpaid.

ACCOUNTING MATTERS

© istock.com/Sturti

High Cost of Credit Card Debt

A 2015 study of more than 18,000 Canadian graduating university students found that 9 out of 10 have at least one credit card, and 3 in 10 have two or more. In fact, the average student surveyed had 3.7 credit cards! While only 56% of the general population pays their credit card balances off in full each month, 77% of students surveyed do so. These students understand the high cost of carrying credit card debt, especially with interest rates on regular Canadian bank credit cards going up to 19.9% and interest rates on nonbank cards reaching as high as 28.8%. This is bad news for those students with unpaid balances on their credit cards, because the average amount they owed was $2,224.[2]

DO IT! ▶8-1   Receivables Transactions

Selected transactions for Holm Corporation follow:

Oct. 29 Sold $10,000 of merchandise to Potter Inc., terms 2/10, n/30. Holm uses a perpetual inventory system and the cost of the goods sold was $6,000.

    31 Added monthly interest charges of 18% per annum (1.5% per month) to various overdue accounts receivable accounts totalling $32,000.

Nov. 1 $500 of merchandise was returned by Potter because it was the wrong size. The cost of the merchandise returned was $300.

    6 Received payment in full from Potter.

    10 Made sales of $5,000 on account, terms n/30. The cost of the goods sold was $3,000.

Record the above transactions on Holm's books, including any cost of goods entries.

Action Plan

✔ Remember that two journal entries are required to record sales of merchandise: (1) to record the sales revenue, and (2) to record the cost of the merchandise sold.

✔ Remember that two journal entries are required to record the return of goods by a customer: (1) to reduce the receivable or record the cash refund, and (2) to return the goods to inventory and reduce cost of goods sold.

✔ Recall that sales returns and discounts use contra accounts rather than affecting the Sales account directly.

✔ Calculate interest by multiplying the interest rate by the overdue account balance, adjusted for the appropriate portion of the year (for example, $1/12$ for one month).

SOLUTION

Try this Do It! Exercise on your own and then check your answer at the end of the chapter.

Related Exercise Material: BE8–1, BE8–2, BE8–3, BE8–4, E8–1, and E8–2.

LEARNING OBJECTIVE ▶2   Account for bad debts.

Once receivables are recorded in the accounts, their collectibility needs to be reviewed regularly. As assets, a company's accounts receivable embody future economic benefits (the cash that will be received upon collection). If there are collectibility concerns, then the company would need to ensure that this is reflected in the amount they are carried at on the statement of financial position. Even though each customer must satisfy the seller's credit requirements before a credit sale is approved, some accounts receivable inevitably become uncollectible. For example, a corporate customer may not be able to pay because of a decline in sales due to a downturn in the economy. Similarly, individuals may be laid off from their jobs or faced with unexpected bills and find themselves unable to pay.

Credit losses from uncollectible receivables are debited to an account called Bad Debts Expense. Note that this new account, Bad Debts Expense, is used instead of debiting a contra sales account as we did for sales returns and allowances because the responsibilities for granting credit and collecting accounts should be separated from sales and marketing. You will recall from Chapter 7 that assigning responsibility (credit authorization versus sales and marketing) is an important feature of a good internal control system.

The key issue in measuring accounts receivable is when to recognize bad debts expense. If the company waits until it knows for sure that a specific account will not be collected, it could end up recording the bad debts expense in a different period than when the revenue from the credit sale was recorded.

Consider the following example. In 2017, Quick Buck Computer Limited decides it could increase its revenues by selling laptops to students without requiring any down payment, and with no credit approval process. The promotion is a success and the company sells 100 computers with a selling price of $400 each. The computers cost Quick Buck Computers $275 each. This promotion increases Quick Buck Computer's receivables and revenues by $40,000 in 2017. Unfortunately, during 2018, nearly 40% of the student customers default on their accounts. Illustration 8-1 shows that the promotion in 2017 was not such a great success after all.

▶Illustration 8-1

Effects of mismatching bad debts

Year 2017

Sales revenue, cost of goods sold, A/R, and profit

Huge sales promotion.
Accounts receivable and
sales increase dramatically.

Year 2018

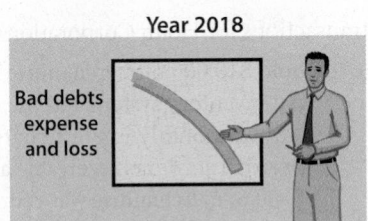

Bad debts expense and loss

Customers default on amounts owed;
accounts receivable plummet.
Bad debts expense increases dramatically.

Quick Buck Computer Limited's income statement is skewed with an overstatement of profit in 2017 and an understatement of profit in 2018 because of mismatched sales revenue and bad debts expense. In addition, accounts receivable in the statement of financial position are not reported at the amount actually expected to be collected at the end of 2017. Consequently, Quick Buck Computer's receivables are overstated in 2018, misrepresenting its statement of financial position.

The allowance method of accounting for bad debts is used by companies to address this issue. Under the **allowance method**, management estimates the uncollectible accounts at the end of each period. This also means that the bad debts expense can be determined each period. This is consistent with the accrual basis of accounting. You will recall that the accrual basis of accounting requires companies to account for transactions that affect their economic resources in the period in which those transactions occur. In other words, transactions such as expected bad debts, which will affect a company's receivables, need to be accounted for in the period in which they arose.

To record bad debts, Bad Debts Expense is debited and the Allowance for Doubtful Accounts is credited. This allowance account is a contra asset account, meaning its normal balance is a credit. It is netted with Accounts Receivable to determine the **carrying amount** of accounts receivable. The carrying amount of accounts receivable is the amount at which the receivables are presented on the statement of financial position and reflects management's estimate of the receivables that will ultimately be collected.

A contra account must be used because bad debt is an estimate and, at the time it is determined, the company does not know which specific accounts will not be paid. If the specific accounts are not known, then no entry can be made in the accounts receivable subsidiary ledger. If this is not possible, then no entry can be made to Accounts Receivable either, because it is the control account.

Illustration 8-2 shows the relationship between Accounts Receivable and Allowance for Doubtful Accounts and how the two are netted to arrive at the carrying amount of accounts receivable. It also illustrates how using the contra account enables companies to keep the balance of the control account (Accounts Receivable) and the total of the accounts receivable subsidiary ledger equal, while achieving the objective of reducing the carrying amount of Accounts Receivable to reflect management's estimate of uncollectible accounts.

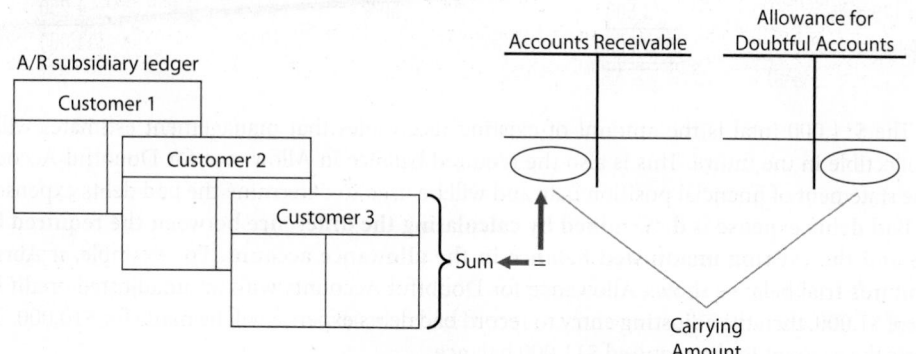

►Illustration 8-2

Carrying amount of accounts receivable

MEASURING AND RECORDING ESTIMATED UNCOLLECTIBLE ACCOUNTS

There are several acceptable methods companies can use to calculate an estimate of their uncollectible accounts. The most common method of determining the allowance for doubtful accounts uses a percentage of outstanding receivables.

Under the **percentage of receivables method**, management estimates what percentage of receivables is likely to be uncollectible. This estimate is normally based on the company's past experience, with the effects of the current economic climate factored in. New companies use industry averages as the basis for their estimate. This percentage can be assigned to receivables in total or, more commonly, accounts receivable are stratified (divided further) by the age of the receivables, with a different percentage assigned to each age group. Stratifying receivables classifies them by the length of time they have been outstanding (unpaid). This improves the reliability of the estimate because it enables management to consider the balances in each age group and how the relative percentage in each age group may have changed relative to previous periods. This stratification process is known as the **aging of accounts receivable method** because of its emphasis on time. Companies disclose information on the aging of their accounts receivable in the notes to their financial statements, generally in a note related to the credit risk of their financial instruments. The North West Company discloses this information in Note 14 to its financial statements.

To illustrate aging the accounts receivable, assume that Abrams Furniture Ltd. has total accounts receivable of $200,000 at December 31. Using the information in the accounts receivable subsidiary ledger, the accounts receivable for each customer are reviewed and grouped by age (number of days outstanding)—this can usually be done easily by the company's accounting software. Note that a customer's receivables balance can be allocated to various age groups if it is made up of amounts that have been outstanding for differing periods of time. Abrams then estimates the likelihood (percentage) of not collecting each group of overdue receivables. Abrams uses five groupings to age its receivables, ranging from those receivables currently due (outstanding 0–30 days) to those 120 days or more overdue. These groupings are very typical, but other companies may use more or fewer groupings, depending on their circumstances.

Abrams presents its aging schedule in Illustration 8-3. In this schedule, the dollar amount in each age group is multiplied by the percentage that it is estimated will be uncollectible to determine its total estimated uncollectible accounts. Note that the longer the receivables are outstanding, the higher the estimated uncollectible percentage. Experience has shown that the longer a receivable is outstanding, the less likely it is to be collected. As a result, the estimated percentage of uncollectible debts increases the longer a receivable has been outstanding.

▶Illustration 8-3
Aging schedule

Number of Days Outstanding	Accounts Receivable	Estimated Percentage Uncollectible	Total Estimated Uncollectible Accounts
0–30 days	$111,500	2%	$ 2,230
31–60 days	41,400	5%	2,070
61–90 days	38,000	10%	3,800
91–120 days	6,600	25%	1,650
Over 120 days	2,500	50%	1,250
Total	$200,000		$11,000

The $11,000 total is the amount of existing receivables that management estimates will be uncollectible in the future. This is also the required balance in Allowance for Doubtful Accounts at the statement of financial position date and will be used to determine the bad debts expense.

Bad debts expense is determined by calculating the difference between the required balance and the existing unadjusted balance in the allowance account. For example, if Abrams Furniture's trial balance shows Allowance for Doubtful Accounts with an unadjusted credit balance of $1,000, then the adjusting entry to record bad debts expense will be made for $10,000. This adjusts the account to the required $11,000 balance.

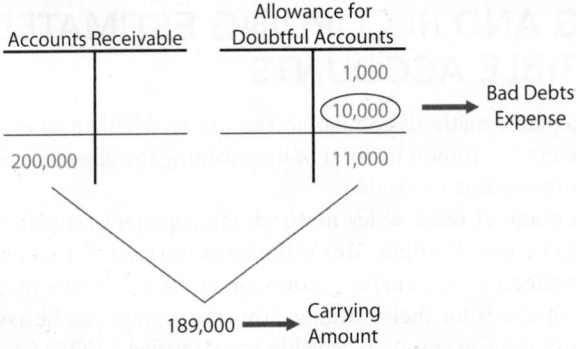

The bad debt adjusting entry would be recorded as follows:

A	=	L	+	SE
−10,000				−10,000

Cash flows: no effect

Dec. 31	Bad Debts Expense	10,000	
	Allowance for Doubtful Accounts		10,000
	(To record estimate of uncollectible accounts)		

It is also possible for the allowance account to have a debit balance before the adjustment. This occurs when write offs during the period exceed previous estimates for bad debts. (We will discuss write offs in the next section.) If there is an opening debit balance, the debit balance is added to the required balance when the adjusting entry is made. That is, if there had been a $1,000 debit balance in Abrams Furniture's allowance account before adjustment, the adjusting entry for bad debts expense would have been for $12,000. This adjusts the allowance account to the required credit balance of $11,000.

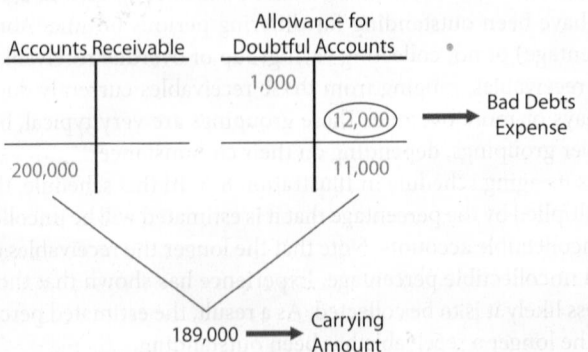

Bad debts expense is reported in the income statement as an operating expense. The balance in Allowance for Doubtful Accounts is deducted from Accounts Receivable in the current assets section of the statement of financial position as shown below:

Accounts receivable	$200,000
Less: Allowance for doubtful accounts	11,000
Carrying amount	$189,000

The $189,000 represents the expected carrying amount, or collectible portion, of the accounts receivable at the statement date.

DO IT! ▶ 8-2a Bad Debts

The following information is available for Chang Wholesalers Corporation about the age of its receivables at December 31, its year end:

Number of days outstanding	0–30	31–60	61–90	over 90
Accounts receivable	$200,000	$120,000	$100,000	$40,000
Estimated percentage uncollectible	2%	5%	10%	20%

(a) Using the above aging schedule, determine the total estimated uncollectible accounts.

(b) Assuming that Allowance for Doubtful Accounts has an unadjusted credit balance of $8,000, prepare the journal entry to record bad debts expense at December 31.

(c) Assuming that Allowance for Doubtful Accounts has an unadjusted debit balance of $4,200, prepare the journal entry to record bad debts expense at December 31.

SOLUTION
Try this Do It! exercise on your own and then check your answer at the end of the chapter.

Related Exercise Material: BE8–5, BE8–6, E8–3, and E8–4.

Action Plan

✔ Apply percentages to outstanding receivables in each age category to determine the total estimated uncollectible accounts.

✔ The estimated uncollectible accounts is the ending balance amount that should appear in the Allowance for Doubtful Accounts.

✔ Determine the difference between the desired balance in the allowance account estimated above and the current balance in that account. Be alert to the possibility that the current balance could be either a debit or a credit while the desired balance in the allowance account after adjustment will always be a credit.

✔ Stop and check your work. Make sure that the balance in the allowance account equals the total estimated uncollectible accounts after all entries have been posted.

WRITING OFF UNCOLLECTIBLE ACCOUNTS

Companies use various methods of collecting past-due accounts, such as letters, phone calls, collection agencies, and legal action. In the feature story, Canadian Tire mentions that it has a large call centre that it uses to deal with some overdue accounts and it outsources other cases to collection agencies. When all ways of collecting a past-due account have been tried and collection appears unlikely, the account should be written off and removed from the allowance because there is no longer any doubt about its collection. Canadian Tire writes off about $350 million a year in bad debts.

To prevent premature or unauthorized write offs, each write off should be formally approved in writing by managers who have been assigned this responsibility. To adhere to the appropriate internal control activity, the responsibility to authorize write offs should not be given to someone who also has daily responsibilities related to cash or receivables, in order to prevent them from misappropriating the cash receipt and writing off the account to hide the theft.

To illustrate a receivables write off, assume that on March 1, Abrams Furniture's vice-president of finance authorizes a write off of the $2,500 balance owed by T. Ebbet, a customer. T. Ebbet's account is more than 120 days overdue. The entry to record the write off is:

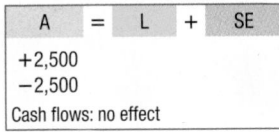

A	=	L	+	SE
+2,500				
−2,500				
Cash flows: no effect				

Mar. 1	Allowance for Doubtful Accounts	2,500	
	Accounts Receivable		2,500
	(Write off of T. Ebbet account)		

Note that bad debts expense is not increased (debited) when the write off occurs. **Under the allowance method, every accounts receivable write off entry is debited to the allowance account and not to bad debts expense.** A debit to bad debts expense would be incorrect because the expense was already recognized when the adjusting entry that estimated the allowance balance was recorded last year.

Notice that the entry to record the write off of an uncollectible account reduces both accounts receivable and allowance for doubtful accounts. After posting, using an assumed Accounts Receivable opening balance of $227,500, the general ledger accounts will appear as follows:

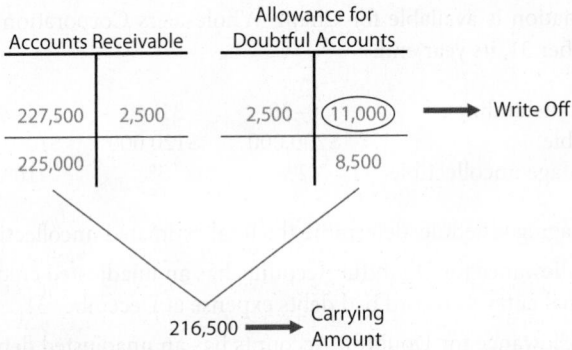

A write off affects only statement of financial position accounts, reducing both Accounts Receivable and Allowance for Doubtful Accounts equally. The carrying amount of accounts receivable on the statement of financial position remains the same, as shown below:

	Before Write Off	After Write Off
Accounts receivable	$227,500	$225,000
Less: Allowance for doubtful accounts	11,000	8,500
Carrying amount	$216,500	$216,500

ACCOUNTING MATTERS

© istock.com/DNY59

Social Media and Debt Collectors

Companies, and collection agencies working on their behalf, go to great lengths to collect amounts owed, including contacting family members and friends of debtors in attempts to locate them. One strategy debt collectors have tried has been to set up a fake profile on Facebook, Twitter, or another social media site and use it to try to "friend" or "follow" someone to determine their whereabouts. One woman successfully sued a debt collector who tried to use Facebook to get her to repay her debt. The court ruled that the debt collector had violated the woman's privacy rights when a collection agency sent messages to her and her family on Facebook to have her call the agency about the debt. The Financial Consumer Agency of Canada, a federal watchdog, says that financial institutions trying to collect debts cannot contact debtors' friends, family, employer, or neighbours, although it does not mention consumer rights when it comes to being contacted by social media.[3]

COLLECTING UNCOLLECTIBLE ACCOUNTS

Even if an account has been written off, a company may still continue with collection efforts, such as having a collection agency continue to try to collect the account. It is also possible that a customer whose account has been written off may wish to make payment as a result of a change in their circumstances. These situations are referred to as a **bad debt recovery**. Two entries are required to record the recovery of a bad debt: (1) reverse the write-off entry to reinstate the customer's account, and (2) record the subsequent cash collection.

To illustrate, assume that on July 1, T. Ebbet's fortunes have changed and he now wants to restore his credit with Abrams Furniture. In order to do so, he has to pay the $2,500 amount that had been written off on March 1. The entries are as follows:

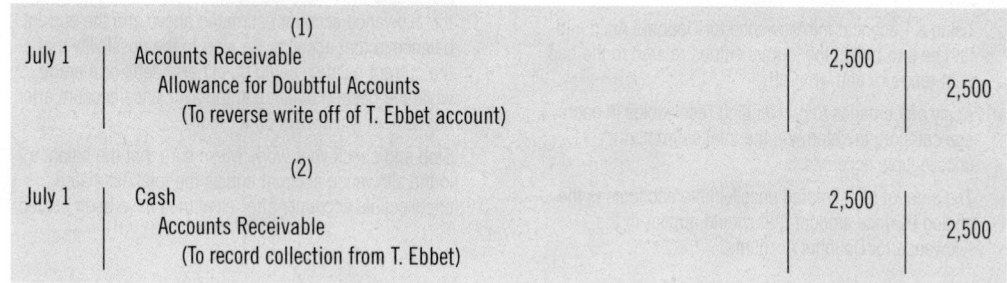

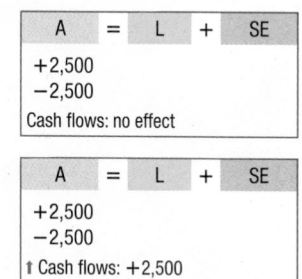

	(1)		
July 1	Accounts Receivable	2,500	
	Allowance for Doubtful Accounts		2,500
	(To reverse write off of T. Ebbet account)		

A = L + SE
+2,500
−2,500
Cash flows: no effect

	(2)		
July 1	Cash	2,500	
	Accounts Receivable		2,500
	(To record collection from T. Ebbet)		

A = L + SE
+2,500
−2,500
↑ Cash flows: +2,500

Note that the recovery of a bad debt, like the write off of a bad debt, affects only statement of financial position accounts. The net effect of the two entries is an increase (a debit) to Cash and an increase (a credit) to Allowance for Doubtful Accounts for $2,500. Instead of making one compound journal entry, Accounts Receivable is debited and later credited in a second entry for two reasons. First, the company should reverse the write off as soon as the receivable is considered collectible. Second, T. Ebbet did pay, and the Accounts Receivable account in the subsidiary and general ledgers should show this collection because it will need to be considered for future credit-granting purposes.

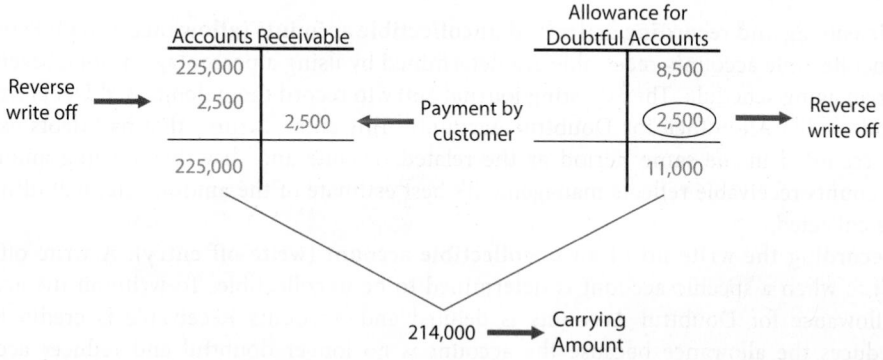

DO IT! ▶ 8-2b   **Write Offs and Recoveries**

Huracan Ltd. began the month of October with a $3,700 credit balance in Allowance for Doubtful Accounts. The company had the following transactions during the month.

Oct. 9   Recovered $3,300 from Telmo Ltd., a customer whose account had been written off in January.
     17   Wrote off the account of Valez Ltd., which owed Huracan $8,200.
     31   Had the following information in its aged A/R subledger:

Classification of Accounts	Amount	Estimated Uncollectible %
Current (<30 days)	$80,000	2%
31–60 days	40,000	5%
61–90 days	10,000	12%
>90 days	20,000	25%

(a) Prepare the journal entries required to record the recovery and write off.

(b) Prepare the journal entry to record bad debts expense at October 31.

Action Plan

✔ Using a T account for Allowance for Doubtful Accounts, update it to reflect the journal entries related to the bad debt recovery and write off.

✔ Apply percentages to outstanding receivables in each age category to determine the total estimated uncollectible accounts.

✔ The amount of estimated uncollectible accounts is the ending balance amount that should appear in the Allowance for Doubtful Accounts.

✔ Determine the difference between the desired balance in the allowance account estimated above and the current balance in that account. Be alert to the possibility that the current balance could be either a debit or a credit while the desired balance in the allowance account after adjustment will always be a credit.

✔ Stop and check your work. Make sure that the balance in the allowance account equals the total estimated uncollectible accounts after all entries have been posted.

SUMMARY OF ALLOWANCE METHOD

In summary, there are three types of transactions when accounts receivable are measured and recorded using the allowance method:

1. **Measuring and recording estimated uncollectible accounts (allowance entry):** Estimated uncollectible accounts receivable are determined by using a percentage of total receivables or an aging schedule. The adjusting journal entry to record them debits Bad Debts Expense and credits Allowance for Doubtful Accounts. This entry ensures that bad debts expense is recorded in the same period as the related revenue and that the carrying amount of accounts receivable reflects management's best estimate of the amount that will ultimately be collected.

2. **Recording the write off of an uncollectible account (write-off entry):** A write off takes place when a specific account is determined to be uncollectible. To write off the account, Allowance for Doubtful Accounts is debited and Accounts Receivable is credited. This reduces the allowance because the account is no longer doubtful and reduces accounts receivable because the account is not collectible. This entry has no effect on the carrying value of accounts receivable.

3. **Recording the recovery of an uncollectible account (recovery entries):** Any recovery of accounts that have previously been written off is recorded using two separate entries. The first reverses the original write off by debiting Accounts Receivable and crediting Allowance for Doubtful Accounts. This re-establishes the receivable. The second entry records the collection of the account by debiting Cash and crediting Accounts Receivable. Note that neither the write off nor the subsequent recovery affects the income statement.

Typical receivables transactions and the above entries are summarized and illustrated in the following T accounts:

Accounts Receivable		Allowance for Doubtful Accounts	
Beginning balance (b) Credit sales	(d) Collections of accounts receivable	(e) Write offs	Beginning balance (f) Subsequent recoveries
(f) Subsequent recoveries	(e) Write offs (g) Collection of subsequent recoveries		Unadjusted balance (h) Bad debts expense
Ending balance			Ending balance

Cash		Bad Debts Expense	
Beginning balance (a) Cash sales	(g) Collection of subse quent recoveries	(h) Bad debts expense	
(d) Collections of accounts receivable		Sales	
(g) Collections of subsequent recoveries			(a) Cash sales (b) Credit sales
Ending balance			Ending balance

Inventory		Cost of Goods Sold	
Beginning balance		(c) Cost of goods sold	
	(c) Cost of goods sold		

LEARNING OBJECTIVE ▶ **3**

Account for notes receivable.

Instead of accepting an account receivable, credit may also be granted in exchange for a formal credit instrument known as a promissory note. A **promissory note** is a written promise to pay a specified amount of money on demand (whenever the payee demands repayment) or at a fixed date in the future. Promissory notes may be used (1) when individuals and companies lend or borrow money, (2) when the amount of the transaction and the length of the credit period exceed normal limits, and (3) to settle an account receivable where payment cannot be made within the established credit period.

In a promissory note, the party making the promise to pay is called the **maker**; the party who will be paid is called the **payee**. For example, if Devon Inc. borrowed money from Scotiabank, Devon would be considered the maker and Scotiabank the payee. For the maker of the note, the note would be classified as a note payable. For the payee of the note, the note would be classified as a note receivable. A note receivable and a note payable are accounted for similarly in each company's records except that the payee's note is an asset while the maker's is a liability.

A promissory note details the names of the maker and the payee, the principal amount or face value of the loan, the loan period, the interest rate, and whether interest is payable monthly or at maturity (the note's due date), along with the principal amount. Other details might include whether any security is pledged as collateral for the loan and what happens if the maker defaults (does not pay).

It is easy to confuse accounts and notes receivable because there are many similarities between them. Like accounts receivable, notes receivable are also financial assets because the company will collect cash in the future. Both notes and accounts are credit instruments. And both are presented on the statement of financial position at their carrying amounts.

However, there are also differences between notes and accounts receivable. A note receivable is a formal promise to pay an amount that bears interest from the time it is issued until it is due. An account receivable is an informal promise to pay that bears interest only after its due date. Because it is less formal, it does not have as strong a legal claim as a note receivable. Most accounts receivable are due within a short period of time, usually 30 days, and are classified as current assets. On the other hand, notes receivable can be due over a longer period than accounts receivable and be classified as current or non-current assets depending on their due date.

> **Alternative Terminology**
> A *note receivable* is sometimes known as a *loan receivable* for the payee of the note, although for the maker of the note it is more common for a *note payable* to be known as a *loan payable*.

The basic issues in accounting for notes receivable are the same as those for accounts receivable: recording notes receivable, estimating and writing off uncollectible notes, and collecting notes receivable.

RECORDING NOTES RECEIVABLE

To illustrate the basic accounting for notes receivable, we will look at a situation in which a customer, Raja Ltd., is unable to pay its account receivable with Tabusintac Inc. by the due date. Let's assume that on May 1, Tabusintac Inc. (the payee) accepts a note receivable in settlement of an account receivable from Raja Ltd. (the maker). The note is for $10,000, with 6% interest due in four months, on September 1.

We record this entry as follows for the receipt of the note by Tabusintac:

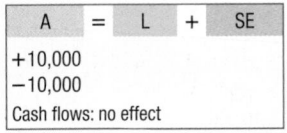

May 1	Notes Receivable	10,000	
	Accounts Receivable		10,000
	(To record acceptance of Raja four-month, 6% note)		

As shown above, notes receivable are recorded at their principal amount, the amount owing on the loan (exclusive of interest). You will note that no interest revenue was recorded when the note was accepted on May 1, because, as we learned in Chapter 4, interest revenue is earned with the passage of time.

Interest Revenue

When recording interest, the principal amount of the note is multiplied by the appropriate interest rate. You will recall that interest rates are always expressed as an **annual** rate of interest. Interest rates may be set as a fixed rate over the period of the note (such as 6% for the duration of the note) or as a floating (variable) rate that changes monthly over the duration of the note. In the situations we describe in this chapter, it would be common for notes to have a fixed interest rate, so you can assume that the interest rate is fixed for the purpose of your assignments. The annual interest rate must be adjusted for the fraction of the year that the note is outstanding. As we did in past chapters, for simplicity we will continue to assume that interest is calculated in months, rather than days.

Interest on the Raja note will total $50 ($10,000 $\times$ 6% $\times$ $^1/_{12}$) a month, or $200 for the four-month period. This interest will be recorded as interest revenue for Tabusintac and interest expense for Raja. If Tabusintac's year end was May 31, the following adjusting journal entry would be required to accrue interest for the month of May:

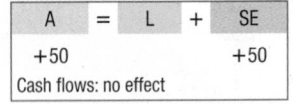

May 31	Interest Receivable	50	
	Interest Revenue		50
	(To accrue interest on Raja note receivable)		

Note that interest on a note receivable is *not* debited to the Notes Receivable account. Instead, as we learned in Chapter 4, a separate account, Interest Receivable, is used. Since the note is a formal credit instrument, the recorded principal amount must remain unchanged.

Uncollectible Notes Receivable

Like accounts receivable, notes receivable are reported at their carrying amount. You will recall that carrying amount is the difference between the balance in the receivables account (Notes Receivable, in this case) and the allowance account. Because companies generally don't have many notes, preparing an aging schedule, as is usually done for accounts receivable, is not the best way to estimate uncollectible notes. Instead, each note should be individually analyzed to determine its probability of collection. If circumstances suggest that eventual collection is in doubt, bad debts expense and an allowance for doubtful notes must be recorded in the same way they are recorded for accounts receivable.

DERECOGNIZING NOTES RECEIVABLE

In the normal course of events, the principal amount of a note receivable and its accrued interest are collected when due and then removed from the books, or **derecognized**. Notes that are collected when due are said to be honoured. In some situations, the maker of the note defaults and an appropriate adjustment must be made. This is known as a dishonoured note. Let's look at each of these possibilities in turn.

Honoured (Collected) Notes Receivable

When a note receivable is collected in full at its maturity date, it is called an **honoured note**. If Raja pays its note when it is due on September 1, the maturity date, the entry by Tabusintac to record the collection is:

Sept. 1	Cash	10,200	
	Notes Receivable		10,000
	Interest Receivable		200
	(To record collection of Raja note and accrued interest)		

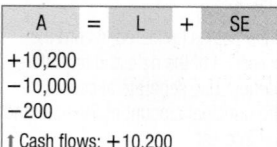

A = L + SE
+10,200
−10,000
−200
↑ Cash flows: +10,200

Recall that one month of interest, $50, was previously accrued on May 31. Additional adjusting entries would have been made at the end of June, July, and August to accrue the interest revenue earned in each month. Consequently, when the note matures and is repaid on September 1, there is no additional interest revenue to be recorded, just the collection of the cash in settlement of the note and interest receivable.

Dishonoured Notes Receivable

A **dishonoured note** is a note that is not paid in full at maturity. A dishonoured note receivable is no longer negotiable. However, the payee still has a claim against the maker of the note for both the principal and any unpaid interest. Therefore, if eventual collection is expected, the Notes Receivable account balance and related interest are transferred to an account receivable by debiting Accounts Receivable for the total of the principal amount of the note and the interest due.

As shown below, the journal entry to record this is identical to the one above where the note was honoured, except that the debit is to Accounts Receivable rather than to Cash:

Sept. 1	Accounts Receivable	10,200	
	Notes Receivable		10,000
	Interest Receivable		200
	(To record dishonoured Raja note; eventual collection expected)		

A = L + SE
+10,200
−10,000
−200
Cash flows: no effect

If management considers that there is no hope of collection, the principal and accrued interest should be written off. Because no allowance has been established for the note (because it was assumed that it would be honoured), bad debts expense would be recorded when it is written off. The entry to write off the amount would be:

Sept. 1	Bad Debts Expense	10,200	
	Notes Receivable		10,000
	Interest Receivable		200
	(To write off dishonoured Raja note)		

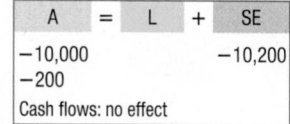

A = L + SE
−10,000   −10,200
−200
Cash flows: no effect

If a company has a material amount of notes receivable or they are a regular feature of the business, then the allowance method would be used to account for them. The accounting treatment would be consistent with how the allowance method is used for accounts receivable. At the end of each accounting period, management would estimate the amount of notes that it expects will be uncollectible. An allowance (allowance for doubtful notes) would be established and bad debts expense would be recorded. When specific notes are subsequently written off, then the allowance would be debited and notes receivable credited.

DO IT! ▶8-3   Notes Receivable

Action Plan

✔ Calculate the accrued interest each month. The formula is: principal amount × annual interest rate × $^1/_{12}$.

✔ If the note is honoured, record the collection of the note and any interest earned. Use separate accounts for the principal amount of the note and the interest.

✔ If the note is dishonoured, record the transfer of the note and any interest earned to an Accounts Receivable account if eventual collection is expected or to Bad Debts Expense if collection is not expected.

Sampson Stores Ltd. accepts from Shiraz Corp. a three-month, 6%, $6,800 note dated May 1 in settlement of Shiraz's overdue account.

(a) What journal entries and adjusting journal entries would be made by Sampson on May 1, May 31, June 30, July 31, and on August 1, the maturity date? Assume that Shiraz pays the note and interest in full at that time and that Sampson made monthly adjusting entries to accrue the interest revenue on the note.

(b) What entry would be made on August 1 if Shiraz could not pay the note but the note is still expected to be collected in the future?

SOLUTION

Try this Do It! exercise on your own and then check your answer at the end of the chapter.

Related Exercise Material: BE8–9, BE8–10, BE8–11, BE8–12, E8–7, and E8–8.

LEARNING OBJECTIVE ▶**4**

Explain the statement presentation of receivables.

Each of the major types of receivables should be identified in the statement of financial position, with supplemental detail included either in the statement or in the supporting notes. In addition, related revenue and expense accounts must be reported in the income statement, as discussed in the following sections.

STATEMENT OF FINANCIAL POSITION

Short-term receivables are reported in the current assets section of the statement of financial position, following cash and held for trading investments if items are presented from most to least liquid. Trade receivables must be reported separately from other types of receivables. Trade receivables are reported at their carrying amount. Both the gross amount of receivables and the allowance for doubtful accounts must be reported either in the statement of financial position or in the notes to the financial statements.

Receivables due more than a year from the statement of financial position date must be presented separately in the non-current assets section of the statement. If a company has a significant risk of uncollectible accounts or other problems with its receivables, it is required to discuss this in the note to the financial statements related to credit risk.

Receivables represent a significant claim for Canadian Tire, making up 43% of its total assets. Illustration 8-4 shows the presentation of receivables for Canadian Tire in its statement of financial position.

▶Illustration 8-4
Presentation of receivables

CANADIAN TIRE CORPORATION
Balance Sheet (partial)
January 2, 2016
(in millions)

Current assets		
Trade and other receivables		$ 915.0
Loans receivable	$4,987.0	
Less: Allowance for credit losses	111.5	4,875.5
Non-current assets		
Loans receivable		628.4
Mortgages receivable		28.0
Other receivables		5.1

The net realizable value of the loans receivable of $4,875.5 million was reported in the current assets section of Canadian Tire's statement of financial position, which it calls "balance sheet." The detail was presented in its notes, but is included in the above illustration for ease of reference. Note that Canadian Tire calls its "allowance for doubtful accounts" an "allowance for credit losses" and reports that its allowance for credit losses is determined by considering an aging schedule, the company's past collection history, as well as economic conditions and trends specific to the company.

In the notes to its statements, Canadian Tire also discloses the components of its loans receivable, which include its credit card loans, dealer loans, and personal loans.

INCOME STATEMENT

Income statement accounts related to receivables can include revenues such as sales or services on account and interest and expenses such as bad debts expense. Sales and service revenue and bad debts expense are reported in the operating expense section of the income statement. Interest revenue is reported separately in the non-operating section. The cost of goods sold would also be reported as an operating expense.

Canadian Tire reported, on its income statement and in the notes to its statements, revenue of $12,279.6 million and bad debts expense (which it called a net impairment loss on loans receivable) of $297.1 million. Its income statement also included interest income on loans receivable of $852.1 million.

DO IT! ▶8-4 Statement Presentation

Beau Resources Limited reports the following selected accounts and balances at December 31, 2018:

Accounts receivable	$ 150,000	Interest revenue	$ 6,000
Advances to employees	5,000	Inventory	110,000
Allowance for doubtful accounts	7,500	Notes receivable (due in 120 days)	25,000
Bad debts expense	10,000	Notes receivable (due in 3 years)	75,000
Cost of goods sold	1,160,000	Salaries expense	405,000
Income tax expense	75,000	Sales	2,000,000
Income tax receivable	7,500	Sales discounts	50,000
Interest receivable	4,000	Sales tax recoverable	2,500

Beau estimates that all its notes receivable are collectible.

(a) Prepare a partial statement of financial position for Beau Resources.

(b) Prepare a multiple-step income statement for Beau Resources.

Action Plan

✔ Determine which accounts are statement of financial position accounts and which are income statement accounts.

✔ Segregate current and non-current assets. Remember that current assets are turned into cash or used up within one year.

✔ Contra accounts offset other accounts and when applied against the related account, reduce it to a net balance.

✔ Refer to Chapter 5 if you need a refresher on the layout of a multiple-step income statement.

SOLUTION

Try this Do It! exercise on your own and then check your answer at the end of the chapter.

Related Exercise Material: BE8–13, E8–9, and E8–10.

Apply the principles of sound accounts receivable management.

There are four key steps in managing accounts receivable:

1. Determine whom to extend credit to.
2. Establish a payment period.
3. Monitor collections.
4. Evaluate the liquidity of receivables.

We will discuss each of these in more detail in the next sections.

EXTENDING CREDIT

A critical part of managing receivables is determining whom the company should extend credit to and whom it should not. If the credit policy is too tight, the company may lose revenue because customers who are denied credit may do business elsewhere. On the other hand, if the credit policy is too loose, the company may end up extending credit to risky customers who pay late or do not pay at all.

Certain steps can be taken to help minimize losses resulting from extending credit. Risky customers might be required to provide letters of credit or bank guarantees. Then, if the customer does not pay, the person or company that provided the guarantee will pay. Particularly risky customers might be required to pay a deposit in advance or cash on delivery. For example, Bombardier Inc., which manufactures transportation equipment (including aircraft, streetcars, and subway cars), reports that it minimizes its credit risk by having a charge over the products sold (so they could be seized if the customer did not pay) or requiring customers to provide cash deposits or letters of credit.

In addition, companies should ask new customers that are seeking credit for references from banks and suppliers to determine their payment history. It is important to check these references and to periodically check the financial health of existing customers. Canadian Tire, in our feature story, calculates credit scores before issuing credit cards. A credit score is a measure of risk of a customer defaulting on an account. Many other resources are available for investigating customers and companies. For example, companies such as Equifax and TransUnion provide credit opinions on companies around the world to aid in lending decisions.

ESTABLISHING A PAYMENT PERIOD

Companies that extend credit should determine the credit term period (the date when payment is due) and advise their customers about these terms. Normally, the credit period would be similar to the period used by competitors. For example, if you require payment in 30 days but your competitors allow payment in 45 days, you may lose sales to your competitors. If you match your competitors' payment period, the slower receipt of cash from customers may require you to carry higher levels of debt. In such situations, you might have to consider options such as allowing up to 45 days to pay but offering a 2% sales discount for customers paying within 15 days (2/15, n/45).

MONITORING COLLECTIONS

An accounts receivable aging schedule should be prepared and reviewed at least monthly. Almost all accounting software programs can generate an aged listing at any time. In addition to its use in estimating the allowance for doubtful accounts, the aging schedule helps estimate the timing of future cash inflows when preparing a cash budget. It also provides information about the company's overall collection experience, and it identifies problem accounts. Canadian Tire uses a variety of different strategies to deal with its problem accounts depending on how big the balance might be, what the payment history has been, and so on.

Credit risk can increase during periods of economic downturn. Credit policies and collection experience must always be monitored not only in comparison with past experience, but also in light of current economic conditions.

EVALUATING LIQUIDITY OF RECEIVABLES

Investors and managers keep a watchful eye on the relationship between sales, accounts receivable, and cash collections. If sales increase, then accounts receivable are also expected to increase. However, if accounts receivable rise faster than sales, this may be an indication of collection problems. Perhaps the company increased its sales by loosening its credit policy, and these receivables may be difficult or impossible to collect, which will affect liquidity. Recall that liquidity is measured by how quickly certain assets can be converted to cash.

The ratio that is used to assess the liquidity of receivables is the **receivables turnover** ratio. This ratio measures the number of times, on average, that receivables are collected during the year. The receivables turnover is calculated by dividing net credit sales by the average gross accounts receivable during the year. Gross accounts receivable is the amount reported in the Accounts Receivable account (before deducting allowance for doubtful accounts). Unless seasonal factors are significant, average gross accounts receivable can be calculated by adding together the beginning and ending balances and dividing by 2.

Unfortunately, companies seldom report the amount of net credit sales in their financial statements. In such instances, net sales (including both cash and credit sales) can be used as a substitute. As long as one consistently chooses the same component to use in a ratio, the resulting ratio will be useful for period-to-period comparisons.

The following data (in millions) are available for Canadian Tire's trade receivables:

	2016	2015	2014
Net sales	$12,279.6	$12,462.9	$11,785.6
Accounts receivable (gross)	915.0	880.2	758.5

The receivables turnover for Canadian Tire is shown in Illustration 8-5. Also included in this illustration is the receivables turnover for Sears, one of its competitors, as well as comparative industry data.

►Illustration 8-5
Receivables turnover

$$\text{RECEIVABLES TURNOVER} = \frac{\text{NET CREDIT SALES}}{\text{AVERAGE GROSS ACCOUNTS RECEIVABLE}}$$

($ in millions)	2016	2015
Canadian Tire	$\dfrac{\$12,279.6}{(\$915.0 + \$880.2) \div 2} = 13.7$	$\dfrac{\$12,462.9}{(\$880.2 + \$758.5) \div 2} = 15.2$
Sears	47.5 times	43.8 times
Industry average	26.7 times	35.6 times

Canadian Tire's receivables turnover was 13.7 times in 2015. The higher the turnover ratio, the more liquid the company's receivables are. The company's turnover ratio declined from 2015, when it was 15.2. Canadian Tire's receivables turnover ratio is much lower than Sears and its industry peers because the company's receivables are primarily from dealers in its network, rather than from individual customers. Canadian Tire extends credit to individual customers through its store credit cards rather than by granting them credit directly.

A popular variant of the receivables turnover is to convert it into an **average collection period** in terms of days. This is done by dividing 365 days by the receivables turnover. The average collection period is frequently used to assess the effectiveness of a company's credit and collection policies. The general rule is that the collection period should not greatly exceed the credit term period (the time allowed for payment).

Illustration 8-6 shows the average collection period for Canadian Tire, Sears, and their industry.

►Illustration 8-6
Average collection period

$$\text{AVERAGE COLLECTION PERIOD} = \frac{365 \text{ DAYS}}{\text{RECEIVABLES TURNOVER}}$$

	2016	2015
Canadian Tire	$\dfrac{365 \text{ days}}{13.7} = 27 \text{ days}$	$\dfrac{365 \text{ days}}{15.2} = 24 \text{ days}$
Sears	8 days	8 days
Industry average	16 days	16 days

▼ HELPFUL HINT

The higher the receivables turnover and lower the average collection period, the more liquid the company's receivables generally are.

This means that, on average, Canadian Tire collected its receivables in approximately 27 days in 2016. The lower the average collection period, the more liquid are a company's receivables. Note that, even though Canadian Tire's receivables turnover and collection period are not as good as those of Sears and the industry, a collection period of 27 days is very good on its own depending on the credit terms granted.

Both the receivables turnover and the average collection period are important components of a company's overall liquidity. Ideally, they should be analyzed along with other information about a company's liquidity, including the current ratio and inventory turnover. Recall from earlier chapters that high receivables and inventory balances due to slow-moving accounts and goods can distort a company's current ratio if the appropriate adjustments to reflect a decline in carrying amount have not been made. In general, the faster the turnover, the more reliable the current ratio is for assessing liquidity.

In addition, in some cases, receivables turnover and collection periods can be misleading. Some large retail chains that issue their own credit cards encourage customers to use these cards for purchases. If customers pay slowly, the stores earn a healthy return on the outstanding receivables in terms of interest revenue earned. Consequently, to interpret these ratios correctly, you must know how a company manages its receivables.

KEEPING AN EYE ON CASH

A company can have strong sales and profits but still have great difficulty paying its liabilities because of poor receivables management. For example, assume that a bank has given a new consulting business an operating line of credit of $20,000 and it used $15,000 of it to pay for rent, damage deposits, and equipment. After the first month of business, the company had earned $18,000 of consulting revenue but collected only $2,000 cash from its clients. It has to pay employees tomorrow and they are owed $9,000 for the salaries incurred this month. Although the company's profit this month is quite healthy ($18,000 − $9,000 − some other expenses), it has only $2,000 in the bank (the amount collected from clients) and it can borrow only another $5,000 on an operating line of credit from the bank to meet payroll. In situations like this, a cash shortage often comes as a surprise and management does not have time to develop solutions to the problem. Businesses should always remember that profit does not equal cash flow and that they always need to find ways to deal with times when liquidity is tight.

DO IT! ▶8-5   Managing Receivables

Action Plan

✔ Assess the steps this company should take in managing its receivables by reviewing the following four steps: (a) determine whom to extend credit to, (b) establish a payment period, (c) monitor collections, and (d) evaluate the liquidity of receivables, and any other steps you think the company should consider.

The Halifax Discount Store (HDS) Ltd. specializes in selling products at discounted prices. Customers can buy products with cash, debit cards, bank credit cards, or the company's own HDS credit card. The HDS card was introduced six months ago and has helped increase sales considerably. Anyone is eligible to receive an HDS credit card as long as they have valid identification and are over the age of 18. Cardholders have up to four months before they are required to pay any amounts due and many customers take the full amount of time to pay. Others take even longer.

HDS has a large outstanding bank loan that has grown this year. The company is concerned that the bank will raise interest rates if the receivables turnover continues to be slow. Consequently, management is looking at ways to speed up the collection of cash and would like you to discuss steps that can be taken to manage receivables more effectively.

SOLUTION

Try this Do It! exercise on your own and then check your answer at the end of the chapter.

Related Exercise Material: BE8–14, BE8–15, E8–11, E8–12, and E8–13.

REVIEW AND PRACTICE

▶ LEARNING OBJECTIVE REVIEW

1. Identify the types of receivables and record accounts receivable transactions. Receivables can include accounts receivable, notes receivable, and other types of receivables. Accounts and notes resulting from sales transactions are called trade receivables. Other receivables include nontrade receivables such as interest receivable, loans to company officers, advances to employees, sales tax recoverable, and income tax receivable.

Accounts receivable arising from sales or services on credit are recorded at the invoice price, and are reduced by any sales returns and allowances. The accounts receivable subsidiary ledger is used to keep track of the account balances of each customer. Accounts Receivable is a control account, meaning it controls the accounts receivable subsidiary ledger. Any entry to the control account must also be made in the subsidiary ledger, and any entry in the subsidiary ledger must also be made in the control account. Normally a single entry is made to the control account for the total of all the entries made to the individual customer accounts in the subsidiary ledger. It is essential that the total of the customer account information in the subsidiary ledger equal the balance in the control account.

When interest is charged on a past-due receivable, interest is added to the Accounts Receivable balance and is realized as interest revenue.

2. Account for bad debts. The allowance method, using a percentage of receivables, is used to ensure that the carrying amount of accounts receivable reflects management's best estimate of the amount that will ultimately be collected. It also results in bad debts expense being recorded in the same period when the revenue from the related credit sales was earned.

Because the specific customer accounts that will become uncollectible are not known at the time the bad debt estimate is made, no entry can be made to Accounts Receivable because it would not be possible to make an entry to the subsidiary ledger. Instead, Allowance for Doubtful Accounts, a contra asset account, is used to record the estimated uncollectible receivables.

A percentage of total receivables, or an aging schedule applying percentages to different age groupings of receivables, is used to estimate the uncollectible accounts (which is also the ending balance in Allowance for Doubtful Accounts). When a specific account receivable is determined to be uncollectible, it is written off and the allowance account reduced. When an account that has previously been written off is collected, the write off is reversed and then the collection is recorded. Bad debts expense is the difference between the estimated total uncollectible accounts (required balance in the allowance account) and the unadjusted balance in the allowance account.

3. Account for notes receivable. Notes receivable are recorded at their principal amount. Interest is earned from the date the note is issued until it matures and is recorded in a separate interest receivable account.

Notes can be held to maturity, at which time the principal plus any unpaid interest is due and the note is removed from the accounts when paid (honoured). In some situations, the maker of the note dishonours the note (defaults). If eventual collection is expected, an account receivable replaces the note receivable and any unpaid interest. If the amount is not expected to be repaid, the note is written off.

4. Explain the statement presentation of receivables. Each major type of receivable should be identified in the statement of financial position, with supplemental detail included in the statement or supporting notes. Companies must report the carrying amount of their receivables on the statement of financial position. The gross amount of receivables and allowance for doubtful accounts can be reported directly on the statement or in the notes. Bad debts expense is reported in the income statement as an operating expense, and interest revenue is shown in the non-operating section of the statement.

5. Apply the principles of sound accounts receivable management. To properly manage receivables, management must (a) determine whom to extend credit to, (b) establish a payment period, (c) monitor collections, and (d) evaluate the liquidity of receivables by calculating the receivables turnover and average collection period.

The receivables turnover is calculated by dividing net credit sales by average gross accounts receivable. The average collection period converts the receivables turnover into days, dividing 365 days by the receivables turnover ratio. A higher receivables turnover or a lower average collection period indicates that the company is doing a good job collecting its accounts and not experiencing collection issues.

▶ KEY TERM REVIEW

The following are key terms defined in this chapter with the corresponding page reference for your review. You will find a complete list of terms and definitions for all chapters in the glossary at the end of this textbook.

Aging of accounts receivable method (p. 419)
Allowance method (p. 418)
Average collection period (p. 431)
Bad debt recovery (p. 423)
Control account (p. 415)
Credit term period (p. 416)

Derecognized (p. 427)
Dishonoured note (p. 427)
Financial assets (p. 414)
Honoured note (p. 427)
Nontrade receivables (p. 414)
Percentage of receivables method (p. 419)

Promissory note (p. 425)
Receivables turnover (p. 431)
Subsidiary ledger (p. 415)
Trade receivables (p. 414)

▶ DECISION TOOLKIT REVIEW

DECISION CHECKPOINTS	INFO NEEDED FOR DECISION	TOOLS TO USE FOR DECISION	HOW TO EVALUATE RESULTS
How has the age mix of accounts receivable changed? How has the allowance for doubtful accounts as a percentage of receivables changed?	Aged receivables information, which can usually be found in the notes to the financial statements discussing the credit risk of financial instruments.	Calculate each age group as a percentage of total accounts receivable. Determine what percentage the allowance for doubtful accounts is of total accounts receivable.	Compare the percentages each age group represents. Increases in the older age groups indicate that the company is having difficulty collecting its receivables. An increase in the allowance as a percentage of accounts receivable suggests concerns with credit granting and collection.
Are collections being made in a timely fashion?	Net credit sales and average gross accounts receivable balance	$$\text{Receivables turnover} = \frac{\text{Net credit sales}}{\text{Average gross accounts receivable}}$$ $$\text{Average collection period} = \frac{365 \text{ days}}{\text{Receivables turnover}}$$	The average collection period should be consistent with corporate credit policy. An increase may suggest a decline in customers' financial health.

▶ PRACTICE USING THE DECISION TOOLKIT

Answers are at the end of the chapter.

There are no direct competitors to Canadian Tire, although Walmart competes in many of the same product lines. Selected financial information for Walmart (in U.S. $ millions) is shown below and can be compared with the information reported for Canadian Tire, Sears, and the industry shown in Illustrations 8-5 and 8-6:

	2016	2015
Net sales	$478,614	$482,229
Accounts receivable (gross)	5,624	6,778

INSTRUCTIONS

Calculate Walmart's receivables turnover and average collection period for 2016. Assume that all sales are made on credit. Comment on the company's accounts receivable management and liquidity compared with that of Canadian Tire, Sears, and the industry.

▶ PRACTICE COMPREHENSIVE DO IT!

Answers are at the end of the chapter.

On February 28, Shawinigan Distributors Ltd. had the following balances in its accounts receivable and allowance accounts. Assume all account balances are normal balances.

Accounts Receivable	$500,000
Allowance for Doubtful Accounts	31,000

The following selected transactions occurred throughout the year. Shawinigan's year end is July 31.

Mar.	1	Sold $30,000 of merchandise to Anderson Ltd., terms 2/10, n/30. Shawinigan uses a perpetual inventory system and the cost of goods sold was $18,000.
	10	Received payment in full from Anderson for balance due.
	15	Made credit sales of $25,000 to Aulac Ltd., terms 2/10, n/30. The cost of goods sold for these sales totalled $15,000.
Apr.	1	Received a payment of $16,000 from Aulac and agreed to accept a two-month note receivable for the balance with interest of 24% per annum (2% per month) for the remaining balance.
	30	Accrued the interest earned on the Aulac note.
May	10	Wrote off as uncollectible $32,000 of accounts receivable.
	31	Accrued the interest earned on the Aulac note.
June	1	Collected the note receivable from Aulac, together with the accrued interest.
July	16	One of the accounts receivable written off in May was received in full, $8,000.
	31	Using an aging schedule, uncollectible accounts are estimated to be $40,000.

INSTRUCTIONS

(a) Record the above transactions.

(b) Open T accounts for the Accounts Receivable and Allowance for Doubtful Accounts general ledger accounts. Post the opening balances as at February 28 as well as the relevant entries from transactions recorded above.

(c) Calculate the carrying amount of the accounts receivable at July 31.

▶ PRACTICE OBJECTIVE-FORMAT QUESTIONS

Answers are given at the end of the chapter.

1. Indicate which of the following statements are correct. (Select as many as are appropriate.)

(a) Accounts receivable and notes receivable are examples of formal instruments of credit, for which a written promise to pay exists.

(b) If a subsidiary ledger is used, it must always remain in balance with the related control account.

(c) Accounts receivable are normally interest-bearing.

(d) Accounts receivable are amounts owed by customers.

(e) Any sales returns made by a customer who purchased goods on credit reduce accounts receivable.

(f) Customers are not charged interest on accounts receivable during the credit period.

(g) Accounts receivable is a control account, which means that its account balance is equal to the balance in the receivables subsidiary ledger.

2. Indicate which of the following statements regarding accounts receivable and bad debts are correct. (Select as many as are appropriate.)

(a) The accounts receivable subsidiary ledger must always equal the balance in Accounts Receivable.

(b) If a company had a debit balance in its Allowance for Doubtful Accounts account prior to the bad debts adjusting entry, it would indicate that the bad debts expense for the prior period was overstated.

(c) When a customer's account is written off, the carrying amount of accounts receivable is reduced.

(d) Allowance for Doubtful Accounts is a temporary account and is closed at the end of each accounting period.

(e) In order to record a write-off entry, the company must know the specific customer whose account is being writtenoff.

(f) Allowance for Doubtful Accounts is a contra asset account and is added to the balance in the Accounts Receivable account to determine the carrying amount of accounts receivable.

(g) When a customer's account is written off, it reduces net income for that period.

3. Indicate the effect (increase, decrease, or no effect) that the following transactions would have on the carrying amount of accounts receivable.

(a) Writing off a customer's account.
(b) Accepting a note receivable in settlement of an outstanding account receivable.
(c) Making a sale of goods to a customer on account.
(d) Recording bad debts expense at the end of an accounting period.
(e) A customer making a payment on its account.
(f) A customer returning merchandise it had purchased on account.
(g) Receiving a payment from a customer whose account had previously been written off.

4. Indicate which of the following accounts would be credited in the journal entry(ies) to record the receipt of a payment by a customer whose account had previously been written off. (Select as many as are appropriate.)

(a) Cash
(b) Bad Debts Expense
(c) Bad Debt Recoveries
(d) Allowance for Doubtful Accounts
(e) Notes Receivable
(f) Accounts Receivable
(g) Interest Receivable

5. Indicate which of the following journal entries would be made by Pro Office Supplies Ltd. (POSL) during the month of May to record the information below. (Select as many as are appropriate.)

POSL uses the aging method for determining its allowance for doubtful accounts. POSL began the month of May with a $6,800 credit balance in Allowance for Doubtful Accounts. The company had the following transactions during the month:

May 7 Wrote off the account of Dig-it Landscaping Ltd, which owed POSL $7,700.
    19 Recovered $3,800 from Al Security Ltd., a customer whose account had been written off in January.
    31 Classified the aged accounts receivable subsidiary ledger as follows:

Classification of Accounts	Amount	Estimated Uncollectible %
Current (<30 days)	$100,000	2%
31–60 days	50,000	4%
61–90 days	15,000	10%
>90 days	20,000	20%

(a) May 31 Bad Debts Expense   6,600
                 Accounts Receivable   6,600

(b) May 19 Accounts Receivable   3,800
                 Allowance for Doubtful Accounts   3,800

(c) May 31 Bad Debts Expense   9,500
                 Allowance for Doubtful Accounts   9,500

(d) May 19 Cash   3,800
                 Bad Debt Recoveries   3,800

(e) May 7 Allowance for Doubtful Accounts   7,700
                 Accounts Receivable   7,700

(f) May 19 Cash   3,800
                 Accounts Receivable   3,800

(g) May 31 Bad Debts Expense   6,600
                 Allowance for Doubtful Accounts   6,600

6. Indicate which of the following journal entries would be made by Primrose Designs on June 1, June 30, and August 1 to record the information below. (Select as many as are appropriate.)

On June 1, Primrose Designs Ltd. made a $5,500 sale related to design services on account. The terms were n/30.

On June 30, the company agreed to accept a note receivable from the customer, which it was unable to pay the account. The note has a one-month term and bears interest at 12%. Primrose makes adjusting entries on a monthly basis.

The customer settled the note in full on the maturity date, August 1.

(a)	Cash	5,500	
	Notes Receivable		5,500
(b)	Notes Receivable	5,500	
	Accounts Receivable		5,500
(c)	Interest Receivable	55	
	Interest Revenue		55
(d)	Cash	5,555	
	Notes Receivable		5,555
(e)	Notes Receivable	55	
	Interest Revenue		55
(f)	Cash	5,555	
	Notes Receivable		5,500
	Interest Receivable		55
(g)	Cash	5,500	
	Accounts Receivable		5,500
	Interest Receivable		55

7. Indicate which of the following statements are correct in relation to notes receivable. (Select as many as are appropriate.)

(a) The maker of a note is the party that will receive cash when the note is repaid.
(b) Promissory notes can be created to replace accounts receivable that customers are unable to pay within the credit period.
(c) Interest accrued on notes receivable is debited to Notes Receivable and credited to Interest Revenue.
(d) The party that will be paid upon the maturity of a note receivable is known as the payee.

(e) If a note is dishonoured, it means that the payee will not pay the amount owing.
(f) Notes receivable usually bear interest from the time the note is issued.
(g) If a note is honoured, then the payee has received payment of principal and interest at maturity.

8. Indicate which of the following accounts would be included in determining the receivables presented as current assets on a company's statement of financial position. (Select as many as are appropriate.)

(a) Mortgage Receivable (due in five years)
(b) Interest Receivable
(c) Accounts Receivable
(d) Notes Receivable (due in two years)

(e) Income Tax Receivable
(f) Allowance for Doubtful Accounts
(g) Advances to Employees

9. Indicate which of the following statements are correct in relation to the information below. (Select as many as are appropriate.)

	2018	2017	2016
Net credit sales	$156,000	$150,000	$120,000
Accounts receivable (gross)	16,000	14,000	10,000

The company's credit terms are n/30.

(a) The receivables turnover for 2018 was 10.4.

(b) The receivables turnover ratio has improved in 2018.

(c) The average collection period in 2017 was 29 days.

(d) The receivables turnover for 2018 was 9.7.

(e) It took less time, on average, for the company to collect its receivables in 2018.

(f) The company collected its receivables within the established credit period in 2018.

(g) It is taking almost six days longer to collect its receivables in 2018 than in 2017.

10. Indicate which of the following statements are correct. (Select as many as are appropriate.)

(a) A high receivables turnover indicates that a company collects its receivables quickly.

(b) If a company's receivables turnover decreases from one year to the next, this is a positive change.

(c) A company's average collection period should be less than the credit terms it establishes with its customers.

(d) A decrease in receivables turnover indicates a company's customers are having more difficulty settling their accounts.

(e) If a company's average collection period increases from one year to the next, this is a positive change.

(f) A significant increase in the average collection period could be an indication that credit-granting policies may be too relaxed.

(g) If a company's receivables turnover increases from one year to the next, this is a positive change.

WileyPLUS

Brief Exercises, Exercises, and many additional resources are available for practice in WileyPLUS.

▶ QUESTIONS

(LO 1) 1. (a) What are the three major types of receivables? (b) Give examples of each type of receivable.

(LO 1) 2. Distinguish between trade receivables and nontrade receivables.

(LO 1) 3. (a) When should a receivable be recorded for a service company? For a merchandising company? (b) Explain how your answer relates to the revenue recognition criteria described in Chapter 4.

(LO 1) 4. **Canadian Tire** accepts credit cards and debit cards. (a) What are the advantages of accepting each type of card? (b) Explain how the accounting differs for each type of card.

(LO 1) 5. (a) What are the advantages of using an accounts receivable subsidiary ledger? (b) Describe the relationship between the general ledger control account and the subsidiary ledger.

(LO 2) 6. (a) What is an aging schedule? (b) How is an aging schedule used to determine total estimated uncollectible accounts?

(LO 2) 7. (a) What is the purpose of the account Allowance for Doubtful Accounts? (b) Although the normal balance of this account is a credit balance, it can sometimes have a debit balance. Explain how and when this can happen.

(LO 2) 8. What does it mean if Allowance for Doubtful Accounts has a debit balance? What does this tell you about the financial statements of the preceding period?

(LO 2) 9. Why is the bad debts expense that is reported on the income statement usually not the same amount as the allowance for doubtful accounts amount reported in the statement of financial position?

(LO 2) 10. Mohamed cannot understand why the carrying amount of accounts receivable does not change when an uncollectible account is written off under the allowance method. Clarify this for Mohamed.

(LO 2) 11. When an account receivable that was previously written off is later collected, two separate journal entries are usually made rather than one compound journal entry. Explain why.

(LO 1, 3) 12. (a) How are accounts receivable and notes receivable alike? (b) How do they differ?

(LO 1, 3) 13. (a) Under what circumstances is interest normally recorded for (1) an account receivable and (2) a note receivable? (b) When interest is accrued, what account is debited for (1) an account receivable and (2) a note receivable? Explain.

(LO 3) 14. Danielle does not understand why a note receivable is not immediately recorded at its maturity amount (principal plus interest), rather than its principal amount. After all, you know you are going to collect both the principal and the interest and you know how much each will be. Clarify this for Danielle.

(LO 3) 15. Cobden Inc. borrowed money from Scotiabank, signing a promissory note. Which company is the maker of the note? The payee? Which company would record a note receivable? A note payable?

(LO 3) 16. What is the difference between honouring a note receivable at maturity and dishonouring a note at maturity?

(LO 3) 17. Athabasca Ltd. has several dozen notes receivable. It expects approximately 10% of these notes to be uncollectible. How should these estimated notes be accounted for?

(LO 4) 18. Indicate how accounts receivable and allowance for doubtful accounts should be presented on the statement of financial position.

(LO 4) 19. Saucier Ltd. has accounts receivable, notes receivable due in three months, notes receivable due in two years, an allowance for doubtful accounts, an allowance for doubtful notes, sales tax recoverable, and income tax receivable.

How should the receivables be reported on the statement of financial position?

(LO 4) 20. (a) Identify three income statement accounts that are related to receivables. (b) Indicate where each account would be reported on the income statement.

(LO 5) 21. What are the four steps in good receivables management?

(LO 5) 22. **High Liner Foods Incorporated**'s receivables turnover was 13.0 times in the 52-week period ended January 2, 2016, and 12.8 times in the 52-week period ended January 3, 2015. Based on this information, has High Liner's receivables management improved or worsened?

(LO 5) 23. The president of Ho Inc. proudly announces that her company has improved its liquidity because its current ratio has increased substantially. (a) Does an increase in the current ratio always indicate improved liquidity? (b) What other ratio or ratios might you review to determine whether or not the increase in the current ratio indicates an improvement in financial health?

(LO 5) 24. Why should a company not want to have a receivables turnover that is significantly higher than those of its competitors? Why would it not want a receivables turnover that is significantly lower than those of its competitors?

▶ BRIEF EXERCISES

BE8–1 Presented below are several receivables transactions. For each transaction, indicate whether the receivables should be reported as accounts receivable, notes receivable, or other receivables on a statement of financial position.
(a) Received a promissory note of $12,200 for services performed.
(b) Sold merchandise on account to a customer for $9,300.
(c) Advanced $5,000 to an employee.
(d) Estimated $5,000 of income tax to be refunded.
(e) Extended a customer's account for six months by accepting a note in exchange for the amount owed on the account.
(f) Sales tax (HST) of $2,500 is recoverable at the end of the quarter.

Identify types of receivables.

(LO 1)

BE8–2 Record the following transactions on the books of Essex Corp., which uses a perpetual inventory system.
(a) On July 1, Essex Corp. sold merchandise on account to Cambridge Inc. for $58,000, terms 2/10, n/30. The cost of the merchandise sold was $32,000.
(b) On July 8, Cambridge returned merchandise worth $6,400 to Essex. Its original cost was $4,320. The merchandise was restored to inventory.
(c) On July 9, Cambridge paid for the merchandise.
(d) Assume now that Cambridge did not pay on July 9, as indicated in transaction (c). At the end of August, Essex added one month's interest to Cambridge's account for the overdue receivable. Essex charges 24% per year on overdue accounts.

Record receivables transactions.

(LO 1)

BE8–3 Record the following transactions on the books of Hernan Ltd., which uses a perpetual inventory system.
(a) Sold $26,000 of merchandise on April 28 to Valez Ltd., terms 2/10, n/30. The goods sold had cost Hernan $18,000.
(b) On May 1, Hernan sold $35,000 of merchandise to Quilmes Ltd., terms 2/10, n/30. The goods sold had cost Hernan $24,000.
(c) On May 3, merchandise with a selling price of $1,200 was returned by Valez. The goods had a cost of $850 and they were restored to inventory.
(d) On May 6, Valez paid its account.
(e) On June 1, Hernan added one month's interest to Quilmes's account for the overdue receivable. Hernan charges 18% per year on overdue accounts.

Record receivables transactions.

(LO 1)

Prepare subsidiary ledger.

(LO 1)

BE8–4 Information related to Bryant Limited is presented below for its first month of operations.

Credit Sales

Jan.	7	Chiu Corp.	$1,800
	15	Elbaz Inc.	6,000
	23	Lewis Corp.	3,700

Cash Collections

Jan.	17	Chiu Corp.	$ 700
	24	Elbaz Inc.	2,000
	29	Lewis Corp.	3,700

Post the above transactions individually to the accounts receivable subsidiary ledger for each customer, and in summary form at the end of the month to the Accounts Receivable control account in the general ledger.

Record bad debts.

(LO 2)

BE8–5 At June 30, Calafate Ltd. prepared the following aging schedule:

Number of Days Outstanding	Accounts Receivable	Estimated Percentage Uncollectible	Total Estimated Uncollectible Accounts
0–45 days	$ 726,000	2%	
46–90 days	248,000	5%	
Over 90 days	112,000	16%	
Total	$1,086,000		

(a) Prepare the adjusting journal entry to record bad debts expense at June 30 assuming that Calafate's allowance for doubtful accounts had a credit balance of $13,175.

(b) Prepare the adjusting journal entry to record bad debts expense at June 30 assuming that Calafate's allowance for doubtful accounts had a debit balance of $8,920 instead of a credit balance.

Complete aging schedule and record bad debts.

(LO 2)

BE8–6 Canton Imports prepared the aging schedule below at December 31. (a) Complete the aging schedule. (b) Prepare the adjusting journal entry at December 31 to record bad debts expense, assuming that the allowance account has a credit balance of $3,600. (c) Prepare the adjusting journal entry at December 31 to record bad debts expense, assuming that the allowance account has a debit balance of $5,400.

Number of Days Outstanding	Accounts Receivable	Estimated Percentage Uncollectible	Total Estimated Uncollectible Accounts
0–30 days	$368,000	1%	
31–60 days	120,000	4%	
61–90 days	72,000	10%	
Over 90 days	40,000	20%	
Total	$600,000		

Record write off and compare carrying amount.

(LO 2)

BE8–7 At the end of 2017, Searcy Corp. has accounts receivable of $480,000 and an allowance for doubtful accounts of $29,000. On January 24, 2018, Searcy learns that its $11,000 receivable from Hutley Inc. is not collectible. Management authorizes a write off. (a) Prepare the journal entry to record the write off. (b) What is the carrying amount of the accounts receivable (1) before the write off and (2) after the write off?

Record recovery of bad debts.

(LO 2)

BE8–8 Assume the same information as in BE8–7, but that on March 4, 2018, Searcy Corp. receives payment in full of $11,000 from Hutley Inc. after the write off. Prepare the required journal entry(ies) to record this transaction.

Record notes receivable transactions.

(LO 3)

BE8–9 On August 1, Belgrano Ltd. accepted a $26,000 note from Borges Ltd. in settlement of an account receivable. The note bears interest of 6% and is due in two months, on October 1. Interest on the note was accrued on August 31 and on September 30. On October 1, Borges paid the note, including the accrued interest. Prepare the journal entries required to record the above transactions.

Record receivables transactions.

(LO 1, 3)

BE8–10 On January 2, Kuril Ltd. sold merchandise on account to R. James for $48,000, terms n/30. The company uses a perpetual inventory system and the merchandise originally cost $32,000. On February 1, R. James gave Kuril a five-month,

7% note in settlement of this account. On April 30, Kuril's year end, annual adjusting entries were made. On July 1, R. James paid the note and accrued interest. Prepare the journal entries for Kuril to record the above transactions.

BE8–11 Stratus Ltd. sells merchandise on April 1, 2017, to Red River Enterprises in return for a 12-month, 9%, $10,000 note, with interest due at maturity. The company uses a perpetual inventory system and the cost of the inventory sold was $6,000. Stratus has a December 31 year end and adjusts its accounts annually. Prepare the journal entries that Stratus will record with regard to this note from April 1, 2017, until the note matures on March 31, 2018.

Record notes receivable transactions.

(LO 3)

BE8–12 Xavier Limited accepts a three-month, 6%, $40,000 note receivable in settlement of an account receivable on April 1, 2018. Interest is due at maturity.
(a) Prepare the journal entries required by Xavier Limited to record the issue of the note on April 1, and the settlement of the note on July 1, assuming the note is honoured and that no interest has previously been accrued.
(b) Repeat part (a) assuming that the note is dishonoured, but eventual collection is expected.
(c) Repeat part (a) assuming that the note is dishonoured and eventual collection is not expected.

Record notes receivable transactions.

(LO 3)

BE8–13 Nias Corporation reported the following selected items at February 28, 2018:

Prepare current assets section.

(LO 4)

Accounts payable	$938,000	Inventory	$380,000
Accounts receivable	470,000	Notes receivable—due November 1, 2018	300,000
Allowance for doubtful accounts	30,000	Notes receivable—due April 1, 2021	400,000
Bad debts expense	24,000	Prepaid rent	8,000
Cash	150,000	Sales tax recoverable	38,000
Held for trading investments	330,000	Unearned revenue	5,000

Prepare the current assets section of Nias's statement of financial position.

BE8–14 Maple Leaf Foods Inc. reported the following selected information (in thousands) for the three years ended December 31, 2015, 2014, and 2013:

Calculate ratios.

(LO 5)

	2015	2014	2013
Trade receivables (gross)	$ 25,537	$ 20,498	$ 37,173
Allowance for doubtful accounts	5	4	80
Sales	3,292,932	3,157,241	2,954,777

(a) Calculate Maple Leaf's receivables turnover and average collection period for 2015 and 2014. (b) Indicate whether each of the receivables turnover and average collection period is better or worse in 2015.

BE8–15 Canfor Corporation reported the following selected information (in millions) for the three years ended December 31, 2015, 2014, and 2013:

Calculate ratios.

(LO 5)

	2015	2014	2013
Trade receivables (gross)	$ 196.3	$ 95.0	$ 115.3
Allowance for doubtful accounts	4.5	3.7	2.7
Net sales	3,925.3	3,347.6	3,194.9

(a) Calculate Canfor's receivables turnover and average collection period for 2015 and 2014. (b) Indicate whether each of the receivables turnover and average collection period is better or worse in 2015.

▶ EXERCISES

E8–1 On January 6, Compton Limited sold merchandise on account to Singh Inc. for $45,200, terms 2/10, n/30. The merchandise originally cost Compton $26,500. On January 15, Singh paid the amount due. Both Compton and Singh use a perpetual inventory system.

Record receivables and payables transactions.

(LO 1)

Instructions

(a)   Prepare the entries on Compton's books to record the sale and related collection.

(b)   Prepare the entries on Singh's books to record the purchase and related payment.

Record receivables trans-
actions; post to subsidiary
and general ledgers.

(LO 1)

E8–2 Selected transactions follow for Discovery Sports Ltd. during the company's first month of business. The company uses a perpetual inventory system.

Feb.   2   Sold $1,140 of merchandise to Andrew Noren on account, terms n/30. The goods had cost Discovery $765.

4   Andrew Noren returned for credit $140 of the merchandise purchased on February 2. The goods had cost Discovery $85 and they were returned to inventory.

5   Sold $760 of merchandise to Dong Corporation on account, terms 2/10, n/30. The goods had cost Discovery $490.

8   Sold $842 of merchandise to Michael Collins for cash. The goods had cost Discovery $622.

10   Sold $920 of merchandise to Rafik Kurji, who paid with a credit card. The goods had cost Discovery $680.

14   Dong Corporation paid its account in full.

17   Andrew Noren purchased an additional $696 of merchandise on account, terms n/30. The goods had cost Discovery $410.

22   Sold $1,738 of merchandise to Batstone Corporation, terms 2/10, n/30. The goods had cost Discovery $1,105.

28   Andrew Noren paid $1,000 on account.

Instructions

(a)   Prepare the journal entries to record each of the above transactions.

(b)   Set up T accounts for the Accounts Receivable general ledger (control) account and for the accounts receivable subsidiary ledger accounts. Post the journal entries to these accounts.

(c)   Prepare a list of customers and the balances of their accounts from the subsidiary ledger. Prove that the total of the subsidiary ledger balances is equal to the control account balance.

Record bad debts.

(LO 2)

E8–3 Chinook Limited's general ledger reports a balance in Accounts Receivable of $360,000 at the end of December.

Instructions

(a)   Assuming that Allowance for Doubtful Accounts has a credit balance of $4,400 and that uncollectible accounts are determined to be $36,000 by aging the accounts, record the adjusting entry at December 31.

(b)   Assuming the same information as in part (a) except that the Allowance for Doubtful Accounts has a debit balance of $2,400, record the adjusting entry at December 31.

Prepare aging schedule;
record bad debts.

(LO 2)

E8–4 Gemini Ltd. has an Accounts Receivable amount of $370,000 and an unadjusted credit balance in Allowance for Doubtful Accounts of $8,800 at March 31. The company's accounts receivable and percentage estimates of its uncollectible accounts are as follows:

Number of Days Outstanding	Accounts Receivable	Estimated Percentage Uncollectible
0–30	$260,000	2%
31–60	50,400	10%
61–90	34,000	30%
Over 90	25,600	50%
Total	$370,000	

Instructions

(a)   Prepare an aging schedule to determine the total estimated uncollectibles at March 31.

(b)   Prepare the adjusting entry at March 31 to record bad debts expense.

(c)   What is the carrying amount of the receivables at March 31?

Record bad debts.

(LO 2)

E8–5 On December 31, 2017, when its accounts receivable were $300,000 and its account Allowance for Doubtful Accounts had an unadjusted debit balance of $2,000, Ceja Corp. estimated that $16,800 of its accounts receivable would become uncollectible, and it recorded the bad debts adjusting entry. On May 11, 2018, Ceja determined that Fei Ya Cheng's account was uncollectible and wrote off $1,900. On November 12, 2018, Cheng paid the amount previously written off.

Instructions

(a) Prepare the required journal entries to record each of the above transactions.

(b) What is the carrying amount of the receivables on (1) December 31, 2017; (2) May 11, 2018; and (3) November 12, 2018, assuming that the total amount of accounts receivable of $300,000 is unchanged on each of these three dates except for any changes recorded in part (a)?

E8–6 At the beginning of March, Paragon Limited, which records adjusting entries at the end of each month, had an Accounts Receivable amount of $30,000 and an Allowance for Doubtful Accounts balance of $5,000. During March, the company had credit sales of $40,000 and collected $35,000 from customers. It also wrote off a certain amount of uncollectible receivables during the month and recorded a certain amount of bad debts expense at the end of the month. No accounts that were written off during the month were subsequently recovered. At the end of March, after all journal entries had been recorded and posted, the balance in Accounts Receivable was $32,000 while Allowance for Doubtful Accounts had a balance of $4,500.

Determine missing amounts and record bad debts.

(LO 2)

Instructions

(a) Prepare T accounts for Accounts Receivable and Allowance for Doubtful Accounts. Post the above transactions and determine the missing amounts for the write off of uncollectible receivables and bad debts expense.

(b) Prepare the journal entry that would have been made by the company to write off uncollectible receivables during March.

(c) Prepare the journal entry that would be made by the company to record bad debts expense for the month of March.

E8–7 Passara Supply Corp. has the following selected transactions for notes receivable.

Record notes receivable transactions.

(LO 3)

Nov.	1	Lent $116,000 cash to A. Bouchard on a one-year, 9% note.
Dec.	1	Sold goods to Wright, Inc., receiving a two-month, 6%, $22,600 note. The goods cost $13,200.
	15	Received a six-month, 6%, $24,000 note in exchange for an account from Aquilina Corporation.
Feb.	1	Collected the amount owing on the Wright note.
	28	Accrued interest on all notes receivable at year end. Interest is calculated to the nearest half month and is due at maturity.
	28	Analyzed each note and estimated that uncollectible notes at year end totalled $18,200.

Instructions

Record the above transactions for Passara Supply Corp.

E8–8 The following selected transactions for notes receivable are for Acre Limited.

Record notes receivable transactions.

(LO 3)

May	1	Received a six-month, 5%, $12,000 note on account from Blackstone Limited. Interest is due at maturity.
June	30	Accrued interest on the Blackstone note on this date, which is Acre's year end.
July	31	Lent $10,000 cash to an employee, Noreen Wong, issuing a three-month, 7% note. Interest is due at the end of each month.
Aug.	31	Received the interest due from Ms. Wong.
Sept.	30	Received the interest due from Ms. Wong.
Oct.	31	Received payment in full for the employee note from Ms. Wong.
Nov.	1	Wrote off the Blackstone note because Blackstone defaulted. Future payment is not expected.

Instructions

Record the above transactions for Acre Limited.

E8–9 **Finning International Inc.** had the following balances in its short-term receivable accounts at December 31, 2015 (in millions): Allowance for Doubtful Accounts $23; Other Receivables $112; Supplier Claims Receivable $76; Value Added Tax Receivable $11; Income Tax Recoverable $1; and Trade Accounts Receivable (gross) $748.

Show statement presentation.

(LO 4)

Instructions

Show the presentation of Finning's receivables in the current assets section of its statement of financial position at December 31.

Show statement presentation.

(LO 4)

E8–10 Apollo Corporation reported the following selected accounts and amounts at November 30, 2018:

Accounts payable	$ 22,600
Accounts receivable	18,200
Advances to employees	2,900
Allowance for doubtful accounts	1,300
Allowance for doubtful notes (current)	5,000
Bad debts expense	2,000
Cash	7,500
Interest expense	2,400
Interest revenue	6,000
Inventory	26,400
Notes receivable (current)	25,000
Notes receivable (non-current)	75,000
Prepaid insurance	1,500
Sales	370,000
Sales discounts	12,000
Sales tax recoverable	3,150

Instructions

(a) Identify which of the above accounts are statement of financial position (SFP) accounts and which are income statement (IS) accounts.

(b) Indicate where each of the income statement accounts would be reported (for example, operating revenue, operating expenses, non-operating expenses, or non-operating revenue).

(c) Prepare the current assets section of Apollo's statement of financial position.

Calculate and evaluate ratios.

(LO 5)

E8–11 The following information (in millions) was taken from the December 31 financial statements of **Canadian National Railway Company (CN)**:

	2015	2014	2013
Accounts receivable, gross	$ 885	$ 937	$ 822
Allowance for doubtful accounts	7	9	7
Accounts receivable, net	878	928	815
Revenues	12,611	12,134	10,575
Total current assets	2,153	1,993	1,977
Total current liabilities	2,998	2,201	2,498

Instructions

(a) For 2015 and 2014, calculate CN's current ratio, receivables turnover, and average collection period.

(b) Comment on any improvement or deterioration in CN's management of its accounts receivable.

Calculate and evaluate ratios.

(LO 5)

E8–12 The following information (in U.S. $ millions) was taken from the December 31 financial statements of **Potash Corporation of Saskatchewan Inc.**:

	2015	2014	2013
Trade accounts receivable, gross	$ 475	$ 715	$ 507
Allowance for doubtful accounts	7	7	7
Trade accounts receivable, net	468	708	500
Revenues	6,279	7,115	7,305
Total current assets	1,553	1,938	2,189
Total current liabilities	1,747	2,198	2,113

Instructions

(a) For 2015 and 2014, calculate Potash's current ratio, receivables turnover, and average collection period.

(b) Comment on any improvement or deterioration in Potash's management of its accounts receivable.

E8–13 The following ratios are for Lin Inc.

Evaluate liquidity.

(LO 5)

	2018	2017
Current ratio	1.5:1	1.3:1
Receivables turnover	10 times	12 times
Inventory turnover	9 times	11 times

Instructions
(a) Is Lin's short-term liquidity improving or deteriorating in 2018? Explain.
(b) Identify any steps Lin might have taken, or wish to take, to improve the management of its accounts receivable and inventory.

▶ PROBLEMS: SET A

P8–1A At January 1, 2018, Underwood Imports Inc. reported the following on its statement of financial position:

Record receivables and bad debts; show statement presentation.

(LO 1, 2, 4)

Accounts receivable	$1,760,000
Allowance for doubtful accounts	118,000

During 2018, the company had the following summary transactions for receivables:
1. Sales on account, $5,400,000; Cost of goods sold, $2,970,000
2. Sales returns and allowances, $80,000; Cost of goods returned to inventory, $44,000
3. Collections of accounts receivable, $5,400,000
4. Interest added to overdue accounts, $400,000
5. Write offs of accounts receivable deemed uncollectible, $160,000
6. Collection of accounts previously written off as uncollectible, $72,000
7. After considering all of the above transactions, total estimated uncollectible accounts, $104,000

Instructions
(a) Prepare journal entries to record each of the above summary transactions.
(b) 1. Prepare T accounts for Accounts Receivable and Allowance for Doubtful Accounts.
    2. Enter the opening balances.
    3. Post the above summary entries.
    4. Determine the ending balances.
(c) Determine the carrying amount of the accounts receivable as at January 1 and December 31.
(d) Show the statement of financial position presentation of the receivables as at December 31.
(e) Show the income statement presentation of the revenue and expense accounts for the year ended December 31.

P8–2A At the beginning of the current period, Azim Enterprises Ltd. had balances in Accounts Receivable of $2.1 million and in Allowance for Doubtful Accounts of $144,000 (credit). During the period, Azim had credit sales of $4.3 million with cost of goods sold of $3.1 million and collections of $5.2 million. It wrote off $185,000 of accounts receivable. However, a $28,000 account written off as uncollectible was recovered before the end of the current period. Uncollectible accounts are estimated to total $85,000 at the end of the period.

Record receivables and bad debts; show statement presentation.

(LO 1, 2, 4)

Instructions
(a) Prepare the entries to record sales and collections during the period.
(b) Prepare the entry to record the write off of the $185,000 of accounts deemed uncollectible during the period.
(c) Prepare the entry(ies) to record the collection of the $28,000 account written off as part of the uncollectible accounts in part (b).
(d) Prepare the entry to record bad debts expense for the period.
(e) 1. Prepare T accounts for Accounts Receivable and Allowance for Doubtful Accounts.
    2. Enter the opening balances.
    3. Post the journal entries prepared in parts (a) through (d).
    4. Determine the ending balances.
(f) Show the statement of financial position presentation of the receivables at the end of the period.

Determine missing amounts.

(LO 2)

P8–3A Wilton Corporation reported the following selected information in its general ledger at December 31:

Accounts Receivable				Sales	
Beg. bal.	18,000				78,000
		55,000			
	(a)	(b)			
End. bal.	(c)				

Allowance for Doubtful Accounts				Bad Debts Expense	
		Beg. bal.	1,800	(f)	
	1,000				
		Unadj. bal.	800		
			(d)		
		End. bal.	(e)		

All sales were on account. Some accounts receivable were collected. One account was written off; there were no subsequent recoveries. At the end of the year, uncollectible accounts were estimated to total $2,000.

Instructions

Using your knowledge of receivables transactions, determine the missing amounts. (*Hint:* You may not be able to solve the above items in alphabetical order. In addition, you may find it helpful to reconstruct the journal entries.)

Prepare aging schedule and record bad debts.

(LO 2)

P8–4A Richibucto Ltd. prepares an aging schedule for its accounts receivable at the end of each month and records bad debts expense monthly. The following selected information is from Richibucto's partial aging schedule at the end of July:

Number of Days Outstanding	Accounts Receivable	Estimated Percentage Uncollectible
0–30 days	$ 780,000	2%
31–60 days	340,000	6%
61–90 days	115,000	12%
Over 90 days	76,000	22%
Total	$1,311,000	

The unadjusted balance in Allowance for Doubtful Accounts is a credit of $12,360.

Instructions

(a) Complete the aging schedule and calculate the total estimated uncollectible accounts from the above information.

(b) 1. Prepare the adjusting journal entry to record the bad debts using the information determined in part (a).

2. Would your journal entry be different if the unadjusted balance in Allowance for Doubtful Accounts were a debit of $12,360?

(c) In August, management determined that $45,730 of the outstanding receivables were specifically uncollectible. Prepare the journal entry to write off the uncollectible amount.

(d) Richibucto subsequently collected $8,850 of the $45,730 that was determined to be uncollectible in part (c). Prepare the journal entry(ies) to record the collection.

Prepare aging schedule; record bad debts for two years.

(LO 2)

P8–5A An aging analysis of Yamoto Limited's accounts receivable at December 31, 2018 and 2017, showed the following:

Number of Days Outstanding	Accounts Receivable		Estimated Percentage Uncollectible
	2018	2017	
0–30 days	$300,000	$320,000	3%
31–60 days	64,000	114,000	6%
61–90 days	86,000	76,000	12%
Over 90 days	130,000	50,000	24%
Total	$580,000	$560,000	

Additional information:

1. At December 31, 2017, the unadjusted balance in Allowance for Doubtful Accounts was a credit of $9,000.

2. In 2018, $42,000 of accounts were written off as uncollectible and $3,000 of accounts previously written off were recovered.

Instructions

(a) Prepare an aging schedule to calculate the estimated uncollectible accounts at December 31, 2017 and 2018. Note that the estimated percentages uncollectible are the same for both years. Comment on the results.
(b) Record the adjusting entry relating to bad debts on December 31, 2017.
(c) Record the write off of uncollectible accounts in 2018.
(d) Record the collection of accounts previously written off in 2018.
(e) Prepare the adjusting entry relating to bad debts on December 31, 2018.
(f) Calculate the carrying amount of Yamoto's accounts receivable at December 31, 2017 and 2018.

P8–6A The following selected transactions occurred for Bleumortier Corporation. The company uses a perpetual inventory system, has a May 31 year end, and adjusts its accounts annually.

Record receivables transactions.

(LO 1, 3)

Feb.	1	Sold merchandise for $8,000 on account (n/30) to Morgan Ltd.. The cost of goods sold was $6,000.
	3	Sold $13,400 of merchandise costing $8,800 to Gauthier Company and accepted Gauthier's two-month, 6% note in payment. Interest is due at maturity.
	26	Sold $12,000 of merchandise to Mathias Corp., terms n/30. The cost of the merchandise sold was $7,600.
Mar.	6	Sold, on account, $4,000 of merchandise that cost $3,000 to Superior Limited.
	27	Accepted a two-month, 7%, $12,000 note from Mathias for the balance due. Interest is due at maturity. (See February 26 transaction.)
Apr.	3	Collected the Gauthier note in full. (See February 3 transaction.)
May	27	The Mathias note of March 27 was dishonoured. It is expected that Mathias will eventually pay the amount owed.
	31	Recorded accrued interest for three months on outstanding interest on the receivable due from Morgan. Interest on unpaid receivables is charged at 24% per annum (2% per month). (See February 1 transaction.)

Instructions

Record the above transactions.

P8–7A On November 1, 2018, Sokos Inc. accepted a three-month, 9%, $60,000 note from Malmo Inc. in settlement of its account. Interest is due on the first day of each month, starting December 1. Both companies' year ends are December 31.

Record notes receivable and payable transactions.

(LO 3)

Instructions

(a) Prepare all journal entries for Sokos over the term of the note. Assume that the note is collected in full on the maturity date.
(b) Prepare all journal entries for Malmo over the term of the note. Assume that the note is paid in full on the maturity date.
(c) Assume that, instead of honouring the note at maturity, Malmo dishonours it. Prepare the necessary journal entry on Sokos's books at the maturity date, February 1, 2019, assuming that eventual collection of the note is (1) expected, and (2) not expected. Interest was last paid by Malmo on January 1.

P8–8A Tardif Corporation adjusts its books monthly. On September 30, 2018, notes receivable include the following:

Record notes receivable transactions; show statement presentation.

(LO 2, 3, 4)

Issue Date	Maker	Principal	Interest	Term
Mar. 31, 2018	RES Inc.	$17,000	6%	7 months
May 31, 2018	Ihara Ltd.	17,500	4%	18 months
Aug. 31, 2018	Dragon Limited	6,000	7%	2 months
Sept. 30, 2018	MGH Corp.	20,500	5%	16 months

Interest is due at maturity for the RES and Dragon notes. Interest is due on the first day of the month for the Ihara and MGH notes. At September 30, the balance in the Allowance for Doubtful Notes account is nil. In October, the following selected transactions were completed.

Oct.	1	Received the interest due from Ihara.
	31	Received notice that Dragon was unable to pay its note as scheduled. It expects to be able to pay in the future.
	31	The RES note matured and was received in full.
	31	Accrued interest on the Ihara and MGH notes.
	31	Analyzed the remaining notes for collectibility. Estimated that $17,500 of notes may not be collectible in the future because of significant labour issues currently being experienced by Ihara.

Instructions
(a) Calculate the balance in the Interest Receivable and Notes Receivable accounts at September 30, 2018.
(b) Record the October transactions.
(c) 1. Prepare T accounts for the Interest Receivable, Notes Receivable, and Allowance for Doubtful Notes accounts.
     2. Enter the opening balances.
     3. Post the entries recorded in part (b).
     4. Determine the ending balances.
(d) Show the statement of financial position presentation of the receivables accounts at October 31.

Prepare assets section.
(LO 4)

P8–9A Canadiana Corporation reports the following selected accounts (in thousands) at December 31, 2018:

Accounts payable	$1,978	Income tax receivable	$ 99
Accounts receivable, gross	1,630	Interest revenue	112
Accumulated depreciation—buildings	960	Inventory	1,902
Accumulated depreciation—equipment	488	Land	1,077
Allowance for doubtful accounts	32	Notes receivable (current)	2,481
Bad debts expense	138	Notes receivable (non-current)	101
Buildings	2,734	Sales	12,637
Cash	592	Sales discounts	341
Cost of goods sold	9,741	Supplies	85
Equipment	737		
Held for trading investments	196		

Instructions
Prepare the assets section of Canadiana's statement of financial position.

Calculate and evaluate ratios.
(LO 5)

P8–10A Presented here is selected information for **Nike, Inc.** (in U.S. $ millions) and **Adidas AG** (in euro millions):

	Nike	Adidas
Net sales	$30,601	€16,915
Allowance for doubtful accounts, beginning of year	54	139
Allowance for doubtful accounts, end of year	41	149
Accounts receivable (gross), beginning of year	3,475	2,085
Accounts receivable (gross), end of year	3,358	2,198

Instructions
(a) Calculate the receivables turnover and average collection period for both companies. The industry average for the receivables turnover was 9.8 times and the average collection period was 37 days.
(b) Comment on the difference in the two companies' collection experiences, and that of their industry counterparts.

Evaluate liquidity.
(LO 5)

P8–11A The following selected ratios are available for Pampered Pets Inc. for the most recent three years:

	2018	2017	2016
Current ratio	2.6:1	2.4:1	2.1:1
Receivables turnover	8.2 times	7.4 times	6.7 times
Inventory turnover	9.9 times	8.7 times	7.5 times

Instructions
(a) Calculate the average collection period and days in inventory for each year.
(b) Is Pampered Pets' liquidity improving or worsening? Explain.
(c) Do changes in turnover ratios affect profitability? Explain.
(d) Do changes in turnover ratios affect cash flow? Explain.
(e) Identify any steps that the company may wish to take in order to improve its management of receivables and inventory.

▶ PROBLEMS: SET B

Record receivables and bad debts; show statement presentation.
(LO 1, 2, 4)

P8–1B At January 1, 2018, Bordeaux Inc. reported the following information on its statement of financial position:

Accounts receivable	$510,000
Allowance for doubtful accounts	42,000

During 2018, the company had the following summary transactions for receivables:

1. Sales on account, $1,800,000; Cost of goods sold, $1,044,000
2. Sales returns and allowances, $280,000; Cost of goods returned to inventory, $162,000
3. Collections of accounts receivable, $1,600,000
4. Interest added to overdue accounts, $125,000
5. Write offs of accounts receivable deemed uncollectible, $51,000
6. Collection of accounts previously written off as uncollectible, $12,000
7. After considering all of the above transactions, total estimated uncollectible accounts, $31,000

Instructions

(a) Prepare the journal entries to record each of the above summary transactions.
(b) 1. Prepare T accounts for Accounts Receivable and Allowance for Doubtful Accounts.
    2. Enter the opening balances.
    3. Post the above summary entries.
    4. Determine the ending balances.
(c) Determine the carrying amount of the accounts receivable as at January 1 and December 31.
(d) Show the statement of financial position presentation of the receivables as at December 31.
(e) Show the income statement presentation of the revenue and expense accounts for the year ended December 31.

P8–2B At the beginning of the current period, Huang Ltd. had balances in Accounts Receivable of $945,000 and in Allowance for Doubtful Accounts of $139,000 (credit). During the period, Huang had credit sales of $4.7 million with cost of goods sold of $2.9 million and collections of $4.8 million. It wrote off $146,000 of accounts receivable. However, a $3,000 account written off as uncollectible was recovered before the end of the current period. Uncollectible accounts are estimated to total $97,000 at the end of the period.

Record receivables and bad debts; show statement presentation.

(LO 1, 2, 4)

Instructions

(a) Prepare the entries to record the sales and collections during the period.
(b) Prepare the entry to record the write off of uncollectible accounts during the period.
(c) Prepare the entry(ies) to record the collection of the $3,000 account written off as uncollectible in part (b).
(d) Prepare the entry to record bad debts expense for the period.
(e) 1. Prepare T accounts for Accounts Receivable and Allowance for Doubtful Accounts.
    2. Enter the opening balances.
    3. Post the journal entries prepared in parts (a) through (d).
    4. Determine the ending balances.
(f) Show the statement of financial position presentation of the receivables at the end of the period.

P8–3B Yasukuni Corporation reported the following selected information in its general ledger at June 30:

Determine missing amounts.

(LO 2)

Accounts Receivable				Sales	
Beg. bal.	(a)				(e)
		(b)			
	225,000	230,000			
End. bal.	22,500				

Allowance for Doubtful Accounts			Bad Debts Expense	
		Beg. bal.	1,000	(f)
	250			
		Unadj. bal.	750	
		(c)		
		End. bal.	(d)	

All sales were on account. Some accounts receivable were collected. One account was written off; there were no subsequent recoveries. At the end of the year, uncollectible accounts were estimated to total $1,150.

Instructions

Using your knowledge of receivables transactions, determine the missing amounts. (*Hint:* You may not be able to solve the above items in alphabetical order. In addition, you may find it helpful to reconstruct the journal entries.)

P8–4B Imagine Corporation prepares an aging schedule for its accounts receivable at the end of each month and records bad debts expense monthly. The following selected information is from Imagine's partial aging schedule at the end of August:

Prepare aging schedule and record bad debts.

(LO 2)

Number of Days Outstanding	Accounts Receivable	Estimated Percentage Uncollectible
0–30 days	$280,000	1%
31–60 days	90,000	3%
61–90 days	45,000	10%
Over 90 days	18,000	15%
Total	$433,000	

The unadjusted balance in Allowance for Doubtful Accounts is a debit of $4,300.

Instructions

(a) Complete the aging schedule and calculate the total estimated uncollectible accounts from the above information.

(b) 1. Prepare the adjusting journal entry to record the bad debts for the month using the information determined in part (a).

   2. Would your journal entry be different if the unadjusted balance in Allowance for Doubtful Accounts were a credit of $4,300?

(c) In September, management determined that $4,200 of the outstanding receivables were uncollectible. Prepare the journal entry to write off the uncollectible amount.

(d) Imagine Corporation subsequently collected $2,300 of the $4,200 that was determined to be uncollectible in part (c). Prepare the journal entry(ies) to record the collection.

Prepare aging schedule; record bad debts for two years.

(LO 2)

P8–5B An aging analysis of Reiko Limited's accounts receivable at December 31, 2018 and 2017, showed the following:

Number of Days Outstanding	Accounts Receivable		Estimated Percentage Uncollectible
	2018	2017	
0–30 days	$240,000	$220,000	3%
31–60 days	104,000	86,000	6%
61–90 days	62,000	52,000	12%
Over 90 days	34,000	22,000	20%
Total	$440,000	$380,000	

Additional information:

1. At December 31, 2017, the unadjusted balance in Allowance for Doubtful Accounts was a credit of $3,000.

2. In 2018, $28,000 of accounts were written off as uncollectible and $3,000 of accounts previously written off were recovered.

Instructions

(a) Prepare an aging schedule to calculate the estimated uncollectible accounts at December 31, 2017 and 2018. Note that the estimated percentages uncollectible are the same for both years. Comment on the results.

(b) Record the adjusting entry relating to bad debts on December 31, 2017.

(c) Record the write off of uncollectible accounts in 2018.

(d) Record the collection of accounts previously written off in 2018.

(e) Prepare the adjusting entry relating to bad debts on December 31, 2018.

(f) Calculate the carrying amount of Reiko's accounts receivable at December 31, 2017 and 2018.

Record receivables transactions.

(LO 1, 3)

P8–6B The following selected transactions occurred for Vu Ltd. The company uses a perpetual inventory system, has a September 30 year end, and adjusts its accounts annually.

Jan.	2	Lent Emily Collis, an employee, $10,000 on a four-month, 8% note. Interest is due at maturity.
	5	Sold $11,000 of merchandise to Asiz Limited, terms n/15. The merchandise cost $6,700.
	20	Accepted Asiz Limited's two-month, 9%, $11,000 note for its balance due. Interest is due each month on the 20th. (See January 5 transaction.)
Feb.	20	Collected interest on the Asiz note. (See January 20 transaction.)
Mar.	20	Collected the Asiz note in full. (See January 20 and February 20 transactions.)
May	2	Collected the Collis note in full. (See January 2 transaction.)
	25	Accepted Thundercloud Inc.'s three-month, 8%, $3,000 note in settlement of a past-due balance on account. Interest is due at maturity.
Aug.	1	Pierpont Ltd. purchased merchandise on account for $6,000 (n/30). The goods had cost Vu $4,000.
	25	The Thundercloud note was dishonoured. Eventual collection is not expected. (See May 25 transaction.)
Sept.	30	Recorded accrued interest for one month on outstanding receivable due from Pierpont. Interest on receivables is charged at 24% per annum (2% per month). (See August 1 transaction.)

Instructions
Record the above transactions.

P8–7B On August 1, 2018, Cappuccitti Limited accepted a two-month, 4%, $30,000 note from Dil-Dil Inc. in settlement of its account. Interest is due on the first day of each month, starting September 1. Both companies' year ends are August 31.

Record notes receivable and payable transactions. (LO 3)

Instructions
(a) Prepare all journal entries for Cappuccitti over the term of the note. Assume that the note is collected in full on the maturity date.
(b) Prepare all journal entries for Dil-Dil over the term of the note. Assume that the note is paid in full on the maturity date.
(c) Assume that, instead of honouring the note at maturity, Dil-Dil dishonours it. Prepare the necessary journal entry on Cappuccitti's books at the maturity date, October 1, 2018, assuming that eventual collection of the note is (1) expected, and (2) not expected. Interest was last paid by Dil-Dil on September 1.

P8–8B Kitimat Corporation adjusts its books monthly. On November 30, 2018, notes receivable include the following:

Record notes receivable transactions; show statement presentation. (LO 2, 3, 4)

Issue Date	Maker	Principal	Interest	Term
Mar. 31, 2018	Kootenay Inc.	$17,000	6%	9 months
May 31, 2018	Cassiar Ltd.	15,000	4%	18 months
Aug. 31, 2018	Namu Limited	6,000	7%	4 months
Sept. 30, 2018	Siska Corp.	20,000	5%	16 months

Interest is due at maturity for the Kootenay and Namu notes. Interest is due on the first day of each month for the Cassiar and Siska notes. At November 30, the balance in the Allowance for Doubtful Notes account is nil. In December, the following selected transactions were completed.

Dec. 1 Received the interest due from Cassiar and Siska.
     31 Received notice that Namu was unable to pay its note as scheduled. It does not expect to be able to pay in the future.
     31 The Kootenay note matured and was received in full.
     31 Accrued interest on the Cassiar and Siska notes.
     31 Analyzed the remaining notes for collectibility. Estimated that $20,000 of notes may not be collectible in the future because of significant economic issues currently being experienced by Siska.

Instructions
(a) Calculate the balance in the Interest Receivable and Notes Receivable accounts at November 30, 2018.
(b) Record the December transactions.
(c) 1. Prepare T accounts for the Interest Receivable, Notes Receivable, and Allowance for Doubtful Notes accounts.
    2. Enter the opening balances.
    3. Post the entries recorded in part (b).
    4. Determine the ending balances.
(d) Show the statement of financial position presentation of the receivables accounts at December 31.

P8–9B Outaouais Inc. reports the following selected accounts (in thousands) at January 31, 2018:

Prepare assets section. (LO 4)

Accounts payable	$ 2,857	Income tax receivable	$ 20
Accounts receivable, gross	2,468	Interest revenue	35
Accumulated depreciation—buildings	250	Inventory	3,000
Accumulated depreciation—equipment	375	Land	200
Allowance for doubtful accounts	268	Notes receivable (current)	50
Bad debts expense	135	Notes receivable (non-current)	300
Bank indebtedness	100	Notes payable (current)	1,000
Buildings	1,000	Sales	29,000
Cost of goods sold	19,000	Sales returns and allowances	800
Equipment	750	Supplies	50
Goodwill	100		

Instructions
Prepare the assets section of Outaouais's statement of financial position.

Calculate and evaluate ratios.

(LO 5)

P8–10B Presented here is selected information (in millions) from the financial statements of **Rogers Communications Inc.** (year ended December 31, 2015) and **Shaw Communications Inc.** (year ended August 31, 2015):

	Rogers	Shaw
Net sales	$13,414	$5,488
Allowance for doubtful accounts, beginning of year	98	32
Allowance for doubtful accounts, end of year	86	26
Accounts receivable (gross), beginning of year	1,689	525
Accounts receivable (gross), end of year	1,878	494

Instructions

(a) Calculate the receivables turnover and average collection period for both companies. The industry average for the receivables turnover was 12.0 times and the average collection period was 30.3 days.

(b) Comment on the difference in the companies' collection experiences, and that of their industry counterparts.

Evaluate liquidity.

(LO 5)

P8–11B The following selected ratios are available for Tianjin Inc. for the most recent three years:

	2018	2017	2016
Current ratio	1.5:1	1.5:1	1.5:1
Receivables turnover	8 times	7 times	6 times
Inventory turnover	6 times	7 times	8 times

Instructions

(a) Calculate the average collection period and days in inventory for each year.

(b) Is Tianjin's liquidity improving or worsening? Explain.

(c) Do changes in turnover ratios affect profitability? Explain.

(d) Do changes in turnover ratios affect cash flow? Explain.

(e) Identify any steps that the company may wish to consider in order to improve its management of receivables and inventory.

ACCOUNTING CYCLE | REVIEW

Record and post transaction, adjusting, and closing journal entries; account for bad debts; account for notes receivable; prepare unadjusted and adjusted trial balances and financial statements.

(LO 1, 2, 3, 4)

ACR8–1 DiTuri Designs Ltd. is an Ottawa-based importer of Italian furniture. The company's post-closing trial balance at December 31, 2017, the end of its fiscal year, is presented below:

DITURI DESIGNS LTD.
Post-Closing Trial Balance
December 31, 2017

	Debit	Credit
Cash	$ 197,000	
Accounts receivable	468,000	
Allowance for doubtful accounts		$ 13,000
Notes receivable	50,000	
Inventory	2,682,000	
Prepaid insurance	14,000	
Interest receivable	900	
Equipment	1,560,000	
Accumulated depreciation—equipment		972,000
Accounts payable		398,000
Salaries payable		16,000
Unearned revenue		44,000
Bank loan payable		800,000
Common shares		600,000
Retained earnings		2,128,900
	$4,971,900	$4,971,900

DiTuri had the following transactions during January 2018:

Jan. 4 Received payments of $236,000 from customers in payment of their accounts.

6 Received a shipment of furniture from a supplier. The invoice for $150,000 indicates that the terms are 2/10, n/30.

8 Collected a note receivable from a customer. The note, which was for $50,000, had been issued to a customer in November 2017. It was a two-month note, with 12% interest. DiTuri had correctly accrued the $900 in interest revenue earned to December 2017.

10 Made sales totalling $198,000 to customers. Of this, $10,000 had been put down as a deposit by the customers when the furniture had been ordered, while the balance was on account (n/30). The furniture had cost DiTuri $102,000.

12 Paid salaries of $26,000, which included the accrued salaries owing at the end of 2017.

14 Wrote off the account of a customer who declared bankruptcy. The customer had owed DiTuri $18,000.

14 Paid the accounts payable related to the furniture received on January 6.

15 Agreed to accept a note receivable from a customer who was unable to pay its account receivable balance. The $20,000 two-month note bears interest at 9%.

17 A customer returned a table that was part of a purchase they had made on account on January 10. The table was returned because it was too big for the customer's dining room. It had a selling price of $4,000, with a cost of $2,400 to DiTuri. The table was in perfect condition and was placed back on the sales floor.

19 Received a $9,000 payment from a customer whose account had been written off in 2017.

23 Made sales of $184,000, of which half was on account and half was cash. The cost of the furniture sold was $98,000.

25 Paid accounts payable that were due to creditors totalling $117,000.

26 Purchased furniture from a supplier in Milan, Italy. The cost of the furniture was $138,000 with freight terms FOB shipping point.

31 Made the monthly payment on the bank loan. The loan bears interest at 3% and requires monthly payments on the last day of the month consisting of principal of $15,000 plus interest.

31 DiTuri's aged accounts receivable subsidiary ledger was classified as follows:

Classification of Accounts	Amount	Estimated Uncollectible %
Current (≤30 days)	$280,000	2%
31–60 days	130,000	5%
61–90 days	40,000	6%
>90 days	20,000	12%

DiTuri reconciles its bank account at the end of every month and makes any necessary journal entries. The following information was gathered from reviewing the company's bank statement for the month of January:
1. The service charges on the account were $128 for the month.
2. There were outstanding cheques of $67,000.
3. A cheque from one of DiTuri's customers for $12,100 that had been deposited during the month was returned by the bank because the customer had insufficient funds in their account.
4. The company's account balance at January 31 was $332,772 according to the bank statement.

DiTuri records adjustments monthly on the last day of the month. Adjusting entries were required for the following:
1. Recorded depreciation on the equipment assuming that DiTuri uses the straight-line method to depreciate its equipment and the equipment is expected to have a useful life of 10 years.
2. The prepaid insurance balance at December 31, 2017, represented eight months of coverage.
3. Accrued salaries payable are $36,000.
4. Accrued the interest receivable on the note receivable from January 15, which had been outstanding for half a month.
5. The estimated income taxes owing for the month of January was $24,000.

Instructions
(a) Record the January transactions.
(b) Set up T accounts, enter the December 31 balances, and post the general journal entries prepared in part (a).
(c) Prepare the bank reconciliation at January 31.
(d) Prepare the journal entries required as a result of the bank reconciliation.
(e) Prepare and post the January adjusting journal entries.
(f) Prepare an adjusted trial balance at January 31.
(g) Prepare an (1) income statement, (2) statement of changes in equity, and (3) statement of financial position for January 31.

EXPAND YOUR | CRITICAL THINKING

CT8-1 Financial Reporting Case

The financial statements of The North West Company Inc. are presented in Appendix A at the end of this book.

Instructions
(a) What types of receivables does The North West Company report in its 2016 balance sheet?
(b) Calculate the receivables turnover and average collection period ratios for accounts receivable for 2016 and 2015. North West's accounts receivable were $70,527 thousand at January 31, 2014. (Assume all sales were credit sales and use the carrying amount for accounts receivable instead of gross receivables.)
(c) What conclusions can you draw about North West's management of its receivables from your answer to part (b)?

CT8-2 Financial Reporting Case

The financial statements of The North West Company Inc. are presented in Appendix A. The financial statements of Sobeys Inc. are presented in Appendix B.

Instructions
(a) Calculate the following for each company for its most recent fiscal year. The industry average is shown in parentheses.
   1. Current ratio (1.18:1)
   2. Receivables turnover (24.2 times) (Assume all sales were credit sales and use net receivables instead of gross receivables.)
   3. Average collection period (15 days)
(b) What conclusions about each company's liquidity and management of its accounts receivable can be drawn from your calculations in part (a)?

CT8-3 Financial Reporting Case

Assume you are an analyst for Big Bank and you are putting together financial information on two clothing manufacturers, Lava Fashions Inc. and Flow Designs Inc., for your boss, to help her monitor Big Bank's loans with those two companies. Lava Fashions is a large public company and Flow Designs is a small private company.

One of the most significant assets for both companies is the accounts receivable from retail customers. You know that your boss will be interested in knowing both the receivables' carrying amount and their exposure to credit risk (the risk that some of the customers won't ultimately pay for the goods they purchased).

You look at the financial statements and find that the information provided is considerably different for each company. Lava Fashions reports the following information related to its receivables:

LAVA FASHIONS INC.
Notes to the Financial Statements
December 31 (in thousands)

Note 14: Trade Receivables

	2018	2017
Trade receivables	$1,854	$1,917
Less: allowance for doubtful accounts	(135)	(124)
Carrying amount	$1,719	$1,793

The aging of gross trade receivables at the end of each year was as follows:

($ in thousands)	2018	2017
Current	$1,322	$1,363
Past due 0–30 days	183	192
Past due 31–60 days	170	167
Past due 61–90 days	50	61
Past due 91–180 days	62	70
Past due > 180 days	67	64
Balance at December 31	$1,854	$1,917

Lava is exposed to normal credit risk with respect to its accounts receivable. It has provided for potential credit losses with an allowance for doubtful accounts. It reduces the potential for such losses because it evaluates a potential customer's creditworthiness before extending credit.

Flow Designs reports the following information related to its receivables:

FLOW DESIGNS INC.
Statement of Financial Position (partial)
December 31 (in thousands)

	2018	2017
Current assets		
Trade receivables, net	$1,720	$2,053

Flow provides credit to its customers in the normal course of its operations. It continually conducts credit checks on its customers and has provided for potential credit losses with an allowance for doubtful accounts although it has not disclosed this information in the notes to its financial statements.

Instructions
(a) Which company's financial statement note provides more useful information about the trade receivables? Why?
(b) Why do you think Lava Fashions provides more information on its receivables than Flow Designs?
(c) What additional information do you think Big Bank would want in order to assess the credit risk in trade receivables for Lava Fashions and Flow Designs?

CT8-4 Financial Analysis Case

This case can be assigned as a group activity. Additional instructions and material for this activity can be found on the Instructor Resource site and in WileyPLUS.

Harry's Hamburgers Ltd. (HHL) is a chain of fast-food restaurants. A few years ago, the company decided it didn't want to own any new restaurants. Rather, when a new restaurant opens up, it is owned by a franchisee rather than the company. A franchisee is an individual investor who owns the land, building, furniture, and other assets and operates the restaurant. In return, the franchisee pays HHL a royalty fee, based on a percentage of sales, for the right to use the HHL name and products under a franchise agreement. If the franchisee needs funds to help build the restaurant, they can borrow money from HHL for a one-year period by signing a note receivable to HHL.

Selected items from the 2018 HHL financial statements along with comparative amounts from 2017 are shown below (in thousands of dollars):

	2018	2017
Cash	$ 1,300	$ 2,900
Accounts receivable	6,000	5,000
Allowance for doubtful accounts	(400)	(500)
Notes receivable	2,700	2,000
Inventory at company-operated stores	1,000	1,100
Total current assets	10,600	10,500
Current liabilities	6,800	5,100
Net credit sales	60,000	50,000

Accounts receivable consist only of royalties receivable from franchisees. During 2018, accounts receivable amounting to $100,000 were written off.

The notes receivable are from franchisees, and are due within one year. During 2018, notes amounting to $1.5 million were received from new franchise operators and these are still outstanding. Also during 2018, notes of $800,000 were collected in full. A number of notes were dishonoured during the year, but the company's new vice-president of finance believes that all of these are recoverable, so no allowance for doubtful notes was set up. In the past, no dishonoured note has ever been collected.

The company's bank requires HHL to maintain a current ratio of 1.5:1.

Instructions

(a) Based on the above information, calculate the company's current ratio for 2018 and 2017. Does it currently meet the bank's requirement?

(b) Reconstruct the Allowance for Doubtful Accounts and Notes Receivable accounts.

(c) Do you believe the allowance is adequate for accounts receivable? Explain.

(d) Do you think that an allowance should be recorded for notes receivable? Why or why not? If you believe that an allowance should be set up, what amount should be recorded? (*Hint:* Calculate the amount of dishonoured notes.)

(e) If an allowance for the doubtful notes was to be recorded based on your answer to part (d), recalculate the company's 2018 current ratio. How do you think the bank would react to this?

(f) Based on a review of the information provided above, do you think that HHL's liquidity has improved or deteriorated in 2018?

CT8–5 Ethics Case

Sam Wong is the controller of Encounter Limited, a publicly traded company. He has completed an aging schedule and determined that the allowance for doubtful accounts should be $100,000 at the end of the current year. Sam has noticed that the average age of receivables this year is older than in prior years. The president of the company, Suzanne Chen, is nervous because the bank expects the company to maintain a current ratio of 2:1. After recording the adjustment for bad debts this year, the current assets total $2,000,000 while current liabilities total $1,025,000. Suzanne recalls from her accounting studies that estimating uncollectible accounts requires judgement. She has asked that Sam review his estimate percentages to reduce the allowance from $100,000 to $40,000. She believes this will better reflect the company's "real" liquidity.

Instructions

(a) Who are the stakeholders in this case?

(b) Why did Suzanne request the adjustment?

(c) Does the president's request pose an ethical dilemma for the controller?

(d) Is the president's reason for reducing the allowance a valid one?

CT8–6 Serial Case

(*Note:* This is a continuation of the serial case from Chapters 1 through 7.)

Most of ABC's sales are paid by cash, debit card, or credit card. However, in a few cases, ABC has been asked to extend credit to select clients. To date, ABC has been giving these clients 30 days to pay for the purchase of products or services. However, a couple of major clients are now taking 45 days to pay each invoice issued. ABC has also been doing more work for Software Solutions, which is now asking for 60 days to pay because it wants to collect the money from its own customers before it pays ABC. As a result, Doug, Bev, and Emily have had to pay close attention to the cash available to purchase additional inventory and pay monthly expenses. Although ABC is happy to have taken on the additional work, it is considering reducing the credit terms it is prepared to offer its clients from 30 days to 15 days. As well, it is attempting to establish a consistent credit policy as it continues to discuss with Software Solutions the possibility of providing a significant amount of support service.

Emily has a meeting scheduled with Michael Richards, operations manager of Software Solutions, to discuss their ongoing business relationship. Michael has wanted to meet because the demand for services continues to increase and is anticipated to double over the next year. He would like to have ABC take on more of these activities but wants to ensure that it can meet the additional demand. Emily believes ABC is now better positioned to take on more of these services but first wants to discuss proposed credit terms with Michael. However, before meeting with Michael, Emily wants to consider all of the possible effects of reducing the credit terms from 30 to 15 days.

Instructions

(a) Identify the advantages and disadvantages of enforcing credit terms for ABC's clients of 30 days.

(b) Do you believe that ABC should reduce its credit terms to 15 days? Discuss the advantages and disadvantages of the company doing so.

(c) If ABC decides to continue providing services to Software Solutions and doubles the number of services it provides, what are some of the effects this will have on ABC's operations and cash flows?

(d) Can you provide other alternatives to ABC to encourage clients to pay quicker and on time?

▶ ANSWERS TO CHAPTER PRACTICE QUESTIONS

DO IT! 8-1
Receivables Transactions

Date	Account	Debit	Credit
Oct. 29	Accounts Receivable	10,000	
	Sales		10,000
	(To record sales on account to Potter Inc., terms 2/10, n/30)		
29	Cost of Goods Sold	6,000	
	Inventory		6,000
	(To record cost of merchandise sold to Potter)		
31	Accounts Receivable	480	
	Interest Revenue ($32,000 \times 18\% \times \frac{1}{12}$)		480
	(To record interest charges on overdue receivables)		
Nov. 1	Sales Returns and Allowances	500	
	Accounts Receivable		500
	(To record sales return by Potter)		
1	Inventory	300	
	Cost of Goods Sold		300
	(To record cost of merchandise returned by Potter)		
6	Cash ($10,000 − $500 − $190)	9,310	
	Sales Discounts ($10,000 − $500) × 2%	190	
	Accounts Receivable ($10,000 − $500)		9,500
	(To record collection of account receivable from Potter)		
10	Accounts Receivable	5,000	
	Sales		5,000
	(To record company credit card sales)		
10	Cost of Goods Sold	3,000	
	Inventory		3,000
	(To record cost of merchandise sold on company credit cards)		

DO IT! 8-2a
Bad Debts

(a)

Number of Days Outstanding	Accounts Receivable	×	Estimated Percentage Uncollectible	=	Total Estimated Uncollectible Accounts
0–30 days	$200,000		2%		$ 4,000
31–60 days	120,000		5%		6,000
61–90 days	100,000		10%		10,000
Over 90 days	40,000		20%		8,000
Total	$460,000				$28,000

(b) An adjusting entry of $20,000 is required to adjust Allowance for Doubtful Accounts from the current credit balance of $8,000 to the desired credit balance of $28,000.

Date	Account	Debit	Credit
Dec. 31	Bad Debts Expense	20,000	
	Allowance for Doubtful Accounts		20,000
	(To record estimate of uncollectible accounts)		

Allowance for Doubtful Accounts		
	Dec. 31	8,000
	31 Adj.	20,000
	Dec. 31 Bal.	28,000

(c) An adjusting entry of $32,200 is required to adjust Allowance for Doubtful Accounts from the current debit balance of $4,200 to the desired credit balance of $28,000.

Dec. 31	Bad Debts Expense	32,200	
	Allowance for Doubtful Accounts		32,200
	(To record estimate of uncollectible accounts)		

Allowance for Doubtful Accounts

Dec. 31	4,200			
		Dec. 31	Adj.	32,200
		Dec. 31	Bal.	28,000

(a)

Oct. 9	Accounts Receivable	3,300	
	Allowance for Doubtful Accounts		3,300
	Cash	3,300	
	Accounts Receivable		3,300
	(To reverse write off of Telmo Ltd.'s account)		
Oct. 31	Allowance for Doubtful Accounts	8,200	
	Accounts Receivable		8,200
	(To write off Valez Ltd.'s account)		

(b) An adjusting entry of $11,000 is required to adjust Allowance for Doubtful Accounts from a debit balance of $1,200 before the adjustment to the desired credit balance of $9,800.

Number of Days Outstanding	Accounts Receivable	×	Estimated Percentage Uncollectible	=	Total Estimated Uncollectible Accounts
0–30 days	$ 80,000		2%		$1,600
31–60 days	40,000		5%		2,000
61–90 days	10,000		12%		1,200
Over 90 days	20,000		25%		5,000
Total	$150,000				$9,800

Oct. 31	Bad Debts Expense	11,000	
	Allowance for Doubtful Accounts		11,000
	(To record estimate of uncollectible accounts)		

Allowance for Doubtful Accounts

		Oct. 1		3,700
Oct. 17	8,200	Oct. 9		3,300
		Oct. 31	Adj.	11,000
		Oct. 31	Bal.	9,800

(a) Note honoured:

May 1	Notes Receivable	6,800	
	Accounts Receivable		6,800
	(To replace account receivable with a 6% note receivable from Shiraz Corp., due August 1)		
May 31	Interest Receivable	34	
	Interest Revenue ($6,800 × 6% × $\frac{1}{12}$)		34
	(To record the accrued interest revenue for May on a 6% note receivable from Shiraz Corp., due August 1)		
June 30	Interest Receivable	34	
	Interest Revenue ($6,800 × 6% × $\frac{1}{12}$)		34
	(To record the accrued interest revenue for June on a 6% note receivable from Shiraz Corp., due August 1)		
July 31	Interest Receivable	34	
	Interest Revenue ($6,800 × 6% × $\frac{1}{12}$)		34
	(To record the accrued interest revenue for July on a 6% note receivable from Shiraz Corp., due August 1)		
Aug. 1	Cash	6,902	
	Notes Receivable		6,800
	Interest Revenue ($6,800 × 6% × $\frac{3}{12}$)		102
	(To record collection of Shiraz note and interest)		

(b) Note dishonoured but collection in future is still likely:

Aug. 1	Accounts Receivable	6,902	
	Notes Receivable		6,800
	Interest Receivable		102
	(To record dishonoured Shiraz note; eventual collection expected)		

DO IT! 8-4

Statement Presentation

(a)

BEAU RESOURCES LIMITED
Statement of Financial Position (partial)
December 31, 2018

Assets

Current assets		
Accounts receivable	$150,000	
Less: Allowance for doubtful accounts	7,500	
Carrying amount	142,500	
Inventory	110,000	
Notes receivable	25,000	
Advances to employees	5,000	
Income tax receivable	7,500	
Interest receivable	4,000	
Sales tax recoverable	2,500	$296,500
Non-current assets		
Notes receivable		75,000

(b)

BEAU RESOURCES LIMITED
Income Statement
Year Ended December 31, 2018

Sales revenue		
Sales		$2,000,000
Less: Sales discounts		50,000
Net sales		1,950,000
Less: Cost of goods sold		1,160,000
Gross profit		790,000
Operating expenses		
Salaries expense	$405,000	
Bad debts expense	10,000	415,000
Income from operations		375,000
Other revenues and expenses		
Interest revenue		6,000
Income before income tax		381,000
Income tax expense		75,000
Net income		$ 306,000

DO IT! 8-5

Managing Receivables

(a) **Extending credit.** The HDS credit card should not be given to just anyone over the age of 18 years. The company should use credit-granting policies similar to those used by banks when issuing credit cards. Although sales have increased due to issuing this new card, it is likely that bad debts expense has increased even more.

(b) **Payment period.** Allowing HDS cardholders to pay after four months is a credit policy that is too loose. It has slowed the collection of receivables and this in turn has probably caused the company to seek more bank financing to meet cash requirements no longer being met by prompt customer collections.

(c) **Monitor collections.** On a monthly basis, management should review the age of the HDS credit card accounts and identify those cardholders who did not pay on time to determine if their receivables are collectible. It is likely that there are many overdue accounts given the ease with which these cards were issued, which makes frequent monitoring of collections even more important.

(d) **Evaluate liquidity.** The receivables turnover ratio and average collection period should be determined and evaluated each month.

Other steps the company might wish to consider to improve the collection of receivables could include cancelling the company credit card and only accepting bank credit cards, or changing the terms on the HDS card. The advantage of the first option is the immediate receipt of cash because bank credit cards are treated as cash by the bank. The disadvantage is the lost interest revenue that could be earned on the HDS card. Although changing the terms of the HDS card will not bring any immediate cash to the company, it may reduce the level of bad debts in the future and still provide a source of interest revenue on overdue accounts as long as they are collectible. Management will have to calculate the effect of these advantages and disadvantages and consider the effect on the timing of cash flows. The company should discuss these options with the bank to ensure that it realizes that steps are being taken to remedy the liquidity problem.

▶ PRACTICE USING THE DECISION TOOLKIT

(in U.S. $ millions)	Walmart	Canadian Tire	Sears	Industry
Receivables turnover	$\dfrac{\$478,614}{(\$5,624 + \$6,778) \div 2} = 77.2$ times	13.7 times	47.5 times	26.7 times
Average collection period	$\dfrac{365 \text{ days}}{77.2} = 5$ days	27 days	8 days	14 days

Based on the above information, Walmart has a higher (better) receivables turnover and lower (better) collection period than all of its competitors. As this means that the company collects its receivables faster, it can more readily pay its current liabilities. Further analysis, including calculating the current ratio and inventory turnover ratio, would be required before finalizing this assessment.

▶ PRACTICE COMPREHENSIVE DO IT!

(a)	Mar. 1	Accounts Receivable	30,000	
		Sales		30,000
		(To record sales on account to Anderson Ltd., terms 2/10, n/30)		
	1	Cost of Goods Sold	18,000	
		Inventory		18,000
		(To record cost of merchandise sold to Anderson)		
	Mar. 10	Cash	29,400	
		Sales Discounts (2% × $30,000)	600	
		Accounts Receivable		30,000
		(To record collection of account receivable from Anderson)		
	15	Accounts Receivable	25,000	
		Sales		25,000
		(To record sales on account to Aulac Ltd.)		
	15	Cost of Goods Sold	15,000	
		Inventory		15,000
		(To record cost of merchandise sold)		
	Apr. 1	Cash	16,000	
		Notes Receivable	9,000	
		Accounts Receivable		25,000
		(To record partial collection of accounts receivable from Aulac and acceptance of two-month, 24% note)		
	30	Interest Receivable ($9,000 × 24% × $\frac{1}{12}$)	180	
		Interest Revenue		180
		(To record accrued interest on note receivable)		
	May 10	Allowance for Doubtful Accounts	32,000	
		Accounts Receivable		32,000
		(To record write off of accounts receivable)		
	May 31	Interest Receivable ($9,000 × 24% × $\frac{1}{12}$)	180	
		Interest Revenue		180
		(To record accrued interest on note receivable)		
	June 1	Cash	9,360	
		Notes Receivable		9,000
		Interest Receivable		360
		(To record collection of note receivable and accrued interest from Aulac)		
	July 16	Accounts Receivable	8,000	
		Allowance for Doubtful Accounts		8,000
		(To reverse write off of account receivable)		
	16	Cash	8,000	
		Accounts Receivable		8,000
		(To record collection of account receivable)		

July 31	Bad Debts Expense ($40,000 – $7,000)	33,000	
	Allowance for Doubtful Accounts		33,000
	(To record estimate of uncollectible accounts [see Allowance for Doubtful Accounts in part (b) to prove calculations])		

(b)

Accounts Receivable						
Feb. 28	Bal.	500,000				
Mar. 1		30,000	Mar. 10			30,000
Mar. 15		25,000	Apr. 1			25,000
July 16		8,000	May 10			32,000
			July 16			8,000
July 31	Bal.	468,000				

Allowance for Doubtful Accounts					
			Feb. 28	Bal.	31,000
May 10		32,000	July 16		8,000
			July 31	Unadj. Bal.	7,000
			31	Adj.	33,000
			July 31	Bal.	40,000

(c)

Accounts receivable	$468,000
Less: Allowance for doubtful accounts	40,000
Carrying amount	$428,000

▶ PRACTICE OBJECTIVE-FORMAT QUESTIONS

1. (b), (d), (e), (f), and (g) are correct.

Feedback
(a) is incorrect. While notes receivable are a formal credit instrument, accounts receivable are not.
(c) is incorrect. Accounts receivable are normally non–interest-bearing during the credit period.

2. (a) and (e) are correct.

Feedback
(b) is incorrect. Allowance for doubtful accounts has a debit balance only when write offs exceed the established allowance. As such, a debit balance prior to the allowance entry would indicate that the value of accounts written off exceeded the established allowance.
(c) is incorrect. This would have no effect on the carrying amount of accounts receivable because the entry would have equal and offsetting effects on Accounts Receivable and Allowance for Doubtful Accounts.
(d) is incorrect. The allowance account is a contra asset account, which is a permanent account.
(f) is incorrect. As a contra asset account, Allowance for Doubtful Accounts is deducted from (netted against) Accounts Receivable in determining the carrying amount (rather than being added to it).
(g) is incorrect. Write offs have no effect on net income, because the entry reduces Accounts Receivable and Allowance for Doubtful Accounts.

3. *Feedback*
(a) No effect. There are equal and offsetting effects to Accounts Receivable and Allowance for Doubtful Accounts.
　　　Allowance for Doubtful Accounts
　　　　　Accounts Receivable
(b) Decrease
　　　Notes Receivable
　　　　　Accounts Receivable
(c) Increase
　　　Accounts Receivable
　　　　　Sales
　　　Cost of Goods Sold
　　　　　Inventory
(d) Decrease. Allowance for Doubtful Accounts is increased at the same time.
　　　Bad Debts Expense
　　　　　Allowance for Doubtful Accounts
(e) Decrease
　　　Cash
　　　　　Accounts Receivable
(f) Decrease
　　　Sales Returns and Allowances
　　　　　Accounts Receivable
　　　Inventory
　　　　　Cost of Goods Sold

(g)   Decrease. While there is an offsetting debit and credit to Accounts Receivable, Allowance for Doubtful Accounts is credited. This decreases the carrying amount of Accounts Receivable.

    Accounts Receivable
        Allowance for Doubtful Accounts
    Cash
        Accounts Receivable

4.   (d) and (f) are correct.

Feedback

The journal entries would be:
   Accounts Receivable
      Allowance for Doubtful Accounts
   Cash
      Accounts Receivable

5.   (b), (e), (f), and (g) are correct.

Feedback

(a)   is incorrect. Bad debts expense is recorded at the time the allowance is established, so it is not used when specific accounts are written off.
(c)   is incorrect. The amount should be $6,600, not $9,500.
(d)   is incorrect. "Bad Debt Recoveries" is not a valid account. Credit should be to Accounts Receivable.

6.   (b), (c), and (f) are correct.

Feedback

(a)   is incorrect. Cash would not be debited because none was received. Instead, an account receivable was exchanged for a note receivable. In addition, Notes Receivable would not be credited—Accounts Receivable would be credited.
(d)   is incorrect. Interest Receivable would be credited, rather than Notes Receivable, because it is important to keep the principal amount of the note intact.
(e)   is incorrect. Interest Receivable would be debited rather than Notes Receivable.
(g)   is incorrect. Notes Receivable would be credited rather than Accounts Receivable.

7.   (b), (d), (f), and (g) are correct.

Feedback

(a)   is incorrect. The "payee" is the party that will receive the cash when the note is repaid.
(c)   is incorrect. Accrued interest is debited to Interest Receivable in order to keep the principal amount of the note intact.
(e)   is incorrect. The payee receives payment; they do not make the payment.

8.   (b), (c), (e), (f), and (g) are correct.

Feedback

(a)   is incorrect. The mortgage receivables are due in five years; therefore, the account is non-current.
(d)   is incorrect. The notes receivable are due in two years; therefore, they are non-current.

9.   (a), (c), and (g) are correct.

Feedback

(b)   is incorrect because the ratio has worsened. It was 12.5 in 2017.
(d)   is incorrect. This calculation failed to use the average Accounts Receivable amount [(opening balance + ending balance) ÷ 2].
(e)   is incorrect. It was taking longer (35 days versus 29 days).
(f)   is incorrect. It was 35.1 days versus the 30-day credit period (n/30).

10.   (a), (c), (d), (f), and (g) are correct.

Feedback

(b)   is incorrect. If a company's receivables turnover decreases from one year to the next it is a negative change.
(e)   is incorrect. If a company's average collection period increases this is a negative change as it is taking longer to collect customer payments.

▶ ENDNOTES

[1] Canadian Tire 2015 Annual Report; "Fast Facts," "About Us," corporate website, http://corp.canadiantire.ca.

[2] Canadian University Survey Consortium, *2015 Graduating University Student Survey: Master Report*, July 2015; "Issue Brief: Credit Cards: Statistics and Facts," Canadian Bankers Association, June 29, 2016, available online at www.cba.ca.

[3] "Debt Collection: Your Rights and Responsibilities," Financial Consumer Agency of Canada, www.fcac-acfc.gc.ca/Eng/forConsumers/topics/yourRights/Pages/Debt-Coll-Recouvre.aspx, accessed September 16, 2016; Carter Dougherty, "Debt Collectors Posing as Facebook Friends Spur Watchdogs," Bloomberg, January 24, 2013; Tamara Lush, "Agency Prohibited from Using Facebook to Collect Debt," Associated Press, March 9, 2011; Alexis Madrigal, "Facebook Warns Debt Collectors about Using Its Service," *The Atlantic*, November 19, 2010.

9

Reporting and Analyzing Long-Lived Assets

CHAPTER PREVIEW

In the last few chapters, we have learned to account for current assets and how they are presented and analyzed. We will now learn how to determine, allocate, and record the cost of long-lived assets, as well as present and analyze this type of asset. For many companies, long-lived assets are the most significant type of asset that they own.

   In this chapter, we focus on the following types of long-lived assets: (1) property, plant, and equipment; (2) intangible assets; and (3) goodwill. Long-lived assets can also include natural resources, investment properties, and biological assets. The accounting for these assets can be complex so we will leave any detailed coverage of such assets for another accounting course.

CHAPTER OUTLINE

LEARNING OBJECTIVES	READ	PRACTICE
1 Determine the cost of property, plant, and equipment.	• Determining cost • To buy or lease?	**DO IT!** 9-1 Cost of an asset
2 Explain and calculate depreciation.	• Depreciation methods • Other depreciation issues	**DO IT!** 9-2 Depreciation
3 Account for the derecognition of property, plant, and equipment.	• Sale of property, plant, and equipment • Retirement of property, plant, and equipment	**DO IT!** 9-3a Sale of a vehicle 9-3b Retirement of equipment
4 Identify the basic accounting issues for intangible assets and goodwill.	• Accounting for intangible assets • Goodwill	**DO IT!** 9-4 Accounting for intangibles
5 Illustrate how long-lived assets are reported in the financial statements.	• Statement of financial position • Income statement • Statement of cash flows	**DO IT!** 9-5 Statement presentation
6 Describe the methods for evaluating the use of assets.	• Return on assets • Asset turnover • Profit margin revisited	**DO IT!** 9-6 Analyze assets

FEATURE STORY

WestJet took to the skies in 1996, promoting lower-cost flights and a culture that treats its passengers as guests. From its beginnings with three planes, five destinations, and 220 employees—called WestJetters—the Calgary-based airline has grown to include over 140 planes and more than 9,200 WestJetters. The airline, in conjunction with its partners, takes guests to more than 160 destinations in Canada, the United States, the Caribbean, Mexico, and Europe.

Of the fleet of more than 140 aircraft, WestJet leases 44 planes and owns the rest. The planes it leases are accounted for as operating leases, with each lease payment recorded as aircraft rental expense on its income statement. The planes it owns are recorded as property and equipment on its statement of financial position. As at December 31, 2015, WestJet had almost $3.5 billion in property and equipment, of which more than $2.7 billion was aircraft.

WestJet's Assets Are for the Long Haul

The aircraft's purchase price and any costs required to get it into service are capitalized (recorded as property and equipment), as are costs incurred after acquisition to overhaul the aircraft. For example, in 2013, WestJet introduced "premium economy" seats with more legroom in a bid to lure business passengers. The cost to reconfigure its planes for this purpose was capitalized. Meanwhile, costs incurred to maintain the plane but not increase its useful life or add a benefit, such as to repair damages, are expensed.

Depreciation of the aircraft is based on a plane's economic useful life, which WestJet has determined is between 15 and 20 years. In addition, WestJet separates the parts of a plane into various components—the engine, airframe, landing gear, and in-flight entertainment equipment, for example. Each component is depreciated separately. While the aircraft may have a useful life of 20 years, the engine may need to be overhauled every 10 years, in which case the engine would be depreciated over 10 years and the airframe would be depreciated over 20 years.

Determining the aircraft's economic useful life involves consultation with the company's technical operations department, observation of the entire industry, and investigation of various external data sources. And although WestJet has been operating for just 20 years, it has disposed of some older planes that had not been purchased brand new.

While the bulk of its fleet are narrow-body Boeing 737s, WestJet has also been buying and leasing smaller and larger aircraft. The smaller aircraft, the Bombardier Q-400 turboprop, serve regional routes in North America as part of the WestJet Encore service. The larger aircraft, including two wide-body Boeing 767s acquired in 2015, serve new international routes, such as London, England. The larger aircraft drive down the cost per seat per mile flown. By 2027, the airline expects to have between 181 and 225 aircraft. The company bases its decision to acquire new airplanes on several factors, including passenger demand, routes and landing rights, the availability of suitable aircraft, and financing options.[1]

Go to the *REVIEW AND PRACTICE* section at the end of the chapter for a targeted summary and exercises with solutions.

Visit **WileyPLUS** for more opportunities.

Determine the cost of property, plant, and equipment.

> **Alternative Terminology**
> *Property, plant, and equipment* are sometimes called *capital assets*; *land, buildings, and equipment*; or *fixed assets*.

Property, plant, and equipment are tangible (have physical substance) long-lived resources that a company controls. They are not intended for sale to customers and are used for the production and sale of goods or services to customers, for rental to others, or for administrative purposes. Unlike current assets, which are used or consumed in the current accounting period, property, plant, and equipment provide economic benefits over many years.

In the following sections, we will learn how to determine the cost of property, plant, and equipment, how to allocate this cost over the asset's useful life through depreciation, and how to account for its disposal either prior to, or at the end of, its useful life.

DETERMINING COST

As we learned in Chapter 2, most companies record property, plant, and equipment at historical cost, which includes the following:

1. The purchase price, including certain kinds of non-refundable taxes and duties, less any discounts or rebates
2. The expenditures necessary to bring the asset to its required location and to make it ready for its intended use
3. An estimate of any future obligations related to dismantling, removing, or restoring the asset at the end of its useful life

Determining which costs to include in property, plant, and equipment and which costs not to include is very important and often requires professional judgement. In general, costs that will benefit only the current period are expensed. Such costs are called **operating expenditures**. Costs that can be measured and will benefit future periods are capitalized (included) in a long-lived asset account and recorded as either property, plant, or equipment. These are called **capital expenditures**.

For example, the cost to purchase an asset such as equipment should be recorded as a capital expenditure, because the asset will benefit future periods. In addition, the cost to insure the asset while it was shipped to the company should also be capitalized because it is part of the cost of obtaining the asset. Insurance paid to insure the asset against fire or theft after it is situated and in use would be expensed because these costs benefit only the current period and were not incurred to obtain the asset. Likewise, any costs incurred to train employees on how to operate the equipment would be expensed and not added to the cost of the equipment because such costs were incurred to get the employees ready to use the equipment rather than getting the equipment itself ready for use.

If there are obligations to dismantle, remove, or restore a long-lived asset when it is retired, these costs must also be estimated and included in the cost of the asset. These capital expenditures are known as **asset retirement costs**. For example, if Encana Corporation has a gas processing plant on which it expects to incur environmental costs to clean up and restore the property at the end of its useful life, these costs must be estimated and added to the cost of the plant when it is acquired and depreciated over the life of the plant. Accounting for asset retirement costs can be complex and we will leave that discussion to a future accounting course. For simplicity, we will assume that asset retirement costs equal zero in the examples used in this chapter.

Property, plant, and equipment are often subdivided into four classes:

1. **Land**, such as a building site
2. **Land improvements**, such as driveways, parking lots, fences, and underground sprinkler systems
3. **Buildings**, such as stores, offices, factories, and warehouses
4. **Equipment**, such as vehicles, computers, office furniture and equipment, and machinery

Note that companies may use more classes (categories) than the ones covered here. How to determine the cost of each of these major classes of property, plant, and equipment is explained in the following sections.

Land

All costs related to the purchase of land, including closing costs such as survey, title search, and legal fees, are added to the Land account. If additional work is required to prepare the land for its intended use, such as clearing, draining, grading, and filling, these costs are also recorded as capital expenditures in the Land account. If the land has a building on it that must be removed to make the site suitable for construction of a new building, all demolition and removal costs, less any proceeds from salvaged materials, are added to the Land account. When land has been purchased to construct a building, all costs that are incurred up to the time of excavation for the new building are considered to be part of the costs that are necessary to prepare the land for its intended use.

To illustrate, assume that Bancroft Corporation purchases real estate for $1.2 million and that the property contains an old warehouse that is torn down at a net cost of $40,000 ($50,000 in costs less $10,000 in proceeds from salvaged materials). Additional expenditures are also incurred for $5,000 of legal fees related to the purchase of the land. The cost of the land would be $1,245,000, calculated as follows:

Cash price of property	$1,200,000
Net cost of removing warehouse ($50,000 − $10,000)	40,000
Legal fees	5,000
Cost of land	$1,245,000

When the acquisition is recorded, Land is debited for $1,245,000 and Cash is credited for $1,245,000 (assuming the expenditures were paid in cash), although these amounts may be recorded in more than one journal entry. Once the land is ready for its intended use, recurring costs, such as property tax, are recorded as operating expenditures. In other words, these costs are reported in the same period (matched) as the revenues that the land helps generate.

Land Improvements

Land improvements are structural additions made to land, such as driveways, sidewalks, fences, lighting, and parking lots. Land improvements, unlike land, decline in service potential over time and require maintenance and eventual replacement. Because of this, land improvements are recorded separately from land and are depreciated over their useful lives.

Many students confuse the cost to get land ready for its intended use with land improvements. Land improvements are typically made after acquisition and can be separately distinguished and removed from the land itself.

Buildings

The cost of a building includes all costs that are directly related to its purchase or construction. When a building is purchased, its cost includes the purchase price and any costs incurred to close (complete) the transaction, such as legal fees, in addition to any costs required to make the building ready for its intended use. This can include expenditures for remodelling rooms and offices, and for replacing or repairing the roof, floors, electrical wiring, and plumbing. All of these costs are capitalized to the Buildings account.

When a new building is constructed, its cost consists of the contract price plus payments made for architect fees, building permits, and excavation costs. In addition, interest costs relating to a loan obtained to finance a construction project (that is, interest that could not be avoided) are also included in the cost of the asset but only up to the date that the asset is ready for its intended use. There are specific rules for determining the amount of interest costs to capitalize; these are not discussed here as they are normally taught in an intermediate accounting course.

If land and a building are purchased together for a single price, as is sometimes the case, the fair (appraised) value of each must be determined and recorded separately. The building must be recorded separately because it will be depreciated, whereas land will not be depreciated.

Equipment

The "equipment" classification is a broad one that can include office equipment, machinery, vehicles, furniture and fixtures, and other such assets. As with land and buildings, the cost of equipment includes the purchase price and all costs that are necessary to get the equipment ready for its intended use. Thus, freight charges, insurance during transit that is paid by the purchaser, and costs incurred to assemble, install, and test the equipment are all charged to the appropriate asset account, such as Equipment or Vehicles.

Because they are recurring expenditures that do not benefit future periods, annual costs such as motor vehicle licences and ongoing insurance are treated as operating expenditures when they are incurred. To illustrate, assume that Perfect Pizzas Ltd. purchases a delivery van for $32,500. Related expenditures are $500 for painting and lettering, $80 for a motor vehicle licence, and $800 for a one-year accident insurance policy. The cost of the delivery van is $33,000, calculated as follows:

Cash price	$32,500
Painting and lettering	500
Cost of delivery van	$33,000

The cost of a motor vehicle licence is treated as a current expense because it is an annual recurring cost. While there are several accounts in which this cost could be recorded, we have chosen to record it in the Vehicles Expense account. Similarly, the cost of the insurance policy is considered a prepaid expense (Prepaid Insurance—a current asset). It will be allocated to Insurance Expense throughout the period covered by the insurance policy. The cost of the van and the cost incurred for painting and lettering are capital expenditures because these costs benefit future periods. Painting and lettering are not recorded as separate assets because they are not separate from the van.

The entry to record the purchase of the van and related expenditures is summarized below. We have recorded this in a single journal entry, although it is possible to record these amounts in several entries (one for the vehicle purchase, one for painting, and so on). Assuming all amounts were paid in cash, the entry is as follows:

A	=	L	+	SE
+33,000				−80
+800				
−33,880				
↓ Cash flows: −33,880				

Vehicles ($32,500 + $500)	33,000	
Vehicles Expense	80	
Prepaid Insurance	800	
Cash ($33,000 + $80 + $800)		33,880
(To record purchase of delivery van and related expenditures)		

Expenditures During Useful Life

Subsequent to the acquisition of a long-lived asset, the same distinction exists between operating and capital expenditures. Operating expenditures generally benefit only the current period. They are required to maintain an asset in its normal operating condition and often recur, although not always annually. Examples include repainting a building or replacing the tires on a truck. These costs would be debited to an expense account, such as Repairs and Maintenance Expense, rather than being debited to an asset account.

Capital expenditures after acquisition include costs that increase the life of an asset or its productivity or efficiency. In other words, they are anticipated to provide future economic benefits. These costs are normally larger than operating expenditures, occur less frequently, and significantly improve the asset. As was mentioned in our chapter-opening feature story, WestJet capitalizes its overhaul costs because they improve the planes' service value or extend their useful lives. Other examples for a different type of business might include the cost to replace the roof on a building or to overhaul an engine in a truck. Determining whether an expenditure is operating or capital can sometimes require significant professional judgement.

TO BUY OR LEASE?

In this chapter, we focus on assets that are purchased, but there is an alternative to purchasing—leasing—that we would like to briefly introduce. In a lease, a party that owns an asset (the **lessor**) agrees to allow another party (the **lessee**) to rent the asset for an agreed period of time at an agreed price.

Instead of borrowing money to buy an asset, many companies choose to lease it instead because less cash is needed to do this initially. For example, many companies lease their photocopiers and other office equipment and, as indicated in the chapter-opening feature story, companies like WestJet lease their airplanes.

Some advantages of leasing an asset rather than purchasing it include the following:

1. **Reduced risk of obsolescence.** Obsolescence is the process by which an asset becomes out of date before it physically wears out. Frequently, lease terms allow the lessee to exchange the asset for a more modern or technologically capable asset if it becomes outdated. This is much easier than trying to sell an obsolete asset and purchasing a new one.
2. **100% financing.** If a company borrows money to purchase an asset, it is usually required to make a down payment. Leasing an asset does not require any down payment, which helps to conserve cash. In addition, rent payments are often fixed for the term of the lease so they are predictable, unlike other financing, which often has an interest rate that can change over time (called a floating interest rate).
3. **Income tax advantages.** When a company owns a depreciable asset, it can only deduct a certain amount of depreciation expense (called *capital cost allowance* for income tax purposes) on its income tax return. (We will learn more about capital cost allowance later in this chapter.) If the company has borrowed funds to purchase an asset, it can also deduct the interest expense on the borrowed funds. When a company leases an asset, it simply deducts the rent paid on its income tax return. In some years, this deduction may be greater than the capital cost allowance that could be taken if the asset was owned, which can reduce the company's income tax expense.

Lease transactions must be accounted for according to their economic substance. This ensures that there is a faithful representation of the transaction in the accounting records as we discussed in Chapter 2. If the risks and rewards of ownership are transferred to the lessee even if legal title has not passed, then the leased asset must be treated by the lessee like an asset purchase financed with a loan provided by the lessor. Consequently, depreciation expense on the asset and interest expense on the loan are recorded and no rent expense is recorded. When a lease is accounted for in this way, it is known as a **finance lease**.

A new International standard, effective January 1, 2019 (or earlier if a company prefers to do so) will require almost all leases with terms greater than one year to be treated as finance leases.

If the risks and rewards of ownership are *not* transferred to the lessee, then the lease is accounted for as an **operating lease**. Under an operating lease, no asset or liability is recorded; rather, each lease payment is recorded as rent (lease) expense on the income statement. Almost a third of WestJet's planes are accounted for under operating leases. Because operating leases are accounted for as rentals, these planes are not recorded as assets and liabilities on its statement of financial position. This is known as off–balance sheet financing, which simply means that an asset and liability have not been recorded when the lease commenced.

Note that under ASPE, a finance lease is also commonly known as a *capital lease*. Furthermore, ASPE does not yet require leases with terms extending beyond a year to be shown as capital leases. To determine if a lease is a capital lease, ASPE looks at several factors, such as the length of the lease term and other criteria that are reviewed in detail in an intermediate accounting course and are not discussed here.

Companies often incur costs when they renovate leased property. These costs are charged to a separate account called **Leasehold Improvements**. Since the leasehold improvements are attached to a leased property, they belong to the lessor at the end of the lease. Because the benefits of these improvements to the lessee will end when the lease expires, they are depreciated over the remaining life of the lease (including any renewal options) or the useful life of the improvements, whichever is shorter.

DO IT! ▶ 9-1 Cost of an Asset

Action Plan

✔ Capitalize expenditures that are made to get the equipment ready for its intended use.

✔ Expense operating costs that benefit only the current period, or that are recurring expenditures.

Assume that $50,000 of equipment was purchased on February 4. A $20,000 down payment was made and a bank loan was obtained to pay for the remaining cost of the equipment. Cash expenditures that relate to this purchase include insurance during shipping, $100; an annual insurance policy, $750; installation and testing costs, $500; and staff training costs for the new equipment, $600. (a) What is the cost of the equipment? (b) Record all the above expenditures in one journal entry on February 4.

SOLUTION

Try this Do It! exercise on your own and then check your answer at the end of the chapter.

Related Exercise Material: BE9–1, BE9–2, BE9–3, and E9–1.

LEARNING OBJECTIVE ▶ 2 Explain and calculate depreciation.

Under International Financial Reporting Standards, companies have two models to choose from when accounting for property, plant, and equipment: the cost model and the revaluation model. The cost model is the most commonly used model under IFRS, and is the only model allowed under ASPE. We will cover the cost model in the following sections of the chapter and refer briefly to the revaluation model in a later section.

The **cost model** records property, plant, and equipment at cost when acquired. Subsequent to acquisition, depreciation is recorded each period and the assets are carried at cost less the accumulated depreciation.

As we learned in Chapter 4, **depreciation is the systematic allocation of the cost of property, plant, and equipment over the asset's useful life**. You will recall that depreciation is recorded in an adjusting journal entry that debits Depreciation Expense and credits Accumulated Depreciation. Depreciation Expense is an income statement account while Accumulated Depreciation appears on the statement of financial position as a contra asset account to the relevant property, plant, or equipment account. The resulting balance, cost less accumulated depreciation, is the carrying amount of a depreciable asset, as defined in Chapter 4.

Of the four classes of property, plant, and equipment we discussed in the last section, only land is not depreciated because its usefulness and revenue-producing ability generally remain intact as long as the land is owned. Its useful life is not limited to a particular time period. In fact, in many cases the usefulness of land increases over time so it is not considered a depreciable asset.

Depreciation begins when the asset is available for use and ends when it is derecognized (removed from the accounts). The cost of the asset is allocated to depreciation expense over the asset's useful life so that expenses are properly matched with the expected use of the asset's future economic benefits.

It is important to understand that **depreciation is a process of allocating cost, not a process of determining an asset's current value**. Under the cost model, an increase in the asset's current value is not considered relevant, because property, plant, and equipment are not held for resale. We will later learn in this chapter that, under the cost model, current values are only relevant when determining if an impairment loss has occurred. As a result, the carrying amount of property, plant, and equipment may be very different from their current value.

It is also important to understand that **depreciation neither uses up nor provides cash to replace the asset**. Accumulated depreciation represents the total amount of the asset's cost that has been allocated to expense to date: it has no effect on cash. Note that cash is neither increased nor decreased by the adjusting entry to record depreciation: debit Depreciation Expense; credit Accumulated Depreciation.

KEEPING AN EYE ON CASH

Depreciation expense is one of the largest differences between accrual-based accounting net income and net cash provided by operating activities that is shown on the statement of cash flows. Depreciation expense reduces net income but does not use up cash. Therefore, to determine net cash provided by operating activities, companies must determine what net income would have been if there had been no depreciation expense. For example, if a company reported net income of $175,000 during the year and had depreciation expense of $40,000, net cash provided by operating activities would be $215,000 ($175,000 + $40,000), assuming no other differences between cash flows and accrual basis revenues and expenses. Note that, to determine what net income would be without depreciation, it must be added to net income. This add-back does not mean that depreciation provides cash.

DEPRECIATION METHODS

In Chapter 4, we learned that depreciation expense is calculated by dividing the cost of the depreciable asset by its useful life. This assumes that the entire cost of the asset is consumed over the useful life. However, if management believes and can estimate that the asset will have a value at the end of its useful life, known as **residual value**, should that residual value be depreciated? No, because that benefit still exists. We therefore must consider three factors when calculating depreciation.

1. **Cost.** The cost of property, plant, and equipment includes the purchase price plus all costs necessary to get the asset ready for use. Cost also includes estimated asset retirement costs, if there are any.
2. **Useful life.** Useful life is expressed as (a) the period of time over which management expects an asset to be available for use or (b) the number of units of production or units of output that management expects to be obtained from an asset. Useful life is an estimate based on such factors as the intended use of the asset and how vulnerable the asset is to wearing out or becoming obsolete. The company's past experience with similar assets is often helpful in estimating a particular asset's useful life.
3. **Residual value.** Residual value is management's estimate of the amount that a company would obtain from the disposal of the asset at the end of its useful life. This portion of the asset's cost is not depreciated, since the amount is expected to be recovered at the end of the asset's useful life and, as such, it will never be an expense to the company.

The difference between a depreciable asset's cost and its residual value is called the **depreciable amount**, which is the total amount to be depreciated over the useful life. Under ASPE, the term *amortization* is often used instead of depreciation, and because of this the depreciable amount is also known as the **amortizable cost**.

Depreciation is generally calculated using one of these three methods:

1. Straight-line
2. Diminishing-balance
3. Units-of-production

While all three methods are used in practice, the majority of Canadian publicly traded companies use the straight-line method of depreciation. WestJet, introduced in our feature story, uses the straight-line method to depreciate its property, plant, and equipment.

How do companies choose which method to use? Management must choose the depreciation method that it believes will best reflect the pattern in which the asset's future economic benefits are expected to be consumed. Once a company chooses the depreciation method, it should apply that method consistently over the useful life of the asset. You will recall from Chapter 2 that comparability is enhanced when the same accounting method is used over multiple years. This does not eliminate the requirement to review the depreciation method, at least annually. And, if the expected pattern of consumption of the future economic benefits changes, then the depreciation method must be changed.

In the sections that follow, the application of each of these depreciation methods is illustrated using the following data for a delivery van purchased by Perfect Pizzas Ltd. on January 1, 2018:

Cost	$33,000
Estimated residual value	$3,000
Estimated useful life (in years)	5
Estimated useful life (in kilometres)	100,000

Straight-Line Method

The straight-line method of depreciation was originally discussed in Chapter 4. We will discuss it again here, this time including the impact of the residual value on this method. Under the **straight-line method**, depreciation per year is calculated by dividing the asset's depreciable amount by its useful life in years. Recall from the previous section that depreciable amount is calculated by subtracting residual value from the cost of the asset.

The calculation of depreciation expense in the first year for Perfect Pizzas' delivery van is shown in Illustration 9-1.

►Illustration 9-1
Formula for straight-line method

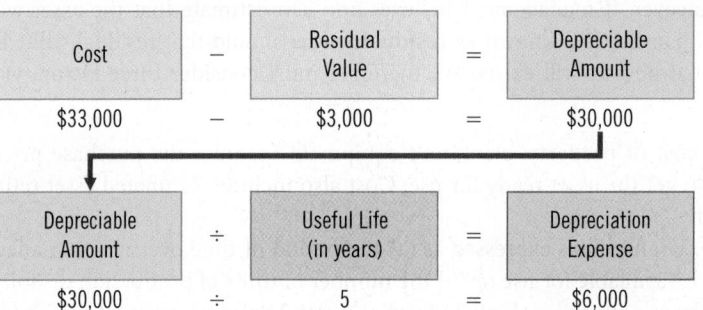

Alternatively, we can calculate a straight-line depreciation rate (expressed as a percentage) to use when determining the delivery van's straight-line annual depreciation expense. First, the depreciation rate is calculated by dividing 100% by the useful life in years.

100%	÷	Useful Life (in years)	=	Straight-Line Depreciation Rate
100%	÷	5 years	=	20%

In Perfect Pizzas' case, the straight-line depreciation rate is 20%. Second, the depreciation expense is calculated by multiplying the asset's depreciable amount by the depreciation rate, as shown in the depreciation schedule in Illustration 9-2.

►Illustration 9-2
Straight-line depreciation schedule

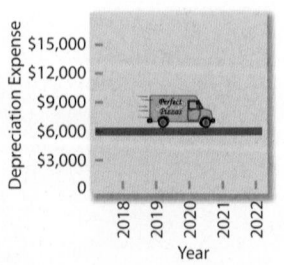

PERFECT PIZZAS LTD.
Straight-Line Depreciation Schedule

Year	Depreciable Amount	×	Depreciation Rate	=	Depreciation Expense	End of Year Accumulated Depreciation	End of Year Carrying Amount
							$33,000
2018	$30,000		20%		$ 6,000	$ 6,000	27,000
2019	30,000		20%		6,000	12,000	21,000
2020	30,000		20%		6,000	18,000	15,000
2021	30,000		20%		6,000	24,000	9,000
2022	30,000		20%		6,000	30,000	3,000
					$30,000		

Note that the depreciation expense of $6,000 is the same each year, and that the carrying amount at the end of the useful life is equal to the estimated $3,000 residual value. Because the depreciation expense is the same each year, a graph showing depreciation per year results in a straight-line pattern, as shown in Illustration 9-2.

What happens to depreciation when an asset is purchased during the year, rather than on January 1 as in our example? In such cases, it is necessary **to prorate the annual depreciation for the part of the year when the asset is available for use**. If Perfect Pizzas' delivery van had been purchased on April 1 rather than January 1, the van would be used for nine months in 2018 (April through December). The depreciation for that year would be $4,500 ($30,000 $\times$ 20% $\times$ $^9/_{12}$). Note that depreciation is normally calculated to the nearest month. Since depreciation is only an estimate, calculating it to the nearest day is not necessary and gives a false sense of accuracy.

To keep things simple, some companies use a convention for partial-period depreciation rather than calculating depreciation monthly. For example, companies may choose to allocate a full year's depreciation in the year of acquisition and none in the year of disposal. Other companies record a half-year's depreciation in the year of acquisition, and a half-year's depreciation in the year of disposal. Whatever company policy is used for partial-year depreciation, the impact is not significant in the long run as long as the policy is used consistently.

The straight-line method is applied to assets that are used uniformly and have a constant decline in usefulness, such as office furniture and fixtures, and buildings.

Diminishing-Balance Method

The **diminishing-balance method** produces a decreasing annual depreciation expense over the asset's useful life, resulting in higher levels of depreciation in the early years of an asset's useful life. It is called the "diminishing-balance" method because the periodic depreciation is calculated using the asset's carrying amount. Recall that the carrying amount is the difference between cost and accumulated depreciation at the beginning of the year, which diminishes each year as accumulated depreciation increases. Annual depreciation expense is calculated by multiplying the carrying amount at the beginning of the year by the depreciation rate. The depreciation rate remains constant from year to year, but the carrying amount that the rate is applied to declines each year.

> **Alternative Terminology**
> The *diminishing-balance* method is also called the *declining-balance* method.

Unlike other depreciation methods, the diminishing-balance method uses the asset's carrying amount, not the depreciable amount (cost – residual value), to calculate depreciation. Thus, **residual value is not used in determining the amount that the diminishing-balance rate is applied to**. Residual value does, however, limit the total depreciation that can be recorded. Depreciation stops when the asset's carrying amount equals its expected residual value.

The diminishing-balance method can be applied using different depreciation rates but these are usually based on multiples of the straight-line depreciation rate expressed in percentage terms. You will find rates such as one time (single), two times (double), and even three times (triple) the straight-line rate of depreciation. A depreciation rate that is often used is double the straight-line rate. This method is referred to as the **double-diminishing-balance method**.

To use this method, we do the following:

1. Determine the straight-line depreciation rate by taking 100% and dividing it by the useful life in years.
2. Multiply the straight-line depreciation rate by the appropriate multiplier (for example, double) to determine the diminishing-balance depreciation rate.
3. Multiply the carrying amount of the asset at the beginning of the period by the diminishing-balance depreciation rate.

If Perfect Pizzas uses double the straight-line depreciation rate, the depreciation rate is 40% (2 multiplied by the straight-line depreciation rate of 20%, which in turn was determined by dividing 100% by the 5-year useful life). Illustration 9-3 presents the formula and calculation of the first year's depreciation on the delivery van using the diminishing-balance method.

► Illustration 9-3
Formula for diminishing-
balance method

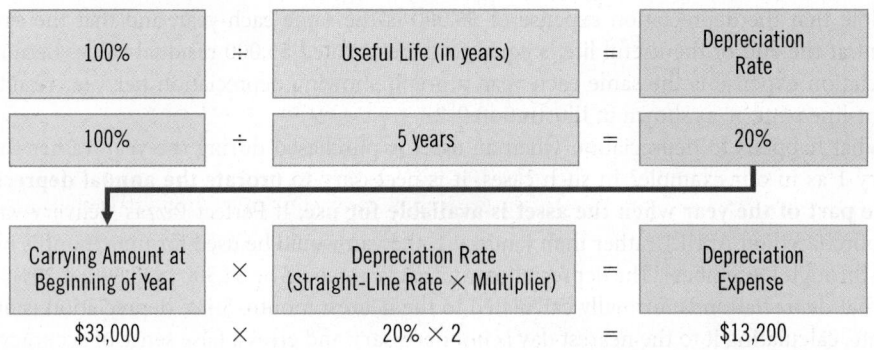

The complete depreciation schedule under this method is shown in Illustration 9-4.

► Illustration 9-4
Double-diminishing-balance
depreciation schedule

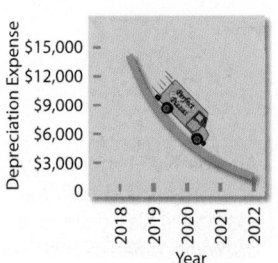

					End of Year	
Year	Carrying Amount Beginning of Year	×	Depreciation Rate	=	Depreciation Expense	Accumulated Depreciation	Carrying Amount
							$33,000
2018	$33,000		40%		$13,200	$13,200	19,800
2019	19,800		40%		7,920	21,120	11,880
2020	11,880		40%		4,752	25,872	7,128
2021	7,128		40%		2,851	28,723	4,277
2022	4,277		40%		1,277*	30,000	3,000
					$30,000		

PERFECT PIZZAS LTD.
Double-Diminishing-Balance Depreciation Schedule

*The calculation of $1,711 ($4,277 × 40%) is adjusted to $1,277 so that the carrying amount will equal the residual value of $3,000.

As explained earlier, depreciation stops in the diminishing-balance method when an asset's carrying amount equals its residual value. Consequently, in 2022, the calculated depreciation expense of $1,711 is restricted to $1,277 ($4,277 − $1,277 = $3,000) to prevent the carrying amount from becoming lower than the residual value. This also results in the total amount of depreciation over the life of the delivery van equalling $30,000—the depreciable amount. The possibility of depreciating an asset fully before the end of its useful life can occur when using diminishing-balance depreciation methods, especially if the asset has a short useful life. Note that although we rounded the depreciation rate to two decimals (for example, 0.40 or 40%) in the above schedule, we have rounded the depreciation expense to the nearest dollar. We will do the same throughout the text and in your homework assignments.

Methods such as the diminishing-balance method that produce higher depreciation expense in the early years than in the later years are known as *accelerated* depreciation methods. For example, in the above illustration, you can see that the delivery equipment is 64% depreciated ($21,120 ÷ $33,000) at the end of the second year. Under the straight-line method, it would be depreciated 36% ($12,000 ÷ $33,000) at that time.

When an asset is purchased during the year, rather than at the beginning of the year as we have illustrated above, it is necessary to prorate the diminishing-balance depreciation in the first year, based on time. For example, if Perfect Pizzas had purchased the delivery van on April 1, 2018, depreciation for 2018 would be $9,900 ($33,000 × 40% × 9/12) if depreciation were calculated based on the number of months in a year that it was used. The carrying amount for calculating depreciation in 2019 then becomes $23,100 ($33,000 − $9,900), and the 2019 depreciation is $9,240 ($23,100 × 40%). Future calculations would follow from these amounts until the carrying amount equalled the residual value.

The diminishing-balance method is applied when more of the asset's economic benefits are used up or consumed in the early years of the asset's useful life than are in later years. Some assets require higher repair and maintenance costs in later periods to maintain usefulness, in which case an advantage of the diminishing-balance method is that it will result in a fairly constant total expense over time (for depreciation plus repairs and maintenance).

Units-of-Production Method

Alternative Terminology
The *units-of-production* method is also called the *units-of-activity* method.

As indicated earlier, useful life can be expressed in ways other than a time period. In the **units-of-production method**, useful life is expressed using a measure of output, such as units produced, or a measure of use, such as machine hours worked, rather than the number of years that the asset is expected to be used. The units-of-production method works well for machinery where production can be measured in terms of units produced or for vehicles where usage can be measured in terms of kilometres driven. Other possible units of measure include tonnes, cubic metres, or hours. The units-of-production method is generally not suitable for such assets as buildings or furniture, because activity levels are less relevant and difficult to measure for these types of assets.

When using the units-of-production method, we do the following:

1. Estimate the units of production in total over the asset's entire useful life.
2. Divide the depreciable amount (cost less residual value) by the estimated units of production to determine the depreciable amount per unit.
3. Multiply the depreciable amount per unit by the units of production during the period and the result is the depreciation expense.

To illustrate, assume that Perfect Pizzas' delivery van is driven 15,000 km in the first year of a total estimated useful life of 100,000 km. Illustration 9-5 presents the formula and calculation of depreciation expense in the first year.

Cost	−	Residual Value	=	Depreciable Amount
$33,000	−	$3,000	=	$30,000

Depreciable Amount	÷	Estimated Total Units of Activity	=	Depreciable Amount per Unit
$30,000	÷	100,000 km	=	$0.30

Depreciable Amount per Unit	×	Units of Activity During the Year	=	Depreciation Expense
$0.30	×	15,000 km	=	$4,500

►Illustration 9-5

Formula for units-of-production method

Illustration 9-6 shows the units-of-production depreciation schedule, using assumed distance data for the years 2018–2022.

PERFECT PIZZAS LTD.
Units-of-Production Depreciation Schedule

Year	Units of Production	Depreciable Amount/Unit	Depreciation Expense	End of Year Accumulated Depreciation	End of Year Carrying Amount
					$33,000
2018	15,000	$0.30	$ 4,500	$ 4,500	28,500
2019	30,000	0.30	9,000	13,500	19,500
2020	20,000	0.30	6,000	19,500	13,500
2021	25,000	0.30	7,500	27,000	6,000
2022	10,000	0.30	3,000	30,000	3,000
	100,000		$30,000		

►Illustration 9-6

Units-of-production depreciation schedule

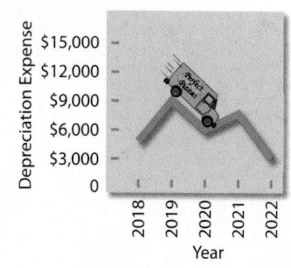

Similar to our calculations in the diminishing-balance method, we have rounded the depreciable amount per unit to two decimal spots (to the nearest cent) in the above schedule and rounded the depreciation expense to the nearest dollar.

The units-of-production method is easy to apply when assets are purchased during the year because adjustments for partial periods of use are already reflected in units produced. For example, if Perfect Pizzas had purchased the delivery van on April 1 instead of January 1, the only kilometres that could have been driven during the year were those driven after April 1 so no multiplication by a ratio pertaining to the portion of year in use is needed to calculate depreciation under this method.

Even though it is often difficult to make a reasonable estimate of total activity, this method is useful for long-lived assets whose productivity varies significantly from one period to another. In this situation, the units-of-production method results in depreciation amounts that match the benefits consumed as the asset is used. The units-of-production method is commonly used in the natural resources industry where production of these resources can vary from year to year. When natural resources are depreciated, the term *depletion* is used instead of depreciation. Further discussion of natural resources is left to an intermediate accounting course.

ACCOUNTING MATTERS

DNY59/iStockphoto

Why does Morris Formal Wear use the units-of-production method to depreciate its tuxedos? The reason is that the Ottawa-based family business wants to track wear and tear on each of its 5,200 tuxedos individually. Each tuxedo has its own bar code. When a tux is rented, a clerk runs its code across an electronic scanner. At year end, the computer adds up the total rentals for each of the tuxedos, then divides this number by the expected total number of uses to calculate the rate. For instance, on a two-button black tux, Morris expects a life of 30 rentals. In one year, the tux was rented 13 times. The depreciation rate for that year was 43% (13 ÷ 30) of the depreciable amount.

Comparison of Depreciation Methods

The following summarizes the three depreciation methods and the calculation of depreciation expense for each method:

Straight-line	$\dfrac{\text{Cost} - \text{Residual Value}}{\text{Useful Life}}$
Diminishing-balance	(Cost − Accumulated Depreciation) × Depreciation Rate (Straight-Line Rate × Multiplier)
Units-of-production	$\dfrac{\text{Cost} - \text{Residual Value}}{\text{Total Estimated Units of Activity}} \times \dfrac{\text{Actual Units of}}{\text{Activity During Year}}$

Using each of the above methods and formulas, we calculated annual and total depreciation expense for Perfect Pizzas for a five-year period earlier in this chapter. The following schedule compares the results under the three different depreciation methods.

	Straight-Line		Diminishing-Balance		Units-of-Production	
Year	Depreciation Expense	Carrying Amount	Depreciation Expense	Carrying Amount	Depreciation Expense	Carrying Amount
2018	$ 6,000	$27,000	$13,200	$19,800	$ 4,500	$28,500
2019	6,000	21,000	7,920	11,880	9,000	19,500
2020	6,000	15,000	4,752	7,128	6,000	13,500
2021	6,000	9,000	2,851	4,277	7,500	6,000
2022	6,000	3,000	1,277	3,000	3,000	3,000
	$30,000		$30,000		$30,000	

As discussed earlier, straight-line depreciation results in the same amount of expense each year on the income statement. Diminishing-balance results in higher expenses, and therefore lower net income, in the early years of the asset's useful life. It also results in lower expenses and higher net income in later years. Results for the units-of-production method vary each year depending on the actual usage of the asset. However, over the entire useful life, total depreciation is the same regardless of the method of depreciation. Note that while each depreciation method may allocate the cost of the asset differently each year, over the life of the asset, all methods allocate the same total amount of asset cost (the depreciable amount) to depreciation expense.

Just as depreciation expense has an inverse relationship with net income, it also has an inverse relationship with the change in the carrying amount. For example, in 2018, the diminishing-balance method, which maximized depreciation compared with the other methods, minimized net income and thus retained earnings, and minimized the carrying amount of the delivery van. Of course, the choice of depreciation method has no impact on cash flow.

OTHER DEPRECIATION ISSUES

There are several other issues related to depreciation that we will briefly introduce here. These include how certain assets are separated into their significant components for depreciation purposes, how assets are depreciated for income tax purposes, how the impairment of assets is recorded when the current value declines, the revaluation model, and under what circumstances depreciation is revised.

Significant Components

When an item of property, plant, and equipment includes individual components that have different useful lives, we need to account for the components (if material) separately rather than for the asset as a whole. This allows each component to be depreciated over different useful lives or even using different depreciation methods if they deliver different patterns of economic benefits. For example, WestJet records the aircraft, engine, airframe, and landing gear separately rather than combining them together into a single aircraft account. In this way, the aircraft can be depreciated over 15 to 20 years, while the engine, airframe, and landing gear are depreciated over 3 to 12 years, all using the straight-line method.

Further discussion of calculating depreciation for the different parts of an asset will be left to a later accounting course. For simplicity, we will assume in this text that all of the components of a depreciable asset have the same useful life and use the same depreciation method, and we will therefore depreciate each asset as a whole.

Depreciation and Income Tax

For accounting purposes, management determines the method of depreciation to use and estimates the useful life and residual value of assets. The Canada Revenue Agency requires that, for income tax purposes, depreciation amounts be determined using tax regulations rather than using management estimates. For this reason, when preparing a tax return and determining taxable income, companies cannot deduct the depreciation expense reported on the income statement. Instead, they must deduct the income tax version of depreciation, which is known as capital cost allowance (CCA). In determining CCA, normally only the diminishing-balance method of depreciation is permitted. In addition, assets are grouped into various classes and the depreciation rates for each asset class are specified for income tax purposes. All management estimates are removed from these calculations.

Impairments

As noted earlier in the chapter, the carrying amount of property, plant, and equipment is rarely the same as their current value. Remember that the cost model assumes that current value is not relevant since property, plant, and equipment are not purchased for resale, but rather for use in operations over the long term. Although the current value of these assets usually exceeds their carrying amount because of depreciation, if the reverse became true, and the current value was less than the carrying amount, it would not be representationally faithful to report assets on the statement of financial position at carrying amounts that were in excess of the future economic benefits expected to flow from that asset. When this happens, the asset is said to be impaired and its carrying amount must be reduced accordingly.

Companies are required to determine if there are indicators of impairment such as asset obsolescence or declining demand for the products produced by an asset on a regular basis. If there are no indicators, further testing for impairment is not required. However, if indicators are present, management is required to perform an impairment test and this involves determining an estimate of the asset's **recoverable amount**. We introduced the concept of the current value of an asset in chapter 2. Current value can be based on fair value or value in use and the recoverable amount is defined as the greater of the asset's fair value (which can be observed in the market) less costs to sell (if known) and the asset's value in use (which is based on future cash flows). In this textbook, we will provide you with the recoverable amount directly and leave the complexities of calculating that amount for a more advanced accounting course.

Property, plant, and equipment are considered impaired if the asset's carrying amount exceeds its recoverable amount. When such an asset is impaired, an **impairment loss** is recorded that is equal to the amount by which the asset's carrying amount exceeds its recoverable amount.

<table>
<tr><td>Carrying Amount
(Cost − Accumulated Depreciation)</td><td>−</td><td>Recoverable
Amount</td><td>=</td><td>Impairment
Loss</td></tr>
</table>

Impairment losses are typically recorded by debiting an Impairment Loss account, which is reported on the income statement as an operating expense, and by crediting the Accumulated Depreciation account. Other methods for recording impairment losses are possible and are covered in more advanced accounting courses. We previously defined an asset's carrying amount as its cost less accumulated depreciation. This is still the case, but accumulated depreciation can now include more than just the depreciation recorded on the asset to date. It will also include accumulated impairment losses, if there have been any.

Most impairment losses can be reversed under IFRS, although this does not occur often. However, impairment losses are not reversed under ASPE. The rules for determining if an asset is impaired are different under ASPE and IFRS. While the details of these differences are left for a future accounting course, note that under ASPE, impairments may be recorded less often.

Impairment losses can create problems for users of financial statements. While asset impairments must be justified, they do involve professional judgement and the determination of an impairment loss usually gives rise to a range of values rather than one correct amount. Management can therefore exercise judgement in determining where in the range the value should be selected from. An unethical accountant may be tempted to record overstated asset impairments in unprofitable years, when they are going to report poor results anyway. This practice is sometimes referred to as "big bath" accounting. Although this lowers net income in the year of the impairment, it means that depreciation expense will be lower in subsequent periods, which results in an artificial improvement of net income at that time.

Revaluation Model

As previously mentioned, under International Financial Reporting Standards, companies can choose to account for property, plant, and equipment under either the cost model or the revaluation model. We have been describing the cost model in this chapter because it is used by most companies. The revaluation model is used on a limited basis—primarily by companies in the financial services and real estate industries where current values are more relevant than cost. It is not allowed under ASPE.

Under the **revaluation model**, the carrying amount of property, plant, and equipment is adjusted to reflect their recoverable amount. This model can be applied only to assets whose current value can be reliably measured. A revaluation is not required each year but must be carried out often enough that the reported carrying amount is not materially different from the asset's current value.

> **Alternative Terminology**
> An *impairment loss* is also known as a *writedown*.

We saw when using the cost model that impairment losses (and any allowable reversals of impairment losses) are recorded on the income statement. With the revaluation model, **revaluation gains** or write-ups are also recorded, but these are not recorded on the income statement. Instead, they must be recorded in other comprehensive income on the statement of comprehensive income. Any reversals of these revaluation gains or write-ups are also recorded in other comprehensive income. Because the application of the revaluation model is relatively complex, and few companies use this model, we will leave further discussion of it to a later accounting course.

Revising Periodic Depreciation

There are several reasons why periodic depreciation may need to be revised during an asset's useful life. These include:

1. **Capital expenditures during the asset's useful life.** While an asset is being used, additional costs relating to it may be incurred. If these are capital expenditures, they will increase the carrying amount of an asset and depreciation calculations from that point onward will have to be revised.
2. **Impairment losses.** As described earlier in the chapter, an impairment loss will reduce an asset's carrying amount. Since the carrying amount is reduced, any future depreciation calculations will also be reduced because the depreciable amount is now lower.
3. **Changes in the estimated useful life or residual value.** Management must review its estimates of useful life and residual value each year. For example, wear and tear or obsolescence might indicate that annual depreciation is not enough. Capital expenditures may increase the asset's useful life and/or its residual value. Impairment losses might signal a reduction in useful life and/or residual value. Regardless of the reason for the change, a change in estimated useful life or residual value will cause a revision to the depreciation calculations.
4. **Changes in the pattern in which the asset's economic benefits are consumed.** As discussed earlier, management must review the choice of depreciation method for a long-lived asset at least annually. If the pattern in which the future benefits will be consumed is expected to change, the depreciation method must change as well, resulting in a revision to depreciation calculations.

Revising depreciation is known as a change in accounting estimate. **Changes in accounting estimates are made in current and future years but not to prior periods.** This is known as prospective treatment. Thus, when a change in depreciation is made, (1) there is no adjustment of previously recorded depreciation expense, and (2) only depreciation expense for current and future years is revised. The rationale for this treatment is that the original calculations were based on the best information known at the time when the asset was purchased. The revision is based on new information that should only affect the current and future periods because that information was not available in the past.

To determine revised depreciation expense, we must first calculate the asset's carrying amount at the time of the change in estimate. This is equal to the asset's original cost less the accumulated depreciation to date plus any capital expenditures. The asset's residual value (either the original amount or a revised amount if it has changed) is deducted from the carrying amount at the time of the change in estimate. This becomes the new depreciable amount and, if using the straight-line method, it is divided by the remaining estimated useful life to determine the revised depreciation expense. We will leave a detailed illustration of a change in the depreciation estimate when using other depreciation methods for another accounting course.

DO IT! ▶9-2 Depreciation

On April 1, 2017, Mountain Ski Corporation purchased a used snow grooming machine for $104,000. The machine was estimated to have a three-year useful life and an $8,000 residual value. It was also estimated to have a total useful life of 6,000 hours. It is used for 1,600 hours in the year ended December 31, 2017, 2,000 hours in the year ended December 31, 2018, 1,900 hours in the year ended December 31, 2019, and 500 hours in the year ended December 31, 2020. How much depreciation expense should Mountain Ski record in each of 2017, 2018, 2019, and 2020 under each depreciation method: (a) straight-line, (b) diminishing-balance using twice the straight-line rate, and (c) units-of-production? What is the total amount of depreciation recorded under each of these methods over this four-year period?

Action Plan

✔ Under straight-line depreciation, annual depreciation expense is equal to the depreciable amount (cost less residual value) divided by the estimated useful life.

✔ Under double-diminishing-balance depreciation, annual depreciation expense is equal to twice the straight-line rate of depreciation times the asset's carrying amount at the beginning of the year. Residual values are not used to calculate depreciation in this method, but you must ensure that the carrying amount does not fall below residual value.

✔ Under the straight-line and diminishing-balance methods, the annual depreciation expense must be prorated if the asset is purchased during the year.

✔ Under units-of-production depreciation, the depreciable amount per unit is equal to the total depreciable amount divided by the total estimated units of production. The annual depreciation expense is equal to the depreciable amount per unit times the actual usage in each year. For partial year use, no proration is required in the calculation because the number of units produced is already prorated.

LEARNING OBJECTIVE **3** Account for the derecognition of property, plant, and equipment.

Property, plant, and equipment are derecognized, or removed from the accounts, when they are disposed of through sale or retired without sale. This can happen during or at the end of the asset's useful life. There are other methods of disposal when the asset is no longer of use to the company, such as exchanges of property, plant, and equipment. However, accounting for these transactions is complex and is covered in a future accounting course.

SALE OF PROPERTY, PLANT, AND EQUIPMENT

A company must perform the following four steps when recording derecognition of property, plant, or equipment. Note that Steps 1 and 2 apply only to depreciable assets and are not required when land is disposed of and derecognized.

Step 1: Update depreciation. Depreciation must be recorded over the entire period of time that an asset is available for use. If the disposal occurs in the middle of an accounting period, depreciation must be updated for the fraction of the year that has passed since the last time depreciation adjusting entries were recorded up to the date of disposal. Note that the update period will never exceed one year, since adjusting entries are made at least annually.

Step 2: Calculate the carrying amount. Calculate the carrying amount at the time of disposal after updating the accumulated depreciation for any partial-year depreciation recorded in Step 1:

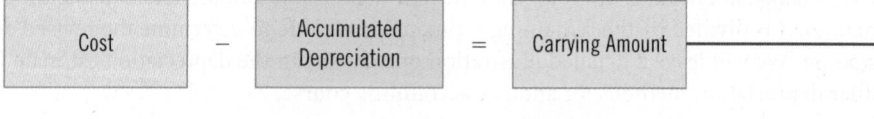

Step 3: Calculate the gain or loss. Determine the amount of the gain or loss on disposal, if any, by comparing the carrying amount with the proceeds received on disposal:

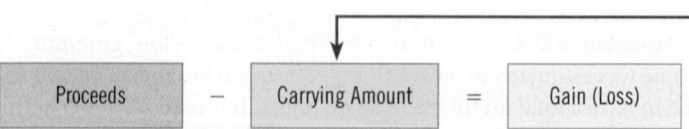

If the proceeds of the sale are more than the carrying amount of the property, plant, or equipment, there is a **gain on disposal**. If the proceeds of the sale are less than the asset's carrying amount, there is a **loss on disposal**.

Step 4: Record the disposal. Record the disposal by removing the cost and accumulated depreciation relating to the disposed asset from each affected account. Remember that this will affect two accounts. The specific asset account (land, land improvements, buildings, or equipment) is decreased with a credit equal to the cost of the asset disposed of while the related Accumulated Depreciation account is decreased with a debit for the portion of the account pertaining to the derecognized asset. The decrease to the Accumulated Depreciation account represents the total amount of depreciation and any impairment losses that have been recorded for the asset up to its disposal date. Record the proceeds (if any), typically with a debit to Cash. Alternatively, the debit may be to a receivable or other asset account. Record the gain or loss on disposal (if any) by crediting a gain account or debiting a loss account for the difference between the proceeds received and the carrying amount of the asset disposed of. A sample journal entry to record a disposal is illustrated below:

Cash	XX	
Accumulated Depreciation	XX	
Loss on Disposal (or credit Gain on Disposal)	XX	or XX
Specific property, plant, or equipment account		XX

In the following pages, we will illustrate the recording of a sale of equipment, using the straight-line depreciation method, first at a gain and then at a loss.

Assume that on July 1, 2018, Keystone Ltd. sells equipment for $25,000 cash. The equipment was purchased three and a half years earlier, on January 1, 2015, at a cost of $60,000. At that time, it was estimated that the equipment would have a residual value of $5,000 and a useful life of five years. Keystone uses the straight-line method of depreciation and makes adjusting entries annually at its year end, December 31.

The first step in recording the sale is to update any unrecorded depreciation. Annual depreciation using the straight-line method is $11,000 [($60,000 − $5,000) ÷ 5]. Depreciation would have already been recorded along with other adjusting entries for each of the years 2015, 2016, and 2017. Depreciation for 2018 will not yet have been recorded because Keystone prepares adjusting entries only once a year.

The journal entry to record depreciation expense and update the accumulated depreciation for the first six months of 2018 up to the disposal date is as follows:

July 1	Depreciation Expense	5,500	
	Accumulated Depreciation—Equipment		5,500
	(To record depreciation expense for the first six months of 2018)		

A	=	L	+	SE
−5,500				−5,500
Cash flows: no effect				

After this journal entry is posted, the Equipment and Accumulated Depreciation accounts appear as follows:

Equipment			Accumulated Depreciation—Equipment		
Jan. 1, 2015	60,000			Dec. 31, 2015	11,000
				Dec. 31, 2016	11,000
				Dec. 31, 2017	11,000
				July 1, 2018	5,500
				Bal.	38,500

Note that the balance in the Accumulated Depreciation account equals 3½ years of depreciation expense ($11,000 × 3.5 = $38,500).

The second step is to calculate the carrying amount on July 1, 2018, the date of disposal:

Cost	−	Accumulated Depreciation	=	Carrying Amount
$60,000	−	$38,500	=	$21,500

The third step is to calculate any gain or loss on disposal. A $3,500 gain is calculated by comparing the proceeds received with the carrying amount:

Proceeds	−	Carrying Amount	=	Gain (Loss)
$25,000	−	$21,500	=	$3,500

The fourth step is to record the sale of the equipment, as follows:

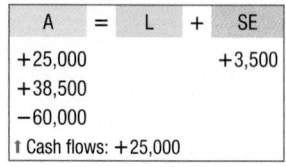

A	=	L	+	SE
+25,000				+3,500
+38,500				
−60,000				
↑ Cash flows: +25,000				

July 1	Cash	25,000	
	Accumulated Depreciation—Equipment	38,500	
	Equipment		60,000
	Gain on Disposal		3,500
	(To record sale of equipment at a gain)		

Note that the carrying amount of $21,500 does not appear in the above journal entry because the carrying amount is the net amount of two account balances: the equipment's cost ($60,000) and the accumulated depreciation ($38,500) and is calculated to determine the gain or loss. It is not a single account to be debited or credited.

Assume now that, instead of selling the equipment for $25,000, Keystone sells it for $20,000. In this case, a loss of $1,500 results:

Proceeds	−	Carrying Amount	=	Gain (Loss)
$20,000	−	$21,500	=	$(1,500)

The entry to record the sale of the equipment at a loss is:

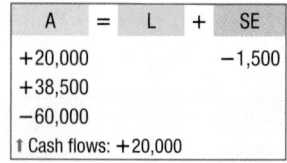

A	=	L	+	SE
+20,000				−1,500
+38,500				
−60,000				
↑ Cash flows: +20,000				

July 1	Cash	20,000	
	Accumulated Depreciation—Equipment	38,500	
	Loss on Disposal	1,500	
	Equipment		60,000
	(To record sale of equipment at a loss)		

DO IT! ▶ 9-3a   Sale of a Vehicle

Action Plan

✔ Record depreciation for the portion of the year that the asset was used.

✔ Calculate the carrying amount.

✔ Compare the proceeds with the carrying amount to determine whether any gain or loss has occurred.

✔ Record any proceeds that are received and any gain or loss. Make sure that all accounts (cost and accumulated depreciation) related to the disposed asset are derecognized (removed).

Overland Trucking Ltd. has a truck that it purchased on January 1, 2014, for $90,000. This purchase was recorded in the Vehicles account at the time. The truck has since been depreciated on a straight-line basis with no residual value and a useful life of six years. Overland has a December 31 year end and prepares adjusting entries annually.

Assume each of the following three independent situations: (a) the truck is sold on September 1, 2018, for $21,000 cash; and (b) the truck is sold on September 1, 2018, for $18,000 cash. What journal entry should Overland make to record each scenario?

SOLUTION

Try this Do It! exercise on your own and then check your answer at the end of the chapter.

Related Exercise Material: BE9–10, E9–5, E9–6, and E9–7.

RETIREMENT OF PROPERTY, PLANT, AND EQUIPMENT

If a company is finished using an asset and there is no market for it (it cannot be sold), then the company will retire it. The journal entry for a retirement is very similar to the ones shown above for the sale of an asset except that there are usually little or no proceeds to record. Let's continue with the Keystone example introduced in the last section, and assume that the equipment is retired at the end of its useful life, on January 1, 2020. In this scenario, depreciation expense would have been recorded for the full five years of the equipment's useful life. The Equipment and the Accumulated Depreciation accounts would be as follows on January 1, 2020:

Equipment		Accumulated Depreciation—Equipment	
Jan. 1, 2015 60,000		Dec. 31, 2015	11,000
		Dec. 31, 2016	11,000
		Dec. 31, 2017	11,000
		Dec. 31, 2018	11,000
		Dec. 31, 2019	11,000
		Bal.	55,000

The equipment is now fully depreciated with a carrying amount of $5,000, as shown below:

Cost	−	Accumulated Depreciation	=	Carrying Amount
$60,000	−	$55,000	=	$5,000

The carrying amount equals the residual value at the end of the useful life. If we assume that Keystone is able to sell the equipment as scrap for $5,000, as originally estimated, the carrying amount will equal the proceeds and there will be no gain or loss on disposal.

Proceeds	−	Carrying Amount	=	Gain (Loss)
$5,000	−	$5,000	=	$0

The cash received on final disposition of an asset may be greater or less than the estimated residual value, because it would be unusual if the estimate was perfect. In that case, a small gain or loss would result.

The final step that is required is an entry to record the retirement:

Jan. 1	Cash	5,000	
	Accumulated Depreciation—Equipment	55,000	
	Equipment		60,000
	(To record retirement of fully depreciated equipment)		

A	=	L	+	SE
+5,000				
+55,000				
−60,000				
↑ Cash flows: +5,000				

Just as we see with any disposal, after this entry is posted, the balance in the Equipment and the Accumulated Depreciation—Equipment accounts will be zero.

If no proceeds were received on disposal, rather than $5,000 as we assumed above, a loss on disposal would result equal to the residual value. The journal entry to record this would be as follows:

Jan. 1	Accumulated Depreciation—Equipment	55,000	
	Loss on Disposal	5,000	
	Equipment		60,000
	(To record retirement of fully depreciated equipment)		

A	=	L	+	SE
+55,000				−5,000
−60,000				
Cash flows: no effect				

Note that, even if the asset had a carrying amount of zero, had no residual value, and no proceeds were received upon disposal, a journal entry would still be required to remove the asset and its related accumulated depreciation from the books to prevent them from being overstated.

What happens if a company is still using a fully depreciated asset? In this case, the asset and its accumulated depreciation are not derecognized and continue to be reported on the statement of financial position, without further depreciation, until the asset is retired or sold. Reporting the asset and related depreciation on the financial statements informs the reader of the financial statements that the asset is still being used by the company. Once an asset is fully depreciated, even if it is still being used, no additional depreciation should be taken. Accumulated depreciation on a piece of property, plant, and equipment can never be more than the asset's cost.

DO IT! ▶ 9-3b Retirement of Equipment

Action Plan

✔ Record depreciation for the portion of the year that the asset was used.

✔ Calculate the carrying amount.

✔ Make sure that all accounts (cost and accumulated depreciation) related to the disposed asset are derecognized (removed) and record a loss equal to the carrying amount of the equipment at the time of retirement.

Glendale Manufacturing Ltd. owns equipment that was purchased on January 1, 2015, for $100,000. The equipment, which has a 10-year useful life and no residual value, has since been depreciated using the diminishing-balance method at double the straight-line depreciation rate. Glendale has a December 31 year end and prepares adjusting entries annually.

On October 1, 2018, it was determined that the equipment had become obsolete and it was replaced with a more efficient model. The old equipment could not be sold so it was retired and disposed of for no consideration. What journal entries should Glendale record in 2018 regarding the retirement of this equipment?

SOLUTION

Try this Do It! exercise on your own and then check your answer at the end of the chapter.

Related Exercise Material: BE9–11.

LEARNING OBJECTIVE ▶4

Identify the basic accounting issues for intangible assets and goodwill.

Property, plant, and equipment are similar to intangible assets and goodwill in that they are long-lived resources used in business operations, and are not intended for sale to customers. All three types of assets provide economic benefits in future periods.

A key distinction between these types is that while property, plant, and equipment are *tangible* assets, which have physical substance, *intangible* assets and goodwill have no physical substance. In other words, intangible assets involve rights, privileges, and/or competitive advantages that are not physical things. Despite this, they do generate future economic benefits, such as revenue from the sale of products or services or cost savings resulting from the company's use of the asset. For some companies, intangible assets are the most valuable assets they have. Some widely known intangibles are Coca-Cola's patents, Tim Hortons' franchises, Apple's trade names, and Google's trademarks.

ACCOUNTING FOR INTANGIBLE ASSETS

An intangible asset must be identifiable, which means it must meet one of the two following criteria: (1) it can be separated from the company and sold, whether or not the company intends to do so, or (2) it is based on contractual or legal rights, regardless of whether or not it can be separated from the company. Because goodwill cannot be separated from a company and sold nor is it based on contractual or legal rights, there are differences in the accounting for goodwill compared with other intangible assets, so we will discuss goodwill in the next section.

Similar to property, plant, and equipment, **intangible assets are recorded at cost**. Cost includes all the costs of acquisition and other costs that are needed to make the intangible asset ready for its intended use, including legal fees and similar charges.

As with property, plant, and equipment, companies have a choice of following the cost model or the revaluation model when accounting for an intangible asset subsequent to acquisition. The majority of companies use the cost model so we will leave further study of the revaluation model as it applies to intangible assets for a later accounting course.

Intangible assets are categorized as having either a **finite (limited) life** or an **indefinite (unlimited) life**. If an intangible asset has a finite life, its cost must be systematically allocated to an expense over its useful life. We called this *depreciation* when discussing property, plant, and equipment. With intangible assets, we use the term **amortization** to describe the process of allocating cost to expense. Under ASPE, *amortization* is often the word used to describe both depreciation of property, plant, and equipment and amortization of intangible assets. Intangible assets with indefinite lives are not amortized.

For an intangible asset with a finite life, its **amortizable amount** (its cost less its residual value) should be allocated over the shorter of (1) the estimated useful life and (2) the legal life. Intangible assets, by their nature, rarely have any residual value, so the amortizable amount is normally equal to the cost. In addition, the useful life of an intangible asset is usually shorter than its legal life, as we will see later, so useful life is most often used as the amortization period. Similar to depreciable assets, the amortization method and useful lives must be disclosed in the notes to the financial statements.

Amortization begins when the intangible asset is ready to be used as intended by management. Similar to depreciation, the company must use the amortization method that best matches the pattern in which the asset's future economic benefits are expected to be consumed. If that pattern cannot be reliably determined, which occurs most of the time, the straight-line method should be used.

A sample journal entry to record amortization is as follows:

Amortization Expense	XX	
Accumulated Amortization		XX
(To record amortization)		

As was the case with depreciation, amortization expense is recognized on the income statement as an operating expense. Companies often combine depreciation and amortization expenses in a single amount for reporting purposes. The Accumulated Amortization account is a contra asset account to the specific intangible asset being amortized, and reported on the statement of financial position.

Recall from earlier in this chapter that an asset is impaired if its recoverable amount falls below its carrying amount. Just as must be done for property, plant, and equipment, companies must determine if there are indicators of impairment on intangible assets with finite lives. If there are indicators, an impairment test is performed. Under IFRS, intangible assets with indefinite lives must be tested annually even if no indications of impairment are present (under ASPE this is done only if indicators of impairment are present). If any impairment is evident, the asset must be written down to its recoverable amount and an impairment loss recorded and reported in the operating expenses section of the income statement. If the impaired asset is a finite-life intangible asset, the Accumulated Amortization account is credited, similar to our practice of recording impairment losses in the Accumulated Depreciation account for depreciable assets. If the impaired asset is an indefinite-life intangible, then the asset account is credited directly because there is no accumulated amortization account available to credit.

Under IFRS, an impairment can be reversed for intangible assets just as it can be reversed for property, plant, and equipment. Under ASPE, reversals are not permitted.

Similar to depreciation, amortization is revised when there is a change in cost or useful life, or an impairment loss, and the revision is treated as a change in estimate. At disposal, just as with property, plant, and equipment, the intangible asset's carrying amount is derecognized with the asset and its related accumulated amortization if applicable brought to nil, and a gain or loss, if any, is recorded.

In the next two sections, we will look in more detail at the accounting for intangibles with finite lives and those with indefinite lives.

Intangible Assets with Finite Lives

Examples of intangible assets with finite lives include patents and copyrights. We also include research and development costs in this section because these costs often lead to the creation of patents and copyrights. WestJet, in our feature story, has intangible assets with limited lives, including software, landing rights, and development costs.

PATENTS   A **patent** is an exclusive right issued by the Canadian Intellectual Property Office of Industry Canada that allows the patent holder to manufacture, sell, or otherwise control an invention for a period of 20 years from the date of the application. A patent cannot be renewed, but a patent's legal life can be extended if the patent holder obtains new patents for improvements or other changes in the basic design.

The initial cost of a patent is the price paid to acquire it. Subsequent to acquisition, costs to register the patent, along with legal costs incurred to successfully defend it in any infringement suit, would also be included in the cost of the patent and amortized over time.

The cost of a patent should be amortized over its 20-year legal life or its useful life, whichever is shorter. When a company estimates the useful life of a patent (or any finite-life intangible asset), it must consider factors such as how long the company expects to use the asset, when it may become obsolete, the level of demand for products or services it produces, and other factors that can diminish the economic benefits produced by the patent. For example, suppose a computer hardware manufacturer obtained a patent on a new computer chip that it developed. From experience, we know that the useful life of a computer chip is rarely more than three years because new, superior chips are developed so rapidly that existing chips quickly become obsolete.

COPYRIGHTS   A **copyright** is granted by the Canadian Intellectual Property Office, giving the owner the exclusive right to reproduce and sell an artistic or published work. Copyrights are valid for the life of the creator plus 50 years (with some extensions for sound recordings). Generally, a copyright's useful life is significantly shorter than its legal life, and the copyright is therefore amortized over its useful life.

ACCOUNTING MATTERS

JB Lacroix/Getty Images, Inc.

Songwriters Sue Justin Bieber for Copyright Infringement

In 2013, two American songwriters filed a $10-million lawsuit alleging that Canadian pop star Justin Bieber and his collaborator, Usher, infringed copyright by using parts of their song in the hit "Somebody to Love." The songwriters, Devin Copeland and Mareio Overton, claimed that Bieber's and Usher's versions used the same beat, chords, and lyrics as their song of the same name. The songwriters also sued Vivendi SA's Universal Music Publishing Group and Sony Corp's Sony/ATV Music Publishing. In 2015, an appeals court in Virginia allowed the suit to continue, saying that the two songs' "choruses are similar enough and also significant enough that a reasonable jury could find the songs intrinsically similar." That court ruled that it didn't matter that the Bieber and Usher versions were "dance pop" while the original song was R&B. Artists' copyright must be protected or else musicians could profit by reinterpreting other songwriters' songs in a different genre, the court found. The case was expected to go to trial in the fall of 2016.[2]

The cost of the copyright consists of the cost of acquiring and defending it. The cost may be quite low and be composed of only the cost to acquire and register the copyright, or it may amount to a great deal more if a copyright infringement suit is involved.

RESEARCH AND DEVELOPMENT COSTS Research and development (R&D) costs are not intangible assets on their own, but may lead to patents, copyrights, or other intangible assets. Many companies spend considerable sums of money on research and development in an ongoing effort to develop new products or processes. For example, Rogers Communications usually spends over $400 million on research and development each year.

When a company develops intangible assets internally rather than acquiring them from another party, two accounting problems arise: (1) It is sometimes difficult to determine the costs related to a specific project; and (2) it is hard to know if future benefits will be generated, and if so, when. To help resolve these issues, accounting distinguishes between a research phase and a development phase.

During the research phase, expenditures are made but it is not yet known if these costs will have any future benefit. Consequently, they are expensed and recorded in the account **Research Expenses**.

The development phase begins when certain criteria are met that indicate that the project being developed will have future benefit. All of the following criteria must be met:

1. The project is technically feasible.
2. The company intends to complete development.
3. The product developed can be used or sold by the company.
4. The company has adequate resources to complete development.
5. The company can reliably measure the costs incurred.
6. A market exists for the product that will provide future economic benefits.

Once all of the above conditions are met, future expenditures on the project that specifically relate to its development will be capitalized and recorded in the asset account **Development Costs**. During the development phase, if expenditures incurred relate to another specific asset, such as equipment or a patent, then those costs are recorded in their respective accounts rather than in Development Costs. The development phase ends when commercial production begins. At that time, the amortization of development costs over the useful life of the product or process developed would commence.

Intangible Assets with Indefinite Lives

Just as land is considered to have an indefinite life, there are also intangible assets with indefinite lives. An intangible asset is considered to have an indefinite life when there is no foreseeable limit to the length of time over which the asset is expected to generate economic benefits for the company. Examples of intangible assets with indefinite lives include trademarks, trade names, and brands; certain franchises; and licences, although some of these assets can also have definite lives. If they do, they would be amortized over the shorter of their legal lives and useful lives. It is more usual, however, for these intangible assets to have indefinite lives, so they are not amortized.

TRADEMARKS (TRADE NAMES) A **trademark** (**trade name**) is a word, phrase, jingle, or symbol that distinguishes or identifies a particular business or product. Trade names like Blue Jays, Big Mac, Nike, and CBC create immediate brand recognition and generally help the sale of the product or service. Each year, Interbrand ranks the world's best brands. In 2015, the most valuable brand was Apple, valued at U.S. $170 billion, followed by Google at U.S. $120 billion. The most valuable Canadian brand was Thomson Reuters at U.S. $6 billion.

A creator or original user may obtain the exclusive legal right to a trademark or trade name by registering it with the Canadian Intellectual Property Office. This registration provides continuous protection and may be renewed every 15 years as long as the trademark or trade name is in use. In most cases, companies continuously renew their trademarks or trade names. Consequently, as long as the trademark or trade name continues to be marketable, it will have an indefinite useful life.

If the trademark or trade name is purchased, the cost is the purchase price. If it is developed internally rather than purchased, it cannot be recognized as an intangible asset on the statement of financial position. The reason is that expenditures on internally developed trademarks cannot be distinguished from the cost of developing the business as a whole and consequently cannot be measured.

FRANCHISES AND LICENCES   When you purchase a Civic from a Honda dealer, fill up your tank at the corner Irving station, attend an Ottawa Senators hockey game, or order a double-double at Tim Hortons, you are likely dealing with franchises. A **franchise** is a contractual arrangement under which the franchisor grants the franchisee the right to sell certain products, to provide specific services, or to use certain trademarks or trade names, usually within a designated geographic area.

Licences, which grant the holder operating rights, are another type of intangible asset. These include licences for a bus line or taxi service; the use of public land for telephone, power, and cable television lines; and the use of airwaves for wireless devices, radio, or TV broadcasting. These can have finite or indefinite lives and can be valuable. They can also be granted by various levels of government or other organizations. For example, in 2013 the National Hockey League (NHL) signed a 13-year deal for $5.2 billion with Rogers Communications giving it the right to broadcast NHL games in Canada.

GOODWILL

Goodwill is an asset representing the future economic benefits arising from the purchase of a business that are not individually identified and separately recognized. It represents the value of favourable attributes such as exceptional management, a desirable location, good customer relations, skilled employees, high-quality products, fair pricing policies, and harmonious relations with labour unions. Unlike other assets, which can be sold *individually* in the marketplace, goodwill can be identified only with the business *as a whole*. Because it cannot be separated from the company and is not separately identifiable, goodwill is not considered an intangible asset and is reported separately in the assets section of the statement of financial position.

If goodwill can only be identified with the business as a whole, how can its value be determined? Certainly a number of businesses have many of the factors cited above (exceptional management, a desirable location, and so on). If these factors are generated internally, measuring the value of this goodwill would be difficult and subjective, which would not contribute to the reliability of the financial statements. For this reason, goodwill is recorded only when it is purchased, not when it is internally generated. Goodwill is recorded only when it can be measured objectively and this occurs only when there is a purchase of an entire business, at which time an independent valuation of the entire business can be determined.

Goodwill is measured by comparing the amount paid to acquire the business (purchase price) with the fair value of its net identifiable assets (assets less liabilities). Identifiable assets and liabilities are tangible and intangible assets and liabilities that can be specifically identified. If the amount paid to acquire the business is greater than its net identifiable assets, the resulting difference is the purchased goodwill, which can be measured as follows and recorded as an asset.

Because goodwill has an indefinite life, just as the company has an indefinite life, it is not amortized. However, every year an impairment test is performed on goodwill under IFRS, and, if impairment losses are recorded, they cannot be reversed because to do so would be to recognize internally generated goodwill and we only recognize goodwill when it is paid for and can be objectively measured. Under ASPE an impairment test of goodwill is performed only if indicators of impairment exist. Note that goodwill cannot be negative and we will leave the coverage of situations where the purchase price of a business is less than the fair value of net identifiable assets to a more advanced accounting course.

DO IT! ▶9-4 Accounting for Intangibles

Gatineau Ltd. purchased a copyright on a new book series for $15,000 cash on August 1, 2017. The books are anticipated to have a saleable life of three years. One year later, on August 1, 2018, the company spent an additional $6,000 cash to successfully defend the copyright in court. The company's year end is July 31 and it prepares adjusting entries annually. Record (a) the purchase of the copyright on August 1, 2017; (b) the amortization at July 31, 2018; and (c) the legal costs incurred on August 1, 2018.

SOLUTION

Try this Do It! exercise on your own and then check your answer at the end of the chapter.

Related Exercise Material: BE9–13, E9–8, and E9–9.

Action Plan

✔ Amortize intangible assets with limited lives over the shorter of their useful life and legal life. (The legal life of a copyright is the life of the author plus 50 years.)

✔ Treat costs to successfully defend an intangible asset as capital expenditures because they benefit future periods.

LEARNING OBJECTIVE 5

Illustrate how long-lived assets are reported in the financial statements.

In the last few sections, we've looked at three categories of long-lived assets: property, plant, and equipment; intangible assets; and goodwill. They are summarized below:

Classification	Definition	Examples
Property, plant, and equipment	Assets that have physical substance that are used in the operations of a business and are not intended for sale to customers	Land, land improvements, buildings, equipment, furniture
Intangible assets	Assets without physical substance that represent rights, privileges, and/or competitive advantages. They are used in the operations of a business and are not intended for sale to customers.	Patents, copyrights, trademarks, trade names, franchises, licences
Goodwill	The value of favourable attributes related to a company as a whole (cannot be separately identified) when one business acquires another and pays more than the fair value of the net identifiable assets	Goodwill

The long-lived assets listed above have an impact on three financial statements: the statement of financial position, income statement, and statement of cash flows. In addition, if a company chooses to use the revaluation model, any revaluation gains will affect other comprehensive income on the statement of comprehensive income. This statement will be illustrated in Chapter 12.

STATEMENT OF FINANCIAL POSITION

Long-lived assets are normally reported in the statement of financial position under the headings "Property, Plant, and Equipment," "Intangible Assets," and "Goodwill."

Either on the statement of financial position or in the notes to the financial statements, the cost of each of the major classes of assets, such as land and buildings, must be disclosed, as well as the accumulated depreciation or amortization affecting the related assets. In addition, the company must specify which depreciation and amortization methods it uses and the useful lives or rates. This is usually done in the summary of significant accounting policies note. Companies must also disclose their policy for testing for impairments as well as any significant changes in methods or rates that result in a revision of depreciation or amortization.

Under International Financial Reporting Standards, companies also have to disclose if they are using the cost or the revaluation model for each class of assets, and include a reconciliation of the carrying amount at the beginning and end of the period for each class of long-lived assets. This means they must show all of the following for each class of long-lived assets: (1) additions, (2) disposals, (3) depreciation or amortization, (4) impairment losses, and (5) reversals of impairment losses. ASPE does not require disclosure of these details.

Illustration 9-7 shows how WestJet reports summary information related to property, plant, and equipment and intangible assets in its statement of financial position. WestJet does not have any goodwill because it has not purchased any goodwill. Any goodwill that the company has from developing strong relationships with its customers is internally generated goodwill and because this cannot be adequately measured, it is not recorded.

▶Illustration 9-7
WestJet's statement of financial position

WESTJET AIRLINES LTD.
Statement of Financial Position (partial)
December 31, 2015
(in thousands)

Non-current assets	
Property and equipment (Note 6)	$3,473,262
Intangible assets (Note 7)	63,549

The notes to its financial statements report further detail, as shown in Illustration 9-8.

▶Illustration 9-8
WestJet's notes to the financial statements

WESTJET AIRLINES LTD.
Notes to Financial Statements (partial)
December 31, 2015
(in thousands)

Note 6. Property and equipment	Cost	Accumulated Depreciation	Carrying Amount
Aircraft	$3,912,617	$1,170,643	$2,741,974
Ground property and equipment	183,828	111,652	72,176
Spare engines and rotables	240,893	73,447	167,446
Buildings	136,783	30,419	106,364
Leasehold improvements	22,104	11,730	10,374
Other	374,928	—	374,928
	$4,871,153	$1,397,891	$3,473,262

Note 8. Intangible assets	Cost	Accumulated Amortization	Carrying Amount
Software	$ 85,348	$55,707	$29,641
Landing rights	17,781	3,186	14,595
Assets under development	13,704	—	13,704
Other	5,836	227	5,609
	$122,669	$59,120	$63,549

Although information for only 2015 was included in the illustration above, WestJet includes information for 2015 and 2014 in its 2015 financial statements, including a detailed reconciliation of the changes between years. Furthermore, WestJet's statement of significant accounting policies note reports that the company uses the cost model and straight-line depreciation and amortization for all of its long-lived assets over periods ranging from 3 to 40 years for its property and equipment and 5 to 20 years for its intangible assets. The notes to its financial statements also explain how significant components of property, plant, and equipment are accounted for as well as its policy on testing its long-lived assets for impairment, even though there were no impairments recorded in 2015.

INCOME STATEMENT

Depreciation expense, gains and losses on disposal, and impairment losses are presented in the operating expenses section of the income statement. Why this section rather than the other revenues and expenses section of the income statement for gains and losses? Recall that depreciation expense is an estimate. If depreciation is overestimated, a gain on disposal is more likely and, if it is underestimated, a loss on disposal is more likely. Because of this, gains and losses are a function of the depreciation recorded in the past and as such should be recorded in the same section of the income statement as depreciation. Gains would essentially reduce operating expenses, while losses would increase operating expenses.

WestJet reported $264,921 thousand for depreciation and amortization in the operating expenses section of its income statement for the year ended December 31, 2015. It also reported a $1,860 thousand loss from the disposal of property and equipment.

STATEMENT OF CASH FLOWS

The cash flows from the purchase and sale of long-lived assets are reported in the investing activities section of the statement of cash flows. Illustration 9-9 shows the investing activities section of WestJet's statement of cash flows.

►Illustration 9-9
WestJet's statement of cash flows

WESTJET AIRLINES LTD.
Statement of Cash Flows (partial)
Year Ended December 31, 2015
(in thousands)

Investing activities	
Aircraft additions	$(841,491)
Aircraft disposals	83,348
Other property and equipment and intangible additions	(64,789)
Net cash used in investing activities	(822,932)

WestJet is in a growth cycle. The company's purchases of long-lived assets are much greater than the proceeds from the sale of such assets.

Although not shown above, when determining its operating cash flows, WestJet would ensure that depreciation was not considered in this calculation because depreciation is not "paid" like most expenses. Depreciation is an allocation of asset costs to expenses, but when paid, these asset costs would be shown as an investing activity cash payment.

DO IT! ▶9-5 Statement Presentation

For each item listed below, state whether it can be found on the income statement (IS) or on the statement of financial position (SFP). Indicate where it would be classified on each statement.

Accumulated Amortization—Patents
Accumulated Depreciation—Buildings
Accumulated Depreciation—Equipment
Amortization Expense
Assets under Finance Leases

Buildings

Depreciation Expense
Development Costs
Equipment
Gain on Disposal
Goodwill

Impairment Loss

Interest Expense
Land
Loss on Disposal
Patents
Repairs and Maintenance Expense
Research Expenses

Action Plan

✔ Identify which accounts are income statement accounts and which are statement of financial position accounts.

✔ Review the classifications on the multiple-step income statement and distinguish between operating and non-operating items.

✔ Review the classifications of long-lived assets among property, plant, and equipment; intangible assets; and goodwill.

SOLUTION
Try this Do It! exercise on your own and then check your answer at the end of the chapter.

Related Exercise Material: BE9–12, BE9–14, BE9–15, E9–10, and E9–11.

▶6

Describe the methods for evaluating the use of assets.

The presentation of financial statement information about long-lived assets allows decision makers to analyze a company's use of its total assets. We will use two ratios to analyze assets: the return on assets and asset turnover. We will also show how the profit margin relates to both.

RETURN ON ASSETS

The **return on assets** ratio measures overall profitability. This ratio is calculated by dividing net income by average total assets. Recall that average total assets are calculated by adding the beginning and ending amounts of the assets and dividing by 2. The return on assets ratio indicates the amount of net income generated by each dollar invested in assets. The higher the return on assets, the more profitable the company is.

The following information (in thousands) is provided for WestJet Airlines Ltd.:

	2015	2014	2013
Net sales	$4,029,265	$3,976,552	$3,662,197
Net income	367,530	283,957	268,722
Total assets	5,129,024	4,646,433	4,143,463

The return on assets for WestJet is shown in Illustration 9-10. This illustration also shows this ratio for Air Canada, WestJet's major competitor, as well as the industry average.

▶Illustration 9-10
Return on assets

$$\text{RETURN ON ASSETS} = \frac{\text{NET INCOME}}{\text{AVERAGE TOTAL ASSETS}}$$		
($ in thousands)	2015	2014
WestJet	$\dfrac{\$367,530}{(\$5,129,024 + \$4,646,433) \div 2} = 7.5\%$	$\dfrac{\$283,957}{(\$4,646,433 + \$4,143,464) \div 2} = 6.5\%$
Air Canada	2.6%	1.0%
Industry average	2.9%	2.3%

As the illustration shows, WestJet's return on assets improved in 2015 compared with 2014. From this ratio, we can see that for every dollar WestJet invested in assets, it was able to generate $0.075 in net income. In both years, it was above the industry average, while Air Canada's return on assets, although improving, was not above the industry average in either year.

ASSET TURNOVER

The **asset turnover** ratio indicates how efficiently a company uses its assets; that is, how many dollars of sales are generated by each dollar invested in assets. It is calculated by dividing net sales by average total assets. When we compare two companies in the same industry, the one with the higher asset turnover ratio is generally perceived to be operating more efficiently because it is generating more sales for every dollar invested in assets.

The asset turnover ratios of WestJet, Air Canada, and their industry for 2015 and 2014 are presented in Illustration 9-11.

▶Illustration 9-11
Asset turnover

($ in thousands)	$\text{ASSET TURNOVER} = \dfrac{\text{NET SALES}}{\text{AVERAGE TOTAL ASSETS}}$	
	2015	2014
WestJet	$\dfrac{\$4,029,265}{(\$5,129,024 + \$4,646,433) \div 2} = 0.8$ times	$\dfrac{\$3,976,552}{(\$4,646,433 + \$4,143,464) \div 2} = 0.9$ times
Air Canada	1.2 times	1.3 times
Industry average	1.0 times	0.9 times

The asset turnover ratios in the illustration indicate that for each dollar invested in assets in 2015, WestJet generated sales of $0.80 and Air Canada $1.20. WestJet's asset turnover was lower than Air Canada's, and slightly lower than the industry average.

The main reason for WestJet's lower asset turnover ratio was not a lower numerator but a higher denominator as WestJet made a significant amount of aircraft purchases in 2015. Note that, in calculating the asset turnover ratio, we assume that the age of the depreciable assets is about the same for each company. If this assumption is not valid, the company with the newer, less depreciated assets will tend to have a lower turnover ratio, as we found with WestJet.

PROFIT MARGIN REVISITED

For a complete picture of the sales-generating ability of assets, it is also important to look at a company's profit margin ratio. In Chapter 5, you first learned about the profit margin. Profit margin is calculated by dividing net income by net sales. It tells how effective a company is in turning its sales into income; that is, how much net income is generated by each dollar of sales.

Together, the profit margin and asset turnover explain the return on assets ratio. Illustration 9-12 shows how return on assets can be calculated from the profit margin and asset turnover ratios for WestJet in 2015.

▶Illustration 9-12
Composition of WestJet's 2015
return on assets (in thousands)

PROFIT MARGIN	×	ASSET TURNOVER	=	RETURN ON ASSETS
$\dfrac{\text{Net Income}}{\text{Net Sales}}$	×	$\dfrac{\text{Net Sales}}{\text{Average Total Assets}}$	=	$\dfrac{\text{Net Income}}{\text{Average Total Assets}}$
$\dfrac{\$367,530}{\$4,029,265}$ $= 9.1\%$	×	$\dfrac{\$4,029,265}{(\$5,129,024 + \$4,646,433) \div 2}$ $= 0.8$ times	=	$\dfrac{\$367,530}{(\$5,129,024 + \$4,646,433) \div 2}$ $= 7.5\%$

You can see the mathematical connections in the above illustration in that net sales in the denominator of the profit margin calculation cancels the net sales in the numerator of the asset turnover calculation when we calculate return on assets. That said, if you multiply 9.1% by 0.8, you get a result of 7.3% and not 7.5%. This is simply because of rounding differences—we have chosen to present results rounded to one decimal place in this text. If you use unrounded numbers in your calculations, this equation works perfectly.

The relationship of asset turnover and profit margin to the return on assets has important implications for management. From Illustration 9-12, we can see that, if a company wants to increase its return on assets, it can do so either by increasing the margin it generates from each dollar of goods that it sells (profit margin), or by increasing the volume of goods or services that it sells (asset turnover).

Let's evaluate WestJet's return on assets for 2015 again, but this time by evaluating the ratio's components: the profit margin and asset turnover ratios. WestJet has a profit margin of 9.1%.

Compared with an industry average for the profit margin of 2.9%, WestJet is far more profitable. Two possible explanations could be higher ticket prices or better control of costs. Given that WestJet is a discount airline, its superior profitability comes from low costs. This advantage is offset by lower asset turnover. Despite this, WestJet still maintains a higher overall return on assets than its nearest competitor, Air Canada.

DO IT! ▶9-6 Analyze Assets

Action Plan

✔ Recall the formulas for each ratio: Profit margin = net income ÷ net sales; asset turnover = net sales ÷ average total assets; return on assets = net income ÷ average total assets.

✔ If the ratio changed compared with the prior year, determine if the change is a result of the numerator or the denominator changing the most.

✔ Remember how the profit margin and asset turnover ratios are components of the return on assets ratio so use them in order to explain the return on assets ratio.

Saluda Enterprises Ltd. and Unami Corporation are competitors that manufacture household appliances. Early in 2018, Saluda's management team found a Mexican company that could supply some of the components used in their appliances at a reduced cost. They decided to pass some, but not all, of these savings on to customers so they lowered their prices in an effort to boost the number of appliances sold. Unami reacted to this strategy in late 2018 when it bought the Mexican company that was supplying Saluda with products.

Listed below are selected amounts taken from the financial statements of these competitors. Calculate the (a) profit margin, (b) asset turnover, and (c) return on assets. (d) Explain whether ratios improved or deteriorated, and why, between 2017 and 2018. Assume that for each company, there was no change in total assets between 2017 and 2016.

($ in thousands)	Saluda		Unami	
	2018	2017	2018	2017
Net sales	$1,200	$1,000	$1,800	$2,000
Net income	110	80	170	200
Total assets	540	500	1,200	800

SOLUTION

Try this Do It! exercise on your own and then check your answer at the end of the chapter.

Related Exercise Material: BE9–16, BE9–17, E9–12, and E9–13.

REVIEW AND PRACTICE

▶ LEARNING OBJECTIVE REVIEW

1. Determine the cost of property, plant, and equipment. The cost of land, land improvements, buildings, and equipment includes all expenditures that are necessary to acquire these assets and make them ready for their intended use. After acquisition, costs incurred that benefit future periods (capital expenditures) are also included in the cost of the asset, whereas costs that benefit only the current period (operating expenditures) are expensed. When applicable, cost also includes asset retirement costs.

If a company leases an asset, it may be accounted for as an operating lease or a finance lease. An operating lease results in rent expense on the income statement. A finance lease results in recording the leased asset as if it were purchased, with a corresponding liability for the future lease payments to be made. This gives rise to depreciation on the asset and interest on the liability for the payments being recorded in the future. Under IFRS, most leases with a term greater than 12 months are to be accounted for as finance leases starting in 2019. The ASPE criteria for determining whether a leased asset is operating or not are covered in intermediate accounting courses.

2. Explain and calculate depreciation. Depreciation is the process of allocating the cost of a long-lived asset to expense over the asset's useful (service) life in a systematic way. There are three commonly used depreciation methods: straight-line, diminishing-balance, and units-of-production.

Method	Annual Depreciation Pattern	Calculation
Straight-line	Constant amount	(Cost – residual value) ÷ estimated useful life (in years)
Diminishing-balance	Diminishing amount	Carrying amount at beginning of year × depreciation rate (straight-line rate × multiplier)
Units-of-production	Varying amount	(Cost – residual value) ÷ estimated total units of activity × actual activity during the year

Other accounting issues related to depreciation include (1) identifying significant components of a long-lived asset for which different depreciation methods or rates may be appropriate; (2) capital cost allowance (CCA) used for income tax purposes; (3) testing long-lived assets for impairment; (4) accounting for property, plant, and equipment using the cost or revaluation model; and (5) circumstances under which a revision of depreciation is required.

3. Account for the derecognition of property, plant, and equipment. The procedure for accounting for the disposal of property, plant, and equipment through sale or retirement is:

Step 1: Update depreciation for any partial period.
Step 2: Calculate the carrying amount.
Step 3: Calculate any gain (proceeds less carrying amount). If the carrying amount is greater than proceeds, then there is a loss on disposal.
Step 4: Derecognize (remove) the asset and accumulated depreciation accounts related to the sold or retired asset. Record the proceeds received and the gain or loss (if any).

4. Identify the basic accounting issues for intangible assets and goodwill. Intangible assets (which we have assumed are accounted for under the cost model) are initially reported at cost, which includes all expenditures that are necessary to prepare the asset for its intended use. An intangible asset with a finite life is amortized over the shorter of its useful life or legal life, usually on a straight-line basis. Like property, plant, and equipment, intangible assets with finite lives are tested for impairment only if indicators of impairment are present. Intangible assets with indefinite lives are not amortized and must be tested for impairment annually under IFRS but only when indicators of impairment are present under ASPE. Impairment losses can be reversed under IFRS but not under ASPE.

Goodwill, which is the difference between the price paid for a business and the fair value of the identifiable assets less liabilities of the business, is not considered an intangible asset because it is not separately "identifiable." Only purchased, not internally generated, goodwill can be recorded. Goodwill has an indefinite life and is not amortized. Impairment tests for goodwill are similar to those for intangibles with indefinite lives. Goodwill impairment losses are never reversed.

5. Illustrate how long-lived assets are reported in the financial statements. In the statement of financial position, land, land improvements, buildings, and equipment are usually combined and shown under the heading "Property, Plant, and Equipment." Intangible assets with finite and indefinite lives are sometimes combined under the heading "Intangible Assets" or are listed separately. Goodwill must be presented separately.

Either on the statement of financial position or in the notes to the financial statements, the cost of the major classes of long-lived assets is presented. The depreciation and amortization methods and rates must also be described in the notes to the statements. The accumulated depreciation and amortization of depreciable/amortizable assets and carrying amount by major classes are also disclosed, including a reconciliation of the carrying amount at the beginning and end of each period for companies reporting under IFRS. The company's impairment policy and any impairment losses should be described and reported. The company must disclose whether it is using the cost or revaluation model.

Depreciation expense, any gain or loss on disposal, and any impairment losses are reported as operating expenses in the income statement. In the statement of cash flows, any cash flows from the purchase or sale of long-lived assets are reported as investing activities.

6. Describe the methods for evaluating the use of assets. The use of assets may be analyzed using the return on assets and asset turnover ratios. Return on assets (net income ÷ average total assets) indicates how well assets are used to generate net income. Return on assets can be determined by multiplying two ratios: asset turnover (net sales ÷ average total assets), which indicates how efficiently assets are used to generate revenue, and profit margin (net income ÷ net sales), which measures the net income made on each sale.

▶ KEY TERM REVIEW

The following are key terms defined in this chapter with the corresponding page reference for your review. You will find a complete list of terms and definitions for all chapters in the glossary at the end of this textbook.

Amortizable amount (p. 483)
Amortization (p. 483)
Asset retirement costs (p. 464)
Asset turnover (p. 490)
Capital expenditures (p. 464)
Copyright (p. 484)
Cost model (p. 468)
Depreciable amount (p. 469)
Development costs (p. 485)

Diminishing-balance method (p. 471)
Finance lease (p. 467)
Franchise (p. 486)
Goodwill (p. 486)
Impairment loss (p. 476)
Licences (p. 486)
Operating expenditures (p. 464)
Operating lease (p. 467)
Patent (p. 484)

Research Expenses (p. 485)
Residual value (p. 469)
Return on assets (p. 490)
Revaluation model (p. 476)
Straight-line method (p. 470)
Trademark (trade name) (p. 485)
Units-of-production method (p. 473)

▶ COMPARING IFRS AND ASPE REVIEW

Key Differences	International Financial Reporting Standards (IFRS)	Accounting Standards for Private Enterprises (ASPE)
Terminology	Leases that are essentially the purchase of an asset are called *finance leases*. *Depreciation* is used to describe cost allocation for property, plant, and equipment.	Leases that are essentially the purchase of an asset are known as *capital leases*. *Amortization* may be used instead of *depreciation* for property, plant, and equipment.
Models for valuing property, plant, and equipment	Choice of cost model or revaluation model.	Only cost model allowed.
Impairment requirements for property, plant, and equipment and intangible assets with finite lives	Must determine each year if indicators of impairment are present and, if so, perform an impairment test. Reversals of impairment losses are allowed.	Impairment tests differ between IFRS and ASPE. Reversals of impairment losses are not allowed.
Disclosure	Must provide a reconciliation of the opening and closing carrying amounts of each class of long-lived assets.	Reconciliation not required.

▶ DECISION TOOLKIT REVIEW

DECISION CHECKPOINTS	INFO NEEDED FOR DECISION	TOOLS TO USE FOR DECISION	HOW TO EVALUATE RESULTS
What is the impact of the choice of depreciation method?	Depreciation policy	Income statement, statement of financial position, and accounting policy note to the statements	In the early years, straight-line depreciation results in lower depreciation and higher net income compared with the diminishing-balance method. The opposite is true in later years. It also results in higher total assets and higher shareholders' equity on the statement of financial position. Results under the units-of-production method will vary. Depreciation does not affect cash flows.
Are the company's long-lived assets over- or undervalued?	Impairment loss; carrying amount of long-lived assets	Compare the carrying and recoverable amounts in light of current business conditions and company performance.	If assets have been adjusted for impairment, depreciation will be lower in the future. If assets are substantially impaired, be cautious when interpreting ratios that use carrying amounts, because these ratios may not be comparable with those of other companies.
Should the company use the cost model or the revaluation model?	Cost and current value of assets	Compare the cost and current value amounts, as well as the cost of determining the current value amounts.	If using the revaluation model would assist users' decision-making, it should be adopted, although the cost of doing so should be considered.
Is the company's amortization of intangibles reasonable?	The estimated useful lives of intangibles with finite lives from notes to the financial statements of both the company and its competitors	If the company's estimated useful lives are significantly higher than those of its competitors, or do not seem reasonable in light of the circumstances, the reason for the difference should be investigated.	Too high an estimated useful life will result in understating amortization expense and overstating net income and assets.
Is the company's goodwill overvalued?	Impairment loss; carrying amount and current value of the company	Determine if an impairment loss has been recorded and what circumstances led to the impairment.	If goodwill is significant and values are fluctuating, consider excluding goodwill from ratio analysis.

DECISION CHECKPOINTS	INFO NEEDED FOR DECISION	TOOLS TO USE FOR DECISION	HOW TO EVALUATE RESULTS
How efficient is the company at generating profit from its assets?	Net income and average total assets	Return on assets = $\dfrac{\text{Net income}}{\text{Average total assets}}$	Indicates the net income generated per dollar of assets. A high value suggests that the company is efficient in using its resources to generate net income.
How efficient is the company at generating sales from its assets?	Net sales and average total assets	Asset turnover = $\dfrac{\text{Net sales}}{\text{Average total assets}}$	Indicates the sales dollars generated per dollar of assets. A high value suggests that the company is efficient in using its resources to generate sales.

▶ PRACTICE USING THE DECISION TOOLKIT

Answers are at the end of the chapter.

Transat A.T. Inc. is an international, publicly traded company, headquartered in Canada. It owns an air carrier (Air Transat) and provides holiday travel packages to numerous countries. Selected information from its statement of financial position follows:

TRANSAT A.T. INC.
Statement of Financial Position (partial)
October 31
(in thousands)

Assets	2015	2014
Property, plant and equipment	$ 133,502	$ 128,560
Intangible assets	79,863	72,769
Goodwill	99,527	95,601
Total assets	1,513,764	1,375,030

Selected information from Transat's income statement follows:

	2015	2014
Revenues	$3,566,368	$3,752,198
Depreciation expense	37,314	35,001
Amortization expense	12,417	10,711
Impairment of goodwill	—	369
Net income	46,964	26,066

INSTRUCTIONS

(a) Similar to WestJet, Transat depreciates its property, plant, and equipment using the straight-line method. It also separates its long-lived assets into significant components in the same manner as WestJet. However, where WestJet depreciates its aircraft over 15 to 20 years, Transat depreciates its aircraft over seven to 10 years. (1) What is a reason why Transat might use a different useful life than WestJet? (2) Assuming all other factors are equal, what impact would this difference in useful lives have on your comparison of the depreciation expense and net income (or loss) of each company?

(b) Transat reports two different kinds of intangible assets with finite lives: software and customer lists. It amortizes these on a straight-line basis over their useful lives. It also reports trademarks as an intangible asset, which it does not amortize. Why do you think that Transat is not amortizing its trademarks?

(c) Goodwill is not amortized but is tested annually for impairment. In 2014, Transat recorded a $369,000 impairment loss, primarily due to the restructuring of its operations. Business conditions improved in 2015 but the goodwill impairment was not reversed. Why?

(d) Calculate Transat's return on assets and asset turnover ratios for 2015 and compare them with those of WestJet, Air Canada, and the industry information given in the chapter.

▶ PRACTICE COMPREHENSIVE DO IT!

Answers are at the end of the chapter.

Dulcimer Ltd. purchased equipment at a cost of $68,000 on June 1, 2018. Dulcimer paid $1,200 to ship the equipment to the company's location, $800 to install the equipment, and $1,500 to train a staff member to operate the equipment. The equipment was expected to have a residual value of $6,000 at the end of its four-year useful life. Dulcimer has a December 31 year end and prepares adjusting entries annually.

During its useful life, the equipment was expected to be used for 10,000 hours. Anticipated annual hourly use was as follows: 1,300 hours in 2018, 2,800 hours in 2019, 3,300 hours in 2020, 1,900 hours in 2021, and 700 hours in 2022.

INSTRUCTIONS

(a) Prepare the cost of the equipment and prepare depreciation schedules showing the expected depreciation expense for 2018 to 2022 using the following methods: (1) straight-line, (2) diminishing-balance using double the straight-line rate, and (3) units-of-production.

(b) Prepare the journal entry to record the retirement of the equipment on June 1, 2022, assuming that the straight-line depreciation method was used and the equipment was retired at the end of its useful life for no proceeds. Then redo the journal entry assuming that the equipment was sold for $9,000 cash.

▶ PRACTICE OBJECTIVE-FORMAT QUESTIONS

Answers are at the end of the chapter.

1. Colby Ltd. purchased equipment and incurred the costs listed below. For each of the costs shown below, determine if it is correct to capitalize the cost and include it in the Equipment account balance. (Select as many as are appropriate.)

(a) Costs incurred to test the equipment
(b) Installation costs
(c) Insurance on equipment while in transit
(d) Training workers to use the equipment
(e) Cost of additional electricity used by the equipment after it was installed

(f) Freight to ship equipment to Colby, FOB shipping point
(g) Annual premium for insurance on the equipment after it is acquired

2. Which of the following items is correct with regard to having an operating lease rather than purchasing an asset with borrowed funds from a bank loan? (Select as many as are appropriate.)

(a) There is a reduced risk of obsolescence with a lease.
(b) Less cash is paid out initially with a lease when the asset is received.
(c) Whether the asset is leased or purchased, legal title will pass to the party that is using the asset.
(d) A large long-term liability for future rent payments is not shown on the statement of financial position with an operating lease.

(e) The rented asset will appear on the statement of financial position when an operating lease is entered into.
(f) There is no effect on current liabilities if an operating lease is entered into and payments are made when due.
(g) Depreciation is not recorded on an asset with an operating lease.

3. A company just hired an accountant. It turns out the accountant is unethical and wants to increase the company's net income because her bonus is based on net income. The company has some equipment that was recently purchased and should be depreciated using the straight-line method. Estimates for residual value and useful life were determined before the accountant was hired. In an effort to increase net income, the accountant might do which of the following? (Select as many as are appropriate.)

(a) Increase the residual value of the equipment
(b) Use the diminishing-balance method to record depreciation
(c) Decrease the useful life of the equipment
(d) Expense a major addition to the equipment that was just incurred

(e) Capitalize repair costs on the equipment that were just incurred
(f) Increase the useful life of the equipment
(g) Decrease the residual value of the equipment

4. Which of the following items would most likely be depreciated using the straight-line method? (Select as many as are appropriate.)

(a) Snow removal equipment
(b) Heavy duty automotive equipment that requires significant repairs as it ages
(c) Buildings
(d) Leasehold improvements

(e) Helicopters that require more "down time" for maintenance and safety inspections as they age
(f) Furniture
(g) Lawn maintenance equipment

5. Which of the following statements is correct? (Select as many as are appropriate.)

(a) When calculating depreciation under the units-of-production method, if the related asset was used for only part of the year, we would have to multiply the depreciation rate times units produced by the portion of the year that the asset was used.
(b) The straight-line method takes into consideration the amount of residual value that the asset will have.
(c) If a company purchases equipment this year and uses a depreciation method that determines depreciation expense to be the lowest amount of all possible methods that could be used, choosing this method will give the highest amount of total assets and the highest amount of total equity of all possible methods.
(d) In the final year of an asset's useful life, depreciation under a diminishing-balance

method would most likely be higher than depreciation under the straight-line method.
(e) If a company using the straight-line method overestimated the amount of an asset's residual value, depreciation expense will be understated.
(f) If a company recorded depreciation for equipment expecting it to have a useful life of six years and the equipment was then sold after four years at a larger-than-expected loss, this may indicate that the estimated useful life was too long.
(g) Because the diminishing-balance method does not consider the residual value of an asset when calculating depreciation expense, it is appropriate to depreciate the asset to a carrying amount that is lower than its residual value.

6. A company has equipment that was purchased on January 1, 2014, for $12,000. The company has a December 31 year end and uses the straight-line method of depreciation. Management estimated the useful life of the equipment at five years and its residual value at $2,000. The equipment was sold on October 1, 2018, for $3,200. Which of the following statements shown below are correct? (Select as many as are appropriate.)

(a) Depreciation expense for 2018 would be $2,000.
(b) A gain on disposal would be recorded in 2018 for $1,200.
(c) When recording the disposal, a debit to Cash of $3,200 would be recorded.
(d) When recording the disposal, Accumulated Depreciation would be debited by $10,000.

(e) The carrying amount of the equipment when it was disposed would have been $2,500.
(f) When recording the disposal, the Equipment account would be credited by $12,000.
(g) The gain on disposal is shown below the income from operations subtotal on the income statement.

7. Pierce Inc. incurred $300,000 of costs in January 2018 to develop a new product that met the criteria for capitalization. In the following month, on February 2, $10,000 was paid to register a patent on the product but the patent application was denied. To make the new product, a machine costing $80,000 was purchased on April 1, 2018, and production of the new product began immediately. No product was sold until July of that year. The machine can be operated for 10 years, after which it would have no residual value. However, the machine is very specialized (no other company would want to use it) and will only be used to produce the new product, which is expected to sell for six years. Pierce has a December 31 year end and uses the straight-line method when depreciating and amortizing assets. Which of the following statements is correct? (Select as many as are appropriate.)

(a) Depreciation expense on the machine for 2018 is $8,000.
(b) An impairment loss of $10,000 will be recorded on the patent.
(c) Development costs will be amortized by $37,500 in 2018.
(d) The development costs should not be amortized until products are sold.

(e) The machine should be depreciated over a six-year period.
(f) If the machine is used for six years, it will have a residual value at that time.
(g) The cost of the patent should be capitalized as part of the development costs because it was still incurred regardless of its lack of success.

8. Which items shown below are correct? (Select as many as are appropriate.)

(a) The type and cost of each major type of long-lived asset is usually shown on the statement of financial position or in the notes to the financial statements.

(b) The method of depreciation must be disclosed in the notes to the financial statements but the duration of useful life does not have to be mentioned.

(c) Goodwill must be shown on the statement of financial position separately from intangible assets.

(d) Under IFRS, it is typical to prepare a note detailing the effects of additions and disposals on the cost of each major type of long-lived asset.

(e) Property, plant, and equipment are not normally combined with intangible assets when presenting amounts on the statement of financial position.

(f) Depreciation is usually shown as a separate expense in the income statement.

(g) Gains and losses from the disposal of property, plant, and equipment are shown below income from operations on the income statement.

9. An accountant has just prepared some draft financial statements for a company. After reviewing the statements, an auditor explained that the accountant made two errors: First of all, he assumed that equipment that was purchased at the beginning of the current year had a residual value when it had none. Second, he estimated that the useful life of that same equipment was six years instead of four years. Because of these errors, which of the following statements is correct? (Select as many as are appropriate.)

(a) Depreciation expense is overstated.

(b) The carrying amount of equipment is understated.

(c) The asset turnover is understated.

(d) The profit margin ratio is overstated.

(e) Net income is overstated.

(f) Income from operations is understated.

(g) Retained earnings are overstated.

10. Which of the following statements would cause the asset turnover to increase and the profit margin to decrease compared with the prior year? (Select as many as are appropriate.)

(a) Revenues have risen due to greater demand for the products sold but net income has remained the same while assets have fallen.

(b) Revenues and assets have remained the same but the company has cut costs so net income has increased.

(c) Revenues have not changed but the company has purchased more assets and implemented better cost controls so expenses have fallen.

(d) Revenues have fallen due to lower demand for products and the company has kept its assets at the same level as last year and has cut expenses, resulting in increased net income.

(e) Revenues have risen even though assets and net income have remained unchanged.

(f) Despite an increase in assets, revenues have fallen but expenses have been cut significantly and the company's net income has risen.

(g) The economy is not strong and revenues are the same as last year while assets are falling and expenses are rising.

WileyPLUS

Brief Exercises, Exercises, and many additional resources are available for practice in WileyPLUS.

▶ QUESTIONS

(LO 1) 1. (a) Susan Leung is uncertain about how to determine the cost of property, plant, and equipment. Explain this for her. (b) Susan also wants you to explain the difference between a capital and an operating expenditure and (c) tell her what an asset retirement cost is and how that affects the cost of property, plant, and equipment.

(LO 1) 2. What are land improvements? Should the cost of clearing and grading land be recorded as a land improvement? Why or why not?

(LO 1) 3. Explain the difference between an operating lease and a finance lease. What accounts are recorded on the financial statements for each type of lease?

(LO 2) 4. Contrast the effects of the three depreciation methods on (1) depreciation expense, (2) net income, (3) accumulated depreciation, and (4) carrying amount in each of the following: (a) the early years of an asset's life, and (b) over the total life of the asset.

(LO 2) 5. Why is the depreciable amount (the asset's cost less residual value) used in the straight-line and units-of-production methods but not in the diminishing-balance method?

(LO 2) 6. Why must the calculation of depreciation be adjusted for any fraction of a year after the purchase when the straight-line and diminishing-balance methods are used, but no adjustment is needed when the units-of-production method is used?

(LO 2) 7. (a) What factors should a company consider when choosing among the straight-line, diminishing-balance, or units-of-production depreciation methods? (b) When choosing between the cost model or revaluation model?

(LO 2) 8. (a) How is an impairment loss calculated? Recorded? (b) How can impairment losses create problems for users in comparing the financial results of a company over multiple years?

(LO 2) 9. In a recent news release, the president of Franklin Company asserted that "something has to be done about depreciation." The president said, "Depreciation does not come close to accumulating the cash needed to replace the asset at the end of its useful life." What is your response to the president?

(LO 3) 10. If equipment is sold in the middle of a fiscal year, why does depreciation have to be updated for the partial period? Doesn't the journal entry to record the sale subsequently remove the accumulated depreciation from the books anyway?

(LO 3) 11. How is a gain or loss on the disposal of property, plant, or equipment calculated? Is the calculation the same for the retirement of property, plant, or equipment?

(LO 3) 12. Rashid Corporation owns a machine that is fully depreciated but is still being used. How should Rashid account for this asset and report it in the financial statements?

(LO 2, 4) 13. What are the similarities and differences between accounting for tangible and intangible assets?

(LO 4) 14. Why are intangible assets with a finite life amortized, but intangible assets with an indefinite life are not?

(LO 4) 15. Heflin Corporation has been amortizing its finite-life intangible assets over their legal lives. The company's accountant argues that this is appropriate because an intangible asset's legal life is known with certainty, but the useful life of an intangible asset is subjective. (a) Is the accountant's argument valid? Why or why not? (b) What impact might using the legal life instead of the useful life have on the company's financial statements?

(LO 4) 16. In what way does goodwill differ from an intangible asset? In what way are they similar? Why is goodwill not amortized?

(LO 4) 17. Two years ago, Pesowski Corp. purchased a patent for $5 million that allows the company to produce and sell a special video game controller. During the year, the company determined that Sucha Ltd. was producing and selling a similar game controller. Pesowski spent $100,000 on legal fees to successfully enforce its rights under the patent. How should Pesowski account for the legal fees and why?

(LO 4) 18. Bob Leno, a business student, is working on a case for one of his classes. The company in the case needs to raise cash to market a new product it has developed. His roommate, Saul Cain, an engineering student, takes one look at the company's statement of financial position and says, "This company has an awful lot of goodwill. Why don't you recommend that they sell some of it to raise cash?" How should Bob respond to Saul?

(LO 5) 19. Explain how long-lived assets and transactions relating to them should be reported on the (a) statement of financial position, (b) income statement, and (c) statement of cash flows.

(LO 5) 20. What information about long-lived assets should be disclosed in the notes to the financial statements for a company reporting under IFRS? Under ASPE?

(LO 5) 21. Why are gains and losses on disposal of property, plant, and equipment presented in the operating section of the income statement rather than the non-operating section?

(LO 6) 22. Would an accounting firm be characterized by (a) a high asset turnover and low profit margin, or (b) a low asset turnover and high profit margin? What about a company that operated a chain of grocery stores?

(LO 6) 23. How can the profit margin and asset turnover ratios be used to help explain the return on assets?

(LO 6) 24. In 2015, **Shaw Communications Inc.** reported net sales of $5,488 million, net income of $880 million, and average total assets of $13,907 million. In 2014, its net sales were $5,421 million, net income was $887 million, and average total assets were $12,991 million. Did the company's return on assets and asset turnover ratios improve or deteriorate in 2015?

▶ BRIEF EXERCISES

BE9–1 These expenditures were incurred by Shumway Ltd. in purchasing land: cash price $450,000; legal fees $8,500; removal of old building $25,000; cost of clearing and grading $6,500; installation of fence $3,000. What is the cost of the land?

Determine cost.
(LO 1)

BE9–2 Basler Ltd. incurred these expenditures when purchasing a truck: invoice price $42,000; installation of a trailer hitch $1,000; one-year accident insurance policy $900; motor vehicle licence $150; painting and lettering $750. What is the cost of the truck?

Determine cost.
(LO 1)

BE9–3 Indicate whether each of the following items is an operating expenditure (O) or a capital expenditure (C). If the expenditure is neither, write NA for "not applicable" in the space provided.

Identify operating and capital expenditures.
(LO 1)

(a) _____ Repaired building roof, $1,500
(b) _____ Replaced building roof, $27,500
(c) _____ Purchased building, $480,000
(d) _____ Purchased insurance on equipment in transit, $350
(e) _____ Purchased truck, $55,000
(f) _____ Purchased oil and gas for truck, $155
(g) _____ Replaced tires on truck, $500
(h) _____ Anticipated retirement costs for plant, $500,000
(i) _____ Added new wing to building, $250,000
(j) _____ Painted interior of building, $6,500

Calculate straight-line depreciation.
(LO 2)

BE9–4 Buckingham Ltd. purchased a delivery truck on January 1, 2018, at a cost of $80,000. The truck is expected to have a residual value of $8,000 at the end of its four-year useful life. Buckingham has a December 31 year end. Calculate the depreciation using the straight-line method (a) for each year of the truck's life, and (b) in total over the truck's life.

Calculate partial-year straight-line depreciation.
(LO 2)

BE9–5 Depreciation information for Buckingham Ltd. is given in BE9–4. Assuming the delivery truck was purchased on May 1 instead of January 1 and that the company records depreciation to the nearest month, calculate the depreciation expense using the straight-line method for 2018 and 2019.

Calculate diminishing-balance depreciation.
(LO 2)

BE9–6 Depreciation information for Buckingham Ltd. is given in BE9–4. Using the diminishing-balance method and assuming the depreciation rate is equal to double the straight-line rate, calculate the depreciation (a) for each year of the truck's life, and (b) in total over the truck's life.

Calculate partial-year diminishing-balance depreciation.
(LO 2)

BE9–7 Depreciation information for Buckingham Ltd. is given in BE9–4. Assuming the delivery truck was purchased on May 1 instead of January 1, calculate the depreciation expense using the diminishing-balance method for 2018 and 2019. Assume the depreciation rate is equal to one time the straight-line rate.

Calculate units-of-production depreciation.
(LO 2)

BE9–8 Speedy Taxi Service uses the units-of-production method to calculate depreciation on its taxicabs. Each cab is expected to be driven 325,000 km over its life. Taxi 10 was purchased on March 1, 2017, for $33,000 and is expected to have a residual value of $500. Taxi 10 was driven 125,000 km in 2017 and 105,000 km in 2018. Speedy Taxi Service has a December 31 year end. Calculate the depreciation expense on Taxi 10 for 2017 and 2018.

Calculate carrying amount and impairment loss.
(LO 2)

BE9–9 Tibble Corporation uses straight-line depreciation, prepares adjusting entries annually, and has a December 31 year end. It purchased equipment on January 1, 2017, for $200,000. The equipment had an estimated useful life of five years and a residual value of $20,000. On December 31, 2018, the company tests for impairment and determines that the equipment's recoverable amount is $100,000. (a) Assuming annual depreciation has already been recorded at December 31, calculate the equipment's carrying amount at December 31, 2018. (b) Calculate the amount of the impairment loss, if any.

Record sale of equipment.
(LO 3)

BE9–10 Goo-Yeong Limited sells equipment on September 30, 2018, for $42,000 cash. The equipment originally cost $144,000 when purchased on January 1, 2016. It has an estimated residual value of $4,000 and a useful life of five years. Depreciation was last recorded on December 31, 2017, the company's year end. Prepare the journal entries to (a) update depreciation using the straight-line method to September 30, 2018, and (b) record the sale of the equipment.

Record retirement of equipment.
(LO 3)

BE9–11 Ruiz Ltd. retires equipment that cost $42,000. No proceeds were received. Prepare journal entries to record the transaction if accumulated depreciation is (a) $42,000, and (b) $40,000.

Record patent transactions; show statement presentation.
(LO 4, 5)

BE9–12 Surkis Corporation purchased a patent for $180,000 cash on April 2, 2018. Its legal life is 20 years and its estimated useful life is 5 years. The company's year end is December 31 and it prepares adjusting entries annually. (a) Prepare the journal entry to record the (1) purchase of the patent on April 2, 2018, and (2) amortization for the first year ended December 31, 2018. (b) Show how the patent would be reported on the statement of financial position at December 31.

Record trademark transactions.
(LO 4)

BE9–13 A company manufacturing hockey bags registered trademarks for $1,000 cash for its revolutionary RackDri hockey bags on June 1, 2018. On December 1, 2018, it paid $10,000 cash for legal costs to successfully defend its trademarks in court. (a) Prepare the journal entry to record the (1) registration of the trademarks on June 1, and (2) legal costs on December 1. (b) Should the cost of the trademarks be amortized? Explain.

Classify long-lived assets.
(LO 5)

BE9–14 Indicate whether each of the following items should be recorded as property, plant, and equipment (PP&E) or an intangible asset (I) on the statement of financial position. If the asset does not fit either of these categories, write NA for "not applicable" in the space provided.

(a)	_____ Accumulated amortization		(j)	_____ Land improvements
(b)	_____ Asset retirement cost for a factory		(k)	_____ Leasehold improvements
(c)	_____ Assets under finance lease		(l)	_____ Licence right
(d)	_____ Building		(m)	_____ Operating lease
(e)	_____ Franchise		(n)	_____ Patent
(f)	_____ Inventory		(o)	_____ Research costs
(g)	_____ Common shares		(p)	_____ Residual value on building
(h)	_____ Impairment loss		(q)	_____ Trademark
(i)	_____ Land			

BE9–15 Saputo Inc. reported the following selected information about long-lived assets at March 31, 2015 (in millions):

Prepare partial statement of financial position.

(LO 5)

Accumulated depreciation—buildings	$ 218
Accumulated depreciation—furniture, machinery, and equipment	887
Accumulated amortization—finite-life intangible assets	57
Buildings	759
Furniture, machinery, and equipment	2,339
Goodwill	2,125
Indefinite-life intangible assets	318
Finite-life intangible assets	246
Land	66

Prepare the long-lived assets section of the statement of financial position for Saputo Inc.

BE9–16 The Coca-Cola Company and PepsiCo reported the following selected ratios in a recent year:

Compare ratios.

(LO 6)

	Coke	Pepsi
Return on assets	7.8%	8.8%
Asset turnover	0.5 times	0.9 times

(a) Identify which company has the better (1) return on assets ratio and (2) asset turnover ratio. (b) Based on these two ratios, calculate the profit margin of each company and comment on which one has the better profit margin.

BE9–17 Gildan Activewear Inc. reported the following selected financial information (all in U.S. $ millions): net sales of $2,415 in 2015, $2,360 in 2014, and $2,184 in 2013. The company also reported net income of $237 in 2015, $360 in 2014, and $320 in 2013. Assets at the end of 2015 were $2,911; at the end of 2014, $2,593; and at the end of 2013, $2,044. (a) Calculate Gildan's (1) asset turnover, (2) profit margin, and (3) return on assets for 2015 and 2014. (b) Comment on whether the return on assets changed primarily due to a changing asset turnover or a changing profit margin.

Calculate and evaluate ratios.

(LO 6)

▶ EXERCISES

E9–1 The following expenditures relating to property, plant, and equipment were made by Bachinski Ltd.:

1. Paid $1.2 million for a plant site.
2. Paid $8,000 of legal fees on the purchase of the plant site.
3. Paid $39,000 to demolish an old building on the plant site; residual materials were sold for $7,000.
4. Paid $55,000 for paving the parking lot on the plant site.
5. Paid $57,600 in architect fees for the design of the new plant.
6. Promised to pay $150,000 in restoration costs when the company is finished using the plant site.
7. Paid $80,000 for a new delivery truck.
8. Paid $3,000 to have the company name and advertising slogan painted on the new truck.
9. Paid a $400 motor vehicle licence fee on the new truck.
10. Paid $2,800 for a one-year accident insurance policy on the new truck.

Classify expenditures.

(LO 1)

Instructions

(a) Explain what types of expenditures should be included in determining the cost of property, plant, and equipment.
(b) List the numbers of the above transactions, and beside each number write the account title that the expenditure should be debited to.

Calculate cost and depreciation; recommend method.

(LO 1, 2)

E9–2 Hohnberger Enterprises purchased equipment on March 15, 2018, for $75,000. The company also paid the following amounts: $500 for freight charges; $200 for insurance while the equipment was in transit; $1,800 for a one-year insurance policy; $2,100 to train employees to use the new equipment; and $2,800 for testing and installation. The equipment was ready for use on April 1, but the company did not start using it until May 1.

Hohnberger has estimated the equipment will have a 10-year useful life with no residual value. It expects to consume the equipment's future economic benefits evenly over the useful life. The company has a December 31 year end.

Instructions
(a) Calculate the cost of the equipment.
(b) When should the company begin depreciating the equipment: March 15, April 1, or May 1? Why?
(c) Which depreciation method should the company use? Why?
(d) Using the method chosen in part (c), calculate the depreciation on the equipment for 2018.

Calculate and compare depreciation under different methods.

(LO 2)

E9–3 Cirrus Ltd. purchased a new machine on April 4, 2014, at a cost of $172,000. The company estimated that the machine would have a residual value of $16,000. The machine is expected to be used for 10,000 working hours during its four-year life. Actual machine usage was 1,500 hours in 2014; 2,200 hours in 2015; 2,300 hours in 2016; 2,100 hours in 2017; and 1,900 hours in 2018. Cirrus has a December 31 year end.

Instructions
(a) Calculate depreciation for the machine under each of the following methods: (1) straight-line, (2) diminishing-balance using double the straight-line rate, and (3) units-of-production for 2014 through to 2018.
(b) Which method results in the highest depreciation expense over the life of the asset? Highest net income? Highest cash flow?

Calculate straight-line depreciation; discuss revision of estimate.

(LO 2)

E9–4 At the beginning of 2018, Lindy Weink, the controller of Lafrenière Inc., reviewed the expected useful life and residual value of two of the company's machines and proposed changes as follows:

Machine	Date Acquired	Cost	Useful Life (in years)		Residual Value	
			Original	Proposed	Original	Proposed
#1	Jan. 1, 2008	$800,000	20	25	$40,000	$62,000
#2	Jan. 1, 2016	120,000	5	4	5,000	3,600

Instructions
(a) Calculate the annual depreciation for each asset using the straight-line method and the original useful life and residual value.
(b) Calculate the accumulated depreciation and carrying amount of each asset on December 31, 2017.
(c) If the company accepts Lindy's proposed changes in useful life and residual value, will depreciation expense for each asset in 2018 be higher or lower than depreciation expense in 2017? Explain.

Reconstruct equipment transactions.

(LO 2, 3)

E9–5 Shown below are the T accounts relating to equipment that was purchased for cash by a company on the first day of the current year. The equipment was depreciated on a straight-line basis with an estimated useful life of 10 years and a residual value of $100. Part of the equipment was sold on the last day of the current year for cash proceeds while the remaining equipment that was not sold became impaired.

Cash	
	Jan. 1 (a)
Dec. 31 450	

Equipment	
Jan. 1 1,100	
	Dec. 31 440

Accumulated Depreciation—Equipment	
	Dec. 31 100
Dec. 31 40	31 55

Depreciation Expense	
Dec. 31 (b)	

Gain on Disposal	
	Dec. 31 (c)

Impairment Loss	
Dec. 31 (d)	

Instructions
Reconstruct the journal entries to record the following and derive the missing amounts:
(a) Purchase of equipment on January 1. What was the cash paid?
(b) Depreciation recorded on December 31. What was the depreciation expense?
(c) Sale of part of the equipment on December 31. What was the gain on disposal?
(d) Impairment loss on the remaining equipment on December 31. What was the impairment loss?

Determine effect of depreciation method over life of asset.

(LO 2, 3)

E9–6 Rahim Corporation purchased a boardroom table for $17,000. The company planned to keep it for four years, after which it was expected to be sold for $1,000.

Instructions

(a) Calculate the depreciation expense for each of the first three years under (1) the straight-line method, and (2) the double-diminishing-balance method assuming the table was purchased early in the first month of the first year.

(b) Assuming Rahim sold the table for $5,800 at the end of the third year, calculate the gain or loss on disposal under each depreciation method.

(c) Determine the impact on net income (total depreciation of the table plus any loss on disposal or less any gain on disposal) of each method over the entire three-year period.

(d) Which method of depreciation do you believe is the most appropriate for a boardroom table? Why?

E9–7 Presented here are selected transactions for Spector Limited for 2018. Spector uses straight-line depreciation and records adjusting entries annually.

       Record disposal of equipment.

       (LO 3)

Jan. 1   Sold a delivery truck for $18,000 cash. The truck cost $62,000 when it was purchased on January 1, 2015, and was depreciated based on a four-year useful life with a $6,000 residual value.

Sept. 1   Sold computers that were purchased on January 1, 2016. They cost $10,980 and had a useful life of three years with no residual value. The computers were sold for $500 cash.

Dec. 30   Retired equipment that was purchased on January 1, 2009. The equipment cost $150,000 and had a useful life of 10 years with no residual value. No proceeds were received.

Instructions

(a) Record the above transactions.

(b) Assume that, when the delivery truck was sold on January 1, the accountant only recorded a debit to Cash and a credit to Miscellaneous Revenue. Because of this, also assume that the accountant recorded depreciation on this asset for 2018. Discuss what accounts are now overstated or understated as a result of these errors.

E9–8 A co-op student, Toni Johnston, encountered the following situations at Chin Corporation, a publicly traded company:

       Apply accounting concepts.

       (LO 2, 4)

1. Toni learned that Chin is depreciating its buildings and equipment, but not its land. She could not understand why land was omitted, so she prepared journal entries to depreciate all the company's property, plant, and equipment, including land, for the current year.

2. Toni determined that Chin's amortization policy on its intangible assets was wrong. The company was amortizing its patents but not its trademarks. Because of this, she recorded amortization relating to trademarks in an adjusting entry at the end of the year. She told a fellow student that she felt she had improved the consistency of the company's accounting policies by making these changes.

3. Chin has a building still in use that has a zero carrying amount but a substantial current value. Toni felt that this practice did not benefit the company's users and so she wrote the building up to its current value. After all, she reasoned, you can write down assets if current values are lower. Writing them up if current value is higher is yet another example of the improved consistency that her employment has brought to the company's accounting practices.

Instructions

Explain whether or not the accounting treatment in each of the above situations is appropriate. If not, explain what the appropriate accounting treatment should be.

E9–9 Amarista Corporation has the following selected transactions during the year ended December 31, 2018:

       Record intangible asset transactions.

       (LO 4)

Jan. 1   Purchased a copyright for $120,000 cash. The copyright has a useful life of six years and a remaining legal life of 30 years.

Mar. 1   Acquired a franchise with a contract period of nine years for $540,000; the expiration date is March 1, 2027. Paid cash of $40,000 and borrowed the remainder from the bank.

Sept. 1   Purchased a trademark for $75,000 cash. As the purchase was being finalized, spent $35,000 cash in legal fees to successfully defend the trademark in court.

Instructions

(a) Prepare the entries to record the above transactions.

(b) Prepare the entries to record any amortization at December 31.

E9–10 Collins Ltd. has these transactions related to intangible assets and goodwill in 2018, its first year of operations:

       Record intangible asset transactions; show statement presentation.

       (LO 4, 5)

Jan. 2   Purchased a patent with an estimated useful life of five years for $40,000. The company that sold the patent to Collins registered the patent 10 years ago.

Apr. 1   Acquired another company and recorded goodwill of $300,000 as part of the purchase.

July 1   Acquired a franchise for $250,000. The franchise agreement is renewable without charge and not expected to expire.

Sept.	1	Incurred research costs of $150,000.
	30	Incurred development costs of $50,000. A marketable product has been identified and resources have been secured so that production will start next year.
Dec.	31	Recorded annual amortization.
	31	Tested the intangible assets for impairment. Recoverable amounts exceeded carrying amounts for all intangible assets. Also tested goodwill and determined that it had a recoverable amount of $270,000.

Instructions

(a) Prepare the entries to record the above transactions. Assume all costs incurred during January through September were incurred for cash.

(b) Show the presentation of the intangible assets and goodwill on the statement of financial position at December 31.

Classify long-lived accounts; prepare partial statement of financial position.

(LO 5)

E9–11 **Reitmans (Canada) Limited** reported the following selected information as at January 31, 2015 (in thousands):

Accumulated amortization—software	$ 8,184
Accumulated depreciation—buildings	19,096
Accumulated depreciation—fixtures and equipment	68,010
Accumulated depreciation—leasehold improvements	83,299
Amortization expense	3,999
Buildings	45,633
Depreciation expense	42,410
Fixtures and equipment	131,073
Goodwill	42,426
Impairment loss	8,276
Land	5,860
Leasehold improvements	140,188
Operating leases	376,372
Reversal of impairment loss	775
Software (intangible assets)	28,261
Trademarks	499

Instructions

(a) Identify in which financial statement (statement of financial position, income statement, or neither) and which section of the statement each of the above items should be reported.

(b) Prepare the long-lived assets section of the statement of financial position.

Compare ratios.

(LO 6)

E9–12 The following selected ratios have been chosen for two companies in different industries:

	Return on Assets	Asset Turnover	Profit Margin
Company A	7.2%	3.5 times	2.1%
Company B	3.4%	0.5 times	6.8%

One company is **Costco Wholesale Corporation** in the retail industry; the other is **Suncor Energy Inc.** in the oil and gas industry.

Instructions

Identify whether Company A or Company B is likely Costco, operating in the retail industry. Explain.

Calculate and evaluate ratios.

(LO 6)

E9–13 Ajax Limited reported the following information (in millions) at December 31, 2018: net sales $14,000; net income $550; total assets at December 31, 2018, $7,200; and total assets at December 31, 2017, $6,800.

Instructions

(a) Calculate the following ratios for the year: (1) return on assets, (2) asset turnover, and (3) profit margin.

(b) By showing the appropriate calculation (using unrounded numbers), prove mathematically how the profit margin and asset turnover work together to explain the return on assets.

(c) On average, the ratio values for Ajax's competitors are return on assets 4.5%, asset turnover 1.5 times, and profit margin 3.0%. Compare these with those of Ajax and determine if Ajax is performing better than the industry.

▶ **PROBLEMS: SET A**

Classify expenditures.

(LO 1)

P9–1A The transactions that follow are expenditures related to property, plant, and equipment:

1. Operator controls on equipment were replaced for $7,000, because the original control devices were not adequate.

2. A total of $4,600 was spent for decorative landscaping (planting flowers and shrubs, etc.).

3. A new air conditioning system for the office was purchased for $16,000.
4. Windows broken in a labour dispute were replaced for $2,400.
5. A fee of $1,500 was paid for adjusting and testing new machinery before its use.
6. Machinery damaged by a forklift was repaired for $5,000.
7. The transmission in a delivery truck was repaired for $2,500.
8. Expenditures totalling $3,000 were incurred to repaint the exterior of the building.
9. Paid $20,000 to convert the company's delivery vehicles from gasoline to propane to increase fuel efficiency.
10. Paid $10,000 to replace the company's light bulbs with more energy-efficient bulbs.

Instructions

For each of the transactions listed above, indicate the title of the account that you think should be debited in recording the transaction. Briefly explain your reasoning.

P9–2A For the year ended December 31, 2018, Westlake Ltd. had the following transactions related to the purchase of property. Assume all transactions are for cash unless otherwise stated.

Determine cost; record property transactions.

(LO 1, 2)

Feb. 7 Purchased real estate for $1.1 million, paying $300,000 cash and signing a mortgage payable for the balance. The site had an old building on it and the current values of the land and building were $1 million and $100,000, respectively. The old building will be demolished and a new apartment building will be constructed on the site.

9 Paid legal fees of $22,000 on the real estate purchase of February 7.

15 Paid $60,000 to demolish the old building and make the land ready for the construction of the apartment building.

16 Received $16,000 from the sale of material from the demolished building.

28 Paid $4,000 to grade the land in preparation for the construction of the apartment building.

Mar. 2 Paid architect fees of $72,000 to design the apartment building.

July 2 The full cost for construction of the apartment building was $2.6 million. Paid $680,000 cash and signed a bank loan payable for the balance.

3 Purchased a one-year insurance policy on the finished building for $10,000.

Aug. 29 Paid $48,000 for the paving of sidewalks and a parking lot for the building.

Instructions

(a) Record the above transactions.
(b) Determine the cost of the land, land improvements, and building that will appear on Westlake's December 31 statement of financial position.
(c) When would depreciation begin on the depreciable assets recorded above?

P9–3A Mazlin Limited purchased a machine on account on April 2, 2018, at an invoice price of $360,000. On April 4, it paid $2,000 for delivery of the machine. A one-year, $4,000 insurance policy on the machine was purchased on April 5. On April 18, Mazlin paid $8,000 for installation and testing of the machine. The machine was ready for use on April 30.

Determine cost; calculate depreciation under different methods.

(LO 1, 2)

Mazlin estimates the machine's useful life will be five years or 6,200 units with a residual value of $80,000. Assume the machine produces the following numbers of units each year: 940 units in 2018; 1,460 units in 2019; 1,400 units in 2020; 1,300 units in 2021; and 1,100 units in 2022. Mazlin has a December 31 year end.

Instructions

(a) Determine the cost of the machine.
(b) Calculate the annual depreciation and total depreciation over the asset's life using (1) the straight-line method, (2) the double-diminishing-balance method, and (3) the units-of-production method. Round the depreciation cost per unit to the nearest cent. Which method causes net income to be lower in the early years of the asset's life?
(c) Assume instead that, when Mazlin purchased the machine, there was no residual value and the company had a legal obligation to ensure that the machine would be recycled at the end of its useful life. The cost of the recycling will be significant. Would this have an impact on the answer to part (a) above? Explain.

P9–4A Valmont Limited purchased equipment on March 27, 2018, at a cost of $244,000. Management is contemplating the merits of using the diminishing-balance or units-of-production method of depreciation instead of the straight-line method, which it currently uses for other equipment. The new equipment has an estimated residual value of $4,000 and an estimated useful life of either four years or 80,000 units. Demand for the products produced by the equipment is sporadic so the equipment will be used more in some years than in others. Assume the equipment produces the following number of units each year: 14,800 units in 2018; 20,400 units in 2019; 19,800 units in 2020; 20,000 units in 2021; and 5,000 units in 2022. Valmont has a December 31 year end.

Calculate and compare depreciation under different methods.

(LO 2)

Instructions

(a) Prepare separate depreciation schedules for the life of the equipment using (1) the straight-line method, (2) the double-diminishing-balance method, and (3) the units-of-production method.

(b) Compare the total depreciation expense and accumulated depreciation under each of the three methods over the life of the equipment.
(c) What estimates were used in determining the depreciation amounts in part (a)? How accurate do you think these estimates are?
(d) How does each method of depreciation affect the company's cash flows?
(e) Which method do you recommend? Why?

Calculate depreciation and effects of disposals.
(LO 2, 3)

P9–5A On January 1, 2016, Penaji Corporation acquired equipment costing $80,000. It was estimated at that time that the equipment would have a useful life of eight years and no residual value. The company uses the straight-line method of depreciation for its equipment, and its year end is December 31.

Instructions
(a) Calculate the equipment's accumulated depreciation and carrying amount at the beginning of 2018.
(b) What is the amount of the gain or loss that would arise when a quarter of the equipment was sold on January 1, 2018, for cash proceeds of $18,000?
(c) What is the depreciation expense for January 1, 2018, to October 31, 2018?
(d) On November 1, 2018, the company purchased additional equipment for $10,000 that also had a useful life of eight years and no residual value. What is the depreciation for the two months ending December 31, 2018?
(e) On December 31, 2018, the company sold some equipment for a loss of $3,000. After recording the sale, the balances in the Equipment account and Accumulated Depreciation account were $58,000 and $16,208, respectively. Based on this information, what were the proceeds received when this equipment was sold?

Record acquisition, depreciation, and disposal of equipment.
(LO 2, 3)

P9–6A Altona Limited purchased delivery equipment on March 1, 2016, for $130,000 cash. At that time, the equipment was estimated to have a useful life of five years and a residual value of $10,000. The equipment was disposed of on November 30, 2018. Altona uses the diminishing-balance method at one time the straight-line depreciation rate, has an August 31 year end, and makes adjusting entries annually.

Instructions
(a) Record the acquisition of equipment on March 1, 2016.
(b) Record depreciation at August 31, 2016, 2017, and 2018.
(c) Record the disposal of the equipment on November 30, 2018, under each of the following independent assumptions:
  1. It was sold for $60,000.
  2. It was sold for $80,000.
  3. It was retired for no proceeds.

Record and determine effect of depreciation method over life of asset.
(LO 2, 3)

P9–7A Yukon Productions Corp. purchased equipment on March 1, 2018, for $70,000. The company estimated the equipment would have a useful life of three years and produce 12,000 units, with a residual value of $10,000. During 2018, the equipment produced 4,900 units. On November 30, 2019, the machine was sold for $18,000 and had produced 5,600 units that year.

Instructions
(a) Record all the necessary journal entries for the years ended December 31, 2018 and 2019, using the following depreciation methods: (1) straight-line, (2) double-diminishing-balance, and (3) units-of-production.
(b) Complete the following schedule for each method of depreciation and compare the total expense over the two-year period.

	Straight-Line	Double-Diminishing-Balance	Units-of-Production
Depreciation expense			
2018			
2019			
Total depreciation expense for two years			
+ Loss (or − gain) on disposal			
= Net expense for two years			

Record property, plant, and equipment transactions; prepare partial statement of financial position.
(LO 2, 3, 5)

P9–8A At January 1, 2018, Youngstown Limited reported the following property, plant, and equipment accounts:

Accumulated depreciation—buildings	$ 62,200,000
Accumulated depreciation—equipment	54,000,000
Buildings	97,400,000
Equipment	150,000,000
Land	20,000,000

The company uses straight-line depreciation for buildings and equipment, its year end is December 31, and it makes adjusting entries annually. The buildings are estimated to have a 40-year useful life and no residual value; the equipment is estimated to have a 10-year useful life and no residual value.

During 2018, the following selected transactions occurred:

Apr. 1   Purchased land for $4.4 million. Paid $1.1 million cash and issued a three-year, 6% mortgage payable for the balance. Interest on the mortgage is payable annually each April 1.

May 1   Sold equipment for $300,000 cash. The equipment cost $2.8 million when originally purchased on January 1, 2010.

June 1   Sold land for $3.6 million. Received $900,000 cash and accepted a three-year, 5% note for the balance. The land cost $1.4 million when purchased on June 1, 2012. Interest on the note is due annually each June 1.

July 1   Purchased equipment for $2.2 million cash.

Dec. 31   Retired equipment that cost $1 million when purchased on January 1, 2009. No proceeds were received.

31   Tested land for impairment and found that its recoverable value was $20 million.

Instructions
(a) Record the above transactions.
(b) Record any adjusting entries required at December 31.
(c) Prepare the property, plant, and equipment section of the company's statement of financial position at December 31.

P9–9A The following is a list of items that might or might not be classified as intangible assets or goodwill:
1. Goodwill recorded in the purchase of a business
2. Equipment obtained under an operating lease
3. Cost of purchasing a copyright
4. Cost of purchasing a trademark
5. Research costs involving tests of chemicals to use in a new medication that has not yet been developed
6. Goodwill generated internally
7. Aircraft acquired using a finance lease
8. Cost of purchasing a patent
9. Legal costs incurred to unsuccessfully defend a patent (see item 8)
10. Development costs incurred to manufacture a sample product that can and will be sold in the future

Identify intangible assets and goodwill.
(LO 4)

Instructions
(a) Identify which of the above items would be reported as intangible assets or goodwill on the statement of financial position.
(b) For those items in part (a) reported as intangible assets or goodwill, identify the specific account title that would be used to record the asset.
(c) For those items in part (a) reported as intangible assets or goodwill, identify which ones would likely be amortized.
(d) For any of the above items that are not intangible assets or goodwill, identify the specific account title, financial statement, and classification under which it would be reported. If it would not be reported on any financial statement, state so.

P9–10A The intangible assets and goodwill reported by Ghani Corporation at December 31, 2017, follow:

Record intangible asset transactions; prepare partial statement of financial position.
(LO 4, 5)

Copyrights	$36,000	
Less: Accumulated amortization	18,000	$ 18,000
Trademarks		54,000
Goodwill		125,000
Total		$197,000

A copyright (#1) was acquired on January 1, 2016, and has a useful life of four years. The trademarks were acquired on January 1, 2014, and are expected to have an indefinite life. The company has a December 31 year end and prepares adjusting journal entries annually.

The following cash transactions may have affected intangible assets and goodwill during 2018:

Jan. 5   Paid $7,000 in legal costs to successfully defend the trademarks against infringement by another company.

July 1   Developed a new product, incurring $210,000 in research and $50,000 in development costs with probable future benefits. The product is expected to have a useful life of 20 years.

Sept. 1   Paid $60,000 to a popular hockey player to appear in commercials advertising the company's products. The commercials will air in early September.

Oct. 1   Acquired another copyright (#2) for $180,000. The new copyright has a useful life of four years.

Dec. 31   Determined the recoverable amount of the goodwill to be $90,000. There was no indication that the copyrights or trademarks were impaired.

Instructions

(a) Prepare journal entries to record the transactions.

(b) Prepare any adjusting journal entries required at December 31.

(c) Show the presentation of the intangible assets and goodwill on the statement of financial position at December 31, 2018.

Calculate and evaluate ratios.

(LO 4, 6)

P9–11A **Walmart Stores Inc.** and **Target Corp.** reported the following information in 2015 (excluding Target's discontinued operations):

	Walmart (in U.S. $ millions)	Target (in U.S. $ millions)
Total assets, 2015	$203,706	$78,315
Total assets, 2014	204,751	79,651
Net sales, 2015	482,229	72,618
Net income, 2015	16,363	2,449

Industry averages were as follows: profit margin, 2.7%; asset turnover, 3.7 times; and return on assets, 10.0%.

Instructions

(a) For each company, calculate the (1) profit margin, (2) asset turnover, and (3) return on assets ratios for 2015.

(b) Based on your calculations in part (a), comment on how effectively each company is using its assets to generate sales and earn net income.

(c) What additional information about long-lived assets would assist you in your comparison of these two companies?

Calculate and evaluate ratios.

(LO 6)

P9–12A **Delicious Limited** competes in the fast food industry with **Scrumptious Limited.** Delicious embarked on a major expansion in 2018, borrowing a large amount of money and acquiring a small competitor. The acquisition doubled the number of restaurants that Delicious has. Scrumptious, on the other hand, took a more conservative approach and did not buy any new assets, focusing instead on a strategy of making existing operations more efficient.

Data for the two companies are provided below (in thousands of dollars):

	2018	2017	2016
Delicious			
Total assets	$2,000	$1,100	$1,000
Net sales	3,100	1,500	1,600
Net income	350	150	140
Scrumptious			
Total assets	800	900	1,000
Net sales	1,900	1,700	2,000
Net income	180	200	210

Instructions

(a) Calculate the (1) profit margin, (2) asset turnover, and (3) return on assets ratios for each company in 2017 and 2018.

(b) Provide an explanation for the year-over-year changes in the ratios calculated in part (a).

▶ PROBLEMS: SET B

Classify expenditures.

(LO 1)

P9–1B The following expenditures are for a forklift:

1. Rebuilding of the diesel engine, $10,000
2. New tires, $2,000
3. New safety cab, $5,000
4. Replacement of the windshield, $800
5. Training a new operator, $1,600
6. New paint job, $2,000
7. One-year accident insurance policy, $1,110
8. Payment to an operator for overtime when using the forklift to reorganize where items were stored in the warehouse to increase efficiency, $2,400
9. Added air conditioning for the operator's comfort, $2,000
10. Completed annual maintenance inspection, $500

Instructions

For each of the transactions listed above, indicate the title of the account that you think should be debited in recording the transaction. Briefly explain your reasoning.

P9–2B For the year ended December 31, 2018, Kadmen Ltd. incurred the following transactions related to the purchase of a property. Assume all transactions are for cash unless otherwise stated.

Determine cost; record property transactions.

(LO 1, 2)

Jan. 22 Purchased real estate for a future plant site for $880,000, paying $220,000 cash and signing a mortgage payable for the balance. There was an old building on the site and the current values of the land and building were $680,000 and $200,000, respectively. The old building will be demolished and a new plant will be constructed on the site.

24 Paid legal fees of $18,000 on the real estate purchase of January 22.

31 Paid $100,000 to demolish the old building to make room for the new plant.

Feb. 13 Graded and filled the land at a cost of $32,000 in preparation for the construction.

28 Received $30,000 from the sale of material from the demolished building.

Mar. 14 Paid $136,000 in architect fees for the building plans.

Apr. 20 Paid excavation costs for the new building of $68,000.

June 15 Received a bill from the building contractor for half of the cost of the new building, $1.2 million. Paid $300,000 cash and signed a bank loan payable for the balance.

Sept. 28 Received a bill for the remaining $1.2 million owed to the building contractor to complete the construction of the new building. Paid $400,000 cash and signed a bank loan payable for the balance.

Oct. 1 Paved the parking lots, driveways, and sidewalks for $168,000.

Instructions

(a) Record the above transactions.

(b) Determine the cost of the land, land improvements, and building that will appear on Kadmen's December 31 statement of financial position.

(c) When would depreciation begin on the depreciable assets recorded above?

P9–3B Mouskori Limited purchased a machine on September 3, 2018, at a cash price of $187,800. On September 4, it paid $1,200 for delivery of the machine. A one-year, $1,950 insurance policy on the machine was purchased on September 6. On September 20, Mouskori paid $7,000 for installation and testing of the machine. The machine was ready for use on September 30.

Determine cost; calculate depreciation under different methods.

(LO 1, 2)

Mouskori estimates the machine's useful life will be four years, or 40,000 units, with no residual value. Assume the equipment produces the following number of units each year: 2,500 units in 2018; 10,300 units in 2019; 9,900 units in 2020; 8,800 units in 2021; and 8,500 units in 2022. Mouskori has a December 31 year end.

Instructions

(a) Determine the cost of the machine.

(b) Calculate the annual depreciation and the total depreciation over the asset's life using (1) straight-line depreciation, (2) double-diminishing-balance depreciation, and (3) units-of-production depreciation. Which method causes net income to be lower in the early years of the asset's life?

(c) Assume instead that, when Mouskori Corporation purchased the machine, there was no residual value and the company had a legal obligation to ensure that the machine would be recycled at the end of its useful life. The cost of this recycling will be significant. Would this have an impact on the answer to part (a) above? Explain.

P9–4B Fast Arrow Ltd. purchased a new bus on October 3, 2018, at a total cost of $165,000. Management is contemplating the merits of using the diminishing-balance or units-of-production methods of depreciation instead of the straight-line method, which it currently uses for its other buses. The new bus has an estimated residual value of $15,000, and an estimated useful life of either four years or 300,000 km. Use of the bus will be sporadic so it could be much higher in some years than in other years. Assume the new bus is driven as follows: 7,500 km in 2018; 100,000 km in 2019; 62,500 km in 2020; 95,000 km in 2021; and 35,000 km in 2022. Fast Arrow has an October 31 year end.

Calculate and compare depreciation under different methods.

(LO 2)

Instructions

(a) Prepare separate depreciation schedules for the life of the bus using the (1) straight-line method, (2) double-diminishing-balance method, and (3) units-of-production method.

(b) Compare the total depreciation expense and accumulated depreciation under each of the three methods over the life of the bus.

(c) What estimates were used in determining the depreciation amounts in part (a)? How accurate do you think these estimates are?

(d) How does each method of depreciation affect the company's cash flows?

(e) Which method do you recommend? Why?

P9–5B On January 1, 2016, Bérubé Ltée acquired equipment costing $60,000. It was estimated at that time that the equipment would have a useful life of five years and no residual value. The straight-line method of depreciation is used by Bérubé for its equipment, and its year end is December 31.

Calculate depreciation and effects of disposals.

(LO 2, 3)

Instructions

(a) Calculate the equipment's accumulated depreciation and carrying amount at the beginning of 2018.

(b) What is the amount of the gain or loss that would arise when one third of the equipment was sold on January 1, 2018, for cash proceeds of $17,000?

(c) What is the depreciation expense from January 1, 2018, to September 30, 2018, and what is the carrying amount of the equipment at September 30, 2018?

(d) On October 1, the company bought more equipment costing $10,000 that also had a useful life of five years and no residual value. What is the depreciation for the three months ending December 31, 2018?

(e) On the last day of 2018, the company sold some equipment for a loss of $2,000. After recording the sale, the balances in the Equipment and the Accumulated Depreciation accounts were $38,000 and $18,000, respectively. Based on this information, what were the proceeds received when this equipment was sold?

Record acquisition, depreciation, and disposal of equipment.

(LO 2, 3)

P9–6B Balmoral Limited purchased equipment on January 1, 2016, for $170,000 on account. At that time, the equipment was estimated to have a useful life of five years and a $2,000 residual value. The equipment was disposed of on August 1, 2018, when the company relocated to new premises. Balmoral uses the diminishing-balance method at one time the straight-line depreciation rate, has a September 30 year end, and makes adjusting entries annually.

Instructions

(a) Record the acquisition of the equipment on January 1, 2016.

(b) Record the depreciation at September 30, 2016 and 2017.

(c) Record the disposal of the equipment on August 1, 2018, under each of the following independent assumptions:
1. It was sold for $115,000.
2. It was sold for $80,000.
3. It was retired for no proceeds.

Record and determine effect of depreciation method over life of asset.

(LO 2, 3)

P9–7B PEI Productions Ltd. purchased equipment on February 1, 2018, for $50,000. The company estimated the equipment would have a useful life of three years and would produce 10,000 units, with a residual value of $10,000. During 2018, the equipment produced 4,000 units. On October 31, 2019, the machine was sold for $12,000; it had produced 5,000 units that year.

Instructions

(a) Record all the necessary entries for the years ended December 31, 2018 and 2019, for the following depreciation methods: (1) straight-line, (2) double-diminishing-balance, and (3) units-of-production.

(b) Complete the following schedule for each method of depreciation and compare the total expense over the two-year period.

	Straight-Line	Double-Diminishing-Balance	Units-of-Production
Depreciation expense			
2018			
2019			
Total depreciation expense for two years			
+ Loss (or − gain) on disposal			
= Net expense for two years			

Record property, plant, and equipment transactions; prepare partial statement of financial position.

(LO 2, 3, 5)

P9–8B At January 1, 2018, Hammersmith Limited reported the following property, plant, and equipment accounts:

Accumulated depreciation—buildings	$24,200,000
Accumulated depreciation—equipment	30,000,000
Buildings	57,000,000
Equipment	96,000,000
Land	8,000,000

The company uses straight-line depreciation for buildings and equipment, its year end is December 31, and it makes adjusting entries annually. The buildings are estimated to have a 40-year life and no residual value; the equipment is estimated to have a 10-year useful life and no residual value.

During 2018, the following selected transactions occurred:

Apr. 1   Purchased land for $3.8 million. Paid $950,000 cash and issued a 10-year, 6% mortgage payable for the balance. Interest is payable at maturity.

May 1   Sold equipment for $700,000 cash. The equipment cost $1.5 million when it was originally purchased on January 1, 2014.

June 1   Sold land for $2.4 million. Received $760,000 cash and accepted a 6% note for the balance. The note is due at maturity. The land cost $600,000 when purchased on June 1, 2008.

July	1	Purchased equipment for $2 million on account, terms n/60.
Sept.	2	Paid amount owing on account for purchase of equipment on July 1.
Dec.	31	Retired equipment that cost $940,000 when purchased on January 1, 2009. No proceeds were received.
	31	Tested land for impairment and found that its recoverable value was $11 million.

Instructions
(a) Record the above transactions.
(b) Record any adjusting entries required at December 31.
(c) Prepare the property, plant, and equipment section of the company's statement of financial position at December 31.

P9–9B The following is a list of items that might or might not be classified as intangible assets or goodwill:
1. Goodwill recorded in the purchase of a business
2. Equipment acquired using a finance lease
3. Cost of purchasing a five-year software licensing agreement
4. Cost of purchasing a patent
5. Legal costs incurred to unsuccessfully defend a patent (see item 4)
6. Goodwill generated internally
7. Vehicles acquired using an operating lease
8. Cost of registering a trademark
9. Legal costs incurred to successfully defend a trademark (see item 8)
10. Research costs incurred to identify a cure for cancer

Identify intangible assets and goodwill.
(LO 4)

Instructions
(a) Identify which of the above items would be reported as intangible assets or goodwill on the statement of financial position.
(b) For those items in part (a) reported as intangible assets or goodwill, identify the specific account title that would be used to record the asset.
(c) For those items in part (a) reported as intangible assets or goodwill, identify which ones would likely be amortized.
(d) For any of the above items that are not intangible assets or goodwill, identify the specific account title, financial statement, and classification under which it would be reported. If it would not be reported on any financial statement, state so.

P9–10B The intangible assets and goodwill reported by Ip Corp. at December 31, 2017, follow:

Record intangible asset transactions; prepare partial statement of financial position.
(LO 4, 5)

Patents	$70,000	
Less: Accumulated amortization	14,000	$ 56,000
Copyrights	$48,000	
Less: Accumulated amortization	28,800	19,200
Goodwill		210,000
Total		$285,200

The patents were acquired in January 2016 and have a useful life of 10 years. A copyright (#1) was acquired in January 2012 and also has a useful life of 10 years. The company has a December 31 year end and prepares adjusting journal entries annually.

The following cash transactions may have affected intangible assets and goodwill during 2018:

Jan.	2	Paid $22,500 in legal costs to successfully defend the patents against infringement by another company. Determined that the revised annual amortization for the patents will be $9,812.
July	1	Developed a new product, incurring $220,000 in research costs and $60,000 in development costs with probable future benefits. The useful life of the new product is equal to 20 years.
Sept.	1	Paid $11,000 to an Olympic rower to appear in commercials advertising the company's products. The commercials will air in September.
Oct.	1	Acquired a second copyright for $16,000. Copyright #2 has a useful life of five years.
Dec.	31	Determined the recoverable amount of the goodwill to be $175,000. There was no indication that the patents or copyrights were impaired.

Instructions
(a) Prepare the journal entries to record the above transactions.
(b) Prepare any adjusting journal entries required at December 31.
(c) Show the presentation of the intangible assets and goodwill on the statement of financial position at December 31, 2018.

P9–11B Dollarama Inc. and Hudson's Bay Company are two competitors in the retail industry. They reported the following information in 2015 (in millions of dollars):

Calculate and evaluate ratios.
(LO 6)

	Dollarama	Hudson's Bay
Total assets, 2015	$1,567	$7,942
Total assets, 2014	1,701	9,072
Net sales, 2015	2,331	8,169
Net income, 2015	295	238

Industry averages are as follows: profit margin, 0.9%; asset turnover, 1.6 times; and return on assets, 1.4%.

Instructions
(a) For each company, calculate the profit margin, asset turnover, and return on assets ratios for 2015.
(b) Based on your calculations in part (a), comment on how effectively each company is using its assets to generate sales and earn net income.
(c) What additional information about long-lived assets would assist you in your comparison of these two companies?

Calculate and evaluate ratios.
(LO 6)

P9–12B Two brewing companies that compete against each other are Northern Ale Ltd. (NAL) and Brew Right Inc. (BRI). The industry is experiencing a slump and each company has undertaken a different strategy to adapt to this situation. NAL has adopted an expansion strategy by borrowing funds to purchase another company. This has boosted 2018 sales by 67% and 2018 net income by 47%, which the company CEO has mentioned in several press releases. BRI has decided to streamline operations and cut costs by looking at more efficient ways to operate the business.

Data for the two companies are listed below (in thousands of dollars):

	2018	2017	2016
Northern Ale			
Total assets	$2,500	$1,100	$1,000
Net sales	2,500	1,500	1,600
Net income	220	150	160
Brew Right			
Total assets	1,100	1,050	1,000
Net sales	1,800	1,500	1,400
Net income	250	150	140

Instructions
(a) Calculate the net income margin, asset turnover, and return on assets ratios for each company in 2017 and 2018.
(b) Provide an explanation for the year-over-year changes in the ratios calculated in part (a).
(c) Comment on which company has been more successful in executing its strategy.

ACCOUNTING CYCLE | REVIEW

Record and post transaction and adjusting journal entries; prepare adjusted trial balance and financial statements.
(LO 2, 3, 4, 5)

ACR9–1 Clear Images Ltd. has been in operation for several years. It wholesales furniture to its customers. The company's post-closing trial balance at July 31, 2018, the end of its fiscal year, is presented below:

CLEAR IMAGES LTD.
Post-Closing Trial Balance
July 31, 2018

	Debit	Credit
Cash	$ 170,000	
Accounts receivable	2,700,000	
Allowance for doubtful accounts		$ 300,000
Inventory	500,000	
Equipment	194,000	
Accumulated depreciation—equipment		73,669
Accounts payable		1,009,000
Bank loan payable		350,000
Common shares		300,000
Retained earnings		1,531,331
	$3,564,000	$3,564,000

The company had a limited amount of business activity in August 2018 because of holidays for both the company and its major customers. You have been hired on a temporary basis to update the company's records for August. The August transactions and adjustments are presented below:

Aug. 1 Paid $20,000 for office expenses and $3,600 for the August rent.

2 Accepted a six-month, 8% note in exchange for Chen Enterprises' overdue account receivable of $100,000.

3 Sale on account to Chavier Ltd. for $500,000, terms 2/10, n/30. Cost of goods sold, $270,000. The company uses a perpetual inventory system.

8 Determined that an account receivable from Densmore Ltd. of $70,000 is uncollectible.

9 A $300,000 partial payment on account was received from Chavier (see August 3 transaction).

10 Old equipment was sold for $6,000. The equipment's original cost was $44,000; accumulated depreciation to the date of disposal was $36,169.

14 Paid a $10,000 income tax instalment.

21 Purchased a patent for $24,000 cash. The estimated useful life of the patent is five years; the legal life, 20 years.

31 Recorded cash received from sales of digital library images for the month, $75,000. The cost of goods sold is $35,000.

31 The monthly bank statement revealed the following unrecorded items: interest on bank loan, $1,500, and bank service charges, $1,130.

31 Reviewed outstanding accounts receivable. Determined, through an aging of accounts, that doubtful accounts totalled $320,000 at month end.

31 Recorded depreciation for the month on the remaining equipment that cost $150,000 and is still in use. Useful life of all equipment is estimated to be four years with no residual value. The straight-line method of depreciation is used and depreciation is calculated to the nearest month.

31 Recorded and paid salaries for the month $100,000.

31 Accrued interest on the Chen Enterprises note receivable (see August 2 transaction).

31 Recorded amortization on the patent (see August 21 transaction). A full month's amortization is recorded on any intangible assets acquired during the month.

Instructions

(a) Record the August transactions and adjustments.
(b) Set up T accounts, enter the July 31 opening balances, and post the journal entries prepared in part (a).
(c) Prepare an adjusted trial balance at August 31.
(d) Prepare a (1) income statement, (2) statement of changes in equity, and (3) statement of financial position for August.

EXPAND YOUR | CRITICAL THINKING

CT9–1 Financial Reporting Case

The financial statements of The North West Company Inc. are presented in Appendix A at the end of this textbook.

Instructions

(a) What depreciation method does North West use? (*Hint*: Look in the note accompanying the financial statements that explains significant accounting policies.)

(b) Identify the following amounts for the five largest components of the company's property and equipment at each of January 31, 2016, and January 31, 2015: (1) cost, (2) accumulated depreciation, (3) impairment losses, and (4) carrying amount (which the company calls "net book value"). (*Hint*: Look in the note accompanying the financial statements that deals with property and equipment.)

(c) Using the amounts determined in part (b) above, what is the difference between the accumulated depreciation (the company refers to this as "accumulated amortization") reported at the end of January 2016 and 2015? What was the amount of amortization expense reported for property and equipment for the year ended January 31, 2016? (*Hint*: Use the property and equipment note used above.) Why is the change in accumulated amortization not equal to amortization expense?

(d) Does North West have any goodwill at January 31, 2016? If so, how much?

(e) What kinds of intangible assets does the company report at January 31, 2016? Did it have any impairment losses for its intangibles for the year ended January 31, 2016? Were any fully depreciated intangibles written off during the year? (*Hint*: See the note pertaining to goodwill and intangibles.)

CT9–2 Financial Analysis Case

The Rosewood Resort and the Blaze Mountain Resort are located in the same four-season resort area. Rosewood is a publicly traded company that follows IFRS. Blaze Mountain, owned by a small group of Canadian private investors, follows ASPE. Both companies use the cost model when accounting for property, plant, and equipment and have a December 31 year end.

From 2012 to 2015, both resorts experienced a period of decline where the number of visitors to the area dwindled. Because of this, at the end of the 2015 fiscal year, each company recorded an impairment loss of $1 million on its buildings because the recoverable amount of these assets did not exceed their carrying amount at that time.

Between 2015 and 2018, the number of visitors to each resort has risen steadily. Resort bookings have dramatically increased because the country's largest developer of destination resorts has opened a ski village, chalets, lodges, and a golf resort in the area. As a result, by the end of 2018, the recoverable amount of the buildings of each resort now exceeds their carrying amount, as shown below, along with other pertinent information.

	Rosewood	Blaze Mountain
Net sales	$2,250,000	$ 2,500,000
Net income	180,000	200,000
Average total assets	9,000,000	10,000,000
Carrying amount of buildings	5,000,000	6,000,000
Recoverable amount of buildings	7,000,000	6,500,000
What the carrying amount of buildings would have been had the impairment not occurred in 2015	5,800,000	6,700,000

Instructions

(a) At the end of 2018, can Rosewood reverse some or all of the impairment loss recorded in 2015? If so, how much?

(b) At the end of 2018, can Blaze Mountain reverse some or all of the impairment loss recorded in 2015? If so, how much?

(c) Calculate the (1) profit margin, (2) asset turnover, and (3) return on assets ratios for both companies based on the amounts provided above. Recalculate each ratio after taking into account any impairment loss reversals determined in parts (a) and (b), if applicable.

(d) Based on the ratios calculated in part (c), after taking into effect any impairment loss reversals, which company is performing better? Why?

(e) If different accounting standards produce different account balances on financial statements, what additional information may users want to have in order to evaluate the nature and performance of long-lived assets?

CT9–3 Professional Judgement Case

This case can be assigned as a group activity. Additional instructions and material for this activity can be found on the Instructor Resource site and in WileyPLUS.

The Peace River Drilling Company (PRD) is a private company, and has just completed its first year of operations. The company drills oil and gas wells. Because rigs are easier to move across dry or frozen ground, most of the drilling done by PRD occurs in the summer and winter. PRD has a part-time accountant who has been responsible for recording most of the company's transactions; he is about to prepare the draft financial statements and needs some advice from you. The company has four major types of tangible assets: land, buildings, drilling rigs, and furniture. PRD has also just developed a new drill bit and has obtained a patent for it because of its unique design. The company has entered into a contract with a drill bit manufacturer that gives the manufacturer the right to use the unique design when producing its products in exchange for a royalty from the sale of these drill bits. The agreement expires in five years. The company plans to do a public issue of shares sometime in the next three years.

Instructions

(a) The accountant would like your advice on the method of depreciation that should be used for each tangible asset. Recommend a method with support.

(b) The accountant would like to know if intangible assets have to be amortized. If this is required, explain why, and describe the method that should be used and length of time over which the patent should be amortized.

(c) PRD has yet to decide if its financial statements will be prepared in accordance with IFRS or ASPE. Which set of accounting standards would you recommend the company choose and why?

(d) If PRD wanted to obtain a bank loan, which type of asset would the bank probably want to use for security on the loan? Which type of asset is least likely to be used as security? Why?

(e) Because the drilling industry is in a mild recession, the company is not planning on buying any rigs or other major assets next year. Industry experts expect most drilling companies to maintain a level volume of sales revenue next year. What do you think will happen to the company's asset turnover ratio next year? How would you interpret this change in the ratio?

CT9–4 Ethics Case

Imporia Container Ltd. is suffering from declining sales of its main product, non-biodegradable plastic cartons. The president, Benny Benson, instructs his controller, Yeoh Siew Hoon, to change estimates relating to a processing line of automated plastic extruding equipment, purchased for $3 million in January 2016. The equipment was originally estimated to have a useful life of five years and a residual value of $200,000 and straight-line depreciation has been recorded for two years on that basis. Benny wants the estimated useful life changed to a total of seven years and the residual value raised to $500,000 in order to reduce the annual depreciation expense.

Yeoh Siew is hesitant to make the change, believing it inappropriate to "manage" profits in this way. Benny says, "I'm under a lot of pressure from the shareholders to maximize net income. Don't you want your bonus, which is based on net income, to be as high as possible? Just go ahead and make the change—the useful life and residual value are only an estimate, anyway."

Instructions

(a) Who are the stakeholders in this situation?

(b) Will Benny Benson's proposed change increase, decrease, or not affect net income in 2017? 2018?

(c) What impact will the proposed change in useful life and residual value have on the company's profit margin and asset turnover ratios?

(d) Discuss whether the proposed change described above is unethical or simply a good business practice by an astute president.

CT9–5 Financial Analysis Case

On January 1, 2018, two companies, Luxor Ltd. and Cale Inc., were incorporated. Each company operates a restaurant and had identical revenues during the year of $3 million but Luxor bought its building for $1.7 million and the related land for $800,000. The company estimated that the building would have a useful life of 20 years with no residual value. Luxor uses the straight-line method of depreciation. Because of the building purchase, Luxor had an outstanding 4% bank loan during the year amounting on average to $2.8 million.

Cale, however, did not buy a building. Instead it rented a building under a five-year operating lease starting on January 1, 2018, for $17,000 per month. Because of this, the company had to install leasehold improvements for $100,000, which were completed in the first few days of January. Because Cale did not have to buy a building, its outstanding 4% bank loan during 2018 averaged only $350,000.

The income tax rate for both companies is 22%. Assume both companies had identical revenues and expenses except for the items noted above.

Instructions

(a) If Luxor had net income of $175,000 for the year ended December 31, 2018, what net income did Cale have?

(b) If Luxor had total assets of $3,025,000 as at December 31, 2018, and the only differences between the assets of Luxor and Cale related to land, buildings, and leasehold improvements, the latter being depreciated over the term of the lease, what are the total assets for Cale at the end of 2018?

(c) Calculate the asset turnover ratio for both companies for 2018. (*Hint*: Because this is the first year of operations, you can use the year-end asset balance rather than the average asset balance for the denominator.) Explain why the ratios are different.

(d) Calculate the profit margin ratio for both companies for 2018. Explain why they are different.

(e) Calculate the return on assets ratio for both companies for 2018. (*Hint*: Because this is the first year of operations, you can use the year-end asset balance rather than the average asset balance for the denominator.) Explain why the ratios are different using your answers in parts (c) and (d) above.

(f) What information relating to Cale is not reflected in the financial statements that may be relevant to assessing its financial position and profitability?

(g) Would adopting the revaluation method under IFRS change the values of any of the three ratios covered above? Would those ratios improve or not?

(h) If new rules for treating operating leases beyond one year as capital leases are adopted in 2019, what impact will this have on Cale's asset turnover ratio?

CT9–6 Student View Case

You are starting your own delivery business and wish to purchase a delivery truck. You have two options available: (1) borrow $25,000 to purchase the truck and repay the loan over three years, or (2) lease the truck over three years and purchase the truck at the end of the lease term for $7,500. You have determined the following:

Interest rate for both purchase and leasing	6.0%
Monthly payment (option 1—purchase)	$760.54
Monthly payment (option 2—lease)	$608.43

Instructions

(a) If you chose option 1 and purchased the vehicle, what is the total cost that you will incur? What will be your costs of financing? (*Hint*: What is the difference between the cost of the vehicle and the total of all of your monthly payments?)

(b) If you chose option 2 and leased the vehicle, and decided not to purchase the vehicle at the end of the lease term, what is the total cost that you will incur?

(c) If you chose option 2 and leased the vehicle, and decided to purchase the vehicle at the end of the lease term, what is the total cost that you will incur?

(d) Compare the three alternatives.

CT9–7 Serial Case

(*Note*: This is a continuation of the serial case from Chapters 1 through 8.)

After meeting with Software Solutions, as described in Chapter 8, Emily was able to negotiate a continuation of existing credit terms of 30 days and decided to take on the additional work offered by Software Solutions. In order to better handle this work, ABC decided to upgrade its computer equipment and hire two additional employees. After some research and much discussion, the computer upgrades and costs were determined to be as follows:

1. Old server will be retired and donated to the community centre. It was originally purchased for $15,000 on January 3, 2014. It is being depreciated on a

straight-line basis over a five-year useful life with no residual value.

2. Purchase of a new server, including installation, $25,000.
3. Purchase of computing equipment for the new employees at a cost of $4,500.
4. Purchase of additional yearly software usage licences for the two new employees at a cost of $1,000 each.
5. Purchase of additional office furniture at a cost of $2,500, plus delivery and shipping costs of $500.
6. Additional insurance is required, $1,000 per year.
7. Rearranging the office space and repainting the office to "freshen things up" at a cost of $2,850.

Doug, Bev, and Emily anticipate that the cost of the upgrade can be financed with cash the company currently has in the bank. The upgrades will take place between Christmas and New Year's when the sales at the business

are a little slower. If all goes smoothly, the new equipment will be installed and ready for use by January 2, 2018.

Emily is concerned about how to record these transactions in the accounting records. She is not certain which costs should be capitalized and which should be expensed.

Instructions
(a) Identify which of the above costs should be capitalized and which should be expensed.
(b) Prepare the journal entry(ies) to record the retirement of the old server (item 1) on January 2, 2018, for no proceeds. The last time depreciation was recorded was on June 30, 2017.
(c) Prepare the journal entry(ies), if any, required to record items 2 through 7 above. Assume all transactions are cash transactions and occurred on January 2, 2018.

▶ ANSWERS TO CHAPTER PRACTICE QUESTIONS

DO IT! 9-1
Cost of an Asset

(a) The cost of the equipment is $50,600 ($50,000 + $100 + $500).

(b)
Feb. 4	Equipment	50,600	
	Prepaid Insurance	750	
	Salaries Expense	600	
	Cash ($20,000 + $100 + $750 + $500 + $600)		21,950
	Bank Loan Payable ($50,000 − $20,000)		30,000
	(To record purchase of equipment and related expenditures)		

DO IT! 9-2
Depreciation

	2017	2018	2019	2020	Total
Straight-line	$24,000	$32,000	$32,000	$8,000	$96,000
Diminishing-balance	52,000	34,667	9,333	0	96,000
Units-of-production	25,600	32,000	30,400	8,000	96,000

(a) Straight-line: ($104,000 − $8,000) ÷ 3 years = $32,000 per year; for the partial period in 2017: $32,000 × $^9/_{12}$ = $24,000; for the full year in 2018 and 2019: $32,000; and for the partial period in 2020: $32,000 × $^3/_{12}$ = $8,000

(b) Diminishing-balance: 100% ÷ 3 years = 33 $^1/_3$% straight-line depreciation rate; so we double this: 33 $^1/_3$% × 2 = 66 $^2/_3$%

2017:	$104,000 × 66$^2/_3$% × $^9/_{12}$ = $52,000
2018:	($104,000 − $52,000) × 66$^2/_3$% = $34,667
2019:	($104,000 − $86,667) × 66$^2/_3$% = $11,556 but this is too much depreciation to record. At the beginning of 2019, the carrying amount was $17,333 ($104,000 − $86,667) and since the residual value is $8,000, we should only record depreciation of $9,333 ($17,333 − $8,000) this year.
2020:	No depreciation is recorded because the asset's carrying amount has been reduced to its residual value in 2019.

(c) Units-of-production: ($104,000 − $8,000) ÷ 6,000 hours = $16 per hour

2017:	1,600 × $16 = $25,600
2018:	2,000 × $16 = $32,000
2019:	1,900 × $16 = $30,400
2020:	500 × $16 = $8,000

Notice that, with all methods used above, the total depreciation recorded over the useful life of the machine was $96,000 but that, in any particular year, the depreciation expense for each of these methods was different.

DO IT! 9-3a
Sale of a Vehicle

Annual depreciation expense: $90,000 ÷ 6 years = $15,000

(a) Sale of the truck at a gain:

Sept. 1, 2018	Depreciation Expense ($15,000 × $^8/_{12}$)	10,000	
	Accumulated Depreciation—Vehicles		10,000
	(To record depreciation for eight months)		

	Cash		21,000	
	Accumulated Depreciation—Vehicles [($15,000 × 4 years) + $10,000]		70,000	
	Gain on Disposal [$21,000 − ($90,000 − $70,000)]			1,000
	Vehicles			90,000
	(To record sale of a truck at a gain)			

(b) Sale of the truck at a loss:

Sept. 1, 2018	Depreciation Expense ($15,000 × 8/12)		10,000	
	Accumulated Depreciation—Vehicles			10,000
	(To record depreciation for eight months)			
	Cash		18,000	
	Accumulated Depreciation—Vehicles [($15,000 × 4 years) + $10,000]		70,000	
	Loss on Disposal [$18,000 − ($90,000 − $70,000)]		2,000	
	Vehicles			90,000
	(To record sale of a truck at a loss)			

Annual depreciation rate: (1 ÷ 10 years) × 2 = 20%

Depreciation recorded in prior years:

2015:	$100,000 × 20% = $20,000
2016:	($100,000 − $20,000) × 20% = $16,000
2017:	($100,000 − $36,000) × 20% = $12,800
2018:	($100,000 − $48,800) × 20% × 9/12 = $7,680

Total depreciation recorded prior to retirement is $56,480 ($20,000 + $16,000 + $12,800 + $7,680) and the carrying amount at date of retirement is $43,520 ($100,000 − $56,480).

Oct. 1, 2018	Depreciation Expense		7,680	
	Accumulated Depreciation—Equipment			7,680
	(To record depreciation for nine months)			
	Accumulated Depreciation—Equipment		56,480	
	Loss on Disposal		43,520	
	Equipment			100,000
	(To record retirement of equipment)			

(a) Aug. 1, 2017	Copyrights		15,000	
	Cash			15,000
	(To record purchase of copyright)			
(b) July 31, 2018	Amortization Expense ($15,000 ÷ 3)		5,000	
	Accumulated Amortization—Copyrights			5,000
	(To record amortization expense)			
(c) Aug. 1, 2018	Copyrights		6,000	
	Cash			6,000
	(To record costs incurred to defend copyright)			

Account Title	Financial Statement	Classification
Accumulated Amortization—Patents	SFP	Intangible assets: patents (contra asset account)
Accumulated Depreciation—Buildings	SFP	Property, plant, and equipment: buildings (contra asset account)
Accumulated Depreciation—Equipment	SFP	Property, plant, and equipment: equipment (contra asset account)
Amortization Expense	IS	Operating expense
Assets under Finance Leases	SFP	Property, plant, and equipment: assets under finance leases
Buildings	SFP	Property, plant, and equipment: buildings
Depreciation Expense	IS	Operating expense
Development Costs	SFP	Intangible assets: development costs
Equipment	SFP	Property, plant, and equipment: equipment
Gain on Disposal	IS	Operating expenses (reduction)
Goodwill	SFP	Goodwill
Impairment Loss	IS	Operating expenses
Interest Expense	IS	Non-operating expenses (other revenues and expenses)
Land	SFP	Property, plant, and equipment: land
Loss on Disposal	IS	Operating expenses
Patents	SFP	Intangible assets: patents
Repairs and Maintenance Expense	IS	Operating expenses
Research Expenses	IS	Operating expenses

DO IT! 9-6
Analyze Assets

	Saluda		Unami	
	2018	2017	2018	2017
(a) Profit margin	$\dfrac{\$110}{\$1,200} = 9.2\%$	$\dfrac{\$80}{\$1,000} = 8.0\%$	$\dfrac{\$170}{\$1,800} = 9.4\%$	$\dfrac{\$200}{\$2,000} = 10.0\%$
(b) Asset turnover	$\dfrac{\$1,200}{(\$540 + \$500) \div 2} = 2.3 \text{ times}$	$\dfrac{\$1,000}{(\$500 + \$500) \div 2} = 2.0 \text{ times}$	$\dfrac{\$1,800}{(\$1,200 + \$800) \div 2} = 1.8 \text{ times}$	$\dfrac{\$2,000}{(\$800 + \$800) \div 2} = 2.5 \text{ times}$
(c) Return on assets	$\dfrac{\$110}{(\$540 + \$500) \div 2} = 21.2\%$	$\dfrac{\$80}{(\$500 + \$500) \div 2} = 16.0\%$	$\dfrac{\$170}{(\$1,200 + \$800) \div 2} = 17.0\%$	$\dfrac{\$200}{(\$800 + \$800) \div 2} = 25.0\%$

(d) Profit margin analysis: Saluda's profit margin improved in 2018. It was able to find a cheaper source for components, which enabled it to earn higher net income while at the same time reducing the components' selling price, which allowed it to sell more products. This hurt Unami, causing its sales to drop. Unami was unable to cut expenses as fast as sales were falling, which caused its net income to fall. Consequently, despite reporting an overall lower profit margin than Unami, Saluda's profit margin improved in 2018 while Unami's deteriorated.

Asset turnover analysis: Saluda's asset turnover improved in 2018. Its increased sales did not create the need for a significant increase in assets, so turnover rose. Unami's asset turnover fell for two reasons: (1) sales volumes dropped because Saluda was taking away customers seeking lower prices, and (2) because of the acquisition of the Mexican company, assets increased with no corresponding increase in revenues because the acquisition was so late in 2018.

Return on assets: Saluda's return on assets ratio improved in 2018. This ratio is a function of the two preceding ratios. Because Saluda's profit margin and asset turnover ratios increased in 2018, the result was a higher return on assets. For Unami, it was both the lower profit margin and the lower asset turnover that caused the drop in the return on assets.

▶ **PRACTICE USING THE DECISION TOOLKIT**

(a) 1. Transat's planes may have been purchased used, compared with WestJet's, which may have been purchased as new planes. If this was the case, then Transat's remaining useful lives would be shorter.

   2. Because Transat uses a shorter useful life on its aircraft, it will report relatively higher depreciation expense and lower net income than WestJet.

(b) Transat's trademarks likely have an indefinite life. In this case, trademarks are not amortized but are tested for impairment at least annually.

(c) Impairment losses on goodwill cannot be subsequently reversed.

(d)

Ratio	Transat	WestJet	Air Canada	Industry
Return on assets	$\dfrac{\$46,964}{(\$1,513,764 + \$1,375,030) \div 2} = 3.3\%$	7.5%	2.6%	2.9%
Asset turnover	$\dfrac{\$3,566,368}{(\$1,513,764 + \$1,375,030) \div 2} = 2.5 \text{ times}$	0.8 times	1.2 times	1.0 times

Transat has a reasonable return on assets, slightly higher than the industry average. The major reason for this is its above-average asset turnover ratio, which is considerably higher than the industry average and the asset turnover of its competitors. One possible reason for this may be the lower cost of its planes. You will recall that we speculated in part (a) (1) above that Transat may be purchasing used planes while WestJet may be purchasing newer planes, which would result in a lower cost of planes for Transat compared with WestJet.

▶ **PRACTICE COMPREHENSIVE DO IT!**

(a) The cost of the equipment is $70,000, representing the purchase price of $68,000 plus the costs incurred to get the equipment ready for use, which included the shipping cost of $1,200 and the installation cost of $800. The training costs would not be capitalized.

1

DULCIMER LTD.
Straight-Line Depreciation Schedule

					End of Year	
Year	Depreciable Amount	×	Depreciation Rate	=	Depreciation Expense	Accumulated Depreciation	Carrying Amount
							$70,000
2018	$64,000[a]		25%[b] × 7/12		$ 9,333	$ 9,333	60,667
2019	64,000		25%		16,000	25,333	44,667
2020	64,000		25%		16,000	41,333	28,667
2021	64,000		25%		16,000	57,333	12,667
2022	64,000		25% × 5/12		6,667	64,000	6,000

[a]$70,000 − $6,000 = $64,000

[b]100% ÷ 4 years = 25%

2.

DULCIMER LTD.
Diminishing-Balance Depreciation Schedule

Year	Carrying Amount Beginning of Year	×	Depreciation Rate	=	Depreciation Expense	Accumulated Depreciation	Carrying Amount
							$70,000
2018	$70,000		50%[a] × 7/12		$20,417	$20,417	49,583
2019	49,583		50%		24,792	45,209	24,791
2020	24,791		50%		12,396	57,605	12,395
2021	12,395		50%		6,198	63,803	6,197
2022	6,197		50%		197[b]	64,000	6,000

[a] 25% × 2
[b] Adjusted to $197 because the ending carrying amount should not be less than the expected residual value.

3.

DULCIMER LTD.
Units-of-Production Depreciation Schedule

Year	Units of Activity	×	Depreciable Amount/Unit	=	Depreciation Expense	Accumulated Depreciation	Carrying Amount
							$70,000
2018	1,300		$6.40[a]		$ 8,320	$ 8,320	61,680
2019	2,800		6.40		17,920	26,240	43,760
2020	3,300		6.40		21,120	47,360	22,640
2021	1,900		6.40		12,160	59,520	10,480
2022	700		6.40		4,480	64,000	6,000

[a] $70,000 − $6,000 = $64,000 ÷ 10,000 total units = $6.40/unit

(b) If the equipment is retired, the following journal entries would be recorded:

June 1, 2022	Depreciation Expense	6,667	
	Accumulated Depreciation—Equipment		6,667
	(To record depreciation for January 1–June 1)		
	Accumulated Depreciation—Equipment	64,000	
	Loss on Disposal	6,000	
	Equipment		70,000
	(To record retirement of equipment)		

If the equipment is sold for $9,000, the following journal entries would be recorded:

June 1, 2022	Depreciation Expense	6,667	
	Accumulated Depreciation—Equipment		6,667
	(To record depreciation for January 1–June 1)		
	Cash	9,000	
	Accumulated Depreciation—Equipment	64,000	
	Equipment		70,000
	Gain on Disposal		3,000
	(To record sale of equipment)		

▶ PRACTICE OBJECTIVE-FORMAT QUESTIONS

1. (a), (b), (c), and (f) are correct

Feedback
The correct items represent costs that should be capitalized as part of the cost of the equipment because they were incurred to get the equipment ready for use. Training costs were not incurred to get the equipment ready for use—they were incurred to get employees ready to operate the equipment. The additional electricity and the annual insurance are period costs and were not incurred to get the equipment ready for use.

2. (a), (b), (d), (f), and (g) are correct

Feedback
With an operating lease, the only transaction recorded would be the payment of rent, which gives rise to rent expense. The leased asset and a liability for the future payments are not recorded as they would be if an asset were purchased using a bank loan.
(c) Is incorrect because title to an asset that is being leased remains with the party collecting the rent (the lessor).
(e) Is incorrect because with operating leases, control of the benefits of the asset is not obtained and therefore the asset is not recorded.

3.   (a), (e), and (f) are correct

Feedback
(a)   Is correct because, with a higher residual value, less depreciation will be recorded in the current year, thereby increasing net income.
(b)   Is incorrect. Because the asset was recently purchased, depreciation using double-diminishing-balance method will be higher than when the straight line method is used and this will increase the depreciation expense and decrease net income.
(c)   Is incorrect because, if the useful life is decreased, depreciation each year will be higher and this will decrease net income.
(d)   Is incorrect. By expensing an asset, net income will fall in the current year and this will more than offset the fact that depreciation on the asset would not be recorded in the current year.
(e)   Is correct. By capitalizing an item that should be expensed in the current year, repair expenses will fall, thereby increasing net income despite the fact that depreciation will rise slightly due to the higher asset cost.
(f)   Is correct because, if the useful life is increased, depreciation each year will be lower and this will increase net income.
(g)   Is incorrect because, with a lower residual value, more depreciation will be recorded in the current year, thereby decreasing net income.

4.   (c), (d), and (f) are correct

Feedback
(a)   and (g) are incorrect because these assets are not used evenly throughout the year and would best be depreciated using the units-of-production method.
(b)   and (e) are incorrect because these assets would be prone to diminishing use over the years as more repairs are performed so they would best be depreciated using the diminishing-balance method.
(c), (d), and (f) are correct because these assets are used evenly over their useful lives.

5.   (b), (c), (e), and (f) are correct

Feedback
(a)   Is incorrect because the number of units produced is already prorated for the portion of the year that the asset was used so there is no need to multiply the depreciation by the portion of the year in use.
(b)   Is correct because the residual value is subtracted from the cost of the asset to determine the depreciable amount and it is this portion of the cost that is depreciated.
(c)   Is correct. If the method chosen gives the lowest possible depreciation, then the accumulated depreciation will be lower and the carrying amount will be higher, making total assets also higher. Because depreciation expense was the lowest possible amount, net income and equity will be the highest possible amounts.
(d)   Is incorrect because, when using the diminishing-balance method, depreciation is higher in the early years of an asset's useful life compared with the straight-line method and the reverse is true in the later years of the asset's life.
(e)   Is correct because, if the residual value was overestimated, the depreciable amount (cost less residual value) would be understated and this would lead to an understatement of depreciation expense.
(f)   Is correct because, if the useful life was overstated, not enough depreciation is recorded each year and the carrying amount of the asset would be higher than it should be. When such an asset is sold, because of the overstatement of its carrying amount, a loss on disposal is more likely.
(g)   Is incorrect because the amount of depreciation taken on an asset should never cause the carrying amount to fall below the residual value of the asset under any method of depreciation.

6.   (c), (e), and (f) are correct

Feedback
Annual depreciation under the straight-line method would be [($12,000 – $2,000) ÷ 5 years] = $2,000. For nine months of use in 2018, depreciation of $1,500 should be recorded. On the date of disposal, the equipment should have accumulated depreciation pertaining to four years and nine months of use, which would be $9,500. Therefore, the carrying amount of the equipment when sold is $12,000 – $9,500 = $2,500 and because the proceeds were $3,200, the gain on disposal is $700. The gain would appear above income from operations. The journal entries that should be recorded for these transactions are:

Depreciation Expense ($2,000 × $9/_{12}$)	1,500	
Accumulated Depreciation—Equipment		1,500
(To record depreciation for nine months in 2018)		
Cash	3,200	
Accumulated Depreciation	9,500	
Equipment		12,000
Gain on Disposal		700

7.   (c) and (e) are correct

Feedback
(a)   and (f) are incorrect and (e) is correct. The machine should be depreciated over its useful life of six, not 10 years. Its residual value will be zero even at the end of six years because the machine cannot be sold at that time. Furthermore, depreciation should start when the machine begins to be used, which is on April 1. Depreciation for the current year is $80,000 ÷ 6 years × $9/_{12}$ = $10,000.
(b)   and (g) are incorrect because the patent application was unsuccessful, so no benefit exists from this activity and the amount spent must be recorded as an expense. Recording this cost as an impairment loss is incorrect because there was never an asset recorded that could become impaired. If the patent had been filed successfully, the cost would have been recorded in a separate patent asset account.
(c)   Is correct and (d) is incorrect. The development costs are capitalized (they were not referred to as research costs so they are not expensed) and amortization of the development costs should start when the production of the product begins, not when sales occur. Amortization is $300,000 ÷ 6 years × $9/_{12}$ = $37,500.

8.   (a), (c), (d), (e) and (f) are correct

Feedback

(b)   Is incorrect because the useful life of an asset must also be disclosed.

(g)   Is incorrect because gains and losses on the disposal of property, plant, and equipment are used to determine income from operations and would be shown above that subtotal in the income statement.

9.   (c), (d), (e), and (g) are correct

Feedback

(a)   and (f) are incorrect because increasing the residual value lowers the depreciable amount and reduces depreciation expense. Increasing the useful life also reduces depreciation expense and this in turn means that that income from operations and net income are overstated, which will also overstate retained earnings, so this makes (e) and (g) correct.

(b)   Is incorrect. Because depreciation is understated, the carrying amount of the equipment is overstated. (Note that the statement of financial position is always balanced—the overstatement of the carrying amount of equipment is offset by an overstatement in retained earnings.)

(c)   Is correct. The error does not affect net sales so when asset turnover is calculated, the numerator is correct, but the average assets denominator will be overstated, thereby reducing the value of the ratio.

(d)   Is correct. Net income is the numerator for this ratio and it is overstated, while the net sales denominator is correct, so this ratio will be overstated.

10.   (a), (e), and (g) are correct

Feedback

		Revenues A	Net Income B	Average Assets C	Asset Turnover A ÷ C	Profit Margin B ÷ A
(a)	Correct	Increased	Unchanged	Decreased	Increased	Decreased
(b)	Incorrect	Unchanged	Increased	Unchanged	Unchanged	Increased
(c)	Incorrect	Unchanged	Increased	Increased	Decreased	Increased
(d)	Incorrect	Decreased	Increased	Unchanged	Decreased	Increased
(e)	Correct	Increased	Unchanged	Unchanged	Increased	Decreased
(f)	Incorrect	Decreased	Increased	Increased	Decreased	Increased
(g)	Correct	Unchanged	Decreased	Decreased	Increased	Decreased

▶ ENDNOTES

[1]Ross Marowits, The Canadian Press, "WestJet Going after Business Travellers with Premium Seating," CBC.ca, September 9, 2015; "WestJet Breaks from Its No-Frills Roots with New Business Perks," *The Globe and Mail*, August 1, 2012; WestJet 2015 annual report; WestJet corporate website, www.westjet.com.

[2]Eriq Gardner, "Justin Bieber Attorneys Fight to Save Their Experts after Missing Deadline in Copyright Lawsuit," *Hollywood Reporter*, April 4, 2016; Paul Chavez and Associated Press, "Justin Bieber and Mentor Usher Must Face Jury Trial in $10 Million Copyright Lawsuit after Federal Appeals Court Revives Case," *Daily Mail*, June 19, 2015; Jonathan Stempel, "Justin Bieber, Usher Ordered to Face Copyright Lawsuit," Reuters.com, June 18, 2015.

10

Reporting and Analyzing Liabilities

CHAPTER PREVIEW

In the last few chapters, we have learned how to account for, and report, current and non-current assets. Just as it is important to understand the nature of a company's assets, it is equally important to know why, and when, a company has to borrow money to finance these assets.

In this chapter, we will review some of the current liabilities you have learned about in past chapters and introduce other types of current liabilities most companies have. We will also introduce some of the different types of liabilities companies use to borrow for the long term, such as mortgages and bonds. We will learn how to use assets and liabilities to analyze a company's liquidity, which is its ability to repay short-term obligations as they come due, and solvency, which is the ability to survive on a long-term basis.

CHAPTER OUTLINE

LEARNING OBJECTIVES	READ	PRACTICE
1 Account for current liabilities.	• Operating line of credit • Sales taxes • Property taxes • Payroll • Short-term notes payable • Current maturities of non-current debt • Provisions and contingent liabilities	**DO IT!** 10-1a Current liabilities 10-1b Provisions and contingent liabilities
2 Account for instalment notes payable.	• Fixed principal payments plus interest • Blended principal and interest payments • Current and non-current portions	**DO IT!** 10-2a Instalment mortgage payable—Fixed payments 10-2b Instalment mortgage payable—Blended payments
3 Identify the requirements for the financial statement presentation and analysis of liabilities.	• Presentation • Analysis	**DO IT!** 10-3a Presentation 10-3b Liquidity and solvency
4 Account for bonds payable (Appendix 10A).	• Accounting for bond issues • Accounting for bond interest expense • Accounting for bond retirements • Determining the issue price of bonds	**DO IT!** 10-4a Bond transactions 10-4b Determining the price of bonds

Richard Lautens/Getty Images

Canada Post Borrows for Future Gains

The Canada Post Group of Companies—a group of related businesses including Canada Post Corporation and non-wholly owned subsidiaries Purolator Holdings Ltd. (Canada's largest courier company), SCI Group Inc., and Innovapost Inc.—employs approximately 65,000 people. In 2015, Canada Post delivered about 9 billion pieces of mail to more than 15 million residential and business addresses across the country.

Like any business, Canada Post Corporation's current liabilities include accounts payable and accrued liabilities, as well as salaries payable to its employees. Current liabilities also include income tax payable, unearned (deferred) revenue, outstanding money orders, and the current portion of its non-current debt. The contractual maturities of these liabilities are less than 12 months.

The Crown corporation also has sizeable long-term or non-current liabilities—those due in over a year—in the form of debts that it uses to finance its operations. There are basically three forms of financing, explains Wayne Cheeseman, Canada Post's chief financial officer. "There's internally generated funds, the equity market, or the debt capital markets. Being a Crown corporation, the equity markets aren't open to us. We do generate funds internally, but it won't be sufficient when we look at our long-term plans. So we looked to the debt capital markets and raised money there, obviously with a plan to pay that off over time."

In 2010, Canada Post raised $1 billion in the Canadian capital markets by issuing two series of bonds—the first series or tranche of $500 million, maturing July 2025 and bearing interest at 4.08%, payable semi-annually;

and the second tranche of $500 million, maturing July 2040 and bearing interest at 4.36%, payable semi-annually, explained Mr. Cheeseman.

The outstanding bonds were part of the "loans and borrowings" item that Canada Post reported as one of its non-current liabilities at the end of 2015. The largest non-current liability on its statement of financial position was "Pension, other post-employment and other long-term benefit liabilities," amounting to $6.4 billion as at December 31, 2015. Like many corporations, Canada Post has a large liability to provide pensions and other post-employment benefits to retired employees, and that's likely to grow. The corporation expected that around 15,000 employees would retire or leave by 2020.

Faced with such large liabilities, declining letter mail volumes, and increased competition in the parcel business, Canada Post launched an action plan in 2014 to cut costs, increase revenues, and modernize its services. As part of the plan, it began to convert millions of urban addresses with delivery at the door to community mailboxes. It also streamlined operations, using more automation for sorting, among other things, which saved more than 2 million labour hours in 2014. "We basically have two goals—to provide an acceptable level of service to all Canadians while remaining financially self-sufficient," says Mr. Cheeseman.

With these long-term plans, Canada Post hopes to remain viable and relevant in Canada's changing and technologically advancing society.[1]

Go to the *REVIEW AND PRACTICE* section at the end of the chapter for a targeted summary and practice questions with solutions.

Visit **WileyPLUS** for more opportunities.

Account for current liabilities.

In Chapter 2, we defined liabilities as present obligations that result from past transactions. These obligations (debts) must be paid sometime in the future by the transfer of assets or through the provision of services. This future date (either the date when assets will be transferred or the date when the services will be provided) determines whether the liability will be a current liability or a non-current liability.

One type of liability is a **financial liability**. These types of liabilities have contractual obligations to pay cash in the future. While most liabilities are financial liabilities, one example of a liability that is not a financial liability is unearned revenue because this will be settled by providing goods or services in the future.

A **current liability** is a liability that will be paid or settled within one year from the date on the statement of financial position or within one operating cycle. Current liabilities also include amounts received from customers in advance for goods to be delivered or services to be performed within one year or operating cycle. A current liability is settled through payment by cash, through the transfer of goods or services, or through the creation of other current liabilities. Most companies pay current liabilities with current assets such as cash rather than by creating other liabilities (for example, paying an account payable by issuing a note payable). All other liabilities are classified as **non-current** or **long-term liabilities**.

Financial statement users want to know whether a company's obligations are current or non-current. This is important since a company that has more current liabilities than current assets often lacks liquidity, which is the ability to pay current liabilities on time. Users must also look at both current and non-current liabilities in total to assess a company's solvency—its ability to pay its interest and total debt, both current and non-current, when due.

Common types of current liabilities include bank indebtedness arising from operating lines of credit; accounts payable; accrued liabilities relating to income tax, salaries, and interest; unearned revenue; notes; and the current portion of long-term liabilities. Entries for many of these liabilities have been explained in previous chapters. In this section, we discuss in more detail operating lines of credit, sales taxes, property taxes, payroll, notes payable, and current portions of long-term liabilities.

The above examples of current liabilities have a known payee (the party that is receiving payment), due date, and amount payable, and are said to be "certain" liabilities. We will also introduce liabilities in this section that have uncertainties regarding the payee, amount, and/or timing of payment. These types of "uncertain" liabilities are known as provisions or contingent liabilities.

OPERATING LINE OF CREDIT

For a variety of reasons, the amount of cash a company has available may be less than it requires. Consequently, companies may borrow cash from banks or other financial institutions by obtaining an **operating line of credit**, also known as a credit facility, to help them manage temporary cash shortfalls. This means that the company has been pre-authorized by the bank to borrow money, up to a pre-set limit, when it is needed. Interest is usually charged at a floating interest rate on any amounts used from the line of credit. A **floating** (or **variable**) **interest rate** is one that is not fixed and is usually based on the prime borrowing rate. The prime rate is the interest rate that banks charge their best customers. For other customers, banks will usually charge interest at the prime rate plus a specified percentage that takes into consideration the risk of lending to that customer.

Security, called **collateral**, is often required by banks as protection against a possible default on the loan by the borrower. Collateral for an operating line of credit normally includes some of the company's current assets (such as accounts receivable or inventory) but may also include some non-current assets (such as investments or property, plant, and equipment).

Line of credit borrowings are normally on a short-term basis, and are repayable immediately upon request—that is, on demand—by the bank. In reality, repayment is rarely demanded without notice. Borrowing from a line of credit is easy to administer because the bank simply allows the borrower to use funds up to the approved line of credit limit.

Amounts that are drawn on an operating line of credit result in a negative or overdrawn cash balance. No special entry is required to record the overdrawn amount. The normal credits to cash will simply accumulate and are reported as **bank indebtedness** in the current liabilities section of the statement of financial position. A note to the financial statements is also prepared describing the interest rate, collateral, and limit applicable to the line of credit.

It is important to look not only at any amounts drawn on the operating line of credit, but also at any unused capacity because this indicates the financial flexibility a company has in terms of what is available for future needs. For example, Canada Post has a line of credit of $100 million but had not drawn on it (used any of the amount) as at December 31, 2015.

SALES TAXES

As consumers, we are well aware that many of the products and services sold to us are subject to sales tax. Sales tax is expressed as a percentage of the sales price. Sales tax may take the form of the Goods and Services Tax (GST), Provincial Sales Tax (PST), or Harmonized Sales Tax (HST), which is a combination of GST and PST. In Quebec, the PST is known as the Quebec Sales Tax (QST).

At the time of writing this textbook, the federal GST was assessed at a rate of 5% across Canada. Provincial sales tax rates varied from 0% to 10% across Canada. In all provinces that are subject to GST and PST, GST is charged on the selling price of the item before PST is applied, thus avoiding GST being charged on PST.

In several provinces, including the Atlantic provinces and Ontario, the PST and GST have been combined into one Harmonized Sales Tax. In 2016, the HST rate ranged from 13% to 15% in these provinces.

When a sale occurs, the retailer collects the sales tax from the customer and periodically (normally monthly) remits (sends) the sales tax collected to the designated federal and provincial collecting authorities. If a customer pays in advance (or purchases a gift card), giving rise to unearned revenue, no sales tax is recorded until later when the revenue is earned. In the case of GST and HST, collections are netted against GST and HST payments made by the company on its own eligible purchases. Only the net amount (that is, GST or HST collected less GST or HST paid) owing or recoverable will be paid or refunded.

The amount of the sale and the amount of the sales tax collected are usually recorded separately by crediting two accounts: Sales, and Sales Tax Payable. For example, assume that on March 25, Islander Corporation had sales of $10,000 and also collected Harmonized Sales Tax of $1,300. (The sale was made in a province where the HST rate is 13%.) The entry is:

Mar. 25	Cash	11,300	
	Sales		10,000
	Sales Tax Payable ($10,000 × 13%)		1,300
	(To record sales and sales taxes)		

A	=	L	+	SE
+11,300		+1,300		+10,000
↑ Cash flows: +11,300				

If, instead of being subject to HST, Islander was located in a province subject to federal GST of $500 (GST rate of 5%) and provincial sales tax of $700 (PST rate of 7%), the entry would be:

Mar. 25	Cash	11,200	
	Sales		10,000
	Sales Tax Payable [($10,000 × 5%) +		1,200
	($10,000 × 7%)]		
	(To record sales and sales taxes)		

A	=	L	+	SE
+11,200		+1,200		+10,000
↑ Cash flows: +11,200				

For simplicity, we use one account—Sales Tax Payable—although many companies use separate accounts for GST Payable and PST Payable. When sales taxes are eventually remitted, the

Sales Tax Payable account is debited and Cash is credited. Note that Islander Corporation is acting as a collection agent for the government. All sales tax it collects from customers will later be remitted to either the federal or provincial government. Amounts collected are a liability until they are remitted.

Accounting for sales tax can be complicated because of different rates in each province, because these rates can change, and because not all goods and services are taxed. Fortunately, point-of-sale computer programs and accounting software can automatically determine and record the correct sales tax rate, or rates, for each good or service provided. Nonetheless, it is still important to make sure all of the relevant sales tax regulations in your jurisdiction are clearly understood before recording sales tax.

PROPERTY TAXES

Businesses that own property pay property taxes each year. These taxes are charged by municipal and provincial governments, and are calculated at a specified rate for every $100 of the assessed value of the property (the land and any buildings). Property taxes are generally for a calendar year, although bills are not usually issued until the spring of each year. In other words, even though a property tax bill may cover the period of January through December, it is not usually issued until March—well after the property tax year has begun.

To illustrate, assume that Tantramar Management Ltd. owns land and a building in the city of Regina. Tantramar's year end is December 31 and it makes adjusting entries annually. Tantramar receives its property tax bill of $6,000 for the calendar year on March 1, payable on May 31.

In March, when Tantramar receives the property tax bill, two months have passed in the year. No entry relating to property taxes for January and February has yet been recorded because this company records adjusting entries annually. The company must now record the property tax expense for the months of January and February and set up the liability owed at that point in time as follows:

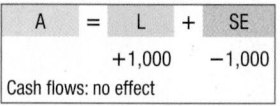

A	=	L	+	SE
		+1,000		−1,000
Cash flows: no effect				

Mar. 1	Property Tax Expense ($6,000 × $^2/_{12}$)	1,000	
	Property Tax Payable		1,000
	(To record property tax expense for January		
	and February)		

In May, when Tantramar records the payment of its property taxes, it is not only paying off the liability recorded on March 1 but also prepaying the property taxes relating to the rest of the year. Since no expense has been recorded yet for property taxes relating to the months of March, April, and May (remember that adjusting entries are not made monthly for this company), the expense for these three months must be recorded at the payment date. Furthermore, since payment is being made for the remaining seven months of the year from June to December, a prepaid asset relating to these months is also recorded, as shown in the following entry:

A	=	L	+	SE
+3,500		−1,000		−1,500
−6,000				
↓ Cash flows: −6,000				

May 31	Property Tax Payable	1,000	
	Property Tax Expense ($6,000 × $^3/_{12}$)	1,500	
	Prepaid Property Tax ($6,000 × $^7/_{12}$)	3,500	
	Cash		6,000
	(To record payment of property tax for		
	January through December)		

After the payment of the property tax, Tantramar has a zero balance in its liability account but does have a prepaid asset. Since Tantramar only makes adjusting entries annually, it would not adjust the Prepaid Property Tax account until year end on December 31. At that time, it would make the following entry to record the expense for the months of June to December:

Dec. 31	Property Tax Expense	3,500	
	Prepaid Property Tax		3,500
	(To record property tax expense for		
	June through December)		

A	=	L	+	SE
−3,500				−3,500

Cash flows: no effect

There are other acceptable ways to record and adjust property taxes. Some companies might debit Property Tax Expense initially when the bill is recorded on March 1 to avoid making adjusting entries later. As we learned in Chapter 4, it is better for control purposes to use a statement of financial position account such as a prepaid when recording cash payments that pertain to expenses relating to subsequent periods of time. We recommend you continue to do so for your assignments.

In addition, companies may prepare monthly or quarterly adjusting entries. In the above example, if Tantramar was recording adjusting journal entries monthly, property taxes would be recorded in January and February based on estimated amounts using historical information. When the property tax notice was received in March, the monthly recording of property tax expense could then be based on actual amounts. Regardless, at year end, whatever way is used, the company should have zero balances in the Prepaid Property Tax and Property Tax Payable accounts and the Property Tax Expense account should have a balance of $6,000. Below is what Tantramar's T accounts look like after the above entries have been posted:

Property Tax Expense				Property Tax Payable			
Mar. 1	1,000			May 31	1,000	Mar. 1	1,000
May 31	1,500					May 31 Bal.	0
Dec. 31	3,500						
Dec. 31 Bal.	6,000			Prepaid Property Tax			
				May 31	3,500	Dec. 31	3,500
				Dec. 31 Bal.	0		

PAYROLL

As employees perform services for their employer, the employer incurs three types of liabilities related to the employees' salaries or wages: (1) the amount owed to employees, (2) employee payroll deductions, and (3) employer payroll obligations.

The first type of liability is the amount of salaries or wages owed to employees. Management and administrative personnel are generally paid **salaries**, which are expressed as a specific amount per week (weekly), per two weeks (biweekly), per month (monthly), or per year (annually). Part-time employees or employees paid on an hourly basis or by the work produced (an amount per unit of product) are normally paid **wages**. The total amount of salaries or wages earned by the employee is called **gross pay**.

The second type of liability is the amount of employee **payroll deductions** required by law to be deducted (withheld) from employees' gross pay. For example, if an employee worked 40 hours during a week, earning $20 per hour, their gross pay would be $800 (40 × $20). The employer is required to withhold amounts, known as payroll deductions, from the employee's gross pay, which are then remitted (paid) to various other parties.

Some payroll deductions are mandatory, while others are voluntary. Mandatory payroll deductions include amounts withheld for federal and provincial income taxes on the employee's earnings. In this way, the government receives income taxes from employees every time the employees are paid. Other deductions include Canada Pension Plan (CPP) contributions and employment insurance (EI) premiums. Companies might also withhold voluntary deductions for benefits such as health and pension plans, union dues, and charitable donations, and for other purposes.

The employee's paycheque will be equal to their gross pay, or total earnings, less any payroll deductions withheld. This amount is known as **net pay**. This is the amount that the company (the employer) must pay to the employee. As all employees will learn, gross pay is very different from net pay.

> **Alternative Terminology**
> *Payroll deductions* are also commonly referred to as *source deductions* because they are being withheld from the employee at the "source" of the payment.

Illustration 10-1 summarizes the types of payroll deductions that most companies normally have and that are responsible for the difference between gross and net pay.

►Illustration 10-1
Payroll deductions

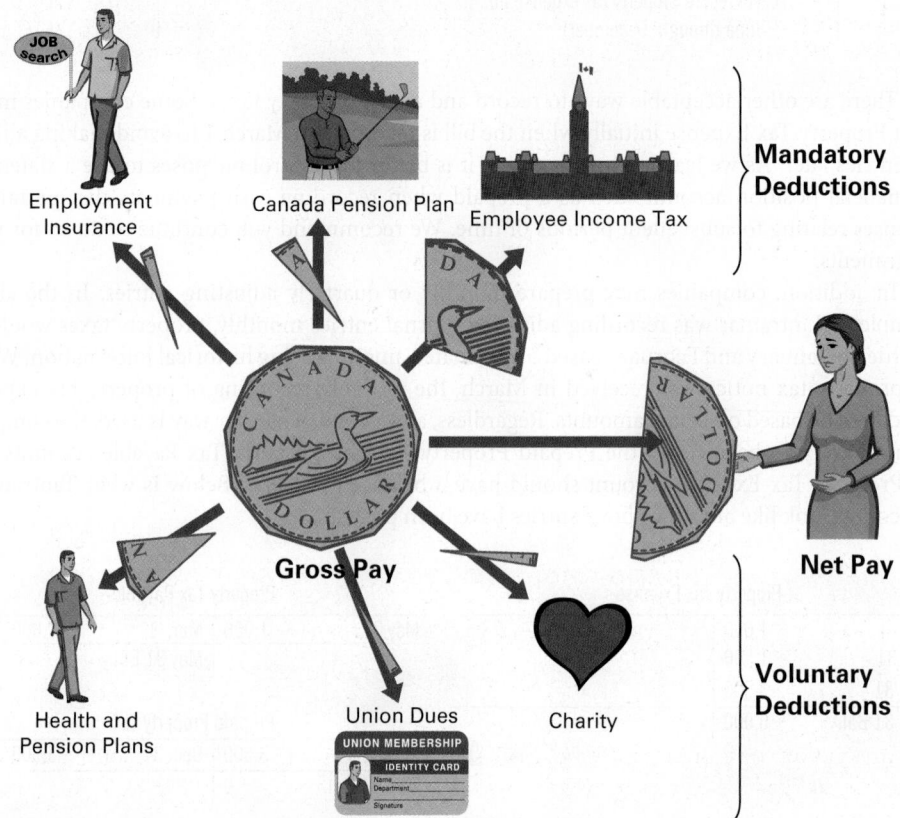

The third type of liability is employer (not employee) payroll obligations. In addition to the liabilities incurred as a result of employee payroll deductions, the employer is also obligated to pay into programs such as CPP and EI and into provincial government programs such as workers' compensation plans. All of these amounts, plus any items pertaining to employer-sponsored health plans and pensions and compensated absences (such as statutory holidays and vacation pay), are referred to together as **employee benefits**. These are not amounts withheld from an employee's pay but instead are additional expenses incurred by the employer.

In summary, companies incur salary expenses and must withhold payroll deductions from their employees on behalf of the government and other third parties. In addition, they also incur various employee benefits expenses. Until these payroll deductions and employee benefits are remitted to the third parties responsible for the related programs, they are reported as current liabilities on the statement of financial position.

To illustrate the recording of payroll, let's assume that an employer accrues salaries of $100,000 for the week ending March 9. The required journal entry, using assumed amounts for the payroll deductions, would be as follows:

A	=	L	+	SE
		+4,950		−100,000
		+1,880		
		+20,427		
		+2,395		
		+1,037		
		+69,311		

Cash flows: no effect

Mar. 9	Salaries Expense	100,000	
	CPP Payable		4,950
	EI Payable		1,880
	Employee Income Tax Payable		20,427
	United Way Payable		2,395
	Union Dues Payable		1,037
	Salaries Payable		69,311
	(To record salaries and employee deductions for the week ending March 9)		

In the above journal entry, the employer records $100,000—the gross pay amount—as salaries expense. The net pay of $69,311 that is owed to employees is recorded as salaries payable. In addition, the employer also records liabilities for the amounts it withheld from the employees' pay for CPP, EI, and employee income tax owed to the government, charitable contributions made on behalf of the United Way, and dues owed to the union. Note that the Employee Income Tax Payable account holds only the amounts withheld from employees' pay regarding amounts that employees owe for their own personal income tax. This account has nothing to do with the income tax that the company (the employer) owes the government for corporate income tax on the income of the company. The account that pertains to income tax owed by the company on its income is called Income Tax Payable.

As noted previously, employers are also required to make contributions to programs such as CPP and EI. They may also make contributions to health plans, pensions, and other programs. These employer payroll costs are not recorded as salaries expense. Instead, these costs are debited to a separate expense account called Employee Benefits Expense. Based on the $100,000 payroll in our example, and using assumed amounts, the following entry would be made to record the employer's expense and liability for its share of the payroll costs, or employee benefits:

Mar. 9	Employee Benefits Expense	12,087	
	CPP Payable		4,950
	EI Payable		2,632
	Workers' Compensation Payable		1,575
	Health Insurance Benefits Payable		2,930
	(To record employer's payroll costs on March 9 payroll)		

A	=	L	+	SE
		+4,950		−12,087
		+2,632		
		+1,575		
		+2,930		
Cash flows: no effect				

In addition to recording the employer's share of CPP and EI in the above journal entry, we have also recorded the employer costs for workers' compensation and health care. In this example, we have assumed that the health care benefits are paid by the employer and are not shared between the employer and the employee, as is sometimes the case.

When the employer pays the employees by direct deposit or by distributing paycheques, the company will record the following entry:

Mar. 9	Salaries Payable	69,311	
	Cash		69,311
	(To record payment of the March 9 payroll)		

A	=	L	+	SE
−69,311		−69,311		
⬇ Cash flows: −69,311				

Although we have recorded the accrual of the payroll and payment of the payroll in separate journal entries above, they could also be combined and recorded in one compound entry—especially if employees are paid on the same day as the accrual is recorded.

Note that in the entry above, the employer is only paying its employees but is not remitting the payroll deductions to the government. Employee payroll deductions and the employer payments for employee benefits will be remitted later in the month when they are due to government authorities or other third parties. In this case, the remittance was made on March 23 and the entry is as follows:

Mar. 23	CPP Payable ($4,950 + $4,950)	9,900	
	EI Payable ($1,880 + $2,632)	4,512	
	Employee Income Tax Payable	20,427	
	United Way Payable	2,395	
	Union Dues Payable	1,037	
	Cash		38,271
	(To record remittance of employee deductions and benefits)		

A	=	L	+	SE
−38,271		−9,900		0
		−4,512		
		−20,427		
		−2,395		
		−1,037		
⬇ Cash flows: −38,271				

Normally payroll deductions must be remitted no later than the 15th day of the month following the monthly pay period. Depending on the size of the payroll deductions, however, the employer's remittance deadline could be different.

ACCOUNTING MATTERS

Understanding Employee Benefits

The new manager at a manufacturing plant is about to hire a new supervisor. The budget only allows $150,000 to be spent on this position each year, so when the manager found a good candidate and was about to offer her a salary of $150,000 per year, the payroll supervisor told her that the most she could offer the new supervisor was a salary of $135,000. The manager did not understand that, in addition to paying the salary, the company was also responsible for spending an extra $15,000 each year on employee benefits consisting of the company's contribution to CPP and EI along with over $8,000 of contributions to the employee's pension plan. So all managers need to understand that a salary is not the only cost incurred when hiring staff.

SHORT-TERM NOTES PAYABLE

A promissory note, or note payable, is a promise to repay a specified amount of money, either at a fixed future date or on demand. Notes payable are often used instead of accounts payable because they give the lender written documentation of the obligation, which helps if legal action is needed to collect the debt. Accounts payable and notes payable that result from transactions with suppliers are often called **trade payables**. Notes payable are also frequently issued to meet short-term financing needs.

Notes can be issued for varying periods of time. Notes that are due for payment within one year of the statement of financial position date are classified as current liabilities. Most notes are interest-bearing, with interest normally due monthly or at maturity. While short-term notes can have floating interest rates, similar to that described earlier for an operating line of credit or credit facility, it is more usual for them to have a fixed interest rate. A **fixed interest rate** is a constant rate for the entire term of the note.

There are differences between an account payable and a note payable. An account payable is supported by an invoice and gives an informal promise to pay, while a note payable is a formal written promise to pay that gives the payee a stronger legal claim. An account payable arises only from credit purchases (amounts owed to suppliers). A note payable can also be used for credit purchases, but is more typically used to extend an account payable beyond normal amounts or due dates or to borrow money. An account payable is usually due within a short period of time (such as 30 days) while a note payable is usually outstanding for longer periods. Finally, an account payable does not incur interest unless the account is overdue, while a note payable usually bears interest for the entire period it is outstanding.

To illustrate the accounting for a note payable, assume that HSBC Bank (the payee) lends $100,000 to Williams Ltd. (the payer) on March 1. Because this note constitutes a loan from a bank, it is commonly referred to as a bank loan payable. The terms *notes* and *loans* are often used interchangeably. The loan is due in four months, on July 1, and bears interest at 3%. Both the principal amount ($100,000) of the loan and the related interest are payable at maturity.

Williams makes the following journal entry when it receives the $100,000:

Alternative Terminology
Notes payable are also commonly referred to as *loans payable*, and *interest expense* is also referred to as *finance costs*.

▼ HELPFUL HINT
Notes payable are the opposite of notes receivable and the accounting is similar.

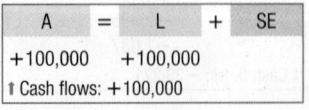

A	=	L	+	SE
+100,000		+100,000		

↑ Cash flows: +100,000

Mar. 1	Cash	100,000	
	Bank Loan Payable		100,000
	(To record receipt of four-month, 3% bank loan from HSBC)		

Interest accrues over the life of the bank loan and must be recorded periodically as it is incurred. If Williams has a March 31 year end and records adjusting entries annually, an adjusting entry is required to recognize the interest expense and interest payable of $250 ($100,000 × 3% × $^1/_{12}$) at March 31. Recall from Chapter 4 that interest is calculated for short-term notes (loans) by multiplying the principal amount by the annual interest rate and by the fraction of the year in which the interest was incurred. Because interest rates are expressed in annual percentages, they must be adjusted for the portion of the year that pertains to the time that interest was incurred.

The adjusting entry is:

▼ HELPFUL HINT
Interest rates are always expressed as an annual (one-year) rate, regardless of the term of the note or loan.

Mar. 31	Interest Expense	250	
	Interest Payable		250
	(To accrue interest for March on HSBC bank loan)		

A	=	L	+	SE
		+250		−250

Cash flows: no effect

In the March 31 year-end financial statements, the current liabilities section of the statement of financial position will show a bank loan payable of $100,000, and interest payable of $250. In addition, interest expense of $250 will be reported in the "other revenues and expenses" section of the income statement.

At maturity on July 1, Williams Ltd. must pay the principal amount of the loan ($100,000) plus $1,000 interest ($100,000 × 3% × $^4/_{12}$). One month of this interest has already been accrued: $250 for the month of March. Interest must also be updated for $750 ($100,000 × 3% × $^3/_{12}$) for the three additional months—April through June—since interest was last recorded. (Recall that adjusting entries for this company are made only annually.) This can be done in two separate entries as shown below, or in one compound entry to record the interest and payment of the note.

July 1	Interest Expense	750	
	Interest Payable		750
	(To accrue interest for April, May, and June on HSBC bank loan)		

A	=	L	+	SE
		+750		−750

Cash flows: no effect

July 1	Bank Loan Payable	100,000	
	Interest Payable ($250 + $750)	1,000	
	Cash ($100,000 + $1,000)		101,000
	(To record payment of HSBC bank loan and interest at maturity)		

A	=	L	+	SE
−101,000		−100,000		
		−1,000		

⬇ Cash flows: −101,000

It is important to watch dates carefully before preparing any transaction or adjusting journal entry. For example, in this particular situation, interest is payable at maturity. If the interest is instead payable monthly, the journal entries above would change. Regardless of whether interest is due periodically or at maturity, when the bank loan matures and is repaid, there should be zero balances remaining in the Bank Loan Payable and Interest Payable accounts. It is always a good idea to prepare T accounts and check that your adjusting entries result in the desired amounts.

How does the accounting for notes receivable differ from the accounting for notes payable? The accounting for notes receivable was covered in Chapter 8. In Illustration 10-2, we compare the journal entries shown above that have been made by Williams Ltd., the payer of the bank loan, with those that would be made by HSBC, the payee of the bank loan.

►Illustration 10-2
Comparison of notes receivable
and payable

		HSBC (Payee)			WILLIAMS LTD. (Payer)		

Acceptance of loan	Mar. 1	Bank Loan Receivable
		  Cash
			100,000	100,000	Cash
					  Bank Loan Payable
						100,000	100,000

Accrual of interest	Mar. 31	Interest Receivable
		  Interest Revenue
			250	250	Interest Expense
					  Interest Payable
						250	250

Record remaining interest	July 1	Interest Receivable
		  Interest Revenue
			750	750	Interest Expense
					  Interest Payable
						750	750

Settlement	July 1	Cash
		  Interest Receivable
		  Bank Loan Receivable
			101,000	1,000
				100,000
					Bank Loan Payable
					Interest Payable
					  Cash
						100,000
						1,000
							101,000

CURRENT MATURITIES OF NON-CURRENT DEBT

Companies often have a portion of non-current (long-term) debt that is due in the current year. For example, Canada Post reports $76 million as the "current portion of long-term debt" at December 31, 2015.

To illustrate, assume that Cudini Construction borrows $25,000 on January 1, 2018, for five years. The terms of the loan specify that each January 1, starting on January 1, 2019, $5,000 of the note will be repaid. When financial statements are prepared on December 31, 2018, $5,000 should be reported as a current liability and $20,000 as a non-current liability.

It is not necessary to prepare an adjusting entry to recognize the current maturities of non-current debt or to have a separate account for the current maturities of non-current debt (although some companies do). We simply recognize the current portion when the statement of financial position is prepared.

DO IT! ►10-1a   Current Liabilities

Action Plan

✔ Record sales separately from sales tax. Recall that sales tax is a liability until remitted.

✔ When the property tax notice is received, record the property tax expense and the property tax payable for the amounts incurred to date. Record the prepaid property tax at the time of payment for any amounts paid in advance.

✔ Record both the employees' portion of the payroll and the benefits owed by the employer. Remember that employee deductions are not an expense for the employer.

✔ Recall that interest rates are expressed on an annual basis, so the formula for interest is: principal value × annual interest rate × time.

Prepare all transaction and adjusting journal entries required to record the following transactions. Assume that the company's year end is December 31 and that it records adjusting entries annually.

1. Pre-tax cash sales on April 2 totalled $256,000. The HST rate is 13%. Record the sales and sales tax.

2. A property tax bill for the calendar year of $12,000 is received on May 1 and is due June 30. No journal entries were recorded for property tax prior to May 1. Record the entries for May 1, for June 30 when the tax is paid, and for December 31, the company's year end.

3. A company's gross salary amounts to $10,000 for the week ended July 11. Amounts deducted from the employees' salaries are CPP of $495, EI of $188, and employee income tax of $3,465. The employer's portion of CPP is $495 and of EI, $263. Record the weekly payroll on July 11, assuming cash is paid to the employees but the payroll deductions have yet to be remitted. On July 18, the company remits payment for all payroll deductions from the weekly payroll of July 11.

4. On December 1, the company borrowed $10,000 on a three-month note payable. Interest on the note is 3% and is payable of the first of each month. Record the journal entries to record the acceptance of this note on December 1; the accrual of interest on December 31, the company's year end; the monthly payments for December, January, and February; and the repayment of the note and interest on March 1.

PROVISIONS AND CONTINGENT LIABILITIES

Liabilities can either be certain (definitely determinable) or uncertain. Liabilities with a known payee, due date, and amount payable are **certain liabilities**. Examples of these include accounts payable, sales tax payable, property tax payable, salaries payable, notes payable, and the other types of liabilities we have covered so far in this section.

Other liabilities are considered uncertain liabilities when a company is not sure to whom an obligation is owed, when that obligation may have to be settled, and/or what amount is needed to settle it. Such *uncertain liabilities* are known as provisions or contingent liabilities. **Provisions** are liabilities of uncertain timing or amount; however, there is no uncertainty about the fact that a liability should be recorded, only that its value and settlement date are uncertain. They are recorded because (1) their outcome is probable and (2) the amount owed can be estimated. Under IFRS, probable is defined as "more likely than not," which is normally interpreted to mean more than a 50% probability of occurring. For example, Canada Post has some buildings with asbestos insulation. Problems with this type of insulation only arise when the asbestos is disturbed. Since some of the buildings are expected to be renovated, the cleanup of asbestos in these buildings is probable and can be estimated, so Canada Post has recorded a provision for this.

Other examples of provisions include product warranties, gift cards, and customer loyalty programs. Let's look at liabilities arising from a product warranty to further illustrate provisions. When a company offers a warranty on its products, it knows it is probable that it will incur an expense for products returned for repair or refund under the warranty. However, it doesn't know exactly when the returns will take place or what they will cost. Still, because these costs can be estimated, a provision is recorded in the same period that the related sale occurred because the warranty obligation arose at the point of sale.

If the outcome is not considered probable or determinable or if the outcome cannot be estimated, no provision would be recorded. Instead, a note to the financial statements would be prepared indicating the details of this unrecorded item. Such unrecorded items are known as **contingent liabilities**. For example, Canada Post has been sued under several lawsuits but is unable to estimate the damages for these, so no provision has been recorded. However, details regarding these lawsuits are shown in a note to the financial statements.

In some circumstances, when the possibility of an outflow of resources (settlement through payment) is remote, a contingent liability is not even disclosed. This is what Canada Post did with regard to the asbestos in the buildings that were not going to be renovated. Because the asbestos was not going to be disturbed, the obligation to fix this problem was remote at the time of its annual report, so no disclosure regarding this was made.

Accounting Standards for Private Enterprises use different terminology and criteria regarding uncertain liabilities. In the questions and problems in this text, we will use the IFRS terms described above. Under ASPE, however, the term *contingent liability* is used instead of the word *provision*. A contingent liability (along with the related contingent loss) is recorded when two conditions are met: (1) it is likely that a future event will confirm that a liability has been incurred and (2) the amount of the related loss can be estimated. If such a loss is likely to occur but cannot be estimated, note disclosure of this contingent loss is made rather than recording it in the accounts. If the loss was unlikely to occur, it would not be recorded or disclosed in the notes to the financial statements. Under ASPE, *likely* has a higher degree of probability than the term *probable* used under IFRS.

▼ **HELPFUL HINT**
Provisions are recorded but contingent liabilities are not. Contingent liabilities are disclosed in the notes to the financial statements except when the possibility of an outflow of resources is remote.

DO IT! ▶10-1b Provisions and Contingent Liabilities

A list of provisions and contingent liabilities follows for a company reporting under IFRS. Identify whether each of the following is a provision or a contingent liability. If a contingent liability, identify whether it should be disclosed or not reported.

1. City council has passed a motion to expropriate some land owned by a company so that a roundabout can be built in the centre of a busy intersection. Negotiations have not yet started to determine the amount that the city will pay the company for the land.

2. A company has been sued for $1 million for alleged gender discrimination in the workplace. The company denies the claim and maintains that it follows appropriate human resources practices in its workplace despite the fact that several employees have launched the suit. Court proceedings are anticipated to start next year.

3. A company has guaranteed a loan for one of its subsidiary companies. The subsidiary has never defaulted on a loan payment in the past.

4. A company sells gift cards during the holiday season. It is not sure when or even if the cards will be redeemed but it does have customer data available from last year's sale of gift cards.

5. A company is facing a nuisance lawsuit and believes that any possibility of paying damages is remote.

SOLUTION

Try this Do It! exercise on your own and then check your answer at the end of the chapter.

Related Exercise Material: BE10–5 and E10–4.

LEARNING OBJECTIVE ▶2 Account for instalment notes payable.

A **non-current liability** is an obligation that is expected to be paid after one year or more. Common examples of non-current liabilities include instalment notes payable, bonds payable, finance leases, deferred income taxes, and pension liabilities. Instalment notes payable are explained in this section, while bonds payable are explained in Appendix 10A. You will recall that finance leases were briefly introduced in Chapter 9. Discussion of deferred income taxes and pension liabilities is left for coverage in an intermediate accounting course.

Using long-term notes payable or loans in debt financing is common. Long-term notes payable are similar to short-term notes payable except that the terms of the notes are for more than one year. Long-term notes may have fixed or floating interest rates. In periods of unstable interest rates, it is common for notes to have a floating interest rate that changes as the prime borrowing rate changes. For example, a company may have long-term debt on which it pays interest at the Bank of Canada prime rate plus 1%.

Long-term notes and loans may be secured or unsecured. A secured note pledges title (ownership) to specific assets as collateral or security for the loan. A note or loan that has property as collateral is known as a mortgage. These are widely used by individuals to purchase homes and by many companies to acquire buildings. Unsecured notes and loans offer no collateral to the lender and are issued against the general credit of the borrower.

ACCOUNTING MATTERS

MORTGAGE APPLICAT...

Mustilk/Getty Images, Inc.

Personal Mortgages

The average mortgage on a Canadian home is over $190,000. Household debt is now 163% of annual household income. This means the average household has roughly $1.63 of debt for every dollar they earn.

Nearly a third of mortgage holders would default on their mortgage payments if they were unemployed for more than three months. This is also a real possibility for younger borrowers who earn less money, have stagnant incomes, and live in provinces where they paid a high amount to purchase a house in a hot housing market, which is now cooling off. It is not surprising that the Bank of Canada has stated that household debts are still a top risk to the nation's financial system.[2]

As with short-term notes, the terms *notes* and *loans* are often used interchangeably. While short-term notes are normally repayable in full at maturity, most long-term notes are repayable in a series of periodic payments. These payments are known as **instalments** and are paid monthly, annually, or at other defined intervals of time. Each instalment payment consists of a mix of (1) interest on the unpaid balance of the loan, and (2) a repayment of a portion of the loan principal. The actual instalment payments generally take one of two forms: (1) fixed principal payments plus interest, or (2) blended principal and interest payments. Let's look at each of these payment patterns in more detail.

FIXED PRINCIPAL PAYMENTS PLUS INTEREST

Instalment loans with fixed principal payments are repayable in **equal periodic amounts plus interest**. As mentioned earlier, interest rates may be either fixed or floating. For simplicity, we will assume a fixed interest rate. To illustrate, assume that on January 1, 2018, Belanger Ltée borrows $120,000 from the bank for a five-year period at a 4% interest rate to finance a research laboratory. The entry to record the loan is as follows:

Jan. 1	Cash	120,000	
	Bank Loan Payable		120,000
	(To record receipt of five-year, 4% bank loan)		

A	=	L	+	SE
+120,000		+120,000		
↑ Cash flows: +120,000				

The terms of the loan provide for equal monthly principal payments of $2,000 that can be calculated by taking the initial loan amount and dividing it by the number of periods covered by the loan term ($120,000 ÷ 60 monthly periods). This loan requires payments on the first of each month, plus interest of 4% on the outstanding principal balance.

Monthly interest expense is calculated by multiplying the outstanding principal balance at the beginning of the period by the interest rate. Because a portion of the principal balance is repaid each month, the outstanding principal balance will decrease each month. This is different from what we observed in the calculation of interest on short-term loans, where the principal balance does not change throughout the term of a short-term loan.

For Belanger, the first payment date is February 1, and the interest expense is $400 ($120,000 × 4% × $1/12$). Similar to short-term loans, the 4% is an annual interest rate and must be adjusted for the monthly time period. The cash payment of $2,400 is the total of the principal payment of $2,000, plus the interest of $400.

The entry to record the first instalment payment on February 1 is as follows:

Feb. 1	Interest Expense ($120,000 × 4% × $1/12$)	400	
	Bank Loan Payable	2,000	
	Cash ($2,000 + $400)		2,400
	(To record instalment payment on bank loan)		

A	=	L	+	SE
−2,400		−2,000		−400
↓ Cash flows: −2,400				

An instalment payment schedule is a useful tool to help organize this information and to provide information that helps prepare journal entries. A partial instalment payment schedule for the first few months for Belanger Ltée, with amounts rounded to the nearest dollar, is shown in Illustration 10-3.

▶Illustration 10-3
Instalment payment schedule—
fixed principal payments

	BELANGER LTÉE			
	Instalment Payment Schedule—Fixed Principal Payments Plus Interest			
Interest Period	(A) Cash Payment (B + C)	(B) Interest Expense (D × 4% × ¹⁄₁₂)	(C) Reduction of Principal ($120,000 ÷ 60)	(D) Principal Balance (D − C)
Jan. 1				$120,000
Feb. 1	$2,400	$400	$2,000	118,000
Mar. 1	2,393	393	2,000	116,000
Apr. 1	2,387	387	2,000	114,000

Column A, the cash payment, is the total of the principal payment, $2,000, plus the interest. The cash payment changes each period because the interest changes. Column B determines the interest expense by multiplying the principal at the beginning of the period by the interest rate. Each period, interest expense decreases because the principal balance, on which interest is calculated, decreases. Column C is the principal repayment amount of $2,000. This payment is constant each period in a "fixed principal payment plus interest" pattern. Column D is the principal balance, which decreases each period by the amount of the principal repayment of $2,000 each period.

In summary, with fixed principal payments plus interest, the interest decreases each period as the principal decreases. The portion applied to the reduction of the loan principal stays constant, but because of the decreasing interest, the total cash payment decreases.

DO IT! ▶10-2a | Instalment Mortgage Payable—Fixed Payments

On December 31, 2017, Harbin Inc. borrowed $400,000 after signing a 10-year, 4% mortgage. The terms provide for semi-annual fixed principal payments plus interest on June 30 and December 31 each year. (a) Calculate the amount of the semi-annual payment. (b) Prepare an instalment payment schedule for the first year of the mortgage through to December 31, 2018. (c) Prepare the journal entries required to record the receipt of the mortgage loan on December 31, 2017, and the first two instalment payments on June 30, 2018, and December 31, 2018.

Action Plan

✔ To calculate the semi-annual payment, divide the mortgage amount by the number of semi-annual periods. Remember, semi-annual means every six months.

✔ Prepare an instalment payment schedule. Round all amounts to the nearest dollar.

✔ Multiply the semi-annual interest rate by the principal balance at the beginning of the period to determine the interest expense.

✔ Record the instalment payments, recognizing that each payment consists of (1) interest on the unpaid mortgage balance, and (2) a reduction of the mortgage principal (the payment calculated in part (a)).

BLENDED PRINCIPAL AND INTEREST PAYMENTS

Instalment loan payments can also be made on a blended basis whereby the total payment each period does not change as it does with fixed principal payment arrangements. Blended principal and interest payments are made in **equal periodic** amounts. The periodic payment still has a portion relating to interest and a portion to principal but as the loan balance decreases, the interest portion of the payment also decreases. Since the loan payment is constant each period, the decreasing interest portion of each payment means that there is an increasing portion of each payment that is applied to reduce the principal balance of the loan. Therefore, in contrast to fixed principal payment loans, with a blended payment loan, the portion of the payment applied to the loan principal increases each period. Most consumer and mortgage loans use blended payments rather than fixed principal payments plus interest.

To illustrate this arrangement, assume that instead of fixed principal payments plus interest, Belanger Ltée repays its bank loan in equal monthly blended principal and interest instalments of $2,210. As with the fixed payments illustrated above, monthly interest expense is calculated by multiplying the outstanding principal balance by the interest rate. For the first payment date—February 1—interest expense is $400 ($120,000 × 4% × $^{1}/_{12}$). The instalment payment of $2,210 is fixed for each month, but the interest and principal components of each payment will vary. In February, the principal balance will be reduced by $1,810, which is the difference between the instalment payment of $2,210 and the interest amount of $400.

The entry to record the borrowing of the money from the bank on January 1 is the same as in the previous section. The entry to record the instalment payment uses the same accounts but different amounts (except that interest expense is the same amount for the first month). The first instalment payment on February 1 is recorded as follows:

Feb. 1	Interest Expense ($120,000 × 4% × $^{1}/_{12}$)	400	
	Bank Loan Payable ($2,210 − $400)	1,810	
	Cash		2,210
	(To record instalment payment on bank loan)		

A	=	L	+	SE
−2,210		−1,810		−400

↓ Cash flows: −2,210

An instalment payment schedule can also be prepared for blended principal and interest payments. Illustration 10-4 shows a partial instalment payment schedule for the first few months for Belanger Ltée, with amounts rounded to the nearest dollar.

BELANGER LTÉE				
Instalment Payment Schedule—Blended Principal and Interest Payments				
Interest Period	(A) Cash Payment	(B) Interest Expense (D × 4% × $^{1}/_{12}$)	(C) Reduction of Principal (A − B)	(D) Principal Balance (D − C)
Jan. 1				$120,000
Feb. 1	$2,210	$400	$1,810	118,190
Mar. 1	2,210	394	1,816	116,374
Apr. 1	2,210	388	1,822	114,552

►Illustration 10-4
Instalment payment schedule—blended payments

Column A, the cash payment, is specified and is the same for each period. The amount of this cash payment can actually be calculated mathematically, but you will cover this in more advanced courses.

Column B determines the interest expense, which decreases each period because the principal balance that the interest is calculated on decreases. Column C shows how much the principal is reduced by. This is the difference between the cash payment of $2,210 and the interest for the period. Consequently, this amount will increase each period. Column D is the principal balance, which decreases each period by a varying amount; that is, by the reduction of the principal amount from Column C. When we prepare this schedule, we determine the interest portion of the payment and then subtract this from the total payment to determine the portion of the payment that relates to the reduction of principal.

In summary, with blended payments, the interest decreases each period as the principal decreases. The total cash payment stays constant, but because of the decreasing interest, the reduction of principal increases.

Illustration 10-5 summarizes the differences between the two types of instalment payment patterns:

►Illustration 10-5
Differences between two types of instalment payment patterns

Instalment Payment Pattern	Principal	Interest	Total Cash Payment
Fixed principal plus interest	Constant: Portion of loan payment applied to reduce principal is equal each period	Decreases: Interest expense decreases each period	Decreases: Total cash payment decreases each period as interest expense decreases each period
Blended principal and interest	Increases: Portion of loan payment applied to reduce principal increases each period	Decreases: Interest expense decreases each period	Constant: Total cash payment equal each period

CURRENT AND NON-CURRENT PORTIONS

With both types of instalment loans, the principal portion of the loan that will be paid off within the next year must be reported as a current liability. The balance of the outstanding principal is classified as a non-current liability.

For example, consider the blended payment schedule in Illustration 10-6 for a $51,000 loan where $11,456 payments are made at the end of each year and the interest rate is 4%:

▶Illustration 10-6

Blended payment schedule—liability classification

Interest Period	Cash Payment	Interest Expense	Reduction of Principal	Principal Balance
Issue Date				$51,000
2017	$11,456	$2,040	$9,416	41,584
2018	11,456	1,663	9,793	31,791
2019	11,456	1,272	10,184	21,607
2020	11,456	864	10,592	11,015
2021	11,456	441	11,015	0

If financial statements were being prepared at the end of 2018, the company would report $31,791 as its total liability for the bank loan, shown in the principal balance column. Of this, $10,184—the amount of principal to be repaid within the next year (2019), which is highlighted above in red—would be reported as a current liability. Meanwhile, the remaining portion of the loan, which is $21,607, would be reported as a non-current liability. This amount, too, is highlighted in red in the above table. Note that, when the current portion ($10,184) and the non-current portion ($21,607) are added together, the amount should agree with the total amount owing at the end of 2018, $31,791. Note as well that, because payments occur at the end of the year, there is no interest payable to report on the financial statements.

DO IT! ▶10-2b | Instalment Mortgage Payable—Blended Payments

SOLUTION

Try this Do It! exercise on your own and then check your answer at the end of the chapter.

Related Exercise Material: BE10–8, BE10–9, E10–5, E10–6, and E10–7.

On December 31, 2017, Harbin Inc. borrowed $400,000 after signing a 10-year, 4% mortgage. The terms provide for semi-annual blended principal and interest payments of $24,463 (principal and interest) on June 30 and December 31. (a) Prepare an instalment payment schedule for the first two years of the mortgage through to December 31, 2019. (b) Prepare the journal entries required to record the receipt of the mortgage loan on December 31, 2017, and the first two instalment payments on June 30, 2018, and December 31, 2018. (c) Show the presentation of the mortgage liability on the statement of financial position at December 31, 2018.

Action Plan

✔ Prepare an instalment payment schedule. Round all amounts to the nearest dollar.

✔ Multiply the semi-annual interest rate by the principal balance at the beginning of the period to determine the interest expense. Remember, semi-annual means every six months.

✔ The reduction of principal is the difference between the cash payment and the interest expense.

✔ Record the instalment payments, recognizing that each payment consists of (1) interest on the unpaid mortgage balance, and (2) a reduction of the mortgage principal.

✔ The current portion of the mortgage payable as at December 31, 2018, is the amount of principal that will be repaid in the next year (2019). Because of this, the instalment payment schedule prepared in part (a) must be prepared up to December 31, 2019. The non-current portion is the total liability as at December 31, 2019 (or the total liability as at December 31, 2018, less the current portion).

LEARNING OBJECTIVE 3 | Identify the requirements for the financial statement presentation and analysis of liabilities.

Many companies finance a significant portion of their assets with liabilities so existing and potential creditors and shareholders want to understand the details and characteristics of liabilities in order to assess the liquidity and solvency of these companies. We will look at the presentation and analysis of liabilities in this section.

PRESENTATION

The presentation of liability-related accounts in the income statement is fairly straightforward. You will recall from Chapter 5 when we learned to prepare a multiple-step income statement that interest expenses are separately reported in the "other revenues and expenses" section of the statement. The presentation in the statement of financial position is a bit more involved, so we will look at this in more detail.

Current Liabilities

As discussed previously, liabilities are shown as current or non-current on the statement of financial position, with current liabilities generally reported as the first category in the liabilities section. Each of the primary types of current liabilities can be listed separately within this category or detailed in the notes to the financial statements. In addition, the terms of any operating lines of credit and notes (loans) payable are disclosed in the notes to the financial statements.

Current liabilities are generally listed in the order in which they are due (that is, the liability that will be repaid first is listed first). Bank indebtedness (operating line of credit) is usually listed first, followed by accounts payable and other types of payables in the estimated order that they will be paid. These in turn are followed by unearned revenue and the current portions of any loans. However, this can be difficult to do because some liability accounts listed on the statement of financial position can be composed of a number of liabilities with different due dates.

Illustration 10-7 shows how Canada Post presents its current liabilities in its statement of financial position.

CANADA POST Statement of Financial Position (partial) December 31, 2015 (in millions)	
Current liabilities	
Trade and other payables	$ 530
Salaries and benefits payable	434
Provisions	65
Income tax payable	65
Unearned revenue	124
Current portion of loans	76
Other long-term benefit liabilities	62
Total current liabilities	1,356

▶Illustration 10-7
Canada Post current liabilities

Non-Current Liabilities

Non-current or long-term liabilities are usually reported separately, immediately following current liabilities. There is no generally prescribed order within the non-current liability classification.

The presentation of Canada Post's non-current liabilities is shown in Illustration 10-8.

CANADA POST Statement of Financial Position (partial) December 31, 2015 (in millions)	
Non-current liabilities	
Loans and borrowings	$1,059
Pension, other post-employment and other long-term benefit liabilities	6,398
Other liabilities	31
Total non-current liabilities	7,488

▶Illustration 10-8
Canada Post non-current liabilities

Generally, non-current liabilities are measured and reported at the amount due when the liability is expected to be paid. There are exceptions to this, but these typically relate to bonds that are reported at their amortized cost. Bonds are covered in Appendix 10A of this chapter. The fair value of the non-current debt should also be disclosed in the notes to the financial statements if it is possible to estimate it. In limited circumstances, there is an option to value financial liabilities at fair value, but this option is used rarely in practice. Valuing financial liabilities at fair value normally applies only to complex financial instruments, which are beyond the scope of an introductory accounting course and are not discussed here.

Full disclosure of non-current debt is very important. Summary data are usually presented in the statement of financial position. Detailed information (such as interest rates, maturity dates, assets pledged as collateral, and fair value, if available) is shown in the notes to the financial statements along with a list showing the amount of non-current debt that is scheduled to be paid off in each of the next five years. Canada Post's disclosure about its non-current liabilities fills 10 pages in the notes to its financial statements.

DO IT! 10-3a   Presentation

Action Plan

✔ Review the definition of a liability: an obligation that must be paid in the future by a transfer of assets or provision of goods or services.

✔ Understand the difference between current and non-current liabilities. Current liabilities are expected to be paid within the year; all other liabilities are non-current.

Identify which of the items listed below are likely current liabilities and which are likely non-current liabilities. Identify any items that are not liabilities and explain where, if anywhere, each item should be classified or disclosed.

Accounts payable
Bonds payable
Current portion of mortgage payable
Employee benefits expense
Employee income tax payable
Interest expense
Loan guarantee

Mortgage payable
Operating leases
Prepaid property tax
Salaries payable
Sales tax payable
Unused operating line of credit
Warranty provision

SOLUTION
Try this Do It! exercise on your own and then check your answer at the end of the chapter.

Related Exercise Material: BE10–10 and E10–8.

ANALYSIS

A careful examination of debt obligations makes it easier to assess a company's ability to pay its current obligations. It also helps determine whether a company can obtain long-term financing in order to grow.

Liquidity

Liquidity ratios measure a company's short-term ability to pay its maturing obligations and to meet unexpected needs for cash within the next year. You will recall that we learned about liquidity ratios such as the current ratio (current assets ÷ current liabilities) in Chapter 2, the inventory turnover ratio (cost of goods sold ÷ average inventory) in Chapter 6, and the receivables turnover ratio (net credit sales ÷ average gross accounts receivable) in Chapter 8. We will not illustrate these ratios again here.

In recent years, many companies have intentionally reduced their less liquid current assets (such as accounts receivable and inventory) because these assets cost too much to hold. Companies that keep fewer liquid assets on hand must rely on other sources of liquidity. One such source is an operating line of credit, as discussed earlier in this chapter, which can be drawn upon when a cash shortfall exists. Consequently, it is important to interpret a company's liquidity ratios in the context of any unused lines of credit, which add to a company's short-term financing flexibility.

You may recall that we discussed Canada Post's operating line of credit earlier in the chapter. This corporation has access to $100 million from a line of credit, but none of this has been used or drawn on to date.

Solvency

Solvency ratios, such as the debt to total assets and times interest earned ratios, measure a company's ability to repay its long-term debt and survive over a long period of time. Most companies, like Canada Post, go into debt in order to grow a business. However, debt must be carefully monitored to ensure that it does not hurt a company's solvency. We will review the debt to total assets ratio next, and then introduce a related ratio, the times interest earned ratio.

DEBT TO TOTAL ASSETS   In Chapter 2, you learned that one measure of a company's solvency is **debt to total assets**. It is calculated by dividing total liabilities by total assets. This ratio indicates the extent to which a company's assets are financed by debt. Let's review this ratio by applying it to Canada Post.

Using the following selected information (in millions) from Canada Post's statement of financial position, the company's debt to total assets ratios for 2015 and 2014 are calculated in Illustration 10-9. The illustration also shows summary ratios for United Parcel Service (UPS), Canada Post's closest competitor (recall that Canada Post owns Purolator Inc.), as well as industry averages.

	2015	2014
Total assets	$7,720	$7,584
Total liabilities	8,844	9,595

►Illustration 10-9
Debt to total assets

$$\text{DEBT TO TOTAL ASSETS} = \frac{\text{TOTAL LIABILITIES}}{\text{TOTAL ASSETS}}$$		
(in millions)	2015	2014
Canada Post	$\frac{\$8,844}{\$7,720} = 114.6\%$	$\frac{\$9,595}{\$7,584} = 126.5\%$
UPS	93.6%	93.9%
Industry average	54.4%	38.6%

Whereas for liquidity ratios, higher values generally indicate that a company has a greater ability to meet its current obligations, for the debt to total assets ratio, a lower value indicates that the company has not used as much debt to finance its assets. This reduces the risk of not being able to pay back that debt along with the related interest if economic conditions worsen or interest rates rise.

Canada Post's debt to total assets ratio improved in 2015 from 126.5% to 114.6%. This occurred because a portion of its liabilities were paid down in 2015.

Canada Post's debt to total assets is, however, much worse (higher) than that of UPS in both 2015 and 2014. The reason why Canada Post's debt to total assets exceeds 100% is because its liabilities are greater than its assets. This has occurred because its equity is negative due to a deficit (negative retained earnings) caused by losses in prior years. Note that it is difficult to compare Canada Post fully with UPS because UPS does not deliver letter mail. Canada Post is the sole mail provider in Canada. Still, a significant portion of both companies' business consists of package delivery. Both companies' debt to total assets ratios are much higher than the industry average. This is partly due to the fact that many companies in the industry are owned by governments and are not financed with significant amounts of debt.

Debt to total assets varies across industries because different financing options are appropriate for different industries. For example, the average debt to total assets ratio for the oil and gas pipeline industry was 58% in 2015. The average debt to total assets ratio for the semiconductor industry for the same period was lower, at 19.3%. Industries with lower debt levels are often industries that cannot provide lenders with reliable forms of collateral. The major asset for a pipeline company is property and equipment that can be seized and sold if the company fails to pay its debts on time but a semiconductor company's assets are often intangible in nature so its lenders require more equity financing than other industries.

TIMES INTEREST EARNED   The **times interest earned** ratio gives an indication of a company's ability to meet interest payments as they come due. The higher this ratio, the more able a company is to pay its interest charges. This ratio should be compared with the debt to total assets ratio because, even if a company has a high debt to total assets ratio, it may still be able to easily cover its interest payments if the times interest earned ratio is also high. Alternatively a company may have a low debt to total assets ratio but despite this relatively low level of debt, the company may struggle to cover its interest payments as indicated by a low times interest earned ratio.

The times interest earned ratio is calculated by dividing the sum of net income, interest expense, and income tax expense by interest expense. It uses net income or earnings before interest and taxes (often abbreviated as **EBIT**) because this number best represents the amount that is available to cover interest.

EBIT can be found directly on the income statement or calculated by adding interest expense and income tax expense to net income. These are amounts that were originally deducted to determine net income. They are added back now to *remove* them from net income, and give the amount of net income before interest and taxes.

Illustration 10-10 uses the following selected information (in millions) from Canada Post's income statement to calculate its times interest earned ratios for 2015 and 2014. The illustration also shows summary ratios for UPS and industry averages.

	2015	2014
Interest expense	$50	$ 53
Income tax expense	37	71
Net income	99	198

▶Illustration 10-10
Times interest earned

$$\text{TIMES INTEREST EARNED} = \frac{\text{NET INCOME} + \text{INTEREST EXPENSE} + \text{INCOME TAX EXPENSE}}{\text{INTEREST EXPENSE}}$$

(in millions)	2015	2014
Canada Post	$\frac{\$99 + \$50 + \$37}{\$50} = 3.7$ times	$\frac{\$198 + \$53 + \$71}{\$53} = 6.1$ times
UPS	22.5 times	14.1 times
Industry average	9.4 times	5.9 times

Contrary to the debt to total assets ratio, a higher times interest earned ratio is better because it measures a company's ability to pay its interest expense. Although the interest expense changed only slightly in 2015 compared with 2014, Canada Post's falling profit in 2015 decreased this ratio. Consequently, its times interest earned ratio was much lower than the corresponding value for UPS, which increased its profitability in 2015 by more than 50%. Canada Post's declining profitability also gave it a much lower times interest earned ratio compared to the industry average.

OPERATING LEASES   You will recall that leases were introduced in Chapter 9. For accounting purposes, operating leases are treated as periodic rentals—only rent expense is recorded and no asset or liability related to the future rent payments is shown on the company's statement of financial position. Finance or capital leases, on the other hand, are treated like debt-financed asset purchases, which are recorded on the statement of financial position along with a liability for the future payments to be made under the lease.

Operating leases are often short-term, such as a lease for the rental of a car or an apartment. If, however, an operating lease covers a long period of time, it may be viewed as "off–balance sheet financing." Off–balance sheet financing simply refers to the fact that, with an operating lease, the rented asset and its related liability are not recorded on the statement of financial position.

Many believe that some companies will choose to structure a lease arrangement as an operating lease rather than a finance lease simply to avoid recording a large liability for future rent payments. In their opinion, if an operating lease results in the long-term use of an asset and an unavoidable obligation, it should be recorded as an asset and a liability rather than as a periodic rental expense.

You may also recall from Chapter 9 that an updated standard on accounting for leases under IFRS has been issued, which becomes effective January 1, 2019, or earlier if a company chooses. Under the new standard, leases with terms longer than one year will be treated as finance leases.

Companies are required to report, in notes to their financial statements, all operating lease commitments. Canada Post reports a total commitment of $914 million over the entire term of its operating leases for facilities, transportation equipment, and other assets.

This information allows analysts and other financial statement users to adjust a company's ratios for these unrecorded commitments if they feel that the inclusion of these future lease payments would have a significant effect on the interpretation of a company's solvency. Canada Post's operating lease commitments are about 10.3% of its total liabilities, so they may be considered to be significant to a user's decision-making. Because the adjustments required to analyze the effects of operating leases on solvency ratios are complex, they are left to a financial statement analysis course.

CREDIT RATINGS   Credit-rating agencies, such as the Dominion Bond Rating Service (DBRS), provide opinions about a company's ability to make timely payments (of principal and interest) on its short- and long-term debt. Short-term debt is rated using an "R" scale, with R-1 being the highest credit quality. Within this scale, the rating is further divided as R-1 (high), R-2 (middle), and R-3 (low) to further distinguish between high, superior, and satisfactory credit quality. Short-term debt rated as R-4 or R-5 is considered to be "speculative," which is a term used to describe a high degree of risk.

Long-term debt is rated using a different letter scale than short-term debt. The highest-quality long-term debt is rated as AAA, superior quality as AA, and good quality as A. The credit scale descends to the D, or default, category. Generally, long-term debt rated below BBB is referred to as speculative and non-investment grade, with a higher risk of default. Canada Post's long-term debt is rated AAA—the highest rating possible by DBRS.

KEEPING AN EYE ON CASH

Cash is critical with respect to debt. Companies must not only be able to generate enough cash to pay their interest charges when due but also to repay any principal amounts due at various dates throughout the term of the loan or at maturity. If a company fails to make payment (defaults) on any of these due dates, it can have serious consequences for its credit rating.

Debt covenants help lenders monitor the risk of default. Most borrowing agreements include restrictions called debt covenants that restrict a company's ability to invest, pay dividends, or make other decisions that might adversely affect the company's ability to pay interest and principal on its outstanding debt.

As well, the statement of cash flows helps provide information about how much cash is being used for debt purposes. Cash paid for interest expense is usually reported in the operating activities section of the cash flow statement. Information on payments of the principal portion of debt and the taking out of new debt are reported in the financing activities section of the statement. We will learn about using the statement of cash flows to calculate debt coverage ratios in Chapter 13.

DO IT! ▶10-3b   Liquidity and Solvency

Action Plan

✔ Determine total current assets and total current liabilities. Divide current assets by current liabilities to calculate the current ratio.

✔ Determine total liabilities. Divide total liabilities by total assets to calculate the debt to total assets ratio.

✔ Divide the net income before interest and income tax expense by the interest expense to calculate the times interest earned ratio. If the only item in the other revenues or expenses section of the income statement is interest expense, then EBIT is the same as income from operations.

✔ Recall that if the current ratio and interest coverage ratios are higher, then the company's liquidity and ability to make interest payments have improved. If the debt to total assets ratio is higher, the company is undertaking a greater level of risk with regard to its financing.

SOLUTION

Try this Do It! exercise on your own and then check your answer at the end of the chapter.

Related Exercise Material: BE10–11, BE10–12, E10–9, and E10–10.

O'Leary Ltd. reported the following information in its financial statements.

O'LEARY LTD.
Financial Information
December 31

	2018	2017
Assets		
Cash	$ 11,000	$ 10,000
Inventory	38,000	31,000
Prepaid expenses	6,000	5,000
Equipment	210,000	93,600
Total assets	$265,000	$139,600
Liabilities and shareholders' equity		
Accounts payable	$ 19,400	$ 23,800
Interest payable	6,400	2,800
Bonds payable	160,000	70,000
Common shares	12,000	8,000
Retained earnings	67,200	35,000
Total liabilities and shareholders' equity	$265,000	$139,600
Revenue	$320,000	$180,000
Operating expenses	260,000	151,000
Income from operations	60,000	29,000
Interest expense	12,800	5,600
Income tax expense	15,000	8,000
Net income	$ 32,200	$ 15,400

(a) Calculate the company's current, debt to total assets, and times interest earned ratios for each year.

(b) Identify if the change in each ratio from 2017 to 2018 is an improvement or a deterioration and provide an explanation for this.

LEARNING OBJECTIVE ▶4

Appendix 10A: Account for bonds payable.

Like other kinds of non-current debt, a **bond** is a promise to repay a specified amount of money (a face value) at a fixed future date in addition to periodic interest payments throughout the term of the bond. A bond is often used instead of other types of debt when the amount of financing needed is too large for one lender. When a company issues bonds for a large amount, say $100 million, this is done by issuing numerous bonds in different denominations, typically with the smallest one being $1,000, although this can vary. This makes it possible for more than one lender to participate in the bond offering. Whereas both small and large organizations issue notes, typically only large corporations and governments issue bonds (although some universities have, too).

In Canada in 2014, there were over $1 trillion in government bonds outstanding and over $460 billion in corporate bonds outstanding.[3]

Accounting for notes and bonds is quite similar. Both have a fixed maturity date and pay interest. Although both can have a fixed or floating interest rate, most bonds have a fixed interest rate. This rate, which determines the amount of interest to pay to bondholders, is known as the **coupon interest rate** and is always quoted as an annual rate. Bond interest is normally paid semi-annually, although some bonds pay interest monthly, quarterly, or annually, similar to notes. Like notes, bonds may be unsecured or secured. Unsecured bonds are also known as debentures. Both notes and bonds can be payable at maturity or in instalments.

> **Alternative Terminology**
> The *face value* is also known as the *par value*.

> **Alternative Terminology**
> The *coupon interest rate* is also known as the *contractual interest rate* or the *stated interest rate*.

ACCOUNTING FOR BOND ISSUES

A significant difference between notes and bonds is that bonds can be traded on a public exchange in the same way that shares trade. Notes are seldom traded on exchanges. **Bond prices are quoted as a percentage of the face value of the bonds.** For example, if the bond price is stated as 100, this means that the bonds will sell at 100% of the face value. If the face value is $1,000, then the bonds will sell for $1,000 ($1,000 × 100%). For our purposes, you can assume that bonds are issued in $1,000 denominations unless you are told otherwise.

However, we need to be aware that the coupon interest rate may differ from the **market interest rate**, which is the rate investors demand to earn for lending their money. This rate is also commonly known as the effective interest rate. Market interest rates change daily. They are influenced by the type of bond issued, the company's financial position and performance, the state of the economy, and current industry conditions, among other factors.

> **Alternative Terminology**
> The *market interest rate* and the *effective interest rate* are also known as the *yield*.

Let us assume that Candlestick Inc. issues 5%, $1 million bonds on January 1, 2018, with semi-annual interest payments. The bonds mature in two years. Notice that the coupon rate on these bonds is 5%. That amount of interest will be paid in two semi-annual payments on July 1 and January 1, with the first payment being made on July 1, 2018. Most bonds have a much longer term than two years, but we are using this shorter time frame for simplicity. The bonds will be sold to public investors. If those investors believe that the coupon rate on the bond is fair, they will pay Candlestick Inc. $1 million for the bonds on January 1, 2018, and be content to receive the interest payments on these bonds for the next two years along with the return of the $1 million face amount for these bonds on January 1, 2020. In this case, the bond is said to be sold at face value. The coupon rate will be considered fair if it is equal to the market interest rate for other investments with the same level of risk and term at the time the bonds are sold. However, this is not always the case given that coupon rates are fixed while market interest rates fluctuate. As a result, sometimes bonds are sold when coupon rates are below or above market interest rates.

If Candlestick sold these bonds when the market interest rate was greater than 5%, the bond purchaser (investor) would not be content and would want more consideration from Candlestick to compensate for the lower coupon rate. Since the interest payments and maturity amount are fixed, the only way that this consideration can be given to the investor is if they pay less than face value for the bond. When this occurs, the bond is sold at a **discount**. In this case, the investor will receive interest payments based on the coupon rate plus, on maturity of the bond, they will receive the face value of the bond which is now greater than the price paid for the bonds. In this way both the discount and the interest payments are the return received by the investor for owning the bond. For Candlestick, both the discount and the interest payments represent the cost of borrowing money by issuing bonds and both of these costs are reported as interest expense over the term that the bonds are outstanding.

Alternatively, if Candlestick issued these bonds when the market rate was lower than 5%, the company would realize that it is making interest payments to bond investors at a rate that is higher than the market expects. This is not fair to Candlestick, but since the interest payments and maturity amount are fixed, the only way that Candlestick can make the issue of these bonds fair will be to sell them for more than their face value. In this case, the investor is paying an additional amount for the bonds to compensate Candlestick for the fact that the company is paying out interest at a rate that is higher than the market rate. When Candlestick does this, it is issuing the bonds at a **premium**. The investor will receive interest payments based on the coupon rate. At maturity, the investor would only receive the face value of the bonds, which is less than the amount that they paid to purchase them. As such, the investor's actual return is lowered by the amount of the premium they paid when the bonds were purchased. For Candlestick, the premium represents a reduction in interest expense over the two years that the bonds are outstanding.

Issuing bonds at an amount different from face value is quite common. By the time a company prints the bond certificates (which provide the legal documentation for the bonds) and markets the bonds, it is unlikely that the market interest rate and the coupon rate are the same. Thus, the issue of bonds at a discount does not mean there is doubt about the financial strength of the issuer. Conversely, the sale of bonds at a premium does not indicate that the financial strength of the issuer is exceptional.

The actual calculation of bond prices and the amount of any discount or premium from the issue of bonds will be considered later. For now, let us review the journal entries that would be made under the following three scenarios:

1. The bonds are sold at face value (price quote would be 100) because market interest rates are at 5%.
2. The bonds are sold at a discount for $981,417 (price quote would be 98.1417) because market interest rates are 6%.
3. The bonds are sold at a premium for $1,019,043 (price quote would be 101.9043) because market interest rates are 4%.

The relationship between interest rates and whether a bond is sold at a discount, or at face value, or at a premium is shown in Illustration 10A-1.

▶Illustration 10A-1
Interest rates and bond prices

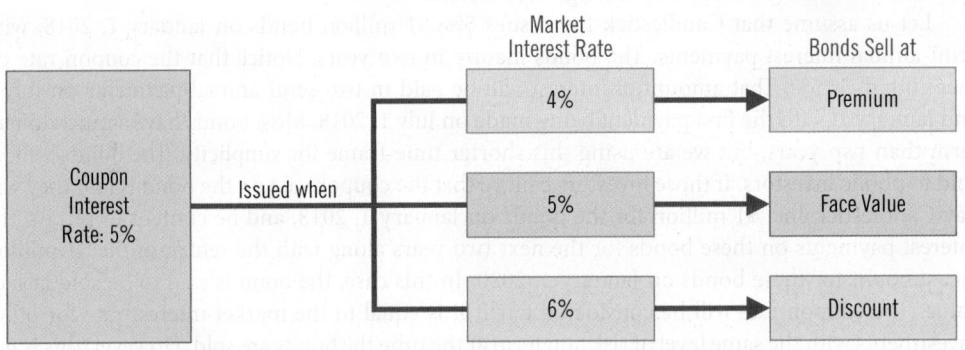

When the bonds are issued under each of these scenarios, the following journal entries would be recorded as shown in Illustration 10A-2.

▶Illustration 10A-2
Journal entries for bond issues

	Face Value		Discount		Premium	
Jan. 1, 2018	Cash 1,000,000		Cash 981,417		Cash 1,019,043	
	Bonds Payable	1,000,000	Bonds Payable	981,417	Bonds Payable	1,019,043

ACCOUNTING FOR BOND INTEREST EXPENSE

A discount or premium on a bond is essentially a form of additional interest (in the case of a discount) or interest saving (in the case of a premium) to the company issuing the bond. This additional interest or interest saving should be reflected as an increase or decrease in interest expense over the bond's term through a process called amortization. This process allocates the discount or premium amount within the Bonds Payable account to interest expense over time. The most common way to do this is by using the **effective-interest method**. In this method, the interest expense is calculated by multiplying the carrying amount of the bonds by the market interest rate when the bonds were sold, as this reflects the reality of the marketplace. The **carrying amount** of a bond is its face value less any unamortized discount, or plus any unamortized premium—in other words, the balance in the Bonds Payable account. At the date of issue, the carrying amount equals the bond's issue price but over time the carrying amount will become equal to the bond's face value. When we determine interest expense using the effective-interest method, it will be different from the interest paid (which is based on the face value and coupon interest rate) if there is a discount or premium on the bonds. The difference between the interest expense and the interest paid is the amount of discount or premium that is being amortized. As amortization occurs, the carrying amount of the bonds will change by the amount amortized and the carrying amount will move closer to the face value of the bonds over time. Because this liability account is changing each period, the interest expense will also change. Nonetheless, when using this method, interest expense will always represent a constant percentage (the market or effective interest rate) of the bond's carrying amount.

The calculation of amortization using the effective-interest method is shown in Illustration 10A-3.

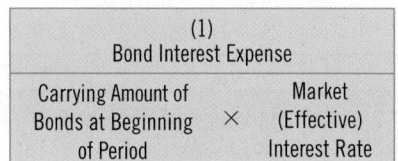 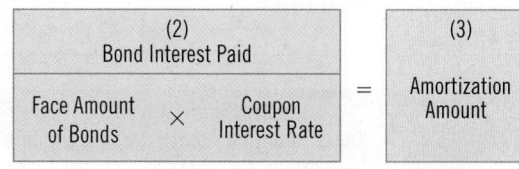

▶Illustration 10A-3
Calculation of amortization using effective-interest method

Returning to our example of Candlestick Inc., if these bonds were issued at face value, the interest expense and interest paid are the same. Interest expense and interest paid are calculated by multiplying $1,000,000 \times 5\% \times {}^6/_{12}$, which equals $25,000.

However, if the bonds, which offer a coupon rate of 5%, were issued when the market interest rate was 6%, they would be issued at a discount for $981,417, as stated earlier. In this case, the interest expense should reflect market conditions on the issue date and will be based on the market interest rate rather than the coupon rate. Furthermore, the market interest rate will be multiplied by the carrying amount to determine the interest expense, which will be $981,417 \times 6\% \times {}^6/_{12} = \$29,443$. Consequently, interest expense will be higher than the interest paid. This reflects the fact that the issuer's borrowing cost is effectively 6% rather than the coupon rate of 5%.

If the Candlestick bonds are instead sold when the market interest rate is 4%, the bonds are more attractive to investors because they offer a coupon interest rate that is higher than the market interest rate. The bonds will sell at a premium for $1,019,043, as calculated earlier. Similar to that illustrated earlier for discounts, the interest expense must reflect the market conditions that created the premium in the first place. Once again, interest will be calculated by multiplying the carrying amount of the bonds by the market interest rate. Interest expense will be $1,019,043 \times 4\% \times {}^6/_{12} = \$20,381$. The interest payments are still calculated by multiplying the carrying amount by the coupon rate and will amount to $25,000. When there is a premium, the interest expense will be less than the interest paid. This reflects the fact that the issuer's borrowing costs are reduced by the premium received on issuance, resulting in a reduction in interest expense over the term of the bond.

The journal entries required to record interest on bonds selling at face value, at a discount, or at a premium are shown in Illustration 10A-4.

▶Illustration 10A-4
Bond interest payment entries

	Face value			Discount			Premium		
July 1, 2018	Interest Expense	25,000		Interest Expense	29,443		Interest Expense	20,381	
	Cash		25,000	Bonds Payable		4,443	Bonds Payable		4,619
				Cash		25,000	Cash		25,000

An amortization table can be prepared to show the calculation of interest expense and the amount of discount or premium amortization for each period. Regardless of what period it is, the interest expense is always equal to the carrying amount of the bonds at the beginning of the period multiplied by the market interest rate. Tables for Candlestick are shown in Illustration 10A-5.

CANDLESTICK INC.
Bond Discount Amortization Schedule

Semi-Annual Interest Period	(A) Interest Payment ($1,000,000 × 5% × 6/12)	(B) Interest Expense (Preceding Bond Carrying Amount × 6% × 6/12)	(C) Discount Amortization (B − A)	(D) Unamortized Discount (D − C)	(E) Bond Carrying Amount ($1,000,000 − D)
Issue date (Jan. 1, 2018)				$18,583	$ 981,417
1 (July 1, 2018)	$ 25,000	$ 29,443	$ 4,443	14,140	985,860
2 (Jan. 1, 2019)	25,000	29,576	4,576	9,564	990,436
3 (July 1, 2019)	25,000	29,713	4,713	4,851	995,149
4 (Jan. 1, 2020)	25,000	29,851*	4,851	0	1,000,000
	$100,000	$118,583	$18,583		

*Adjusted for rounding differences.

CANDLESTICK INC.
Bond Premium Amortization Schedule

Semi-Annual Interest Period	(A) Interest Payment ($1,000,000 × 5% × 6/12)	(B) Interest Expense (Preceding Bond Carrying Amount × 4% × 6/12)	(C) Premium Amortization (A − B)	(D) Unamortized Premium (D − C)	(E) Bond Carrying Amount ($1,000,000 + D)
Issue date (Jan. 1, 2018)				$19,043	$1,019,043
1 (July 1, 2018)	$ 25,000	$20,381	$ 4,619	14,424	1,014,424
2 (Jan. 1, 2019)	25,000	20,288	4,712	9,712	1,009,712
3 (July 1, 2019)	25,000	20,194	4,806	4,906	1,004,906
4 (Jan. 1, 2020)	25,000	20,094*	4,906	0	1,000,000
	$100,000	$80,957	$19,043		

*Adjusted for rounding differences.

▶Illustration 10A-5
Amortization tables for bonds issued with discount and premium

From the tables shown above, we can see that the bond's carrying amount always moves toward its face value over time. For bonds with discounts, each period the interest expense rises, because the carrying amount of the bond is rising. For bonds with premiums, as the carrying amount falls, the interest expense also falls. In both cases, the carrying amount of the bonds will be equal to their face value at maturity.

Using the information from the above tables we can record the adjusting entry needed on December 31, Candlestick's year end, to accrue the interest expense that is due to be paid on January 1, as shown in Illustration 10A-6.

▶Illustration 10A-6
Bond interest accrual entries

Face value			Discount			Premium		
Dec. 31, 2018	Interest Expense	25,000	Interest Expense	29,576		Interest Expense	20,288	
	Interest Payable	25,000	Bonds Payable		4,576	Bonds Payable		4,712
			Interest Payable		25,000	Interest Payable		25,000

The interest payable on the bonds is classified as a current liability at December 31, 2018, because it is scheduled for payment within the next year. The bonds payable are reported in the non-current liability section of the statement of financial position because their maturity date is January 1, 2020 (more than one year away). When the interest is paid on January 1, 2019, Interest Payable is decreased (debited) and Cash is also decreased (credited) for $25,000.

The effective-interest method is required for companies reporting under IFRS. Private companies reporting using ASPE can choose to use either the effective-interest method or other methods (usually a straight-line method) if they do not differ materially from the effective-interest method. Because the use of the effective-interest method is prevalent, we focus on this method in the chapter.

ACCOUNTING FOR BOND RETIREMENTS

Bonds are retired either (1) when they mature, or (2) when the issuing corporation purchases them on the open market before they mature. Some bonds have special redemption provisions that allow them to be retired before they mature. Bonds that can be retired at a specified price before maturity at the option of the company (the issuer) are known as **redeemable (or callable) bonds**.

Why would a company want to have the option to retire its bonds early? If interest rates drop, it can be financially advantageous to retire the bond issue and replace it with a new bond issue at a lower interest rate. Or a company may become financially able to repay its debt earlier than expected. In this textbook, we will cover bond retirements only at maturity, leaving coverage of bond retirements prior to maturity for an intermediate accounting course.

Regardless of the issue price of bonds, their carrying amount at maturity will equal their face value because by that time, any discount or premium will have been fully amortized. Assuming that the journal entry for the last interest payment is recorded, the entry to record the redemption of the Candlestick bonds at maturity, on January 1, 2020, is:

Jan. 1, 2020	Bonds Payable	1,000,000	
	Cash		1,000,000
	(To record redemption of bond at maturity)		

A	=	L	+	SE
−1,000,000		−1,000,000		
↓ Cash flows: −1,000,000				

DO IT! ▶10-4a   Bond Transactions

On January 1, 2018, Selkirk Ltd. issued $800,000 of five-year, 4% bonds to yield a market interest rate of 5%, which resulted in an issue price of 95.6241. Interest is paid semi-annually on January 1 and July 1. (a) Calculate the proceeds received when the bonds are issued. (b) Prepare the entries to record (1) the issue of the bonds on January 1, 2018; (2) the payment of interest and amortization of any bond discount or premium on July 1, 2018; (3) the accrual of interest on December 31, 2018, which is Selkirk's year end; (4) the payment of interest on January 1, 2019; and (5) the final entry that would be made after the last payment of interest when the bonds mature on January 1, 2023. Round all amounts to the nearest dollar.

Action Plan

✔ Apply the issue price as a percentage, in this case, 95.6241%, to the face value of the bonds to determine the proceeds received.

✔ Recall that the amortization of a bond discount increases the Interest Expense account and makes it higher than the cash paid out for interest while the amortization of a bond premium reduces the Interest

Expense account and makes it lower than the cash paid out for interest.

✔ Amortization of bond discounts (and premiums) occurs even when accruing interest expense at year end.

✔ To record the retirement of the bond at maturity, simply bring the balance in the Bonds Payable account, which would now equal its face value, to zero by debiting this account by its carrying amount with an offsetting credit to cash.

SOLUTION

Try this Do It! exercise on your own and then check your answer at the end of the chapter.

Related Exercise Material: *BE10–13, *E10–11, *E10–12, and *E10–13.

DETERMINING THE ISSUE PRICE OF BONDS

In the examples above, the price of the bond was provided but, if you worked for Candlestick and were asked how much your bonds would sell for, how would you determine that amount? We will now look at how bond prices can be calculated by first assuming that Candlestick Inc. wants to issue zero-interest bonds (a bond that pays no interest) with a face value of $1 million due in two years. For these bonds, the only cash an investor would receive is $1 million at the end of two years. Would investors pay $1 million for these bonds today? No, because giving up $1 million today and receiving the exact same amount two years later would mean that no interest is earned. Therefore, as we saw with discounts earlier, Candlestick will only be able to sell these bonds if interest is incurred and since a discount is a form of interest expense, the bonds will sell at a discount. When these bonds are sold initially, their value is lower than it will be at maturity.

This concept of an increasing bond value over time occurs because of **the time value of money**, which simply means that over time money can become more valuable because it earns interest (and this bond is earning interest for the investor and incurring interest for Candlestick). For example, we know that the Candlestick bond will be worth less than $1 million on the day it is issued but it will be worth $1 million on the day it matures. The value of a bond (or any future cash flow) today is known as a **present value** while the value at a future date (such as the maturity date) of a bond is known as a **future value**.

The present value of a bond is the amount that it sells for in the marketplace today. The issue price (present value), therefore, depends on three factors: (1) the dollar amounts to be received in the future, such as the maturity amount and interest (if any is paid); (2) the length of time until the amounts are received; and (3) the market interest rate. The process of finding the present value is referred to as discounting the future cash flows (that is, the interest payments that will be received over the term of the bond plus the amount to be received on maturity).

To illustrate, using our earlier example, on January 1, 2018, Candlestick Inc. issues $1 million of 5% bonds, due in two years, with interest payable semi-annually on January 1 and July 1. Unlike the bonds above that paid no interest, this time Candlestick will be making two types of future cash flows: (1) the face value or principal amount of $1 million to be paid at maturity, and (2) four interest payments of $25,000 ($1,000,000 \times 5\% \times {}^6/_{12}$ months) over the term of the bonds.

The issue price of a bond is equal to the present value of all the future cash flows relating to the bond, namely the face value of the bond at maturity and periodic interest payments promised by the bond. There are standardized present value tables available that give us factors that can be multiplied by the amount of each type of future cash flow (interest and maturity value) relating to a bond to determine the present value of each cash flow. When the present values of each cash flow are added together, the result is the bond price. These present value tables are reproduced below for your reference as we outline the procedures for calculating the present value of a bond.

1. To calculate the present value of the face value, take the applicable factor from Table 1 (the present value of $1) and multiply it by the principal or face value of the bond. In Candlestick's

TABLE 1: PRESENT VALUE OF $1 $\left(PV = \dfrac{1}{(1+i)^n} \right)$

(n) Periods	1%	1.5%	2%	2.5%	3%	3.5%	4%	4.5%	5%	6%	7%	8%	9%	10%
1	0.99010	0.98522	0.98039	0.97561	0.97087	0.96618	0.96154	0.95694	0.95238	0.94340	0.93458	0.92593	0.91743	0.90909
2	0.98030	0.97066	0.96117	0.95181	0.94260	0.93351	0.92456	0.91573	0.90703	0.89000	0.87344	0.85734	0.84168	0.82645
3	0.97059	0.95632	0.94232	0.92860	0.91514	0.90194	0.88900	0.87630	0.86384	0.83962	0.81630	0.79383	077218	0.75131
4	0.96098	0.94218	0.92385	0.90595	0.88849	0.87144	0.85480	0.83856	0.82270	0.79209	0.76290	0.73503	0.70843	0.68301
5	0.95147	0.92826	0.90573	0.88385	0.86261	0.84197	0.82193	0.80245	0.78353	0.74726	0.71299	0.68058	0.64993	0.62092
6	0.94205	0.91454	0.88797	0.86230	0.83748	0.81350	0.79031	0.76790	0.74622	0.70496	0.66634	0.63017	0.59627	0.56447
7	0.93272	0.90103	0.87056	0.84127	0.81309	0.78599	0.75992	0.73483	0.71068	0.66506	0.62275	0.58349	0.54703	0.51316
8	0.92348	0.88771	0.85349	0.82075	0.78941	0.75941	0.73069	0.70319	0.67684	0.62741	0.58201	0.54027	0.50187	0.46651
9	0.91434	0.87459	0.83676	0.80073	0.76642	0.73373	0.70259	0.67290	0.64461	0.59190	0.54393	0.50025	0.46043	0.42410
10	0.90529	0.86167	0.82035	0.78120	0.74409	0.70892	0.67556	0.64393	0.61391	0.55839	0.50835	0.46319	0.42241	0.38554
11	0.89632	0.84893	0.80426	0.76214	0.72242	0.68495	0.64958	0.61620	0.58468	0.52679	0.47509	0.42888	0.38753	0.35049
12	0.88745	0.83639	0.78849	0.74356	0.70138	0.66178	0.62460	0.58966	0.55684	0.49697	0.44401	0.39711	0.35553	0.31863
13	0.87866	0.82403	0.77303	0.72542	0.68095	0.63940	0.60057	0.56427	0.53032	0.46884	0.41496	0.36770	0.32618	0.28966
14	0.86996	0.81185	0.75788	0.70773	0.66112	0.61778	0.57748	0.53997	0.50507	0.44230	0.38782	0.34046	0.29925	0.26333
15	0.86135	0.79985	0.74301	0.69047	0.64186	0.59689	0.55526	0.51672	0.48102	0.41727	0.36245	0.31524	0.27454	0.23939
16	0.85282	0.78803	0.72845	0.67362	0.62317	0.57671	0.53391	0.49447	0.45811	0.39365	0.33873	0.29189	0.25187	0.21763
17	0.84438	0.77639	0.71416	0.65720	0.60502	0.55720	0.51337	0.47318	0.43630	0.37136	0.31657	0.27027	0.23107	0.19784
18	0.83602	0.76491	0.70016	0.64117	0.58739	0.53836	0.49363	0.45280	0.41552	0.35034	0.29586	0.25025	0.21199	0.17986
19	0.82774	0.75361	0.68643	0.62553	0.57029	0.52016	0.47464	0.43330	0.39573	0.33051	0.27651	0.23171	0.19449	0.16351
20	0.81954	0.74247	0.67297	0.61027	0.55368	0.50257	0.45639	0.41464	0.37689	0.31180	0.25842	0.21455	0.17843	0.14864

case, this is a single payment of $1 million to be paid at the end of the bond term, two years from now. Locate the appropriate factor at the intersection of the number of periods (n) and the interest rate (i).

When interest is paid semi-annually, the number of periods and the interest rate must relate to six-month periods of time. In the Candlestick example, the two-year term of the bonds means that there are four semi-annual interest periods. In addition, the annual market interest rate of 5% becomes 2.5% ($5\% \times {}^{6}/_{12}$) when adjusted for the semi-annual period. The present value factor to be used for the face value for $n = 4$ and $i = 2.5\%$ is 0.90595.

2. To calculate the present value of the interest payments, use Table 2 (the present value of an annuity of $1) to determine the factor to use to calculate the present value of the bond interest. In Candlestick's case, $25,000 of interest ($1,000,000 \times 2.5\%$) is to be paid every six months for the next two years, or four semi-annual periods. A series of payments like this is called an annuity. The present value factor to be used for the interest for $n = 4$ and $i = 2.5\%$ is 3.76197.

$$\text{TABLE 2: PRESENT VALUE OF AN ANNUITY OF } \$1 \left(PV \frac{1 - \frac{1}{(1+i)^n}}{i} \right)$$

(n) Periods	1%	1.5%	2%	2.5%	3%	3.5%	4%	4.5%	5%	6%	7%	8%	9%	10%
1	0.99010	0.98522	0.98039	0.97561	0.97087	0.96618	0.96154	0.95694	0.95238	0.94340	0.93458	0.92593	0.91743	0.90909
2	1.97040	1.95588	1.94156	1.92742	1.91347	1.89969	1.88609	1.87267	1.85941	1.83339	1.80802	1.78326	1.75911	1.73554
3	2.94099	2.91220	2.88388	2.85602	2.82861	2.80164	2.77509	2.74896	2.72325	2.67301	2.62432	2.57710	2.53129	2.48685
4	3.90197	3.85438	3.80773	3.76197	3.71710	3.67308	3.62990	3.58753	3.54595	3.46511	3.38721	3.31213	3.23972	3.16987
5	4.85343	4.78264	4.71346	4.64583	4.57971	4.51505	4.45182	4.38998	4.32948	4.21236	4.10020	3.99271	3.88965	3.79079
6	5.79548	5.69719	5.60143	5.50813	5.41719	5.32855	5.24214	5.15787	5.07569	4.91732	4.76654	4.62288	4.48592	4.35526
7	6.72819	6.59821	6.47199	6.34939	6.23028	6.11454	6.00205	5.89270	5.78637	5.58238	5.38929	5.20637	5.03295	4.86842
8	7.65168	7.48593	7.32548	7.17014	7.01969	6.87396	6.73274	6.56589	6.46321	6.20979	5.97130	5.74664	5.53482	5.33493
9	8.56602	8.36052	8.16224	7.97087	7.78611	7.60769	7.43533	7.26879	7.10782	6.80169	6.51523	6.24689	5.99525	5.75902
10	9.47130	9.22218	8.98259	8.75206	8.53020	8.31661	8.11090	7.91272	7.72173	7.36009	7.02358	6.71008	6.41766	6.14457
11	10.36763	10.07112	9.78685	9.51421	9.25262	9.00155	8.76048	8.52892	8.30641	7.88687	7.49867	7.13896	6.80519	6.49506
12	11.25508	10.90751	10.57534	10.25776	9.95400	9.66333	9.38507	9.11858	8.86325	8.38384	7.94269	7.53608	7.16073	6.81369
13	12.13374	11.73153	11.34837	10.98318	10.63496	10.30274	9.98565	9.68285	9.39357	8.85268	8.35765	7.90378	7.48690	7.10336
14	13.00370	12.54338	12.10625	11.69091	11.29607	10.92052	10.56312	10.2283	9.89864	9.29498	8.74547	8.24424	7.78615	7.36669
15	13.86505	13.34323	12.84926	12.38138	11.93794	11.51741	11.11839	10.73955	10.37966	9.71225	9.10791	8.55948	8.06069	7.60608
16	14.71787	14.13126	13.57771	13.05500	12.56110	12.09412	11.65230	11.23402	10.83777	10.10590	9.44665	8.85137	8.31256	7.82371
17	15.56225	14.90765	14.29187	13.71220	13.16612	12.65132	12.16567	11.70719	11.27407	10.47726	9.76322	9.12164	8.54363	8.02155
18	16.39827	15.67256	14.99203	14.35336	13.75351	13.18968	12.65930	12.15999	11.68959	10.82760	10.05909	9.37189	8.75563	8.20141
19	17.22601	16.42617	15.67846	14.97889	14.32380	13.70984	13.13394	12.59329	12.08532	11.15812	10.33560	9.60360	8.95011	8.36492
20	18.04555	17.16864	16.35143	15.58916	14.87747	14.21240	13.59033	13.00794	12.46221	11.46992	10.59401	9.81815	9.12855	8.51356

Using the above factors, we can calculate the present values of the face value and the annuity of interest payments as follows:

Present value of $1,000,000 received in 4 periods	
$1,000,000 \times 0.90595 ($n = 4$, $i = 2.5\%$)	$ 905,950
Present value of $25,000 received for each of 4 periods	
$25,000 \times 3.76197 ($n = 4$, $i = 2.5\%$)	94,050
Present value (issue price) of bonds	$1,000,000
Where n = number of interest periods and i = interest rate	

Note that the face value of the bonds and the coupon interest rate are always used to calculate the interest payment—$25,000 in this case. However, the market interest rate is always used to determine the appropriate factor to be used for the present value because it clearly has an impact on the bond price. When the present value (issue price) of the bond equals the face value, these two rates are the same (both are 5% per annum), as is the case in our Candlestick example above. The journal entry to record the issue of these bonds at face value was shown in Illustration 10A-2.

The present value can also be determined mathematically using a financial calculator or spreadsheet program. The same principles are involved as described above, but with a calculator, we can input values in order to have the calculator determine the present value. There are four values to enter into the calculator: (1) the future value (FV), which is the face value of the bond; (2) the market interest rate per period (i); (3) the number of payment periods (n); and (4) the interest payment per period (PMT).

In the Candlestick example, the future value (FV) is $1 million, the interest rate (i) is 2.5%, the number of periods (n) is 4, and the interest payment (PMT) is $25,000, which is calculated as above by multiplying the future value by the coupon rate. Some calculators may require you to enter the payment amount and future value amount as a minus (for example, –25,000) and you may also have to input the information that the interest payments occur at the end (not the beginning) of each period.

We will not illustrate how to use a financial calculator or spreadsheet program here as the methodology for each can vary. You should be aware that the present value amounts calculated with a financial calculator or spreadsheet program will most likely differ by a few dollars from those calculated using the factors in the present value tables as we have illustrated above. This is because the factors in the present value tables are rounded to five decimal places whereas your own calculations are likely not rounded at all, or are rounded to the number of decimal places you specify.

If the bonds were issued when the market interest rate was 6%, the bonds would be less attractive and they would sell for a lower amount, as calculated below using factors found in the present value tables or by using a calculator with all of the same input values used before, except that the interest rate used is now 3% instead of 2.5%:

Present value of $1,000,000 received in 4 periods	
$1,000,000 × 0.88849 ($n = 4$, $i = 3\%$)	$888,490
Present value of $25,000 received for each of 4 periods	
$25,000 × 3.71710 ($n = 4$, $i = 3\%$)	92,927
Present value (issue price) of bonds	$981,417

The issue price of $981,417 gives rise to a bond discount of $18,583 ($1,000,000 − $981,417). Note that the carrying amount of the bonds, $981,417, will always be lower than the face value, $1,000,000, when bonds are issued at a discount. The journal entry to record the issue of these bonds at a discount was shown in Illustration 10A-2. If you want to use a calculator or spreadsheet to determine this bond price, you would input $1,000,000 for FV, $25,000 for PMT, 4 for N, and 3 for I/Y and the present value calculated would be $981,415, slightly different from the present value calculated with the table factors above.

Now let us assume that when these bonds were sold, market interest rates were only 4% rather than the coupon interest rate of 5%. These bonds would be very attractive to investors in the market because the coupon rate is higher than expected, and because of this, Candlestick Inc. will be able to sell these bonds at a premium. The issue price of these bonds can be calculated using factors found in the present value tables or by using a calculator with all of the same input values used before except that the interest rate used is now 2% (4% × $^6/_{12}$) instead of 2.5%:

Present value of $1,000,000 received in 4 periods	
$1,000,000 × 0.92385 ($n = 4$, $i = 2\%$)	$ 923,850
Present value of $25,000 received for each of 4 periods	
$25,000 × 3.80773 ($n = 4$, $i = 2\%$)	95,193
Present value (issue price) of bonds	$1,019,043

This issue price of $1,019,043 gives rise to a premium of $19,043 ($1,019,043 − $1,000,000). Notice that this time the carrying amount of the bonds, $1,019,043, is greater than their face value, $1,000,000, as will always be the case when bonds are issued at a premium. The journal entry to record the issue of these bonds at a premium was shown in Illustration 10A-2. If you want to use a calculator or spreadsheet to determine this bond price, you would input $1,000,000 for *FV*, $25,000 for *PMT*, 4 for *N*, and 2 for *I/Y* and the present value calculated would be $1,019,039, slightly different from the present value calculated with the table factors above.

Now that we have a better understanding of the relationship between present values and bond prices, if you refer to the discount and premium amortization tables shown in Illustration 10A-5, you will notice that the carrying amount of a bond is always equal to its present value. Because of this, if you were asked what the carrying amount of the Candlestick bonds would be at the end of a certain period, you could either prepare an amortization schedule or calculate the present value of the bond at the end of the specified period, where *n* is the number of interest periods remaining. Notice that the change in the carrying amount of the bonds is equal to the change in their present value. In other words, the amount of any premium or discount amortized is simply equal to the change in the present value of the bonds.

DO IT! ▶10-4b   Determining the Price of Bonds

On January 1, 2018, Copperthorne Ltd. issued bonds with a face value of $500,000 and a coupon interest rate of 4%. Interest is paid semi-annually. (a) Calculate the price that these bonds would sell for if they matured in five years and the market interest rate on January 1, 2018, was (1) 5% and (2) 3%. (b) Calculate the price assuming these were 10-year bonds and the market interest rate on the date of issue was (1) 5% and (2) 3%. (c) Explain the effect that market interest rates have on bond prices. (d) Determine if the effect that market interest rates have on bond prices is more or less significant as the term of the bond gets longer. Round all amounts to the nearest dollar.

Action Plan

✔ Determine the price of the bond by determining its present value using four items: the number of periods in which interest is paid, the amount of each interest payment, the market interest rate, and the face value of the bond. These values can be used to find factors in present value tables or to enter into a financial calculator.

✔ The interest payment is calculated by multiplying the face value of the bond by the coupon interest rate.

✔ If the market interest rate exceeds the coupon interest rate, you should expect the bond to sell below its face value (at a discount) and if the coupon interest rate exceeds the market interest rate, you should expect the bond to sell above its face value (at a premium).

SOLUTION
Try this Do It! exercise on your own and then check your answer at the end of the chapter.

Related Exercise Material: *BE10–14, *BE10–15, *BE10–16, *BE10–17, and *E10–14.

REVIEW AND PRACTICE ▶

▶ LEARNING OBJECTIVE REVIEW

1. Account for current liabilities.   A current liability is a debt that will be paid (1) from existing current assets or through the creation of other current liabilities, and (2) within one year or operating cycle. An example of a current liability is an operating line of credit that results in bank indebtedness. Current liabilities also include sales taxes, payroll deductions, and employee benefits, all of which the company collects on behalf of third parties. Other examples include property tax and interest on notes or loans payable, which must be accrued until paid. The portion of non-current debt that is due within the next year must be deducted from the non-current debt and reported as a current liability.

All of the above are "certain" or determinable liabilities. Provisions are "uncertain" liabilities that are recorded because their outcome is considered probable and can be measured. A contingent liability is an uncertain liability that is not recorded because it does not meet the two conditions necessary for recognition as a provision or because its outcome cannot be determined. The terms and nature of each recorded provision and contingent liability should be described in the notes accompanying the financial statements unless the probability of an outflow of resources arising from a contingent liability is remote.

2. Account for instalment notes payable. Long-term notes payable are usually repayable in a series of instalment payments. Each payment consists of (1) interest on the unpaid balance of the note, and (2) a reduction of the principal balance. These payments can be either (1) fixed principal payments plus interest or (2) blended principal and interest payments. With fixed principal payments plus interest, the reduction of principal is constant but the cash payment and interest expense decrease each period as the principal decreases. With blended principal and interest payments, the reduction of principal increases while the interest expense decreases each period. In total, the cash payment (principal and interest) remains constant each period.

3. Identify the requirements for the financial statement presentation and analysis of liabilities. In the income statement, interest expense (finance cost) is reported under "other revenues and expenses." In the statement of financial position, current liabilities are usually reported first, followed by non-current liabilities. Within the current liability section, items are listed in the order they fall due. Typically bank indebtedness (operating lines of credit) is listed first, followed by accounts payable and other types of payables, followed by unearned revenue and the current portions of any loans.

The liquidity of a company may be analyzed by calculating the current ratio, in addition to the receivables and inventory turnover ratios. The solvency of a company may be analyzed by calculating the debt to total assets and times interest earned ratios. Another factor to consider is the impact of unrecorded debt, such as operating lease obligations, when interpreting these ratios.

4. Account for bonds payable (Appendix 10A). When bonds are issued, the Cash account is debited and the Bonds Payable account is credited for the issue price of the bonds.

Bond discounts and bond premiums represent the difference between a face value and price of the bonds. They are amortized to interest expense over the life of the bonds using the effective-interest method of amortization. Amortization is calculated as the difference between the interest paid and the interest expense. Interest paid is calculated by multiplying the face value of the bonds by the coupon interest rate. Interest expense is calculated by multiplying the carrying amount of the bonds (which is equal to their present value at that time) at the beginning of the interest period by the market interest rate when the bonds were issued. The amortization of a bond discount increases interest expense and the bond's carrying amount. The amortization of a bond premium decreases interest expense and the bond's carrying amount.

When bonds are retired at maturity, Bonds Payable is debited and Cash is credited. There is no gain or loss at retirement.

▶ KEY TERM REVIEW

The following are key terms defined in this chapter with the corresponding page reference for your review. You will find a complete list of terms and definitions for all chapters in the glossary at the end of this textbook.

Bond (p. 544)	Effective-interest method (p. 546)	Operating line of credit (p. 524)
Collateral (p. 524)	Employee benefits (p. 528)	Payroll deductions (p. 527)
Contingent liabilities (p. 533)	Financial liability (p. 524)	Premium (p. 545)
Coupon interest rate (p. 545)	Gross pay (p. 527)	Provisions (p. 533)
Discount (p. 545)	Market interest rate (p. 545)	Times interest earned (p. 542)
EBIT (p. 542)	Net pay (p. 527)	

▶ COMPARING IFRS AND ASPE REVIEW

Key Standard Differences	International Financial Reporting Standards (IFRS)	Accounting Standards for Private Enterprises (ASPE)
Contingent liability	The definition of probability used to record a provision is "probable." Under IFRS, a contingent liability is not recorded but disclosed.	The definition of probability used to record a contingent liability is "likely," which is a higher level of certainty than the "probable" measure under IFRS. ASPE does not use the term *provision* so a contingent liability could be either recorded or disclosed.
Bonds (Appendix 10A)	Must use the effective-interest method to amortize any bond premium or discount.	Normally will use the effective-interest method to amortize any bond premium or discount but permitted to use alternative methods if the results do not differ materially from the effective-interest method.

▶ DECISION TOOLKIT REVIEW

DECISION CHECKPOINTS	INFO NEEDED FOR DECISION	TOOLS TO USE FOR DECISION	HOW TO EVALUATE RESULTS
Does the company have any provisions or contingent liabilities?	Knowledge of events with uncertain but possibly negative outcomes.	Financial statements and notes to the financial statements.	If negative outcomes are probable and can be estimated, record a provision. If the likelihood is not probable or determinable and/or cannot be estimated, disclose a contingent liability in the notes to the financial statements. If a negative outcome is considered to be remote, there is no need to disclose the contingent liability.
Can the company obtain short-term financing when necessary?	Liquidity ratios, available lines of credit from notes to the financial statements.	Compare available lines of credit with current liabilities. Also evaluate liquidity ratios.	If liquidity ratios are low, lines of credit should be high to compensate.
Can the company meet its obligations in the long term?	Total liabilities, total assets, net income, interest expense, and income tax expense.	$$\text{Times interest earned} = \frac{\text{Net income} + \text{Interest expense} + \text{Income tax expense (EBIT)}}{\text{Interest expense}}$$ Compare the times interest earned ratio with the debt to total assets ratio.	A high times interest earned ratio indicates there is enough net income available to cover annual interest payments. A low debt to total assets ratio is preferable, but a high debt to total assets ratio along with a high times interest earned ratio is acceptable.
Does the company have significant unrecorded obligations, such as operating leases?	Information on unrecorded obligations, such as operating lease payments disclosed in the notes to the financial statements.	Compare liquidity and solvency ratios with and without unrecorded obligations included.	If ratios differ significantly after including unrecorded obligations, these obligations should not be ignored in analysis.

▶ PRACTICE USING THE DECISION TOOLKIT

Answers are at the end of the chapter.

Royal Mail plc is comparable with Canada Post. Royal Mail is the national postal service in the United Kingdom. It also owns Parcelforce, a parcel delivery company, similar to Canada Post's Purolator.

Selected financial information for Royal Mail follows:

ROYAL MAIL HOLDINGS plc Selected Financial Information March 26, 2016 (in £ millions)	
Statement of financial position	
Non-current assets	6,180
Current assets	1,420
Non-current liabilities	1,142
Current liabilities	1,991
Income statement	
Interest expense	16
Income tax expense	45
Net income	248

Additional information:
The company had an unused operating line of credit at March 31, 2016.

INSTRUCTIONS

(a) Canada Post's current ratio is 1.8:1. Calculate Royal Mail's current ratio, and compare its liquidity with that of Canada Post and the industry average of 1.0:1.

(b) Calculate Royal Mail's debt to total assets and times interest earned ratios, and compare its solvency ratios with those of Canada Post, which are 114.6% and 3.7 times respectively, and the industry averages of 54.4% and 9.4 times, respectively.

(c) Because Royal Mail has an unused line of credit, how would that affect the assessment of its liquidity?

▶ PRACTICE COMPREHENSIVE DO IT!

Answers are at the end of the chapter.

Snyder Software Inc. successfully developed a new computer program. To produce and market the program, the company needed to raise $1 million. On December 31, 2017, Snyder borrowed $1 million from the bank for 15 years at 6%. The terms of the bank loan provide for semi-annual blended principal and interest payments of $51,019 on June 30 and December 31.

INSTRUCTIONS

(a) 1. Prepare an instalment payment schedule for the first four instalment payments. Round all amounts to the nearest dollar.

2. Record the receipt of the bank loan on December 31, 2017.

3. Record the first instalment payment on June 30, 2018.

4. Indicate the current, non-current, and total amounts that would be presented in the statement of financial position for the bank loan payable at December 31, 2018.

5. Explain how the pattern of payments would change if the instalment payments were based on fixed principal payments plus interest rather than blended principal and interest payments.

6. In 2018, the company's times interest earned ratio rose. How would you interpret this when considering the additional bank loan taken out by the company at the end of 2017?

(b) When the new software programs are to be sold, HST of 13% will be applicable on each sale. Record the journal entry that would be made if a program that was held in inventory at a cost of $75 was sold for $200 on credit on January 3, 2018.

(c) 1. Additional employees will be hired to sell the new programs. If a new salesperson was hired at a salary of $3,000 per month and was paid at the end of each month, record the journal entry that would be made to record this payment to the employee on January 31, 2018. The following deductions were taken in arriving at the net pay for this employee: Canada Pension Plan $135, employment insurance $56, and income tax $385.

2. Record the journal entry that would be made on January 31, 2018, to record the employer's contributions for the Canada Pension Plan of $135 and employment insurance of $84 pertaining to the payment above. Payment of these amounts will occur later.

3. Record the journal entry for the remittance on February 7, 2018, of employee income tax, CPP, and EI pertaining to the employee's pay as described above.

▶ PRACTICE OBJECTIVE-FORMAT QUESTIONS

Answers are at the end of the chapter.

Note: All questions below with an asterisk (*) relate to material in Appendix 10A.

1. Restouche Ltd. is about to record the sale on account of some inventory for $5,000 before considering the effect of HST. The inventory cost the company $3,000. The company is required to collect HST of 13% on every sale it makes. Indicate which of the following statements are correct with regard to the recording of this sale. (Select as many as are appropriate).

(a) The Sales account will be credited for $5,000.

(b) No HST needs to be recorded until the sale proceeds are collected.

(c) The Sales Tax Payable account will be debited for $650.

(d) The Accounts Receivable account will be debited for $5,000.

(e) The HST pertaining to this sale should be recorded as an expense.

(f) The Cost of Goods Sold account will be debited for $3,000.

(g) The Inventory account will be credited for $3,000.

2. Wapiti Ltd. is assessed for its property taxes on a calendar year basis. On March 31, the company received its property tax invoice, which amounted to $18,000 for that calendar year. The assessed amount was not due until

---

May 31 of that year, at which time payment was made. Indicate which of the following statements are correct. (Select as many as are appropriate.)

(a) On March 31, when the assessment was received, the company recorded a journal entry. The entry should have debited Property Tax Expense for $4,500 and credited Property Tax Payable for $4,500.

(b) On March 31, when the assessment was received, the company recorded a journal entry. The entry should have debited Prepaid Property Tax for $18,000 and credited Property Tax Payable for $18,000.

(c) On May 31, when the property taxes were paid, the journal entry to record that event should have included a debit to Prepaid Property Tax for $18,000.

(d) When recording the journal entry for the payment of the property taxes on May 31, Property Tax Expense should have been debited for $18,000.

(e) When the company records adjusting entries on December 31, Prepaid Property Taxes will be credited by $18,000.

(f) On the December 31 statement of financial position, the Property Tax Payable account would have a balance of $4,500.

(g) On the December 31 statement of financial position, the Prepaid Property Tax account will have a balance of zero.

3. Jane Chan works for the Blue Door Corporation at a salary of $700 per week. She is paid every two weeks. For this pay period, the company has calculated that the following items should be deducted from her biweekly pay: income tax of $185, CPP of $60, and EI premiums of $25. In addition to the employee contributions to CPP and EI, the company is also required to pay CPP of $60 and EI premiums of $35 for this same pay period. Indicate which of the following statements are correct with regard to Jane's biweekly pay. (Select as many as are appropriate.)

(a) Jane's net pay for this period is $1,130.

(b) The salary expense for this period would be $1,400.

(c) The employee benefits expense for this period is $285.

(d) Immediately before making any payments to the government, the company will have a balance of $60 in its CPP Payable account.

(e) Immediately before making any payments to the government, the company will have a balance of $185 in its Employee Income Tax Payable account.

(f) The total payment remitted to the government for amounts withheld from Jane's gross pay and for employee benefits pertaining to employer contributions to CPP and EI will be $355.

(g) The EI Payable, CPP Payable, and Employee Income Tax Payable accounts are not considered current liabilities because companies usually retain their employees for longer than one year.

4. In order to obtain some needed funds on May 1, Irving Holdings Ltd. issued a 5% short-term note payable for $120,000 that is due on August 31. Interest is due at maturity. The company's year end is June 30 and it makes adjusting entries annually. Indicate which of the following statements are correct. (Select as many as are appropriate.)

(a) When the note is issued, Irving recorded a debit to Cash for $120,000.

(b) On the company's statement of financial position on June 30, the interest payable on the note would amount to $3,000.

(c) On the company's statement of financial position on June 30, all current liabilities relating to the note would total $121,000.

(d) On its income statement for the year ended June 30, the interest expense pertaining to the note would amount to $1,000.

(e) On August 31, the company would pay the payee of the note cash amounting to $122,000.

(f) The repayment of the note and interest on August 31 would be recorded with a debit to Interest Payable of $1,000.

(g) The repayment of the note and interest on August 31 would be recorded with a debit to Interest Expense of $2,000.

5. Columbia Ltd. has a bank loan payable outstanding with the following payment schedule. Payments are made on December 31 of each year, which is also the company's year end.

Interest Period	Cash Payment	Interest Expense	Reduction of Principal	Principal Balance
Jan. 1, 2018				$500,000
Dec. 31, 2018	$45,000	$20,000	$25,000	475,000
Dec. 31, 2019	44,000	19,000	25,000	450,000
Dec. 31, 2020	43,000	18,000	25,000	425,000
Dec. 31, 2021	42,000	17,000	25,000	400,000

Indicate which of the following statements are correct regarding the bank loan. (Select as many as are appropriate.)

(a) The bank loan will be fully paid off on December 31, 2037.

(b) On its December 31, 2018, statement of financial position, the current portion of the bank loan payable will be $25,000.

(c) The interest rate on the bank loan is 3%.

(d) On its December 31, 2020, statement of financial position, the non-current portion of the bank loan payable will be $425,000.

(e) On its December 31, 2021, statement of financial position, the Interest Payable account balance pertaining to the bank loan will be $17,000.

(f) The interest expense declines each year because the interest rate on the bank loan is falling over time.

(g) If the company prepared interim financial statements on June 30, 2018, and recorded appropriate adjusting entries at that time, the total of all liabilities pertaining to the bank loan at the time would be $500,000.

6. Manitoba Inc. has a bank loan outstanding with the following payment schedule. Payments are made on December 31 of each year, which is also the company's year end.

Interest Period	Cash Payment	Interest Expense	Reduction of Principal	Principal Balance
Jan. 1, 2018				$600,000
Dec. 31, 2018	$50,000	$30,000	$20,000	580,000
Dec. 31, 2019	50,000	29,000	21,000	559,000
Dec. 31, 2020	50,000	27,950	22,050	536,950
Dec. 31, 2021	50,000	26,848	23,152	513,798

Indicate which of the following statements are correct regarding the bank loan. (Select as many as are appropriate.)

(a) The loan is being paid off with blended principal and interest payments.

(b) On its December 31, 2018, statement of financial position, the current portion of the loan will be $50,000.

(c) The interest rate for this loan is 5%.

(d) On its December 31, 2020, statement of financial position, the non-current portion of the loan will be $513,798.

(e) On its December 31, 2021, statement of financial position, the Interest Payable account balance pertaining to the loan will be $26,848.

(f) The interest expense declines each year because the outstanding balance of the loan is falling over time.

(g) If the company prepared monthly financial statements on January 31, 2018, and recorded appropriate adjusting entries at that time, the total of all liabilities pertaining to the loan at that time would be $600,000.

7. Indicate which of the following statements are correct. (Select as many as are appropriate.)

(a) The total payment including both principal and interest portions for a loan that has blended principal and interest payments will remain the same each period.

(b) For a loan with fixed principal payments plus interest each period, the total payment will become smaller over time.

(c) For a loan that has blended principal and interest payments, we would expect the current portion of that loan payable to fall over time.

(d) For a loan that has fixed principal payments plus interest, we would expect the current

portion of that loan to remain the same until the loan is paid off in full.

(e) The principal portion of a payment for a loan with blended principal and interest payments is determined by dividing the original amount of the loan by the number of loan payments that will be made.

(f) The interest portion of a payment made on a loan requiring blended principal and interest payments will remain constant over time.

(g) The interest portion of a payment on a loan requiring fixed principal payments plus interest will rise over time.

8. Indicate which of the following statements are correct. (Select as many as are appropriate.)

(a) In the notes to financial statements, the amount of principal to be paid on non-current debt in each of the next three years is disclosed.

(b) Amounts drawn on an operating line of credit will be reported as bank

indebtedness on the statement of financial position.

(c) Companies have a higher degree of liquidity if inventory is turning over slower and accounts receivable are collected more quickly.

(d) Most companies in Canada list their liabilities in order of their due date, starting with those liabilities that are due first.

(e) Solvency, like liquidity, addresses a company's ability to settle its current liabilities within one year.

(f) Credit rating agencies will assign an AA rating to organizations that have the greatest ability to pay off non-current liabilities.

(g) When an operating lease is entered into, the leased asset and the amount owed under the leasing agreement are recorded on the statement of financial position.

9. Indicate which of the following statements are correct. (Select as many as are appropriate.)

(a) A company with a high debt to total assets ratio will have a more difficult time being profitable.

(b) A company with a high debt to total assets ratio is taking on more risk.

(c) A company with a high times interest earned ratio is better able to make its interest payments.

(d) A company with a low times interest earned ratio should take on more debt.

(e) A company that has an increasing debt to total assets ratio and a decreasing times

interest earned ratio is most likely earning a significant amount of additional income from borrowed funds.

(f) A company that has an increasing debt to total assets ratio but an even faster increasing times interest earned ratio is most likely more profitable even with the higher levels of debt.

(g) A company with a decreasing debt to assets ratio and an increasing times interest earned ratio may want to consider taking on more debt if it wants to grow.

*10. On January 1 of the current year, Gamma Ltd. issued $200,000 five-year bonds bearing coupon interest at 4%. Interest is paid on December 31 each year. The bonds sold at 96. Indicate which of the following statements are correct. (Select as many as are appropriate.)

(a) The bonds sold for $192,000.

(b) The bonds sold at a discount because the market interest rate was below 4%.

(c) The interest expense recorded each year will be higher than $8,000.

(d) If the market interest rate is 5%, the interest expense for the current year is $10,000.

(e) If the market rate is 5%, the balance in the Bonds Payable account on December 31 of the current year will be $193,600.

(f) The interest expense in the current year will be lower than the interest expense recorded in the following year.

(g) If the bond had sold at a premium, the price would be in excess of 100.

WileyPLUS

Brief Exercises, Exercises, and many additional resources are available for practice in WileyPLUS.

Note: All questions, exercises, and problems below with an asterisk (*) relate to material in Appendix 10A.

▶QUESTIONS

(LO 1) 1. Identify the similarities and differences between accounts payable and short-term notes payable.

(LO 1) 2. What is the difference between an operating line of credit and a short-term bank loan payable?

(LO 1) 3. Your roommate says, "Sales tax is a part of the operating activities of a business and should be reported in the revenue section of the income statement." Do you agree? Explain.

(LO 1) 4. If a company has sold gift cards to customers, what should be recorded at the time of sale? What should be recorded

when the gift cards are redeemed? Should anything be recorded if the card is not redeemed?

(LO 1) 5. What criteria must be met before an uncertain liability can be recorded as a provision? How do these criteria differ depending on whether the company is a public company using IFRS or a private company using ASPE?

(LO 1, 2) 6. Explain how to determine the current and non-current portions of debt for presentation in the liabilities section of the statement of financial position.

(LO 2)   7. Identify the similarities and differences between short-term notes payable and long-term instalment notes payable.

(LO 2)   8. Distinguish between instalment notes payable with fixed principal payments plus interest and those with blended principal and interest payments.

(LO 2)   9. When students borrow money for their post-secondary education under the Canada Student Loans Program, they can choose a fixed interest rate of prime plus 5% or a floating interest rate of prime plus 2.5%. (a) Explain the difference between these two types of interest rates. (b) Which interest rate—fixed or variable—do you think you would prefer? Explain.

(LO 2)   10. Doug Bareak, a friend of yours, has recently purchased a home for $200,000. He paid $20,000 down and financed the remainder with a 20-year, 5% mortgage that is payable in blended payments of principal and interest of $1,290 per month. At the end of the first month, Doug received a statement from the bank indicating that only $540 of the principal was paid during the month. At this rate, he calculated that it would take about 28 years to pay off the mortgage. Explain why Doug is incorrect.

(LO 3)   11. In general, what are the requirements for the financial statement presentation of (a) current liabilities and (b) non-current liabilities?

(LO 3)   12. Distinguish between liquidity and solvency. Provide an example of two ratios that can be used to measure each and indicate whether an increase in each ratio from one year to the next would be considered an improvement or a deterioration.

(LO 3)   13. Explain how an operating line of credit can help a company's liquidity and why it is considered more flexible than most bank loans such as mortgages.

(LO 3)   14. Explain why the debt to total assets ratio should never be interpreted without referring to the times interest earned ratio.

(LO 3)   15. Explain why it is important to know if a company has significant operating lease commitments and why an operating lease is often considered "off–balance sheet financing."

(LO 4)   *16. Identify the similarities and differences between bonds payable and (a) instalment notes payable, and (b) common shares.

(LO 4)   *17. Is there a difference between the interest expense recorded in the income statement and the interest paid during the year when a bond is sold (a) at a discount and (b) at a premium? Explain.

▶ BRIEF EXERCISES

Record sales taxes.
(LO 1)

BE10–1 Abbotsford Bikes Ltd. reports cash sales of $6,000 on October 1. (a) Record the sales assuming they occurred in Ontario and are subject to 13% HST (charged on selling price only). (b) Record the sales assuming they occurred in Quebec and are subject to 5% GST and 9.975% QST (charged on selling price before GST).

Record property tax.
(LO 1)

BE10–2 Pierce Corp. has a December 31 year end. It received its property tax invoice of $36,000 for the calendar year on April 30. The invoice is payable on July 15. Prepare the journal entries to record the property tax on (a) April 30, (b) July 15, and (c) December 31, assuming the company adjusts its accounts annually.

Record payroll.
(LO 1)

BE10–3 Zerbe Consulting Inc.'s gross salaries for the biweekly period ended August 24 were $15,000. Deductions included $743 for CPP, $282 for EI, and $6,258 for income tax. The employer's payroll costs were $743 for CPP and $395 for EI. Prepare journal entries to record (a) the payment of salaries on August 24; (b) the employer payroll costs on August 24, assuming they will not be remitted to the government until September; and (c) the payment to the government on September 3 of all amounts owed.

Record short-term loan.
(LO 1)

BE10–4 Romez Limited borrowed $60,000 from National Bank on July 1 for three months; 5% interest is payable the first of each month, starting August 1. Romez's year end is August 31 and the company records adjusting entries only at that time. Prepare journal entries to record (a) the receipt of the bank loan on July 1; (b) (1) the payment of interest on August 1, (2) the accrual of interest on August 31, (3) the payment of interest on September 1, and (4) the payment of interest on October 1; and (c) the payment of the bank loan at maturity on October 1.

Account for contingencies.
(LO 1)

BE10–5 For each of the following independent situations, indicate whether a provision should be recorded or a contingent liability disclosed for a publicly traded company reporting under IFRS. Indicate if your answer would change if the company were a private company reporting under ASPE.

(a) A pending lawsuit for which a negative outcome has been estimated and determined to be "likely" as well as "probable"

(b) A pending lawsuit, about which the outcome cannot be determined

(c) A nuisance lawsuit, which the company is not anticipated to lose

(d) A loan guarantee for a subsidiary company that has a credit rating of AA

(e) A pending lawsuit for which a negative outcome has been determined as "likely" as well as "probable" but an estimate of the outflow of resources cannot be made

BE10–6 Assume that you qualify for a $25,000 loan from the Canada Student Loans Program to help finance your education. You are considering whether to repay this loan on graduation with a fixed interest rate of prime plus 5% or a floating interest rate of prime plus 2.5%. Assuming you start repaying your loan immediately upon graduation, information related to your loan options follows:

Discuss fixed and floating rates of interest.

(LO 2)

	Fixed Interest Rate	Floating Interest Rate
Amount of loan	$25,000	$25,000
Prime interest rate assumed	2.75%	2.75%
Number of months to repay loan	120 months	120 months
Monthly instalment payment	$300	$268
Total interest payable over life of loan	$11,003	$7,188

(a) Identify the advantages and disadvantages of each interest rate option. (b) Explain which option you think is best for you and why.

BE10–7 Assad Inc. issued a five-year, 7% instalment note payable, with fixed principal payments plus interest, due annually. The following instalment payment schedule is partially completed:

Complete instalment payment schedule; identify current and non-current portions.

(LO 2)

Interest Period	Cash Payment	Interest Expense	Reduction of Principal	Principal Balance
Issue date				$50,000
1	$13,500	$ [1]	[2]	40,000
2	12,800	2,800	[3]	[4]
3	[5]	2,100	[6]	[7]
4	11,400	1,400	[8]	10,000
5	10,700	700	[9]	[10]

(a) Fill in the missing amounts for items [1] through [10]. Round all amounts to the nearest dollar. (b) What are the current and non-current portions of the note at the end of period 3?

BE10–8 Hyatt Inc. issued a five-year, 7% instalment loan payable, with blended principal and interest payments due annually. The following instalment payment schedule is partially completed:

Complete instalment payment schedule; identify current and non-current portions.

(LO 2)

Interest Period	Cash Payment	Interest Expense	Reduction of Principal	Principal Balance
Issue date				$50,000
1	$12,195	$ [1]	$ 8,695	41,305
2	[2]	2,891	[3]	32,001
3	[4]	[5]	9,955	[6]
4	[7]	1,543	[8]	11,394
5	[9]	801*	11,394	[10]

*Adjusted for rounding differences.

(a) Fill in the missing amounts for items [1] to [10]. Round all amounts to the nearest dollar. (b) What are the current and non-current portions of the loan at the end of period 3?

BE10–9 Eyre Inc. signs a 10-year, 4%, $300,000 mortgage payable on November 30, 2017, to obtain financing for a new building. The terms provide for payments at the end of each month. Prepare the entries to record the mortgage on November 30, 2017, and the first two payments on December 31, 2017, and January 31, 2018, assuming the payment is (a) a fixed principal payment of $2,500, plus interest, and (b) a blended principal and interest payment of $3,037. Round all amounts to the nearest dollar.

Record mortgage payable.

(LO 2)

BE10–10 Identify which of the following transactions would be classified as a current liability and which would be classified as a non-current liability. For those that are neither, identify where they should be classified or disclosed.
(a) A bank loan payable due in two years, with principal due at maturity and interest due the first of each month
(b) Cash received in advance by Air Canada for airline tickets on flights leaving next month
(c) HST collected on sales
(d) Unused amount of operating line of credit
(e) Provision relating to a lawsuit settlement expected to be paid next month
(f) Obligations due under operating leases

Identify current and non-current liabilities.

(LO 3)

(g) Bonds payable, due in 10 years
(h) Payroll deductions withheld from the employees' weekly pay
(i) Prepaid property tax
(j) A $75,000 mortgage payable, of which $5,000 is due in the next year
(k) An uncertain liability the outcome of which is considered to be remote

Calculate liquidity and solvency ratios.

(LO 3)

BE10–11 Leon's Furniture Ltd. financial statements recently reported the following selected data (in $ millions):

Total current assets	$ 443
Total current liabilities	424
Total assets	1,563
Total liabilities	1,014
Income tax expense	28
Interest expense	19
Net income	76

Calculate Leon's (a) current ratio, (b) debt to total assets ratio, and (c) times interest earned ratio.

Analyze solvency.

(LO 3)

BE10–12 The following solvency ratios are available for Fromage Corporation:

	2018	2017
Debt to total assets	40%	52%
Times interest earned	7 times	11 times

(a) Identify whether the change in each ratio is an improvement or deterioration. (b) Did the company's overall solvency improve or deteriorate in 2018?

Record bond transactions.

(LO 4)

*BE10–13 Hopkins Ltd. issued five-year bonds with a face value of $200,000 on January 1. The bonds have a coupon interest rate of 6% and interest is paid semi-annually on June 30 and December 31. The market interest rate was 7% when the bonds were issued at a price of 96. Using this information, determine (a) the proceeds received by the company when the bonds were issued, (b) the interest expense recorded for the six months ending June 30 when the first interest payment is made, and (c) the balance in the Bonds Payable account immediately following the first interest payment.

Record bond transactions.

(LO 4)

*BE10–14 Green Hills Ltd. issued five-year bonds with a face value of $100,000 on January 1. The bonds have a coupon interest rate of 5% and interest is paid semi-annually on June 30 and December 31. The market interest rate was 3% when the bonds were issued at a price of 109. Using this information, determine (a) the proceeds received by the company when the bonds were issued, (b) the interest expense recorded for the six months ending June 30 when the first interest payment is made, and (c) the balance in the Bonds Payable account immediately following the first interest payment.

Calculate present value.

(LO 4)

*BE10–15 On January 1, 2018, Carvel Corp. issued five-year bonds with a face value of $500,000 and a coupon interest rate of 6%, with interest payable semi-annually. How much would Carvel receive from the sale of these bonds if the market interest rate was (a) 5%, (b) 6%, and (c) 7%?

Prepare bond amortization tables.

(LO 4)

*BE10–16 Using the information from BE10–15, prepare a partial bond amortization table for the first two interest payments assuming that interest is paid on July 1 and January 1 and that the bonds sold when the market interest rate was (a) 5%, (b) 6%, and (c) 7%.

Record bond transactions.

(LO 4)

*BE10–17 Using the information from BE10–16, assume that the company has a December 31 year end and records adjusting entries annually. Record the journal entries relating to the bonds on January 1, July 1, and December 31, assuming that when the bonds were sold, the market interest rate was (a) 5%, (b) 6%, and (c) 7%.

▶ **EXERCISES**

Determine impact of current liability transactions.

(LO 1)

E10–1 A list of transactions follows.
1. Purchased inventory (perpetual system) on account.
2. Extended payment terms of the account payable in item 1 by replacing the accounts payable with the issue of a nine-month, 5% note payable.
3. Recorded accrued interest on the note payable from item 2.
4. Recorded repayment of the note and accrued interest from items 2 and 3.
5. Recorded cash received from sale of services, plus HST.
6. Recorded salaries expense and employee payroll deductions, and paid employees.

7. Recorded employer's share of employee benefits.
8. Recorded property tax expense and property tax payable when bill was received.
9. Recorded a receipt of cash for services that will be performed in the future.
10. Recorded the performance of services for item 9.

Instructions

Set up a table using the format that follows. Indicate the effect of each of the above transactions on the financial statement categories in the table: use "+" for increase, "–" for decrease, and "NE" for no effect. The first one has been done for you as an example.

	Assets	Liabilities	Shareholders' Equity	Revenues	Expenses	Net Income
1.	+	+	NE	NE	NE	NE

E10–2 Chen Wholesalers Ltd. incurred the following transactions related to current liabilities.

1. Chen's cash register showed the following totals at the end of the day on March 17: pre-tax sales $50,000, GST $2,500, and PST $3,500.
2. Chen received its property tax bill for the calendar year for $52,800 on May 1, payable July 1.
3. Chen's gross payroll for the week of August 15 was $81,000. The company deducted $4,010 for CPP, $1,523 for EI, $6,400 for pension, and $16,020 for income tax from the employees' pay. The employer portions of CPP and EI for the week were $4,010 and $2,132, respectively.
4. On August 22, all amounts owing for employee income taxes, CPP, and EI pertaining to the payroll in transaction 3 above were paid.
5. On October 1, Chen borrowed $100,000 from First Bank for a six-month period; 4% interest on the bank loan is payable on April 1.

Record current liabilities.
(LO 1)

Instructions

(a) Record journal entries for the transactions above.
(b) Assuming that Chen's year end is December 31 and that it makes adjusting entries annually, prepare any adjusting entries required for the property tax in transaction 2 and the interest in transaction 5.
(c) Record the journal entry for the settlement of the bank loan in transaction 5 on April 1.

E10–3 Dougald Construction Ltd. borrowed $250,000 from TD Bank on October 1, 2017, for a nine-month period; 5% interest is payable at maturity. Both companies have a December 31 year end and make adjusting entries annually.

Record short-term loans.
(LO 1)

Instructions

(a) For Dougald Construction, record (1) the receipt of the bank loan on October 1, 2017; (2) the accrual of interest on December 31, 2017; and (3) the payment of the loan on July 1, 2018.
(b) For the TD Bank, record (1) the issue of the bank loan on October 1, 2017; (2) the accrual of interest on December 31, 2017; and (3) the collection of the loan on July 1, 2018. (*Hint:* The TD Bank uses a Notes Receivable account to record its loans.)

E10–4 WestJet Airlines Ltd. leases aircraft and, when doing so, the company must perform scheduled maintenance on these aircraft.

Discuss contingent liabilities.
(LO 1)

Instructions

(a) The company records a provision for aircraft maintenance when the aircraft are acquired. Why is the provision recognized at that time rather than when the maintenance will actually be performed?
(b) In what way does a provision for aircraft maintenance differ from an account payable?

E10–5 Ste. Anne Corp. obtained a 10-year, 5%, $150,000 mortgage loan to finance the purchase of a building at December 31, 2017. The terms provide for semi-annual instalment payments on June 30 and December 31.

Record mortgage payable.
(LO 2)

Instructions

(a) Record the obtaining of the mortgage payable on December 31, 2017.
(b) Record the first two instalment payments on June 30, 2018, and December 31, 2018, assuming the payment is (1) a fixed principal payment of $7,500, plus interest, and (2) a blended principal and interest payment of $9,622. Round all amounts to the nearest dollar.
(c) Explain why interest expense is the same regardless of whether the payment is blended or based on fixed payments for the six months ended June 30 but different for the six months ended December 31.

E10–6 On July 1, 2017, Granville Ltd. borrowed $15,000 by signing a two-year, 4% note payable. The note is payable in two annual blended principal and interest instalments of $7,953 on June 30. Adjusting journal entries are recorded annually at year end on December 31.

Record instalment note payable; identify current and non-current portions.
(LO 2)

Instructions

(a) Prepare an instalment payment schedule for the term of the note. Round all amounts to the nearest dollar.
(b) Record (1) the issue of the note on July 1, 2017; (2) the accrual of interest on December 31, 2017; and (3) the first payment on June 30, 2018.
(c) What amounts would be reported as current and non-current in the liabilities section of Granville's statement of financial position on December 31, 2018?

Analyze instalment payment schedule.

(LO 2)

E10–7 The following instalment payment schedule is for a long-term bank loan payable:

Interest Period	Cash Payment	Interest Expense	Reduction of Principal	Principal Balance
Issue date				$100,000.00
1	$23,097.48	$5,000.00	$18,097.48	81,902.52
2	23,097.48	4,095.13	19,002.35	62,900.17
3	23,097.48	3,145.01	19,952.47	42,947.70
4	23,097.48	2,147.38	20,950.10	21,997.60
5	23,097.48	1,099.88	21,997.60	0

Instructions

(a) Is the above schedule a fixed principal plus interest or blended principal and interest payment schedule?
(b) Assuming payments are made annually, what is the interest rate on the bank loan?
(c) Prepare the journal entry to record the first instalment payment.
(d) What are the current and non-current portions of the bank loan after the payment at the end of period 2?

Prepare liabilities section.

(LO 3)

E10–8 Dollarama Inc. reported the following liabilities (in thousands) in its February 1, 2015, financial statements (in thousands):

Long-term debt	$560,641	Income taxes payable	$ 25,427
Deferred income taxes	122,184	Accounts payable and accrued liabilities	175,739
Current portion of long-term debt	3,846	Deferred (unearned) tenant deposits	60,475
Finance lease obligations	1,566	Dividends payable	10,480

Instructions

(a) Identify which of the above liabilities are likely current and which are likely non-current. State whether any item fits in either category. Explain the reasoning for your selections.
(b) Prepare the liabilities section of Dollarama's statement of financial position.

Analyze liquidity.

(LO 3)

E10–9 The following selected information (in thousands) was taken from Fruition Collections Ltd.'s December 31 statement of financial position:

	2018	2017
Current assets		
Cash	$1,074	$1,521
Accounts receivable	2,147	1,575
Inventories	1,201	1,010
Other current assets	322	192
Total current assets	$4,744	$4,298
Total current liabilities	$3,011	$2,989

Instructions

(a) Calculate the current ratio for each of the two years. (1) Based only on this information, would you say that the company's liquidity is improving or getting weaker in 2018? (2) What additional information should you request to complete your assessment of liquidity?
(b) Suppose that Fruition Collections used $1 million of its cash to pay off $1 million of its accounts payable. How would this transaction change the current ratio for 2018?
(c) At December 31, 2018, Fruition Collections had an unused operating line of credit of $4 million. Does this information affect the assessment of the company's short-term liquidity that you made in part (a) above?

Analyze solvency.

(LO 3)

E10–10 Open Text Corporation's financial statements contain the following selected data (in U.S. $ millions):

	2015	2014
Total assets	$4,388	$3,900
Total liabilities	2,559	2,258
Net income	234	218
Income tax expense	32	58
Interest expense	55	28

Instructions

(a) Calculate the debt to total assets and times interest earned ratios for 2015 and 2014. Did Open Text's solvency improve or deteriorate in 2015?

(b) The notes to Open Text's financial statements show that the company has an operating line of credit (credit facility) of $300 million that can be drawn on at any time and repaid at any time. However, no portion of this credit facility has been drawn on. What does this mean and how is this shown in the financial statements?

*E10–11 The following information about two independent bond issues was reported in the financial press.

1. **Province of Manitoba** 2.50% bonds, maturing January 1, 2020, were trading at a price of 99.9 to yield a market interest rate of 3.06%.

2. **Loblaw Companies Limited** 8.75% bonds, maturing November 23, 2033, were trading at a price of 144.09 to yield a market interest rate of 5.02%.

Analyze and record bond issue.

(LO 4)

Instructions

(a) Are the Province of Manitoba bonds trading at a premium or a discount?

(b) Are the Loblaw bonds trading at a premium or a discount?

(c) If these bonds were issued today by the Province of Manitoba and Loblaw, record the issue of $100,000 of each of these two bonds.

(d) Is it likely that these bonds were issued at a value closer to their face value? If so, how does the issuer do this?

(e) What is the major reason for the change in the price of the bonds since they were issued?

*E10–12 On October 1, 2018, Spooner Corporation issued $800,000 of 10-year, 5% bonds at 100. Interest is payable semi-annually on October 1 and April 1. Spooner's year end is December 31 and the company records adjusting entries annually.

Record bond transactions; identify current and non-current portions.

(LO 4)

Instructions

(a) Prepare journal entries to record the following:
   1. The issue of the bonds on October 1, 2018
   2. The accrual of interest on December 31, 2018
   3. The payment of interest on April 1, 2019

(b) Identify what amounts, if any, would be reported as a current liability and non-current liability with respect to the bond and bond interest accounts on December 31, 2018.

*E10–13 A partial bond amortization schedule follows for Hwee Corporation:

Complete bond amortization schedule; answer questions.

(LO 4)

Semi-Annual Interest Period	Interest Payment	Interest Expense	Discount/Premium Amortization	Unamortized Discount/Premium	Bond Carrying Amount
Issue date (Oct. 31)				$74,387	$925,613
1 (Apr. 30)	$25,000	[1]	$2,768	[2]	928,381
2 (Oct. 31)	25,000	$27,851	[3]	68,768	[4]
3 (Apr. 30)	[5]	27,937	[6]	[7]	934,169

Instructions

(a) Fill in the missing amounts for items [1] to [7].

(b) What is the face value of the bonds?

(c) Were the bonds issued at a discount or at a premium?

(d) What is the coupon interest rate on the bonds? The market interest rate?

(e) Explain why interest expense is greater than interest paid.

(f) Explain why interest expense will increase each period.

(g) What will be the bonds' carrying amount on their maturity date?

*E10–14 Tarawa Limited issued $1 million of 10-year, 5% bonds on January 1, 2018, when the market interest rate was 6%. Tarawa received $925,617 when the bonds were issued. Interest is payable semi-annually on July 1 and January 1. Tarawa has a December 31 year end.

Calculate present value; record bond transactions.

(LO 4)

Instructions

(a) Record the issue of the bonds on January 1.

(b) Record the payment of interest on July 1.

(c) Record the accrual of interest on December 31.

(d) Prove the amount of cash received when the bonds were sold by determining the bonds' present value (issue price) on January 1, 2018. Prove the carrying amount of the bonds, one year later, by determining the present value of the bonds at that time.

▶ PROBLEMS: SET A

Record and present current liabilities.

(LO 1, 3)

P10–1A On February 28, 2018, Molega Ltd.'s general ledger contained the following liability accounts:

Accounts payable	$42,500
CPP payable	2,680
EI payable	1,123
Sales tax payable	5,800
Employee income tax payable	5,515
Unearned revenue	15,000

The following selected transactions occurred during the month:

Mar.	2	Issued a three-month, 6% note payable in exchange for an account payable in the amount of $10,000. Interest is due at maturity.
	5	Sold inventory for cash totalling $40,000, plus 13% HST. The cost of goods sold was $24,000. Molega uses a perpetual inventory system.
	9	Received the property tax bill of $18,000 for the calendar year. It is payable on May 1.
	12	Provided services for customers who had made advance payments of $11,300 including HST, which is not payable until the related sale occurs.
	13	Paid $5,800 HST to the Receiver General for sales tax collected in February.
	16	Paid $9,318 to the Receiver General for amounts owing from the February payroll for employee payroll deductions of $7,323 (CPP $1,340, EI $468, and employee income tax $5,515) and for employee benefits of $1,995 (CPP $1,340 and EI $655).
	27	Paid $30,000 to trade creditors on account.
	30	Paid employees for the month. Gross salaries totalled $16,000 and payroll deductions included CPP of $792, EI of $301, and employee income tax of $5,870. Employee benefits included CPP of $792 and EI of $421.

Instructions

(a) Record the above transactions.

(b) Record any required adjusting entries at March 31.

(c) Prepare the current liabilities section of the statement of financial position at March 31.

Record and present short-term notes.

(LO 1, 3)

P10–2A Cling-on Ltd. sells rock-climbing products and also operates an indoor climbing facility for climbing enthusiasts. On July 1, 2018, Cling-on received a three-month $12,000 bank loan from City Credit Union due on September 30, 2018, and bearing interest at 3%. Interest is payable at maturity. Note that the company records adjusting entries annually at its year end, December 31.

During the next four months, Cling-on incurred the following:

Sept.	1	Purchased inventory on account for $15,000 from Black Diamond, terms n/30. The company uses a perpetual inventory system.
	30	Repaid the $12,000 bank loan payable to City Credit Union (see opening balance), as well as any interest owed.
Oct.	1	Issued a six-month, 4%, $15,000 note payable to Black Diamond in exchange for the account payable (see September 1 transaction). Interest is payable on the first of each month.
	2	Borrowed $25,000 from Montpelier Bank for 12 months at 3% to finance the building of a new climbing area for advanced climbers. (Use the asset account Buildings.) Interest is payable monthly on the first of each month.
Nov.	1	Paid interest on the Black Diamond note and Montpelier Bank loan.
Dec.	1	Paid interest on the Black Diamond note and Montpelier Bank loan.

Dec. 3   Purchased a vehicle for $28,000 from Auto Dealer Ltd. to transport clients to nearby climbing sites. Paid $8,000 as a down payment and borrowed the remainder from Atlantic Bank for 12 months at 3%. Interest is payable quarterly, at the end of each quarter.

     31   Recorded accrued interest for the Black Diamond note and the Montpelier and Atlantic loans.

Instructions

(a) Record the above transactions.

(b) Open T accounts for the Interest Expense, Interest Payable, Bank Loans Payable, and Notes Payable accounts and enter any opening balances. Post the above entries.

(c) Assuming there is no other interest expense than that recorded in the transactions above, show the income statement presentation of interest expense for the year ended December 31.

(d) Show the current liability section of the statement of financial position as at December 31, listing balances of accounts affected by the above transactions.

P10–3A On September 30, 2017, Coldwater Corporation purchased equipment for $1.1 million. The equipment was purchased with a $100,000 down payment and a three-year, 4%, $1-million bank loan for the balance. The terms provide for payment of the bank loan with quarterly fixed principal payments of $83,333, plus interest, starting on December 31. Coldwater has a November 30 year end and records adjusting entries annually.

Record instalment note.
(LO 2)

Instructions

(a) Record the purchase of equipment on September 30, 2017.

(b) Record the accrual of interest expense on November 30, 2017. Round to the nearest dollar.

(c) Record the first two instalment payments, on December 31, 2017, and March 31, 2018. Round all amounts to the nearest dollar.

(d) Repeat parts (b) and (c) assuming that the terms provide for quarterly blended principal and interest payments of $88,849, rather than fixed principal payments of $83,333, plus interest.

P10–4A Starlight Graphics Ltd. signed a 10-year, 6.5%, $700,000 mortgage on June 30, 2017, to help finance a new research laboratory. The mortgage terms provide for semi-annual blended principal and interest payments of $48,145. Payments are due on December 31 and June 30. The company's year end is June 30.

Prepare instalment payment schedule; record and present instalment note.
(LO 2, 3)

Instructions

(a) Prepare an instalment payment schedule for the first two years. Round all amounts to the nearest dollar.

(b) Record the receipt of the mortgage loan on June 30, 2017.

(c) Record the first two instalment payments, on December 31, 2017, and June 30, 2018.

(d) Show the statement of financial position presentation of the mortgage payable at June 30, 2018.

P10–5A Hussein Hage has just approached a venture capitalist for financing for his new restaurant, Bistro Sally. The lender is willing to loan Bistro Sally Inc. $240,000 at a high-risk interest rate of 9%. The loan is payable over three years in fixed principal payments each quarter of $20,000, plus interest. Hussein signed a note payable and received the loan on April 30, 2018. He made the first payment on July 31. The company's year end is October 31.

Prepare instalment payment schedule; record and present instalment note.
(LO 2, 3)

Instructions

(a) Prepare an instalment payment schedule for the three years. Round all amounts to the nearest dollar.

(b) Record the receipt of the loan on April 30.

(c) Record the first two instalment payments, on July 31 and October 31.

(d) Show the statement of financial position presentation of the note payable at October 31, 2018.

(e) Explain how the quarterly and total cash payments would change if the note had been payable in blended principal and interest payments of $23,044, rather than fixed principal payments plus interest.

P10–6A The following transactions occurred in Wendell Corporation, which has a December 31 year end.

Classify liabilities.
(LO 1, 3)

1. Property taxes of $40,000 were assessed on March 1 for the calendar year. They are payable by May 1.

2. Wendell signed a five-year, 7%, $200,000 instalment note payable on July 1. The note requires fixed principal payments of $40,000, plus interest annually on each June 30 for the next five years.

3. Wendell purchased inventory for $120,000 on December 23 on account, terms n/30, FOB shipping point. The inventory was shipped on December 28 and received by Wendell on January 2.

4. Wendell received $10,000 from customers on December 21 for services to be performed in January.

5. On December 31, Wendell sold inventory for $8,000, plus 13% HST. The cost of goods sold was $5,000. The company uses a perpetual inventory system.

6. Weekly salaries of $18,000 are paid every Friday for a five-day workweek (Monday to Friday). This year, December 31 is a Monday. Payroll deductions for the one day of pay before the end of the year include CPP of $175, EI of $68, and employee income tax of $1,200. Employee benefits to be paid by the employer include CPP of $175 and EI of $95. Payroll deductions will be paid on January 15.

7. Wendell, which reports under IFRS, is the defendant in a negligence lawsuit. Wendell's legal counsel estimates that Wendell may suffer a $75,000 loss if it loses the suit. In legal counsel's opinion, however, it cannot be determined at this time whether or not the case will be lost.

8. After the preparation of its corporate income tax return at year end, Wendell determined that total corporate income tax payable for the year was $50,000 but $45,000 of this amount was paid during the year when the company paid tax instalments.

9. Wendell reported non-current debt of $250,000 at December 31, of which $30,000 was due within the next year.

10. Wendell has a $100,000 operating line of credit available, on which no funds have yet been drawn.

Instructions

(a) Identify which of the above transactions gave rise to amounts that should be reported in the current liabilities section or the non-current liabilities section of Wendell's statement of financial position as at December 31. Identify the account title(s) and amount(s) for each reported liability.

(b) Indicate any information that should be disclosed in the notes to Wendell's financial statements.

Analyze liquidity and solvency.

(LO 3)

P10–7A You have been presented with the following selected information from the financial statements of one of Canada's largest dairy producers, **Saputo Inc.** (in millions):

	2015	2014	2013
Statement of financial position			
Accounts receivable	$ 785	$ 807	$ 625
Inventory	1,006	933	770
Total current assets	1,962	1,896	1,513
Total assets	6,800	6,357	5,194
Current liabilities	1,179	1,725	1,227
Total liabilities	3,172	3,518	2,888
Income statement			
Net sales	$10,658	$9,223	$7,298
Cost of goods sold	7,688	6,518	5,136
Interest expense	73	69	34
Income tax expense	237	225	186
Net income	613	534	482

Instructions

(a) Calculate each of the following ratios for 2015 and 2014. Industry ratios are shown in parentheses.
  1. Current ratio (2015, 1.9:1; 2014, 1.7:1)
  2. Receivables turnover (2015, 13.4 times; 2014, 14.0 times)
  3. Inventory turnover (2015, 5.9 times; 2014, 6.1 times)
  4. Debt to total assets (2015, 58.0%; 2014, 54.0%)
  5. Times interest earned (2015, 3.7 times; 2014, 3.0 times)

(b) Based on your results in part (a), comment on Saputo's liquidity and solvency.

(c) Saputo had a $1.1-billion operating line of credit, of which $170 million was used at March 31, 2015. Most of the bank debt held by the company was in U.S. dollars, which rose in value relative to the Canadian dollar in 2015. Discuss the implications of this information for your analysis.

(d) Saputo had operating lease commitments totalling $27 million in 2016 and $21 million in 2017. Discuss the implications of this information for your analysis.

Analyze liquidity and solvency.

(LO 3)

P10–8A The following selected liquidity and solvency ratios are available for two companies operating in the petroleum industry:

	Petro-Zoom	Sun-Oil	Industry Average
Current ratio	1.3:1	1.2:1	1.4:1
Receivables turnover	12 times	13 times	13 times
Inventory turnover	16 times	10 times	19 times
Debt to total assets	41%	39%	34%
Times interest earned	21 times	24 times	26 times

Instructions

Assume that you are the credit manager of the local bank. Answer the following questions, using relevant ratios to justify your answer.

(a) Both Petro-Zoom and Sun-Oil have applied for a short-term loan from your bank. Which of the two companies is more liquid and should get more consideration for a short-term loan? Explain.

(b) Both Petro-Zoom and Sun-Oil have applied for a long-term loan from your bank. Are you concerned about the solvency of either company? Explain why or why not.

*P10–9A When market interest rates were 6%, three companies issued bonds on January 1, 2018. Each company has a December 31 year end and each company issued bonds with a face value of $100,000 that pay interest annually on December 31. Able Limited sold its bonds at 100 and offered a coupon interest rate of 6%, while Beta Corp. sold its bonds at 94 and offered a coupon interest rate of 4%, and Charles Inc. sold its bonds at 105 and offered a 7% coupon interest rate.

Record bond transactions.

(LO 4)

Instructions

(a) Record the issue of the bonds by each company on January 1, 2018.

(b) Prepare the entry that each company would record for the payment of interest on December 31, 2018.

(c) Explain why some of the companies are not recording an interest expense on the bonds that is equal to the interest that was actually paid.

(d) Determine the balance in each company's Bonds Payable account on December 31, 2018.

*P10–10A On July 1, 2017, Global Satellites Corporation issued $1.5 million of 10-year, 7% bonds to yield a market interest rate of 6%. The bonds pay semi-annual interest on July 1 and January 1. Global has a December 31 year end. When the bonds were issued, Global received $1,611,587.

Prepare an amortization schedule; record and present bond transactions.

(LO 3, 4)

Instructions

(a) Prepare an amortization table through January 1, 2019 (three interest periods) for this bond issue. Round all amounts to the nearest dollar.

(b) Record the issue of the bonds on July 1.

(c) Prepare the adjusting entry on December 31, 2018, to accrue the interest on the bonds.

(d) Show the statement of financial position presentation of the liabilities at December 31, 2018.

(e) Record the payment of interest on January 1, 2019.

(f) Prove the issue proceeds of the bonds on July 1, 2017, by calculating the present value of the bonds at that time.

▶ PROBLEMS: SET B

P10–1B On January 1, 2018, Burlington Inc.'s general ledger contained these opening balances for its liability accounts:

Record and present current liabilities.

(LO 1, 3)

Accounts payable	$52,000	Sales tax payable	18,000
CPP payable	3,810	Employee income tax payable	7,700
EI payable	1,598	Unearned revenue	16,000

The following selected transactions occurred during the month.

Jan. 5 Sold inventory for cash totalling $20,000, plus 5% GST and 7% PST. The cost of goods sold was $14,000. Burlington uses a perpetual inventory system.

13 Paid $18,000 ($7,500 GST to the Receiver General and $10,500 PST to the provincial Minister of Finance) for sales taxes collected in December.

14 Paid $13,108 to the Receiver General for amounts owing from the December payroll for the employee payroll deductions of $10,271 (CPP $1,905, EI $666, and employee income tax $7,700) and employee benefits of $2,837 (CPP $1,905 and EI $932).

15 Borrowed $18,000 from HSBC Bank for three months; 6% interest is payable monthly on the 15th of each month.

19 Provided services for customers who had made advance payments of $11,200. This amount includes applicable GST and PST, which is not payable until the related revenue is earned.

22 Paid $32,000 to trade creditors on account.

28 Received assessment of property taxes of $4,200 for the calendar year. They are payable on March 1.

29 Paid employees for the month. Gross salaries totalled $40,000 and payroll deductions included CPP of $1,980, EI of $752, and employee income tax of $9,474. Employee benefits included CPP of $1,980 and EI of $1,053.

Instructions

(a) Record the above transactions.

(b) Record any required adjusting entries at January 31.

(c) Prepare the current liabilities section of the statement of financial position at January 31.

Record and present short-term notes.

(LO 1, 3)

P10–2B Sparky's Mountain Bikes Ltd. markets mountain-bike tours to clients vacationing in various locations in the mountains of British Columbia. On October 1, 2017, Sparky's issued a six-month, 5% note to Easy Finance Corp. due in six months on March 31, 2018. All of the interest on the note is payable at maturity. Note that the company records adjusting entries annually at its year end, June 30.

In preparation for the upcoming summer biking season, Sparky's engaged in the following transactions in 2018:

Mar.	2	Purchased Cannondale bikes for use as rentals by borrowing $16,000 from the Western Bank for a three-month period; 3% interest is payable at maturity.
	31	Paid the $30,000 note payable to Easy Finance Corp. (see opening balance), as well as any interest owed.
Apr.	1	Issued a nine-month, 4%, $50,000 note to Mountain Real Estate for the purchase of mountain property on which to build bike trails. Interest is payable at the first of each month.
May	1	Paid interest on the Mountain Real Estate note (see April 1 transaction).
	2	Borrowed $36,000 from National Bank for a four-month period. The funds will be used for working capital for the beginning of the season; 3% interest is payable at maturity.
June	1	Paid interest on the Mountain Real Estate note (see April 1 transaction).
	2	Paid principal and interest to the Western Bank (see March 2 transaction).
	29	Purchased trailers for $10,000 to transport the bikes from one location to another. (*Hint:* Use the Vehicles account.) Paid $1,000 as a down payment and borrowed the remainder from the Provincial Bank for a 12-month period; 3% interest is payable quarterly, at the end of each quarter, starting September 30.
	30	Recorded accrued interest for the Mountain Real Estate note and the National Bank loan.

Instructions

(a) Record the above transactions.

(b) Open T accounts for the Interest Expense, Interest Payable, Bank Loans Payable, and Notes Payable accounts and enter any opening balances. Post the above entries.

(c) Assuming there is no other interest expense than that recorded in the transactions above, show the income statement presentation of the interest expense for the year ended June 30.

(d) Show the current liability section of the statement of financial position as at June 30, listing balances of accounts affected by the above transactions.

Record instalment note.

(LO 2)

P10–3B On July 31, 2018, Myron Corporation purchased equipment for $750,000. The equipment was purchased with a $50,000 down payment and with a four-year, 4%, $700,000 bank loan payable for the balance. The terms provide for the bank loan to be repaid with monthly blended principal and interest instalment payments of $15,805 starting on August 31. Myron has a September 30 year end.

Instructions

(a) Record the purchase of equipment and the receipt of the bank loan on July 31.

(b) Record the first two instalment payments, on August 31 and September 30. Round all amounts to the nearest dollar.

(c) Repeat part (b) assuming that the terms provide for monthly fixed principal payments of $14,583, plus interest, rather than blended payments of $15,805.

Prepare instalment payment schedule; record and present instalment note.

(LO 2, 3)

P10–4B Beaumont Building Supplies Limited signed a 10-year, 8%, $1-million mortgage on December 31, 2017, to help finance a plant expansion. The terms of the mortgage provide for semi-annual fixed principal payments of $50,000, plus interest. Payments are due on June 30 and December 31.

Instructions

(a) Prepare an instalment payment schedule for the first two years. Round all amounts to the nearest dollar.

(b) Record the issue of the mortgage payable on December 31, 2017.

(c) Record the first two instalment payments, on June 30, 2018, and December 31, 2018.

(d) Show the statement of financial position presentation of the mortgage payable at December 31, 2018.

Prepare instalment payment schedule; record and present instalment note.

(LO 2, 3)

P10–5B The owner of Alpine Golf Course Ltd., a local golf course, has just approached a venture capitalist for financing for its new business venture, the development of another course. On April 1, 2017, the venture capitalist lent the company $200,000 at an interest rate of 8%. The loan is payable over four years in annual blended principal and interest instalments of $60,384, due annually on March 31. The first payment is due March 31, 2018. The golf course's year end is March 31.

Instructions

(a) Prepare an instalment payment schedule for the loan period. Round all amounts to the nearest dollar.

(b) Record the receipt of the loan on April 1, 2017.

(c) Record the first two instalment payments, on March 31, 2018, and March 31, 2019.

(d) Show the statement of financial position presentation of the loan payable as at March 31, 2019.

(e) Explain how the annual and total interest expense would change if the loan had been payable in fixed principal payments of $50,000, plus interest, rather than in blended principal and interest payments.

P10–6B The following transactions are for Iqaluit Ltd., which has an April 30 year end.

Classify liabilities.

(LO 1, 3)

1. Received property taxes assessment of $12,000 on March 1 for the calendar year. They are payable by May 1.
2. Purchased equipment for $35,000 on April 1 by making a $5,000 down payment and borrowing the remainder from the bank for a six-month period; 6% interest is payable on the first of each month.
3. Purchased inventory for $7,000 on April 27 on account, terms 2/10, n/30.
4. Sold inventory on April 28 for $15,000, plus 5% GST. (There is no PST in Nunavut, where Iqaluit Ltd. is based.) The cost of the goods sold was $10,500. The company uses a perpetual inventory system.
5. Received $25,000 from customers on April 29 for services to be performed in May.
6. Weekly salaries of $40,000 are paid every Friday for a five-day workweek (Monday to Friday). This year, April 30 is a Monday. Payroll deductions for the one day of this period that falls before the end of the year include CPP of $393, EI of $150, and employee income tax of $3,200. Employee benefits to be paid by the employer include CPP of $393 and EI of $210. Payroll deductions will be paid on May 15.
7. Iqaluit, which reports under IFRS, was named in a lawsuit alleging negligence for an oil spill that leaked into the neighbouring company's water system. Iqaluit's legal counsel estimates that it is probable that the company will lose the suit but the amount of the loss cannot be determined yet.
8. Iqaluit paid income tax instalments of $80,000 throughout the year. After the preparation of its year-end corporate income tax return, it was determined that the total corporate income tax payable for the year was $95,000.
9. Iqaluit reported non-current liabilities of $150,000 at April 30, of which $15,000 was due within the next year.
10. Iqaluit has a $50,000 operating line of credit available, on which no funds have yet been drawn.

Instructions

(a) Identify which of the above transactions give rise to amounts that should be reported in the current liabilities section or the non-current liabilities section of Iqaluit's statement of financial position as at April 30. Identify the account title(s) and amount(s) for each reported liability.

(b) Indicate any information that should be disclosed in the notes to Iqaluit's financial statements.

P10–7B The following selected information was taken from the financial statements of one of the world's largest convenience store operators, Montreal-based **Alimentation Couche-Tard Inc.** (in U.S. $ millions):

Analyze liquidity and solvency.

(LO 3)

	2015	2014	2013
Statement of financial position			
Accounts receivable	$ 1,195	$ 1,726	$ 1,616
Inventory	860	848	846
Total current assets	2,707	3,215	3,281
Total assets	10,838	10,545	10,546
Current liabilities	2,415	2,663	3,138
Total liabilities	6,931	6,568	7,329
Income statement			
Net sales	$34,530	$37,962	$35,543
Cost of goods sold	29,262	32,974	30,934
Interest expense	92	111	118
Income tax expense	306	134	74
Net income	933	812	573

Instructions

(a) Calculate each of the following ratios for 2015 and 2014. Industry ratios are shown in parentheses.
1. Current ratio (2015, 1.7:1; 2014, 1.5:1)
2. Receivables turnover (2015, 29.2 times; 2014, 30.8 times)
3. Inventory turnover (2015, 10.7 times; 2014, 14.9 times)
4. Debt to total assets (2015, 44.0%; 2014, 40.0%)
5. Times interest earned (2015, 12.0 times; 2014, 9.0 times)

(b) Based on your results in part (a), comment on Alimentation Couche-Tard's liquidity and solvency.

(c) Alimentation Couche-Tard has an unused operating line of credit of over U.S. $3 billion. Why would a bank be willing to provide such a large line of credit?

P10–8B The following selected liquidity and solvency ratios are available for two companies operating in the fast food industry:

Analyze liquidity and solvency.

(LO 3)

	Grab 'N Gab	Chick 'N Lick	Industry Average
Current ratio	0.8:1	0.7:1	0.9:1
Receivables turnover	46 times	38 times	34 times
Inventory turnover	39 times	45 times	31 times
Debt to total assets	49%	40%	39%
Times interest earned	10 times	5 times	7 times

Instructions

Assume that you are the credit manager of the local bank. Answer the following questions, using relevant ratios to justify your answer.

(a) Both Grab 'N Gab and Chick 'N Lick have applied for a short-term loan from your bank. Which of the two companies is more liquid and should get more consideration for a short-term loan? Explain.

(b) Both Grab 'N Gab and Chick 'N Lick have applied for a long-term loan from your bank. Are you concerned about the solvency of either company? Explain why or why not.

Record bond transactions.
(LO 4)

*P10–9B When market interest rates were 5%, three companies issued bonds on January 1, 2018. Each company has a December 31 year end and each company issued bonds with a face value of $200,000 that pay interest annually on December 31. Delta Limited sold its bonds at 100 and offered a coupon interest rate of 5%, while Founders Corp. sold its bonds at 94 and offered a coupon interest rate of 3%. Grand Inc. sold its bonds at 108 and offered a 7% coupon interest rate.

Instructions

(a) Record the issue of the bonds by each company on January 1, 2018.

(b) Prepare the entry that each company would record for the payment of interest on December 31, 2018.

(c) Explain why some of the companies are not recording an interest expense on the bonds that is equal to the interest that was actually paid.

(d) Determine the balance in each company's Bonds Payable account on December 31, 2018.

Prepare an amortization schedule; record and present bond transactions.
(LO 3, 4)

*P10–10B On July 1, 2017, Ponasis Corporation issued $1 million of 10-year, 6% bonds at a price to yield a market interest rate of 7%. The bonds pay semi-annual interest on July 1 and January 1. Ponasis has a December 31 year end. When the bonds were issued, Ponasis received $928,942.

Instructions

(a) Prepare an amortization table through January 1, 2019 (three interest periods) for this bond issue. Round all amounts to the nearest dollar.

(b) Record the issue of the bonds on July 1.

(c) Prepare the adjusting entry on December 31, 2018, to accrue the interest on the bonds.

(d) Show the statement of financial position presentation of the liabilities at December 31, 2018.

(e) Record the payment of interest on January 1, 2019.

(f) Prove the issue proceeds on the bonds on July 1, 2017, by calculating the present value of the bonds at that time.

ACCOUNTING CYCLE | REVIEW

Record and post transactions; prepare trial balance and financial statements; calculate ratios.
(LO 1, 2, 3)

ACR10–1 Wascana Ltd. is a small wholesaler of restaurant supplies. The company's post-closing trial balance at December 31, 2017, the end of its fiscal year, is presented below:

WASCANA LTD.
Post-Closing Trial Balance
December 31, 2017

	Debit	Credit
Cash	$ 80,000	
Accounts receivable	480,000	
Allowance for doubtful accounts		$ 24,000
Inventory	356,000	
Equipment	1,800,000	
Accumulated depreciation—equipment		480,000
Accounts payable		321,000
Interest payable		4,000
Employee income tax payable		52,000
CPP payable		28,000
EI payable		12,000
Provisions		35,000
Unearned revenue		12,000
Bank loan payable		1,200,000
Common shares		60,000
Retained earnings		488,000
	$2,716,000	$2,716,000

The company had the following transactions during January 2018. When recording these transactions, use the item number listed in lieu of the date and also use that same item number if recording a subsequent adjustment pertaining to that item.

1 The bank loan bears interest at 4% and requires monthly payments on the first day of the month consisting of a fixed principal, payment of $8,000, plus interest, which was properly accrued at the end of 2017. A loan payment was made on January 1, 2018.

2 Accrue interest on the bank loan for the month of January 2018.

3 Early in January 2018, the company paid for a one-year insurance policy on equipment for $24,000.

4 Equipment has a useful life of five years and is depreciated on a double-diminishing-balance basis.

5 All of the payroll-related liabilities were paid off in early January 2018.

6 At the end of January, salaries for that month were paid out. Gross salaries were $290,000 and amounts withheld from the employees' paycheques included the related employee income tax of $52,000, CPP of $14,000, and EI of $5,452. In addition to these amounts, the employer was required to contribute $14,000 to CPP and $7,633 to EI. The salaries were paid but no amounts were remitted to the government regarding the salaries for January.

7 Paid a $9,000 income tax instalment.

8 Sales for the month of January were $745,000 and the cost of the inventory sold was $270,000. The company uses a perpetual inventory system. All sales were on credit.

9 Accounts receivable collected during the month were $780,000.

10 A customer owing the company $16,000 went bankrupt during January.

11 Reviewed outstanding accounts receivable. Determined, through an aging of accounts, that doubtful accounts were $30,000 at month end.

12 Inventory costing $250,000 was purchased in January on credit. Also, office expenses of $49,000 were incurred on credit.

13 During the month of January, accounts payable amounting to $350,000 were paid.

14 The provisions at December 31, 2017, consisted of estimated damages from a lawsuit. In January, legal counsel felt that an additional $20,000 of damages had become probable that month. Any expenses relating to these damages are recorded in administrative expenses.

15 Unearned revenue consists of deposits from customers received in advance. No new deposits were received in January, but by the end of the month, management has estimated that unearned revenue at that time should be $7,000. Products sold to these customers that paid deposits cost 25% of the price they were sold at.

16 The company declared and paid out dividends amounting to $4,000 in January.

Instructions
(a) Prepare T accounts and enter the December 31 balances.
(b) Record the January transactions and adjustments.
(c) Post the journal entries from part (b) to the T accounts.
(d) Prepare an adjusted trial balance at January 31, 2018.
(e) Prepare a (1) income statement and (2) statement of changes in equity for the month ended January 31, 2018, and (3) statement of financial position at January 31, 2018.

EXPAND YOUR | CRITICAL THINKING

CT10–1 Financial Reporting Case

The financial statements of **The North West Company Inc.** are presented in Appendix A at the end of the book.

Instructions
(a) What types of current and non-current liabilities were reported in The North West Company's statement of financial position (balance sheet) at January 31, 2016?

(b) By looking at the details provided in the long-term debt note to the financial statements, determine what is the most significant component of the current portion of long-term debt and the most significant component of the long-term debt balances.

(c) The company has issued some senior notes, some of which have fixed interest rates while others have floating rates. What could be a reason for issuing notes with both of these types of interest rates?

CT10–2 Financial Analysis Case

The financial statements of The North West Company Inc. are presented in Appendix A followed by the financial statements for **Sobeys Inc.** in Appendix B.

Instructions
(a) Based on the information contained in the financial statements, calculate the following ratios for each company for the latest fiscal year. Industry ratios are shown in parentheses.
1. Current ratio (1.3:1)
2. Receivables turnover (37.1 times) (Assume all sales were on credit.)
3. Inventory turnover (9.5 times)
4. Debt to total assets (60.6%)
5. Times interest earned (10.8 times)

(b) What conclusions about the companies' liquidity and solvency can you draw from the ratios calculated in part (a)? What ratios do you think are more important for your assessment?

CT10–3 Financial Analysis Case

This case can be assigned as a group activity. Additional instructions and material for this activity can be found on the Instructor Resource site and in WileyPLUS.

Atlas Limited operates a small private wholesale company selling imported foods to grocery retailers on Prince Edward Island. The company began operations on January 1, 2017, and has just completed its second year of operations. In January 2018, the company moved to a new location and now rents a much larger facility. When the move occurred, additional bank loans were taken out to finance the purchase of some new equipment. The CEO of the business, Jim O'Sullivan, negotiated with the bank to have principal payments (not interest) on any bank loan delayed until 2020. Jim has asked you to review information from the company's financial statements shown below and to accompany him to the bank. He wants you to help him convince his banker to give the company an operating line of credit.

The banker has some misgivings. Jim is not sure why, because the current ratio has risen and the debt to total assets ratio has fallen slightly. He did tell you that a contingent liability relating to a lawsuit launched against the company will be disclosed in the financial statements, but it has not been recorded because an estimate could not be determined.

Shown below are amounts extracted from the financial statements (in thousands).

	2018	2017
Statement of Financial Position Information		
Cash	$ 2,000	$10,000
Accounts receivable	20,000	5,000
Inventory	30,000	7,500
Property, plant, and equipment, net	60,000	50,000
Accounts payable	30,930	16,550
Bank loan, non-current	40,000	30,000
Common shares	13,000	13,000
Retained earnings	28,070	12,950
Income Statement Information		
Sales	$100,000	$50,000
Cost of goods sold	50,000	20,000
Operating expenses	26,000	10,000
Interest expense	2,400	1,500
Income tax expense	6,480	5,550

Instructions

(a) Calculate the current, receivables turnover, inventory turnover, debt to total assets, and times interest earned ratios. Assume year-end amounts equal average amounts for the purpose of your calculations.

(b) Discuss how the ratios calculated in part (a) have changed in 2018 compared with 2017 and identify possible underlying reasons for these changes.

(c) Explain to Jim why his banker may not want to give the company an operating line of credit.

CT10–4 Financial Analysis Case

At the beginning of 2014, **Baytex Energy Corp.** had assets of $2.7 billion and liabilities of $1.4 billion. Expecting oil prices to remain high, the company expanded significantly in the first half of 2014, and by the end of that year, total assets had risen to $6.2 billion. To finance this growth, the company borrowed heavily, and at one point during the expansion in early 2014, total liabilities were at $5.3 billion. However, shortly after the expansion, total liabilities fell and they were $3.7 billion by year end. In the last half of 2014, oil prices dropped dramatically and the company had a loss of $0.4 billion for that year. However, by December 31, 2014, shareholders' equity had risen to $2.5 billion and most of this rise occurred in the middle of the year.

Instructions

(a) What is the most likely explanation for the increase in shareholders' equity given the loss that occurred during 2014?

(b) If liabilities were highest during the year, why did they fall by year end?

(c) Do you think that the company was under pressure to reduce its liabilities once oil prices began to fall? Why or why not?

(d) The company's share price was over $45 when the expansion occurred but it fell to less than $20 by the end of the year. If the company issued any shares during the year, when do you think this happened and did the company choose the right time of year to issue shares?

CT10–5 Financial Analysis Case

Citizens Bank has just received draft financial statements from ABC Wholesalers, one of its clients. In the loan agreement between the bank and ABC, there is a covenant that requires the company to have a debt to assets ratio that does not exceed 50% and a times interest earned ratio that exceeds 5.0 times. Alex Scullion, the controller of ABC, prepared the draft statement of financial position at year end that indicated that total assets were $100,000 and total liabilities were $45,000. The draft income statement for the year showed income from operations of $120,000 and interest expense of $20,000. The income tax rate is 30%. After receiving the draft financial statements, the bank was informed by Alex's boss, Jennifer Woo, that three errors were made when the draft financial statements were prepared. They were: (1) interest of $2,500 was not accrued on a loan payable, (2) a loan payment was debited completely to the bank loan liability account when $1,800 of the payment related to interest, and (3) proceeds of $2,700 from the sale of gift cards were recorded as revenue even though the gift cards have not yet been redeemed (*Hint:* Use the Unearned Revenue account.)

Instructions

(a) Calculate the ratio values used for the bank's covenant tests based on the information in the original draft statements.

(b) Each one of the errors described above affects two accounts. For each error, explain which accounts are affected and by how much. In doing this, also describe if the error has caused an overstatement or understatement in those accounts.

(c) Based on your analysis in part (b) above, determine if there is any error in the Income Tax Expense and Income Tax Payable account balances.

(d) Calculate the ratio values used for the bank's covenant tests based on revised information in the financial statements assuming that all of the errors analyzed above have been corrected.

(e) Based on your answer to part (d) above, did ABC fail to meet either of the loan's covenant tests?

(f) Do you think that the errors made by Alex could be intentional? Why or why not?

CT10–6 Ethics Case

Crown Point Inc. is arranging a long-term lease for the company's equipment. The company has dismissed the option of borrowing money from the bank and buying the equipment and is now trying to decide between structuring the lease as an operating lease or a finance lease. Lise Ranier, the company's CEO, strongly urges the controller to structure the lease as an operating lease. "That way," she says, "we won't add debt that might create problems with our existing debt covenants at the bank."

Instructions

(a) Who are the stakeholders in this situation?

(b) Explain generally how an operating lease affects the financial statements of a company, compared with a finance lease.

(c) Is it unethical to deliberately structure a lease as an operating lease just to keep the debt off the financial statements?

(d) Do you think analysts will be able to distinguish between the financial impacts of purchasing equipment by borrowing from a bank compared with leasing it on an operating lease or a finance lease?

CT10–7 Serial Case

(*Note:* This is a continuation of the serial case from Chapters 1 through 9.)

You will recall from Chapter 9 that Emily, Bev, and Doug had originally thought that the equipment upgrade that ABC decided to undertake could be paid for with cash in the bank. Unfortunately, there was not enough cash and an operating line of credit was required. At January 31, 2018, the balance used on the new line of credit, and recorded in the Bank Indebtedness account, was $25,000.

At June 25, 2018, the balance of the 5% mortgage payable was $49,050. Monthly blended principal and interest instalment payments are $667, paid on the 25th of each month.

The mortgage is up for renewal on November 25, 2018, and Bev, Doug, and Emily would like to reduce the mortgage term to five years, instead of the seven years remaining. The current interest rate is 4%. They are considering transferring the balance of the line of credit onto the mortgage payable balance outstanding instead of trying to pay the balance owed on the line of credit from cash generated from operations. The bank has agreed to accommodate this request and has estimated the monthly blended principal and interest instalment payments would be $1,320 for the combined amounts, starting on December 25, 2018.

Instructions

(a) If the amount of mortgage owing was $49,050 on June 25, and blended payments are $667 per month as indicated above, what is the amount of the mortgage owing at November 25, 2018, immediately before it is renegotiated? Round all amounts to the nearest dollar.

(b) Assume that ABC increases the mortgage payable amount you determined in part (a) by $25,000, which is the amount of the line of credit still outstanding at November 25, 2018. What is the revised amount of the mortgage payable at November 25, 2018? Record the increase in the mortgage payable on November 25.

(c) Prepare an instalment payment schedule using the blended instalment payments of $1,320, from December 25, 2018, to June 25, 2020. Round all amounts to the nearest dollar.

(d) Record the first two instalment payments for December 25, 2018, and January 25, 2019.

(e) From the information provided in part (c), show the presentation of the current and non-current portions of the mortgage payable on ABC's statement of financial position at June 30, 2019.

▶ ANSWERS TO CHAPTER PRACTICE QUESTIONS

1.	Apr. 2	Cash ($256,000 + $33,280)	289,280		DO IT! 10-1a
		Sales		256,000	Current Liabilities
		Sales Tax Payable ($256,000 × 13%)		33,280	
		(To record sales and sales tax)			

2.	May 1	Property Tax Expense ($12,000 × $^{4}/_{12}$)	4,000	
		Property Tax Payable		4,000
		(To record property tax expense for January to April and amount owing)		
	June 30	Property Tax Payable	4,000	
		Property Tax Expense ($12,000 × $^{2}/_{12}$)	2,000	
		Prepaid Property Tax ($12,000 × $^{6}/_{12}$)	6,000	
		Cash		12,000
		(To record payment of property tax for January through December)		
	Dec. 31	Property Tax Expense	6,000	
		Prepaid Property Tax		6,000
		(To record the expiry of the prepaid property tax and property tax expense for the last six months of the year)		
3.	July 11	Salaries Expense	10,000	
		CPP Payable		495
		EI Payable		188
		Employee Income Tax Payable		3,465
		Cash		5,852
		(To record payroll and employee deductions)		
	11	Employee Benefits Expense	758	
		CPP Payable		495
		EI Payable ($188 × 1.4)		263
		(To record employee benefits)		
	18	CPP Payable ($495 + $495)	990	
		EI Payable ($188 + $263)	451	
		Employee Income Tax Payable	3,465	
		Cash		4,906
		(To record remittance of employee deductions and benefits)		
4.	Dec. 1	Cash	10,000	
		Note Payable		10,000
		(To record receipt of three-month, 3% note payable)		
	Dec. 31	Interest Expense ($10,000 × 3% × $^{1}/_{12}$)	25	
		Interest Payable		25
		(To accrue interest for December on note payable)		
	Jan. 1	Interest Payable	25	
		Cash		25
		(To record payment of interest for December on note payable)		
	Feb. 1	Interest Expense	25	
		Cash		25
		(To record payment of interest for January on note payable)		
	Mar. 1	Interest Expense	25	
		Note Payable	10,000	
		Cash		10,025
		(To record repayment of note payable and interest for February)		

DO IT! 10-1b

Provisions and Contingent Liabilities

1. Contingent liability—Probable but amount not determinable. Disclose.
2. Contingent liability—It is not yet determinable whether the company will win or lose the lawsuit, nor is an amount, if any, estimable. Disclose.
3. Contingent liability—Disclose as not probable. No provision is recorded until the subsidiary defaults on the loan.
4. Provision—Record using an estimated amount from past experience.
5. Contingent liability—No disclosure is required because the possibility of an outflow of resources is remote.

DO IT! 10-2a

Instalment Mortgage Payable—Fixed Payments

(a) Semi-annual payment:
10 years × 2 semi-annual periods per year = 20 periods
$400,000 ÷ 20 periods = $20,000

(b) Instalment payment schedule:

Interest Period	Cash Payment	Interest Expense (4% × $^{6}/_{12}$)	Reduction of Principal	Principal Balance
Dec. 31, 2017				$400,000
June 30, 2018	$28,000	$8,000	$20,000	380,000
Dec. 31, 2018	27,600	7,600	20,000	360,000

(c) Journal entries:

2017			
Dec. 31	Cash	400,000	
	Mortgage Payable		400,000
	(To record receipt of 10-year, 4% mortgage payable)		
2018			
June 30	Interest Expense ($400,000 × 4% × 6/12)	8,000	
	Mortgage Payable	20,000	
	Cash ($8,000 + $20,000)		28,000
	(To record semi-annual instalment payment on mortgage)		
Dec. 31	Interest Expense [($400,000 − $20,000) × 4% × 6/12]	7,600	
	Mortgage Payable	20,000	
	Cash ($7,600 + $20,000)		27,600
	(To record semi-annual instalment payment on mortgage)		

DO IT! 10-2b

Instalment Mortgage Payable—Blended Payments

(a) Instalment payment schedule:

Interest Period	Cash Payment	Interest Expense (4% × 6/12)	Reduction of Principal	Principal Balance
Dec. 31, 2017				$400,000
June 30, 2018	$24,463	$8,000	$16,463	383,537
Dec. 31, 2018	24,463	7,671	16,792	366,745
June 30, 2019	24,463	7,335	17,128	349,617
Dec. 31, 2019	24,463	6,992	17,471	332,146

(b) Journal entries:

2017			
Dec. 31	Cash	400,000	
	Mortgage Payable		400,000
	(To record receipt of 10-year, 4% mortgage payable)		
2018			
June 30	Interest Expense ($400,000 × 4% × 6/12)	8,000	
	Mortgage Payable ($24,463 − $8,000)	16,463	
	Cash		24,463
	(To record semi-annual instalment payment on mortgage)		
Dec. 31	Interest Expense [($400,000 − $16,463) × 4% × 6/12]	7,671	
	Mortgage Payable ($24,463 − $7,671)	16,792	
	Cash		24,463
	(To record semi-annual instalment payment on mortgage)		

(c) Presentation:

HARBIN INC.
December 31, 2018
Statement of Financial Position (partial)

Current liabilities	
Current portion of mortgage payable ($17,128 + $17,471)	$ 34,599
Non-current liabilities	
Mortgage payable	332,146
Total liabilities	$366,745

Item	Classification	Financial Statement
Accounts payable	Current liability	Statement of financial position
Bonds payable	Non-current liability	Statement of financial position
Current portion of mortgage payable	Current liability	Statement of financial position
Employee benefits expense	Operating expense	Income statement
Employee income tax payable	Current liability	Statement of financial position
Interest expense	Other expense	Income statement
Loan guarantee	Not recorded; disclosed	Notes to the financial statements
Mortgage payable	Non-current liability	Statement of financial position
Operating leases	Not recorded; disclosed	Notes to the financial statements
Prepaid property tax	Current asset	Statement of financial position
Salaries payable	Current liability	Statement of financial position
Sales tax payable	Current liability	Statement of financial position
Unused operating line of credit	Not recorded, disclosed	Notes to the financial statements
Warranty provision	Current liability	Statement of financial position

DO IT! 10-3a

Presentation

DO IT! 10-3b
Liquidity and Solvency

	(a)		(b)
	2018	2017	
Current ratio	$\dfrac{\$11,000 + \$38,000 + \$6,000}{\$19,400 + \$6,400} = 2.1{:}1$	$\dfrac{\$10,000 + \$31,000 + \$5,000}{\$23,800 + \$2,800} = 1.7{:}1$	Improvement
Debt to total assets	$\dfrac{\$19,400 + \$6,400 + \$160,000}{\$265,000} = 70.1\%$	$\dfrac{\$23,800 + \$2,800 + \$70,000}{\$139,600} = 69.2\%$	Deterioration
Times interest earned	$\dfrac{\$32,200 + \$12,800 + \$15,000}{\$12,800} = 4.7 \text{ times}$	$\dfrac{\$15,400 + \$5,600 + \$8,000}{\$5,600} = 5.2 \text{ times}$	Deterioration

The company's assets grew considerably in 2018 but so did the debt, resulting in very little change (a slight increase) in the debt to total assets ratio. The growth in assets allowed the company to generate more sales and operating income but this did not grow as fast as the interest expense, so the times interest earned ratio deteriorated. As the company grew, inventory levels increased, but accounts payable were paid down more rapidly and this improved the current ratio.

DO IT! 10-4a
Bond Transactions

(a) Proceeds received when bond is issued = $800,000 × 0.956241 = $764,993

(b)

2018

1. Jan. 1	Cash	764,993	
	Bonds Payable		764,993
	(To record issue of five-year, 4% bonds at a discount)		
2. July 1	Interest Expense ($764,993 × 5% × %₁₂)	19,125	
	Bonds Payable ($19,125 − $16,000)		3,125
	Cash ($800,000 × 4% × %₁₂)		16,000
	(To record semi-annual bond interest payment and amortization of discount)		
3. Dec. 31	Interest Expense [($764,993 + $3,125) × 5% × %₁₂]	19,203	
	Bonds Payable ($19,203 − $16,000)		3,203
	Interest Payable ($800,000 × 4% × %₁₂)		16,000
	(To accrue interest at year end)		

2019

4. Jan. 1	Interest Payable	16,000	
	Cash		16,000
	(To record the payment of interest)		

2023

5. Jan. 1	Bonds Payable	800,000	
	Cash		800,000
	(To record redemption of five-year, 4% bonds at maturity)		

DO IT! 10-4b
Determining the Price of Bonds

(a) The interest paid on a semi-annual basis will be $500,000 × 2% = $10,000. Assuming maturity in five years after 10 interest payment periods have elapsed, we can calculate the present value of the bond as follows:

1. Assuming a market interest rate of 5% or 2.5% semi-annually, the present value of the maturity amount (face value) is:
   $500,000 × 0.78120 ($n = 10$, $i = 2.5\%$) $390,600

   The present value of the semi-annual interest payments is:
   $10,000 × 8.75206 ($n = 10$, $i = 2.5\%$)   87,521
                                          $478,121

2. Assuming a market interest rate of 3% or 1.5% semi-annually, the present value of the maturity amount (face value) is:
   $500,000 × 0.86167 ($n = 10$, $i = 1.5\%$) $430,835

   The present value of the semi-annual interest payments is:
   $10,000 × 9.22218 ($n = 10$, $i = 1.5\%$)   92,222
                                           $523,057

(b) Assuming maturity in 10 years after 20 interest payment periods have elapsed, we can calculate the present value of the bond as follows:

1. Assuming a market interest rate of 5% or 2.5% semi-annually, the present value of the maturity amount (face value) is:

$500,000 × 0.61027 (n = 20, i = 2.5%) $305,135

The present value of the semi-annual interest payments is:
$10,000 × 15.58916 (n = 20, i = 2.5%)   155,892
                                                                                             $461,027

2. Assuming a market interest rate of 3% or 1.5% semi-annually, the present value of the maturity amount (face value) is:

$500,000 × 0.74247 (n = 20, i = 1.5%) $371,235

The present value of the semi-annual interest payments is:
$10,000 × 17.16864 (n = 20, i = 1.5%)   171,686
                                                                                             $542,921

Note that present value amounts may vary if a financial calculator is used instead of present value table factors.

(c) Market interest rates and bond prices have an inverse relationship. The price of the bond was higher when market interest rates were lower and the price of the bond was lower when market interest rates were higher.

(d) The discount or premium on a bond becomes larger when the term of the bond becomes longer. As we can see from above, the lowest bond price and the highest bond price that were calculated pertained to the 10-year bonds, not the five-year bonds.

▶ PRACTICE USING THE DECISION TOOLKIT

(a) Liquidity:

(in millions)	Royal Mail	Canada Post	Industry Average
Current ratio	$\frac{£1,420}{£1,991} = 0.7:1$	1.8:1	1.0:1

Royal Mail's current ratio of 0.7:1 means that it has £0.70 of current assets for each £1 of current liabilities. In other words, its current liabilities exceed its current assets. Although its available line of credit improves its liquidity position, its liquidity is still not good and is significantly below that of Canada Post and the industry.

(b) Solvency:

(in millions)	Royal Mail	Canada Post	Industry Average
Debt to total assets	$\frac{£3,133}{£7,600} = 41.2\%$	114.6%	54.4%
Times interest earned	$\frac{£309}{£16} = 19.3$ times	3.7 times	9.4 times

Royal Mail's debt to total assets ratio of 41.2% is significantly better (lower) than that of Canada Post and also better than the industry average. Royal Mail's times interest earned ratio is also better (higher) than Canada Post's ratio and the industry average because of its higher net income.

(c) Royal Mail's unused operating line of credit improves its liquidity and may help reduce any concerns that its short-term lenders and creditors may have.

▶ PRACTICE COMPREHENSIVE DO IT!

(a) 1.

Interest Period	(A) Cash Payment	(B) Interest Expense (D × 6% × 6/12)	(C) Reduction of Principal (A − B)	(D) Principal Balance (D − C)
Issue date (Dec. 31, 2017)				$1,000,000
1 (June 30, 2018)	$51,019	$30,000	$21,019	978,981
2 (Dec. 31, 2018)	51,019	29,369	21,650	957,331
3 (June 30, 2019)	51,019	28,720	22,299	935,032
4 (Dec. 31, 2019)	51,019	28,051	22,968	912,064

2.

Dec. 31, 2017	Cash	1,000,000	
	Bank Loan Payable		1,000,000
	(To record receipt of 15-year, 6% bank loan)		

3.

June 30, 2018	Interest Expense	30,000	
	Bank Loan Payable	21,019	
	Cash		51,019
	(To record semi-annual instalment payment on bank loan)		

4. The current liability is $45,267 ($22,299 + $22,968). The non-current liability is $912,064. The total liability is the balance of $957,331 at the end of the second period, December 31, 2018.

5. In a fixed principal payment plus interest situation, the reduction of the principal is constant while the interest expense and total cash payment decrease. The total cash payment would decrease each period. However, this does not change the nature of the journal entry because the same accounts will be debited and credited; it is just the amounts that will change.

6. When the times interest earned ratio increases, it signals an improvement. In this case, the company's earnings before interest and income tax rose faster than interest expense. This indicates that the borrowed funds from the bank were spent wisely, resulting in increased profitability, which makes the company more able to pay interest on loans.

(b)

Jan. 3, 2018	Accounts Receivable	226	
	Sales		200
	Sales Tax Payable ($200 × 13%)		26
	(To record sale of software program)		
Jan. 3, 2018	Cost of Goods Sold	75	
	Inventory		75
	(To record the cost of goods sold on the above sale)		

(c) 1.

Jan. 31, 2018	Salaries Expense	3,000	
	CPP Payable		135
	EI Payable		56
	Employee Income Tax Payable		385
	Cash		2,424
	(To record the payment of salary to an employee)		

2.

Jan. 31, 2018	Employee Benefits Expense	213	
	CPP Payable		135
	EI Payable ($56 × 1.4)		78
	(To record the employer's share of payroll costs)		

3.

Feb. 7, 2018	CPP Payable ($135 + $135)	270	
	EI Payable ($56 + $78)	134	
	Employee Income Tax Payable	385	
	Cash		789
	(To record remittance of employee deductions and benefits)		

▶ PRACTICE OBJECTIVE-FORMAT QUESTIONS

1.   (a), (f), and (g) are correct

Feedback
The journal entries that should be recorded for this transaction are shown below:

Accounts Receivable	5,650	
Sales		5,000
Sales Tax Payable		650
(To record the sale and applicable sales tax)		
Cost of Goods Sold	3,000	
Inventory		3,000
(To record the cost of goods sold)		

(a)   Is correct because sales revenue of $5,000 is earned at this date, as shown in the first journal entry above.
(b)   Is incorrect because sales taxes are levied on the sale date, not the collection date.
(c)   Is incorrect because the Sales Tax Payable account should be credited, not debited.

(d) Is incorrect because the Accounts Receivable account should include not just the price of the product sold but also the sales tax that needs to be collected.

(e) Is incorrect because sales tax is collected from the customer on behalf of the government so it is not an expense for the company earning revenue; rather the amount is a liability owed to the government.

(f) Is correct because sales tax is applied to sales only so the cost of goods sold is not affected by sales taxes.

(g) Is correct because inventory has decreased by $3,000 since it is sold, as shown in the second journal entry above.

2. (a) and (g) are correct

Feedback

Property taxes for the year amounted to $18,000 or $1,500 per month ($18,000 ÷ 12 = $1,500). The journal entries that should be recorded throughout the year on the dates referred to are shown below:

Mar. 31	Property Tax Expense ($1,500 × 3 months)	4,500	
	Property Tax Payable		4,500
	(To record property tax expense incurred for January to March)		
May 31	Property Tax Expense ($1,500 × 2 months)	3,000	
	Property Tax Payable (from above)	4,500	
	Prepaid Property Tax ($1,500 × 7 months)	10,500	
	Cash		18,000
	(To record the property tax payment)		
Dec. 31	Property Tax Expense ($1,500 × 7 months)	10,500	
	Prepaid Property Tax		10,500
	(To record the property tax expense at year end; all of the prepaid tax has now expired)		

(a) Is correct because by the time the assessment is received, only three months have passed in the current year and property taxes relating to these three months ($1,500 × 3 months) should be recorded now that the amount of the property taxes can be determined. Since the property taxes have not been paid, a corresponding payable is also recorded.

(b) Is incorrect because a prepaid should only be recorded when a payment has been made.

(c) Is incorrect because when the payment was made on May 31, there are only seven months remaining in the year so when the property taxes are paid in full, only $10,500 ($1,500 × 7 months) is prepaid at that time.

(d) Is incorrect because by the payment date of May 31, five months of the year have passed and since property tax expense pertaining to the first three of those months was recorded on March 31, only two more months of property tax expense amounting to $3,000 ($1,500 × 2 months) would be recorded on May 31.

(e) Is incorrect because prior to recording this entry on December 31, the balance in the Prepaid Property Tax account is $10,500 and since it is fully expired by the end of the year, the most this account would be credited by would be the full amount of $10,500, not $18,000.

(f) Is incorrect because no property taxes have been payable since May 31 when they were paid in full.

(g) Is correct because by the end of the year, no prepaid property tax asset exists as it is fully expired.

3. (a), (b), and (e) are correct

Feedback

The journal entries that should be recorded for these transactions are:

Salary Expense		1,400	
Employee Income Tax Payable			185
CPP Payable			60
EI Payable			25
Cash			1,130
(To record the payment of salary)			
Employee Benefits Expense		95	
CPP Payable			60
EI Payable			35
(To record the employer share of CPP and EI)			
Employee Income Tax Payable		185	
CPP Payable ($60 + $60)		120	
EI Payable ($25 + $35)		60	
Cash			365
(To record payment of amounts owing to government)			

(a) Is correct because the net pay represents the amount paid out to an employee after taking various withholdings away from the gross pay.

(b) Is correct because the salary expense represents the gross pay for the period and is the amount incurred but not necessarily paid.

(c) Is incorrect because the employee benefits expense is equal to the employer contributions to CPP and EI, which total $95 ($60 + $35).

(d) Is incorrect because the CPP payable owing just prior to payment will be $120, consisting of the $60 contribution from the employee withheld by the company along with the amount owed by the company of $60.

(e) Is correct because, as shown in the entries above, the Employee Income Tax Payable account has a balance of $185 just prior to the payment of that amount to the government.

(f) Is incorrect because the amount paid is $365. See the third journal entry shown above.
(g) Is incorrect because all of these accounts are current liabilities because they are required to be paid shortly after they arise, usually within one month.

4.   (a), (c), (d), (e), and (f) are correct

Feedback
The journal entries that should be recorded for these transactions are:

May 1	Cash	120,000	
	Note Payable		120,000
	(To record the issue of the note)		
June 30	Interest Expense ($120,000 $\times$ 5% $\times$ $^2/_{12}$)	1,000	
	Interest Payable		1,000
	(To accrue interest on note for two months)		
Aug. 31	Note Payable	120,000	
	Interest Payable	1,000	
	Interest Expense ($120,000 $\times$ 5% $\times$ $^2/_{12}$)	1,000	
	Cash		122,000
	(To record payment of note plus interest at maturity)		

(a) Is correct as that is the amount of cash received when the note was issued.
(b) Is incorrect because interest rates always pertain to an annual rate. The $3,000 amount for interest is not the interest for half of the duration of the note (two months). Instead, it is the interest for half of a year on the note, which is incorrect.
(c) Is correct because, at that time, the principal owed is $120,000 along with interest of $1,000.
(d) Is correct because, after two months, interest amounting to $1,000 ($120,000 $\times$ 5% $\times$ $^2/_{12}$) has been incurred.
(e) Is correct because, by that time, interest of $2,000 ($120,000 $\times$ 5% $\times$ $^4/_{12}$) has been incurred and is due along with the principal of $120,000.
(f) Is correct because, although $2,000 of interest is being paid on August 31, $1,000 of this amount was accrued on June 30, establishing an interest payable of $1,000, which is settled on August 31. This causes a debit to Interest Payable for $1,000 at that time.
(g) Is incorrect because, when the adjusting entry was made on June 30, the interest expense for the period May 1 to June 30 of $1,000 was recorded. Therefore, there is no need to record that expense again as is implied by the $2,000 amount in this part of the question, which pertains to all of the interest on the note for the four months ended August 31.

5.   (a) and (b) are correct

Feedback
(a) Is correct because each year $25,000 of the principal is repaid and it will therefore take 20 years to pay off the loan ($500,000 $\div$ $25,000), which means the last payment will be on December 31, 2037.
(b) Is correct because the current portion is the amount of principal that will be paid in the next year, which with the payment pattern shown in the question means that the current portion will always be $25,000 at the end of each year until maturity.
(c) Is incorrect because the interest rate on the bank loan is 4%, which is determined by taking the interest for any year and dividing it by the bank loan balance at the beginning of that year ($20,000 $\div$ $500,000).
(d) Is incorrect because the entire bank loan balance on December 31, 2020, is $425,000 and $25,000 of this will be paid in the following year, so the non-current portion of the note is $400,000.
(e) Is incorrect because no interest payable is outstanding on December 31 of any year because all outstanding interest for each year is paid on that day.
(f) Is incorrect because each year the interest expense is always 4% of the bank loan balance at the beginning of the year. The interest expense falls each year because the bank loan balance (the principal balance) is falling each year.
(g) Is incorrect because on June 30, 2018, interest pertaining to the first half of that year of $10,000 ($20,000 $\times$ $^6/_{12}$) would be accrued and that amount plus the principal balance on the bank loan of $500,000 would result in a total liability relating to the bank loan of $510,000 being shown on the statement of financial position as at June 30.

6.   (a), (c), (d), and (f) are correct

Feedback
(a) Is correct because the total payment is the same each year even though the interest and principal portions of the payment change each year.
(b) Is incorrect because the current portion of a loan is the amount of principal that will be paid off in the following year—in this case, only $21,000. The $50,000 is the entire amount of the payment that will be made next year and it includes interest of $29,000, which has not yet been incurred and is not owing at the end of 2018.
(c) Is correct because the interest each year is 5% of the loan balance at the beginning of each year ($30,000 $\div$ $600,000 = 5%).
(d) Is correct because at the end of 2020, the total loan outstanding is $536,950 but $26,848 will be paid in the following year, leaving a non-current portion of $513,798.
(e) Is incorrect because no interest payable is outstanding on December 31 of any year because all outstanding interest for each year is paid on the last day of the year.
(f) Is correct because, even though the interest rate is unchanged, as the loan balance falls, interest expense will also fall.
(g) Is incorrect because interest for the month of January would be accrued amounting to $2,500 ($600,000 $\times$ 5% $\times$ $^1/_{12}$) and that amount along with the principal outstanding of $600,000 would mean that the total liability relating to this loan would be $602,500 on January 31, 2018.

7.   (a), (b), and (d) are correct

Feedback
(a) Is correct because, with blended principal and interest payments, the payment is constant. This allows parties to better predict cash flows in the future.
(b) Is correct because, although the principal payment is fixed, the interest portion of the payment will fall each period as the loan balance is also falling.

(c)   Is incorrect because, with blended principal and interest payments, the amount paid each period is constant but the portion pertaining to interest falls as the loan balance falls. Since the total payment is fixed but the interest portion is falling, that means that the principal portion of each payment rises over time so therefore the current portion of the loan will also rise over time.

(d)   Is correct because, if the same amount of principal is paid each period, the current portion of the loan will remain the same each period.

(e)   Is incorrect. The description provided in the question is the method used to determine the principal portion of a loan payment when fixed principal plus interest payments are required, not when blended principal and interest payments are required.

(f)   Is incorrect because, as the loan balance is paid off over time, the interest portion of any loan payment will also fall.

(g)   Is incorrect because, as mentioned above, if the loan balance is falling each period, the interest portion of payments will also fall over time.

8.   (b) and (d) are correct

Feedback

(a)   Is incorrect because payments for the next five years are disclosed.

(b)   Is correct because a line of credit represents an amount owing to a bank with no fixed repayment terms and as such is shown as a current liability.

(c)   Is incorrect because inventory needs to turn over (be sold) quickly to enhance liquidity.

(d)   Is correct because this form of ranking allows readers of the financial statements to better understand which liabilities must be paid first.

(e)   Is incorrect because solvency deals with a company's ability to settle all of its liabilities, including non-current ones.

(f)   Is incorrect because the top rating is AAA.

(g)   Is incorrect because the leased asset and the amounts owing under the lease agreement are not recorded. Only rent expense would be recorded over the lease term. Consequently, operating leases are often referred to as "off–balance sheet" financing arrangements.

9.   (b), (c), (f), and (g) are correct

Feedback

(a)   Is incorrect. Just because a company has a high level of debt does not mean that it will be less profitable. Even though its interest expense is higher, the borrowed funds may have been used to invest in assets that generated even higher operating profits.

(b)   Is correct because with a high level of debt, a company must now make higher fixed loan payments and if business conditions deteriorate, there is a greater possibility of defaulting on these loan payments.

(c)   Is correct because the numerator of this ratio shows how much income before interest and income tax is available to pay interest, which is shown in the denominator. The higher this ratio, the more able the company is to pay this interest.

(d)   Is incorrect because a company with a low times interest earned ratio is less able to cover its interest payments and that will make it less likely to be able to take on more debt.

(e)   Is incorrect because this company increased its debt levels but the borrowed funds did not boost income as expected and consequently the times interest earned ratio is falling.

(f)   Is correct because the increasing debt to total assets ratio indicates that the company most likely is increasing its debt level. But at the same time, income before interest and income tax is increasing faster than interest expense, as indicated by the increasing times interest earned ratio. Therefore, taking on the extra debt has made the company more profitable.

(g)   Is correct because in this case, the company appears to be reducing its debt and is increasingly able to cover its interest payments. When this occurs, the company can take on more debt because of its ability to cover the interest if doing so would allow the company to grow faster.

*10.   (a), (c), (e), (f), and (g) are correct

Feedback

(a)   Is correct as the bonds will sell for $200,000 \times 96\% = \$192,000$.

(b)   Is incorrect because, if the market rate was below 4%, the bonds, which offer 5%, would be attractive to investors and the price for the bonds would be above face value, not below.

(c)   Is correct because the discount on the bond is amortized into interest expense each period and this will cause that expense to exceed the cash paid out for interest.

(d)   Is incorrect because the interest expense will be $9,600 ($192,000 \times 5\%$), which is determined by multiplying the carrying amount of the bond by the market interest rate.

(e)   Is correct. The entry to record interest would debit the Interest Expense account by $9,600, with a credit to the Cash account for $8,000 ($200,000 \times 4\%$), and the difference between the two previous amounts of $1,600 would be credited to the Bonds Payable account, increasing it from $192,000 to $193,600.

(f)   Is correct. When this bond sold at a discount, its carrying amount was only $192,000 net of an $8,000 discount. As the discount is amortized over time and added to interest expense, the discount falls, which in turn increases the bond's carrying amount. Over time, the carrying amount will rise until it is at $200,000 when the bond matures. Since the bond liability is rising over time, so too will the interest expense, so interest expense this year is lower than it will be in the following year.

(g)   Is correct because, when a bond sells at a premium, its price will exceed 100% of the face value of the bond and that price will be expressed as a value greater than 100.

▶ ENDNOTES

[1] Canada Post 2015 annual report; "Canada Post's Five-Point Action Plan: Our Progress to Date," Canada Post, March 2015.

[2] Jane Gerster, "Canadian Homeowners Carrying Average of $154,090 in Mortgage Debt," *The Wall Street Journal,* June 16, 2015.

[3] Ontario Securities Commission, "The Canadian Fixed Income Market 2014."

11

Reporting and Analyzing Shareholders' Equity

CHAPTER PREVIEW

In the last few chapters, we have learned about assets and liabilities. Now our attention will turn to the nature of shareholders' equity, which is a major source of funding for many corporations.

In this chapter, we will look at the essential features of a corporation. You will recall from Chapter 1 that corporations are the dominant form of business organization in Canada in terms of revenue, net income, and number of employees. We will review and expand upon the accounting for, and reporting of, the different components that make up shareholders' equity that were introduced in prior chapters. We will discuss the accounting for dividends and conclude by reviewing dividend and earnings measures of performance.

CHAPTER OUTLINE

LEARNING OBJECTIVES	READ	PRACTICE
1 Identify and discuss the major characteristics of a corporation.	• Characteristics of a corporation • Share issue considerations	**DO IT!** 11-1 Corporation characteristics
2 Record share transactions.	• Common shares • Preferred shares	**DO IT!** 11-2 Share transactions
3 Prepare the entries for cash dividends, stock dividends, and stock splits, and understand their financial impact.	• Cash dividends • Stock dividends • Stock splits • Comparison of effects	**DO IT!** 11-3 Stock dividend and split effects
4 Indicate how shareholders' equity is presented in the financial statements.	• Statement of financial position • Statement of changes in equity • Statement of retained earnings • Summary of shareholders' equity transactions	**DO IT!** 11-4 Statement of changes in equity
5 Evaluate dividend and earnings performance.	• Dividend record • Earnings performance	**DO IT!** 11-5a Payout ratio and dividend yield 11-5b Basic earnings per share 11-5c Return on common shareholders' equity

FEATURE STORY

Owning Shares Is a Family Affair

When Ablan Leon bought his son a mattress as a wedding gift, he leaned it outside his general store in Welland, Ontario, after it was delivered. A customer offered to buy it, so he added on a few dollars' profit and resold it. That accidental shopper is what turned The A. Leon Company, founded in 1909, into the Leon's Furniture chain, which today is one of Canada's largest retailers, selling furniture, major appliances, electronics, and, of course, mattresses.

After Ablan Leon died in 1942, his children took over the furniture business and expanded the company into Toronto and other southern Ontario locations. Knowing the company needed an injection of capital to fund its growth, the family took the business public in 1969 when its shares became listed on the Toronto Stock Exchange (TSX). The Leon family retained a 65% majority ownership of the shares in Leon's Furniture Limited, and continue to do so today.

The sale of shares allowed Leon's to continue to grow. In 1973, the company opened Canada's first "big box" store, a furniture showroom and warehouse in suburban Toronto. In 2013, it acquired a competitor, The Brick Ltd., for over $700 million. Leon's operates more than 300 stores across Canada—about 100 owned by franchisees—under banners including Leon's and The Brick. It also sells products through its website. In 2015, the company had revenues of more than $2.0 billion and total assets of almost $1.6 billion.

At the end of 2015, Leon's had 71.4 million common shares issued. The company pays common shareholders an annual dividend of $0.40 per share (or $0.10 every quarter). This amount was decided upon by Leon's board of directors. Although a company is not required to pay dividends to its shareholders, many do. A dividend cannot be paid out unless a company's board of directors declares such a dividend to be paid. It is upon this declaration that a company becomes legally required to pay the dividend. In 2015, Leon's paid a total of nearly $28.5 million in dividends.

Receiving dividends is one reason the public wants to own shares in companies like Leon's. Another reason is the possibility of selling shares for more than they paid for them. During 2015, Leon's shares traded as low as $12.61 and as high as $19.38. Someone who was fortunate enough to buy a share on the day when the price was at its lowest point during 2015 and sell it when the share was trading at its highest value would have earned $6.77 for a return of over 53%. Once shares trade on a public stock exchange like the TSX, companies like Leon's have no control over the share price and do not earn any money from the trading activity on the exchange. However, the company wants to ensure it provides good returns for investors, including members of the Leon family, several of whom are executives. You could say they want to be able to sleep well knowing the mattress business is making money.[1]

Go to the *REVIEW AND PRACTICE* section at the end of the chapter for a targeted summary and practice questions with solutions.

Visit **WileyPLUS** for more practice opportunities.

Identify and discuss the major characteristics of a corporation.

A **corporation** is a legal entity that is separate and distinct from its owners, who are known as shareholders. You will recall from Chapter 1 that a **public corporation** may have thousands of shareholders, and its shares are publicly traded or held. As we have learned in previous chapters, public corporations must follow International Financial Reporting Standards (although some, like Canadian Pacific Railway, can follow U.S. GAAP because their shares are listed on a U.S. stock exchange). In contrast, a **private corporation**—often called a privately held corporation—usually has only a few shareholders and does not offer its shares for sale to the general public. A private corporation has the choice of following IFRS or Accounting Standards for Private Enterprises. Leon's Furniture Limited, in our feature story, was a privately held corporation until it offered its shares for sale to the public in 1969, after which it became a publicly traded company.

CHARACTERISTICS OF A CORPORATION

Many characteristics distinguish corporations—whether public or private—from proprietorships and partnerships. Recall from Chapter 1 that a proprietorship is a business owned by one person, and a partnership is owned by two or more people who are associated as partners. We also discussed some of the distinguishing characteristics of a corporation in Chapter 1, and we review them again here.

Separate Legal Existence

As a legal entity that is separate and distinct from its owners, a corporation acts under its own name rather than in the name of its shareholders. Leon's, for example, may buy, own, and sell property, borrow money, and enter into legally binding contracts in its own name. It may also sue or be sued. And it pays income tax as a separate entity.

In contrast to a proprietorship or partnership, which is bound by the owners' actions, a corporation is not bound by the actions of its owners (shareholders) unless these owners are also agents of the corporation. For example, if you owned Leon's shares, you would not have the right to purchase or lease a new building for the company unless you were designated as an agent of the corporation.

Limited Liability of Shareholders

The liability of shareholders is limited to their investment in the shares of the corporation. This means that, in the event that a corporation is unable to pay its liabilities, its creditors can seize the assets of only the corporation to settle these claims; creditors cannot require shareholders to pay for the company's liabilities using their personal assets. Consequently, the maximum amount of loss that a shareholder could incur would be the amount that they have invested in the shares of the company. They will not lose *more* than their investment.

Limited liability is a significant advantage for the corporate form of organization. However, in smaller private corporations, creditors may demand a personal guarantee from the controlling shareholder. This has the effect of making the controlling shareholder's personal assets available, if required, to satisfy the creditor's claim—which, of course, reduces or eliminates the advantage of limited liability. Nonetheless, even if personal guarantees are required, many private corporations are still formed because of income tax advantages, which are covered later.

Transferable Ownership Rights

A shareholder obtains an ownership interest in a corporation by purchasing its shares. Shareholders can dispose of part or all of their interest in a corporation simply by selling their shares. With a public corporation, the transfer of shares is entirely up to the shareholder and is normally done without the approval of either the corporation or other shareholders. In contrast, many private corporations impose limitations on the sale or transfer of shares by shareholders.

Whether public or private, the transfer of ownership rights between shareholders has no effect on a corporation's financial position. Such a transaction occurs between shareholders and does not involve the corporation, whose assets, liabilities, or shareholders' equity are unchanged. Because of this, the company does not record a journal entry for this type of transaction. A journal entry is recorded by the corporation only when it issues shares to new investors and receives cash or other assets in exchange for these shares. We will cover how a company records the sale of shares the first time they are offered for sale in the next section.

Ability to Acquire Capital

Most individuals will never have an opportunity to invest in a private corporation, but even with a limited amount of funds, many of us can purchase the shares of a public company and become shareholders. Public corporations usually have many shareholders (their shares are said to be "widely held") and became publicly listed in order to raise large amounts of capital for expansion.

Continuous Life

Corporations have an unlimited life. Because a corporation is a separate legal entity, its continuance as a going concern is not affected by the withdrawal, death, or incapacity of a shareholder, employee, or officer. As a result, a successful corporation can have a very long, if not indefinite, life. For example, there are about 5,500 companies throughout the world that have been in business for more than 200 years. Canada's oldest corporation is the Hudson's Bay Company, which was formed in 1670. In contrast, proprietorships end if anything happens to the proprietor and partnerships normally reform if anything happens to one of the partners.

Corporation Management

Shareholders can invest in a corporation without having to manage it personally. Although shareholders legally own the corporation, they manage it indirectly through a board of directors they elect. The board, in turn, sets the broad strategic objectives for the company. The board also selects officers, such as the CEO, to execute policy and to perform daily management functions.

Government Regulations

Canadian companies may be incorporated federally, under the terms of the Canada Business Corporations Act, or provincially, under the terms of a provincial business corporations act. Federal and provincial laws state the requirements for issuing and reacquiring shares and distributing dividends. Similarly, the regulations of provincial securities commissions control the sale of public company shares.

There are additional reporting and disclosure requirements by corporations, particularly by publicly traded corporations. When a corporation's shares are listed and traded on foreign securities markets, the corporation must also comply with the reporting requirements of these exchanges. For example, Canadian Pacific Railway shares are listed on both the Toronto Stock Exchange in Canada and the New York Stock Exchange in the United States. Complying with federal, provincial, and securities regulations, whether in one or multiple jurisdictions, increases the cost and complexity of the corporate form of organization.

Income Tax

Proprietorships and partnerships do not pay income tax as separate entities. Instead, each owner's (or partner's) share of net income from these organizations is reported on his or her personal income tax return. Income tax is then paid on this amount by the individual. Corporations, on the other hand, must pay federal and provincial income taxes as separate legal entities. Income tax rates vary based on the type of income and by province. In general, however, corporate income tax rates are lower than the rate individuals would pay on the same amount of income, and especially so for small corporations.

Summary

The following list summarizes the advantages and disadvantages of the corporate form of business organization:

Advantages	Disadvantages
• Separate legal entity • Limited liability of shareholders • Ease of transferring ownership rights (shares) • Ability to acquire capital (cash) by issuing shares • Continuous life • Separation of management and ownership • Potential for reduced income tax	• Increased cost and complexity to follow government regulations • Increased reporting and disclosure requirements

The above advantages pertain to large, publicly traded corporations. As noted earlier, some of these advantages may not apply to small publicly traded or private corporations. For example, limited liability advantages are not always available for smaller corporations where creditors require personal loan guarantees. It is also not always easy for small corporations to issue or transfer shares.

SHARE ISSUE CONSIDERATIONS

After incorporation, a corporation sells ownership rights in the form of shares. The shares of the company are divided into different classes, such as Class A, Class B, and so on. The rights and privileges for each class of shares are stated in articles of incorporation, which form the "constitution" of the company. The different classes are usually identified by the generic terms *common shares* and *preferred shares*. Combined, they form the **share capital** of the company. When a corporation has only one class of shares, that class has the rights and privileges of common shares. As mentioned in Chapter 2, common shares are also known internationally as *ordinary shares*.

Common shareholders are considered to be the "owners" of the corporation. Only common shareholders have the right to vote on certain matters, such as the election of the board of directors and appointment of external auditors. Each shareholder normally has one vote for each common share owned.

Authorized Share Capital

The amount of share capital that a corporation is authorized to sell is indicated in its articles of incorporation. It may be specified as either an unlimited amount or a specific number (for example, 1 million shares authorized). Most companies in Canada have an unlimited amount of **authorized shares**. If a specific number of shares is authorized, that amount normally anticipates a company's initial and later capital needs.

Leon's has an unlimited number of common shares authorized. The authorization of share capital does not result in a journal entry, because the event has no effect on either corporate assets or shareholders' equity. It is the issue (sale) of shares by the corporation that results in a transaction that must be journalized, and not the authorization of shares. Some companies will also authorize an unlimited number of preferred shares. This type of share almost always pays out a dividend but holders of these shares usually have no voting rights. Leon's does not feel that it is necessary to have preferred shares so none have been authorized. We will learn more about preferred shares in the next section of this chapter.

Issue of Shares

The first time a corporation's shares are offered for sale to the public, the offer is called an **initial public offering (IPO)**. Leon's went public in 1969. The largest IPO to date was the offering by the

Alibaba Group (a diversified e-commerce company), which raised over U.S. $21 billion. The largest IPO in Canada occurred in 2000 when Sun Life raised $1.8 billion, but more recently, Hydro One (Ontario's largest electricity transmission and distribution company) went public, raising $1.7 billion. When a company issues shares through an IPO, it receives the cash (less any financing or issue fees) from the sale of the shares. The company's assets (cash) increase, and its shareholders' equity (share capital) also increases; consequently, this transaction requires a journal entry to be made by the company.

Issued shares are authorized shares that have been sold. Leon's had 71.4 million common shares issued at the end of 2015. Once the shares have been issued and sold by the company through an IPO, they then trade on the secondary market. That is, investors buy and sell shares from each other rather than from the company, using a stock exchange such as the Toronto Stock Exchange. As mentioned earlier in the chapter, when shares are sold among investors, there is no impact on the company's financial position. The company receives no additional assets, and it issues no additional shares. The only change in the company records is the name of the shareholder, not the number of shares issued.

ACCOUNTING MATTERS

Mario Beauregard/The Canadian Press

DAVIDs TEA IPO

After opening over 130 stores in Canada and 25 stores in the United States, Montreal-based DAVIDs TEA decided to become a public corporation and chose to do so by listing its shares on the New York Stock Exchange. The initial share price was U.S. $19 per share for 5.1 million shares. The day after going public, the shares were trading above U.S. $27 per share on June 24, 2015.

A company that offers shares in the public market must prepare a document called a prospectus, which provides information about the company's past performance and future plans. In its prospectus, DAVIDs TEA reported net income of U.S. $11.4 million for the year ending January 31, 2015. However, in the nine months following, the company reported a net loss of over U.S. $145 million. Even though the company had grown revenues by over 25% and most of the loss did not arise from operations, the share price dropped below U.S. $11 by the end of 2015.

Fair Value of Shares

After the initial issue of new shares, the share price changes according to the interaction between buyers and sellers. In general, the price follows the trend of a company's net income, dividends, and future prospects but other factors can affect share prices. Some factors that are beyond a company's control (such as a drop in oil prices, an economic recession, changes in interest rates, the outcome of an election, and acts of violence) can also influence share prices. Understanding share prices is complex and the subject of advanced finance courses.

For each listed security, the financial press reports the highest and lowest prices that the shares sold at for the year, the annual dividend rate, the high and low prices for the day, and the net change over the previous day. The total volume of shares traded on a particular day, the dividend yield, and the price-earnings ratio are also reported. A listing for Leon's common shares on the Toronto Stock Exchange at the end of 2015 follows:

365-day		stock	sym	div	high	low	close	chg	vol (000)	yld	p/e
high	low										
19.38	12.61	Leon's Furniture	LNF	0.40	$14.55	$14.15	$14.55	$0.05	13	2.75	15.67

Leon's shares traded as high as $19.38 and as low as $12.61 during the year. The stock's ticker symbol is "LNF." Leon's pays an annual dividend of $0.40 per share, as indicated in the "div" column. The high and low share prices for the date shown were $14.55 and $14.15 per share, respectively. The closing share price was $14.55, an increase of $0.05 from the previous day. The trading volume was 13,000 shares.

The dividend yield ("yld") was 2.75%. The dividend yield reports the rate of return an investor earned from dividends, calculated by dividing the dividend per share by the share price. Investors wishing to earn dividend income will compare this yield with yields of other companies when deciding which company to invest in. We will learn more about this ratio later in the chapter. Leon's shares are currently trading at a price-earnings ("p/e") ratio (share price divided by basic earnings per share) of 15.67 times earnings. You will recall that the price-earnings ratio was introduced in Chapter 2 and measures the relationship between the stock price and its basic earnings per share. This ratio is often used to determine how much investors favour a company.

One commonly reported measure of the fair value of a company's total equity is its market capitalization. **Market capitalization** is calculated by multiplying the number of shares issued by the share price at any given date. Leon's market capitalization in December 2015 was $1.2 billion. The largest market capitalization for any company in Canada was that of the Royal Bank of Canada, whose market capitalization at the time of writing was $110 billion.

Legal Capital

The shareholders' equity section of a corporation's statement of financial position includes both share capital (common shares and preferred shares, if any) and retained earnings, in addition to other items we will discuss later in this chapter. The distinction between retained earnings and share capital is important from both a legal and an economic point of view. Retained earnings can be distributed to shareholders as dividends or retained in the company for operating needs. On the other hand, share capital of most types of shares issued is **legal capital** that cannot be distributed to shareholders unless the shares are returned to the corporation and cancelled. Most shares are commonly known as **no par value shares**, which simply means that the shares have no predetermined value. Rather, the amount received by the company when issuing shares is considered to be legal capital that must remain invested in the company for the protection of corporate creditors.

Although there are circumstances when other types of shares are issued for which the entire proceeds received do not form the legal capital of the company, these types of shares are rare in Canada and we do not discuss them in this textbook.

DO IT! ▶11-1   Corporation Characteristics

Action Plan

✔ Review the characteristics of a corporation.

✔ Understand the difference between authorized and issued shares.

Indicate whether each of the following statements is true or false:

_____ 1. Shareholders of large, publicly traded corporations have unlimited liability.

_____ 2. It is relatively easy for a large, publicly traded corporation to obtain capital through the issue of shares.

_____ 3. The journal entry to record the authorization of share capital includes a credit to the appropriate preferred or common share account.

_____ 4. The journal entry to record the sale of common shares by one shareholder to another involves a credit to the Common Shares account.

_____ 5. The proceeds received from the sale of shares is known as a company's legal capital.

_____ 6. It is possible to authorize a certain number of shares but then not issue any of them.

_____ 7. Although various classes of shares can be issued, there is at least one class that has the characteristics of common shares that have voting rights.

_____ 8. Shares in Canada usually have a par value.

_____ 9. One way to determine the overall value of a public company is to calculate its market capitalization by multiplying the number of shares issued by their share price.

_____ 10. Normally the legal capital of a company cannot be withdrawn by shareholders but the retained earnings can be withdrawn through the use of dividends.

SOLUTION

Try this Do It! exercise on your own and then check your answer at the end of the chapter.

Related Exercise Material: BE11–1 and E11–1.

LEARNING OBJECTIVE ▶ **2**   **Record share transactions.**

Contributed capital is the amount shareholders paid, or contributed, to the corporation in exchange for shares of ownership. This includes **share capital**, which can consist of both common and preferred shares. All corporations must issue common shares because these shares have voting rights and major decisions affecting the corporation must be approved through shareholder voting. For example, common shareholders typically have the right to vote for the board of directors and external auditors, in addition to certain other matters of significance to the corporation. Some corporations also issue preferred shares and we will discuss below the reasons for doing this.

Contributed capital can also include other sources of capital known as **contributed surplus**, which can result from certain types of equity transactions, including the reacquisition of shares. We will learn about contributed surplus in the next, and later, sections of this chapter.

> **Alternative Terminology**
> *Contributed surplus* is also known as *additional contributed capital*.

COMMON SHARES

In addition to issuing shares to investors, companies can also buy back their own shares. We will look at the issue of shares in some detail, and then cover the concept of reacquiring shares.

Issue of Common Shares

We first learned about issuing common shares in Chapter. 1. To review the accounting for the issue of shares, assume that Hydro-Slide, Inc. is authorized to issue an unlimited number of common shares and that it issues 15,000 of these shares for $2 per share on January 12.

No journal entry is required to record the *authorization* of shares. The entry to record the *issue* of the shares is:

Jan. 12	Cash	30,000	
	Common Shares		30,000
	(To record issue of 15,000 common shares)		

A	=	L	+	SE
+30,000				+30,000

↑ Cash flows: +30,000

Common shares are usually issued in exchange for cash, especially in large corporations. However, they may also be issued for a consideration other than cash, such as services (for example, compensation to lawyers or consultants) or noncash assets (for example, land, buildings, or equipment). **When shares are issued for a noncash consideration, they should be recorded at the fair value of the consideration received** (for example, goods or services). If the fair value of the consideration received cannot be reliably determined, then the fair value of the consideration given up would be used instead.

For example, assume that 5,000 common shares were issued by Hydro-Slide in exchange for a parcel of land on January 27. The shares were trading at $3.50 per share and the land was valued at $20,000 on the date of the acquisition. The transaction is recorded using the value of the land ($20,000)—the consideration received—rather than the value of the common shares ($17,500 = 5,000 × $3.50)—the consideration given up, unless the value of the land cannot be determined and only the value of the shares is known.

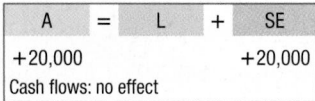

A	=	L	+	SE
+20,000				+20,000
Cash flows: no effect				

Jan. 27	Land	20,000	
	Common Shares		20,000
	(To record issue of 5,000 common shares in exchange for land)		

Noncash considerations tend to be found more often in private companies than in large publicly traded companies. When shares are issued for a noncash consideration in a private company following ASPE, they should be recorded at the more reliable of the fair value of the consideration received or the fair value of the consideration given up. Quite often the fair value of the consideration received is the more reliable value because a private company's shares seldom trade and therefore do not have a ready fair value.

Reacquisition of Common Shares

After shares have been issued, companies may later decide to repurchase their own shares on the open (secondary) market. This can be done for a number of reasons. The company may want to buy back shares in an effort to increase their price. If the number of shares is reduced, the values of certain ratios, such as basic earnings per share, will rise. Some companies issue shares to their employees as a form of compensation and, if the company wishes to maintain the number of issued shares at a constant amount, it will reacquire the same number of shares in the open market that it is issuing to employees. Lastly, some companies will buy back shares from hostile shareholders who disagree with the strategic direction of the company.

The reacquisition of shares for a public company is often called a **normal course issuer bid**. In a normal course issuer bid, a company is allowed to repurchase up to a certain percentage of its shares subject to regulatory approval. It can purchase the shares gradually over a period of time, such as one year. This repurchasing strategy allows the company to buy when its shares are favourably priced.

For federally incorporated companies, and most provincially incorporated companies, repurchased shares must be retired (cancelled). This effectively restores the shares to the status of authorized but unissued shares. In some Canadian provinces, in the United States, and internationally, reacquired shares do not have to be retired and can be held in the "treasury" for subsequent reissue. We will not discuss the accounting for treasury shares in further detail here, but leave it for an intermediate accounting course.

To record a reacquisition and retirement of common shares (or preferred shares), the following steps are required:

1. **Remove the cost of the shares from the share capital account:** Recall that when a non-current asset is retired, the cost of the asset must be deleted (credited) from the appropriate asset account. Similarly, the **average cost per share** of the common or preferred shares that are reacquired and retired must be determined and this amount is then removed (debited) from the Common Shares account.

   In order to determine the average cost of the shares reacquired, we divide the dollar amount in the applicable share capital account by the related number of shares immediately before the acquisition of the shares.

2. **Record the cash paid:** The Cash account is credited for the amount paid to reacquire the shares.

3. **Record the "gain" or loss" on reacquisition:** The difference between the price paid to reacquire the shares and their average cost is basically a "gain" or "loss" on reacquisition. However, because companies cannot realize a gain or incur a loss from share transactions with their own shareholders, these amounts are not reported on the income statement. They are seen instead

as an excess or deficiency that belongs to the remaining shareholders and as such, are recorded (most of the time) directly into the shareholders' equity account Contributed Surplus.

You will recall that you were first introduced to contributed surplus in Chapter 2. It has a normal credit balance, similar to other shareholders' equity accounts, such as Common Shares, Preferred Shares, and Retained Earnings. While a company may have multiple sources of contributed surplus and different accounts under this classification, we will discuss only one source of contributed surplus in this chapter. Accordingly, we will record any gains or losses on reacquisition of shares directly to the Contributed Surplus account. If different classes of shares are affected, it is usual to have two separate contributed surplus accounts—one for common shares and one for preferred shares.

The accounting for the reacquisition and retirement of shares is different depending on whether the shares are reacquired by paying less than average cost or more than average cost. We will illustrate both situations in the next two sections.

REACQUISITION BELOW AVERAGE COST   To illustrate the reacquisition of common shares at a price less than their average cost, assume based on entries recorded previously that Hydro-Slide, Inc. now has a total of 20,000 common shares issued and a balance in its Common Shares account of $50,000. The average cost of Hydro-Slide's common shares, immediately before the reacquisition, is $2.50 per share ($50,000 ÷ 20,000).

On September 23, Hydro-Slide reacquired and retired 5,000 of its common shares at a price of $1.50 per share. Since the average cost of the shares was $2.50 per share, a $1.00 per share ($2.50 – $1.50) addition to contributed surplus results, as shown below:

Sept. 23	Common Shares (5,000 × $2.50)	12,500	
	Contributed Surplus (5,000 × $1.00)		5,000
	Cash (5,000 × $1.50)		7,500
	(To record reacquisition and retirement of 5,000 common shares)		

A	=	L	+	SE
−7,500				−12,500
				+5,000

↓ Cash flows: −7,500

After this entry, Hydro-Slide still has an unlimited number of shares authorized, but only 15,000 (20,000 – 5,000) shares issued, and a balance of $37,500 ($50,000 – $12,500) in its Common Shares account. The difference between the average cost of the shares and the amount paid to repurchase them is credited to the Contributed Surplus account because a "gain" was made on the share reacquisition. A "gain" or credit results because the amount paid to buy back and retire the shares was less than the average amount that these shares were sold at.

REACQUISITION ABOVE AVERAGE COST   Following the above transaction, Hydro-Slide decided to retire another 4,000 of its common shares on November 12 but this time, the company paid $4.00 per share. Recall that the average cost that the shares were issued at was $2.50, which remains unchanged ($37,500 ÷ 15,000). Because the company is paying more to buy back the shares than the average cost that they were issued at, this difference must be recorded directly into a shareholders' equity account. If there is any balance in the Contributed Surplus account from previous transactions related to the retirement of shares from the same class, this amount would first be reduced (debited).

Note that the Contributed Surplus account cannot be reduced beyond any previously existing balance. In other words, the Contributed Surplus account can never have a negative, or debit, balance. Instead, any excess deficiency amount remaining after bringing the Contributed Surplus account to zero would be debited to Retained Earnings.

The journal entry to record the reacquisition and retirement of Hydro-Slide's common shares at a price of $4.00 per share, where the excess paid above the average cost per share is $1.50 ($4.00 − $2.50), is as follows:

Nov. 12	Common Shares (4,000 × $2.50)	10,000	
	Contributed Surplus (see balance above)	5,000	
	Retained Earnings ($6,000 − $5,000)	1,000	
	Cash (4,000 × $4.00)		16,000
	(To record reacquisition and retirement of 5,000 common shares)		

A	=	L	+	SE
−16,000				−10,000
				−5,000
				−1,000

↓ Cash flows: −16,000

In this entry, Hydro-Slide applied the $6,000 difference between the amount paid to reacquire and retire the shares of $16,000 (4,000 × $4.00) and the average cost that the shares were issued at of $10,000 (4,000 × $2.50) against the balance in the Contributed Surplus account, reducing it to zero. The remaining difference was allocated to the Retained Earnings account, decreasing it by $1,000 ($6,000 − $5,000).

In summary, the only difference in the accounting for reacquisitions at prices below or above the average cost has to do with recording the difference between the amount paid to repurchase the shares and their average cost. If the shares are reacquired at a price below their average cost, the difference is credited to the Contributed Surplus account. If the shares are reacquired at a price above the average cost, the difference is debited first to the Contributed Surplus account if it has a balance, and then any remaining difference is applied to reduce the Retained Earnings account.

PREFERRED SHARES

To appeal to a larger segment of potential investors, a company may issue an additional class of shares, called preferred shares. **Preferred shares** have contractual provisions that give them a preference, or priority, over common shares in certain areas.

Issue of Preferred Shares

Like common shares, preferred shares may be issued for cash or for noncash considerations. To illustrate, assume that Hydro-Slide, Inc. issues 500 preferred shares for $100 per share for a total consideration of $50,000 (500 × $100) on July 7. The entry to record this transaction is as follows:

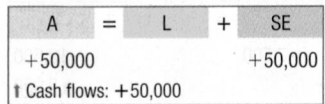

	A	=	L	+	SE
	+50,000				+50,000
↑ Cash flows: +50,000					

July 7	Cash	50,000	
	Preferred Shares		50,000
	(To record issue of 500 preferred shares)		

Note that, when a company has more than one class of shares, separate account titles should be used (for example, Preferred Shares, Common Shares).

Preferred shares can also be issued for noncash considerations. The entry for a noncash transaction is similar to the entry shown earlier for common shares, so it is not illustrated here. Preferred shares can also be reacquired, although it is not as typical to do so as with common shares.

We will discuss the key features of preferred shares, including dividend and liquidation preferences, in the next section.

Preferential Features of Preferred Shares

Typically, preferred shareholders have priority over common shareholders regarding the distribution of dividends and, in the event of liquidation, over the distribution of assets. However, they do not usually have the voting rights that the common shareholders have. We will discuss these and other contractual provisions that give preferred shares a preference, or priority, over common shares next.

DIVIDEND PREFERENCE Preferred shares are usually issued with a specified dividend rate, which makes them attractive to investors who wish to earn dividend income. In contrast, common shares do not have a specified dividend associated with them, although the company may choose to pay dividends to common shareholders. For example, Leon's pays dividends on its common shares but this was not specified when these shares were issued.

A dividend preference simply means that the **preferred shareholders must be paid dividends before any are paid to the common shareholders**. For example, if Hydro-Slide's preferred shares have a $5 annual dividend rate, common shareholders will not receive any dividends in the current year until preferred shareholders have received $5 per share. Preferred shares such as these would be called "$5 preferred," with the $5 indicating the annual dividend rate. Even though the dividend rate is reported as an annual dollar amount per share, it is usual to pay dividends quarterly. For example, if Hydro-Slide paid a quarterly dividend it would be $1.25 per share ($5.00 ÷ 4) per share.

A preferred claim to dividends does not guarantee that dividends will be paid to the preferred shareholders. The payment of dividends depends on a number of factors, including having sufficient cash in the case of a cash dividend. In addition, all dividends must be formally declared (approved) by the board of directors. We will learn more about these factors in the section on Retained Earnings later in this chapter.

Preferred shares with a dividend preference may contain a **cumulative** dividend feature. This right means that when dividends are declared to be payable, preferred shareholders must be paid both current-year dividends and any unpaid prior-year dividends before common shareholders receive dividends. Preferred shares without this feature are called **noncumulative**. A dividend that is not paid on noncumulative preferred shares in any particular year is lost forever. The majority of preferred shares issued in Canada are noncumulative.

When preferred shares are cumulative, preferred dividends that are not declared in a period are called **dividends in arrears**. No distribution can be made to common shareholders until this entire cumulative preferred dividend is paid. In other words, dividends cannot be paid to common shareholders while any preferred share dividends are in arrears. It is unusual for a company to have any dividends in arrears.

It is important to understand that, if a company does have dividends in arrears, they would *not* be considered a liability. No obligation exists until a dividend is declared by the board of directors and without the existence of an obligation, no liability can be recorded. However, the amount of dividends in arrears should be disclosed in the notes to the financial statements. This allows investors to evaluate the potential impact of this commitment on the corporation's financial position.

Even though there is no requirement to pay an annual dividend, companies that are unable to meet their dividend obligations—whether cumulative or noncumulative—are not looked upon favourably by the investment community. Even announcements of dividend reductions tend to cause significant reductions in a company's share price.

LIQUIDATION PREFERENCE In addition to having a priority claim over common shares on any distribution of dividends, preferred shareholders also have a priority claim over common shareholders regarding the distribution of corporate assets if the corporation fails or liquidates. This means that if the company ceases to operate, preferred shareholders will get their capital back before common shareholders do. The preference on assets may be for the legal value of the shares or for a specified liquidating value. Although creditors rank above all shareholders in terms of preference in liquidations, preferred shareholders rank above common shareholders. This is important because the money usually runs out before everyone gets paid.

Sometimes a company will liquidate even if it is not going bankrupt. For example, assume that a small corporation's preferred shares are owned by the parents of a family, while the common shares are held by the children. For various reasons, the company is to be liquidated. This is done by selling all of the assets and settling all of the liabilities. After this, the statement of financial position shows the following: Cash $1,000,000, Preferred Shares $200,000, Common Shares $100,000, and Retained Earnings $700,000. Because of their preferences, upon liquidation, the parents will receive $200,000 for their preferred shares from the company and all of the remaining equity of $800,000 will be given to the children. It is important to understand that the retained earnings of a company accrue to the common shareholders and, because of this, the price for the common shares will rise over time if a company is profitable and fall if it is not. Therefore the price for a common share is usually more volatile than the price for preferred shares. The major factor affecting the common share price is the profitability of the company whereas the major factor affecting the preferred share price is the level of dividends paid on these shares.

OTHER PREFERENCES The attractiveness of preferred shares as an investment is sometimes increased by adding a conversion privilege. Convertible preferred shares allow the exchange of preferred shares for common shares at a specified ratio. Convertible preferred shares are purchased by investors who want the greater security of preferred shares, but who also desire the option of conversion if the value of the common shares increases significantly.

A significant number of preferred shares are issued with the right for a corporation to reset the dividend rate on their preferred shares. These are known as **rate- or fixed-reset preferred shares**. Normally when preferred shares are issued, the dividend rate is specified because investors usually purchase these shares for the primary purpose of earning dividends. Almost 60% of the issued preferred shares in Canada reset their dividends on predetermined dates. The reset dividend rate is usually a function of the interest rate, so if interest rates fall before the reset date, the dividend rate will also fall when it is reset.

Most preferred shares are also issued with a redemption or call feature. **Redeemable (or callable) preferred shares** give the issuing corporation the right to purchase the shares from shareholders at specified future dates and prices. The redemption feature offers some flexibility to a corporation by enabling it to eliminate this type of equity security when it is advantageous to do so.

Retractable preferred shares are similar to redeemable or callable preferred shares, in that they both include a right to purchase shares at specified future dates and prices. However, in the case of retractable preferred shares, it is at the *shareholder's* option, rather than the corporation's option, that the shares can be redeemed. Less than 5% of preferred shares issued in Canada currently have this feature.

Comparison of Preferred Shares and Liabilities

Preferred shares can have similar characteristics to liabilities. For example, preferred shares and bond liabilities are both issued at fixed values that are used to determine the amount of dividends to be declared or interest payments to be made, respectively. Both bond and preferred share prices will typically have an inverse relationship with changes in interest rates. Preferred shares can be given credit ratings similar to those used for debt and sometimes both bonds and preferred shares can be converted into common shares. Nonetheless, the key reason why a preferred share is not treated as a liability is because there is no contractual obligation to make periodic cash payments for dividends, unlike the requirement to pay interest on non-current liabilities.

Some financial instruments are structured to have features of both debt and equity but coverage of these is left for an intermediate accounting course.

Summary Comparison of Preferred Shares and Common Shares

Preferred shares are similar to common shares in many ways. Both are equity instruments that can be used to declare and pay dividends and, regardless of the type of share issued, there is no legal requirement to declare dividends.

However, there are many differences between common and preferred shares. Preferred shareholders do not have the right to vote at annual general meetings but they do have preferences over common shareholders with regard to dividend payments and a priority claim over the assets of the company when liquidating. While both types of shares have the potential for price appreciation, the prices for preferred shares tend to be less volatile than for common shares because any income not distributed through dividends accrues to the common shareholders, as do any losses.

DO IT! ▶11-2   Share Transactions

Action Plan

✔ Credit the appropriate share account for the entire proceeds received in a share issue.

✔ When shares are issued for a noncash consideration, record the transaction at the fair value of the consideration received, if available.

✔ Keep a running total of the number of shares issued to date.

At January 1, 2018, MasterMind Corporation, a publicly traded company, had an unlimited number of common shares authorized, of which 120,000 had been issued for $960,000. It also had 100,000 shares of $2, cumulative preferred shares authorized, of which 10,000 shares were issued for $250,000. On July 2, the company issued 1,000 common shares to its lawyers in settlement of their bill for $8,000. At that time, the shares had a fair value of $8 per share. On October 1, the company issued an additional 2,500 preferred shares for $30 per share. On December 3, the company reacquired and retired 5,000 common shares at $7 per share. On December 18, a further 10,000 common shares were reacquired and retired at $9 per share.

(a) Record the issue of the common shares on July 2.

(b) Record the issue of the preferred shares on October 1.

(c) Calculate the average cost of the common shares prior to the reacquisition transactions in December.

(d) Record the reacquisition of the common shares on December 3.

(e) Record the reacquisition of the common shares on December 18.

(f) Calculate the number of preferred shares issued at December 31.

(g) Assuming dividends are paid quarterly and that all requirements have been met to declare a dividend, calculate the amount of the dividend that MasterMind paid its preferred shareholders for the fourth quarter of 2018.

Action Plan (cont'd)

✔ Recall that the dividend rate given on preferred shares is always expressed as an annual amount. Divide the dividend rate by 4 to determine the quarterly dividend rate.

SOLUTION

Try this Do It! exercise on your own and then check your answer at the end of the chapter.

Related Exercise Material: BE11–2, BE11–3, BE11–4, BE11–5, E11–2, E11–3, and E11–4.

 LEARNING OBJECTIVE 3

Prepare the entries for cash dividends, stock dividends, and stock splits, and understand their financial impact.

A **dividend** is a pro rata (equal) distribution of a portion of a corporation's retained earnings to its shareholders. "Pro rata" means that the dividends are allocated to each shareholder based on the proportion of the shares that is owned by each shareholder. So if you own, say, 10% of the common shares, you will receive 10% of the common share dividends.

Dividends are discretionary and many high-growth companies, such as Facebook, do not pay dividends, choosing instead to use spare cash to grow their business. Investors purchase shares in companies like Facebook with the hope that the share price will increase in value and they will realize a gain when they sell their shares. Other investors purchase shares of established companies with the hope of earning dividends (and profiting from some share price appreciation when they sell their shares).

Paying dividends with cash is most common in practice but stock dividends are also declared on occasion. Stock splits, which are similar to stock dividends, also occur with some frequency. All three of these have varying impacts on a company's share capital and retained earnings, which are discussed in the next sections.

CASH DIVIDENDS

A **cash dividend** is a distribution that can be paid to preferred and common shareholders. If dividends are paid to both the preferred and common shareholders, the preferred shareholders have to be paid first.

For a corporation to declare and pay a cash dividend, it must meet a two-part solvency test under the Canada Business Corporations Act:

1. It must have sufficient cash or resources to be able to pay its liabilities as they become due after the dividend is declared and paid, and
2. The net realizable value of its assets must exceed the total of its liabilities and share capital.

Under some provincial legislation, a company must also have enough retained earnings before it can pay a dividend. You will recall from past chapters that retained earnings are increased by net income and decreased by net losses and declared dividends, as shown below:

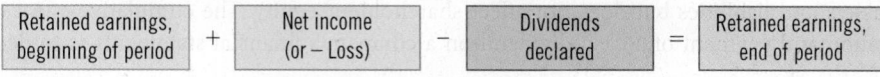

| Retained earnings, beginning of period | + | Net income (or − Loss) | − | Dividends declared | = | Retained earnings, end of period |

Because dividends are a distribution of retained earnings, it makes sense that sufficient retained earnings are required so that, when dividends are declared, the resulting reduction in retained earnings is not so large that it creates a deficit (negative retained earnings). However, it is not illegal to do so if the two conditions listed above in the Canada Business Corporations Act are met.

There are three important dates to consider when a company wants to pay cash dividends. They are: (1) the declaration date, (2) the record date, and (3) the payment date. Normally, there are several weeks between each date and the next one. For example, on November 12, 2015 (the declaration date), the board of Leon's Furniture declared a quarterly dividend of $0.10 per share payable to its common shareholders. On December 8, 2015 (the record date), holders of common shares became entitled to receive the dividend and on January 8, 2016 (the payment date), the company paid out the dividends to those common shareholders.

To illustrate a cash dividend to preferred shareholders, assume that on December 1, 2018, the directors of IBR Inc. declared a $0.50 per share quarterly cash dividend on the company's 100,000 $2 preferred shares, payable on January 20 to shareholders of record on December 22. IBR's dividend is $50,000 (100,000 × $0.50). On the first of the three dates, December 1, which is the **declaration date**, the board of directors formally authorized the cash dividend and announced it to shareholders. Because the declaration creates a legal obligation for the company, a journal entry must be recorded as follows:

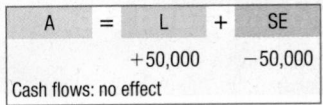

		Declaration Date		
Dec. 1	Dividends declared		50,000	
	Dividends Payable			50,000
	(To record declaration of cash dividend)			

In prior chapters, we assumed that the dividend was declared and paid on the same day for simplicity. In this chapter, we illustrate the separation of the declaration of the dividend and the payment of the dividend by recording journal entries on two different dates—the declaration date and the payment date. As we learned in Chapter 4, the Dividends Declared account will be closed into, and reduce, the Retained Earnings account at the end of the fiscal year. Dividends Payable is a current liability: it will normally be paid within the next month or so on the payment date, which is January 20 in this particular example.

On December 22, which is the **record date**, ownership of the shares is determined. As mentioned earlier, individual shareholders may change as shares are bought and sold frequently on the secondary market. Although transactions between shareholders do not affect the company's financial position, the company does have to maintain shareholder records identifying individual owners so it knows who to pay the dividend to. In the interval between the declaration date and the record date, the company updates its share ownership record. No journal entry is required on the record date, because the corporation's liability that was recognized on the declaration date is unchanged.

On January 20, which is the **payment (distribution) date**, dividends are paid to the shareholders. The journal entry is:

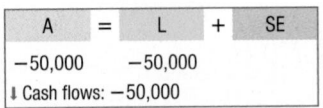

		Payment Date		
Jan. 20	Dividends Payable		50,000	
	Cash			50,000
	(To record payment of cash dividend)			

As shown below in Illustration 11-1, the declaration of a cash dividend increases liabilities and reduces shareholders' equity (through retained earnings). There is no journal entry recorded on the record date, but on the payment date a journal entry is recorded because the payment reduces both assets and liabilities but does not affect shareholders' equity. The cumulative effect of the declaration and payment of a cash dividend on a company's financial statements is to decrease both assets (through cash) and shareholders' equity (through retained earnings). In the illustration below, "+" means increase, "−" means decrease, and "NE" means "no effect."

	Assets	Liabilities	Shareholders' Equity	
			Share Capital	Retained Earnings
Declaration date	NE	+	NE	−
Record date	NE	NE	NE	NE
Payment date	−	−	NE	NE
Cumulative effect of declaration and payment of cash dividend	−	NE	NE	−

▶ Illustration 11-1

Effects of cash dividends

STOCK DIVIDENDS

A **stock dividend** is a distribution of the corporation's own shares rather than cash to shareholders. Whereas a cash dividend is paid in cash, a stock dividend is distributed (paid) in shares. And, while a cash dividend decreases assets (through the Cash account) and shareholders' equity (through the Retained Earnings account), a stock dividend does not change assets, liabilities, or total shareholders' equity. No cash has been paid, and no liabilities have been assumed. A stock dividend affects share capital because either common or preferred shares are increased when new shares are issued for the dividend. A stock dividend also affects retained earnings, which are decreased because a dividend was declared. However, these changes offset each other and there is no overall change to shareholders' equity.

Because a stock dividend does not result in a distribution of assets, investors are not actually receiving anything they did not already own. In a sense, it is like asking for two pieces of pie instead of one piece and having your host take one piece of pie and cut it into two smaller pieces. You now have two pieces of pie, but you still have the same amount of pie.

What, then, are the purposes and benefits of a stock dividend? A corporation generally issues a stock dividend for one or more of the following reasons:

1. To satisfy shareholders' dividend expectations while conserving cash.
2. To increase the marketability of the shares. When the number of shares increases, the share price decreases on the stock market so decreasing the market price of the shares makes them more affordable and there are now more issued shares that can be purchased by investors.
3. To emphasize that a portion of shareholders' equity has been permanently reinvested in the legal capital of the business and is unavailable for dividends. Because of its effects, a stock dividend is often referred to as *capitalizing retained earnings*.

Similar to a cash dividend, stock dividends can be declared for either preferred or common shares, although they are usually done with common shares. Just as cash dividends have three key dates, so too do stock dividends: (1) the declaration date, (2) the record date, and (3) the distribution (payment) date.

To illustrate the accounting for stock dividends, assume that CIS Inc. has 50,000 common shares with a balance of $500,000 in Common Shares and $300,000 in Retained Earnings. On June 30, the board declares a 10% stock dividend to shareholders of record at July 20, to be distributed to shareholders of record on August 5. The share price on June 30 (declaration date) is $15 per share; on July 20 (record date), $16 per share; and on August 5 (distribution date), $14 per share.

The number of shares to be issued is 5,000 (50,000 × 10%). Notice that the 10% is applied to the number of shares, not the dollar value of those shares. The Canada Business Corporations Act requires that stock dividends be recorded at **fair value** (market price per share) because this is what the corporation would have paid if the shares had been issued for cash rather than as a stock dividend. So the total amount to be debited to CIS's Dividends Declared account is $75,000 (5,000 × $15). Note that it is the fair value at the declaration date that is relevant for this transaction, and not the fair value on the record date or distribution date.

The entry to record the declaration of the stock dividend on June 30 is as follows:

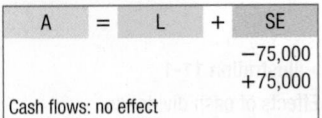

	Declaration Date		
June 30	Dividends Declared	75,000	
	Stock Dividends Distributable		75,000
	(To record declaration of 10% stock dividend)		

Note that the credit entry uses the word *Distributable*, not *Payable*, in the account title. Unlike the Dividends Payable account, Stock Dividends Distributable is not a liability account; it is a shareholders' equity account. It is not a liability, because assets will not be used to pay the dividend; instead, common shares will be used. If a statement of financial position is prepared before the dividend shares are issued, the distributable account is reported along with other share capital in the shareholders' equity section of the statement of financial position. As was the case with any dividend, the Dividends Declared account will be closed into, and reduce, the Retained Earnings account at the end of the year.

Similar to cash dividends, there is no entry at the record date. When the dividend shares are issued on August 5, the account Stock Dividends Distributable is decreased (debited) and the account Common Shares is increased (credited), as follows:

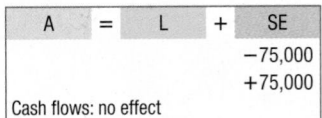

	Distribution Date		
Aug. 5	Stock Dividends Distributable	75,000	
	Common Shares		75,000
	(To record issue of 5,000 common shares in 10% stock dividend)		

Neither of the above entries changes shareholders' equity in total. However, the composition of shareholders' equity changes because a portion of retained earnings, $75,000, is transferred to the Common Shares account. The number of shares also increases by 5,000 (50,000 × 10%). These effects are shown below for CIS:

	Before Stock Dividend	Change	After Stock Dividend
Shareholders' equity			
Common shares	$500,000	+$75,000	$575,000
Retained earnings	300,000	−75,000	225,000
Total shareholders' equity	$800,000	$ 0	$800,000
Number of shares	50,000	+5,000	55,000

STOCK SPLITS

Although stock splits are not dividends, we discuss them in this section because of their similarities to stock dividends. A **stock split**, like a stock dividend, involves the issue of additional shares to shareholders according to their percentage ownership. However, a stock split is usually much larger than a stock dividend. For example, a stock dividend might result in an additional 10% of common shares issued, whereas a stock split could result in 100% more common shares issued. This is because the main purpose of a stock split is to increase the marketability of the shares by lowering the share price. Normally it is only common shares that are split because preferred shares are usually purchased primarily for the dividend income and do not significantly rise in value.

The effect of a stock split on the share price is inversely proportional to the size of the split; that is, in a 2-for-1 stock split, the number of shares will double and the share price will halve. For example, a company that has 100,000 common shares trading at $20 per share (total value is 100,000 × $20 = $2 million) before the split issues an additional 100,000 common shares to have a total of 200,000 common shares (100,000 × 2). Because the company does not receive or pay out cash when the stock is split, the total value of its common shares trading in the market should still be $2 million, but because there are now 200,000 common shares, each share will now trade at only $10.

As with a stock dividend, a shareholder is not initially better off after a stock split, because although they own more shares, the split has reduced the value of these shares. Quite often, due to increased investor interest, the share price may climb more rapidly because stock splits are usually done for shares that have grown significantly in value and many investors think that stock splits are indicative of more growth. For the company, a stock split does not have any effect on total share capital, retained earnings, or total shareholders' equity. Only the number of shares increases. Because a stock split does not affect the balances in any shareholders' equity accounts, **a stock split is not journalized**. Only a memo entry explaining the effect of the split (that is, the change in the number of shares) is needed.

These effects are shown below for CIS Inc., assuming that instead of issuing a 10% stock dividend, it split its 50,000 common shares on a 2-for-1 basis:

	Before Stock Split	Change	After Stock Split
Shareholders' equity			
Common shares	$500,000	$0	$500,000
Retained earnings	300,000	0	300,000
Total shareholders' equity	$800,000	$0	$800,000
Number of shares	50,000	+50,000	100,000

Note that, after the stock split, CIS has 100,000 common shares issued. Don't forget that, if a dividend is declared after a stock split, there are now more shares outstanding and this will affect the amount of the dividend. It is helpful to keep a running total of the number of shares when doing your assignments so that you can properly calculate the amount of any subsequent dividends declared as well as basic earnings per share, which we will see later in this chapter.

Although we will not cover this in any detail in this text, reverse stock splits (the opposite of a stock split) can occur if a company's share price falls to a very low level. Many stock exchanges require listed companies to have a minimum share price and a common way to increase that price is to combine several existing shares into one new share. This can be very common during a recession. In just the last week of June 2016, six public companies did reverse splits including Confederation Minerals, which did a 1:10 reverse split which made ten "old" shares equal to one "new" share.

ACCOUNTING MATTERS

Bloomberg/Getty Images

Netflix Shares Soar

When Netflix went public in 2002, the company raised $83 million by selling over 5.5 million shares at $15 each. When the price hit $73 in February 2004, the company split the shares on a 2-to-1 basis to make the shares more affordable to ordinary investors. Over the next 10 years, the price continued to rise but the company did not split the shares again until July 2015, when the price soared to more than $700 per share. At that time, the shares were split on a 7-to-1 basis, so after the split the share price fell to around $100.

If you want to determine how much the share price has risen, you need to take the effect of splits into account. If you bought one share of Netflix in 2002 for $15, by July 2015 you would have had 14 shares worth $100 each, for a total value of $1,400. Not a bad rate of return for an investment!

COMPARISON OF EFFECTS

A cash dividend, stock dividend, and stock split have differing overall impacts on a company's financial position. The cumulative effect of these differences is shown in Illustration 11-2. In the illustration, "+" means increase, "−" means decrease, and "NE" means "no effect."

▶Illustration 11-2
Effects of cash dividends, stock dividends, and stock splits

	Assets	=	Liabilities	+	Shareholders' Equity			
					Share Capital	Retained Earnings	Total Shareholders' Equity	Number of Shares
Cash dividend	—		NE		NE	—	—	NE
Stock dividend	NE		NE		+	—	NE	+
Stock split	NE		NE		NE	NE	NE	+

Cash dividends reduce cash when paid and reduce the balance in the Retained Earnings account (after the Dividends Declared account is closed into Retained Earnings). Stock dividends increase share capital, usually the Common Shares account, when distributed and decrease retained earnings when the Dividends Declared account is closed. Stock splits do not affect any of the accounts. However, both a stock dividend and a stock split increase the number of shares issued.

Although a stock dividend does not usually have a significant effect on the number of outstanding shares compared with the effect of a stock split, if the stock dividend is very large, it may cause the same increase in the number of outstanding shares that a stock split would. For example, if a company declares a 100% stock dividend whereby one share would be received as a dividend for every share held, this would double the number of outstanding shares even though the company did not officially split the shares. Companies that opt for such large stock dividends rather than stock splits do so for a variety of legal and tax reasons, which you may cover in more advanced courses.

DO IT! ▶ 11-3   Stock Dividend and Split Effects

SOLUTION
Try this Do It! exercise on your own and then check your answer at the end of the chapter.

Related Exercise Material: BE11–6, BE11–7, BE11–8, BE11–9, E11–5, and E11–6.

Over the past five years since its formation, when it listed its shares on a public stock exchange, Sing Corporation has had significant increases in its net income. Due to this success, the price of its 500,000 common shares tripled from $20 per share to $60. During this period, the Common Shares account remained the same at $10 million. Retained Earnings increased from $2 million to $13 million. President Andrea Helston is considering either (1) a 10% stock dividend or (2) a 2-for-1 stock split. She asks you to show the before-and-after effects of each option on common shares, retained earnings, total shareholders' equity, and the number of shares.

Action Plan

✔ Calculate the stock dividend effects by multiplying the stock dividend percentage by the number of existing shares to determine the number of new shares to be issued. Multiply the number of new shares by the price (fair value) of each share at the declaration date.

✔ A stock dividend increases the number of shares and affects both the Common Shares and Retained Earnings accounts.

✔ A stock split increases the number of shares but does not affect the Common Shares or Retained Earnings accounts.

LEARNING OBJECTIVE 4

Indicate how shareholders' equity is presented in the financial statements.

Shareholders' equity is reported in the statement of financial position and statement of changes in equity for companies using IFRS. Companies using ASPE can prepare a statement of retained earnings rather than a statement of changes in equity. Equity transactions are not reported in the income statement, although the income statement is linked to shareholders' equity through net income or loss, which affects retained earnings.

STATEMENT OF FINANCIAL POSITION

In the shareholders' equity section of the statement of financial position, the following are reported: (1) contributed capital, (2) retained earnings, and (3) accumulated other comprehensive income, if any. These categories have been introduced previously. We will review each of them briefly here.

Contributed Capital

Contributed capital represents amounts contributed by shareholders. It includes share capital and contributed surplus, if any:

1. **Share capital.** This category consists of preferred and common shares. Because of the additional rights they give, preferred shares are shown before common shares. Information about the legal capital, number of shares authorized, number of shares issued and amount received for them, and any particular share preferences (such as a dividend rate) is reported for each class of shares either directly in the shareholders' equity section of the statement of financial position or in a note to the financial statements. Note also that any stock dividends distributable that exist at year end are also reported under share capital.

2. **Contributed Surplus.** This category includes equity amounts other than share capital not arising from sources of income. Contributed surplus can arise in a number of ways, including from the excess received when reacquiring and retiring shares at an amount less than they were originally issued at, as we discussed earlier in this chapter. Other sources of contributed surplus will be covered in more advanced accounting courses. For many companies, however, there is no contributed surplus. In this case, the caption "share capital" would be used on the statement of financial position rather than "contributed capital."

Retained Earnings

While contributed capital is provided by the shareholders, retained earnings are often called "earned" capital because they arise from a company's profitable operations. You will recall that retained earnings are the cumulative net incomes (or net losses) since incorporation that have been retained in the company (that is, not distributed to shareholders). Each year, net income is added (or a net loss is deducted) to retained earnings at the beginning of the year and any dividends declared are then deducted, resulting in the ending retained earnings amount. If the retained earnings become negative due to unprofitable operations, the balance in that account becomes known as a deficit.

Note that it is only the amount of dividends *declared* that is deducted from retained earnings, not the amount of dividends *paid*. Dividends can be declared in one year and paid in the next; consequently, dividends declared and dividends paid are not always the same amounts. When they are unequal, a current liability account, Dividends Payable, will be seen on the statement of financial position.

Other deductions from retained earnings can also occur, as we saw earlier in this chapter, when shares are reacquired at a price above their average cost. This difference after first being applied to reduce the Contributed Surplus account, is then applied to reduce the Retained Earnings account. There are other examples of deductions from, and additions to, retained earnings, most notably due to changes in accounting policies. When a company changes accounting policies, such as switching from first-in, first-out to average cost when determining the cost of inventory, the change must be accounted for on a retrospective basis. This means that, after adopting the policy change, inventory and cost of goods sold shown on any prior year's financial statements have to be adjusted to show their proper balances under the new policy. Because cost of goods sold in prior years has now changed, so too have retained earnings (because the cost of goods sold for that year has been closed into retained earnings), and this effect will be shown in the statement of changes in equity. The detailed methods used for the retrospective treatment of policy changes will be covered in more advanced accounting courses.

Recall that it is only the end-of-period balance of retained earnings that is presented in the shareholders' equity section of the statement of financial position, not the detailed changes that are presented in the statement of changes in equity. We will review the statement of changes in equity in more detail later in this chapter.

Retained Earnings is a shareholders' equity account that would normally have a credit balance. If a deficit (negative retained earnings with a debit balance) exists, it is reported as a deduction from shareholders' equity.

In some cases, **retained earnings restrictions** make a portion of the balance in the Retained Earnings account unavailable for dividends. The most common reason for a restriction is the requirement under a loan agreement (known as a **covenant**) to limit the amount of retained earnings that can be distributed as dividends. Restricting retained earnings does not mean that cash is set aside; rather, it is meant to inform users that a portion of retained earnings is not available for dividend payments. No journal entry is necessary to record a retained earnings restriction, but such restrictions are disclosed in the notes to the financial statements.

Accumulated Other Comprehensive Income (IFRS)

Most revenues, expenses, gains, and losses are included in net income. However, certain gains and losses bypass net income and are recorded in **other comprehensive income (OCI)**.

There are several examples of these unique gains and losses being recorded in other comprehensive income or loss. One example that we learned about in Chapter 9 is gains on revaluing property, plant, and equipment using the revaluation model. Another example that we will learn about in the next chapter is unrealized gains and losses on certain types of investments. You will learn about other items that can be included in OCI (loss) in more advanced accounting courses.

Companies will typically add OCI (loss) to net income (loss) and the sum of these two items is **comprehensive income (loss)**. Comprehensive income (loss) therefore includes (1) the revenues, expenses, gains, and losses included in net income, *and* (2) the gains and losses that are reported in OCI, as shown in Illustration 11-3.

►Illustration 11-3
Comprehensive income

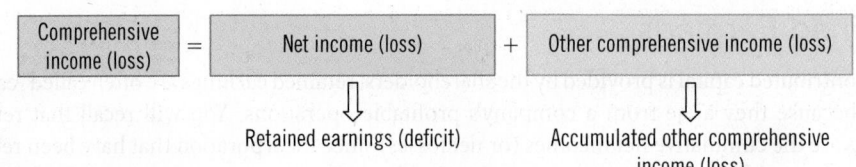

As we learned in Chapter 4, net income (loss) is closed into retained earnings at the end of the year. Likewise, OCI (loss) is closed out at the end of the year but not into retained earnings. Rather, it is closed out into another equity account known as **accumulated other comprehensive income (AOCI)**. In other words, AOCI starts with the balance at the beginning of the period and is increased by other comprehensive income and decreased by other comprehensive losses during the period, to arrive at the ending balance. It is this ending balance that is reported in the shareholders' equity section of the statement of financial position. If AOCI becomes negative because of accumulated other comprehensive losses, it is shown as accumulated other comprehensive loss. Further discussion and illustration of closing entries related to other comprehensive income are left to an intermediate accounting course.

Only companies using IFRS have to report other comprehensive income. Companies using ASPE do not because OCI is not used under these standards. Of course, not all companies using IFRS will have transactions affecting other comprehensive income. However, if they do, they must report comprehensive income in a statement of comprehensive income, and movements affecting accumulated other comprehensive income in the statement of changes in equity. The balance in AOCI at the end of the period would be shown in the shareholders' equity section of the statement of financial position.

Illustration of Shareholders' Equity Section

Leon's reports contributed capital comprising common shares and contributed surplus and earned capital comprising retained earnings and accumulated other comprehensive income in the shareholders' equity section of its statement of financial position, as shown in Illustration 11-4.

LEON'S FURNITURE LIMITED
Statement of Financial Position (partial)
December 31, 2015
(in thousands)

	2015	2014
Shareholders' equity		
Contributed capital		
Common shares. Authorized: unlimited shares.		
Issued, 71,404 and 71,057, respectively	$ 34,389	$ 31,169
Contributed surplus - equity component of debentures	7,089	7,089
Total contributed capital	41,478	38,258
Retained earnings	558,526	510,398
Accumulated other comprehensive income	398	449
	$600,402	$549,105

►Illustration 11-4
Leon's Furniture statement of financial position—shareholders' equity section

Leon's has an unlimited number of common shares authorized, with 71,404 thousand issued at December 31, 2015, and 71,057 thousand at December 31, 2014. It also has contributed surplus of $7,089 thousand on both December 31, 2015, and December 31, 2014, relating to an equity component of convertible debentures. A debenture is a type of liability (similar to a bond) that arises when funds are borrowed directly from lenders. In this case, the debentures can be converted into common shares and the value of that conversion right is shown in equity. This source of contributed surplus was not illustrated in this chapter and is discussed in intermediate accounting courses. Leon's total contributed capital is $41,478 thousand at the end of 2015, and $38,258 thousand at the end of 2014.

Leon's reported a retained earnings balance of $558,526 thousand in 2015, an increase over the retained earnings balance of $510,398 thousand in 2014. The company reported accumulated other comprehensive income of $398 thousand in 2015 and $449 thousand in 2014. Total shareholders' equity for the company was $600,402 thousand in 2015 and $549,105 thousand in 2014.

STATEMENT OF CHANGES IN EQUITY (IFRS)

As we learned in Chapter 1, the **statement of changes in equity** discloses changes in total shareholders' equity for the period, as well as changes in each individual shareholders' equity account, including share capital, contributed surplus, retained earnings, and accumulated other comprehensive income. It is a required statement for companies reporting under IFRS.

A simplified form of Leon's statement of equity (statement of changes in equity) is shown in Illustration 11-5.

Alternative Terminology
The *statement of changes in equity* is also known as the *statement of shareholders' equity* or *statement of equity*.

►Illustration 11-5
Leon's Furniture statement of changes in equity

LEON'S FURNITURE LIMITED
Statement of Changes in Equity
Year Ended December 31, 2015
(in thousands)

	Contributed Capital		Retained Earnings	Accumulated Other Comprehensive Income	Total
	Common Shares	Contributed Surplus			
Balance, January 1	$31,169	$7,089	$510,398	$449	$549,105
Issued common shares	3,220				3,220
Declared dividends			(28,501)		(28,501)
Comprehensive income					
Net income			76,629		76,629
Other comprehensive loss				(51)	(51)
Balance, December 31	$34,389	$7,089	$558,526	$398	$600,402

Leon's details the changes in each of its shareholders' equity accounts, starting with the account balances at the beginning of the 2015 fiscal year (January 1, 2015) and ending with the account balances at the end of the fiscal year (December 31, 2015). Although not included in Illustration 11-5, the company also includes the same information for the 2014 fiscal year for comparative purposes in its actual financial statements. Leon's declared only cash dividends in 2015, but if stock dividends had also been declared, they could have been shown separately in the statement or included in the declared dividends amount above and disclosed in notes to the financial statements.

Note that all of the dollar amounts as at December 31, 2015, that are shown in the above illustration were reported in the shareholders' equity section of Leon's statement of financial position shown in Illustration 11-4. We recommend that you now trace the opening and ending balances, and the total shareholders' equity amounts shown in Illustration 11-5, to those shown in Illustration 11-4.

STATEMENT OF RETAINED EARNINGS (ASPE)

Private companies that report using ASPE usually have a less complex capital structure, with few share transactions, which can more easily be disclosed in the notes to the financial statements. Consequently, private companies are not required to prepare a statement of changes in equity but instead prepare a statement of retained earnings. In contrast to the statement of changes in equity, which shows the amounts and causes of changes in all of the shareholders' equity accounts, the statement of retained earnings shows only the changes in the Retained Earnings account. This statement can be prepared as a separate statement or combined with the income statement.

A **statement of retained earnings** shows the amounts and causes of changes in retained earnings during the period. Similar to the statement of changes in equity, a statement of retained earnings must be prepared after the income statement is prepared, because net income is a key component of retained earnings.

The beginning retained earnings amount is shown on the first line of the statement of retained earnings. Then net income is added and dividends declared are deducted to calculate the retained earnings at the end of the period. If a company has a net loss, it is deducted (rather than added) and if Retained Earnings has a debit (negative) balance it is referred to as a deficit rather than as retained earnings. The statement will also list any effects on retained earnings arising from the reacquisition of shares and other adjustments beyond the scope of this textbook. This statement covers the same period of time as the income statement.

A sample statement of retained earnings is shown in Illustration 11-6 for Graber Inc., using assumed data:

▶Illustration 11-6
Statement of retained earnings

GRABER INC.	
Statement of Retained Earnings	
Year Ended December 31, 2018	
Balance, January 1	$1,068,000
Add: Net income	262,800
	1,330,800
Less: Dividends declared	58,000
Balance, December 31	$1,272,800

SUMMARY OF SHAREHOLDERS' EQUITY TRANSACTIONS

The table that follows includes a brief overview of some of the common transactions or items that have been discussed in this chapter, indicating which shareholders' equity account is affected, and on which statement the account is reported for public companies following IFRS and private companies following ASPE.

	Statement	
Transaction	IFRS	ASPE
Share capital		
Issue (sale) of share capital	Statement of changes in equity	Disclosed in the notes
Ending balance of share capital	Statement of changes in equity; Statement of financial position	Statement of financial position
Contributed surplus		
Changes arising from reacquisition and retirement of shares	Statement of changes in equity	Disclosed in the notes because changes in contributed surplus are not shown in the statement of retained earnings
Ending balance of contributed surplus	Statement of changes in equity; Statement of financial position	Statement of financial position
Retained earnings		
Net income (loss)	Statement of changes in equity	Statement of retained earnings
Dividends declared	Statement of changes in equity	Statement of retained earnings
Changes arising from the reacquisition and retirement of shares	Statement of changes in equity	Statement of retained earnings
Stock split	Disclosed in notes	Disclosed in notes
Dividends in arrears	Disclosed in notes	Disclosed in notes
Ending balance of retained earnings	Statement of changes in equity; Statement of financial position	Statement of retained earnings; Statement of financial position
Restriction of retained earnings	Disclosed in notes	Disclosed in notes
Accumulated other comprehensive income		
Other comprehensive income (loss)	Statement of changes in equity	Not reported
Ending balance of accumulated other comprehensive income (loss)	Statement of changes in equity; Statement of financial position	Not reported

DO IT! 11-4 Statement of Changes in Equity

Grand Lake Corporation had the following shareholders' equity balances at January 1, 2018:

Common shares, unlimited number authorized, 500,000 issued	$1,000,000
Retained earnings	600,000
Accumulated other comprehensive income	100,000

The following selected information is available for the year ended December 31, 2018:

1. Issued 100,000 common shares for $300,000 on January 1.
2. Declared and paid dividends of $0.10 per share in December.
3. Reported net income of $360,000 for the year.
4. Reported other comprehensive loss of $25,000 for the year.

Prepare a statement of changes in equity.

Action Plan

✔ The statement of changes in equity covers a period of time, starting with the opening balances and ending with the ending balances for the period.

✔ Explain the changes in each shareholders' equity account, as well as total shareholders' equity.

SOLUTION
Try this Do It! exercise on your own and then check your answer at the end of the chapter.

Related Exercise Material: BE11–10, BE11–11, BE11-12, E11–7, E11–8, E11–9, and E11–10.

Evaluate dividend and earnings performance.

Investors are interested in both a company's dividend record and its profitability. Although they are often parallel, sometimes they are not. Each item should therefore be investigated separately.

The information in Illustration 11-7 will be used throughout this section to calculate a number of ratios, including the payout ratio, dividend yield, basic earnings per share, and return on common shareholders' equity for Leon's in 2015 and 2014:

▶Illustration 11-7
Selected information for Leon's

(in thousands, except for per-share information)	2015	2014
Net income	$ 76,629	$ 75,524
Shareholders' equity	600,402	549,105
Dividends declared	28,465	28,328
Weighted average number of common shares	71,218	70,899
Dividends declared per common share	0.40	0.40
Market price per common share	14.08	17.90

Leon's has no preferred shares issued.

DIVIDEND RECORD

One way that companies reward investors for their investment is to pay them dividends. The **payout ratio** measures the percentage of a company's net income distributed as cash dividends. It is calculated by dividing the cash dividends declared by net income. It can also be calculated using per-share information rather than total information. In that case, dividends declared per share would be divided by basic earnings per share (which will be discussed in the next section).

Using selected information from Illustration 11-7, Leon's payout ratio follows in Illustration 11-8. We have also included the payout ratios for BMTC Group Inc., one of Leon's competitors, which operates furniture and electronics stores in Quebec including Brault & Martineau, and their industry for comparison.

▶Illustration 11-8
Payout ratio

	$$\text{PAYOUT RATIO} = \frac{\text{CASH DIVIDENDS DECLARED}}{\text{NET INCOME}}$$	
($ in thousands)	2015	2014
Leon's	$$\frac{\$28,465}{\$76,629} = 37.1\%$$	$$\frac{\$28,328}{\$75,524} = 37.5\%$$
BMTC	21.9%	22.2%
Industry average	27.8%	29.2%

In 2015, Leon's paid 37.1% of its net income back to its common shareholders, just slightly less than the 37.5% that was paid out in 2014. BMTC had a payout ratio of 21.9% in 2015, lower than Leon's and down slightly from 22.2% in 2014. Unlike Leon's, BMTC had a payout ratio that was lower than the industry average in both 2015 and 2014.

Unlike some ratios, where a higher value is considered to be good, interpreting a higher payout ratio, like Leon's, depends on an investor's perspective and the company's strategy. Investors seeking dividend income rather than growth in a company's share price will tend to prefer companies with a higher payout ratio. On the other hand, companies that have a higher payout ratio will have less funds available for growth. Consequently, their share price may not rise as rapidly as other companies in the industry. Therefore, investors interested in share price appreciation may not like to invest in companies that have high payout ratios.

You must also be careful when analyzing payout ratios to understand the causes of changes in the ratio. If a company's payout ratio rises, one often assumes this occurred because dividends were increased but it may have occurred because net income fell. For most companies, changes in net income are more likely to occur than changes in dividends declared because most boards of directors believe it is responsible to maintain dividend stability. Consequently, an increase in net income can cause the payout ratio to drop, which is what happened to Leon's in 2015. This decrease should not be interpreted as a reduction in the dividends paid out by the company.

Another dividend measure that interests shareholders is the dividend yield. The **dividend yield** is calculated by dividing the dividend declared per share by the market price per share. Using selected information from Illustration 11-7, the dividend yield is shown in Illustration 11-9 for Leon's. BMTC and the industry average have been included for comparison.

	DIVIDEND YIELD $= \dfrac{\text{DIVIDENDS DECLARED PER SHARE}}{\text{MARKET PRICE PER SHARE}}$	
($ in thousands)	2015	2014
Leon's	$\dfrac{\$0.40}{\$14.08} = 2.8\%$	$\dfrac{\$0.40}{\$17.90} = 2.2\%$
BMTC	1.7%	1.5%
Industry average	1.9%	1.5%

▶Illustration 11-9
Dividend yield

Leon's dividend yield was 2.8% at the end of 2015, an improvement over its yield of 2.2% at the end of 2014 and higher than the industry average in both years. It is also significantly higher than the dividend yield for BMTC. Notice, however, that the amount of dividends paid out by Leon's was unchanged in 2015 compared with 2014, so the increase in the yield was caused not by the numerator of this ratio but by the denominator, which indicates a decrease in Leon's stock price in 2015. This same effect was felt by both BMTC and the industry overall as the increase in the dividend yield throughout the industry arose due to a drop in share prices rather than a change in dividends paid.

The dividend yield is, in essence, a measure of a shareholder's return on his or her investment. In Leon's case, an investor who purchased common shares at the end of 2015 paid $14.08 to purchase each share. Based on the annual dividend of $0.40 per share, the investor earned a return of 2.8% on this investment.

Of course, dividend income is only one part of an investor's return on an investment in shares. Investors also hope to also earn a return from increases in the market price of their shares when they are ready to sell them. Consequently, investors purchasing shares in order to earn dividend income would look for companies with high dividend yields and high payout ratios. Investors purchasing shares for growth purposes (price appreciation) would look for companies with lower dividend yields and low payout ratios.

Illustration 11-10 shows the payout ratios and dividend yields of selected companies in a recent year.

	Payout Ratio	Dividend Yield
BCE (Bell Canada Enterprises)	87.2%	4.7%
Costco	28.7%	1.0%
lululemon athletica	0.0%	0.0%
Royal Bank of Canada	45.8%	4.3%
WestJet	19.1%	2.8%

▶Illustration 11-10
Payout ratios and dividend yields

As explained above, companies that have high growth rates tend to be characterized by low payout ratios and dividend yields because they reinvest most of their net income back into the business. For example, lululemon's payout ratio and dividend yield are zero in Illustration 11-10. The company's dividend policy is stated in the annual report: "We have never declared or paid any cash dividends on our common stock and do not anticipate paying any cash dividends on our common stock at this time. We anticipate that we will retain all of our available funds for use in the operation and expansion of our business."

DO IT! ▶11-5a Payout Ratio and Dividend Yield

Action Plan

✔ Recall that the payout ratio is calculated by dividing cash dividends declared by net income.

✔ Recall that the dividend yield is calculated by dividing the dividends declared per share by the share price.

✔ Determine the reasons for the changes in each ratio over the years.

SOLUTION

Try this Do It! exercise on your own and then check your answer at the end of the chapter.

Related Exercise Material: BE11–13, BE 11-14, and E11–11.

You are helping a conservative investor who has just retired and is interested in purchasing shares in companies that will provide a consistent level of dividends in the future. She is looking at buying shares in either Westbrook Ltd. or Eastglen Inc. and she believes that Westbrook Ltd. are probably the better shares to buy because their yield is higher. To help her make her investment decision, you have gathered the information shown below:

	2018	2017	2016
Westbrook Ltd.			
Net income	$90,000	$110,000	$100,000
Dividends declared	89,000	90,000	80,000
Dividends per share	1.11	1.13	1.00
Share price	24.00	30.00	38.00
Eastglen Inc.			
Net income	$70,000	$60,000	$50,000
Dividends declared	29,000	27,000	25,000
Dividends per share	3.63	3.38	3.13
Share price	92.00	85.00	80.00

(a) Calculate the payout ratio and dividend yield for each year and for each company.

(b) Based on your results in part (a), recommend whether the investor should purchase shares in Westbrook or Eastglen to ensure a consistent level of dividend income in the future. Explain the rationale for your choice.

EARNINGS PERFORMANCE

The earnings performance, or profitability, of a company is measured in several different ways. In Chapter 2, we learned about the basic earnings per share ratio. In this section, we will revisit the calculation of this ratio and introduce a new profitability ratio, the return on common shareholders' equity.

Basic Earnings per Share

Using selected information shown earlier in Illustration 11-7, Leon's basic earnings per share ratio is illustrated below. Comparative information for the industry has not been included because basic earnings per share are not comparable between companies since they issued a different number of common shares.

▶Illustration 11-11
Basic earnings per share

	INCOME AVAILABLE TO COMMON SHAREHOLDERS (NET INCOME − PREFERRED DIVIDENDS)	
BASIC EARNINGS PER SHARE =	WEIGHTED AVERAGE NUMBER OF COMMON SHARES	
(in thousands)	2015	2014
Leon's	$\frac{\$76,629 - \$0}{71,218} = \$1.08$	$\frac{\$75,524 - \$0}{70,899} = \$1.07$
BMTC	$0.99	$1.08
Industry average	n/a	n/a

In Chapter 2, the value of both the numerator and denominator were provided to you in order to calculate basic earnings per share. Now, in this chapter you can determine the value of these items on your own. The numerator, **income available to common shareholders**, is calculated by subtracting any preferred dividends declared from net income. This is because preferred shareholders have preferential rights to receive these dividends before the common shareholders can share in any remaining amounts. Note that cumulative preferred dividends are deducted from net income whether declared or not; noncumulative preferred dividends are deducted only if declared. In Leon's case, no preferred shares have been issued so its income available to common shareholders is the same as its net income.

For the denominator of the basic earnings per share calculation, the weighted average number of shares is used. It is important to understand that Leon's weighted average numbers of common shares, which were 71,218 thousand in 2015 and 70,899 thousand in 2014, are not the same as the numbers of common shares outstanding at the end of each year, which were 71,404 thousand in 2015 and 71,057 thousand in 2014. You will recall that, whenever we calculate a ratio with an amount that measures something over a period of time (such as net income) and an end-of-period amount (such as the number of common shares), we always average the end-of-period amount so that the numerator and denominator in the calculation represent the same period of time. However, we do not use a straight average in the calculation of the number of common shares as we do in some other ratio calculations. For example, we do not take the beginning and ending balances of the number of common shares, add them together, and divide the result by two.

Instead, we use a **weighted average number of common shares** because this considers the impact of shares issued and reacquired at different times throughout the year. This is done because changes in the number of issued shares affects the amount of assets on which net income can be generated. If there is no change in the number of common shares during the year, the weighted average number of shares will be the same as the ending balance. If new shares are issued or existing shares are reacquired throughout the year, then these shares are adjusted for the fraction of the year remaining since they were issued or reacquired to determine the weighted average number of shares.

To illustrate the calculation of the weighted average number of common shares, assume that a company had 100,000 common shares on January 1. It issued an additional 7,500 shares on July 1 and 10,000 shares on October 1. Then, on December 1, 6,000 shares were reacquired and retired. The weighted average number of shares for the year ended December 31 would be calculated as follows:

Date	Actual Number		Weighted Average
Jan. 1	100,000	$\times$ $12/12$ =	100,000
July 1	7,500	$\times$ $6/12$ =	3,750
Oct. 1	10,000	$\times$ $3/12$ =	2,500
Dec. 1	(6,000)	$\times$ $1/12$ =	(500)
	111,500		105,750

As indicated in the "Actual Number" column above, 111,500 shares were actually issued by the end of the year. Of these, 100,000 were issued for the full year and are allocated a full weight, or 12 months out of 12 months. The 7,500 new shares issued on July 1 have only been issued for six months (from July 1 to December 31) and are weighted for $6/12$ of the year, to result in 3,750 weighted shares. Another 10,000 shares have been issued for three months (from October 1 to December 31) and are weighted for $3/12$ of the year, to result in 2,500 weighted shares, and finally, the reacquired shares are weighted for $1/12$ and shown as a reduction in arriving at the weighted average number of shares, which is 105,750 for the year.

Leon's basic earnings per share ratio has improved slightly in 2015, from $1.07 to $1.08, while BMTC's basic earnings per share has deteriorated. As mentioned earlier, we cannot compare BMTC's basic earnings per share with that of Leon's or the industry.

When a corporation has securities that may be converted into common shares, it has what is called a complex capital structure. One such example is the convertible debentures issued by Leon's. When these debentures are converted into common shares, the additional common shares will result in a reduced, or diluted, basic earnings per share figure.

When a company has a complex capital structure, it must not only calculate **basic earnings per share** as shown in Illustration 11-11 of $1.08 in 2015 and $1.07 in 2014, but it must also present **diluted earnings per share**. Leon's diluted earnings per share are $0.97 in 2015 and $0.96 in 2014. The calculation of diluted earnings per share is complex and is a hypothetical calculation of earnings per share assuming that the convertible items that make the capital structure complex have been converted into common shares even though that has not yet happened. We focus only on basic earnings per share in this chapter and leave further discussion of diluted earnings per share and other complexities to an intermediate accounting course.

The disclosure of earnings per share is required for companies reporting using IFRS. This ratio is considered to be so important that it must be reported directly on the income statement (or the statement of comprehensive income).

DO IT! ▶ 11-5b Basic Earnings per Share

SOLUTION
Try this Do It! exercise on your own and then check your answer at the end of the chapter.

Related Exercise Material: BE11–15, BE11–16, BE 11–17, and E11–12.

The Shoten Corporation reported net income of $249,750 for the year ended October 31, 2018. The shareholders' equity section of its statement of financial position reported 3,000 $2 cumulative preferred shares and 58,800 common shares issued. Of the common shares, 40,000 had been outstanding since the beginning of the year on November 1, 2017, 15,000 were issued on March 1, and 5,000 were issued on August 1. On October 1, 1,200 common shares were reacquired and retired. Calculate Shoten's basic earnings per share.

Action Plan
✔ Subtract any preferred dividends from net income to determine the income available for common shareholders.

✔ Note that cumulative preferred dividends are deducted from net income whether declared or not; noncumulative preferred dividends are deducted only if declared.

✔ Adjust the shares for the fraction of the year issued to determine the weighted average number of common shares.

✔ Divide the income available for common shareholders by the weighted average number of common shares to calculate basic earnings per share.

Return on Equity

A widely used ratio that measures profitability from the common shareholders' viewpoint is the **return on common shareholders' equity**. This ratio shows how many dollars were earned for each dollar invested by common shareholders. It is calculated by dividing income available to common shareholders by average common shareholders' equity. As we just learned, the income available to common shareholders is equal to net income less preferred dividends. Common shareholders' equity is total shareholders' equity less the legal capital of any preferred shares. Recall that every other component of shareholders' equity belongs to the common, or residual, shareholders.

We can calculate a return on common shareholders' equity for Leon's using the information shown in Illustration 11-7. In addition, we will require the shareholders' equity amount for 2013, which was $497,764 thousand, in order to calculate average common shareholders' equity for 2014. As we mentioned earlier, Leon's common shareholders' equity is the same as its total shareholders' equity because it does not have any preferred shares.

Leon's return on common shareholders' equity ratios are calculated for 2015 and 2014 in Illustration 11-12, with comparative information included for BMTC and the industry.

	INCOME AVAILABLE TO COMMON SHAREHOLDERS	
RETURN ON COMMON SHAREHOLDERS' EQUITY =	$\dfrac{\text{(NET INCOME} - \text{PREFERRED DIVIDENDS)}}{\text{AVERAGE COMMON SHAREHOLDERS' EQUITY}}$	
(in thousands)	2015	2014
Leon's	$\dfrac{\$76,629 - \$0}{(\$600,402 + \$549,105) \div 2} = 13.3\%$	$\dfrac{\$75,524 - \$0}{(\$549,105 + \$497,764) \div 2} = 14.4\%$
BMTC	19.4%	21.5%
Industry average	4.8%	5.4%

▶Illustration 11-12
Return on common shareholders' equity

In 2015, Leon's return on common shareholders' equity was 13.3%, slightly lower than in 2014. Both years' returns were lower than those of BMTC but significantly better than the industry average. Although Leon's return on equity was quite good, BMTC's superior return on equity was due to higher profit margins and higher asset turnover ratios.

The Effect of Debt on the Return on Shareholders' Equity

When a company has no liabilities, its assets are equal to its shareholders' equity and because of this, its returns on assets and shareholders' equity will be equal. Because most companies have liabilities, their assets will be greater than shareholders' equity and this in turn will cause their return on assets to be different from their return on common shareholders' equity. When a company has liabilities and is using these to finance a portion of newly acquired assets, it is using *leverage*. Because of leverage, interest expense will rise. However, if the newly acquired assets improve profitability despite the higher interest expense, then the increased net income will cause a larger increase in the return on common shareholders' equity than in the return on assets. (This is because common shareholders' equity is smaller than assets.) In this case, the leverage will be advantageous. However, if a company takes on too much debt to purchase new assets and cannot cover the additional interest expense with additional income from the new assets, the leverage will be detrimental and will cause the return on common shareholders' equity to be less than the return on assets.

For example, let's assume that a company with average assets and average common shareholders' equity of $10 million operates a hotel that has net income of $1.5 million for a return on assets of 15%. If the company has no liabilities, its return on common shareholders' equity (assuming no preferred shares are issued) is also 15% because in this case, assets are equal to common shareholders' equity. Management decides to open up a second hotel and will pay for this expansion using $10 million of borrowed funds at 5% after income tax. Assuming both hotels have the same level of assets and are equally profitable, they will both generate net income of $1.5 million for a return on assets of 15% before taking into consideration the interest on the borrowed funds to obtain the second hotel. After considering the effect of interest, which amounts to $500,000 ($10 million × 5%), the net income of the second hotel will fall to $1 million, giving a return on that asset of 10%. However, this return was earned without any additional equity and it will accrue to common shareholders, increasing their total return on equity from 15% to 25%. Clearly in this case, using debt to finance an expansion was a good idea. **In general, as long as the return on assets (15% in this case) exceeds the interest rate paid on debt (5% in this case), a company can increase its return on shareholders' equity by using leverage.** This is shown below in Illustration 11-13.

	Hotel 1	Hotel 2	Total Company
Net income	$ 1,500,000	$ 1,000,000	$ 2,500,000
Average assets	10,000,000	10,000,000	20,000,000
Average liabilities	0	10,000,000	10,000,000
Average equity	10,000,000	0	10,000,000
Return on assets	15.0%	10.0%	12.5%
Return on common shareholders' equity	15.0%	n/a	25.0%

▶Illustration 11-13
Effect of return on assets and leverage on return on shareholders' equity

However, if the second hotel was unprofitable and had a 0% return on assets before considering interest, a net loss would arise because interest of $500,000 would still be incurred. Therefore, the second hotel would have a return on assets of negative 5% after considering interest. In this case the company borrowed funds and was not able to earn a return on them that exceeded 5%. The effect of these ratios can be seen in illustration 11-14.

▶ Illustration 11-14

Effect of return on assets and leverage on return on shareholders' equity

	Hotel 1	Hotel 2	Total Company
Net income (loss)	$ 1,500,000	$ (500,000)	$ 1,000,000
Average assets	10,000,000	10,000,000	20,000,000
Average liabilities	0	10,000,000	10,000,000
Average equity	10,000,000	0	10,000,000
Return on assets	15.0%	(5.0)%	5.0%
Return on common shareholders' equity	15.0%	n/a	10.0%

If the expansion had not been done, the company would have had a 15% return on shareholders' equity. Using leverage can cause that return to vary. Consequently, using leverage is *risky*. This increased risk may or may not be considered an advantage of debt financing.

In addition to the effects of leverage, some advantages of debt financing compared with equity financing include the following:

1. When debt is used, the ownership interests of current shareholders remain the same and are not decreased or diluted by new equity from new shareholders.
2. When financing with debt, interest expense is tax deductible whereas dividends paid are not.

Some disadvantages of debt financing compared with equity financing include:

1. Interest payments are legally binding and if not paid, litigation by creditors can arise, whereas dividends to shareholders are discretionary and are not legally binding if they are not declared.
2. The principal portion of loans must be paid back to creditors whereas the amount received from the sale of shares does not have to be returned to shareholders until the company is liquidated.

Summary of Ratios

In summary, we have covered four ratios in this chapter—all of which are profitability ratios. Their formulas are summarized below, as is the desired result. Of course, we must be cautious in interpreting one ratio on its own. Ratios should always be considered in light of other ratios, as seen above with the return on common shareholders' equity ratio and the return on asset ratio. Furthermore, ratios must be interpreted in conjunction with available financial and non-financial information.

Ratio	Formula	Desired Result
Payout ratio	$\dfrac{\text{Cash dividends declared}}{\text{Net income}}$	Higher is better for investors seeking dividend income.
Dividend yield	$\dfrac{\text{Dividends declared per share}}{\text{Market price per share}}$	Lower is better for investors seeking growth.
Basic earnings per share	$\dfrac{\text{Income available to common shareholders}}{\text{(Net income − Preferred dividends)}}{\text{Weighted average number of common shares}}$	Higher
Return on common shareholders' equity	$\dfrac{\text{Income available to common shareholders}}{\text{(Net income − Preferred dividends)}}{\text{Average common shareholders' equity}}$	Higher

DO IT! ▶ 11-5c ┃ Return on Common Shareholders' Equity

Pierce Enterprises Ltd. and Darrow Inc. operate in the same retail industry. Pierce is growth oriented and has used leverage to expand the number of stores it operates significantly whereas Darrow Inc. prefers to expand through the use of internally generated funds. You are trying to decide which of these two companies you would like to invest in and you realize that comparing the return on common shareholders' equity of these two companies is an important consideration in making your investment decision. Neither company has any preferred shareholders. You have gathered the following information (in thousands):

	Pierce	Darrow
Average assets	$2,000,000	$1,000,000
Average liabilities	1,200,000	200,000
Average common shareholders' equity	800,000	800,000
Net income	200,000	100,000
Return on assets	10%	10%

(a) Calculate the return on common shareholders' equity and compare your results with the return on assets provided above for both companies.

(b) Based on your results in part (a), identify which company you would like to invest in. Explain the rationale for your choice.

Action Plan

✔ Recall that return on common shareholders' equity is calculated by dividing income available to common shareholders by average common shareholders' equity.

✔ Determine if there is a significant difference between these two ratios. If there is, the effect is caused by leverage. Determine if the leverage is an advantage or a disadvantage for these companies.

SOLUTION

Try this Do It! exercise on your own and then check your answer at the end of the chapter.

Related Exercise Material: BE11–18, E11–13, E11–14, and E11–15.

REVIEW AND PRACTICE

▶ LEARNING OBJECTIVE REVIEW

1. Identify and discuss the major characteristics of a corporation. The major characteristics of a corporation are separate legal existence, limited liability of shareholders, transferable ownership rights, the ability to acquire capital, continuous life, separation of corporation management from ownership, increased cost and complexity of government regulations, and the possibility of reduced corporate income tax. Some of these characteristics may differ depending on the size of the corporation.

Corporations issue shares for sale to investors. The proceeds received from the issue of shares become the company's legal capital. Shares then trade among investors on the secondary stock market and do not affect the company's financial position.

2. Record share transactions. If only one class of shares is issued, they are considered to be common shares. Common shareholders have the right to vote and, as such, are the "owners" of the company. When shares are issued for noncash goods or services in a company using IFRS, the fair value of the goods or services received is used to record the transaction if it can be

reliably determined. If not, the fair value of the common shares is used. For a private company following ASPE, the more reliable of the two fair values should be used, which is usually also the fair value of the goods or services received.

When shares are reacquired, the Common Shares (or Preferred Shares) account is reduced by the average cost of these shares immediately prior to the reacquisition. If the price paid to reacquire the shares is lower than their average cost, the difference is recorded as an increase to the Contributed Surplus account. If the price paid to reacquire the shares is greater than their average cost, the difference is first applied to any Contributed Surplus previously recorded from acquisitions of shares of the same class and any remaining difference is then applied to reduce the Retained Earnings account.

The accounting for preferred shares is similar to the accounting for common shares. Preferred shares do not have the right to vote—only common shares have voting rights—but have contractual provisions that give them preference over common shares for dividends and assets in the event of liquidation. Dividends are quoted at an annual rate (such as $5 preferred), but are normally paid quarterly (such as $1.25 per quarter). In addition, preferred shares may have other preferences, such as the right to redeem or to periodically reset dividend rates based on changes in interest rates.

3. Prepare the entries for cash dividends, stock dividends, and stock splits, and understand their financial impact. Entries for both cash and stock dividends are required at the declaration date and the payment or distribution date. There is no entry (other than a memo entry) for a stock split. The overall impact of a cash dividend is to reduce assets (cash) and shareholders' equity (retained earnings). Stock dividends increase common shares and decrease retained earnings but do not affect assets, liabilities, or shareholders' equity in total. Stock splits also have no impact on assets, liabilities, or shareholders' equity. The number of shares increases with both stock dividends and stock splits.

4. Indicate how shareholders' equity is presented in the financial statements. In the shareholders' equity section of the statement of financial position for companies using IFRS, share capital, retained earnings, and accumulated other comprehensive income, if any, are reported separately. If contributed surplus exists, then the caption "contributed capital" is used for share capital (preferred and common shares) and contributed surplus that may have been created from various sources. A statement of changes in equity explains the changes in each shareholders' equity account, and in total, for the reporting period. Notes to the financial statements explain details about authorized and issued shares, restrictions on retained earnings, and dividends in arrears, if there are any.

For private companies reporting using ASPE, comprehensive income is not reported and a statement of changes in equity is not required. Instead, a statement of retained earnings is prepared that explains the changes in the Retained Earnings account for the reporting period. Changes to share capital and any other equity items are disclosed in the notes to the statements.

5. Evaluate dividend and earnings performance. A company's dividend record can be evaluated by looking at the dividend payout ratio (cash dividends declared divided by net income), which measures what percentage of net income it chooses to pay out in dividends, and by the dividend yield ratio (dividends per share divided by the share price), which measures dividends as a percentage of the share price.

Earnings performance can be measured by two profitability ratios: basic earnings per share (net income less preferred dividends divided by the weighted average number of common shares) and the return on common shareholders' equity ratio (net income less preferred dividends divided by average common shareholders' equity).

The return on shareholders' equity is affected by the extent to which a company uses debt or equity to finance the acquisition of its assets. Taking on more debt is risky because the company is legally bound to make principal and interest payments on debt, but on the other hand, the ownership interests of existing shareholders are not diluted when greater debt is assumed. Furthermore, any excess income generated from assets financed with debt accrues to the shareholders, not the creditors.

▶ KEY TERM REVIEW

The following are key terms defined in this chapter with the corresponding page reference for your review. You will find a complete list of terms and definitions for all chapters in the glossary at the end of this textbook.

Accumulated other comprehensive income (AOCI) (p. 604)
Authorized shares (p. 588)
Cash dividend (p. 597)
Contributed capital (p. 591)
Contributed surplus (p. 591)
Cumulative (p. 595)
Declaration date (p. 598)
Dividend yield (p. 609)
Dividends in arrears (p. 595)

Income available to common shareholders (p. 611)
Initial public offering (IPO) (p. 588)
Issued shares (p. 589)
Legal capital (p. 590)
Market capitalization (p. 590)
Noncumulative (p. 595)
Normal course issuer bid (p. 592)
Other comprehensive income (OCI) (p. 604)
Payment (distribution) date (p. 598)

Payout ratio (p. 608)
Preferred shares (p. 594)
Record date (p. 598)
Retained earnings restrictions (p. 604)
Return on common shareholders' equity (p. 612)
Statement of retained earnings (p. 606)
Stock dividend (p. 599)
Stock split (p. 600)
Weighted average number of common shares (p. 611)

▶ COMPARING IFRS AND ASPE REVIEW

Key Differences	International Financial Reporting Standards (IFRS)	Accounting Standards for Private Enterprises (ASPE)
Issue of shares for a noncash consideration	When shares are issued for a noncash consideration, they should be recorded at the fair value of the consideration (for example, goods or services) received. If the fair value of the consideration received cannot be reliably determined, then the fair value of the consideration given up would be used instead.	When shares are issued for a noncash consideration, they should be recorded at the most reliable of the two values—the fair value of the consideration (for example, goods or services) received or the fair value of the consideration given up.

Key Differences	International Financial Reporting Standards (IFRS)	Accounting Standards for Private Enterprises (ASPE)
Comprehensive income	Must present other comprehensive income and net income to determine comprehensive income. Must present accumulated other comprehensive income in the statement of financial position and detail changes in other comprehensive income in the statement of changes in equity.	Disclosure of comprehensive income is not required because other comprehensive income is not reported.
Statement of changes in equity/retained earnings	Changes in all shareholders' equity accounts are presented in a statement of changes in equity.	Changes in retained earnings are presented in a statement of retained earnings. Changes in share capital and other accounts are presented in the notes to the financial statements.
Earnings per share	Required to present in the income statement (or statement of comprehensive income).	Not required to present in the income statement.

▶ DECISION TOOLKIT REVIEW

DECISION CHECKPOINTS	INFO NEEDED FOR DECISION	TOOLS TO USE FOR DECISION	HOW TO EVALUATE RESULTS
Should the company incorporate?	Capital needs, growth expectations, type of business, income tax status	Corporations have limited liability, greater ability to raise capital, and professional managers. In addition, there is a potential for reduced income tax, especially for smaller corporations. However, there is increased cost and complexity from complying with government regulations.	Carefully weigh the costs and benefits in light of the particular circumstances.
What portion of its net income does the company pay out in dividends?	Net income and total cash dividends declared	$\text{Payout ratio} = \dfrac{\text{Cash dividends declared}}{\text{Net income}}$	A high payout ratio is considered desirable for investors seeking income. A low ratio suggests that the company is retaining its net income for investment in future growth and would be preferred by investors seeking growth.
What percentage of the share price is the company paying in dividends?	Dividends declared and share price	$\text{Dividend yield} = \dfrac{\text{Dividends declared per share}}{\text{Market price per share}}$	A high dividend yield is considered desirable for investors seeking income. It may mean that the company is paying out, rather than retaining, its net income, and it may be indicative of a decline in the market price per share.
How does the company's net income compare with previous years?	Income available to common shareholders and weighted average number of common shares	$\text{Basic earnings per share} = \dfrac{\text{Net income} - \text{Preferred dividends}}{\text{Weighted average number of common shares}}$	A higher measure suggests improved performance. Values should not be compared across companies.
What is the company's return on its common shareholders' investment?	Income available to common shareholders and average common shareholders' equity	$\text{Return on common shareholders' equity} = \dfrac{\text{Net income} - \text{Preferred dividends}}{\text{Average common shareholders' equity}}$	A high measure suggests a strong earnings performance from the common shareholders' perspective.

▶ PRACTICE USING THE DECISION TOOLKIT

Answers are at the end of the chapter.

The following selected information (in U.S. $ millions, except per-share information) is available for **Ethan Allen Interiors Inc.**, one of Leon's competitors. Ethan Allen has had a well-established presence in Canada for more than 40 years, in addition to in the United States and elsewhere in the world. Note that, similar to Leon's, Ethan Allen does not have any preferred shares.

	2015	2014
Net income	$ 37.1	$ 42.9
Dividends declared and paid	14.5	11.6
Shareholders' equity	370.5	367.5
Weighted average number of shares	28.9	28.9
Dividends per share	0.50	0.40
Market price per share	26.34	24.74

INSTRUCTIONS

(a) Using the above information, calculate the (1) payout ratio, (2) dividend yield, (3) basic earnings per share, and (4) return on common shareholders' equity for Ethan Allen for 2015.

(a) Contrast the company's (1) dividend record and (2) earnings performance with those of Leon's and the industry, which are given in the chapter.

▶ PRACTICE COMPREHENSIVE DO IT!

Hutchings Limited is authorized to issue an unlimited number of common shares and 250,000 $1 cumulative preferred shares. At January 1, 2018, it had the following opening equity balances: Preferred shares, nil; Common Shares, 400,000 shares issued, $2.4 million; Contributed Surplus, $80,000; Retained Earnings, $1,820,000; and Accumulated Other Comprehensive Income, $90,000. The contributed surplus arose from the reacquisition of common shares in prior years.

During the year ended December 31, 2018, the company had the following share transactions:

Jan.	10	Issued 50,000 common shares at $9.24 per share.
July	2	Issued 40,000 preferred shares at $25 per share.
Sept.	4	Declared a 4% stock dividend to common shareholders of record on September 14, distributable September 28. The price of the common shares was $10 per share on September 4, $12 per share on September 14, and $11 per share on September 28.
Nov.	1	Issued 10,000 preferred shares at $25 per share.
	3	Reacquired and retired 20,000 common shares for $11 per share.
Dec.	21	Declared an annual cash dividend to preferred shareholders of record on January 15, payable January 31.
	31	A loan agreement entered into on December 31 contains a restrictive covenant that limits the payment of future dividends to 15% of net income.

In addition, Hutchings reported net income of $512,000 for the year.

INSTRUCTIONS

(a) Record the above transactions, including any entries required to close dividends and net income.

(a) Prepare the statement of changes in equity and the shareholders' equity section of the statement of financial position, including any required note disclosure.

▶ PRACTICE OBJECTIVE-FORMAT QUESTIONS

Answers are at the end of the chapter.

1. Which of the following is a characteristic of a corporation? (Select as many as are appropriate.)

(a) It is easy to transfer ownership in a large, publicly traded corporation.

(b) The assets and liabilities of a corporation are not legally distinct from the assets and liabilities of the shareholders.

(c) The liability of the shareholders for amounts owed by the corporation to others is usually limited to just the interest that the shareholders have in the corporation and does not extend to other assets they hold personally.

(d) The shares of all companies incorporated in Canada are required by law to trade on public stock exchanges.

(e) The common shareholders of a corporation directly manage the operations of that corporation because their shares have voting rights.

(f) Private corporations in Canada do not have to comply with the provisions of the Canada Business Corporations Act or their provincial equivalent.

(g) Small corporations in Canada are usually subject to a lower rate of income tax than the rate applicable to individuals.

2. Which of the following statements is correct? (Select as many as are appropriate.)

(a) The authorized number of shares is the maximum number of shares that a corporation can issue.

(b) The number of issued shares must always be equal to the number of authorized shares.

(c) An initial public offering occurs when a corporation is listed on a stock exchange and sells its shares to the public for the first time.

(d) A normal course issuer bid is the amount that shareholders bid when buying their shares.

(e) Dividends can fall into arrears on common shares only when the board of directors refuses to pay dividends on these shares.

(f) A public corporation that has issued only common shares can determine its market capitalization by multiplying the number of issued common shares by the current market value of these shares.

(g) The legal capital of a corporation is usually equal to the proceeds received by the corporation when these shares were issued.

3. Which of the following statements is correct regarding preferred shares? (Select as many as are appropriate.)

(a) Preferred shareholders are entitled to receive dividends before the common shareholders receive their dividends.

(b) Some preferred shares can be converted into common shares.

(c) A redeemable (callable) feature on a preferred share gives the corporation that issued these shares the right to buy them back from shareholders by a specific date and at a specific price.

(d) Preferred shareholders have voting rights at shareholder meetings.

(e) Some preferred shares have cumulative dividend rights, which means that the accumulated dividends paid out by the corporation to preferred shareholders can be used to buy special voting shares.

(f) A dividend in arrears can arise only on shares with a cumulative dividend right.

(g) Retractable preferred shares allow those shareholders to sell their shares back to the company at a stated price and within a certain period of time.

4. Which of the following statements pertaining to dividends is correct? (Select as many as are appropriate.)

(a) When cash dividends are declared, a liability to pay them arises and a journal entry is recorded.

(b) On the record date, cash dividends are paid out to shareholders who owned the shares on the day that the related dividends were declared.

(c) If a cash dividend is declared and paid on the same day, the entry to record this will debit Dividends Declared and credit Cash.

(d) When cash dividends are paid that were previously declared, the journal entry to record this payment would debit Dividends Declared and credit Cash.

(e) Like interest expense, cash dividends become payable through the passage of time.

(f) If we want to determine the amount of dividends that have been declared by a company, we can find this on the income statement.

(g) On the payment date, cash dividends are paid out to those shareholders who owned the shares on the record date.

5. Which of the following statements pertaining to stock splits and stock dividends is correct? (Select as many as are appropriate.)

(a) When a stock dividend is distributed, total equity will fall.

(b) A stock split is done to lower the price of a company's shares in order to make them more marketable.

(c) When a stock split occurs, no journal entry is recorded.

(d) A stock split will lower basic earnings per share.

(e) When a stock dividend is declared but not distributed, a current liability is recorded.

(f) When a stock dividend is declared on a common share, it will lower the return on common shareholders' equity.

(g) When a common stock dividend is distributed after being declared earlier, the entry to record the distribution will debit Stock Dividends Distributable and credit Common Shares.

6. Which of the following statements pertaining to the presentation of equity in financial statements is correct? (Select as many as are appropriate.)

(a) Accumulated other comprehensive income is a component of contributed capital.

(b) Contributed surplus is also known as retained earnings.

(c) Other comprehensive income is closed out to retained earnings at the end of each year.

(d) Under ASPE, the statement of changes in equity is used instead of a statement of retained earnings.

(e) Both preferred and common shares are examples of contributed capital.

(f) When the Retained Earnings account falls into a credit balance, it is usually referred to as a Deficit.

(g) The effect that both stock and cash dividends have on retained earnings can be seen in the income statement.

7. Greenwich Limited had 80,000 common and 50,000 $1 cumulative preferred shares at the beginning of the current year. Halfway through the year, another 40,000 common shares were issued. The company declared and paid all the required dividends on the preferred shares and $80,000 on the common shares this year. Also during the year, the company had net income of $200,000 and other comprehensive income of $30,000. Based on the above, which of the following statements is correct regarding basic earnings per share for the year? (Select as many as are appropriate.)

(a) The denominator for basic earnings per share this year will be 150,000 shares.

(b) The denominator for basic earnings per share this year will be 100,000 shares.

(c) The amount of dividends that will be subtracted in determining the income available to common shareholders will be $130,000.

(d) The amount of preferred share dividends that will be subtracted in determining the income available to common shareholders will be $50,000.

(e) Preferred share dividends should be subtracted from comprehensive income of $230,000 when arriving at income available to common shareholders.

(f) Preferred share dividends should be subtracted from net income of $200,000 when arriving at income available to common shareholders.

(g) Basic earnings per share this year will be $1.50 per share.

8. During the current year, a company's board of directors doubled the dividend that the company paid to its common shareholders. The company has no preferred shares. This was done even though net income had only risen during that year by 10%. Even after the dividend increase, the dividends were still lower than the current year's net income. Despite the increase in the dividend, the price of the company's shares fell during the current year. As a result of the above events, which of the following statements is correct? (Select as many as are appropriate.)

(a) The payout ratio will increase.

(b) The return on common shareholders' equity will decrease.

(c) The dividend yield will increase.

(d) Shareholders' equity will decrease.

(e) Retained earnings will increase.

(f) If the dividend increase did not occur, the dividend yield would have increased.

(g) If the dividend increase did not occur, the payout ratio would have increased.

9. Which of the following statements is correct? (Select as many as are appropriate.)

(a) Investors who are retired and need dividend income to maintain their standard of living will prefer to invest in shares that have a high dividend yield.

(b) A stock split will cause the return on common shareholders' equity to decrease.

(c) If there is an increase in the cash dividends declared in a year when net income has decreased, the payout ratio will increase.

(d) When a company with no preferred shares increases its leverage by taking on more debt, the difference between the return on

assets and the return on common shareholders' equity will usually become smaller.

(e) A company with a very low payout ratio is less likely to be following a strategy that will grow the size of the business.

(f) If a company lowers its dividends per share by 10% when its share price has decreased by 20%, the company's dividend yield will increase.

(g) The basic earnings per share of one company should always be compared with the basic earnings per share of other companies.

10. Which of the following statements is correct regarding the financing of an asset acquisition with debt rather than issuing common shares? (Select as many as are appropriate.)

(a) Interest payments on debt must be made on predetermined dates and this is an

advantage of financing with debt because the company knows when interest is due.

(b) Amounts raised from the issue of shares must be repaid to shareholders at predetermined dates and this is a disadvantage of raising funds by issuing shares.

(c) Interest payments are tax deductible and this is an advantage to financing with debt.

(d) No dividend payments are legally required to be made to common shareholders unless declared and this is an advantage when raising funds by selling common shares.

(e) Principal payments on debt must be made on predetermined dates and this is a disadvantage of debt financing.

(f) When using debt financing, there is dilution of existing ownership interests and this is a disadvantage because the company has fewer shareholders.

(g) Dividend payments to shareholders are tax deductible and this is an advantage of raising funds by selling shares.

WileyPLUS

Brief Exercises, Exercises, and many additional resources are available for practice in WileyPLUS.

▶QUESTIONS

(LO 1) 1. Pat Kabza, a student, asks for your help in understanding the different corporation characteristics. (a) Explain the following characteristics to Pat and identify whether they are an advantage or a disadvantage for a large, publicly traded corporation: (1) separate legal existence, (2) limited liability of shareholders, (3) transferable ownership rights, (4) ability to acquire capital, (5) continuous life, (6) separation of management and ownership, (7) government regulations, and (8) income tax. (b) Would your answers to part (a) change if you were commenting about the advantages and disadvantages for a small, private corporation rather than a large, publicly traded corporation? Explain.

(LO 1) 2. Letson Corporation is authorized to issue 100,000 common shares. During its first two years of operation, Letson issued 60,000 shares. (a) After this transaction, how many more shares is Letson able to issue? (b) Are both authorized and issued shares recorded in the general journal?

(LO 1) 3. Richard Boudreault purchased 100 **lululemon athletica** common shares for $18 a share from the company's initial public offering. A few years later, Richard purchased 200 more lululemon shares for $71 each on the Toronto Stock Exchange. Explain the impact of each of these transactions on lululemon's assets, liabilities, and shareholders' equity.

(LO 1) 4. The market capitalization of **Dollarama Inc.** was $11.6 billion at the end of its fiscal year in 2014 and $7.9 billion at the end of 2015. Explain what "market capitalization" means and describe the effect of this decrease in market capitalization between 2014 and 2015 on Dollarama's assets, liabilities, and shareholders' equity.

(LO 1) 5. (a) What is legal capital? (b) How is the value of the legal capital determined? (c) In Canada, does legal capital usually take the form of par value or no par value shares? (d) Why is legal capital reported separately from retained earnings in the shareholders' equity section of the statement of financial position?

(LO 2) 6. (a) Compare the rights of preferred shareholders with those of common shareholders. Include in your answer the areas in which preferred shares are given priority over common shares. (b) Why would a company issue preferred shares when common shares are already issued?

(LO 2) 7. When common and preferred shares are issued for a consideration other than cash (for example, goods or services), at what value should the shares be recorded for a publicly traded company using IFRS? Would your answer change if it were a private company using ASPE?

(LO 2) 8. (a) What is a normal course issuer bid? (b) Why might a company wish to reacquire some of its own shares?

(LO 2) 9. Why is a gain or a loss not recorded in the income statement when a company reacquires its shares and buys them back for an amount that is different from their average cost?

(LO 2) 10. When reacquiring shares, under what circumstances would the Contributed Surplus account be affected? The Retained Earnings account? Would the effect caused by the circumstances described above result in an increase or a decrease in these accounts?

(LO 2) 11. The **Royal Bank of Canada** has a noncumulative class of preferred shares with an annual dividend rate of $1.18. David Chen owns 1,000 of these shares. If the Royal Bank declares and pays a quarterly dividend on these shares, how much cash can David expect to receive for the quarter? If these preferred shares have a feature to reset the dividend rate, does that make these shares more or less appealing as an investment for David?

(LO 2) 12. (a) What is the difference between a redeemable and a retractable preferred share? (b) What is the difference between cumulative and noncumulative preferred shares? (c) Can dividends in arrears arise on both cumulative and noncumulative preferred shares? Explain.

(LO 3) 13. What conditions must be met before a cash dividend on a common share can be declared?

(LO 3) 14. Contrast the effects of the (a) declaration date, (b) record date, and (c) payment date for a cash dividend on a company's (1) assets, (2) liabilities, (3) share capital, (4) retained earnings, (5) total shareholders' equity, and (6) number of shares.

(LO 3) 15. Contrast the effects of a (a) cash dividend, (b) stock dividend, and (c) stock split on a company's (1) assets, (2) liabilities, (3) share capital, (4) retained earnings, (5) total shareholders' equity, and (6) number of shares.

(LO 3) 16. Bella Corporation has 10,000 common shares issued when it announces a 3-for-1 split. Before the split, the shares were trading for $120 per share. (a) After the split, how many shares will be issued? (b) After the split, what will be the likely share price?

(LO 3) 17. When a company declares a cash or stock dividend, a journal entry is recorded but this does not happen when a stock split takes place. Why?

(LO 4) 18. Indicate how each of the following should be reported in (a) the statement of changes in equity and (b) the shareholders' equity section of the statement of financial position: (1) preferred shares, (2) common shares, (3) stock dividends distributable, (4) contributed surplus, (5) retained earnings, and (6) accumulated other comprehensive income.

(LO 4) 19. For what reason might a company restrict its retained earnings? How is a restriction reported in the financial statements?

(LO 4) 20. Distinguish between other comprehensive income and accumulated other comprehensive income. Include in your answer how and where each is reported in the financial statements.

(LO 4) 21. (a) What is the difference between a statement of changes in equity and statement of retained earnings? (b) How do each of these relate to the shareholders' equity section of the statement of financial position?

(LO 4) 22. Distinguish between the content of the (a) shareholders' equity sections and (b) financial statements of a publicly traded company using IFRS and a private company using ASPE.

(LO 5) 23. Indicate whether each of the following is generally considered favourable or unfavourable by a potential investor:
(a) A decrease in the payout ratio
(b) An increase in the dividend yield
(c) A decrease in the return on common shareholders' equity
(d) An increase in basic earnings per share

(LO 5) 24. **The Coca-Cola Company** recently reported dividends per share of U.S. $1.32 and a dividend yield of 2.9%. **PepsiCo Inc.** reported dividends per share of U.S. $2.76 and a dividend yield of 2.7% for the same period. Can you determine which company had the higher share price?

(LO 5) 25. In the calculation of basic earnings per share, why is the weighted average number of common shares used instead of the number of common shares at the end of the year?

(LO 5) 26. Why do the basic earnings per share and return on common shareholders' equity ratios use income available to common shareholders in their numerator rather than net income?

(LO 5) 27. Company A has a payout ratio of 30% and a dividend yield of 2%. Company B has a payout ratio of 50% and a dividend yield of 3%. (a) Which company's shares would be of more interest to an investor wanting a steady dividend income? (b) Would your answer change if the investor had purchased the shares for growth rather than for income?

(LO 5) 28. Company A has a return on assets of 8% but a return on common shareholders' equity of 15%. Company B has the same return on assets of 8% but a return on common shareholders' equity of 9%. How can both of these companies, neither of which has any preferred shares, have the same return on assets but a different return on common shareholders' equity?

▶ BRIEF EXERCISES

Evaluate impact of share issue.
(LO 1)

BE11–1 In November 2015, **Hydro One Limited** issued an IPO on the Toronto Stock Exchange. Shares purchased under the IPO were sold at $20.50 per share. If a shareholder purchased Hydro One's shares in March 2016, they would have paid $24 per share. Explain the impact on Hydro One's financial position of the shares sold (a) under the IPO in November 2015 for $20.50 and (b) on the Toronto Stock Exchange in March 2016 for $24.

Record issue of shares.
(LO 2)

BE11–2 On May 1, Armada Corporation incorporated and authorized 200,000 preferred shares and an unlimited number of common shares. On May 2, Armada issued 2,000 common shares for $15 per share. On June 15, it issued an additional 1,000 common shares for $17 per share. On November 1, Armada issued 200 preferred shares for $30 per share. On December 15, it issued an additional 200 preferred shares for $35 per share. (a) Record the share transactions. (b) Indicate how many shares are authorized and how many are issued at the end of the year for the (1) preferred shares and (2) common shares.

Record the issue and reacquisition of shares.
(LO 2)

BE11–3 On June 8, Dieppe Ltd was incorporated and issued 60,000 common shares for $300,000. On August 19, an additional 15,000 shares were issued for $90,000. On November 2, the company paid $28,800 to reacquire 6,000 common shares and on December 7 it paid $52,000 to reacquire 8,000 common shares. (a) Calculate the average cost of the common shares on June 8, August 19, November 2, and December 7. (b) Prepare the journal entries to record the above transactions.

Record issue of shares for cash and noncash consideration.
(LO 2)

BE11–4 On March 8, Daschen Inc., a publicly traded company, issued 5,000 preferred shares for cash of $30 per share. On April 20, when the shares were trading at $35, the company issued an additional 3,000 preferred shares in exchange for land with a fair value of $110,000. (a) Prepare the journal entries for each transaction. (b) Would your answer change if you were unable to determine the land's fair value on April 20? (c) Would your answer change if Daschen Inc. was a private company using ASPE?

BE11–5 Canaan Limited had 20,000 $2 cumulative preferred shares issued. It was unable to pay any dividend to the preferred shareholders in the current year. (a) What are the dividends in arrears? (b) How would the dividends in arrears be reported in the financial statements? (c) Would your answer to part (a) change if the preferred shares were noncumulative rather than cumulative?

Determine dividends in arrears.
(LO 2)

BE11–6 The Seabee Corporation has 60,000 $2 noncumulative preferred shares that have been issued. It declares a quarterly cash dividend on November 15 to shareholders of record on December 10. The dividend is paid on December 31. Prepare the entries on the appropriate dates to record the cash dividend.

Record cash dividend.
(LO 3)

BE11–7 Satina Corporation has 100,000 common shares that have been issued. It declares a 5% stock dividend on December 1 to shareholders of record on December 20. The shares are issued on January 10. The share price is $15 on December 1, $14.50 on December 20, and $14.75 on January 10. Prepare the entries on the appropriate dates to record the stock dividend.

Record stock dividend.
(LO 3)

BE11–8 In April 2015, **Richelieu Hardware Ltd.** completed a 3-for-1 stock split. Immediately before the split, the company had 19.5 million issued common shares trading at $67.30 per share. (a) How many shares did it have after the stock split? (b) What was the most likely price of the shares after the stock split? (c) How would Richelieu record or report this stock split?

Analyze impact of stock split.
(LO 3)

BE11–9 Indicate whether each of the following transactions would increase (+), decrease (−), or have no effect (NE) on total assets, total liabilities, total shareholders' equity, and the number of shares:

Compare cash dividend, stock dividend, and stock split.
(LO 3)

	Assets	Liabilities	Shareholders' Equity	Number of Shares
(a) Declared cash dividend.				
(b) Paid cash dividend declared in part (a).				
(c) Declared stock dividend.				
(d) Distributed stock dividend declared in part (c).				
(e) Split stock 2-for-1.				

BE11–10 Luxat Corporation reported the following statement of changes in equity accounts for the year ended December 31, 2018.

Determine missing amounts in statement of changes in equity.
(LO 4)

LUXAT CORPORATION
Statement of Changes in Equity
Year Ended December 31, 2018

	Contributed Capital		Retained Earnings	Accumulated Other Comprehensive Income	Total
	Common Shares	Contributed Surplus			
Bal., Jan. 1	$1,500,000	$500,000	$3,000,000	$100,000	$5,100,000
Issued common shares	[1]				[2]
Declared and issued stock dividend	110,000		[3]		[4]
Declared cash dividends			(135,000)		(135,000)
Comprehensive income					
Net income			750,000		[5]
Other comprehensive income				[6]	25,000
Bal., Dec. 31	$2,050,000	$ [7]	$3,505,000	$125,000	$ [8]

Determine the missing amounts for items [1] to [8].

BE11–11 Refer to the data given in BE11–10 for Luxat Corporation. Luxat had an unlimited number of common shares authorized and 550,000 shares issued at December 31. Prepare the shareholders' equity section of its statement of financial position at December 31, 2018.

Prepare shareholders' equity section.
(LO 4)

BE11–12 For the year ended December 31, 2018, Stirling Farms Limited, a private company, reported net income of $150,000. The company declared dividends of $90,000 and paid $80,000 of these dividends during the year. (a) Prepare a statement of retained earnings for the year, assuming the balance in Retained Earnings on January 1, 2018, was $490,000. (b) How would this statement change if Stirling Farms were a publicly traded company?

Prepare statement of retained earnings.
(LO 4)

Evaluate payout ratio.
(LO 5)

BE11–13 Paul Schwartz, president of Schwartz Corporation, believes that it is good practice to maintain a constant pay-out of dividends relative to net income. Last year, net income was $600,000, and the company paid $60,000 in dividends. This year, due to some unusual circumstances, the company had a net income of $2 million. Paul expects next year's net income to be about $700,000. (a) What was Schwartz Corporation's payout ratio last year? (b) If it is to maintain the same payout ratio, what amount of dividends would it pay this year? (c) Is this a good idea? In other words, what are the pros and cons of trying to maintain a constant payout ratio?

Calculate dividend yield.
(LO 5)

BE11–14 **Canadian National Railway** and **Canadian Pacific Railway** have a dividend of $1.25 per common share and $1.40 per common share, respectively. The market price of their shares is $80 per share and $168 per share, respectively. (a) Calculate the dividend yield for each company. (b) Which company would investors prefer if they wished to purchase shares for the purpose of dividend income?

Calculate weighted average number of shares.
(LO 5)

BE11–15 Messier Inc. had 34,000 common shares on January 1, 2018. On May 1, 3,000 common shares were reacquired and retired. On August 31 and November 30, 9,000 and 6,000 common shares were issued, respectively. Calculate (a) the number of common shares issued at December 31, 2018, and (b) the weighted average number of common shares for 2018.

Calculate basic earnings per share.
(LO 5)

BE11–16 Refer to the data for Messier Inc. given in BE11–15. Messier reported net income of $370,000. Messier also had 10,000 $2 cumulative preferred shares, on which the dividend for the current year was declared and paid. Calculate the basic earnings per share.

Calculate basic earnings per share.
(LO 5)

BE11–17 Castera Inc. reported a net income of $800,000 and a weighted average number of common shares of 300,000 for the year. It also had 50,000 $2 preferred shares. Calculate basic earnings per share assuming (a) the preferred shares are cumulative and the dividend was not paid, (b) the preferred shares are noncumulative and the dividend was paid, and (c) the preferred shares are noncumulative and the dividend was not paid.

Calculate return on common shareholders' equity.
(LO 5)

BE11–18 Salliq Ltd. reported the following selected information for the year ended January 31, 2018: net income, $14,000; beginning shareholders' equity, $104,000; and ending shareholders' equity, $122,000. Salliq has no preferred shares. (a) Calculate the return on common shareholders' equity. (b) Explain how your calculation in part (a) would change if Salliq had preferred shares and had paid the preferred shareholders a dividend.

▶ EXERCISES

Interpret stock market listing.
(LO 1)

E11–1 The following is a recent stock market listing for **Metro Inc.** common shares:

365-day		stock	sym	div	high	low	close	chg	vol	yld	p/e ratio
High	low										
44.56	32.87	Metro	MRU	0.56	43.59	43.11	43.56	0.19	216,740	1.29	20.33

Instructions
(a) What is the highest price Metro's shares traded at during the year? The lowest? If you had bought 100 common shares of this company at its lowest price during the year and then sold them at the highest price during the year, what would your income be from such a trade?
(b) What is the annual per-share dividend paid on these shares?
(c) If you had purchased 1,000 common shares at Metro's closing price of the day in the above listing, what would be the total cost of your share purchase?
(d) What was the closing price of Metro's common shares on the previous day?
(e) How many of Metro's common shares were sold on the trading day of the listing?

Record issue of shares.
(LO 2)

E11–2 Santiago Corp., a publicly traded company, had 2,500 preferred shares issued with a balance of $55,000 and 140,000 common shares issued with a balance of $700,000 at the beginning of the year. The following share transactions occurred during the year:

June 12   Issued 50,000 common shares for $6 per share.
July 11   Issued 1,000 preferred shares for $25 per share.
Oct. 1   Issued 10,000 common shares in exchange for land. The common shares were trading for $7 per share on that date. The fair value of the land was estimated to be $75,000.
Nov. 15   Issued 25,000 preferred shares for $28 per share.

Instructions
(a)   Record the above transactions.
(b)   Calculate the number of shares and balance in the account for each of the preferred and common shares at the end of the year.

E11–3   Moosonee Ltd. was incorporated as a private company on January 2, 2018, and is authorized to issue an unlimited number of common shares and $1 preferred shares. The company had the following share transactions in its first month of operations:

Record issue and reacquisition of shares.
(LO 2)

Jan.	6	Issued 200,000 common shares for $1.50 per share.
	12	Issued 50,000 common shares for $1.75 per share.
	17	Issued 10,000 preferred shares for $25 per share.
	18	Issued 500,000 common shares for $2 per share.
	24	Reacquired 200,000 common shares at $1.90 per share.
	31	Issued 10,000 common shares in exchange for $15,000 of legal services.

Instructions
(a)   Record the above transactions.
(b)   What is the number and average cost of the preferred and common shares at the end of January?
(c)   If Moosonee were a publicly traded company, how might the journal entry to record the noncash transaction on January 31 change?

E11–4   Marsh Corporation issued 400,000 $2 cumulative preferred shares. In its first year of operations, it paid $600,000 of dividends to its preferred shareholders. In its second year, the company paid dividends of $400,000 to its preferred shareholders.

Determine dividends in arrears.
(LO 2)

Instructions
(a)   What is the total annual preferred dividend supposed to be for the preferred shareholders?
(b)   Calculate any dividends in arrears in years 1 and 2.
(c)   Explain how dividends in arrears should be reported in the financial statements.
(d)   If the preferred shares were noncumulative rather than cumulative, what is the amount of dividends that the company would be obligated to pay its preferred shareholders in each year?
(e)   Do you think that it is easier for a company to sell preferred shares that pay dividends on a noncumulative or cumulative basis?

E11–5   On January 1, 2018, Tarow Corporation had 80,000 common shares, recorded at $600,000, and retained earnings of $1 million. During the year, the following transactions occurred:

Record and post share and dividend transactions.
(LO 2, 3)

Apr.	2	Issued 5,000 common shares at $20 per share.
June	15	Declared a cash dividend of $0.25 per share to common shareholders of record on June 30, payable on July 10.
Aug.	21	Declared a 5% stock dividend to common shareholders of record on September 5, distributable on September 20. The shares were trading for $22 a share on August 21, $24 on September 5, and $26 on September 20.
Nov.	1	Issued 3,000 common shares at $25 per share.
Dec.	20	Declared a cash dividend of $0.30 per share to common shareholders of record on December 31, payable on January 10.

Instructions
(a)   Record the above transactions for 2018. (*Note*: Closing entries are not required.)
(b)   What is the number of common shares at the end of the year?

E11–6   Laine Inc. is considering one of the three following courses of action: (1) paying a $0.50 cash dividend, (2) distributing a 5% stock dividend, or (3) effecting a 2-for-1 stock split. The current share price is $14 per share.

Compare cash dividend, stock dividend, and stock split.
(LO 3)

Instructions
Help Laine make its decision by completing the following chart (treat each possibility independently):

	Before Action	(1) After Cash Dividend	(2) After Stock Dividend	(3) After Stock Split
Total assets	$1,250,000			
Total liabilities	$ 250,000			
Shareholders' equity				
Common shares	600,000			
Retained earnings	400,000			
Total shareholders' equity	1,000,000			
Total liabilities and shareholders' equity	$1,250,000			
Number of common shares	100,000			

Indicate impact of transactions on shareholders' equity.

(LO 2, 3, 4)

E11–7 Milford Corporation had the following transactions and events:

1. Issued preferred shares for cash.
2. Declared a cash dividend on the preferred shares.
3. Paid the cash dividend declared in transaction (2).
4. Issued common shares for cash.
5. Issued common shares for a noncash exchange of assets.
6. Completed a 2-for-1 stock split of the common shares.
7. Declared a stock dividend on the common shares.
8. Distributed the stock dividend declared in transaction (7).
9. Restricted retained earnings.
10. Reported other comprehensive income from an unrealized gain on investments.

Instructions

Indicate whether each of the above transactions would increase (+), decrease (−), or have no effect (NE) on assets, liabilities, and key categories within shareholders' equity, as shown in the following table. The first one has been done for you as an example.

			Shareholders' Equity			
	Assets	Liabilities	Share Capital	Retained Earnings	Accumulated Other Comprehensive Income	Total Shareholders' Equity
1.	+	NE	+	NE	NE	+

Classify accounts.

(LO 4)

E11–8 The general ledger of Val d'Or Corporation contains the following selected accounts and information:

1. Cash
2. Common shares
3. Other comprehensive income—Revaluation gain from revaluing property, plant, and equipment to fair value
4. Long-term investments
5. Preferred shares
6. Retained earnings
7. Gain on disposal
8. Dividends declared
9. Stock split
10. Stock dividends distributable

Instructions

Indicate whether each of the above accounts should be reported in the statement of changes in equity. If yes, indicate whether the account should be reported in the share capital, retained earnings, or accumulated other comprehensive income section of the statement. If not, indicate in which financial statement (statement of financial position or income statement) and in which section the account should be reported, or write NE (no effect) if the statement is not affected. The first account has been done for you as an example.

		Statement of Changes in Equity				
	Account	Share Capital	Retained Earnings	Accumulated Other Comprehensive Income	Other Financial Statement	Classification
1.	Cash	NE	NE	NE	Statement of financial position	Current assets

Prepare shareholders' equity section.

(LO 4)

E11–9 The following accounts appear in the ledger of Ozabal Inc. after the books are closed at December 31, 2018:

Accumulated other comprehensive loss	$ 50,000
Common shares (unlimited number of shares authorized, 250,000 shares issued)	500,000
Stock dividends distributable	50,000
Contributed surplus	25,000
Preferred shares ($1.25 noncumulative, 100,000 shares authorized, 10,000 shares issued)	250,000
Retained earnings (of which $100,000 is restricted for a plant expansion)	900,000

Instructions

Prepare the shareholders' equity section of Ozabal's statement of financial position, including any required note disclosure.

E11–10 The Blue Canoe Limited reported the following changes to its shareholders' equity accounts for the year ended December 31, 2018.

Prepare statement of changes in equity and shareholders' equity section.

(LO 4)

Accumulated other comprehensive income:		Retained earnings:	
Balance, Jan. 1	$ 90,000	Balance, Jan. 1	$1,500,000
Other comprehensive income	(25,000)	Net income	400,000
Balance, Dec. 31	$ 65,000	Dividends declared	(70,000)
Contibuted surplus:		Balance, Dec. 31	$1,830,000
Balance, Jan. 1	$540,000	Common shares:	
Common shares reaquired	(40,000)	Balance, Jan. 1	$ 800,000
Balance, Dec. 31	$500,000	Shares issued	180,000
		Shares reacquired	(200,000)
		Balance, Dec. 31	$ 780,000

Instructions
(a) Prepare a statement of changes in equity for the year.
(b) Prepare the shareholders' equity section of the balance sheet at December 31.

E11–11 The following selected information is available for two competitors, **Nike, Inc.** and **Adidas AG**:

Calculate and evaluate dividend record.

(LO 5)

(in millions, except for per-share information)	Nike (in U.S. $)	Adidas (in euros)
Market price per share	$62.50	€89.91
Dividends declared and paid	931	320
Dividends per share	1.08	1.60
Net income	3,273	634

Instructions
(a) Calculate the (1) payout and (2) dividend yield ratios for each company.
(b) Which company would investors favour for dividend income purposes? Explain.

E11–12 Chinook Corporation started the year ended November 30, 2018, with 180,000 common shares and no preferred shares issued. The following changes in share capital occurred during the year:

Calculate basic earnings per share.

(LO 5)

Feb. 28 Issued 45,000 common shares for $775,000.
Sept. 4 Issued 60,000 $1 cumulative preferred shares for $1.5 million.
Nov. 1 Issued 18,000 common shares in exchange for land. The shares were trading for $20 on this date and the fair value of the land was $345,000.
  30 Reported net income of $963,750.
  30 Declared the quarterly cash dividend to the preferred shareholders of record on December 14, payable on December 31.

Instructions
(a) Calculate the income available for the common shareholders.
(b) Calculate the weighted average number of common shares for the year.
(c) Calculate the basic earnings per share for the year.

E11–13 Selected financial information (in millions, except per-share information) is available for **CIBC** at October 31:

Calculate and evaluate ratios.

(LO 5)

	2015	2014	2013
Dividends declared and paid to common shareholders	$ 1,708	$ 1,567	$ 1,523
Dividends declared per common share	$ 4.30	$ 3.94	$ 3.81
Income available to common shareholders (equals net income)	$ 3,531	$ 3,131	$ 3,253
Common shareholders' equity	$20,360	$17,588	$16,546
Market price per common share	$100.28	$102.89	$ 88.70
Weighted average number of common shares	397	398	401

Instructions
(a) Calculate the (1) payout, (2) dividend yield, (3) basic earnings per share, and (4) return on common shareholders' equity ratios for the common shareholders for 2015 and 2014.
(b) Using the information in part (a), comment on CIBC's dividend record and earnings performance over the two-year period.

Evaluate ratios.

(LO 5)

E11–14 Selected ratios are shown below for two competing toolmakers, **Stanley Black & Decker, Inc.** and **Snap-On Incorporated.**

	Stanley Black & Decker	Snap-On
Payout ratio	35.9%	26.1%
Dividend yield	2.1%	1.4%
Basic earnings per share (in U.S. dollars)	$5.96	$8.24
Return on common shareholders' equity	14.4%	20.2%

Instructions

Which of the two companies' shares would you prefer to purchase if you were looking for an income-oriented investment to supplement your income? Explain which ratios you used to support your answer. Based on just the information above, which company's shares may have the best chance for future price appreciation?

Evaluate impact of debt on ratios.

(LO 5)

E11–15 You are about to form a corporation that will need $500,000 to start operations. One option (the no-debt option) for the corporation is to raise the $500,000 by selling 50,000 common shares to you. Another option (the debt option) for the corporation would be to borrow $250,000 from you at 4% and to sell you 25,000 common shares for $250,000. You expect the corporation to earn income from operations this year of $80,000 and to incur income tax at a 30% rate. You also expect total assets to remain at $500,000 throughout the year and liabilities to remain at an amount equal to the funds you lent the corporation because no new liabilities will be assumed. Furthermore, any net income will immediately be distributed to you through the payment of dividends. Consequently, retained earnings will be zero at year end.

Instructions

Complete the following information:

	No-Debt Option	Debt Option
Income from operations	$80,000	$80,000
Interest expense (4%)	0	[7]
Income before income tax	[1]	[8]
Income tax expense (30%)	[2]	[9]
Net income	[3]	[10]
Average total assets	$500,000	$500,000
Average common shareholders' equity	$500,000	$250,000
Number of common shares	50,000	25,000
Basic earnings per share	[4]	[11]
Dividends declared	[3]	[10]
Payout ratio	[5]	[12]
Return on common shareholders' equity	[6]	[13]

(a) Calculate the missing amounts for items [1] through [13].
(b) Explain why many of the ratio values you have calculated above are different with each financing option.

► PROBLEMS: SET A

Show impact of transactions on accounts.

(LO 2, 3, 4)

P11–1A The following shareholders' equity accounts are reported by Talty Inc. on January 1, 2018:

Preferred shares ($6 cumulative, 6,000 issued)	$ 600,000
Common shares (500,000 issued)	4,000,000
Retained earnings	1,958,000
Accumulated other comprehensive income	25,000

The following selected transactions, given in chronological order, occurred during the year:
1. Reacquired and retired 20,000 common shares for $12 per share.
2. Issued 10,000 common shares for $14 per share.
3. Issued 5,000 common shares in exchange for equipment. The fair value of the shares was $14 per share. The current value of the equipment could not be reliably determined.
4. Issued 1,000 preferred shares for $100 per share.
5. The annual preferred share cash dividend was declared and paid during the year.
6. Determined that the company had an other comprehensive loss of $5,000 arising from the reversal of a previously recorded revaluation gain on land.

Instructions

For each of the above transactions, indicate its impact on the items in the table that follows. Indicate if the item will increase (+) or decrease (−), and by how much, or if there will be no effect (NE). The first transaction has been done for you as an example.

			Shareholders' Equity			
			Share Capital			Accumulated Other
	Assets	Liabilities	Preferred Shares	Common Shares	Retained Earnings	Comprehensive Income
1.	−$240,000	NE	NE	−$160,000	−$80,000	NE

P11–2A Remmers Corporation, a publicly traded company, was organized on January 1, 2018. It is authorized to issue an unlimited number of $3 noncumulative preferred shares and an unlimited number of common shares. The following share transactions were completed during the company's first year of operations:

Record and post equity transactions; prepare shareholders' equity section.

(LO 2, 3, 4)

Jan.	10	Issued 1,000,000 common shares for $2 per share.
Mar.	1	Issued 20,000 preferred shares for $50 per share.
May	1	Issued 250,000 common shares for $3 per share.
June	1	Reacquired and retired 10,000 common shares at $2 per share. Determine the average cost of each reacquired share to the nearest cent before recording this transaction.
July	24	Issued 33,500 common shares for $120,000 cash and used equipment. The equipment originally cost $30,000. It now has a carrying amount of $15,000 and a current value of $16,000. The common shares were trading for $4 per share on this date.
Sept.	4	Issued 10,000 common shares for $5 per share.
Nov.	1	Issued 4,000 preferred shares for $50 per share.
	20	Reacquired and retired 15,000 common shares at $4 per share. Determine the average cost of each reacquired share to the nearest cent before recording this transaction.
Dec.	14	Declared a $72,000 cash dividend to the preferred shareholders, to shareholders of record on December 31, payable on January 10.
	31	Reported net income of $1.3 million for the year.

Instructions

(a) Record the above transactions for 2018, including any required entries to close dividends declared and net income.
(b) Open T accounts and post to the shareholders' equity accounts.
(c) Prepare the shareholders' equity section of the statement of financial position at December 31.

P11–3A Largent Corporation, a publicly traded company, is authorized to issue 200,000 $4 cumulative preferred shares and an unlimited number of common shares. On January 1, 2018, the general ledger contained the following shareholders' equity accounts:

Record and post equity transactions; prepare statements.

(LO 2, 3, 4)

Preferred shares (8,000 shares issued)	$ 440,000
Common shares (70,000 shares issued)	1,050,000
Contributed surplus	25,000
Retained earnings	800,000
Accumulated other comprehensive income	10,000

The following equity transactions occurred in 2018:

Feb.	6	Issued 10,000 preferred shares for $600,000.
Apr.	6	Issued 20,000 common shares for $570,000.
	27	Reacquired and retired 3,000 common shares at $17 per share.
May	29	Declared a semi-annual cash dividend to the preferred shareholders of record at June 12, payable July 1.
Aug.	22	Issued 9,000 common shares in exchange for a building. At the time of the exchange, the building was valued at $165,000 and the common shares at $150,000.
Dec.	14	The board of directors decided there were insufficient funds to declare the semi-annual dividend to the preferred shareholders.
	31	Net income for the year was $582,000.

Instructions

(a) Record the above transactions, including any entries required to close dividends and net income.
(b) Open T accounts and post to the shareholders' equity accounts.
(c) Prepare the statement of changes in equity for the year.
(d) Prepare the shareholders' equity section of the statement of financial position at December 31, including any required note disclosure.

*Record and post equity
transactions; prepare
statements under ASPE.*

(LO 2, 3, 4)

P11–4A On January 1, 2018, Conway Ltd., a private company, had the following shareholders' equity accounts:

Preferred shares, $1 noncumulative, unlimited number authorized, none issued
Common shares, unlimited number authorized, 3 million issued $3,000,000
Retained earnings   3,800,000

The following selected transactions occurred during 2018:

Jan.	2	Issued 200,000 preferred shares at $25 per share.
Feb.	8	Issued 100,000 common shares in exchange for land. On this date, the current value of the land was $210,000. The common shares have not recently traded, but the last time they traded, they sold for $2.50 per share.
Mar.	5	Declared the quarterly cash dividend to preferred shareholders of record on March 20, payable April 2.
Apr.	18	Issued 400,000 common shares at $3 per share.
June	5	Declared the quarterly cash dividend to preferred shareholders of record on June 20, payable July 1.
Sept.	5	Declared the quarterly cash dividend to preferred shareholders of record on September 20, payable October 1.
Oct.	4	Issued 40,000 preferred shares at $25 per share.
Dec.	5	Declared the quarterly cash dividend to preferred shareholders of record on December 20, payable January 1.
	14	Declared a cash dividend of $0.50 per share to the common shareholders of record on December 31, payable January 10.
	31	Net income for the year was $1 million.

Instructions
(a) Record the above transactions for 2018, including any entries required to close dividends declared and net income to Retained Earnings.
(b) Open T accounts and post to the shareholders' equity accounts.
(c) Prepare a statement of retained earnings for the year.
(d) Prepare the shareholders' equity section of the statement of financial position at December 31.
(e) Conway is a private company following ASPE. If it followed IFRS instead, how might your answers in parts (a) through (d) change?

*Reproduce equity
accounts; prepare
shareholders' equity
section.*

(LO 2, 3, 4)

P11–5A The general ledger of Robichaud Corporation, a publicly traded company, contained the following shareholders' equity accounts in 2018:

	January 1	December 31
Preferred shares (10,000 and 20,000 shares issued, respectively)	$ 500,000	$1,000,000
Common shares (320,000 and 370,000 shares issued, respectively)	2,700,000	3,700,000
Stock dividends distributable	0	407,000
Retained earnings	2,980,000	3,345,000

A review of the accounting records for the year ended December 31, 2018, reveals the following information:
1. On January 1, 10,000 additional $5 noncumulative preferred shares were issued for $50 each. An unlimited number are authorized.
2. On October 1, 50,000 common shares were sold for cash at $20 per share. An unlimited number are authorized.
3. The annual preferred shareholders' cash dividend was declared and paid during the year.
4. On December 31, a 5% stock dividend was declared on common shares when the share price was $22. The stock dividend is distributable on January 20.
5. Net income for the year was $872,000.
6. On December 31, the board of directors authorized a $500,000 restriction on retained earnings for a plant expansion.

Instructions
(a) Using T accounts, determine the transactions that explain the movement in the Preferred Shares, Common Shares, Dividends Declared, Stock Dividends Distributable, and Retained Earnings general ledger accounts for the year. (*Hint*: Although not required, you may find it helpful to prepare journal entries.)
(b) Prepare the shareholders' equity section of the statement of financial position at December 31, including any required note disclosure.

*Compare impact of cash
dividend, stock dividend,
and stock split.*

(LO 3)

P11–6A The condensed statement of financial position of Laporte Corporation reports the following amounts:

LAPORTE CORPORATION
Statement of Financial Position (partial)
June 30, 2018

Total assets		$16,000,000
Total liabilities		$ 6,000,000
Shareholders' equity		
Common shares, unlimited number authorized, 400,000 issued	$2,000,000	
Retained earnings	8,000,000	10,000,000
Total liabilities and shareholders' equity		$16,000,000

The common shares are currently trading for $30 per share. Laporte wants to assess the impact of three possible alternatives:
1. Payment of a $1.50 per share cash dividend
2. Distribution of a 5% stock dividend
3. A 3-for-2 stock split

Instructions
(a) Determine the impact of each alternative on (1) assets, (2) liabilities, (3) common shares, (4) retained earnings, (5) total shareholders' equity, and (6) the number of shares.
(b) Identify the advantages and disadvantages of each alternative for the company.

P11–7A On January 1, 2018, Wirth Corporation, a publicly traded company, had these shareholders' equity accounts:

Common shares (unlimited number of shares authorized, 220,000 shares issued)	$2,200,000
Retained earnings	1,080,000
Accumulated other comprehensive income	120,000

Record and post dividend transactions; prepare statements.

(LO 3, 4)

During the year, the following transactions occurred:
Jan. 15 Declared a $1 per share cash dividend to shareholders of record on January 31, payable February 15.
Apr. 16 Declared a 10% stock dividend to shareholders of record on April 30, distributable May 15. On April 16, April 30, and May 15, the share prices were $15, $13.50, and $14, respectively.
Oct. 1 Effected a 2-for-1 stock split. On October 1, the share price was $20.
Dec. 31 Determined that net income for the year was $700,000.

Instructions
(a) Record the above transactions, including any required entries to close dividends and net income.
(b) Open T accounts as required and post to the shareholders' equity accounts.
(c) Prepare a statement of changes in equity for the year.
(d) Prepare the shareholders' equity section of the statement of financial position at December 31.

P11–8A Gualtieri Inc.'s shareholders' equity accounts were as follows at the beginning of the current fiscal year, August 1, 2017:

Calculate basic earnings per share.

(LO 5)

$1 noncumulative preferred shares (100,000 shares issued)	$2,500,000
Common shares (350,000 shares issued)	3,500,000
Retained earnings	2,500,000
Total shareholders' equity	$8,500,000

During the year, the following selected transactions occurred:
Oct. 1 Reacquired 24,000 common shares for $20 per share.
Dec. 1 Issued 60,000 common shares for $25 per share.
Feb. 1 Issued 10,000 common shares for $26 per share.
June 20 Declared the annual preferred cash dividend to shareholders of record on July 10, payable on July 31.
July 31 Net income for the year ended July 31, 2018, was $1,280,000.

Instructions
(a) Calculate the weighted average number of common shares for the year.
(b) Calculate the basic earnings per share.
(c) Why is it important to use a weighted average number of shares in the calculation of basic earnings per share? Why not just use the number of shares issued at year end?
(d) Would your answer to part (b) change if the preferred share dividend had not been declared on June 20? Explain.

Evaluate ratios.

(LO 5)

P11–9A The following summary of the payout, dividend yield, and basic earnings per share ratios is available for four years ended December 31 for **Cineplex Inc.**:

	2015	2014	2013	2012
Payout ratio	72.3%	122.3%	106.0%	67.2%
Dividend yield	3.2%	3.3%	3.2%	4.18%
Basic earnings per share	$2.13	$1.21	$1.33	$1.98

Instructions

(a) Determine the common dividends per share in each of the years shown above. What are some possible reasons that Cineplex's dividend payout ratio and its dividend yield ratio declined in 2015?

(b) Why do you think Cineplex's payout ratio rose so much in 2013?

(c) If you were one of Cineplex's creditors, what would you think about the company paying out dividends in 2013 and 2014 that exceeded basic earnings per share? Explain.

(d) Derive the company's share price for 2015 and 2014 by using the common dividends per share calculated in part (a) above. How did investors trading Cineplex shares react to the change in the basic earnings per share in 2015?

Calculate and evaluate ratios.

(LO 5)

P11–10A The following selected information (in millions, except for per-share information) is available for **National Bank of Canada** for the year ended October 31:

	2015	2014
Weighted average number of common shares	333.1	331.1
Income available to common shareholders (equals net income)	$1,574	$1,498
Dividends declared and paid per common share	2.04	1.88
Dividends declared and paid on common shares	672	616
Average common shareholders' equity	9,806	8,778
Market price per common share	43.31	52.68
Industry averages were as follows:		
Payout ratio	45.5%	44.8%
Dividend yield	4.3%	3.8%
Basic earnings per share	n/a	n/a
Return on common shareholders' equity	13.6%	14.7%

Instructions

(a) Calculate the following ratios for the common shareholders for each fiscal year:
1. Payout ratio
2. Dividend yield
3. Basic earnings per share
4. Return on common shareholders' equity

(b) Comment on the above ratios for 2015 in comparison with the prior year, and in comparison with the industry.

Evaluate profitability ratios.

(LO 5)

P11–11A Selected ratios for two companies operating in the energy industry follow, along with the industry averages:

	Petro-Boost	World Oil	Industry Average
Profit margin	10.0%	8.4%	10.9%
Return on common shareholders' equity	15.1%	29.6%	11.3%
Return on assets	11.0%	12.6%	5.5%
Asset turnover	1.1 times	1.5 times	0.5 times
Basic earnings per share	$4.06	$4.38	n/a
Price-earnings ratio	14.2 times	17.1 times	13.0 times
Payout ratio	12.3%	9.9%	0.2%
Dividend yield	1.9%	0.7%	1.2%

Instructions

(a) Explain, using the asset turnover and profit margin ratios, why World Oil has a higher return on assets than Petro-Boost and the industry average. (*Hint*: You might find it helpful to review how these three ratios are related in Chapter 9.)

(b) What is the most likely reason that World Oil has the largest difference between its return on common shareholders' equity and its return on assets?

(c) You would like to invest in the shares of one of the two companies. Your goal is to have regular income from your investment that will help pay your tuition fees for the next few years. Which of the companies is a better choice for you? Explain.

(d) Assume that, instead of looking for regular income, you are looking for growth in the share value so that you can resell the shares at a gain in the future. Now which of the two companies is better for you? Explain.

▶ PROBLEMS: SET B

P11–1B The following shareholders' equity accounts are reported by Branch Inc. on January 1, 2018:

Preferred shares ($4 noncumulative, 35,000 issued)	$ 350,000
Common shares (150,000 issued)	2,400,000
Retained earnings	1,276,000
Accumulated other comprehensive income	15,000

Show impact of transactions on accounts.

(LO 2, 3, 4)

The following selected transactions, given in chronological order, occurred during the year:
1. Reacquired and retired 20,000 common shares for $26 per share.
2. Issued 10,000 common shares for $30 per share.
3. Issued 500 preferred shares for $100 per share.
4. Issued 1,000 common shares in exchange for land. The fair value of the shares was $30 per share. The current value of the land was $29,000.
5. Declared and paid the preferred shareholders a $2 per share cash dividend.
6. Determined that the company had other comprehensive income of $5,000 from the revaluation of land.

Instructions
For each of the above transactions, indicate its impact on the items in the table below. Indicate if the item will increase (+) or decrease (−), and by how much, or if there will be no effect (NE). The first transaction has been done for you as an example.

			Shareholders' Equity			
			Share Capital			Accumulated Other
	Assets	Liabilities	Preferred Shares	Common Shares	Retained Earnings	Comprehensive Income
1.	−$520,000	NE	NE	−$320,000	−$200,000	NE

P11–2B Wetland Corporation, a publicly traded company, was organized on June 1, 2017. It is authorized to issue an unlimited number of $4 cumulative preferred shares and an unlimited number of common shares. The following share transactions were completed during the company's first year of operations:

Record and post equity transactions; prepare shareholders' equity section.

(LO 2, 3, 4)

June	5	Issued 240,000 common shares for $4 per share.
Aug.	21	Issued 15,000 preferred shares for $100 per share.
Sept.	15	Issued 60,000 common shares in exchange for land. The asking price of the land was $300,000 and the current value was $285,000. The common shares were trading for $4.25 per share on this date.
Oct.	20	Reacquired and retired 20,000 common shares for $4 per share.
Nov.	20	Issued 220,000 common shares for $4.95 per share.
Mar.	9	Reacquired and retired 25,000 common shares for $5 per share. Determine the average cost of each reacquired share to the nearest cent before recording this transaction.
Apr.	16	Issued 6,000 preferred shares for $100 per share.
May	15	Declared the annual preferred cash dividend to the preferred shareholders, to shareholders of record on May 30, payable on June 10.
	31	Reported net income of $250,000 for the year.

Instructions
(a) Record the above transactions for the year ended May 31, 2018, including any required entries to close dividends declared and net income.
(b) Open T accounts and post to the shareholders' equity accounts.
(c) Prepare the shareholders' equity section of the statement of financial position at May 31.

P11–3B Ujjal Corporation, a publicly traded company, is authorized to issue an unlimited number of $5 noncumulative preferred shares and an unlimited number of common shares. On February 1, 2018, the general ledger contained the following shareholders' equity accounts:

Record and post equity transactions; prepare statements.

(LO 2, 3, 4)

Preferred shares (44,000 shares issued)	$ 440,000
Common shares (70,000 shares issued)	1,050,000
Contributed surplus	75,000
Retained earnings	1,000,000
Accumulated other comprehensive income	65,000

The following equity transactions occurred during the year ended January 31, 2019:

Feb.	28	Issued 1,500 preferred shares for $150,000.
Apr.	11	Issued 100,000 common shares for $3.5 million.
May	25	Issued 2,500 common shares in exchange for land. At the time of the exchange, the land was valued at $85,000 and the common shares at $87,500.
Nov.	26	Reacquired and retired 10,000 common shares for $24 each. Determine the average cost of each reacquired share to the nearest cent before recording this transaction.
Dec.	31	Declared a $2.50 per share cash dividend to the preferred shareholders of record at January 15, payable February 1.
Jan.	31	Incurred a net loss of $5,000 for the year.

Instructions

(a) Record the above transactions for the year ended January 31, 2019, including any entries required to close dividends declared and net loss.
(b) Open T accounts and post to the shareholders' equity accounts.
(c) Prepare the statement of changes in equity for the year.
(d) Prepare the shareholders' equity section of the statement of financial position at January 31, 2019.

Record and post equity transactions; prepare statements under ASPE.

(LO 2, 3, 4)

P11–4B On January 1, 2018, Schipper Ltd., a private company, had the following shareholders' equity accounts:

Preferred shares, $2 noncumulative, unlimited number authorized, none issued	
Common shares, unlimited number authorized, 200,000 issued	$300,000
Retained earnings	990,000

The following selected transactions occurred during 2018:

Jan.	2	Issued 20,000 preferred shares for $50 per share.
Mar.	10	Declared the quarterly cash dividend to preferred shareholders of record on March 22, payable April 2.
June	10	Declared the quarterly cash dividend to preferred shareholders of record on June 22, payable July 2.
Aug.	12	Issued 10,000 common shares for $7.30 per share.
Sept.	10	Declared the quarterly cash dividend to preferred shareholders of record on September 22, payable October 1.
Oct.	8	Issued 10,000 preferred shares at $50 per share.
	15	Issued 2,000 common shares in exchange for equipment. The common shares had not traded recently but were valued at $7.60 per share on the last date they had traded. The value of the equipment was $15,000 on October 15.
Dec.	10	The fourth-quarter cash dividend to preferred shareholders was not declared or paid.
	31	A net loss of $50,000 was reported for the year.

Instructions

(a) Record the above transactions for 2018, including any required entries to close dividends and net loss.
(b) Open T accounts and post to the shareholders' equity accounts.
(c) Prepare a statement of retained earnings for the year.
(d) Prepare the shareholders' equity section of the statement of financial position at December 31.
(e) Schipper is a private company following ASPE. If it followed IFRS instead, how might your answers in parts (a) through (d) change?

Reproduce equity accounts; prepare shareholders' equity section.

(LO 2, 3, 4)

P11–5B The general ledger of Maggio Corporation, a publicly traded company, contained the following shareholders' equity accounts in 2018:

	January 1	December 31
Preferred shares (15,000 and 15,000 shares issued, respectively)	$ 750,000	$ 750,000
Common shares (255,000 and 291,500 shares issued, respectively)	3,210,000	3,857,000
Retained earnings	980,000	1,373,000

A review of the accounting records for the year ended December 31, 2018, reveals the following information:

1. On March 1, 20,000 common shares were sold for $17.50 per share. An unlimited number are authorized.
2. On August 18, a 6% stock dividend was declared for 16,500 common shares when the share price was $18. The stock dividend was distributed on September 25.
3. The preferred shares are $4 cumulative. An unlimited number of preferred shares are authorized. The quarterly preferred shareholders' cash dividend was declared and paid on the last day of each quarter.
4. Net income for the year was $750,000.
5. On December 31, the directors authorized a $200,000 restriction on retained earnings in accordance with a debt covenant.

Instructions

(a) Using T accounts, determine the transactions that explain the movement in the Preferred Shares, Common Shares, Dividends Declared, Stock Dividends Distributable, and Retained Earnings general ledger accounts for the year. (*Hint:* Although not required, you may find it helpful to prepare journal entries.)

(b) Prepare the shareholders' equity section of the statement of financial position at December 31, including any required note disclosure.

P11–6B The condensed statement of financial position of Erickson Corporation reports the following amounts:

Compare impact of cash dividend, stock dividend, and stock split.

(LO 3)

ERICKSON CORPORATION
Statement of Financial Position (partial)
January 31, 2019

Total assets		$9,000,000
Total liabilities		$2,500,000
Shareholders' equity		
Common shares, unlimited number authorized, 500,000 issued	$3,000,000	
Retained earnings	3,500,000	6,500,000
Total liabilities and shareholders' equity		$9,000,000

The common shares are currently trading for $15 per share. Erickson wants to assess the impact of three possible alternatives on the corporation and its shareholders:

1. Payment of a $1 per share cash dividend
2. Distribution of a 5% stock dividend
3. A 2-for-1 stock split

Instructions

(a) Determine the impact of each alternative on (1) assets, (2) liabilities, (3) common shares, (4) retained earnings, (5) total shareholders' equity, and (6) the number of shares.

(b) Identify the advantages and disadvantages of each alternative for the company.

P11–7B On January 1, 2018, Stengel Corporation, a publicly traded company, had these shareholders' equity accounts:

Record and post dividend transactions; prepare statements.

(LO 3, 4)

Common shares (unlimited number of shares authorized, 150,000 issued)	$3,400,000
Retained earnings	1,800,000
Accumulated other comprehensive loss	250,000

During the year, the following transactions occurred:

Feb.	1	Declared a $1 per share cash dividend to shareholders of record on February 15, payable March 1.
Apr.	2	Effected a 3-for-1 stock split. On April 2, the share price was $36.
July	2	Declared a 5% stock dividend to shareholders of record on July 16, distributable July 31. On July 2, July 16, and July 31, the share prices were $14, $13.50, and $13.75, respectively.
Dec.	31	Determined that net income for the year was $800,000.

Instructions

(a) Record the above transactions, including any entries required to close dividends and net income.

(b) Open T accounts as required and post to the shareholders' equity accounts.

(c) Prepare a statement of changes in equity for the year.

(d) Prepare the shareholders' equity section of the statement of financial position at December 31.

P11–8B Blue Bay Logistics Ltd.'s shareholders' equity accounts were as follows at the beginning of the current fiscal year, April 1, 2017:

Calculate basic earnings per share.

(LO 5)

$1 cumulative preferred shares (78,000 shares issued)	$1,950,000
Common shares (500,000 shares issued)	3,750,000
Retained earnings	1,500,000
Total shareholders' equity	$7,200,000

During the year, the following selected transactions occurred:

May	1	Reacquired and retired 12,000 common shares for $11 per share.
June	1	Issued 6,000 common shares for $12 per share.
July	1	Issued 50,000 common shares for $13 per share.
Feb.	28	Declared the annual preferred cash dividend to shareholders of record on March 12, payable on April 1.
Mar.	31	Net income for the year ended March 31, 2018, was $1,016,750.

Instructions

(a) Calculate the weighted average number of common shares for the year.

(b) Calculate the basic earnings per share.

(c) Why is it important to use income available to common shareholders in the calculation of basic earnings per share? Why not just use net income?

(d) Would your answer to part (b) change if the preferred share dividend had not been declared on February 28? Explain.

Evaluate ratios.

(LO 5)

P11–9B The following summary of the payout, dividend yield, and basic earnings per share ratios is available for a three-year period for **Gildan Activewear Inc.**:

	2015	2014	2013
Payout ratio	32.7%	15.5%	13.6%
Dividend yield	0.84%	0.75%	0.75%
Basic earnings per share (U.S. $)	$1.01	$1.48	$1.32

Instructions

(a) Using the information provided above, determine the dividends declared and paid per common share in each year (assume there were no preferred share dividends). Why do you think dividends declared and paid per common share changed each year? (*Hint:* You can determine dividends per share by using basic earnings per share and the payout ratio).

(b) Do you think most companies would reduce dividends declared on common shares when basic earnings per share is declining? Why or why not?

(c) Derive the company's market share price at the end of each of the three years shown above by using the common dividends per share calculated in part (a) above and the dividend yield provided. Why do you think that the company's dividend yield increased in 2015?

(d) If you were an investor looking for dividend income, would you be happy with Gildan's dividend policy? Explain.

Calculate and evaluate ratios.

(LO 5)

P11–10B The following selected information (in millions, except for per-share information) is available for **Bank of Nova Scotia** for the year ended October 31:

	2015	2014
Weighted average number of common shares	1,210	1,214
Income available to common shareholders (equals net income)	$7,213	$7,298
Dividends declared and paid per common share	2.72	2.56
Dividends declared and paid on common shares	3,289	3,110
Average common shareholders' equity	47,025	42,565
Market price per common share	61.49	69.02
Industry averages were as follows:		
Payout ratio	45.5%	44.8%
Dividend yield	4.3%	3.8%
Basic earnings per share	n/a	n/a
Return on common shareholders' equity	13.6%	14.7%

Instructions

(a) Calculate the following ratios for the common shareholders for each fiscal year:

1. Payout ratio
2. Dividend yield
3. Basic earnings per share
4. Return on common shareholders' equity

(b) Comment on the above ratios for 2015 in comparison with the prior year, and in comparison with the industry.

Evaluate profitability ratios.

(LO 5)

P11–11B Selected ratios for two retailers follow, along with the industry averages:

	Bargain Hunters	Discount Paradise	Industry Average
Profit margin	6.8%	3.5%	3.7%
Return on common shareholders' equity	24.9%	22.4%	20.8%
Return on assets	10.2%	8.8%	9.2%
Asset turnover	1.5 times	2.5 times	2.5 times
Basic earnings per share	$3.30	$2.49	n/a
Price-earnings ratio	12.3 times	17.0 times	16.3 times
Payout ratio	9.4%	25.0%	19.3%
Dividend yield	0.8%	2.5%	1.2%

Instructions

(a) Explain, using the asset turnover and profit margin ratios, why Bargain Hunters has a higher return on assets than Discount Paradise and the industry average. (*Hint:* You might find it helpful to review how these three ratios are related in Chapter 9.) What is the most likely reason Bargain Hunters has the largest difference between its return on common shareholders' equity and its return on assets?

(b) You would like to invest in the shares of one of the two companies. Your goal is to have regular income from your investment that will help pay your tuition fees for the next few years. Which of the two companies is a better choice for you? Explain.

(c) Assume that, instead of looking for regular income, you are looking for growth in the share value so that you can resell the shares at a gain in the future. Now which of the two companies is better for you? Explain.

ACCOUNTING CYCLE | REVIEW

ACR11–1 Hampton Corporation's statement of financial position at December 31, 2017, is presented below.

Prepare and post transaction, adjusting, and closing entries; prepare adjusted trial balance; prepare financial statements.

(LO 2, 3, 4)

HAMPTON CORPORATION
Statement of Financial Position
December 31, 2017

Cash	$ 24,000	Accounts payable	$ 55,600
Accounts receivable	45,500	Mortgage payable	80,000
Allowance for doubtful accounts	(1,500)	Common shares, unlimited number	
Inventory	70,000	authorized, 3,000 issued	30,000
Supplies	4,400	Retained earnings	127,400
Land	40,000	Accumulated other comprehensive	
Buildings	142,000	income	9,400
Accumulated depreciation	(22,000)		
	$302,400		$302,400

During 2018, the following transactions occurred.

1. Hampton issued 500 shares of $2.80 cumulative preferred shares for $50,000. Hampton is authorized to issue 50,000 preferred shares.
2. Hampton also issued 500 common shares for $30,000.
3. Hampton sold inventory for $320,000 on account and $100,000 for cash. Hampton uses a perpetual inventory system and its cost of goods sold for this total transaction was $250,000.
4. Hampton collected $296,000 from customers on account.
5. Hampton bought $35,100 of supplies on account.
6. Purchased $330,000 of inventory on account, terms 2/10, n/30.
7. Hampton paid $322,000 on accounts payable related to purchases of merchandise in transaction 6, within the 10-day discount period.
8. Paid salaries of $88,200.
9. An account receivable of $1,700, which originated in 2017, was written off as uncollectible.
10. Paid $2,000 on the mortgage principal during the year, and $4,000 of interest.
11. Near the end of the current fiscal year, Hampton declared the annual preferred share cash dividend of $1,400 and a $4,200 common share cash dividend, to shareholders of record on January 13, 2019, payable on January 31, 2019.

Adjustment data:

1. A count of supplies indicates that $5,900 of supplies remain unused at year end.
2. Estimated uncollectible accounts were $3,500 at year end.
3. Depreciation is recorded on the building on a straight-line basis based on a 30-year life and a residual value of $10,000.
4. Interest of $350 is owed on the mortgage at year end. The current portion of the mortgage due is $2,500.
5. The bank statement included a service charge of $3,000.
6. Income tax of $6,000 is estimated to be due.

Instructions

(a) Record the 2018 summary transactions numbered (1) through (11).
(b) Set up T accounts, enter any opening balances, and post the general journal entries prepared in part (a).
(c) Record and post the adjusting journal entries (1) through (6) shown above at December 31, assuming adjusting entries are prepared annually.

(d) Prepare an adjusted trial balance as at December 31.
(e) Prepare (1) an income statement, (2) a statement of changes in equity, and (3) a statement of financial position.
(f) Prepare and post any required closing journal entries.

EXPAND YOUR | CRITICAL THINKING

CT11–1 Financial Reporting Case

The financial statements of **The North West Company Inc.** are presented in Appendix A at the end of this book.

Instructions
(a) Using the statement of earnings (income statement), answer the following questions:
  1. What amount did the company report as basic earnings per share for the years ending January 31, 2016 and 2015?
  2. What was its weighted average number of shares for each year?
(b) Review Note 15: Share Capital and answer the following questions:
  1. How many common shares and preferred shares has the company authorized?
  2. How many common shares had been issued on January 31, 2016 and 2015? How does the number of issued shares compare with the weighted average number of shares determined in part (a) (2) above?
  3. On average, what amount did the company receive for each common share that it has issued as at January 1, 2016?
(c) Using the statement of changes in shareholders' equity, answer the following questions:
  1. Did North West report other comprehensive income or loss for the years ended January 31, 2016 and 2015? If so, how much?
  2. Did the company declare any dividends for the years ended January 31 2016, and 2015? If so, how much?

CT11–2 Financial Analysis Case

Boston Pizza Royalties Income Fund is a public company that has over 340 Boston Pizza locations in Canada. **Pizza Pizza Limited** is a privately held company that has over 500 locations in Canada.

Instructions
(a) Why do you think the two companies chose different types of ownership structure?
(b) When Boston Pizza or Pizza Pizza purchases new restaurants, part of the payment may be in shares of the company. How would Boston Pizza determine the fair value of its shares (which it calls units) for this purpose? How would Pizza Pizza determine the fair value of its shares? Which fair value measure would be the more reliable?
(c) Because Boston Pizza is a public company, it uses IFRS and is required to disclose basic earnings per share. Pizza Pizza uses ASPE and is not required to

report basic earnings per share. Why do you think the standard setters do not require private companies to disclose their basic earnings per share?

CT11–3 Professional Judgement Case

This case can be assigned as a group activity. Additional instructions and material for this activity can be found on the Instructor Resource site and in WileyPLUS.

Depinder Singh is a friend of yours who has worked at a number of restaurants. He has always wanted to own his own business and his dream can now come true because he just won $1 million in a lottery. There are two restaurants (one is small and one is large) currently operating that are available for purchase on January 1. Regardless of which one he buys, Depinder will set up a business that will have a December 31 year end. The business will be financed with his winnings from the lottery and the business will then buy all of the assets of one of the two restaurants. Depinder is not sure if the money he puts into the business should consist completely of debt or equity. He believes that the assets will cost $1 million for the small restaurant and $2 million for the large restaurant. Revenues for the first year are expected to be equal to the value of the assets purchased. Operating expenses are expected to be 85% of sales, and the corporate income tax rate is calculated at 25% of income before income tax. Interest on any loans (whether from Depinder or from the bank) will be 6% and any net income earned by the corporation will be paid out as dividends.

Depinder needs your help in assessing the following three options:

1. His business is formed as a corporation with $1 million of common shares and no debt. The assets of the small restaurant are then purchased by the business.
2. His business is formed as a corporation with $1 of common shares and a $999,999 loan from Depinder. The assets of the small restaurant are then purchased by the business.
3. His business is formed as a corporation with $1 million of common shares and a $1-million loan from the bank. The assets of the large restaurant are then purchased.

Instructions
(a) For each of the three options listed above, prepare the income statement that you would expect to see for the first year of the company's operations.
(b) Calculate the return on common shareholders' equity for the first year for each option above. Which option results in the best return? Explain why.

(c) Based on your results in part (a) above, how much cash (before personal income tax) would Depinder have personally (not in the corporation) under each option if all of the net income earned by the company is paid out to him at the end of the year as a dividend?

(d) Without calculating any amounts, what do you think would happen to the return on common shareholders' equity if the operating expenses were 110% of revenue and the company suffered a loss? Would the return be better or worse if the company had more debt?

(e) Without calculating any amounts, how would the income statement change if Depinder did not borrow $1 million from the bank, but obtained those funds from an uncle who bought preferred shares in the corporation and wanted a 5% dividend yield?

(f) Following from part (e) above, if the uncle insisted on being able to sell the preferred shares back to the company at a time of his (the uncle's) choosing, would the preferred shares be classified as debt or equity on the statement of financial position?

(g) Without doing any calculations, if Depinder bought the small restaurant, operated it as a proprietorship rather than incorporating it, and did not borrow any money, how would the projected income statement change from that indicated in your answer to Option 1 in part (a) above?

CT11–4 Ethics Case

Flambeau Corporation has paid 60 consecutive quarterly cash dividends (15 years' worth). The past six months have been a real cash drain on the company, however, as profit margins have been greatly narrowed by increasing competition. With a cash balance that is only enough to meet day-to-day operating needs, the president, Vince Ramsey, has decided that a stock dividend instead of a cash dividend should be declared. He tells Flambeau's financial vice-president, Janice Rahn, to issue a press release stating that the company is extending its consecutive dividend record with the declaration of a 5% stock dividend. "Write the press release convincing the shareholders that the stock dividend is just as good as a cash dividend," he orders. "Just watch our share price rise when we announce the stock dividend; it must be a good thing if that happens."

Instructions

(a) Who are the stakeholders in this situation?

(b) What is the effect of a stock dividend on a corporation's shareholders' equity accounts?

(c) Will the share price rise if a stock dividend is declared, as the president expects?

(d) Is there anything unethical about President Ramsey's intentions or actions?

CT11–5 Financial Analysis Case

John Applewood is evaluating some financing alternatives that are available to his company as it begins its operations. The company has already issued 500 common shares at $100 per share. Now John's accountant has prepared projected year-end financial statements using three different alternatives to obtain an additional $50,000: (1) borrow $50,000 at the beginning of the year with repayment terms of $10,000 per year and interest at 6% per year; (2) issue 500 common shares for $100 per share ($50,000 in total) at the beginning of the year; and (3) issue 500 $6 noncumulative preferred shares for $100 per share ($50,000 in total) at the beginning of the year.

Selected information related to each of these three alternatives follows:

	Alternative 1 (Borrow $50,000)	Alternative 2 (Issue $50,000 common shares)	Alternative 3 (Issue $50,000 preferred shares)
Total assets, end of year	$195,280	$207,680	$204,680
Total liabilities, end of year	$ 71,980	$ 31,980	$ 31,980
Total shareholders' equity			
Preferred shares, beg. of year	$ 0	$ 0	$ 0
Issue of 500 shares			50,000
Preferred shares, end of year	0	0	50,000
Common shares, beg. of year	50,000	50,000	50,000
Issue of 500 shares	0	50,000	0
Common shares, end of year	50,000	100,000	50,000
Retained earnings, beg. of year	51,700	51,700	51,700
Add: Net income	21,600	24,000	24,000
Less: Preferred dividends declared	0	0	3,000
Retained earnings, end of year	73,300	75,700	72,700

Instructions

(a) Using the information provided above, assist John by calculating the debt to total assets, return on common shareholders' equity, and basic earnings per share ratios for each alternative at the end of year.

(b) Based upon your calculations in part (a), which alternative provides for the least amount of debt? Why?

(c) Which alternative provides for the highest return on common shareholders' equity? The highest basic earnings per share?

(d) If you were John, at the beginning of the year, which alternative would you choose? Why?

CT11–6 Serial Case

(*Note:* This is a continuation of the serial case from Chapters 1 through 10.)

Doug, Bev, and Emily are thrilled with the success of ABC. That success, however, has meant that the Anthonys have had no time to enjoy personal interests. When Emily was hired, Doug and Bev believed that they would have more time to take holidays, leaving Emily in charge. Because of the growth in the business and the service contract with Software Solutions Inc., that has not happened.

Software Solutions has increased the volume of services required on a monthly basis, and the business is trying to keep up with the demand. Doug, Bev, and Emily recognize that additional help is needed with running the business. Currently, each of them owns 100 shares of the 300 common shares issued.

Emily's brother, Daniel, has worked in sales and marketing in an international city for a number of years. After being away from Canada for over a decade, he has a keen interest in returning home and getting involved in the family business. He believes that his sales and marketing experience will prove to be a great resource that ABC can rely upon as it continues to experience significant growth. Daniel would like to purchase a 25% interest in the company in exchange for cash.

The share capital and retained earnings of ABC Ltd. at July 1, 2017, are as follows:

Share capital
  $6 cumulative preferred shares, 10,000
    shares authorized, none issued
  Common shares, unlimited number of
    shares authorized, 300 shares issued $ 300
Retained earnings   177,834

Net income for the year ended June 30, 2018, was $156,069. In addition, a dividend of $60,000 was declared on June 15, 2018, to common shareholders of record on June 20, payable on June 30. ABC decides to issue 100 common shares to Daniel for $1,250 per share, effective at the close of business on June 30, 2018. After the issue of shares to Daniel, each member of the Anthony family will hold a 25% interest in the common shares of ABC.

Instructions
(a) Prepare the journal entries required for the dividend declared on June 15, 2018, and paid on June 30. Who will receive the dividend to be paid on June 30, and for what amount?
(b) Prepare the journal entry to record the issue of common shares to Daniel on June 30, 2018, in exchange for $1,250 cash per share.
(c) Prepare a statement of retained earnings for the year ended June 30, 2018. If ABC followed IFRS rather than ASPE, would it still have to prepare a statement of retained earnings? Explain.
(d) Prepare the shareholders' equity section of the statement of financial position at June 30, 2018.

▶ ANSWERS TO CHAPTER PRACTICE QUESTIONS

DO IT! 11-1
Corporation
Characteristics

1. False. The liability of shareholders is normally limited to their investment in the corporation.
2. True.
3. False. The authorization of share capital does not result in a journal entry; only the actual issue of shares by the company results in a journal entry.
4. False. The company makes no journal entry to record the sale of common shares owned by one shareholder to another. It only records the change of ownership.
5. True.
6. True.
7. True.
8. False. In general, Canadian companies have shares with no par value, which means that the amount recorded for them is equal to the proceeds received when the shares were issued rather than some predetermined value.
9. True.
10. True.

DO IT! 11-2
Share Transactions

(a)	July 2	Professional Fees Expense		8,000	
		Common Shares			8,000
		(To record issue of 1,000 common shares in payment of legal bill)			
(b)	Oct. 1	Cash (2,500 × $30)		75,000	
		Preferred Shares			75,000
		(To record issue of 2,500 preferred shares)			

(c) Number of common shares: 120,000 (Jan. 1) + 1,000 (July 2) = 121,000
Balance in Common Shares account: $960,000 (Jan. 1) + $8,000 (July 2) = $968,000
Average cost = $968,000 ÷ 121,000 shares = $8 per share. Note that this average cost will not change after shares are reacquired. The average cost can only change if more shares are issued at a price that is not $8 or if a stock split or dividend occurs.

(d)	Dec. 3	Common Shares (5,000 × $8)		40,000	
		Cash (5,000 × $7)			35,000
		Contributed Surplus			5,000
		(To record reacquisition and retirement of 5,000 common shares)			

(e) Dec. 18

Common Shares (10,000 × $8)		80,000	
Contributed Surplus		5,000	
Retained Earnings		5,000	
Cash (10,000 × $9)			90,000
(To record reacquisition and retirement of 10,000 common shares)			

(f) Preferred shares: 10,000 (Jan. 1) + 2,500 (Oct. 1) = 12,500

(g) Oct. 1 − Dec. 31, 2018 dividend = 12,500 × $2 ÷ 4 = $6,250

---

1. With a 10% stock dividend, the stock dividend amount is $3 million (500,000 × 10% = 50,000 × $60). Prior to the declaration and distribution of the stock dividend, the balance in the Common Shares account was $10 million (500,000 × $20) and after the declaration and distribution, the balance will be $13 million ($10 million + $3 million) and Retained Earnings is now $10 million ($13 million − $3 million). The number of shares is now 550,000 (500,000 + 50,000).

2. With a stock split, the account balances in Common Shares and Retained Earnings after the stock split are the same as they were before: $10 million and $13 million, respectively. The number of shares is now 1,000,000 (500,000 + 500,000).

DO IT! 11-3
Stock Dividend and Split Effects

The effects on the shareholders' equity accounts of each option are as follows:

	Original Balances	After Stock Dividend	After Stock Split
Common shares	$10,000,000	$13,000,000	$ 10,000,000
Retained earnings	13,000,000	10,000,000	13,000,000
Total shareholders' equity	$23,000,000	$23,000,000	$23,000,000
Number of shares	500,000	550,000	1,000,000

GRAND LAKE CORPORATION
Statement of Changes in Equity
Year Ended December 31, 2018

DO IT! 11-4
Statement of Changes in Equity

	Common Shares	Retained Earnings	Accumulated Other Comprehensive Income	Total
Balance, January 1	$1,000,000	$600,000	$100,000	$1,700,000
Issued common shares	300,000			300,000
Dividends declared		(60,000)*		(60,000)
Comprehensive income				
Net income		360,000		360,000
Other comprehensive loss			(25,000)	(25,000)
Balance, December 31	$1,300,000	$900,000	$75,000	$2,275,000

*(500,000 + 100,000) × $0.10 = $60,000

(a)

DO IT! 11-5a
Payout Ratio and Dividend Yield

	2018	2017	2016
Westbrook Ltd.			
Payout ratio (dividends declared ÷ net income)	98.9%	81.8%	80.0%
Dividend yield (dividend per share ÷ market price per share)	4.6%	3.8%	2.6%
Eastglen Inc.			
Payout ratio (dividends declared ÷ net income)	41.4%	45.0%	50.0%
Dividend yield (dividend per share ÷ market price per share)	3.9%	4.0%	3.9%

(b) Westbrook has a much higher payout ratio than Eastglen so, when net income drops as it did in 2018, even though the dividend per share was decreased from $1.13 per share to $1.11 per share, the payout ratio rose to almost 99%. If net income stays at this same level in 2019, the company may be forced to cut its dividend because it is unlikely that it will want to maintain such a high payout ratio. The major reason for the increase in dividend yield for this company is the drop in share price, so the increased dividend yield should not be interpreted as an increased ability to pay out dividends.

Eastglen has been increasing its dividends per share each year while at the same time decreasing the payout ratio and retaining more funds for growth. Investors seem pleased with this strategy because the stock price has grown nicely each year. This company has not had a decline in net income during the past three years and the dividend yield is stable. Based on the ratios just analyzed, it appears that Eastglen shares should be purchased because the company is more capable of making dividend payments in the future.

DO IT! 11-5b
Basic Earnings per Share

Preferred dividends: 3,000 × $2 = $6,000

Weighted average number of common shares:

Date	Actual Number		Weighted Average
Nov. 1	40,000	× $^{12}/_{12}$=	40,000
Mar. 1	15,000	× $^{8}/_{12}$ =	10,000
Aug. 1	5,000	× $^{3}/_{12}$ =	1,250
Oct. 1	(1,200)	× $^{1}/_{12}$ =	(100)
	58,800		51,150

Basic earnings per share $\dfrac{\$249,750 - \$6,000}{51,150} = \$4.77$

DO IT! 11-5c
Return on Common Shareholders' Equity

(a)

	Pierce		Darrow	
Return on common shareholders' equity	$\dfrac{\$200,000 - \$0}{\$800,000}$	= 25.0%	$\dfrac{\$100,000 - \$0}{\$800,000}$	= 12.5%
Return on assets (provided in problem)	10%		10%	

(b) Both companies have a higher return on common shareholders' equity than their return on assets of 10%. This is because of leverage. For every dollar of debt taken out by these companies, they are able to earn additional income. Under these conditions, the company that takes on more debt will therefore have higher net income and higher return on common shareholders' equity. Because Pierce has financed 60% of its assets ($1,200,000 ÷ $2,000,000) with its liabilities but Darrow financed only 20% of its assets ($200,000 ÷ $1,000,000) with liabilities, Pierce has a much higher return on common shareholders' equity.

Although Pierce's higher leverage gave it a superior return on common shareholders' equity, it is worthwhile to note that, if the company had a net loss rather than net income, a negative return on common shareholders' equity would have resulted and this negative return (like the positive return seen above) would also be significantly more negative than Darrow's return.

We can therefore conclude that investing in Pierce is riskier but the risk may be worthwhile as long as we believe that the company will be able to earn a rate of return on its assets that can cover the interest rate charged on its liabilities.

▶ PRACTICE USING THE DECISION TOOLKIT

(a)

(in U.S. $ millions, except per-share information)	Ethan Allen		Leon's	Industry
1. Payout ratio	$\dfrac{\$14.50}{\$37.10}$	= 39.1%	37.1%	27.8%
2. Dividend yield	$\dfrac{\$0.50}{\$26.34}$	= 1.9%	2.8%	1.9%
3. Basic earnings per share	$\dfrac{\$37.10 - \$0}{28.9}$	= $1.28	$1.08	n/a
4. Return on common shareholders' equity	$\dfrac{\$37.10 - \$0}{(\$370.50 + \$367.50) ÷ 2}$	= 10.1%	13.3%	4.8%

(b) 1. Dividend record: Ethan Allen's payout ratio is higher than both Leon's and the industry average while its dividend yield is equal to the industry average but lower than Leon's. Ethan Allen's payout is higher due in part to lower net income while its yield is lower compared with Leon's because its share price has risen during the year while Leon's has fallen, primarily due to better economic conditions in the United States, where a significant number of Ethan Allen stores are located.

2. Earnings performance: It is not possible to compare basic earnings per share between companies, because of the different size of each company's operations and the different number of shares that each company has. Ethan Allen's return on common shareholders' equity, although higher than the industry average, is lower than that of Leon's.

▶ PRACTICE COMPREHENSIVE DO IT!

(a)

Jan. 10	Cash (50,000 × $9.24)		462,000	
	Common Shares			462,000
	(To record issue of 50,000 common shares)			
July 2	Cash (40,000 × $25)		1,000,000	
	Preferred Shares			1,000,000
	(To record issue of 40,000 preferred shares)			
Sept. 4	Dividends Declared (400,000 + 50,000 = 450,000 × 4% = 18,000 × $10)		180,000	
	Stock Dividends Distributable			180,000
	(To record declaration of 4% stock dividend)			
14	Record date—no entry required			
28	Stock Dividends Distributable		180,000	
	Common Shares			180,000
	(To record issue of 18,000 common shares in a 4% stock dividend)			

Nov. 1	Cash (10,000 × $25)	250,000	
	Preferred Shares		250,000
	(To record issue of 10,000 preferred shares)		
3	Common Shares (20,000 × $6.50)	130,000	
	Contributed Surplus	80,000	
	Retained Earnings	10,000	
	Cash (20,000 × $11)		220,000
	(To record the reacquisition and retirement of 20,000 common shares)		

Balance in Common Shares account prior to reacquisition:

($2,400,000 + $462,000 + $180,000) = $3,042,000

Number of shares prior to reacquisition: 400,000 + 50,000 + 18,000 = 468,000

Average cost of a common share: $3,042,000 ÷ 468,000 = $6.50

Dec. 21	Dividends Declared (40,000 + 10,000 = 50,000 × $1)	50,000	
	Dividends Payable		50,000
	(To record declaration of annual preferred cash dividend of $1 per share)		
31	No entry required for restriction of retained earnings—disclosure only		
31	Retained Earnings	230,000	
	Dividends Declared ($180,000 + $50,000)		230,000
	(To close dividends declared)		
31	Income Summary	512,000	
	Retained Earnings		512,000
	(To close net income)		

(b)

HUTCHINGS LIMITED
Statement of Changes in Equity
Year Ended December 31, 2018

| | Contributed Capital | | | | Accumulated Other | |
| | Share Capital | | Contributed Surplus | Retained Earnings | Comprehensive Income | Total |
	Preferred Shares	Common Shares				
Balance, Jan. 1		$2,400,000	$ 80,000	$1,820,000	$90,000	$4,390,000
Issued preferred shares	$1,250,000[1]					1,250,000
Issued common shares		462,000				462,000
Reacquired common shares		(130,000)	(80,000)	(10,000)		(220,000)
Net income				512,000		512,000
Declared and issued stock dividend		180,000		(180,000)		–0–
Declared cash dividend				(50,000)		(50,000)
Balance, Dec. 31	$1,250,000	$2,912,000	$ –0–	$2,092,000	$90,000	$6,344,000

HUTCHINGS LIMITED
Statement of Financial Position (partial)
December 31, 2018

Shareholders' equity
  Contributed capital
    Share capital

Preferred shares, 250,000 $1 cumulative authorized, 50,000[2] shares issued	$1,250,000
Common shares, unlimited number of shares authorized, 448,000[3] shares issued	2,912,000
Total contributed capital	4,162,000
Retained earnings (Note x)	2,092,000
Accumulated other comprehensive income	90,000
Total shareholders' equity	$6,344,000

Note x: A loan agreement contains a restrictive covenant that limits the payment of future dividends to 15% of net income.

[1] $1,000,000 + $250,000 = $1,250,000
[2] 40,000 + 10,000 = 50,000
[3] 400,000 + 50,000 + 18,000 − 20,000 = 448,000

▶ PRACTICE OBJECTIVE-FORMAT QUESTIONS

1.   (a), (c), and (g) are correct

Feedback
(b)   Is incorrect because a corporation is an entity that is distinct from its shareholders under law.
(d)   Is incorrect because most corporations in Canada are privately held by a small number of shareholders and as such, the shares do not trade on a stock exchange.
(e)   Is incorrect because one of the significant advantages of a corporation is that the shareholders do not have to manage the company. In this way, share capital can be raised from a large number of shareholders and the company will have the resources to hire professional managers.
(f)   Is incorrect because all corporations must comply with these acts.

2.   (a), (c), (f), and (g) are correct

Feedback
(b)   Is incorrect because the authorized shares are the maximum number of shares that can be issued by the corporation (this can be "unlimited") while the issued shares are the ones sold by the corporation to its shareholders.
(d)   Is incorrect because a normal course issuer bid is used by a public corporation to buy back some of its issued shares on a stock exchange.
(e)   Is incorrect because dividends can only fall into arrears on cumulative preferred shares. On these shares, if dividends are not declared, the right to receive them still exists. With common shares or noncumulative preferred shares, if the board of directors does not declare a dividend for a particular period of time, the right to receive that dividend later does not exist.

3.   (a), (b), (c), (f), and (g) are correct

Feedback
(d)   Is incorrect because only common shareholders will usually have voting rights at shareholder meetings.
(e)   Is incorrect because a cumulative dividend right simply means that, if the board of directors does not declare a dividend on cumulative preferred shares, the holders of these shares do not lose the right to receive the dividend (which is now in arrears) in the future.

4.   (a), (c), and (g) are correct

Feedback
(b)   Is in correct because the record date is simply the date on which the list of shareholders on record is determined. No journal entry is recorded on that date because no transaction has occurred. Shareholders will receive their dividends later on the payment date, at which time a journal entry will be recorded for this payment.
(d)   Is incorrect because when the dividends are declared, a legal obligation to pay these dividends exists, so on the declaration date, a journal entry will be recorded to debit Dividends Declared and credit Dividends Payable. Later, on the payment date, the entry that will be recorded at that time will debit Dividends Payable and credit Cash.
(e)   Is incorrect because dividends become payable when they are declared and do not accrue (become a liability) until they are declared.
(f)   Is incorrect because dividends are shown on the statement of changes in equity for companies using IFRS or on the statement of retained earnings for companies using ASPE.

5.   (b), (c), (d), and (g) are correct

Feedback
(a)   Is incorrect because stock dividends reduce retained earnings and increase share capital by equal amounts so there is no overall change to shareholders' equity.
(e)   Is incorrect because when a stock dividend is declared, a debit to Dividends Declared is recorded along with a credit to Stock Dividends Distributable, which is an equity account shown in the share capital section and not a liability account. It is not a liability account because a liability is an obligation that is typically settled with an asset like cash or through the provision of services, not with equity.
(f)   Is incorrect because the numerator for return on common shareholders' equity is net income minus preferred share dividends. This will not change regardless of the type of common stock dividend that is declared. The denominator for return on common shareholders' equity is also unaffected by common stock dividends. If a stock dividend is declared on common shares, Retained Earnings is decreased and Common Shares is increased. This does not change common shareholders' equity. Therefore, a stock dividend on a common share has no effect on return on common shareholders' equity.

6.   (d) and (e) are correct

Feedback
(a)   Is incorrect because other comprehensive income was not contributed by shareholders; it arises from gains and losses that are not recorded in net income and it is reported separately from contributed capital.
(b)   Is incorrect because contributed surplus arises from equity-related transactions that do not affect net income. Because net income is closed out into retained earnings, contributed surplus is not the same as retained earnings.
(c)   Is incorrect because other comprehensive income is closed out into accumulated other comprehensive income and not retained earnings.
(f)   Is incorrect because, when the Retained Earnings account has a debit balance, it is referred to as a Deficit.
(g)   Is incorrect because the effect of dividends on retained earnings can be seen in the statement of changes in equity under IFRS or in the statement of retained earnings under ASPE.

7.   (b), (d), (f), and (g) are correct

Feedback

$$\text{Basic earnings per share} = \frac{\text{Net income} - \text{Prefered dividends}}{\text{Weighted average number of common shares}}$$

Net income does not include other comprehensive income and is equal to $200,000.
The preferred share dividends declared this year were $1 × 50,000 shares = $50,000; dividends declared for common shares do not affect this ratio.
The weighted average number of common shares is $(80,000 \times {}^{12}/_{12}) + (40,000 \times {}^{6}/_{12}) = 100,000$ shares.

$$\text{Basic earnings per share} = \frac{\$200,000 - \$50,000}{100,000} = \$1.50 \text{ per share}$$

(a) Is incorrect because the denominator should include only common shares, not preferred shares. If preferred shares were included, the denominator would incorrectly be calculated at 150,000 shares.

(c) Is incorrect because only the preferred dividends of $1 per share or $50,000 should be deducted from net income. We do not subtract common share dividends because they are attributed to the common shareholders.

(e) Is incorrect because net income, not comprehensive income, is used in determining basic earnings per share.

8. (a), (c), (e), and (f) are correct

Feedback

(a) Is correct because the payout ratio is calculated by dividing cash dividends by net income. Because the dividends doubled and net income rose by only 10%, the payout ratio will increase.

(b) Is incorrect because the return on common shareholders' equity is calculated by dividing income available to common shareholders (which increased by 10%) by the average common shareholders' equity, which increased only slightly during the year (retained earnings would have increased only by the excess of net income over dividends declared, unlike the numerator which rose by the full amount of net income), so the return on common shareholders' equity would have increased this year.

(c) Is correct because the dividend yield is determined by dividing the dividends per common share by the market price of a common share. Because the dividends increased and the market price of the shares fell, the yield would increase.

(d) Is incorrect because even though net income rose by 10% and the dividends paid out doubled, the amount of the dividend paid out was still less than net income. Because some of the net income was retained and not paid out through dividends, shareholders' equity will increase.

(e) Is correct because even though the dividend doubled, it is still less than net income so a portion of net income is still retained and will cause retained earnings to increase.

(f) Is correct because, if the dividend did not change, assuming the market price of the shares still fell, the dividend yield would have increased but only because the market price fell.

(g) Is incorrect because, if the dividends remained unchanged, net income would still have risen and this would cause the payout ratio to decrease.

9. (a), (c), and (f) are correct

Feedback

(a) Is correct because shares with a high dividend yield tend to provide investors with larger amounts of dividends relative to the amount invested, so they are attractive to investors needing dividend income to replace the salaries they no longer receive.

(b) Is incorrect because, when shares are split, no journal entry is recorded so there will be no change to any component of the return on shareholders' equity ratio.

(c) Is correct because both the increase in the cash dividends declared and the decrease in net income will cause the payout ratio to increase.

(d) Is incorrect because, when a company has no leverage (no liabilities), its assets and common shareholders' equity will be equal and this in turn will make the return on assets and the return on common shareholders' equity equal. As leverage increases, however, assets will become larger compared with common shareholders' equity and this in turn will cause a greater difference between the return on assets and the return on common shareholders' equity.

(e) Is incorrect because, when a company has a low payout ratio, a lower portion of net income is being paid to shareholders through dividends. This means that more net income is retained by the company, which in turn will make it more likely to grow.

(f) Is correct because dividend yield is calculated by dividing dividends per share by the market price of its shares. Although the dividends per share numerator of this ratio is 10% lower, because the denominator has decreased even more, the overall value of the ratio will rise.

(g) Is incorrect because comparing the basic earnings per share of two companies is not useful because it does not take into consideration the number of shares that each company has issued. For example, assume two companies of comparable size have equal amounts of net income but one of the companies has issued 10 times as many common shares as the other. The company with the higher number of issued common shares will have a basic earnings per share that is one tenth of the earnings per share of the other company. Comparing the basic earnings per share of these two companies would be misleading because one may think that one of the companies is ten times more profitable when it is not.

10. (c), (d), and (e) are correct

Feedback

(a) Is incorrect because, when financing with debt, a company is legally required to pay interest on certain due dates. Because there is no flexibility on when these payments must be made, this is a disadvantage compared with equity financing, where no set payment dates for dividends exist.

(b) Is incorrect because, when shares are sold, there is no predetermined date or requirement that the shares have to be bought back by the company. This is a major advantage to financing with shares rather than debt because the amount raised is not due for repayment.

(f) Is incorrect because when issuing debt there is no dilution of existing ownership interests because the number of shareholders would not change. This is not a disadvantage to these shareholders.

(g) Is incorrect because dividends are not an expense and are therefore not deductible on a tax return when determining taxable income.

► ENDNOTE

[1]Sources: Francine Kopun, "Leon's Buys The Brick in $700-Million Deal," *Toronto Star*, November 11, 2012; "Leon's Through the Years," *The Globe and Mail online*, November 12, 2012; Leon's Furniture Limited corporate website, www.leons.ca; Leon's Furniture Limited 2015 annual report.

12

Reporting and Analyzing Investments

CHAPTER PREVIEW

Over the past few chapters, we have learned a great deal about various types of assets. We have also covered how a company obtains financing from both equity investors and lenders. In this chapter, we are going to learn how those investors and lenders account for the investments they have made in other companies. Investments can be made by purchasing equity securities issued by corporations or by purchasing debt securities issued by corporations or governments. Investments can be either non-strategic, where the goal is to generate investment income, or strategic, where the goal is to influence the decisions made by the company invested in. As you will see in this chapter, the way in which a company accounts for each of these investments is determined by several factors, including whether the investment is non-strategic or strategic.

New standards for the accounting for investments were recently issued in IFRS 9, which is effective on January 1, 2018. This chapter covers these new standards in addition to their ASPE equivalents.

CHAPTER OUTLINE

LEARNING OBJECTIVES	READ	PRACTICE
1 Identify reasons to invest, and classify investments.	• Non-strategic investments • Strategic investments	**DO IT!** 12-1 Investment classifications
2 Account for non-strategic investments.	• Valuation of non-strategic investments • Using fair value models	**DO IT!** 12-2 Non-strategic investments
3 Account for strategic investments.	• Using the equity method • Using the cost model	**DO IT!** 12-3 Strategic investments
4 Explain how investments are reported in the financial statements.	• Income statement • Statement of comprehensive income • Statement of changes in equity • Statement of financial position	**DO IT!** 12-4 Reporting investments
5 Compare the accounting for a bond investment and a bond payable (Appendix 12A)	• Recording a bond investment for the investor • Recording a bond for investor and investee	**DO IT!** 12-5 Investments in bonds with discounts and premiums

Scotiabank

FEATURE STORY

Vince Talotta/Getty Images

Like all large organizations, the Bank of Nova Scotia (Scotiabank) manages its money through a number of investment vehicles. It has two main areas of investments: its regular banking operations and strategic acquisitions.

"In banks, we're always changing the mix of financial assets, looking for different opportunities," says Sean McGuckin, Group Head and Chief Financial Officer, "whereas for non-financial institutions, financial assets may not be their primary assets. It could be property, plant, and equipment, oil in the ground, what have you. So they may take a longer-term view on some of their investments." Scotiabank is like an individual investor who reviews and rebalances his or her portfolio regularly, rather than one who buys stocks and holds them over time with little adjustment.

In its regular banking operations, Scotiabank holds investments in trading portfolios and treasury portfolios. In its trading environment, Scotiabank buys and sells securities primarily to facilitate customer requests and invests in certain securities to adjust its trading risk profile. These may be debt instruments such as bonds, or equity instruments such as common and preferred shares. Scotiabank's treasury investments strengthen the organization's liquidity profile by having some assets on hand that it could quickly convert into cash if needed. The bank also uses various investments in fixed-term securities or variable-rate securities to help adjust its interest rate exposure. These investments can be held for a few days or longer. As well, the bank may also invest in long-term instruments; for example, five-year government bonds.

Managing Money for Clients and the Company

Scotiabank also invests strategically by acquiring all or a portion of other companies. "Our strategy, like most companies, is to grow," Mr. McGuckin explains. "You can grow either organically over time by continuing to build out your business, or you can acquire growth by buying a company." If a business fits within Scotiabank's overall strategy, it may buy shares in that company or acquire an equity interest.

For example, Scotiabank has made several recent deals to acquire an equity stake in the credit card business of major retailers. In 2015, Scotiabank acquired 51% of the financial services business of Cencosud, a major retailer in Chile, for about US$280 million, allowing it to manage the company's 2.5 million credit cards for 15 years. That same year, the bank announced it would buy the Canadian credit-card portfolio of JPMorgan Chase Bank, which includes the credit cards associated with Sears Canada Inc., for an undisclosed amount. In 2014, Scotiabank purchased a 20% equity stake in Canadian Tire Corporation's financial services business, for $500 million in cash. Canadian Tire was Canada's eighth-largest credit card issuer, with 1.8 million customers and $4.4 billion in receivables. These types of strategic investments allow Scotiabank to diversify into different revenue streams.

In fact, there are many reasons and ways by which organizations make investments, whether they are non-strategic investments to earn a higher return on extra cash than from a bank account, or strategic investments to influence or control another company, such as a competitor, supplier, or complementary business that their customers may benefit from.[1]

Go to the *REVIEW AND PRACTICE* section at the end of the chapter for a targeted summary and practice questions with solutions.

Visit **WileyPLUS** for more practice opportunities.

▶1 Identify reasons to invest, and classify investments.

Recall that in Chapter 8 you were introduced to the concept of financial assets. These are assets that consist of cash and other assets such as receivables and investments that have a contractual right to receive cash. It is common practice for corporations to purchase financial assets, such as debt and equity investments, for investment purposes. **Debt investments** include low-risk guaranteed investment certificates or term deposits, as well as bonds, commercial paper, and a large variety of other debt securities available for purchase. They earn interest revenue over time, and in most cases, the borrower has an obligation to return the original amount (principal) of the investment on a fixed maturity date. **Equity investments** usually consist of either preferred or common shares of other corporations in the expectation of generating revenue from dividends or earning a gain on future sale. Unlike debt investments, equity investments are riskier because they have no requirement to receive any form of revenue through dividends over time or to receive a return of the original amount invested.

As mentioned above, investments are often made to earn income from interest, dividends, and gains upon the sale of the investment. An investment made for these reasons is known as a **non-strategic investment**. However, sometimes an investment is made for the additional purpose of influencing or controlling the operations of another company. Such an investment is known as a **strategic investment**. Both types of investments are covered in the next two sections.

NON-STRATEGIC INVESTMENTS

There are several reasons for a company to purchase debt or equity securities of another company as a non-strategic investment. A corporation may have **excess cash** that it does not immediately need. This is particularly true for companies that have seasonal fluctuations in their sales levels, which can lead to having excess cash balances after high sales periods. These excess funds should be invested to earn a greater return than would be realized by just holding the funds in the company's chequing account.

When investing excess cash for short periods of time, corporations generally invest in debt securities that have low risk and high liquidity. Examples include guaranteed investment certificates, bankers' acceptances, term deposits, and treasury bills. It is usually not wise to invest short-term excess cash in equity securities such as common shares of other companies because share prices can fluctuate significantly over the short term. If the share price drops just before the company needs the cash again, the company will be forced to sell its investment at a loss. Most debt securities do not change significantly in value and are purchased only for the interest revenue they generate.

If a company has excess cash for a prolonged period of time, and wants a low-risk investment, bonds or preferred shares may be purchased because their values do not fluctuate very much. Although a company is not required to pay out a dividend, as discussed in Chapter 11, it is common to do so for preferred shares. Investments of this nature usually generate steady amounts of dividend revenue over time.

A company can also invest in debt and equity securities with the hope of selling them later at a higher price and benefiting from their price appreciation. The resulting gain is called a capital gain, which receives preferential income tax treatment in Canada because only half of the gain is usually taxed. Non-strategic investments that are held for the purpose of earning capital gains are called **held for trading investments**.

Non-strategic investments can be further classified as **short-term investments** (current assets) or **long-term investments** (non-current assets), depending on how liquid the investment is and how long management wants to hold it. Later in this chapter, we will learn about the classification and methods of accounting for non-strategic investments.

STRATEGIC INVESTMENTS

Although both debt and equity securities can be purchased as non-strategic investments, only equity securities (normally common shares) can be purchased for the strategic purpose of influencing relationships between companies. This is because, for most companies, only common shareholders have voting rights and the ability to influence or control the company's major decisions. Preferred shareholders generally do not have voting rights, and therefore they have no influence or control.

The degree of influence determines how a strategic investment is classified. More details about the degree of influence and how it affects the accounting for that investment will be discussed later in this chapter. While non-strategic investments can be either short-term or long-term, strategic investments are usually long-term.

To summarize, the reasons corporations make non-strategic and strategic investments are shown in Illustration 12-1.

►Illustration 12-1
Why corporations invest

Reason	Purpose	Type of Investment
Non-strategic investment	To generate investment income (interest, dividends, appreciation in share prices)	Debt securities (guaranteed investment certificates, bonds, bankers' acceptances, term deposits, treasury bills) and equity securities (preferred and common shares)
Strategic investment	To influence or control another company	Equity securities (common shares)

DO IT! ►12-1   Investment Classifications

For each investment below, determine:

(a) whether the investment is a debt or equity instrument.

(b) whether the investment is non-strategic or strategic.

(c) the purpose for making the investment.

1. Investment in 120-day treasury bills, purchased with excess cash

2. Investment in Canadian Pacific Railway common shares, intended to be sold when the price rises 10% above cost

3. Investment in Royal Bank of Canada 20-year bonds, intended to be held until maturity

4. Investment in 40% of the common shares of Ajax Limited, a supplier, for the purpose of influencing its relationship with Ajax

SOLUTION
Try this Do It! exercise on your own and then check your answer at the end of the chapter.

Related Exercise Material: BE12–1 and E12–1.

Action Plan

✔ Distinguish between debt and equity investments:

  ✔ Debt investments are securities that have fixed due dates to receive interest revenue and a maturity date on which the investment's original amount (principal) is returned.

  ✔ Equity investments give the owner a portion of equity in a company and are usually made by buying preferred or common shares.

✔ Distinguish between non-strategic and strategic investments:

  ✔ Non-strategic investments are debt or equity investments that are purchased to earn interest or dividend revenue and/or to earn gains from the appreciation in the value of the investment.

  ✔ Strategic investments are equity investments that represent a large enough portion of a company's issued common shares so that the investor can influence or control the decisions made by that company.

Account for non-strategic investments.

At acquisition, debt and equity investments are recorded at their purchase cost. Although an investment's fair value is equal to its cost when purchased, fair value may rise and fall greatly during the time debt and equity investments are held. For example, when oil prices fell in 2015, the share prices of dozens of Canadian companies fell. Scotiabank, which was mentioned in our feature story, often invests in companies like these for the purpose of trading their shares for a profit and, because the bank had invested in oil companies, its share price also fell.

Recall that we first learned about fair value in Chapter 2. Fair value is more commonly used when discussing investments than current value, so we use that term in this chapter.

Volatility of share prices presents investors with an opportunity for trading profits. If prices can change so much, an important question arises: should non-strategic investments be valued at the statement of financial position date at fair value or at cost or at some other value? The next sections will discuss the valuation models for non-strategic investments.

ACCOUNTING MATTERS

imagestock/iStockphoto

Non-Strategic Investments for Individuals

Most Canadians, when they invest in the shares of public companies, are buying non-strategic investments rather than strategic ones. These individuals may trade these shares frequently or not, depending on their investment strategies. Studies have shown that investors with smaller portfolios of non-strategic investments usually have a higher return on their investments if they resist the urge to frequently trade them. One reason for this is the cost of commissions, which increases with trading activity. Another reason is the fact that income tax is paid on gains only once the investment is sold, so delaying the sale of an investment also delays the payment of any income tax on these gains.

In another form of non-strategic investment, Canadians over the age of 18 have been allowed to contribute to a tax-free savings account (TFSA). Currently, the limit that can be paid into this account each year is $5,500. Any income earned in this account is not taxed. Let's assume someone opens up a TFSA when they are 18 years old and contributes $5,500 each year into the account for the next 42 years until they are 60 years old. Let's also assume that the investments made by the funds placed in the account earn 5% per year and would compound annually. By the time that person is 60 years old, the value of the account would be $743,000. If no more contributions were made into the account but it continued to grow by 5% per year until the person was 85 years old, the value of the account would be over $2.7 million . . . quite a nest egg to spend or to leave to their family, even accounting for inflation.

VALUATION OF NON-STRATEGIC INVESTMENTS

There are four major models that can be used for valuing non-strategic investments, as outlined below:

1. **Fair value through profit or loss model.** Under this model, investments are adjusted upward or downward to reflect their fair value at the end of an accounting period. Fair value, for this purpose, means the price that would be received to sell an asset in an orderly transaction between market participants at the measurement date. This adjustment (the difference between the investment's fair value and carrying amount) to reflect fair value is known as an **unrealized gain or loss**. It is recorded in the income statement along with any interest or dividend revenue. When the investment is sold, the resulting gain or loss, which is known as a **realized gain or loss**, is also shown in the income statement.

2. **Fair value through other comprehensive income (OCI) model**. This is a variation of the fair value through profit or loss model where both unrealized and realized gains and losses are recorded in other comprehensive income rather than in the income statement. This is done because these types of gains and losses are not critical to the evaluation of management and therefore do not need to be reflected in net income. However, after these gains and losses are realized they are reclassified to net income for debt investments and to retained earnings for equity investments. These reclassifications are complex and are not covered in this textbook.

3. **Amortized cost model**. Under this model, which applies only to debt investments, the investment's carrying amount is not adjusted to reflect fair value (unless it is impaired, similar to the way we would record an impairment loss on property). Consequently, no unrealized gains and losses are recorded. The term *amortized* is used because, if the investment was purchased at a discount or a premium, as is often the case when purchasing bond investments, the discount or premium would be gradually amortized over the period of time until the bond matures. You learned about bond premium and discount amortization in the appendix to Chapter 10 when accounting for bond liabilities and you will review this concept again with regard to bond investments in Appendix 12A in this chapter. Because this model requires amortization over the remaining term of the investment, it is used for debt investments rather than equity investments. Any interest revenue or realized gains or losses on this type of investment are reported in the income statement.

4. **Cost model**. This model (often referred to as the *cost method*) is very similar to the amortized cost model except that it is used for equity investments. Again, no adjustments are made to the investments to record them at fair value. Because this type of investment does not give rise to a discount or premium (because there is no period to maturity for an equity investment), the concept of amortization does not apply to this model. Investment revenue under this model consists of dividend revenue along with realized gains and losses that would be reported in the income statement. Although the name is identical to the cost model used when accounting for depreciation in Chapter 9, the use of this term in this chapter is different and it relates only to investments.

A summary of these models is shown in Illustration 12-2.

▶Illustration 12-2

Summary of valuation models for non-strategic investments

	Fair Value Through Profit or Loss	Fair Value Through Other Comprehensive Income	Amortized Cost	Cost
Used for	Debt or equity investments	Debt or equity investments	Debt investments	Equity investments
Investment valued at	Fair value	Fair value	Amortized cost	Cost
Interest revenue	Income statement	Income statement	Income statement	Not applicable
Dividend revenue	Income statement	Income statement	Not applicable	Income statement
Unrealized gains and losses	Income statement	Other comprehensive income	Not recorded	Not recorded
Realized gains and losses	Income statement	Other comprehensive income, but for debt investments, reclassified to the income statement and for equity investments reclassified to retained earnings.	Income statement	Income statement

The items listed above that are shown on the income statement are typically listed as other revenues and expenses below net income from operations.

We will look at the fair value models (the first two models described above) in the next section. We will look at the third model, the amortized cost model, in the appendix to this chapter and the fourth model, the cost model, later in the chapter when we discuss strategic investments. We will also review when these models are used under both IFRS and ASPE when we cover learning objective 4, which deals with reporting investments.

USING FAIR VALUE MODELS

We will now look in greater detail at how each of the fair value models described earlier—the fair value through profit or loss model and the fair value through OCI model—is used.

Fair Value Through Profit or Loss

As mentioned earlier, because this model requires an adjustment to the investment to reflect it at fair value, a corresponding unrealized gain or loss is recorded when the investment is adjusted upward or downward, respectively to reflect changes in fair value. An unrealized gain or loss is recorded because the investment has not actually been sold. It is only when the investment is sold that a gain or loss is "realized."

Gains and losses on investments are calculated similarly to the calculation of gains and losses on the disposal of property, plant, and equipment. In the case of property, plant, and equipment, gains and losses are determined by comparing proceeds with the asset's carrying amount. In the case of investments, gains and losses are determined by comparing fair value with the asset's carrying amount. If the fair value exceeds the carrying amount, a gain results. If the fair value is less than the carrying amount, a loss results. The formula for calculating gains or losses is:

$$\text{Fair value } - \text{ Carrying amount } = \text{ Unrealized/realized gain (loss)}$$

To illustrate the valuation of held for trading investments accounted for under the fair value through profit or loss model, assume that on December 31, 2018, Plano Corporation has the following costs and fair values for its debt and equity securities:

Held for Trading Investments	Cost	Fair Value	Unrealized Gain (Loss)
BCE shares	$ 50,000	$ 48,000	$(2,000)
Norbord bonds	90,000	95,000	5,000
Total	$140,000	$143,000	$ 3,000

Plano has an overall unrealized gain on its total investments of $3,000 because the total fair value of $143,000 is $3,000 greater than the total cost of $140,000. Its held for trading investments would be reported at $143,000 at December 31 in the current assets section of the statement of financial position. In addition, Plano would report a net unrealized gain of $3,000 in its income statement. **Note that unrealized gains and losses for held for trading investments under the fair value through profit or loss model are reported in exactly the same way as realized gains and losses.**

The adjustment of the held for trading investments to fair value and the recognition of any unrealized gain or loss are usually done through an adjusting journal entry. The adjusting entry for Plano is:

A	=	L	+	SE
+3,000				+3,000

Cash flows: no effect

Dec. 31	Held for Trading Investments ($5,000 − $2,000)	3,000	
	Unrealized Gain on Held for Trading Investments		3,000
	(To record unrealized net gain on held for trading investments)		

We have combined the BCE shares and Norbord bonds into a single Held for Trading Investments account in the above journal entry and maintain a subsidiary ledger containing the details of individual investments. This entry also nets an unrealized loss of $2,000 on the BCE shares with an unrealized gain of $5,000 on the Norbord bonds. Although we have chosen to net the two held for trading investment securities and their respective gains and losses here, it would also be correct to record them separately.

If, early in January, Plano sells its BCE shares for $48,000, the following journal entry would be recorded:

A	=	L	+	SE
+48,000				
−48,000				

↑ Cash flows: +48,000

Jan. 5	Cash	48,000	
	Held for Trading Investments		48,000
	(To record sale of BCE shares)		

The BCE shares originally cost $50,000, but because they were written down to their fair value of $48,000 on December 31, the new carrying amount is $48,000. Consequently, the investment account is credited for that amount. Although it could be argued that the $2,000 unrealized loss recorded in the prior year has now been realized, for simplicity we are not going to reclassify an unrealized loss from one period into a realized loss in another period because such a reclassification has no impact on the net income reported in either period.

If the shares had been sold for $47,000 instead of $48,000, then a realized loss of $1,000 ($48,000 − $47,000) would have been recorded, representing the difference between the carrying amount of the investment on the date of sale and the proceeds received from that sale. This would be done as follows:

Jan. 5	Cash	47,000	
	Realized Loss on Held for Trading Investments	1,000	
	Held for Trading Investments		48,000
	(To record a realized loss on BCE shares)		

A	=	L	+	SE
+47,000				−1,000
−48,000				
↑ Cash flows: +47,000				

Fair Value Through Other Comprehensive Income (OCI)

When we use fair value models, we attempt to show users of the financial statements relevant information regarding the value of investments. Under the fair value through profit or loss model, as the investments fluctuate in value, any corresponding unrealized gains or losses are shown in the income statement. This is because we are trying to evaluate the company's ability to manage these investments.

However, sometimes we are not trying to measure management's ability to manage investments, especially if there is no intention of trading them frequently. In this case, management can designate an investment as fair value through OCI. With this method, the investment is recorded at its fair value but any unrealized gains and losses are recorded in other comprehensive income instead of in the income statement. When the investment is sold, any realized gain or loss arising from the sale is recorded in other comprehensive income. If the investment sold is a debt investment, the realized gain or loss is reclassified to the income statement while such gains are reclassified to retained earnings for equity investments.

Once an investment is accounted for under this approach, it cannot be changed. Because fair value through OCI is not used widely, and because of the complexity involved with the reclassifications mentioned above, detailed coverage of this topic is left for an intermediate accounting course.

DO IT! 12-2 Non-Strategic Investments

Wang Corporation had the following transactions:

Sept. 2 Purchased 1,000 Jenkins Corp. common shares for $70,000 with the intention of trading them.
Oct. 12 Received a dividend on the Jenkins shares of $0.90 per share.
22 Sold half of the investment in Jenkins shares at $67 per share.
Dec. 30 Jenkins declares a dividend of $0.95 per share, payable next year.

(a) Record the above transactions.

(b) Prepare the adjusting entry for the valuation of the investment on December 31, Wang's year end, assuming the remaining Jenkins shares are worth $65 each on December 31.

(c) Identify where each account would be reported and on what financial statement.

Action Plan

✔ Use the fair value through profit or loss model for held for trading investments.

✔ Record the held for trading investment initially at cost and adjust for changes in fair value.

✔ When the investment is adjusted for any change in value, record any difference between the shares' carrying amount and fair value as an unrealized gain or loss in the income statement.

Action Plan (cont'd)

✔ Report dividend revenue in the income statement.

✔ When the investment is sold, record any difference between the carrying amount of the shares and the proceeds as a realized gain or loss in the income statement

SOLUTION

Try this Do It! exercise on your own and then check your answer at the end of the chapter.

Related Exercise Material: BE12–2, BE12–3, BE12–4, BE12–5, E12–3, and E12–4.

LEARNING OBJECTIVE ▶ 3

Account for strategic investments.

A company that purchases (owns) securities is known as the **investor**, whereas the company that issues (sells) the securities is known as the **investee**. An investor that owns common shares has the potential to strategically influence the investee if enough shares are owned. The accounting for equity investments in common shares is based on how much influence the investor has over the investee's operating, investing, and financial affairs. That influence is often measured by the percentage of common shares of the investee that are owned by the investor, but these percentages are just guidelines because other qualitative factors are used to determine the degree of influence.

▶Illustration 12-3
Accounting guidelines for strategic investments

Investor's Ownership Interest in Investee's Common Shares	Presumed Influence over Investee	Method to Account for Investment
Less than 20%	Insignificant	Fair value
20% to 50%	Significant	Equity method
More than 50%	Control	Equity or cost method (and consolidation of financial statements)

As noted in Illustration 12-3, we assume that, if the investor owns less than 20% of the investee's common shares, then they are unable to influence or control the investee. In this case, the investment is accounted for using one of the fair value models. Remember that, although this usually means using the fair value through profit or loss model, an election can be made to account for the investment using the fair value through OCI model, as discussed earlier in this chapter.

When an investor owns 20% or more of the common shares of another company but does not have control (less than 50% of the common shares), the investor is generally presumed to have a **significant influence** over the decisions of the investee company. When an investee can be significantly influenced, it is known as an **associate**.

The presumption of significant influence may not be valid if other evidence exists to refute it. For example, a company that purchases a 25% interest in another company in a "hostile" acquisition may not have any significant influence over the investee. As another example, if less than 20% ownership is held, there is a presumption that significant influence does not exist but evidence could suggest otherwise. For example, if a highly respected investor with 18% ownership has board membership and plays a key role in forming company strategy, then significant influence could exist.

Among the questions that should be considered in determining an investor's influence are the following:

1. Does the investor have representation on the investee's board of directors?
2. Does the investor participate in the investee's policy-making process?
3. Are there material transactions between the investor and the investee?
4. Are the investor and investee exchanging managerial personnel?
5. Is the investor providing key technical information to the investee?

Companies are required to use judgement instead of blindly following the percentage guidelines mentioned above.

If the investor has more than 50% of the investee's voting shares, it is assumed that the investor controls the investee. In this case, the investee is considered to be a **subsidiary company** of the investor or **parent company**. Even though the investee is a separate legal entity, it is part of a group of corporations controlled by the parent company. For example, Sobeys Inc., one of the two feature companies used throughout this textbook, is a wholly owned subsidiary company. Its parent company is Empire Company Limited.

In order to show shareholders and other users of the parent's financial statements the full extent of the group's operations, the financial statements of all entities within the group are combined, resulting in **consolidated financial statements**. The process of consolidating financial statements is quite complex and will be left for an advanced accounting course, but in essence, the investment account is replaced with the subsidiary's assets and liabilities. Prior to consolidation, the investment in the subsidiary is usually accounted for using either the equity method or the cost model. In certain circumstances for companies following ASPE, alternatives to consolidation exist that will be covered later in this chapter.

ACCOUNTING MATTERS

Ashley Cooper/Getty Images

Suncor Reaches $4.2-Billion Deal with Canadian Oil Sands

Sometimes companies will take extraordinary steps to gain significant influence over the operations of another company. Take Suncor Energy Inc., for example. That company had a 12% interest in Syncrude Canada Ltd., which is a major producer of oil from the oil sands. Syncrude has a production capacity of 350,000 barrels per day but was only producing 248,300 barrels per day in early 2016. Its cost to produce a barrel was over $40. Suncor also operated its own production facilities nearby, producing oil at a lower cost per barrel. Suncor believed that, if it could have a greater influence over the operations of Syncrude, it could lower its operating costs and make Syncrude more efficient.

Another company, Canadian Oil Sands Ltd., had a 37% interest in Syncrude. In an effort to boost its ownership of Syncrude, Suncor made a hostile takeover bid for Canadian Oil Sands. Initially the bid was rejected but, after some modifications, the Canadian Oil Sands board of directors approved the $4.2-billion takeover offer in January 2016. With this 37% interest added to their 12% stake in Syncrude, Suncor planned to influence decisions at Syncrude and improve its operations.[2]

USING THE EQUITY METHOD

When an investor exercises significant influence over an associate, the investee company, to some extent, becomes an extension of the investor company. Consequently, such an investment is recorded using the equity method.

Under the **equity method**, the investment is initially recorded at cost in an account called Investment in Associates. After that, the Investment in Associates account is adjusted annually to show how the investor's equity in the associate has changed. In this way, the movement in the investment account reflects the changes that are occurring to the associate's retained earnings. When the associate reports net income, the investor will increase the investment account for its share of that net income. When the associate declares a dividend, resulting in the reduction of its

▼ HELPFUL HINT
Under the equity method, revenue is recognized on the accrual basis, so when it is earned by the investee, it is also earned by the investor.

retained earnings, the investor's investment account will be decreased. It would be wrong to delay recognizing the investor's share of net income until a cash dividend is received. This is because that approach would ignore the fact that the investor and associate are, in some sense, one company, and that the investor therefore benefits from the income earned by the associate, which should be recorded when it is earned rather than when it is received as a dividend.

To keep its records up to date, each year the investor adjusts the investment account to:

1. **Record its share of the associate's net income (loss)**: When the associate reports net income, the investor records its share of that net income by increasing (debiting) the Investment in Associates account and increasing (crediting) a revenue account called Income from Associate. Conversely, when the associate has a net loss, the investor increases (debits) a Loss from Associate account and decreases (credits) the Investment in Associates account for its share of the associate's loss.
2. **Record the dividends declared by the associate**: This is done by increasing (debiting) Dividends Receivable (or debiting Cash if the dividend is declared and paid) and decreasing (crediting) the Investment in Associates account for the amount of any dividends earned. The investment account is reduced for dividends declared because the associate's shareholders' equity is decreased when a dividend is declared.

We will now illustrate the equity method, using two fictitious companies, Millar Corporation and Beck Inc.

Recording Acquisition of Shares

Beck Inc. has 10,000 common shares issued in total. Assume that on January 1, 2018, Millar Corporation (the investor) acquires 30%, or 3,000 common shares, of Beck (the associate) for $120,000 cash or $40 per share. Millar is assumed to have significant influence over Beck and will use the equity method to account for this transaction. If Millar had more than one associate, we would add the associate's name to the investment account name, or maintain a subsidiary ledger of associates similar to that discussed earlier in the Using Fair Value Models section with respect to held for trading investments. The entry to record this investment is:

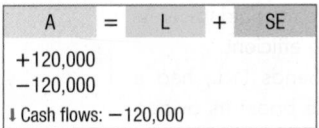

A	=	L	+	SE
+120,000				
−120,000				
↓ Cash flows: −120,000				

Jan. 1	Investment in Associates	120,000	
	Cash		120,000
	(To record the purchase of Beck common shares)		

Recording Income from Associates

Now assume that for the year ended December 31, 2018, Beck reports net income of $100,000 and declares and pays a $40,000 cash dividend. At December 31, 2018, Beck's common shares were trading at $42 each. Millar is required to record (1) its share of Beck's net income, $30,000 (30% × $100,000), and (2) the reduction in the investment account for the dividends declared, $12,000 ($40,000 × 30%). If Millar had owned the Beck shares for only a portion of the year, the revenue recorded from the Beck investment would be prorated for that portion. The entries are as follows:

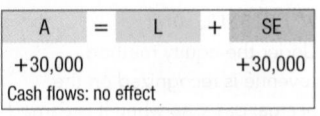

A	=	L	+	SE
+30,000				+30,000
Cash flows: no effect				

	(1)		
Dec. 31	Investment in Associates	30,000	
	Income from Associates		30,000
	(To record 30% share in Beck's net income)		

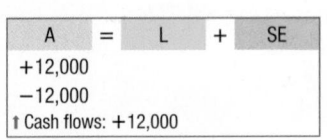

A	=	L	+	SE
+12,000				
−12,000				
↑ Cash flows: +12,000				

	(2)		
Dec. 31	Cash	12,000	
	Investment in Associates		12,000
	(To record dividends declared and received from Beck)		

No entry is required under the equity method for the increase in the shares' fair value (from $40 to $42 per share). After the above transactions are posted, the investment and revenue accounts show the following:

Investment in Associates						Income from Associates		
Jan. 1	120,000	Dec. 31	12,000				Dec. 31	30,000
Dec. 31	30,000							
Bal. Dec. 31	138,000							

During the year, the investment account has increased by $18,000 ($30,000 − $12,000). This $18,000 is Millar's 30% share of the $60,000 increase in Beck's retained earnings ($100,000 − $40,000). In addition, Millar will report $30,000 of income from its investment, which is 30% of Beck's net income of $100,000.

The income recorded under the equity method can be significant. Illustration 12-4 compares the journal entries recorded above under the equity method with the journal entries that would have been recorded if significant influence did not exist and the fair value through profit or loss model were used to account for the investment, assuming that it was held for trading. This is done on the left-hand side of the illustration. On the right-hand side of the illustration, we assume that Millar did have significant influence over Beck and used the equity method (as just illustrated in this section).

►Illustration 12-4

Comparison of fair value through profit or loss and equity methods

Fair Value Through Profit or Loss Model			Equity Method		
Acquisition			**Acquisition**		
Held for Trading Investments	120,000		Investment in Associates	120,000	
Cash		120,000	Cash		120,000
Investee reports net income			*Associate reports net income*		
No entry			Investment in Associates	30,000	
			Income from Associates		30,000
Investee declares and pays dividends			*Associate declares and pays dividends*		
Cash	12,000		Cash	12,000	
Dividend Revenue		12,000	Investment in Associates		12,000
Adjustment to fair value			*Adjustment to fair value*		
Held for Trading Investments	6,000		No entry		
Unrealized Gain on Held for Trading Investments		6,000			

Using the fair value through profit or loss model, the investment is reported as a held for trading investment of $126,000. Dividend revenue of $12,000 is recognized in the income statement, as is an unrealized gain of $6,000 (3,000 shares × $2 [$42 fair value less $40 purchase price] per share). Using the equity method of accounting, the investment account is reported as $138,000 and income from associates of $30,000 is recognized on the income statement. Notice how the use of different methods can affect net income and the carrying amount of investments. The decision as to whether an investee can be significantly influenced is therefore a very critical one.

USING THE COST MODEL

Under certain circumstances that we will cover later, the cost model may be used when accounting for strategic investments. This model can also be used for non-strategic equity investments under certain circumstances. Under the cost model, the equity investment is recorded initially at cost and is not subsequently adjusted for any changes in fair value until sold. When the investee declares a dividend, the investor will record dividend revenue. The equity investment is reported on the statement of financial position at cost. Details regarding these transactions are covered below.

Alternative Terminology
The *cost model* is also known as the *cost method.*

Recording the Acquisition of Shares

At acquisition, the cost of the investment is the price paid to acquire it. Assume, for example, that on July 1, 2018, Passera Corporation (the investor) acquires 1,000 common shares of Beal Corporation (the investee) at $40 per share. Beal is a private corporation and its shares are now held by only two individuals and Passera. If Beal has a total of 10,000 common shares, then Passera has a 10% (1,000 ÷ 10,000) ownership interest in Beal. When a company uses the cost model, it is usually not for investments that are held for trading or investments in which there is significant influence. It is usually used when the fair value of the investment is difficult to determine. Consequently, the investment account when using this method is often just referred to as Long-Term Investments. The assumption here is that the Beal shares are the only long-term investment held by Passera. If there were others, we would distinguish them by adding the name of the investee to the account name or maintaining a subsidiary ledger.

The entry to record the acquisition of the Beal shares is as follows:

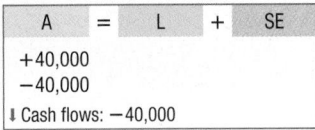

July 1	Long-Term Investments	40,000	
	Cash		40,000
	(To record purchase of 1,000 common shares of Beal)		

This investment would be reported as a non-current asset on the statement of financial position.

Recording Dividend Revenue

During the time the shares are held, entries are required for any cash dividends that the investee declares. If a $2-per-share dividend is declared and paid by Beal Corporation on October 1, the entry that Passera would record is:

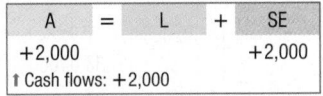

Oct. 1	Cash (1,000 × $2)	2,000	
	Dividend Revenue		2,000
	(To record receipt of cash dividend)		

Recording the Sales of Shares

When shares are sold, the difference between the net proceeds from the sale and the cost of the shares is recognized as a realized gain or realized loss. Assume that Passera Corporation receives net proceeds of $39,000 on the sale of its Beal Corporation shares on December 10. Because the shares cost $40,000, a loss of $1,000 has been realized. The entry to record the sale is:

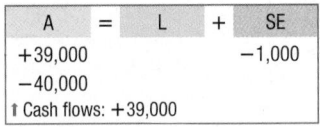

Dec. 1	Cash	39,000	
	Realized Loss on Long-Term Investments	1,000	
	Long-Term Investments		40,000
	(To record sale of Beal common shares)		

DO IT! ▶ 12-3   Strategic Investments

CJW Inc. purchased 20% of North Sails Ltd.'s 300,000 common shares for $15 per share on January 2, 2018. On April 15, North Sails declared and paid a cash dividend of $180,000. On December 31, North Sails reported net income of $300,000 for the year and had a share value of $16. Prepare all necessary journal entries assuming the following:

(a) CJW plans to trade the investment and uses the fair value through profit or loss model.

(b) This is a strategic investment with significant influence accounted for using the equity method.

(c) This is neither a held for trading investment nor one that has given CJW significant influence. Furthermore, a quoted share price for North Sails Ltd.'s shares is unavailable, so the company has used the cost model.

Action Plan

✔ Under the fair value through profit or loss model, recognize dividend revenue when dividends are declared. Adjust the investment's carrying amount to fair value, recognizing an unrealized gain or unrealized loss at year end that is recorded in the income statement.

✔ Under the equity method, recognize income when the associate reports net income. The declaration of dividends is not income; rather, it reduces the Investment in Associates account.

✔ Under the cost model, only dividend revenue and realized gains and losses are recognized and these items are recognized in the income statement.

SOLUTION

Try this Do It! exercise on your own and then check your answer at the end of the chapter.

Related Exercise Material: BE12–6, BE12–7, E12–6, E12–7, and E12–8.

Explain how investments are reported in the financial statements.

This section will explain when the valuation models we have covered are used under both IFRS and ASPE. This will be done as we cover the presentation of investments in the income statement, statement of comprehensive income, statement of changes in equity, and statement of financial position.

INCOME STATEMENT

Under most models, if applicable, any gains and losses along with dividend and interest revenue and income from associates are shown in the "other revenues and expenses" section of the income statement. One exception is the accounting for dividend revenue under the equity method, which is shown as a reduction in the investment rather than in the income statement. Other exceptions occur under the fair value through OCI model but we will leave coverage of this model to a more advanced course. Illustration 12-5 summarizes the above.

▶Illustration 12-5

Treatment of investment income items under valuation models

Item Earned	Fair Value Through Profit or Loss (Debt or Equity Investments)	Equity (Equity Investments)	Amortized Cost (Debt Investments)	Cost (Equity Investments)
Realized gains and losses	Income statement	Income statement	Income statement	Income statement
Unrealized gains and losses	Income statement	Not recorded	Not recorded	Not recorded
Interest revenue	Income statement	Not applicable	Income statement	Not applicable
Dividend revenue	Income statement	Reduces investment	Not applicable	Income statement
Income from associates	Not recorded	Income statement	Not applicable	Not recorded

Scotiabank, introduced in our chapter-opening feature story, reported various types of income from investments totalling $3,151 million in its income statement for the year ended October 31, 2015, as shown in Illustration 12-6.

▶Illustration 12-6

Income statement

BANK OF NOVA SCOTIA Income Statement (partial) Year Ended October 31, 2015 (in millions)	
Other operating income	
Trading revenues (primarily unrealized gains and losses)	$1,185
Net realized gain on sale of investments	639
Income from associates	405
Interest revenue	922
	$3,151

STATEMENT OF COMPREHENSIVE INCOME

You learned in Chapter 11 that the **statement of comprehensive income** includes not only net income reported on the income statement but also "other comprehensive income" transactions. You learned about other comprehensive income in past chapters. You will recall that revaluations of property, plant, and equipment under the revaluation model are recorded in OCI. In this chapter, you learned that gains and losses are recorded in OCI when using the fair value through OCI model. Under ASPE, OCI is not reported, so a statement of comprehensive income is not prepared when using these standards.

Companies can present the items included in other comprehensive income in a separate statement or at the bottom of the income statement in a combined statement of comprehensive income.

Scotiabank presents its net income in an income statement and then prepares a separate statement of comprehensive income by listing net income and then adding other comprehensive income (or subtracting other comprehensive loss) elements to (from) net income to arrive at comprehensive income, as Illustration 12-7 shows.

►Illustration 12-7
Statement of comprehensive income

BANK OF NOVA SCOTIA Statement of Comprehensive Income (partial) Year Ended October 31, 2015 (in millions)		
Net income		$7,213
Other comprehensive income (loss), net of tax		
Unrealized losses on investments using the fair value through OCI model	$ (480)	
Unrealized foreign currency gains	1,855	
Other	61	1,436
Comprehensive income		$8,649

The bank's net income of $7,213 million was increased by the other comprehensive income of $1,436 million, resulting in overall comprehensive income of $8,649 million. As we can see, other comprehensive income included an unrealized loss on investments accounted for under the fair value through OCI model of $480 million along with unrealized gains on foreign currencies and other minor items. Note that adjustments to comprehensive income are reported net of income tax. For simplicity, we are ignoring the income tax implications of comprehensive income in this chapter.

STATEMENT OF CHANGES IN EQUITY

As you learned in prior chapters, the statement of changes in equity presents the changes in each component of shareholders' equity each period. This includes changes in share capital, retained earnings, accumulated other comprehensive income (loss), and any other equity items that a company might report. While net income increases retained earnings, other comprehensive income (loss) increases (or decreases) accumulated other comprehensive income.

An extract from Scotiabank's statement of changes in equity, detailing the determination of accumulated other comprehensive income, is shown in Illustration 12-8. Note that detailed calculations of the changes in share capital have been omitted in the illustration for simplicity. Illustration 12-8 shows the movements in retained earnings and accumulated other comprehensive income only.

It is important to understand that the other comprehensive income of $1,436 million shown in Illustration 12-8 is not the same amount reported as the ending comprehensive income amount on the bank's statement of comprehensive income, which was $8,649 million. This is because comprehensive income shown in Illustration 12-7 comprises both net income ($7,213 million) and other comprehensive income ($1,436 million). Similar to how ending retained

►Illustration 12-8
Statement of changes in equity

BANK OF NOVA SCOTIA Statement of Changes in Equity (partial) Year Ended October 31, 2015 (in millions)		
Share capital (not detailed)		$18,075
Retained earnings		
Balance at beginning of year	$28,609	
Net income	7,213	
Dividends	(3,289)	
Other	(1,217)	
Balance at end of year		31,316
Accumulated other comprehensive income		
Balance at beginning of year	$ 949	
Other comprehensive income	1,436	
Other	70	
Balance at end of year		2,455
Other (not detailed)		1,633
Total shareholders' equity		$53,479

earnings are determined, the current period's other comprehensive income of $1,436 million is added to the opening accumulated other comprehensive income balance to determine the ending balance. This resulted in an ending accumulated other comprehensive income of $2,455 million, as shown in Illustration 12-8. It is this amount that is reported in the shareholders' equity section of the statement of financial position.

Closing Entries for Other Comprehensive Income

As we saw in Chapter 4, revenues and expenses are closed to the Retained Earnings account through the Income Summary account. This was done because we wanted to add net income earned (or deduct net loss incurred) during the year to (from) retained earnings to update the balance in that account. Just as net income (loss) for the year updates retained earnings, other comprehensive income (loss) must also be closed out into the Accumulated Other Comprehensive Income (Loss) account at the end of the year. For Scotiabank this would be done by decreasing the individual components of other comprehensive income and recording an offsetting total credit of $1,436 million to Accumulated Other Comprehensive Income (Loss) to increase the balance in that account.

STATEMENT OF FINANCIAL POSITION

Before we look at the ways investments are reported on the statement of financial position, we need to determine when the various models we have been covering are used under both IFRS and ASPE.

Accounting for Investments under IFRS

With regard to non-strategic investments, a company determines how an investment is accounted for based on its business model and the nature of the investment's cash flows. If the business model is not based on held for trading investments, and the investment is held to earn contractual cash flows relating to principal and interest payments rather than price appreciation, the investment (which would be a debt investment) is accounted for using the amortized cost model, although an option to use fair value is allowed. If the investment is held only for the purpose of selling it later (trading) and not held to earn contractual cash flows, then the investment (which could be debt or equity) is accounted for using the fair value through profit or loss model. However, if the investment is held to earn principal and interest payments and for the purpose of selling it later to earn a gain, then the investment (which would be a debt investment) would be accounted for using the fair value through other comprehensive income model. This model would also be used for an equity investment that was not held for trading. IFRS also allows companies that have non-strategic investments not accounted for under the fair value through profit or loss model as described above to elect to use the fair value through profit or loss model. However, that election is irrevocable.

For strategic investments, IFRS requires a company to prepare consolidated financial statements if it has achieved control over the investee. If significant influence but no control exists, then the investment is accounted for using the equity method. If neither control nor significant influence exists, then the investment is considered non-strategic.

Illustration 12-9 summarizes the above. Notice that the cost model is not listed in Illustration 12-9 because IFRS does not anticipate a situation where the fair value of an investment cannot be determined, but if that were to occur, the cost rather than the fair value of the investment would be used if applicable.

▶Illustration 12-9

Accounting for investments on the statement of financial position under IFRS

Accounting for Non-Strategic Investments Under IFRS				
Objective	Model Used for Debt Investment	Model Used for Equity Investment	Statement of Financial Position Classification	Name of Account Used in This Text
To receive interest and principal payments	Amortized cost model*	Not applicable	Current or non-current based on maturity date of investment	If current, usually a specific name is used, such as Note Receivable (see Chapter 8), and if non-current, Long-Term Investments
To receive interest and principal payments and to sell	Fair value through OCI model*	Not applicable	Current or non-current based on maturity date of investment	Held for Trading Investments
To hold investment for sale only	Fair value through profit or loss model	Fair value through profit or loss model	Current	Held for Trading Investments
Other objective not shown above	Not applicable	Fair value through OCI model*	Current or non-current based on intended holding period	If current, Held for Trading Investments If non-current, Long-Term Investments

*Option exists to account for investment using the fair value through profit or loss model.

Accounting for Strategic Investments Under IFRS				
Control	Not applicable	Use consolidation	Because consolidated financial statements are prepared, the investment account is not shown. It is replaced with the specific assets and liabilities of the subsidiary.	Not applicable
Significant influence	Not applicable	Equity method	Non-current	Investment in Associates

Accounting for Investments under ASPE

Under ASPE, for non-strategic investments, one first determines if an investment is an equity investment that has a quoted price in an active market. An example of this would be shares in a public company that trade on a stock exchange. For these investments, the fair value through profit or loss model is used. For all other non-strategic investments, the amortized cost (for debt investments) or cost model (for equity investments) would be used. However, if a debt investment had a quoted price in an active market, an option to use fair value through profit or loss can be taken. Because other comprehensive income is not measured under ASPE, the fair value through OCI model is not applicable at any time.

For strategic investments, if control is exercised, the investor can prepare consolidated financial statements or choose not to consolidate and use instead the fair value through profit or loss model or the equity method. These options are available because quite often there are a limited number of users of private company financial statements and, if they are not interested in reading consolidated financial statements, these statements do not have to be prepared. The cost model can also be used if there is no quoted price in an active market. If control is not achieved but significant influence can be exercised, then the equity method or fair value through profit or loss model can be used, again depending on what the users of the financial statements prefer. However, the cost model can be used if a quoted value of the associate's shares cannot be obtained. Illustration 12-10 summarizes the above.

▶Illustration 12-10

Accounting for investments on the statement of financial position under ASPE

	Criteria	Valuation Model	Statement of Financial Position Classification	Name of Account Used in This Text
Non-strategic investments	Equity investment has a quoted price in an active market.	Fair value through profit or loss	Current or non-current based on management's intentions	Held for Trading Investments or Long-Term Investments
	Investment is not an equity investment, or it is but there is no quoted price in an active market.	Amortized cost if debt or cost model if equity (can choose fair value through profit or loss on debt investment)	Current or non-current based on management's intentions	Held for Trading Investments or Long-Term Investments
Strategic investments	Investor has control.	(a) Consolidation, or (b) if fair value is known, can choose equity method or fair value through profit or loss, or (c) if fair value is not known, can choose equity method or cost model	If consolidated financial statements are prepared, the investment account is not shown because it is replaced with the specific assets and liabilities of the subsidiary. However, under ASPE, consolidation is not mandatory.	Not applicable if consolidation takes place. If no consolidation, then Long-Term Investments.
	Investor has significant influence but not control.	If fair value is known, can choose equity method or fair value through profit or loss. If fair value is not known, can choose equity method or cost model.	Non-current	Investment in Associates

Classifying Investments on the Statement of Financial Position

Many companies, including Scotiabank, view highly liquid investments that have insignificant risk and that are near maturity (usually less than three months) as cash equivalents. You will recall that we first learned about cash equivalents in Chapter 7.

Other short-term investments rank next in order of liquidity. As you learned earlier, held for trading investments are always classified as current assets, whereas non-strategic investments that are not held for trading may be either current or non-current, depending on when management intends to sell them or is able to sell them. Regardless of their classification, these types of investments are carried at fair value if this can be determined.

Illustration 12-11 shows how Scotiabank reports its held for trading investments, and for illustration purposes only, we are showing the amounts that appeared in the notes to the financial statements.

For most companies, no distinction is usually made between debt and equity securities on the face of the statement of financial position. These securities are often combined and reported as one portfolio amount on that statement. Most companies will then provide further details in notes to the financial statements.

▶Illustration 12-11
Presentation of short-term
investments

BANK OF NOVA SCOTIA Statement of Financial Position (partial) October 31, 2015 (in millions)	
Current assets	
Trading securities—equity	$35,704
Trading securities—debt	42,676
	$78,380

Long-term investments include debt securities held to earn interest revenue until they mature, and consequently they are reported at amortized cost. Any portion that is expected to mature within the year is classified as a current asset. Long-term investments also include equity securities that are purchased to have significant influence or control. If an investment is not large enough to exercise either significant influence or control, but is still being held for long-term purposes, it will typically be accounted for using the fair value through profit or loss model unless the option to use the fair value through other comprehensive income model is taken. Investments recorded using fair value through OCI have been called *available-for-sale securities* but this term will be discontinued when IFRS 9 is adopted in 2018. Under IFRS, it is possible to report long-term debt investments using the fair value through profit or loss model even though they would normally be accounted for using the amortized cost model. Scotiabank did this with some of its debt investments.

Scotiabank reports its long-term investments as shown in Illustration 12-12.

▶Illustration 12-12
Presentation of long-term
investments

BANK OF NOVA SCOTIA Statement of Financial Position (partial) October 31, 2015 (in millions)	
Assets	
Non-current assets	
Available-for-sale investments	$42,565
Investment in associates	4,033
Investments at fair value through profit or loss	320
Debt investments held using amortized cost	651
	$47,569

In the notes to its financial statements, Scotiabank provides further details about these investments.

Accumulated Other Comprehensive Income (Loss)

Accumulated other comprehensive income (or loss) is presented in the shareholders' equity section of the statement of financial position. Scotiabank reported accumulated other comprehensive income of $2,455 million, as shown earlier in Illustration 12-8.

Illustration 12-13 reviews the interrelationships among the income statement, statement of comprehensive income, statement of changes in equity, and statement of financial position. Note that changes in share capital have not been detailed in the illustration but the statement of changes in equity would include this information as well as changes in retained earnings, accumulated other comprehensive income, and any other equity items.

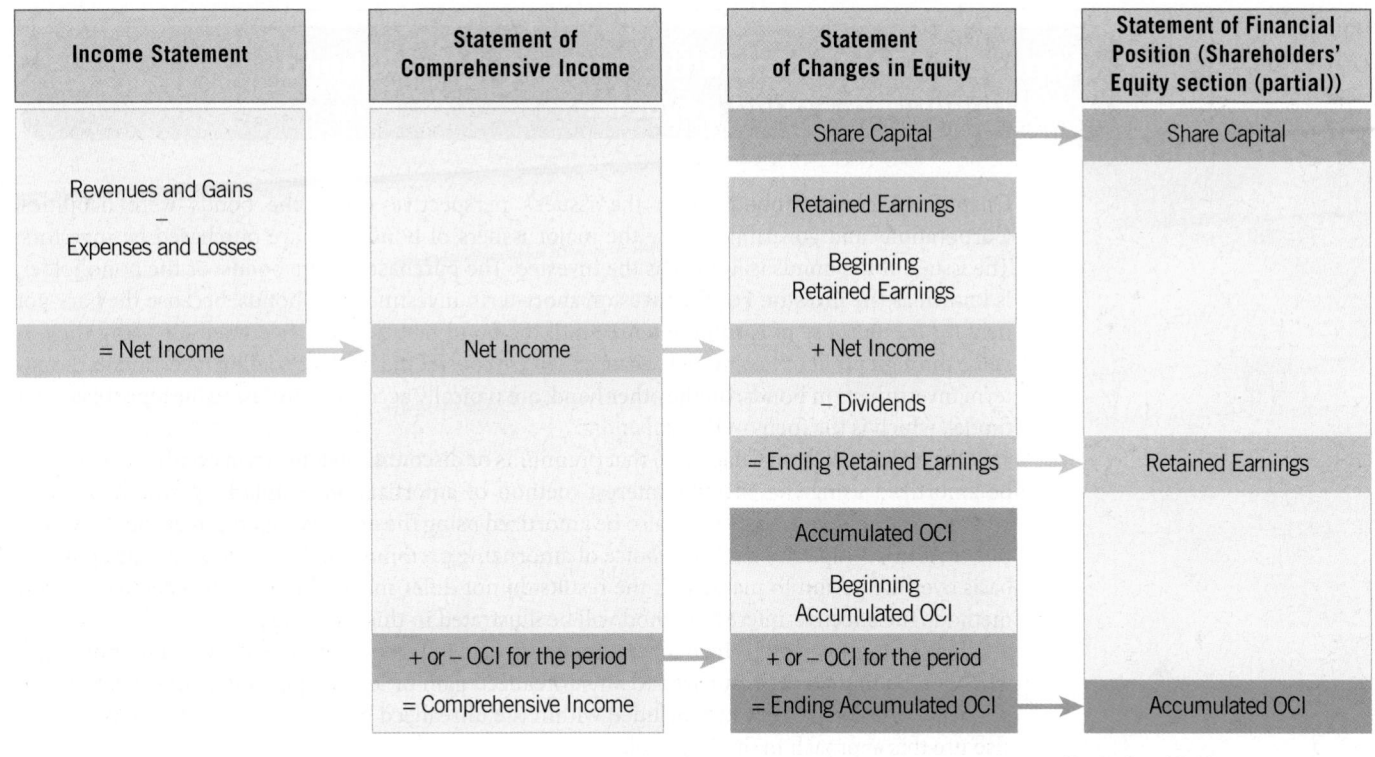

▶Illustration 12-13
Financial statement
interrelationships

Although we have chosen not to illustrate the statement of cash flows, you will recall from earlier chapters that the purchase and sale of investments are generally reported in the investing activities section of the statement. You will learn more about this in the next chapter.

DO IT! ▶12-4 Reporting Investments

Zaboschuk Corporation has the following selected accounts, listed in alphabetical order:

Accumulated other comprehensive income
Cash
Common shares
Dividend revenue
Held for trading investments
Income from associates
Interest revenue

Investment in associates
Realized gain or loss on sale of investment
    using the fair value through profit or loss
    model
Unrealized gain or loss on investment using
    the fair value through OCI model
Unrealized gain or loss on investment using
    the fair value through profit or loss model

Assume that Zaboschuk reports net income and other comprehensive income in separate statements. For each account listed above determine whether the account would be reported on the income statement, statement of comprehensive income (OCI portion), or the statement of financial position. Also determine what section of each statement the account is shown in.

SOLUTION
Try this Do It! exercise on your own and then check your answer at the end of the chapter.

Related Exercise Material: BE12–8, BE12–9, BE12–10, BE12–11, BE12–12, BE12–13, E12–2, E12–5, E12–9, and E12–10.

Action Plan

✔ Determine whether each account belongs on the income statement, the statement of comprehensive income, or statement of financial position.

✔ Identify the classifications on each statement, such as:

  ✔ current assets, non-current assets, current liabilities, non-current liabilities, share capital, retained earnings, accumulated other comprehensive income, and the like on the statement of financial position;

  ✔ other revenues and other expenses on the income statement; and

  ✔ other comprehensive income on the statement of comprehensive income.

Appendix 12A: Compare the accounting for a bond investment and a bond payable.

Chapter 10 covered bonds from the issuer's perspective where the bonds were liabilities. Corporations and governments are the major issuers of bonds that are purchased by investors. The issuer of the bonds is known as the investee. The purchaser of the bonds, or the bondholder, is known as the investor. For the investor, short-term investments in bonds, because they are not held for the purpose of earning interest until the bond matures, are accounted for using the fair value through profit or loss model because they are considered held for trading investments. Long-term investments in bonds, on the other hand, are typically accounted for using the amortized cost model, which is the focus of this appendix.

You will recall from Chapter 10 that premiums or discounts on long-term bonds payable must be amortized using the effective-interest method of amortization. Similarly, premiums or discounts on bond investments must also be amortized using the effective-interest method. However, under ASPE, companies have the choice of amortizing premiums and discounts on a straight-line basis over the period to maturity if the results do not differ materially from the effective-interest method. The effective-interest method will be illustrated in this appendix.

If a bond investment is held for trading purposes, any amortization of a premium or discount will often be immaterial compared to any unrealized gain or loss so quite often amortization will not be recorded separately but included within the unrealized gain or loss. For simplicity, we will also use this approach in this textbook.

While the amortization of discounts and premiums on bonds payable was recorded in an Interest Expense account, the amortization of discounts and premiums on a bond investment is recorded in an Interest Revenue account. If there is a bond premium on a long-term bond investment, the Interest Revenue account and carrying amount of the investment are *reduced* by the amortization amount to reflect the effect of the additional cost of the bond premium over the term of the bond. If there is a bond discount, the Interest Revenue account and carrying amount of the investment are *increased* by the amortization amount to reflect the benefit of the discount over the term on the bond.

RECORDING A BOND INVESTMENT FOR THE INVESTOR

This section will illustrate the recording of a bond investment using an example for Kuhl Corporation, the bond purchaser, and Doan Inc., the bond issuer. It will then compare Kuhl's recording of its bond investment with Doan Inc.'s recording of its bond liability. Assume that Kuhl Corporation acquires $50,000 of Doan 10-year, 6% bonds on January 1, 2018, for $49,000. This means that the bonds sold at a discount of $1,000 ($50,000 – $49,000). The price of $49,000 was based on a market, or effective, rate of interest of 6.272%. The bonds pay interest semi-annually, on July 1 and January 1. We will use the account Long-Term Investments because this investment is not going to be held for trading purposes nor is it an investment in an associate. If more than one such investment was held, we would add the company's specific name to the end of the account name or use a subsidiary ledger to track each investment. Assuming that Kuhl is intending to hold these bonds until maturity and is therefore using the amortized cost model, the entry to record the investment is as follows:

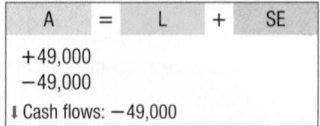

A	=	L	+	SE
+49,000				
−49,000				
↓ Cash flows: −49,000				

Jan. 1	Long-Term Investments	49,000	
	Cash		49,000
	(To record purchase of Doan bonds)		

In the above entry, the bonds are recorded at their acquisition cost of $49,000. Similar to a bond liability, the $1,000 discount on the bonds is not recorded separately but rather is netted with the cost in the investment account. Therefore, the balance in the Long-Term Investments account really consists of a credit relating to the discount of $1,000 and a debit relating to the bond's maturity value of $50,000. Over time, the credit pertaining to the discount will be amortized. This process transfers a portion of this credit into the Interest Revenue account in the income statement each period and increases it to reflect the benefit of buying the bond at a discount.

Interest to be received in cash is calculated by multiplying the face value of the bond investment by the coupon (stated) interest rate per semi-annual period. Kuhl will collect interest of $1,500 ($50,000 $\times$ 6% $\times$ $^6/_{12}$) semi-annually on July 1 and January 1.

Interest revenue will differ from the cash received by the amount of discount that is to be amortized. The interest revenue is calculated by multiplying the carrying amount of the bond investment by the market (effective) rate of interest per semi-annual interest period. Kuhl's interest revenue is $1,537 ($49,000 $\times$ 6.272% $\times$ $^6/_{12}$) for the first interest period. Interest revenue is then compared with the interest received to determine the amount by which to amortize the discount— in this case, the portion of the $1,000 discount that is amortized in this six-month period. The amortization is $37 ($1,537 − $1,500) in this case, and is debited to the bond investment account. Notice that the interest revenue of $1,537 is higher than the interest received in cash of $1,500 because the company is recognizing the benefit of purchasing the bond at a discount over the period that it intends to hold the bond.

The entry to record the receipt of interest on July 1 is:

July 1	Cash ($50,000 $\times$ 6% $\times$ $^6/_{12}$)	1,500	
	Long-Term Investments	37	
	Interest Revenue ($49,000 $\times$ 6.272% $\times$ $^6/_{12}$)		1,537
	(To record receipt of interest on Doan bonds)		

A	=	L	+	SE
+1,500				+1,537
+37				
↑ Cash flows: +1,500				

After amortization, the investment's carrying amount will increase to $49,037, which is the bond's present value on July 1. This is shown in the following T account:

Long-Term Investments		
Jan. 1	49,000	
July 1	37	
Bal. July 1	49,037	

If the bonds are later sold before their maturity date, it is necessary to (1) update any unrecorded interest, (2) debit Cash for the proceeds received, (3) credit the investment account for the cost of the bonds, and (4) record any gain or loss realized on the sale. Any difference between the proceeds from the sale and their original cost is recorded as a realized gain or loss.

Assume, for example, that Kuhl receives proceeds of $50,500 plus accrued interest on the sale of the Doan bonds on September 1, 2018. First, record the interest entry for the two months from July 1 to September 1.

Sept. 1	Cash ($50,000 $\times$ 6% $\times$ $^2/_{12}$)	500	
	Long-Term Investments	13	
	Interest Revenue ($49,037 $\times$ 6.272% $\times$ $^2/_{12}$)		513
	(To record receipt of interest on Doan bonds)		

A	=	L	+	SE
+500				+513
+13				
↑ Cash flows: +500				

The difference between the cash, $500, and the interest revenue, $513, is the amortization of the discount, $13 ($513 − $500). The investment's carrying amount is now $49,050, as shown here:

Long-Term Investments		
Jan. 1	49,000	
July 1	37	
Sept. 1	13	
Bal. Sept. 1	49,050	

Because the investment has been sold for $50,500, a gain of $1,450 has been realized ($50,500 − $49,050). The entry to record the sale is:

A	=	L	+	SE
+50,500				+1,450
−49,050				
↑ Cash flows: +50,500				

Sept. 1	Cash	50,500	
	Long-Term Investments		49,050
	Realized Gain on Long-Term Investments		1,450
	(To record sale of Doan bonds)		

Because the last two journal entries occur on the same day, most companies would simply combine them together, as follows:

A	=	L	+	SE
+51,000				+513
−49,037				+1,450
↑ Cash flows: +51,000				

Sept. 1	Cash	51,000	
	Long-Term Investments		49,037
	Interest Revenue		513
	Realized Gain on Long-Term Investments		1,450
	(To record sale of Doan bonds)		

RECORDING A BOND FOR INVESTOR AND INVESTEE

With a few exceptions, recording a debt investment in bonds (an asset) for an investor is essentially the opposite of recording bonds payable (a liability) for an investee, which was discussed in Chapter 10. Using the Kuhl Corporation example, Illustration 12A-1 compares the recording of the bonds as an investment for Kuhl and as a liability for Doan.

▶Illustration 12A-1

Comparison of a bond investment using the amortized cost model and a bond liability

Kuhl Corporation (Investor)

	Acquisition of bonds		
Jan. 1	Long-Term Investments	49,000	
	Cash		49,000
	Receipt of interest and amortization of discount		
July 1	Cash	1,500	
	Long-Term Investments	37	
	Interest Revenue		1,537
	Sale of investment		
Sept. 1	Cash	500	
	Long-Term Investments	13	
	Interest Revenue		513
1	Cash	51,000	
	Long-Term Investments		49,037
	Interest Revenue		513
	Realized Gain on Long-Term Investments		1,450

Doan Inc. (Investee)

	Issue of bonds		
	Cash	49,000	
	Bonds Payable		49,000
	Payment of interest and amortization of discount		
	Interest Expense	1,537	
	Bonds Payable		37
	Cash		1,500
	No entry because the interest that Kuhl receives is paid by the party that purchases the bond from Kuhl.		

Assuming that Kuhl sold its bonds on the open market, the issuer, Doan, is not affected by this transaction because it took place between Kuhl and another company. Doan would only be affected if it decided to buy back (redeem) its bonds from Kuhl.

DO IT! ▶12-5 Investments in Bonds with Discounts and Premiums

Apollo Limited purchased a 4%, 5-year, $800,000 Genstar bond on January 1, 2018, for $765,000 with the intention of holding it until maturity. At that time, market interest rates were 5%. The bond matures on January 1, 2023, and pays interest on July 1 and January 1 each year. Apollo has a December 31 year end.

(a) Explain why the bond was purchased by Apollo Limited at a discount.

(b) Record the journal entries that Apollo would make in 2018 on January 1, July 1, and December 31.

(c) Explain why a different amount of interest revenue is recorded on July 1 and December 31, 2018.

(d) Record the journal entry that Apollo would make on January 1, 2019, when the interest payment is received.

(e) If market interest rates rise, will bond prices fall? Why or why not?

(f) Assume that the market value of the bond on January 1, 2019, was $780,000 and because of this, Apollo decided to sell the bond immediately after receiving the interest payment that day. Record the journal entry that the company would make to record this sale.

SOLUTION

Try this Do It! exercise on your own and then check your answer at the end of the chapter.

Related Exercise Material: *BE12–14 and *E12–11.

Action Plan

✔ Record bond investments at their cost when acquired.

✔ Calculate the interest revenue on a bond by multiplying the carrying amount of the bond at the beginning of the period by the market interest rate when the bond was purchased.

✔ Calculate the cash payment received for interest on the bond by multiplying the face or maturity value of the bond by the coupon interest rate.

✔ If the bond is to be held until maturity, any premium or discount is amortized over time. The amount to be amortized is the difference between the interest revenue earned and the interest revenue received or receivable. Over time, the carrying amount of a bond investment will move toward its maturity value as the discount or premium on the bond is amortized.

✔ When a bond investment is sold, the difference between its carrying amount and the proceeds received from its sale is the realized gain or loss on the sale of the bond.

REVIEW AND PRACTICE

▶ LEARNING OBJECTIVE REVIEW

1. Identify reasons to invest, and classify investments. Corporations generally purchase investments in debt and equity securities for a variety of reasons. The investment may be purchased for a strategic reason in order to influence or control the operations of another company. Alternatively, an investment may be made for non-strategic reasons. Non-strategic debt investments may be purchased for trading purposes or to receive interest payments until maturity. Non-strategic equity investments can be held for trading purposes or to earn dividend revenue and can be held for any length of time.

2. Account for non-strategic investments. Non-strategic investments include investments in debt and equity securities. There are four major models that can be used to account for some of these investments. (1) The fair value through profit or loss model reports debt or equity investments at their fair values on the statement of financial position while all related investment income, such as interest, dividends, and both unrealized and realized gains and losses, are reported in the income statement

under other revenues and expenses. (2) The fair value through other comprehensive income model is very similar to the above except that both unrealized gains and losses are reported in other comprehensive income rather than on the income statement. Depending on whether the investment is a debt or equity security, the treatment of realized gains and losses and previously recorded unrealized gains and losses can be accounted for in different ways under this model that are covered in more advanced accounting courses. (3) The amortized cost model is used for debt investments that have premiums or discounts that need to be amortized over time. Under this model, if interest is received, it is recorded in the income statement, as is the effect of any amortization. The investment is not adjusted to reflect fair value so no unrealized gains or losses are recorded. Any realized gains and losses arising on the sale of the investment are recorded in the income statement. (4) The cost model is identical to the amortized cost model but would be used on an equity investment rather than a debt investment.

3. Account for strategic investments. When an investor company makes a strategic investment, it is usually done to influence or control the investee. Significant influence is usually achieved when at least 20% of the investee's shares are acquired. However, qualitative factors (board representation, participation in investee's decisions, material transactions with investee, interchange of managerial personnel, and provision of technical information) are the major criteria used to determine the existence of significant influence. If the investor is not able to exert significant influence over the investee company, the investment is accounted for as if it were a non-strategic equity investment. When significant influence exists, the equity method can be used. The equity method records investment income from an associate (a significantly influenced investee) based on the investor's proportion of the associate's income. If the investor receives dividends from the associate, they reduce the carrying amount of the investment account because that investee's equity has fallen.

When the investor obtains control (usually more than 50% of the shares) of the investee, the investee is referred to as a subsidiary whose financial statements are normally consolidated into those of the parent company.

4. Explain how investments are reported in the financial statements. Realized gains and losses, unrealized gains and losses, dividend revenue, and interest revenue are shown in the income statement as other revenues and expenses, with two exceptions. The first exception arises when using the equity method, where dividend revenue is not recorded in the income statement but is instead shown as a reduction to the investment account. The second exception applies to investments accounted for under the fair value through OCI model, where gains and losses are not shown in the income statement but are instead reported in OCI. (Realized gains and losses are then reclassified out of OCI, but this treatment goes beyond the scope of this textbook.)

Under both IFRS and ASPE, non-strategic equity investments are usually held for trading purposes and would be shown in the current assets section of the statement of financial position using the fair value through profit or loss model. If a non-strategic equity investment is not held for trading, it may be shown as a long-term investment on the statement of financial position and can be accounted for using the fair value through OCI model under IFRS (an option to use fair value through profit or loss is available), but because ASPE does not use other comprehensive income, use of the fair value through OCI model is not available

under ASPE. Debt investments that are held to earn interest revenue until maturity may be shown as current assets or long-term investments, depending on their maturity date. Under both IFRS and ASPE, these debt investments would be accounted for under the amortized cost model, although under IFRS, there is an option to use fair value through profit or loss if the investment is also held for trading purposes. Under ASPE or IFRS, if fair value cannot be measured, the cost model for equity investments or the amortized cost model for debt investments would be used.

Strategic investments in significantly influenced associates are shown as long-term investments. Under IFRS, they are accounted for using the equity method. Under ASPE, if fair value is known, they are accounted for using the equity method or fair value through profit or loss method. If fair value is not known, they can be accounted for using the equity method or cost model.

Under IFRS, when a company has a strategic investment in a subsidiary where control has been obtained, the preparation of consolidated financial statements is required. In this case, the investment account is replaced by the specific assets and liabilities of the subsidiary. Under ASPE, parent companies can choose to use consolidation or, if the fair value of the investment is known, the investment can be accounted for using the fair value through profit or loss model or the equity method. If the fair value of the investment is not known, then in addition to consolidating financial statements, the investment can be accounted for using either the cost model or the equity method.

Accumulated other comprehensive income is presented in the shareholders' equity section of the statement of financial position. Other comprehensive income is closed out at the end of the year into accumulated other comprehensive income.

Changes in share capital, retained earnings, and accumulated comprehensive income are shown in the statement of changes in equity.

5. Compare the accounting for a bond investment and a bond payable (Appendix 12A). The accounting for a bond investment is similar to that of a bond payable in that any premium or discount is amortized using the effective-interest method of amortization. Companies using ASPE can choose to use the straight-line method instead if the results do not materially differ from the effective-interest method. Premiums and discounts are not amortized for non-strategic investments that are held for trading purposes and would normally be accounted for under the fair value through profit or loss model.

▶ KEY TERM REVIEW

The following are key terms defined in this chapter with the corresponding page reference for your review. You will find a complete list of terms and definitions for all chapters in the glossary at the end of this textbook.

Amortized cost model (p. 651)

Associate (p. 654)

Consolidated financial statements (p. 655)

Cost model (also known as cost method) (p. 651)

Debt investment (p. 648)

Equity investment (p. 648)

Equity method (p. 655)

Fair value through other comprehensive income (OCI) model (p. 651)

Fair value through profit or loss model (p. 650)

Investee (p. 654)

Non-strategic investment (p. 648)

Parent company (p. 655)

Realized gain or loss (p. 650)

Significant influence (p. 654)

Statement of comprehensive income (p. 660)

Strategic investment (p. 648)

Subsidiary company (p. 655)

Unrealized gain or loss (p. 650)

COMPARING IFRS AND ASPE REVIEW

Key Standard Differences	International Financial Reporting Standards (IFRS)	Accounting Standards for Private Enterprises (ASPE)
Fair value through OCI	Allowed.	Not allowed because other comprehensive income is not reported.
Accounting for investments in associates	Must use the equity method.	Choice of using the equity method or cost model if shares do not have quoted prices. If they are quoted, the equity method or the fair value through profit or loss model may be chosen.
Consolidation of financial statements	Consolidation required if investor controls investee.	Consolidation is optional. If consolidation is not used, there is a choice of using the equity method or cost model if shares do not have quoted prices. If share prices are quoted, the equity method or the fair value through profit or loss model may be chosen.

DECISION TOOLKIT REVIEW

DECISION CHECKPOINTS	INFO NEEDED FOR DECISION	TOOLS TO USE FOR DECISION	HOW TO EVALUATE RESULTS
Should a company reporting under IFRS elect to use the fair value through profit or loss model for non-strategic investments accounted for using amortized cost or fair value through other comprehensive income?	Need to know how management is evaluated on the performance of an investment and whether the fair value of an investment is essential to measuring performance.	If an investment is to be held on a longer-term basis, or held only for the purposes of earning cash flows like interest payments, management is less likely to be evaluated on unrealized gains. Excluding unrealized items from the income statement makes sense, especially if management receives bonuses based on net income. In these circumstances, the investment should not be accounted for using the fair value through profit or loss model.	Review the financial statements to see the extent to which investments are recorded using the fair value through OCI model and whether debt investments are valued at amortized cost. This will give an indication of how the company views the importance of measuring short-term fluctuations in the fair value of investments in the income statement. It may also provide some insight into the relationship between investment performance and bonus calculations.
Given the options that are available under ASPE when accounting for investments, what model should be used?	Need to know what the users of the financial statements are using the information regarding these investments for. Also need to know if the fair value of the investment can be determined from an active market.	If the shareholders of the parent company want detailed information about the assets and liabilities of subsidiaries, then statements will be consolidated. If not, then determine if recording a share of the investee's income is needed to evaluate the performance of the subsidiary. A similar question would be asked of associates. If it is needed, then the equity method should be used. If it is not needed, then the fair value through profit or loss model must be used, unless fair value cannot be determined, in which case the cost model would be used. For debt investments, fair value would be used if it was considered more relevant to users than amortized cost.	Review the financial statements to see the extent to which subsidiaries have been consolidated. Then determine if income from associates or subsidiaries is being reported on the income statement. This will give an indication of how the company views the importance of measuring the performance of subsidiaries and associates. Then determine if any strategic investments are carried at fair value or cost because this will give an indication of how actively the shares of the investee are traded.

► PRACTICE USING THE DECISION TOOLKIT

Answers are at the end of the chapter.

The Simmons Foundation was established to hold a number of investments on behalf of a university and allocates the investment income to a number of worthy projects undertaken by the university. The foundation reports under IFRS, given its high public profile, and consults with several financial advisors who ensure that it has an appropriate mix of debt and equity investments in its portfolio. Some of the debt investments mature in less than a few years while others mature in 10 or 20 years. All of the debt investments are typically held to maturity in order to earn interest revenue. Other investments include non-strategic equity investments, which are actively traded.

INSTRUCTIONS

(a) What reasons does the foundation have for purchasing both debt and equity investments?

(b) Why would debt investments with different maturities be purchased?

(c) How should each type of investment be accounted for?

(d) The foundation is considering a strategic investment that would attain significant influence without achieving control. How would this be accounted for and presented on the statement of financial position? How would the net income and dividends relating to this investment be reported?

► PRACTICE COMPREHENSIVE DO IT!

Answers are at the end of the chapter.

In 2018, its first year of operations, Northstar Finance Ltd., which reports under IFRS, had the following transactions regarding its investments:

May	1	Purchased 600 Sandburg Ltd. common shares for $60 per share. This investment is held for trading purposes.
June	1	Purchased 1,000 bonds of Gladstone Inc. at $100 each. These bonds bear interest at 6%, which is paid semi-annually on November 30 and May 31 each year. They were also purchased for trading purposes.
July	1	Purchased 4,000 Lansdowne Ltd. common shares for $70 per share. This represents 25% of the issued common shares. Because of this investment, the directors of Lansdowne have invited a Northstar executive to sit on their board.
Sept.	1	Received a $1-per-share cash dividend from Lansdowne.
Nov.	1	Sold 200 Sandburg common shares for $63 per share.
	30	Interest on the Gladstone bonds was received.
Dec.	15	Received a $0.50-per-share cash dividend on Sandburg common shares.
	31	On this date, the fair values per share were $55 for Sandburg and $73 for Lansdowne. The fair value of the Gladstone bonds was $101 each. Lansdowne reported net income for the year ended December 31, 2018, of $100,000.

INSTRUCTIONS

(a) Record the above transactions.

(b) Prepare the adjusting entries required to report the investments at their fair value and accrue any investment revenue.

(c) Show the presentation of each investment and the related investment income in the statement of financial position and income statement.

(d) Without recording any entries or presenting financial statements, discuss how your answer could change if Northstar used ASPE.

▶ PRACTICE OBJECTIVE-FORMAT QUESTIONS

Answers are at the end of the chapter. Note: All questions below with an asterisk (*) relate to material in Appendix 12A.

1. Which of the following is a valid reason for a corporation's managers to make a strategic investment? (Select as many as are appropriate.)

(a) To exert influence over the decisions of the investee company.

(b) To invest excess cash for short periods of time to earn more interest revenue than would be earned if the funds were simply held in the company's chequing account.

(c) To invest excess cash for the long term to generate dividend revenue.

(d) To earn a capital gain from the appreciation of a stock over the short term.

(e) To gain control over a competitor.

(f) To invest excess cash to earn interest revenue over the long term.

(g) To gain control over a supplier.

2. Which of the following is a non-strategic investment? (Select as many as are appropriate.)

(a) Equity investment held for the purpose of trading in the short term.

(b) Debt investment held for the purpose of trading in the short term.

(c) Debt investment intended to be held to maturity.

(d) Debt investment purchased to earn contractual cash flows (interest) and to trade in the short term.

(e) Equity investment representing 30% of the issued common shares with the intention of holding the shares for a number of years.

(f) Equity investment representing 55% of the issued common shares with the intention of holding the shares for a number of years.

(g) Equity investment purchased with the intention of earning dividend revenue.

3. A company uses the fair value through profit or loss model and purchased 1,000 shares in Ace Ltd. for $23,000. Later that year, Ace declared and paid dividends of $1 per share. Following the receipt of the dividend, the company sold 600 shares of Ace Ltd. for $27 each. By the end of the year, Ace Ltd. shares were trading at $30 per share. Based on the information above, which statements listed below are correct with regard to amounts that will appear on the company's year-end financial statements? (Select as many as are appropriate.)

(a) The investment in Ace will appear as a long-term investment at the end of the year because a portion of that investment was not sold during the year.

(b) The realized gain on the investment in Ace will be $2,400 and will appear on the income statement.

(c) The unrealized gain on the investment in Ace will be $2,800 and will appear on the statement of other comprehensive income.

(d) Cash received during the year from the investment in Ace will be $16,200.

(e) Dividend revenue on the income statement will be $1,000.

(f) The investment in Ace is considered a held for trading investment and will be shown as a current asset.

(g) The investment in Ace will have a balance of $9,200 at the end of the year.

4. On the financial statements of Acadia Investments Ltd. for the year ended December 31, 2018 (its first year of operation), the following account balances were listed: Dividend Revenue $1,000, Dividend Receivable $250, Unrealized Losses on Held for Trading Investments $5,000, and Realized Gains on Held for Trading Investments $3,000. Acadia holds only held for trading investments and uses the fair value through profit or loss model. During the first week of 2018, Acadia purchased shares in three companies: Georgian Ltd. (2,000 shares), Baxter Inc. (500 shares), and Chen Enterprises Inc. (1,000 shares). Georgian Ltd. was the only investee to declare dividends in 2018 and its shares had a fair value of $19 at the end of 2018. Each share of Chen Enterprises Inc. had a fair value of $9 at the end of the year. During the year, no other investments were purchased and all of the shares of Baxter Inc. were sold. Select the statements below that are correct. (Select as many as are appropriate.)

(a) Georgian Ltd. declared dividends of $0.50 per share this year.

(b) Acadia Investments Ltd. received cash dividends of $750 this year.

(c) If Baxter Inc. shares were purchased at $32 per share, they were sold at $37 per share.

(d) If an unrealized loss of $2,000 was recorded on Georgian Ltd. shares in 2018, they must have had a fair value at the beginning of 2018 of $20 per share.

(e) If an unrealized loss of $2,000 was recorded on the Georgian Ltd. shares in 2018, an unrealized loss of $3,000 must have been recorded on the Chen Enterprises Inc. shares.

(f) If the Chen Enterprises Inc. shares had a fair value of $9 at the beginning of the year, they must have had a fair value at the end of the year of $7 per share.

(g) The realized and unrealized gains and losses and the dividend revenue for this year would all be shown in the income statement under other revenues and expenses.

5. For a company reporting under IFRS, would it be correct to use the equity method of accounting in each of the following situations? (Select as many as are appropriate.)

(a) The investor owns 19% of the investee's common shares, but has been welcomed onto the investee's board of directors.

(b) The investor owns 22% of the investee's common shares but has obtained these shares against the wishes of all other shareholders of the investee company.

(c) The investor owns 18% of the investee's common shares but has material transactions with the investee and has provided the investee with essential technical information.

(d) The investor owns all of the investee's bonds.

(e) The investor owns 17% of the investee's common shares but has exchanged managerial personnel with the investee company and consults frequently with the investee company's management team.

(f) The investor owns 24% of the investee's common shares but intends to sell these shares to a larger investor who is trying to obtain control of the investee company.

(g) The investor owns 4% of the investee's common shares and has done a small amount of business with the investee in the past and is unsure if the shares will be sold soon.

6. Big K Ranch, which reports under IFRS, purchased 30,000 of the 100,000 issued common shares of Little L Ranch on July 1, 2018, for $600,000. Managers from Big K Ranch now sit on the board of Little L Ranch. For the year ending December 31, 2018, Little L Ranch reported net income of $200,000, which was earned evenly throughout that year. In December 2018, the board of Little L Ranch declared and paid annual dividends of $70,000. On December 31, 2018, the common shares of Little L Ranch were trading at $25 each. Based on the preceding information, determine which of the following statements is correct with regard to Big K Ranch's financial statements for the year ending December 31, 2018. (Select as many as are appropriate.)

(a) Dividend revenue reported on the income statement will be $21,000.

(b) Income from associates reported on the income statement will be $60,000.

(c) An unrealized gain of $150,000 will be reported in other comprehensive income.

(d) Because the dividends from Little L Ranch were received in cash, the Investment in Associates account will fall to $579,000 at the end of 2018.

(e) When the dividends from Little L Ranch are declared, Big K Ranch should reduce its Investment in Associates account, even if the dividends have not yet been received in cash.

(f) The balance in the Investment in Associates account at the end of the year would be $609,000.

(g) The total amount of investment income from all sources from Little L Ranch reported on the income statement of Big K Ranch for 2018 would be $51,000.

7. Which of the following statements is correct if Lesage Ltd. uses IFRS? (Select as many as are appropriate.)

(a) If Lesage has an investment in bonds that it holds only for trading and the fair value of the bonds is readily obtainable, Lesage must account for the bonds using the fair value through profit and loss method.

(b) If Lesage holds 2% of the shares of a publicly listed corporation but does not intend to trade the shares, Lesage should use the fair value through other comprehensive income model but can also choose to use the fair value through profit or loss model.

(c) If Lesage holds 40% of the shares of another corporation and has a seat on the board of the investee, Lesage will account for this investment using the fair value

through other comprehensive income model.

(d) If Lesage has an investment in the bonds of another corporation and intends to hold these bonds to maturity, Lesage will use the amortized cost model for this investment, although an option to use the fair value through profit or loss model is also allowed.

(e) If Lesage has an insignificant investment in the shares of a publicly listed corporation and intends to actively trade these shares, it should use the equity method when accounting for these shares.

(f) If Lesage holds 70% of the shares of a publicly listed corporation, Lesage should prepare consolidated financial statements, which would include the accounts of this subsidiary regardless of how Lesage accounts for the investment prior to consolidation.

(g) If Lesage has an investment in bonds and has made this investment not only to earn interest revenue but also to sell the bonds before maturity, it should account for the bonds using the fair value through other comprehensive income model but it can also elect to use the fair value through profit and loss model.

8. Which of the following statements is correct if Dundas Ltd. uses ASPE? (Select as many as are appropriate.)

(a) If Dundas has an investment in the shares of a company that are held for sale (held for trading investments) but the fair value of the shares cannot be determined, Dundas can account for the investment using the equity method.

(b) If Dundas has an investment in bonds that are held for trading, even if the fair value of the bonds is known, the investment must be accounted for using the amortized cost model.

(c) If Dundas owns enough shares of another company to exercise significant influence over that company, then that investment must be accounted for using the equity method only.

(d) If Dundas owns shares in another company but does not control or significantly influence that company and does not want to trade these shares in the near term, then Dundas should account for these shares using the fair value through

other comprehensive income model if the fair value of the investment cannot be determined.

(e) If Dundas purchased enough shares in another company and now controls that company, Dundas must now prepare consolidated financial statements and include the accounts of the new subsidiary in its consolidated financial statements.

(f) If Dundas owns bonds and plans to hold them to maturity, Dundas can account for these bonds using the amortized cost model or the fair value through profit or loss model if the fair value of the bonds can be determined.

(g) If Dundas acquires shares in a publicly listed company but does not have control or significant influence over that company, and does not intend to trade these shares, then Dundas must use the fair value through profit or loss model on this investment.

9. Which of the following statements is correct regarding the presentation in the financial statements of the items mentioned below? (Select as many as are appropriate.)

(a) Held for trading investments would be shown as a current asset.

(b) Comprehensive income is equal to net income plus other comprehensive income.

(c) Other comprehensive income is closed out at the end of each year into retained earnings.

(d) Investment in associates would be shown as a current asset.

(e) A bond investment held for the purpose of receiving interest revenue over the long term would be shown as a long-term investment.

(f) Comprehensive income is closed out at the end of the year into retained earnings.

(g) Accumulated other comprehensive income is an equity account on the statement of financial position.

*10. Which of the following statements is correct with regard to recording bonds under the amortized cost model? (Select as many as are appropriate.)

(a) Unrealized gains and losses are recorded through adjusting entries at the end of the period.

(b) A bond purchased at a premium will result in the amount of interest received exceeding the amount of interest revenue recorded.

(c) Premiums and discounts are not recorded separately for the investor but are included in the investment account.

(d) The investor records the bonds initially at acquisition cost rather than at their maturity value.

(e) The amortization of a discount will decrease interest revenue.

(f) If a bond is held to maturity, there will be no realized gain or loss recorded when the bond matures.

(g) When amortizing the bond premium or discount under the effective-interest method, the interest revenue for the period will always represent the same percentage of the face value of the bond at the beginning of the period in every period that the bond is held.

WileyPLUS

Brief Exercises, Exercises, and many additional resources are available for practice in WileyPLUS.

Note: All questions, exercises, and problems below with an asterisk (*) relate to material in Appendix 12A.

▶QUESTIONS

(LO 1)   1. What are the reasons why corporations invest in debt and equity securities?

(LO 1)   2. Explain the differences between non-strategic and strategic investments.

(LO 1, 4)   3. Cumby Corporation is an equipment retailer that owns 1,000 common shares of Suncor Energy Inc. It intends to sell these shares if it needs cash. (a) Is the investment in Suncor considered a non-strategic investment or a strategic investment? Explain your reasoning. (b) Would the investment be classified as a current asset or a non-current asset on Cumby's statement of financial position?

(LO 2)   4. When an investment is accounted for at fair value, how is that value determined? How does this value differ from the net realizable value used when accounting for inventories or accounts receivable?

(LO 2)   5. At what amount—cost, amortized cost, or fair value—is each of the following most likely to be reported at on a statement of financial position: (a) common shares in a publicly traded company that will probably be sold within a year, (b) bond investments that will be held until maturity, and (c) shares in a private company that do not have a determinable fair value?

(LO 2)   6. Why might management prefer to account for a bond investment at amortized cost rather than fair value?

(LO 2)   7. What is the difference between realized gains (losses) and unrealized gains (losses)?

(LO 2)   8. Communications Inc. reported held for trading investments at their fair value of $255,000 on its year-end statement of financial position. These securities were purchased earlier in the year at a cost of $245,000. (a) How should the difference between these two amounts be recorded and reported? (b) Would your answer differ if the fair value of these securities could not be determined?

(LO 2)   9. Timmerman Ltd. purchased $1 million of 10-year bonds at face value (100) in 2018. The bonds were trading on December 31, 2018, at 105. (Recall that a bond price in this case means that the bond trades at 105% of its maturity value.) (a) At what amount would the bonds be reported in the December 31, 2018, statement of financial position if management accounted for the bonds using the fair value through profit or loss model? (b) How would any related interest revenue be reported?

(LO 2)   10. Why might management account for an equity investment using the fair value through other comprehensive model rather than using the fair value through profit or loss model?

(LO 3)   11. Identify and explain what is included in the carrying amount of a strategic equity investment using the (a) cost model, (b) equity method, and (c) fair value through profit or loss model.

(LO 3)   12. Why is the equity method used when significant influence exists?

(LO 3)   13. Explain how, and why, investment revenue differs when a strategic long-term equity investment is accounted for using the (a) cost model, (b) equity method, and (c) fair value through profit or loss model.

(LO 3)   14. (a) What constitutes (1) "significant influence" and (2) "control"? (b) Is it always safe to conclude that there is significant influence when a company owns 20% of the common shares of another company and control when a company owns 50% of the common shares of another company?

(LO 3)   15. Why are financial statements consolidated when control over a subsidiary is achieved?

(LO 4)   16. Indicate how (a) held for trading investments, (b) investment in associates, and (c) debt investments held to maturity are classified on the statement of financial position.

(LO 4)   17. Identify the proper statement presentation of the following accounts: (a) Unrealized Gain on Held for Trading Investments, (b) Realized Loss on Held for Trading Investments, (c) Income from Associates, and (d) Investment in Associates.

(LO 4)   18. Distinguish between other comprehensive income and accumulated other comprehensive income. Indicate how each is reported in the financial statements. Explain how closing entries for other comprehensive income differ from closing entries for net income.

(LO 4)   19. Explain how the income statement, statement of comprehensive income, statement of changes in equity, and statement of financial position are interrelated.

(LO 3, 4)   20. **George Weston Ltd.** owns 63% of the common shares of **Loblaw Companies Ltd.** After Loblaw acquired Shoppers' Drug Mart, George Weston's ownership percentage of Loblaw dropped to 46%. (a) When George Weston owned 63% of the Loblaw shares, what method do you think it used to account for its investment in Loblaw? (b) At that time, which company was the parent and which company was the subsidiary? (c) What kind of financial statements did George Weston Ltd. prepare to properly present this investment?(d) When George Weston's ownership interest fell to 46%, how would it account for its investment in Loblaw? (e) Is Loblaw still a subsidiary of George Weston?

(LO 5) *21. Compare the accounting for a debt investment in bonds with the accounting for a bond liability.

(LO 2, 5) *22. Explain why premiums and discounts on bond investments must be amortized when using the amortized cost model and why no amortization occurs when using the fair value through profit or loss model.

(LO 5) *23. When bonds mature, a journal entry is recorded on the books of both the investor and the investee (issuer). However, when bonds are sold by the investor prior to maturity on the open market, the sale of the bond investment results in a journal entry on the books of the investor, but not on the books of the investee (issuer). Explain why.

▶BRIEF EXERCISES

BE12–1 Identify whether each of the following is most likely (a) a debt or equity investment, and (b) a non-strategic or strategic investment. (c) Identify the most likely reason (such as earning gains, interest, dividends, obtaining influence or control) for making the investment.

Classify investments.
(LO 1)

	(a) Debt or Equity Investment?	(b) Non-Strategic or Strategic Investment?	(c) Reason for Making the Investment?
1. 120-day treasury bill			
2. A few common shares of a small oil company purchased with a temporary surplus of cash that will be held temporarily			
3. 30% of the common shares of a company purchased in order to obtain a position on the board of directors			
4. Bonds purchased with a temporary cash surplus that will not be held to maturity			
5. 100% of the common shares of a company purchased to combine its operations with those of the investor			
6. Five-year bonds intended to be held for the entire term of the bonds			

BE12–2 On January 1, 2018, Columbia Ltd. purchased $200,000 of 10%, 10-year bonds at face value (100) with the intention of selling the bonds early the next year. Interest is received semi-annually on July 1 and January 1. At December 31, 2018, which is the company's fiscal year end, the bonds were trading in the market at 97 (this means 97% of maturity value). Using the fair value through profit or loss model, prepare the journal entries to record (a) the purchase of the bonds on January 1, (b) the receipt of the interest on July 1, and (c) any adjusting entries required at December 31.

Record non-strategic investment.
(LO 2)

BE12–3 Using the data presented in BE12–2, assume that the bonds were sold for $194,000 on January 2, 2019. Record the sale of the bonds.

Record non-strategic investment.
(LO 2)

BE12–4 On August 1, 2018, McLellan Ltd. purchased 1,000 Datawave Inc. common shares for $45,000 cash with the intention of trading the shares and using the fair value through profit or loss model. Datawave declared a dividend of $1 per common share, which McLellan received on December 28, 2018. On December 31, 2018, McLellan's year end, the shares' fair value was $49,000. Prepare the journal entry to record (a) the purchase of this investment on August 1, (b) the receipt of the dividend on December 28, and (c) any adjusting journal entry required at December 31.

Record non-strategic investment.
(LO 2)

BE12–5 Using the data presented in BE12–4, assume that the shares were sold on February 1, 2019. Record the sale under two different assumptions: (a) the shares sold for $47,000, and (b) the shares sold for $44,000.

Record non-strategic investment.
(LO 2)

BE12–6 On January 1, Rook Corporation, a publicly traded company, purchased 25% of Hook Ltd. common shares for $800,000. At December 26, Hook declared a $40,000 dividend (Rook received its share that day) and reported net income of $80,000. The shares' fair value at December 31 was $840,000. (a) Record each of these transactions, assuming Rook has significant influence over Hook and is using the equity method to account for this investment. (b) How much income would be reported by Rook because of its investment in Hook?

Record strategic investment.
(LO 3)

Record strategic investment.

(LO 3)

BE12–7 Using the data presented in BE12–6, assume that Rook Corporation reports under ASPE and has chosen to account for its investment in Hook Ltd. using the cost model because the shares do not trade in an active market. (a) Record each of the transactions given in BE12–6 under this assumption. (b) How much revenue would be reported by Rook in this situation? (c) Explain why this differs from your answer in BE12–6.

Determine investment account balances; indicate statement presentation.

(LO 2, 3, 4)

BE12–8 Chan Inc., a publicly traded company, purchased 20% of Dong Ltd.'s common shares for $225,000 on January 1. During the year, Dong reported net income of $350,000 and declared and paid dividends of $40,000. The investment's fair value at December 31 was $275,000, the company's year end. (a) Assuming there is significant influence, indicate the balance in the investment account at year end and where it would be reported in the statement of financial position if Chan uses the equity method. (b) Assuming Chan does not have significant influence, determine the balance in the investment account at year end and where it would be reported in the statement of financial position if the fair value through profit or loss model is used. (c) Assuming Chan reports under ASPE and chooses the cost model because fair value cannot be determined on December 31, determine the balance in the investment account at year end and where it would be reported in the statement of financial position.

Determine the effect on the income statement when using different models.

(LO 2, 3, 4)

BE12–9 Using the data presented in BE12–8, determine the accounts and balances that would appear on the income statement at the end of the current year, and identify where those accounts are presented on that statement assuming (a) there is significant influence and the equity method is used, (b) the investment is accounted for under the fair value through profit or loss model, and (c) the investment is accounted for under the cost model.

Indicate statement presentation.

(LO 4)

BE12–10 Indicate on which financial statement (the statement of financial position, income statement, or statement of changes in equity) each of the following accounts would be reported. Also give the appropriate financial statement classification (such as current assets, non-current assets, shareholders' equity, and other revenues and expenses). Assume all held for trading investments are accounted for using the fair value through profit or loss model.

	Financial Statement	Classification
A bond investment that will mature next year		
Dividend revenue from a held for trading investment		
Investment in associates		
Investment of a few hundred common shares in a large publicly traded company that is held for trading purposes		
A bond investment that management intends to hold for 10 years		
Realized gain on a held for trading investment		
Unrealized gain on a held for trading investment		
Dividends received from a strategic investment accounted for using the equity method		
Interest earned on a held for trading investment		

Classify items as net income or OCI.

(LO 4)

BE12–11 Rosewater Corporation, a publicly traded company, reported a realized gain in the year ended April 30, 2018, on the sale of a long-term bond investment that was held to earn interest revenue. For the same year, the company also had an unrealized loss of $28,000 on its equity investments that were held for trading and $17,000 of revenue relating to its share of the net income of an associate. The accountant was not sure if these items should have been included in net income or in other comprehensive income. Identify whether each of the above items should be included in net income or OCI.

Prepare partial statement of financial position.

(LO 4)

BE12–12 Sabre Corporation, which reports under IFRS, has the following investments at December 31, 2018:
1. Held for trading investments: common shares of National Bank, cost $38,000, fair value $45,000.
2. Investment in an associate (40% ownership): common shares of Sword Corp., cost $220,000, fair value cannot be determined because the shares do not trade publicly. The investment was purchased on January 1, 2018. For the year ended December 31, 2018, Sword Corp. reported net income of $50,000 and declared and paid dividends of $16,000.
3. Equity investment: common shares of Epee Inc. (18% ownership) purchased on July 1, 2018, cost $420,000, fair value at December 31, 2018, $550,000. Management intends to purchase more shares of Epee in two years. Epee earned $42,000 for the year ended December 31, 2018, and declared and paid dividends of $2,000, which were received at the end of each quarter in 2018.

4. Bond investment that is to be held to maturity: bonds of Ghoti Ltd., purchased at a cost equal to its maturity value of $320,000, fair value $344,000.

Prepare a partial statement of financial position for Sabre Corporation at December 31, 2018.

BE12–13 Brookfield Asset Management Inc., a publicly traded company, reported in its financial statements for the year ended December 31, 2015, the following information: purchases of investments in associates, $4,136 million; share of net income of associates, $1,695 million; dividends received from associates, $480 million; investment in associates at year end, $23,216 million. Explain how each of these amounts should be reported in Brookfield's financial statements.

Indicate statement presentation.
(LO 4)

*BE12–14 On June 30, $150,000 of five-year, 10% Orbit bonds are issued at $138,960 to yield a market interest rate of 12%. Interest is payable semi-annually each June 30 and December 31. (a) Record the purchase of these bonds on June 30 and the receipt of the first interest payment on December 31 on the books of the investor assuming the bonds are to be held to maturity. (b) Record the issue of the bonds on June 30 and the first interest payment on December 31 on the books of the investee (issuer).

Record bonds for investor and investee.
(LO 5)

► EXERCISES

E12–1 Gleason Telecommunications Ltd. has several investments in debt and equity securities of other companies:
1. 15% of the common shares of Morrison Telecommunications Inc., with the intent of purchasing at least 10% more of the common shares. Gleason has already been allowed to appoint one of its executives to a seat on Morrison's board of directors.
2. 100% of the 15-year bonds issued by Li Internet Ltd., intended to be held for 15 years
3. 95% of the common shares of Barlow Internet Services Inc.
4. 120-day treasury bills, purchased for interest revenue
5. 10% of the common shares of Talk to Us Ltd., to be sold next month if the share price increases

Classify investments.
(LO 1)

Instructions
Indicate whether each of the above investments is a (a) debt or equity investment, and (b) non-strategic or strategic investment.

E12–2 Kroshka Holdings Corporation has several investments in debt and equity securities of other companies:
1. 10-year BCE bonds, intended to be held until the bonds mature
2. 10-year GE bonds, intended to be sold if interest rates go down
3. 5-year Government of Canada bonds, intended to be sold if cash is needed, which is likely
4. 180-day treasury bill
5. Bank of Montreal preferred shares, purchased for the dividend income
6. Common shares, purchased to sell in the near term at a profit. These shares are part of an investment portfolio that is actively traded.

Classify investments.
(LO 1, 4)

Instructions
(a) Indicate whether each of the above investments is a non-strategic or strategic investment.
(b) For each investment that you classified as non-strategic in part (a), indicate whether it is a held for trading investment, an investment that will be held until maturity to earn interest, or an investment that does not relate to these two categories.
(c) Indicate whether each of the above investments would be classified as a current or non-current asset on Kroshka Holdings' statement of financial position.

E12–3 Matthews Ltd. purchased $1 million of 10-year, 4% bonds on July 1, 2018, at 108.5 (this means 108.5% of maturity value). Interest is received semi-annually on January 1 and July 1. The bonds were trading at 107 at December 31, 2018. Matthews intends to trade the bonds in the near future and is using the fair value through profit or loss model.

Record non-strategic investment.
(LO 2)

Instructions
(a) Record the purchase of the bonds.
(b) Record any required adjusting journal entries at December 31.

E12–4 During the year ended December 31, 2018, and in the following months of January and February 2019, McCormick Inc. had the following transactions pertaining to its held for trading investments:
Apr.	1	Purchased 2,000 Starr Corporation $5, preferred shares for $210,000 cash.
July	1	Received quarterly cash dividend.
	2	Sold 500 Starr shares for $57,000 cash.

Record non-strategic investment.
(LO 2)

Oct.	1	Received quarterly cash dividend.
Nov.	22	Starr declared the quarterly dividend on November 22, to preferred shareholders of record on December 15, payable on January 1.
Dec.	31	Starr's shares were trading at $115 per share.
Jan.	31	Due to an urgent need for cash, 700 Starr Corporation shares were sold despite a drop in the share price to $89 per share.
Feb.	15	McCormick sold an additional 500 Starr shares after the market recovered to $117 per share.

Instructions

(a)   Record the above transactions, using the fair value through profit or loss model.

(b)   Prepare any required adjusting entries at December 31. If no adjusting entries are required, explain why.

(c)   How many Starr shares does McCormick own after the sale of shares on February 15, 2019? What are the cost and fair value of its investment on this date?

Record non-strategic investments; indicate statement presentation.

(LO 2, 4)

E12–5 At December 31, 2018, the held for trading investments for Yanik Inc. are as follows:

Security	Cost	Fair Value
A	$18,500	$21,000
B	12,500	14,000
C	21,000	19,000
Totals	$52,000	$54,000

Instructions

(a)   Prepare the adjusting entry at December 31 to report the held for trading investment portfolio at fair value.

(b)   Show the financial statement presentation of the held for trading investments and any related accounts at December 31, 2018.

(c)   On March 22, 2019, Yanik sold security A for $22,000 cash. Record the sale of the security.

Record investments.

(LO 2, 3)

E12–6 Aurora Cosmetics Ltd. acquired 40% of Diner Corporation's 60,000 common shares for $16 per share on January 1, 2018. On June 15, Diner declared a cash dividend of $140,000 to all of its shareholders and Aurora received its share of the dividend on the same day. On December 31, Diner reported net income of $300,000 for the year. At December 31, Diner's shares were trading at $20 per share. Aurora accounts for this investment using the equity method.

Aurora Cosmetics also acquired 15% of the 400,000 common shares of Bell Fashion Ltd. for $28 per share on March 18, 2018. On June 30, Bell declared a $300,000 dividend to all of its shareholders and Aurora received its share of these dividends on that day. On December 31, Bell reported net income of $640,000 for the year. At December 31, Bell's shares were trading at $26 per share. Aurora intends to hold onto the Bell shares as a long-term investment for the dividend income. Aurora uses the fair value through profit or loss model for this investment.

Instructions

Record the above transactions for the year ended December 31, 2018.

Record strategic investments.

(LO 3)

E12–7 Lovell Corporation purchased 200,000 of the 1 million common shares of Abacus Ltd. on October 1, 2018, at $2.50 per share. Near the end of the fourth quarter ended December 31, Abacus declared dividends on its common shares of $80,000 but payment will not be made until 2019. Abacus also announced that it had net income for the quarter ended December 31, 2018, of $200,000.

Instructions

Record the journal entries that Lovell would make during the last quarter ended December 31, 2018, under the following assumptions:

(a)   Lowell has significant influence over Abacus and uses the equity method to account for this investment.

(b)   Lowell does not have significant influence over Abacus and uses the cost model to account for this investment.

Determine investment account balances.

(LO 2, 3, 4)

E12–8 Young & Price Ltd. is an investment management firm that had, at the beginning of the current year on January 1, 2018, a balance of $120,000 in its Held for Trading Investments account (using the fair value through profit or loss model) and a balance of $500,000 in its Investment in Associates account (using the equity method). At the end of the year, these account balances were $130,000 and $600,000, respectively. During the year, dividends of $60,000 were received from associates while $10,000 were received from held for trading investments. In addition, the company purchased investments in associates and held for trading investments for cash of $120,000 and $50,000, respectively. Also during 2018, the company received $45,000 when it sold investments held for trading that were carried at $30,000.

Instructions

(a)   List the accounts that Young & Price will show on its 2018 income statement pertaining to its investments. Indicate where these accounts will appear on the income statement.

(b)   Determine the balances in each of these accounts at December 31.

E12–9 Grimsby Holdings Ltd., a publicly traded company, has two portfolios of investments: held for trading invest- *Determine investment*
ments using the fair value through profit or loss model and investments in associates using the equity method. *account balances; indicate*
Information regarding these two portfolios is shown below: *statement presentation.*

(LO 2, 3, 4)

	Held for Trading Investments	Investment in Associates
Balance, beginning of year	$100,000	$300,000
Purchases of investments during the year	30,000	40,000
Proceeds from sale of investments during the year	55,000	32,000
Realized gain (loss) on sale of investments	12,000	(10,000)
Dividends received	3,000	8,000
Share of associates' net income		43,000
Fair value of portfolio, end of year	94,000	350,000

Instructions
(a) Calculate the ending balance for each investment category at the end of the year.
(b) Record the journal entries for each event described in the table above.
(c) Present the amounts that would be reported on the income statement and statement of financial position at year end.

E12–10 **Cameco Corp.**, a publicly traded company and the world's largest producer of uranium concentrates, has several *Identify valuation model.*
long-term investments. These include a 100% investment in Cameco Europe, a 20.3% investment in UEX Corporation *(LO 4)*
(a publicly traded company that Cameco does not want to trade), a 24% interest in GE-Hitachi Global Laser Enrichment
LLC (a private corporation with no determinable fair value that Cameco does not wish to trade), and an insignificant
investment in an unnamed public company that the company intends to hold over the long term.

Instructions
(a) Indicate whether each of the above investments should be accounted for using the cost model, the fair value through
profit or loss model, or the equity method, and explain why.
(b) Which of the above investments, if any, should be consolidated with Cameco's operations?

*E12–11 On July 2, 2018, Imperial Inc. purchased $500,000 of Acme Corp. 5% bonds at a price to yield a market interest *Record bonds for investor*
rate of 6%. The bonds pay interest semi-annually on July 1 and January 1, and mature on July 1, 2028. Imperial plans to *and investee.*
hold this investment until it matures. At December 31, 2018, which is the year end for both companies, the bonds were *(LO 5)*
trading at 93 (this means 93% of maturity value).

Instructions
(a) Calculate the present value (issue price) of the bonds on July 2, 2018.
(b) For Imperial, the investor, record
    1. the purchase of the bonds on July 2, 2018,
    2. the accrual of interest on December 31, 2018,
    3. the receipt of interest on January 1, 2019, and
    4. the receipt of interest on July 1, 2019.
(c) For Acme, the investee (issuer), record
    1. the issue of the bonds on July 2, 2018,
    2. the accrual of interest on December 31, 2018,
    3. the payment of interest on January 1, 2019, and
    4. the payment of interest on July 1, 2019.
(d) Explain how your responses to parts (a) and (b) would differ if Imperial classified the bond investment as a held for
trading investment instead of one that would be held until maturity.

▶ PROBLEMS: SET A

P12–1A The following Givarz Corporation transactions are for bonds that were purchased as a held for trading invest- *Record non-strategic*
ment for the year ended December 31, 2018: *investment; show*
statement presentation.

Feb.	1	Purchased $200,000 of Leslye Corporation 3% bonds at 104 (this means 104% of maturity value).
		Interest is received semi-annually on August 1 and February 1. The bonds mature on February 1, 2020.
Aug.	1	Received interest on Leslye bonds.
	2	Sold $80,000 of the Leslye bonds at 102.
Dec.	31	Accrued interest on the remaining bonds.
	31	The fair value of the remaining bonds was 100 on this date.

(LO 2, 4)

Instructions

(a) Record the above transactions, using the fair value through profit or loss model, including required adjusting entries (if any).

(b) Show how the investment would be presented on the statement of financial position at December 31, 2018.

(c) Determine the balance in each of the income statement accounts that are affected in the transactions above and indicate how they would be presented on the income statement for the year ended December 31, 2018.

Record non-strategic investments; show statement presentation.

(LO 2, 4)

P12–2A During 2018, Kakisa Financial Corporation had the following held for trading investment transactions:

Feb.	1	Purchased 600 CBF common shares for $36,000.
Mar.	1	Purchased 800 RSD common shares for $24,000.
Apr.	1	Purchased 7% MRT bonds at face value, for $60,000. Interest is received semi-annually on April 1 and October 1.
July	1	Received a cash dividend of $3 per share on the CBF common shares.
Aug.	1	Sold 200 CBF common shares at $58 per share.
Sept.	1	Received a cash dividend of $1.50 per share on the RSD common shares.
Oct.	1	Received the semi-annual interest on the MRT bonds.
	1	Sold the MRT bonds for $62,000.
Dec.	31	The market prices of the CBF and RSD common shares were $55 and $31 per share, respectively.

Instructions

(a) Record the above transactions, including any required adjusting entries, using the fair value through profit or loss model.

(b) Show how the investments would be presented on the statement of financial position at December 31, 2018.

(c) Determine the balance in each of the income statement accounts that are affected in the transactions above and indicate how they would be presented on the income statement for the year ended December 31, 2018.

Record non-strategic investments for second year; show statement presentation.

(LO 2, 4)

P12–3A Data for Kakisa Financial's held for trading investments in 2018 are presented in P12–2A. Kakisa had the following held for trading investment transactions in 2019:

Mar.	1	Sold 400 CBF common shares for $23,600.
June	1	Purchased 2,000 KEF common shares for $28,000.
Sept.	1	Received a cash dividend of $1.50 per share on the RSD common shares.
Oct.	1	Sold 400 RSD common shares for $12,500.
Dec.	1	The market prices of the RSD and KEF common shares were $33 and $11 per share, respectively.

Instructions

(a) Record the above transactions including any required adjusting entries, continuing the use of the fair value through profit or loss model.

(b) Show how the investments would be presented on the statement of financial position at December 31, 2019.

(c) Determine the balance in each of the income statement accounts that are affected in the transactions above and indicate how they would be presented on the income statement for the year ended December 31, 2019.

Determine valuation of investments; indicate statement presentation.

(LO 2, 4)

P12–4A On December 31, 2018, Val d'Or Ltée held the following debt and equity investments:

	Quantity	Cost per Unit	Fair Value per Unit
Debt Securities			
Dominion bonds	4,000	$100	$ 97
Government of Canada bonds	2,000	100	135
Equity Securities			
Bank of Calgary	4,000	55	61
Matco Inc.	10,000	29	32
Argenta Corp.	10,000	36	40

Instructions

(a) Calculate the cost and fair value of Val d'Or's investment portfolio at December 31.

(b) 1. If Val d'Or considers its entire portfolio to be held for trading investments, at what value should the investments be reported on the statement of financial position at December 31 if it uses the fair value through profit or loss model?

   2. At what amount, and where, should any unrealized gains or losses on these securities be reported?

(c) 1. If Val d'Or intends to hold the debt securities until maturity and uses the amortized cost model, at what value should the debt investments be reported on the statement of financial position at December 31?

   2. At what amount, and where, should any unrealized gains or losses be reported?

(d) If all of the investments held by Val d'Or related to private companies and no fair value information relating to these securities could be obtained, what would be the impact on the income statement and on the statement of financial position?

P12–5A Lai Inc. had the following investment transactions:

Identify impact of investment transactions.

(LO 2, 3, 4)

1. Purchased Chang Corporation preferred shares as a held for trading investment and accounts for them using the fair value through profit or loss model.
2. Received a cash dividend on the Chang preferred shares.
3. Purchased Government of Canada bonds for cash, intending to hold them until maturity and accounts for them using the amortized cost model.
4. Accrued interest on the Government of Canada bonds.
5. Sold half of the Chang preferred shares at a price less than originally paid.
6. Purchased 25% of Xing Ltd.'s common shares, which was enough to achieve significant influence and accounts for the investment using the equity method.
7. Received Xing's financial statements, which reported a net loss for the year.
8. Received a cash dividend from Xing.
9. The fair value of Chang's preferred shares was lower than cost at year end.
10. The fair value of the Government of Canada bonds was higher than amortized cost at year end and the fair value of Xing Ltd.'s common shares was unknown.

Instructions

(a) Using the following table format, indicate whether each of the above transactions would result in an increase (+), a decrease (−), or have no effect (NE) on the specific element in the statement. The first one has been done for you as an example.

Statement of Financial Position			Income Statement		
Assets	Liabilities	Shareholders' Equity	Other Revenues	Other Expenses	Net Income
1. (+/−) NE	NE	NE	NE	NE	NE

(b) If the company were reporting under IFRS, would any alternative(s) to the models chosen be allowed? Explain.
(c) If the company were reporting under ASPE, would any alternative(s) to the models that were initially chosen be allowed? Explain.

P12–6A Drummond Services Ltd. acquired 25% of the common shares of Bella Roma Ltd. on January 1, 2018, by paying $3.6 million for 200,000 shares. Bella Roma declared a $0.50-per-share cash dividend in each quarter that was received on March 15, June 15, September 15, and December 15. Bella Roma reported net income of $2.2 million for the year. At December 31, the market price of the Bella Roma shares was $17 per share.

Record strategic investment.

(LO 2, 3, 4)

Instructions

(a) Prepare the journal entries for Drummond Services for 2018, assuming Drummond cannot exercise significant influence over Bella Roma and uses the fair value through profit or loss model.
(b) Prepare the journal entries for Drummond Services for 2018, assuming Drummond can exercise significant influence over Bella Roma and uses the equity method.
(c) What factors help determine whether a company has significant influence over another company?
(d) Prepare the journal entries for Drummond Services for 2018, assuming that the company reports under ASPE and has chosen to account for its investment using the cost model.
(e) Under ASPE, why do you think companies can choose to use the cost model?
(f) For parts (a), (b), and (d), calculate the ending balance in each account affected by this investment. You may omit the Cash account.

P12–7A Hat Limited has a total of 200,000 common shares issued. On October 3, 2017, CT Inc. purchased a block of these shares in the open market at $50 per share to hold as a long-term equity investment. Hat reported net income of $575,000 for the year ended September 30, 2018, and CT received a $0.25-per-share dividend on that date. Hat's shares were trading at $53 per share at September 30, 2018.

Record strategic investment; indicate statement presentation.

(LO 2, 3, 4)

This problem assumes three independent situations related to the accounting for this investment by CT:

Situation 1: CT purchased 25,000 Hat common shares.
Situation 2: CT purchased 70,000 Hat common shares.
Situation 3: CT purchased 200,000 Hat common shares.

Instructions

(a) 1. For situation 1, is it likely that significant influence has been achieved? If it has not been achieved, record all journal entries relating to the investment for the year ended September 30, 2018, using the fair value through profit or loss model. If significant influence is met, use the equity method to record these transactions.
   2. From the journal entries prepared in (1), calculate the ending balance in the investment account and any related investment revenue accounts.

(b) 1. For situation 2, is it likely that significant influence has been achieved? If it has not been achieved, record all journal entries relating to the investment for the year ended September 30, 2018, using the fair value through profit or loss model. If significant influence is met, use the equity method to record these transactions.

   2. From the journal entries prepared in (1), calculate the ending balance in the investment account and any related investment revenue accounts.

(c) When significant influence is achieved, does the investment have to be accounted for using the equity method if the investor is reporting under IFRS? Does this change if the investor is reporting under ASPE?

(d) For situation 3, is consolidation required? Why or why not? Do alternatives to consolidation exist under IFRS? Do alternatives exist under ASPE?

(e) What does consolidation mean? What happens to the investment account when consolidation occurs? Whose name will be on the consolidated financial statements?

(f) What accounting models would most likely be used for each of the situations listed above if CT Inc. reported under ASPE and the fair value of the Hat shares was unknown?

Analyze strategic investment.

(LO 2, 3, 4)

P12–8A Sandhu Travel Agency Ltd. has 400,000 common shares authorized and 120,000 shares issued on December 31, 2017. On January 2, 2018, Kang Inc. purchased shares of Sandhu Travel Agency for $40 per share. Kang intends to hold these shares as a long-term investment.

Kang's accountant prepared a trial balance at December 31, 2018, under the assumption that Kang could not exercise significant influence over Sandhu Travel Agency. Under this assumption, the trial balance included the following accounts and amounts related to the Sandhu investment:

Long-term investments	1,320,000
Dividend revenue	90,000
Unrealized gain on long-term investments	120,000

Instructions

(a) How many shares of Sandhu Travel Agency did Kang purchase on January 2? (*Hint:* Subtract the unrealized gain from the investment account.)

(b) What percentage of Sandhu Travel Agency's shares does Kang own?

(c) What was the amount of the cash dividend per share that Kang received from Sandhu Travel Agency in 2018?

(d) What was the fair value per share of the Sandhu Travel Agency shares at December 31, 2018?

(e) Assume that, after closely examining the situation, Kang's auditors determine that it does have significant influence over Sandhu Travel Agency and the equity method should be used. Accordingly, the investment account balance is adjusted to $1.4 million at December 31, 2018. What was the net income reported by Sandhu Travel Agency for the year ended December 31, 2018?

(f) Assuming that Kang does use the equity method, what amount will it report on its income statement for 2018 with regard to this investment?

(g) How would your answer to part (f) change if Kang reported under ASPE and chose to use the cost model when accounting for its investment in Sandhu because the shares did not trade in an active market?

Determine investment account balances.

(LO 2, 3, 4)

P12–9A The accountant for Ajax Holdings Ltd. has prepared the following table in order to explain to the company's board of directors the transactions that caused various investment accounts to increase and decrease during the past year. The company uses the fair value through profit or loss model for all held for trading investments, the equity method for investments in associates, and the cost method for equity investments that are not traded actively and have no determinable fair value.

	Held for Trading Investments	Investments in Associates	Long-Term Investments (at cost)
Balance, beginning of year	$50,000	$250,000	$30,000
Dividends earned and received	1,000	7,000	800
Interest earned and received	1,200	0	0
Realized gain (loss)	4,000	0	(2,000)
Unrealized gain (loss)	(3,500)	(7,300)	1,900
Proceeds received on sale of investment	10,000	0	6,300
Share of income (loss)	(4,000)	22,000	3,100
Balance, end of year	$58,700	$271,700	$40,100

Instructions

Although each of the amounts in the above table is correct, in determining the balance at the end of the year, the accountant may have included amounts that should not be included and may have added rather than subtracted (or vice versa) amounts.

(a) Prepare a revised table and calculate the correct year-end balances in the three investment accounts.
(b) Prepare a table showing the amounts that would be reported on the income statement.

*P12–10A On January 1, 2018, Jackson Corp. purchased $1.6 million of 6-year, 3% bonds for $1,515,397 to yield a market interest rate of 4%. Interest is received semi-annually on July 1 and January 1. Jackson's year end is September 30. Jackson intends to hold the bonds until January 1, 2024, the date the bonds mature. The bonds' trading value was $1,532,000 on September 30, 2018.

Record bond investment; show statement presentation.

(LO 5)

Instructions
(a) Record the purchase of the bonds on January 1, 2018.
(b) Prepare a bond amortization schedule for the term of the bonds. Round all amounts on the table to the nearest dollar.
(c) Prepare the entry to record the receipt of interest on July 1, 2018.
(d) Prepare any adjusting entries required at September 30, 2018.
(e) Show the financial statement presentation of the bonds at September 30, 2018.
(f) Prepare the entry to record the maturity of the bonds on January 1, 2024.

*P12–11A The following bond transactions occurred during 2018 for the University of Higher Learning (UHL) and Otutye Ltd.:

Record bonds for investor and investee.

(LO 5)

Feb.	1	UHL issued $10 million five-year, 4% bonds at 96 (this means 96% of maturity value) at a price to yield a market interest rate of 4.9%. The bonds pay interest semi-annually on August 1 and February 1.
	1	Otutye Ltd. purchased $3 million of UHL's bonds at 96 as a long-term investment that was to be held to maturity.
Aug.	1	The semi-annual interest on the bonds was paid.

Instructions
(a) Prepare all required journal entries for Otutye Ltd., the investor, to record the above transactions.
(b) How would the journal entries for Otutye Ltd. change if the investment had been purchased for trading purposes?
(c) Prepare all required entries for UHL, the investee, to record the above transactions.
(d) Comment on the differences in recording that you observe between the investor and the investee.

▶ PROBLEMS: SET B

P12–1B The following Liu Corporation transactions are for bonds that were purchased as held for trading investments for the year ended December 31, 2018:

Record non-strategic investment; show statement presentation.

(LO 2, 4)

Jan.	1	Purchased $200,000 of RAM Corporation 3% bonds at 96 (this means 96% of maturity value). Interest is received semi-annually on July 1 and January 1. The bonds mature on January 1, 2020.
July	1	Received interest on the RAM bonds.
	2	Sold $50,000 of RAM bonds at 99.
Dec.	31	Accrued interest on the remaining bonds.
	31	The fair value of the remaining bonds was 101 on this date.

Instructions
(a) Record the above transactions, including any required adjusting entries, using the fair value through profit or loss model.
(b) Show how the investment would be presented on the statement of financial position at December 31, 2018.
(c) Determine the balance in each of the income statement accounts that are affected in the transactions above and indicate how they would be presented on the income statement for the year ended December 31, 2018.

P12–2B During 2018, Cheque Mart Ltd. had the following held for trading investment transactions:

Record non-strategic investments; show statement presentation.

(LO 2, 4)

Feb.	1	Purchased 1,000 IBF common shares for $30,000.
Mar.	1	Purchased 500 RST common shares for $29,000.
Apr.	1	Purchased 6% CRT bonds at face value, for $90,000. Interest is received semi-annually on April 1 and October 1.
July	1	Received a cash dividend of $2 per share on the IBF common shares.
Aug.	1	Sold 350 IBF common shares at $33 per share.
Sept.	1	Received a cash dividend of $1.50 per share on the RST common shares.
Oct.	1	Received the semi-annual interest on the CRT bonds.
	1	Sold the CRT bonds for $86,000.
Dec.	31	The market prices of the IBF and RST common shares were $28 and $62 per share, respectively.

Instructions

(a) Record the above transactions, including any required adjusting entries, using the fair value through profit or loss model.

(b) Show how the investments would be presented on the statement of financial position at December 31, 2018.

(c) Determine the balance in each of the income statement accounts that are affected in the transactions above and indicate how they would be presented on the income statement for the year ended December 31, 2018.

Record non-strategic investments for second year; show statement presentation.

(LO 2, 4)

P12–3B Data for Cheque Mart's held for trading investments in 2018 are presented in P12–2B. Cheque Mart had the following held for trading investment transactions in 2019:

Mar.	1	Sold 650 IBF common shares for $22,100.
June	1	Purchased 2,000 DEF common shares for $18,000.
Sept.	1	Received a cash dividend of $1.50 per share on the RST common shares.
Oct.	1	Sold 250 RST common shares for $14,250.
Dec.	31	The market prices of the RST and DEF common shares were $56 and $12 per share, respectively.

Instructions

(a) Record the above transactions, including any required adjusting journal entries, continuing the use of the fair value through profit or loss model.

(b) Show how the investments would be presented on the statement of financial position at December 31, 2019.

(c) Determine the balance in each of the income statement accounts that are affected in the transactions above and indicate how they would be presented on the income statement for the year ended December 31, 2019.

Determine valuation of investments; indicate statement presentation.

(LO 2, 4)

P12–4B On January 1, 2018, Sturge Enterprises Inc. held the following debt and equity investments:

Security	Quantity	Cost per Unit
Ajax Ltd. Shares	3,000	$12
Beta Corp. shares	4,000	7

During the year, Sturge made the following purchases:

Security	Quantity	Cost per Unit
Ajax Ltd. shares	2,400	$ 11
Ajax Ltd. shares	2,000	9
Ajax Ltd. shares	2,000	10
Beta Corp. shares	1,000	8
Citrus Inc. bonds	600	100

There were no differences between cost and fair value at January 1, 2018. The market prices of the various securities at year end, December 31, 2018, were as follows: Ajax shares $6; Beta shares $9; and Citrus bonds $107 (this means 107% of maturity value).

Instructions

(a) Calculate the cost and fair value of Sturge Enterprises' investment portfolio at December 31.

(b) 1. If Sturge Enterprises considers its entire portfolio to be held for trading investments and uses the fair value through profit or loss model, at what value should these investments be reported on the statement of financial position at December 31?

2. At what amount, and where, should any unrealized gains or losses be reported?

(c) 1. If Sturge Enterprises intends to hold the Citrus bonds until they mature and uses the amortized cost model, at what value should these bonds be reported on the statement of financial position at December 31?

2. At what amount, and where, should any unrealized gains or losses on the bonds be reported?

(d) If all of the investments held by Sturge Enterprises related to private companies and no fair value information related to these securities could be obtained, what would be the impact on the income statement and on the statement of financial position?

Identify impact of investment transactions.

(LO 2, 3, 4)

P12–5B Olsztyn Inc. had the following investment transactions:

1. Purchased Arichat Corporation common shares as a held for trading investment and accounts for them using the fair value through profit or loss model.

2. Received a cash dividend on Arichat common shares.

3. Purchased Bombardier bonds intending to hold them to maturity and accounts for them using the amortized cost model.

4. Received interest on Bombardier bonds.

5. Sold half of the Bombardier bonds at a price greater than originally paid.

6. Purchased 40% of LaHave Ltd.'s common shares, which was enough to achieve significant influence, and accounts for the investment using the equity method.
7. Received LaHave's financial statements, which reported net income for the year.
8. Received a cash dividend from LaHave.
9. The fair value of Arichat's common shares was higher than cost at year end.
10. The fair value of Bombardier's bonds was lower than their amortized cost at year end and the fair value of LaHave Ltd.'s common shares was unknown.

Instructions

(a) Using the following table format, indicate whether each of the above transactions would result in an increase (+), a decrease (−), or have no effect (NE) on the specific element on the statement. The first one has been done for you as an example.

Statement of Financial Position			Income Statement		
Assets	Liabilities	Shareholders' Equity	Other Revenues	Other Expenses	Net Income
1. (+/−) NE	NE	NE	NE	NE	NE

(b) If the company were reporting under IFRS, would any alternative(s) to the models chosen above be allowed? Explain.
(c) If the company were reporting under ASPE, would any alternative(s) to the models that were initially chosen be allowed? Explain.

P12–6B Cassidy Concrete Corp. acquired 20% of Enda Inc.'s common shares on January 1, 2018, by paying $6 million for 200,000 shares. Enda declared a $0.50-per-share cash dividend, which Cassidy received on June 30 and again on December 31. Enda reported net income of $3,360,000 for the year. At December 31, the market price of the Enda shares was $31 per share.

Record strategic investment.

(LO 2, 3, 4)

Instructions

(a) Prepare the journal entries for Cassidy Concrete for 2018, assuming Cassidy cannot exercise significant influence over Enda and uses the fair value through profit or loss model.
(b) Prepare the journal entries for Cassidy Concrete for 2018, assuming Cassidy can exercise significant influence over Enda and uses the equity method.
(c) What factors help determine whether a company has significant influence over another company?
(d) Prepare the journal entries for Cassidy Concrete for 2018, assuming that the company reports under ASPE and has chosen to account for its investment using the cost model because the shares did not trade in an active market.
(e) Under ASPE, why do you think companies can choose to use the cost model?
(f) For parts (a), (b), and (d) above, calculate the ending balance in each account affected by this investment. You may omit the Cash account.

P12–7B Sub Corporation has a total of 500,000 common shares issued. On January 2, 2018, Partridge Inc. purchased a block of these shares in the open market at $10 per share to hold as a long-term investment. At the end of 2018, Sub Corporation reported net income of $350,000 and Partridge received a $0.50-per-share dividend from Sub. Sub Corporation's shares were trading at $12 per share at December 31, 2018.

Record strategic investment; indicate statement presentation.

(LO 2, 3, 4)

This problem assumes three independent situations related to the accounting for this investment by Partridge:

Situation 1: Partridge purchased 60,000 Sub common shares.
Situation 2: Partridge purchased 125,000 Sub common shares.
Situation 3: Partridge purchased 500,000 Sub common shares.

Instructions

(a) 1. For situation 1, is it likely that significant influence has been achieved? If it has not been achieved, record all journal entries relating to the investment for the year ended December 31, 2018, using the fair value through profit or loss model. If significant influence is met, use the equity method to record these transactions.
   2. From the journal entries prepared in (1), calculate the ending balance in the investment account and any related investment revenue accounts.
(b) 1. For situation 2, is it likely that significant influence has been achieved? If it has not been achieved, record all journal entries relating to the investment for the year ended December 31, 2018, using the fair value through profit or loss model. If significant influence is met, use the equity method to record these transactions.
   2. From the journal entries prepared in (1), calculate the ending balance in the investment account and any related investment revenue accounts.
(c) When significant influence is achieved, does the investment have to be accounted for using the equity method if the investor is reporting under IFRS? Does this change if the investor is reporting under ASPE?

(d) For situation 3, is consolidation required? Why or why not? Do alternatives to consolidation exist under IFRS? Do alternatives exist under ASPE?

(e) What does consolidation mean? What happens to the investment account when consolidation occurs? Whose name will be on the consolidated financial statements?

(f) What accounting models would most likely be used for each of the situations listed above if Partridge Corporation reported under ASPE and the fair value of the Sub shares was unknown?

Analyze strategic investment.

(LO 2, 3, 4)

P12–8B On January 2, 2018, Hadley Inc. purchased shares of Letourneau Cycles Corp. for $10 per share. Hadley intends to hold these shares as a long-term investment. During 2018, Letourneau Cycles reported net income of $1 million and declared and paid dividends of $200,000. The investment's fair value at December 31, 2018, was $950,000.

Hadley's accountant prepared a trial balance at December 31, 2018, under the assumption that Hadley should use the equity method because it could exercise significant influence over Letourneau Cycles. Under this assumption, the trial balance included the following accounts and amounts:

Investment in associates	$960,000
Income from associates	200,000

Instructions

(a) What percentage of the Letourneau Cycles shares does Hadley own? (*Hint*: The ownership percentage can be determined using the investment revenue and Letourneau's net income.)

(b) What was the amount of the cash dividend that Hadley received from Letourneau Cycles during 2018?

(c) How many shares of Letourneau Cycles did Hadley purchase on January 2?

(d) What questions need to be asked to determine if Hadley has significant influence over Letourneau Cycles?

(e) Assume that, after closely examining the situation, Hadley's auditors determine that it does not have significant influence over Letourneau Cycles. What amount should be reported on Hadley's statement of financial position at December 31 for its investment in Letourneau Cycles, assuming that the fair value through profit or loss model was used? What will be reported on Hadley's income statement for 2018?

(f) How would your answer to part (e) change if Hadley reported under ASPE and chose to use the cost model when accounting for its investment in Letourneau assuming that the shares did not trade in an active market?

Determine investment account balances.

(LO 2, 3, 4)

P12–9B The accountant for Comet Holdings Ltd. has prepared the following table in order to explain to the company's board of directors the transactions that caused various investment accounts to increase and decrease during the past year. The company uses the fair value through profit or loss model for all held for trading investments, the equity method for investments in associates, and the cost method for equity investments that are not traded actively and have no determinable fair value.

	Held for Trading Investments	Investments in Associates	Long-Term Investments (at cost)
Balance, beginning of year	$100,000	$500,000	$60,000
Dividends earned and received	3,000	15,000	1,200
Interest earned and received	2,800	0	0
Realized gain (loss)	9,000	0	(5,000)
Unrealized gain (loss)	(8,200)	(14,400)	4,200
Proceeds received on sale of investment	21,000	0	12,600
Share of income (loss)	(8,100)	37,000	5,300
Balance, end of year	$119,500	$537,600	$78,300

Instructions

Although each of the amounts in the above table is correct, in determining the balance at the end of the year, the accountant may have included amounts that should not be included and may have added rather than subtracted (or vice versa) amounts.

(a) Prepare a revised table and calculate the correct year-end balances in the three investment accounts.

(b) Prepare a table showing the amounts that would be reported on the income statement.

Record bond investment; show statement presentation.

(LO 5)

*P12–10B On January 1, 2018, Morissette Inc. purchased $900,000 of 6-year, 2% bonds for $850,916 to yield a market interest rate of 3%. Interest is received semi-annually on July 1 and January 1. Morissette's year end is October 31. Morissette intends to hold the bonds until January 1, 2024, the date the bonds mature. The bonds' fair value on October 31, 2018, was $860,000.

Instructions

(a) Record the purchase of the bonds on January 1, 2018.

(b) Prepare a bond amortization schedule for the term of the bonds. Round all amounts on the table to the nearest dollar.

(c) Prepare the entry to record the receipt of interest on July 1, 2018.

(d) Prepare any adjusting entries required at October 31, 2018.

(e) Show the financial statement presentation of the bonds at October 31, 2018.

(f) Prepare the entry to record the maturity of the bonds on January 1, 2024.

*P12–11B On January 1, 2018, CASB Incorporated issued $1 million of 5-year, 4% bonds at 102 (this means 102% of maturity value) at a price to yield a market interest rate of 3.5%. The bonds pay interest semi-annually on June 30 and December 31. On January 1, Densmore Consulting Ltd. purchased $200,000 of CASB bonds at 102 as a held for trading investment. On July 1, after receiving the bond interest, Densmore Consulting sold its CASB bonds at 103. Both companies have a December 31 year end.

Record bonds for investor and investee.

(LO 5)

Instructions

(a) Prepare all required entries for Densmore Consulting, the investor, to record the above transactions.

(b) How would the journal entries for Densmore Consulting change if the investment had been purchased with the intent of holding it to maturity?

(c) Prepare all required entries for CASB, the investee, to record the above transactions.

(d) Comment on the differences in recording that you observe between the investor and the investee.

EXPAND YOUR | CRITICAL THINKING

CT12–1 Financial Reporting Case

The financial statements of **The North West Company Inc.** are presented in Appendix A at the end of this textbook.

Instructions

(a) Does North West report any investments on its statement of financial position or in the notes to its financial statements? If so, are they debt or equity investments? Non-strategic or strategic investments? (*Hint*: Look at Note 10 and Note 23.)

(b) Note 23 to the financial statements lists a number of subsidiaries owned by the company. Why aren't investment accounts relating to these subsidiaries shown on the statement of financial position?

CT12–2 Financial Analysis Case

The financial statements of **The North West Company Inc.** are presented in Appendix A, followed by the financial statements for **Sobeys Inc.** in Appendix B.

Instructions

(a) Compare the statements of financial position of the two companies.

1. North West has an "other asset" that includes an investment in a jointly controlled (significantly influenced) entity. What model or method of accounting do you think the company should use for this investment?

2. Sobeys has an investment in an associate (affiliate) that is a private company with no determinable fair value and there is no intention of trading these shares. What model or method of accounting do you think the company should use for this investment?

(b) Compare the income statements of each company. Why does neither of these companies report any items on the income statement pertaining to its investments?

(c) Which company had the largest other comprehensive income? Although this other comprehensive income did not relate to investments, to what account was this OCI closed out at the end of the year?

CT12–3 Professional Judgement Case

Two brothers, Adam and Robert Merkle, began A&R Plumbing Ltd. (ARP), a private company, approximately five years ago. Adam performs all administrative tasks (inventory ordering, accounting, payroll, and so on) while Robert provides the skills of the trade. In January 2018, ARP purchased 20,000 common shares of Canadian Plumbing Supplies Ltd (CPS). CPS is a plumbing supply distributor and its shares were acquired for $100,000. The shares represent a 20% ownership holding of CPS and the shares are traded actively on the Toronto Stock Exchange. Since the purchase, neither Adam nor Robert has been actively involved in any decisions related to CPS's operations. However, next year when Robert has more free time, he plans on using ARP's 20% share to obtain a seat on the CPS board of directors. He wants to use his board position to develop a referral system whereby CPS will refer customers to ARP for plumbing services. At the same time, he hopes to obtain additional financing from his bank to expand ARP further. The banker is very interested in ARP's profitability. At December 31, 2018, CPS's shares were trading for $4.50 each.

CPS's year end is December 31. For the year ended December 31, 2018, CPS reported a loss of $30,000. CPS did not declare any dividends. Adam had accounted for the investment in CPS using the cost model.

Instructions

(a) Robert has come to you, an independent public accountant, for advice. He would like you to assess the accounting choice that Adam has made for the investment in CPS.

1. Describe the acceptable accounting policy choices available under ASPE to account for ARP's investment in CPS. Is the cost model an acceptable method under ASPE for this investment?

2. Which accounting policy choice do you think Robert would prefer? Why?

(b) Explain how the accounting policy choices available to ARP for its investment in CPS might be different if it reported its financial results in accordance with IFRS.

CT12–4 Professional Judgement Case

At the beginning of 2018, Bering Limited purchased three investments:

1. Government of Alberta bonds, which are to be held to maturity.
2. Common shares in Atlas Inc., representing only 1% of the shares of this company, that are expected to be traded soon.
3. 40% of the common shares in CH Resources Ltd.

The cost and the fair value at December 31, 2018, for each of these investments are shown below:

Security	Cost	Fair Value
Government of Alberta bonds	$100,000	$ 90,000
Atlas Inc. common shares	100,000	105,000
CH Resources Ltd. common shares	100,000	111,000

During 2018, interest revenue of $3,000 was earned and received on the Government of Alberta bonds. CH Resources reported net income in 2018 of $10,000, and declared and paid dividends of $2,000. No dividends were received on the Atlas shares.

Instructions

(a) The board of directors of Bering Limited is considering the use of IFRS and is aware that there are choices that can be made when accounting for investments using these standards. The board would like you to choose the appropriate model for each type of investment that will maximize Bering's financial position and profitability and determine the amounts that would appear on the December 31, 2018, financial statements given these choices.

(b) Assuming that the company may prefer to use ASPE rather than IFRS, address the issues raised in part (a) above but do this in an ASPE context.

CT12–5 Ethics Case

This case can be assigned as a group activity. Additional instructions and material for this activity can be found on the Instructor Resource site and in WileyPLUS.

Kreiter Financial Services Ltd. recently purchased a portfolio of debt and equity securities. Financial vice-president Vicki Lemke and controller Ula Greenwood are in the process of classifying the securities in the portfolio.

Lemke suggests accounting for both debt and equity securities expected to increase in value during the year using the fair value through profit or loss model in order to increase net income. She wants to account for all securities that are expected to decline in value using the cost model for equity securities and the amortized cost model for debt securities so that no decline in the value of the investment will ever be shown.

Greenwood disagrees. She recommends accounting for all equity securities that are expected to increase in value using the equity method and using the amortized cost model for all debt securities and the cost model for equity securities expected to fall in value to avoid recording the decline. Greenwood argues that the fair value of an equity investment is more volatile and, if the equity method were used instead, there would be a "smoother" buildup in the value of the investment.

Instructions

(a) Prepare arguments against the position taken by Lemke. What flaws are there in her arguments? Are any of her proposals reasonable? Does she understand the implications that each method has for the financial statements?

(b) Prepare arguments against the position taken by Greenwood. What flaws are there in her arguments? Are any of her proposals reasonable? Does she understand the implications that each method has for the financial statements?

(c) Assume that Lemke and Greenwood classify the portfolio properly. If Kreiter sold all of its held for trading investments that had risen in value just prior to year end and sold all of its held for trading investments that declined in value immediately after year end, would these decisions allow the company to manipulate net income?

CT12–6 Serial Case

(*Note:* This is a continuation of the serial case from Chapters 1 through 11.)

The year ended June 30, 2019, has been another successful year for ABC. The success, however, has meant that Doug, Bev, Emily, and Daniel have spent many long hours in the business accommodating their clients, both large and small. Doug and Bev have still not had much time to enjoy any of their successes and are considering retiring from the business.

The Anthony family has come to know the executives at Software Solutions, a public corporation, and at Compuhelp Limited, a private corporation. Both of these organizations have been pleased with the service and products that ABC has provided over the years. Joey Vosburgh, the president of Software Solutions, wishes to strengthen the relationship between ABC and Software Solutions. He recognizes that Doug and Bev are considering retirement. He has put forward an offer for Software Solutions to purchase all of the shares that are currently held by the Anthony family. He has also guaranteed employment to both Emily and Daniel for the next two years.

Ali Rashid, the president of Compuhelp, learned about the offer put forward by Software Solutions and is concerned that the relationship his company has developed with ABC will not be maintained if it is purchased by Software Solutions. As a result, he has offered to purchase the shares held by Doug and Bev, leaving Emily and Daniel with their 50% ownership interest and the responsibility for running the business. You will recall from Chapter 11 that 100 common shares are owned by each family member, for a total of 400 common shares.

Instructions

(a) If Software Solutions were to succeed in the offer to purchase all of the shares of ABC, describe how this investment would be accounted for, and reported, in the accounting records of Software Solutions. ABC shares do not trade in an active market. Would a change in the manner in which ABC's accounting records are maintained have to be undertaken? Why or why not?

(b) If Compuhelp were to succeed in the offer to purchase Bev and Doug's shares (50%) of ABC, describe how this investment would be accounted for in the accounting records of Compuhelp. Would a change in the manner in which ABC's accounting records are maintained have to be undertaken? Why or why not?

(c) Identify some of the advantages and disadvantages to Bev, Doug, Emily, and Daniel of each of these offers.

▶ ANSWERS TO CHAPTER PRACTICE QUESTIONS

DO IT! 12-1
Investment Classifications

	(a)	(b)	(c)
1.	Debt	Non-strategic	Interest revenue for 120 days
2.	Equity	Non-strategic	Share price appreciation (capital gain)
3.	Debt	Non-strategic	Interest revenue over the long term
4.	Equity	Strategic	Influence the company or other shareholders with a large block of voting common shares

DO IT! 12-2
Non-Strategic Investments

(a)

Date	Account	Debit	Credit
Sept. 2	Held for Trading Investments	70,000	
	Cash		70,000
	(To record purchase of Jenkins Corp. shares)		
Oct. 12	Cash ($0.90 × 1,000)	900	
	Dividend Revenue		900
	(To record receipt of dividend on Jenkins Corp. shares)		
22	Cash ($67 × 500 shares)	33,500	
	Realized Loss on Held for Trading Investments	1,500	
	Held for Trading Investments ($70,000 × ½)		35,000
	(To record sale of half of Jenkins Corp. shares)		
Dec. 30	Dividends Receivable	475	
	Dividend Revenue ($0.95 × 500)		475
	(To record dividends earned)		

(b)

Date	Account	Debit	Credit
Dec. 31	Unrealized Loss on Held for Trading Investments	2,500	
	($70 − $65) × 500 shares		
	Held for Trading Investments		2,500
	(To record unrealized loss on Jenkins shares)		

(c) The Cash and Held for Trading Investments accounts would be reported as current assets on the statement of financial position. The Dividend Revenue, Realized Loss, and Unrealized Loss accounts would be reported as other revenues and expenses on the income statement.

DO IT! 12-3
Strategic Investments

(a) Fair value through profit or loss model

Date	Account	Debit	Credit
Jan. 2	Held for Trading Investments (20% × 300,000 × $15)	900,000	
	Cash		900,000
	(To record purchase of 60,000 [20% × 300,000] North Sails shares)		
Apr. 15	Cash	36,000	
	Dividend Revenue (20% × $180,000)		36,000
	(To record receipt of cash dividend)		
Dec. 31	No entry for investee net income		
31	Held for Trading Investments	60,000	
	Unrealized Gain on Held for Trading Investments		60,000
	(60,000 × [$16 − $15])		
	(To record unrealized gain on North Sails shares)		

(b) Equity method

Jan. 2	Investment in Associates (20% × 300,000 × $15)		900,000	
	Cash			900,000
	(To record purchase of 60,000 [20% × 300,000] North Sails shares)			
Apr. 15	Cash		36,000	
	Investment in Associates (20% × $180,000)			36,000
	(To record receipt of cash dividend)			
Dec. 31	Investment in Associates (20% × $300,000)		60,000	
	Income from Associates			60,000
	(To record 20% equity in North Sails' net income)			
31	No entry to record change in fair value			

(c) Cost model

Jan. 2	Long-Term Investments (20% × 300,000 × $15)		900,000	
	Cash			900,000
	(To record purchase of 60,000 [20% × 300,000] North Sails shares)			
Apr. 15	Cash		36,000	
	Dividend Revenue (20% × $180,000)			36,000
	(To record receipt of cash dividend)			
Dec. 31	No entry to record share of investee net income or change in fair value			

DO IT! 12-4

Reporting Investments

Account	Financial Statement	Classification
Accumulated other comprehensive income	Statement of financial position	Accumulated OCI section; shareholders' equity
Cash	Statement of financial position	Current assets
Common shares	Statement of financial position	Share capital; shareholders' equity
Dividend revenue	Income statement	Other revenues and expenses
Held for trading investments	Statement of financial position	Current assets
Income from associates	Income statement	Other revenues and expenses
Interest revenue	Income statement	Other revenues and expenses
Investment in associates	Statement of financial position	Non-current assets
Realized gain or loss on sale of investment using the fair value through profit or loss model	Income statement	Other revenues and expenses
Unrealized gain or loss on investment using the fair value through OCI model	Statement of comprehensive income	Other comprehensive income
Unrealized gain or loss on investment using the fair value through profit or loss model	Income statement	Other revenues and expenses

---

DO IT! 12-5

Investments in Bonds with Discounts and Premiums

(a) A bond will typically sell at a price that is equal to the present value of its future cash flows determined by using market interest rates on the date that the investment is acquired. In this case, since the bond offers a coupon interest rate that is lower than the market interest rate, the bond is less attractive to investors, and the price of the bond will fall to a value where its effective interest rate will then be equal to the market rate. A bond discount can be considered an additional benefit that is obtained when an investment is purchased, which is recognized over time until maturity through increases in interest revenue in a process known as amortization.

(b) Journal entries for the events described above are shown below:

Jan. 1	Long-Term Investments		765,000	
	Cash			765,000
	(To record purchase of Genstar bond)			
Jul. 1	Cash (4% × $800,000 × $^6/_{12}$)		16,000	
	Long-Term Investments		3,125	
	Interest Revenue (5% × $765,000 × $^6/_{12}$)			19,125
	(To record interest revenue on Genstar bond)			
Dec. 31	Interest Receivable (4% × $800,000 × $^6/_{12}$)		16,000	
	Long-Term Investments		3,203	
	Interest Revenue (5% × ($765,000 + $3,125) × $^6/_{12}$)			19,203
	(To record interest revenue on Genstar bond)			

(c) Every time interest revenue is recorded, the discount on the bond is amortized. This in turn increases the bond's carrying amount (as it moves over time to its maturity amount), as a portion of the discount is allocated to interest revenue. Since the interest revenue earned is a function of the carrying amount, which is rising each period, the interest revenue in turn will increase in each period.

(d) The journal entry to record the receipt of interest is as follows:

Jan. 1	Cash	16,000	
	Interest Receivable		16,000
	(To record interest received on Genstar bond)		

(e) If market interest rates rise, the bond becomes less attractive to potential investors as its interest rate is locked in at 4%. Consequently, the bond price will fall, which is what happened before this bond investment was purchased. Therefore, bond prices are inversely related to changes in market interest rates.

(f) The journal entry that would be recorded for the sale of this bond would be

Dec. 31	Cash	780,000	
	Long-Term Investments ($765,000 + $3,125 + $3,203)		771,328
	Realized Gain on Long-Term Investments		8,672
	(To record sale of Genstar bond)		

▶ PRACTICE USING THE DECISION TOOLKIT

(a) When the Simmons Foundation purchases debt investments, they are held to maturity and this is done for the purpose of earning interest revenue. These types of investments on average are less risky than equity investments and typically earn a lower return. The equity investments are held for trading purposes to earn dividend income and realize gains on the sale of these investments.

(b) Debt investments, such as bonds, with shorter periods to maturity are chosen so that, if interest rates change, the foundation will not be "locked in" and earn a specific interest rate over the long term that may now be too low. Debt investments, such as bonds, with longer terms are purchased so that interest revenue will be stable for a number of years, which makes it easier to prepare budgets and predict cash flows. In addition, the university may be trying to match the maturity date of investments to dates when large cash expenditures are planned.

(c) If the criterion to measure the performance of a debt investment is the interest revenue it will earn to maturity, the amortized cost model should be used when accounting for such an investment. This model does not measure unrealized gains and losses, as these are not relevant to the objectives for investing in such a security. The equity investments were most likely purchased for their potential price appreciation, given that they are actively traded. In this case, the fair value through profit or loss model should be used. This model recognizes unrealized gains and losses directly in the income statement and carries the investment at its fair value.

(d) A strategic investment is an equity investment where the investor obtains a significant portion of the voting shares of an investee or associate, usually 20% or more of the shares. Undertaking such an investment requires the investor's commitment to become more involved with the associate's operations and the foundation must take this into consideration before making the investment. If 20% to 50% of the shares are purchased, it is likely that significant influence is achieved, although other qualitative factors may have to be considered. Given that the foundation uses IFRS, an investment of this size would be accounted for using the equity method. It would be reported as a non-current asset that would be increased by the foundation's share of the associate's net income (with a corresponding increase in investment revenue) and decreased by its share of the associate's dividends (with a corresponding increase in cash).

▶ PRACTICE COMPREHENSIVE DO IT!

(a)

May 1	Held for Trading Investments	36,000	
	Cash (600 × $60)		36,000
	(To record purchase of 600 Sandburg common shares)		
June 1	Held for Trading Investments	100,000	
	Cash (1,000 × $100)		100,000
	(To record purchase of 1,000 Gladstone bonds)		
July 1	Investment in Associates	280,000	
	Cash (4,000 × $70)		280,000
	(To record purchase of Lansdowne common shares)		
Sept. 1	Cash (4,000 × $1)	4,000	
	Investment in Associates		4,000
	(To record dividend received from associate, Lansdowne, of $1 per share)		
Nov. 1	Cash (200 × $63)	12,600	
	Held for Trading Investments (200 × $60)		12,000
	Realized Gain on Held for Trading Investments		600
	(To record sale of 200 Sandburg shares)		

30	Cash (6% × $100,000 × $^6/_{12}$)		3,000	
	Interest Revenue			3,000
	(To record interest received on Gladstone bonds)			
Dec. 15	Cash [(600 − 200) × $0.50]		200	
	Dividend Revenue			200
	(To record dividend received of $0.50 per share from Sandburg)			
(b) Dec. 31	Unrealized Loss on Held for Trading Investments		1,000	
	Held for Trading Investments [400 × ($55 − $60)] − [1,000 × ($101 − $100)]			1,000
	(To record net unrealized loss on Sandburg shares and Gladstone bonds)			
31	No entry is made for the change in the fair value of Lansdowne shares because the equity method is used for this investment.			
31	Interest Receivable (6% × $100,000 × $^1/_{12}$)		500	
	Interest Revenue			500
	(To accrue interest revenue on Gladstone bonds for December)			
31	Investment in Associates		12,500	
	Income from Associates (25% × $100,000 × $^6/_{12}$)			12,500
	(To record Northstar's share of Lansdowne's net income since the date of acquisition of July 1, which was six months ago)			

(c)   Supporting calculations:

	Held for Trading Investment— Sandburg Shares	Held for Trading Investment— Gladstone Bonds	Total Held for Trading Investments	Investment in Associates
At acquisition	$36,000	$100,000	$136,000	$280,000
Dividends received				(4,000)
Carrying amount of shares sold	(12,000)		(12,000)	
Adjustment to fair value	(2,000)	1,000	(1,000)	
Share of associate's net income				12,500
Carrying amount, December	$22,000	$101,000	$123,000	$288,500

NORTHSTAR FINANCE LTD.
Statement of Financial Position (partial)
December 31, 2018

Assets

Current assets	
Held for trading investments	$123,000
Interest receivable	500
Non-current assets	
Investment in associates	288,500

NORTHSTAR FINANCE LTD.
Income Statement (partial)
Year Ended December 31, 2018

Other revenues and expenses	
Income from associates	$12,500
Interest revenue ($3,000 + $500)	3,500
Realized gain on held for trading investments	600
Dividend revenue	200
Unrealized loss on held for trading investments	1,000

(d)   If Northstar reported using ASPE, it could account for the investment in Lansdowne Corporation using either the equity method or the fair value through profit or loss model (because a fair value for Lansdowne shares can be obtained). If the fair value through profit or loss model were used, other revenue would be increased from the $12,500 share of Lansdowne's income to $16,000. Other revenue would consist of dividend revenue of $4,000 and an unrealized gain of $12,000 arising from the difference in the fair value of the investment of $292,000 (4,000 shares at $73 each) and the carrying amount of $280,000. Therefore, the total change in net income would be an increase of $3,500 ($16,000 – $12,500). On the statement of financial position, the investment would be shown at its fair value of $292,000 rather than the amount shown above of $288,500 under the equity method. So in summary, both net income and the carrying amount of the investment account would be higher by $3,500.

▶ **PRACTICE OBJECTIVE-FORMAT QUESTIONS**

1. (a), (e), and (g) are correct

Feedback
A strategic investment is made with the intent of achieving control or significant influence and not for earning trading gains, interest, or dividends.
(b)   Is incorrect because strategic investments are made to control or influence investees, not to earn a higher short-term return on excess cash.
(c)   Is incorrect because, although the investment is made for a longer term, its purpose is to earn dividend revenue, not to control or influence an investee.
(d)   Is incorrect because the investment is made over a short term for the purpose of earning a trading gain and not influencing or controlling an investee.
(f)   Is incorrect because the goal is to earn interest revenue and not control or influence an investee.

2. (a), (b), (c), (d), and (g) are correct

Feedback
A non-strategic investment is one that is held to earn dividend or interest revenue or trading gains. A strategic investment, by contrast, must be an equity investment that gives the investor significant influence or control over the investee.
(e)   Is incorrect because the intent of owning the shares is strategic. The shares were purchased to obtain significant influence. (In the absence of more information, it is appropriate to assume that a 30% ownership of the investee's shares would allow the investor to influence the investee.)
(f)   Is incorrect because the shares were purchased for a strategic reason (to obtain control), which in turn implies that it is to be held for the long term.

3. (b), (e), and (f) are correct

Feedback
(a)   Is incorrect because the investment is a current asset because it is held for the purpose of trading.
(b)   Is correct because 600 shares were purchased at $23 per share and then sold at $27 per share, for a gain of $4 per share and a total realized gain on the 600 shares of $2,400.
(c)   Is incorrect because, although the unrealized gain is $2,800 (400 shares increased in value by $7 ($30 – $23) per share during the year), under the fair value through profit or loss model, such an unrealized gain would be shown on the income statement, not in other comprehensive income.
(d)   Is incorrect because the total cash received would be $1,000 (1,000 shares × $1 per share) for dividends plus the proceeds from the sale of the shares of $16,200 (600 shares × $27 per share) for a total amount of cash received during the year of $17,200.
(e)   Is correct because the total dividends received are $1,000 (1,000 shares × $1 per share) and under the fair value through profit or loss model, this would be reported as dividend revenue in the income statement.
(f)   Is correct; the investment is a current asset because the investor does not intend to hold the Ace Ltd. shares over the long term.
(g)   Is incorrect because, under the fair value through profit or loss model, the investment, which consists of 400 shares, would be reported at its fair value of $12,000 (400 shares × $30 per share).

4. (a), (b), (d), (e), and (g) are correct

Feedback
(a)   Is correct because Georgian Ltd. is the only investee to declare dividends, so the dividend revenue is attributable to that investee. Since the dividend revenue is $1,000 and 2,000 shares of Georgian Ltd. are owned, the dividend declared per share must have been $0.50 ($1,000 ÷ 2,000 shares).
(b)   Is correct because, if dividend revenue is $1,000 and a dividend receivable for $250 exists, then only $750 of the dividend revenue would have been received in cash.
(c)   Is incorrect; since the sale of 500 Baxter Inc. shares gave rise to the only realized gain for the year, each share sold must have realized a gain of $6 ($3,000 ÷ 500 shares). Because the Baxter shares were purchased at $32 per share, they must have been sold at a price that is $6 higher, which is $38, not $37.
(d)   Is correct; because Acadia owned 2,000 shares of Georgian Ltd., the unrealized loss per share would be $1 per share ($2,000 ÷ 2,000 shares). If the fair value of a share at the end of the year was $19, they must have been purchased at $20 to have an unrealized loss of $2,000.
(e)   Is correct; because Acadia sold the Baxter Inc. shares, this investment could not have given rise to an unrealized gain or loss during the year, so the only investment other than the Georgian Ltd. shares that could have caused an unrealized loss to occur would be the Chen Enterprises Inc. shares. Because the total unrealized loss was $5,000 and $2,000 of this was attributable to Georgian Ltd., the remaining unrealized loss of $3,000 must be attributable to Chen Enterprises Inc.
(f)   Is incorrect; because the unrealized loss on Chen Enterprises Inc. shares was $3,000 [see (e)] or $3 per share ($3,000 ÷ 1,000 shares) and their fair value at the beginning of the year was $9 per share, the shares must have a fair value of $6 per share at the end of the year in order to have an unrealized loss of $3 per share.
(g)   Is correct because all of these items are recorded on the income statement as other revenues and expenses when using the FVTPL model.

5. (a), (c), and (e) are correct

Feedback
(a)   Is correct because, even though the 20% ownership threshold has not been reached, significant influence has been attained through board membership.
(b)   Is incorrect because, even though the 20% ownership threshold has been exceeded, no influence is exercised because the investment in the company has not been welcomed by other shareholders.
(c)   Is correct because, even though the 20% ownership threshold has not been reached, significant influence has been attained because of the material transactions and sharing of essential technical information.
(d)   Is incorrect because an investment in bonds is a debt investment and does not give the investor any significant influence in the company because the bonds do not have any voting rights at board and shareholder meetings.

(e)   Is correct because, even though the 20% ownership threshold has not been reached, significant influence has been attained because of the exchange of managerial personnel and the consultations that are taking place.
(f)   Is incorrect; because the investment was acquired for trading purposes rather than to achieve significant influence, it would be more appropriate to use the fair value through profit or loss model.
(g)   Is incorrect because, given the small percentage of common shares acquired, it is unlikely that significant influence could be achieved, so a fair value model would be used instead.

6.   (e) and (f) are correct

Feedback
In the absence of any other detailed information, it is likely Big K Ranch has significant influence over Little L Ranch given that Big K Ranch owns 30% of the shares of Little L Ranch, so the equity method would be used to account for this investment.
(a)   Is incorrect because, under the equity method, dividends earned are recorded as a reduction in the investment account (dividends reduce the value of the associate) rather than as revenue. Because under the equity method, income from associates is recorded on the income statement, recording dividends on the income statement essentially records this income twice.
(b)   Is incorrect because the investor's share of the income of the investee for the six months ending December 31 (since the investment was purchased on July 1) is $30,000 ($200,000 × 30% × $6/12$), not $60,000.
(c)   Is incorrect; no unrealized gain is recorded under the equity method because the investment is not reported at fair value; rather it is adjusted to reflect the investor's share of changes in the associate's retained earnings.
(d)   Is incorrect although the investor's share of the dividends is 30% (30,000 of 100,000 shares owned) of $70,000, which is $21,000, this amount would reduce the investment account from $600,000 to $579,000. However, this would not be the balance in the investment account at the end of the year because that account would also be adjusted when recording the income from associates.
(e)   Is correct because dividends are recorded by Big K Ranch as soon as Little L Ranch declares them regardless of whether the dividend is received. If the dividend is declared but not yet paid, Big K Ranch would debit Dividends Receivable and credit Investment in Associates. Under the equity method, dividends are not recorded as revenue because the income that they pertain to would have already been recognized by Big K Ranch in its Income from Associates account.
(f)   Is correct because the original balance of $600,000 would be increased by Big K's share of Little L's income, which is 30% × $200,000 × $6/12$ = $30,000, but then reduced by the amount of dividends earned, which is 30% × $70,000 = $21,000. Notice that the dividend is not prorated because Big K owned the shares when the dividend was declared. (Dividends are earned upon declaration, not throughout the year.) So the balance at the end of the year is $609,000 ($600,000 + $30,000 − $21,000).
(g)   Is incorrect because the amount of $51,000 relates to Big K's share of Little L's income, which was $30,000 (30% × $200,000 × $6/12$), plus Big K's share of the Little L dividend, which was $21,000 (30% × $70,000). However, the dividend is not reported on Big K's income statement. Rather, it is shown as a reduction in the investment account balance. So the income from associates would be $30,000, not $51,000.

7.   (a), (b), (d), (f), and (g) are correct

Feedback
(c)   Is incorrect because under IFRS, when significant influence has been achieved, the equity method must be used to account for the investment.
(e)   Is incorrect; because the intent of owning the shares is to trade them actively, this is not a strategic investment where significant influence or control is achieved, so the fair value through profit or loss model must be used because the fair value can be measured.

8.   (f) and (g) are correct

Feedback
(a)   Is incorrect; because the intent is to trade the shares, obtaining significant influence or control is not likely. Because the fair value of the shares cannot be determined, the only option under ASPE is to use the cost model.
(b)   Is incorrect because under ASPE, such an investment would normally be accounted for using the amortized cost model, but an option to use the fair value through profit and loss model is also available.
(c)   Is incorrect because ASPE allows alternatives to the equity method when significant influence is achieved. If the fair value of the shares can be determined, the investor can also use the fair value through profit or loss model and if the fair value cannot be determined, the cost model can be used instead of the equity method.
(d)   Is incorrect because ASPE does not use other comprehensive income, so in this case, the cost model would be used.
(e)   Is incorrect because consolidated financial statements can be prepared but ASPE does not make this mandatory. The investment could be accounted for using the equity method. Also, if the fair value of the shares can be determined, the investor can use the fair value through profit or loss option, and if the fair value cannot be determined, the cost model can also be used.

9.   (a), (b), (e), and (g) are correct

Feedback
(c)   Is incorrect because other comprehensive income is closed out into accumulated other comprehensive income at the end of the year.
(d)   Is incorrect because an investment in associates means that the investor has significant influence. If an investment of that size was made to accomplish this objective, the investment is usually not held for trading but held for a number of years. Therefore, it would be a non-current asset.
(f)   Is incorrect because comprehensive income consists of two parts: net income, which is closed out to retained earnings, and other comprehensive income, which is closed out into accumulated other comprehensive income.

*10.   (b), (c), (d), and (f) are correct

Feedback
(a)   Is incorrect because under the amortized cost model, investments are not carried at fair value, so no unrealized gains or losses are recorded.
(b)   Is correct because a bond premium is an additional cost paid to acquire a bond investment and that cost is allocated to interest revenue over the time to maturity. Allocating such a cost against a revenue account will reduce it and make it lower than the amount of cash interest received. In this way, interest revenue is based on the market interest rate when the bond was purchased rather than the coupon rate.

(e) Is incorrect because a bond discount implies that the bond was purchased at a cost less than face value. The benefit of such a discount, which is initially embedded in the bond investment, will be amortized to interest revenue and will cause interest revenue to increase to an amount that exceeds the cash interest received. In this way, interest revenue becomes based on the market interest rate when the bond was purchased rather than on the coupon rate.

(f) Is correct because, by the time the bond matures, any premium or discount would have been fully amortized, so the balance in the investment account on the date of maturity will simply be the face value of the bond. Since that exact amount will be collected in cash upon the maturity of the bond, no gain or loss will be recorded upon maturity.

(g) Is incorrect because the interest revenue will always be the same percentage of the balance in the investment account (not its face value) at the beginning of the period. That percentage will be the market interest rate on the day that the bond was purchased. In other words, the interest revenue is equal to the bond investment at the beginning of the period times the market interest rate when the bond was purchased.

▶ ENDNOTES

[1] The Canadian Press, "Scotiabank Buys Canada Credit Card Portfolio from JPMorgan Chase, Includes Sears," CTVNews.ca, October 15, 2015; "Scotiabank and Cencosud Finalize Strategic Alliance in Chile," Scotiabank news release, May 1, 2015; "Canadian Tire Corporation and Scotiabank Enter Strategic Business Partnership That Includes Scotiabank Acquiring 20% of Canadian Tire's Financial Services Business," Scotiabank news release, May 8, 2014; John Greenwood, "Would You Like Canadian Tire Money with That Mortgage?", *Financial Post*, May 8, 2014; Scotiabank 2014 and 2015 annual reports.

[2] Jeff Lewis, "Suncor Reaches $4.2-Billion Deal with Canadian Oil Sands," *The Globe and Mail*, January 18, 2016.

13

Statement of Cash Flows

CHAPTER PREVIEW

Throughout the preceding chapters of this book, we have learned how to report and analyze assets, liabilities, and shareholders' equity. We will now return to the statement of cash flows to learn more about how the information in that statement can complement the accrual-based information in the statement of financial position, income statement, statement of comprehensive income, and statement of changes in equity. We will see how the statement of cash flows gives greater insight into a company's operating, investing, and financing activities and how we can use this information to better understand a company's financial condition.

CHAPTER OUTLINE

LEARNING OBJECTIVES	READ	PRACTICE
1 Describe the content and format of the statement of cash flows.	• Classification of cash flows • Format of the statement of cash flows • Preparation of the statement of cash flows	**DO IT!** 13-1 Cash flow activities
2 Prepare the operating activities section of a statement of cash flows using the indirect method.	• Noncash expenses • Losses and gains • Changes in current asset and current liability accounts • Summary of conversion to net cash provided (used) by operating activities—indirect method	**DO IT!** 13-2 Operating activities—indirect method
3 Prepare the investing and financing activities sections and complete the statement of cash flows.	• Investing activities • Financing activities • Completing the statement of cash flows	**DO IT!** 13-3a Investing activities 13-3b Financing activities 13-3c Statement of cash flows—indirect method
4 Use the statement of cash flows to evaluate a company.	• Corporate life cycle and cash flows • Free cash flow	**DO IT!** 13-4 Corporate life cycle and free cash flow
5 Prepare the operating activities section of a statement of cash flows using the direct method (Appendix 13A).	• Cash receipts • Cash payments • Summary of conversion to net cash provided (used) by operating activities—direct method	**DO IT!** 13-5 Operating activities—direct method

FEATURE STORY

The up-and-down movement of commodities prices can wreak havoc on the cash flow of companies like Teck Resources, Canada's largest diversified resource company, headquartered in Vancouver. In 2006, metal prices were riding high, but by late 2008, the global financial crisis was in full swing, resulting in "unprecedented volatility for the world economy and for the mining sector," according to Don Lindsay, Teck President and CEO.

During this economic turmoil in late 2008 and early 2009, Teck had to implement a multi-step program to manage its debt. This included suspending dividends, reducing planned capital expenditures, withdrawing from a copper project in Panama, reducing refined zinc production, selling assets, and reducing its global workforce by 13%. Any free cash flow went toward servicing the company's debt.

Teck's financial position continued to be volatile in the following years. In 2010 and 2011, strong commodity prices yielded record revenues and net income for Teck, but in 2012, prices began to fall again. For example, copper was selling at over U.S. $4.00 per pound in 2011, but by 2015, it had fallen to U.S. $2.50 per pound. Because of this, the company's operating cash flows, which were $3.4 billion in 2012, had fallen to only $1.9 billion by the end of 2015. Teck had cash and short-term investments of $3.2 billion in 2012, but by 2015, this had fallen to $1.9 billion.

The company had to implement strategies to react to these declining cash flows. One approach included deferring about $1.5 billion in capital spending. Other spending cuts on operating activities saved $640 million by 2014 because of the implementation of a cost-reduction program. Another strategy undertaken by the company was to sell off some of its investments to improve its cash position. In 2012, the company received only $51 million from the sale of investments, but by 2013, that increased to $502 million, and by 2015, the company received proceeds of $1,222 million from this source. Despite these problems, Teck still undertook new investment opportunities.

In 2013, with Alberta's oil sector booming, Teck announced it would proceed with a joint venture with Suncor and Total E&P Canada to develop a bitumen mine near Fort McMurray. Teck's 20% stake in the project, called Fort Hills, was expected to cost the company more than $2.9 billion in capital investments over four years. Noting that the Fort Hills mine was expected to last more than 50 years, Mr. Lindsay said at the time that the project fit with Teck's strategy of developing long-lived assets in diversified commodities. "With Fort Hills and our other oil sands assets, we are building a new division within Teck that will create value, significant cash flow and diversification for our business for decades to come."

Cash Flow Can Be a Rocky Road

But the company was not just focused on raising operating cash flows and reducing expenditures on investing activities. To conserve cash, Teck reduced its dividends from $0.90 per share in 2014 to $0.20 per share in 2015. In the company's 2015 annual report, noting the bankruptcy of some of Teck's major competitors, Mr. Lindsay told shareholders, "We are experiencing some of the worst business conditions of our lifetime." As it looked to the expected opening of Fort Hills in 2017, Teck was keeping a close eye on cash flow in the hopes that the company could continue to weather fluctuating oil and other commodity prices as it had successfully done for more than a century.[1]

Go to the *REVIEW AND PRACTICE* section at the end of the chapter for a targeted summary and practice questions with solutions.

Visit **WileyPLUS** for more practice opportunities.

Describe the content and format of the statement of cash flows.

The financial statements that we have studied so far present only partial information about a company's cash flows because these statements are prepared on an accrual basis rather than a cash basis. For example, comparative statements of financial position show the increase in property, plant, and equipment during the year, but they do not show how the additions were financed or paid for. The income statement reports net income for the year, but this amount rarely equals the amount of cash received or used by operating activities. The statement of changes in equity shows cash dividends declared but not the cash dividends paid during the year. None of these statements presents a detailed summary of where cash came from and how it was used.

Consequently, the statement of cash flows plays an important role in helping users of financial statements assess a company's ability to generate cash from its operating activities, and determine if other cash flows regarding investing and financing activities were received or used. Along with the other financial statements, the statement of cash flows helps users evaluate a company's ability to generate future cash flows and its presentation is required for both publicly traded and private corporations.

Before we learn how to prepare the statement of cash flows, we must first understand what it includes and why. We will begin by discussing how cash receipts and payments are classified within the statement and then review the content and format of the statement.

> **Alternative Terminology**
> The *statement of cash flows* is also commonly known as the *cash flow statement*.

CLASSIFICATION OF CASH FLOWS

The statement of cash flows is often prepared using **cash and cash equivalents** as its basis rather than just cash. You will recall from Chapter 7 that cash equivalents are short-term, highly liquid held for trading investments that have insignificant risk and are readily convertible to cash within a very short period of time. Generally, only debt investments due within three months qualify as cash equivalents under this definition. An example of a cash equivalent is a term deposit maturing in less than 90 days. Cash equivalents can also consist of liabilities such as bank overdrafts and loans that are repayable on demand. These items are deducted from the cash balances on hand or on deposit to arrive at the amount of cash and cash equivalents.

Activities Reported on the Statement of Cash Flows

The statement of cash flows reports the cash receipts and cash payments during the accounting period, in a format that reconciles the beginning and ending balances of cash (and cash equivalents if there are any). These cash receipts and cash payments are classified into three types of activities within the statement: (1) operating, (2) investing, and (3) financing. The transactions that are found within each type of activity include the following:

1. **Operating activities** include a company's principal income-producing activities and all other activities that are not investing or financing activities. They arise from the cash effects of transactions that create revenues and expenses.
2. **Investing activities** include the acquisition and disposal of non-current assets. They involve (a) purchasing and disposing of long-lived assets and investments not held for trading, and (b) lending money and collecting the loans. Investing activities, for the most part, affect non-current asset accounts.
3. **Financing activities** are those that result in changes in the size and composition of the equity and borrowings of a company. They include (a) obtaining cash from issuing debt and repaying the amounts borrowed, and (b) cash received from issuing shares and cash paid for dividends and buying back shares. Financing activities generally affect non-current liability and shareholders' equity accounts.

Illustration 13-1 lists typical cash receipts and cash payments in each of the three activities.

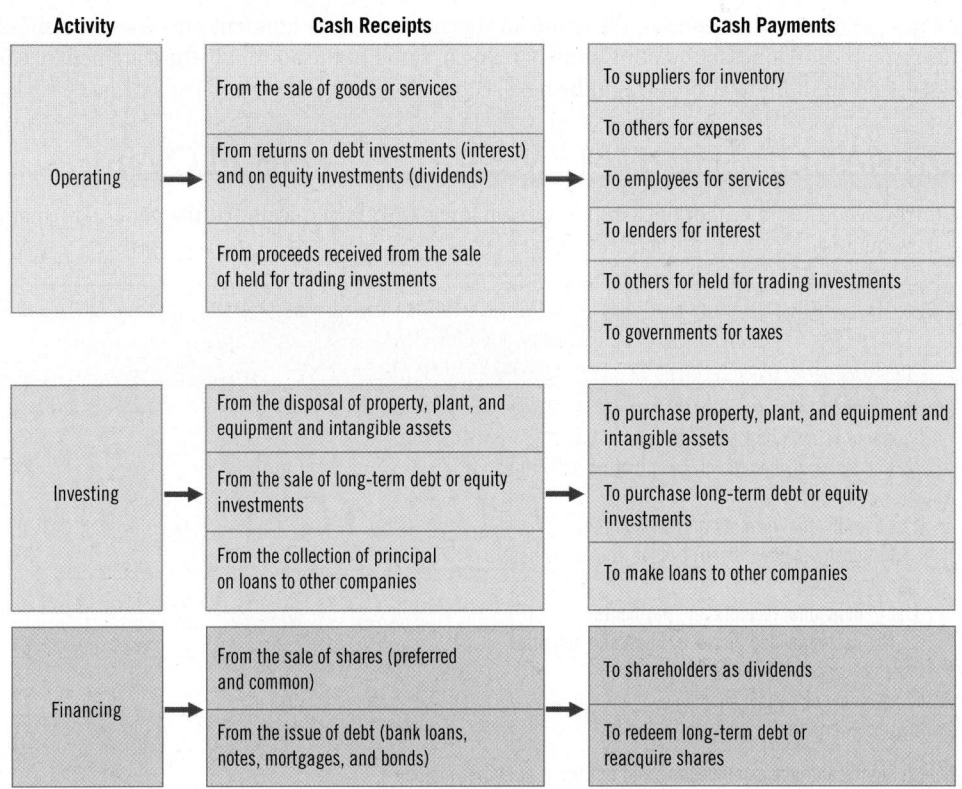

Cash receipts and payments classified by activity

As you can see above, some cash flows that an average person may consider to be investing or financing activities are actually shown as operating activities. For example, receipts of investment revenue (interest and dividends) are classified in the above illustration as operating activities. So are payments of interest to lenders. Why are these considered operating activities? It is because these items are reported in the income statement where results of operations are shown.

Although we've shown interest received and paid and dividends received as operating activities and dividends paid as financing activities in the above illustration, it is important to note that companies reporting under IFRS have some flexibility when reporting these items. For example, interest and dividends received may be classified as either an operating or investing activity, while interest and dividends paid may be classified as either an operating or financing activity. Once the choice is made, it must be applied consistently.

In contrast, private companies reporting under ASPE do not have this flexibility. They classify interest received and paid and dividends received as operating activities. Dividends declared and paid, which are reported on the statement of changes in equity rather than in the income statement, are shown as financing activities. Most North American companies, whether they follow IFRS or ASPE, classify any dividends received or interest received or paid as operating activities because these items are reported on the income statement. For this reason, this classification is the one shown in Illustration 13-1 and the one we recommend you use when completing assignments in this text.

Activities Not Reported on the Statement of Cash Flows

It is important to recognize that not all of a company's significant investing and financing activities involve cash and therefore some are not reported on the statement of cash flows. Examples of noncash investing and financing activities include:

1. Issue of shares to purchase assets or to reduce liabilities
2. Conversion of debt into equity
3. Exchanges of property, plant, and equipment

Significant investing and financing activities that do not affect cash are not reported in the body of the statement of cash flows. However, because they are significant, details about these activities are disclosed in notes to the financial statements. For assignment purposes, you should present significant noncash investing and financing in a note at the bottom of the statement of cash flows, as shown in Illustration 13-2 in the next section.

FORMAT OF THE STATEMENT OF CASH FLOWS

We introduced the statement of cash flows in Chapter 1. You will recall that the general format of the statement is as shown in Illustration 13-2.

► Illustration 13-2
Format of the statement of cash flows

COMPANY NAME Statement of Cash Flows Period Covered		
Operating activities		
(Prepared using indirect or direct method)	XX	
Net cash provided (used) by operating activities		XX
Investing activities		
(List of individual receipts and payments)	XX	
Net cash provided (used) by investing activities		XX
Financing activities		
(List of individual receipts and payments)	XX	
Net cash provided (used) by financing activities		XX
Net increase (decrease) in cash		XX
Cash, beginning of period		XX
Cash, end of period		XX
Note x: Significant noncash investing and financing activities include …		

The statement covers the same period of time as the income statement, statement of comprehensive income, and statement of changes in equity (such as for the year ended on a given date [?]). Cash receipts and payments are reported in three separate sections: operating, investing, and financing activities.

The section that reports cash flows from operating activities usually appears first. There are two acceptable ways to prepare the operating activities section of the statement of cash flows. One way is to use the **indirect method**, which converts net income from an accrual basis to a cash basis. When the indirect method is used, we start with net income and adjust the accrual-based net income to remove any revenues and expenses that do not generate operating cash flows. An alternative to the indirect method of presentation is the **direct method**. With this method, rather than listing net income and then adjusting it for noncash items, we simply make the operating section look like a cash basis income statement. It will therefore list first not revenues but cash received from customers, followed not by expenses but cash paid for various operating activities.

To expand on the general format of the operating activities section of the statement of cash flows shown in Illustration 13-2, the indirect and direct methods would look somewhat like the following:

Indirect Method			Direct Method		
Operating activities			Operating activities		
Net income		XX	Cash receipts from customers		XX
Adjustments to reconcile net income to net cash			Cash payments		
provided (used) by operating activities			To suppliers	XX	
(List of individual adjustments)	XX	XX	For operating expenses	XX	
Net cash provided (used) by operating			To employees	XX	
activities		XX	For interest	XX	
			For income tax	XX	XX
			Net cash provided (used) by operating activities		XX

Regardless of whether the indirect or direct method is used, the result—net cash provided or used by operating activities—will be exactly the same. While both the indirect and direct methods are permissible choices to present cash flows from operating activities for both publicly traded and private companies, the direct method is encouraged, although not required, by standard setters. The direct method is considered to be more informative for users and is easier to compare with other financial statements. Despite this preference, most companies use the indirect method because it is easier to prepare and it reveals less company information to competitors. Teck, introduced in our chapter-opening story, and its competitors use the indirect method.

The operating activities section—whether prepared using the indirect or direct method—is followed by the investing activities section and then the financing activities section. Each of these sections reports a subtotal showing net cash either provided from or used by each activity. These subtotals are totalled to determine the net increase or decrease in cash for the period. This amount is then added to (if a net increase) or subtracted from (if a net decrease) the beginning-of-period cash balance to obtain the end-of-period cash balance. The end-of-period cash balance should agree with the cash balance reported on the statement of financial position. Note that, although we use the term "cash" here for simplicity, if any cash equivalents exist, then we would use "cash and cash equivalents" instead.

PREPARATION OF THE STATEMENT OF CASH FLOWS

Where do we find the information to prepare the statement of cash flows? There are no specific accounts in the general ledger for the types of operating activities, investing activities, or financing activities shown in Illustration 13-1. This is because the statement of cash flows is prepared differently from the other financial statements in that it is not prepared from an adjusted trial balance. The statement of cash flows requires detailed information about the changes in account balances that occurred over a period of time. An adjusted trial balance will not provide the necessary data. The information to prepare this statement usually comes from three sources:

1. The **comparative statement of financial position** is examined to determine the amounts of the changes in assets, liabilities, and shareholders' equity from the beginning of the period to its end.
2. The **income statement** and related noncash current asset and current liability accounts from the statement of financial position are used to determine the amount of cash provided or used by operating activities during the period.
3. **Additional information** is usually needed to determine how cash was provided or used during the period. We will also use selected information from the statement of changes in equity and other sources to help us complete the statement of cash flows and the notes to the financial statements.

There are four steps to prepare the statement of cash flows from these data sources, as shown in Illustration 13-3.

▶Illustration 13-3

Steps in preparing the statement of cash flows

Step 1: Prepare operating activities section.
Determine the net cash provided (used) by operating activities by converting net income from an accrual basis to a cash basis. To do this, analyze the current year's income statement, relevant current asset and current liability accounts from the comparative statement of financial position, and selected information.

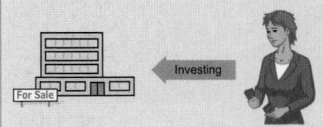

Step 2: Prepare investing activities section.
Determine the net cash provided (used) by investing activities by analyzing changes in non-current asset accounts from the comparative statement of financial position and selected information.

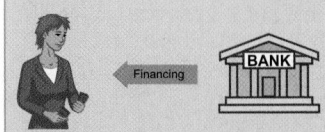

Step 3: Prepare financing activities section.
Determine the net cash provided (used) by financing activities by analyzing changes in non-current liability and equity accounts from the comparative statement of financial position and selected information.

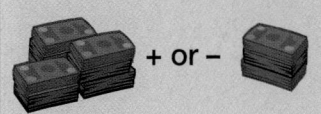

Step 4: Complete the statement of cash flows.
Determine the net increase (decrease) in cash. Compare the net change in cash reported on the statement of cash flows with the change in cash reported on the statement of financial position to make sure the amounts agree.

To explain and illustrate these steps in the preparation of a statement of cash flows in the next sections, we will use financial information from Computer Services Corporation. Illustration 13-4 presents Computer Services' current- and previous-year statement of financial position, its current-year income statement, and related financial information.

▶ Illustration 13-4

Financial information for Computer Services Corporation

COMPUTER SERVICES CORPORATION Statement of Financial Position December 31			
	2018	2017	Increase (Decrease)
Assets			
Current assets			
Cash	$ 55,000	$ 33,000	$ 22,000
Accounts receivable	20,000	30,000	(10,000)
Inventory	15,000	10,000	5,000
Prepaid expenses	5,000	1,000	4,000
Property, plant, and equipment			
Land	140,000	30,000	110,000
Buildings	160,000	40,000	120,000
Accumulated depreciation—buildings	(11,000)	(5,000)	6,000
Equipment	27,000	10,000	17,000
Accumulated depreciation—equipment	(3,000)	(1,000)	2,000
Total assets	$408,000	$148,000	
Liabilities and Shareholders' Equity			
Liabilities			
Current liabilities			
Accounts payable	$ 17,000	$ 10,000	7,000
Dividends payable	2,000	1,000	1,000
Income tax payable	6,000	8,000	(2,000)
Current portion of mortgage payable	15,000	6,000	9,000
Non-current liabilities			
Mortgage payable	124,000	15,000	109,000
Shareholders' equity			
Common shares	70,000	50,000	20,000
Retained earnings	164,000	48,000	116,000
Accumulated other comprehensive income	10,000	10,000	-0-
Total liabilities and shareholders' equity	$408,000	$148,000	

COMPUTER SERVICES CORPORATION Income Statement Year Ended December 31, 2018		
Sales revenue		$507,000
Cost of goods sold		150,000
Gross profit		357,000
Operating expenses		
Other operating expenses	$141,000	
Depreciation expense	9,000	
Loss on disposal of equipment	3,000	153,000
Income from operations		204,000
Interest expense		12,000
Income before income tax		192,000
Income tax expense		47,000
Net income		$145,000

Additional information for 2018:

1. The company uses a perpetual inventory system.

2. Assume that prepaid expenses relate to other operating expenses and accounts payable relates only to purchases of inventory on account.

3. The company acquired land by paying cash of $95,000 and by issuing common shares worth $15,000. Other common shares were issued for $5,000 cash.

4. Equipment costing $25,000 was purchased for cash.

5. The company sold equipment with a carrying amount of $7,000 (cost of $8,000, less accumulated depreciation of $1,000) for $4,000 cash.

6. Depreciation expense consists of $6,000 for the buildings and $3,000 for equipment.

7. The company received a $124,000 mortgage loan during the year and paid off $6,000 of the loan.

8. The company declared a $29,000 cash dividend.

9. There was no other comprehensive income reported in 2018.

Before we even begin to prepare the statement of cash flows, we can determine the company's net cash flow by simply looking at how its cash (or cash and equivalents) has changed during the year. For Computer Services Corporation, the cash flow for 2018 is $22,000 because cash increased from $33,000 to $55,000. If we know this, why don't we prepare the statement of cash flows by simply listing this single amount of $22,000? Because we need to know *why* the cash flow for the year is $22,000 and this is answered by providing a detailed list of the types of activities that generated this cash flow.

In the next two sections, we will apply the four steps shown in Illustration 13-3 and prepare the statement of cash flows using the information provided in Illustration 13-4 for Computer Services Corporation. We will start by learning how to prepare the operating activities section using the more popular indirect method. The direct method is explained in Appendix 13A. We will then illustrate the investing and financing activities sections of the statement of cash flows, which are prepared the same way regardless of whether the indirect or direct method is used for operating activities.

DO IT! ▶13-1   Cash Flow Activities

Plano Moulding Corp. had the following cash transactions:

(a) Issued common shares.

(b) Sold a long-term debt investment.

(c) Purchased a tractor-trailer truck.

(d) Paid interest on the bank loan.

(e) Collected cash for services provided.

(f) Acquired equipment by issuing common shares.

(g) Paid salaries to employees.

Classify each of these transactions by type of cash flow activity. Indicate whether the transaction would be reported as a cash receipt or cash payment, or as a noncash activity.

Action Plan

✔ Report as operating activities the cash effects of transactions that create revenues and expenses and are used to determine net income.

✔ Report as investing activities the transactions that (a) acquire and dispose of long-lived assets, and (b) lend money and collect loans.

✔ Report as financing activities the transactions that (a) obtain cash by issuing debt or repay the amounts borrowed, and (b) obtain cash from shareholders or pay them dividends or amounts for the buyback of their shares.

SOLUTION

Try this Do It! exercise on your own and then check your answer at the end of the chapter.

Related Exercise Material: BE13–1, BE13–2, BE13–3, E13–1, and E13–2.

2   Prepare the operating activities section of a statement of cash flows using the indirect method.

1. Prepare operating activities section—indirect method.   2. PREPARE INVESTING ACTIVITIES SECTION.   3. PREPARE FINANCING ACTIVITIES SECTION.   4. COMPLETE THE STATEMENT OF CASH FLOWS.

The first step in the preparation of a statement of cash flows begins with the operating activities section. To determine the net cash provided (used) by operating activities under the indirect method, net income must be adjusted for items that do not affect cash. You will recall, from Chapter 4, that generally accepted accounting principles require companies to use the accrual basis of accounting. As you have learned, accrual accounting requires that a company record revenue when the performance obligation is satisfied and record expenses when incurred. For example, revenues include credit sales for which the company has not yet collected cash. Expenses include some items that have not been paid in cash. Thus, under the accrual basis of accounting, net income is not the same as net cash and companies must convert accrual-based net income to a cash basis.

Illustration 13-5 identifies three types of adjustments that are made to adjust net income to net cash provided or used by operating activities under the indirect method.

► Illustration 13-5

Adjustments to convert net income to net cash provided (used) by operating activities

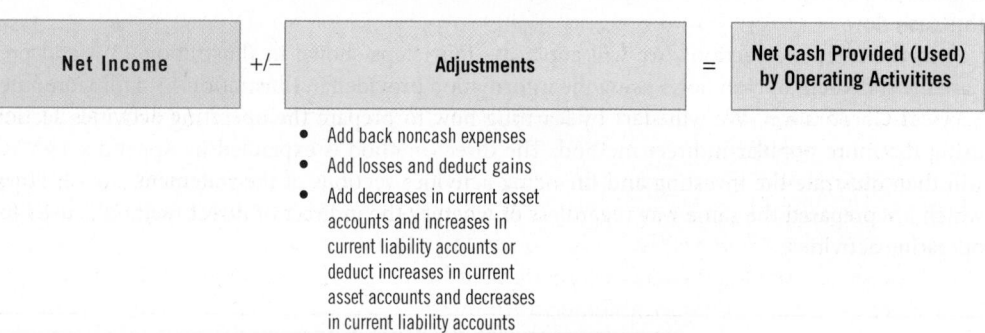

Net Income	+/–	Adjustments	=	Net Cash Provided (Used) by Operating Activitites

- Add back noncash expenses
- Add losses and deduct gains
- Add decreases in current asset accounts and increases in current liability accounts or deduct increases in current asset accounts and decreases in current liability accounts

The first two types of adjustment—noncash expenses, losses, and gains—are found on the income statement. The last type of adjustment—changes (increases or decreases) in certain current asset and current liability accounts—are found on the statement of financial position. The next three sections explain each type of adjustment.

NONCASH EXPENSES

The income statement includes expenses that do not use cash, such as depreciation and amortization expense. For example, Computer Services' income statement reports depreciation expense of $9,000. Although depreciation expense reduces net income, it does not reduce cash. Recall that the entry to record depreciation is:

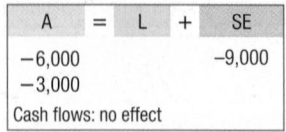

A	=	L	+	SE
−6,000				−9,000
−3,000				
Cash flows: no effect				

Depreciation Expense	9,000	
Accumulated Depreciation—Buildings		6,000
Accumulated Depreciation—Equipment		3,000

This entry has no effect on cash, so although it reduced net income, it did not reduce cash. Since the indirect method starts with net income, depreciation expense is added back to net income in order to arrive at net cash provided (used) by operating activities. It is important to understand that depreciation expense is not added to operating activities as if it were a source of cash. As shown in the journal entry above, depreciation does not involve cash. It is simply added to net income to cancel out the effect it has on that amount.

The following is a partial operating activities section of the statement of cash flows for Computer Services. The addition of the noncash expense to net income is highlighted in red.

Operating activities	
Net income	$145,000
Adjustments to reconcile net income to net cash provided (used) by operating activities	
Depreciation expense	9,000

Similar to depreciation expense, amortization expense for intangible assets is also added to net income to arrive at net cash provided (used) by operating activities. Another example of a non-cash expense is the amortization of bond discounts and premiums. Since this topic was covered in the appendices to Chapters 10 and 12, we will not cover them in this chapter.

If a company has noncash revenues (see Chapter 12), such as income from associates, they would be deducted from net income when determining cash provided (used) by operating activities. We do not cover these types of revenues in this chapter.

LOSSES AND GAINS

Cash received from the disposal of long-lived assets should be reported in the investing activities section of the statement of cash flows. Since these cash receipts are recorded in the investing section, any amounts relating to the disposal of these assets must be excluded from other sections of the statement of cash flows. Since the operating section lists net income as its starting amount, all losses and gains from asset disposals, which are included in net income, must be eliminated from this section. To understand this more fully, let us review the accounting for the disposal of property, plant, and equipment.

The disposal of property, plant, and equipment is recorded by (1) recognizing the cash proceeds that are received, (2) removing the asset and accumulated depreciation accounts from the books, and (3) recognizing any loss or gain on the disposal.

To illustrate, recall that Computer Services' income statement reported a $3,000 loss on the disposal of equipment. With the additional information provided for Illustration 13-4, we can reconstruct the journal entry to record the disposal of equipment:

Cash	4,000	
Accumulated Depreciation	1,000	
Loss on Disposal	3,000	
Equipment		8,000

A	=	L	+	SE
+4,000				−3,000
+1,000				
−8,000				

↑ Cash flows: +4,000

The receipt of cash proceeds of $4,000 is considered an investing activity. Selling equipment is not part of the company's primary activities. **There is therefore no cash receipt (or payment) from operating activities.** Logically, then, to calculate the net cash provided (used) by operating activities, we have to eliminate the loss or gain on the disposal of an asset from net income.

To eliminate the $3,000 loss on the disposal of the equipment, we have to add the loss back to net income to cancel the original deduction made for this loss in the income statement. We can then arrive at net cash provided (used) by operating activities, as shown in the following partial statement of cash flows for Computer Services:

Operating activities	
Net income	$145,000
Adjustments to reconcile net income to net cash provided (used) by operating activities	
Depreciation expense	9,000
Loss on disposal of equipment	3,000

If a gain on disposal occurs, the gain is deducted from net income in order to determine net cash provided (used) by operating activities. For both a loss and a gain, the actual amount of cash received from the sale is reported as a cash receipt in the investing activities section of the statement of cash flows.

Gains and losses can arise in other circumstances and will always result in an adjustment to net income if the gain or loss was recorded in the income statement. Examples include unrealized gains and losses on investments that are recorded when the carrying amount of an investment is adjusted to fair value but it is not sold. Other examples include realized gains and losses on investments and the early settlement of debt. Again, these gains and losses, which would have been recorded on the income statement, would have to be eliminated from net income in order to calculate net cash provided (used) by operating activities.

CHANGES IN CURRENT ASSET AND CURRENT LIABILITY ACCOUNTS

Another type of adjustment in converting net income to net cash provided (used) by operating activities involves examining the changes (increases or decreases) in certain noncash current asset and current liability accounts, also known as noncash working capital accounts. You will recall that working capital is the difference between current assets and current liabilities.

Not all noncash working capital accounts affect operating activities, however. One such example is short-term loans or notes receivable that have been issued for lending purposes rather than for trade. The issue and repayment of loans or notes such as these are shown instead in the investing section of the statement of cash flows. Similarly, the receipt and repayment of short-term loans or notes payable that have been incurred for lending purposes rather than trade are shown in the financing section of the statement of cash flows. Furthermore, the declaration and payment of dividends may affect the Dividends Payable account, but these activities are financing in nature rather than operating in nature.

So what types of noncash working capital accounts affect operating activities? In this course, you will find that all of them—other than those referred to above relating to loans, notes, and dividends—can affect operating activities. For example, portions of some revenues and expenses may have been recorded not because of a cash transaction but because of noncash events such as a service or sale made on account or the incurring of an expense on credit. Even though these events are reflected in the income statement, they do not affect cash. These events caused a change in noncash working capital accounts, such as accounts receivable and accounts payable. To the extent that these changes occurred, they pertain to the noncash portion of their related revenue and expense accounts and so they will be removed from net income as we determine net cash provided (used) by operating activities. On the other hand, some working capital accounts relating to prepayments, such as prepaid insurance and unearned revenue, are created when cash is paid or received, yet these operating cash events are not reflected in net income. To the extent that we have changes in these prepayment-related accounts, we need to reflect the related cash flow by adjusting net income for these items.

In addition, cash paid to purchase held for trading investments and cash received upon the sale of these investments would be considered operating activities.

Changes in Current Assets

We will now analyze the changes in Computer Services' current asset accounts to determine how each change affects net income and cash. The adjustments that are required for changes in noncash current asset accounts that affect operating activities are as follows: increases in current asset accounts are deducted from net income, and decreases in current asset accounts are added to net income, to arrive at net cash provided (used) by operating activities.

ACCOUNTS RECEIVABLE   Computer Services' accounts receivable decreased by $10,000 (from $30,000 to $20,000) during the year. When accounts receivable decrease during the year, cash collected from customers is greater than the amount of sales to those customers. In other words, revenues on an accrual basis are lower than revenues on a cash basis. For Computer Services, this means that cash receipts were $10,000 higher than revenues.

Illustration 13-4 shows that Computer Services had $507,000 in sales revenue reported on its income statement. To determine how much cash was collected in connection with this revenue, it is useful to analyze the Accounts Receivable account:

Accounts Receivable						
Jan.	1	Balance	30,000			
		Sales on account	507,000	Receipts from customers	517,000	
Dec.	31	Balance	20,000			

} $10,000 net decrease (add to net income)

If sales revenue (assumed to be sales on account) recorded during the period was $507,000 (debit Accounts Receivable; credit Sales Revenue), and the change in Accounts Receivable during the period was a decrease of $10,000, then cash receipts from customers must have been $517,000 (debit Cash; credit Accounts Receivable), which we can derive as shown in red above.

When we use the indirect method, we first list net income, which would include the $507,000 sales on account amount seen above. However, because the cash received from customers was actually $10,000 higher than this—as indicated by the decrease in accounts receivable—this amount would have to be added to net income to determine net cash provided by operating cash flows.

What happens if accounts receivable increase rather than decrease? When the Accounts Receivable account increases during the year, this means that revenues on an accrual basis are higher than cash receipts. Therefore, the amount of the increase in accounts receivable is deducted from net income to arrive at net cash provided (used) by operating activities. Notice how an increase in an asset like accounts receivable results in a reduction to net income in arriving at net cash provided by operations. All increases to noncash current assets related to operating activities would have the same effect. Conversely, decreases in these assets would result in additions made to net income.

If Computer Services collected deposits from customers in advance, the company would be using an Unearned Revenue account. Changes in this account during the year would indicate that cash received from customers differed from the amount of revenue recorded, and this change would have to be taken into consideration when determining net cash provided (used) by operating activities.

INVENTORY Computer Services' inventory increased by $5,000 (from $10,000 to $15,000) during the year. When inventory increases during the year, the cost of goods purchased is greater than the cost of goods sold expense recorded in the income statement. In other words, Computer Services must have purchased $5,000 more inventory than it sold in order for inventory levels to increase. To determine how much inventory was purchased, it is useful to analyze the Inventory account:

Inventory						
Jan.	1	Balance	10,000			
		Purchases	155,000	Cost of goods sold	150,000	
Dec.	31	Balance	15,000			

} $5,000 net increase (deduct from net income)

In a perpetual inventory system, the Inventory account is increased by the cost of goods purchased (debit Inventory and credit Accounts Payable) and decreased by the cost of goods sold (debit Cost of Goods Sold and credit Inventory). Because Computer Services reported $150,000 of cost of goods sold on its income statement (as shown in Illustration 13-4), purchases of merchandise during the year must have been $155,000 which can be derived as shown above.

To convert net income, which includes the Cost of Goods Sold of $150,000, to net cash provided (used) by operating activities, the $5,000 increase in Inventory must be deducted from net income. As explained above, the increase in inventory means that the cash-based expense must be increased. We do this by deducting this increase from net income in arriving at net cash provided by operating activities.

The deduction of an increase in inventory from net income does not completely convert an accrual-based figure to a cash-based figure. It does not tell us how much cash was paid for the goods purchased. It just converts the cost of goods sold to the cost of goods purchased during the year. The analysis of accounts payable—shown later in this section—completes this analysis by converting the cost of goods purchased from an accrual basis to a cash basis.

PREPAID EXPENSES   Computer Services' prepaid expenses increased by $4,000 (from $1,000 to $5,000) during the year. When prepaid expenses increase during the year, it means that the amount of cash spent on prepayments and their related other operating expenses (cash basis operating expenses) exceeds the accrual-based operating expenses shown on the income statement.

Computer Services' other operating expenses, other than its depreciation expense and loss from the disposal of equipment, have been combined in one summary account in Illustration 13-4. These other operating expenses would include administrative and selling expenses, among other types of expenses. To determine how much cash was paid relative to these expenses, the Prepaid Expenses account must be analyzed. Other operating expenses, as reported on the income statement, are $141,000. If we assume that all expenses are prepaid, payments for expenses as shown below must have been $145,000:

			Prepaid Expenses		
Jan.	1	Balance	1,000		
		Payments for expenses	145,000	Other operating expenses	141,000
Dec.	31	Balance	5,000		

$4,000 net increase (deduct from net income)

To adjust net income to net cash provided (used) by operating activities, the $4,000 increase in prepaid expenses must be deducted from net income to determine the cash paid for expenses. If prepaid expenses decrease during the year, rather than increase, expenses reported on an accrual-based income statement would be higher than expenses on a cash basis. Decreases in prepaid expenses would be added to net income rather than deducted as we did above for an increase in prepaid expenses.

If Computer Services Corporation had any accrued liabilities pertaining to operating expenses not yet paid, the change in these accrued liabilities would have to be considered in determining the cash paid for other operating expenses.

Changes in Current Liabilities

We will now look at the changes in Computer Services' current liability accounts to determine the impact that each change has on net income and cash. The adjustments that are required for changes in current liability accounts are as follows: increases in current liability accounts are added to net income. An increase in a liability means that the company has not paid it and this improves operating cash flows. Likewise, decreases in current liability accounts are deducted from net income, to arrive at net cash provided (used) by operating activities. A decrease in a liability means that it was paid down and this decreases operating cash flows. The only exception to the above involves changes in current liability accounts that have no effect on the income statement and these are typically the Dividends Payable account and the Current Portion of Mortgage Payable account. Because changes in these accounts do not affect the income statement, these changes are considered to be financing, not operating, activities, and we will deal with them later.

ACCOUNTS PAYABLE   In some companies, the Accounts Payable account is used only to record purchases of merchandise on account. Other payable accounts are used to record the credit entries for other expenditures made on account. In other companies, the Accounts Payable account is used to record all credit purchases. For simplicity in this chapter, we have assumed that Accounts Payable is used only to record purchases of inventory on account.

Computer Services' accounts payable increased by $7,000 (from $10,000 to $17,000) during the year. When accounts payable increase during the year, expenses on an accrual basis are higher than expenses on a cash basis because the difference caused accounts payable to increase. For Computer Services, this means that it received $7,000 more in goods than it actually paid for.

To illustrate, recall that Computer Services' Accounts Payable account is increased by purchases of merchandise (debit Inventory; credit Accounts Payable) and decreased by payments to suppliers (debit Accounts Payable; credit Cash). We determined the amount of purchases made by Computer Services in the analysis of the Inventory account earlier: $155,000. Using this figure, we can now determine that payments to suppliers must have been $145,000.

Accounts Payable				
		Jan.	1	Balance	10,000
Payments to suppliers	148,000			Purchases	155,000
		Dec.	31	Balance	17,000

$7,000 net increase (add to net income)

To convert net income to net cash provided (used) by operating activities, the $7,000 increase in accounts payable must be added to net income. The increase in accounts payable means that less cash was paid for the purchases than was deducted in the accrual-based expenses section of the income statement. The addition of $7,000 completes the adjustment required to convert the cost of goods purchased to the cash paid for these goods.

Decreases in accounts payable mean that more cash was paid for purchases than was recorded as an expense. As a result, decreases in accounts payable are deducted from net income.

In summary, the conversion of the cost of goods sold on the accrual-based income statement to the cash paid for goods purchased involves two steps: (1) The change in the Inventory account adjusts the cost of goods sold to the accrual-based cost of goods purchased. (2) The change in the Accounts Payable account adjusts the accrual-based cost of goods purchased to the cash-based payments to suppliers.

INCOME TAX PAYABLE   A change in the Income Tax Payable account reflects the difference between the income tax expense incurred and the income tax actually paid during the year.

Computer Services' Income Tax Payable account has decreased by $2,000 (from $8,000 to $6,000) during the year. This means that the $47,000 of income tax expense reported on the income statement in Illustration 13-4 was $2,000 less than the $49,000 of taxes paid during the period, as shown in the following T account:

Income Tax Payable				
		Jan.	1	Balance	8,000
Payments for income tax	49,000			Income tax expense	47,000
		Dec.	31	Balance	6,000

$2,000 net decrease (deduct from net income)

To adjust net income to net cash provided (used) by operating activities, the $2,000 decrease in income tax payable must be deducted from net income. If the amount of income tax payable had increased during the year, the increase would be added to net income to reflect the fact that income tax expense deducted on the accrual-based income statement was higher than the cash paid during the period.

The partial statement of cash flows in Illustration 13-6 shows the impact on operating activities of the changes in the current asset and current liability accounts. (The changes are highlighted in red.) It also shows the adjustments that were described earlier for noncash expenses and revenues and losses and gains. The operating activities section of the statement of cash flows is now complete.

►Illustration 13-6
Net cash provided (used)
by operating activities—
indirect method

COMPUTER SERVICES CORPORATION		
Statement of Cash Flows—Indirect Method (partial)		
Year Ended December 31, 2018		
Operating activities		
Net income		$145,000
Adjustments to reconcile net income to net cash		
provided (used) by operating activities		
Depreciation expense	$ 9,000	
Loss on disposal of equipment	3,000	
Decrease in accounts receivable	10,000	
Increase in inventory	(5,000)	
Increase in prepaid expenses	(4,000)	
Increase in accounts payable	7,000	
Decrease in income tax payable	(2,000)	18,000
Net cash provided by operating activities		163,000

▼ HELPFUL HINT
Whether the indirect or direct
method is used, net cash
provided (used) by operating
activities will be the same.

In summary, the operating activities section of Computer Services' statement of cash flows shows that the accrual-based net income of $145,000 resulted in net cash provided by operating activities of $163,000, after adjustments for noncash items.

SUMMARY OF CONVERSION TO NET CASH PROVIDED (USED) BY OPERATING ACTIVITIES— INDIRECT METHOD

As shown in the previous section, the statement of cash flows prepared by the indirect method starts with net income. Selected adjustments to net income to determine cash provided (used) by operating activities are then made. They are summarized here:

Noncash expenses	Depreciation expense (property and equipment)	Add
	Amortization expense (intangible assets)	Add
Losses and gains	Losses including impairment losses	Add
	Gains and reversal of impairment losses	Deduct
Changes in certain noncash current asset and current liability accounts	Increase in current asset account	Deduct
	Decrease in current asset account	Add
	Increase in current liability account	Add
	Decrease in current liability account	Deduct

Notice that increases in current liability accounts are added in the table above while decreases are deducted, meaning that the effects are directly related to cash flow. However, an increase in a current asset account is deducted while decreases are added, meaning that the effects are inversely related.

ACCOUNTING MATTERS

Why Does the Indirect Method Persist?

Both IFRS and ASPE encourage companies to prepare the statement of cash flows using the direct method rather than the indirect method. Standard setters prefer the direct method because its presentation is easier to understand for the average financial statement user. Despite this, the vast majority of companies continue to use the indirect method. The primary reason is that it is easier to prepare. Changes in

noncash current asset and liability accounts do not have to be split up to relate to inventory purchases and other operating expenses. However, some analysts prefer the use of the indirect method because users can see in one place how management of noncash working capital can affect cash flow. Furthermore, users can also see to what extent net income has been created by noncash items. For most companies, when preparing the statement using the indirect method, after adding back depreciation to net income, operating cash flow is higher than net income. Taking into consideration the changes in noncash working capital, there may be a slight decrease in operating cash flows because the rise in accounts receivable and inventory may be higher than the increase in accounts payable for a healthy, growing company.

The effect of changes in noncash working capital is usually not significant. However, consider the following information relating to the first six months of a fiscal year for Calgary-based Poseidon Concepts Corp. (in thousands):

	Current Period	Prior Period
Net income	$31,183	$ 6,341
Depreciation and other noncash expenses	8,224	9,627
Operating cash flow before the following	39,407	15,968
Changes in noncash working capital	(31,467)	(3,878)
Net cash from operating activities	$ 7,940	$12,090

When we use the indirect method, we can see that the change in the noncash working capital, which represented a 24% ($3,878 ÷ $15,968) decline in operating cash flows (before considering changes in noncash working capital) in the prior period, grew to represent an 80% decline in the current period. Despite net income rising almost fivefold, net cash from operating activities declined. Why? It is because of the changes in noncash working capital. If you dug deeper into the reason for this, you would have discovered a very large increase in accounts receivable because this company was having difficulty collecting receivables. Consequently, Poseidon Concepts, which supplied storage tanks to the oil and gas sector, later declared bankruptcy.

DO IT! ▶13-2 Operating Activities—Indirect Method

Selected financial information follows for Denham Ltd. at December 31. Prepare the operating activities section of the statement of cash flows using the indirect method.

	2018	2017	Increase (Decrease)
Current assets			
Cash	$61,000	$37,000	$24,000
Accounts receivable	68,000	26,000	42,000
Inventory	54,000	10,000	44,000
Prepaid expenses	4,000	6,000	(2,000)
Current liabilities			
Accounts payable	35,000	55,000	(20,000)
Accrued liabilities	4,000	5,000	(1,000)
Salaries payable	6,000	4,000	2,000
Income tax payable	20,000	10,000	10,000

DENHAM LTD.
Income Statement
Year Ended December 31, 2018

Sales revenue		$890,000
Cost of goods sold		465,000
Gross profit		425,000
Operating expenses		
Administrative expenses	$196,000	
Depreciation expense	33,000	
Loss on disposal of equipment	4,000	233,000
Income from operations		192,000
Interest expense		12,000
Income before tax		180,000
Income tax expense		36,000
Net income		$144,000

Action Plan

✔ Start with net income to determine the net cash provided (used) by operating activities.

✔ Examine the income statement: Add back noncash expenses and losses because, although these items are included in net income, they have no effect on cash flows and must therefore be removed from our determination of cash flow. For the same reasons, we would deduct any gains recorded in net income.

✔ Analyze the noncash current assets and liabilities on the statement of financial position: Add decreases in related noncash current asset accounts and increases in related noncash current liability accounts. Deduct increases in related noncash current asset accounts and decreases in related noncash current liability accounts.

SOLUTION

Try this Do It! exercise on your own and then check your answer at the end of the chapter.

Related Exercise Material: BE13–4, BE13–5, E13–3, and E13–4.

Prepare the investing and financing activities sections and complete the statement of cash flows.

Unlike the operating activities section, which can be prepared using either the indirect or direct method, the investing and financing activities are measured and reported in the same way regardless of which method is used to report operating activities. We will illustrate investing activities first, followed by financing activities, and then explain how to combine all three activities together when completing the statement of cash flows.

INVESTING ACTIVITIES

1. PREPARE OPERATING ACTIVITIES SECTION.	2. Prepare investing activities section.	3. PREPARE FINANCING ACTIVITIES SECTION.	4. COMPLETE THE STATEMENT OF CASH FLOWS.

The second step in the preparation of a statement of cash flows involves investing activities. Investing activities measure cash flows relating to non-current asset accounts, such as long-term investments; property, plant, and equipment; and intangible assets. Note that only the purchase and sale of investments not held for trading purposes are considered investing activities. Cash flows relating to investments in debt or equity securities that are held specifically for trading purposes are classified as operating activities rather than as investing activities. This is because they relate to revenue-producing activities of the company, similar to inventory purchased for resale. You will recall that held for trading investments were discussed in Chapter 12.

Although it is primarily non-current asset accounts that give rise to investing activities, there are some current asset account transactions that may also be classified as investing activities. For example, short-term notes receivable obtained from lending funds rather than from revenue-producing transactions would be classified as an investing activity rather than an operating activity. The point of mentioning exceptions such as this is to advocate caution about applying general guidelines too widely.

We will use the statement of financial position and additional information provided in Illustration 13-4 to determine what effect, if any, the change in each relevant current asset and non-current asset account had on investing activities. Computer Services did not have any affected current asset accounts but does have three non-current asset accounts that must be analyzed: Land, Buildings, and Equipment.

Land

Land increased by $110,000 during the year, as reported in Computer Services' statement of financial position in Illustration 13-4. The additional information provided states that this land was purchased by paying cash of $95,000 and by issuing common shares worth $15,000. Because a portion of the land was acquired by issuing shares rather than by paying cash, this portion of the purchase transaction is a noncash investing activity (acquisition of land), as well as a noncash financing activity (issuing shares). Such noncash activities are disclosed in a note to the statement of cash flows even though these amounts are not listed in the actual statement of cash flows. Consequently, the investing activities section of the statement will show a payment of only $95,000.

Buildings

The Buildings account increased by $120,000 during the year, as reported in Illustration 13-4. What caused this increase? No additional information has been provided regarding this change. Whenever unexplained differences in non-current accounts occur, we assume the transaction was for cash. That is, we would assume in this case that a building was acquired, or expanded, for $120,000 cash and report this cash payment as an investing activity.

ACCUMULATED DEPRECIATION—BUILDINGS Accumulated Depreciation increased by $6,000 during the year, as shown in Illustration 13-4. As explained in the additional information, this increase resulted from the $9,000 of depreciation expense reported on the income statement, of which $6,000 related to buildings:

Accumulated Depreciation—Building				
	Jan.	1	Balance	5,000
			Depreciation expense	6,000
	Dec.	31	Balance	11,000

} $6,000 net increase

Depreciation expense is a noncash expense and does not affect the statement of cash flows. Adding it back to net income in the operating section of the statement when we used the indirect method or just ignoring depreciation expense when using the direct method means that we have recognized its noncash nature. Therefore, it does not need to be dealt with in the investing activity section.

Equipment

Computer Services' Equipment account increased by $17,000, as reported in Illustration 13-4. The additional information provided in this illustration explains that this was a net increase resulting from two different transactions: (1) a purchase of equipment for $25,000 cash, and (2) a disposal of equipment that cost $8,000 for $4,000 cash. The following entries reproduce these two equipment transactions:

Equipment	25,000	
Cash		25,000

A	=	L	+	SE
+25,000				
−25,000				
↓ Cash flows: −25,000				

Cash	4,000	
Accumulated Depreciation	1,000	
Loss on Disposal	3,000	
Equipment		8,000

A	=	L	+	SE
+4,000				−3,000
+1,000				
−8,000				
↑ Cash flows: +4,000				

The T account that follows summarizes the changes in the Equipment account during the year:

Equipment					
Jan.	1	Balance	10,000		
		Purchase of equipment	25,000	Cost of equipment sold	8,000
Dec.	31	Balance	27,000		

} $17,000 net increase

In the above example, you were given information about both the purchase and the disposal of equipment. Often, in analyzing accounts, you will not be given all of the information needed to determine what caused the change in an account balance. You need to know four things about a non-current asset account when preparing the investing section. They are the opening and closing balances, and the upward and downward movement in the account. If you know three of these four amounts, you can always derive the fourth and usually it will be an upward or downward movement that you will have to determine. For example, if you knew the beginning and ending balances of the Equipment account were $10,000 and $27,000, respectively, as well as the fact that the cost of the equipment sold was $8,000, you could determine that the cost of the equipment purchased must have been $25,000.

Each upward or downward movement in an applicable account should be reported separately in the investing section even though the net movement is often reported for accounts applicable to the operating section. In this particular case, the purchase of equipment should be reported as a $25,000 cash payment. The disposal of equipment should be reported as a $4,000 cash receipt. (We do not show the loss or the cost of the equipment sold because these are not cash flows.) We do not net the cash paid for equipment with the cash received on the disposal of equipment; instead, we show them separately because this information is useful.

ACCUMULATED DEPRECIATION—EQUIPMENT The accumulated depreciation for equipment increased during the year by $2,000. This change does not represent the overall depreciation expense for the year. This is important to remember: the change in the Accumulated Depreciation account is only equal to depreciation expense if there were no disposals of related assets during the period, and this is very rare. The additional information in Illustration 13-4 reported that depreciation expense was $9,000 in total, of which $3,000 related to the equipment.

We can use the journal entry shown earlier for the disposal of the equipment and the information about the amount of the depreciation expense recorded for the year to help us understand why the Accumulated Depreciation account increased by $2,000, and not $3,000:

Accumulated Depreciation—Equipment					
		Jan.	1	Balance	1,000
Disposal of equipment	1,000			Depreciation expense	3,000
		Dec.	31	Balance	3,000

$2,000 net increase

The $2,000 net increase is composed of two different amounts: (1) a reduction in accumulated depreciation of $1,000 as a result of the disposal of equipment described above, and (2) an increase in accumulated depreciation of $3,000 as a result of depreciation expense for the current period. Neither of these amounts, however, is shown on the statement of cash flows because they do not represent an amount of cash received or paid, so their effects are eliminated from net income by adding back depreciation expense and losses on disposal and deducting gains on disposal from net income.

As we have seen, the disposal of the equipment affected a number of accounts: one account on Computer Services' income statement (Loss on Disposal) and three accounts on its statement of financial position (Cash, Equipment, and Accumulated Depreciation). In the statement of cash flows, it is important to combine the effects of this disposal in one place: the investing activities section. The overall result, then, is that the loss on the disposal of the equipment is removed from net income in the operating activities section of the statement of cash flows and the cash proceeds received from the disposal of the equipment are shown in the investing activities section.

Investments

Although Computer Services has no investment accounts, it is important to remember to remove any noncash transactions when analyzing changes in any long-term investment and investment-related accounts. Similar to the disposal of equipment discussed above, items reported for investments in a statement of cash flows should consist only of amounts paid when purchasing the investments and amounts received when selling investments. These amounts are not netted together but are shown separately.

The investing activities section of Computer Services' statement of cash flows is shown in Illustration 13-7. It reports the purchase of a building as well as the purchase and disposal of equipment.

Computer Services also reports in the accompanying notes to the statement any significant noncash investing and financing activities, such as the issue of common shares to purchase part of the land.

COMPUTER SERVICES CORPORATION
Statement of Cash Flows (partial)
Year Ended December 31, 2018

Investing activities		
Purchase of building	$(120,000)	
Purchase of land	(95,000)	
Purchase of equipment	(25,000)	
Proceeds from disposal of equipment	4,000	
Net cash used by investing activities		$(236,000)
Note x: Significant noncash investing and financing activities		
Portion of land cost purchased by issuing common shares		$15,000

▶Illustration 13-7
Net cash provided (used)
by investing activities

DO IT! ▶13-3a   Investing Activities

In its Equipment account, Umiujaq Corporation reported an opening balance of $146,000 and an ending balance of $135,000 while the Accumulated Depreciation—Equipment account had an opening balance of $47,000 and an ending balance of $62,000. During the year, it sold equipment with a cost of $21,000 and a carrying amount of $5,000 for cash, for a gain on the disposal of $1,000. It also purchased equipment for cash. It recorded depreciation expense on the equipment of $31,000.

(a) Prepare the journal entries that would have been made to record the sale of the equipment, the purchase of the equipment, and the depreciation expense. [*Note*: Some amounts may have to be determined from the T accounts prepared in part (b).]

(b) Set up T accounts for the Equipment and Accumulated Depreciation—Equipment accounts, enter the opening and ending balances, and post the relevant portions of the journal entries prepared in part (a).

(c) Identify the amount of cash received from the disposal of equipment and the amount of cash paid for equipment that would appear in the investing section of the statement of cash flows.

Action Plan

✔ Use journal entries and T accounts, and your knowledge of account relationships, to reconstruct the transactions affecting the Equipment and Accumulated Depreciation accounts. Fill in the information given and use this to determine any missing information (for example, the cost of equipment purchased and the accumulated depreciation on the equipment that was disposed).

✔ Remember that the carrying amount of equipment is its cost less accumulated depreciation and that gains result when the cash proceeds exceed the carrying amount.

SOLUTION
Try this Do It! exercise on your own and then check your answer at the end of the chapter.

Related Exercise Material: BE13–6 and BE13–7.

FINANCING ACTIVITIES

1. PREPARE OPERATING ACTIVITIES SECTION.	2. PREPARE INVESTING ACTIVITIES SECTION.	**3. Prepare financing activities section.**	4. COMPLETE THE STATEMENT OF CASH FLOWS.

The third step in preparing a statement of cash flows is to prepare the financing activities section by analyzing the changes in non-current liability and equity accounts. In addition, changes involving current liability accounts, such as dividends payable and short-term loans or notes payable (if incurred for lending purposes rather than for trade), should also be reported in the financing activities section. Computer Services has two current liability accounts affected (Dividends Payable and the Current Portion of Mortgage Payable), one non-current liability account (Mortgage Payable), and three shareholders' equity accounts (Common Shares, Retained Earnings, and Accumulated Other Comprehensive Income), as shown in Illustration 13-4.

Bank Loan and Mortgage Payable

Computer Services does not have any bank loans, but it has a mortgage payable, which was increased by $118,000 [$9,000 current + $109,000 non-current]. As we saw with non-current asset movements, we show the effects on cash of both increases and decreases in non-current liability accounts. Given the nature of bank loans and mortgages, it is common to have these items split into current and non-current liabilities. When disclosing the movement in these items, they should be combined. Thus we show the total loan received regardless of whether it affected the current or non-current portion of the loan and the total loan principal payments made regardless of which portion, current or non-current, changed as a result of this payment.

For Computer Services, the entire mortgage balance (both current and non-current portions) amounted to $21,000 ($6,000 + $15,000) at the beginning of 2018. During the year, a new mortgage loan was received for $124,000, while payments pertaining to the principal of the mortgage were made for $6,000.

Note that any interest paid would be recorded in the operating activities section, as covered earlier. As we see with many investing and financing activities, we disclose separately the increases and decreases in cash pertaining to a particular asset or liability. We do not net these movements together, which is why you will see both the receipts of cash from loans and their repayment in the financing section.

Share Capital

Share capital can include both preferred and common shares. Computer Services does not have any preferred shares, but does have a balance of $70,000 in Common Shares at the end of 2018. According to Illustration 13-4, the company's Common Shares account increased by $20,000. We know from the additional information provided that $15,000 of these shares were issued to acquire land. Because this is a noncash transaction, neither the issue of the shares nor the acquisition of the portion of the land acquired by these shares is shown on the statement of cash flows (although note disclosure of these noncash transactions is made). However, the issue of shares for $5,000 would be reported as a cash receipt under the financing activities on the statement of cash flows. Just as we did with investing activities, if we are aware of what caused an account to rise and fall, we would show both movements separately rather than netting them together.

If the company had reacquired shares, the amount of cash paid to reacquire the shares would be reported as a cash payment in the financing activities section of the statement of cash flows.

Retained Earnings

What caused the net increase of $116,000 in Retained Earnings reported in Illustration 13-4? This increase can be explained by two factors. First, net income increased retained earnings by $145,000. Second, the additional information provided in Illustration 13-4 indicates that a dividend of $29,000 was declared.

This information could also have been determined by analyzing the T account:

	Retained Earnings				
Dividends declared	29,000	Jan.	1	Balance	48,000
				Net income	145,000
		Dec.	31	Balance	164,000

$116,000 net increase {

These two changes—net income and the cash dividend—must be reported separately. If using the indirect method, the net income is reported in the operating activities section of the statement of cash flows, although it is later adjusted to a cash basis net income amount. If using the direct method, the net income is reported by listing revenues and expenses on a cash basis.

With respect to reporting the cash dividends, it is important to note that the Retained Earnings account above only reports the dividends declared. We need to report the dividends paid in the financing activities section. This will differ from the dividends declared if there is a change in the Dividends Payable account and this year, that account increased by $1,000. Because of this, the dividends paid amount on the statement will be lower than the dividends declared and is equal to

$28,000, representing the amount of the dividend declared less the increase in the Dividends Payable account. This can be seen by viewing the activity in the Dividends Payable account as shown below:

			Dividends Payable		
			Jan.	1	Balance	1,000
Dividends paid	28,000			Dividends declared	29,000
			Dec.	31	Balance	2,000

} $1,000 net increase

Notice that the change in the Dividends Payable account is not shown as a separate item on the statement of cash flows. Rather, we use the change in the Dividends Payable account to convert the accrual-based dividends declared into the cash-based dividends paid.

Accumulated Other Comprehensive Income

Computer Services had no changes in its accumulated other comprehensive income during 2018. That is why it did not prepare a statement of comprehensive income, only an income statement for that year. If accumulated other comprehensive income had increased or decreased in the current year, it would not affect the statement of cash flows because there are no cash flow effects in any of the sources of other comprehensive income. That is why the starting point for the operating activities of the statement of cash flows is net income and not comprehensive income.

The financing activities section of Computer Services' statement of cash flows is shown in Illustration 13-8 and reports the issue of common shares and payment of a dividend. It also reports in the accompanying notes to the statement the significant noncash investing and financing activities. This is the same note shown in Illustration 13-7. It is not a new note; it has been included here for completeness only.

▶Illustration 13-8
Net cash provided (used) by financing activities

COMPUTER SERVICES CORPORATION
Statement of Cash Flows (partial)
Year Ended December 31, 2018

Financing activities	
Additions to mortgage payable	$124,000
Repayments of mortgage payable	(6,000)
Issue of common shares	5,000
Payment of cash dividend	(28,000)
Net cash provided by financing activities	$95,000
Note x: Significant noncash investing and financing activities	
Portion of land cost purchased by issuing common shares	$15,000

DO IT! ▶13-3b   Financing Activities

Selected financial information for La Tuque Ltd. at December 31 is shown below.

	2018	2017
Current liabilities		
Dividends payable	$ 2,000	$ 1,000
Current portion of bank loan	5,000	4,000
Non-current liabilities		
Bank loan payable	55,000	48,000
Shareholders' equity		
Common shares	121,000	103,000
Retained earnings	72,000	57,000

Action Plan

✔ Use journal entries and T accounts, and your knowledge of account relationships, to reconstruct the transactions affecting the accounts listed above. Fill in the information given and use this to determine any missing information.

✔ Based on the journal entries and T accounts used above, list the amounts that would appear in the financing section of the statement of cash flows.

During the year, the company had net income of $27,000. It received bank loans of $17,000 and repaid a portion of other outstanding bank loans. It issued new common shares and did not reacquire any. Calculate and present the net cash provided by financing activities for 2018.

COMPLETING THE STATEMENT OF CASH FLOWS

| 1. PREPARE OPERATING ACTIVITIES SECTION. | 2. PREPARE INVESTING ACTIVITIES SECTION. | 3. PREPARE FINANCING ACTIVITIES SECTION. | **4. Complete the statement of cash flows.** |

The last step in preparing the statement of cash flows is to complete the statement, combining the operating, investing, and financing activities sections to determine the net increase or decrease in cash for the period. Using the partial information shown in Illustration 13-6 for operating activities, in Illustration 13-7 for investing activities, and in Illustration 13-8 for financing activities, we can now combine the sections and present a complete statement of cash flows for Computer Services Corporation, as shown in Illustration 13-9.

▶Illustration 13-9
Statement of cash flows—
indirect method

COMPUTER SERVICES CORPORATION Statement of Cash Flows Year Ended December 31, 2018		
Operating activities		
Net income		$145,000
Adjustments to reconcile net income to net cash provided (used)		
by operating activities		
Depreciation expense	$ 9,000	
Loss on disposal of equipment	3,000	
Decrease in accounts receivable	10,000	
Increase in inventory	(5,000)	
Increase in prepaid expenses	(4,000)	
Increase in accounts payable	7,000	
Decrease in income tax payable	(2,000)	18,000
Net cash provided by operating activities		163,000
Investing activities		
Purchase of building	$(120,000)	
Purchase of land	(95,000)	
Purchase of equipment	(25,000)	
Proceeds from disposal of equipment	4,000	
Net cash used by investing activities		(236,000)
Financing activities		
Additions to mortgage payable	$ 124,000	
Repayment of mortgage payable	(6,000)	
Issue of common shares	5,000	
Payment of cash dividend	(28,000)	
Net cash provided by financing activities		95,000
Net increase in cash		22,000
Cash, January 1		33,000
Cash, December 31		$ 55,000
Note x: Significant noncash investing and financing activities		
Portion of land cost purchased by issuing common shares		$15,000

The statement of cash flows begins with the operating activities section, prepared using the indirect method in Illustration 13-9. The operating activities section using the direct method, illustrated in Appendix 13A, could be substituted in this illustration, if desired. Regardless of whether the indirect or direct method has been used, the operating activities section would disclose that cash was provided by operating activities in the amount of $163,000.

The statement continues with investing activities, reporting that investing activities used $236,000 of cash. Financing activities follow, providing $95,000 cash. The statement concludes with the net change in cash, reconciled to the beginning- and end-of-period cash balances. The comparative statement of financial position in Illustration 13-4 indicates that the net change in cash during the period was an increase of $22,000. The $22,000 net increase in cash reported in the statement of cash flows above agrees with this change.

Additional disclosures are required to complete the statement of cash flows. As we previously discussed, significant noncash investing and financing activities must be reported in the notes to the financial statements. In addition, if a company has combined cash equivalents with its cash, it must disclose the components of its cash equivalents along with a reconciliation of the amounts reported on the statement of cash flows with those reported on the statement of financial position. There are other disclosures required, but we will leave discussion of these to a future accounting course.

DO IT! ▶13-3c   Statement of Cash Flows—Indirect Method

Selected information follows for Denham Ltd. at December 31:

	2018	2017	Increase (Decrease)
Cash	$ 61,000	$ 37,000	$24,000
Property, plant, and equipment			
Land	45,000	70,000	(25,000)
Buildings	200,000	200,000	-0-
Accumulated depreciation—buildings	(21,000)	(11,000)	10,000
Equipment	193,000	68,000	125,000
Accumulated depreciation—equipment	(28,000)	(10,000)	18,000
Liabilities and shareholders' equity			
Bank loan payable	110,000	150,000	(40,000)
Common shares	200,000	60,000	140,000
Retained earnings	201,000	112,000	89,000

Additional information:

1. Net cash provided by operating activities was $88,000 for the year.

2. Equipment was purchased for cash. Equipment with a cost of $41,000 and a carrying amount of $36,000 was sold at a loss of $4,000. Land was sold for an amount equal to its cost.

3. Bank loans amounting to $65,000 were paid off this year while some new loans were obtained.

4. Common shares were issued for cash; no shares were reacquired during the year.

5. Net income was $144,000.

6. A cash dividend was declared and paid.

Prepare a statement of cash flows, excluding the detail normally required for the operating activities section.

Action Plan

✔ Begin with the operating activities section.

✔ Determine the net cash provided (used) by investing activities. Investing activities generally relate to changes in non-current asset accounts.

✔ Determine the net cash provided (used) by financing activities. Financing activities generally relate to changes in non-current liabilities and shareholders' equity accounts.

✔ Determine the net increase (decrease) in cash. Reconcile to the end-of-period cash balance reported on the statement of financial position ($61,000 in this case).

SOLUTION

Try this Do It! exercise on your own and then check your answer at the end of the chapter.

Related Exercise Material: E13-5 and E13–7.

Use the statement of cash flows to evaluate a company.

Throughout this book, we have been using ratios to evaluate the performance of a business. These ratios were typically based on amounts from accrual basis financial statements but in this next section we will use amounts from the statement of cash flows instead.

CORPORATE LIFE CYCLE AND CASH FLOWS

Just as products have a life cycle, so do companies. The **corporate life cycle** consists of four phases: introductory, growth, maturity, and decline. Each phase, as indicated in the following graph, can help us understand what to expect for a company's cash flow from its operating, investing, and financing activities.

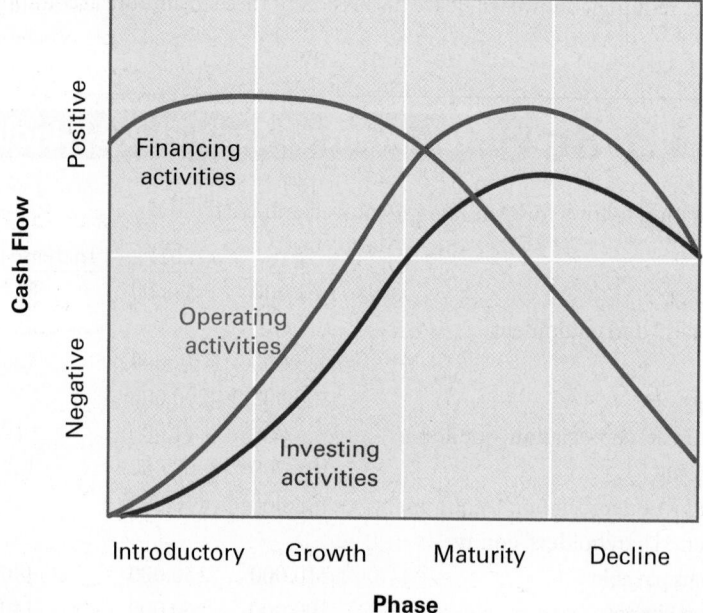

In the introductory and growth phases, we don't usually expect to see a company generate positive cash from its operating activities. Because the company is making significant investments in its long-lived assets, cash will be used by investing activities. In contrast, cash generated by financing activities is usually positive because debt and equity are issued to pay for the investments and cover the operating activities shortfall.

As companies move to the maturity and decline phases of their life cycle, these patterns tend to reverse. The company is usually able to generate positive cash from its operating activities as it reaches maturity, which is used to cover its investing activities. At this point in their life cycle, companies can start to declare and pay dividends, retire debt, and/or buy back shares, so their cash flows from financing activities move toward the negative. In the decline phase, cash from operating activities decreases. Cash from investing activities is positive as the company sells off its excess assets, before starting to decline. Cash is used for financing activities as the company continues to pay off its debt.

At times, some companies do not experience the phases of the corporate life cycle as described above. An example of such a time is when a company is undergoing financial difficulties. Under these circumstances, cash provided by operating activities is usually declining (or negative with cash used by operating activities) while cash is used for financing activities as creditors demand loan repayments. At times like this, a company may need to sell off non-current assets to obtain the cash to make these payments to lenders. Understanding the relationship between the categories of cash flows is therefore critical in gaining a better insight into the nature of a company's activities.

ACCOUNTING MATTERS

Emre YILDIZ/Getty Images

Analyze Statement of Cash Flows with Care

When we prepare an income statement, we use estimates, such as the useful life of a building or the amount of the allowance for doubtful accounts. Furthermore, due to accrual accounting concepts, revenue is recorded even though the related cash from that activity may not yet have been received. Because of these estimates and uncertainty regarding the collection of revenue, some analysts believe that cash flow from operating activities is a better indicator of a company's success than net income. They believe that, because cash flow measures what has actually happened and is not based on estimates or accruals, it is a superior indicator of performance.

Although this viewpoint certainly has some merit, we have to be careful when analyzing the statement of cash flows. Some operating cash flows are nonrecurring, and although they cause an immediate increase in cash flow, this is not sustainable. For example, what would happen if a company, just prior to the end of the year, sold its accounts receivable? There would be an immediate jump in operating cash flows. However, one year later, if the accounts receivable that existed at that time were not sold, the increase in accounts receivable over that year would cause a large drop in operating cash flows, reversing out the increase recorded in the prior year.

Although overall cash flows are hard to manipulate, their classification within the statement can sometimes be distorted. For example, assume that a company had a major repair on a building and there was some doubt about whether the expenditure should be expensed or capitalized. If the company wanted to maximize its operating cash flows, the decision would be made to capitalize the amount spent on the building because this would be treated as a cash payment in the investing section rather than the operating section. In summary, as with all financial statements, we need to understand and question the decisions that were made regarding the underlying events that affect amounts recorded on the statement.

FREE CASH FLOW

In the statement of cash flows, net cash provided by operating activities is an indication of the company's cash-generating capability. Analysts have noted, however, that cash provided by operating activities fails to take into account the fact that a company must invest in new capital equipment just to maintain its current level of operations. Companies usually maintain dividends at current levels to satisfy investors. One measure of a company's cash-generating ability is free cash flow. Free cash flow helps creditors and investors understand how much discretionary cash flow a company has left from its operating activities that can be used to expand operations, reduce debt, or pay additional dividends.

Although there are different concepts of free cash flow, a commonly used one is to deduct net capital expenditures and dividends paid from cash provided or used by operating activities to determine **free cash flow**. Net capital expenditures—representing amounts paid for the acquisition of property, plant, and equipment less any recoveries from the disposal of these assets—can be found in the investing activities section of the statement of cash flows. Dividends paid, if any, are reported in the financing activities section of the statement of cash flows.

We will use the following selected information (in millions) to calculate free cash flow for Teck, featured in our chapter-opening story:

	2015	2014
Net cash provided by operating activities	$1,951	$2,278
Net capital expenditures	1,104	2,223
Cash dividends	374	518

Illustration 13-10 presents the free cash flow numbers for Teck, along with comparative results for Freeport-McMoRan Inc., one of Teck's key competitors.

► Illustration 13-10
Free cash flow

FREE CASH FLOW =	NET CASH PROVIDED (USED) BY OPERATING ACTIVITIES	−	NET CAPITAL EXPENDITURES	− DIVIDENDS PAID
(in millions)		2015		2014
Teck (in C$ millions)		$1,951 − $1,104 − $374 = $473		$2,278 − $2,223 − $518 = $(463)
Freeport-McMoRan (in U.S. $ millions)		$(3,751)		$101

The free cash flow for Teck increased in 2015 and became positive, while the free cash flow for Freeport-McMoRan declined in 2015 and became negative. Both companies sell commodities and the prices for these dropped significantly in 2015. In that year, despite a decrease in Teck's cash flows from operating activities, the company reduced capital expenditures and dividends, which successfully increased free cash flow. Freeport-McMoRan reduced dividends in 2015, but unlike Teck, this company actually increased capital expenditures and acquired assets at historically low prices.

DO IT! ► 13-4   Corporate Life Cycle and Free Cash Flow

Action Plan

✔ Recall the four phases of the corporate life cycle—introductory, growth, maturity, and decline—and whether each category of cash flow is likely positive or negative at each of these cycles.

✔ Recall the formula for free cash flow: Net cash provided (used) by operating activities − net capital expenditures − cash dividends.

Speyside Inc. reported the following selected information:

	2018	2017	2016
Net cash provided by operating activities	$43,000	$ 69,000	$ (2,000)
Net capital expenditures	(9,000)	(17,000)	(5,000)
Cash dividends	(6,000)	(4,000)	-0-
Receipt (repayments) of long-term debt	(4,000)	(1,000)	15,000

(a) In each of the years shown above, what phase of the corporate life cycle do you think the company is in? For the purpose of this question, use the information provided above for net capital expenditures as a proxy for net cash used by investing activities and dividends and long-term debt as a proxy for net cash provided or used by financing activities.

(b) Calculate the company's free cash flow for 2018 and 2017.

(c) Explain why the free cash flow changed in 2018 compared with 2017.

SOLUTION

Try this Do It! exercise on your own and then check your answer at the end of the chapter.

Related Exercise Material: BE13–10, BE13–11, E13–8, E13–9, E13–10, and E13–11.

LEARNING
OBJECTIVE **5**

Appendix 13A: Prepare the operating activities section of a statement of cash flows using the direct method.

1. Prepare operating activities section—direct method.   2. PREPARE INVESTING ACTIVITIES SECTION.   3. PREPARE FINANCING ACTIVITIES SECTION.   4. COMPLETE THE STATEMENT OF CASH FLOWS.

To explain and illustrate the direct method of preparing the operating activities section, we will use the transactions of Computer Services Corporation for 2018 to prepare a statement of cash flows. You will find Computer Services' financial information in Illustration 13-4, presented earlier in the chapter.

Similar to the indirect method, net cash provided (used) by operating activities using the direct method is determined by adjusting the income statement from the accrual basis of accounting to the cash basis of accounting. Whereas the indirect method adjusts total net income, the direct method adjusts each individual revenue and expense item in the income statement so that the result looks like a cash basis income statement rather than a list of adjustments to net income.

To simplify and condense the operating activities section, only major classes of operating cash receipts and cash payments are reported. The difference between the cash receipts and cash payments for these major classes is the net cash provided (used) by operating activities.

These relationships are shown in Illustration 13A-1.

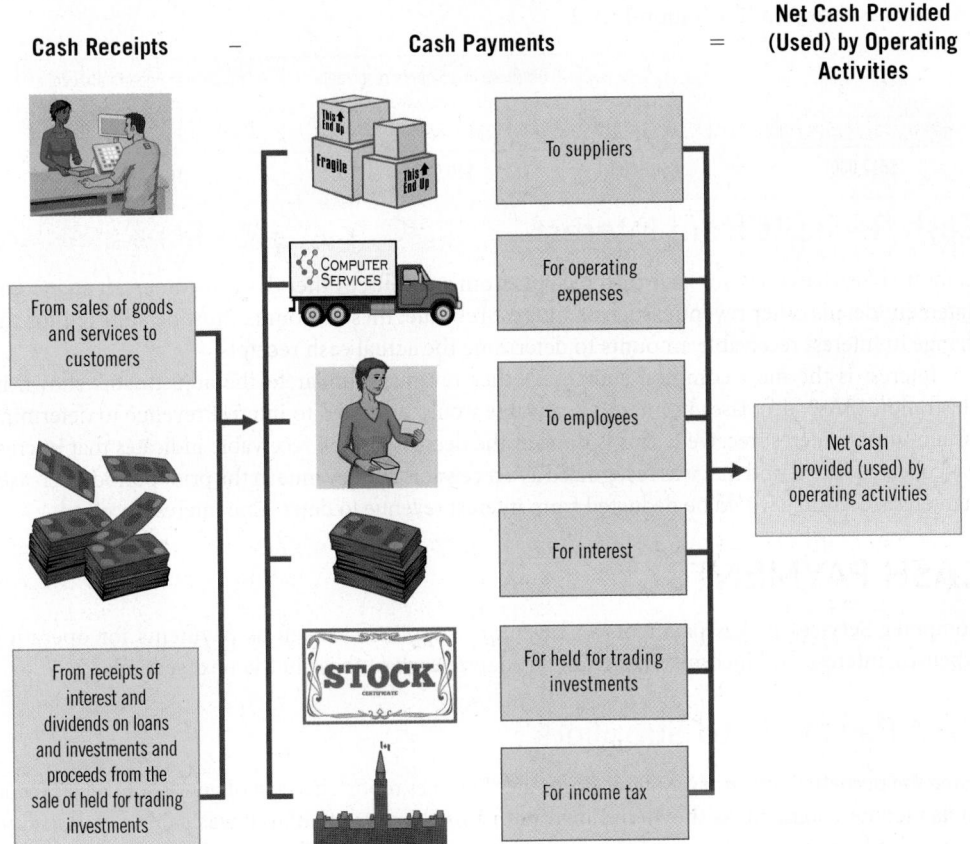

► Illustration 13A-1
Major classes of cash receipts and payments

CASH RECEIPTS

We will now look at Computer Services' cash receipts. Note that it has only one source of cash receipts: the sale of goods to its customers.

Cash Receipts from Customers

The income statement shown in Illustration 13-4 for Computer Services reported sales revenue from customers of $507,000. How much of that was received in cash? To answer that, we need to look at the change in accounts receivable during the year.

Computer Services' accounts receivable decreased by $10,000 (from $30,000 to $20,000) during the year. When accounts receivable decrease during the year, this means that the company has collected more cash during the year than the amount of revenues earned. In this case, accrual basis revenues are lower than cash basis revenues. In other words, more cash was collected during the year than was recorded as revenue and this caused accounts receivable to decrease. To determine the amount of cash receipts, the decrease in accounts receivable is added to sales revenue.

Alternatively, when the Accounts Receivable account balance increases during the year, revenues on an accrual basis are higher than cash receipts. In other words, revenues have increased, but not all of these revenues resulted in cash receipts. Therefore, the amount of the increase in accounts receivable is deducted from sales revenues to arrive at cash receipts from customers.

Although Computer Services does not collect deposits from customers, if it did, the company would have an Unearned Revenue account and changes in this account would also affect the determination of cash receipts from customers. For example an increase in Unearned Revenue would indicate that cash receipts were greater than revenue, while a decrease would indicate the opposite effect.

For Computer Services, cash receipts from customers were $517,000, or $10,000 higher than revenues, as shown in Illustration 13A-2.

►Illustration 13A-2
Formula to calculate cash receipts from customers

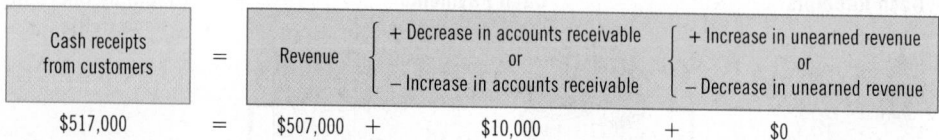

Cash Receipts from Interest

Computer Services does not have cash receipts from any source other than customers. If an income statement details other revenue, such as interest revenue, these amounts must be adjusted for the change in interest receivable amounts to determine the actual cash receipts.

Interest is the most common source of other revenue. Similar to the adjustments shown in Illustration 13A-2, decreases in interest receivable would be added to interest revenue to determine the amount of interest received. This is done as the decrease in the receivable indicates that interest was collected this period that was recognized as a receivable and revenue in the prior period. Increases in interest receivable would be deducted from interest revenue to determine interest received.

CASH PAYMENTS

Computer Services makes payments to inventory suppliers, as well as payments for operating expenses, interest, and income taxes. We will analyze each of these in the next sections.

Cash Payments to Suppliers

Using the perpetual inventory system, Computer Services reported a cost of goods sold of $150,000 on its income statement, as shown in Illustration 13-4. How much of that was paid in cash to suppliers (also known as creditors)? To answer that, it is necessary to first calculate the cost of goods purchased for the year. After the cost of goods purchased is calculated, cash payments to suppliers can be determined.

1. **Cost of goods purchased:** To calculate the cost of goods purchased, the cost of goods sold must be adjusted for any change in inventory. When the Inventory account increases during the year, the cost of goods purchased is higher than the cost of goods sold. To determine the cost of goods purchased, the increase in inventory is added to the cost of goods sold. Computer Services' inventory increased by $5,000, so its cost of goods purchased is $155,000.

Cost of goods sold	$150,000
Add: Increase in inventory	5,000
Cost of goods purchased	155,000

Any decrease in inventory would be deducted from the cost of goods sold.

2. **Cash payments to suppliers:** After the cost of goods purchased is calculated, cash payments to suppliers can be determined. This is done by adjusting the cost of goods purchased for the change in accounts payable. In some companies, the Accounts Payable account is used only to record purchases of merchandise on account. An accrued liability account such as Accrued Expenses Payable or some similar account is used to record other credit purchases. In other

companies, the Accounts Payable account is used to record all credit purchases. For simplicity, we have assumed in this chapter that Accounts Payable is used only to record purchases of inventory on account.

Consequently, when accounts payable increase during the year, cash payments to suppliers will be lower than the cost of goods purchased. To determine cash payments to suppliers, an increase in accounts payable is deducted from the cost of goods purchased. For Computer Services, cash payments to suppliers were $148,000.

Cost of goods purchased (from item 1 above)	$155,000
Less: Increase in accounts payable	7,000
Cash payments to suppliers	148,000

On the other hand, there may be a decrease in accounts payable. That would occur if cash payments to suppliers amounted to more than purchases. In that case, the decrease in accounts payable is added to the cost of goods purchased.

The narrative above is shown in formula format in Illustration 13A-3.

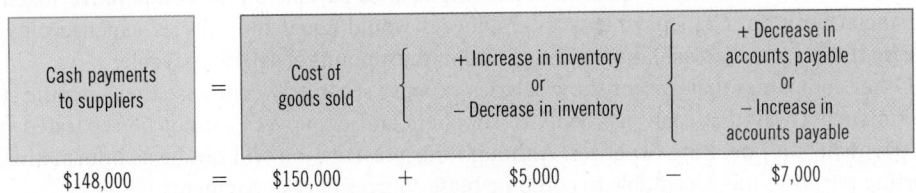

► Illustration 13A-3

Formula to calculate cash payments to suppliers

Cash Payments for Operating Expenses

Computer Services' income statement shown in Illustration 13-4 includes $141,000 of other operating expenses. In this particular case, other operating expenses are total operating expenses exclusive of the noncash depreciation expense and the loss on the disposal of equipment, which have been reported separately for our convenience. If these amounts had been combined, we would have first had to remove the noncash expenses before determining how much of the $141,000 of other operating expenses was paid in cash. Then, this amount would be adjusted for any changes in prepaid expenses and accrued liabilities.

If prepaid expenses increase during the year, the cash paid for operating expenses will be higher than the operating expenses reported on the income statement because cash was spent not only to pay for the related expense but also to build up the prepaid balance. To adjust operating expenses to determine cash payments for services, any increase in prepaid expenses must be added to operating expenses. On the other hand, if prepaid expenses decrease during the year, the decrease must be deducted from operating expenses, because the expense that arose when the prepaid expense expired was not paid in cash.

Operating expenses must also be adjusted for changes in other liability accounts such as accrued expenses payable. While for simplicity we have assumed in this chapter that accrued liabilities are recorded separately from accounts payable, some companies do combine them with accounts payable. This is one reason why the direct method can be difficult to use in practice. If accrued liabilities and accounts payable are combined and recorded in one account, you have to determine what proportion of accounts payable relates to purchases of inventory, and what relates to other payables, in order to determine the cash payments to suppliers and cash payments for operating expenses.

At this time, Computer Services does not have any accrued liabilities related to its operating expenses. If it did, any changes in these accounts would affect cash payments for operating expenses. When an accrued liability account increases during the year, operating expenses on an accrual basis are higher than they are on a cash basis. This happens because some of the operating expenses have not yet been paid, which is why the liability increased. To determine cash payments for operating expenses, an increase in the accrued liability account is deducted from operating expenses. On the other hand, a decrease in an accrued liability account is added to operating expenses because the cash payments are greater than the operating expenses.

Computer Services' cash payments for operating expenses were $145,000, calculated as in Illustration 13A-4.

►Illustration 13A-4
Formula to calculate cash payments for operating expenses

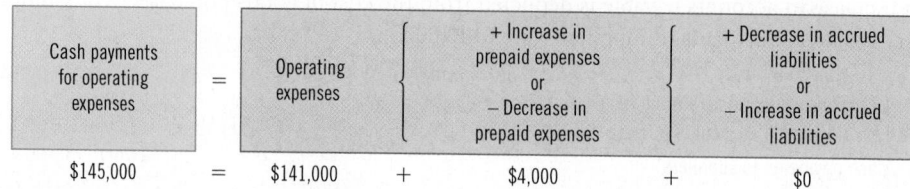

Cash Payments to Employees

Some companies report payments to employees separately, removing these payments from their operating expenses. To determine payments to employees, you would have to know the salaries expense amount on the income statement and any salaries payable on the comparative statement of financial position. Cash payments to employees would equal the salaries expense plus any decrease (or less any increase) during the period in the amount of salaries payable.

Other companies that do not show salaries expense separately condense their income statement in such a way that cash payments to suppliers and employees cannot be separated from cash payments for operating expenses. Although this presentation will not be as informative, for reporting purposes it is acceptable to combine these sources of cash payments.

Cash Payments for Interest

Computer Services reported $12,000 of interest expense on its income statement in Illustration 13-4. This amount equals the cash paid, since the comparative statement of financial position indicated no interest payable at the beginning or end of the year. If there was any interest payable, decreases in the Interest Payable account would be added to, or increases would be deducted from, the Interest Expense account to determine cash payments for interest.

Cash Payments for Income Tax

Computer Services reported income tax expense of $47,000 on its income statement shown in Illustration 13-4. Income tax payable, however, decreased by $2,000 (from $8,000 to $6,000) during the year. This means that income tax paid was more than the income tax reported in the income statement; otherwise, the income tax payable would not have fallen. Decreases in income tax payable are added to income tax expense, to determine the cash payments for income tax. This would be $49,000 for Computer Services.

The relationship among cash payments for income tax, income tax expense, and changes in income tax payable is shown in Illustration 13A-5.

►Illustration 13A-5
Formula to calculate cash payments for income tax

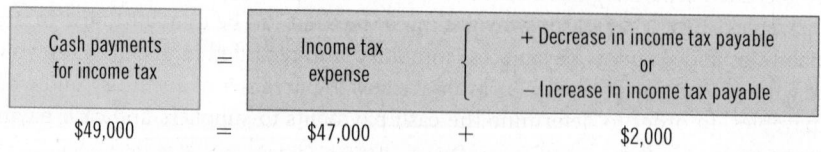

All of the revenues and expenses in Computer Services' income statement have now been adjusted to a cash basis. The operating activities section of the statement of cash flows is shown in Illustration 13A-6. Note that positive numbers in the statement of cash flows prepared using the direct method indicate cash receipts (inflows) and negative numbers, shown in parentheses, indicate cash payments (outflows).

COMPUTER SERVICES CORPORATION
Statement of Cash Flows (partial)
Year Ended December 31, 2018

Operating activities		
Cash receipts from customers		$517,000
Cash payments		
To suppliers	$(148,000)	
For operating expenses	(145,000)	
For interest	(12,000)	
For income tax	(49,000)	(354,000)
Net cash provided by operating activities		163,000

▶ Illustration 13A-6
Net cash provided (used) by operating activities—direct method

▼ **HELPFUL HINT**
Whether the direct or indirect method is used, net cash provided (used) by operating activities will be the same.

Compare the operating activities section prepared using the direct method in Illustration 13A-6 with the operating activities section prepared using the indirect method in Illustration 13-6. You will see that both arrive at the same net cash provided by operating activities amount of $163,000, although the presentation of the detail differs.

SUMMARY OF CONVERSION TO NET CASH PROVIDED (USED) BY OPERATING ACTIVITIES—DIRECT METHOD

As shown on the previous pages, revenues and expenses reported on the income statement are reviewed to determine if any cash receipts and cash payments relate to them. Noncash revenues and expenses are excluded. Any revenue and expense accounts with cash effects are included, after adjusting them for changes (increases or decreases) in the related current asset and current liability accounts to determine cash receipts and cash payments in the operating activities section.

The adjustments that are required to convert individual revenues and expenses from an accrual basis of accounting to a cash basis of accounting are summarized here:

	Cash Receipts (Revenues)	Cash Payments (Expenses)
Current assets		
Increase in account balance	Deduct (−)	Add (+)
Decrease in account balance	Add (+)	Deduct (−)
Current liabilities		
Increase in account balance	Add (+)	Deduct (−)
Decrease in account balance	Deduct (−)	Add (+)

Note that, while the adjustments to revenues shown above are in the same direction as those we discussed in the indirect section, the adjustments to expenses move in the opposite direction. This is because, in the indirect method, we are adjusting net income (in which expenses are deductions). In the direct method, we are adjusting each expense account, which will later be deducted in the calculation of operating activities.

Before we move on, let's review the relationship between the amounts shown in the income statement and the effect they have on assets and liabilities in the indirect and direct methods. This is done in Illustration 13A-7.

We know that the amounts shown in red in Illustration 13A-7 are the amounts that appeared on the statement of cash flows when using the indirect method and that these amounts totalled $163,000 ($145,000 + $18,000) for the net cash provided by operating activities. However, if we were to take a different approach and use individual items from the income statement rather than the total net income amount and then make adjustments to each of these items to arrive at cash flows (the items shown in blue in Illustration 13A-7), we would be preparing the operating activities section of the statement of cash flows using the direct method. Regardless of the method used, the net cash provided by operating activities is $163,000.

▶Illustration 13A-7
Comparison of indirect
and direct methods

	Income Statement Account—Cash Flow Effect	Components of Income Statement Accounts Not Reflected in Cash	Amount of Adjustment Needed (Shown in Indirect Method)	Net Cash Flow (Shown in Direct Method)
Sales	$507,000	Decrease in accounts receivable	$10,000	$517,000
Cost of goods sold	(150,000)	Increase in inventory	(5,000)	
		Increase in accounts payable	7,000	(148,000)
Other operating expenses	(141,000)	Increase in prepaid expenses	(4,000)	(145,000)
Depreciation expense	(9,000)	Entire amount is noncash	9,000	0
Loss on disposal of equipment	(3,000)	Entire amount is noncash	3,000	0
Interest expense	(12,000)	No change		(12,000)
Income tax expense	(47,000)	Decrease in income tax payable	(2,000)	(49,000)
Net income	$145,000			
Net cash provided by operating activities			$18,000	$163,000

DO IT! ▶ 13-5   Operating Activities—Direct Method

Action Plan

✔ Do not include any noncash expenses or revenues.

✔ Determine the net cash provided (used) by operating activities by adjusting each revenue and expense item for changes in the related current asset or current liability account.

✔ To adjust revenues for changes in related noncash working capital accounts, add decreases in noncash current asset accounts and increases in noncash current liability accounts. Deduct increases in these asset accounts and decreases in these liability accounts. To adjust expenses, add increases in these asset accounts and decreases in these liability accounts. Deduct decreases in these asset accounts and increases in these liability accounts.

✔ Assume that the accounts payable relate to suppliers.

✔ Assume that the prepaid expenses and accrued payables relate to administrative expenses.

✔ Report cash receipts and cash payments by major sources and uses: (1) cash receipts from customers, and (2) cash payments to suppliers, for administrative expenses, to employees, for interest, and for income tax.

Selected financial information follows for Denham Ltd. at December 31. Prepare the operating activities section of the statement of cash flows using the direct method.

	2018	2017	Increase (Decrease)
Current assets			
Cash	$61,000	$37,000	$24,000
Accounts receivable	68,000	26,000	42,000
Inventory	54,000	10,000	44,000
Prepaid expenses	4,000	6,000	(2,000)
Current liabilities			
Accounts payable	35,000	55,000	(20,000)
Accrued expenses payable	4,000	5,000	(1,000)
Salaries payable	6,000	4,000	2,000
Income tax payable	20,000	10,000	10,000

DENHAM LTD.
Income Statement
Year Ended December 31, 2018

Sales revenue		$890,000
Cost of goods sold		465,000
Gross profit		425,000
Operating expenses		
Salaries expense	$150,000	
Administrative expenses	46,000	
Depreciation expense	33,000	
Loss on disposal of equipment	4,000	233,000
Income from operations		192,000
Interest expense		12,000
Income before income tax		180,000
Income tax expense		36,000
Net income		$144,000

REVIEW AND PRACTICE

▶ LEARNING OBJECTIVE REVIEW

1. Describe the content and format of the statement of cash flows. The statement of cash flows provides information about the cash receipts and cash payments resulting from the operating, investing, and financing activities of a company during a specific period.

Operating activities include the cash effects of transactions that create revenues and expenses used in the determination of net income. Operating activities are affected by noncash items in the income statement and changes in certain current asset and current liability accounts in the statement of financial position. Investing activities involve cash flows resulting from changes in non-current asset items. Financing activities involve cash flows resulting from changes in non-current liabilities and shareholders' equity items. These are general guidelines, to which there are a few exceptions.

The statement of cash flows begins with the operating activities section, which can be prepared using either the indirect or direct method. Both end up with the same net cash provided or used by operating activities but differ in the detail provided in this section. Investing and financing activities follow. The statement concludes by reporting the net change in cash for the period, and reconciles it to the beginning and ending cash (or cash and cash equivalents) balances reported on the statement of financial position. Significant noncash transactions are reported in a note to the financial statements.

2. Prepare the operating activities section of a statement of cash flows using the indirect method. The first step in the preparation of a statement of cash flows is to determine the net cash provided (used) by operating activities. In the indirect method, net income is converted from an accrual basis to a cash basis. To do this, noncash expenses and losses, decreases in certain current asset accounts, and increases in certain current liability accounts are added back to net income. Noncash revenues and gains, increases in certain current asset accounts, and decreases in certain current liability accounts are deducted from net income.

3. Prepare the investing and financing activities sections and complete the statement of cash flows. The second step in the preparation of a statement of cash flows is to analyze the changes in certain non-current asset accounts and record them as investing activities, or disclose them as significant noncash transactions. The third step is to analyze the changes in non-current liability (and any related current portions) and equity accounts and record them as financing activities, or disclose them as significant noncash transactions. In addition to this, changes in the Dividends Payable account should be considered in determining the amount of dividends paid.

The fourth and final step in the preparation of a statement of cash flows is to determine the overall net cash flow for the year and add it to the opening amount of cash (and cash equivalents) to determine the ending amount. This result should agree to the cash (and cash equivalents) reported on the statement of financial position.

4. Use the statement of cash flows to evaluate a company. When using the statement of cash flows to appreciate the nature of a company, we must understand what phase of its corporate life cycle a company is in. In the introductory and growth phases, financing cash flows are needed to offset the cash used in operating and investing activities. However, by the time a company enters the maturity phase, operating cash flows are usually sufficient to cover cash used in investing activities and to begin to pay down debt and use cash for financing activities. When the company is in the decline phase, this trend continues but, as cash from operating activities declines, so does the amount of cash used in investing and financing activities.

Free cash flow (net cash provided or used by operating activities minus net capital expenditures minus dividends paid) is a measure of solvency. It indicates the amount of cash a company generated during the period that is available for increases in the payment of dividends, expansion, or the reduction of debt.

5. Prepare the operating activities section of a statement of cash flows using the direct method (Appendix 13A). In the direct method of determining net cash provided or used by operating activities, each individual revenue and expense account is converted from an accrual basis to a cash basis. These cash flows are then combined into the major classes of cash receipts and cash payments and reported in the operating activities section.

▶ KEY TERM REVIEW

The following are key terms defined in this chapter with the corresponding page reference for your review. You will find a complete list of terms and definitions for all chapters in the glossary at the end of this textbook.

Corporate life cycle (p. 722)　　　　Free cash flow (p. 723)
Direct method (p. 702)　　　　　　Indirect method (p. 702)

▶ COMPARING IFRS AND ASPE REVIEW

Key Standard Differences	International Financial Reporting Standards (IFRS)	Accounting Standards for Private Enterprises (ASPE)
Classification of activities	Interest and dividends received may be classified as operating or investing activities. Interest and dividends paid may be classified as operating or financing activities. Once the choice is made, it must be applied consistently.	Interest and dividends received are classified as operating activities. Interest paid is classified as an operating activity. Dividends paid are classified as a financing activity.

▶ DECISION TOOLKIT REVIEW

DECISION CHECKPOINTS	INFO NEEDED FOR DECISION	TOOLS TO USE FOR DECISION	HOW TO EVALUATE RESULTS
Can the company meet its long-term obligations?	Net cash provided or used by operating activities, net capital expenditures, and cash dividends	Free cash flow = Net cash provided (used) by operating activities − Net capital expenditures − Dividends paid	Free cash flow indicates the potential to finance new investments, reduce debt, or pay more dividends.

▶ PRACTICE USING THE DECISION TOOLKIT

Answers are at the end of the chapter.

Stantec Inc., headquartered in Edmonton, is a professional consulting services company with employees in more than 160 offices throughout North America. Stantec's statement of cash flows for the most recent three years follows:

STANTEC INC.
Statement of Cash Flows
Years Ended December 31
(in thousands)

	2015	2014	2013
Operating activities			
Cash receipts from clients	$ 2,967,720	$ 2,599,190	$ 2,225,332
Cash paid to suppliers	(1,023,416)	(871,696)	(646,719)
Cash paid to employees	(1,664,563)	(1,438,417)	(1,247,723)
Interest received	2,377	2,422	1,774
Interest and finance costs paid	(13,699)	(11,316)	(11,721)
Income taxes paid	(73,211)	(75,667)	(61,201)
Income taxes recovered	10,311	2,705	12,387
Net cash provided by operating activities	205,519	207,221	272,129

Investing activities			
Business acquisitions	(203,461)	(123,713)	(43,539)
Cash held in escrow	(8,646)	—	—
Dividends from investments in joint ventures and associates	2,931	2,472	2,685
Purchase of investments held for self-insured liabilities	(7,487)	(19,597)	(25,129)
Decrease in investments and other assets	4,922	3,531	4,681
Proceeds from lease inducements	560	8,884	—
Purchase of intangible assets	(3,591)	(3,365)	(4,490)
Purchase of property and equipment	(38,084)	(42,706)	(52,639)
Proceeds on disposition of property and equipment	462	176	998
Net cash used by investing activities	(252,394)	(174,318)	(117,433)
Financing activities			
Repayment of bank debt	(135,854)	(136,823)	(70,924)
Proceeds from bank debt	135,758	140,320	36,319
Repayment of acquired bank indebtedness	(1,986)	—	—
Payment of finance lease obligations	(13,360)	(5,174)	(6,271)
Proceeds from issue of share capital	9,480	10,587	16,504
Payment of dividends to shareholders	(38,334)	(33,641)	(29,782)
Net cash provided (used) by financing activities	(44,296)	(24,731)	(54,154)
Other (foreign exchange gain [loss])	4,809	2,502	1,780
Net increase (decrease) in cash and cash equivalents	(86,362)	10,674	102,322
Cash and cash equivalents, beginning of the year	153,704	143,030	40,708
Cash and cash equivalents, end of the year	$ 67,342	$ 153,704	$ 143,030

INSTRUCTIONS

(a) Does Stantec use the indirect or direct method to prepare its operating activities section?

(b) Calculate Stantec's free cash flow for 2015 and 2014 and comment on whether it changed and why.

(c) Comment on any significant changes in Stantec's cash flows over the last three years.

▶ PRACTICE COMPREHENSIVE DO IT!

Answers are at the end of the chapter.

The income statement for Kosinski Inc. contains the following condensed information:

KOSINSKI INC. Income Statement Year Ended December 31, 2018	
Sales	$6,583,000
Cost of goods sold	3,427,000
Gross profit	3,156,000
Operating expenses	2,349,000
Income from operations	807,000
Interest expense	124,000
Income before income tax	683,000
Income tax expense	203,000
Net income	$ 480,000

The following selected current asset and current liability balances are reported on Kosinski's comparative statement of financial position at December 31:

	2018	2017	Increase (Decrease)
Cash	$150,000	$ 30,000	$120,000
Accounts receivable	775,000	610,000	165,000
inventory	834,000	867,000	(33,000)
Accounts payable	521,000	501,000	20,000
Income tax payable	53,000	25,000	28,000

Additional information:
1. The company uses a perpetual inventory system.
2. Operating expenses include salaries expense of $1 million, depreciation expense of $300,000, amortization expense of $80,000, and a loss on the disposal of machinery of $24,000.
3. Machinery was sold for $270,000, at a loss of $24,000.
4. New machinery was purchased during the year for $1,250,000. It was partially financed by a bank loan payable issued for $400,000.
5. Dividends paid in 2018 totalled $100,000.

INSTRUCTIONS

(a) Prepare the statement of cash flows using the indirect method.

(b) If Kosinski had prepared the statement of cash flows using the direct method, rather than the indirect method, what similarities and differences would you expect to see compared with your answer in part (a)?

▶ PRACTICE OBJECTIVE-FORMAT QUESTIONS

Note: All questions marked with an asterisk (*) relate to material in Appendix 13A. Answers are at the end of the chapter.

1. Which of the events listed below will affect the net cash flows provided (used) by operating activities of a company? (Select as many as are appropriate.)

(a) Increased borrowing from banks.
(b) Difficulty in selling inventory.
(c) Replacing manufacturing facilities damaged by fire.
(d) Delayed payments to suppliers of inventory.

(e) Slowing collection of accounts receivable.
(f) Increased dividends paid to shareholders.
(g) Salary increases arising from contract negotiations.

2. Which of the following items is added to net income when determining cash provided (used) by operating activities when using the indirect method? (Select as many as are appropriate.)

(a) Decrease in accounts receivable.
(b) Decrease in accounts payable.
(c) Increase in dividends payable.
(d) Decrease in term deposits maturing in 60 days.

(e) Decrease in prepaid insurance.
(f) Increase in inventory.
(g) Increase in common shares.

3. At the beginning of the year, a company had balances of $500,000, $1.4 million, and $300,000, respectively, in its Land, Buildings, and Accumulated Depreciation—Buildings accounts. At the end of the year, there were balances of $750,000, $2.2 million, and $270,000, respectively, in these same three accounts. During the year, the company had a gain of $100,000 when it sold half of its land. Also during the year, the company sold one of its small buildings that cost $200,000 and had accumulated depreciation of $150,000, for a loss of $10,000. Based on the above, one would expect to see which of the following items in the investing activities section of the statement of cash flows? (Select as many as are appropriate.)

(a) Payment for purchase of land for $500,000.
(b) Payment for the purchase of buildings for $1 million.
(c) Proceeds received from the sale of land for $350,000.
(d) Proceeds received from the sale of a building for $35,000.

(e) Loss on sale of building for $10,000.
(f) Gain on sale of land for $100,000.
(g) Depreciation expense on buildings of $120,000.

4. In preparing the statement of cash flows for 2018, the following account balances were obtained:

	Dec. 31	Jan. 1
Accounts Receivable	$ 400	$ 700
Inventory	2,400	2,100
Prepaid Insurance	150	100
Accounts Payable	300	400
Income Taxes Payable	70	40
Dividends Payable	50	10
Current Portion of Mortgage Payable	350	280

If the company prepares the statement of cash flows using the indirect method, which items listed below would appear in the operating activities section of that statement? (Select as many as are appropriate.)

(a) Add increase in Prepaid Insurance, $50.
(b) Deduct increase in Dividends Payable, $40.
(c) Deduct increase in Inventory, $300.
(d) Deduct decrease in Accounts Payable, $100.
(e) Add increase in Current Portion of Mortgage, $70.
(f) Add increase in Income Taxes Payable, $30.
(g) Add decrease in Accounts Receivable, $300.

5. When determining the net cash provided (used) by financing activities for the current year, an accountant obtained the following information: the Current Portion of Mortgage Payable increased by $5,000, Interest Payable increased by $2,000, Dividends Payable decreased by $1,000, and the Mortgage Payable account (non-current portion) increased by $70,000. Mortgage payments made during the year were $36,000, of which $5,000 consisted of interest on the mortgage. Net income was $100,000, which included interest expense of $7,000. The Retained Earnings account increased by $88,000 during the year and the company also declared dividends during the year. The Common Shares account increased by $15,000 when some shares were sold to new shareholders. Based on the preceding, what items would appear in the financing activities section of the company's statement of cash flows for the current year? (Select as many as are appropriate.)

(a) Mortgage payments made, $36,000.
(b) Mortgage loans obtained, $106,000.
(c) Interest paid, $7,000.
(d) Dividends paid, $13,000.
(e) Common shares issued, $15,000.
(f) Dividends paid, $12,000.
(g) Interest paid, $5,000.

6. The following information was taken from the financial statements of a company that reports under ASPE:

Proceeds from land disposal	$100,000
Issue of common shares for cash	70,000
Issue of common shares to acquire land	40,000
Payment of cash dividends	50,000
Purchase of equipment	110,000
Gain on sale of land	20,000
Interest received from bond investments	15,000
Payment of interest	10,000

Based on the information above, determine which of the statements below are correct. (Select as many as are appropriate.)

(a) Cash provided by financing activities is $60,000.
(b) Cash used by investing activities is $35,000.
(c) Cash provided by financing activities is $20,000.
(d) Cash used by investing activities is $10,000.
(e) If the company reports under IFRS, the receipt of interest can be reported as either an investing or an operating activity.
(f) If the company reports under IFRS, the payment of cash dividends can be reported as either a financing or an investing activity.
(g) If the company had purchased an investment that was held for trading rather than purchasing equipment, the cash spent on the investment could be reported as an operating activity.

7. In late December 2018, a private company borrowed $12 million from a bank in order to use those funds to expand its operations. One week later, on the last day of 2018, the company increased its dividend payments by $1 million and paid $9 million for some vacant land to use for future development. Interest charges on the bank loan do not start until 2019. Furthermore, the loan does not require any principal payments for three years. Based on only the preceding transactions, choose the statements below that correctly describe these changes. (Select as many as are appropriate.)

(a) Cash provided by operating activities for the current year will remain unchanged.
(b) Cash used by investing activities for the current year will decrease.
(c) Cash provided by financing activities for the current year will increase.
(d) Free cash flow will increase by $2 million because that is the amount of cash left over after increasing the dividends and paying for the land.
(e) The increased dividend payment has no effect on free cash flow because it is not an operating activity.
(f) Free cash flow will decrease because of the land purchase.
(g) Free cash flow will increase by $12 million because that is the amount of financing obtained from the bank.

8. After reviewing draft financial statements for the current year, a CEO has asked her accountants to correct an error that recorded an expenditure costing $100,000 as a repair expense instead of recording it as an equipment purchase. In addition to this, the CEO has informed the accountants that she forgot to tell them that, on the last day of the year, common shares were issued in exchange for land costing $150,000. Taking into consideration the two items mentioned above, which of the following statements regarding the corrections made to the company's statement of cash flows is correct? (Select as many as are appropriate.)

(a) The cash provided by operating activities will now be higher by $100,000.
(b) The cash provided by operating activities will be unchanged.
(c) The cash used by investing activities will now be lower by $150,000.
(d) The cash used by investing activities will now be higher by $50,000.
(e) The cash used by investing activities will be unchanged.
(f) The cash provided by financing activities will be unchanged.
(g) The cash provided by financing activities will now be higher by $150,000.

9. Standard Inc. is an unprofitable retailer that has had to sell assets in order to avoid defaulting on its bank loan payments. General Ltd. is a start-up company with sales that have not reached sufficient levels to cover operating expenses. However, it has developed a very popular software program and has just completed its initial public offering of shares. Which of the following statements is correct regarding the statements of cash flows for these two companies? (Select as many as are appropriate.)

(a) Standard Inc. will show cash provided by operating activities and cash used by investing activities.
(b) General Ltd. will show cash provided by operating activities and cash used by financing activities.
(c) Standard Inc. will show cash used by investing activities and cash used by financing activities.
(d) General Ltd. will show cash used by operating activities and cash used by investing activities.
(e) Standard Inc. will show cash provided by investing activities and cash used by financing activities.
(f) General Ltd. will show cash used by investing activities and cash provided by financing activities.
(g) Standard Inc. will show cash used by operating activities and cash used by financing activities.

*10. Which of the following items represents a cash flow that would appear in the operating activities section of a statement of cash flows when using the direct method of presentation? (Select as many as are appropriate.)

(a) Depreciation expense.
(b) Cash from customers.
(c) Income tax expense.
(d) Interest paid.

(e) Amortization of a patent.
(f) Gain on disposal of equipment.
(g) Dividends paid to shareholders.

WileyPLUS

Brief Exercises, Exercises, and many additional resources are available for practice in WileyPLUS.

Note: All questions, exercises, and problems below with an asterisk (*) relate to material in Appendix 13A.

▶ QUESTIONS

(LO 1) 1. What is a statement of cash flows and why do some users of the financial statements, especially creditors, find it useful?

(LO 1) 2. What are "cash equivalents"? Should a company combine cash equivalents with cash when preparing the statement of cash flows? Explain why or why not.

(LO 1) 3. Explain the differences among the three categories of activities—operating, investing, and financing—reported in the statement of cash flows.

(LO 1) 4. Private companies following ASPE can classify interest and dividends differently than can companies following IFRS. Explain how these classifications can differ and identify the most commonly used classification(s).

(LO 1) 5. Masood and Adriana were discussing where they should report significant noncash investing and financing transactions in Rock Candy Corp.'s statement of cash flows. Give two examples of these transactions and describe where they should be reported.

(LO 1) 6. Goh Corporation changed its method of reporting operating activities from the indirect method to the direct method in order to make its statement of cash flows more informative to its readers. Will this change increase, decrease, or not affect the net cash provided (used) by operating activities?

(LO 1) 7. (a) Identify whether each of the following is used in the preparation of a statement of cash flows: (1) the adjusted trial balance, (2) the statement of financial position, (3) the income statement, (4) the statement of comprehensive income, and (5) the statement of changes in equity. (b) Explain how each of the items identified in part (a) is used in the preparation of the statement of cash flows.

(LO 2) 8. Describe the indirect method for determining net cash provided (used) by operating activities.

(LO 2) 9. In 2015, **Clearwater Seafoods Incorporated,** one of Canada's largest seafood companies, reported a loss of $20,671 thousand. During the same period, its cash provided by operating activities was $68,494 thousand, despite the loss experienced by the company. Explain how this could occur.

(LO 2) 10. Why and how is depreciation and amortization expense reported in the operating activities section of a statement of cash flows prepared using the indirect method?

(LO 2) 11. The gain on the disposal of equipment is deducted from net income when calculating net cash provided (used) by operating activities in the indirect method. Jacques doesn't understand why gains aren't added, rather than deducted, on the statement of cash flows since they result in an increase in net income on the income statement. He also doesn't understand why only the gain and not the proceeds

from the entire disposal of the equipment is reported in the operating activities section. Help Jacques understand the reporting of the disposal of equipment on the statement of cash flows.

(LO 2) 12. Denis says, "I understand that operating activities are affected by changes in current asset and current liability accounts. I also know that held for trading investments are current assets and that the purchase and sale of these investments are recorded as operating activities. What I don't understand is why the purchase and sale of investments that are not held for trading are usually classified as investing activities." Help Denis understand the classification of investments.

(LO 3) 13. Laurel says, "I know that the current portion of a bank loan is a current liability but we never seem to see the change in this account shown on the statement of cash flows. Why?" Explain to Laurel why this is the case.

(LO 3) 14. If a company declared cash dividends during the year of $40,000 but you noticed that the Dividends Payable account had increased from $8,000 at the beginning of the year to $10,000 at the end of the year, what amount pertaining to dividends would appear on the statement of cash flows?

(LO 3) 15. Explain how the statement of cash flows interrelates with the other financial statements.

(LO 4) 16. (a) What are the phases of the corporate life cycle? (b) What effect does each phase have on the amounts reported on a statement of cash flows?

(LO 4) 17. In general, would you expect a growing, healthy company to report cash provided by or used by its operating, investing, and financing activities? Explain.

(LO 4) 18. A company's free cash flow has been declining steadily over the last five years. What does this decline likely mean to creditors and investors?

(LO 4) 19. How is it possible for a company to report positive net cash provided by operating activities but have a negative free cash flow?

(LO 5) *20. Describe the direct method for determining net cash provided (used) by operating activities.

(LO 5) *21. Under the direct method, why is depreciation and amortization expense not reported in the operating activities section?

(LO 5) *22. Explain how (a) the disposal of equipment at a gain, and (b) the loss on disposal of land are reported on a statement of cash flows using the direct method.

▶ BRIEF EXERCISES

BE13–1 For each of the following transactions, indicate whether it will result in an increase (+), decrease (−), or have no effect (NE) on cash flows:

Indicate impact of transactions on cash.

(LO 1)

(a) _____ Repayment of mortgage payable
(b) _____ Payment of interest on mortgage
(c) _____ Purchase of land in exchange for common shares
(d) _____ Issue of preferred shares for cash
(e) _____ Payment for the purchase of a held for trading investment that is not a cash equivalent
(f) _____ Collection of accounts receivable
(g) _____ Declaration of cash dividend
(h) _____ Payment of cash dividend
(i) _____ Cash purchase of inventory
(j) _____ Recording of depreciation expense
(k) _____ Purchase and cancellation of common shares

Classify activities.
(LO 1)

BE13–2 Classify each of the transactions listed in BE13–1 as an operating (O), investing (I), financing (F), or significant noncash investing and financing (NC) activity. If a transaction does not belong in any of these classifications, explain why.

Classify activities.
(LO 1)

BE13–3 Linamar Corporation reported the following items on its statement of cash flows:
1. _____ Repayments of long-term debt
2. _____ Depreciation of property, plant, and equipment
3. _____ Payments for purchase of property, plant, and equipment
4. _____ Dividends to shareholders
5. _____ Proceeds from long-term debt
6. _____ Changes in noncash operating working capital items

(a) Indicate in which section each of the above items was reported in Linamar's statement of cash flows—operating activity (O), investing activity (I), or financing activity (F). (b) Does Linamar use the indirect or direct method of preparing the operating activities section of its statement of cash flows? Explain how you came to your conclusion.

Indicate impact on operating activities—indirect method.
(LO 2)

BE13–4 Indicate whether each of the following items would be added to (+) or subtracted from (−) net income to calculate net cash provided (used) by operating activities using the indirect method. If a transaction is not shown in the operating cash flows section of the statement of cash flows, indicate that it is NA (not applicable).
(a) _____ Depreciation expense
(b) _____ Increase in accounts receivable
(c) _____ Decrease in inventory in the perpetual inventory system
(d) _____ Increase in accounts payable
(e) _____ Interest expense
(f) _____ Decrease in income tax payable
(g) _____ Gain on disposal of equipment
(h) _____ Loss on sale of long-term investment
(i) _____ Decrease in dividends payable
(j) _____ Impairment loss for goodwill
(k) _____ Decrease in 60-day term deposit

Calculate operating activities—indirect method.
(LO 2)

BE13–5 The comparative statement of financial position for Dupigne Corporation shows the following noncash current asset and liability accounts at March 31:

	2018	2017
Accounts receivable	$60,000	$40,000
Inventory	75,000	70,000
Accounts payable	35,000	40,000
Dividends payable	1,000	2,000

Dupigne's income statement reported the following selected information for the year ended March 31, 2018: net income was $275,000, depreciation expense was $60,000, and a loss on the disposal of land was $15,000. Dupigne uses a perpetual inventory system. Calculate net cash provided (used) by operating activities using the indirect method.

Calculate cash received from disposal of equipment.
(LO 3)

BE13–6 The T accounts for equipment and accumulated depreciation for Trevis Ltd. are shown here:

Equipment					Accumulated Depreciation—Equipment			
Beg. bal.	80,000	Disposals	20,000		Disposals	5,500	Beg. bal.	44,500
Acquisitions	40,000						Depreciation	20,000
End bal.	100,000						End bal.	59,000

In addition, Trevis's income statement reported a $1,500 loss on the disposal of equipment. (a) What amount was reported on the statement of cash flows as "cash provided by disposal of equipment"? (b) In what section of the statement of cash flows would the effects of this disposal transaction be reported?

Prepare investing activities section.
(LO 3)

BE13–7 Holmes Corporation reported the following information (in thousands) at December 31, 2018:

	2018	2017
Long-term investments	$150	$100
Land	200	200
Buildings	300	300
Accumulated depreciation—buildings	90	75
Equipment	500	400
Accumulated depreciation—equipment	200	200

Additional information:

1. Long-term investments were purchased during the year; none were sold.
2. Equipment was purchased during the year. In addition, equipment with a cost of $100 and a carrying amount of $50 was sold at a gain of $10.

Prepare the investing activities section of Holmes's statement of cash flows for the year.

BE13–8 Canadian Tire Corporation, Limited reported net income of $735.9 million for the year ended January 2, 2016. Its retained earnings were $4,075.1 million at the beginning of the year and $4,172.0 million at the end of the year. It had no dividends payable at the beginning or end of the year. Assuming no other changes to retained earnings, what amount of dividends did Canadian Tire pay during the year? Would your answer change if you knew that the Dividends Payable account increased during the year?

Calculate cash paid for dividends.

(LO 3)

BE13–9 Nicoloff Corporation reported the following information (in thousands) at December 31, 2018:

Prepare financing activities section.

(LO 3)

	2018	2017
Dividends payable	$ 15	$ 10
Bank loan payable—current portion	200	200
Bank loan payable—non-current portion	400	300
Common shares	600	400
Retained earnings	700	500

Additional information:

1. The bank loan was increased by additional borrowings of $300 to partially finance the purchase of new equipment that cost $500. The bank loan was decreased by repayments.
2. Common shares were issued during the year. None were reacquired.
3. Dividends were paid during the year.
4. Net income for the year was $400.

Prepare the financing activities section of Nicoloff's statement of cash flows for the year.

BE13–10 Jain Corporation reported net cash provided by operating activities of $325,000, net cash used by investing activities of $250,000, and net cash provided by financing activities of $70,000. In addition, cash spent for net capital expenditures during the period was $200,000, and $25,000 of dividends were paid. (a) Calculate Jain's free cash flow. (b) Explain why free cash flow often provides better information than net cash provided by operating activities?

Calculate free cash flow.

(LO 4)

BE13–11 Apple Inc. reported the following amounts (in U.S. $ millions) in its financial statements:

Evaluate life cycle and free cash flow.

(LO 4)

	2015	2014
Cash provided by operating activities	$81,266	$59,713
Cash used by investing activities	(56,274)	(22,579)
Cash used by financing activities	(17,716)	(37,549)
Capital expenditures	11,831	9,571
Dividends paid	11,561	11,126

(a) Based on the change in Apple's cash flows between 2014 and 2015, which phase of its corporate life cycle do you think the company is most likely in?
(b) Calculate the company's free cash flow for each of 2015 and 2014.
(c) If you were a shareholder of the company, would you be pleased with the answer calculated in part (b)? Why or why not?
(d) Why do you think the amount of dividends paid is greater than the amount of capital expenditures in 2014?

*BE13–12 Idol Corporation has accounts receivable of $14,000 at January 1, and of $24,000 at December 31. Sales revenues were $170,000 for the year. What amount of cash was received from customers?

Calculate cash receipts from customers—direct method.

(LO 5)

*BE13–13 Columbia Sportswear Company reported cost of goods sold of U.S. $1,252,680 thousand on its 2015 income statement. It also reported an increase in inventory of U.S. $88,987 thousand and an increase in accounts payable of U.S. $2,955 thousand. What amount of cash was paid to suppliers, assuming that the company uses a perpetual inventory system and that accounts payable relate to merchandise creditors?

Calculate cash payments to suppliers—direct method.

(LO 5)

Calculate cash payments
for operating expenses—
direct method.
(LO 5)

*BE13–14 Excellence Corporation reports operating expenses of $200,000, including depreciation expense of $30,000, amortization expense of $5,000, and a gain of $1,000 on the disposal of equipment during the current year. During this same period, prepaid expenses increased by $13,200 and accrued expenses payable decreased by $4,800. Calculate the cash payments for operating expenses.

Calculate cash payments
for income tax—direct
method.
(LO 5)

*BE13–15 Home Grocery Limited reported income tax expense of $50,000 for the year. (a) Calculate the cash payments for income tax assuming income tax payable increased by $4,000 during the year. (b) Repeat part (a), assuming income tax payable decreased by $3,000 during the year.

Calculate operating
activities—direct method.
(LO 5)

*BE13–16 The comparative statement of financial position for Baird Corporation shows the following noncash current asset and liability accounts at March 31:

	2018	2017
Accounts receivable	$60,000	$40,000
Inventory	64,000	70,000
Prepaid expenses	6,000	4,000
Accounts payable	35,000	40,000
Income tax payable	10,000	5,000

Baird's income statement reported the following selected information for the year ended March 31, 2018: sales were $850,000, cost of goods sold was $475,000, operating expenses were $230,000 (which included depreciation expense of $20,000), and income tax expense was $15,000. Calculate net cash provided (used) by operating activities using the direct method.

▶ EXERCISES

Classify activities.
(LO 1)

E13–1 Eng Corporation had the following transactions:

	(a) Cash Effect	(b) Classification
1. Issued common shares for $50,000.		
2. Purchased a machine for $30,000. Made a $5,000 down payment and issued a long-term note payable for the remainder.		
3. Collected $16,000 of accounts receivable.		
4. Paid a $25,000 cash dividend.		
5. Sold a long-term investment with a carrying amount of $15,000 for $18,000.		
6. Sold inventory for $1,000.		
7. Paid $18,000 on accounts payable.		
8. Purchased a held for trading investment (equity securities) for $100,000.		
9. Purchased inventory for $28,000 on account.		
10. Collected $1,000 in advance from customers.		
11. Paid $25,000 to reacquire and retire common shares.		

Instructions

(a) In the above table, indicate by how much each transaction increases (+) or decreases (−) cash. If the transaction has no effect (NE) on cash, say so.
(b) Identify whether the transaction should be classified as an operating activity (O), investing activity (I), financing activity (F), or noncash investing and financing activity (NC).

Evaluate noncash items.
(LO 1)

E13–2 Crown Point Limited reports the following noncash transactions:
1. Recorded an impairment loss on goodwill.
2. Recorded depreciation expense.
3. Recorded an unrealized gain on a held for trading investment carried at fair value through profit or loss.
4. Reduced inventory to net realizable value.
5. Declared and distributed a stock dividend.
6. Completed a 2-for-1 stock split.
7. Converted an account receivable to a note receivable.
8. Acquired equipment by issuing common shares.

Instructions

For each of the above transactions, explain why it does not involve cash and where it should be reported (as an operating, investing, or financing activity), if at all, on the statement of cash flows or accompanying notes.

E13–3 He Corporation had the following transactions:

Indicate impact of transactions on net income and operating activities.

(LO 2)

	(a) Net Income	(b) Cash Provided (Used) by Operating Activities
1. Sold inventory for cash at a higher price than its cost.	+	+
2. Collected cash in advance from a customer for a service to be provided in the future.		
3. Purchased inventory on account in a perpetual inventory system.		
4. Declared and paid dividends.		
5. Recorded and paid salaries.		
6. Recorded income tax payable.		
7. Accrued interest receivable.		
8. Recorded depreciation expense.		
9. Paid an amount owing on account to a supplier.		
10. Collected an amount owing from a customer.		

Instructions

Complete the above table, indicating whether each transaction will increase (+), decrease (−), or have no effect (NE) on (a) net income and (b) cash provided (used) by operating activities. The first one has been done for you as an example.

E13–4 Selected information from Juno Ltd.'s statement of financial position and income statement is as follows:

Prepare operating activities section— indirect method.

(LO 2)

JUNO LTD.
Statement of Financial Position (partial)
December 31

	2018	2017
Current assets		
Accounts receivable	$7,000	$12,000
Inventory	5,900	4,500
Prepaid expenses	3,000	2,500
Current liabilities		
Accounts payable	3,750	2,500
Income tax payable	1,200	800
Accrued liabilities	2,500	1,500
Bank loan payable—current portion	5,000	10,000

JUNO LTD.
Income Statement
Year Ended December 31, 2018

Net sales	$190,000
Cost of goods sold	114,000
Gross profit	76,000
Operating expenses	50,000
Income from operations	26,000
Interest expense	1,200
Income before income tax	24,800
Income tax expense	3,800
Net income	$ 21,000

Additional information:

1. The bank loan was issued to finance the purchase of equipment.
2. Operating expenses included depreciation expense of $11,000 and a loss of $5,000 on the disposal of equipment.

Instructions

Prepare the operating activities section of the statement of cash flows, using the indirect method.

Classify activities—indirect method.

(LO 2, 3)

E13–5 The following is a list of transactions that occurred during the year.

	Operating Activities	Investing Activities	Financing Activities	Noncash Activities
1. Purchased inventory for cash.	−	NE	NE	NE

2. Sold inventory on account.
3. Sold equipment for cash at a loss.
4. Recorded depreciation on equipment.
5. Paid dividends.
6. Recorded an unrealized loss on a long-term equity investment carried at fair value through profit or loss.
7. Collected an account from a customer.
8. Signed and received a mortgage payable.
9. Paid, in full, the current portion of a mortgage payable.
10. Purchased land by issuing common shares.

Instructions

Complete the above table, indicating in which classification(s) each transaction would appear in a statement of cash flows prepared using the indirect method, and whether the transaction would be added to (+), deducted from (−), or have no effect (NE) on the category you have chosen. The first one has been done for you as an example.

Calculate investing and financing activities.

(LO 3)

E13–6 The following selected accounts are from Dupré Corp.'s general ledger:

Land

Jan.	1	Bal.	500,000				
Dec.	1		6,000				
Dec.	31	Bal.	506,000				

Equipment

Jan.	1	Bal.	160,000				
July	31		70,000				
Sept.	2		53,000	Nov.	10		39,000
Dec.	31	Bal.	244,000				

Accumulated Depreciation—Equipment

				Jan.	1	Bal.	71,000
Nov.	10		30,000	Dec.	31		48,000
				Dec.	31	Bal.	89,000

Dividends Payable

				Jan.	1	Bal.	1,000
				Dec.	23		4,000
				Dec.	31	Bal.	5,000

Bank Loan Payable

				Jan.	1	Bal.	0
				Sept.	2		43,000
				Dec.	31	Bal.	43,000

Retained Earnings

				Jan.	1	Bal.	105,000
Dec.	23		4,000	Dec.	31		60,000
				Dec.	31	Bal.	161,000

Additional information:

July 31 Equipment with a cost of $70,000 was purchased for cash.

Sept. 2 Equipment with a cost of $53,000 was purchased and partially financed through the issue of a long-term bank loan payable.

Nov. 10 A loss of $3,000 was incurred on the disposal of equipment.

Dec. 1 Acquired a small parcel of adjoining land.

23 A $4,000 cash dividend was declared to shareholders of record on December 31, payable on January 10.

31 Depreciation expense of $48,000 was recorded for the year.

31 Net income for the year was $60,000.

Instructions

From the postings in the above accounts and additional information provided, indicate what information would be reported in the investing and/or financing activities sections of, and notes to, the statement of cash flows.

E13–7 The comparative unclassified statement of financial position for Puffy Ltd. follows:

Prepare statement of cash flows—indirect method.

(LO 2, 3)

PUFFY LTD.
Statement of Financial Position
December 31

	2018	2017
Assets		
Cash	$ 53,000	$ 22,000
Accounts receivable	80,000	76,000
Inventory	185,000	189,000
Long-term investments	70,000	100,000
Equipment	265,000	200,000
Accumulated depreciation	(66,000)	(32,000)
Total assets	$587,000	$555,000
Liabilities and Shareholders' Equity		
Accounts payable	$ 39,000	$ 47,000
Bank loan payable	150,000	200,000
Common shares	199,000	174,000
Retained earnings	199,000	134,000
Total liabilities and shareholders' equity	$587,000	$555,000

Additional information:

1. Net income was $115,000.
2. Sales were $978,000.
3. Cost of goods sold was $751,000.
4. Operating expenses were $43,000, exclusive of depreciation expense.
5. Depreciation expense was $34,000.
6. Interest expense was $14,000.
7. Income tax expense was $26,000.
8. Long-term investments were sold at a gain of $5,000.
9. No equipment was sold during the year.
10. $50,000 of the bank loan was repaid during the year.
11. Common shares were issued for $25,000.

Instructions

Prepare a statement of cash flows using the indirect method.

E13–8 The comparative statement of financial position for Charmaine Retailers Ltd. follows:

Prepare and evaluate statement of cash flows—indirect method.

(LO 2, 3, 4)

CHARMAINE RETAILERS LTD.
Statement of Financial Position
December 31

	2018	2017
Assets		
Cash	$ 18,000	$ 9,000
Accounts receivable	50,000	42,000
Inventory	168,000	143,000
Furniture	163,000	80,000
Accumulated depreciation	(45,000)	(24,000)
Total assets	$354,000	$250,000
Liabilities and Shareholders' Equity		
Accounts payable	$ 45,000	$ 35,000
Bank loan payable (noncurrent)	103,000	76,000
Common shares	60,000	55,000
Retained earnings	146,000	84,000
Total liabilities and shareholders' equity	$354,000	$250,000

Additional information:

1. Net income was $62,000 in 2018.
2. Depreciation expense was $21,000 in 2018.
3. Payments made to the bank pertaining to the bank loan were $10,000 in 2018. Some new loans were obtained that year.
4. Common shares were issued in 2018 and no shares have been bought back by the company.
5. In 2018, no furniture was sold.

Instructions

(a) Prepare a statement of cash flows using the indirect method for 2018.
(b) Assess the strength of the company's cash flows for that year.

Prepare and evaluate statement of cash flows— indirect method.

(LO 2, 3, 4)

E13–9 The comparative statement of financial position for Dagenais Retailers Ltd. follows:

DAGENAIS RETAILERS LTD.
Statement of Financial Position
December 31

	2018	2017
Assets		
Cash	$ -0-	$ 18,000
Accounts receivable	77,000	50,000
Inventory	219,000	168,000
Furniture	130,000	163,000
Accumulated depreciation	(35,000)	(45,000)
Total assets	$391,000	$354,000
Liabilities and Shareholders' Equity		
Bank overdraft	$ 10,000	$ -0-
Accounts payable	68,000	45,000
Bank loan payable (noncurrent)	90,000	103,000
Common shares	50,000	60,000
Retained earnings	173,000	146,000
Total liabilities and shareholders' equity	$391,000	$354,000

Additional information:

1. Net income was $32,000 in 2018.
2. Depreciation expense was $19,000 in 2018.
3. In 2018, no new bank loans were received.
4. In 2018, no furniture was purchased, but some furniture was sold for $6,000, which resulted in a gain on this disposal of $2,000.
5. No common shares were issued during the year but some were reacquired at the cost at which they were originally issued.
6. In 2018, dividends were declared and paid.

Instructions

(a) Prepare a statement of cash flows using the indirect method for 2018.
(b) Assess the strength of the company's cash flows for that year.

Compare cash flows for three companies.

(LO 4)

E13–10 Condensed net income and cash flow information follow for three companies operating in the same industry:

	Company A	Company B	Company C
Net income	$ 75,000	$ 25,000	$(50,000)
Net cash provided (used) by operating activities	100,000	(25,000)	(25,000)
Net cash provided (used) by investing activities	(50,000)	(25,000)	35,000
Net cash provided (used) by financing activities	(25,000)	75,000	15,000
Net increase in cash	25,000	25,000	25,000

Instructions

(a) Assuming each company has the same amount of depreciation expense, which company is best at managing its non-cash working capital?
(b) Why would Company C have cash provided by investing activities?
(c) Which company is most likely to have sufficient cash flows to pay down debt or pay out dividends?
(d) Which company is more capable of growing the size of its business operations?

E13–11 A company is experiencing some cash management issues. The senior management team has proposed four strategies to improve the success of the company. Each strategy is listed in the table below.

Evaluate impact of decisions on cash flow categories.

(LO 4)

	Category of Cash Flow Affected	Impact on Cash Flow (Increase or Decrease)
Collect accounts receivable more quickly and use the cash received to buy equipment.		
Pay accounts payable more slowly and use the cash saved to pay dividends.		
Issue common shares and use the proceeds to pay down bank loans.		
Sell non-current bond investments and use the proceeds to pay a larger bonus to employees to improve retention rates.		

Instructions

Complete the above table by identifying the categories (operating, investing, or financing) of cash flows affected by each strategy and the impact (increase or decrease) that the strategy will have on each category.

*E13–12 The following is a list of income statement accounts that must be converted from the accrual basis to the cash basis in order to calculate cash provided (used) by operating activities using the direct method:

Convert operating activities from accrual to cash basis—direct method.

(LO 5)

		Part (a)	Part (b)
Income Statement Account	Change in Current Asset/ Current Liability Account	Add to (+) or Deduct from (−) Income Statement Account	Related Cash Receipt or Payment
1. Sales revenue	Decrease in accounts receivable	+	Cash receipts from customers
2. Dividend revenue	Increase in dividends receivable		
3. Interest revenue	Decrease in interest receivable		
4. Rent revenue	Decrease in unearned rent		
5. Cost of goods sold	Decrease in inventory		
6. Cost of goods sold	Decrease in accounts payable		
7. Insurance expense	Decrease in prepaid insurance		
8. Salaries expense	Decrease in salaries payable		
9. Interest expense	Increase in interest payable		
10. Income tax expense	Decrease in income tax payable		

Instructions

Do the following for each of the above income statement accounts. The first one has been done for you as an example.
(a) Identify if the change in the current asset or current liability account stated in the second column should be added to (+) or deducted from (−) the income statement account in order to convert the accrual-based number to a cash-based number.
(b) Identify the title of the resulting cash receipt or payment on the statement of cash flows.

*E13–13 The following selected information is taken from the general ledger of Carnival Limited:

Calculate cash flows—direct method.

(LO 5)

(a) Sales revenue	$160,000	(c) Salaries expense	$45,000
Accounts receivable, January 1	16,000	Salaries payable, January 1	2,500
Accounts receivable, December 31	14,000	Salaries payable, December 31	3,675
Unearned revenue, January 1	2,000		
Unearned revenue, December 31	5,000	(d) Operating expenses	$50,000
		Accrued expenses payable, January 1	4,200
(b) Cost of goods sold	$85,000	Accrued expenses payable, December 31	3,900
Inventory, January 1	11,200	Prepaid expenses, January 1	2,600
Inventory, December 31	12,900	Prepaid expenses, December 31	2,150
Accounts payable, January 1	2,500		
Accounts payable, December 31	5,700		

Instructions

Using the above information and the direct method, calculate the (a) cash receipts from customers, (b) cash payments to suppliers, (c) cash payments to employees, and (d) cash payments for operating expenses.

Prepare operating activities section—direct method.

(LO 5)

*E13–14 Selected information from Juno Ltd.'s statement of financial position and income statement is found in E13–4. In addition to the information contained in these statements, note the following:

1. Prepaid expenses and accrued liabilities relate to operating expenses.
2. Accounts payable relate to purchases of merchandise.
3. Operating expenses included depreciation expense of $11,000 and a loss of $5,000 on the disposal of equipment.

Instructions

Prepare the operating activities section of the statement of cash flows, using the direct method.

Prepare statement of cash flows—direct method.

(LO 3, 5)

*E13–15 Refer to the financial information given in E13–7 for Puffy Ltd.

Instructions

Prepare a statement of cash flows using the direct method.

▶ PROBLEMS: SET A

Classify activities.

(LO 1)

P13–1A The following is a list of transactions that took place during the year:

	(a) Classification	(b) Cash Flow	(c) Net Income
1. Paid salaries to employees.	O	–	–
2. Sold land for cash, at a gain.			
3. Purchased a building by making a down payment in cash and signing a mortgage payable for the balance.			
4. Made a principal repayment on the mortgage.			
5. Paid interest on the mortgage.			
6. Issued common shares for cash.			
7. Purchased shares of another company to be held as a long-term non-strategic investment.			
8. Paid dividends to shareholders.			
9. Sold inventory on account, at a price greater than cost. The company uses a perpetual inventory system.			
10. Wrote down the cost of the remaining inventory to its net realizable value.			

Instructions

(a) Classify each of the above transactions as an operating activity (O), investing activity (I), financing activity (F), or noncash investing and financing activity (NC). If it does not fit into one of these classifications, indicate that there is no effect (NE). The first one has been done for you as an example.

(b) Specify if the transaction will result in a cash receipt (+), cash payment (−), or have no effect on cash (NE).

(c) Indicate if the transaction will increase (+), decrease (−), or have no effect (NE) on net income.

(d) Explain how it is possible for the same transaction to affect cash and net income differently.

Prepare operating activities section—indirect method.

(LO 2)

P13–2A The income statement for Whistler Ltd., a private company following ASPE, is presented here:

WHISTLER LTD.	
Income Statement	
Year Ended November 30, 2018	
Sales	$8,000,000
Cost of goods sold	5,000,000
Gross profit	3,000,000
Operating expenses	2,000,000
Income from operations	1,000,000
Interest expense	100,000
Income before income tax	900,000
Income tax expense	300,000
Net income	$ 600,000

Additional information:

1. Operating expenses include $75,000 of depreciation expense and a $100,000 impairment loss on property, plant, and equipment.
2. Accounts receivable increased by $190,000.
3. Inventory decreased by $50,000.
4. Prepaid expenses related to operating expenses increased by $40,000.
5. Accounts payable to suppliers of merchandise decreased by $180,000.
6. Accrued liabilities related to operating expenses decreased by $90,000.
7. Interest payable decreased by $10,000.
8. Unearned revenue that was received from customers decreased by $17,000.
9. Income tax payable increased by $20,000.

Instructions

(a) Prepare the operating activities section of the statement of cash flows, using the indirect method.
(b) Would your answer in part (a) change if Whistler were a public company following IFRS?

P13–3A The following selected account balances relate to the property, plant, and equipment accounts of Katewill Inc.:

Calculate and classify cash flows for property, plant, and equipment.

(LO 3, 4)

	2018	2017
Accumulated depreciation—buildings	$337,500	$300,000
Accumulated depreciation—equipment	144,000	96,000
Depreciation expense—buildings	37,500	37,500
Depreciation expense—equipment	60,000	48,000
Land	100,000	60,000
Buildings	750,000	750,000
Equipment	300,000	240,000
Gain on disposal (equipment)	5,000	–0–

Additional information:

1. Purchased $40,000 of land for cash.
2. Purchased $75,000 of equipment for a $10,000 down payment, financing the remainder with a bank loan. Equipment was also sold during the year.

Instructions

(a) Calculate any cash receipts or payments related to the property, plant, and equipment accounts in 2018.
(b) Indicate where each of the cash receipts or payments identified in part (a) would be classified on the statement of cash flows or accompanying notes.
(c) Would you expect a growing company like Katewill to be generating or using cash for its investing activities? Explain.

P13–4A The following selected account balances relate to the shareholders' equity accounts of Valerio Corp. at year end:

Calculate and classify cash flows for shareholders' equity.

(LO 3, 4)

	2018	2017
Preferred shares, 3,250 shares in 2018; 2,750 in 2017	$325,000	$275,000
Common shares, 55,000 shares in 2018; 40,000 in 2017	550,000	400,000
Retained earnings	500,000	300,000
Cash dividends declared (preferred shares)	16,250	13,750
Dividends payable	4,062	3,438

Additional information:

1. During the year, 500 preferred shares were issued. No preferred shares were repurchased.
2. During the year, 25,000 common shares were issued after 10,000 common shares were repurchased at $11 per share.

Instructions

(a) Determine the amounts of any cash receipts or payments related to the shareholders' equity accounts in 2018.
(b) Indicate where each of the cash receipts or payments identified in part (a) would be classified on the statement of cash flows or accompanying notes.
(c) Would you expect a growing company like Valerio to be generating or using cash for its financing activities? Explain.

Prepare statement of cash flows (indirect method) and comment.

(LO 2, 3)

P13–5A The income statement and unclassified statement of financial position for E-Perform, Inc. follow:

E-PERFORM, INC.
Statement of Financial Position
December 31

	2018	2017
Assets		
Cash	$ 97,800	$ 48,400
Held for trading investments	128,000	114,000
Accounts receivable	75,800	43,000
Inventory	122,500	92,850
Prepaid expenses	18,400	26,000
Equipment	270,000	242,500
Accumulated depreciation	(50,000)	(52,000)
Total assets	$662,500	$514,750
Liabilities and Shareholders' Equity		
Accounts payable	$ 93,000	$ 77,300
Accrued liabilities	11,500	7,000
Bank loan payable	110,000	150,000
Common shares	200,000	175,000
Retained earnings	248,000	105,450
Total liabilities and shareholders' equity	$662,500	$514,750

E-PERFORM, INC.
Income Statement
Year Ended December 31, 2018

Sales		$492,780
Cost of goods sold		185,460
Gross profit		307,320
Operating expenses		116,410
Income from operations		190,910
Other revenues and expenses		
Unrealized gain on held for trading investments	$14,000	
Interest expense	(4,730)	9,270
Income before income tax		200,180
Income tax expense		45,000
Net income		$155,180

Additional information:
1. Prepaid expenses and accrued liabilities relate to operating expenses.
2. An unrealized gain on held for trading investments of $14,000 was recorded.
3. New equipment costing $85,000 was purchased for $25,000 cash and a $60,000 long-term bank loan payable.
4. Old equipment having an original cost of $57,500 was sold for $1,500.
5. Accounts payable relate to merchandise creditors.
6. Some of the bank loan was repaid during the year.
7. A dividend was paid during the year.
8. Operating expenses include $46,500 of depreciation expense and a $7,500 loss on disposal of equipment.

Instructions
(a) Prepare the statement of cash flows, using the indirect method.
(b) E-Perform's cash position more than doubled between 2017 and 2018. Identify the primary reason(s) for this significant increase.

Prepare statement of cash flows (indirect method) and answer questions.

(LO 2, 3)

P13–6A The comparative, unclassified statement of financial position for Sylvester Ltd. shows the following balances at December 31:

	2018	2017
Assets		
Cash	$ 23,000	$ -0-
Accounts receivable	25,000	36,000
Inventory	34,000	55,000
Land	100,000	110,000
Buildings	527,000	263,000
Accumulated depreciation—buildings	(67,000)	(100,000)
Equipment	85,000	40,000
Accumulated depreciation—equipment	(18,000)	(10,000)
Total assets	$709,000	$394,000
Liabilities and Shareholders' Equity		
Bank overdraft	$ -0-	$ 8,000
Accounts payable	43,000	26,000
Income tax payable	3,000	2,000
Interest payable	6,000	7,000
Dividends payable	3,000	1,000
Bank loan payable—current portion	26,000	20,000
Bank loan payable—non-current portion	380,000	212,000
Common shares	198,000	88,000
Retained earnings	50,000	30,000
Total liabilities and shareholders' equity	$709,000	$394,000

Additional information regarding 2018:
1. Net income was $57,000.
2. A gain of $7,000 was recorded on the disposal of a small parcel of land. No land was purchased during the year.
3. A gain on disposal of $38,000 was recorded when an old building was sold for $50,000 cash. A new building was purchased for $364,000 and depreciation expense on buildings for the year was $55,000.
4. Equipment costing $65,000 was purchased while a loss of $4,000 was recorded on equipment that was sold for $5,000. The equipment that was sold late in the year had accumulated depreciation of $11,000.
5. The company took out $210,000 of new bank loans during the year.
6. Dividends were declared and paid and no common shares were bought back by the company.

Instructions
(a) Prepare the statement of cash flows using the indirect method.
(b) Did the company manage its noncash working capital effectively?
(c) How could the company afford to buy a new building?

P13–7A The comparative, unclassified statement of financial position for Alton Ltd. shows the following balances at December 31:

Prepare statement of cash flows (indirect method) and answer questions.

(LO 2, 3)

	2018	2017
Assets		
Cash	$ 5,000	$ 36,000
Term deposits (maturing in 60 days)	-0-	42,000
Accounts receivable	75,000	40,000
Inventory	101,000	70,000
Land	180,000	230,000
Buildings	923,000	524,000
Accumulated depreciation—buildings	(136,000)	(190,000)
Equipment	100,000	70,000
Accumulated depreciation—equipment	(41,000)	(20,000)
Total assets	$1,207,000	$802,000
Liabilities and Shareholders' Equity		
Accounts payable	$ 29,000	$ 72,000
Income tax payable	3,000	5,000
Interest payable	18,000	13,000
Bank loan payable—current portion	56,000	40,000
Bank loan payable—non-current portion	891,000	420,000
Common shares	160,000	180,000
Retained earnings	50,000	72,000
Total liabilities and shareholders' equity	$1,207,000	$802,000

Additional information regarding 2018:

1. Net income was $10,000.
2. A loss of $21,000 was recorded on the disposal of a small parcel of land. No land was purchased during the year.
3. A gain on disposal of $15,000 was recorded when an old building was sold for $40,000 cash. A new building was purchased for $520,000 and depreciation expense on buildings for the year was $42,000.
4. Equipment costing $72,000 was purchased while a loss of $11,000 was recorded on equipment that originally cost $42,000 and was sold for $21,000.
5. The company received $512,000 from new bank loans during the year.
6. Dividends were declared and paid during the year.
7. No common shares were issued during the year but some were bought back and retired at the amount they were originally issued at.

Instructions

(a) Prepare the statement of cash flows using the indirect method.
(b) Did the company manage its noncash working capital effectively?
(c) The company's banker is worried. Why?

Calculate and compare free cash flow.

(LO 4)

P13–8A Selected information (in thousands) for **Reitmans (Canada) Limited** and **Le Château Inc.** for fiscal 2015 follows:

	Reitmans	Le Château
Net cash provided (used) by operating activities	$34,770	$(14,161)
Net capital expenditures	33,291	9,115
Dividends paid	12,782	-0-

Instructions

(a) Calculate the free cash flow for each company. Which company has the better free cash flow? Why?
(b) If a company has a negative free cash flow, does that necessarily imply that overall cash flow will be negative, too? Why or why not?

Compare cash flows for two companies.

(LO 4)

P13–9A Condensed net income and cash flow information follow for a recent year for two coffee companies, **The Second Cup Ltd.** and **Starbucks Corporation**, follow:

	Second Cup (in C$ millions)	Starbucks (in U.S. $ millions)
Net income (loss)	$ (1.2)	$2,757.4
Net cash provided by operating activities	$ 0.2	$3,749.1
Net cash used by investing activities	(2.9)	(1,520.3)
Net cash used by financing activities	(5.1)	(2,407.1)
Net decrease in cash	(7.8)	(178.3)
Cash, beginning of year	10.9	1,708.4
Cash, end of year	$ 3.1	$1,530.1

Instructions

(a) Compare the cash provided or used in each of the three activities by each company.
(b) Based on the information provided above, which company appears to be in the stronger position? Explain the reasoning behind your decision.

Prepare operating activities section (indirect and direct methods) and discuss methods.

(LO 2, 5)

*P13–10A The income statement for Tremblant Limited is presented here:

TREMBLANT LIMITED Income Statement Year Ended December 31, 2018	
Service revenue	$925,000
Operating expenses	701,000
Income from operations	224,000
Interest expense	75,000
Income before income tax	149,000
Income tax expense	37,250
Net income	$111,750

Tremblant's statement of financial position contained these comparative data at December 31:

	2018	2017
Accounts receivable	$57,000	$47,000
Prepaid expenses	12,000	15,000
Accounts payable	36,000	41,000
Salaries payable	19,500	20,000
Unearned revenue	12,000	9,000
Interest payable	6,250	5,000
Income tax payable	4,000	9,250

Additional information:

1. Operating expenses include depreciation expense, $50,000; amortization expense, $15,000; administrative expenses, $110,000; salaries expense, $500,000; and loss on the disposal of equipment, $26,000.
2. Unearned revenue is received from customers.
3. Prepaid expenses and accounts payable relate to operating (administrative) expenses.

Instructions

(a) Prepare the operating activities section of the statement of cash flows, using (1) the indirect method, and (2) the direct method.
(b) Which method—indirect or direct—do you recommend that this company use to prepare its operating activities section? Explain your reasoning.

*P13–11A Refer to the financial information presented in P13–2A for Whistler Ltd., a private company following ASPE.

Instructions

(a) Prepare the operating activities section of the statement of cash flows, using the direct method.
(b) Would your answer in part (a) change if Whistler were a public company following IFRS?

Prepare operating activities section—direct method.

(LO 5)

*P13–12A Refer to the financial statements presented in P13–5A for E-Perform, Inc.

Instructions

(a) Prepare the statement of cash flows using the direct method.
(b) E-Perform's cash position doubled between 2017 and 2018. Identify the primary reason(s) for this significant increase.

Prepare statement of cash flows (direct method) and comment.

(LO 5)

▶ PROBLEMS: SET B

P13–1B The following is a list of transactions that took place during the year:

Classify activities.

(LO 1)

	(a) Classification	(b) Cash Flow	(c) Net Income
1. Collected an account receivable.	O	+	NE
2. Sold equipment for cash, at a loss.			
3. Recorded an unrealized gain on a held for trading investment.			
4. Acquired land by issuing common shares.			
5. Expired prepaid insurance.			
6. Paid dividends to preferred shareholders.			
7. Recorded depreciation expense.			
8. Issued preferred shares for cash.			
9. Purchased inventory for cash. The company uses a perpetual inventory system.			
10. Provided services on account.			

Instructions

(a) Classify each of the above transactions as an operating activity (O), investing activity (I), financing activity (F), or noncash investing and financing activity (NC). If it does not fit into one of these classifications, indicate that there is no effect (NE). The first one has been done for you as an example.
(b) Specify if the transaction will result in a cash receipt (+), cash payment (−), or have no effect on cash (NE).
(c) Indicate if the transaction will increase (+), decrease (−), or have no effect (NE) on net income.
(d) Explain how it is possible for the same transaction to affect cash and net income differently.

Prepare operating activities section—indirect method.

(LO 2)

P13–2B The income statement for Gum San Ltd., a private company following ASPE, is presented here:

GUM SAN LTD.
Income Statement
Year Ended December 31, 2018

Sales	$4,500,000
Cost of goods sold	2,390,000
Gross profit	2,110,000
Operating expenses	1,070,000
Income from operations	1,040,000
Interest expense	12,000
Income before income tax	1,028,000
Income tax expense	260,000
Net income	$ 768,000

Additional information:
1. Operating expenses include $150,000 of depreciation expense and a $12,000 gain on disposal of equipment.
2. Accounts receivable increased by $500,000.
3. Inventory decreased by $220,000.
4. Prepaid expenses related to operating expenses increased by $170,000.
5. Accounts payable to suppliers of merchandise increased by $50,000.
6. Accrued liabilities related to operating expenses decreased by $165,000.
7. Interest payable increased by $5,000.
8. Unearned revenue that is received from customers increased by $8,000.
9. Income tax payable decreased by $16,000.

Instructions
(a) Prepare the operating activities section of the statement of cash flows, using the indirect method.
(b) Would your answer in part (a) change if Gum San were a public company following IFRS?

Calculate and classify cash flows for property, plant, and equipment.

(LO 3, 4)

P13–3B The following selected account balances relate to the property, plant, and equipment accounts of Bird Corp.

	2018	2017
Accumulated depreciation—buildings	$ 675,000	$ 600,000
Accumulated depreciation—equipment	288,000	192,000
Depreciation expense—buildings	75,000	75,000
Depreciation expense—equipment	128,000	96,000
Land	250,000	200,000
Buildings	1,250,000	1,250,000
Equipment	500,000	480,000
Loss on disposal (equipment)	4,000	-0-

Additional information:
1. Purchased land for $50,000, making a $20,000 down payment and financing the remainder with a mortgage payable.
2. Equipment was purchased for $80,000 cash. Equipment was also sold during the year.

Instructions
(a) Calculate any cash receipts or payments related to the property, plant, and equipment accounts in 2018.
(b) Indicate where each of the cash receipts or payments identified in part (a) would be classified on the statement of cash flows or accompanying notes.
(c) Would you expect a growing company like Bird to be generating or using cash for its investing activities? Explain.

Calculate and classify cash flows for shareholders' equity.

(LO 3, 4)

P13–4B The following selected account balances relate to the shareholders' equity accounts of Mathur Corp. at year end:

	2018	2017
Preferred shares, 6,000 shares in 2018, 5,000 shares in 2017	$150,000	$125,000
Common shares, 18,700 shares in 2018, 20,000 in 2017	190,400	200,000
Retained earnings	259,600	250,000
Cash dividends declared—preferred	7,500	6,250
Stock dividends declared—common shares	20,400	-0-

Additional information:
1. During 2018, the company sold 1,000 preferred shares. No shares were reacquired by the company.
2. All cash dividends pertained to the preferred shares and were declared and paid during the same year. There were no dividends payable at the end of 2017 or 2018.

3. At the beginning of the year, 3,000 common shares were bought back and retired at a price of $10 per share. Later in the year, a 10% stock dividend was declared and distributed when the fair value of the shares was $12 per share.

4. Net income was $37,500 in 2018.

Instructions

(a) Determine the amounts of any cash receipts or payments related to the shareholders' equity accounts in 2018.

(b) Indicate where each of the cash receipts or payments identified in part (a) would be classified on the statement of cash flows or accompanying notes.

(c) Would you expect a growing company like Mathur to be generating or using cash for its financing activities? Explain.

P13–5B The income statement and unclassified statement of financial position for Nackawic Inc. follow:

Prepare statement of cash flows (indirect method) and comment.

(LO 2, 3)

NACKAWIC INC.
Statement of Financial Position
December 31

	2018	2017
Assets		
Cash	$ 82,700	$ 47,250
Accounts receivable	80,800	37,000
Inventory	131,900	102,650
Long-term investments	94,500	107,000
Equipment	290,000	205,000
Accumulated depreciation	(49,500)	(40,000)
Total assets	$630,400	$458,900
Liabilities and Shareholders' Equity		
Accounts payable	$ 62,700	$ 48,280
Accrued liabilities	12,100	18,830
Bank loan payable	140,000	70,000
Common shares	240,000	200,000
Retained earnings	175,600	121,790
Total liabilities and shareholders' equity	$630,400	$458,900

NACKAWIC INC.
Income Statement
Year Ended December 31, 2018

Sales		$317,500
Cost of goods sold		99,460
Gross profit		218,040
Operating expenses		82,120
Income from operations		135,920
Other revenues and expenses		
Interest expense	$12,940	
Realized loss on sale of long-term investments	7,500	20,440
Income before income tax		115,480
Income tax expense		27,670
Net income		$ 87,810

Additional information:

1. Long-term investments were sold for $5,000, resulting in a realized loss of $7,500.
2. New equipment costing $141,000 was purchased for $71,000 cash and a $70,000 bank loan payable.
3. Equipment costing $56,000 was sold for $15,550, resulting in a gain of $8,750.
4. Accounts payable relate to merchandise creditors; accrued liabilities relate to operating expenses.
5. A dividend was paid during the year.
6. Operating expenses include $58,700 of depreciation expense and an $8,750 gain on disposal of equipment.

Instructions

(a) Prepare the statement of cash flows, using the indirect method.

(b) Nackawic's cash position increased by 75% between 2017 and 2018. Identify the primary reason(s) for this significant increase.

Prepare statement of cash flows (indirect method) and answer questions.

(LO 2, 3)

P13–6B The comparative, unclassified statement of financial position for Anderson Ltd. shows the following balances at December 31:

	2018	2017
Assets		
Cash	$ -0-	$ 36,000
Accounts receivable	38,000	20,000
Inventory	49,000	35,000
Land	95,000	110,000
Buildings	477,000	263,000
Accumulated depreciation—buildings	(67,000)	(100,000)
Equipment	135,000	40,000
Accumulated depreciation—equipment	(18,000)	(10,000)
Total assets	$709,000	$394,000
Liabilities and Shareholders' Equity		
Bank overdraft	$ 5,000	$ -0-
Accounts payable	9,000	35,000
Income tax payable	3,000	2,000
Interest payable	6,000	7,000
Bank loan payable—current portion	26,000	20,000
Bank loan payable—non-current portion	520,000	212,000
Common shares	90,000	88,000
Retained earnings	50,000	30,000
Total liabilities and shareholders' equity	$709,000	$394,000

Additional information regarding 2018:
1. Net income was $53,000.
2. A gain of $14,000 was recorded on the disposal of a small parcel of land. No land was purchased during the year.
3. A gain on disposal of $28,000 was recorded when an old building was sold for $40,000 cash. A new building was purchased for $304,000 and depreciation expense on buildings for the year was $45,000.
4. Equipment costing $125,000 was purchased while a loss of $5,000 was recorded on equipment that originally cost $30,000 and was sold for $4,000.
5. The company took out $350,000 of new bank loans during the year.
6. Dividends were declared and paid during the year.
7. Common shares were issued for $10,000. Some common shares were also reacquired at the price at which they were originally issued.

Instructions
(a) Prepare the statement of cash flows using the indirect approach.
(b) Did the company manage its noncash working capital effectively?
(c) The company's banker is worried. Why?

Prepare statement of cash flows (indirect method) and answer questions.

(LO 2, 3)

P13–7B The comparative, unclassified statement of financial position for Summerville Ltd. shows the following balances at December 31:

	2018	2017
Assets		
Cash	$ 17,000	$ 12,000
Term deposits (matures in 30 days)	52,000	-0-
Accounts receivable	50,000	60,000
Inventory	68,000	110,000
Land	200,000	220,000
Buildings	943,000	466,000
Accumulated depreciation—buildings	(130,000)	(150,000)
Equipment	190,000	80,000
Accumulated depreciation—equipment	(36,000)	(20,000)
Total assets	$1,354,000	$778,000

Liabilities and Shareholders' Equity		
Accounts payable	$ 86,000	$ 68,000
Income tax payable	6,000	4,000
Interest payable	18,000	14,000
Dividends payable	3,000	2,000
Bank loan payable—current portion	52,000	40,000
Bank loan payable—non-current portion	673,000	418,000
Common shares	396,000	172,000
Retained earnings	120,000	60,000
Total liabilities and shareholders' equity	$1,354,000	$778,000

Additional information for 2018:

1. Net income was $89,000.
2. A gain of $7,000 was recorded on the disposal of a small parcel of land. No land was purchased during the year.
3. A gain on disposal of $78,000 was recorded when an old building was sold for $90,000 cash. A new building was purchased for $564,000 and depreciation expense on buildings for the year was $55,000.
4. Equipment costing $140,000 was purchased while a loss of $10,000 was recorded on equipment that was sold for $15,000. The equipment that was sold late in the year had accumulated depreciation of $5,000.
5. The company took out $300,000 of new bank loans during the year.
6. Dividends were declared during the year.
7. Common shares were bought back by the company for $26,000, which was the amount at which they were originally issued, and additional shares were issued during the year.

Instructions
(a) Prepare the statement of cash flows using the indirect approach.
(b) Did the company manage its noncash working capital effectively?
(c) How could the company afford to buy a new building?

P13–8B Selected information (in U.S. $ millions) for **Google Inc.** and **Microsoft Corp.** for 2015 and 2016, respectively, follows:

Calculate and compare free cash flow.

(LO 4)

	Google	Microsoft
Net cash provided by operating activities	$26,024	$33,325
Net capital expenditures	9,915	23,950
Dividends paid	-0-	11,006

Instructions
(a) Calculate the free cash flow for each company. Which company has the better free cash flow? Why?
(b) Why do you think Microsoft has paid out dividends while Google has not?

P13–9B Condensed net income and cash flow information (in U.S. $ millions) follow for a recent year for two fast food companies: **McDonald's Corporation** and **Wendy's/Arby's Group, Inc.**:

Compare cash flows for two companies.

(LO 4)

	McDonald's	Wendy's
Net income	$4,529.3	$ 161.1
Net cash provided by operating activities	$6,539.1	$212.5
Net cash provided (used) by investing activities	(1,420.0)	35.4
Net cash provided (used) by financing activities	735.3	(175.7)
Other (foreign exchange gain [loss])	(246.8)	(12.2)
Net increase in cash and cash equivalents	5,607.6	60.0
Cash and cash equivalents, beginning of year	2,077.9	267.2
Cash and cash equivalents, end of year	$7,685.5	$ 327.2

Instructions
(a) Compare the cash provided or used in each of the three activities by each company.
(b) Based on the information provided above, which company appears to be in the stronger position? Explain the reasoning behind your decision.

Prepare operating activities section (indirect and direct methods) and discuss methods.

(LO 2, 5)

*P13–10B The income statement for Hanalei International Inc. is presented here:

HANALEI INTERNATIONAL INC.
Income Statement
Year Ended December 31, 2018

Fees earned	$565,000
Operating expenses	365,000
Income from operations	200,000
Interest expense	10,000
Income before income tax	190,000
Income tax expense	47,500
Net income	$142,500

Hanalei's statement of financial position contained the following account balances:

	2018	2017
Accounts receivable	$50,000	$60,000
Prepaid insurance	5,000	8,000
Accounts payable	40,000	31,000
Unearned revenue	10,000	14,000
Salaries payable	10,000	7,000
Interest payable	1,000	1,000
Income tax payable	4,000	3,000

Additional information:

1. Operating expenses include depreciation expense, $45,000; amortization expense, $5,000; administrative expenses, $40,000; salaries expense, $300,000; and gain on disposal of equipment, $25,000.
2. Unearned revenue is received from customers.
3. Prepaid insurance and accounts payable relate to operating (administrative) expenses.

Instructions

(a) Prepare the operating activities section of the statement of cash flows, using (1) the indirect method, and (2) the direct method.

(b) Which method—indirect or direct—do you recommend that this company use to prepare its operating activities section? Explain your reasoning.

Prepare operating activities section—direct method.

(LO 5)

*P13–11B Refer to the financial information presented in P13–2B for Gum San Ltd., a private company following ASPE.

Instructions

(a) Prepare the operating activities section of the statement of cash flows, using the direct method.

(b) Would your answer in part (a) change if Gum San were a public company following IFRS?

Prepare statement of cash flows (direct method) and comment.

(LO 3, 5)

*P13–12B Refer to the financial statements presented in P13–5B for Nackawic Inc.

Instructions

(a) Prepare the statement of cash flows using the direct method.

(b) Nackawic's cash position increased by 75% between 2017 and 2018. Identify the primary reason(s) for this significant increase.

EXPAND YOUR CRITICAL THINKING

CT13–1 Financial Reporting Case

The financial statements of **The North West Company Inc.** are presented in Appendix A at the end of this book.

Instructions

(a) Does North West use the indirect or direct method of calculating operating activities?

(b) What was the amount of net operating cash flows reported for 2015? For 2014?

(c) From your analysis of the 2015 statement of cash flows, what was the most significant investing activity? Financing activity?

(d) What amount was reported as the increase or decrease in cash on the statement of cash flows for 2015? 2014?

(e) Did North West increase its capital expenditures? How could the company afford to do this and still maintain its dividend payments?

(f) By comparing operating, investing, and financing cash flows for 2015, describe how North West spent its operating cash flows. Was this a different approach than the one taken in 2014?

CT13–2 Financial Analysis Case

Action Carpets Ltd. recently became publicly traded. A few years ago, the company reported under ASPE and it did not really change the way that it presented the statement of cash flows when it adopted IFRS upon going public. The CEO of Action has just read a newspaper article comparing her company with Discount Carpets Ltd., which is another public company. She is angry because the article claimed that Discount was "better" because it had higher net cash flows from operating activities. As the CFO of Action, you have been asked to explain to your boss how the author of the newspaper article may be mistaken because he is unaware of the choices that can be made under IFRS when presenting the statement of cash flows. You are pretty sure that the choices made by Discount were ones that would maximize its operating cash flow.

Instructions (CT13-2)
(a) Using your understanding of the differences between IFRS and ASPE with regard to the presentation of information on the statement of cash flows, explain the choices that Discount Ltd. management probably made when preparing this statement for their company.
(b) Based on your answer to part (a) above, explain how each difference you covered would affect the free cash flow of these companies.

CT13–3 Professional Judgement Case

This case can be assigned as a group activity. Additional instructions and material for this activity can be found on the Instructor Resource site and in WileyPLUS.

Listed below are statements of cash flows for three companies in millions of dollars. Each company went public in 2017 and then began operations by acquiring a number of restaurants. Despite the identical incomes and cash flows of each company, there are some differences in the way that each company manages its cash flows.

	A Limited 2018	A Limited 2017	B Limited 2018	B Limited 2017	C Limited 2018	C Limited 2017
Operating activities						
Net income	$ 800	$ 800	$ 800	$ 800	$ 800	$ 800
Depreciation	300	200	220	200	210	200
Loss (gain) on disposal of non-current assets	(10)	-0-	(20)	-0-	70	-0-
	1,090	1,000	1,000	1,000	1,080	1,000
Increase in accounts receivable	(50)	(80)	(20)	(80)	(150)	(80)
Increase in inventory	(50)	(50)	(10)	(50)	(200)	(50)
Increase in accounts payable	40	60	10	60	90	60
Net cash provided by operating activities	1,030	930	980	930	820	930
Investing activities						
Proceeds from disposal of property, plant, and equipment	50	-0-	50	-0-	120	-0-
Purchases of property, plant, and equipment	(2,350)	(2,000)	(830)	(2,000)	(430)	(2,000)
Net cash used by investing activities	(2,300)	(2,000)	(780)	(2,000)	(310)	(2,000)
Financing activities						
Bank loans received	-0-	700	-0-	-0-	-0-	1,050
Bank loan payments made	(50)	(50)	-0-	-0-	(425)	(115)
Common share sale proceeds	1,500	500	-0-	1,200	-0-	200
Dividends paid	(100)	(20)	(120)	(70)	(5)	(5)
Net cash provided (used) by financing activities	1,350	1,130	(120)	1,130	(430)	1,130
Net increase in cash	80	60	80	60	80	60
Cash, January 1	60	-0-	60	-0-	60	-0-
Cash, December 31	$ 140	$ 60	$ 140	$ 60	$ 140	$ 60

Instructions
(a) Which company may have too much debt?
(b) Which company has some problems with its operating cash flows? What is causing these problems?
(c) Why do you think that C Limited had to pay down its bank loans so much in 2018?
(d) If you were a shareholder wanting to receive dividends but were not too interested in owning shares for a long time, which company's shares might you consider buying?
(e) Which company is the most committed to growth? Do you think that this company is growing too quickly?
(f) Which company has the highest free cash flow in 2018?
(g) Based on the above, which company would you like to own or lend cash to?

CT13–4 Financial Analysis Case

Shown below is some information pertaining to **Apple Inc.'s** financial statements over a 10-year period. All amounts are shown in U.S. $ millions.

	2015	2010	2005
Cash provided by operating cash flows	$ 81,266	$ 18,595	$ 2,535
Cash used by investing cash flows	(56,274)	(13,854)	(2,556)
Cash provided (used) by financing cash flows	(17,716)	1,257	543
Capital expenditures paid during the year	11,831	2,759	281
Dividends paid during the year	11,561	–0–	–0–

Instructions

(a) Based on the information provided above, assess what stage of its corporate life cycle Apple was at in each of the years shown above.

(b) Calculate the free cash flow for each year. Calculate free cash flow as a percentage of operating cash flow. Is the change in free cash flow as a percentage of operating cash flow consistent with your response to part (a) above?

CT13–5 Ethics Case

Onwards and Upwards Corporation has paid cash dividends to its shareholders for eight consecutive years. The board of directors' policy requires that, in order for a dividend to be declared, cash provided by operating activities as reported in the current year's statement of cash flows must exceed $1 million. The job of president Phil Monat is secure so long as Phil produces annual operating cash flows to support the usual dividend.

At the end of the current year, controller Leland Yee informs president Monat of some disappointing news. The net cash provided by operating activities is only $970,000. The president says to Leland, "We must get that amount above $1 million. Isn't there some way to increase this amount?" Leland answers, "These figures were prepared by my assistant. I'll go back to my office and see what I can do." The president replies, "I know you won't let me down, Leland."

Upon close scrutiny of the statement of cash flows, Leland concludes that he can get net cash provided by operating activities above $1 million by reclassifying interest paid from the operating activities section, where it has been classified in the past, to the financing activities section. The company is a publicly traded company using IFRS. Leland knows that sometimes a major repair can be recorded as an asset rather than an expense. He returns to the president and exclaims, "You can tell the board to declare their usual dividend. Our cash flow provided by operating activities is $1,030,000." Excited, the president exclaims, "Good job, Leland! I knew I could count on you."

Instructions

(a) Should any other factors, besides net cash provided by operating activities, be considered by the board in setting the company's dividend policy? If so, what factors?

(b) Who are the stakeholders in this situation?

(c) Was there anything unethical about the president's actions? Was there anything unethical about the controller's actions?

(d) Because the company reported under IFRS, could there be other ways to change the cash flow provided by operating activities? Are these options available under ASPE?

CT13–6 Student View Case

Your friend and colleague has been working for about a year since graduating from university. He has come to you for advice on his saving and spending habits. You have accumulated the following information on his savings and spending that has occurred over the past year:

Salary received over the last year, net of income tax	$45,000
Rent and utilities paid	16,600
Car expenses paid	4,800
Credit card debt at the start of the year	1,000
Food, entertainment, recreation paid	6,000
Credit card debt at the end of the year	2,500
Line of credit at the start of the year	2,500
Line of credit at the end of the year	1,200
Purchase of car	20,000
Car loan at the end of the year	15,000
Cash account at the beginning of the year	500
Cash received from disposal of motorcycle	1,000
Cash received from disposal of computer	100
Cash account at the end of the year	1,000
Purchase of investments	5,500
Student loan at the beginning of the year	15,000
Student loan at the end of the year	10,000
Purchase of new computer	1,500
Interest expense paid	1,400

Instructions

(a) Prepare a statement of cash flow for your friend from information provided above using the direct method.

(b) Can you provide some advice to your friend on how he could improve his cash flow strategies, such as managing debt levels and terms of payment?

CT13–7 Serial Case

(*Note:* This is a continuation of the serial case from Chapters 1 through 12.)

The Anthonys have met with representatives of Software Solutions Inc., a public company, and Compuhelp Limited, a private company. Both companies have offered to purchase some or all of the shares of ABC Ltd. The financial statements, including the statement of cash flows, for ABC have been prepared for analysis and the

Anthonys are meeting to discuss the results of these financial statements with representatives of both of these companies. These meetings will enable Doug and Bev to decide upon the best alternative as they move forward with their decision to sell their shares. Emily and Daniel have been offered employment at each of these organizations and want to ensure these companies can continue to operate.

Selected information for ABC, Software Solutions, and Compuhelp for 2019 follow:

	ABC Ltd.	Software Solutions Inc.	Compuhelp Limited
Net income	$ 199,629	$ 2,628,000	$ 89,900
Net cash provided by operating activities	$ 225,279	$ 6,821,000	$ 159,400
Net cash used by investing activities	(57,071)	(3,397,000)	(144,800)
Net cash used by financing activities	(157,833)	(1,762,000)	(89,000)
Net increase (decrease) in cash	10,375	1,662,000	(74,400)
Cash, beginning of year	9,068	2,252,000	97,600
Cash, end of year	$ 19,443	$ 3,914,000	$ 23,200
Net capital expenditures	$ 54,000	$ 3,414,000	$ 144,800
Dividends declared and paid	80,000	580,000	-0-

Instructions

(a) Calculate the free cash flow for each company.

(b) Compare the cash provided and used in each of the three activities by each company.

(c) Based on the information provided in parts (a) and (b), identify why Software Solutions and Compuhelp are likely pursuing an investment in ABC.

(d) Based on the information provided in parts (a) and (b), identify some of the issues the Anthonys should consider before deciding whether to sell their shares and/or to be employed by one of these companies.

ANSWERS TO CHAPTER PRACTICE QUESTIONS

(a) Financing activity, cash receipt

(b) Investing activity, cash receipt

(c) Investing activity, cash payment

(d) Operating activity, cash payment

(e) Operating activity, cash receipt

(f) Noncash activity (noncash investing activity for equipment and noncash financing activity for common shares) so not shown on statement, just in a note

(g) Operating activity, cash payment

DO IT! 13-1
Cash Flow Activities

DENHAM LTD.
Statement of Cash Flows (partial)
Year Ended December 31, 2018

Operating activities		
Net income		$144,000
Adjustments to reconcile net income to net cash provided (used) by operating activities		
Depreciation expense	$ 33,000	
Loss on disposal of equipment	4,000	
Increase in accounts receivable	(42,000)	
Increase in inventory	(44,000)	
Decrease in prepaid expenses	2,000	
Decrease in accounts payable	(20,000)	
Decrease in accrued liabilities	(1,000)	
Increase in salaries payable	2,000	
Increase in income tax payable	10,000	(56,000)
Net cash provided by operating activities		88,000

DO IT! 13-2
Operating Activities—
Indirect Method

DO IT! 13-3a
Investing Activities

(a)

Cash	6,000	
Accumulated Depreciation—Equipment ($21,000 − $5,000)	16,000	
Gain on Disposal		1,000
Equipment		21,000
Equipment (see T account to determine amount)	10,000	
Cash		10,000
Depreciation Expense	31,000	
Accumulated Depreciation—Equipment		31,000

(b)

Equipment

Opening balance	146,000		
Purchase of equipment	10,000	Disposal of equipment	21,000
Ending balance	135,000		

Accumulated Depreciation—Equipment

		Opening balance	47,000
Sale of equipment	16,000	Depreciation expense	31,000
		Ending balance	62,000

(c) Cash received from disposal of equipment = $6,000
Cash paid for equipment = $10,000

DO IT! 13-3b
Financing Activities

Bank loans received would have been recorded as follows:

Cash	17,000	
Bank Loan Payable		17,000

We will combine both accounts relating to the bank loan and analyze the movement in these accounts in one T account. The opening balance is therefore $52,000 ($4,000 + $48,000) while the ending balance is $60,000 ($5,000 + $55,000). We know that the amount of new loans received is $17,000, so we can derive the loan payments as follows:

Current and Non-Current Bank Loan Payable

		Opening balance	52,000
Loan payments	9,000	Loans received	17,000
		Ending balance	60,000

The entry that would have been recorded for the bank loan payments would have been:

Bank Loan Payable	9,000	
Cash		9,000

Because we know the opening and closing balance in the Common Shares account and that only one transaction (the issue of shares) affected the account during the year, we can determine the amount for which the shares were issued.

Common Shares

		Opening balance	103,000
		Shares issued	18,000
		Ending balance	121,000

The entry to record the issue of common shares would have been:

Cash	18,000	
Common Shares		18,000

Because we know the net income and the opening and ending Retained Earnings account balances, we can determine the dividends declared as follows:

Retained Earnings

		Opening balance	57,000
Dividends declared	12,000	Net income	27,000
		Ending balance	72,000

The journal entry to record the declaration of these dividends would have been:

Dividends	12,000	
Dividends Payable		12,000

Knowing what dividends were declared, we can now determine the amount of dividends that were paid by analyzing the movement in the Dividends Payable account as follows:

Dividends Payable

		Opening balance	1,000
Dividends paid	11,000	Dividends declared	12,000
		Ending balance	2,000

The entry to record dividends paid would be:

Dividends Payable	11,000	
Cash		11,000

LA TUQUE LTD.
Statement of Cash Flows (partial)
Year Ended December 31, 2018

Financing activities	
Bank loans received	$ 17,000
Bank loan payments	(9,000)
Issue of common shares	18,000
Payment of dividend	(11,000)
Net cash provided by financing activities	15,000

DENHAM LTD.
Statement of Cash Flows
Year Ended December 31, 2018

Operating activities		
Net cash provided by operating activities		$ 88,000
Investing activities		
Disposal of land	$ 25,000	
Disposal of equipment	32,000[1]	
Purchase of equipment	(166,000)[2]	
Net cash used by investing activities		(109,000)
Financing activities		
Bank loan payments made	$ (65,000)	
New bank loans received	25,000[3]	
Issue of common shares	140,000	
Payment of dividends	(55,000)[4]	
Net cash provided by financing activities		45,000
Net increase in cash		24,000
Cash, January 1		37,000
Cash, December 31		$ 61,000

DO IT! 13-3c
Statement of Cash Flows—
Indirect Method

[1]Proceeds on disposal of equipment: $36,000 (carrying amount) − $4,000 (loss) = $32,000

[2]Purchase of equipment: $68,000 (opening account balance) − $41,000 (disposal of equipment) + $166,000 (purchase of equipment) = $193,000 (ending account balance)

[3]New loans received: $150,000 (opening account balance) − $65,000 (loan payments made) + $25,000 (new loans received) = $110,000 (ending account balance)

[4]Payment of dividends: $112,000 (opening account balance) + $144,000 (net income) − $55,000 (dividends declared and paid) = $201,000 (ending account balance)

(a) In 2016, the company is in its growth phase and financing cash flows are used to expand the business. By 2017, the company has reached maturity and operating cash flows are now large enough to fund capital expenditures and dividends and begin to pay down debt. But by 2018, decline is beginning and operating cash flows decline along with cash used in investing activities.

DO IT! 13-4
Corporate Life Cycle and
Free Cash Flow

(b)

	2018	2017
Free cash flow	$43,000 − $9,000 − $6,000 = $28,000	$69,000 − $17,000 − $4,000 = $48,000

(c) Cash flow decreased as the company entered the decline phase.

DO IT! 13-5
Operating Activities—
Direct Method

DENHAM LTD.
Statement of Cash Flows (partial)
Year Ended December 31, 2018

Operating activities		
Cash receipts from customers		$ 848,000[1]
Cash payments		
To suppliers	$(529,000)[2]	
For administrative expenses	(45,000)[3]	
To employees	(148,000)[4]	
For interest	(12,000)	
For income tax	(26,000)[5]	(760,000)
Net cash provided by operating activities		88,000

Calculations:
[1]Cash receipts from customers: $890,000 – $42,000 (accounts receivable) = $848,000
[2]Payments to suppliers: $465,000 + $44,000 (inventory) + $20,000 (accounts payable) = $529,000
[3]Payments for administrative expenses: $46,000 – $2,000 (prepaid expenses) + $1,000 (accrued expenses payable) = $45,000
[4]Payments to employees: $150,000 – $2,000 (salaries payable) = $148,000
[5]Payments for income tax: $36,000 – $10,000 (income tax payable) = $26,000

▶ **PRACTICE USING THE DECISION TOOLKIT**

(a) Stantec uses the direct method to prepare the operating activities section of its statement of cash flows.

(b) (in thousands)

	2015	2014
Free cash flow	$205,519 – ($38,084 – $462) – $38,334 = $129,563	$207,221 – ($42,706 – $176) – $33,641 = $131,050

Stantec's free cash flow is relatively unchanged in 2015 compared with 2014. In 2015, reductions in capital expenditures were offset by increases in dividend payments.

(c) Cash from operating activities dropped significantly in 2014 compared with 2013 because cash paid to suppliers and employees increased by more than the increase in cash from customers. Cash from operating activities in 2015 decreased slightly compared with 2014. Increases in cash from customers were mostly offset by increases in payments to suppliers and employees.

Cash used in investing activities increased in each year primarily due to business acquisitions, even though these were offset by reductions in the purchases of investments and in property, plant, and equipment.

Cash used in financing activities decreased in 2014 compared with 2013 as net payments to banks declined. This decline was offset in part by lower proceeds from the sale of shares and increased dividend payments. In 2015, cash used in financing activities rose primarily due to increased dividend and lease payments and lower proceeds from the sale of shares.

In both 2013 and 2014, the cash provided by operating cash flows exceeded the cash used in investing activities. In both years, cash was used in financing activities but overall, cash flow increased. However, in 2015, cash used in investing activities exceeded the cash provided by operating activities primarily because of business acquisitions. This excess caused an overall cash flow decrease and decline in cash and equivalent balances in that year.

▶ **PRACTICE COMPREHENSIVE DO IT!**

(a)

KOSINSKI INC.
Statement of Cash Flows—Indirect Method
Year Ended December 31, 2018

Operating activities		
Net income		$480,000
Adjustments to reconcile net income to net cash provided by operating activities		
Depreciation expense	$ 300,000	
Amortization expense	80,000	
Loss on disposal of machinery	24,000	
Increase in accounts receivable	(165,000)	
Decrease in inventory	33,000	
Increase in accounts payable	20,000	
Increase in income tax payable	28,000	320,000
Net cash provided by operating activities		800,000
Investing activities		
Proceeds from disposal of machinery	$ 270,000	
Purchase of machinery (see Note x)	(850,000)	
Net cash used by investing activities		(580,000)

Financing activities		
Payment of dividends	$(100,000)	
Net cash used by financing activities		(100,000)
Net increase in cash		120,000
Cash, January 1		30,000
Cash, December 31		$150,000

Note x: Machinery was purchased for $1,250,000 and partially financed by the issue of a $400,000 bank loan payable.

(b) Both the indirect and direct methods would report the same net cash provided by operating activities, but include different detail within each section. Both methods would report the same totals and detail for the investing and financing activities section. Both methods arrive at the same change in cash for the period and ending cash balances.

▶ **PRACTICE OBJECTIVE-FORMAT QUESTIONS**

1.   (b), (d), (e), and (g) are correct

Feedback
Operating activities include a company's principal income-producing activities, such as selling inventory, collecting receivables, and paying wages.
(a)   and (f) are incorrect because borrowing from a bank and paying dividends are financing activities.
(c)   Is incorrect because purchasing non-current assets is an investing activity.

2.   (a) and (e) are correct

Feedback
When we use the indirect method for determining cash provided (used) by operations, we list net income first and then we need to adjust this accrual-based amount for the effects of any noncash revenues and expenses to determine cash flows provided (used) by operating activities.
(a)   and (e) are correct because a decrease in an asset such as accounts receivable indicates that more cash was collected from customers than the amount of sales recorded, thereby increasing cash flows from operating activities. Meanwhile, a decrease in prepaid insurance means that a portion of insurance expense arose not from a cash payment but from the expiry of a prepaid. Therefore, cash paid for insurance was less than insurance expense, thereby increasing cash flows from operating activities.
(b)   Is incorrect because a decrease in accounts payable would cause cash provided by operating activities to decrease because it was used to repay such a liability.
(c)   Is incorrect because dividend-related payments and movements in dividends payable accounts affect financing cash flows.
(d)   Is incorrect because term deposits maturing within 90 days are a cash equivalent and the statement of cash flows reports the reasons for cash and equivalent changes by reporting the "other side" of cash transactions. For example, if the term deposit was decreased, the funds may have been spent on equipment. However, this effect would be reported in the investing section of the cash flow statement as an equipment purchase. Therefore, there is no need to separately report the change in the term deposit because doing so would be double-counting the effect of this cash flow.
(f)   Is incorrect because an increase in inventory would cause a reduction in cash flows and therefore this effect would be deducted from net income to arrive at cash provided (used) by operating activities.
(g)   Is incorrect because changes in common shares are a financing activity.

3.   (a), (b), and (c) are correct

Feedback
Given the information provided in the question, we can create T accounts to understand these items as follows:

Land		Buildings		Accumulated Depreciation	
500,000		1,400,000			300,000
	250,000		200,000	150,000	
(1)		(2)			(3)
750,000		2,200,000			270,000

As we can see from the above, information pertaining to increases in these three accounts is missing but we can derive that information as follows:
(1)   Land purchases are $500,000 ($500,000 − $250,000 + Purchases = $750,000)
(2)   Building purchases are $1,000,000 ($1,400,000 − $200,000 + Purchases = $2,200,000)
(3)   Depreciation expense is $120,000 ($300,000 − $150,000 + Depreciation expense = $270,000)

Other missing information that needs to be derived are the proceeds from the sale of the land and the building:

Gain from land sale = Proceeds − Cost of land sold
$100,000 = Proceeds − $250,000
Proceeds = $350,000

Loss from building sale = Carrying amount of building sold − Proceeds
$10,000 = ($200,000 − $150,000) − Proceeds
Proceeds = $40,000

(d) Is incorrect because the amount is incorrect—the proceeds from the sale of the building are $40,000. Note, however, that the correct amount of the proceeds from the sale of the building would be classified as an investing activity.

(e) and (f) are incorrect because even though they have been calculated properly, a loss or a gain would be shown in the operating activities section of the statement when using the indirect method and not shown at all if using the direct method.

(g) Is incorrect because depreciation would be shown in the operating activities section of the statement when using the indirect method and not shown at all if using the direct method.

4.   (c), (d), (f), and (g) are correct

Feedback

Operating activities include the cash effects of transactions that create revenues and expenses.

(a) Is incorrect because an increase in a current asset such as prepaid insurance means that cash was spent to increase that prepaid balance. Therefore, this change to the prepaid insurance should be deducted in determining cash provided (used) by operating activities.

(b) Is incorrect because changes in dividends payable relate to financing activities.

(c) Is correct because cash is used to increase inventory balances so this should be shown as a reduction in cash provided (used) by operating activities.

(d) Is correct because cash is used in order to reduce accounts payable so it is appropriate to deduct such a change in arriving at cash provided (used) by operating activities.

(e) Is incorrect because movements in mortgage-related accounts are financing, not operating, activities.

(f) Is correct because when an increase in income tax payable arises, it occurs because a portion of income tax expense is not paid. Therefore, this will increase operating cash flows and this effect would be added to net income in arriving at cash provided (used) by operating cash flows.

(g) Is correct because a decrease in accounts receivable occurs when cash received from customers exceeds sales revenue. Therefore, it is appropriate to add this change to net income in arriving at cash provided (used) by operating activities.

5.   (b), (d), and (e) are correct

Feedback

Cash flows pertaining to changes in non-current liabilities and their related current portions as well as changes to equity not shown in comprehensive income are typically shown as financing activities. Cash flows pertaining to income statement items are considered operating activities.

(a) Is incorrect because the portion of the mortgage payment relating to interest is an operating activity. Only the portion pertaining to the principal would be treated as a financing activity in the statement of cash flows.

(b) Is correct. When we explain cash receipts and payments pertaining to the mortgage in the statement of cash flows, we determine this information on an aggregate basis, combining movements in the current and non-current portions. In this case, we know that the current and non-current mortgage balances increased in total by $75,000 and that $31,000 of the principal portion of the mortgage was paid down. Therefore, new mortgages amounting to $106,000 must have been received during the year in order for these accounts to increase by $75,000 in total.

(c) Is incorrect because interest payments are operating activities. Note also that the amount calculated is also incorrect. Interest expense was $7,000 but only $5,000 of it was paid, which caused the Interest Payable account to increase by $2,000.

(d) Is correct. If retained earnings increased by $88,000 during the year and net income was $100,000, we can assume that dividends declared must have accounted for the difference of $12,000. To decrease the dividends payable by $1,000, the company must have paid out dividends that exceeded the amount declared by $1,000, which is equal to $13,000. This would have been shown as a financing activity.

(e) Is correct. The amount is stated in the question and it is a financing cash flow.

(f) Is incorrect; see the answer to part (d).

(g) Is incorrect. Although the amount of interest paid is correct, this payment is an operating activity, not a financing activity.

6.   (c), (d), (e), and (g) are correct

Feedback

The totals for each section of the statement of cash flows can be determined as follows. Note that under ASPE, interest received from a bond investment would be considered an operating activity, although under IFRS, this could also be classified as an investing activity.

	Investing Activities	Financing Activities	Other
Proceeds from land disposal	$100,000		
Issue of common shares for cash		$70,000	
Issue of common shares to acquire land			Disclosed only
Payment of cash dividends		(50,000)	
Purchase of equipment	(110,000)		
Gain on sale of land			Not a cash flow
Interest received from bond investments			Operating activity
Payment of interest			Operating activity
Total	$ (10,000)	$20,000	

(a) and (b) are incorrect; see the above calculations.

(f)　Is incorrect because IFRS allows the payment of dividends to be shown as an operating activity or as a financing activity.

7.　(a), (c), and (f) are correct

Feedback
Borrowing funds to buy land causes an increase in cash provided by financing activities and causes an increase in cash used by investing activities. There is no impact on operating activities in 2018, although next year, the interest expense on the loan will be treated as an operating activity (or possibly a financing activity if IFRS is used). Free cash flow is equal to operating cash flows less capital expenditures and dividends. Therefore, these transactions will cause free cash flow to fall by the amounts paid for the land and for the increase in dividends, which in total is $10 million.
(a)　Is correct because the purchase of the land and the receipt of the loan have no effect on operating cash flows this year.
(b)　Is incorrect because the cash used by investing activities will increase because of the purchase of land.
(c)　Is correct because cash provided by financing activities will increase because of the receipt of the bank loan.
(d)　Is incorrect because free cash flow will decrease by $10 million.
(e)　Is incorrect. Because of the increased dividend payment, free cash flow will decrease.
(f)　Is correct because the land purchase is a capital expenditure and this transaction will decrease free cash flow.
(g)　Is incorrect because free cash flow increases when operating cash flows increase or through reductions in capital expenditures and dividends, which is not occurring.

8.　(a) and (f) are correct

Feedback
When the repair expense is corrected, net income will increase and this will increase cash provided by operating activities and increase cash used by investing activities. (The fact that depreciation will rise is irrelevant because it is not a cash flow.) When the land was exchanged for common shares, no cash flow occurred. Therefore, the effect of this transaction is not shown on the statement of cash flows but would be disclosed in a note instead.
(a)　Is correct because the repair expense is removed from net income and this in turn will cause cash flows from operating activities to increase by $100,000.
(b)　Is incorrect; see the answer to part (a).
(c)　Is incorrect because the equipment was paid for with cash. Therefore, cash used by investing activities will increase by $100,000, not by the $150,000 pertaining to land, because this asset was not paid for using cash but by issuing common shares.
(d)　Is incorrect. Cash used by investing activities will increase by $100,000; see the answer to part (c).
(e)　Is incorrect. Cash used by investing activities will increase by $100,000; see the answer to part (c).
(f)　Is correct. The common shares were issued in exchange for land so there is no financing cash flow effect at all.
(g)　Is incorrect. If the common shares had been issued for cash, this would be correct, but they were issued for land so no cash flows were affected.

9.　(d), (e), (f), and (g) are correct

Feedback
Standard Inc. will have net cash used by operating activities because it is unprofitable, which has caused the difficulty with the bank. The company will have net cash provided by investing activities because it is selling its assets and it will have net cash used by financing activities because payments are being made to the bank, they are not being received from the bank. Because General Ltd. just went public, it will report net cash provided by financing activities, and because its revenues are not high enough, the company will have net cash used by operating activities. It will most likely use the IPO proceeds to invest in non-current assets, so it will report net cash used by investing activities.

10.　(b) and (d) are correct

Feedback
When we use the direct method for determining cash provided (used) by operating activities, we essentially list an income statement presented on a cash basis.
(a), (e), and (f) are incorrect because depreciation, amortization, and gains on disposals are not items that give rise to a cash payment or cash receipt.
(b)　and (d) are correct because these items report information from the income statement on a cash basis (not on an accrual basis) so they are correctly shown on a direct-method statement of cash flows.
(c)　Is incorrect because, even though income tax expense is eventually paid, the amount of income taxes paid may differ from income tax expense, thereby giving rise to changes in income tax payable. When using the direct method, we must report the expenses paid directly.
(g)　Is incorrect because dividend payments are a financing activity (although under IFRS they can also be treated as an operating activity).

▶ ENDNOTE

[1] "Teck Announces Partners Proceeding with Fort Hills Oil Sands Project," Teck Resources Limited news release, October 30, 2013; Teck Resources Limited annual reports, 2009 to 2015.

14

Performance Measurement

CHAPTER PREVIEW

Throughout many chapters in this textbook, you have been introduced to ratios that can be used to gain a better understanding of the solvency, liquidity, and profitability of a company. We will use all of these ratios in this chapter. We will also introduce you to other analysis techniques, such as horizontal and vertical analysis, as we analyze Hudson's Bay Company and compare its performance with another Canadian retailer, Dollarama Inc., and their industry. This will give you a comprehensive look at the financial analysis tools a company's stakeholders use to help them make decisions. This chapter will also help you to appreciate the limits that stakeholders face when performing such analysis.

CHAPTER OUTLINE

LEARNING OBJECTIVES	READ	PRACTICE
1 Explain and apply comparative analysis.	• Horizontal analysis • Vertical analysis • Ratio analysis	**DO IT!** 14-1a Horizontal analysis 14-1b Vertical analysis
2 Calculate and interpret ratios that are used to analyze liquidity.	• Working capital • Current ratio • Receivables turnover • Inventory turnover • Liquidity conclusion • Summary of liquidity ratios	**DO IT!** 14-2 Liquidity analysis
3 Calculate and interpret ratios that are used to analyze solvency.	• Debt to total assets • Times interest earned • Free cash flow • Solvency conclusion • Summary of solvency ratios	**DO IT!** 14-3 Solvency analysis
4 Calculate and interpret ratios that are used to analyze profitability.	• Gross profit margin • Profit margin • Asset turnover • Return on assets • Return on common shareholders' equity • Basic earnings per share • Price-earnings (P-E) ratio • Payout ratio • Dividend yield • Profitability conclusion • Summary of profitability ratios	**DO IT!** 14-4 Profitability analysis
5 Understand the limitations of financial analysis.	• Diversification • Alternative accounting policies and estimates • Other comprehensive income • Discontinued operations • Nonrecurring items	**DO IT!** 14-5 Limitations of financial analysis

FEATURE STORY

The Canadian Press Images/Francis Vachon

In its first two centuries, the Hudson's Bay Company, created by a royal charter from King Charles II in 1670, was largely a fur trader. The company had outposts in the interior of what would become Canada almost 200 years after the company was formed. The company would trade goods such as kettles and blankets for furs. Employees in charge of the trading posts sent an annual letter to the headquarters in London, England, tallying the year's activities and enclosing their financial account books. With only a yearly update, head office did not have the financial information needed to react quickly to changing market conditions and opportunities. Its business strategy was simply to expand its trading territory, which eventually stretched from sea to sea to sea.

After leaving the fur trading business and evolving into a department store in the late 1800s, today the Hudson's Bay Company or HBC, the oldest continuing corporation in North America, electronically tracks its accounts daily. Its head office, now in Toronto, has instant access to financial information and uses it for decision-making, including decisions about how to position itself in the highly competitive retail industry.

In recent years, HBC's ownership has changed hands several times. In 2006, the company was purchased by American businessman Jerry Zucker, who died in 2008. Shortly after Zucker's death, the company was bought by a U.S. equity group owned by U.S. real estate investor Richard Baker. In 2012, HBC became a publicly traded corporation with a $365-million initial public offering to raise money to pay down debt and return some ownership to Canadian hands.

From the Fur Trade to Fifth Avenue

HBC's recent strategy has been to specialize in the high-end market. Two years before buying HBC, Mr. Baker purchased U.S. luxury department store Lord & Taylor, which is now part of Hudson's Bay Company. In 2011, HBC started moving away from the discount retail business by announcing it would sell the leases for most of its Zellers and Fields discount stores for $1.8 billion to U.S.-based Target Corporation.

In mid-2013, HBC announced a deal to purchase iconic American luxury retailer Saks Inc. for U.S. $2.9 billion. As of the time of writing, HBC had opened two Saks stores and four Saks Off Fifth discount luxury stores in Canada. In 2015, HBC bought Galeria Holdings, which operates department stores in Germany and Belgium. That same year, HBC sold some of its valuable real estate to establish joint ventures with real estate companies, which allowed it to pay down $1 billion of debt on its balance sheet. In 2016, HBC bought American online luxury retailer Gilt Groupe.

HBC has 90 Hudson's Bay department stores across Canada, along with 69 Home Outfitters stores that sell home decor items. With its openings of Saks and Lord & Taylor stores in Canada, HBC plans to compete in the high-end market with competitors such as U.S. department store Nordstrom, which began to open stores in Canada in 2014. Hudson's Bay Company and its shareholders and potential investors will be relying on financial information to measure its performance in the changing retail landscape.[1]

Go to the *REVIEW AND PRACTICE* section at the end of the chapter for a targeted summary and practice questions with solutions.

Visit **WileyPLUS** for more practice opportunities.

LEARNING
OBJECTIVE ▶1

Explain and apply comparative analysis.

Investors, lenders, and other creditors are interested in making comparisons about a company's past and current financial performance and position in order to better determine future expectations about that company. These comparisons are called comparative analysis.

Various tools are available to help users make comparisons of a company's financial data. We will explain and illustrate horizontal and vertical analysis, two commonly used tools in comparative analysis. But first, we should note that, while a company's financial statement data are usually the starting point in any analysis, it is important to review nonfinancial information as well. Nonfinancial information includes information found in a company's annual report, such as its mission, strategy, goals and objectives, and management discussion and analysis (MD&A). Understanding this information is important when interpreting financial performance, as we learned in our feature story about HBC.

As we know from the feature story, HBC's strategy is to operate several different types of retail chains (or banners) in different geographic areas. The company operates Hudson's Bay Company and Saks stores in Canada, Lord & Taylor and Saks stores in the United States, and the Galeria group in Europe. HBC acquired Saks in November 2013 and the Galeria group in September 2015. In 2014, the HBC board of directors believed that the real estate assets of the company were not "core" assets needed by a retailer, so starting in 2014 and more extensively in 2015, the company sold off some of its significant real estate holdings to various joint ventures in exchange for either cash or an interest in these joint ventures. In 2015, the company began to earn income from these ventures.

HORIZONTAL ANALYSIS

Horizontal analysis, also called **trend analysis**, is a technique to determine the change (increase or decrease) over time that has taken place in a series of financial statement data. This change can be expressed as either an amount or a percentage.

Horizontal analysis is used in intracompany comparisons. You will recall from earlier chapters that intracompany comparisons involve financial data *within* a company, comparing current financial data with those of one or more prior periods, usually years. Comparisons within a company are often useful to detect significant trends. For example, annual net sales for a four-year period for HBC are shown in Illustration 14-1 in dollars (in millions) and percentages.

▼ **HELPFUL HINT**
The term *horizontal analysis* means that we view financial statement data from left to right (or right to left) across time.

▶Illustration 14-1
Horizontal analysis for Hudson's Bay Company sales

	2015	2014	2013	2012
Net sales	$11,162	$8,169	$5,223	$4,077
% of base-year (2012) amount	273.8%	200.4%	128.1%	100.0%
% change for the year	36.6%	56.4%	28.1%	—

Using 2012 as the base year, we can express net sales in each year as a percentage of the base-year (or period if less than a year) amount shown on the second line of Illustration 14-1. We call this a **horizontal percentage of a base-period amount**. This percentage is calculated by dividing the amount for the specific year (or period) we are analyzing by the base-year (or period) amount, as shown in Illustration 14-2.

▶Illustration 14-2
Horizontal percentage of a base-period amount formula

$$\text{Horizontal Percentage of Base-Period Amount} = \text{Analysis-Period Amount} \div \text{Base-Period Amount}$$

We can use horizontal analysis on the Hudson's Bay Company's sales shown in Illustration 14-1 to determine that net sales in 2015 were 273.8% of net sales in 2012. We do this by dividing $11,162 million by $4,077 million. In other words, sales in 2015 were 173.8% greater than sales four years earlier in 2012.

Reviewing the percentages of base-year amounts shown in the second row of Illustration 14-1, we can easily see the trend of the company's net sales, which have steadily improved since 2012. You should remember, however, that it would be difficult to properly interpret the company's past performance over this time period without fully understanding the strategic decisions it made and the underlying economic environment. For example, Hudson's Bay acquired Saks in late 2013 so the large increase in sales in 2014 occurred mainly because Saks's sales were included in sales for that year. If we review detailed information provided by HBC in its MD&A about its sales, we can determine that over 60% of the sales increase in 2015 occurred because the Galeria group's sales for the last quarter of 2015 were now included in the sales amounts and over 30% of the remaining increase came from Saks stores, not Hudson's Bay stores in Canada.

We can also use horizontal analysis to measure the percentage change for the year or period (between any two periods of time) by calculating a **horizontal percentage change for the period**. This is calculated by dividing the dollar amount of the change between the specific year (or period) under analysis and the prior year (or period) by the prior-year (or period) amount, as shown in Illustration 14-3.

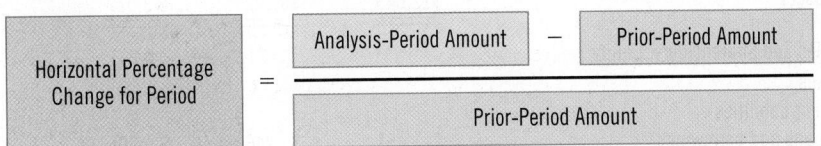

►Illustration 14-3
Horizontal percentage change for period formula

For example, we can determine that Hudson's Bay's sales increased by $2,993 million ($11,162 − $8,169) in 2015 compared with 2014. This increase can then be expressed as a percentage by dividing the amount of the change between the two years of $2,993 million by the amount in the prior year, the 2014 net sales of $8,169 million. Thus, in 2015, sales increased by 36.6% compared with 2014. The horizontal percentage change in sales for each of the last four years is presented in the last row of Illustration 14-1. Note that no change can be calculated for the first year in our example, 2012, because 2011 data were not included.

We will apply horizontal analysis, calculating the percentage change for each year, to compare HBC's statement of financial position and income statement in the next sections. We will also use other financial and nonfinancial information found in the company's annual report to help us understand some of the reasons for the changes we will observe by comparing these statements.

Statement of Financial Position

Condensed statements of financial position, which the company chooses to call the balance sheet, for fiscal 2015 (as at January 30, 2016) and for fiscal 2014 (as at January 31, 2015), showing dollar and percentage changes for the two-year period, are shown in Illustration 14-4.

Note that in a horizontal analysis, while the amount column of the increase or decrease is additive (the total change in assets is an increase of $3,527 million), the percentage column is not additive. That is, 38.7% is not a total but just the percentage change in the total.

The horizontal analysis of Hudson's Bay's comparative statement of financial position shows that several changes occurred between 2015 and 2014. As stated earlier, no interpretation of amounts in financial statements can be done without an understanding of the strategic decisions and key transactions undertaken by the company. After the Galeria group was acquired in 2015, we would expect an increase in most assets because the entire company has grown in size due to this acquisition. Another strategic decision made by Hudson's Bay in 2015 was to sell many of its real estate assets to real estate joint ventures in exchange for a percentage ownership in those joint ventures.

In the current assets section, cash increased by 201.8%. It is helpful to look at the statement of cash flows to determine the cause of key changes in cash during the year. After reviewing this statement (not illustrated here), we learn that the increase in cash is primarily because less cash was required for financing activities in 2015 than in the prior year.

▶Illustration 14-4

Horizontal analysis of balance sheet (percentage change for year)

HUDSON'S BAY COMPANY
Balance Sheet
January 30, 2016, and January 31, 2015
(in millions)

	2015	2014	Increase (Decrease) Amount	Percentage
Assets				
Current assets				
Cash	$ 507	$ 168	$ 339	201.8%
Trade and other receivables	512	212	300	141.5%
Inventories	3,415	2,319	1,096	47.3%
Other current assets	194	100	94	94.0%
Total current assets	4,628	2,799	1,829	65.3%
Property, plant, and equipment	5,154	4,606	548	11.9%
Intangible assets	1,774	1,313	461	35.1%
Other assets	1,093	404	689	170.5%
Total assets	$12,649	$9,122	$ 3,527	38.7%
Liabilities and Shareholders' Equity				
Liabilities				
Current liabilities				
Loans and borrowings	$ 451	$ 246	$ 205	83.3%
Trade payables and accrued liabilities	2,514	1,548	966	62.4%
Unearned revenue	132	130	2	1.5%
Provisions and other	299	220	79	35.9%
Total current liabilities	3,396	2,144	1,252	58.4%
Non-current liabilities	6,154	4,504	1,650	36.6%
Total liabilities	9,550	6,648	2,902	43.7%
Shareholders' equity	3,099	2,474	625	25.3%
Total liabilities and shareholders' equity	$12,649	$9,122	$ 3,527	38.7%

The analysis also shows that accounts receivable increased by $300 million, or 141.5%. We will look at the income statement in the next section to determine if sales and accounts receivable changed by the same percentage. Inventories increased by $1,096 million, or 47.3%. Similar to accounts receivable, we will look at the income statement to determine if cost of goods sold and inventory increased by the same percentage. We will also review the receivables and inventory turnover ratios in later sections to assess the company's ability to collect its receivables and sell its merchandise.

With respect to non-current assets, property, plant, and equipment increased by $548 million, or 11.9%, due to the acquisition of the Galeria group. However, this effect was partially offset by reductions as real estate assets were sold off. Intangible assets rose by $461 million, or 35.1%, due to the Galeria acquisition. Other assets consist primarily of investments in real estate joint ventures, which increased by $689 million or 170.5% as the company sold real estate in exchange for an interest in these joint ventures.

In 2015, Hudson's Bay's total current liabilities increased by $1,252 million for a number of reasons. Current bank borrowings increased by $205 million or 83.3% because it made more bank borrowings to finance the purchase of the Galeria group. Furthermore, trade payables and accrued liabilities increased by $966 million or 62.4% because Galeria payables are now included in this amount. The company's non-current liabilities increased by $1,650 million or 36.6%, as funds were borrowed for the Galeria acquisition.

The company's total shareholders' equity increased by $625 million or 25.3% in 2015 due to increased net income, causing a corresponding increase in retained earnings less dividends. We will see below why net income increased.

Income Statement

Illustration 14-5 presents a horizontal analysis of HBC's condensed income statement for the fiscal years 2015 and 2014.

▶Illustration 14-5
Horizontal analysis of income statement (percentage change for year)

HUDSON'S BAY COMPANY
Statement of Earnings
Years Ended January 30, 2016, and January 31, 2015
(in millions)

			Increase (Decrease)	
	2015	2014	Amount	Percentage
Net sales	$11,162	$ 8,169	$ 2,993	36.6%
Cost of sales	6,638	4,901	1,737	35.4%
Gross profit	4,524	3,268	1,256	38.4%
Operating expenses	(4,526)	(3,103)	1,423	45.9%
Other operating income	684	308	376	122.1%
Income from operations	682	473	209	44.2%
Other revenues and expenses				
Interest expense	(225)	(218)	(7)	3.2%
Other	62	(44)	106	240.9%
Income before income tax	519	211	308	146.0%
Income tax benefit (expense)	(132)	22	(154)	(700.0)%
Net income	$ 387	$ 233	$ 154	66.1%

A horizontal analysis of the income statement (HBC calls it a statement of earnings) shows that net sales increased by $2,993 million, or 36.6%. Over 30% of this increase came from higher sales in Saks stores in the United States and over 60% of the increase came from the sales of the Galeria group, which are now included in Hudson's Bay's results. A similar increase occurred with cost of goods sold (or cost of sales as HBC calls it), which increased by $1,737 million or 35.4%. This is slightly less than the increase in net sales in percentage terms.

HBC's operating expenses increased by $1,423 million, or 45.9%, primarily because of the inclusion of the Galeria group's expenses. However, this increase is greater than the sales increase because operating expenses also include some one-time expenses for the acquisition of the Galeria group. Other operating income has more than doubled because of gains arising from the sale of real estate assets to joint ventures. Interest expense, on the other hand, has not changed significantly. Other revenues and expenses, which relate primarily to income from joint ventures, have increased because of the increased investment in these joint ventures. Because the company was not taxable in 2014, it received income tax refunds shown on the income statement as an income tax benefit. In 2015, however, the company was taxable and a tax expense was recorded.

The measurement of changes in percentages from period to period is fairly straightforward and quite useful. However, the calculations can be affected by complications. For example, if an item has a small value in a base year and a large value in the next year, the percentage change, although large, may not be meaningful. Look at the 122.1% increase in other operating income in Illustration 14-5. This is because the base-year amount was relatively low. In addition, if an item has no value in a base year and a value in the next year, no percentage change can be determined. Finally, if a negative amount appears in the base-year and a positive amount in the following year, or vice versa, the percentage change will exceed 100% as it does above with the change in other revenues and expenses. In many cases, such a percentage change should not be calculated, although we did so above for illustration purposes only.

We have not done a horizontal analysis of the Hudson's Bay Company statement of comprehensive income (which it presents separately from its income statement), statement of changes in equity, and statement of cash flows because analyses of these statements are not as useful as horizontal analyses pertaining to the statement of financial position and income statement. The amounts presented in these other statements already give details of the changes between two periods.

DO IT! ▶14-1a Horizontal Analysis

Action Plan

✔ Horizontal percentage of the base-year amount: Set the base-year (2015) dollar amounts at 100%. Express each subsequent year's amount as a percentage of the base-period amount by dividing the dollar amount for the year under analysis by the base-year amount.

✔ Horizontal percentage change for year: Divide the dollar amount of the change between the current and prior years by the prior-year amount.

Selected condensed information (in thousands) from Bonora Ltd.'s income statement for four years ended June 30 follows:

	2018	2017	2016	2015
Net sales	$37,600	$36,500	$38,700	$40,500
Cost of goods sold	14,900	14,200	13,800	15,300
Gross profit	22,700	22,300	24,900	25,200
Operating expenses	18,500	17,400	16,200	17,600
Income from operations	4,200	4,900	8,700	7,600
Income tax expense	1,050	1,225	2,175	1,900
Net income	$ 3,150	$ 3,675	$ 6,525	$ 5,700

Using horizontal analysis, calculate (a) the percentage of the base-year amount for each year, assuming that 2015 is the base year, and (b) the percentage change for each year (that is, between each of the following sets of years: 2018 and 2017, 2017 and 2016, and 2016 and 2015).

SOLUTION

Try this Do It! exercise on your own and then check your answer at the end of the chapter.

Related Exercise Material: BE14–1, BE14–2, and E14–1.

VERTICAL ANALYSIS

Vertical analysis, also called **common size analysis**, is a technique that expresses each item in a financial statement as a percentage of a total (base) amount within the same financial statement. Note that while horizontal analysis compares data across more than one year, vertical analysis compares data within the same year.

Vertical analysis expresses account balances in percentage terms known as the **vertical percentage of a base amount**. These percentages are calculated by dividing the financial statement amount under analysis by the base amount in that particular financial statement, as shown in Illustration 14-6.

▶Illustration 14-6

Vertical percentage of a base amount formula

Vertical Percentage of Base Amount	=	Analysis Amount	÷	Base Amount

▼ **HELPFUL HINT**

The term *vertical analysis* means that we view rows of financial statement data from up to down (or down to up) within the same period of time.

The base amount commonly used for the statement of financial position is *total assets* (or total liabilities and shareholders' equity, which equals total assets) because that is the largest amount on the statement. For example, we might say that current assets are 43.8% of total assets (total assets being the base amount). The base amount for the income statement is usually *revenues* for a service company and *net sales* for a merchandising company, again, because that is usually the largest amount on that statement. Because of this, we might say that cost of goods sold is 61.0% of net sales (net sales being the base amount).

Vertical analysis is used in both intracompany and intercompany comparisons. Vertical analysis is helpful to compare financial data both *within* a company and *between* one or more competitor companies, especially if the competitor is much larger or smaller, because vertical analysis expresses all items on a common base of total assets or total revenues (net sales).

Statement of Financial Position

Illustration 14-7 presents a vertical analysis of HBC's comparative statement of financial position.

►Illustration 14-7
Vertical analysis of statement of financial position

HUDSON'S BAY COMPANY
Balance Sheet
January 30, 2016, and
January 31, 2015
(in millions)

	2015		2014	
	Amount	Percentage	Amount	Percentage
Assets				
Current assets				
Cash	$ 507	4.0%	$ 168	1.8%
Trade and other receivables	512	4.0%	212	2.3%
Inventories	3,415	27.0%	2,319	25.4%
Other current assets	194	1.5%	100	1.1%
Total current assets	4,628	36.6%	2,799	30.7%
Property, plant, and equipment	5,154	40.7%	4,606	50.5%
Intangible assets	1,774	14.0%	1,313	14.4%
Other assets	1,093	8.6%	404	4.4%
Total assets	$12,649	100.0%	$9,122	100.0%
Liabilities and Shareholders' Equity				
Liabilities				
Current liabilities				
Loans and borrowings	$ 451	3.6%	$ 246	2.7%
Trade payables and accrued liabilities	2,514	19.9%	1,548	17.0%
Unearned revenue	132	1.0%	130	1.4%
Provisions and other	299	2.4%	220	2.4%
Total current liabilities	3,396	26.8%	2,144	23.5%
Non-current liabilities	6,154	48.7%	4,504	49.4%
Total liabilities	9,550	75.5%	6,648	72.9%
Shareholders' equity	3,099	24.5%	2,474	27.1%
Total liabilities and shareholders' equity	$12,649	100.0%	$9,122	100.0%

In contrast to the percentage changes shown in the horizontal analysis section, the percentage changes in the vertical analysis are additive. That is, if you add the vertical percentages in the 2015 and 2014 columns above, they should sum to 100.0%. However, because the percentage changes shown above have been rounded to one decimal place not all the percentage columns add perfectly. This is due solely to rounding discrepancies.

Vertical analysis shows the relative size of each item in the statement of financial position compared with a base amount. It can be prepared for one or more years, as we have shown in Illustration 14-7. It is also useful to compare vertically prepared information for multiple periods with similar information provided earlier in our horizontal analysis. In 2015, the most significant change affecting Hudson's Bay's assets was a decrease in property, plant, and equipment, which fell from 50.5% to 40.7% of total assets. Even though Galeria was acquired, some real estate assets were sold to joint ventures in exchange for an interest in these joint ventures and this caused the decrease in property, plant, and equipment percentage. The increase in other assets from 4.4% to 8.6% of total assets was caused by increases from investments in these joint ventures.

We also see that current liabilities increased from 23.5% to 26.8% of total assets, due primarily to increases in trade payables, but this was also offset by increases in cash, indicating that payables were not paid as quickly as in 2014. Non-current liabilities have changed very little.

Shareholders' equity decreased from 27.1% to 24.5% of total assets. This decrease is primarily due to the fact that, although 100% of the assets of Galeria are now included in Hudson's Bay's statement of financial position, retained earnings were only increased by Galeria's income since the date it was acquired, which was September 30, 2015. As a result, Galeria's impact on assets and liabilities was more significant than its impact on retained earnings and shareholders' equity.

Income Statement

Illustration 14-8 presents a vertical analysis of Hudson's Bay's comparative income statement for fiscal 2015 and 2014.

▶Illustration 14-8
Vertical analysis of income statement

		HUDSON'S BAY COMPANY Statement of Earnings Years Ended January 30, 2016, and January 31, 2015 (in millions)		
	2015		2014	
	Amount	Percentage	Amount	Percentage
Net sales	$11,162	100.0%	$8,169	100.0%
Cost of sales	6,638	59.5%	4,901	60.0%
Gross profit	4,524	40.5%	3,268	40.0%
Operating expenses	(4,526)	(40.5)%	(3,103)	(38.0)%
Other operating income	684	6.1%	308	3.8%
Income from operations	682	6.1%	473	5.8%
Other revenues and expenses				
Interest expense	(225)	(2.0)%	(218)	(2.7)%
Other	62	0.6%	(44)	(0.5)%
Income before income tax	519	4.7%	211	2.6%
Income tax benefit (expense)	(132)	(1.2)%	22	0.3%
Net income	$ 387	3.5%	$ 233	2.9%

Percentage changes in horizontal analysis tend to be larger than percentage changes in vertical analysis but often reflect the same events. As we saw in our horizontal analysis shown in Illustration 14-5, both net sales and cost of sales rose significantly because of the acquisition of Galeria and higher sales from Saks. In the vertical analysis above, we can see that the gross profit as a percentage of sales remained relatively unchanged. This indicates that the growth strategy, although it increased the number of stores owned by the company, and total net sales, did not have a significant impact on the gross profit as a percentage of sales.

Similar to the vertical percentages shown in Illustration 14-7, the percentages shown in Illustration 14-8 should add vertically. However, minor rounding discrepancies may prevent this from occurring in some cases.

Although vertical analysis can also be performed on the other period statements—comprehensive income, changes in equity, and cash flows—this is seldom done. As mentioned earlier, these statements, by their very nature, provide an analysis of changes during the year.

Intercompany Comparisons

Vertical analysis also makes it easier to compare different companies. As we mentioned earlier, one of Hudson's Bay's competitors is Dollarama. We are going to compare these two companies to gain a better understanding of their performance. Dollarama's operations are different from HBC's in several areas, which we need to understand before analyzing the financial statements of each company. These differences include:

1. HBC has grown by buying other banners such as Saks in 2014 and the Galeria group in 2015. Dollarama has grown internally and has not acquired stores from other companies.
2. HBC owns the land and buildings of many of its stores. Dollarama owns some warehouses but its retail store locations are rented, not owned. In 2015, HBC sold some of its real estate assets to joint ventures, giving rise to large gains in return for an ownership interest in these entities. Consequently, HBC is earning investment income (rent) from these joint ventures. Dollarama has had no significant gains from the sale of its assets and does not have any investment income from real estate.
3. HBC operates 451 stores with 65.4 million square feet (about 6 million square metres) of retail space. Dollarama operates 1,030 stores with 10.6 million square feet (about 1 million square metres) of retail space. This means that the average Dollarama store is much smaller and the company tries to maximize its sales per square foot, which it does very effectively. In fact,

Dollarama generates $268 of sales per year for every square foot of space in its stores compared with $170 per square foot for Hudson's Bay.

Even though HBC is much larger than Dollarama, by using vertical analysis, we can make a more meaningful comparison of the condensed income statements of both of these companies. As shown in Illustration 14-9, vertical analysis reduces each financial statement item to a percentage that can be compared more easily than large differences in dollar amounts.

► Illustration 14-9
Intercompany comparison by vertical analysis

HUDSON'S BAY COMPANY AND DOLLARAMA INC.
Statements of Earnings
Year Ended January 30, 2016, and January 31, 2016
(in millions)

	Hudson's Bay		Dollarama	
	Amount	Percentage	Amount	Percentage
Net sales	$11,162	100.0%	$2,650	100.0%
Cost of sales	6,638	59.5%	1,617	61.0%
Gross profit	4,524	40.5%	1,033	39.0%
Operating expenses	(4,526)	(40.5)%	(484)	(18.3)%
Other operating income	684	6.1%	-0-	0.0%
Income from operations	682	6.1%	549	20.7%
Other revenues and expenses				
Interest expense	(225)	(2.0)%	(21)	(0.8)%
Other	62	0.6%	-0-	0.0%
Income before income tax	519	4.7%	528	19.9%
Income tax expense	(132)	(1.2)%	(143)	(5.4)%
Net income	$ 387	3.5%	$ 385	14.5%

For their fiscal years shown above, Hudson's Bay had a higher gross profit percentage, 40.5%, than Dollarama at 39.0%. Unlike Dollarama, Hudson's Bay has pursued a strategy of selling products with higher quality and prices. Normally one would expect such products to generate a higher gross profit, which they usually do, but Dollarama does a very good job at purchasing the products it sells at a very low cost.

It is interesting to note that Hudson's Bay's operating expenses are higher than Dollarama's, representing 40.5% of sales compared with Dollarama's 18.3%. This indicates that the management of Dollarama has either been very successful in keeping these expenses as low as possible or they have been very successful generating sales relative to operating expenses. Both of these reasons are true. Dollarama controls its operating costs more effectively, and as stated earlier, that company also generates more sales per square foot than HBC does.

Hudson's Bay's other operating income arose from one-time sales of real estate assets to joint ventures. Dollarama had no corresponding types of gains. It is important to understand that, without these gains that gave rise to higher other operating income, HBC would have reported a net loss in 2015.

Interest expense for Hudson's Bay was 2.0% of net sales compared with Dollarama at 0.8%. Both companies financed their assets with approximately the same level of debt, so their interest expense, relative to the size of each company, is comparable. The difference between these two percentages is caused by the fact that Dollarama generates more sales relative to its size than HBC. We can see this same effect with operating expenses, Dollarama simply generates more sales per square foot than Hudson's Bay does; therefore its operating expenses as a percentage of sales are also lower.

In dollar amounts, HBC's income before income tax and also its income tax expense are almost the same as Dollarama's. However, Dollarama's tax expense as a percentage of sales is much larger given its lower level of sales.

In summary, we can conclude from our comparative vertical analysis that other income played a major role in making HBC profitable and that Dollarama's control over its operating costs was essential in making that company profitable.

Without reference to the percentages shown in our vertical analysis, we can see that the net income of both companies is approximately the same. However, in order to earn that level of net income, HBC had significant gains from the sale of its real estate assets and it also had merchandise sales that were more than four times as high as Dollarama's.

Vertical analysis can also be used to compare two companies' statements of financial position, in addition to the income statement as we did above. We have not done so here because the information that would be obtained from doing this can also be derived from ratio analysis, which we will cover next.

DO IT! ▶14-1b   Vertical Analysis

Action Plan

✔ Set the base amount as net sales in an income statement.

✔ Vertical percentage of a base amount: Find the relative percentage by dividing the specific income statement amount by the base amount (net sales) for each year. Round your results to one decimal spot. Recall that, although the vertical percentage columns should add, minor rounding discrepancies may prevent this from happening.

Selected condensed information (in thousands) from Bonora Ltd.'s income statement for four years ended June 30 follows:

	2018	2017	2016	2015
Net sales	$37,600	$36,500	$38,700	$40,500
Cost of goods sold	14,900	14,200	13,800	15,300
Gross profit	22,700	22,300	24,900	25,200
Operating expenses	18,500	17,400	16,200	17,600
Income from operations	4,200	4,900	8,700	7,600
Income tax expense	1,050	1,225	2,175	1,900
Net income	$ 3,150	$ 3,675	$ 6,525	$ 5,700

Using vertical analysis, calculate the percentage of a base amount for each year.

> ### SOLUTION
> Try this Do It! exercise on your own and then check your answer at the end of the chapter.
>
> Related Exercise Material: BE14–3, BE14–4, BE14–5, E14–2, and E14–3.

RATIO ANALYSIS

Throughout many chapters in this textbook you have been introduced to the calculation of ratios. Similar to horizontal and vertical analyses, ratio analysis is also a comparative tool used to evaluate the significance of a company's financial data. However, ratio analysis is much broader than the other tools, because it can be used in all three types of comparisons (intracompany, intercompany, and industry) discussed in this text.

The first step in any comprehensive ratio analysis is to perform a horizontal and vertical analysis. This helps users understand some of the reasons for changes in financial position and performance, as well as identify further areas for investigation. Calculating and interpreting the meaning of ratios completes our overall analysis.

In the next three sections, we provide an example of comprehensive ratio analysis using the liquidity, solvency, and profitability ratios presented in past chapters. This analysis uses three categories of comparisons:

▼ **HELPFUL HINT**

A summary of ratios can be found on the back inside cover of this textbook.

1. intracompany, comparing two years of ratios for Hudson's Bay Company for 2015 and 2014;
2. intercompany, comparing ratios for Hudson's Bay Company and Dollarama Inc. for 2015 and 2014; and
3. industry, comparing ratios for both companies with industry averages for 2015 and 2014.

You will recall that Hudson's Bay's statement of financial position (which it calls a balance sheet) was presented earlier in the chapter in Illustration 14-4 and its income statement (which it calls a statement of earnings) in Illustration 14-5. We will use the information in these two financial statements, in addition to the following data, to calculate the Hudson's Bay Company's ratios:

(in millions, except for per-share data)	2015	2014
Net cash provided by operating activities	$ 18	$ 547
Net capital expenditures	$ 610	$ 426
Total cash dividends	$ 36	$ 36
Dividends per share	$ 0.20	$ 0.20
Market price per share	$17.30	$23.42
Weighted average number of shares	182	182

Note that HBC does not have any preferred shares.

Detailed calculations of the ratios that follow are not shown but you can use the above data and the statement of financial position and income statement data shown earlier in the chapter to recalculate the ratios for Hudson's Bay to make sure you understand where the numbers came from.

LEARNING
OBJECTIVE ▶2

Calculate and interpret ratios that are used to analyze liquidity.

Liquidity ratios measure a company's short-term ability to pay its maturing obligations and to meet unexpected needs for cash. Short-term lenders and other creditors, such as bankers and suppliers, are particularly interested in assessing liquidity. Liquidity ratios include working capital, the current ratio, receivables turnover, average collection period, inventory turnover, and days in inventory.

WORKING CAPITAL

Working capital is the difference between current assets and current liabilities. It is one measure of liquidity. However, as we learned in Chapter 2, the current ratio, which expresses current assets and current liabilities as a ratio rather than as an amount, is a more useful indicator of liquidity. Consequently, we will not illustrate working capital again here, and will focus instead on the current ratio.

CURRENT RATIO

The current ratio expresses the relationship of current assets to current liabilities, and is calculated by dividing current assets by current liabilities. It is widely used for evaluating a company's liquidity and short-term debt-paying ability.

The 2015 and 2014 current ratios for HBC, Dollarama, and the industry are shown below. Note that in the following ratio comparison, and in all ratios that follow, there is a column titled "Comparison with Prior Year," indicating whether the 2015 result is better or worse than the 2014 result shown for each of HBC, Dollarama, and the industry.

	CURRENT RATIO = $\dfrac{\text{CURRENT ASSETS}}{\text{CURRENT LIABILITIES}}$		
	2015	2014	Comparison with Prior Year
Hudson's Bay Company	1.4:1	1.3:1	Better
Dollarama	2.7:1	2.5:1	Better
Industry average	1.9:1	2.0:1	Worse

What does the current ratio actually mean? The 2015 ratio of 1.4:1 means that, for every dollar of current liabilities, Hudson's Bay has $1.40 of current assets. Hudson's Bay's current ratio increased marginally between 2015 and 2014 but is below that of Dollarama and its industry peers.

In assessing the current ratio, it is important to look at its components. The major components of current assets for retailers are cash and inventory. In 2014, HBC had a lower amount of cash and this contributed to its lower ratio in that year. We will analyze inventory more thoroughly below. The major component of current liabilities is accounts payable. In 2015 HBC had a higher level of these payables because of its acquisition of the Galeria group and this was the major reason for its current ratio to be lower than that of its peers in that year.

ACCOUNTING MATTERS

How to Manage the Current Ratio

The apparent simplicity of the current ratio can have real-world limitations because adding equal amounts to both the numerator and the denominator causes the ratio to decrease.

Assume, for example, that a company has $2 million of current assets and $1 million of current liabilities. Its current ratio is 2:1. If it purchases $1 million of inventory on account, it will have $3 million of current assets and $2 million of

current liabilities. Its current ratio decreases to 1.5:1. If, instead of buying inventory, the company pays off $500,000 of its current liabilities, it will have $1.5 million of current assets and $500,000 of current liabilities. Its current ratio increases to 3:1. Thus, any horizontal or ratio analysis should be done with care because the ratio is susceptible to sudden changes and is easily influenced by management's decisions.

RECEIVABLES TURNOVER

We mentioned in earlier chapters that a high current ratio is not always a good indication of liquidity. For example, a high current ratio can exist because of increased receivables resulting from uncollectible accounts. The ratio that is used to assess the liquidity of receivables is the receivables turnover. It measures the number of times, on average, that receivables are collected during the period. The receivables turnover is calculated by dividing net credit sales (sales on account less sales returns and allowances and discounts) by average gross accounts receivable (before the allowance for doubtful accounts is deducted) during the year.

Recall that a receivables turnover ratio that is significantly higher than the industry average may indicate that a company's credit-granting policies are too strict or "tight" and this may reduce sales to customers. Conversely, a receivables turnover ratio that is significantly lower than the industry average usually indicates a collection problem.

The 2015 and 2014 receivables turnover ratios for Hudson's Bay, Dollarama, and the industry are shown below.

$$\text{RECEIVABLES TURNOVER} = \frac{\text{NET CREDIT SALES}}{\text{AVERAGE GROSS ACCOUNTS RECEIVABLE}}$$

	2015	2014	Comparison with Prior Year
Hudson's Bay Company	30.8 times	46.8 times	Worse
Dollarama	251.0 times	292.0 times	Worse
Industry average	110.6 times	115.2 times	Worse

Because companies do not normally disclose the proportion of their sales that were made for cash and for credit, we assume that all sales are credit sales. In addition, not all companies report gross and net accounts receivable separately. In such cases, it is appropriate to use net accounts receivable. The important thing is to be consistent when choosing amounts to use in your calculations so that ratios are comparable.

Because many sales made by retailers are not on credit, the receivables turnover for the companies we are analyzing will be quite high given the low level of accounts receivable that these companies have. Even small changes in the receivables balance can cause the value of this ratio to change significantly. HBC's turnover is lower because it has credit card receivables, which Dollarama does not have because it does not accept credit cards. The industry average, which includes companies that have credit card receivables and those that do not, also worsened in 2015 but not as much as it did for HBC and Dollarama.

Average Collection Period

A variant of the receivables turnover is the average collection period. It is calculated by converting it into a collection period stated in days. This is done by dividing 365 days by the receivables turnover. The 2015 and 2014 average collection period for Hudson's Bay, Dollarama, and the industry are shown below.

AVERAGE COLLECTION PERIOD $= \dfrac{\text{365 DAYS}}{\text{RECEIVABLES TURNOVER}}$			
	2015	2014	Comparison with Prior Year
Hudson's Bay Company	12 days	8 days	Worse
Dollarama	1 day	1 day	Same
Industry average	3 days	3 days	Same

Analysts frequently use the average collection period to assess the effectiveness of a company's credit and collection policies. The general rule is that the collection period for receivables should not greatly exceed the credit period (the time allowed for payment of payables). While we do not know Hudson's Bay's credit period, the company appears to have been worse at collecting its accounts receivable in 2015 than in 2014. As stated previously, receivables are insignificant for Dollarama so even though the receivables turnover fell, the collection period is essentially unchanged. The same is true of the industry average. The average collection period for HBC is worse than the industry average because this company has receivables from its own credit card operations.

INVENTORY TURNOVER

Slow-moving inventory can also have an effect on the current ratio so we can calculate the inventory turnover ratio to see how a company's management of its inventory is affecting its liquidity. This ratio measures the number of times on average that the inventory is sold during the period, and is calculated by dividing the cost of goods sold by the average inventory.

An inventory turnover ratio that is significantly higher than the industry average may indicate that a company is maintaining inventory levels that are too low. This increases the risk of having no inventory available for customers when needed. (This lack of inventory is called a stockout.) Conversely, an inventory turnover ratio that is significantly lower than the industry average usually indicates difficulty selling that inventory and the likelihood of incurring higher than average storage costs.

The 2015 and 2014 inventory turnover ratios for Hudson's Bay, Dollarama, and the industry are shown below.

INVENTORY TURNOVER $= \dfrac{\text{COST OF GOODS SOLD}}{\text{AVERAGE INVENTORY}}$			
	2015	2014	Comparison with Prior Year
Hudson's Bay Company	2.3 times	2.2 times	Better
Dollarama	3.7 times	3.8 times	Worse
Industry average	3.3 times	3.4 times	Worse

HBC's inventory turnover improved in 2015 as the company concentrated efforts to offer more popular product lines. Dollarama, on the other hand, has an inventory turnover ratio that exceeds the industry average and this is a function of the company's much higher sales per square foot of retail space. Dollarama's inventory turnover ratio fell slightly in 2015, in part due to the opening of a number of stores during the year that had slower inventory turnover than more established stores.

Days in Inventory

A variant of the inventory turnover ratio is days in inventory, which measures the average number of days it takes to sell the inventory. It is calculated by dividing 365 days by the inventory turnover.

The 2015 and 2014 days in inventory for Hudson's Bay, Dollarama, and the industry are shown below.

DAYS IN INVENTORY = $\dfrac{365 \text{ DAYS}}{\text{INVENTORY TURNOVER}}$			
	2015	2014	Comparison with Prior Year
Hudson's Bay Company	159 days	166 days	Better
Dollarama	99 days	96 days	Worse
Industry average	111 days	107 days	Worse

Hudson's Bay's 159 days in inventory means that in 2015, on average, it took 159 days to sell merchandise. Dollarama sells its inventory faster. Generally, the faster inventory is sold, the less cash is tied up in inventory and the less chance there is of inventory becoming obsolete.

If we relate the current ratio to the receivables and inventory turnover ratios, we must first understand that, for retailers like HBC and Dollarama, the effect of receivables turnover is insignificant given that receivables, unlike inventory, represent a small percentage of current assets. For Dollarama, both the days in inventory and the current ratio increased. For Hudson's Bay, the days in inventory declined yet the current ratio rose. We can conclude that this increase was not caused by slow-moving or obsolete inventory.

It is worth noting that the above interpretations are based not only on financial data, but also on the knowledge gained from an understanding of the underlying nature of these companies and of the significant events that occurred during the year, all of which are disclosed in annual reports and other publicly available information. As mentioned earlier in the chapter, nonfinancial information is important in interpreting financial results.

LIQUIDITY CONCLUSION

In an intracompany comparison, we have noticed that in 2015 HBC's receivables turnover ratio worsened; that is, the average collection period was higher. However, its inventory turnover ratio improved; that is, its days in inventory were lower. Because inventory is a more significant asset for HBC, the improvement in inventory turnover helped to increase the current ratio.

> ▼ **HELPFUL HINT**
> An explanation for changes in the current ratio should be linked to changes in the receivables and inventory turnover ratios.

One item in the current ratio that was not analyzed in the inventory and receivables turnover is accounts payable. HBC's current ratio is also lower than Dollarama's due to higher payables arising from the Galeria acquisition. In an intercompany and industry comparison, we can conclude that Hudson's Bay's liquidity ratios are worse than those of Dollarama and the industry average.

SUMMARY OF LIQUIDITY RATIOS

Illustration 14-10 summarizes the liquidity ratios we have used in this chapter, and throughout the textbook. We have included the chapter number where each ratio was discussed in detail for your review. In addition to the ratio formula and what it measures, the desired direction (higher or lower) of the ratio result is included.

▶ **Illustration 14-10**
Liquidity ratios

Chapter	Ratio	Formula	What the Ratio Measures	Desired Result
2	Working capital	Current assets − Current liabilities	Short-term debt-paying ability	Higher
2	Current ratio	$\dfrac{\text{Current assets}}{\text{Current liabilities}}$	Short-term debt-paying ability	Higher
8	Receivables turnover	$\dfrac{\text{Net credit sales}}{\text{Average gross accounts receivable}}$	Liquidity of receivables	Higher
8	Average collection period	$\dfrac{365 \text{ days}}{\text{Receivables turnover}}$	Number of days receivables are outstanding	Lower
6	Inventory turnover	$\dfrac{\text{Cost of goods sold}}{\text{Average inventory}}$	Liquidity of inventory	Higher
6	Days in inventory	$\dfrac{365 \text{ days}}{\text{Inventory turnover}}$	Number of days inventory is on hand	Lower

To summarize, a higher result is generally considered to be better for the working capital, current, receivables turnover, and inventory turnover ratios. For those ratios that use turnover ratios in their denominators—the average collection period and days in inventory—a lower result is better. That is, you want to take fewer days to collect receivables and have fewer days of inventory on hand.

However, before concluding any assessment of liquidity, we need to understand the relationship between the inventory and receivables turnover ratios and the current ratio, as well as other components within current assets and current liabilities. Generally, as the turnover ratios increase, cash flow improves and cash balances will rise. If the cash balance rises by the same amount that a receivables balance falls, as can happen when the receivables turnover increases, the current ratio will not change. Yet clearly, the company has greater liquidity. If the cash or receivables balance rises because sales have increased and inventory has been reduced (inventory turnover has been rising), the current ratio will increase. This is because the increase in cash or receivables will be greater than the decrease in inventory (assuming the sales price exceeded the cost of the inventory sold). It is important to also understand that a current ratio can be artificially high at times because of higher balances of receivables and inventory included in current assets that are the result of uncollectible receivables or slow-moving inventory.

We must also understand how the current ratio is affected by cash balances and current liabilities. For example, a company could have a higher-than-normal cash balance because it just sold some land or common shares. This would increase liquidity (and the current ratio) but it has no effect on inventory or the receivables turnover. If a company lost a lawsuit and recorded a current liability for the damages to be paid, the current ratio would fall but this is not related to inventory or accounts receivable.

The above discussion highlights why it is important never to conclude an assessment of liquidity based only on the current ratio. We should also use the receivables and inventory turnover ratios in our assessment. Furthermore, we also have to assess the significance of each item in current assets and current liabilities and their effect on the current ratio. As we saw with Hudson's Bay and Dollarama, inventory was much more significant than receivables.

DO IT! ▶ 14-2   Liquidity Analysis

Liquidity ratios for two companies follow:

	Wasis Corporation	Rita Limited
Current ratio	1.6:1	1.9:1
Receivables turnover	27.0 times	22.6 times
Inventory turnover	6.8 times	5.6 times

(a) For each company, calculate the average collection period and days in inventory ratios.

(b) Identify whether Wasis or Rita has the "better" current ratio, receivables turnover ratio, average collection period, inventory turnover ratio, and days in inventory.

(c) Which company is more liquid? Explain.

Action Plan

✔ Review the formula for each ratio so you understand how it is calculated and how to interpret it.

✔ The current ratio should always be interpreted along with the receivables and inventory turnover ratios.

✔ Remember that for liquidity ratios, a higher result is usually better unless the current ratio has been artificially inflated by slow-moving receivables or inventory.

SOLUTION
Try this Do It! exercise on your own and then check your answer at the end of the chapter.

Related Exercise Material: BE14–6, BE14–7, BE14–8, E14–5, E14–6, and E14–7.

LEARNING
OBJECTIVE

3   Calculate and interpret ratios that are used to analyze solvency.

While liquidity ratios measure a company's ability to pay its current liabilities, **solvency ratios** measure the ability to pay total liabilities. The debt to total assets and times interest earned ratios allow us to better assess the company's ability to pay its interest. In addition, free cash flow gives information about the company's discretionary cash flow that is available to expand operations, invest in new business ventures, or pay additional dividends, among other alternatives.

DEBT TO TOTAL ASSETS

The debt to total assets ratio measures the percentage of the total assets that have been financed by creditors. It is calculated by dividing total liabilities (both current and non-current) by total assets. This ratio indicates the extent to which a company's assets are financed with debt. When this ratio is high, the company has a high level of debt and there is greater risk that it will be unable to pay its maturing obligations. If the debt to total assets ratio is low, the company has less debt and there is less concern about being able to pay off the debt and its interest charges. So, from the creditors' point of view, a low ratio of debt to total assets is good. However, if the ratio is too low, it may indicate that management is missing an opportunity to grow the business by obtaining financing from lenders. Furthermore, although a having a high debt to total assets ratio is risky, the risk may be justified if the interest on the debt is much lower than the return earned on the amounts borrowed.

The 2015 and 2014 debt to total assets ratios for Hudson's Bay, Dollarama, and the industry are shown below.

$$\text{DEBT TO TOTAL ASSETS} = \frac{\text{TOTAL LIABILITIES}}{\text{TOTAL ASSETS}}$$

	2015	2014	Comparison with Prior Year
Hudson's Bay Company	75.5%	72.9%	Worse
Dollarama	74.3%	56.5%	Worse
Industry average	70.1%	62.9%	Worse

HBC's debt to total assets ratio of 75.5% in 2015 means that creditors have provided financing that covers 75.5% of the company's total assets. The inverse means that shareholders have provided equity to cover 24.5% (100% − 75.5%) of the company's total assets.

Hudson's Bay's solvency, as measured by the debt to total assets ratio, worsened between 2015 and 2014, increasing from 72.9% to 75.5%. According to Illustration 14-4, presented earlier in the chapter, total assets increased by 38.7% in 2015 while total liabilities increased by 43.7%. Consequently, liabilities have increased faster than assets, causing the debt to total assets ratio to increase. Debt levels increased in order to finance the acquisition of the Galeria group. Because these companies are operating during a time when interest rates are falling, this has created an opportunity to borrow funds to acquire other companies, as HBC did. Dollarama also increased its debt to total assets ratio in 2015 to finance the opening of more locations. This trend was found in the entire industry, as shown in the increase in the industry average ratio as well.

Another ratio with a similar meaning to the debt to total assets ratio is the debt to equity ratio. It shows the use of borrowed funds relative to the investments by shareholders. The debt to equity ratio is calculated by dividing total liabilities by total shareholders' equity. When the debt to total assets ratio equals 50%, the debt to equity ratio is 100% (because total liabilities plus shareholders' equity equals total assets).

Using this definition, Hudson's Bay's debt to equity ratio for 2015 is 308.2% ($9,550 million ÷ $3,099 million). This means that Hudson's Bay has financed its operations with 3.1 times as much debt as equity, which is quite high compared with the industry. Such a strategy of increasing debt (which the entire industry did as well) may prove successful if the income earned from these borrowed funds exceeds the interest expense incurred on them. We can measure this by examining the times interest earned ratio in the next section.

TIMES INTEREST EARNED

While a company's debt level is important, its ability to service the debt—that is, pay the interest—is of equal or greater importance. The times interest earned ratio (also called interest coverage) indicates the company's ability to meet interest payments as they come due. The numerator in this ratio consists of income (earnings) before interest expense and income tax. This is often abbreviated as EBIT, which stands for earnings before interest and tax. EBIT is then divided by interest expense to determine this ratio's value. The ratio therefore measures how many times higher EBIT is than interest expense. The higher the ratio, the more EBIT there is available to cover interest.

The 2015 and 2014 times interest earned ratios for Hudson's Bay, Dollarama, and the industry are shown below.

TIMES INTEREST EARNED $= \dfrac{\text{NET INCOME + INTEREST EXPENSE + INCOME TAX EXPENSE (EBIT)}}{\text{INTEREST EXPENSE}}$			
	2015	2014	Comparison with Prior Year
Hudson's Bay Company	3.3 times	2.0 times	Better
Dollarama	25.7 times	21.2 times	Better
Industry average	8.4 times	7.9 times	Better

HBC's times interest earned ratio rose in 2015, primarily due to an increase in net income in 2015 from the sale of real estate assets to joint ventures and increased income from Saks. Although the company's debt levels rose, this increase did not occur until late in the year so it had almost no impact on interest expense for that year. Dollarama's times interest earned ratio also rose but not by as much as HBC's. The increasing times interest earned was indicative of the industry overall. Dollarama still maintained a much larger ratio value than HBC due to its more profitable operations.

Times interest earned should always be interpreted along with the debt to total assets ratio. We saw earlier that both companies increased their debt to total assets ratio because more debt was assumed in 2015 to finance expansion. This strategy appears to have been successful given the increase in the times interest earned ratio, which implies that despite the higher debt levels, these companies are now more capable of paying the interest on this debt because of increased net income.

FREE CASH FLOW

Another indication of a company's solvency is the amount of free cash flow that it generates. Free cash flow is measured as the amount of cash left over from operating cash flows after investing some of this to maintain current productive capacity and after paying current dividends.

Free cash flow for 2015 and 2014 for Hudson's Bay and Dollarama is shown below.

FREE CASH FLOW $= \dfrac{\text{NET CASH PROVIDED (USED) BY OPERATING ACTIVITIES − NET CAPITAL}}{\text{EXPENDITURES − DIVIDENDS PAID}}$			
(in millions)	2015	2014	Comparison with Prior Year
Hudson's Bay Company	$(628)	$ 85	Worse
Dollarama	$ 322	$241	Better
Industry average	n/a	n/a	n/a

There are no industry average amounts available. Hudson's Bay's free cash flow worsened considerably in 2015 compared with 2014. This happened for two reasons. First, although HBC had higher net income in 2015 of $387 million, included in that amount was other operating income of $684 million (see Illustration 14-9) that arose from the sale of real estate assets to joint ventures. Although HBC owns part of these ventures and did earn $62 million of other income from them, without the large gain from the sale of these assets, HBC would have reported a loss. This is reflected in a very low operating cash flow compared with 2014. (Such a gain does not affect operating cash flows, because the proceeds for real estate sales are an investing activity.) Second, capital expenditures rose significantly in 2015 due to the larger number of stores now operated by the company. Consequently, free cash flow fell from a positive to a negative amount for HBC. Dollarama, on the other hand, has always operated stores on a profitable basis and, as the number of stores grew in 2015, so too did its free cash flow. The lack of free cash flow for HBC means that it is not generating sufficient cash from its operations to grow its business. Proof of this can be seen when the Galeria group was acquired. This purchase was not paid for from free cash but instead by increasing debt and raising cash by selling off real estate assets.

SOLVENCY CONCLUSION

In an intracompany comparison, except for the times interest earned ratio, Hudson's Bay's solvency ratios worsened in 2015. Its debt to total assets ratio rose, but despite the higher level of debt, its times interest earned ratio improved due to higher profitability. However, that profitability was primarily earned by a one-time gain from the sale of real estate assets and the proceeds for such sales improve investing, not operating, cash flows. Consequently, operating cash flows decreased at a time when net capital expenditures increased, which in turn caused free cash flows to decline in 2015.

Like HBC, Dollarama's and the industry's average debt to total assets ratio worsened. Also like HBC, this resulted in an improved times interest earned ratio for both Dollarama and the industry average. However, Dollarama had an increase in its free cash flow, which HBC did not. Consequently, we can conclude that HBC's solvency is below average and much worse than Dollarama's solvency.

SUMMARY OF SOLVENCY RATIOS

Illustration 14-11 summarizes the solvency ratios discussed above, and throughout this textbook.

▶ Illustration 14-11
Solvency ratios

Chapter	Ratio	Formula	What the Ratio Measures	Desired Result
2, 10	Debt to total assets	$\dfrac{\text{Total liabilities}}{\text{Total assets}}$	Percentage of total assets provided by creditors	Lower
10	Times interest earned	$\dfrac{\text{Net income + Interest expense + Income tax expense (EBIT)}}{\text{Interest expense}}$	Ability to meet interest payments	Higher
13	Free cash flow	Net cash provided (used) by operating activities − Net capital expenditures − Dividends paid	Cash available from operating activities for discretionary purposes	Higher

For the debt to total assets ratio, a lower result is generally considered to be better. Having less debt reduces a company's dependence on debt financing, minimizes the impact that rising interest rates can have on profitability, and offers more flexibility for future financing alternatives. For times interest earned and free cash flow, a higher result is better.

It is important to interpret the debt to total assets and times interest earned ratios together. If a company uses debt to become more profitable, its times interest earned ratio will rise despite having a higher debt to total assets ratio. If taking on additional debt did not lead to greater profitability, then the times interest earned ratio will fall. If a company reduces its debt to total assets ratio and this reduces interest expense and improves profitability, we would see an increase in the times interest earned ratio. Consequently, one should always interpret a company's solvency after considering the interrelationship of these two ratios.

DO IT! ▶14-3   Solvency Analysis

Selected information from the financial statement of the Home Affairs Corporation follows:

	2018	2017
Total assets	$1,000,000	$1,015,000
Total liabilities	737,700	809,000
Interest expense	59,000	40,500
Income tax expense	48,400	50,500
Net income	193,600	202,000

(a) For each company, calculate the debt to total assets and times interest earned ratios.

(b) Comment on whether Home Affairs' overall solvency has improved or deteriorated in 2018.

Action Plan

✔ Review the formula for each ratio so you understand how it is calculated and how to interpret it.

✔ The debt to total assets ratio should always be interpreted together with the times interest earned ratio.

✔ Remember that for debt to total assets, a lower result is better. For other solvency ratios, a higher result is better.

SOLUTION

Try this Do It! exercise on your own and then check your answer at the end of the chapter.

Related Exercise Material: BE14–9, E14–8, E14–9, and E14–10.

LEARNING OBJECTIVE ▶4

Calculate and interpret ratios that are used to analyze profitability.

Profitability ratios measure a company's operating success for a specific period of time. To be successful, assets must be used efficiently and generate enough sales at an appropriate price to cover all of the company's expenses. Consequently, profitability ratios focus mainly on the relationships between income statement items and statement of financial position items. Understanding these relationships can help management determine where to focus efforts on improving profitability.

Illustration 14-12 shows these relationships and will guide our discussion of Hudson's Bay's profitability. Profitability ratios include the gross profit margin, profit margin, asset turnover, return on assets, and return on common shareholders' equity ratios, as shown in Illustration 14-12.

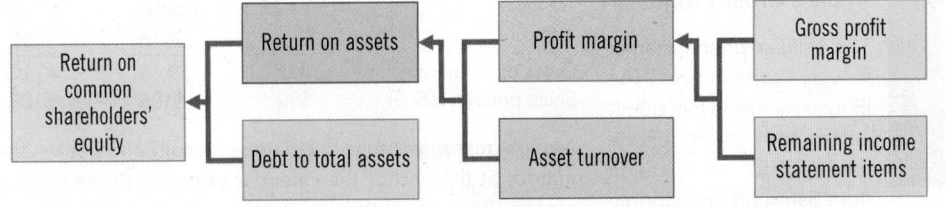

▶Illustration 14-12

Relationships among profitability measures

As shown in Illustration 14-12, the return on common shareholders' equity ratio is affected by the return on assets and debt to total assets ratios. If a company wants to increase its return on common shareholders' equity, it can either increase its return on assets or increase its reliance on debt financing. In fact, as long as the return on assets is higher than the interest rate paid on debt, the return on common shareholders' equity will be increased by the use of debt. You will recall that this concept is known as leverage, which we first learned about in Chapter 11.

The return on assets ratio is affected by the profit margin and asset turnover. If a company wants to increase its return on assets, it can do this by either increasing its return (profit margin) or increasing its asset utilization (asset turnover). It is very rare for a company to do both so management usually pursues a strategy to maximize one of these ratios. For example, years ago Hudson's Bay decided to maximize asset turnover by acquiring discount stores like Zellers. These stores operate on a low-price, high-volume basis, which means in effect that they are prepared to reduce profit margins in order to improve asset turnover. However, with new ownership and management, Hudson's Bay reversed that strategy and decided that it was more effective to boost return on assets with the higher profit margins that come with the sale of higher-quality goods.

The profit margin is in turn affected by the gross profit margin and the amount, or percentage, of operating expenses (assuming there are no other revenues or expenses), interest, and income taxes. (These last three items are components of profit margin but not gross profit margin.) If a company wants to increase its profit margin, it can increase its gross profit margin (by either raising selling prices or reducing its cost of goods sold), or reduce its operating expenses, interest expense, or income tax expense.

We will now look at each of these ratios in turn and examine their relationships. In addition, before we conclude this section, we will also review the basic earnings per share, price-earnings, payout, and dividend yield ratios.

GROSS PROFIT MARGIN

The gross profit margin is calculated by dividing gross profit (net sales less cost of goods sold) by net sales. This ratio indicates a company's ability to maintain an adequate selling price above its cost of goods sold. The 2015 and 2014 gross profit margin ratios for Hudson's Bay, Dollarama, and the industry are shown below.

GROSS PROFIT MARGIN = $\dfrac{\text{GROSS PROFIT}}{\text{NET SALES}}$			
	2015	2014	Comparison with Prior Year
Hudson's Bay Company	40.5%	40.0%	Better
Dollarama	39.0%	36.9%	Better
Industry average	39.4%	38.7%	Better

Hudson's Bay's gross profit margin increased slightly in 2015. Meanwhile, Dollarama's gross profit margin increased substantially, due primarily to cost savings from Asian suppliers because of foreign currency fluctuations. (Asian currencies fell in value so their products were cheaper to buy.) This same effect contributed to the change in the industry average.

ACCOUNTING MATTERS

Andrew F. Kazmierski/Shutterstock

Apple's Gross Profit

The cellular phone market is very competitive. The iPhone by Apple Inc. dominated the smart phone market until competition from Samsung and Google began to cut into its market share. To combat this competition, Apple needed not only to be more innovative but also to be more price-competitive while at the same time trying to maintain the healthy gross profits that investors had come to expect.

Listed below are the gross profit margin and share price for all Apple products for three consecutive quarters:

	June 25, 2016	Mar. 26, 2016	Dec. 26, 2015
Gross profit margin	38.0%	39.4%	40.1%
Share price (in U.S. $)	$92	$106	$108

Apple's quarterly results fluctuate seasonally and peak in the quarter at the end of the calendar year due to the holiday season. Because of this, sales always decline after the last quarter in the calendar year. However, when investors noticed that Apple's gross profit margin had fallen for three quarters in a row, the share price fell dramatically in June 2016. Only time will tell if the reaction in the stock market was too extreme or not, but this clearly illustrates the importance of gross profit margins to share prices.

PROFIT MARGIN

The profit margin is calculated by dividing net income by net sales for the period. This ratio is significantly affected by the gross profit margin ratio because gross profit is a major component of net income. The profit margin ratio, in addition to measuring the effect of the gross profit margin, also indicates how effective the company is at controlling operating expenses and how interest expense and income tax expense have affected net income. In some instances, this ratio can also indicate the impact of other items on net income, such as significant gains and losses, as is the case with HBC.

The 2015 and 2014 profit margin ratios for Hudson's Bay, Dollarama, and the industry are shown below.

PROFIT MARGIN $= \dfrac{\text{NET INCOME}}{\text{NET SALES}}$			
	2015	2014	Comparison with Prior Year
Hudson's Bay Company	3.5%	2.9%	Better
Dollarama	14.5%	12.7%	Better
Industry average	3.2%	2.8%	Better

We know that Hudson's Bay has a lower gross profit margin than Dollarama. Because of this, we might expect to see this company with a lower profit margin ratio as well, and this is certainly the case. However, because some items are included in the profit margin that are not included in the gross profit margin, we need to understand these items. For HBC, they include operating expenses, other operating income, interest expense, other revenues and expenses, and income tax expense. Of these, operating expenses and other operating income were significant for HBC. We know from the vertical analysis performed earlier that Hudson's Bay's operating expenses are considerably higher relative to sales than those of Dollarama. However, the negative impact of this was offset by other operating income that was earned from the sale of some HBC real estate assets. (Dollarama had no such corresponding item.) We can conclude that Dollarama's higher profit margin was due to its higher gross profit margin and its lower operating expenses. HBC had a positive profit margin, despite its higher operating expenses, because of its other operating income. Without this other operating income, HBC would have had a negative profit margin in both 2015 and 2014. Compared with the industry average, HBC and Dollarama had higher profit margins in both 2015 and 2014.

ASSET TURNOVER

The asset turnover ratio measures how efficiently a company uses its assets to generate sales. It is calculated by dividing net sales by average total assets for the period. The resulting number shows the dollars of sales produced by each dollar invested in assets.

The 2015 and 2014 asset turnover ratios for Hudson's Bay, Dollarama, and the industry are shown below.

ASSET TURNOVER $= \dfrac{\text{NET SALES}}{\text{AVERAGE TOTAL ASSETS}}$			
	2015	2014	Comparison with Prior Year
Hudson's Bay Company	1.0 times	1.0 times	Same
Dollarama	1.5 times	1.4 times	Better
Industry average	0.9 times	0.9 times	Same

The asset turnover ratio shows that HBC generated $1.00 of sales in 2015 for each dollar it had invested in assets. The asset turnover remained the same as 2014; it is lower than Dollarama's asset turnover but slightly higher than that of the industry. One reason why HBC has a lower asset turnover ratio is because Dollarama generates more sales per square foot of retail space. We normally believe that the higher this ratio is, the more efficient a company is at generating sales with a certain amount of assets. However, we can only draw that conclusion if the assets are comparable.

For HBC and Dollarama, their non-current assets are not comparable and this affects the value of their respective asset turnover ratios. HBC has a much larger asset base, consisting primarily of property, plant, and equipment, because it owns most of its store locations. Dollarama does not, preferring instead to rent these facilities. Furthermore, if we look carefully at the notes to Dollarama's financial statements, we see that accumulated depreciation at the end of fiscal 2015 represented 44% of the cost of its depreciable assets. For HBC, this amount was only 17% because many of its assets were acquired recently (hence the lower level of accumulated depreciation) with its purchase of Saks and the Galeria group. Consequently, the denominator in this ratio is higher for Hudson's Bay and its asset turnover is lower.

For some companies, current assets may represent significant portions of their assets and have an impact on the asset turnover ratio. For HBC and Dollarama, this is true with regard to inventory. HBC's lower inventory turnover ratio is also a contributing factor to its lower asset turnover ratio.

RETURN ON ASSETS

Return on assets measures the overall profitability of assets in terms of how much is earned on each dollar invested in assets. You may recall that we first learned in Chapter 9 that the return on assets ratio is affected by the profit margin and asset turnover. By multiplying the profit margin and asset turnover ratios, we can calculate the return on assets ratio as illustrated below:

$$\text{Return on Assets} = \text{Profit Margin} \times \text{Asset Turnover}$$

$$\frac{\text{Net income}}{\text{Average total assets}} = \frac{\text{Net income}}{\text{Net sales}} \times \frac{\text{Net sales}}{\text{Average total assets}}$$

Notice that when we cancel out the net sales term in the profit margin and asset turnover ratios, we have the return on assets ratio, which is net income divided by average total assets.

The 2015 and 2014 return on assets ratios for Hudson's Bay, Dollarama, and the industry are shown below.

RETURN ON ASSETS = $\dfrac{\text{NET INCOME}}{\text{AVERAGE TOTAL ASSETS}}$			
	2015	2014	Comparison with Prior Year
Hudson's Bay Company	3.6%	2.7%	Better
Dollarama	21.9%	18.1%	Better
Industry average	2.9%	2.5%	Better

The return on assets ratio for Hudson's Bay can also be calculated by multiplying the profit margin by the asset turnover. For 2015 this is 3.5% × 1.0 times = 3.5%, which is slightly less than the amount shown above due to rounding. For Dollarama, the corresponding amounts are 14.5% × 1.5 times = 21.8% (approximately equal to the direct calculation used in the table above due to rounding). Notice how the higher asset turnover experienced by Dollarama "boosts" the return on assets higher.

We know that in 2015, the asset turnover for HBC and Dollarama changed very little, so the change in the return on assets ratio for each company was caused mainly by changes in the profit margin. This means that profitability was the primary driver in each company's return on assets rather than asset utilization (turnover). We can therefore understand the reasons for the change in the return on assets ratio by understanding the reasons for the changes to the profit margin ratio.

RETURN ON COMMON SHAREHOLDERS' EQUITY

A widely used measure of profitability from the common shareholders' view point is the return on common shareholders' equity. This ratio shows how many dollars of net income were earned for each dollar invested by the common shareholders. It is calculated by dividing net income available to common shareholders (net income – preferred dividends declared) by average common shareholders' equity (total shareholders' equity – preferred shares).

▼ **HELPFUL HINT**
An explanation for changes in the return on assets ratio should be linked to changes in the profit margin and asset turnover ratios.

The 2015 and 2014 return on common shareholders' equity ratios for Hudson's Bay, Dollarama, and the industry are shown below.

RETURN ON COMMON SHAREHOLDERS' EQUITY = $\dfrac{\text{NET INCOME} - \text{PREFERRED DIVIDENDS DECLARED}}{\text{AVERAGE COMMON SHAREHOLDERS' EQUITY}}$			
	2015	2014	Comparison with Prior Year
Hudson's Bay Company	13.9%	10.3%	Better
Dollarama	63.8%	36.8%	Better
Industry average	9.6%	6.8%	Better

The return on common shareholders' equity is a ratio that is affected by other ratios, as discussed above. It is determined in part by the company's use of leverage (the debt to total assets ratio) and the return on assets, which in turn is determined by the profit margin and the asset turnover. We know from examining solvency ratios that Hudson's Bay and Dollarama have very similar levels of debt relative to assets and equity and that these levels are slightly above the industry average. As long as the income made on these borrowed funds exceeds the interest incurred on the funds, then the return on common shareholders' equity will rise.

We can see the effect of this leverage by comparing the company's return on assets with its return on equity. In 2015, the return on assets for HBC was 3.6%, but because a large amount of the company's assets was financed with debt, the equity was much smaller than assets. As a result, when we take the net income less preferred dividends of nil and divide it by a smaller average common shareholders' equity amount compared with average total assets, we get a higher return on common shareholders' equity of 13.9%. This shows the advantage of leverage, which, as it increases, magnifies the difference between the return on common shareholders' equity and the return on assets. In 2014, this same effect occurred, with the return on common shareholders' equity being much higher than the return on assets.

Dollarama and the industry in general also used leverage to boost their return on common shareholders' equity. In 2015, Dollarama had a return on assets of 21.9% but this was further magnified by leverage to provide a return on common shareholders' equity of 63.8%.

▼ **HELPFUL HINT**
An explanation for changes in the return on common shareholders' equity ratio should be linked to changes in the return on assets ratio and the debt to total assets ratio.

BASIC EARNINGS PER SHARE

Basic earnings per share is a measure of net income available to common shareholders that is realized on each common share. It is calculated by dividing net income available to common shareholders (net income – preferred dividends) by the weighted average number of common shares. Basic earnings per share is widely used by current and potential investors. It is the only ratio that must be presented on the income statement or statement of comprehensive income by companies following IFRS. As we learned in Chapter 11, basic earnings per share is not required to be reported by companies following ASPE.

Basic earnings per share for 2015 and 2014 for Hudson's Bay, Dollarama, and the industry are shown below.

BASIC EARNINGS PER SHARE = $\dfrac{\text{NET INCOME} - \text{PREFERRED DIVIDENDS}}{\text{WEIGHTED AVERAGE NUMBER OF COMMON SHARES}}$			
	2015	2014	Comparison with Prior Year
Hudson's Bay Company	$2.13	$1.28	Better
Dollarama	$3.03	$2.22	Better
Industry average	n/a	n/a	n/a

Note that no industry average is included above. Comparisons with the industry average, or with Dollarama's basic earnings per share, are not meaningful, because of the different financing structures. For example, one company could have more debt than the other. Furthermore, there are wide variations in numbers of shares issued by companies. The only meaningful basic earnings per share comparison would be an intracompany one. Hudson's Bay's basic earnings per share increased, from $1.28 in 2014 to $2.13 in 2015. As we have seen earlier, this was attributable primarily to the sale of real estate assets. Dollarama's basic earnings per share increased primarily from the growth in the number of stores it operates and its control of operating expenses.

PRICE-EARNINGS (P-E) RATIO

The price-earnings (P-E) ratio is often quoted as a measure of the relationship of the market price of each common share to the basic earnings per share. It is commonly known as a market measure because it uses a company's share price, which reflects the stock market's (investors') expectations for the company.

While basic earnings per share is not comparable on an intercompany or industry basis, the price-earnings ratio is. The 2015 and 2014 price-earnings ratios for Hudson's Bay, Dollarama, and the industry are shown below.

PRICE-EARNINGS $= \dfrac{\text{MARKET PRICE PER SHARE}}{\text{BASIC EARNINGS PER SHARE}}$			
	2015	2014	Comparison with Prior Year
Hudson's Bay Company	8.1 times	18.3 times	Lower
Dollarama	24.8 times	27.2 times	Lower
Industry average	20.6 times	17.2 times	Higher

As we learned in Chapter 2, the P-E ratio indicates what investors expect of a company's future profitability. For that reason, we have not described the comparison with the prior year above using the qualitative terms of "better" or "worse." Instead, we have used the quantitative terms of "lower" or "higher." If investors believe that a company will have significant growth in its profitability, they will bid the price of that company's shares up and its price-earnings ratio will rise. If that ratio is too high, it may indicate that the share price is overvalued rather than indicating an accurate expectation of a company's future profitability. Ideally, an investor would like to buy shares in a company before the price-earnings ratio rises, because if that ratio is still low, the share price is quite inexpensive. However, investors seeking price appreciation will still look for companies with increasing, or the potential for increasing, price-earnings ratios.

At the end of its fiscal 2014 year, Hudson's Bay's shares were trading at a price of $23.42 and one year later, even after reporting higher net income and improved returns on its assets and common shareholders' equity, the price had fallen to $17.30. One never knows all the reasons for the change in a share's price but it is likely that the major reason for this decline was that the company would not have been profitable in 2015 without the sale of real estate assets. Because that type of transaction cannot occur every year, investors may have been expecting HBC to have a loss in the future. So even though the earnings per share rose in 2015, the share price fell and the price-earnings ratio declined significantly due to future expectations of the company's performance.

On the other hand, Dollarama's share price went from $60.35 at the end of fiscal 2014 to $75.17 at the end of fiscal 2015. This most likely occurred because investors have confidence that the company's increased profitability and its above-average return on common shareholders' equity will continue in the future. The price-earnings ratio fell slightly in 2015 because the share price did not increase as rapidly as the basic earnings per share. Dollarama's higher than average price-earnings ratio reflects investors' optimism about the future profitability of this company.

Investors felt more optimistic about the future profitability of the industry in 2015, as indicated by the increase in the price-earnings ratio for the industry.

Some investors carefully study price-earnings ratios over time to help them determine when to buy or sell shares. They may buy shares when the P-E ratio is low in the belief that this indicates that the shares are inexpensive. However, a low P-E ratio may also indicate that the market believes that the company will be less profitable in the future and because of that, the share price may decline further. Investors must therefore be very cautious when interpreting price-earnings ratios.

PAYOUT RATIO

The payout ratio measures the percentage of net income that is distributed as cash dividends. It is calculated by dividing cash dividends by net income. Companies that have high growth rates usually have low payout ratios because they reinvest most of their income back into the company by using those funds to purchase more assets rather than paying out dividends to shareholders. Investors seeking dividend income usually look for companies with a high payout ratio. Investors seeking price appreciation look for companies with a low payout ratio.

The 2015 and 2014 payout ratios for Hudson's Bay, Dollarama, and the industry are shown below.

PAYOUT RATIO $= \dfrac{\text{CASH DIVIDENDS DECLARED}}{\text{NET INCOME}}$			
	2015	2014	Comparison with Prior Year
Hudson's Bay Company	9.3%	15.5%	Lower
Dollarama	11.7%	14.2%	Lower
Industry average	14.4%	15.5%	Lower

The amount of dividends that a company will declare each year is at the discretion of the board of directors and is directly related to the company's growth strategy. Companies interested in retaining cash for future growth will have no payout ratio while companies less interested in retaining cash for growth will reward shareholders with cash dividends. For this reason, we have not described the comparison with the prior-year amounts in the table above as "better" or "worse."

Because companies that adopt a policy of paying out dividends do not want to disappoint shareholders with dividend reductions, the amount of dividends paid out each year will be kept fairly constant or will increase slightly over time. Consequently, the value for the numerator in the payout ratio is less likely to change than the net income amount in the denominator. If net income is volatile, it will cause the payout ratio to fluctuate even if the company has not changed the amount of dividends it is paying out. Therefore, it is important to understand that a change in the payout ratio does not mean that dividends paid are necessarily changing; it is more likely that net income is changing.

HBC has a lower than average dividend payout compared with its peers, in order to free up cash so that it can acquire new banners. However, the company has kept its dividend payments constant at $0.20 per common share in 2014 and 2015. The dividend payout ratio for this company fell because of the increase in net income in 2015.

The industry average and Dollarama's payout ratio fell in 2015 for the same reason: its net income rose faster than its cash dividends declared even though, unlike HBC, it increased its dividends per share from $0.31 to $0.35. This $0.04 per share increase may seem insignificant but it represents a 12.9% increase in dividends received by shareholders and that in turn makes the shares more attractive to investors. This is another factor that explains why Dollarama has a higher price-earnings ratio than HBC.

DIVIDEND YIELD

The dividend yield supplements the payout ratio. The dividend yield reports the rate of return a shareholder earned from dividends during the year as a percentage of the share price. It is calculated by dividing the dividends per share by the market price per share. Similar to the price-earnings ratio, this ratio is also known as a market measure, because of the use of the share price in its calculation.

The dividend yields for 2015 and 2014 for Hudson's Bay, Dollarama, and the industry are shown below.

DIVIDEND YIELD $= \dfrac{\text{DIVIDENDS DECLARED PER SHARE}}{\text{MARKET PRICE PER SHARE}}$			
	2015	2014	Comparison with Prior Year
Hudson's Bay Company	1.2%	0.9%	Higher
Dollarama	0.5%	0.5%	Same
Industry average	0.8%	0.8%	Same

A company's dividend yield can change because the company has changed the amount of dividends declared per share or because there has been a change in the company's share price. For

HBC, the dividends declared were the same in 2015 and 2014 but its share price fell in 2015 and this explains the increase in its dividend yield. Dollarama increased its dividends in 2015 by over 11% and its share price rose by almost 25%. However, because its payout ratio is quite low, the difference between these two increasing amounts did not cause the dividend yield to change if we round the yield to one decimal place.

Investors often compare the dividend yield they can earn from a particular share with the rate of return they could earn from a conservative investment like a bond or term deposit. If the dividend yield is lower than the return on these alternative investments, which is the case with this industry in general and Dollarama in particular, an investor's primary reason for buying those shares will be for price appreciation rather than dividend yield. Consequently, whether an increase in dividend yield is better or worse depends on the investor's perspective. If they are looking to buy a particular company's shares for dividend income, they would prefer a higher dividend yield. If they are looking to buy a share for price appreciation, they would prefer a lower dividend yield.

PROFITABILITY CONCLUSION

In an intracompany comparison, all of Hudson's Bay's profitability ratios increased from 2014 to 2015 except for asset turnover, which remained the same, and the price-earnings ratio and payout ratio, which decreased. The higher profitability ratios were caused by an improving gross profit from Saks and increases in gains from the sale of real estate assets in 2015, which followed a year when there were gains from similar types of transactions. If we were to exclude the effects of these gains in 2015 and 2014, HBC would have shown losses in both years. HBC maintained the same level of dividend payments in both years but the rise in net income in 2015 caused the payout ratio to fall while the decline in the company's share price in 2015 caused the P-E ratio to fall and the dividend yield to rise.

In an intercompany comparison, HBC's profitability in 2015 was lower than that of Dollarama despite the gains from real estate asset sales. Dollarama increased sales not just at each existing store but by opening new stores, and it was very effective at controlling its operating expenses. All of Dollarama's profitability ratios increased in 2015 except for its payout ratio, which fell because the company did not increase dividends to the same extent that net income increased. Also, the P-E ratio fell because the company's share price did not rise as much as the basic earnings per share.

HBC outperformed the industry average on most profitability ratios due to the sale of its real estate assets but it had a lower-than-average payout ratio because it retained more cash to finance expansion. Because of the decline in its share price in 2015, HBC had a higher dividend yield and a lower P-E ratio than the industry average.

SUMMARY OF PROFITABILITY RATIOS

Illustration 14-13 summarizes the profitability ratios discussed above, and throughout this textbook.

▶Illustration 14-13
Profitability ratios

Chapter	Ratio	Formula	What the Ratio Measures	Desired Result
5	Gross profit margin	$\dfrac{\text{Gross profit}}{\text{Net sales}}$	Margin between selling price and cost of goods sold	Higher
5	Profit margin	$\dfrac{\text{Net income}}{\text{Net sales}}$	Net income generated by each dollar of sales	Higher
9	Asset turnover	$\dfrac{\text{Net sales}}{\text{Average total assets}}$	How efficiently assets are used to generate sales	Higher
9	Return on assets	$\dfrac{\text{Net income}}{\text{Average total assets}}$	Overall profitability of assets	Higher

11	Return on common shareholders' equity	$\dfrac{\text{Net income} - \text{Preferred dividends}}{\text{Average common shareholders' equity}}$	Profitability of shareholders' investment	Higher
2, 11	Basic earnings per share	$\dfrac{\text{Net income} - \text{Preferred dividends}}{\text{Weighted average number of common shares}}$	Net income earned on each common share	Higher
2	Price-earnings ratio	$\dfrac{\text{Market price per share}}{\text{Earnings per share}}$	Relationship between market price per share and basic earnings per share	Based on market expectations
11	Payout ratio	$\dfrac{\text{Cash dividends declared}}{\text{Net income}}$	Percentage of net income distributed as cash dividends	Based on growth strategy
11	Dividend yield	$\dfrac{\text{Dividend declared per share}}{\text{Market price per share}}$	Income generated for the shareholder by each share, based on the market price per share	Higher for investors seeking dividends; lower for investors seeking price appreciation

▶Illustration 14-13
(*Continued*)

For the profitability ratios shown above, a higher result is generally considered to be better. However, there are some investor-related considerations with respect to the price-earnings and payout ratios that must be understood. A higher price-earnings ratio generally means that investors favour that company and have high expectations of future profitability, which is why its share price is relatively higher than its basic earnings per share.

Investors interested in purchasing a company's shares to earn dividend income (for example, retired persons who have no salary) are interested in companies with a high payout ratio and high dividend yield. Investors more interested in purchasing a company's shares for price appreciation (for example, those who do not need to earn dividend income because they have salaries) are likely to prefer companies with lower payout ratios and lower dividend yields. They would prefer to see the company retain its income rather than pay it out.

We have shown liquidity, solvency, and profitability ratios in separate sections above. However, it is important to recognize that analysis should not focus on one type of ratio without considering the others. Liquidity, solvency, and profitability are closely interrelated in most companies. For example, a company's profitability is affected by the availability of financing and its liquidity. Similarly, a company's solvency not only requires satisfactory liquidity but is also affected by its profitability.

It is also important to recognize that the ratios shown in Illustrations 14-10, 14-11, and 14-13 are only examples of commonly used ratios. There are many different and additional ratios and groupings that financial analysts use. Users should therefore determine which ratios best suit the decisions they need to make. Analysts often use ratios that are specific to an industry. For example, in the retail sector, because growing companies open new stores every year, growing sales are expected, so looking at sales growth is not as important as same-store sales or sales per square foot of retail space.

Finally, it is important to remember that ratios give clues about underlying conditions that may not be seen from an inspection of the individual components of a particular ratio. A single ratio by itself is not very meaningful. Accordingly, ratios must be interpreted in conjunction with information that has been gained from a detailed review of the financial information, including horizontal and vertical analyses, as well as relevant nonfinancial information.

This ends our comprehensive analysis illustration using Hudson's Bay Company. What can be practically covered in this textbook shows only a small portion of the types of financial information available and the ratios that are used by various industries. The availability of information is not a problem. The real challenge is to be discriminating enough to choose relevant data for comparisons and analyses.

DO IT! ▶14-4   Profitability Analysis

Selected information from the financial statements of two companies competing in the same industry follows:

	De Marchi Corporation	Bear Limited
Total assets, beginning of year	$388,000	$372,000
Total assets, end of year	434,000	536,000
Total liabilities, beginning of year	119,000	76,000
Total liabilities, end of year	97,000	135,000
Total common shareholders' equity, beginning of year	269,000	296,000
Total common shareholders' equity, end of year	337,000	401,000
Net sales	660,000	780,000
Gross profit	175,000	248,000
Net income	68,000	105,000

(a) For each company, calculate the following ratios: debt to total assets, gross profit margin, profit margin, asset turnover, return on assets, and return on common shareholders' equity.

(b) Which company is more profitable? Explain.

(c) What is the key driver of Bear Limited's return on common shareholders' equity ratio—return on assets or debt to total assets—when compared with that of De Marchi Corporation? Explain.

SOLUTION

Try this Do It! exercise on your own and then check your answer at the end of the chapter.

Related Exercise Material: BE14–10, BE14–11, BE14–12, BE14–13, E14–4, E14–11, E14–12, E14–13, and E14–14.

LEARNING OBJECTIVE ▶5   Understand the limitations of financial analysis.

Before relying on the information you have gathered through your horizontal, vertical, and ratio analyses, you must understand the limitations of these tools and of the financial statements they are based on. Some of the factors that can limit the usefulness of your analysis include the degree to which a company is diversified, the use of different accounting policies and estimates, the exclusion of events reported in other comprehensive income (loss), gains or losses arising from discontinued operations, and the effects of nonrecurring items.

DIVERSIFICATION

Diversification in Canadian industry can limit the usefulness of financial analysis. Many companies today are so diversified that they cannot be classified by industry, which makes it difficult to compare them with their peers. Canadian Tire, for example, sells selected grocery, home, car, clothing, sports, and leisure products. In addition, it is the country's largest independent gasoline retailer. Consequently, deciding what industry a company like Canadian Tire is in can be one of the main challenges to effectively evaluating its results.

Other companies may appear to be comparable but are not. McCain Foods and Irving-owned Cavendish Farms compete in the frozen potato product category. Yet McCain produces other food products besides french fries, and Irving has many other interests, including oil, newspapers, tissue products, transportation, and ship building.

Because of this diversification, analysts must be careful in interpreting consolidated financial statements. You will recall that we learned about consolidated financial statements in Chapter 12. Consolidated statements include financial information about a parent company and each of its subsidiaries. The parent company may have a strong debt to total assets ratio, and the subsidiary a weak one. However, because these statements are consolidated, the combined results may show that the debt to total assets ratio is close to the industry average. The fact that the subsidiary may have solvency problems is hidden from the general public because of the consolidated reporting of the financial information. Of course, such a situation would not be hidden from management because it has access to the statements of each subsidiary company even though the general public does not.

When companies have significant operations in different lines of business, they are required to report additional disclosures in a segmented information note to their financial statements. IFRS has specific revenue, income, and asset tests to determine if a company is required to report segmented information or not. (You will learn more about this in an intermediate accounting course.) If a company has reportable operating segments, it must disclose relevant information about revenues, operating income, and/or identifiable assets by products and services, by geographic area, and by major customer. For example, HBC discloses information for its Canadian, U.S., and European banners.

Note that segments are not as common in private companies as they are in large public companies and consequently there are no requirements for the disclosure of segments in ASPE.

ALTERNATIVE ACCOUNTING POLICIES AND ESTIMATES

Variations among companies in their use of alternative accounting policies can lessen the comparability of their statements. For example, it is difficult to compare the financial statements of a company that determines its inventory costs using FIFO with another company that uses average cost. Different accounting policy choices can result in differing account balances and net incomes, which again affect how easily their results can be compared.

Although Hudson's Bay Company and Dollarama both use the average method for determining the cost of their inventory, this is not true of all retailers. If we tried to compare Hudson's Bay's inventory balances and cost of goods sold with those of a company that used FIFO instead of average, we would need to adjust one of the company's amounts to make them comparable with the other. Note that although cost of goods sold may be different because of the use of a different policy, this is really just an artificial, or timing, difference. While there may be differences year by year, in total, over time, there is no difference.

Policy choices are even more pronounced if the two companies we are comparing use different sets of accounting standards, like ASPE instead of IFRS. For example, if we wanted to compare the performance of Hudson's Bay with Walmart, this would be just as difficult, because Walmart prepares its financial statements using U.S. GAAP and HBC uses IFRS. Although differences in accounting policies might be detectable from reading the notes to the financial statements, adjusting the financial data to compensate for the different policies is difficult, if not impossible, in some cases.

OTHER COMPREHENSIVE INCOME

When calculating financial ratios that require the use of net income, have you noticed that we do not use total comprehensive income? By using net income rather than comprehensive income, we exclude the impact of other comprehensive income from the analysis. Profitability ratios, including industry averages, generally use data from the income statement and not from the statement of comprehensive income, which includes both net income and other comprehensive income. In fact, there are no standard ratio formulas incorporating comprehensive income.

Nonetheless, it is important to review a company's sources of comprehensive income in any financial analysis. For example, Hudson's Bay reported net income of $387 million for the year ended January 30, 2016. During the same year, it reported other comprehensive income of $248 million, which resulted in total comprehensive income of $635 million ($387 + $248). Currency translation adjustments were the main cause of the other comprehensive income. They are not reported on the income statement because they do not deal directly with the company's operations, but clearly the company benefited from these currency gains.

HBC's profit margin, illustrated earlier in the chapter, was $387 million ÷ $11,162 million = 3.5%. However, if the other comprehensive income had been included in this ratio as well as the other profitability ratios we covered in this chapter, those ratios would have indicated much better performance than originally shown. For example, Hudson's Bay's profit margin would have been $635 million ÷ $11,162 million = 5.7%.

In cases like this, where other comprehensive income is significant, and depending on the source of the income, some analysts will adjust profitability ratios to incorporate the effect of total comprehensive income. Of course, you will recall from past chapters that private companies following ASPE do not report comprehensive income, so this limitation would apply only to private and public companies following IFRS.

DISCONTINUED OPERATIONS

Discontinued operations are any components of an entity that have been disposed of or are available for sale. A component of an entity, for the purpose of discontinued operations, represents a separate major line of business or major geographical area of operations that has been disposed of or is held for sale. It must be clearly distinguishable operationally and financially from the rest of the company.

We often use net income to calculate ratios but sometimes net income will include gains or losses from discontinued businesses. Such gains or losses do not occur frequently and because of this, they are shown separately on the income statement, usually as the last item before determining net income. Why? Users of an income statement are looking at this historical information to predict future performance. By segregating the gains or losses from discontinued businesses (which most likely will not be operating in the future) from the net income or loss from continuing operations, it is easier to predict what net income may be in the future. Because of this, we exclude the effects of discontinued business operations when performing financial analysis and calculating ratios.

When HBC made a strategic decision to sell its interest in Zellers stores several years ago, this business became a discontinued operation. Illustration 14-14 shows the information pertaining to Zellers that HBC reported on its income statement (which it calls statement of earnings) in fiscal 2014.

▶Illustration 14-14

Presentation of discontinued operations on income statement

HUDSON'S BAY COMPANY Statement of Earnings (partial) Year Ended February 1, 2014 (in millions)	
Income (loss) from continuing operations before income tax	$(254.2)
Income tax benefit	78.5
Income (loss) from continuing operations	(175.7)
Discontinued operations	
Loss from discontinued operations, net of income tax	(111.1)
Gain on disposal of discontinued operations, net of income tax	28.7
Loss from discontinued operations, net of income tax	(82.4)
Net loss	$(258.1)

Notice that when a discontinued business gain or loss (more likely to be an overall loss than a gain) is reported, there is a new subtotal that is also shown for income (loss) from continuing operations because this amount is useful for predicting net income or loss in the future. Also notice that income tax relating to discontinued operations is shown within the discontinued operations section of the income statement and is not included in the income tax expense that pertains to continuing operations.

Discontinued operations on the income statement can consist of two parts: (1) the income (loss) earned from the discontinued operations during the period, net of any income tax expense or benefit, and (2) the gain (loss) on the disposal of the component, net of any income tax expense or benefit. Of course, if the component of an entity has not yet been disposed of but is being held for sale, only the first part (the income or loss from the discontinued operations) will be reported on the income statement until the actual disposal occurs.

Notice that there were gains on the disposal of assets of the Zellers business for the year ended February 1, 2014. These gains arose primarily from the sale of leasehold interests in the Zellers stores. These stores operated that year with a net loss of $111.1 million, which is one of the reasons why management made the decision to sell them.

In addition, although not illustrated here, basic earnings per share must be reported separately for continuing operations and for discontinued operations so that investors can clearly see the impact that both types of operations have on this ratio. The impact of the discontinued operations on cash flows must also be reported separately on the statement of cash flows.

Any assets and liabilities pertaining to discontinued businesses are segregated on the statement of financial position and are usually shown as current items. This is because the assets are available for sale and are expected to be sold within a year and the liabilities will be settled as soon as the sale of assets occurs.

NONRECURRING ITEMS

A nonrecurring item is a significant item that is recorded in the income statement but is not expected to occur again. Gains and losses from a discontinued business operation are considered to be nonrecurring items. Because these items are well defined and shown separately, it is easy to exclude their effects when calculating ratios and performing financial analysis. But sometimes there may be events such as a large gain on the sale of land that are not related to a discontinued operation but may not occur again for many years. Should such a gain be excluded from ratio analysis? Usually not, because it is not reported separately as a discontinued item and because its impact on income tax may be difficult to determine, whereas the tax impact of a discontinued business loss is included in that loss.

The determination of whether an item is nonrecurring requires the use of professional judgement. For example, some companies will report impairment losses or writedowns of inventory to net realizable value, but it may be difficult to determine to what extent they are truly nonrecurring. Unpredictable economic events such as steep declines in oil prices or changes in interest rates may or may not result in nonrecurring events. Consequently, because of this lack of certainty, we include these items in net income when calculating profitability ratios even though they can cause significant fluctuations in these ratio values. An example of this was the sale of real estate assets for HBC that we included in the determination of many of the ratios we covered in this chapter.

When management feels that accounting standards define key measures of performance such as net income too rigidly, they will disclose **non-GAAP measures**, which are management-defined measures of financial performance that are not included in accounting standards. For example, HBC discusses normalized net earnings, which includes net income adjusted for items that management feels are nonrecurring. HBC also measures performance using adjusted earnings before income tax and depreciation (adjusted EBITDA) to exclude the effects of tax refunds and depreciation (because it is based on estimates and has no effect on cash flows). When management uses non-GAAP measures such as normalized earnings, they must provide an explanation as to how these measures differ from well-defined IFRS terms like *net income* and must also provide a reconciliation between the two amounts.

DO IT! ▶14-5   **Limitations of Financial Analysis**

Action Plan

✔ Recall the formula for profit margin: Net income ÷ Net sales. Substitute total comprehensive income instead of net income to determine the impact of other comprehensive income on profitability.

✔ Recall the formula for return on assets: Net income ÷ Average total assets. Substitute total comprehensive income instead of net income to determine the impact of other comprehensive income on profitability.

✔ To determine the significance of other comprehensive income, compare the ratios with and without other comprehensive income and assess whether the change in the ratios is significant enough to affect decision-making.

✔ Recall that inventory turnover is equal to cost of goods sold divided by average inventory.

✔ Recall that asset turnover is equal to net sales divided by average total assets.

Linamar Corporation which is located in Guelph, Ontario, is Canada's second-largest auto parts manufacturer. The company reported the following selected information (in millions) for the year ended December 31, 2015:

Average total assets	$3,374
Total revenue	5,162
Net income	437
Other comprehensive income	173
Total comprehensive income	610

(a) Calculate the profit margin and return on assets ratios using (1) net income as the numerator, and (2) total comprehensive income as the numerator.

(b) Do you think other comprehensive income is a significant factor in the analysis of Linamar's profitability?

(c) Linamar has a significant amount of inventory, which it accounts for at average cost. If the cost of this inventory was rising during the year and many of the company's competitors determined their inventory costs using FIFO, how would this affect the comparability of the company's inventory turnover ratio to the industry average?

(d) Linamar depreciates its buildings using a diminishing-balance method. If the rest of the industry used a straight-line method and most buildings were relatively new, how would this affect the comparability of the asset turnover ratio?

(e) If Linamar had a loss from a discontinued business, what impact would this have on the determination of the profit margin ratio?

SOLUTION

Try this Do It! exercise on your own and then check your answer at the end of the chapter.

Related Exercise Material: BE14–14, BE14–15, E14–15, and E14–16.

REVIEW AND PRACTICE

▶ LEARNING OBJECTIVE REVIEW

1. Explain and apply comparative analysis. Horizontal analysis is a technique for evaluating a series of data, such as line items in a company's financial statements, by expressing them as percentage increases or decreases over two or more years (or periods of time). The horizontal percentage of a base-period amount is calculated by dividing the amount in a specific year (period) by a base-year (period) amount. This percentage calculation normally covers multiple years (periods).

The horizontal percentage change for the period is calculated by dividing the dollar amount of the change between two years (or periods) by the prior-year (period) amount. This percentage calculation normally covers two years (or periods) only.

Vertical analysis is a technique for evaluating data within one year (or period) by expressing each item in a financial statement as a percentage of a relevant total (base amount) in that same financial statement. For example, the vertical percentage of a base amount can be determined by expressing each item on the income statement as a percentage of revenue (or net sales) or each item on the statement of financial position as a percentage of total assets by dividing the financial statement amount under analysis by the base amount for that particular financial statement.

2. Calculate and interpret ratios that are used to analyze liquidity. Liquidity ratios include working capital, the current ratio, receivables turnover and average collection period, and inventory turnover and days in inventory. The formula, what it measures, and desired result of each liquidity ratio are presented in Illustration 14-10.

3. Calculate and interpret ratios that are used to analyze solvency. Solvency ratios include debt to total assets, times interest earned, and free cash flow. The formula, what it measures, and desired result of each solvency ratio are presented in Illustration 14-11.

4. Calculate and interpret ratios that are used to analyze profitability. Profitability ratios include gross profit margin, profit margin, asset turnover, return on assets, return on common shareholders' equity, basic earnings per share, price-earnings, payout, and dividend yield. The formula, what it measures, and desired result of each profitability ratio are presented in Illustration 14-13.

5. Understand the limitations of financial analysis. The comparability of a company's financial results with those of its peers can be affected by the level of diversification undertaken by the company, the accounting policies it has chosen from acceptable

alternatives, and management's professional judgement when determining estimated amounts in financial statements. Companies using IFRS may report significant amounts of other comprehensive income in their financial statements while those using ASPE do not. Furthermore, accounting policy choices within IFRS may lead to differences in how or if other comprehensive income is reported. Consequently, if other comprehensive income is significant, it should be taken into consideration when performing financial analysis. Gains or losses from discontinued operations are presented separately from continuing operations on the income statement, net of income tax, to highlight their infrequent nature. Assets and liabilities pertaining to these operations are also segregated on the statement of financial position. Normally, the effects of discontinued operations are ignored when undertaking financial analysis because they are not expected to be present in the future. When management believes that accounting standards do not produce effective amounts to measure performance or financial position, they will provide adjusted measures of selected financial statement items such as net income. These are called non-GAAP measures and will often exclude items that management believes are nonrecurring or not relevant.

▶ KEY TERM REVIEW

The following are key terms defined in this chapter with the corresponding page reference for your review. You will find a complete list of terms and definitions for all chapters in the glossary at the end of this textbook.

Discontinued operations (p. 796)
Horizontal analysis (p. 768)
Horizontal percentage change for the period (p. 769)

Horizontal percentage of a base-period amount (p. 768)
Non-GAAP measures (p. 797)
Vertical analysis (p. 772)

Vertical percentage of a base amount (p. 772)

▶ COMPARING IFRS AND ASPE REVIEW

Key Standard Differences	International Financial Reporting Standards (IFRS)	Accounting Standards for Private Enterprises (ASPE)
Comprehensive income	If other comprehensive income is significant, selected profitability ratios can be recalculated using total comprehensive income rather than net income.	Comprehensive income is not reported.
Segmented reporting	There are specific revenue, income, and asset tests to determine if information must be reported in the notes to the financial statements for segments.	There are no disclosure requirements for reporting segment information.

▶ DECISION TOOLKIT REVIEW

DECISION CHECKPOINTS	INFO NEEDED FOR DECISION	TOOLS TO USE FOR DECISION	HOW TO EVALUATE RESULTS
How do the company's financial position and operating results compare with those of previous periods?	Statement of financial position and income statement	Comparative financial statements should be prepared over at least two years, with the first year reported as the base year. Changes in each line item relative to the base year should be presented both by amount and by percentage. This is called horizontal analysis.	A significant change should be investigated to determine what caused it.

DECISION CHECKPOINTS	INFO NEEDED FOR DECISION	TOOLS TO USE FOR DECISION	HOW TO EVALUATE RESULTS
How do the relationships between items in this year's financial statements compare with last year's relationships or those of competitors?	Statement of financial position and income statement	Each line item on the statement of financial position should be presented as a percentage of total assets (total liabilities and shareholders' equity). Each line item on the income statement should be presented as a percentage of revenues (or net sales). This is called vertical analysis.	Any difference, either across years or between companies, should be investigated to determine the cause.
Does the company report other comprehensive income?	Statement of income and comprehensive income	Determine source and amount of other comprehensive income.	If other comprehensive income is significant, selected profitability ratios can be recalculated using total comprehensive income rather than net income.
Has the company sold, or is it holding for sale, a component of an entity?	Discontinuation of, or plans to discontinue, a component of an entity	Discontinued operations section of the statement of financial position, income statement, and/or statement of cash flows.	If a component of an entity has been discontinued, its results in the current period should not be included in assessing the company's financial position or in estimating its future profit or cash flows.
Are efforts to evaluate the company hampered by diversification, alternative accounting policies, the use of estimates, and nonrecurring items?	Financial statements as well as other information that is disclosed	Review segmented information. Review accounting policies and estimates for comparability and reasonableness. Understand significant events including economic ones that affected the company's performance.	If there are any comparability issues or irregularities, the analysis should be relied on with caution.

▶ PRACTICE USING THE DECISION TOOLKIT

Answers are at the end of the chapter.

Walmart Stores Inc. and Target Corporation are U.S.-based retailers. Selected liquidity, solvency, and profitability ratios follow for the two companies and their industry for a recent year:

	Walmart	Target	Industry
Liquidity			
Current ratio	1.0:1	1.1:1	1.1:1
Average collection period	5 days	Not applicable	4 days
Days in inventory	45 days	59 days	46 days
Solvency			
Debt to total assets	57.8%	67.8%	54.5%
Times interest earned	10.9 times	9.2 times	11.1 times
Profitability			
Gross profit margin	24.3%	29.5%	29.6%
Profit margin	3.3%	4.6%	2.2%
Asset turnover	2.4 times	1.8 times	2.5 times
Return on assets	7.9%	8.3%	5.5%
Return on common shareholders' equity	19.6%	25.0%	12.1%

INSTRUCTIONS

(a) Which company is more liquid? Why? Is the company you chose more liquid than the industry average?

(b) Which company is more solvent? Explain. Is the company you chose more solvent than the industry average? Why does Target have more leverage?

(c) Why does Walmart have a lower return on assets than Target?

(d) Why does Walmart have a lower return on common shareholders' equity than Target?

► PRACTICE COMPREHENSIVE DO IT!

Answers are at the end of the chapter.

Green Ltd. and Gold Corp. operate in the same segment of the manufacturing industry and have roughly the same amount of sales. Ratios for both companies have been determined for the year ending December 31, 2018, and are listed below:

	Green	Gold
Current ratio	2.1:1	1.2:1
Receivables turnover	12.2 times	8.1 times
Inventory turnover	10.3 times	6.4 times
Debt to total assets	25.2%	50.3%
Times interest earned	3.1	2.2
Gross profit margin	40.0%	50.0%
Profit margin	10.0%	15.0%
Asset turnover	1.5 times	1.0 times
Return on assets	15.0%	15.0%
Return on common shareholders' equity	20.1%	30.2%
Payout ratio	75.0%	50.0%
Dividend yield	5.0%	2.5%
Price-earnings ratio	15	20

INSTRUCTIONS

(a) Which company does a better job of collecting its accounts receivable faster and turning its inventory over more quickly? Explain.

(b) The company you selected in part (a) above should have relatively lower accounts receivable and inventory balances, so if it had a higher current ratio than the other company, what could be a reason for this?

(c) One of the companies has an aggressive growth strategy and is taking on more debt in order to finance this expansion. Which company is doing this? Explain.

(d) One of the companies has a foreign supplier that is selling goods to the company at a much lower cost than its competitors. Which company is this? Explain.

(e) Both companies pay income taxes at the same rate but one of the companies has higher operating expenses and higher interest expenses relative to its sales. Which company is this? Explain.

(f) Both companies own their property, plant, and equipment, so depreciable assets are the major assets owned by each company, but one company has acquired some of these assets more recently. Which company is that? Explain.

(g) Neither company has preferred shares outstanding. What is the primary reason for Gold having a higher return on common shareholders' equity?

(h) The shareholders of which company would be more interested in receiving dividend income from the company? Why?

(i) Provide some reasons why Gold's price-earnings ratio is higher than Green's ratio.

► PRACTICE OBJECTIVE-FORMAT QUESTIONS

Answers are at the end of the chapter.

1. Assuming all other items remain unchanged on the financial statements, which events shown below (which are mutually exclusive) would most likely increase the current ratio for a company that has more current assets than current liabilities? (Select as many as are appropriate.)

(a) An increase in the receivables turnover ratio.

(b) A decrease in the number of days in inventory.

(c) A more conservative estimate of the allowance for doubtful accounts.

(d) A write off of accounts receivable from bankrupt customers that was previously estimated when the allowance for doubtful accounts was recorded.

(e) An increase in sales discounts from 2% to 3% that successfully increases credit sales by 10%.

    (f) An increase in the payout ratio even though there is no change to net income.

    (g) Paying down a large account payable sooner than expected.

2. Which of the following items would affect the determination of free cash flow? (Select as many as are appropriate.)

    (a) Dividends declared and paid on preferred shares

    (b) An increase in depreciation expense

    (c) The purchase of equipment

    (d) The collection of an account receivable

    (e) The payment of the principal portion of a bank loan

    (f) Dividends declared on common shares but not yet paid

    (g) The gain on the sale of land

3. Which of the following statements are correct? (Select as many as are appropriate.)

    (a) Most of the time, an increasing current ratio indicates that a company's liquidity is getting worse.

    (b) The profit margin will decrease if the gross profit margin is increasing and interest expense, operating expenses, and income tax expense are decreasing.

    (c) Increasing dividends paid will cause free cash flow to decrease.

    (d) Asset turnover will decrease if a company does not replace any of its depreciable assets.

    (e) Receivables turnover will increase if a company is collecting its accounts receivable more quickly.

    (f) When the payout ratio increases, and net income remains unchanged, the company must have decreased cash dividends.

    (g) Inventory turnover will decrease when a company is selling its inventory more quickly.

4. What items listed below are included in the profit margin ratio but are not included in the gross profit margin ratio? (Select as many as are appropriate.)

    (a) Cost of goods sold

    (b) Operating expenses

    (c) Sales

    (d) Gains on disposal of equipment

    (e) Interest expense

    (f) Other comprehensive income

    (g) Income tax expense

5. At the beginning of the current fiscal year, a company began purchasing inventory from a new supplier at a cost that was 5% lower than it paid in the past. When the inventory was sold on account to customers, the company did not change the price it sold these products at because demand for the products grew by 15%. The company was able to handle this increased demand without borrowing money and without moving to new premises or hiring additional staff and the company was able to maintain the same number of inventory units on hand that it had in the past. The company does not pay out any dividends. Because of the events described above we should expect which of the following effects to occur? (Select as many as are appropriate.)

    (a) Gross profit margin will increase.

    (b) Inventory turnover will decrease.

    (c) Receivables turnover will increase.

    (d) Profit margin will decrease.

    (e) Times interest earned will remain unchanged.

    (f) Free cash flow will increase.

    (g) Days in inventory will decrease.

6. Worried about the risk of rising interest rates, the management of a company decided to sell its retail stores early in the year for $10 million and use the proceeds received from these sales to pay off $8 million of its non-current mortgages on these properties. The $2-million difference was paid out to shareholders as a dividend, the first time the company has paid a dividend. The sale resulted in a gain of $4 million. The company then rented its store locations. When analyzing its income statement at the end of the year, the new rent expense was $1 million greater than the interest expense, depreciation, and other occupancy costs incurred on the retail stores in the previous year. Because of this, cash is lower at the end of the year than at the beginning. Assuming all other items on the financial statements were the same this year as in prior years, which of the following statements are correct? (Select as many as are appropriate.)

    (a) Gross profit margin will increase.

    (b) Profit margin will increase.

    (c) Times interest earned will increase.

    (d) Return on assets will increase.

    (e) Dividend payout will decrease.

    (f) Working capital will decrease.

    (g) Inventory turnover will decrease.

7. Interest rates have been falling throughout the year on loans held by a company. No new loans have been received during the year but existing ones have been partially paid down. Which of the following statements are correct, assuming no other events have changed? (Select as many as are appropriate.)
   (a) Gross profit margin will increase.
   (b) Profit margin will decrease.
   (c) Times interest earned will increase.
   (d) Return on common shareholders' equity will increase.
   (e) Inventory turnover will decrease.
   (f) Debt to total assets will decrease.
   (g) Free cash flow will increase.

8. A company has just completed its most profitable year ever. Net income and net cash provided (used) by operating activities has increased by 25% and the board has increased dividends on common shares by 10%. Investors have reacted favourably to this news and the share price has risen by 17%. Because of these events, which of the following statements are correct? (Select as many as are appropriate.)
   (a) Dividend yield will decrease.
   (b) Price-earnings ratio will increase.
   (c) Payout ratio will increase.
   (d) Profit margin will increase.
   (e) Return on assets will decrease.
   (f) Return on common shareholders' equity will increase.
   (g) Free cash flow will decrease.

9. At the beginning of the current year, a new accountant for a company estimated that the residual value of equipment that was being depreciated on a straight-line basis was lower than originally determined and he also estimated that damages for a lawsuit against the company that might be paid out next year needed to be increased. When these estimate changes are adopted in the current year, we would expect which of the following statements to be correct? (Select as many as are appropriate.)
   (a) Gross profit margin will decrease.
   (b) Profit margin will decrease.
   (c) The current ratio will decrease.
   (d) Debt to total assets will increase.
   (e) Free cash flow will decrease.
   (f) Times interest earned will decrease.
   (g) Asset turnover will decrease.

10. Which of the following items would normally be excluded from net income when determining the return on assets or common shareholders' equity? (Select as many as are appropriate.)
   (a) Other comprehensive income
   (b) Gains from the sale of equipment
   (c) Losses from discontinued operations
   (d) Income tax expense pertaining to continuing businesses
   (e) Gains for the sale of assets pertaining to discontinued operations
   (f) Losses arising from uninsured fire damage
   (g) Interest expense

WileyPLUS

Brief Exercises, Exercises, and many additional resources are available for practice in WileyPLUS.

▶ QUESTIONS

(LO 1) 1. Explain how a horizontal analysis is affected if an account (a) has no value in a base year and a value in the next year, or (b) has a negative value in the base year and a positive value in the next year.

(LO 1) 2. Two methods of financial statement analysis are horizontal analysis and vertical analysis. Explain how these two methods are similar, and how they differ.

(LO 1) 3. Explain how the (a) horizontal percentage of a base-period amount, (b) horizontal percentage change for a period, and (c) vertical percentage of a base amount are calculated.

(LO 1) 4. **Davids TEA** became a public corporation in June 2015. Can a meaningful horizontal and vertical analysis be prepared for its first two years of operations? Why or why not?

(LO 1) 5. What base amount is usually assigned a 100% value in a vertical analysis of the (a) statement of financial position and (b) income statement?

(LO 1) 6. Can vertical analysis be used to compare two companies of different sizes and using different currencies, such as **Anheuser-Busch In Bev SA/NV**, the world's largest brewer, headquartered in Belgium, and **SAB Miller plc**, the second-largest brewer, headquartered in the United Kingdom? Explain.

(LO 1, 2) 7. (a) Distinguish among the following bases of comparison: intracompany, intercompany, and industry average. (b) Explain which analysis technique(s)—horizontal analysis, vertical analysis, or ratio analysis—is normally used with each base of comparison.

(LO 2) 8. Is a high current ratio always a good indicator of a company's liquidity? Describe two situations in which a high current ratio might be hiding liquidity problems.

(LO 2) 9. Identify for which liquidity ratios a lower result might be better, and explain why.

(LO 2) 10. If a company increases its receivables turnover ratio and its inventory turnover ratio (assuming nothing else changes), what impact will this have on the current ratio?

(LO 3) 11. Identify for which solvency ratios a higher result or a lower result might be better, and explain why.

(LO 3) 12. **Magna International Inc.** reported a debt to total assets ratio of 22.4% and times interest earned ratio of 56.6 times at the end of its fiscal 2015 year. The industry averages at the time were 35.1% and 5.9 times, respectively. Is Magna's solvency better or worse than that of the industry? Why?

(LO 3) 13. Amber Ltd. increased its debt to total assets ratio from 40% to 60% over the past year and its times interest earned ratio rose from 3.0 times to 3.8 times. Meanwhile, Baxter Inc. also increased its debt to total assets ratio by the same amount but its times interest earned ratio fell. Explain how this is possible.

(LO 4) 14. How do the profit margin and the asset turnover ratio help to explain the return on assets ratio?

(LO 4) 15. How do the return on assets ratio and the debt to total assets ratio help to explain the return on common shareholders' equity ratio?

(LO 4) 16. **CIBC's** return on assets was 0.8% in 2015. During the same year, CIBC reported a return on common shareholders' equity of 18.7%. Has CIBC made effective use of leverage? Explain.

(LO 4) 17. (a) If you were an investor interested in buying the shares of a company with growth potential, what ratio(s) would you primarily look at to help you make your decision? (b) How would your answer change if you were interested in buying shares with an income potential?

(LO 2, 3, 4) 18. Identify the ratio(s) that should be used to help answer each of these questions.
(a) How efficient is the company in using its assets to produce sales?
(b) How near to sale is the inventory on hand?
(c) How profitable was the company relative to the amount invested by shareholders?
(d) How able is the company to pay interest charges as they come due?
(e) How able is the company to repay a short-term loan?
(f) How much of a company's net income is being distributed as dividends?
(g) Are the shares of a company trading at a price that is higher relative to its basic earnings per share?

(LO 5) 19. Identify and explain the factors that can limit the usefulness of financial analysis.

(LO 5) 20. If a company adopted a more conservative approach when estimating expenses, how would this affect the profit margin ratio?

(LO 5) 21. (a) What are discontinued operations? (b) What is a component of an entity?

(LO 5) 22. Is other comprehensive income included or excluded in the determination of profitability ratios?

(LO 5) 23. **McCain Foods** and **Cavendish Farms** are both private companies. McCain Foods uses IFRS and Cavendish Farms uses ASPE. What impact do these differing standards have on financial analysis?

(LO 5) 24. Explain how management communicates what it considers to be more effective measures of performance than ones that are typically measured by IFRS or ASPE.

(LO 4, 5) 25. In 2015, **Potash Corporation of Saskatchewan** reported a profit margin of 20.2% using net income in the numerator. Had the profit margin been based on total comprehensive income, instead of net income, the revised profit margin would have decreased to 12.0%. In 2014, its profit margin was 21.6% using net income and 17.7% using total comprehensive income. (a) Has Potash's profitability improved or deteriorated in 2015? (b) Which profit margin—without other comprehensive income or with other comprehensive income—is the most appropriate ratio to use in this particular case for analysis purposes? Explain.

▶ BRIEF EXERCISES

Prepare horizontal analysis.

(LO 1)

BE14–1 Selected data from the comparative statements of financial position of Rioux Ltd. are shown below:

	2018	2017	2016
Cash	$ 150,000	$ 175,000	$ 75,000
Accounts receivable	600,000	400,000	450,000
Inventory	780,000	600,000	700,000
Property, plant, and equipment	3,130,000	2,800,000	2,850,000
Intangible assets	90,000	100,000	0
Total assets	$4,750,000	$4,075,000	$4,075,000

(a) Using horizontal analysis, calculate the percentage of a base-year amount, assuming 2016 is the base year.

(b) Using horizontal analysis, calculate the percentage change for each year.

BE14–2 Selected horizontal percentages of a base-year amount from Coastal Ltd.'s income statement are listed here:

	2018	2017	2016
Net sales	110%	101%	100%
Cost of goods sold	105%	111%	100%
Operating expenses	99%	112%	100%
Income tax expense	136%	60%	100%

Use horizontal analysis to determine change in net income.
(LO 1)

Assuming that Coastal did not have any non-operating or irregular items, did its net income increase, decrease, or remain unchanged over the period from 2016 to 2018? Explain.

BE14–3 Comparative data from the statement of financial position of Elke Ltd. are shown below. (a) Using horizontal analysis, calculate the percentage of the base-year amount, using 2016 as the base year. (b) Using vertical analysis, calculate the percentage of the base amount for each year.

Prepare horizontal and vertical analyses.
(LO 1)

	2018	2017	2016
Current assets	$1,530,000	$1,175,000	$1,225,000
Property, plant, and equipment	3,130,000	2,800,000	2,850,000
Goodwill	90,000	100,000	-0-
Total assets	$4,750,000	$4,075,000	$4,075,000

BE14–4 Selected data (in thousands) from the income statement of JTI Inc. are shown below. Using vertical analysis, calculate the percentage of the base amount for each year.

Prepare vertical analysis.
(LO 1)

	2018	2017
Net sales	$1,914	$2,073
Cost of goods sold	1,612	1,674
Gross profit	302	399
Operating expenses	218	210
Income before income tax	84	189
Income tax expense	17	38
Net income	$ 67	$ 151

BE14–5 Vertical analysis percentages from Waubon Corp.'s income statement are listed here:

Use vertical analysis to determine change in net income.
(LO 1)

	2018	2017	2016
Net sales	100.0%	100.0%	100.0%
Cost of goods sold	59.4%	60.5%	60.0%
Operating expenses	19.6%	20.4%	20.0%
Income tax expense	4.2%	3.8%	4.0%

Assuming that Waubon did not have any non-operating or irregular items, did its net income as a percentage of sales increase, decrease, or remain unchanged over the three-year period? Explain.

BE14–6 Selected financial data for Shumway Ltd. are shown below. (a) Calculate for each of 2018 and 2017 the (1) current ratio, (2) receivables turnover ratio, and (3) inventory turnover ratio. (b) Based on these ratios, what conclusion(s) can be drawn about the company's liquidity?

Calculate and evaluate liquidity.
(LO 2)

	2018	2017	2016
Accounts receivable (gross)	$ 850,000	$ 750,000	$ 650,000
Inventory	1,020,000	980,000	840,000
Total current assets	2,100,000	2,000,000	1,700,000
Total current liabilities	1,000,000	1,100,000	1,250,000
Net credit sales	6,420,000	6,240,000	5,430,000
Cost of goods sold	4,540,000	4,550,000	3,950,000

BE14–7 At the beginning of 2018, the new CEO of Optimus Ltd. introduced two new initiatives to improve the company's performance. First of all, she introduced "blowout" sales offering prices at deep discounts to reduce inventory levels. Second, she extended the period of time that customers had to pay the company from 30 days to 50 days. Although the

Assess liquidity ratios.
(LO 2)

new initiatives allowed the company to sell more products and reduce inventory, price decreases were so steep that overall sales decreased. What changes would you expect to see in the receivables and inventory turnover ratios? Explain why.

Evaluate liquidity.
(LO 2)

BE14–8 Holysh Inc. reported a current ratio of 1.5:1 in the current fiscal year, which is higher than its current ratio last year of 1.2:1. It also reported a receivables turnover of 9 times, which is less than last year's receivables turnover of 12 times, and an inventory turnover of 6 times, which is less than last year's inventory turnover of 9 times. Is Holysh's liquidity improving or deteriorating? Explain.

Evaluate solvency.
(LO 3)

BE14–9 New Flyer Industries Inc. reported the following measures for 2015 and 2014:

	2015	2014
Debt to total assets	72.7%	60.1%
Times interest earned	9.4 times	5.2 times
Free cash flow (in U.S. $ millions)	$34	$35

Is New Flyer's solvency improving or deteriorating? Explain.

Evaluate solvency and profitability.
(LO 3, 4)

BE14–10 A company changed its strategic direction and undertook an aggressive growth strategy, acquiring a significant amount of new assets early in the current fiscal year. The purchase of these assets was financed by increased levels of debt, and that strategy proved to be very successful as net income increased at a significantly higher rate than the increase in interest expense. (a) Because of this strategy, explain how the following ratios would most likely change during the year: (1) debt to total assets, (2) interest coverage, and (3) free cash flow (the company does not pay out dividends). (b) When a company takes on new amounts of debt and profitability rises because of this, what happens to the relationship between the return on assets ratio and the return on common shareholders' equity ratio?

Evaluate profitability.
(LO 4)

BE14–11 Wolastoq Corp. reported the following ratios for 2018 and 2017:

	2018	2017
Return on common shareholders' equity	17.4%	19.1%
Return on assets	10.8%	9.2%
Debt to total assets	38.0%	52.0%
Profit margin	9.8%	6.1%
Asset turnover	1.1 times	1.5 times

(a) What changes in the ratios above may have increased or decreased the company's return on assets in 2018?
(b) What is the key reason driving the change in Wolastoq's return on common shareholders' equity in 2018? Explain.

Evaluate market measures.
(LO 4)

BE14–12 Recently, the price-earnings ratio of **Amazon.com, Inc.** was 191.7 times, and the price-earnings ratio of **Bank of Montreal** was 12.1 times. The dividend yield of each company was 0.0% and 3.9%, respectively. Which company's shares would you purchase for growth? For income? Explain.

Evaluate profitability ratios.
(LO 4)

BE14–13 In 2018, Ajax Ltd. completed a very successful year with an increase in its net income of over 20%. Most of this increase occurred because a new manufacturing plant was built almost exclusively through the use of borrowed funds. To conserve cash for further expansion, the board of directors increased the dividend in 2018 by only 3%. Because of this, the company's share price rose by only 6% in that year. (a) What ratio increased the most in 2018: return on assets or return on common shareholders' equity? Why? (b) Did the payout, price-earnings, and dividend yield ratios increase or decrease in 2018? Why?

Calculate impact of other comprehensive income on profit margin.
(LO 4, 5)

BE14–14 **Thomson Reuters Corporation** reported the following selected information (in U.S. $ millions):

	2015	2014	2013
Revenues	$12,209	$12,607	$12,702
Net income	1,311	1,959	185
Other comprehensive income (loss)	(496)	(1,866)	202
Total comprehensive income	815	93	387

(a) Calculate the profit margin with and without the other comprehensive income (loss) for each year.
(b) Which of the two profit margin ratios that you calculated in part (a) should you rely upon for your financial analysis? Explain.

BE14–15 You are analyzing the financial statements of Able Ltd. and read in the notes to its financial statements that the company uses FIFO rather than an average cost formula when accounting for inventories. Inventory costs in the industry have been rising steadily for the past two years. You also learn that Able and the industry both use straight-line depreciation but Able estimates that its equipment has a useful life of 10 years compared with the industry average of eight years. Able's ratios would be very similar to the industry average if it were not for the differences mentioned above. What is the impact of Able's different accounting policies and estimates on its (a) inventory turnover, (b) asset turnover, (c) profit margin, (d) return on assets, and (e) return on common shareholders' equity compared with the industry average?

Determine impact of accounting policies and estimates on ratios.

(LO 5)

▶ EXERCISES

E14–1 Condensed data from the comparative statement of financial position of Dressaire Inc. follow:

Prepare horizontal analysis.

(LO 1)

	2018	2017	2016
Current assets	$115,000	$110,000	$100,000
Non-current assets	400,000	330,000	300,000
Current liabilities	110,000	100,000	95,000
Non-current liabilities	90,000	110,000	120,000
Common shares	110,000	100,000	100,000
Retained earnings	205,000	130,000	85,000

Instructions
(a) Using horizontal analysis, calculate the percentage of a base-year amount, using 2016 as the base year.
(b) Using horizontal analysis, calculate the percentage change for each year.
(c) Using the information prepared above, do you think the company's shareholders would be pleased by the trends shown in your analysis? Why?

E14–2 Condensed data from the income statement for Fleetwood Corporation follow:

Prepare vertical analysis.

(LO 1)

	2018	2017
Net sales	$800,000	$600,000
Cost of goods sold	550,000	375,000
Gross profit	250,000	225,000
Operating expenses	155,000	125,000
Income before income tax	95,000	100,000
Income tax expense	15,000	20,000
Net income	$ 80,000	$ 80,000

Instructions
(a) Using vertical analysis, calculate the percentage of the base amount for each year.
(b) Comment on three trends that can be noticed in the vertical analysis that you prepared in part (a).

E14–3 The income statement for Labelle Ltd. is shown below:

Prepare horizontal and vertical analyses of income statement.

(LO 1)

LABELLE LTD.
Income Statement
Year Ended December 31
(in millions)

	2018	2017	2016
Sales	$1,600	$1,400	$1,200
Cost of goods sold	900	750	600
Gross profit	700	650	600
Operating expenses	520	410	400
Income from operations	180	240	200
Interest expense	80	50	40
Income before income tax	100	190	160
Income tax expense	25	48	40
Net income	$ 75	$ 142	$ 120

Instructions
(a) Using horizontal analysis, calculate the horizontal percentage of a base-year amount, assuming 2016 is the base year.
(b) Using vertical analysis, calculate the percentage of the base amount for each year.
(c) Identify any significant changes from 2016 to 2018. Explain the trends in your analysis that management should be concerned about and the trends that management would be pleased to see.

Classify ratios.

(LO 2, 3, 4)

E14–4 The following is a list of the ratios and values we have calculated in this text:

(a)	(b)	
_____	_____	Asset turnover
_____	_____	Average collection period
_____	_____	Basic earnings per share
_____	_____	Current ratio
_____	_____	Days in inventory
_____	_____	Debt to total assets
_____	_____	Dividend yield
_____	_____	Free cash flow
_____	_____	Gross profit margin
_____	_____	Inventory turnover
_____	_____	Payout ratio
_____	_____	Price-earnings ratio
_____	_____	Profit margin
_____	_____	Receivables turnover
_____	_____	Return on assets
_____	_____	Return on common shareholders' equity
_____	_____	Times interest earned
_____	_____	Working capital

Instructions
(a) Classify each of the above ratios as a liquidity (L), solvency (S), or profitability (P) ratio.
(b) For each of the above ratios, indicate whether a higher result is generally considered better (B), worse (W), or (N) not determinable.

Calculate and compare liquidity ratios.

(LO 2)

E14–5 Selected comparative financial statement data for Kigio Inc. are shown below.

KIGIO INC.
Statement of Financial Position (partial)
December 31
(in thousands)

	2018	2017	2016
Current assets			
Cash	$ 30	$ 91	$ 60
Held for trading investments	55	60	40
Accounts receivable, net	676	586	496
Inventory	628	525	575
Prepaid expenses	41	52	29
Total current assets	$1,430	$1,314	$1,200
Total current liabilities	$ 890	$ 825	$ 750

Additional information:

(in thousands)	2018	2017	2016
Allowance for doubtful accounts	$ 50	$ 45	$ 40
Net credit sales	4,190	3,940	3,700
Cost of goods sold	2,900	2,650	2,350

Instructions
(a) Calculate all possible liquidity ratios for 2018 and 2017.
(b) Indicate whether each of the liquidity ratios calculated in part (a) is better or worse in 2018.

E14–6 The following selected ratios are available for Pampered Pets Inc. for the three most recent years:

Evaluate liquidity.

(LO 2)

	2018	2017	2016
Current ratio	2.7:1	2.4:1	2.1:1
Receivables turnover	6.7 times	7.4 times	8.2 times
Inventory turnover	7.7 times	8.6 times	9.9 times

Instructions

(a) Has the company's collection of its receivables improved or deteriorated over these three years?

(b) Is the company selling its inventory faster or slower than in past years?

(c) Overall, has the company's liquidity improved or deteriorated over these three years? Explain.

E14–7 Shown below are liquidity ratios for several companies.

Assess liquidity ratios.

(LO 2)

	Company #1	Company #2	Company #3	Company #4	Industry Average
Current ratio	1.5:1	1.6:1	1.3:1	2.9:1	1.2:1
Average collection period	29 days	57 days	39 days	52 days	45 days
Days in inventory	71 days	20 days	50 days	65 days	60 days

Instructions

For each of the following questions, choose the appropriate company and explain why you chose that company by referring to the ratios shown above.

(a) Which company sold common shares recently and has not yet invested all of the cash raised from the share issue? Why?

(b) Which company has had difficulty obtaining products from its suppliers? Why?

(c) Which company may have a credit policy that is too tight? Why?

(d) Which company is managing its working capital most effectively? Why?

E14–8 The following selected information (in thousands) is available for Tukai Limited:

Calculate and compare solvency ratios.

(LO 3)

	2018	2017
Total assets	$3,890	$3,700
Total liabilities	2,175	1,960
Interest expense	15	25
Income tax expense	175	150
Net income	405	375
Cash provided by operating activities	850	580
Net capital expenditures	400	300
Dividends paid on common shares	110	90

Instructions

(a) Calculate all possible solvency ratios for 2018 and 2017.

(b) Indicate whether each of the solvency ratios calculated in part (a) is better or worse in 2018.

E14–9 The following selected ratios are available for Ackabe Inc. for the three most recent years:

Evaluate solvency.

(LO 3)

	2018	2017	2016
Debt to total assets	50.0%	45.5%	40.3%
Times interest earned	1.8 times	1.4 times	1.0 times

Instructions

(a) Has the debt to total assets improved or deteriorated over these three years?

(b) Has the times interest earned improved or deteriorated over these three years? What do you think is a possible explanation for this?

(c) Overall, has the company's solvency improved or deteriorated over these three years? Explain.

Evaluate solvency.

(LO 3)

E14–10 Shown below are solvency ratios for three companies.

	Company #1		Company #2		Company #3	
	2018	2017	2018	2017	2018	2017
Debt to total assets	30.3%	42.1%	59.8%	48.2%	54.3%	33.4%
Times interest earned	4.2 times	2.9 times	1.9 times	3.2 times	5.1 times	3.7 times
Free cash flow (in millions)	75	41	65	75	92	67

Instructions

For each of the following questions, choose the appropriate company and explain why you chose that company by referring to the ratios shown above.

(a) Which company was concerned about its high debt levels and high interest expense and took steps to reduce that debt? Was this strategy successful?

(b) Which company adopted a new growth strategy this year and executed it with success?

(c) Which company's solvency decreased the most in 2018? Why?

Calculate and compare profitability ratios.

(LO 4)

E14–11 The following selected information is for Karatu Corporation:

	2018	2017	2016
Total assets	$350,000	$275,000	$274,000
Total shareholders' equity	133,500	100,000	50,000
Net sales	500,000	400,000	300,000
Cost of goods sold	375,000	290,000	180,000
Net income	33,500	30,000	20,000

Karatu had no preferred shares.

Instructions

(a) Calculate the gross profit margin, profit margin, asset turnover, return on assets, and return on common shareholders' equity ratios for 2018 and 2017.

(b) Indicate whether each of the profitability ratios calculated in part (a) is better or worse in 2018.

Evaluate profitability.

(LO 4)

E14–12 The following selected profitability ratios are available for two companies, BetaCom Corporation and Top Corporation, for a recent fiscal year:

	BetaCom	Top	Industry
Gross profit margin	37.5%	48.2%	37.9%
Profit margin	5.2%	4.9%	4.8%
Asset turnover	1.1 times	1.1 times	1.0 times
Return on assets	5.7%	5.4%	4.8%
Return on common shareholders' equity	9.5%	6.4%	6.0%

Instructions

Which company is more profitable? Explain, making sure to refer to the industry ratios where appropriate.

Identify drivers of profitability.

(LO 4)

E14–13 Selected information for **Metro Inc.** for the most recent three years is as follows (dollar amounts are in millions):

	2015	2014	2013
Net income	$506	$447	$712
Assets, beginning of year	$5,280	$5,064	$5,155
Assets, end of year	$5,387	$5,280	$5,064
Sales	$12,224	$11,590	$11,403
Return on common shareholders' equity	19.1%	16.3%	26.7%
Return on assets	9.5%	8.6%	13.9%
Debt to total assets	50.9%	49.5%	44.7%
Asset turnover	2.3 times	2.2 times	2.2 times
Profit margin	4.1%	3.9%	6.2%

Instructions

(a) What event most likely caused the high amount of profitability in 2013?

(b) What was the main driver of the company's return on assets over these three years? Explain.

(c) What was the main driver of the company's return on common shareholders' equity over these three years? Explain.

E14–14 The following selected ratios are available for a recent year for Archers Post Limited and Nyarboro Corporation:

Evaluate liquidity, solvency, and profitability.

(LO 2, 3, 4)

	Archers Post	Nyarboro	Industry Average
Liquidity			
Current ratio	0.8:1	0.6:1	1.0:1
Receivables turnover	8.7 times	10.4 times	15.2 times
Inventory turnover	6.7 times	29.9 times	65.3 times
Solvency			
Debt to total assets	66.7%	59.0%	68.9%
Times interest earned	4.1 times	3.4 times	3.6 times
Profitability			
Gross profit margin	88.2%	45.2%	55.8%
Profit margin	12.6%	11.2%	2.0%
Return on assets	8.7%	3.9%	1.0%
Return on common shareholders' equity	32.8%	16.2%	4.6%
Price-earnings ratio	13.8 times	20.6 times	26.5 times

Instructions

(a) Which company is more liquid? Explain.

(b) Which company is more solvent? Explain.

(c) Which company is more profitable? Explain.

(d) Which company do investors favour, given that neither company pays out dividends? Is this consistent with your findings in parts (a) to (c)? Investors would be more interested in buying the shares of which company?

E14–15 The following independent events occurred at Ike Inc. during the year:

Identify impact of nonrecurring items on profitability ratios.

(LO 5)

1. A realized gain on the sale of long-term investments
2. A loss caused by a labour strike
3. Other comprehensive income arising from the revaluation of a building
4. An operating loss from a discontinued component of an entity, held for immediate and probable sale
5. An impairment loss on goodwill

Instructions

(a) Identify which of the above items would be excluded from net income when determining profitability ratios. Why?

(b) If management felt that items above that had to be included in net income distorted the measurement of the company's performance, what alternative measures of performance might management adopt?

E14–16 The following are events experienced by a company in the past fiscal year and some common ratios used to analyze company performance.

Identify impact of events on ratios.

(LO 5)

(1) Event	(2) Ratio	Effect
Increased estimate of allowance for doubtful accounts.	Receivables turnover Current ratio Profit margin	
Increased useful life of equipment.	Asset turnover Gross profit margin Profit margin	
Recorded an increase in other comprehensive income when adjusting an investment to its fair value.	Profit margin Return on assets	

Instructions

For each independent event listed in column (1) above, determine if each ratio listed in column (2) above will increase, decrease, or remain unchanged (the effect).

▶ PROBLEMS: SET A

P14–1A **TWC Enterprises Limited** is Canada's largest golf course and resort owner. The following selected information is available for three recent fiscal years:

Prepare horizontal analysis.

(LO 1)

TWC ENTERPRISES LIMITED
Statement of Financial Position
December 31
(in thousands)

	2015	2014	2013
Assets			
Current assets	$ 33,418	$ 12,127	$ 9,650
Non-current assets	678,647	661,208	649,029
Total assets	$712,065	$673,335	$658,679
Liabilities and Shareholders' Equity			
Liabilities			
Current liabilities	$108,480	$103,044	$ 49,280
Non-current liabilities	378,395	369,735	416,106
Total liabilities	486,875	472,779	465,386
Shareholders' equity	225,190	200,556	193,293
Total liabilities and shareholders' equity	$712,065	$673,335	$658,679

TWC ENTERPRISES LIMITED
Statement of Comprehensive Income
Year Ended December 31
(in thousands)

	2015	2014	2013
Revenue	$227,309	$213,050	$213,711
Operating expenses	190,350	181,519	174,765
Income from operations	36,959	31,531	38,946
Other revenues and expenses			
Interest expense	19,659	20,573	20,577
Other expense	9,960	6,181	135
Income before income tax	7,340	4,777	18,234
Income tax expense	3,081	1,312	5,080
Net income	4,259	3,465	13,154
Other comprehensive income	20,375	8,680	5,527
Comprehensive income	$ 24,634	$ 12,145	$ 18,681

Instructions

(a) Using horizontal analysis, calculate the percentage of the base-year amount for each of the statement of financial position and income statement items, assuming 2013 is the base year.

(b) Identify the key components in TWC's statement of financial position and income statement that are primarily responsible for the change in the company's financial position and performance over the three-year period.

Prepare vertical analysis.
(LO 1)

P14–2A The following condensed information is available for **Brick Brewing Company Ltd.**:

BRICK BREWING COMPANY LTD.
Statement of Financial Position
January 31
(in thousands)

	2016	2015	2014
Assets			
Cash	$ 394	$ 595	$ -0-
Accounts receivable	6,176	6,492	5,865
Inventory	3,291	3,401	3,951
Prepaids	355	350	396
Assets held for sale	-0-	-0-	3,406
Current assets	10,216	10,838	13,618
Non-current assets	38,624	34,096	32,751
Total assets	$48,840	$44,934	$46,369

Liabilities and Shareholders' Equity
Liabilities

Current liabilities	$ 6,855	$ 6,335	$ 9,302
Non-current liabilities	6,460	4,217	4,554
Total liabilities	13,315	10,552	13,856
Shareholders' equity	35,525	34,382	32,513
Total liabilities and shareholders' equity	$48,840	$44,934	$46,369

BRICK BREWING COMPANY LTD.
Income Statement
Year Ended
January 31
(in thousands)

	2016	2015	2014
Net sales	$37,610	$36,333	$37,674
Cost of goods sold	27,076	26,136	27,857
Gross profit	10,534	10,197	9,817
Operating expenses	8,008	8,075	8,399
Gain on sale of non-current assets	(205)	(436)	-0-
Income from operations	2,731	2,558	1,418
Interest expense	479	535	692
Income before income tax	2,252	2,023	726
Income tax expense	658	628	201
Net income	$ 1,594	$ 1,395	$ 525

Instructions

(a) Using vertical analysis, calculate the percentage of the base amount for the statement of financial position and income statement for each year.

(b) Identify the key components in Brick Brewing's statement of financial position and income statement that are primarily responsible for the change in the company's financial position and performance over the three-year period.

P14–3A A horizontal and vertical analysis of the income statement for a service company providing consulting services is shown below:

Interpret horizontal and vertical analysis.

(LO 1)

SERVICE CORPORATION
Horizontal Income Statement
Year Ended December 31

	2018	2017	2016	2015
Revenue	120.0%	110.0%	114.0%	100.0%
Operating expenses	118.6%	111.4%	114.3%	100.0%
Income from operations	123.3%	106.7%	113.3%	100.0%
Other revenues and expenses				
Interest expense	40.0%	60.0%	80.0%	100.0%
Other revenue	240.0%	140.0%	140.0%	100.0%
Income before income tax	166.8%	130.2%	131.7%	100.0%
Income tax expense	166.8%	130.2%	131.7%	100.0%
Net income	166.8%	130.2%	131.7%	100.0%

SERVICE CORPORATION
Vertical Income Statement
Year Ended December 31

	2018	2017	2016	2015
Revenue	100.0%	100.0%	100.0%	100.0%
Operating expenses	69.2%	70.9%	70.2%	70.0%
Income from operations	30.8%	29.1%	29.8%	30.0%
Other revenues and expenses				
Interest expense	3.3%	5.4%	7.0%	10.0%
Other revenue	(1.0)%	(0.6)%	(0.9)%	(0.5)%
Income before income tax	28.5%	24.3%	23.7%	20.5%
Income tax expense	5.7%	4.9%	4.8%	4.1%
Net income	22.8%	19.4%	18.9%	16.4%

Instructions

(a) How effectively has the company controlled its operating expenses over the four-year period?

(b) In a horizontal analysis, the company's income tax expense has changed exactly the same as net income (66.8%) over the four-year period. Yet, in a vertical analysis, the income tax percentage is different than the net income percentage in each period. Explain how this is possible.

(c) Identify any other key financial statement components that have changed over the four-year period for the company.

(d) Identify any additional information that might be helpful to you in your analysis of this company over the four-year period.

Calculate and evaluate ratios.

(LO 2, 3, 4)

P14–4A Condensed statement of financial position and income statement data for Pronghorn Ltd. are shown below:

PRONGHORN LTD.
Statement of Financial Position
December 31
(in thousands)

	2018	2017	2016
Assets			
Current assets			
Cash	$ 30	$ 80	$ 200
Accounts receivable	900	700	500
Inventory	1,200	800	500
Total current assets	2,130	1,580	1,200
Property, plant, and equipment (net)	4,100	3,800	3,200
Total assets	$6,230	$5,380	$4,400
Liabilities and Shareholders' Equity			
Liabilities			
Current liabilities	$ 600	$ 550	$ 500
Non-current liabilities	3,070	2,320	1,500
Total liabilities	3,670	2,870	2,000
Shareholders' equity			
Common shares	1,000	1,000	1,000
Retained earnings	1,560	1,510	1,400
Total shareholders' equity	2,560	2,510	2,400
Total liabilities and shareholders' equity	$6,230	$5,380	$4,400

PRONGHORN LTD.
Income Statement
Year Ended December 31
(in thousands)

	2018	2017	2016
Sales (all on credit)	$4,500	$4,000	$3,600
Cost of goods sold	2,500	2,100	1,800
Gross profit	2,000	1,900	1,800
Operating expenses	1,450	1,475	1,490
Income from operations	550	425	310
Interest expense	190	130	70
Income before income tax	360	295	240
Income tax expense	90	75	60
Net income	$ 270	$ 220	$ 180

Instructions

(a) Calculate the receivables turnover ratio, inventory turnover ratio, and current ratio for all three years. Assume that the accounts receivable and inventory balances at the end of 2015 were equal to the balances at the end of 2016. The company does not have an allowance for doubtful accounts and all sales are on credit. Conclude on whether the company's liquidity has improved or worsened over this three-year period and support your explanation by relating the results of the turnover ratios to the current ratio.

(b) Calculate the gross profit margin for each year. The costs paid for inventory purchased from suppliers have changed little over the three years but there is significant competition in the industry. How has this affected this ratio?

(c) Calculate the profit margin ratio. Why has this ratio changed over the three years? Incorporate in your answer any conclusions you made when analyzing the gross profit margin in part (b) above.

(d) Calculate the debt to total assets ratio and the times interest earned ratio for all three years. What strategy pertaining to leverage has the company pursued? Is the company more or less solvent in 2018 than it was in 2016?

(e) The company paid all dividends as soon as they were declared and has only issued common shares. There are no preferred shares. Retained earnings at the beginning of 2016 were $1.3 million. Calculate the cash dividends declared and dividend payout ratio for each year. Why has the payout ratio changed? Do you think that the dividend payout has affected the company's liquidity? Why or why not?

(f) Calculate the asset turnover for each of the three years. Assume that total assets at the end of 2015 were equal to total assets at the end of 2016. Multiply the asset turnover for each year by the profit margin for each year from part (c) above to determine the return on assets for each year. What is the major driver of the company's return on assets?

(g) Calculate the return on common shareholders' equity for each year. Assume that common shareholders' equity at the end of 2015 was equal to that amount for 2016. Why is the return on common shareholders' equity different from the return on assets? Why does the difference between these two ratios change?

P14–5A Condensed statement of financial position and income statement data for Pitka Corporation follow:

Calculate and evaluate ratios.

(LO 2, 3, 4)

PITKA CORPORATION
Statement of Financial Position
December 31

	2018	2017	2016
Assets			
Current assets			
Cash	$ 25,000	$ 20,000	$ 18,000
Accounts receivable (net)	55,000	45,000	48,000
Inventory	100,000	85,000	64,000
Total current assets	180,000	150,000	130,000
Long-term investments	55,000	70,000	45,000
Property, plant, and equipment (net)	500,000	370,000	258,000
Total assets	$735,000	$590,000	$433,000
Liabilities and Shareholders' Equity			
Liabilities			
Current liabilities	$ 85,000	$ 80,000	$ 30,000
Non-current liabilities	155,000	85,000	20,000
Total liabilities	240,000	165,000	50,000
Shareholders' equity			
Common shares	330,000	300,000	300,000
Retained earnings	165,000	125,000	83,000
Total shareholders' equity	495,000	425,000	383,000
Total liabilities and shareholders' equity	$735,000	$590,000	$433,000

PITKA CORPORATION
Income Statement
Year Ended December 31

	2018	2017
Sales	$740,000	$500,000
Less: Sales returns and allowances	40,000	50,000
Net sales	700,000	450,000
Cost of goods sold	450,000	300,000
Gross profit	250,000	150,000
Operating expenses	150,000	84,000
Income from operations	100,000	66,000
Interest expense	10,000	4,000
Income before income tax	90,000	62,000
Income tax expense	18,000	12,400
Net income	$ 72,000	$ 49,600

Additional information:
1. The allowance for doubtful accounts was $4,800 in 2016, $4,500 in 2017, and $5,000 in 2018.
2. All sales were credit sales.
3. Net cash provided by operating activities was $119,600 in 2017 and $102,000 in 2018.
4. Net capital expenditures were $150,000 for 2017 and $180,000 for 2018.

Instructions

(a) Calculate the following ratios for 2017 and 2018:
1. Current ratio
2. Receivables turnover
3. Inventory turnover
4. Debt to total assets
5. Times interest earned
6. Free cash flow
7. Gross profit margin
8. Profit margin
9. Asset turnover
10. Return on assets

(b) Identify whether each ratio calculated in part (a) was better, worse, or unchanged between 2017 and 2018.

(c) Explain whether overall (1) liquidity, (2) solvency, and (3) profitability improved, deteriorated, or remained the same between 2017 and 2018.

Calculate and evaluate ratios.

(LO 2, 3, 4)

P14–6A Condensed statement of financial position and comprehensive income statement data for Clack Ltd. follow:

CLACK LTD.
Statement of Financial Position
December 31

	2018	2017
Assets		
Cash	$ 70,000	$ 65,000
Accounts receivable (net)	95,000	90,000
Inventory	130,000	125,000
Prepaid expenses	24,000	23,000
Long-term investments	45,000	40,000
Property, plant, and equipment (net)	390,000	305,000
Total assets	$754,000	$648,000
Liabilities and Shareholders' Equity		
Liabilities		
Accounts payable	$ 45,000	$ 42,000
Accrued liabilities	30,000	40,000
Bank loan payable (current)	110,000	100,000
Bonds payable, due 2025	200,000	150,000
Total liabilities	385,000	332,000
Shareholders' equity		
Common shares (20,000 shares issued)	200,000	200,000
Retained earnings	172,000	116,000
Accumulated other comprehensive loss	(3,000)	-0-
Total shareholders' equity	369,000	316,000
Total liabilities and shareholders' equity	$754,000	$648,000

CLACK LTD.
Statement of Comprehensive Income
Year Ended December 31

	2018	2017
Sales	$900,000	$840,000
Cost of goods sold	600,000	575,000
Gross profit	300,000	265,000
Operating expenses	184,000	160,000
Income from operations	116,000	105,000
Interest expense	30,000	20,000
Income before income tax	86,000	85,000
Income tax expense	22,000	20,000
Net income	64,000	65,000
Other comprehensive loss	(3,000)	-0-
Total comprehensive income	$ 61,000	$ 65,000

Additional information:
1. The allowance for doubtful accounts was $4,000 in 2017 and $5,000 in 2018.
2. Accounts receivable at the beginning of 2017 were $88,000, net of an allowance for doubtful accounts of $3,000.
3. Inventory at the beginning of 2017 was $115,000.
4. Total assets at the beginning of 2017 were $630,000.
5. Total current liabilities at the beginning of 2017 were $180,000.
6. Total liabilities at the beginning of 2017 were $371,000.
7. Shareholders' equity at the beginning of 2017 was $259,000.
8. Seventy-five percent of the sales were on account.
9. Net cash provided by operating activities was $85,000 in 2017 and $96,000 in 2018.
10. Net capital expenditures were $50,000 in 2017 and $125,000 in 2018.
11. In each of 2017 and 2018, $8,000 of dividends were paid to the common shareholders.

Instructions
(a) Do we normally include the effects of other comprehensive income in the calculation of profitability ratios?
(b) Calculate all possible liquidity, solvency, and profitability ratios for 2017 and 2018.
(c) Identify whether each liquidity, solvency, and profitability ratio (except for any market measures) calculated in part (a) was better, worse, or unchanged between 2017 and 2018. Use higher, lower, or unchanged for any market measures calculated in part (a).
(d) Explain whether overall (1) liquidity, (2) solvency, and (3) profitability improved, deteriorated, or remained the same between 2017 and 2018.

P14–7A Selected ratios for the current year for two companies in the office supplies industry, Bureau Nouveau Inc. and Supplies Unlimited Corp., follow:

Evaluate ratios.

(LO 2, 3, 4)

	Bureau Nouveau	Supplies Unlimited
Asset turnover	2.6 times	2.2 times
Average collection period	31 days	35 days
Basic earnings per share	$3.50	$2.40
Current ratio	1.7:1	2.0:1
Days in inventory	61 days	122 days
Debt to total assets	45.5%	30.8%
Dividend yield	0.3%	0.5%
Gross profit margin	22.6%	30.7%
Payout ratio	8.0%	19.2%
Price-earnings ratio	29 times	45 times
Profit margin	5.5%	4.7%
Return on assets	14.3%	10.3%
Return on common shareholders' equity	26.1%	12.9%
Times interest earned	4.2 times	8.6 times

Instructions
(a) Both companies offer their customers credit terms of net 30 days. Indicate which ratio(s) should be used to assess how well the accounts receivable are managed. Comment on how well each company appears to be managing its accounts receivable.
(b) Indicate the ratio(s) used to assess inventory management. Which company is managing its inventory better?
(c) Supplies Unlimited's current ratio is higher than that of Bureau Nouveau. Identify two possible reasons for this.
(d) Which company is more solvent? Identify the ratio(s) used to determine this, and defend your choice.
(e) You notice that Supplies Unlimited's gross profit margin is higher and its profit margin lower than those of Bureau Nouveau. Identify two possible reasons for this.
(f) What is mostly responsible for Bureau Nouveau's higher return on assets: profit margin or asset turnover? Explain.
(g) What is mostly responsible for Bureau Nouveau's higher return on common shareholders' equity: return on assets or use of debt? Explain.
(h) Bureau Nouveau's payout ratio is lower than Supplies Unlimited's. Indicate one possible reason for this.
(i) What is the market price per share of each company's common shares?
(j) Which company do investors appear to believe has greater prospects for growing in future (for price appreciation)? Indicate the ratio(s) you used to reach this conclusion, and explain your reasoning.

P14–8A The following ratios are available for fast-food competitors and their industry, for a recent year:

Evaluate ratios.

(LO 2, 3, 4)

	Mac's Burgers	King's Burgers	Industry Average
Liquidity			
Current ratio	1.5:1	0.9:1	1.2:1
Receivables turnover	21.5 times	28.3 times	34.8 times
Inventory turnover	33.6 times	42.3 times	35.2 times

Solvency

Debt to total assets	44.6%	40.1%	44.8%
Times interest earned	16.5 times	6.7 times	11.4 times

Profitability

Gross profit margin	40.0%	33.1%	36.9%
Profit margin	20.6%	7.5%	10.8%
Asset turnover	0.8 times	0.9 times	1.2 times
Return on assets	16.5%	6.8%	13.0%
Return on common shareholders' equity	34.5%	17.8%	22.4%
Price-earnings ratio	19.6 times	17.6 times	19.9 times
Dividend yield	3.0%	1.0%	1.6%

Instructions

(a) Which company is more liquid? Explain.

(b) Which company is more solvent? Explain.

(c) Which company is more profitable? Explain.

(d) Which company do investors favour for growing in the future (price appreciation)? Is your answer consistent with your findings in parts (a) to (c)?

Discuss impact of accounting policies and estimates on financial analysis.

(LO 5)

P14–9A You are in the process of analyzing two similar companies in the same industry. You learn that they have different accounting practices and policies, as follows:

1. Company A, which has the same type of inventory as Company B, uses the FIFO cost formula while Company B uses average. Prices have generally been rising in this industry.

2. Company A uses the double-diminishing-balance depreciation method for most of its buildings, while Company B uses the straight-line method for its buildings.

Instructions

(a) Considering only the impact of the choice of inventory cost formula, determine which company will report a higher (1) current ratio, (2) debt to total assets ratio, and (3) profit margin ratio, or whether the choice of cost formula will have no impact. This is the first year of operations for both companies.

(b) Considering only the impact of the choice of depreciation method, determine which company will report a higher (1) current ratio, (2) debt to total assets ratio, and (3) profit margin ratio, or whether the choice of depreciation method will have no impact. This is the first year of operations for both companies.

(c) Will the use of different accounting estimates and policies affect your analysis? Explain.

(d) When researching information about these companies, you find that each has prepared a non-GAAP measure called normalized net income. Why might these companies calculate such a measure of performance?

(e) Identify two other limitations of financial analysis that an analyst should watch for when analyzing financial statements.

▶ PROBLEMS: SET B

Prepare horizontal analysis.

(LO 1)

P14–1B lululemon athletica inc. has seen a significant amount of growth over the three years shown below. The following selected information is available for three recent fiscal years:

LULULEMON ATHLETICA INC.
Statement of Financial Position
January 31
(in U.S. $ millions)

	2016	2015	2014
Assets			
Current assets	$ 917	$ 951	$ 943
Non-current assets	397	345	307
Total assets	$1,314	$1,296	$1,250
Liabilities and Shareholders' Equity			
Liabilities			
Current liabilities	$ 226	$ 160	$ 114
Non-current liabilities	61	47	39
Total liabilities	287	207	153
Shareholders' equity	1,027	1,089	1,097
Total liabilities and shareholders' equity	$1,314	$1,296	$1,250

LULULEMON ATHLETICA INC.
Statement of Comprehensive Income
Year Ended January 31
(in U.S. $ millions)

	2016	2015	2014
Net revenue	$2,060	$1,797	$1,591
Cost of goods sold	1,063	883	751
Gross profit	997	914	840
Operating expenses	628	538	449
Income from operations	369	376	391
Other income (expense)	(1)	7	6
Income before income tax	368	383	397
Income tax expense	102	144	117
Net income	266	239	280
Other comprehensive loss	65	105	90
Comprehensive income	$ 201	$ 134	$ 190

Instructions

(a) Using horizontal analysis, calculate the percentage of the base-year amount for each of the statement of financial position and income statement, assuming 2014 is the base year.

(b) Identify the key components in lululemon's statement of financial position and income statement that are primarily responsible for the change in the company's financial position and performance over the three-year period.

P14–2B The following condensed information is available for **Canadian Pacific Railway Limited**, Canada's oldest railway: *Prepare vertical analysis.* (LO 1)

CANADIAN PACIFIC RAILWAY LIMITED
Statement of Financial Position
December 31
(in millions)

	2015	2014	2013
Assets			
Cash	$ 650	$ 226	$ 887
Accounts receivable	645	702	580
Supplies and other	242	293	562
Current assets	1,537	1,221	2,029
Non-current assets	18,100	15,329	15,031
Total assets	$19,637	$16,550	$17,060
Liabilities and Shareholders' Equity			
Liabilities			
Current liabilities	$ 1,447	$ 1,411	$ 1,378
Non-current liabilities	13,394	9,529	8,585
Total liabilities	14,841	10,940	9,963
Shareholders' equity	4,796	5,610	7,097
Total liabilities and shareholders' equity	$19,637	$16,550	$17,060

CANADIAN PACIFIC RAILWAY LIMITED
Statement of Comprehensive Income
Year Ended December 31
(in millions)

	2015	2014	2013
Revenues	$6,712	$6,620	$6,133
Operating expenses	4,024	4,281	4,713
Income from operations	2,688	2,339	1,420
Interest expense	394	282	278
Other expense	335	19	17
Income before income tax	1,959	2,038	1,125
Income tax expense	607	562	250
Net income	1,352	1,476	875
Other comprehensive income (loss)	742	(716)	1,265
Comprehensive income	$2,094	$ 760	$2,140

Instructions

(a) Using vertical analysis, calculate the percentage of the base amount for the statement of financial position and income statement for each year.

(b) Identify the key components in Canadian Pacific's statement of financial position and income statement that are primarily responsible for the change in the company's financial position and performance over the three-year period.

Interpret horizontal and vertical analysis.

(LO 1)

P14–3B A horizontal and vertical analysis of the income statement for a retail company selling a wide variety of general merchandise is shown below:

RETAIL CORPORATION
Horizontal Income Statement
Year Ended January 31

	2018	2017	2016	2015
Revenue	140.0%	111.0%	114.0%	100.0%
Cost of goods sold	148.3%	113.3%	116.7%	100.0%
Gross profit	127.5%	107.5%	110.0%	100.0%
Operating expenses	171.4%	133.1%	126.9%	100.0%
Income from operations	93.3%	87.6%	96.9%	100.0%
Other revenues and expenses				
Interest expense	40.0%	60.0%	80.0%	100.0%
Other revenue	240.0%	140.0%	200.0%	100.0%
Income before income tax	140.0%	110.8%	113.8%	100.0%
Income tax expense	160.0%	116.0%	124.0%	100.0%
Net income	135.2%	109.5%	111.4%	100.0%

RETAIL CORPORATION
Vertical Income Statement
Year Ended January 31

	2018	2017	2016	2015
Revenue	100.0%	100.0%	100.0%	100.0%
Cost of goods sold	63.6%	61.2%	61.4%	60.0%
Gross profit	36.4%	38.8%	38.6%	40.0%
Operating expenses	21.4%	21.0%	19.5%	17.5%
Income from operations	15.0%	17.8%	19.1%	22.5%
Other revenues and expenses				
Interest expense	(2.9)%	(5.4)%	(7.0)%	(10.0)%
Other revenue	0.9%	0.6%	0.9%	0.5%
Income before income tax	13.0%	13.0%	13.0%	13.0%
Income tax expense	2.9%	2.6%	2.7%	2.5%
Net income	10.1%	10.4%	10.3%	10.5%

Instructions

(a) How effectively has the company controlled its cost of goods sold over the four-year period?

(b) In a vertical analysis, the company's income before income tax has remained unchanged at 13% of revenue over the four-year period. Yet, in a horizontal analysis, income before income tax has grown 40% over that period of time. Explain how this is possible.

(c) Identify any other key financial statement components that have changed over the four-year period for the company.

(d) Identify any additional information that might be helpful to you in your analysis of this company over the four-year period.

Calculate and evaluate ratios.

(LO 2, 3, 4)

P14–4B Condensed statement of financial position and income statement data for St. Lawrence Ltd. are shown below:

ST. LAWRENCE LTD.
Statement of Financial Position
December 31
(in thousands)

	2018	2017	2016
Assets			
Current assets			
Cash	$ 380	$ 230	$ 80
Accounts receivable	600	550	500
Inventory	700	700	800
Total current assets	1,680	1,480	1,380
Property, plant, and equipment (net)	4,600	3,900	3,200
Total assets	$6,280	$5,380	$4,580
Liabilities and Shareholders' Equity			
Liabilities			
Current liabilities	$ 600	$ 500	$ 400
Non-current liabilities	2,870	2,310	1,780
Total liabilities	3,470	2,810	2,180
Shareholders' equity			
Common shares	1,000	1,000	1,000
Retained earnings	1,810	1,570	1,400
Total shareholders' equity	2,810	2,570	2,400
Total liabilities and shareholders' equity	$6,280	$5,380	$4,580

ST. LAWRENCE LTD.
Income Statement
Year Ended December 31
(in thousands)

	2018	2017	2016
Sales (all on credit)	$4,500	$4,000	$3,600
Cost of goods sold	2,000	1,900	1,800
Gross profit	2,500	2,100	1,800
Operating expenses	1,970	1,680	1,490
Income from operations	530	420	310
Interest expense	100	80	70
Income before income tax	430	340	240
Income tax expense	110	90	60
Net income	$ 320	$ 250	$ 180

Instructions

(a) Calculate the receivables turnover ratio, inventory turnover ratio, and current ratio for all three years. Assume that the accounts receivable and inventory balances at the end of 2015 were equal to the balances at the end of 2016. The company does not have an allowance for doubtful accounts and all sales are on credit. Conclude on whether the company's liquidity has improved or worsened over this three-year period and support your explanation by relating the results of the turnover ratios to the current ratio.

(b) Calculate the gross profit margin for each year. The price charged to customers has changed little over the three years but the company has entered into new contracts with inventory suppliers. How has this affected this ratio?

(c) Calculate the profit margin ratio. Why has this ratio changed over the three years? Incorporate in your answer any conclusions you made when analyzing the gross profit margin in part (b) above.

(d) Calculate the debt to total assets ratio and the times interest earned ratio for all three years. What strategy pertaining to leverage has the company pursued? Is the company more or less solvent in 2018 than it was in 2016?

(e) The company paid all dividends as soon as they were declared and has only issued common shares. There are no preferred shares. Retained earnings at the beginning of 2016 were $1.3 million. Calculate the cash dividends declared and dividend payout ratio for each year. Why has the payout ratio changed? Do you think that the dividend payout has affected the company's liquidity? Why or why not?

(f) Calculate the asset turnover for each of the three years. Assume that total assets at the end of 2015 were equal to total assets at the end of 2016. Multiply the asset turnover for each year by the profit margin for each year from part (c) above to determine the return on assets for each year. What is the major driver of the company's return on assets?

(g) Calculate the return on common shareholders' equity for each year. Assume that common shareholders' equity at the end of 2015 was equal to that amount for 2016. Why is the return on common shareholders' equity different from the return on assets? Why does the difference between these two ratios change?

Calculate and evaluate ratios.

(LO 2, 3, 4)

P14–5B Condensed statement of financial position and income statement data for Colinas Corporation follow:

COLINAS CORPORATION
Statement of Financial Position
December 31

	2018	2017	2016
Assets			
Cash	$ 30,000	$ 24,000	$ 10,000
Accounts receivable (net)	80,000	50,000	53,000
Inventory	85,000	45,000	50,000
Other current assets	70,000	75,000	62,000
Long-term investments	100,000	76,000	50,000
Property, plant, and equipment (net)	595,000	345,000	315,000
Total assets	$960,000	$615,000	$540,000
Liabilities and Shareholders' Equity			
Liabilities			
Current liabilities	$ 63,500	$ 51,000	$ 65,000
Non-current liabilities	245,000	65,000	70,000
Total liabilities	308,500	116,000	135,000
Shareholders' equity			
Common shares	416,500	319,000	275,000
Retained earnings	235,000	180,000	130,000
Total shareholders' equity	651,500	499,000	405,000
Total liabilities and shareholders' equity	$960,000	$615,000	$540,000

COLINAS CORPORATION
Income Statement
Year Ended December 31

	2018	2017
Sales	$950,000	$840,000
Less: Sales returns and allowances	60,000	40,000
Net sales	890,000	800,000
Cost of goods sold	490,000	450,000
Gross profit	400,000	350,000
Operating expenses	266,000	260,000
Income from operations	134,000	90,000
Interest expense	27,750	8,750
Income before income tax	106,250	81,250
Income tax expense	21,250	16,250
Net income	$ 85,000	$ 65,000

Additional information:

1. The allowance for doubtful accounts was $2,400 in 2016, $2,750 in 2017, and $3,650 in 2018.
2. Assume all sales were credit sales.
3. Net cash provided by operating activities was $91,000 in 2017 and $107,500 in 2018.
4. Net capital expenditures were $75,000 for 2017 and $325,000 for 2018.

Instructions

(a) Calculate the following ratios for each of 2017 and 2018:

    1. Current ratio   6. Free cash flow

    2. Receivables turnover   7. Gross profit margin

    3. Inventory turnover   8. Profit margin

    4. Debt to total assets   9. Asset turnover

    5. Times interest earned   10. Return on assets

(b) Indicate whether each ratio calculated in part (a) was better, worse, or unchanged between 2017 and 2018.

(c) Explain whether overall (1) liquidity, (2) solvency, and (3) profitability improved, deteriorated, or remained the same between 2017 and 2018.

P14–6B Condensed statement of financial position and comprehensive income statement data for Track Ltd. *Calculate and evaluate* follow: *ratios.*

(LO 2, 3, 4)

TRACK LTD.
Statement of Financial Position
December 31

	2018	2017
Assets		
Cash	$ 50,000	$ 42,000
Accounts receivable (net)	100,000	87,000
Inventories	400,000	300,000
Prepaid expenses	25,000	31,000
Long-term investments	80,000	50,000
Land	125,000	75,000
Buildings and equipment (net)	560,000	400,000
Total assets	$1,340,000	$985,000
Liabilities and Shareholders' Equity		
Liabilities		
Notes payable	$ 150,000	$ 50,000
Accounts payable	245,000	190,000
Current portion of mortgage payable	48,750	25,000
Mortgage payable, due 2025	200,000	125,000
Total liabilities	643,750	390,000
Shareholders' equity		
Common shares (100,000 shares issued)	400,000	400,000
Retained earnings	292,250	195,000
Accumulated other comprehensive income	4,000	-0-
Total shareholders' equity	696,250	595,000
Total liabilities and shareholders' equity	$1,340,000	$985,000

TRACK LTD.
Statement of Comprehensive Income
Year Ended December 31

	2018	2017
Net sales	$1,100,000	$950,000
Cost of goods sold	650,000	635,000
Gross profit	450,000	315,000
Operating expenses	285,000	215,000
Income from operations	165,000	100,000
Interest expense	30,000	10,000
Income before income tax	135,000	90,000
Income tax expense	33,750	22,500
Net income	101,250	67,500
Other comprehensive income	4,000	-0-
Total comprehensive income	$ 105,250	$ 67,500

Additional information:
1. The allowance for doubtful accounts was $5,000 in 2017 and $10,000 in 2018.
2. Accounts receivable at the beginning of 2017 were $80,000, net of an allowance for doubtful accounts of $3,000.
3. Inventories at the beginning of 2017 were $320,000.
4. Total assets at the beginning of 2017 were $1,075,000.
5. Current liabilities at the beginning of 2017 were $250,000.
6. Total liabilities at the beginning of 2017 were $543,500.
7. Total shareholders' equity at the beginning of 2017 was $531,500.
8. All sales were on account.
9. Net cash provided by operating activities was $135,500 in 2017 and $223,000 in 2018.
10. Net capital expenditures were $50,000 in 2017 and $92,000 in 2018.
11. In each of 2017 and 2018, $4,000 of dividends were paid to the common shareholders.

Instructions

(a) Do we normally include the effects of other comprehensive income in the calculation of profitability ratios?

(b) Calculate all possible liquidity, solvency, and profitability ratios for each of 2017 and 2018.

(c) Indicate whether each liquidity, solvency, and profitability ratio (except any market measures) calculated in part (a) was better, worse, or unchanged between 2017 and 2018. Use higher, lower, or unchanged for any market measures calculated in part (a).

(d) Explain whether Track's overall (1) liquidity, (2) solvency, and (3) profitability improved, deteriorated, or remained the same between 2017 to 2018.

Evaluate ratios.

(LO 2, 3, 4)

P14–7B Selected ratios for the current year for two companies in the beverage industry, Refresh Corp. and Flavour Limited, follow:

	Refresh	Flavour
Asset turnover	1.0 times	1.0 times
Basic earnings per share	$0.98	$1.37
Current ratio	2.2:1	1.6:1
Debt to total assets	56%	72%
Dividend yield	0.2%	1.1%
Gross profit margin	73.8%	60.0%
Inventory turnover	5.8 times	9.9 times
Payout ratio	10.0%	20.5%
Price-earnings ratio	14.3 times	20.3 times
Profit margin	9.3%	10.2%
Receivables turnover	9.8 times	10.4 times
Return on assets	9.3%	10.2%
Return on common shareholders' equity	25.7%	29.8%
Times interest earned	12.3 times	6.9 times

Instructions

(a) Both companies offer their customers credit terms of net 30 days. Indicate which ratio(s) should be used to assess how well the accounts receivable are managed. Comment on how well each company appears to be managing its accounts receivable.

(b) Indicate the ratio(s) used to assess inventory management. Which company is managing its inventory better?

(c) Refresh's current ratio is higher than that of Flavour. Identify two possible reasons for this.

(d) Which company, Refresh or Flavour, is more solvent? Identify the ratio(s) used to determine this, and defend your choice.

(e) You notice that Refresh's gross profit margin is higher and its profit margin lower than those of Flavour. Identify two possible reasons for this.

(f) What is mostly responsible for Flavour's higher return on assets: profit margin or asset turnover? Explain.

(g) What is mostly responsible for Flavour's higher return on common shareholders' equity: return on assets or use of debt? Explain.

(h) Refresh's payout ratio is significantly lower than that of Flavour. Indicate one possible reason for this.

(i) What is the market price per share of each company's common shares?

(j) Which company, Refresh or Flavour, do investors appear to believe has greater prospects for future growth (price appreciation)? Indicate the ratio(s) you used to reach this conclusion, and explain your reasoning.

Evaluate ratios.

(LO 2, 3, 4)

P14–8B The following ratios are available for toolmakers Best Tools Inc. and Snappy Tools Incorporated, and their industry, for a recent year:

	Best Tools	Snappy Tools	Industry Average
Liquidity			
Current ratio	1.8:1	2:1	2.6:1
Receivables turnover	8.7 times	6.1 times	7.4 times
Inventory turnover	6.7 times	4.8 times	3.9 times
Solvency			
Debt to total assets	32.9%	45.7%	22.5%
Times interest earned	3.2 times	6.1 times	7.6 times
Profitability			
Gross profit margin	35.1%	45.7%	33.3%
Profit margin	2.4%	7.0%	3.0%

Asset turnover	0.8 times	0.7 times	0.9 times
Return on assets	1.9%	4.9%	2.7%
Return on common shareholders' equity	4.4%	13.9%	4.9%
Price-earnings ratio	8.1 times	19.2 times	15.4 times
Payout ratio	11.5%	38.2%	17.4%
Dividend yield	0.8%	2.0%	1.2%

Instructions

(a) Which company is more liquid? Explain.

(b) Which company is more solvent? Explain.

(c) Which company is more profitable? Explain.

(d) Which company do investors favour for future growth (price appreciation)? Is your answer consistent with your findings in parts (a) to (c)? Explain.

P14–9B You are in the process of analyzing two similar companies in the same industry. You learn that they have different accounting practices and policies, as follows:

Discuss impact of accounting policies on financial analysis.

(LO 5)

1. Company A, which has the same type of equipment as Company B, uses the straight-line method of depreciation while Company B uses diminishing-balance. This is the first year of operations for both companies.

2. Company A is a private company and does not report other comprehensive income. Company B is a publicly traded company that generates and reports other comprehensive income from the revaluation of property, plant, and equipment.

Instructions

(a) Considering only the impact of the choice of depreciation method, determine which company will report a higher (1) current ratio, (2) debt to total assets ratio, and (3) profit margin ratio, or if the depreciation method will have no impact.

(b) Considering only the impact of total comprehensive income, determine which company will report a higher (1) current ratio, (2) debt to total assets ratio, and (3) profit margin ratio, or if the other comprehensive income will have no impact.

(c) Will the use of different accounting practices and policies affect your analysis? Explain.

(d) When researching information about these companies, you find that each has prepared a non-GAAP measure called normalized net income. Why might these companies calculate such a measure of performance?

(e) Identify two other limitations of financial analysis that an analyst should watch for when analyzing financial statements.

ACCOUNTING CYCLE | REVIEW

ACR14–1 Manutech Ltd.'s industrial product sales were down in 2017. Fortunately, after investing in a customer relationship management system, it was able to turn its operations around in 2018. Selected financial statements follow:

Prepare vertical analysis; calculate and evaluate ratios; prepare statement of cash flows.

(LO 1, 2, 3, 4)

MANUTECH LTD.
Income Statement
Year Ended December 31

	2018	2017
Net sales	$1,470,000	$1,100,000
Cost of goods sold	735,000	655,000
Gross profit	735,000	445,000
Operating expenses	313,500	270,000
Income from operations	421,500	175,000
Interest expense	61,500	53,600
Income before income tax	360,000	121,400
Income tax expense	90,000	30,350
Net income	$ 270,000	$ 91,050

MANUTECH LTD.
Statement of Financial Position
December 31

	2018	2017
Assets		
Current assets		
Cash	$ 30,000	$ 79,500
Accounts receivable	150,000	105,000
Inventory	112,000	90,000
Total current assets	292,000	274,500
Property, plant, and equipment (net)	1,100,000	965,000
Intangible assets	120,000	120,000
Total assets	$1,512,000	$1,359,500
Liabilities and Shareholders' Equity		
Liabilities		
Current liabilities		
Accounts payable	$ 65,000	$ 72,500
Accrued liabilities	15,000	20,000
Bank loan payable	85,000	-0-
Mortgage payable—current portion	20,000	20,000
Total current liabilities	185,000	112,500
Mortgage payable	630,000	650,000
Total liabilities	815,000	762,500
Shareholders' equity		
Common shares, 10,000 shares issued	100,000	100,000
Retained earnings	597,000	497,000
Total shareholders' equity	697,000	597,000
Total liabilities and shareholders' equity	$1,512,000	$1,359,500

Additional information for 2018:
1. Assume all sales were credit sales.
2. Manutech has no bad debts and no allowance for doubtful accounts.
3. Property, plant, and equipment increased in 2018 by the $300,000 cost of a new customer relationship management system and decreased by additional accumulated depreciation for the year of $165,000.
4. $20,000 of the mortgage was repaid in 2018.
5. Cash dividends paid during the year amounted to $170,000.

Instructions
(a) Using vertical analysis, calculate the percentage of the base amount for the income statement for 2017 and 2018. Use the results to answer the following question from management: "We know that the sales volume has increased, but we don't know if gross profit and net income are increasing in proportion to sales." Identify the primary reason(s) for the change between the two years.
(b) Calculate the various liquidity ratios for 2018 and compare the company's results with the industry average. The industry average for the current ratio is 2.0:1, for the average collection period it is 28 days, and for days in inventory it is 40 days.
(c) Calculate the various solvency ratios for 2018 and compare the company's results with the industry average. The industry average for debt to total assets is 50% and that for times interest earned is 5.0 times.
(d) Calculate the various profitability ratios for 2018 and compare the company's results with the industry average. The industry average for gross profit margin is 44.5%, and for the profit margin it is 15.1%. Similarly, the industry average for asset turnover is 0.8 times and for return on assets it is 12.5%.
(e) After a review of the financial statements, the vice-president is surprised that the cash balance reported on the statement of financial position at year end is not higher, since financial performance improved and net cash provided by operating activities was determined to be $355,500. Prepare the investing and financing activities sections of the statement of cash flows for 2018 to explain where the cash has been used.

EXPAND YOUR CRITICAL THINKING

CT14–1 Financial Reporting Case

The financial statements of **The North West Company Inc.** are presented in Appendix A at the end of this book. The following selected condensed information (in thousands) has been taken from these, and the prior years', financial statements:

	Year Ended January 31		
	2016	2015	2014
Income Statement			
Sales	$1,796,035	$1,624,400	$1,543,125
Cost of goods sold	1,273,421	1,160,182	1,088,071
Gross profit	522,614	464,218	455,054
Selling, operating, and administrative expenses	415,293	366,752	354,994
Income from operations	107,321	97,466	100,060
Interest expense	6,210	6,673	7,784
Income tax expense	31,332	27,910	28,013
Net income	$ 69,779	$ 62,883	$ 64,263
Statement of Financial Position			
Current assets	$ 335,581	$ 315,840	$ 299,071
Non-current assets	458,214	408,459	371,441
Current liabilities	155,501	146,275	209,738
Non-current liabilities	280,682	248,741	138,334
Shareholders' equity	357,612	329,283	322,440

Instructions

(a) Using horizontal analysis, calculate the percentage of the base-year amount for the information shown above, assuming 2014 is the base year.

(b) Using vertical analysis, calculate the percentage of a base amount for each of the (1) income statement and (2) statement of financial position, shown above for each year.

(c) Comment on any significant changes you observe from your calculations in parts (a) and (b).

CT14–2 Financial Analysis Case

The financial statements of **The North West Company Inc.** are presented in Appendix A, followed by the financial statements for **Sobeys Inc.** in Appendix B.

Instructions

(a) Calculate the liquidity ratios for the current fiscal year that you believe are relevant for each company. Assume

all sales are on credit and that there is no allowance for doubtful accounts. Which company is more liquid?

(b) Calculate the solvency ratios for the current fiscal year that you believe are relevant for each company. Which company is more solvent?

(c) 1. Sobeys reported a loss from operations and a net loss for the year ended May 7, 2016. Do you believe it is still appropriate to calculate and compare profitability ratios for North West when that company reported income from operations and net income for its current fiscal year? Explain.

    2. Do you believe it would be appropriate to exclude certain nonrecurring items from your analysis to improve the comparison? If so, identify which, if any, nonrecurring items you would remove for North West and Sobeys.

(d) Identify information that is not included in the financial statements that might also be useful for comparing North West and Sobeys.

CT14–3 Financial Analysis Case

Fine Leather Ltd. (FLL) is a retailer of various leather goods. Its major competitor is Deluxe Leatherwear Ltd. (DLL). During the past year, Fine Leather has recorded a large loss in other comprehensive income while DLL reported no other comprehensive income or loss. FLL has also reversed an impairment loss on some equipment, accrued a provision relating to a salary dispute, and adjusted some of its equipment up to fair value. DLL has recorded no similar transactions. FLL uses the FIFO inventory cost formula while DLL uses average cost. Both companies are experiencing rising costs for inventory and both companies have more current assets than current liabilities.

Instructions

(a) One of the companies described above prepares financial statements using IFRS while the other uses ASPE. Which one complies with IFRS and which one with ASPE?

(b) Do all of the differences between the two companies relate to IFRS and ASPE differences?

(c) For each of the following ratios, determine if FLL could be expected to have a higher or lower ratio based on the different approach that it takes when preparing financial statements: current ratio, inventory turnover, debt to total assets, profit margin, and asset turnover.

CT14–4 Professional Judgement Case

This case can be assigned as a group activity. Additional instructions and material for this activity can be found on the Instructor Resource site and in WileyPLUS.

Listed below is a vertical analysis of selected information from the financial statements of five publicly traded Canadian companies:

	A	B	C	D	E
Sales	100.0%	100.0%	100.0%	100.0%	100.0%
Cost of goods sold	(82.3)%	(58.1)%	(76.5)%	(43.2)%	(60.1)%
Gross profit	17.7%	41.9%	23.5%	56.8%	39.9%
Selling and administrative expenses	(1.4)%	(19.1)%	(17.2)%	(10.3)%	(31.4)%
Research and development	-0-	(13.6)%	-0-	-0-	-0-
Interest	(1.4)%	-0-	(1.4)%	(2.3)%	-0-
Depreciation	(5.4)%	(6.5)%	(2.5)%	(26.7)%	(2.1)%
Other	0.3%	(13.7)%	0.3%	(1.4)%	3.2%
Income (loss) before income tax	9.8%	(11.0)%	2.7%	16.1%	9.6%
Income tax	(2.9)%	5.2%	(0.7)%	(4.4)%	(2.5)%
Net income (loss)	6.9%	(5.8)%	2.0%	11.7%	7.1%
Cash	37.6%	20.2%	10.0%	0.1%	37.9%
Accounts receivable	1.0%	24.5%	15.4%	2.4%	5.2%
Inventories	1.0%	4.6%	11.2%	1.1%	14.7%
Other current assets	4.1%	4.7%	0.6%	0.3%	0.8%
Total current assets	43.7%	54.0%	37.2%	3.9%	58.6%
Property, plant, and equipment	53.0%	18.2%	50.5%	95.2%	38.7%
Intangible assets	1.3%	26.2%	5.9%	-0-	2.5%
Other non-current assets	2.0%	1.6%	6.4%	0.9%	0.2%
Total assets	100.0%	100.0%	100.0%	100.0%	100.0%
Current liabilities	31.7%	26.2%	30.0%	8.1%	19.8%
Non-current liabilities	29.0%	2.0%	34.2%	42.3%	3.0%
Shareholders' equity	39.3%	71.8%	35.8%	49.6%	77.2%
Total liabilities and shareholders' equity	100.0%	100.0%	100.0%	100.0%	100.0%

One of the companies included in the vertical analysis above operates a chain of grocery stores and has its own private labels. The other four companies are a furniture retailer that has operated for over 100 years, an oil and gas producer with facilities in the oil sands in a year when oil prices were high, a discount airline, and a developer of high-tech communications equipment that does not sell its products directly to consumers.

Instructions
By analyzing the relationships between the amounts shown, match the descriptions of the companies provided to the applicable company A through E shown above.

CT14–5 Ethics Case

Vern Fairly, president of Flex Industries Inc., wants to issue a press release to boost the company's image and its share price, which has been gradually falling. As controller, you have been asked to provide a list of horizontal percentages and financial ratios for Flex Industries' first-quarter operations.

Two days after you provide the ratios and data requested, you are asked by Anne Saint-Onge, Flex's vice-president of communications, to review the accuracy of the financial and operating data contained in the press release written by the president and edited by Anne. In the news release, the president highlights the sales increase of 10% over last year's first quarter and the positive change in the current ratio from 1.1:1 last year to 1.5:1 this year. He also emphasizes that production was up 15% over last year's first quarter.

You note that the release contains only positive or improved ratios and none of the negative or worsening ratios. For instance, there is no mention of the fact that, although the current ratio improved, the debt to total assets ratio has increased from 35% to 45%. Nor is there any mention that the reported net income for the quarter would have been a loss if excess machinery had not been sold at a gain.

Instructions
(a) Who are the stakeholders in this situation?
(b) Is there anything unethical in President Fairly's actions?
(c) As controller, should you remain silent? Why or why not? Does Anne have any responsibility?

CT14–6 Student View Case

You have just won $2 million in a lottery. Realizing how fortunate you are, you have spent some of this money on a car, a house, some guaranteed investment certificates, and some highly diversified mutual funds. You would like to take $100,000 of the remaining money and invest it in the shares of one publicly traded Canadian company. You seek advice on which company to invest in from one of your friends, who is a computer programmer. She tells you to invest in a new software company that just went public. It develops new online games and receives fees from players along with advertising revenue. This company has not had very many sales yet, but expects to in the future due to the popularity of its products. Its price-earnings ratio is 80 times earnings, its return on common shareholders' equity is 2.0%, and its return on assets is 1.8%. Your uncle, on the other hand, suggests that you purchase shares in a large bank that has consistently paid dividends for over 100 years and has increased its dividend every year for the past 45 years. This bank has a price-earnings ratio of 11 times earnings but unlike the software company, it has a dividend yield of 3.0%. The bank's net income has barely risen over the past two years but its return on common shareholders' equity is 10.2% while its return on assets is 2.7%.

Instructions

(a) Why would the price-earnings ratio be higher for the software company?

(b) Why would the bank have a dividend yield and the software company would not?

(c) Why would the software company have lower returns on both assets and equity?

(d) Why would a bank have such a large difference between its return on common shareholders' equity and its return on assets?

(e) Which company would you invest in? Explain your reasoning.

CT14–7 Serial Case

(*Note:* This is a continuation of the serial case from Chapters 1 through 13.)

Doug, Bev, Emily, and Daniel have sold their shares of ABC Ltd. to Software Solutions Inc., a public company. One of the terms of the sale agreement was that Emily and Daniel remain employees of Software Solutions for the next two years and continue to operate the business. Emily and Daniel are now operating ABC as a wholly owned subsidiary of Software Solutions.

Daniel and Emily have received a sizable amount of cash from the sale of their shares of ABC. As a result, they are considering where they should invest this money. They recognize how profitable ABC continues to be as a subsidiary of Software Solutions and are considering investing some of their excess cash in Software Solutions. They have accumulated a number of ratios for Software Solutions Inc., and Micro Inc. (a publicly traded competitor of Software Solutions), in addition to the overall industry to enable them to make a decision on whether or not they should invest in Software Solutions.

Ratio	Software Solutions Inc.	Micro Inc.	Industry Ratio
Current ratio	1.9:1	1.1:1	1.5:1
Receivables turnover	5.2 times	6.3 times	6.1 times
Inventory turnover	13.3 times	17.9 times	18.0 times
Debt to total assets	35.8%	31.5%	35.0%
Times interest earned	10.8 times	11.7 times	12.4 times
Gross profit margin	43.0%	24.0%	24.9%
Profit margin	20.9%	14.3%	13.2%
Return on assets	11.3%	9.6%	8.9%
Return on common shareholders' equity	21.9%	17.9%	16.5%
Dividend yield	1.7%	1.3%	1.5%
Price-earnings ratio	12.5 times	14.8 times	9.5 times

Instructions

(a) Which company is more liquid? Explain.

(b) Which company is more solvent? Explain.

(c) Which company is more profitable? Explain.

(d) If an investor was more interested in receiving dividend income than in appreciation of the share price, which company's shares would they prefer to buy?

(e) If an investor was more interested in appreciation of the share price than receiving dividend income, which company's shares would they prefer to buy?

(f) Emily and Daniel are familiar with ASPE from their previous experience with Anthony Business Company as a private company. Software Solutions and Micro use IFRS. Are there any particular differences Emily and Daniel should be aware of that might affect their analysis of these two companies?

(g) What other factors must Emily and Daniel consider before making an investment in any public company?

▶ ANSWERS TO CHAPTER PRACTICE QUESTIONS

(a) Horizontal percentage of base-year amount

DO IT! 14-1a
Horizontal Analysis

	2018	2017	2016	2015
Net sales	92.8%	90.1%	95.6%	100.0%
Cost of goods sold	97.4%	92.8%	90.2%	100.0%
Gross profit	90.1%	88.5%	98.8%	100.0%
Operating expenses	105.1%	98.9%	92.0%	100.0%
Income from operations	55.3%	64.5%	114.5%	100.0%
Income tax expense	55.3%	64.5%	114.5%	100.0%
Net income	55.3%	64.5%	114.5%	100.0%

(b)   Horizontal percentage change for year

	2018	2017	2016	2015
Net sales	3.0%	(5.7)%	(4.4)%	—
Cost of goods sold	4.9%	2.9%	(9.8)%	—
Gross profit	1.8%	(10.4)%	(1.2)%	—
Operating expenses	6.3%	7.4%	(8.0)%	—
Income from operations	(14.3)%	(43.7)%	14.5%	—
Income tax expense	(14.3)%	(43.7)%	14.5%	—
Net income	(14.3)%	(43.7)%	14.5%	—

DO IT! 14-1b

Vertical Analysis

	2018	2017	2016	2015
Net sales	100.0%	100.0%	100.0%	100.0%
Cost of goods sold	39.6%	38.9%	35.7%	37.8%
Gross profit	60.4%	61.1%	64.3%	62.2%
Operating expenses	49.2%	47.7%	41.9%	43.5%
Income from operations	11.2%	13.4%	22.5%	18.8%
Income tax expense	2.8%	3.4%	5.6%	4.7%
Net income	8.4%	10.1%	16.9%	14.1%

DO IT! 14-2

Liquidity Analysis

(a)

Wasis	Rita

Average collection period

$$\frac{365 \text{ days}}{27.0} = 14 \text{ days} \qquad \frac{365 \text{ days}}{22.6} = 16 \text{ days}$$

Days in inventory

$$\frac{365 \text{ days}}{6.8} = 54 \text{ days} \qquad \frac{365 \text{ days}}{5.6} = 65 \text{ days}$$

(b)   Rita has the better (higher) current ratio, ignoring any potential inflation due to slow-moving receivables and inventory. Wasis has the better (higher) receivables and inventory turnover ratios. It also has the better (lower) average collection period and days in inventory ratios.

(c)   Wasis is the more liquid of the two companies, because it collects its receivables and sells its inventory sooner than does Rita. This could help explain Rita's higher current ratio, although this is unlikely given the small differential between the two companies' liquidity ratios. In addition, it is noteworthy that, even though Wasis has a better receivables turnover and average collection period than Rita, both companies are collecting their receivables in a timely fashion—far less than 30 days. It is safe to assume that neither company has a large proportion of receivables and they most likely sell their goods for cash more often than on account.

DO IT! 14-3

Solvency Analysis

(a)

2018	2017	Comparison with Prior Year

Debt to total assets

$$\frac{\$737,700}{\$1,000,000} = 73.8\% \qquad\qquad \frac{\$809,000}{\$1,015,000} = 79.7\% \qquad\qquad \text{Better}$$

Times interest earned

$$\frac{\$193,600 + \$59,000 + \$48,400}{\$59,000} = 5.1 \text{ times} \qquad \frac{\$202,000 + \$40,500 + \$50,500}{\$40,500} = 7.2 \text{ times} \qquad \text{Worse}$$

(b)   Overall, solvency has deteriorated in 2018. While the debt to total assets ratio has improved in 2018, total liabilities are still a very high percentage of total assets. Of greater concern is the proportionally greater decline in the times interest earned ratio in 2018. The company is no longer able to handle its interest payments as well as in the past, even though it is still able to cover its interest payments 5.1 times. Taken together, this leads us to conclude that overall solvency has deteriorated.

DO IT! 14-4

Profitability Analysis

(a)

De Marchi	Bear

Debt to total assets

$$\frac{\$97,000}{\$434,000} = 22.4\% \qquad\qquad\qquad \frac{\$135,000}{\$536,000} = 25.2\%$$

Gross profit margin

$$\frac{\$175,000}{\$660,000} = 26.5\% \qquad\qquad \frac{\$248,000}{\$780,000} = 31.8\%$$

Profit margin

$$\frac{\$68,000}{\$660,000} = 10.3\% \qquad\qquad \frac{\$105,000}{\$780,000} = 13.5\%$$

Asset turnover

$$\frac{\$660,000}{(\$388,000 + \$434,000) \div 2} = 1.6 \text{ times} \qquad \frac{\$780,000}{(\$372,000 + \$536,000) \div 2} = 1.7 \text{ times}$$

Return on assets

$$\frac{\$68,000}{(\$388,000 + \$434,000) \div 2} = 16.5\% \qquad \frac{\$105,000}{(\$372,000 + \$536,000) \div 2} = 23.1\%$$

Return on common shareholders' equity

$$\frac{\$68,000}{(\$269,000 + \$337,000) \div 2} = 22.4\% \qquad \frac{\$105,000}{(\$296,000 + \$401,000) \div 2} = 30.1\%$$

(b) Bear is more profitable than De Marchi on all profitability ratios.

(c) Bear has the higher return on common shareholders' equity ratio primarily because of its higher return on assets ratio because there is not a large difference between the two companies' debt to total assets ratios. Drilling down, the factor most influencing Bear's higher return on assets ratio and ultimately its return on common shareholders' equity ratio is its profit margin. Bear has the higher profit margin of the two companies, much higher than its asset turnover.

(a)

DO IT! 14-5
Limitations of
Financial Analysis

($ in millions)	(1)	(2)
Profit margin	$\dfrac{\$437}{\$5,162} = 8.5\%$	$\dfrac{\$610}{\$5,162} = 11.8\%$
Return on assets	$\dfrac{\$437}{\$3,374} = 13.0\%$	$\dfrac{\$610}{\$3,374} = 18.1\%$

(b) The inclusion of other comprehensive income in the calculation of the profitability ratios is most likely significant enough to make a difference in a user's decision-making. In Linamar's case, the major reason for other comprehensive income was from foreign currency gains on the company's assets in the United States, which in turn were caused by a rising U.S. dollar.

(c) Under FIFO, the industry cost of goods sold would likely be lower because older, less costly inventory items would be included in that amount, while ending inventory would have a higher proportion of more costly items in ending inventory. Consequently, the industry average inventory turnover would be lower because the cost of goods sold numerator would be lower and the denominator of average inventory would be higher. Therefore this ratio would be less comparable because of this accounting policy difference.

(d) By depreciating its buildings using a dimishing-balance method, because the buildings are relatively new, Linamar would record more depreciation and its buildings would have a lower carrying amount than the industry average. Therefore its asset turnover would be higher than the industry average because of the relatively lower denominator in this ratio.

(e) A discontinued business loss should be excluded from net income and only income from continuing operations should be used in profitability analysis. Consequently, this loss would have no impact on the profit margin ratio because it is excluded from the numerator of net income. This is to be consistent with the practice of segregating these items on the income statement because it is not helpful to consider discontinued business losses when predicting future performance.

▶ **PRACTICE USING THE DECISION TOOLKIT**

(a) Because the current ratios of Walmart and Target are almost the same and because accounts receivable is not reported by Target and is insignificant for Walmart, the liquidity of these companies is best assessed by looking at the inventory turnover ratio. The most significant current asset for both of these companies is inventory. The company that turns its inventory faster, which is Walmart, will more likely have lower inventory and higher cash balances despite having a slightly lower current ratio. Therefore, Walmart is more liquid. Furthermore, Walmart's inventory turnover is just slightly higher than the industry average indicating that it has above average liquidity.

(b) Walmart is more solvent than Target because it has a lower debt to total assets ratio and a higher times interest earned ratio. However, the industry on average has a higher times interest earned ratio, most likely due to a lower average debt to total assets ratio. Target has a higher debt to total assets ratio, indicating that it has more leverage and has financed a higher portion of its assets with debt than Walmart. The decision to do this would be at the discretion of the company because management must have believed that the interest on this debt would be lower than the income earned from these borrowed funds.

(c) The return on assets ratio can be determined by multiplying the profit margin by the asset turnover ratio. Although Walmart has a lower profit margin than Target (in part due to its lower gross profit margin), it tries to compensate for this by having a higher asset turnover, which it does. Despite this, Target's return on assets is higher due to its much higher profit margin (which also exceeds the industry average).

(d) The return on common shareholders' equity is a function of the return on assets and the use of leverage. Because Target has a return on assets that is higher than the return earned by Walmart and the industry average and because it is using more leverage, Target has a much higher return on common shareholders' equity.

When leverage is used, the difference between the return on assets ratio and the return on common shareholders' equity ratio will widen. This occurs because Target is taking advantage of the fact that it can earn a return on borrowed funds that exceeds the interest on those funds. This boosts income and the return on common shareholders' equity.

▶ PRACTICE COMPREHENSIVE DO IT!

(a) Green collects receivables and sells its inventory faster than Gold because its receivables turnover and inventory turnover ratios are higher than Gold's ratios.

(b) The current ratio numerator, which is current assets, consists primarily of cash, accounts receivable, and inventory. If Green's current ratio is higher because of its numerator, it would most likely be due to higher levels of cash because less cash is tied up in accounts receivable and inventory due to its higher turnover. The major item in the denominator of the current ratio is accounts payable and a lower balance in accounts payable could also explain why Green has a higher current ratio. It may be that Green is paying off its accounts payable more quickly because it receives cash sooner than Gold due to its higher receivables and inventory turnover.

(c) Gold is taking on more debt, as indicated by its higher debt to total assets ratio and its lower times interest earned ratio (likely lower due to higher interest expense).

(d) Gold is likely the company with the supplier that provides goods at a lower cost due to its higher gross profit margin ratio.

(e) Although Gold has a higher gross profit margin (10 percentage points higher than Green's), the advantage of this lessens when we look at the profit margin ratio, where Gold's profit margin is only 5 percentage points higher than Green's. The most likely explanation for this would be Gold having higher operating expenses and interest expense relative to its sales than Green has.

(f) The company that acquired property, plant, and equipment most recently would have a higher carrying amount for these assets than a company that had older, more depreciated assets. As both of these companies have the same amount of sales, the company with the newer property, plant, and equipment would most likely have a lower asset turnover ratio and that is Gold. This is consistent with the fact that this company increased its debt levels, most likely to purchase these newer assets.

(g) The return on common shareholders' equity is a function of the return on assets and the company's strategy of taking on debt to increase its return on common shareholders' equity. Although both of these companies have the same return on assets, Gold is able to earn a higher return on common shareholders' equity because it is more highly leveraged. It borrows more funds and invests them in assets that provide a return of 15% while the interest paid out on these borrowed funds is lower than 15%, so the difference that is earned increases the return on common shareholders' equity. This increase is greater for Gold because it has borrowed more extensively.

(h) Current and future investors in Green shares are more likely to prefer dividend income because the payout ratio of that company is higher (the board is committed to distributing a higher portion of its income to shareholders through dividends) and the dividend yield is higher.

(i) Gold's higher P-E ratio indicates that investors are paying a higher price for that company's shares relative to its basic earnings per share when compared with Green. They are doing this because they are anticipating greater growth in the income of Gold than Green. This is reasonable given that Gold has a higher return on common shareholders' equity and lower payout ratio, indicating that more cash is retained in the business to finance expansion.

▶ PRACTICE OBJECTIVE-FORMAT QUESTIONS

1.   (b), (e), and (g) are correct.

Feedback
The current ratio is determined by dividing current assets by current liabilities.

(a)   is incorrect because, when the receivables turnover increases, it means that receivables are collected more quickly so cash will increase and receivables will decrease but by the same amount, so there is no overall change to the amount of current assets or the current ratio.

(b)   is correct because a decrease in the days in inventory means that inventory is selling more quickly. When that happens, inventory decreases by the amount of its cost but accounts receivable or cash increases by a higher amount (the price the inventory is sold at) and this means that, overall, current assets will increase along with the current ratio.

(c)   is incorrect because, when the allowance for doubtful accounts increases (even though this does not affect receivables turnover), current assets will decrease and so will the current ratio.

(d)   is incorrect because this transaction would reduce both the accounts receivable and the allowance for doubtful accounts by an equal amount, resulting in no change to net accounts receivable or current assets.

(e)   is correct because the discount policy has increased sales by more than the amount of the discount, so overall sales are rising and this in turn would initially cause an increase in accounts receivable and current assets.

(f)   is incorrect because, if net income is unchanged and the payout ratio increased, this can only occur if the amount of the dividends paid has been increased and this would reduce cash, current assets, and the current ratio.

(g)   is correct because, even though cash is decreased, so is accounts payable. One might assume that because both current assets and current liabilities are decreased by the same amount, the current ratio will remain unchanged, but this is only the case when both of these items are equal, which in this case they are not. Because current assets were greater than current liabilities, a change of equal amount to both of these items will change the value of the current ratio. Because the change has a greater percentage effect on the smaller amount (current liabilities), the denominator in this case is falling by a greater percentage, causing the current ratio to rise. For example, assume that, before paying a $25 current liability, the current ratio was 2:1 with current assets of $100 and current liabilities of $50. After the payment, the current ratio is 3:1 ($75 ÷ $25).

2.   (a), (c), and (d) are correct.

Feedback
Free cash flow is equal to net cash flow provided (used) by operating activities − net capital expenditures − dividends paid.

(a) is correct because the payment of both preferred and common dividends is considered when determining free cash flow.
(b) is incorrect because depreciation is not a cash flow.
(c) is correct because such a purchase is included in net capital expenditures and this would decrease free cash flow.
(d) is correct because receivables collections increase cash flow from operating activities.
(e) is incorrect because the payment of the principal portion of a loan is a financing activity.
(f) is incorrect because no dividend was paid, so this had no impact on free cash flow.
(g) is incorrect because a gain is not a cash flow. (The proceeds from the sale would be an investing cash flow.)

3. (c) and (e) are correct.

Feedback
(a) is incorrect because the current ratio is calculated by dividing current assets by current liabilities. As that ratio rises, there are more current assets relative to current liabilities and that indicates better, not worse, liquidity.
(b) is incorrect because, if the gross profit margin is increasing, that will increase net income and since all other expenses not included in the gross profit are also decreasing, all of these effects will tend to increase net income and increase the profit margin ratio.
(c) is correct because dividends paid is subtracted from free cash flow so as dividends paid increases, free cash flow will decrease.
(d) is incorrect because, when depreciable assets are not replaced, their carrying amount will decrease over time and this in turn will cause the denominator of the asset turnover ratio to decrease, causing (assuming no other changes) the asset turnover to increase.
(e) is correct because, when a company collects receivables more quickly, the balance in the Accounts Receivable account will fall and this in turn will cause an increase in the receivables turnover ratio.
(f) is incorrect because the payout ratio measures what portion of net income was distributed to shareholders as dividends. If the payout ratio is increasing while net income remains unchanged, then the amount of dividends paid must have increased.
(g) is incorrect because a decreasing inventory turnover ratio indicates that the company is selling its inventory more slowly because, relative to cost of goods sold, the company has more inventory on hand.

4. (b), (d), (e), and (g) are correct.

Feedback
Profit margin uses net income in the numerator so all income statement items are included in this ratio, whereas the gross profit margin ratio uses only sales and cost of goods sold in its numerator. Therefore, items in profit margin that are not in the gross profit margin are all items in net income except sales and cost of goods sold.
(a) and (c) are incorrect because both sales and cost of goods sold are in both ratios.
(f) is incorrect because other comprehensive income is not included in either ratio.

5. (a), (f), and (g) are correct.

Feedback
This company not only experienced an increase in the volume of items sold but each item sold for a higher gross profit and there was no corresponding increase in operating expenses, so operating income and net income both increased.
(a) is correct because gross profit rose when the inventory cost was reduced.
(b) is incorrect because, even though the cost of inventory fell by 5%, the volume increased by 15%, so cost of goods sold increased while the inventory units on hand remained the same (with a lower cost). Because cost of goods sold increased and inventory decreased, inventory turnover would increase.
(c) is incorrect because, although sales increased, accounts receivable increased at the same rate, so the receivables turnover would remain the same.
(d) is incorrect because profit margin would increase due to the higher gross profit and the fact that most operating expenses were unchanged.
(e) is incorrect because net income before interest and income tax expense would be higher and there is no reason to assume that interest expense would change, so the times interest earned ratio should increase.
(f) is correct because the only component of free cash flow that is changing would be net cash flow provided (used) by operating activities, which would increase due to higher profitability.
(g) is correct because of the reasons given in (b) above. Days in inventory will fall because the volume of sales and cost of goods sold has risen while the cost of inventory on hand has fallen.

6. (b), (c), (d), and (f) are correct.

Feedback
This company has a significant increase in net income due to the gain on the sale of stores and a large decrease in its non-current debt. Its cash levels would have remained unchanged because the leftover cash from the store sales was paid out through dividends. However, the costs of renting stores turned out to be higher and this decreased cash.
(a) is incorrect because there has been no change in the price or costs of inventory sold, so the gross profit would have remained unchanged.
(b) is correct because the profit margin, although declining because of increased rent, would have been increased to a greater extent by the gain on the sale of the stores.
(c) is correct because net income before interest expense and income tax expense would have increased due to the gain on the store sales (offset slightly by the higher store rent) while interest expense would decline because of lower debt levels.
(d) is correct because net income increased and assets decreased because the stores were sold.
(e) is incorrect because this is the first time that the company paid out a dividend so the payout ratio would increase.
(f) is correct because any cash increase as a result of the store sale was distributed as a dividend and, when the stores were sold, non-current rather than current liabilities were paid off, so it seems that the sale had no effect on working capital. However, the cost of renting rather than owning the stores was higher than expected and this diminished cash, so working capital is lower.
(g) is incorrect because the transactions described had no effect on inventory or cost of goods sold.

7.   (c), (d), (f), and (g) are correct.

Feedback

As both interest rates and loan levels decline, interest expense will decrease and net income will increase. These effects, however, have no impact on gross profit.

(a)   is incorrect because gross profit does not include interest expense, so a change in this item has no impact on gross profit.

(b)   is incorrect because the profit margin will increase because the net income in its numerator has increased due to lower interest expense while the sales in the denominator of this ratio is unchanged.

(c)   is correct because, even though the numerator (net income before interest expense and income tax expense) is unchanged, the denominator is lower (interest expense has decreased), so the ratio will increase.

(d)   is correct because of the increase in net income, which is the numerator for this ratio.

(e)   is incorrect because inventory and cost of goods sold are unaffected by the events described.

(f)   is correct because debt levels were paid down.

(g)   is correct because interest expense is lower and this will cause net cash flow provided (used) by operating activities to increase, which in turn will increase free cash flow.

8.   (a), (d), and (f) are correct.

Feedback

Because net income has increased, return on assets and common shareholders' equity will also increase. Because the dividends did not increase to the same extent as net income, the payout ratio will decrease. Because the share price increased by more than the dividends, the dividend yield will fall, and because the share price did not increase as rapidly as net income, the price-earnings ratio will decrease. Because net cash provided (used) by operating activities increased, free cash flow will also increase.

9.   (b), (c), (d), and (f) are correct.

Feedback

Lowering the residual value of equipment will increase operating expenses (depreciation) and lowering the carrying amount of the equipment while accruing damages for the lawsuit will increase operating expenses and increase current liabilities.

(a)   is incorrect because gross profit is not affected by changes in operating expenses.

(b)   is correct because the profit margin will decrease because operating expenses have increased.

(c)   is correct because current liabilities have increased, thereby lowering this ratio.

(d)   is correct because liabilities were increased (increases numerator of ratio) when the damages were accrued and the carrying amount of depreciable assets will be lower (decreases denominator of this ratio) due to higher amounts of depreciation.

(e)   is incorrect because neither the increased depreciation nor the accrual for the damages has caused any change to cash flows yet.

(f)   is correct because income before interest expense and income tax expense is lower due to higher operating expenses while interest expense remains unchanged, so the ratio will decrease.

(g)   is incorrect because net sales are not affected but the average total assets will be lower because of the higher amount of depreciation and this will cause the ratio to increase.

10.   (a), (c), and (e) are correct.

Feedback

Accounting standards clearly segregate discontinued business gains and losses and other comprehensive income (loss) from other items on the income statement and, because of this, these items are excluded from our determination of net income for ratios that we analyze. All other items shown above would therefore be included in net income even if the item may be nonrecurring, such as the loss from the fire. Although such a loss is included in net income, its occurrence would have to be understood and its impact explained when interpreting changes in ratio values. Gains from the sale of equipment, income tax expense pertaining to continuing businesses, and interest expense are all recurring items and would not be excluded from net income.

▶ ENDNOTE

1 HBC corporate website, "Our History," www.hbcheritage.ca; David Friend, The Canadian Press, "HBC Joins New Real Estate Ventures Worth about $4.2B," CTV.ca, February 25, 2015; "Hudson's Bay Company to Acquire Saks Incorporated for US$16 per Share, Bringing Together Three Iconic Retail Brands," HBC news release, July 29, 2013; Marina Strauss, "HBC Snaps Up Saks for $2.9-Billion, Plans Canadian Rollout," *The Globe and Mail*, July 28, 2013; Theresa Tedesco, "HBC's US$2.9-Billion Deal for Saks Banks on Big Spenders," *Financial Post*, July 29, 2013; CBC News, "Hudson's Bay to Bring Saks to Canada in $2.9B Takeover," CBC.ca, July 29, 2013; "Hudson's Bay Company Completes $365 Million Initial Public Offering," HBC news release, November 26, 2012; CBC News, "Target Buys Zellers Leases for $1.8B," CBC.ca, January 13, 2011; CTV News, "Hudson's Bay Company Sold to NRDC Equity," CTVNews.ca, July 16, 2008; HBC 2015 annual report.

Appendix A

Specimen Financial Statements: The North West Company Inc.

In this appendix and the next, we illustrate current financial reporting with two different sets of corporate financial statements that are prepared in accordance with International Financial Reporting Standards. We are grateful for permission to use the actual financial statements of The North West Company Inc. in Appendix A.

The financial statement package for North West includes the consolidated statement of financial position (which North West calls balance sheet), income statement (which North West calls statement of earnings), statement of comprehensive income, statement of changes in equity (which North West calls statement of changes in shareholders' equity), and statement of cash flows. The financial statements are preceded by two reports: management's responsibility for the financial statements and the auditor's report on these statements.

Only selected notes to the financial statements related to the topics included in this textbook have been included in this appendix. The complete set of financial statements and annual report for North West can be found on *WileyPLUS*. In addition, material about working with annual reports, including the financial statements, is included on *WileyPLUS*.

We encourage you to scan North West's financial statements to familiarize yourself with the contents of this appendix. You will also have the opportunity to use these financial statements in conjunction with relevant chapter material in the textbook. As well, these statements can be used to solve the Financial Reporting and Financial Analysis cases in the Expand Your Critical Thinking section of the end of chapter material. As you near the end of your financial accounting course, we challenge you to reread North West's financial statements to see how much greater your understanding of them has become.

Management's Responsibility for Financial Statements

The management of The North West Company Inc. is responsible for the preparation, presentation and integrity of the accompanying consolidated financial statements and all other information in the annual report. The consolidated financial statements have been prepared by management in accordance with International Financial Reporting Standards as issued by the International Accounting Standards Board and include certain amounts that are based on the best estimates and judgment by management.

In order to meet its responsibility and ensure integrity of financial information, management has established a code of business ethics, and maintains appropriate internal controls and accounting systems. An internal audit function is maintained that is designed to provide reasonable assurance that assets are safeguarded, transactions are authorized and recorded and that the financial records are reliable.

Ultimate responsibility for financial reporting to shareholders rests with the Board of Directors. The Audit Committee of the Board of Directors, consisting of independent Directors, meets periodically with management and with the internal and external auditors to review the audit results, internal controls and accounting policies. Internal and external auditors have unlimited access to the Audit Committee. The Audit Committee meets separately with management and the external auditors to review the financial statements and other contents of the annual report and recommend approval by the Board of Directors. The Audit Committee also recommends the independent auditor for appointment by the shareholders.

PricewaterhouseCoopers LLP, an independent firm of auditors appointed by the shareholders, have completed their audit and submitted their report as follows.

Edward S. Kennedy
PRESIDENT & CEO
THE NORTH WEST COMPANY INC.

John D. King
EXECUTIVE VICE-PRESIDENT &
CHIEF FINANCIAL OFFICER
THE NORTH WEST COMPANY INC.

April 8, 2016

Independent Auditor's Report   pwc

To the Shareholders of The North West Company Inc.:

We have audited the accompanying consolidated financial statements of The North West Company Inc. and its subsidiaries, which comprise the consolidated balance sheets as at January 31, 2016 and January 31, 2015 and the consolidated statements of earnings, comprehensive income, changes in shareholders' equity and cash flows for the years then ended, and the related notes, which comprise a summary of significant accounting policies and other explanatory information.

Management's responsibility for the consolidated financial statements

Management is responsible for the preparation and fair presentation of these consolidated financial statements in accordance with International Financial Reporting Standards, and for such internal control as management determines is necessary to enable the preparation of consolidated financial statements that are free from material misstatement, whether due to fraud or error.

Auditor's responsibility

Our responsibility is to express an opinion on these consolidated financial statements based on our audits. We conducted our audits in accordance with Canadian generally accepted auditing standards. Those standards require that we comply with ethical requirements and plan and perform the audit to obtain reasonable assurance about whether the consolidated financial statements are free from material misstatement.

An audit involves performing procedures to obtain audit evidence about the amounts and disclosures in the consolidated financial statements. The procedures selected depend on the auditor's judgment, including the assessment of the risks of material misstatement of the consolidated financial statements, whether due to fraud or error. In making those risk assessments, the auditor considers internal control relevant to the entity's preparation and fair presentation of the consolidated financial statements in order to design audit procedures that are appropriate in the circumstances, but not for the purpose of expressing an opinion on the effectiveness of the entity's internal control. An audit also includes evaluating the appropriateness of accounting policies used and the reasonableness of accounting estimates made by management, as well as evaluating the overall presentation of the consolidated financial statements.

We believe that the audit evidence we have obtained in our audits is sufficient and appropriate to provide a basis for our audit opinion.

Opinion

In our opinion, the consolidated financial statements present fairly, in all material respects, the financial position of The North West Company Inc. and its subsidiaries as at January 31, 2016 and January 31, 2015 and their financial performance and their cash flows for the years then ended in accordance with International Financial Reporting Standards.

PricewaterhouseCoopers LLP

CHARTERED PROFESSIONAL ACCOUNTANTS
WINNIPEG, CANADA

April 8, 2016

Consolidated Balance Sheets

($ in thousands)	January 31, 2016	January 31, 2015
CURRENT ASSETS		
Cash	$ 37,243	$ 29,129
Accounts receivable (Note 5)	79,373	72,506
Inventories (Note 6)	211,736	204,812
Prepaid expenses	7,229	9,393
	335,581	315,840
NON-CURRENT ASSETS		
Property and equipment (Note 7)	345,881	311,692
Goodwill (Note 8)	37,260	33,653
Intangible assets (Note 8)	32,610	22,485
Deferred tax assets (Note 9)	29,040	28,074
Other assets (Note 10)	13,423	12,555
	458,214	408,459
TOTAL ASSETS	$ 793,795	$ 724,299
CURRENT LIABILITIES		
Accounts payable and accrued liabilities	$ 152,136	$ 138,834
Current portion of long-term debt (Note 11)	—	6,271
Income tax payable	3,365	1,170
	155,501	146,275
NON-CURRENT LIABILITIES		
Long-term debt (Note 11)	225,489	195,125
Defined benefit plan obligation (Note 12)	33,853	36,556
Deferred tax liabilities (Note 9)	2,630	2,392
Other long-term liabilities	18,710	14,668
	280,682	248,741
TOTAL LIABILITIES	436,183	395,016
SHAREHOLDERS' EQUITY		
Share capital (Note 15)	167,910	167,460
Contributed surplus	2,620	2,831
Retained earnings	156,664	140,527
Accumulated other comprehensive income	30,418	18,465
TOTAL EQUITY	357,612	329,283
TOTAL LIABILITIES & EQUITY	$ 793,795	$ 724,299

See accompanying notes to consolidated financial statements.

Approved on behalf of the Board of Directors

"Eric L. Stefanson, FCPA, FCA"

DIRECTOR

"H. Sanford Riley"

DIRECTOR

Consolidated Statements of Earnings

($ in thousands, except per share amounts)	Year Ended January 31, 2016	Year Ended January 31, 2015
SALES	$ **1,796,035**	$ 1,624,400
Cost of sales	**(1,273,421)**	(1,160,182)
Gross profit	**522,614**	464,218
Selling, operating and administrative expenses (Notes 16, 17)	**(415,293)**	(366,752)
Earnings from operations	**107,321**	97,466
Interest expense (Note 18)	**(6,210)**	(6,673)
Earnings before income taxes	**101,111**	90,793
Income taxes (Note 9)	**(31,332)**	(27,910)
NET EARNINGS FOR THE YEAR	$ **69,779**	$ 62,883
NET EARNINGS PER SHARE (Note 20)		
Basic	$ **1.44**	$ 1.30
Diluted	$ **1.43**	$ 1.29
WEIGHTED-AVERAGE NUMBER OF SHARES OUTSTANDING (000's)		
Basic	**48,509**	48,432
Diluted	**48,783**	48,709

See accompanying notes to consolidated financial statements.

Consolidated Statements of Comprehensive Income

($ in thousands)	Year Ended January 31, 2016	Year Ended January 31, 2015
NET EARNINGS FOR THE YEAR	$ **69,779**	$ 62,883
Other comprehensive income/(expense), net of tax:		
Items that may be reclassified to net earnings:		
Exchange differences on translation of foreign controlled subsidiaries	**11,953**	11,384
Items that will not be subsequently reclassified to net earnings:		
Remeasurements of defined benefit plans (Note 12)	**4,583**	(11,968)
Remeasurements of defined benefit plan of equity investee	**(15)**	30
Total other comprehensive income, net of tax	**16,521**	(554)
COMPREHENSIVE INCOME FOR THE YEAR	$ **86,300**	$ 62,329

See accompanying notes to consolidated financial statements.

Consolidated Statements of Changes in Shareholders' Equity

($ in thousands)	Share Capital	Contributed Surplus	Retained Earnings	AOCI[(1)]	Total
Balance at January 31, 2015	$ 167,460	$ 2,831	$ 140,527	$ 18,465	$ 329,283
Net earnings for the year	—	—	69,779	—	69,779
Other comprehensive income (Note 12)	—	—	4,583	11,953	16,536
Other comprehensive income of equity investee	—	—	(15)	—	(15)
Comprehensive income	—	—	74,347	11,953	86,300
Equity settled share-based payments	—	124	—	—	124
Dividends (Note 19)	—	—	(58,210)	—	(58,210)
Issuance of common shares (Note 15)	450	(335)	—	—	115
	450	(211)	(58,210)	—	(57,971)
Balance at January 31, 2016	**$167,910**	**$ 2,620**	**$156,664**	**$ 30,418**	**$357,612**
Balance at January 31, 2014	$ 166,069	$ 3,528	$ 145,762	$ 7,081	$ 322,440
Net earnings for the year	—	—	62,883	—	62,883
Other comprehensive income (Note 12)	—	—	(11,968)	11,384	(584)
Other comprehensive income of equity investee	—	—	30	—	30
Comprehensive income	—	—	50,945	11,384	62,329
Equity settled share-based payments	—	373	—	—	373
Dividends (Note 19)	—	—	(56,180)	—	(56,180)
Issuance of common shares	1,391	(1,070)	—	—	321
	1,391	(697)	(56,180)	—	(55,486)
Balance at January 31, 2015	$ 167,460	$ 2,831	$ 140,527	$ 18,465	$ 329,283

(1) Accumulated Other Comprehensive Income

See accompanying notes to consolidated financial statements.

Consolidated Statements of Cash Flows

($ in thousands)	Year Ended January 31, 2016	Year Ended January 31, 2015
CASH PROVIDED BY (USED IN)		
Operating activities		
Net earnings for the year	$ 69,779	$ 62,883
Adjustments for:		
Amortization (Note 7, 8)	44,026	40,372
Provision for income taxes (Note 9)	31,332	27,910
Interest expense (Note 18)	6,210	6,673
Equity settled share option expense (Note 13)	386	373
Taxes paid	(30,659)	(32,881)
Loss / (Gain) on disposal of property and equipment	350	(294)
	121,424	105,036
Change in non-cash working capital	5,904	9,225
Change in other non-cash items	5,659	825
Cash from operating activities	132,987	115,086
Investing activities		
Purchase of property and equipment (Note 7)	(63,179)	(49,101)
Intangible asset additions (Note 8)	(12,804)	(3,228)
Proceeds from disposal of property and equipment	170	2,017
Cash used in investing activities	(75,813)	(50,312)
Financing activities		
Increase in long-term debt (Note 11)	13,081	78,572
Repayments of long-term debt (Note 11)	—	(75,950)
Dividends (Note 19)	(58,210)	(56,180)
Interest paid	(5,160)	(5,713)
Issuance of common shares	115	321
Cash used in financing activities	(50,174)	(58,950)
Effect of changes in foreign exchange rates on cash	1,114	952
NET CHANGE IN CASH	8,114	6,776
Cash, beginning of year	29,129	22,353
CASH, END OF YEAR	$ 37,243	$ 29,129

See accompanying notes to consolidated financial statements.

Notes to Consolidated Financial Statements

($ IN THOUSANDS, EXCEPT PER SHARE AMOUNTS) JANUARY 31, 2016 AND 2015

1. ORGANIZATION

The North West Company Inc. (NWC or the Company) is a corporation amalgamated under the Canada Business Corporations Act (CBCA) and governed by the laws of Canada. The Company, through its subsidiaries, is a leading retailer of food and everyday products and services. The address of its registered office is 77 Main Street, Winnipeg, Manitoba.

These consolidated financial statements have been approved for issue by the Board of Directors of the Company on April 8, 2016.

2. BASIS OF PREPARATION

(A) **Statement of Compliance** These consolidated financial statements have been prepared in accordance with International Financial Reporting Standards (IFRS), as issued by the International Accounting Standards Board (IASB).

(B) **Basis of Measurement** The consolidated financial statements have been prepared on a going concern basis, under the historical cost convention, except for the following which are measured at fair value, as applicable:

- Liabilities for share-based payment plans (Note 13)
- Defined benefit pension plan (Note 12)
- Assets and liabilities acquired in a business combination

The methods used to measure fair values are discussed further in the notes to these financial statements.

(C) **Functional and Presentation Currency** The presentation currency of the consolidated financial statements is Canadian dollars, which is the Company's functional currency. All financial information is presented in Canadian dollars, unless otherwise stated, and has been rounded to the nearest thousand.

3. SIGNIFICANT ACCOUNTING POLICIES

The accounting policies set out below have been applied to all years presented in these consolidated financial statements, and have been applied consistently by both the Company and its subsidiaries using uniform accounting policies for like transactions and other events in similar circumstances.

(A) **Basis of Consolidation** Subsidiaries are entities controlled, either directly or indirectly, by the Company. Control is established when the Company has rights to an entity's variable returns, and has the ability to affect those returns through its power over the entity. Subsidiaries are fully consolidated from the date on which control is transferred to the Company until the date that control ceases. The Company assesses control on an ongoing basis.

A joint arrangement can take the form of a joint operation or a joint venture. Joint ventures are those entities over which the Company has joint control of the rights to the net assets of the arrangement, rather than rights to its assets and obligations for its liabilities. The Company's 50% interest in the jointly controlled entity Transport Nanuk Inc. has been classified as a joint venture. Its results are included in the consolidated statements of earnings using the equity method of accounting. The consolidated financial statements include the Company's share of both earnings and other comprehensive income from the date that that it ceases. Joint ventures are carried in the consolidated balance sheets at cost plus post-acquisition changes in the Company's share of net assets of the entity, less any impairment in value.

All significant inter-company amounts and transactions have been eliminated.

[. . .]

(C) **Revenue Recognition** Revenue on the sale of goods is recorded at the time the sale is made to the customer, being when the significant risks and rewards of ownership have transferred to the customer, recovery of the consideration is probable, and the amount of revenue can be measured reliably. Sales are presented net of tax, returns and discounts and are measured at the fair value of the consideration received or receivable from the customer for the products sold or services supplied. Service charges on customer account receivables are accrued each month on balances outstanding at each account's billing date.

(D) **Inventories** Inventories are valued at the lower of cost and net realizable value. The cost of warehouse inventories is determined using the weighted-average cost method. The cost of retail inventories is determined primarily using the retail method of accounting for general merchandise inventories and the cost method of accounting for food inventories on a first-in, first-out basis. Cost includes the cost to purchase goods net of vendor allowances plus other costs incurred in bringing inventories to their present location and condition. Net realizable value is estimated based on the amount at which inventories are expected to be sold, taking into consideration fluctuations in retail prices due to obsolescence, damage or seasonality.

Inventories are written down to net realizable value if net realizable value declines below carrying amount. When circumstances that previously caused inventories to be written down below cost no longer exist or when there is clear evidence of an increase in selling price, the amount of the write-down previously recorded is reversed.

[. . .]

(F) **Property and Equipment** Property and equipment are stated at cost less accumulated amortization and any impairment losses. Cost includes any directly attributable costs, borrowing costs on qualifying construction projects, and the costs of dismantling and removing the items and restoring the site on which they are located. When major components of an item of property and equipment have different useful lives, they are accounted for as separate items. Amortization is calculated from the dates assets are available for use using the straight-line method to allocate the cost of assets less their residual values over their estimated useful lives as follows:

Buildings	3% – 8%
Leasehold improvements	5% – 20%
Fixtures and equipment	8% – 20%
Computer equipment	12% – 33%

[. . .]

Amortization methods, useful lives and residual values are reviewed at each reporting date and adjusted if appropriate. Assets under construction and land are not amortized.

(P) **Provisions** A provision is recognized if, as a result of a past event, the Company has a present legal or constructive obligation that can be estimated reliably, and it is probable that an outflow of economic benefits will be required to settle the obligation.

[. . .]

6. INVENTORIES

Retail inventories are valued at the lower of cost and net realizable value. Valuing retail inventories requires the Company to use estimates related to: adjusting to cost inventories valued at retail; future retail sales prices and reductions; and inventory losses during periods between the last physical count and the balance sheet date. Included in cost of sales for the year ended January 31, 2016, the Company recorded $1,392 (January 31, 2015 - $4,223) for the write-down of inventories as a result of net realizable value being lower than cost. The decrease in the write-down of inventories is due to the clearance of discontinued under-performing general merchandise inventory in the northern Canada stores last year. There was no reversal of inventories written down previously that are no longer estimated to sell below cost during the year ended January 31, 2016 or 2015.

7. PROPERTY & EQUIPMENT

January 31, 2016	Land	Buildings	Leasehold improvements	Fixtures & equipment	Computer equipment	Construction in process	Total
Cost							
Balance, beginning of year	$ 16,041	$ 377,061	$ 51,845	$ 265,706	$ 73,151	$ 16,459	$ 800,263
Additions	—	28,613	10,863	20,422	2,715	566	63,179
Disposals	—	(365)	(747)	(367)	(13)	—	(1,492)
Effect of movements in foreign exchange	894	11,873	2,094	9,161	1,289	50	25,361
Total January 31, 2016	$ 16,935	$ 417,182	$ 64,055	$ 294,922	$ 77,142	$ 17,075	$ 887,311
Accumulated amortization							
Balance, beginning of year	$ —	$ 209,584	$ 30,296	$ 186,617	$ 62,074	$ —	$ 488,571
Amortization expense	—	17,593	3,806	14,591	4,226	—	40,216
Disposals	—	(206)	(509)	(251)	(7)	—	(973)
Effect of movements in foreign exchange	—	5,231	1,218	6,047	1,120	—	13,616
Total January 31, 2016	$ —	$ 232,202	$ 34,811	$ 207,004	$ 67,413	$ —	$ 541,430
Net book value January 31, 2016	$ 16,935	$ 184,980	$ 29,244	$ 87,918	$ 9,729	$ 17,075	$ 345,881

January 31, 2015	Land	Buildings	Leasehold improvements	Fixtures & equipment	Computer equipment	Construction in process	Total
Cost							
Balance, beginning of year	$ 15,692	$ 350,924	$ 45,576	$ 245,863	$ 65,327	$ 9,120	$ 732,502
Additions	—	16,917	4,001	14,363	6,540	7,280	49,101
Disposals	(700)	(4,402)	(148)	(4,858)	(200)	—	(10,308)
Effect of movements in foreign exchange	1,049	13,622	2,416	10,338	1,484	59	28,968
Total January 31, 2015	$ 16,041	$ 377,061	$ 51,845	$ 265,706	$ 73,151	$ 16,459	$ 800,263
Accumulated amortization							
Balance, beginning of year	$ —	$ 191,439	$ 25,798	$ 171,321	$ 57,069	$ —	$ 445,627
Amortization expense	—	16,565	3,275	13,034	3,903	—	36,777
Disposals	—	(4,047)	(82)	(4,321)	(135)	—	(8,585)
Effect of movements in foreign exchange	—	5,627	1,305	6,583	1,237	—	14,752
Total January 31, 2015	$ —	$ 209,584	$ 30,296	$ 186,617	$ 62,074	$ —	$ 488,571
Net book value January 31, 2015	$ 16,041	$ 167,477	$ 21,549	$ 79,089	$ 11,077	$ 16,459	$ 311,692

The Company reviewed its property and equipment for indicators of impairment. No assets were identified as impaired.

Interest capitalized

Interest attributable to the construction of qualifying assets was capitalized using an average rate of 2.86% and 3.66% for the years ended January 31, 2016 and 2015 respectively. Interest capitalized in additions amounted to $275 (January 31, 2015 - $274). Accumulated interest capitalized in the cost total above amounted to $1,438 (January 31, 2015 - $1,163).

8. GOODWILL & INTANGIBLE ASSETS

Goodwill	January 31, 2016	January 31, 2015
Balance, beginning of year	$ 33,653	$ 29,424
Effect of movements in foreign exchange	3,607	4,229
Balance, end of year	$ 37,260	$ 33,653

Goodwill Impairment Testing

The goodwill asset balance relates to the Company's acquired subsidiary, Cost-U-Less, and is allocated to the International Operations operating segment. The value of goodwill was tested by means of comparing the recoverable amount of the operating segment to its carrying value. The recoverable amount is the greater of its value in use or its fair value less costs of disposal. Recoverable amount was estimated from the product of financial performance and trading multiples observed for comparable public companies. Values assigned to the key assumptions represent management's best estimates and have been based on data from both external and internal sources. The fair value measurement was categorized as a Level 3 fair value based on the inputs in the valuation technique used. Key assumptions used in the estimation of enterprise value are as follows:

- Financial performance was measured with actual and budgeted earnings based on sales and expense growth specific to each store and the Company's administrative offices. Financial budgets and forecasts are approved by senior management and consider historical sales volume and price growth;
- The ratio of enterprise value to financial performance was determined using a range of market trading multiples from comparable companies;
- Costs to sell have been estimated as a fixed percentage of enterprise value. This is consistent with the approach of an independent market participant.

No impairment has been identified on goodwill, and management considers reasonably foreseeable changes in key assumptions are unlikely to produce a goodwill impairment.

Intangible assets				
January 31, 2016	Software	Cost-U-Less banner	Other	Total
Cost				
Balance, beginning of year	$ 28,376	$ 8,902	$ 7,989	$ 45,267
Additions	12,654	—	150	12,804
Effect of movements in foreign exchange	—	954	225	1,179
Total January 31, 2016	$ 41,030	$ 9,856	$ 8,364	$ 59,250
Accumulated Amortization				
Balance, beginning of year	$ 17,032	$ —	$ 5,750	$ 22,782
Amortization expense	3,558	—	252	3,810
Effect of movements in foreign exchange	—	—	48	48
Total January 31, 2016	$ 20,590	$ —	$ 6,050	$ 26,640
Net book value January 31, 2016	$ 20,440	$ 9,856	$ 2,314	$ 32,610

11. LONG-TERM DEBT

	January 31, 2016	January 31, 2015
Current:		
Notes payable	$ —	$ 72
Finance lease liabilities	—	55
Revolving loan facilities(1)	—	6,144
	$ —	$ 6,271
Non-current		
Revolving loan facilities(1)	$ 7,946	$ —
Revolving loan facilities(2)	—	27,977
Revolving loan facilities(3)	119,193	78,367
Senior notes(4)	98,350	88,779
Finance lease liabilities	—	2
	$ 225,489	$ 195,125
Total	$ 225,489	$ 201,396

(1) In July 2015, the Company completed the refinancing of the US $30,000 loan facility maturing October 31, 2015. The new increased, committed, revolving U.S. loan facility provides the International Operations with up to US$40,000 for working capital requirements and general business purposes. This facility matures October 31, 2020, bears a floating rate of interest based on U.S. LIBOR plus a spread and is secured by certain accounts receivable and inventories of the International Operations. At January 31, 2016, the International Operations had drawn US$5,643 (January 31, 2015 – US$4,831) on this facility.

(2) The US$52,000 committed, revolving loan facilities in the International Operations mature December 31, 2018 and bear interest at LIBOR plus a spread. These loan facilities are secured by certain assets of the Company and rank *pari passu* with the US$70,000 senior notes and the $200,000 Canadian Operations loan facilities. At January 31, 2016, the Company had drawn US$NIL (January 31, 2015 – US$22,000) on these facilities. See Note 25, Subsequent Event.

(3) These committed, revolving loan facilities provide the Company's Canadian Operations with up to $200,000 for working capital requirements and general business purposes. The facilities mature December 31, 2018 and are secured by certain assets of the Company and rank *pari passu* with the US$70,000 senior notes and the US$52,000 loan facilities in International Operations. These facilities bear a floating interest rate based on Bankers Acceptances rates plus stamping fees or the Canadian prime interest rate. See Note 25, Subsequent Event.

(4) The Company refinanced the US$70,000 senior notes that matured on June 15, 2014. The maturing senior notes had a fixed interest rate of 6.55% on US$42,000 and a floating interest rate based on US LIBOR plus a spread on US$28,000. The new US$70,000 senior notes, which mature on June 16, 2021, have a fixed interest rate of 3.27% on US $55,000 and a floating interest rate on US$15,000 based on US LIBOR plus a spread. The floating interest rate on US$15,000 based on certain assets of the Company and rank *pari passu* with the $200,000 Canadian Operations loan facilities and the US$52,000 loan facilities in the International Operations.

[. .]

15. SHARE CAPITAL

Authorized – The Company has an unlimited number of shares.

	Shares	Consideration
Balance at January 31, 2015	48,497,199	$ 167,460
Issued under option plans (Note 13)	26,142	450
Balance at January 31, 2016	48,523,341	$ 167,910

[. .]

23. SUBSIDIARIES AND JOINTLY CONTROLLED ENTITIES

The Company's principal operating subsidiaries are set out below.

	Activity	Country of Organization	Proportion of voting rights held by:	
			Company	Subsidiary
NWC GP Inc.	General Partner	Canada	100%	
North West Company Holdings Inc.	Holding Company	Canada	100%	
The North West Company LP	Retailing	Canada	100% (less one unit)	
NWC (U.S.) Holdings Inc.	Holding Company	United States	100%	
The North West Company (International) Inc.	Retailing	United States	100%	
The North West Finance Company Coöperatie U.A.	Finance Company	Netherlands	99%	1%

The investment in jointly controlled entities comprises a 50% interest in a Canadian Arctic shipping company, Transport Nanuk Inc. At January 31, 2016, the Company's share of the net assets of its jointly controlled entity amount to $10,119 (January 31, 2015 - $9,244), comprised assets of $11,277 (January 31, 2015 - $10,462) and liabilities of $1,158 (January 31, 2015 - $1,218). During the year ended January 31, 2016 the Company purchased freight handling and shipping services from Transport Nanuk Inc. and its subsidiaries of $7,274 (January 31, 2015 - $7,462). The contract terms are based on market rates for these types of services on similar arm's length transactions.

[. .]

Intangible assets

January 31, 2015

Cost	Software	Cost-U-Less banner	Other	Total
Balance, beginning of year	$ 25,218	$ 7,783	$ 7,987	$ 40,988
Additions	3,158	—	70	3,228
Write off of fully amortized assets	—	—	(731)	(731)
Effect of movements in foreign exchange	—	1,119	663	1,782
Total January 31, 2015	$ 28,376	8,902	7,989	$ 45,267
Accumulated Amortization				
Balance, beginning of year	$ 14,272	$ —	$ 5,202	$ 19,474
Amortization expense	2,760	—	835	3,595
Write off of fully amortized assets	—	—	(731)	(731)
Effect of movements in foreign exchange	—	—	444	444
Total January 31, 2015	$ 17,032	$ —	5,750	22,782
Net book value January 31, 2015	$ 11,344	$ 8,902	$ 2,239	$ 22,485

Work in process

As at January 31, 2016, the Company had incurred $6,037 (January 31, 2015 - $468) for intangible assets that were not yet available for use, and therefore not subject to amortization.

Intangible Asset Impairment Testing

The Company determines the fair value of the Cost-U-Less banner using the Relief from Royalty approach. This method requires management to make long-term assumptions about future sales, terminal growth rates, royalty rates and discount rates. Sales forecasts for the following financial year together with medium and terminal growth rates ranging from 2% to 5% are used to estimate future sales, to which a royalty rate of 0.5% is applied. The present value of this royalty stream is compared to the carrying value of the asset. No impairment has been identified on intangible assets and management considers reasonably foreseeable changes in key assumptions are unlikely to produce an intangible asset impairment.

[. .]

10. OTHER ASSETS

	January 31, 2016	January 31, 2015
Investment in jointly controlled entity (Note 23)	$ 10,356	$ 9,482
Other	3,067	3,073
	$ 13,423	$ 12,555

Appendix B

Specimen Financial Statements: Sobeys Inc.

In this appendix, we illustrate current financial reporting using the financial statements of Sobeys Inc., one of Canada's leading grocery chains.

The financial statements included in this appendix contain the consolidated statement of financial position (which Sobeys calls balance sheet), income statement (which Sobeys calls statement of earnings), statement of comprehensive income, statement of changes in equity (which Sobeys calls statement of changes in shareholders' equity), and statement of cash flows. The complete set of financial statements for Sobeys, including the auditor's report and notes to the financial statements, can be found on sedar.com in the Issuer Profiles/Companies/S section.

We encourage you to use these financial statements in conjunction with relevant chapter material in the textbook.

SOBEYS INC. Consolidated Balance Sheets As At (in millions of Canadian dollars)	May 7 2016	May 2 2015
ASSETS		
Current		
Cash and cash equivalents	$ 258.8	$ 295.6
Receivables	489.4	499.7
Inventories (Note 4)	1,287.3	1,260.3
Prepaid expenses	117.2	120.3
Loans and other receivables (Note 5)	26.1	19.4
Income taxes receivable	6.4	18.5
Assets held for sale (Note 6)	396.2	43.9
	2,581.4	2,257.7
Loans and other receivables (Note 5)	93.0	87.9
Investment in affiliate	48.0	48.0
Other assets (Note 7)	42.8	48.4
Property and equipment (Note 8)	3,096.8	3,448.4
Investment property (Note 9)	90.4	102.3
Intangibles (Note 10)	654.1	677.6
Goodwill (Note 11)	716.3	3,501.5
Deferred tax assets (Note 12)	637.8	89.2
	$7,960.6	$10,261.0
LIABILITIES		
Current		
Accounts payable and accrued liabilities	$2,180.2	$ 2,245.4
Income taxes payable	16.8	21.4
Provisions (Note 13)	169.0	114.3
Long-term debt due within one year (Note 14)	341.4	32.4
	2,707.4	2,413.5
Provisions (Note 13)	125.1	138.5
Long-term debt (Note 14)	1,922.6	2,229.6
Other long-term liabilities (Note 15)	107.9	106.9
Employee future benefits (Note 16)	326.9	341.2
Deferred tax liabilities (Note 12)	41.0	52.9
	5,230.9	5,282.6
SHAREHOLDERS' EQUITY		
Capital stock (Note 17)	2,752.9	2,752.9
Contributed surplus	93.0	93.0
(Deficit) retained earnings	(172.1)	2,086.5
Accumulated other comprehensive loss	(3.2)	(7.1)
	2,670.6	4,925.3
Non-controlling interest	59.1	53.1
	2,729.7	4,978.4
	$7,960.6	$10,261.0

See accompanying notes to the consolidated financial statements.

B-1

SOBEYS INC.
Consolidated Statements of (Loss) Earnings
53 and 52 Weeks Ended
(in millions of Canadian dollars)

	May 7 2016	May 2 2015
Sales	$24,618.8	$23,928.8
Other (loss) income, net (Note 18)	(14.2)	88.2
Operating expenses		
Cost of sales	18,661.2	17,966.3
Selling and administrative expenses	5,416.1	5,403.0
Impairments of goodwill and long-lived assets (Note 8 and 11)	2,975.3	–
Operating (loss) income	(2,448.0)	647.7
Finance costs, net (Note 20)	134.6	150.7
(Loss) earnings before income taxes	(2,582.6)	497.0
Income tax (recovery) expense (Note 12)	(463.4)	130.3
Net (loss) earnings	$ (2,119.2)	$ 366.7
(Loss) earnings for the year attributable to:		
Non-controlling interest	$ 16.4	$ 17.9
Owners of the Company	(2,135.6)	348.8
	$ (2,119.2)	$ 366.7

See accompanying notes to the consolidated financial statements.

SOBEYS INC.
Consolidated Statements of Comprehensive (Loss) Income
53 and 52 Weeks Ended
(in millions of Canadian dollars)

	May 7 2016	May 2 2015
Net (loss) earnings	$(2,119.2)	$366.7
Other comprehensive income (loss)		
Items that will be reclassified subsequently to net (loss) earnings		
Unrealized gains (losses) on derivatives designated as cash flow hedges (net of taxes of $(1.5) (2015 – $1.8))	3.8	(4.6)
Reclassification of losses on derivatives designated as cash flow hedges to net (loss) earnings (net of taxes of $(0.1) (2015 – $(0.2))	0.1	0.4
	3.9	(4.2)
Items that will not be reclassified subsequently to net (loss) earnings		
Actuarial gains (losses) on defined benefit plans (net of taxes of $(2.7) (2015 – $15.9)) (Note 16)	7.3	(45.6)
Total comprehensive (loss) income	$(2,108.0)	$316.9
Total comprehensive (loss) income for the year attributable to:		
Non-controlling interest	$ 16.4	$ 17.9
Owners of the Company	(2,124.4)	299.0
	$(2,108.0)	$316.9

See accompanying notes to the consolidated financial statements.

SOBEYS INC.
Consolidated Statements of Changes in Shareholders' Equity
(in millions of Canadian dollars)

	Capital Stock	Contributed Surplus	Accumulated Other Comprehensive Loss	Retained Earnings (Deficit)	Total Attributable to Owners of the Company	Non-controlling Interest	Total Equity
Balance at May 3, 2014	$2,752.9	$93.0	$(2.9)	$1,902.5	$ 4,745.5	$41.0	$ 4,786.5
Dividends declared on common shares	–	–	–	(119.2)	(119.2)	–	(119.2)
Capital transactions with structured entities	–	–	–	–	–	(5.8)	(5.8)
Transactions with owners	–	–	–	(119.2)	(119.2)	(5.8)	(125.0)
Net earnings	–	–	–	348.8	348.8	17.9	366.7
Other comprehensive loss	–	–	(4.2)	(45.6)	(49.8)	–	(49.8)
Total comprehensive income for the year	–	–	(4.2)	303.2	299.0	17.9	316.9
Balance at May 2, 2015	$2,752.9	$93.0	$(7.1)	$2,086.5	$ 4,925.3	$53.1	$ 4,978.4
Dividends declared on common shares	–	–	–	(130.3)	(130.3)	–	(130.3)
Capital transactions with structured entities	–	–	–	–	–	(10.4)	(10.4)
Transactions with owners	–	–	–	(130.3)	(130.3)	(10.4)	(140.7)
Net loss	–	–	–	(2,135.6)	(2,135.6)	16.4	(2,119.2)
Other comprehensive income	–	–	3.9	7.3	11.2	–	11.2
Total comprehensive loss for the year	–	–	3.9	(2,128.3)	(2,124.4)	16.4	(2,108.0)
Balance at May 7, 2016	$2,752.9	$93.0	$(3.2)	$ (172.1)	$ 2,670.6	$59.1	$ 2,729.7

See accompanying notes to the consolidated financial statements.

SOBEYS INC.
Consolidated Statements of Cash Flows
53 and 52 Weeks Ended
(in millions of Canadian dollars)

	May 7 2016	May 2 2015
Operations		
Net (loss) earnings	$(2,119.2)	$ 366.7
Adjustments for:		
Depreciation	380.5	393.6
Income tax (recovery) expense	(463.4)	130.3
Finance costs, net (Note 20)	134.6	150.7
Amortization of intangibles	86.0	81.7
Loss (gain) on disposal of assets	45.9	(56.8)
Impairment of non-financial assets, net	17.6	1.5
Impairments of goodwill and long-lived assets (Notes 8 and 11)	2,975.3	—
Amortization of deferred items	12.5	12.4
Employee future benefits	(4.3)	(4.2)
Increase in long-term lease obligation	6.7	5.8
Decrease in long-term provisions	(27.6)	(44.5)
Stock option plan	3.6	4.0
Restructuring	—	103.0
Net change in non-cash working capital	(116.6)	6.2
Income taxes paid, net	(93.9)	(84.0)
Cash flows from operating activities	837.7	1,066.4
Investment		
Property, equipment and investment property purchases	(616.2)	(497.2)
Proceeds on disposal of property, equipment and investment property	136.7	778.8
Additions to intangibles	(55.5)	(39.8)
Loans and other receivables	(11.8)	(19.8)
Other assets and other long-term liabilities	5.1	(18.0)
Business acquisitions (Note 21)	(90.7)	(11.7)
Interest received	1.0	4.2
Cash flows (used in) from investing activities	(631.4)	196.5
Financing		
Issue of long-term debt	582.7	374.4
Debt financing costs	(1.4)	(0.9)
Repayment of long-term debt	(594.4)	(1,511.8)
Interest paid	(89.3)	(117.3)
Dividends paid, common shares	(130.3)	(119.2)
Non-controlling interest	(10.4)	(5.8)
Cash flows used in financing activities	(243.1)	(1,380.6)
Decrease in cash and cash equivalents	(36.8)	(117.7)
Cash and cash equivalents, beginning of year	295.6	413.3
Cash and cash equivalents, end of year	$ 258.8	$ 295.6

See accompanying notes to the consolidated financial statements.

Glossary

Account An individual accounting record of increases and decreases in a specific asset, liability, and/or shareholders' equity (common shares, retained earnings, revenue, expense, and dividends declared) item. (p. 115)

Accounting The information system that identifies, records, and communicates the economic events of an organization to users interested in that information. (p. 4)

Accounting cycle A series of nine steps used to account for, and report, transactions: analyze transactions (step 1), journalize transactions (step 2), post transactions (step 3), prepare a trial balance (step 4), journalize and post adjusting entries (step 5), prepare an adjusted trial balance (step 6), prepare financial statements (step 7), journalize and post closing entries (step 8), and prepare a post-closing trial balance. (p. 106)

Accounting equation The equation that states that Assets = Liabilities + Shareholders' Equity. (p. 17)

Accounting information system The system of collecting and processing transaction data and communicating financial information to decision makers. (p. 106)

Accounting transaction An economic event that is recorded in the financial statements because it involves an exchange that affects assets, liabilities, and/or shareholders' equity. (p. 106)

Accounts payable Amounts owed to suppliers for purchases made on credit (on account). (p. 61)

Accounts receivable Amounts owed by customers who purchased products or services on credit (on account). (p. 57)

Accrual basis accounting An accounting basis in which transactions that change a company's financial statements are recorded in the periods in which the events occur, rather than in the periods in which the company receives or pays cash. (p. 172)

Accrued expenses Expenses incurred but not yet paid in cash that are recorded at the end of the period by an adjusting entry. (p. 185)

Accrued revenues Revenues earned but not yet received in cash that are recorded at the end of an accounting period by an adjusting entry. (p. 189)

Accumulated other comprehensive income (AOCI) The cumulative change in shareholders' equity that results from the gains and losses that bypass net income (recorded in OCI) but affect shareholders' equity. (p. 604)

Adjusted trial balance A list of accounts and their balances after all adjusting journal entries have been recorded and posted. (p. 193)

Adjusting entries Journal entries made at the end of an accounting period to update the accounts to ensure the proper recognition of revenues and expenses. (p. 174)

Aging of accounts receivable method A method of determining bad debts expense and allowance for doubtful accounts based on an analysis of customer balances by the length of time they have been outstanding. (p. 419)

Allowance method A method of accounting for bad debts that involves estimating uncollectible accounts at the end of each period. (p. 418)

Amortizable amount The cost of a finite-life intangible asset (for example, patent, copyright) less its residual value, if any. (p. 483)

Amortization The systematic allocation of the amortizable cost of a finite-life intangible asset over the shorter of the asset's legal or useful life. (p. 483)

Amortized cost model A method of valuing debt investments that are held to earn cash flows with specified payment dates in a contract in which the carrying value is adjusted only to the extent that discounts and premiums are amortized and not for the effect of changes in fair value. (p. 651)

Asset retirement costs The amount added to the cost of a long-lived asset that relates to obligations to dismantle, remove, or restore an asset when it is retired. (p. 464)

Asset turnover A measure of how efficiently a company uses its total assets to generate sales. It is calculated by dividing net sales by average total assets [(beginning + ending total assets) ÷ 2]. (p. 490)

Assets The resources owned or controlled by a business that are expected to provide future economic benefits. (p. 11)

Associate An investee that is significantly influenced by an investor. (p. 654)

Authorized shares The amount of share capital that a corporation is authorized to sell. The amount may be unlimited or specified. (p. 588)

Average collection period The average amount of time that a receivable is outstanding. It is calculated by dividing 365 days by the receivables turnover. (p. 431)

Average cost formula An inventory cost formula that assumes that the goods available for sale are homogeneous or non-distinguishable. The cost of goods sold and ending inventory are determined using a weighted average unit cost, calculated by dividing the cost of the goods available for sale by the units available for sale. (p. 309)

Bad debt recovery Accounting for a payment by a customer whose account had previously been written off. (p. 423)

Bank indebtedness A short-term loan, such as an operating line of credit, pre-arranged with a bank to cover cash shortfalls. (p. 61)

Basic earnings per share A measure of profitability showing the income earned by each common share. It is calculated by dividing income available to common shareholders by the weighted average number of common shares. (p. 70)

Bond A type of long-term debt issued by large corporations, universities, and governments that involves a promise to repay a large amount of money at a fixed future date. (p. 544)

Capital expenditures Expenditures that benefit future periods. They are recorded (capitalized) as long-lived assets. (p. 464)

Carrying amount (also known as book value) Amount at which an asset is recognized in the statement of financial position. Can be used to describe the assets of a company as a whole or individual assets such as accounts receivable (cost less allowance for doubtful accounts), depreciable assets (cost less accumulated depreciation), amortizable assets (cost less accumulated amortization), investments, and bonds. (p. 181)

Cash Resources that consist of coins, currency, cheques, and money orders that are acceptable at face value on deposit in a bank or similar institution. (p. 367)

Cash basis accounting An accounting basis in which revenue is recorded only when cash is received, and an expense is recorded only when cash is paid. (p. 172)

Cash dividend A pro rata (proportional) distribution of cash to shareholders. (p. 597)

Cash equivalents Short-term, highly liquid (easily sold) held for trading investments that are subject to an insignificant risk of changes in value. (p. 380)

Chart of accounts A list of a company's accounts and account numbers that identify where the accounts are in the general ledger. (p. 124)

Closing entries Journal entries at the end of an accounting period to transfer the balances of temporary accounts (revenues, expenses, and dividends declared) to the permanent shareholders' equity account Retained Earnings. (p. 197)

Collateral Assets pledged as security for the payment of a debt. (p. 524)

Collusion Two or more individuals working together to get around prescribed control activities. (p. 366)

Comparability An enhancing qualitative characteristic of useful information that enables users to identify and understand similarities in, and differences among, items. (p. 75)

Compensating balance A minimum cash balance that a bank requires a borrower to keep on deposit in support of a bank loan in the event that the borrower fails to make a payment. (p. 381)

Conceptual framework A coherent system of interrelated objectives and fundamentals that can lead to consistent standards and that prescribes the nature, function, and limits of financial accounting statements. (p. 73)

Consigned goods Goods shipped by a consignor, who retains ownership, to a party called the consignee, who holds the goods for sale. (p. 303)

Consignee The party that holds the consigned goods and is responsible for selling them, but does not own the goods. (p. 303)

Consignor The party that owns the consigned goods, but has transferred them to a consignee who is responsible for selling them. (p. 303)

Consolidated financial statements Financial statements that present the assets and liabilities controlled by the parent company and the total profitability of the combined companies (the parent company and the subsidiary companies). (p. 655)

Contingent liabilities Existing or possible obligations arising from past events. The liability is contingent (dependent) on whether or not some uncertain future event occurs that will confirm either its existence or the amount payable, or both. (p. 533)

Contra asset account An account that is offset against (reduces) another related asset account on the statement of financial position. Examples include allowance for doubtful accounts and accumulated depreciation. (p. 59)

Contra expense account An account that is offset against (reduces) an expense account on the income statement. Examples include purchase returns and allowances and purchase discounts. (p. 261)

Contra revenue account An account that is offset against (reduces) a revenue account on the income statement. Examples include sales returns and allowances and sales discounts. (p. 250)

Contributed capital The total amount paid or contributed by shareholders in exchange for shares of ownership. It consists of share capital and additional contributed capital, such as contributed surplus, if any. (p. 591)

Contributed surplus A source of contributed capital that can result from certain types of equity transactions, including the reacquisition of shares. (p. 591)

Control account An account in the general ledger that summarizes the details for a subsidiary ledger and controls it. (p. 415)

Copyright An exclusive right granted by the federal government allowing the owner to reproduce and sell an artistic or published work for a period extending over the life of the creator plus 50 years. (p. 484)

Corporate life cycle The four phases in the life of a business: introductory, growth, maturity, and decline. In each phase, the nature of the company's cash flows changes. (p. 722)

Corporation A company organized as a separate legal entity, with most of the rights and privileges of a person. Shares are evidence of ownership. (p. 7)

Cost constraint The pervasive constraint that ensures that the value of the information provided in financial reporting is greater than the cost of providing it. (p. 76)

Cost model (for investments—also known as the cost method) An accounting model in which an equity investment is recorded at cost because a fair value for the investment cannot be readily determined. This model is also a choice allowed under ASPE for investments in associates. Investment revenue is recognized only when cash dividends are earned. This model should not be confused with the cost model that is used when accounting for property, plant, and equipment in Chapter 9. (p. 651)

Cost model (for long-lived assets) A model for accounting for an asset that carries the asset at its cost less any accumulated depreciation or amortization. (p. 468)

Cost of goods available for sale The sum of beginning inventory and the cost of goods purchased. (p. 243)

Cost of goods purchased The sum of net purchases and freight in. (p. 244)

Cost of goods sold The total cost of inventory sold during the period. In a perpetual inventory system, it is calculated and recorded for each sale. In a periodic inventory system, it is calculated at the end of the accounting period by deducting ending inventory from the cost of goods available for sale. (p. 241)

Coupon interest rate (also known as the contractual or stated interest rate) The rate stated in a bond certificate used to determine the amount of interest the borrower pays and the investor receives. (p. 545)

Credit The right side of an account. (p. 116)

Credit term period The interest-free period (usually 30 days) provided to customers purchasing on credit. (p. 416)

Creditors Users of accounting information, including suppliers, that grant credit (sell on account) to a customer. (p. 5)

Cumulative A feature of preferred shares that entitles the shareholder to receive current-year and unpaid prior-year dividends before common shareholders receive any dividends. (p. 595)

Current assets Assets that are expected to be converted into cash, sold, or used up within one year of the company's financial statement date. (p. 56)

Current liabilities Obligations that will be paid or settled within one year of the company's financial statement date. (p. 61)

Current maturities of long-term debt The portion of a non-current or long-term loan that is repayable within the current year. (p. 61)

Current ratio A measure of liquidity used to evaluate a company's short-term debt-paying ability. It is calculated by dividing current assets by current liabilities. (p. 68)

Current value The price that would be paid to purchase the same asset or paid to settle the same liabilities. (p. 77)

Current value basis of accounting Measurement basis that states that certain assets and liabilities should be recorded at their current value. (p. 77)

Days in inventory A liquidity measure of the average number of days that inventory is held. It is calculated as 365 days divided by the inventory turnover ratio. (p. 320)

Debit The left side of an account. (p. 116)

Debt investments Investments in money-market instruments, bonds, commercial paper, or similar items. (p. 648)

Debt to total assets A measure of solvency showing the percentage of total financing that is provided by lenders and other creditors. It is calculated by dividing total liabilities by total assets. (p. 69)

Declaration date The date the board of directors formally declares (approves) a dividend and announces it to shareholders. (p. 598)

Deficit A negative balance in retained earnings resulting from cumulative net losses exceeding cumulative net income. (p. 16)

Deposits in transit Amounts deposited at a bank and recorded by the depositor that have not yet been recorded by the bank. (p. 373)

Depreciable amount The cost of a depreciable asset (for example, property, plant, and equipment) less its residual value. (p. 469)

Depreciation (also known as amortization) The process of allocating the cost of a depreciable asset (for example, buildings and equipment) over its useful life. (p. 179)

Derecognized The term used when an asset (such as a note receivable, property, plant, and equipment, or an intangible asset) no longer provides any future benefits and is removed from the accounts. (p. 427)

Development costs Expenditures related to the application of research to a plan or design for a new or improved product or process for commercial use. These costs are recorded (capitalized) as long-lived assets. (p. 485)

Diminishing-balance method A depreciation method in which depreciation expense is calculated by multiplying the carrying amount of an asset by a depreciation rate (the straight-line rate, which is 100% divided by the useful life, adjusted for any multiplier effect). This method produces a decreasing periodic depreciation expense over the asset's useful life. (p. 471)

Direct method A method of determining net cash provided (used) by operating activities on the statement of cash flows by adjusting each item in the income statement from the accrual basis to the cash basis. (p. 702)

Discontinued operations The disposal, or availability for sale, of a separate component of an entity. A component is a major line of business or major geographic area of operations. (p. 796)

Discount The difference between a bond's face value and its issue price when it is sold for less than its face value. This occurs when the market interest rate is higher than the coupon interest rate. (p. 545)

Dishonoured note A note that is not paid in full at maturity. (p. 427)

Dividend yield A measure of the percentage of the share price that is paid in dividends. It is calculated by dividing dividends per share by the share price. (p. 609)

Dividends The distribution of retained earnings from a corporation to its shareholders, normally in the form of cash. (p. 10)

Dividends in arrears Dividends that were not declared on cumulative preferred shares during a period. (p. 595)

Double-entry accounting system A system that records the dual effect of each transaction in appropriate accounts. (p. 119)

EBIT Earnings (net income) before interest expense and income tax expense. (p. 542)

Effective-interest method A method of amortizing a bond discount or premium that results in a periodic interest expense that equals a constant percentage (the market or effective interest rate) of the bond's carrying amount. Amortization is calculated as the difference between the interest expense and the interest paid. (p. 546)

Elements of financial statements A set of broad categories or classes used to group financial information for presentation in the financial statements, such as assets, liabilities, equity, income, and expenses. (p. 76)

Employee benefits Payments made by an employer for pension, insurance, health, and/or other benefits paid on behalf of its employees. (p. 528)

Equity investments Investments in the share capital (common and/or preferred shares) of other corporations. (p. 648)

Equity method An accounting method in which the investment in common shares is initially recorded at cost. The investment account is then adjusted (increased for the investor's share of the investee's net income and decreased for dividends received) to show the investor's equity in the investee. (p. 655)

Expense recognition The process of recording an expense when there is a decrease in future economic benefits related to a decrease in an asset or an increase in a liability in the course of ordinary activities. Expense recognition is linked to revenue recognition in that expenses are recognized in the period in which a company makes efforts to generate revenues. (p. 172)

Expenses The decreases in economic benefits that result from the costs of assets consumed or services used in ongoing operations to generate revenue. (p. 12)

External users Users of accounting information that are not involved in managing the organization and do not have access to accounting information other than that which is publicly available, including investors, lenders, and other creditors. (p. 5)

Fair value through other comprehensive income (OCI) model A fair value model for non-strategic investments that can be used only with an election under IFRS (not used under ASPE). It allows investors to record realized and unrealized gains and losses in other comprehensive income rather than in net income. (p. 651)

Fair value through profit or loss model A valuation method that reports non-strategic debt or equity investments that are held for trading at their fair values, resulting in the recording of unrealized gains and losses in the income statement. (p. 650)

Faithful representation A fundamental qualitative characteristic describing information that represents economic reality. It must be complete, neutral, and free from material error. (p. 74)

Finance lease (also known as a capital lease) A long-term agreement allowing one party (the lessee) to use the asset of another party (the lessor). The arrangement is accounted for as a purchase because the risks and rewards of owning the asset have been transferred to the lessee. (p. 467)

Financial assets Receivables and investments that have a contractual right to receive cash or another financial asset. (p. 414)

Financial liability A form of financial instrument, represented by a contractual obligation to pay cash in the future. (p. 524)

Financing activities Activities that report the cash effects of debt or equity financing. These include (1) borrowing or repaying cash from (to) lenders, and (2) issuing or reacquiring shares or paying dividends to investors. (p. 13)

First-in, first-out (FIFO) cost formula An inventory cost formula that assumes that the costs of the earliest (oldest) goods acquired are the first to be recognized as the cost of goods sold. The costs of the latest goods acquired are assumed to remain in ending inventory. (p. 306)

Fiscal year An accounting period that is one year long. (p. 14)

FOB (free on board) destination Freight terms indicating that the seller will pay for the shipping costs of the goods and is responsible for the goods until they arrive at their destination (normally the buyer's place of business). (p. 245)

FOB (free on board) shipping point Freight terms indicating that the seller is responsible for the goods only until they reach their shipping point (normally the seller's place of business). The buyer will pay for the shipping costs of the goods from the shipping point until they arrive at their destination and is responsible for them once they have left the shipping point. (p. 245)

Franchise A contractual arrangement under which the franchisor grants the franchisee the right to sell certain products, to render specific services, or to use certain trademarks or trade names, usually within a designated geographic area. (p. 486)

Fraud Intentional misappropriation of assets or misstatement of financial information. (p. 361)

Free cash flow A cash-based measure used to evaluate solvency. It is calculated by deducting net capital expenditures and cash dividends from net cash provided (used) by operating activities. (p. 723)

Function A method of organizing expenses on the income statement by way of the activity (business function) for which they were incurred (such as cost of goods sold, administrative, and selling). (p. 254)

General journal The book of original entry in which transactions are recorded in chronological (date) order. (p. 122)

General ledger The book of accounts that contains a company's asset, liability, and shareholders' equity (common shares, retained earnings, revenue, expense, and dividends declared) accounts. (p. 123)

Generally accepted accounting principles (GAAP) A general guide, having substantial authoritative support, that describes how economic events should be recorded and reported for financial reporting purposes. (p. 8)

Going concern assumption The assumption that the business will remain in operation for the foreseeable future. (p. 76)

Goodwill The value of favourable, unidentifiable attributes related to a company as a whole. It is calculated when one business acquires another and pays more than the fair value of the company's net identifiable assets. (p. 486)

Gross pay The total compensation (such as salaries or wages) earned by an employee. (p. 527)

Gross profit (also known as gross margin) Sales revenue less cost of goods sold. (p. 241)

Gross profit margin Gross profit expressed as a percentage of sales. It is calculated by dividing gross profit by net sales. (p. 258)

Gross sales Total sales before deducting any sales returns and allowances and sales discounts. (p. 252)

Held for trading investments Investments in debt securities or equity securities of other companies that are bought with the intention of selling them after a short period of time in order to earn income from their price fluctuations. (p. 57)

Historical cost basis of accounting Measurement basis that states that assets and liabilities should be recorded at their cost at the time of acquisition. (p. 77)

Honoured note A note that is paid in full at maturity. (p. 427)

Horizontal analysis (also known as trend analysis) A technique for evaluating a series of financial statement data over a period of time to determine the increase (decrease) that has taken place. This increase (decrease) is expressed as either an amount or a percentage. (p. 768)

Horizontal percentage change for the period (also known as the horizontal percentage change between periods) A percentage measuring the change from one year (or period) to the next year (or period). It is calculated by dividing the dollar amount of the change between the specific year (or period) under analysis and the prior year (or period) by the prior-year amount. (p. 769)

Horizontal percentage of a base-period amount A percentage measuring the change since a base year (or period), normally involving more than one year (or period). It is calculated by dividing the amount for the specific year (or period) under analysis by the base-year (period) amount. (p. 768)

Impairment loss The amount by which the carrying amount of an asset exceeds its recoverable amount. (p. 476)

Income (also known as revenue) The increase in economic benefits that result from the normal operating activities of a business, such as the sale of a product or provision of a service. (p. 12)

Income available to common shareholders Net income less the annual preferred dividend for cumulative preferred shares. The dividend is deducted for noncumulative preferred shares only if declared. (p. 611)

Income from operations The results of a company's normal operating activities. It is calculated as gross profit less operating expenses. (p. 256)

Income statement (also known as statement of earnings or statement of profit and loss) A financial statement that presents the revenues and expenses and resulting net income or loss of a company for a specific period of time. (p. 15)

Income summary A temporary account used in closing revenue and expense accounts. The balance in each individual revenue and expense account is credited or debited and summarized in the Income Summary account before being closed to retained earnings (via the Income Summary account). (p. 198)

Indirect method A method of determining net cash provided (used) by operating activities on the statement of cash flows in which net income is adjusted for items that do not affect cash. (p. 702)

Initial public offering (IPO) The initial offering of a corporation's shares to the public. (p. 588)

Intangible assets Assets of a long-lived nature that do not have physical substance but represent a privilege or a right granted to, or held by, a company. (p. 59)

Internal controls Systems designed to help an organization achieve reliable financial reporting, effective and efficient operations, and compliance with relevant laws and regulations. (p. 304)

Internal users Users of accounting information who have access to an organization's internal accounting information, including company officers, managers, and directors. (p. 4)

Inventory Goods held for sale to customers. (p. 57)

Inventory turnover A liquidity measure of the number of times, on average, that inventory is sold ("turned over") during the period. It is calculated by dividing the cost of goods sold by the average inventory. Average inventory is calculated by adding the beginning and ending inventory balances and dividing the result by 2. (p. 320)

Investee The corporation that issues (sells) the debt or equity securities. (p. 654)

Investing activities Activities that report the cash effects of purchasing and disposing of long-lived assets such as property, plant, and equipment and investments not held for trading. (p. 13)

Investors Users of accounting information that have an ownership interest (owns debt or equity securities) in the organization. (p. 5)

Issued shares The portion of authorized shares that has been sold. (p. 589)

Legal capital The amount per share that must be retained in the business for the protection of corporate creditors. Equal to the proceeds received from the issue of most shares. (p. 590)

Lenders Users of accounting information, including bankers, that extend credit to borrowers. (p. 5)

Liabilities The debts and obligations of a business. Liabilities are claims of lenders and other creditors on the assets of a business. (p. 10)

Licences Operating rights to use an asset that are granted by a government agency or other organization. (p. 486)

Liquidity ratios Measures of a company's short-term ability to pay its maturing obligations (usually current liabilities) and to meet unexpected needs for cash. These include working capital and the current, receivables turnover, average collection period, inventory turnover, and days in inventory ratios. (p. 67)

Long-term investments (also known as investments) Investments in debt securities intended to be held for many years to earn interest, and (2) equity securities of other companies held to generate investment revenue or held for strategic reasons. (p. 58)

Loss (also known as net loss) The amount by which expenses are more than revenues. The opposite of net income. (p. 13)

Lower of cost and net realizable value (LCNRV) A basis for stating inventory at the lower of its original cost and its net realizable value at the end of the period. (p. 317)

Market capitalization A measure of the fair value of a company's equity. It is calculated by multiplying the number of shares by the share price at any given date. (p. 590)

Market interest rate (also known as the effective interest rate) The rate that investors demand for lending funds to a corporation. (p. 545)

Multiple-step income statement An income statement that shows several steps to determine net income or loss by separately reporting net sales, gross profit, income from operations, income before income tax, and net income. (p. 255)

Nature A method of organizing expenses on the income statement by way of their natural classification (such as salaries, transportation, depreciation, and advertising). (p. 254)

Net income (also known as profit or net earnings) The amount by which revenues exceed expenses. (p. 12)

Net pay Gross pay less payroll deductions. (p. 527)

Net purchases Purchases less purchase returns and allowances and purchase discounts. (p. 262)

Net realizable value (NRV) The selling price of an inventory item, less any costs required to make the item saleable. (p. 317)

Net sales Gross sales less sales returns and allowances and sales discounts. (p. 252)

Noncumulative Preferred shares that are entitled to the current dividend, if declared, but not to any undeclared and unpaid amounts from prior years. (p. 595)

Non-current assets (also known as long-term assets) Assets that are not expected to be converted into cash, sold, or used up by the business within one year of the financial statement date. (p. 58)

Non-current liabilities (also known as long-term liabilities) Obligations that are not expected to be paid or settled within one year of the financial statement date. (p. 62)

Non-GAAP measures Management-defined measures of financial performance. (p. 797)

Non-strategic investment A debt or equity investment that is purchased mainly to generate investment income. (p. 648)

Nontrade receivables Receivables (such as interest receivable, loans to company officers, and income tax receivable) that do not result from the operations of the business. (p. 414)

Normal balance The side of an account used to increase the account. Asset accounts have a normal debit balance. Liabilities and shareholders' equity accounts have a normal credit balance. Individual components that make up shareholders' equity have normal balances as follows: common shares, retained earnings, and revenue accounts have normal credit balances. Expense and dividends declared accounts have normal debit balances, as they reduce retained earnings. (p. 116)

Normal course issuer bid The reacquisition of a specified percentage of a company's own shares from the general public for a predetermined price and period, subject to regulatory approval. (p. 592)

Notes payable (also known as loans payable) Amounts owed to suppliers, banks, or others that are normally interest-bearing and supported by a written promise to repay. (p. 61)

Notes receivable (also known as loans receivable) Amounts owed by customers or others that are normally interest-bearing and supported by a written promise to repay. (p. 57)

NSF (not sufficient funds) cheque (also known as a returned cheque) A cheque that has been deposited but is returned by a bank because there are insufficient funds in the bank account of the customer who wrote the cheque. (p. 372)

Objective of financial reporting The provision of financial information about a company that is useful to existing and potential investors, lenders, and other creditors in making decisions about providing resources to the company. (p. 73)

Operating activities Activities that result from day-to-day operations. They report the cash effects of transactions that create revenues and expenses. (p. 13)

Operating cycle Average period of time it takes for a business to pay cash to obtain products or services and then receive cash from customers for these products or services. (p. 56)

Operating expenditures Expenditures that benefit only the current period. They are immediately charged against revenues as an expense. (p. 464)

Operating expenses Expenses incurred in the process of earning sales revenue. They are deducted from gross profit to arrive at income from operations. (p. 241)

Operating lease An arrangement allowing one party (the lessee) to use the asset of another party (the lessor). The arrangement is accounted for as a rental because the risks and rewards of owning the asset have been retained by the lessor. (p. 467)

Operating line of credit (also known as a credit facility) A pre-arranged agreement to borrow money at a bank, up to an agreed-upon amount. (p. 524)

Other comprehensive income (OCI) Gains and losses that affect shareholders' equity but are not shown in net income or loss. They relate to complex transactions such as certain types of gains and losses on investments. (p. 604)

Outstanding cheques Cheques issued (written and distributed) and recorded by a company that have not yet been paid (cleared) by the bank. (p. 373)

Parent company A company that controls (usually owns more than 50% of) the common shares of another company. (p. 655)

Partnership A business owned by more than one person. (p. 7)

Patent An exclusive right issued by the federal government that enables the recipient to manufacture, sell, or otherwise control an invention for a period of 20 years from the date of the application. (p. 484)

Payment (distribution) date The date dividends are paid or distributed to shareholders. (p. 598)

Payout ratio A measure of the percentage of the net income distributed in the form of cash dividends to common shareholders. It is calculated by dividing cash dividends by net income. (p. 608)

Payroll deductions Deductions from gross pay to determine the amount of a paycheque. (p. 527)

Percentage of receivables method A method of determining bad debts expense using a percentage of accounts receivable that are likely to be uncollectible. (p. 419)

Periodic inventory system An inventory system in which detailed records are not maintained and the ending inventory and cost of goods sold are determined only at the end of the accounting period after a physical inventory count has been completed. (p. 243)

Permanent accounts Statement of financial position accounts whose balances are carried forward to the next accounting period. (p. 197)

Perpetual inventory system An inventory system in which the quantity and cost of each inventory item is maintained. The records continuously show the inventory that should be on hand and the cost of the items sold. (p. 241)

Post-closing trial balance A list of permanent accounts and their balances after closing entries have been journalized and posted. (p. 203)

Posting The procedure of transferring journal entries to the general ledger accounts. (p. 124)

Preferred shares Share capital that has contractual preferences over common shares in certain areas. (p. 594)

Premium The difference between the issue price and the face value of a bond when a bond is sold for more than its face value. This occurs when the market interest rate is lower than the coupon interest rate. (p. 545)

Prepaid expenses Costs paid in advance of use that benefit more than one accounting period. They are initially recorded as assets and become expenses only when they are used or consumed and no longer have future benefit. (p. 57)

Price-earnings (P-E) ratio A profitability measure of the ratio of the market price of each common share to the earnings per share. It reflects investors' beliefs about a company's future income potential. (p. 71)

Private corporation A corporation whose shares are not traded on a public stock exchange. (p. 8)

Profit margin Net income expressed as a percentage of net sales. It is calculated by dividing net income by net sales. (p. 259)

Profitability ratios Measures of a company's operating success for a specific period of time. These include the gross profit margin, profit margin, return on assets, return on common shareholders' equity, earnings per share, price-earnings, payout, and dividend yield ratios. (p. 70)

Promissory note A written promise to pay a specified amount of money on demand or at a fixed date in the future. (p. 425)

Property, plant, and equipment Tangible assets, such as land, buildings, and equipment, with relatively long useful lives that are being used to operate the business. (p. 59)

Proprietorship A business owned by one person. (p. 6)

Provisions Liabilities of uncertain timing or amount. They are recorded in the accounts based on reasonable and probable estimates. (p. 533)

Public corporation A corporation whose shares are publicly traded on a stock exchange. (p. 8)

Purchase discount A price reduction, based on the invoice price less any returns and allowances, to encourage customers to make an early payment of a credit purchase. (p. 247)

Purchase returns and allowances A return of goods for cash or credit, or a deduction granted by the seller on the selling price of unsatisfactory merchandise. (p. 246)

Quantity discount A price reduction that reduces the invoice price and is given to the buyer for volume purchases. Quantity discounts are not separately recorded. (p. 251)

Realized gain or loss The difference between fair value and cost (carrying amount) when an investment is actually sold. (p. 650)

Receivables turnover A measure of the liquidity of receivables. It is calculated by dividing net credit sales by the average gross accounts receivable and is expressed as the number of times per year that the accounts receivable are collected. (p. 431)

Record date The date when ownership of shares is determined for dividend purposes. (p. 598)

Relevance A fundamental qualitative characteristic describing information that makes a difference in a user's decision. It should have predictive value, confirmatory value, or both, and be material. (p. 74)

Reporting entity concept The concept that economic activity that can be identified with a particular company must be kept separate and distinct from the activities of the owner(s) and of all other economic entities. (p. 6)

Research expenses Expenditures on an original planned investigation that is done to gain new knowledge and understanding. These costs are expensed because criteria for recording them as assets have not been met. (p. 485)

Residual value An estimate of the amount that a company would obtain from the disposal of an asset at the end of its useful life. (p. 469)

Restricted cash Cash that is not available for general use, but instead is restricted for a particular purpose. (p. 380)

Retained earnings The amount of accumulated net income (less net losses, if any) from the prior and current periods that has been retained and reinvested in the corporation for future use and not distributed to shareholders as dividends. (p. 16)

Retained earnings restrictions Circumstances that make a portion of retained earnings currently unavailable for dividends. (p. 604)

Return on assets A profitability measure that indicates the amount of net income generated by each dollar invested in assets. It is calculated as net income divided by average total assets [(beginning + ending total assets) ÷ 2]. It can also be calculated by multiplying profit margin by asset turnover. (p. 490)

Return on common shareholders' equity A measure of profitability from the shareholders' point of view. It is calculated by dividing net income minus preferred dividends by average common shareholders' equity (total shareholders' equity minus preferred shares). (p. 612)

Revaluation model A model of accounting for a long-lived asset that carries the asset at its current value less accumulated depreciation or amortization. (p. 476)

Revenue (also known as income) The increase in economic benefits that result from the operating activities of a business, such as the sale of a product or provision of a service. (p. 12)

Revenue recognition The process of recording revenue when there is an inflow of future economic benefits that result from an increase in an asset or a decrease in a liability in the course of ordinary activities. In addition, five conditions must be met: a contract must exist, performance obligations identified, the transaction price determined, the transaction price allocated to the performance obligations, and revenue recognized when the performance obligation is satisfied. (p. 170)

Sales discount A price reduction that is based on the invoice price less any returns and allowances and is given by a seller for early payment of a credit sale. (p. 251)

Sales returns and allowances A return of goods or reduction in price due to unsatisfactory merchandise. (p. 250)

Sales revenue The main source of revenue in a merchandising company. (p. 241)

Share capital Shares representing the ownership interest in a corporation. If only one class of shares exists, it is known as common shares. (p. 10)

Shareholders' equity The shareholders' claim on total assets, represented by the investments of the shareholders (share capital) and undistributed earnings (retained earnings) generated by the company. (p. 16)

Significant influence An investor's ability to influence decisions made by an investee, which is assumed to exist when more than 20% but less than 50% of an investee's shares are owned. (p. 654)

Single-step income statement An income statement that shows only one step (revenues less expenses) in determining income before income tax, after which income tax expense is deducted to determine net income (loss). (p. 253)

Solvency ratios Measures of a company's ability to survive over a long period of time by having enough assets to settle its liabilities as they fall due.

These include the debt to total assets and times interest earned ratios and free cash flow. (p. 69)

Specific identification cost formula An inventory cost formula used when goods are unique, identifiable items and not ordinarily interchangeable. It follows the actual physical flow of goods, and individual items are specifically costed to arrive at the cost of goods sold and cost of the ending inventory. (p. 305)

Statement of cash flows A financial statement that provides information about the cash inflows (receipts) and cash outflows (payments) for a specific period of time. (p. 19)

Statement of changes in equity A financial statement that summarizes the changes in total shareholders' equity, as well as each component of shareholders' equity, for a specific period of time. (p. 16)

Statement of comprehensive income A financial statement that presents net income (loss) and other comprehensive income (loss) for a specific period of time. Other comprehensive income items, such as realized and unrealized gains and losses from investments accounted for using the fair value through OCI model, are not reported on the income statement because they are not considered critical to the evaluation of management's performance, but are included in comprehensive income. (p. 660)

Statement of financial position (also known as balance sheet) A financial statement that reports the assets, liabilities, and shareholders' equity at a specific date. (p. 17)

Statement of retained earnings A statement that summarizes the changes in the Retained Earnings account during the period. This statement is issued only by private companies reporting using ASPE. (p. 606)

Stock dividend A pro rata (proportional) distribution of the corporation's own shares to shareholders. (p. 599)

Stock split The issue of additional shares to shareholders accompanied by a reduction in the legal capital per share. (p. 600)

Straight-line method A depreciation method in which depreciation expense is calculated by dividing the depreciable amount of a long-lived asset, such as buildings or equipment, by its useful life. (p. 470)

Strategic investment An equity investment that is purchased to influence or control another company. (p. 648)

Subsidiary company A company whose common shares are controlled (usually more than 50% of the common shares are owned) by another company. (p. 655)

Subsidiary ledger A ledger that is used to manage the detailed information that would be difficult to track in a general ledger account. A control account in the general ledger summarizes the information in the subsidiary ledger. (p. 415)

Supplies Consumable items used in running a business, such as office and cleaning supplies. (p. 57)

T account (also known as a general ledger account) The basic form of an account, with a debit (left) side and a credit (right) side showing the effect of transactions on the account. (p. 116)

Temporary accounts Revenue, expense, and dividends declared accounts whose balances are transferred to Retained Earnings at the end of an accounting period. (p. 197)

Timeliness An enhancing qualitative characteristic of useful information that means that information is available to decision makers in time to be capable of influencing their decisions. (p. 75)

Times interest earned A measure of a company's solvency, calculated by dividing net income (earnings) before interest expense and income tax expense (EBIT) by interest expense. (p. 542)

Trade receivables Accounts and notes receivable that result from sales transactions. (p. 414)

Trademark (trade name) A word, phrase, jingle, or symbol that distinguishes or identifies a particular business or product. (p. 485)

Trial balance A list of general ledger accounts and their balances at a specific time, usually at the end of the accounting period. There are three different kinds of trial balances: unadjusted trial balances (before adjusting entries are made), adjusted trial balances (after adjusting entries are made), and post-closing trial balances (after closing entries are made). (p. 132)

Unadjusted trial balance A list of accounts and their balances before adjusting journal entries have been made. (p. 175)

Understandability An enhancing qualitative characteristic of useful information that means that information is clearly and concisely classified, characterized, and presented. (p. 75)

Unearned revenue Cash received when a customer pays in advance of being provided with a service or product. It is received before revenue is earned and is therefore recorded as a liability until it is earned. (p. 61)

Units-of-production method A depreciation method in which the useful life is expressed in terms of the total units of production or total use expected from the asset. Depreciation expense is calculated by multiplying the depreciable amount by the actual activity during the year divided by the estimated total activity. The method will produce an expense that will vary each period depending on the amount of activity. (p. 473)

Unrealized gain or loss The difference between the fair value and cost (carrying amount) of an investment still held (owned) by the investor. (p. 650)

Useful life The length of service of a depreciable asset. (p. 179)

Verifiability An enhancing qualitative characteristic of useful information that means that different knowledgeable and independent users could reach a consensus that the information is faithfully represented. (p. 75)

Vertical analysis (also known as common size analysis) A technique for evaluating financial statement data that expresses each item in a financial statement as a percentage of a base amount. The base amount is usually net sales in the income statement and total assets in the statement of financial position. (p. 772)

Vertical percentage of a base amount A percentage measuring the proportion of an amount in a financial statement within a year (or period). It is calculated by dividing the financial statement amount under analysis by the base amount for that particular financial statement (such as net sales for the income statement or total assets for the statement of financial position). (p. 772)

Weighted average number of common shares A weighted average of the number of common shares issued during the year. Shares issued or repurchased during the year are weighted by the fraction of the year for which they have been issued. (p. 611)

Weighted average unit cost The average cost of inventory weighted by the number of units purchased at each unit cost. It is calculated as the cost of goods available for sale divided by the number of units available for sale. (p. 309)

Working capital A measure of liquidity used to evaluate a company's short-term debt-paying ability. It is calculated by subtracting current liabilities from current assets. (p. 67)

Company Index

Subject Index

SHAREHOLDERS' EQUITY   (Chapter 11)

Equity Transactions

Transaction	Journal Entry
Issue of shares	Dr. Cash Cr. Common/Preferred Shares

Cash dividends (declaration and payment)	Dr. Dividends Declared
	    Cr. Dividends Payable
	Dr. Dividends Payable
	    Cr. Cash

Stock dividends (declaration and distribution)	Dr. Dividends Declared
	    Cr. Stock Dividends Distributable
	Dr. Stock Dividends Distributable
	    Cr. Common Shares

Comparison of Dividend Effects (after declaration and payment/distribution)

	Assets	=	Liabilities	+	Share Capital	+	Retained Earnings	Number of Shares
					Shareholders' Equity			
Cash dividend	–		NE		NE		–	NE
Stock dividend	NE		NE		+		–	+
Stock split	NE		NE		NE		NE	+

Note: "+" means increase, "–" means decrease, "NE" means no effect.

Comprehensive Income

Comprehensive income (loss) = Net income + Other comprehensive income (loss)

⇓ Net income → Retained earnings (statement of changes in equity and shareholders' equity section of statement of financial position)

⇓ Other comprehensive income (loss) → Accumulated other comprehensive income (loss) (statement of changes in equity and shareholders' equity section of statement of financial position)

INVESTMENTS   (Chapter 12)

Reporting and Valuation of Investments

Method/Model	Used On	Financial Statement Effect
Cost model	Equity investments	Investment carried at cost so no unrealized gains or losses reported. Dividend revenue and realized gains and losses are reported in income.
Amortized cost model	Debt investments	Investment carried at amortized cost so if a premium or discount exists, it is amortized to interest revenue, making it different from interest received. By its maturity date, the investment is carried at its face value. Interest revenue and realized gains and losses are reported in income. No unrealized gains or losses are reported.
Fair value through profit or loss model	Debt and equity investments	Investment carried at fair value. Both unrealized and realized gains and losses are reported in income along with dividend and interest revenue.
Fair value through other comprehensive income (OCI) model	Debt and equity investments	Investment carried at fair value. Unrealized and realized gains and losses are reported in OCI. For equity investments, once sold, gains and losses are reclassified to retained earnings and for debt investments, they are reclassified to net income. Dividend and interest revenue are reported in income.
Equity method	Equity investments when significant influence exists	Investment adjusted for share of associate's income or loss, which is reported in income. Dividends reduce the investment account. Investment is not carried at fair value so no unrealized gains or losses are reported. Realized gains and losses are reported in income.

Comparison of Fair Value through Profit or Loss Model and Equity Method of Accounting for Equity Investments

Transaction	Fair Value (no significant influence)	Equity (significant influence)

Acquisition	Dr. Held for Trading Investments
	    Cr. Cash
		Dr. Investment in Associates
		    Cr. Cash

Investee reports net income	No entry	Dr. Investment in Associates Cr. Income from Associates

Investee declares and pays dividends	Dr. Cash
	    Cr. Dividend Revenue
		Dr. Cash
		    Cr. Investment in Associates

Adjustment for increase in fair value (entry is opposite for decrease)	Dr. Held for Trading Investments Cr. Unrealized Gain on Held for Trading Investments	No entry

Note: The unrealized gain (or loss) on held for trading investments is reported as other revenues and expenses in the income statement.

Comparison of Long-Term Bond Investment and Liability Journal Entries

Transaction	Investor (amortized cost model)	Investee

Purchase/issue of bonds	Dr. Long-Term Investments
	    Cr. Cash
		Dr. Cash
		    Cr. Bonds Payable

Interest receipt/payment and amortization of discount or premium	Dr. Cash
	Dr. Long-Term Investments (Dr. for discount; Cr. for premium)
	    Cr. Interest Revenue
		Dr. Interest Expense
		    Cr. Bonds Payable (Dr. for premium; Cr. for discount)
		    Cr. Cash

Sale of investment	Dr. Cash Dr. Realized Loss (or Cr. Realized Gain) Cr. Long-Term Investments	No entry

STATEMENT OF CASH FLOWS   (Chapter 13)

Business Activities

1. Operating activities: Include a company's principal income-producing activities and all other activities that are not investing or financing activities. They arise from the cash effects of transactions that create revenues and expenses.
2. Investing activities: Include (a) purchasing and disposing of long-term investments and long-lived assets and (b) lending money and collecting the loans. Investing activities generally affect non-current asset accounts.
3. Financing activities: Include (a) obtaining cash from issuing debt and repaying the amounts borrowed and (b) obtaining cash from shareholders and paying them dividends. Financing activities generally affect non-current liability and shareholders' equity accounts.

Steps in Preparing the Statement of Cash Flows

1. Prepare operating activities section: Determine net cash provided (used) by operating activities by converting net income from accrual basis to cash basis using either indirect or direct method (preferred). To do this, analyze the current year's income statement, relevant current asset and current liability accounts from the comparative statement of financial position, and selected information. In the indirect method, this is done by converting total net income from accrual basis to cash basis. In the direct method, this is done by converting each individual revenue and expense account from accrual basis to cash basis (Appendix 13A).
2. Prepare investing activities section: Determine net cash provided (used) by investing activities by analyzing changes in non-current asset accounts from the comparative statement of financial position and selected information.
3. Prepare financing activities section: Determine net cash provided (used) by financing activities by analyzing changes in non-current liability and equity accounts from the comparative statement of financial position and selected information.
4. Complete statement of cash flows: Determine net increase (decrease) in cash. Compare net change in cash reported on statement of cash flows with change in cash reported on the statement of financial position to make sure the amounts agree.

PERFORMANCE MEASUREMENT   (Chapter 14)

Horizontal (Trend) Analysis

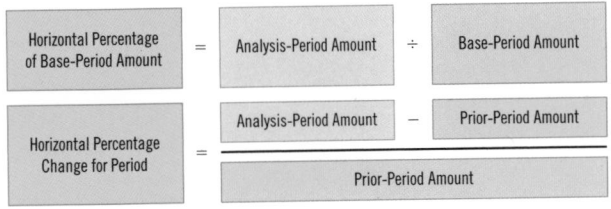

Horizontal Percentage of Base-Period Amount = Analysis-Period Amount ÷ Base-Period Amount

$$\text{Horizontal Percentage Change for Period} = \frac{\text{Analysis-Period Amount} - \text{Prior-Period Amount}}{\text{Prior-Period Amount}}$$

Vertical (Common-Size) Analysis

Vertical Percentage of Base Amount	=	Analysis Amount	÷	Base Amount

Liquidity Ratios

Chapter	Ratio	Formula	What the Ratio Measures	Desired Result
2	Working capital	Current assets − Current liabilities	Short-term debt-paying ability	Higher
2	Current ratio	$\dfrac{\text{Current assets}}{\text{Current liabilities}}$	Short-term debt-paying ability	Higher
8	Receivables turnover	$\dfrac{\text{Net credit sales}}{\text{Average gross accounts receivable}}$	Liquidity of receivables	Higher
8	Average collection period	$\dfrac{365 \text{ days}}{\text{Receivables turnover}}$	Number of days receivables are outstanding	Lower
6	Inventory turnover	$\dfrac{\text{Cost of goods sold}}{\text{Average inventory}}$	Liquidity of inventory	Higher
6	Days in inventory	$\dfrac{365 \text{ days}}{\text{Inventory turnover}}$	Number of days inventory is on hand	Lower

Solvency Ratios

Chapter	Ratio	Formula	What the Ratio Measures	Desired Result
2, 10	Debt to total assets	$\dfrac{\text{Total liabilities}}{\text{Total assets}}$	Percentage of total assets provided by creditors	Lower
10	Times interest earned	$\dfrac{\text{Net income + Interest expense + Income tax expense (EBIT)}}{\text{Interest expense}}$	Ability to meet interest payments	Higher
13	Free cash flow	Net cash provided (used) by operating activities − Net capital expenditures − Dividends paid	Cash available from operating activities for discretionary purposes	Higher

Chapter	Ratio	Formula	What the Ratio Measures	Desired Result
5	Gross profit margin	$\dfrac{\text{Gross profit}}{\text{Net sales}}$	Margin between selling price and cost of goods sold	Higher
5	Profit margin	$\dfrac{\text{Net income}}{\text{Net sales}}$	Net income generated by each dollar of sales	Higher
9	Asset turnover	$\dfrac{\text{Net sales}}{\text{Average total assets}}$	How efficiently assets are used to generate sales	Higher
9	Return on assets	$\dfrac{\text{Net income}}{\text{Average total assets}}$	Overall profitability of assets	Higher
11	Return on common shareholders' equity	$\dfrac{\text{Net income − Preferred dividends}}{\text{Average common shareholders' equity}}$	Profitability of shareholders' investment	Higher
2, 11	Basic earnings per share	$\dfrac{\text{Net income − Preferred dividends}}{\text{Weighted average number of common shares}}$	Net income earned on each common share	Higher
2	Price-earnings ratio	$\dfrac{\text{Market price per share}}{\text{Earnings per share}}$	Relationship between market price per share and earnings per share	Based on market expectations
11	Payout ratio	$\dfrac{\text{Cash dividends declared}}{\text{Net income}}$	Percentage of net income distributed as cash dividends	Based on growth strategy
11	Dividend yield	$\dfrac{\text{Dividend declared per share}}{\text{Market price per share}}$	Income generated for the shareholder by each share, based on the market price per share	Higher for investors seeking dividends; lower for investors seeking price appreciation

SAMPLE FINANCIAL STATEMENTS

Multiple-Step Income Statement (perpetual inventory system)

Name of Company Income Statement Period Ended		
Sales revenues		
Sales		$X
Less: Sales returns and allowances	$X	
Sales discounts	X	X
Net sales		X
Cost of goods sold		X
Gross profit		X
Operating expenses		
(Examples: salaries, advertising, freight, rent, depreciation, utilities, insurance)		X
Income from operations		X
Other revenues and expenses		
(Example: interest)		X
Income before income tax		X
Income tax expense		X
Net income		$X

Income Statement (cost of goods sold detail in periodic inventory system—Appendix 5A)

Cost of goods sold		
Beginning inventory		$X
Purchases	$X	
Less: Purchase returns and allowances	X	
Net purchases	X	
Add: Freight in	X	
Cost of goods purchased		X
Cost of goods available for sale		X
Less: Ending inventory		X
Cost of goods sold		$X

Statement of Comprehensive Income

Name of Company Statement of Comprehensive Income Period Ended	
Net income	$X
Other comprehensive income (loss)	
(Example: revaluations of property, plant, and equipment)	X
Comprehensive income (loss)	$X

Statement of Changes in Equity (IFRS)

Name of Company Statement of Changes in Equity Period Ended					
	Common Shares	Additional Contributed Capital	Retained Earnings	Accumulated Other Comprehensive Income (Loss)	Total
Balance, beginning of period	$X	$X	$X	$X	$X
Issued shares	X				X
Cash dividends declared			(X)		(X)
Stock dividends declared	X		(X)		
Comprehensive income					
Net income			X		X
Other comprehensive income (loss)				X	X
Balance, end of period	$X	$X	$X	$X	$X

Statement of Retained Earnings (ASPE)

Name of Company Statement of Retained Earnings Year Ended December 31, 2018	
Balance, January 1	$X
Add: Net income	X
Less: Dividends declared	X
Balance, December 31	$X

Statement of Financial Position

Name of Company Statement of Financial Position End of the Period			
Assets			
Current assets			
(Examples: cash, held for trading investments, accounts			
receivable, inventory, supplies, prepaid expenses)			$X
Long-term investments			
(Examples: equity investments, debt investments)			X
Property, plant, and equipment			
(Examples: land, land improvements, buildings,			
equipment)		$X	
Less: Accumulated depreciation		X	X
Intangible assets			
Limited life intangibles (Examples: patents, copyrights)	$X		
Less: Accumulated amortization	X	$X	
Indefinite life intangibles (Examples: trademarks, franchises)		X	X
Goodwill			X
Total assets			$X
Liabilities and Shareholders' Equity			
Liabilities			
Current liabilities			
(Examples: accounts payable, accruals, unearned revenues,			
bank loan payable, current portion of non-current liabilities)			$X
Non-current liabilities			
(Examples: mortgage payable, bonds payable)			X
Total liabilities			X
Shareholders' equity			
Contributed capital			
Preferred shares	$X		
Common shares	X		
Contributed surplus	X	$X	
Retained earnings (deficit)		X	
Accumulated other comprehensive income (loss)		X	X
Total liabilities and shareholders' equity			$X

STOP AND CHECK: (1) Total assets on the statement of financial position must equal total liabilities and shareholders' equity, and (2) ending shareholders' equity on the statement of financial position must equal ending shareholders' equity on the statement of changes in equity.

Note: The classifications and ordering within the classifications have been presented in order of liquidity in the above statement of financial position. They may be presented in alternative orders, such as a reverse order of liquidity, as well.

Statement of Cash Flows (Indirect method)

Name of Company Statement of Cash Flows Period Ended			
Operating activities			
Net income			$X
Add:	Noncash expenses (Examples: depreciation, amortization)	$X	
	Losses (Examples: disposal of assets, realized and unrealized		
	losses on investments)	X	
	Decreases in related noncash current assets	X	
	Increases in related noncash current liabilities	X	
Deduct:	Noncash revenues (Example: amortization of bond		
	discount for investor)	(X)	
	Gains (Examples: disposals of assets, realized and unrealized		
	gains on investments)	(X)	
	Increases in noncash current assets	(X)	
	Decreases in related noncash current liabilities	(X)	X
Cash provided (used) by operating activities			X
Investing activities			
(Examples: purchase/sale of non-current assets)			
Cash provided (used) by investing activities			X
Financing activities			
(Examples: issue/repayment of non-current liabilities, issue of shares,			
payment of dividends)			
Cash provided (used) by financing activities			X
Net increase (decrease) in cash			X
Cash, beginning of period			X
Cash, end of period			$X

STOP AND CHECK: Cash, end of the period, on the statement of cash flows must equal cash presented on the statement of financial position.

Statement of Cash Flows (operating activities section in direct method—Appendix 13A)

Operating activities		
Cash receipts from customers		$X
Cash payments		
To suppliers	$X	
For operating expenses	X	
To employees	X	
For interest	X	
For income tax	X	X
Cash provided (used) by operating activities		$X